Nineteenth-Century Literature Criticism

Guide to Thomson Gale Literary Criticism Series

For criticism on	Consult these Thomson Gale series
Authors now living or who died after December 31, 1999	*CONTEMPORARY LITERARY CRITICISM (CLC)*
Authors who died between 1900 and 1999	*TWENTIETH-CENTURY LITERARY CRITICISM (TCLC)*
Authors who died between 1800 and 1899	*NINETEENTH-CENTURY LITERATURE CRITICISM (NCLC)*
Authors who died between 1400 and 1799	*LITERATURE CRITICISM FROM 1400 TO 1800 (LC)* *SHAKESPEAREAN CRITICISM (SC)*
Authors who died before 1400	*CLASSICAL AND MEDIEVAL LITERATURE CRITICISM (CMLC)*
Authors of books for children and young adults	*CHILDREN'S LITERATURE REVIEW (CLR)*
Dramatists	*DRAMA CRITICISM (DC)*
Poets	*POETRY CRITICISM (PC)*
Short story writers	*SHORT STORY CRITICISM (SSC)*
Literary topics and movements	*HARLEM RENAISSANCE: A GALE CRITICAL COMPANION (HR)* *THE BEAT GENERATION: A GALE CRITICAL COMPANION (BG)* *FEMINISM IN LITERATURE: A GALE CRITICAL COMPANION (FL)* *GOTHIC LITERATURE: A GALE CRITICAL COMPANION (GL)*
Asian American writers of the last two hundred years	*ASIAN AMERICAN LITERATURE (AAL)*
Black writers of the past two hundred years	*BLACK LITERATURE CRITICISM (BLC)* *BLACK LITERATURE CRITICISM SUPPLEMENT (BLCS)*
Hispanic writers of the late nineteenth and twentieth centuries	*HISPANIC LITERATURE CRITICISM (HLC)* *HISPANIC LITERATURE CRITICISM SUPPLEMENT (HLCS)*
Native North American writers and orators of the eighteenth, nineteenth, and twentieth centuries	*NATIVE NORTH AMERICAN LITERATURE (NNAL)*
Major authors from the Renaissance to the present	*WORLD LITERATURE CRITICISM, 1500 TO THE PRESENT (WLC)* *WORLD LITERATURE CRITICISM SUPPLEMENT (WLCS)*

ISSN 0732-1864

Volume 183

Nineteenth-Century Literature Criticism

Criticism of the
Works of Novelists, Philosophers, and Other
Creative Writers Who Died between 1800
and 1899, from the First Published Critical
Appraisals to Current Evaluations

Kathy D. Darrow
Russel Whitaker
Project Editors

THOMSON
★
GALE

Detroit • New York • San Francisco • New Haven, Conn. • Waterville, Maine • London

Nineteenth-Century Literature Criticism, Vol. 183

Project Editors
Kathy Darrow and Russel Whitaker

Editorial
Jeffrey W. Hunter, Jelena O. Krstović, Michelle Lee, Thomas J. Schoenberg, Noah Schusterbauer, Lawrence J. Trudeau

Data Capture
Frances Monroe, Gwen Tucker

Indexing Services
Factiva, Inc.

Rights and Acquisitions
Robert McCord, Barbara McNeil, Lista Person

Composition and Electronic Capture
Tracey L. Matthews

Manufacturing
Cynde Bishop

Associate Product Manager
Marc Cormier

LIBRARY OF CONGRESS CATALOG CARD NUMBER 84-643008

ISBN-13: 978-0-7876-9854-6
ISBN-10: 0-7876-9854-7
ISSN 0732-1864

Contents

Preface vii

Acknowledgments xi

Literary Criticism Series Advisory Board xiii

Preface

S ince its inception in 1981, *Nineteenth-Century Literature Criticism* (*NCLC*) has been a valuable resource for students and librarians seeking critical commentary on writers of this transitional period in world history. Designated an "Outstanding Reference Source" by the American Library Association with the publication of is first volume, *NCLC* has since been purchased by over 6,000 school, public, and university libraries. The series has covered more than 500 authors representing 38 nationalities and over 28,000 titles. No other reference source has surveyed the critical reaction to nineteenth-century authors and literature as thoroughly as *NCLC*.

Scope of the Series

NCLC is designed to introduce students and advanced readers to the authors of the nineteenth century and to the most significant interpretations of these authors' works. The great poets, novelists, short story writers, playwrights, and philosophers of this period are frequently studied in high school and college literature courses. By organizing and reprinting commentary written on these authors, *NCLC* helps students develop valuable insight into literary history, promotes a better understanding of the texts, and sparks ideas for papers and assignments. Each entry in *NCLC* presents a comprehensive survey of an author's career or an individual work of literature and provides the user with a multiplicity of interpretations and assessments. Such variety allows students to pursue their own interests; furthermore, it fosters an awareness that literature is dynamic and responsive to many different opinions.

Every fourth volume of *NCLC* is devoted to literary topics that cannot be covered under the author approach used in the rest of the series. Such topics include literary movements, prominent themes in nineteenth-century literature, literary reaction to political and historical events, significant eras in literary history, prominent literary anniversaries, and the literatures of cultures that are often overlooked by English-speaking readers.

NCLC continues the survey of criticism of world literature begun by Thomson Gale's *Contemporary Literary Criticism* (*CLC*) and *Twentieth-Century Literary Criticism* (*TCLC*).

Organization of the Book

An *NCLC* entry consists of the following elements:

- The **Author Heading** cites the name under which the author most commonly wrote, followed by birth and death dates. Also located here are any name variations under which an author wrote, including transliterated forms for authors whose native languages use nonroman alphabets. If the author wrote consistently under a pseudonym, the pseudonym will be listed in the author heading and the author's actual name given in parenthesis on the first line of the biographical and critical information. Uncertain birth or death dates are indicated by question marks. Single-work entries are preceded by a heading that consists of the most common form of the title in English translation (if applicable) and the original date of composition.

- The **Introduction** contains background information that introduces the reader to the author, work, or topic that is the subject of the entry.

- The list of **Principal Works** is ordered chronologically by date of first publication and lists the most important works by the author. The genre and publication date of each work is given. In the case of foreign authors whose works have been translated into English, the list will focus primarily on twentieth-century translations, selecting those works most commonly considered the best by critics. Unless otherwise indicated, dramas are dated by first performance, not first publication. Lists of **Representative Works** by different authors appear with topic entries.

- Reprinted **Criticism** is arranged chronologically in each entry to provide a useful perspective on changes in critical evaluation over time. The critic's name and the date of composition or publication of the critical work are given at the beginning of each piece of criticism. Unsigned criticism is preceded by the title of the source in which it appeared. All titles by the author featured in the text are printed in boldface type. Footnotes are reprinted at the end of each essay or excerpt. In the case of excerpted criticism, only those footnotes that pertain to the excerpted texts are included. Criticism in topic entries is arranged chronologically under a variety of subheadings to facilitate the study of different aspects of the topic.

- A complete **Bibliographical Citation** of the original essay or book precedes each piece of criticism.

- Critical essays are prefaced by brief **Annotations** explicating each piece.

- An annotated bibliography of **Further Reading** appears at the end of each entry and suggests resources for additional study. In some cases, significant essays for which the editors could not obtain reprint rights are included here. Boxed material following the further reading list provides references to other biographical and critical sources on the author in series published by Thomson Gale.

Indexes

Each volume of *NCLC* contains a **Cumulative Author Index** listing all authors who have appeared in a wide variety of reference sources published by Thomson Gale, including *NCLC*. A complete list of these sources is found facing the first page of the Author Index. The index also includes birth and death dates and cross references between pseudonyms and actual names.

A **Cumulative Nationality Index** lists all authors featured in *NCLC* by nationality, followed by the number of the *NCLC* volume in which their entry appears.

A **Cumulative Topic Index** lists the literary themes and topics treated in the series as well as in *Classical and Medieval Literature Criticism, Literature Criticism from 1400 to 1800, Twentieth-Century Literary Criticism,* and the *Contemporary Literary Criticism* Yearbook, which was discontinued in 1998.

An alphabetical **Title Index** accompanies each volume of *NCLC*, with the exception of the Topics volumes. Listings of titles by authors covered in the given volume are followed by the author's name and the corresponding page numbers where the titles are discussed. English translations of foreign titles and variations of titles are cross-referenced to the title under which a work was originally published. Titles of novels, dramas, nonfiction books, and poetry, short story, or essay collections are printed in italics, while individual poems, short stories, and essays are printed in roman type within quotation marks.

In response to numerous suggestions from librarians, Thomson Gale also produces an annual paperbound edition of the *NCLC* cumulative title index. This annual cumulation, which alphabetically lists all titles reviewed in the series, is available to all customers. Additional copies of this index are available upon request. Librarians and patrons will welcome this separate index; it saves shelf space, is easy to use, and is recyclable upon receipt of the next edition.

Citing *Nineteenth-Century Literature Criticism*

When citing criticism reprinted in the Literary Criticism Series, students should provide complete bibliographic information so that the cited essay can be located in the original print or electronic source. Students who quote directly from reprinted criticism may use any accepted bibliographic format, such as University of Chicago Press style or Modern Language Association style.

The examples below follow recommendations for preparing a bibliography set forth in *The Chicago Manual of Style,* 14th ed. (Chicago: The University of Chicago Press, 1993); the first example pertains to material drawn from periodicals, the second to material reprinted from books:

Franklin, J. Jeffrey. "The Victorian Discourse of Gambling: Speculations on *Middlemarch* and *The Duke's Children.*" *ELH* 61, no. 4 (winter 1994): 899-921. Reprinted in *Nineteenth-Century Literature Criticism.* Vol. 168, edited by Jessica Bomarito and Russel Whitaker, 39-51. Detroit: Thomson Gale, 2006.

Frank, Joseph. "*The Gambler*: A Study in Ethnopsychology." In *Freedom and Responsibility in Russian Literature: Essays in Honor of Robert Louis Jackson,* edited by Elizabeth Cheresh Allen and Gary Saul Morson, 69-85. Evanston, Ill.: Northwestern University Press, 1995. Reprinted in *Nineteenth-Century Literature Criticism.* Vol. 168, edited by Jessica Bomarito and Russel Whitaker, 75-84. Detroit: Thomson Gale, 2006.

The examples below follow recommendations for preparing a works cited list set forth in the *MLA Handbook for Writers of Research Papers,* 6th ed. (New York: The Modern Language Association of America, 2003); the first example pertains to material drawn from periodicals, the second to material reprinted from books:

Franklin, J. Jeffrey. "The Victorian Discourse of Gambling: Speculations on *Middlemarch* and *The Duke's Children.*" *ELH* 61.4 (Winter 1994): 899-921. Reprinted in *Nineteenth-Century Literature Criticism.* Eds. Jessica Bomarito and Russel Whitaker. Vol. 168. Detroit: Thomson Gale, 2006. 39-51.

Frank, Joseph. "*The Gambler*: A Study in Ethnopsychology." *Freedom and Responsibility in Russian Literature: Essays in Honor of Robert Louis Jackson.* Eds. Elizabeth Cheresh Allen and Gary Saul Morson. Evanston, Ill.: Northwestern University Press, 1995. 69-85. Reprinted in *Nineteenth-Century Literature Criticism.* Eds. Jessica Bomarito and Russel Whitaker. Vol. 168. Detroit: Thomson Gale, 2006. 75-84.

Suggestions are Welcome

Readers who wish to suggest new features, topics, or authors to appear in future volumes, or who have other suggestions or comments are cordially invited to call, write, or fax the Associate Product Manager:

Associate Product Manager, Literary Criticism Series
Thomson Gale
27500 Drake Road
Farmington Hills, MI 48331-3535
1-800-347-4253 (GALE)
Fax: 248-699-8054

Acknowledgments

The editors wish to thank the copyright holders of the criticism included in this volume and the permissions managers of many book and magazine publishing companies for assisting us in securing reproduction rights. Following is a list of the copyright holders who have granted us permission to reproduce material in this volume of *NCLC*. Every effort has been made to trace copyright, but if omissions have been made, please let us know.

COPYRIGHTED MATERIAL IN *NCLC*, VOLUME 183, WAS REPRODUCED FROM THE FOLLOWING PERIODICALS:

American Literature, v. 47, November, 1975. Copyright © 1975 by Duke University Press. All rights reserved. Used by permission of the publisher.—*American Quarterly,* v. 20, summer, 1968. Copyright © 1968 The Johns Hopkins University Press. Reproduced by permission.—*Deutsche Vierteljahrs Schrift für Literaturwissenschaft und Geistesgeschichte,* v. 77, June, 2003. Copyright © 2003 J. B. Metzlersche Verlagsbuchhandlung und Carl Ernst Poeschel Verlag GmbH in Stuttgart. Reproduced by permission.—*ELH,* v. 39, June, 1972; v. 69, spring, 2002. Copyright © 1972, 2002 by The Johns Hopkins University Press. Both reproduced by permission.—*English,* v. 49, spring, 2000. Copyright © The English Association 2000. Reproduced by permission.—*Genre,* v. 15, winter, 1982 for "*Middlemarch*: The 'Home Epic'" by Kenny Marotta; v. 24, summer, 1991 for "Closure and Escape: The Questionable Comedy of George Eliot's *Middlemarch*" by Laura Mooneyham. Copyright © 1982, 1991 by the University of Oklahoma. Reproduced by permission of *Genre,* the University of Oklahoma and the respective authors.—*The German Quarterly,* v. 58, summer, 1985. Copyright © 1985 by the American Association of Teachers of German. Reproduced by permission.—*The Germanic Review,* v. 51, May, 1976 for "'The Labyrinth of Crime': A Reinterpretation of E. T. A. Hoffmann's 'Das Fräulein von Scuderi'" by Hermann F. Weiss. Copyright © 1976 by Columbia University Press. Reproduced by permission of the author.—*Journal of English and Germanic Philology,* v. 75, October, 1976. Copyright © 1976 by the Board of Trustees of the University of Illinois. Used with permission of the University of Illinois Press.—*Midwest Quarterly,* v. 20, summer, 1979. Copyright © 1979 by *Midwest Quarterly,* Pittsburgh State University. Reproduced by permission.—*Monatshefte,* v. 58, summer, 1966; v. 69, spring, 1977; v. 91, summer, 1999. Copyright © 1966, 1977, 1999 by the Board of Regents of the University of Wisconsin System. All reproduced by permission.—*Mosaic: A Journal for the Interdisciplinary Study of Literature,* v. 18, winter, 1985. Copyright © *Mosaic* 1985. Acknowledgment of previous publication is herewith made.—*Nineteenth-Century Fiction,* v. 9, March, 1955 for "A Preface to *Middlemarch*" by F. George Steiner. Copyright, 1955 by George Steiner. Reprinted by permission of Georges Borchardt, Inc., on behalf of the author./ v. 30, June, 1975 for "*Middlemarch*: An Avuncular View" by U. C. Knoepflmacher. Copyright © 1975 by the Regents of the University of California. Reproduced by permission of the publisher and the author.—*Seminar: A Journal of Germanic Studies,* v. 22, May, 1986. Copyright © 1986 The Canadian Association of University Teachers of German. Reproduced by permission.—*Southern Literary Journal,* v. 11, spring, 1979. Copyright © 1979 by the University of North Carolina Press. Used by permission.—*Southern Quarterly,* v. 21, winter, 1983. Copyright © 1983 by the University of Southern Mississippi. Reproduced by permission.—*Studies in English Literature, 1500-1900,* v. 31, autumn, 1991; v. 44, autumn, 2004. Copyright © 1991, 2004 The Johns Hopkins University Press. Both reproduced by permission.—*Studies in Romanticism,* v. 14, fall, 1975; v. 19, winter, 1980. Copyright © 1975, 1980 by the Trustees of Boston University. Both reproduced by permission.—*Studies in the Novel,* v. 15, spring, 1983. Copyright © 1983 by North Texas State University. Reproduced by permission.—*Style,* v. 32, spring, 1988. Copyright © *Style,* 1988. All rights reserved. Reproduced by permission of the publisher.—*University of Toronto Quarterly,* v. 56, spring, 1987. Copyright © University of Toronto Press 1987. Reproduced by permission of University of Toronto Press Incorporated.

COPYRIGHTED MATERIAL IN *NCLC,* VOLUME 183, WAS REPRODUCED FROM THE FOLLOWING BOOKS:

Auerbach, Nina. From "Dorothea's Lost Dog," in **Middlemarch** *in the Twenty-First Century.* Edited by Karen Chase. Oxford University Press, 2006. Copyright © 2006 by Oxford University Press, Inc. Reproduced by permission of Oxford University Press.—Blair, Walter, and Hamlin Hill. From **America's Humor: From Poor Richard to Doonesbury.** Oxford University Press, 1978. Copyright © 1978 by Oxford University Press. Reproduced by permission of Oxford University Press.—Negus, Kenneth. From **E. T. A. Hoffmann's Other World: The Romantic Author and His 'New Mythology.'** Uni-

Thomson Gale Literature Product Advisory Board

The members of the Thomson Gale Literature Product Advisory Board—reference librarians from public and academic library systems—represent a cross-section of our customer base and offer a variety of informed perspectives on both the presentation and content of our literature products. Advisory board members assess and define such quality issues as the relevance, currency, and usefulness of the author coverage, critical content, and literary topics included in our series; evaluate the layout, presentation, and general quality of our printed volumes; provide feedback on the criteria used for selecting authors and topics covered in our series; provide suggestions for potential enhancements to our series; identify any gaps in our coverage of authors or literary topics, recommending authors or topics for inclusion; analyze the appropriateness of our content and presentation for various user audiences, such as high school students, undergraduates, graduate students, librarians, and educators; and offer feedback on any proposed changes/enhancements to our series. We wish to thank the following advisors for their advice throughout the year.

Middlemarch

George Eliot

The following entry presents criticism of Eliot's novel *Middlemarch: A Study of Provincial Life* (1871-72). For information on Eliot's complete career, see *NCLC,* Volume 4. For additional discussion of *Middlemarch,* see *NCLC,* Volume 13; for discussion of the novel *Daniel Deronda,* see *NCLC,* Volume 23; for discussion of the novel *Silas Marner,* see *NCLC,* Volume 41; for discussion of the novel *The Mill on the Floss,* see *NCLC,* Volume 49; for discussion of the novel *Adam Bede,* see *NCLC,* Volume 89.

INTRODUCTION

George Eliot's *Middlemarch: A Study of Provincial Life* is regarded by some critics as the greatest novel ever written in English. An in-depth portrait of a town and its inhabitants, the work describes the intricate bonds that connect people's lives, exploring the relationship between individual action and the unwieldy, seemingly indeterminate forces that shape society. Eliot employs the metaphor of a web to describe the intertwining of individuals within a community, a network at once orderly and infinitely complex. The novel originated as two separate narratives—one revolving around the character of a doctor, Lydgate, and the other focusing on a female protagonist named Dorothea—which Eliot eventually wove together into a single novel. *Middlemarch* was first serialized in *Blackwood's Magazine,* appearing in eight installments between December 1871 and December 1872; a four-volume book edition was published in 1872.

Although the action of the novel is concentrated within the fictional town of Middlemarch, England, its themes are universal: the individual ambitions of the main characters, set against the complicated social labyrinth of the community, symbolize the struggle of peoples and nations to form societies based on principles of equality, justice, and compassion. At the heart of these struggles, in Eliot's worldview, we find human nature: fickle, vain, and selfish and yet also noble and creative. Eliot's exposure of the frailty of her characters, combined with her broad sympathy for human weakness, lends the work an underlying sense of hope; while people's best intentions are often thwarted by their own personal failings, the striving for improvement, both on the individual level and within the larger community, endures. In its exhaustive, minutely detailed portrayals of its characters and in the ambition and profundity of its themes, *Middlemarch* stands with Leo Tolstoy's *War and Peace* as one of the great epic novels of the nineteenth century.

PLOT AND MAJOR CHARACTERS

Middlemarch is primarily a novel about character and setting. The novel takes place in the early 1830s, a period of significant political and social change in England, and concerns the inhabitants of a small provincial town. Although no one character claims a central role in the novel, Dorothea Brooke, the niece of the opinionated, strong-willed Mr. Brooke, receives the author's closest attention. A religious, thoughtful young woman, Dorothea embodies, in many respects, the idealistic spirit of her age: she is driven by a powerful, albeit vague, desire to perform some great act for society's good, and she clearly has progressive ideas concerning a woman's ability to determine the course of her own life. At the same time, Dorothea's lofty intentions and large spirit lead to a fundamental detachment from everyday life, a rupture that has profound effects on the course of her future. Throughout the first half of the novel, she repeatedly makes poor choices, continually allowing her ideals to obscure reality.

The novel opens with a "Prelude," in which Eliot recounts an anecdote relating to Saint Teresa of Avila. From this brief story Eliot moves into a description of the Brooke household, home of Dorothea, her uncle, and her younger sister, Celia. Two suitors come to visit the sisters: James Chettam, an amiable, well-educated young man, and Edward Casaubon, an older scholar who betrays little emotion. Although Chettam is clearly interested in Dorothea, she rebuffs him, thinking he will make a better match for her sister; indeed, Chettam and Celia eventually marry. Dorothea meanwhile begins to develop a fascination with Casaubon, in spite of his coldness and clumsy social skills. Intrigued by Casaubon's scholarly life—he is engrossed in the writing of an epic study titled "The Key to All Mythologies"—Dorothea imagines her role as his wife, assisting him in his research and enlightening herself in the process. When Casaubon proposes to her in a letter, she immediately decides to accept, ignoring the reservations of her uncle and sister.

As Dorothea and Casaubon search for a house, Eliot introduces the character of Will Ladislaw, Casaubon's younger cousin, whom he is supporting financially. Notwithstanding their family ties, Casaubon and Ladislaw strongly dislike each other. The contrast between the two men is immediately apparent: whereas Casaubon is cold and aloof, Ladislaw is gregarious and good-natured, a young, unemployed artist without specific goals. Ladislaw's initial impression of Dorothea is negative, in part because of her self-effacing manner but also because she is to marry Casaubon. Shortly after the encounter, Ladislaw leaves Middlemarch for a tour of Europe, while Dorothea and Casaubon continue to prepare for their wedding.

At this juncture a new doctor, Tertius Lydgate, moves to Middlemarch. An ambitious and talented physician, Lydgate aspires to become a famous innovator in the field of medicine. He brings several progressive ideas concerning new treatments to the town, which makes him suspect in the eyes of the predominantly provincial, conservative residents. At a dinner party Lydgate meets Rosamond Vincy, the beautiful but materialistic daughter of the mayor. Although their personalities are not compatible, they are attracted to each other: Lydgate admires Rosamond's beauty and charm, while Rosamond sees prestige in marrying a doctor. Though Lydgate remains focused on his career, Rosamond immediately begins to think about marriage.

As the narrative unfolds, Eliot introduces the work's minor characters. Among the most significant are Mr. Bulstrode, a banker and landowner who uses his wealth to manipulate people into doing his bidding; Fred Vincy, Rosamond's profligate brother; Mr. Featherstone, the mean-spirited owner of Stone Court, a large estate, and uncle to Fred and Rosamond; Mary Garth, the kind-hearted and earnest assistant to Mr. Featherstone; and Farebrother, the clergyman. All of the characters' lives are deeply intertwined in one way or another. Fred, plagued by debts, is financially dependent on his Uncle Featherstone, who exploits the situation in order to shame his nephew. Mary Garth develops a fondness for Fred and arranges for her family to lend him money, in spite of his irresponsible ways. Lydgate and Farebrother develop a close friendship, spending long hours talking about politics, science, and books. When Bulstrode and Lydgate become involved in discussions concerning the construction of a new hospital in Middlemarch, a debate arises over the question of the position of hospital chaplain. Most of the townspeople favor the likable, intelligent Farebrother, but Bulstrode intends to wield his influence to give the post to his own man, the sanctimonious, conservative Mr. Tyke. Farebrother urges Lydgate to side with Bulstrode on the issue of the chaplaincy, arguing that it is a political necessity if he hopes to play a role in running the hospital. Although Lydgate at first resolves to support Farebrother, he ultimately realizes that crossing Bulstrode might prove disastrous for his career, and he decides to endorse Tyke.

Following their marriage, Dorothea and Casaubon honeymoon in Rome, where they run into Ladislaw. Casaubon spends his days researching his book, while Dorothea begins to realize the magnitude of her decision to marry. She soon develops a friendship with Ladislaw, who finds that he admires her intelligence and openness. As they become closer, Ladislaw speaks more directly to Dorothea, telling her bluntly that her marriage to Casaubon won't make her happy and that her piety is excessive. Meanwhile, Casaubon becomes jealous of their burgeoning friendship and contrives ways to keep them apart.

Back in Middlemarch, Fred's situation worsens after he rashly decides to use his loan to buy a racehorse that turns out to be lame. As Fred's relations with Mary Garth and her family deteriorate, he suddenly contracts scarlet fever. Fred's parents become angry with the family doctor, Mr. Wrench, for failing to detect the illness and turn to Lydgate for Fred's care. The tension between the two doctors becomes a topic of widespread gossip, sparking debates over the value of new medicine and the importance of loyalty and tradition.

In January, Dorothea and Casaubon return to Middlemarch, where they settle into a loveless married life. As the rift between them widens, Casaubon becomes ill. Dorothea asks her uncle to write to Ladislaw to tell him not to come back to Middlemarch, fearing his presence will exacerbate Casaubon's condition. Mr. Brooke has developed a liking for Ladislaw, however, and instead he invites the young man to write for his new newspaper. During this period Celia becomes engaged to Chettam, while Lydgate and Rosamond move closer to marriage, in spite of Lydgate's resistance. Their imminent union becomes a subject of discussion throughout the town, a factor that further compromises Lydgate's will, and he eventually proposes. The marriage proves disastrous, especially for Lydgate, who soon finds himself forced to take on enormous debt in order to provide Rosamond with the bourgeois comforts she demands, at fatal cost to his own career.

At around this time, Mr. Featherstone dies, inciting speculation about his will. His various descendents in the town expect to inherit substantial wealth; most desperate among them is Fred, who views the large sum he expects to receive as the solution to all his problems. They are shocked when they find out that the will gives everything to Featherstone's illegitimate son, the mysterious Mr. Rigg. Rigg settles into Stone Court with his alcoholic stepfather, Mr. Raffles, and immediately begins to involve himself in town affairs. It emerges that Rigg has had shady business dealings with Bulstrode in the past, a fact he intends to use to blackmail Bulstrode.

At the same time, Casaubon's health deteriorates further. Intensely jealous, he secretly revises his will to stipulate that Dorothea will inherit his assets only if she agrees not to marry Will Ladislaw.

As the novel progresses, themes of disappointment and failure push to the foreground. Lydgate finds increasing resistance among the townspeople to his new hospital, largely because of deep-seated resentment against Bulstrode; Lydgate fails to raise the money he needs to operate the hospital properly, further straining a financial situation already burdened by Rosamond's demands for luxury. Ladislaw encourages Mr. Brooke to run for Parliament, but Brooke's political activism agitates the citizens of Middlemarch, in part because his outspokenness seems inappropriate in a man of his stature but also because his views run contrary to the more conservative leanings of the town, which is predominantly Tory. Ladislaw eventually becomes disillusioned with Brooke's arrogance, and the young man begins to question his involvement with the newspaper. Though Ladislaw and Dorothea find their affection for each other deepening, it is impossible to express themselves openly, as Dorothea's pained relationship with Casaubon weighs on her. When Casaubon dies, Dorothea goes to live with her sister and Chettam, where she discovers the truth about her husband's will. Dorothea is deeply hurt by his stipulation on her inheritance, and the last strand of her emotional bond to him breaks. As she ponders life as a widow, she begins to contemplate her relationship with Ladislaw; they are not able to express their feelings clearly, however, and their struggles to understand each other continue.

Toward the story's conclusion, Eliot begins to reveal the ultimate consequences of her characters' actions. Lydgate, increasingly alienated from the townspeople and overwhelmed by his debts, finds his name linked with Bulstrode's in a scandal involving the death of Rigg's father, Mr. Raffles; although Lydgate is innocent, his reputation as a doctor is ruined. In the midst of her husband's struggles, an unsympathetic Rosamond becomes disenchanted and begins to make overtures toward Ladislaw. Although Ladislaw is clearly not interested, Dorothea discovers them together, deepening her mistrust of Will. Bulstrode, weary of the disdain of his neighbors, decides to leave Middlemarch for good. In the novel's final chapters, the transformation of Dorothea's character becomes apparent: having suffered disappointment in both her marriage and her career ideals, she has gained a clear knowledge of her own weaknesses, as well as of her strengths. At the same time, her empathy for others, particularly Lydgate, Ladislaw, and Rosamond, has given her insight into human nature, further bolstering her resolve to determine the course of her own life. At the end of the novel, Dorothea and Will marry, and Dorothea discovers happiness in exerting a small, but positive, impact on the lives of the townspeople.

MAJOR THEMES

Middlemarch examines the struggle between the individual and the larger social forces that drive modern society. Throughout the work, Eliot elucidates a number of essential dichotomies entrenched in community life: between ideal and reality, ambition and ability, love and pragmatism. The novel's historical context bolsters these themes; set amidst the intense debates surrounding the emerging reform movement of the 1830s, the novel illustrates the minute workings of political and social change by focusing on the day-to-day life of average English citizens. In the provincial town of Middlemarch, backwardness manifests itself in people's reactions against progress, whether scientific, social, or political: many inhabitants of Middlemarch view Lydgate's medical talent with suspicion, in spite of his success treating difficult cases; Mr. Brooke's involvement with the reform movement provokes the ire of a number of his acquaintances. Indeed, the process of reform, increasingly prominent throughout England during the 1830s, threatens the status quo in Middlemarch, rousing the residents' instincts to preserve their traditional ways.

Middlemarchers' attitudes are further shaped by personal biases and long-standing feuds, and emotional factors shape their decisions more than rationality. The town's citizens refuse to donate money to Lydgate's new hospital because of his association with Bulstrode, even though his skill as a doctor is unparalleled. These attitudes continually complicate the efforts of Lydgate, Mr. Brooke, and Bulstrode to implement positive change in the community. Conversely, the egotism of characters like Lydgate and Casaubon also proves an obstacle to their ambition. Although Lydgate possesses a prodigious medical mind, his overinflated sense of his own importance to the field ultimately becomes a distraction, effectively hampering his efforts to attain positive results. In this sense, Eliot suggests, ideals of truth and goodness, though pure in the abstract, are inevitably tainted by human weakness.

CRITICAL RECEPTION

Middlemarch was widely reviewed upon its original publication. Most early critiques of the novel focused on the authenticity and intelligence of Eliot's portrayal of English country life. One prominent early reviewer was Henry James. Reflecting on the centrality of ideas in Eliot's narrative, as well as on the book's loose structure and vague plot, James questioned whether *Mid-*

dlemarch could even be classified as a novel; while he had high praise for the work's details and observations, he described it as an "indifferent whole" and "too copious a dose of pure fiction." Few commentators have agreed with James's assessment, and for more than a century *Middlemarch* has held a preeminent position in scholarship devoted to the novel form. Writing in the 1880s, Mathilde Blind compared Eliot's unconventional plot to a "panorama" that offered a full view of the rich landscape of English life. A number of critics have devoted studies to analyzing Dorothea's character. Valerie Wainwright examined Dorothea's moral stature in the novel, while John Kucich argued that Dorothea's selflessness is in fact a manifestation of sexual repression. Questions of Eliot's narrative approach have played a central role in *Middlemarch* criticism. While some scholars, notably George Steiner in 1955, argued that the work fails on a technical level, later commentators identified an intricate, and highly original, method behind the novel's apparent lack of structure. John L. Tucker has noted a tension inherent in Eliot's style between traditional novelistic techniques and the analytical, historical approach she takes to her major themes. Tucker views this tension as an expression of Eliot's ambivalence toward the novel form in general while arguing that it represents a significant innovation in fictional prose. Since the 1970s a number of feminist readings of the novel have emerged, examining issues of female identity as they are manifest in Dorothea's character, as well as in Eliot's role as a woman novelist.

PRINCIPAL WORKS

The Life of Jesus, Critically Examined [translator; as Marian Evans] (essay) 1846

The Essence of Christianity [translator; as Marian Evans] (essay) 1854

*Scenes of Clerical Life. 2 vols. (novel) 1858

Adam Bede (novel) 1859

The Mill on the Floss (novel) 1860

Silas Marner, the Weaver of Raveloe (novel) 1861

Romola (novel) 1863

Felix Holt, the Radical (novel) 1866

The Spanish Gypsy: A Poem (poetry) 1868

Middlemarch: A Study of Provincial Life (novel) 1871-72

The Legend of Jubal and Other Poems (poetry) 1874

Daniel Deronda (novel) 1876

The Works of George Eliot. 24 vols. (essays, novels, poetry, criticism, and prose) 1878-85

Impressions of Theophrastus Such (essays) 1879

The George Eliot Letters. 9 vols. (letters) 1954-78

Essays of George Eliot (essays) 1963

**This and all of Eliot's other novels were originally published serially in magazines.

CRITICISM

***Quarterly Review* (review date January and April 1873)**

SOURCE: Review of *Middlemarch: A Study of Provincial Life,* by George Eliot. *Quarterly Review* 134, no. 268 (January and April 1873): 336-69.

[*In the following excerpts, the reviewer critiques what he sees as dogmatism and "despondency" in the novel, suggesting that Eliot's emphasis on serious moral themes detracts from the book's value as entertainment.*]

George Eliot is clearly very susceptible to the leadings of philosophical and physical speculations; and she, under the promptings of her scientific interests, once did very nearly lose her artistic perception and her whole capacity for unbiassed observation and statement. *Felix Holt* was a failure. Its perusal led many to fear that its author had passed the zenith of her fame. One could scarcely avoid overlooking its frequent beauties to remember particularly its faults. . . .

Middlemarch rehabilitates George Eliot. 'L'esprit,' it was happily said, 'a sa pudeur comme la beauté,' and our author has quickly discerned and repaired her error. Not that there is in *Middlemarch* any repudiation of principles, which, we need not say, we should have been very glad to see her shake off altogether, but there is no unfair or inartistic prominence given to them; she has her accustomed and conscientious moderation, if, indeed, there does not appear now and again something like the implied acknowledgment that, after all, the system remains for her undiscovered which can furnish any useful key to the riddles of the universe. Nevertheless, we may look upon *Middlemarch* as the most remarkable work of the ablest of living novelists, and, considered as a study of character, as unique, without being blind to the existence in it of evident and even glaring defects.

First among these defects, and more conspicuous, we think, in *Middlemarch* than in any of her previous novels, is a certain want of enthusiasm in the writer, which tells very seriously upon the reader, on behalf of the narrative she has to relate. She does not write, like the great names among her predecessors, for the sake of the story, she feels none of the zest with which, in some degree Dickens and Thackeray, in greater degree Fielding and Goldsmith, above all, Scott, lose themselves in the current on which toss the chances of their heroes, and into which the strained attention of their readers is absorbed. George Eliot comes to novel-writing from strange schooling for a writer of novels. It is always the motive of action which interests her more than the effect, it is only her love for her characters which induces her to follow them through the weariness of their lives.

She wants altogether Scott's elasticity, expansiveness, and exuberance. He is going to fascinate, to transport his reader; it shall be a tale of real life, which shall at the same time cast an ideal and brightening ray upon the lives of those who read it; the exact costume of the period, the exact copy of the landscape shall be caught, but so shall the airy legendary charm which first lured the novelist to the theme; there shall be some freak of fortune, there shall be some fear of fate; he is happy in the prospects, he revels in the progress of the plot, his impatience equals that of the most impulsive among his audience to arrive at and to enjoy the last chapter. And those old-fashioned and simple novels were more perfect and complete as works of art. They gratified and invigorated; one went from them as from the contemplation of some classic example of Greek statuary, or of some well-preserved painting by a serene Venetian master with a delightful sensation of improved taste and satisfied fancy. But George Eliot has none of Walter Scott's passion for, to use his own phrase, his 'occupation as a romancer.' *Middlemarch* will leave all of us, in greater or less measure, restless and distressed. There has been no hero, there has been no romance, there has been no last chapter; the 'finale' repeats the sad note of the 'prelude.'

Again, the authoress is much too eager, in and out of season, to point her moral and to enforce upon her readers certain particular views concerning the great problems of life. Archbishop Whately observed, in one of the earlier numbers of this *Review*, 'Any direct attempt at moral teaching, and any attempt whatever to give scientific information will, we fear, unless managed with the utmost discretion, interfere with what, after all, is the immediate and peculiar object of the novelist, as of the poet, *to please.*'[1] The inclinations he well and wisely censured are far too apparent in *Middlemarch.* We could have accepted Lydgate's scientific education and professional aims on trust. The long explanations of his desire to follow out the discoveries of M. Bichat, and to ascertain 'what was the primitive tissue,' and the disquisitions and meditations upon true and false methods of medical treatment, are tedious in the extreme. It is in a scientific essay, not in a novel, that such a passage as the following should have been placed:—

> That great Frenchman (Bichat) first carried out the conception that living bodies, fundamentally considered, are not associations of organs which can be understood by studying them first apart, and then, as it were, federally; but must be regarded as consisting of certain primary webs or tissues, out of which the various organs— brain, heart, lungs, and so on—are compacted, as the various accommodations of a house are built up in various proportions of wood, iron, stone, brick, zinc, and the rest, each material having its peculiar composition and proportions. No man, one sees, can understand and estimate the entire structure or its parts—what are its frailties and what its repairs, without knowing the nature of the materials. And the conception wrought

out by Bichat, with his detailed study of the different tissues, acted necessarily on medical questions as the turning of gas-light would on a dim oil-lit street, showing new connections and hitherto hidden facts of structure which must be taken into account in considering the symptoms of maladies and the actions of medicaments.

—ii. pp. 263, 264

Here is a sentence, which could scarcely be more obscure; we have vainly sought its veiled meaning:—

> These kinds of inspiration Lydgate regarded as rather vulgar and vinous compared with the imagination that reveals subtle actions inaccessible by any sort of lens, but tracked in that outer darkness through long pathways of necessary sequence by the inward light which is the last refinement of energy, capable of bathing even the ethereal atoms in its ideally illuminated space.

—ii. p. 295

And the ordinary narrative, in its struggle after conciseness, gets sometimes to look like an inexplicable verbal puzzle:—

> What could two men, so different from each other, see in this "brown patch," as Mary called herself? It was certainly not her plainness that attracted them (and let all plain young ladies be warned against the dangerous encouragement given them by society to confide in their want of beauty). A human being, in this aged nation of ours is a very wonderful whole, the slow creation of long interchanging influences; and charm is the result of two such wholes, the one loving and the one loved.

—iv. p. 341

Also we must mention a far more serious blemish, the repetitions of which, if we were to cite them, would fill and, we regret to have to add, would sully many a page. There is an acerbity about her satire with a studied flippancy about her diction, when she chooses to misrepresent amiable weakness and even religious faith, which will have startled and shocked many gentle and candid souls, and which is altogether indefensible in a writer of fiction, who makes personages in order to malign them, and has the whole domain of thought and language to ransack for characters and for expressions.

Further, the humour of *Middlemarch* strikes us as both less independent and less natural than was the case in the earlier books. Not only in the general management of her humorous personages in this work, but even in the verbal construction and in the cadence of continuous bits of description, there is noticeable a resemblance to what we may, we hope without irreverence, term the tricks and mannerisms of the greatest of our recent humourists.

> In the large wainscoted parlour, too, there were constantly pairs of eyes on the watch and own relatives eager to be "sitters up." Many came, lunched and de-

parted, but Brother Solomon, and the lady who had been Jane Featherstone for twenty-five years before she was Mrs. Waule, found it good to be there every day for hours, without other calculable occupation than that of observing the cunning Mary Garth (who was so deep that she could be found out in nothing) and giving occasional dry wrinkly indications of crying—as if capable of torrents in a wetter season—at the thought that they were not allowed to go into Mr. Featherstone's room.

—iii. 150, 1

This, for instance, is a passage, admirable in its way, but clearly, as it seems to us, in the manner of Charles Dickens. And throughout *Middlemarch* George Eliot's wit shows itself rather in the quaint working out of detail than in those spicy, epigrammatic sayings, which gave so much pungency and spirit to her former writings. Thus Mr. Brooke, who at first promised so well, degenerates sadly. He might have been rendered equal to one of Thackeray's charming old gentlemen, but he sinks into a vexatious and infelicitous bore, drawn from Dickens's models, and not first-rate after his kind, for we doubt if even Dickens would have made him reiterate himself so often and labour so hard to become, through the simple absence of originality, an original. We had been informed, quite at the beginning of the first volume (i. p. 58), that Mr. Brooke speaks not 'with any intention;' but 'from his usual tendency to say what he had said before;' we have been much surprised, that the authoress should have thought it necessary to publish, as we vaguely surmise, the bulk of his conversations during several years. We are sorry—and Mr. Brooke shall help us to a phrase—'that she couldn't put the thing better, couldn't put it better, *beforehand, you know.*' (i. p. 63)

We have already praised the structure of the book, and, as a framework to character, we could not well overpraise it, and yet we confess to a suspicion that there has been a change of plot in the course of composition; that the story, as originally conceived, was to have concluded with more startling and exciting incidents (cf. i. 164), but that the author found a less painful narrative sufficient for the analysis of the moral and intellectual characteristics of Lydgate and Dorothea, and dispensed, accordingly, with the more terrible trial, involving more visible and widespread disaster, which had been designed for them.

That inconsequence and incompleteness in *Middlemarch* and its personages, to which we have already made reference, baffles and, we might say, defies criticism. What is the lesson of this book, what its conclusion, not that verbal one on the last page, but the logical inference, when reading is done, and judgment would settle itself? Why must Dorothea marry Casaubon, endow Farebrother, restore Lydgate, on her way to provide and embellish a home for—Ladislaw? Why

should Lydgate and Dorothea be no wiser and better, why should author and reader be no wiser and better, at the end of the story than at the beginning? And can we have more hope for Lydgate's (and Rosamund's) sons than for him—for Dorothea's (and Ladislaw's) daughters than for her? Are we soberly and seriously told to see the whole rich round of private and public life through the spectacles of the malicious gossip, who points to the ill-assorted marriage-column as index, compendium, and supplement of all the rest? There is a pent-up outcry against society throughout the book, which should, anyhow, have made itself articulate. What is George Eliot's new Providence, what her ideal training for scientific men and emotional women? Towards what in earth and heaven does she beckon us on?

We must sum up. Assuredly, unless we have misread this book altogether, it, at all events, is not written as by a person with a mission, who desires converts, plans a Utopia, preaches new dogmas. About none of her other writings was there such a profound despondency. Truly it would be the most melancholy and forlorn historical situation (if actual and historical it were), that in which a reflective reader, rising from a study of George Eliot, might be inclined to place modern society, though, all the while, he would hardly be able to make out to himself how far his hopeless mood had grown directly out of the words of his author or out of his own musings.

We repeat, and lay all possible stress upon, our protest. It is not the moral nor is it the artistic purpose of a work of fiction, (or indeed of sound literature at all) to produce this state of mind and to invite such afterthoughts.

Note

1. See *Quarterly Review,* vol. xxiv. [October 1820/January 1821] p. 358.

***London Times* (review date 7 March 1873)**

SOURCE: Review of *Middlemarch: A Study of Provincial Life,* by George Eliot. *London Times* (7 March 1873): 3-4.

[*In the following review, the critic examines the novel's characterizations, prose style, and major themes. The author expresses high praise for Eliot's insights into English provincial life, observing that the everyday concerns and habits of her characters are "profoundly identical with the issues and mysteries of human life."*]

For a year and more the reading world was kept in suspense while *Middlemarch* appeared in monthly or bi-monthly numbers. According to custom on such high occasions, it was served out a few chapters at a time, and readers were expected to accept with thankfulness the portion vouchsafed to them, to read it, and to go about their business with the equanimity of the Sultan in the *Arabian Nights,* who, instead of threatening to cut off Scheherazade's head if she did not immediately finish her story, was content to wait till the time came round when the watchful sister, whom we may interpret to mean the publisher, suggested that it should be continued. We confess that our patience was not quite so Oriental; but, now that we have the whole book in our hands, we forgive Messrs. Blackwood for tantalizing us, and we feel that the splendid novel which was able to keep us interested for so many months is at least as great a treat in the second reading as in the first. Knowing the story as a whole, we can now begin to study it in every part. There is a new delight in the close observation of its admirable art, in the full understanding of its weighty sentences. It is a luxury to pause upon each passage of fine, well-woven English, never a mere web of words. We do not now look towards the end, wondering whether this or that will happen, but we search the pages for riches we have missed. There are few novels in the language which will repay reading over again so well as *Middlemarch.*

Its name is taken from the town in and about which its scenes are laid. It is "a study of provincial life," and the local colouring, the flavour of the soil of a midland county, is imparted to places and people, to life and manners, with strange felicity and fidelity. Yet these four volumes, as we need hardly say, though provincial in the outward form of their story, have depths and meanings "of the widest" interest. Under George Eliot's pen a few square miles of fields and villages become the world. The game we watch may be played upon the checkers of a small board, but we are conscious all the while that its problems are profoundly identical with the issues and mysteries of human life. The nominal stakes are the fortunes of a few country people, but the pieces stand proxy for the destinies of humanity. With the exception of a short digression, which takes us to Rome for a few chapters, the story never stirs from the isolated life of a provincial neighbourhood about the time of the passing of the first Reform Bill, before railways had broken down the barriers and disturbed the traditions of rural existence. The social formation of Middlemarch, a town of some trade and manufacture, is laid bare in a complete section cut clean from summit to base of its ancient stratifications. From Viney, the hearty, hospitable mayor, with his warehouse, well-spread table, bluff manner, and coursing tastes; Bulstrode, the evangelical banker, worldly and money-getting, but tormented into charity and philanthropy as with a scourge of small cords by religious nervousness and by the memories of a questionable past; Lydgate, the young doctor, enamoured of science and full of a fine enthusiasm for research and discovery, whose wings

are gradually weighted to the ground by the cost of supporting a wife—from these we are gradually conducted down through layers of lawyers, auctioneers, horse-dealers, and the like, even to good Mrs. Dollop, landlady of the Tankard in Slaughter-lane, who, in racily characteristic phrase, throws her weight into the opposition to Lydgate and his new hospital, in which people were to be allowed to die, if not, indeed, to be actually poisoned, for the sake of cutting them up, without saying with your leave or by your leave—"a poor tale for a doctor, who, if he was good for anything, should know what was the matter with you before you died, and not want to pry into your inside after you were gone." But it is in the country, even more than in the town, that George Eliot finds the chief persons of her story. Mr. Brooke, the altogether original and inimitable squire of Tipton Grange, is a man "of miscellaneous opinions," who all his life had been in the habit "of taking too much in the form of ideas," who had tried everything in turn, had, as he says of himself, "taken in all the new ideas at one time, human perfectibility now," but had seen "that it would not do," and had "pulled up" before he had got too far on any of the fifty different roads on which he had started at full gallop. Cadwallader, his neighbour, "the large-lipped, easy rector" of Freshitt, well says of him that "Brooke is a very good fellow, but pulpy; he will run into any mould, but he won't keep shape." His portrait is perfectly and thoroughly painted, and, though less elaborately finished, that of his friend Sir James Chettam, the prim and honourable country baronet, ordering his conduct by a narrow but upright code of social requirements and family honour, is scarcely less admirable and life-like. With all their crotchets these two are thorough gentlemen, as well as marvellously clear pictures of human nature. Casaubon, the rich rector of Lowick, is another masterly painting. All his life he had been busy among his books, collecting notes for a Key to all Mythologies, "chewing a end of erudite mistake about Cush and Mizraim," till, when he began to be about 50 years of age, it occurred to him to take a wife, just "to adorn the remaining quadrant of his course, and be a little moon that would cause hardly a calculable perturbation." This wife is the woman upon whom the interest of the story centres. However out of place as the Rev. Edward Casaubon's satellite, she is well entitled to be the heroine of the book, for a female character more nobly conceived, and executed with art at once more thorough and more exalted, is not to be found even in the whole gallery of George Eliot's novels. She and her sister Celia, who is more of a young lady, and cannot understand Dorothea's enthusiasm, thinking her motives and scruples "like spilt needles, making one afraid of treading, sitting down, or even eating," are nieces to Mr. Brooke, and live with their uncle and guardian at Tipton Grange. Celia's life and love affairs settle themselves easily, for on Sir James failing to win Dorothea she soon becomes Lady Chettam, but Dorothea's troubles are the chief pillars of the story from first to last. There is also Fred Vincy, the mayor's son, a sanguine, rather nerveless young man, full of good feeling and easy selfishness, and Mary Garth, whose sweet, yet sturdy, temperament is delineated with infinite finish and charm. The relations of these two are one of the "love problems" of the book, most admirably worked out, and set in a frame of minor characters. The elder Garth and Peter Featherstone, an old man from whom Fred has expectations, belong to this group.

In reading **Middlemarch,** as in George Eliot's other stories, nothing strikes us more than the topographical power, if we may so call it, of her writing. She bestows upon the places the same attention she bestows upon persons, and the pictures of a county town and a country side created in the imagination of the reader are no less clear and distinct than the pictures of the men and women with whom they are peopled. This "bump of locality" in her genius encircles the persons of the story with a background and scenery the colour and perspective of which double the reality of the drama. By frequent touches, rather than by detailed descriptions, the arrangement and distances of streets and roads, the look of fields and buildings, the relative positions of villages and hamlets, are conveyed to us, so that before we have got far in the novel we are able to find our way from Middlemarch to Lowick, and from Lowick to Freshitt, and have not the bewildering feeling of being taken blind-folded from place to place. The face of the country becomes familiar to us, till we know what sort of things they are which "make the gamut of joy in landscape to midland-bred souls—the things they toddled among, or perhaps learned by heart standing between their father's knees, while he drove leisurely." All this is done without long passages of description; for instance, is not the hamlet of Frick perfectly well known to us when we are told that there "a watermill and some stone-pits made a centre of slow, heavy-shouldered industry?" Clearness in all things is the great characteristic of George Eliot's writing. This is a main cause why no two pictures of the midland life she has so often drawn are the least uninteresting or the least alike, though it would seem on the surface that dull county towns, dull country squires and clergymen must be all uninteresting and all alike. The truth is that squires and rural clergymen are no more fashioned after a traditional type than the rest of mankind. At a little distance every one is like his neighbour, but if you approach closely you perceive an infinite variety. It is just this power of approaching closely to human nature which is the hidden secret we call genius, and which enables George Eliot to construct a story full of novelty and interest out of materials which seem commonplace, and have been used a thousand times by her and others. Nothing can more resemble the course of life than the manner in which the various persons have at first their

separate existences, but are gradually thrown together, their lives, like different streams, falling into the river of the story as it flows to the sea. It is thus only at the close of the last volume, when the interest of most novels collapses like a bubble, that we find how perfect a work of art **Middlemarch** is. For long we do not gather how the circle of Rosamond Vincy's life can possibly touch that of Dorothea Brooke's, yet, before the book is done, they approach and interest each other naturally and inevitably, and the contact determines the course of the plot at its most critical juncture. We give the following extract as bearing upon this point, and as an exposition of the social philosophy of the novel, full of fine thought and observation, embalmed in a stately style:—

> Certainly nothing at present could seem much less important to Lydgate than the turn of Miss Brooke's mind, or to Miss Brooke than the qualities of the woman who had attracted this young surgeon. But any one watching keenly the stealthy convergence of human lots sees a slow preparation of effects from one life on another, which tells like a calculated irony on the indifference or the frozen stare with which we look at our unintroduced neighbour. Destiny stands by sarcastic with our *dramatis personæ* folded in her hand.
>
> Old provincial society had its share of this subtle movement; had not only its striking downfalls, its brilliant young professional dandies, who ended by living up an entry with a drab and six children for their establishment, but also those less marked vicissitudes which are constantly shifting the boundaries of social intercourse, and begetting new consciousness of interdependence. Some slipped a little downward, some got higher footing; people denied aspirates, gained wealth, and fastidious gentlemen stood for boroughs; some were caught in political currents, some in ecclesiastical, and perhaps found themselves surprisingly grouped in consequence; while a few personages or families that stood with rocky firmness amid all this fluctuation, were slowly presenting new aspects in spite of solidity, and altering with the double change of self and beholder. Municipal town and rural parish gradually made fresh threats of connexion; gradually, as the old stocking gave way to the savings bank, and the worship of the solar guinea became extinct; while squires and baronets, and even lords who had once lived blamelessly afar from the civic mind, gathered the faultiness of closer acquaintanceship. Settlers, too, came from distant counties, some with an alarming novelty of skill, others with an offensive advantage in cunning. In fact, much the same sort of movement and mixture went on in old England as we find in older Herodotus, who also, in telling what has been, thought it well to take a woman's lot for his starting point; though Io, as a maiden apparently beguiled by attractive merchandise, was the reverse of Miss Brooke, and in this respect, perhaps, bore more resemblance to Rosamond Vincy, who had excellent taste in costume, with that nymph-like figure and pure blondness which give the largest range to choice in the flow and colour of drapery.

The first and last pages of the novel seem to give us the clue of a purpose, not obtrusively put forward in the body of the story. Yet it must not be supposed that the lustre of this gain-like work is concentrated to one point. Dorothea is the chief heroine, and so far the lesson of her fate is the moral of the tale; but its variety and interest are not subordinated to a single meaning, though a meaning may be expressed at the beginning and the end. The "Prelude" strikes a key-note by reminding us of that early episode in the life of St. Theresa, when the little girl, hand-in-hand with her still smaller brother, toddled out from rugged Avila to seek martyrdom in the country of the Moors. They were turned back from their great resolve "by domestic reality in the shape of uncles," but their child-pilgrimage was a fit beginning.

> Theresa's passionate, ideal nature demanded an epic life. What were many-volumed romances of chivalry, and the social conquests of a brilliant girl to her? Her flame quickly burned up that light fuel, and, fed from within, soared after some illimitable satisfaction.

Dorothea is "a later-born St. Theresa," but the epic life she attempts turns out, at least for a considerable part of it, "a tragic failure." Her vague longings lead her to make very definite mistakes, the chief of which is the marrying of an elderly pedant out of enthusiasm for his musty learning and superannuated researches. She is nevertheless a noble woman, and her blundering life is held up to us as due to "the inconvenient indefiniteness with which the Supreme Power has fashioned the natures of women," permitting exceptions to the general type, for whom the common social lot is not enough.

> Here and there a cygnet is reared uneasily among the ducklings in the brown pond, and never finds the living stream in fellowship with its own oary-footed kind. Here and there is born a St. Theresa, foundress of nothing, whose loving heartbeats and sobs after an unattained goodness tremble off and are dispersed among hindrances, instead of centring in some long-recognizable deed.

There is a certain school which will find satisfaction in thinking that Dorothea's story involves some special impeachment of the fitness of the present female lot. We do not think that this is at all intended, and if it be intended it is certainly not justified. George Eliot gives us a noble portrait and an affecting history of a woman who nearly spoilt her life by attempting to rise above her opportunities, but her failures and mistakes are not due to the fact of her being a woman, but are simply those which belong to the common lot of human life. Just as she married a husband who did not suit her, so a man may marry a wife who does not suit him. The mistakes which arose out of her vague longings, her desire "to shape her thought and deed in noble agreement," were not one whit sillier or more lamentable than those which a young man may fall into under the like circumstances. The fetters she were are too common to humanity, but the weight of them is felt far more by men than by women. Youths more often than girls long after

a life of "far resonant action" and find it not; unsatisfied ambitions are masculine rather than female ills; and, as a matter of fact, women attain contentment and their ideal far oftener than men. Yet, while we demur to any special application of the story of this new St. Theresa, we allow that its pathos and force would be half lost if she were not a woman. In her portrait, womanhood, beauty, and the ardour of a tender, yet masculine, spirit are wrought together with thorough art, and her mistakes, her endurance, her failures, and her triumphs must touch and thrill and fascinate us with a double power, because they are those of a woman. The reader is strangely attracted to this young creature, who knew Pascal and Jeremy Taylor by heart, to whom "the destinies of mankind, seen by the light of Christianity, made the solicitudes of female fashion appear an occupation for Bedlam;" whose soul and eyes were so full of candour, who was possessed by such a frank ardour, such a generous anxiety to do what was right, such a passion for truth and justice in all things, even when the terrible oppression of the adverse circumstances of her life was crushing her spirit. She is drawn with a unity of conception all the more perfect because of the faults with which her physical and mental beauty are slightly and subtly touched. That she should be somewhat short-sighted, and that she should be cold to the influences of art, wandering careless through the galleries of the Vatican, though Rome was not without its "gigantic broken revelations," are traits which seem perfectly in keeping directly they are mentioned. She begins by worshipping her scholastic husband, and we are finely shown how, under the cold contact of his formal nature, her feelings changed "with the secret motion of a watchhand from what they had been in her maiden dream." Many of the finest passages in the novel relate to her. Of these is the account of her interview with Lydgate about her husband's heart disease, wonderful for its concentrated pathos, and for its quick and subtle pursuit of thought and feeling through Dorothea's mind. Not less masterly is the analysis of her feelings and the description of her conduct towards the withered scholar, which ends the second volume; or, in the fourth volume, and after Casaubon's death, the description of her behaviour upon finding Rosamond and Ladislaw together, of "the great draught of scorn" which sustained her through the day, and of the reaction which followed when she was shut up alone in her room:—

> Then came the hour in which the waves of suffering shook her too thoroughly to leave any power of thought. She could only cry in loud whispers, between her sobs, after her lost belief which she had planted and kept alive from a very little seed since the days in Rome—after her lost joy of clinging with silent love and faith to one who, misprized by others, was worthy in her thought; after her lost woman's pride of reigning in his memory; after her sweet dim perspective of hope,

that along some pathway they should meet with un-
changed recognition, and take up the backward years
as a yesterday.

In that hour she repeated what the merciful eyes of
solitude have looked on for ages in the spiritual
struggles of man: she besought hardness and coldness
and aching weariness to bring her relief from the mysterious incorporeal might of her anguish; she lay on the
bare floor and let the night grow cold around her, while
her grand woman's frame was shaken by sobs as if she
had been a despairing child.

Perhaps the finest passage in the whole novel is the description of her second interview with Rosamond, a few
pages further on. Our limits will not suffer us to extract
it, but it must be familiar to most of our readers, and
they will agree with us that George Eliot's works do
not contain a more admirable instance of the intuitive
power which seems to guide her genius along the wind-
ings of the human mind. It would be hard, also, to match
the dramatic effectiveness of the situation, the natural
course of the dialogue, the fine tact, the tenderness and
felicity of touch and expression, the simplicity and
power of the whole writing of the chapter which at last
brings Dorothea and Ladislaw together at the end of the
book.

He was her second husband, and she married him for
love, as she had married Casaubon for learning. His
character is drawn with much care and subtlety, yet
there is a certain indistinctness about his picture; neither does he seem at all worthy of the woman he wins.
This may only be because the reader is in love with her
himself, or because George Eliot altogether declines to
allow a magnificent destiny even to Dorothea. She loses
most of her fortune by her second marriage, and though
in time Ladislaw is successful and gets into Parliament,
we feel that to the last "to love what is great, to try to
reach it, and then to fail," has been Dorothea's lot. As
Ladis law's wife she bore children, and her home was a
happy one; yet the authoress makes us feel that this was
not enough. At the beginning of her career her "great
feelings had resulted in error, her great faith in illusion," and the most that George Eliot is at last able to
say of her is that "her finely-touched spirit had still its
fine issues, though they were not widely visible. Her
full nature, like that river of which Alexander broke the
strength, spent itself in channels which had no great
name on earth."

We have left ourselves too little space to say as much
as we should like of the other characters of the book.
We should like to return to Mr. Brooke, to describe him
as he is described on the Middlemarch hustings, "with a
glass of sherry hurrying like smoke among his ideas,"
and causing him to forget his set speech, and to impro-
vise another, which did not convince the electors, but
which is far more amusing to the reader. Equally de-

lightful is his advice to Casaubon, whom the doctor had
commanded away from his books, to read *Roderick
Random* and to play at backgammon and shuttlecock,
or the melancholy and nervous "well, you're all here
you know," with which he joins Celia and Chettam and
the Cadwalladers on the lawn at Freshitt, and tells them
the unacceptable news of Dorothea's engagement to
Ladislaw, and how he had "put it strongly" to his niece,
but in vain. Neither have we said enough of Casaubon
nor of the truth and impartiality with which George
Eliot invests his feelings, narrow and dried up and unreasonable as they are, with dignity, and his lot with pathos. We see "his black figure, with hands behind and
head bent forward pacing the walk, where the dark yew
trees gave him a mute companionship in melancholy,
and the little shadows of bird or leaf that fleeted across
the isles of sunlight stole along in silence as in the presence of a sorrow," for he knew that there was death at
his heart, and that the Key to all Mythologies was
doomed never to be finished. The course of his creeping malady is traced with great effect and accuracy;
and, indeed, nothing is more remarkable through the
book than George Eliot's medical knowledge. This appears most when she writes of Lydgate, though even at
other times her mind betrays a singular scientific turn,
often, manifested in some clear comparison. Thus the
first quarrels of a man and wife are "a fracture of delicate crystal;" after the enforced renunciation of an ideal,
"life has to be taken upon a lower stage of expectation,
as by men who have lost their limbs," and "a vigorous
error vigorously pursued has kept the embryos of truth
a breathing;" "the quest of gold is a questioning of sub-
stances, the body of chymistry is prepared for its soul,
and Lavoisier is born." Turning from Casaubon, who
was "a believing Christian with some private, scholarly
reservations," to Bulstrode, we find a character most
complex and human, drawn with minuteness and finish,
and not to be described by a random adjective. Nothing
is more common in novels than a man whose religion is
a mask for his knavery. Bulstrode is half a saint and
half a rogue, yet he is thoroughly original. Great pains
are bestowed upon him, for one of George Eliot's characteristics is that her powers are not engrossed or exhausted by a favourite hero or heroine, but turn from
character to character, from subject to subject, with impartial case. She lays down one set of tools and takes
up another, a description of a morning at the Mayor of
Middlemarch's, and an analysis of the feelings which
tear Dorothea's soul being carved with the same grave
art. Her genius bends over all its children. Mrs. Bulstrode, her friend Mrs. Plymdale, and other "well-
meaning women, knowing very little of their own motives," are done in a series of clear vignettes. Mrs.
Bulstrode is sincerely religious, yet not unworldly, being endowed with a double "consciousness of filthy
rags and the best damask." It is a fine touch where, her
husband being disgraced for ever in Middlemarch, she

lays aside her handsome raiment and clothes herself in plain gray, feeling the pride of her life broken; and there is an inimitable page which tells in what manner "the well-meaning women" received her after the crash. Lydgate, the young doctor, oppressed by money troubles, and an unsympathetic wife, is a portrait which looks out from the canvas, firm and clear in all its lines. The heroic and common sides of his character, the paralysis creeping over his enthusiasm, the wearing out of his masculine resolve by the stubborn tenacity of Rosamond, a creature of beauty and seeming softness, and yet hard as iron—all this is wrought with never-failing art. The family of the Garths is a creation wondrously natural and distinct; upon this group the author seems to labour and to linger with an especial love. Caleb Garth is a portrait marvellous in its fine minuteness, and one of the most charming passages in the novel is that which describes Mrs. Garth making pastry while she hears her children their lessons. Another scene, the power of which is owing to its sheer truth and simplicity, is that which shows us Mary Garth by Featherstone's death-bed; and the funeral and will-reading which the old miser, having a vision of "gratification inside his coffin," had arranged for himself, are inimitably described. The character of Farebrother, resembling "those southern landscapes which seem divided between natural grandeur and social slovenliness," is a fine study of human nature, and so also, though less elaborate, is that of Cadwallader, his brother clergyman, who in exciting times could "talk politics with a trout-fisher's dispassionateness;" nor must we omit Vincy, the Middlemarch Mayor, whose spirits were raised by the "seasonable occurrence of the felicitous word 'demise', which made old Featherstone's death assume a merely legal aspect, so that he could tap his snuffbox over it and be jovial," and who counter-ordering the wine at dinner when his son took a fever, "added emphatically 'I shall drink brandy,' as much as to say that this was not an occasion for firing with blank cartridges." The novel a bounds with minor characters, such as Mrs. Taft, "who was always counting stitches, and, gathering her information in misleading fragments, caught between the rows of her knitting, had got it into her head that Mr. Lydgate was a natural son of Bulstrode's, a fact which seemed to justify her suspicions of Evangelical laymen." Even of supernumeraries who only pass across the stage once or twice in the story, and have then only a few words allotted to them, we gain an image clear as a profile cut in silhouette, or as a figure standing still in a flash of lightning.

The remarkable distinctness of George Eliot's men and women is in no small degree owing to the fine perception with which she matches some habit of body with their habit of mind. Of nearly every one in Middlemarch some phrase, gesture, manner, point of costume, or other personal characteristic is related, and stamps its image on the reader's mental retina. Some of these traits, par-

ticularly Rosamond's birdlike movement of head and neck, are so often alluded to as to become tiresome, but they all help us to form an idea of the person, Casaubon's "singsong and dignified bending," Chettam's "exactly" and little frown, Mrs. Vincy's plumage of fluttering cap ribands; the delicate play of Caleb Garth's eyebrows, and his habit of laying the tips of his fingers together when he wanted to be impressive; Dorothea's fine wrist and hand; Celia "settling her arms cosily" and the "quiet staccato" of her voice; Miss Noble's "beaver-like noises" and "small compassionate mewings;" Mrs. Garth's oddities, "which her character sustained, as a very fine wine sustains a flavour of skin"—all these are little details the art-value of which is not insignificant. George Eliot often pauses to give a touch of description. She can paint a picture at one stroke, in a single sentence—as when Brooke seats himself before the wood-fire, "which had fallen into a wondrous mass of glowing dice between the dogs," or when Dorothea walks in the "solemn glory" of an autumn afternoon, "with its long swathes of light between the far-off rows of limes, whose shadows touched each other;" and again when through the open window of the room in which Dorothea sits in angry misery there comes "the serene glory of the afternoon lying in the avenue, where the lime trees cast long shadows." Her reflective power is still greater than her descriptive, and is manifested in **Middlemarch** more often than in any other of her works. We could easily fill a column with sentences remarkable for their flashing thought or fortunate phrase:—

> Those initial chapters to the successive books of his history, in which Fielding seems to bring his arm-chair to the proscenium, and chat with us in all the lusty ease of his fine English.
>
> If we had a keen vision and feeling of all ordinary human life, it would be like hearing the grass grow and the squirrel's heart beat, and we should die of that roar which lies on the other side of silence.
>
> One can begin so many things with a new person—even begin to be a better man!
>
> To be a poet is to have a soul in which knowledge passes instantaneously into feeling, and feeling flashes back into a new organ of knowledge.
>
> One must be poor to know the luxury of giving!
>
> He was a likeable man—sweet-tempered, ready-witted, frank, without grins of suppressed bitterness, or other conversational flavours which make half of us an affliction to our friends.
>
> Our tongues are little triggers which have usually been pulled before general intentions can be brought to bear.
>
> Men and women make sad mistakes about their own symptoms, taking their vague, uneasy longings sometimes for genius, sometimes for religion, and oftener still for a mighty love.

Like Sir Walter Scott, George Eliot writes many of the mottoes to her chapters, giving us in this way short snatches of blank verse and rhyme, and once a whole little poem. These fragments have nearly all of them that depth and beauty of thought which make their author's prose so poetic, and that dry turn of phrase and difficult involutions of a keen meaning which make her verse so prosaic.

No one can close *Middlemarch* without feeling that he has read a great book. He is impressed, and, perhaps, depressed, by its cruel likeness to life; for George Eliot does not bring in the golden age even at the end of the fourth volume, and nothing happens merely in order that the curtain may fall pleasantly. We have seen how to the last circumstances "broke the strength" of Dorothea's full nature. Lydgate, who, had the author consulted the proprieties of romance and the fitness of things, should have married Dorothea, dies before his hair is gray, and Rosamond, who broke down his determination to do good work in the world, and made his life ignoble, finds what she calls "her reward" in a rich second husband. The sober happiness and length of humdrum days accorded to Fred and Mary scarcely lighten the general gray of a sky which novelists usually make it a point of honour to flood with sunshine at the final hour. *Middlemarch* is not without its passages of fun and humour, though these are much fewer and farther between than in *Adam Bede.* As a novel proper it is inferior to the earlier work; its plot is not exciting; it has not the liveliness, variety, and picturesqueness of its great predecessor. In delineation of character it gives us the same round and solid drawing; but it is its philosophical power which is it distinctive and supreme excellence. On every page things small and subtle are seized and fixed under the microscope. Thought and expression is everywhere exact and acute, and the explanations and solutions of moods, feelings, mental processes, and circumstances are clear and true. Through the four volumes we feel that the story moves like the forces of a General who has made all his dispositions beforehand, and has left nothing to chance. It is a thoroughly worked-out and prepared conception which is being unfolded to us page by page. We do not watch the fashioning of the plot and the modelling of the characters; we detect no second thoughts and alterations, the writing of the book has merely been as the drawing of a curtain, and work is turned and shown to us which has been finished in the mind. In her descriptions of various life George Eliot is never at fault, but seems always to speak confidently and out of a fulness of knowledge. We never feel that her writing is the clever literary work that slips from the end of a practised pen, but that it is the *bonâ fide* product of real thought and experience. Her similes and metaphors are admirable and never hackneyed. Her style is clear, and may stand for a specimen of the best written English of the present day. The sequence of her well-appointed sentences is like the march of troops; every word has a firm tread and a proud bearing as it passes before the reader's mind. The majestic effect of the whole is the result of the minutest

art, and reminds us of those ornaments discovered in Greek tombs by Signor Castellani, in which the wondrously rich effect of the leaves and beads is found to be caused by innumerable grains of gold adhering to the surface.

If we are asked, "What, then, are the faults of *Middlemarch*?" we reply that they are very secondary to its excellence. The mysteries about Ladislaw's ancestry and Bulstrode's antecedents may have a mean and common-place effect against the rich texture of better material. The drunken knave Raffles may be quite unworthy of his place in the story, and that he should use his knowledge of Bulstrode's early life to persecute the latter, and get money out of him, until Bulstrode is driven to compass his death, may be a trite device and a "poor tale," as Mrs. Dollop would say, in such a book as *Middlemarch.* We confess, also, that of some pages in the course of these four volumes we are tempted to say, as Byron said of Milton, that though sublime, they are just a little heavy, and a light-minded reader may aver that once or twice the creator of Casaubon is herself guilty of Casaubonism, and may even declare that certain passages have about them something of that "sing-song and dignified bending" which made the learned clergyman so odious to Celia. But *Middlemarch* could well afford its faults, even though they were more than these.

North American Review (review date April 1873)

SOURCE: Review of *Middlemarch: A Study of Provincial Life,* by George Eliot. *North American Review* 116, no. 239 (April 1873): 432-40.

[*In the following review, the critic applauds the universality and moral authority of Eliot's artistic vision.*]

Perhaps the first impression that forces itself upon the reader's mind after he has laid down this remarkable novel [*Middlemarch: A Study of Provincial Life*] is one of profound admiration, almost of reverence, for the mind of a writer who is able to take so comprehensive a view of life, to seize what to most of us is a knot of tangled threads, and unravel it, showing the mutual relations of people to one another, and to the circumstances which encompass them, and, while this is done with breadth of treatment, losing none of even the pettiest links which are forever serving as either clogs or aids. The book has all the multifariousness of life; the author has, as it were, created a world in which we see the diverse feelings, passions, and interests of complicated characters without the veils of self-adulation or of exaggerated distrust with which we view our own lives, or the prejudice with which we regard those of our neighbors. Ordinary terms of praise sound insipid before the excellence with which this task is done. The very truth which this writer possesses seems so like simplicity that we feel inclined to take it for granted as a *sine qua non,* which we ought to accept with as little emotion as we do the air we breathe. But however great the merit of such excellence, and in spite of its rareness, it is so obvious that we may content ourselves with this bare mention.

But it was not the author's intention merely to set before us living pictures: she aimed to tell us the story of certain sorts of human lives, which bear within themselves the elements of tragedy from the incongruity between their aspirations and the possibility of attaining them under the conditions imposed upon them by their surroundings. So much may be said of Dorothea, at least. She, we are told, is one of the "many Theresas who found for themselves no epic life wherein there was a constant unfolding of far-resonant action; perhaps only a life of mistakes, the offspring of a certain spiritual grandeur ill-matched with the meanness of opportunity; perhaps a tragic failure which found no sacred poet and sank unwept into oblivion. With dim lights and tangled circumstance they tried to shape their thought and deed in noble argument; but after all, to common eyes their struggles seemed mere inconsistency and formlessness; for these later-born Theresas were helped by no coherent social faith and order which could perform the function of knowledge for the ardently willing soul. Their ardor alternated between a vague ideal and the common yearning of womanhood; so that the one was disapproved as extravagance, and the other condemned as a lapse." It is only too probable that any woman, born with such lofty yearnings, is unlikely to have them satisfied in a state of society like that of the present time,—we need not speak now of any possibilities in the remote future of the enthusiasts,—in which girls are taught, and by no means entirely repugnantly to their nature, to modify their character and tastes to the selfish demands of men. Indeed, it is the quality of every lofty nature to fall short of its highest ideal, whether from its ignorance, due to too exalted an opinion of conflicting obstacles, or from its clashing with other lofty aims, whose supporters lack sufficient breadth of vision to have perfect sympathy with different work which may be as good, but which they do not comprehend. But the mere possession of such desires, however impossible of attainment, exalts the owner and makes the path easier for others. It is not success only which ennobles the world; it is what the people are who live in it.

Of Dorothea's two marriages—the first with a withered, sensitive, morbid scholar, who is himself more than half conscious of his failure in life, of his incompetency for the vast work he has chosen, and who finds in Dorothea a strong mind judging his own with a certain coldness, which he exaggerates into something like contempt; the

second with a young, superficially attractive, brilliant man, who leaves upon our mind (we can but record our own opinion) the impression of a light-weight—the author says: "Certainly those determining acts of her life were not ideally beautiful. They were the mixed result of young and noble impulse struggling under prosaic conditions. Among the many remarks passed on her mistakes, it was never said in the neighborhood of Middlemarch that such mistakes could not have happened if the society into which she was born had not smiled on propositions of marriage from a sickly man to a girl less than half his own age, on modes of education which make a woman's knowledge another name for motley ignorance, on rules of conduct which are in flat contradiction with its own loudly asserted beliefs. While this is the social air in which mortals begin to breathe, there will be collisions such as those in Dorothea's life, when great feelings will take the aspect of error, and great faith the aspect of illusion. For there is no creature whose inward being is so strong that it is not greatly determined by what lies outside of it."

But with regard to her married life with Mr. Casaubon, it seems to us that the author is far from leaving the impression on the reader's mind which she intended. As it was, Dorothea simply adored him; when she first made his acquaintance, she fancied she saw in him a great man whom she would be able to aid in his difficult studies, and who, from his wider experience, could help her solve the problems of life; she considered him a man who understood the loftiness of her nature, and who shared with her a devotion to all that made life noble; she felt a natural distaste for the young man who merely said, "Exactly," when she expressed her doubts; to her Mr. Casaubon was everything that was opposite to mediocrity. She was young, and perfectly inexperienced. She had seen nothing of the world. Of course she was bitterly disappointed in her married life; instead of all those merits which she had thought she saw, she found only pedantry, the sourness of a mind that is gradually coming to the certainty of its own failure, and a petty nature warped by a sensitiveness which forbade its uttering the explanation that would have done so much toward setting to rights their discordant relations. By the superiority of her mind Dorothea was a keen-eyed critic of her husband's shortcomings, and, seeing them, she felt acutely the shock of surprise at their discovery. She found him an arid recipient of even what interest she could assume with respect to his studies, while all the time she was miserably conscious of the extent of the mistake which she had made. As George Eliot says, Mr. Casaubon deserves our pity; the marriage was a great mistake, but it was a sort of mistake for which the conventionalities of society are not alone to blame. The feeling which each had for the other before marriage was a natural one; and society, or at least the small portion of it which Dorothea saw, certainly did not smile upon the match. In the face of every one she married Mr. Casaubon; and had the opposition been more violent, we may be sure that she would only have persevered the more strongly in her opinion, and have married him in defiance of every attempt to forbid her. That she would have considered glorious, yet her disappointment would have been only the greater. There are cases in which an artificial society encourages such distasteful unions, but can it be fairly said that this was one?

As to the other marriage with Ladislaw, it is not easy to make out the author's opinion, whether it is one of approval or of disapprobation. The same obscurity exists with regard to Ladislaw himself, who seems to be a favorite with the writer to an extent which hardly justifies itself to the mind of the reader. There is, at the best, a certain personal charm about him,—at least such is implied if it is not given; but, notwithstanding, there is room for some disappointment when a Theresa contents herself with the life which this marriage promised her; and this, not because marriage in itself would mar our ideal, but because one cannot help feeling a diminution of reverence for Theresas who can replace their lofty yearnings by what in this case would seem to promise such meagre consolation. If that is the solution of the question, if these loftily aspiring women can rest satisfied with the humble duties of domesticity, men certainly have no need to complain, and society may well pride itself about its eager match-making.

But even if Dorothea is happy in her second marriage, she fails in the main, so far as she had hoped to make her life a different one. She had yearned to be a Saint Theresa, and the result was far different. And here we cannot help thinking that the reader would have drawn a stronger moral if the author had not impressed upon him the comparison to be made with the saint. The book would have been impressive enough simply as a picture of life: the alleged similarity does not add to its force; for a Saint Theresa is not like a spoiled actor who spurns any but the principal *rôles*; she does not impotently yearn, but she puts her hand to the work before her without complaining of its meanness, and ennobles it by the vigor with which she does it. He alone is the truly noble character who takes the world as he finds it, and does what he has to do there without longing for the world to be made over again, when some more glorious lot may fall to his share. Every one will like Dorothea,—but for her own sake, not for any resemblance to the Spanish saint.

In Lydgate, the hero of the story, we see a much sadder failure, because what he had set before him was no vague ideal, but a very thoroughly understood, definite object,—success in his profession. He had every reason to feel confident, he knew fully the excellence of his powers and the advantage which his careful training had given him. It is by no means difficult to imagine

for him a life in which he might have easily attained the success he desired. The "commonness" of his mind, however, as George Eliot somewhat obscurely calls it, which in his case, we take it, means a confidence that what he regards as less important matters will take care of themselves and set themselves right without particular care from him, for the reason that they must be subservient to the greater things with which he occupies himself, and must necessarily adapt themselves to these nobler aims,—this commonness, we say, is the flaw which maims his whole life. While he is intellectually the finest man in the novel, his impatience of others, his lack of high-mindedness in his earlier relations with Bulstrode, his unfortunate choice of a wife, and, moreover, the very fact that he persists in loving her, and, in spite of her antagonism, treats her kindly, combine to bring down upon his head the heavy load of suffering under which he labors. The whole description of his misery is most melancholy reading. While the story is told with much relentlessness, while we see the man sink into debt, severed daily more and more from his wife; and all the time we see the absolute necessity of it, its coherency with his nature, and the mistakes it led him into, we yet feel a profound pity, and perhaps a certain opposition of feeling to the grim resemblance to life which makes the picture so impressive. A redeeming part, a bit of poetic justice (it may be called poetic, for every truly noble action bears to human eyes the stamp of poetry) is found in the scenes of Dorothea's intervention, in the first place to aid Lydgate,—to which, it will be remembered, she made up her mind without that comparison of reasons for and against, with the same feminine, confident certainty which directed all her actions,—and, again, when she visited Rosamond. That chapter and those immediately preceding it are the most beautiful in the book. Dorothea's simplicity, her confidence in right-doing being the only necessity, her resignation, which melts even Rosamond's pettiness, are wonderfully set before us. We see the contrast between the mode of action which is alone possible for so lofty-minded a person as she is, and the way in which others let themselves be overcome by circumstances. She rises superior to them here, and if, as some of her soundest critics say but which we think may be disputed, the book is written to show how character is influenced by circumstances, it should be borne in mind that the writer herself says, "It always remains true, that if we had been greater, circumstance would have been less strong against us." Can it be denied that this is a case in point? And in the matter of invention, a quality for which the novel is by no means remarkable, those scenes are certainly the most prominent. Nowhere does Dorothea so truly justify herself as here. She is not deceived by any illusion; she is free from a certain hardness, or, perhaps, more properly, a certain coldness, which we fancy is to be detected in her relation with Mr. Casaubon after she is awakened to a sense of his inferiority; her conduct is noble in its freedom from conventionality, instead of throwing open a certain opportunity for ridicule on the part of an indifferent world, as was the case with what we are told her sister used to call her "fads."

Perhaps another reason for our liking these chapters is the fact that they come after a long and depressing account of the troubles of all the people; after we have been reading of Lydgate's sordid cares, his debts, and his terrible life with Rosamond; after the grim horrors of Bulstrode's exposure and its implication of Lydgate; in fact, at the end of a long novel in which both the irony and the relentless realism of the writer have given us no relief from a feeling of profound melancholy,—a melancholy which is only the intenser from the admiration which her wonderful genius demands. Up to this point there has been no relief; so far the story has been as sad as life itself appears to us in our gloomiest hours. Dorothea's love for Ladislaw has but a slight hold upon our sympathy; the humor which the author shows so invariably in her treatment of the minor characters, as, for instance, with Trumbull, the auctioneer, in this novel, is far from relieving the intense strain which all the rest causes. Hence, when we see Dorothea's single-mindedness, her simple honesty interfering to maintain her own dignity and bringing a revelation of help to Lydgate in his sore distress, we feel keenly, to be sure, a sense of the mightiness of the tragedy, but it is all exalted into something higher than mere freedom from debt and unjust suspicion; we feel that comfort which can only come from the contemplation of a lofty action. That Dorothea finds from her visit to Rosamond that Ladislaw is and always has been true to her, is but a small matter; our real joy is due to the fact that she is true to the highest impulses of her nature, that she sees so clearly what her course should be, and that she rises above all pettiness in taking it.

It is only here that George Eliot abandons the irony which is so marked in the treatment of the other incidents of the book. It is not so much to an irony of incident that we refer; that is natural enough; and even an author who, apparently, prefers a long and even monotonous narration which shall resemble the uneventfulness of so many days of human life to an artificially rounded story where dramatic effect is sought, deserves no blame for employing what is so common in our experience, namely, the way in which events curtly and grimly belie our wishes and most reasonably formed hopes. We must allow any one who is writing a novel to employ the resources of his art; no one is less guilty of introducing the *deus ex machina* than our author; she lets the events follow one another in direct sequence; and if they seem ironical, it is because they make so clear the difference between man's expectations and his deserts. As a special instance, we would mention Bulstrode's overthrow at the moment when he seemed to

himself to have the best ground for congratulating himself upon his success. It is not to irony of this sort, however, that we would take exception, but to that irony of treatment which is shown in almost the whole of the book. It is wonderful. One must bow down with respect before the intelligence of a human being who can devise such distinct creations, breathe into them such genuine life, and meanwhile, although not without partisanship,—for why should Celia be a greater favorite with the writer than Rosamond?—should keep herself aloof from all, seeing through them, and detecting their littleness with such extraordinary acuteness. But it may be fair to consider the issue of the whole book, to weigh the impression it leaves upon us of the failure of human life, especially of the higher aims of life, and to ask ourselves if this novel attains the highest position among works of art. Not necessarily with regard to execution, though that, too, should be considered, but simply in the matter of final judgment of the book as a whole. The continual presence of this ironical spirit would incline us to give a negative answer. Irony is so barren a method, it seems so like contenting one's self with an easily attained renunciation of the endeavor to ask questions which can never be satisfactorily answered, it is so much the result of a mood, or a fashion of a time, that a comparison of it with other feelings would seem to lead to its condemnation. Not that every one who sets before us distinct problems which baffle us whenever we pause to consider the perplexities of life, is obliged to solve them any more than a man who asks difficult questions of any sort is obliged to answer them himself, nor do we demand a wilfully contrived effort to please us by a joyous ending; but it does seem to be necessary for any work of art to give us lasting pleasure, and before it can take its place among immortal works, that it should give us, not necessarily in the attractiveness of the incidents, but in the treatment, some expression of the hopefulness, of the belief in the existence of something better than what we see, which really forms so great a part of the nature of man, however often it may be overclouded by temporary gloom or even by the prevailing pessimism of a generation. While at the end of the book, as we have said, there is something to redeem the grimness of the earlier part, still it may not be impossible that these strictures may apply to the rest, which is terrible in its realism. Perhaps with the advance of man in enlightenment, idealism will disappear along with other superstitions, and the scientific spirit will demand only complete realism; but we doubt it.

As to the skill with which, in this novel, life is set nakedly before us, there can be but one opinion, nor can the irony ever be called false to itself. But as we in this country, owing to our less exact knowledge of the scenes, circumstances, and people which she describes, may possibly stand in the position of posterity, for whom much will be obscure that is now familiar or as good as familiar to those in the country where the book is written, we may prophesy a lack of interest in the future for what depends so much on the ability of the reader to stamp with his approval what he himself knows to be true. If an exact imitation of certain special modes of life is the chief claim to merit of a great part of the story, if the reader is not able to appreciate the truth he will find the interest of the delineation lacking. Still it is to be remembered that posterity makes up its own mind with but little regard for the prophecies of its forefathers, for whom it is apt to have some contempt. But then this is a rule which may work both ways. Without wishing to usurp any of the privileges of our descendants, we cannot forbear saying that many will find, or, more exactly, many have found the long episode of Featherstone less interesting than other parts; though even here it is not from any failure of the author's power, but rather from the nature of the subject. With time, much may fall into the same category which now we read with no doubt of its lastingness. However this may be, we cannot close without gladly welcoming the novel as one of the most remarkable books of one of the greatest living writers. He is a cautious critic who has left himself words fit to describe its merits. From its wonderful accuracy in depicting life, from the morality of its lesson, from the originality, keenness, and fate-like sternness of the author, we may draw the conclusion that it is a book which every one should read for a wider knowledge of the world. But is this the highest praise that a novel can receive?

Mathilde Blind (essay date 1883)

SOURCE: Blind, Mathilde. "*Felix Holt* and *Middlemarch*." In *George Eliot*, pp. 232-53. Boston: Roberts Brothers, 1883.

[*In the following excerpt, Blind briefly examines the novel's central characters. Blind also discusses the work's lack of conventional structure, comparing Eliot's depiction of English country life to a "panorama."*]

If *Felix Holt* is the most intricately constructed of George Eliot's novels, *Middlemarch,* which appeared five years afterwards, is, on the other hand, a story without a plot. In fact, it seems hardly appropriate to call it a novel. Like Hogarth's serial pictures representing the successive stages in their progress through life of certain typical characters, so in this book there is unrolled before us, not so much the history of any particular individual, as a whole phase of society portrayed with as daring and uncompromising a fidelity to Nature as that of Hogarth himself. In *Middlemarch,* English provincial life in the first half of the nineteenth century is indelibly fixed in words "holding a universe impalpable" for the apprehension and delight of the furthest

generations of English-speaking nations. Here, as in some kind of panorama, sections of a community and groups of character pass before the mind's eye. To dwell on the separate, strongly individualized figures which constitute this great crowd would be impossible within the present limits. But from the county people such as the Brookes and Chettams, to respectable middle-class families of the Vincy and Garth type, down to the low, avaricious, harpy-tribes of the Waules and Featherstones, every unit of this complex social agglomeration is described with a life-like vividness truly amazing, when the number and variety of the characters especially are considered. I know not where else in literature to look for a work which leaves such a strong impression on the reader's mind of the intertexture of human lives. Seen thus in perspective, each separate individuality, with its specialized consciousness, is yet as indissolubly connected with the collective life as that of the indistinguishable zoöphyte which is but a sentient speck necessarily moved by the same vital agency which stirs the entire organism.

Among the figures which stand out most prominently from the crowded background are Dorothea, Lydgate, Casaubon, Rosamond Vincy, Ladislaw, Bulstrode, Caleb, and Mary Garth. Dorothea belongs to that stately type of womanhood, such as Romola and Fedalma, a type which seems to be specifically George Eliot's own, and which has perhaps more in common with such Greek ideals as Antigone and Iphigenia, than with more modern heroines. But Dorothea, however lofty her aspirations, has not the Christian heroism of Romola, or the antique devotion of Fedalma. She is one of those problematic natures already spoken of; ill-adjusted to her circumstances, and never quite adjusting circumstances to herself. It is true that her high aims and glorious possibilities are partially stifled by a social medium where there seems no demand for them: still the resolute soul usually finds some way in which to work out its destiny.

"Many 'Theresas,'" says George Eliot, "have been born who found for themselves no epic life wherein there was a constant unfolding of far-resonant action; perhaps only a life of mistakes, the offspring of a certain spiritual grandeur ill-matched with the meanness of opportunity; perhaps a tragic failure which found no sacred poet, and sank unwept into oblivion. With dim lights and tangled circumstance they tried to shape their thought and deed in noble agreement; but, after all, to common eyes, their struggles seemed mere inconsistency and formlessness; for these later-born 'Theresas' were helped by no coherent social faith and order which could perform the function of knowledge for the ardently willing soul.

"Some have felt that these blundering lives are due to the inconvenient indefiniteness with which the Supreme Power has fashioned the natures of women; if there were one level of feminine incompetence as strict as the ability to count three and no more, the social lot of woman might be treated with scientific certitude. Meanwhile the indefiniteness remains, and the limits of variation are really much wider than any one would imagine from the sameness of women's coiffure, and the favorite love-stories in prose and verse."

Such a life of mistakes is that of the beautiful Dorothea, the ill-starred wife of Casaubon. In his way the character of Casaubon is as great a triumph as that of Tito himself. The novelist seems to have crept into the inmost recesses of that uneasy consciousness, to have probed the most sensitive spots of that diseased vanity, and to lay bare before our eyes the dull labor of a brain whose ideas are stillborn. In an article by Mr. Myers it is stated, however incredible it may sound, that an undiscriminating friend once condoled with George Eliot on the melancholy experience which, from her knowledge of Lewes, had taught her to depict the gloomy character of Casaubon; whereas, in fact, there could not be a more striking contrast than that between the pedant groping amid dim fragments of knowledge, and the vivacious *littérateur* and thinker with his singular mental energy and grasp of thought. On the novelist's laughingly assuring him that such was by no means the case, "From whom, then," persisted he, "did you draw 'Casaubon'?" With a humorous solemnity, which was quite in earnest, she pointed to her own heart. She confessed, on the other hand, having found the character of Rosamond Vincy difficult to sustain, such complacency of egoism, as has been pointed out, being alien to her own habit of mind. But she laid no claim to any such natural magnanimity as could avert Casaubon's temptations of jealous vanity, and bitter resentment.

If there is any character in whom one may possibly trace some suggestions of Lewes, it is in the versatile, brilliant, talented Ladislaw, who held, that while genius must have the utmost play for its spontaneity, it may await with confidence "those messages from the universe which summon it to its peculiar work, only placing itself in an attitude of receptivity towards all sublime chances." But however charming, the impression Ladislaw produces is that of a somewhat shallow, frothy character, so that he seems almost as ill-fitted for Dorothea as the dreary Casaubon himself. Indeed the heroine's second marriage seems almost as much a failure as the stultifying union of Lydgate with Rosamond Vincy, and has altogether a more saddening effect than the tragic death of Maggie, which is how much less pitiful than that death in life of the fashionable doctor, whose best aims and vital purposes have been killed by his wife.

Much might be said of Bulstrode, the sanctimonious hypocrite, who is yet not altogether a hypocrite, but has a vein of something resembling goodness running through his crafty character; of Farebrother, the lax, amiable, genuinely honorable vicar of St. Botolph's; of Mrs. Cadwallader, the glib-tongued, witty, meddling rector's wife, a kind of Mrs. Poyser of high life; of Caleb Garth, whose devotion to work is a religion, and whose likeness to Mr. Robert Evans has already been pointed out; of the whole-hearted, sensible Mary, and of many other supremely vivid characters, whom to do justice to would carry us too far.

John Crombie Brown (essay date 1885)

SOURCE: Brown, John Crombie. *The Ethics of George Eliot's Works,* pp. 76-89. Philadelphia: Arnold and Company, 1885.

[*In the following excerpt, Brown analyzes the character of Dorothea Brooke, focusing on her qualities of humility and self-abnegation. In Brown's reading, Dorothea serves as the moral center of the novel.*]

To not a few of George Eliot's readers, we believe that Dorothea [in ***Middlemarch***] is and will always be a fairer and more attractive form than Dinah Morris or Romola di Bardi, Fedalma or Mirah Cohen. In her sweet young enthusiasm, often unguided or misguided by its very intensity, but always struggling and tending on toward the highest good; in the touching maidenly simplicity with which she at once identifies and accepts Mr. Casaubon as her guide and support toward a higher, less self-contained and self-pleasing, more inclusive and all-embracing life; in the yearning pain with which the first dread of possible disappointment dawns and darkens over her, and the meek humility of her repentance on the one faint betrayal—wrung from her by momentary anguish—of that disappointment; in the tender wifely patience, reticence, forbearance, with which she hides from all, the heart-gnawings of shattered and expiring hope; the sense which she can no longer veil from her own deepest consciousness that in Mr. Casaubon there is no help or stay for her and the unwearied though too soon unhoping earnestness with which she labors to establish true relations between herself and her uncongenial mate; in the patient yet crushing anguish of that long night's heart-struggle which precedes the close—a struggle not against her own higher self, but whether she dare bind down that higher self to a lifelong, narrow, worthless task, and the aching consciousness of what—almost against conscience and right—her answer must be;—there is an inexpressible charm and loveliness in all this which no one, not utterly dead to all that is fairest and best in womanhood, can fail to recognize.

Not less wonderfully depicted is the guileless frankness which, from first to last, characterizes her whole relations to Ladislaw. If there is one flaw in this noble work, it is that Ladislaw on first examination is scarcely equal to this exquisite creation. Yet it might have been nearly as difficult even for George Eliot to satisfy our instinctive cravings in this particular with regard to Dorothea, as in respect to Romola or Fedalma. And when we study her portrait of Ladislaw more carefully, there is a latent beauty and nobleness about him; an innate and intense reverence for the highest and purest, and an unvarying aim and struggle toward it; an utter scorn and loathing of everything mean and base,—that almost makes us cancel the word flaw. We recognize this nobleness of nature almost on his first appearance, in the deep reverence with which he regards Dorothea, the fulness with which he penetrates the guileless candor of the relation she assumes to him, the entireness of his trust in the spotless purity of her whole nature. And in him we have presented all those essential and fundamental elements of nature which give assurance that, Dorothea by his side, he shall be no unfitting helpmeet to her, no drag or hindrance on her higher life; that he shall rise to the elevation and purity of her self-consecration, and shall stand by her side sustaining, guiding, expanding that life of evergrowing fulness and human helpfulness to which each is dedicated.

But the essence of all this moral and spiritual loveliness is its unconsciousness. Self has no place in it. From the first the one absorbing life aim and action is toward others—toward aiding the toils, advancing the well-being, relieving the suffering, elevating the life, of all around her. And this in no spirit of self-satisfied and vainglorious self-estimation, but in that utter unconsciousness which is characteristic of her whole being. Of the social reformer, the purposed philanthropist, the benefactor of the poor, the wretched, and the fallen, there is no trace in Dorothea Brooke. Grant that, as she is first presented to us, that aim is for the time apparently concentrated in improved cottage accommodation for the poor; even here there is no thought of displaying the skill of the design and contriver; there is thought alone of the object she seeks—ameliorating the condition of those she yearns to benefit.

In her very first interview with Casaubon, there is something inexpressibly touching in the humility of childlike trust with which she accepts him and his "great mind," and the innocent purity with which she allows herself to indulge the vision of a life passed by his side; a life which he, by his influence and guidance, is to make more full and free, and delivered from those conventionalities of custom and fashion which restrict it. At last his cold, formal proposal of marriage is made. She sees nothing of its true character—that he is but seeking, not an helpmeet for life and soul in all their higher requirements, but simply and solely a kind of superior, blindly submissive dependant and drudge. In the *impossibility* of marriage presenting itself to her purity of maiden innocence as a mere establishment in life, or in

any of those meaner aspects in which meaner natures regard it, she sees nothing of all this—nothing save that the yearning of her heart is fulfilled, and that henceforth her life shall pass under a high guardianship, sustained by a holier strength, animated by a more self-expansive fulness, guided toward nobler and fuller aims.

Picturing to some extent, in degree as we are capable of entering into a nature like hers, the anguish that such an awakening must be to her, it is exquisitely painful to follow in imagination the slow sure process of her awakening to what this man, who "has no good red blood in his body," really is—a cold, shallow pedant, whose entire existence is bound up in researches, with regard to which he even shrinks from inquiry as to whether all he has for years been vaguely attempting has not been anticipated, and whose intense and absorbing egoism makes the remotest hint of depreciation pierce like a dagger. The first faint dawn of discovery breaks on her almost immediately on their arrival at Rome. Conscious of her want of mere æsthetic culture—neglected in the past as a turning aside from life's highest aims—she has looked forward to his guidance and support for the supply of this want as enlarging her whole being; broadening and deepening, refining and elevating all its sympathies. For all shadow of aid or sympathy here, she finds herself as utterly alone as if she were in a trackless and uninhabited desert. Nay, more: he who sits by her side is as cold and dead to all sensations or emotions that art can enkindle, as the glorious marbles amid which they wander. Soon she finds herself relegated to the society and fellowship of her maid; her husband is less to her, is incapable of being other than less, amid those transcendent treasures of architecture, painting, and sculpture, than a hired guide or cicerone would be.

Soon follows the scene where her timid offer of humble service is thrown back with all the irritation of that absorbing egoism which is the very essence and life-in-death of the man. For the first and only time, a faint cry of conscious irritation escapes her, followed by an anguish of repentance so deep, so meekly, humbly self-accusing, it reveals to us more of her truest and innermost life than pages of elaborate description could do. A single sentence descriptive of her mood even in that first irritation brings before us her deepest soul, and the utter absence of self-isolation and self-insistence there:—"However just her indignation might be, her ideal was not *to claim justice* but *to give tenderness.*"

She meets Ladislaw; and he more than hints to her that the dim, vague labors and accumulations of years which have constituted her husband's nearest approach to life have been labor in vain; that the "great mind" has been toiling, with feeble, uncertain steps, in a path which has already been trodden into firmness and completeness; toiling in wilful and obdurate ignorance that other and abler natures have more than anticipated all he has been painfully and abortively laboring to accomplish. Again a cry bursts from a wounded heart, seemingly of anger against her informant, really of anguish—anguish, not for her own sinking hopes, but for the burden of disappointment and failure which she instinctively perceives must, sooner or later, fall on the husband who is thus throwing away life in vain.

So it goes on, through all the ever-darkening problem of her married, yet unmated, life. Efforts, always more earnest on the part of her yearning, unselfish tenderness, to establish true relations between them; to find in him something of that sweet support, that expansive and elevating force, silently entering into her own innermost life, which her first childlike trust inspired; to become to him, even if no more may be, that to which her childlike humility at first alone aspired—eyes to his weakness, and strength and freedom to his pen. So it goes on; ever-gnawing pain and anguish, as all her yearning love and pity is thrown back, and that dulled insensate heart and all-absorbing egoism can find only irritation in her timid attempts at sympathy, only dread of detection of the half-conscious futility of all his labors, in her humble proffers of even mechanical aid. Not easily can even the most fervid and penetrative imagination conceive what, to a nature like Dorothea's, such a life must be, with its never-ceasing, ever-gathering pain; its longing tenderness not even actively repelled, but simply ignored or misinterpreted; its humblest, equally with its highest yearnings, baffled and shattered against that triple mail of shallowest self-includedness. And all has to be borne in silence and alone. No word, no look, no sign, betrays to other eye the inward anguish, the deepening disappointment, the slow dying away of hope. Nay, for long, on indeed to the bitter close, failure seems to her to be almost wholly on her own side; and repentance and self-upbraiding leave no room for resentment.

Ere long—indeed, very soon—another, and if possible, a still deeper humiliation comes upon her,—another, and, in some respects a keener pang, as showing more intensely how entirely she stands alone, is thrown into her life,—in her husband's jealousy of Ladislaw. Yet jealousy it cannot be called. Of any emotion so comparatively profound, any passion so comparatively elevated, that self-absorbed, self-tormenting nature is utterly incapable. Jealousy, in some degree, presupposes love; love not wholly absorbed in self, but capable to some extent of going forth from our own mean and sordid self-inclusion in sympathetic relation, dependency, and aid towards another existence. In Mr. Casaubon there is no capability, no possibility of this. What in him wears the aspect of jealousy is simply and solely self-love, callous irritation, that any one should—not stand above, but—approach himself in importance with the woman he has purchased as a kind of superior slave.

For long her guileless innocence and purity, her utter inability to conceive such a feeling, leaves her only in doubt and perplexity before it; long after it has first betrayed itself, she reveals this incapability in the fullest extent, and in the way most intensely irritating to her husband's self-love—by her simple-hearted proposal that whatever of his property would devolve on her should be shared with Ladislaw. Then it is that Casaubon is roused to inflict on her the last long and bitter anguish; to lay on her for life—had not death intervened—the cold, soul-benumbing, life-contracting clutch of "the Dead Hand." In the innocence of her entire relations with Ladislaw, not the faintest dawning of thought connects itself with him in her husband's cold, insistent demand on her blind obedience to his will. She thinks alone of his thus binding her to a life-long task, not only hard and ungenial, but one that shall absorb and fetter all her energies, restrain all her faculties, impair and frustrate all her higher and broader aims, make impossible all that better and purer fulness of life for which she yearns. Then follows the long and painful struggle,—a struggle so agonizing to such a nature, that only one nearly akin to her own can adequately conceive or picture it. For it is a struggle not primarily to forego any certain or fancied mere personal good. On one side is ranged tenderest pitifulness over her husband's wasted life and energies, even though she knows those energies have been wasted—that life has been thrown away—on an object in which there is no gain to humanity, no advancement of human well-being, no profit even to himself, save, perchance, a barren and useless notoriety at last; an object that has been already far more fully and ably achieved.

On the other stands her clear undoubting *conscience* of her own truest and highest course,—the course to which every prompting of the Divine within impels her,—that she shall not thus isolate herself within this narrowest sphere, shut herself out from all social sympathies and social outgoings and sacrifice to the Dead Hand that holds her in its cold remorseless clutch every interest that may be intrusted to her. We instinctively shudder at the result; but we never doubt what the answer will be. We know that the tender, womanly, wifely pitifulness, the causeless remorse, will be the nearest and most urgent conscience, and will prevail. The agonized assent is to be given; but it falls on the ear of the dead.

It is scarcely necessary to follow Dorothea minutely through all the details of her widowed relations to Mr. Casaubon. Enough that these are all in touching and beautiful harmony with everything that has gone before. No resentment, no recalcitration against all the ever-gathering perplexity, pain, and anguish he has caused her—nothing but the sweet unfailing pitifulness, the uncalled-for repentance, almost remorse, over her own assumed shortcomings and deficiencies—her failures to be to him what in those first days of her childlike simplicity and innocence she had hoped she might become. Even on the discovery of the worse than treachery, of the mean insulting malignity with which, trusting to her confiding purity and truthfulness, he had sought to grasp her for life in his "Dead Hand" with regard to Ladislaw, and she only escaped the irrevocable bond her own blindly-given pledge would have fixed around her by his death,—the momentary and violent shock of revulsion from her dead husband, who had had hidden thoughts of her, perhaps perverting everything she said or did, *terrified her as if it had been a sin.*

It is not alone, however, toward her husband that this simple, unconscious self-devotion and self-abnegation of Dorothea Brooke displays itself. Toward every one with whom she comes in contact, it steals out unobtrusively and silently, as the dew from heaven on the tender grass, to each and all according to the kind and nearness of that relation. Even for her "pulpy" uncle she has no supercilious contempt—no sense of isolation or separation; not even the consciousness of toleration toward him. Toward Celia, with her delicious commonplace of rather superficial yet *naïve* worldly wisdom, her half-conscious selfishness, her baby-worship, and her inimitable "staccato," she is more than tolerant. She looks up to her as in many respects a superior, even though her own far higher instincts and aims of life cannot accept her as an aid and guidance toward the realization of these. Even at old Featherstone's funeral, her one emotion is of pitiful sorrow over that loveless mockery of all human pity and love; and for the "Frog-faced" there is no feeling but sympathetic compassion for his apparent loneliness amongst strangers, who all stand aloof and look askance on him. Into all Lydgate's plans into the whole question of the hospital and all he hopes to achieve through means of it, she throws herself with swift intelligence, with active, eager sympathy, as a probable instrumentality by which at least one phase of suffering may be redressed or allayed. And in the hour of his deep humiliation, when all others have fallen away from his side, when the wife of his bosom forsakes him in callous and heartless resentment of what was done for her sake alone; when he stands out the mark of scorn and obloquy for all save Farebrother, and scans and all but loathes himself—she, with her artless trust in the best of humanity, in the strength of her instinctive recognition of the merest glimmering of whatever is true and right and high in others, comes to his side, yields him at once her fullest confidence, gives him with frank simplicity her aid, and enables him, so far as determined prejudice and uncharity will allow, to right himself before others.

Reference has already been made to her whole relations, from first to last, with Ladislaw. It is not easy to conceive anything more touchingly beautiful than these, more perfectly in harmony with her whole nature. Of anything approaching either coquetry or prudery she is incapable. The utter absence of all self-consciousness, whether of external beauty or inward loveliness; the ethereal purity, the childlike trustfulness, the instinctive recognition of all that is true and earnest and high in Ladislaw, through all the surface appearance of indecision, of vague uncertain aim and purpose and limited object in life; no thought of what is ordinarily called love toward him, of love on his part toward her—ever dawns upon her guileless innocence. Through all her yearning to do justice to him as regards the property of her dead husband, which she looks upon as fairly and justly his, or at least to be shared with him, there arises before her the determination of her dead husband that it should not be so; and her sweet regretful pitifulness over that meagre wasted life prevails. Anon, when at last through the will she is made aware of the crowning act of that concentrated callousness of heart and soul, and of the true nature of the benumbing grasp it had sought to lay on her for life, and had so far succeeded in doing, then for the first time her "tremulous" maiden purity and simplicity awakens, and for the first time it enters her mind that Ladislaw could, under any circumstances, become her lover; that another had thought of them in that light, and that he himself had been conscious of such a possibility arising. The latter scenes between them are characterized by a quiet beauty, a suppressed power and pathos, compared to which most other love-scenes in fiction appear dull and coarse. The tremulous yearning of her love, as it awakens more and more to distinct consciousness within; the new-born shyness blent with the old, trustful, frank simplicity— bring before us a picture of love, in its purest and most beautiful aspect, such as cannot easily be paralleled in fiction.

Toward her late husband's parishioners there is the same wise instinctive insight as to their true needs, the same thoughtful and provident consideration that characterizes her in every relation into which she is brought. If she at once objects, on their behoof, to Mr. Tyke's so-called "apostolic" preaching, it is that she means by that, sermons about "imputed righteousness and the prophecies in the Apocalypse. I have always been thinking of the different ways in which Christianity is taught, and whenever I find one way that makes it a wider blessing than any other, I cling to that as the truest—I mean that which takes in the most good of all kinds, and brings in the most people as sharers in it." And in her final selection of Mr. Farebrother, she is guided not alone by her sense of his general and essential fitness for the work assigned to him, but also in some degree by her desire to make whist-playing for money, and the comparatively inferior society into which it necessarily draws him, no longer a need of his outer life.

Of all the less prominent relations into which Dorothea Brooke is brought, there is not one more touchingly tender, or in which her whole nature is drawn more beautifully out, than that to Rose Vincy. Between these two, at least on the side of the hard unpenetrable incarnation of self-inclusion and self-pleasing, any approach to harmony or sympathy is impossible. There is not even any true ground of womanhood on which Rosamond can meet Dorothea; for she is nearly as far removed from womanhood as Tito Melema is from manliness or manhood. Yet even here the tender pitifulness of Dorothea overpasses a barrier that to any other would be impassable. In her sweet, instinctive, universal sympathy for human sorrow and pain, she finds a common ground of union; and in no fancied sense of superiority—solely from the sense of common human need—she strives to console, to elevate, to lead back to hope and trust, with a gentle yet steadfast simplicity all her own.

Such, as portrayed by unquestionably the greatest fictionist of the time—is it too much to say, the greatest genius of our English nineteenth century?—is the nineteenth century St. Theresa.

Henry H. Bonnell (essay date 1902)

SOURCE: Bonnell, Henry H. "George Eliot." In *Charlotte Brontë, George Eliot, Jane Austen: Studies in Their Works*, pp. 131-322. New York: Longmans, Green, and Co., 1902.

[*In the following brief excerpt, Bonnell analyzes inconsistencies in Dorothea's character.*]

The treatment of Dorothea [in **Middlemarch**] is clearly an indication [. . .] of a faculty used to excess, for the reader fails to give his sympathy into the keeping of the author's; which, when the reader is in general sympathy with the author,—when he is a sympathetic reader, in short,—suggests, at least, a false note somewhere. The character is built on a sure foundation; namely, the lack of complete ideality in woman; but the superstructure is not convincingly true. "All Dorothea's passion was transferred through a mind struggling toward an ideal life; the radiance of her transfigured girlhood fell on the first object that came within its level." Exactly; but was Casaubon within the level of any such girl as Dorothea? His letter of proposal is nothing more than a bid for an amanuensis. Can it be supposed that a girl like that would not see through such language,—would not feel insulted by the suggestion that their introduction came at a moment when he most needed help for the completion of a life's plan? He is proposing marriage to her, but he is thinking of himself and his book on fish deities and things. The "meanness of opportunity" is what galled Dorothea, but that is a kind of meanness felt by all whose ideals are higher than their surroundings; and it is difficult to conceive of any genuine girl regarding that semi-petrified mummy as in any way a realization of an ideal.

In the concluding chapter of the story, Dorothea is pictured as living happily with Ladislaw, and yet the general opinion seems to be that, spiritually, her marriage with that attractive Bohemian was her *second* mistake. The author acknowledges that it was not ideally beautiful. And she maintains that her first mistake could not have happened if "Society" had not smiled on such propositions. But Dorothea's society did not smile on it. Brooke said all he could for Chettam, although what Brooke said on any subject was not much to the purpose, and she would not have had Chettam, no matter who had spoken for him. Her sister is filled with horror at the thought of the marriage. She has been ridiculing Casaubon before Dorothea, unconscious of her engagement; and when that is announced she is awed with a sense of doom. "There was something funereal in the whole affair, and Mr. Casaubon seemed to be the officiating clergyman, about whom it would be indecent to make remarks." When Chettam hears of the engagement he exclaims—as do all of us—"Good God! It is horrible!" Mrs. Cadwallader's view is that the great soul which Dorothea has discovered in Casaubon is really a great bladder for dried peas to rattle in; and as for Mr. Cadwallader, why should he interfere? It was surely none of his business. George Eliot's horses have run away with her, for once. In the first place, Casaubon is too evident a bag-of-bones to win the warm esteem of any Dorothea; and in the second place, Dorothea's story closes in great happiness, notwithstanding the author's intention to make it plain that it ought not to, in the light of ideal longings. It is a double failure,—the result of an overworked sympathy.

F. George Steiner (essay date March 1955)

SOURCE: Steiner, F. George. "A Preface to *Middlemarch*." *Nineteenth-Century Fiction* 9, no. 4 (March 1955): 262-79.

[*In the following essay, Steiner presents the difficulties in classifying* Middlemarch *within the framework of the nineteenth-century novel. While he concedes that Eliot's loose, unstructured approach to her material lends the work its originality, as well as its unique authenticity, he also argues that her "total lack of technique" fails to provide adequate expression of the novel's major themes. Still, Steiner concludes that the novel is a "fine thing in its own kind" and that it contains real depth of insight and feeling.*]

Middlemarch is often granted a place apart in Victorian fiction. It tends to command, in however discrete a fashion, the respect of close attention, the marshalling of knowledge, historical and critical, which is accorded Stendhal or Dostoevsky, rather than *Jane Eyre* or *David Copperfield*, both of which are splendid novels in their kind. Why should this be so? One might hazard a reply if we knew something about the novel as a genre, about the discipline of approach it requires. But there are no clear poetics of an art which has been described by its most conscious craftsman as "the most independent, most elastic, most prodigious of literary forms." A critic of the novel can refer to no such authority as Aristotle's on drama or Coleridge's on the structure of poetry. Henry James's difficult and precious volume on "The Art of Fiction" and Mr. Forster's elegance in the Clark Lectures on the novel, stand out as much by their uniqueness as by their excellence. We have no standard or scale whereby to fix the rank **Middlemarch** should occupy, but are encumbered with the vague, if steadfast, conviction that there are degrees of seriousness in fiction and orders of excellence. Once we have some notion of what George Eliot set out to accomplish we can hint at the measure of her success.

Confessedly, our voice and mien change as we pass from current romance to Mr. Maugham, for example. It takes on deeper inflection as we approach Thackeray or Balzac, but assumes hesitant and passionate inquiry when confronted with *Madame Bovary, The Possessed* or *The Magic Mountain.* By the mere standard of first reaction it is our suspicion that **Middlemarch** falls short of this latter constellation, and, in fact, belongs to a different kind of literature. But on what system or assumption is such a sentiment grounded? Can a single pattern, however loose, comprise the phenomena of *Moby-Dick,* of Cervantes or of Joyce? The scene is one of confusion, and criticism has contented itself with rough-hewn conclusions about individual works. Obviously much that is labelled fiction is hardly art, and much of what is labelled "supreme" in literature can manifestly be classed as fiction. Under these circumstances it may be permissible to take the problem in reverse. What type of public, what particular discipline of taste does an enjoyment of **Middlemarch** presume? Is the volume picked up in the same fashion as an octavo by Dickens, or laid on our table as might be placed a copy of *The Idiot?*

It will be part of our task to seek points of reference throughout fiction, tuning forks, as it were, by which to determine the area **Middlemarch** most fittingly belongs to. One fact should be borne in mind: George Eliot's novel is a work of considerable scope (in the "World's Classics" edition it runs to 900 pages). It aspires to convey a complex social and psychological image of Midland life. It would be mere knavery to set out and prove that such a book is important and deserves enjoyment. And yet why does it fall so decisively short of that immense stature associated with some French and much Russian fiction in the nineteenth century? It may appear unfortunate to advance a conclusion before evidence is offered, but prefaces should be read after a novel and not before it.

We must first determine what the anatomy of this novel is, and whether there are sections which can, without impairing the whole, be lifted from the context, examined and valued in relationship to other works.

Middlemarch is composed of four plots unequal in emphasis. The most important appears to be Dorothea Casaubon's attempts to exercise in the provincial world a fineness of temper and gift for passionate abstraction, which, however, "tremble off and are dispersed among hindrances, instead of centering in some long-recognisable deed." In both Prelude and Finale this plot rounds the entire novel. Its initial development is so rich and displays so sure a touch as to gain undue weight in the balance of narrative forces.

The career of Tertius Lydgate and his marriage to Rosamond Vincy are equally if not more significant in the overall structure and convey qualities of modernism and analysis singular in Victorian writing. George Eliot's style takes on a shade of Flaubert's irony as she concludes regarding the physician's life, "his acquaintances thought him enviable to have so charming a wife, and nothing happened to shake their opinion."

Both principal plots are case studies in unsuccessful marriage, but whereas the first is somewhat extraordinary in circumstance and refers to Saint Theresa's flight from the modern Avila, the second is perfectly average, is ribbed and buttressed by social approval, and yet shatters inwardly. Lydgate's portrait is that of a gifted man marred by minor weakness and background in which superficial strength or cleverness attract nothing but suspicion. In her handling of Rosamond Vincy, George Eliot attempts a dry style, constantly on the edge of malice. This study of a Middlemarch doll's house contributes to a problem as yet unsolved, that of infatuation sliding into indifference. Though Dorothea is of a far deeper and more valuable nature than Rosamond, her solution is also incomplete, and both plots drift beyond the novel to a middling fate.

They are united for a celebrated instant as both women meet. Chapter 81 has been praised for its delicacy of feeling and fulness of emotion; the author is obviously charmed by her *trouvaille,* by the situation her characters have created. One tends to overlook, however, its inherent irony. Saint Theresa and Miss Vincy out of finishing school are discovered to be profoundly alike. It requires a touch of courage to conceive so, and the novel is brought abruptly, and by chance, to the threshold of importance.

The manner in which these two plots are designed, the background of Celia Brooke's meaningless and blissful marriage to Sir James Chettam and the interesting but undeveloped figure of Will Ladislaw, suggest that the narrator's point of view is substantially masculine and only half challenges or questions accepted norms. How would Stendhal have treated Dorothea's stay in Rome? Instead of cataloguing outward signs of Mrs. Casaubon's terrible disillusion with her husband, he would have conveyed the significance of Ladislaw's appearance, or illustrated by the young proselyte's indifference to Vatican treasures, the decline of her confidence in erudition. In other words, *Middlemarch* squarely poses the problem of woman's place in modern marriage but sedulously avoids using the narrative techniques which could enforce a radical solution.

This gap between thought and style is characteristic of nineteenth-century English fiction. It places a screen of avoidance between author and page. In Dostoevsky's technique of first person narrative, style is thought directly transcribed; in *The Charterhouse of Parma* style is perpendicular to thought. But George Eliot's third person and omniscient narration can avail itself of irony or pathos rather than depth of meaning. With such exceptions as Mr. Turnell's work on French novelists, the study of language in prose fiction is unattempted. Actually it deserves evaluation nearly as minute as that given to word usage in poetry and drama. In the case of much Victorian prose it may detect means magnificently effective along a certain range of emotion, but entirely barred from other modes.

The third and weakest plot is that of Fred Vincy's courtship of Mary Garth and an account of the latter's Arcadian family in which virtue and poverty are united. At its frequent worst this tale evokes Dickensian tears or the Salvation Army manual. It contains the most Gothic scene in the novel: old Featherstone's death and Mary's refusal to carry out his last wild instructions. The latter would have bestowed wealth on her suitor but virtue must out. This powerful night scene shows the art of fiction passing from Rhoda Broughton to Gissing. Fred, the young squire of sterling qualities and good heart but lack of seriousness in financial transactions, is a direct progeny of Tom Jones. He is rewarded by the love of Mary Garth, and the author concludes, somewhat disarmingly, that all will like to know "that these two achieved a solid mutual happiness."

Is this part of the book a concession to Victorian taste for the idyllic and to a belief in the virtues of yeomanry? Perhaps in part. But the figure of Caleb Garth is modelled on Robert Evans, as was Adam Bede. George Eliot's worship of a perfect father, her compulsion toward domestic idylls and homespun goodness, are founded on something more important than a keen feeling for public demand. In a world picture and form of life which included a translation of Strauss's *Leben Jesu* and the conquest of professional status in a man's domain, there had to be areas of private refuge and traditional certainty, of clerical afternoons and Millet's agriculture. Probably we owe to the safety-valve effect of

this plot the extreme quietness and moderation with which problems of feminism or class structure are approached in George Eliot's Midland county.

The fourth part of the book, concentrated in later chapters, involves the disgrace of Vincy's brother-in-law, Bulstrode. Lydgate's probity is severely tested in the course of events, and Ladislaw's background is somewhat artificially related to obscure machinations in the financial underworld. The author's hand is not entirely at ease in these trammels, but the Bulstrode episodes are of extreme importance in the work as a whole. Primarily, they deepen the complexity of Middlemarch as a social world and suggest sudden ramifications which give an illusion of social veracity. They construct a sinister world outside the novel, a continuum in which the narrative covers a mere span. Faulkner is the contemporary master of this illusion through which a novel seems but a brief glance at realities whose existence is totally independent of the author's. Whereas the first three plots are explicit and localized, the decline and fall of Bulstrode convey a sense of geographical scope (London and the resort to which the banker retires) and a sense of secrecy, of knowledge not wholly confided to the narrator. Of equal interest is the actual material with which the plot is ravelled. It is a matter of finance and social prestige in which a parvenu of exalted, if narrow, convictions and honesty is trapped by the class from which he rose. It is a peculiar business brought on by a diabolus ex machina from Bulstrode's past and throws light on the problem of the intrusion of finance into modern fiction.

This relationship of economics to art is a study in itself. Balzac, Zola and Dos Passos are novelists with a strong and partisan grasp of monetary or commercial facts. Ibsen's *Wild Duck* is a good example of drama based on a system of industrial and fiscal relationships. George Eliot has neither the theoretical knowledge nor interest required for *The Big Money,* but attempts in her account of Bulstrode to interpret the effect of a new banking class and commercial mentality on an agrarian, eighteenth-century society.

To some extent, indeed, *Middlemarch* is a book about money. The latter intrudes on each of the four plots with a threat of disaster. Casaubon's will contains a clause forcing Dorothea to choose between affluence and her love for Ladislaw. It is significant that the two lovers are finally joined with the young widow's sobbing declaration, "I will learn what everything costs." Lydgate's marriage, which could have gathered strength and momentum from solid ease, is suddenly imperiled and shown as defective by the menace of poverty. It is the subsequent transaction which leads to Lydgate's involvement in the death of Raffles. Fred Vincy's entire form of life is based on the expectation of a heritage from old Featherstone who dies surrounded by a chorus reminiscent of *Volpone,* that great comedy of finance. Fred's disappointment and destitution lead to his reform and ennobling. In the Garth homestead, money is significant through its absence. In Bulstrode's case, money overcomes its master and drags him from the stage in Morality fashion. But George Eliot shapes her concern with economics in a manner entirely different from that of Stendhal or Zola.

It is the distinction between *Eugénie Grandet* and *Le Père Goriot,* a book intensely disliked by the author of **Adam Bede.** In the first instance, money is important because it affects character and moral situations. It acts as a barrier to natural feeling. In the second, money is a force, an idea obsessing men, ruling Rastignac and to be ruled in turn. Stendhal, influenced by Saint Simon, chronicled the rise of the banking aristocracy with interest and expert detachment. Bulstrode's early career would have held more challenge for him than his somewhat theatrical decline. In Dostoevsky money becomes a symbol and demon. The ruble notes for which old Karamazov is murdered, pervade the novel but are more or less than actual cash. In *The Idiot,* money as the incarnation of evil, is conquered and thrown into the fireplace with mockery. George Eliot's concern with the theme of economics is valuable but incomplete.

In the interweaving of four plots and a host of minor characters, runs the thread of the political crisis associated with the Reform Bill and the Catholic Question. *Middlemarch* devotes little attention to directly political events. Mr. Brooke's Parliamentary campaign and Will Ladislaw's journalism do not influence its essential development, and there is something which rings sincere in the author's remark regarding politics: "there were plenty of dirty-handed men in the world to do dirty business." In the Finale we learn that Will has been returned to the House of Commons "by a constituency who paid his expenses." The Florentine politics of *Romola* are more thoroughly illuminated and characterized than those of *Middlemarch.*

The book is set, however, between 1830 and 1832. Questions involving Reform and Lord Russell crop up in social and domestic scenes. The end of the novel is dated "just after the Lords had thrown out the Reform Bill." The town is clearly divided over Peele's advocacy of Catholics, and much confusion is caused by the Liberal measures of a Tory cabinet. Mr. Vincy, for example, tends to identify the thought of general election with the end of the world. All these shocks to Middlemarch sensibility are part of a much deeper transformation and what George Eliot hints at is the decline of a rural and isolated community life before the intrusion of modernism. The overwhelming importance of this change is disguised by her reserved narration and concern with essentially private experience. In two cases only is the conflict frankly shown. The advance of railroad surveyors ends in a brawl involving Fred Vincy, and Lydgate's real struggle is that of modern experimental pathology against the unholy alliance of country physicians and apothecaries.

The author's notions of scientific research are somewhat rudimentary but her admiration is unstinted. In Balzac research is reserved to art or philosophy. *Middlemarch,* in creating Lydgate, marks a transition to the figure of the scientist, which is so abused in contemporary writing. Lydgate is intensely modern, but there is nothing in the world of Sheridan which would puzzle Rosamond. The Garth family has emigrated directly from Goldsmith's Wakefield, and the victory of their good over Bulstrode's evil is a fine piece of nostalgia. The New Fever Hospital signifies the excellence of modernism. Bulstrode's power represents the vulgarity and ruthlessness of the new era. It is a touch of narrative subtlety that the two be so closely associated.

In her concluding reflections on the transformation of Midland life, George Eliot points out that "the young hopefulness of immediate good" with which Reform began "has been much checked" and tempered. Conservative Middlemarch felt as much from the start and was averse to the entire experiment.

We have sought to indicate that *Middlemarch* consists of four plots, two of which are essentially psychological, and two of which are mainly social in emphasis. These four plots are drawn on a canvas of financial relationships and profound political change symbolized by the crisis in the years 1830 to 1832. This structure has the tangled wealth of life itself and does not aim at too rigid an artistic selection. Whereas Flaubert's picture of provincial existence is the result of a classical discipline, grouping, analyzing, shifting focus in obedience to calculated effect, George Eliot allows her characters and ideas to sprawl into reality. Balzac conceives an entire nation by accumulating evidence and successive points of view, but Middlemarch is a town more loosely built and wandered through with hurried or languid step as the case may be. The result is convincing. Neither Flaubert's *pointillisme* nor Balzac's enormous brush stroke could have conveyed the flavor and calm of Midland life as George Eliot or Trollope succeeded in doing with means far more primitive.

But the novel also aspires to the rank of a psychological document. In so doing it challenges comparison with works on related themes. Dorothea is a case of Romanticism and exaltation. Madame Bovary dreams of passionate adventure, but Mrs. Casaubon, equally disillusioned with marriage, is obsessed with the idea of serving in a transcendent cause. The two forms of sickness are closely allied, but George Eliot's diagnosis is conceived from the outside and eschews a radical or tragic solution, whereas Flaubert focuses his world through Emma's vision and carries off the stroke with lasting brilliance. The total lack of technique on George Eliot's part is the more unfortunate for the fact that her subject is the more important. The question of spirituality and high endeavor with no outlet is at the heart of our social and economic difficulties. It is of far wider significance than a woman's secret hankering after adultery. In *The Bostonians,* Henry James took up the problem with George Eliot's moral seriousness and something of Flaubert's art.

The study of Lydgate's infatuation, his marriage with Rosamond and their gradual estrangement, is clearly psychological in purpose. Admittedly, the task is difficult and involves a question to which our society has given no answer: can a relationship conceived in youth or under special impulse be expected to last through a lifetime, or is it preserved solely by a system of hypocrisy and social values? Lydgate's courtship is handled with perfect control, and his surrender at the end of Chapter 31 is a famous page. It is studded with verbs of motion: shook, thrilled, put, moved, poured. The cloying grace is tinged with irony, and the author slips, as it were, into her characters. It is after the wedding, however, that her difficulties begin, and the tone falters.

By interfering constantly in the narration George Eliot attempts to persuade us of what should be artistically evident. In a single paragraph and through his use of verb tenses, Proust qualifies without the need of commentary or subtitle an entire matrix of emotions. George Eliot has difficulty in creating action and fails to turn into motion the ideas at hand. In the case of Dostoevsky, the fact that a character walks to the window can compel us to the understanding of his most hidden thoughts. This is nowhere the case in *Middlemarch,* and we are told over and over facts which action should communicate in its immediate language. To evoke *Anna Karenina* or Bourget's *Le Divorce* in our context seems palpably unfair. Why should it be if George Eliot's subject matter so clearly challenges comparison with Flaubert, Tolstoy or Henry James? Her failure, if such there be, is of a different order from that of one of the masters. One cannot describe *Middlemarch* as a poor novel by Bourget, though one might characterize *Lohengrin* as Meyerbeer's supreme achievement. Is it because George Eliot, and Victorian fiction, generally, work in a different medium from that of the French or Russian novel?

Before circumscribing a reply, our attention must hinge on problems of technique, because it is technique which stands between the marble and the finished statue, between ideas and their coming alive on the stage. The material is at hand both from a social and psychological point of view, but when placed near masterpieces related in subject and milieu, *Middlemarch* recedes to a secondary ranking. In the hands of a non-English reader

it might be cruelly impaired. Why should this be so? Why should George Eliot invite the sympathies of a reader to whom Proust or Stendhal might prove inaccessible?

English novelists of the nineteenth century, with the possible exception of the Brontës, shared with their readers the conviction that sound sentiment would hold its own without the embellishment of art. Thackeray registered some doubt, but were his sentiments truly sound? His admiration for the structural brilliance of Restoration comedy parallels that of Henry James for the perfectly managed situations of Dumas or Augier. But it hardly affected public taste for morality and tenderness in abundant, if rather shapeless form. In Flaubert's sense there is hardly an English novel before Henry James, Conrad and D. H. Lawrence, a view shared, in fact, by Dr. Leavis.

When George Eliot declared in 1866 that she thought aesthetic teaching "the highest of all teaching," she meant it regarding the substance of her sermon rather than the voice in which it might best be conveyed. Henry James's subtle striving after shades of device and narrative cunning would have seemed quite secondary to her, to Trollope or even to Dickens, though the latter sometimes carries off a brilliant technical stroke by sheer moral indignation. *Middlemarch* shows little trace of the self-tormenting, deliberate wrestling with which Flaubert overcame his material and composed. Perhaps we are nearing the core of our problem, and it is one of considerable difficulty inasmuch as we lack a critical vocabulary for the novel. Several facts emerge, however, independent of where our sympathies may lie.

Drama or poetry, if it aims at survival, cannot ask for the concessions made by the fiction-devouring public. Excellence of structure and command over material are natural exigencies. And yet English novels of the Victorian age, entirely lacking the consciousness of an art form or genre, not only survive, but are widely read, republished every Christmas, and crop up on rainy afternoons. It is the evidence given by wide acclaim and facility of enjoyment which suggests that we are dealing with something quite different from Flaubert or Dostoevsky, something which is narrative prose and fiction rather than a novel. For if we designate by art a singular and individual transformation of immediate material, a transformation which has the quality of becoming universal, a metaphor between relationships hitherto unsuspected, much of Victorian fiction is not art at all.

Unable to commit ourselves at first to any set classification we may have arrived at a fundamental differentiation in the field of fiction. This differentiation allows two orders of excellence and indicates wherein lies the peculiar merit of Dickens, for example, as contrasted with James. A novelist is one whose material need not differ from the storyteller's; it can, in fact, be more modest and commonplace. But he will rely on a very different order of response, on a reader aware of technique, of indirect narration, of point of view; on a reader alert for the tactics used in a single paragraph, and for the over-all strategy whereby the artist demonstrates that he has seen from the inside. The storyteller depends essentially on the nature of his material and on the associations it will evoke in the reader's imagination. Incident is the springboard of this effect, and his characters are marked for easy recognition.

The novel can be carried to excess, as in Gide's *Counterfeiters,* a novel about the technique of the novel, or as in Joyce's *Ulysses,* a novel on the nature of meaning and communication. But the art of the novel reaches magnitude and intensity to which no story, however passionate, fantastic or moving, can aspire. There is nothing in English fiction of the nineteenth century to match Albertine's first visit to the Narrator or the hero's tale in *Notes from the Underground.*

In these instances, as in much of Tolstoy, the novel outplays its own limitations, sometimes tending to lyric verse, sometimes to epic or, as in the case of the Karamazov trial, to drama. The quality which distinguishes these works from the most sublime of stories, and which, to greater or lesser degree, affects *The Magic Mountain, Moby-Dick,* or Cervantes, is a frank acknowledgment that man is in a symbolic structure and a prey to transcendent forces. The English temper, however, is averse to blending good yarns with metaphysics. It claims allegiance to sound morality above and beyond the complexities of individual emotion. The suggestion has been advanced that art, if it is to pass into universality, must attack on a partially metaphysical front. Though we can get no nearer to a general formula, our considerations make it appear that **Middlemarch** is barred from the ranking of great novels. Its author would stake no claim in the Dostoevskyan direction, and her readers would support her discretion, but it is worth bearing in mind that this direction exists and lies upward from the Midlands.

Continuing from the point of view of the attention and depth to be present in the reader, there follows close upon the metaphysical novel a second order of excellence and classicism obviously distinct from storytelling. *Madame Bovary* is supreme in a domain which includes Stendhal, Henry James, Turgeniev and D. H. Lawrence. In this area of the novel daily life is given depth and intensity by the control of art over raw material. This is an effect different from that achieved by a storyteller who rearranges daily life with an emphasis on the exceptional happening or contrived situation. It is in this select and essentially nineteenth-century group that **Middlemarch** might demand inclusion.

For the most part, however, a brief comparison shows it will not do. The metaphysical or epic novel demands genius on the part of the author. The category we are now examining demands perfect technique and artistry. George Eliot clearly has no pretensions to the former. Has she any to the latter?

Our answer requires a closer look at some of her devices. Take, for instance, her use of mottoes at chapterheads, a touch of Sir Walter Scott and something looked for in the *Cornhill.* Sometimes they are ironic comments, volleys of silver laughter discharged by the author on her characters. Dorothea's impression of Casaubon, to cite a case, is equated to Don Quixote's encounter with the helmet of Mambrino. Sometimes the motto sets the tone of the chapter, gay or sad. Often it summarizes the action and appends a moral aphorism. Considered severely, all these are illicit means of persuasion: the author not entirely confident in what she has written, stands behind our chair and whispers advice as to how we should feel about this or that part of her tale. As Emma Bovary leaps from the saddle, we need no syllable of commentary. Active verbs compel our every emotion and the author is never in sight.

At other times, George Eliot adds to her omniscience deliberate comments and summaries of events. It should be noted that omniscience is a novelist's most lazy approach and that personal interference in the action must be compared to what occurs in a Chinese theater where the manager comes on during the play to change props. In a few scenes only does George Eliot triumph over her fatal inclination to storytelling. Dorothea's discovery of Rosamond and Ladislaw, the fall of Lydgate, and some moments in Rome are seen dramatically rather than narratively, are conceived, as it were, by a novelist transforming his material.

The characters in **Middlemarch** are allowed to progress in their own meandering provided marriages conclude their journey. The author seems to be watching with a pleasure closely akin to that of her readers. This makes for charm and useful sentiment but does not lead to the conscious and exacting magic of art. She is so naturally a storyteller that her voice gains or falters, bestowing on **Middlemarch** its unevenness of tone and performance. There are sections in which the writer is nearly as bored as the reader and others in which George Eliot impresses a sense of urgency and delight. This lack of unified texture in Victorian fiction is probably related to serialized publication, but more significantly, is based on the assumption that a story should sound "somewhat like life." This belief in approximate realism pervades the modern public, and it is not our task to examine its full absurdity and irrelevance. In any case, life has stretches of boredom and sermonizing, so why should not a novel, appearing as it does over a year of *Blackwood's* and then in several stout volumes? George Eliot, in fact, insisted on the serialization of *Romola,* since she wished it to be read slowly. The effect may be comforting and convey the ups and downs of daily existence, but has little to do with art. Being assured that a good chapter would compensate for a poor one might fill James or Flaubert with contemptuous astonishment. Yet it is on an over-all similitude to the rhythm of life and her reader's affable memory that George Eliot banks to carry us through many a dull hour.

Moreover, she uses her material with varying insight or polish. Her delight in autobiographical passages is manifest. This is a dangerous compliment for a novelist to receive. The first exchanges between Dorothea and Celia (who is modelled on Christiana Evans) sparkle with warmth and effortless farce. It is evident that Caleb Garth is fondly dwelt on and familiar to the author, whereas Bulstrode, for example, retains an automatic and exterior quality. It is admissible for an author to prefer one character to another, although such is rather the reader's liberty, but in no case should this preference betray itself in ups and downs of style and technique. Such tricks of voice and moral winks are the storyteller's art, not the novelist's.

Had we time or skill it might be worth guessing why the villain in Victorian fiction is so crude a figure. Such magnificent conceptions of mixed evil and suffering as Proust's Charlus, Dostoevsky's Versilov, or Melville's Ahab are beyond the Midland range. The English mind, in fact, harbors the suspicion that Milton must have been of Satan's faction in order to speak so perfectly within his voice. Whereas storytelling remains outside good or evil and comments on both, the art of the novelist lives in them. That is where technique surpasses sentiment.

There are specific blind spots on the retina of many writers. For George Eliot dialogue seems to pose a special problem and usually spills over into lengthy speech. The break between descriptive prose and passages in quotation is often obscured by their similarity. The author speaks through her characters and not in them. Apart from touches of mannerisms, as in the case of Farebrother's household, she hardly attempts to differentiate individual styles of expression. She lowers or raises her storytelling voice but cannot disguise it. There are wonderful passages in Swift or Stendhal to suggest how difficult an art the short dialogue requires, how perfect a sense of language. But the nineteenth-century reader in his parsonage had abundant time.

We have glanced at questions of technique in order to show reason for a refusal to include *Middlemarch* in the category of social or psychological novels as conceived by the masters. Sales such as those registered by Dickens or George Eliot (specifically with *Adam Bede*) are a tribute to the general cultural level and the writer's feeling for public taste, but do not permit much striving after art. The acceptance of Flaubert, Henry James, or Stendhal was notoriously slow, and is, as yet, far from widespread, but the ultimate fate of their works invites no doubt whatever.

Beyond questions of technique, however, *Middlemarch* suffers from a commanding defect: its lack of structural unity, of a narrative center. We are not implying that all novels are to be arrested by a single formula, such as the first person narrative in Dostoevsky or the fixed and limited point of view in *The Ambassadors*; but we are inquiring whether there is in *Middlemarch* a center of gravity, a real mark of penetration into the tangle of incident.

The Jamesian analysis of plot in *The Ring and the Book* is the subtlest inquiry along these lines, but our task is simpler, for George Eliot's novel offers not even that semblance of unity to be detected in Browning. The four plots are distributed in such manifest slices, light and shadows fall so massively as to raise the suspicion that they were separately conceived and tacked together by the loose ends of social chit-chat and chance encounter. The problem could have been approached from several angles. The selection of the years immediately preceding the Reform Bill suggests a novel in the Balzac manner pivoting on the changes operated by London politics on provincial life. The Prelude, on the other hand, strikes a chord of exalted psychological inquiry into the status of woman. For a time this appears to be the central theme, but it becomes entangled in the conventional affair of Dorothea and Ladislaw, or is confused by the more essential emergence of Lydgate as a figure in a moral and historical conflict.

Could a single point of vantage lead to vistas as abundant as those offered by *Middlemarch*? Both Flaubert and Proust warrant an affirmative answer. It is Emma Bovary's partial blindness to life which suffuses the provincial scene in so rich a light, and it is the singular, unique, nonuniversal outlook of the Narrator which encompasses times past. There are only two guiding principles in George Eliot's book, the goal of marriage and a system of reward and punishment meted out to the characters. Lydgate is an interesting exception, for despite his superior worth he is allowed to fail.

When dwelt upon in memory (rather, we fear, than reread) *Middlemarch* is associated with a sentiment of rambling pleasure, rendered precise, to be sure, at this or that moment in the narrative of events. Parts will be glanced at on later occasions and the rest inferred. George Eliot might have asked for no more, but there are elements in her craft which deserve a finer brand of admiration, if not the secret devotion accorded to often-thumbed copies of *The Red and the Black* by an entire generation.

And yet, despite our suspicions regarding its intrinsic worth or claims to permanence, *Middlemarch* is a fine thing in its own kind. Our sole task has been to separate its excellence from that of a related genre, to hint at the barrier between a novel and a story told so charmingly. Few books of fiction care to assume the responsibilities of the novel as art, and Victorian fiction, in particular, must be differentiated from a similar pursuit in Russia or across the Channel. Heard as a series of tales from provincial life, *Middlemarch* has undeniable depth and profuseness. It is generous in providing enjoyment, and creates in Dorothea and Lydgate literary figures which tempt to closer acquaintance. At a time when so many novelists set out either to mystify our ignorance or to terrorize our precarious leisure, it is a privilege to have George Eliot for host and to be invited where neither grief nor exultation assume too disproportionate a significance. The vogue of Trollope and other Victorians in our time testifies to their healing virtue. It would be of bad tone to insist that it is not the task of great art to soothe.

What makes a discussion such as ours so tentative, so dependent, whether avowedly or not, on data of personal taste, is the lack of a standard of reference for the novel, a standard capable of embracing works as short as a *nouvelle* or as prodigiously long as *The Human Comedy.* That is why we have sought to approach our task from the point of view of the reader and of the skills and willingness to affront complexity required on his part. Assuredly it has induced a crude view, but the distinction between the novel and the telling of tales in prose has remained helpful amid varied and shifting examples.

George Eliot may have been asked to bear the onus of invidious comparison, but *Middlemarch* can only profit, its real value can only emerge more clearly, for having been placed in its own system of reference and court of appeal. If a preface, moreover, provokes disagreement, it may lead to a second reading, and that is its true purpose and sole justification.

Brian Swann (essay date June 1972)

SOURCE: Swann, Brian. "*Middlemarch*: Realism and Symbolic Form." *ELH* 39, no. 2 (June 1972): 279-308.

[*In the following essay, Swann discusses Eliot's innovative use of symbolism in* Middlemarch. *In Swann's view, the book's symbolic elements reside not in specific images but in the complex interrelationship of characters, actions, and ideas.*]

I Symbolic Form: General Survey

Unity in essence is multiplicity in existence.

(Feuerbach, *Essence of Christianity*)[1]

"*Middlemarch* is a treasure-house of details, but it is an indifferent whole." Henry James could not see the one quality which all of George Eliot's critics today are agreed on: the amazing unification of meaning and sensibility in *Middlemarch.* James, however, had already decided in *Partial Portraits* that George Eliot's bent was peculiarly intellectual, and when he came to write his review of the novel for *The Galaxy,* he did not meet the new novel as a new experience. "Certainly the greatest minds have the defects of their qualities, and as George Eliot's mind is preeminently contemplative and analytic, nothing is more natural than that her manner should be discursive and expansive. 'Concentration' would doubtless have deprived us of many of the best things in the book. . . ."[2] Blackwood had used the word "panorama" in discussing *Felix Holt,*[3] and James uses the same word when he asks "It is not compact; but when was a panorama compact?" He concludes his 1873 review with these words: "It sets a limit, we think, to the development of the old-fashioned English novel. Its diffuseness, on which we have touched, makes it too copious a dose of pure fiction. If we write novels so, how shall we write History?"[4]

James has raised an important point. The old-fashioned novel did indeed reach a climax in *Middlemarch* and could go no further, but not for the reason James gives, as we shall see later in more detail. At this point we should note that George Eliot as social historian is all the while an artist attempting new forms of art in which to embody her vision. Contemporary nineteenth-century criticism was simply not equipped to deal in critical terminology with that George Eliot was doing in her greatest novel.[5] Today, we are still groping for terms to describe a work which stays so close to the tumultuous surface of life itself that Calvin Bedient can claim that *Middlemarch* is "in effect, all vehicle, all medium, all transparency: dead to itself"; a novel that "wears no aesthetic garment, only the hair shirt of the world." Such an approach which deprecates the "formal mining" of Barbara Hardy and her associates as being "a little like counting the change at Fort Knox," leaves us with a feeling of dissatisfaction. For *Middlemarch* is not a slice of life ("the bare beauty of veracity"), nor is it true to say that "nothing in George Eliot's other novels prepares us for its strong achievement."[6] Only if one insists on a simplistic approach such as Mr. Bedient's can one make out a case for *Middlemarch* as *sui generis.* If, as will be argued later, one sees the real uniqueness of the novel, then one also observes that the poetic texture is related to the realism of *The Mill on the Floss,* for example, or *Felix Holt,* or even *Adam Bede.* In other words, there is a vivid imagination at work which has its eye on the object and on related objects—an "esemplastic" imagination.

The traditional way of looking at such a structure has been in terms of organic unity.[7] George Eliot herself was constantly referring to this aesthetic principle. In a letter to John Blackwood, for instance, she declines to make a change that Lewes had suggested in the *Middlemarch* manuscript. "I don't see how I can leave anything out," she writes, "because I hope there is nothing that will be seen to be irrelevant to my design, which is to show the gradual action of ordinary causes rather than exceptional, and to show this in some directions which have not been from time immemorial the beaten path—the Cremorne walks and shows of fiction."[8] The concept of organic unity had become a commonplace for George Eliot by the time she wrote this sentence. We must look elsewhere for the real and fresh aesthetic essence of *Middlemarch,* a novel which includes and transmutes this ancient Aristotelian ideal of organicism. George Eliot herself provides a clue in the above quotation. She intends to take "directions which have not been from time immemorial the beaten path," and in 1863 she had told Richard Holt Hutton that "It is the habit of my imagination to strive after as full a vision of the medium in which a character moves as of the character itself."[9] In this letter, George Eliot puts her failure in *Romola* down to "excess." The "vision" had been too "full." In *Middlemarch,* however, George Eliot realized her ambition. The concept of organic unity has not so much changed as become more subtle and inclusive. Almost every important word finds its sum of meaning increased to the pitch of symbolism, and the most helpful concept for understanding the enormous richness of *Middlemarch* that I have found is Kenneth Burke's notion of "symbolic action." Before we can discuss its value in detail, however, a word on what we mean by the terms realism and symbolism in the novel, especially in a novel which came well before symbolism, having pervaded poetry, conquered drama and the novel by being "discreetly camouflaged under a deliberate show of realism."[10]

Ursula Brumm has pointed out that the novel is a product of historicism and therefore "agnostic, sceptical, empirical, and secular."[11] Along this line of reasoning, therefore, she claims that the novel was originally anti-symbolic, "for it is opposed to the entire class of elements to which the symbol belongs. The realistic novel owes its origin to rejecting the paradigms that had for centuries determined literary forms: fable, legend, myth, and the traditional, typical stories and characters from the storehouse of world literature that were constantly being reworked (i. e., the 'archetypes' that have become so popular again today)."[12]

It is hard to agree with such a selective approach, for it ignores the actual workings of the artistic mind. Even *Robinson Crusoe,* that "just history of fact," is structured round a whole series of symbolic incidents which, while anchored in spiritual autobiography, float free into the archetypal. The statement applies even less to George Eliot. It is too simplistic to say that the novel is

merely concerned with "the individual and idiosyncratic, that is, the particular in its particular circumstances, with reality as experienced by the individual as constituting the only genuine version of reality." For one, the core of George Eliot's philosophic position is that the voracious ego must accommodate itself to the needs of others. For another, there is a stage in her novels in which, as she told Frederic Harrison, a general idea is more important than "the individual and idiosyncratic,"[13] (we remember that Henry James had observed that "she proceeds from the abstract to the concrete").[14] She aimed at a balance between the two forces, and had set aside *The Spanish Gypsy* because "it was in that stage of Creation or 'Werden,' in which the idea of the characters predominated over the incarnation."[15]

Despite my disagreement with Miss Brumm, it is she, however, who approaches the position I would like to develop when she writes on Ippolito Nievo's forgotten masterpiece of mid-nineteenth century, *Confessions of an Octogenarian.* She asserts that "the great nineteenth-century novel is not the product of an imagination working in symbolic terms. It is a representation of life, but not a symbolic representation."[16] Miss Brumm shows that, in fact, Nievo's novel cannot help becoming a symbolic representation of meaning. Details of the castle of Frata are "components in which the forms that shape" the empirical reality "concentrate and become visible. From this point of view they are seen to concretize the meaning sought in reality." That is, the castle comes close to being a symbol. As Miss Brumm admits, the castle is "the concrete and particular expression of the ideas and forces that shape the reality, and as such it can assume the functions of a symbol. The outstanding difference between such 'realistic' symbols and the symbols of modern literature is that, unlike the latter, the former are not compact images that make a single sensual impact, but are often extensive and not easily delimitable segments of reality."

With George Eliot we have precisely the same case, but there are complications. She, for instance, extends the meaning of historical realism, not only in the direction of the incorporation of strictly accurate historical backgrounds, but by embodying the "mythopoeic aspect of history" which Miss Brumm claims Stendhal, Tolstoy, and other nineteenth-century masters did not concern themselves with. As Jerome Beaty has shown, the Reform movement makes its appearance in *Middlemarch* not only with the physical incidents and structures of the Reform Bill, but is a structural metaphor which symbolizes the efforts of the individuals in the novel to evolve, or reform themselves.[17] A symbol, then, need not only be a thing. It can also be an idea. The "medium" George Eliot strives to realize is not merely objective, but spiritual. Not only is there "no creature whose inward being is so strong that it is not greatly determined by what lies outside it,"[18] but this objective reality is never the simple entity Miss Brumm assumes reality to be. As early as **Adam Bede,** George Eliot had claimed the right to take as reality that which is *selected* by her consciousness. The mind is not merely a mirror, nor is reality simply objective verisimilitude. While denying the transcendentalism implicit and explicit in Carlyle, she would yet have agreed with him that "all visible things are emblems," and that "matter exists only spiritually." Since language is the body of thought, and "metaphors are her stuff," man everywhere "finds himself encompassed with symbols."[19]

Absolute realism in the novel can never exist, for, as José Ortega y Gasset observes, reality "in itself" is "anti-poetic"; its nature is "inert and insignificant." Reality, indeed, can never be the subject of art. Myth comes first, and reality comes from its destruction; reality becomes poetic and hence artistic by "destruction of the myth":

> In this form reality, which is of an inert and insignificant nature, quiet and mute, acquires movement, is changed into an active power of aggression against the crystalline orb of the ideal. The enchantment of the latter broken, it falls into fine, iridescent dust which gradually loses its colours until it becomes an earthy brown. We are present at this scene in every novel. So that strictly speaking, it is not reality that becomes poetic or enters into the work of art, but only that feature or movement of reality in which the ideal is reabsorbed.[20]

Such realism is best summarized for Ortega y Gasset in *Don Quixote* which, because it was written against chivalry, bears all the books of chivalry within it, and hence possesses a quality of poetry which complicates surface realism. One cannot call such a novel realistic. "This is what we call realism: to bring things to a distance, place them under a light, incline them in such a way that the stress falls upon the side which slopes down towards pure materiality." This is death, not art. The life of true realism is myth. "The myth is always the starting point of all poetry, including the realistic, except that in the latter we accompany the myth in its descent, in its fall. The theme of realistic poetry is the crumbling of poetry."[21]

George Eliot began her writing career with a translation of Feuerbach, the whole impetus of whose work was to destroy supernatural myth and place humanistic values on what had once been regarded as transcendental. *Scenes of Clerical Life* and **Adam Bede** are studies, in purely "provincial" terms, of sin (in these cases, not venal sin, but a kind of atrophy of the heart), punishment, repentance, and forgiveness. The religious or liturgical pattern is clear, but the significance has changed. In George Eliot the crumbling of the ideal is the construction of the real, but the tradition of the ideal is transformed and incorporated into a new reality. Christian teleology and epistemology are brought down to earth, and become truly "ideal" in Lewes' sense of the word.[22]

George Eliot's theory and practice of art moved from this "simple" realism, to a complex or true realism which comes close to Ortega y Gasset's position that true realism contains the mythic or poetic. The mythic and poetic are both subsumed in the symbol, and in **Middlemarch,** George Eliot devotes no little space to discussions of the symbolic mode of perception. For instance, Mr. Brooke, who is in many ways a wise fool, a character who often voices dramatically George Eliot's own opinions, says at one point that in Naumann's painting, "Everything is symbolical you know—the higher style of art." Having decided this, he concludes his sentence with "I like that up to a certain point, but not too far—it's rather straining to keep up with, you know. But you are at home in that, Casaubon. And your painter's flesh is good—solidity, transparency, everything of that sort" (241). In a humorous way, George Eliot is indicating her own position. The "natural meaning" is in the "flesh," its "solidity, transparency." A man has been painted, and not an abstraction.

Of course, George Eliot is directing gentle irony at Mr. Brooke also, since we had learned previously of the way Will explained the symbolism of his painting of "Tamburlaine Drawing the Conquered Kings in his Chariot." Tamburlaine, says Will, symbolizes the "tremendous course of the world's physical history lashing on the harnessed dynasties" (158), as well as "earthquakes and volcanoes" and "migrations of races and clearings of forests—and America and the steam-engine." Will is also having fun, of course, but he does not seem to take symbolism seriously, George Eliot, however, regards an ability to respond to proper symbolism as important. Symbolism is concentrated indication of meaning, and we see how Dorothea is beginning to recover from "the gigantic broken revelations" (143) of Rome, when she realizes that the symbolic method is more than "a difficult kind of shorthand" (158). She begins to see meanings below the surface, to grow in aesthetic and intellectual power when she can see significance in "saints with architectural models in their hands, or knives accidentally wedged in their skulls. Some things which had seemed monstrous to her were gathering intelligibility and even a natural meaning" (159).

We can obtain a clearer idea of what George Eliot meant by symbolism as "the higher style of art" when we extend our view, if not as far as Mr. Brooke suggests, from "China to Peru" (370), then over and within the novel itself, and eventually to **"Notes On Form In Art."** George Eliot aimed at creating the complete image, for image-making is the prime function of the imagination.[23] "We are all of us imaginative in some form or other, for images are the brood of desire" (237). In his argument with Naumann, Will defends language against painting on these grounds: "Language gives the fuller image, which is all the better for being vague. After all, the true seeing is within; and painting stares at you with an insistent imperfection" (142). Knowledge passes into feeling "within." The complete image is a spiritually conditioned segment of reality. We have something like George Eliot's aesthetic ideal in the phrase describing "that distinctness which is no longer reflection but feeling—an idea wrought back to the directness of sense, like the solidity of objects" (157). A similar point is made in the later dialogue between Will and Dorothea. To be a poet, Will pontificates, is to have a soul "in which knowledge passes instantaneously into feeling, and feeling flashes back as a new organ of knowledge" (166).[24] Symbolic form is not the same as meddling with symbols, which is what Will does in his painting, and, to a lesser extent, what Naumann the Nazarene does also. Symbolic form is a whole habit of mind in which unity is the object—unity of the person as individual and symbol. Just as knowledge and feeling should be one, so for George Eliot an individual is only fully himself when he sees himself in relation to others. Every part of the organism, whether as idea, perception, or individual, should become what I would wish to term "symbolic" of all the others, by way of what Kenneth Burke calls "synecdoche."[25]

Ortega y Gasset describes the way in which reality becomes poetic (or symbolic) in terms which recall Will's statement of the way in which knowledge is wrought back to the directness of sense. He refers to "that gesture or movement of reality in which the idea is reabsorbed."[26] Kenneth Burke describes this mutuality, this "symbolic act," as "the dancing of an attitude."[27] Language and gesture coincide, and the whole artefact is constructed, in E. K. Brown's terms, of "rhythm,"[28] or as George Eliot has it, "repetition with variation" (7). Reality, says Ortega y Gasset, is a "generic function";[29] that is, a cause and not an end. They way in which it takes its primary part in the evolution of a symbolic form gives it value.

In *Middlemarch,* George Eliot has created a new form of fiction which, with the remarks of Ortega y Gasset and Kenneth Burke in mind, might be called "symbolic realism." As far as organizing "natural everyday incidents" into a "strictly related"[30] whole is concerned, George Eliot did not have to move beyond *Scenes of Clerical Life* and its achievement. But in her first novel, symbolic technique is rudimentary and relatively unsophisticated. There may be a fervor in the bareness, but the event takes precedence and any symbolism is a bonus. Thus, in **"Mr. Gilfil's Love Story,"** we are told explicitly that the remodelling of Cheveral Manor and the growing-up of Tina are meant to be brought together in our mind. In *Middlemarch,* George Eliot speaks occasionally as if a symbol were a kind of substitute for the real event. She can write, for example, that in droughty years, "baptism by immersion could only be performed symbolically" (46). At other times, in her letters, the symbolic seems superior to the empirical or mundane: "It seems to me that the soul of Christianity lies not at all in the facts of an individual life, but in the ideas of which that life was the meeting-point and the new starting-point. We can never have a satisfactory basis for the history of the man Jesus, but that negation does not affect the Idea of the Christ either in its historical influence or its great symbolic meaning."[31] Still again, George Eliot speaks of the symbolic as if it were an adjunct of the ideal (and hence an ambiguous ingredient of any realistic presentation). She explains what she considers the failure of *Romola*: "The various *strands* of thought I had to work out forced me into a more ideal treatment of Romola than I had foreseen at the outset—though the 'Drifting away' and the Village with the Plague belonged to my earliest version of the story and were by deliberate forecast adopted as romantic and symbolical elements."[32] The romantic element, these final scenes, is meant clearly to summarize and symbolize certain strands of the narrative by way of colorful conclusion. The suggestion is that such incidents are climactic, unusual, and therefore a whole novel could not consist of such a symbolic technique. By the time George Eliot wrote *Middlemarch,* however, matters had become more complex.

A symbol is without meaning in itself (as George Eliot realized by having the final scenes in *Romola* gather all that had gone before). To complicate the matter, a symbol's "many-sidedness"[33] is hazardous to strict accuracy, and the meaning of a symbol is not ascertainable, since if it were there would be no need for the symbol. To read *Middlemarch* correctly, one must be able to hear nuances, reverberations of a word from context to context, for in this novel everything is part of symbolic form or action, down to the metaphors themselves. As Mark Schorer has demonstrated, George Eliot's metaphors "tend always to be, or to become, explicit symbols of psychological or moral conditions, and they actually function in such a way as to give symbolical value to much action, as Dorothea's pleasure in planning buildings ('a kind of work which she delighted in') and Casaubon's desire to construct a 'Key to all Mythologies.' Their significance lies, then, not so much in the area of choice (as 'commerce,' or 'natural elements' and 'animals') as in the choice of function, and one tests them not by their field, but by their conceptual portent."[34]

In a later essay, Mr. Schorer admits that his classification of verbs of unification and progressive movement which symbolize on a verbal level the movement of the plot ("endless vistas of unending good," "the religion of progress"), *is* a classification: "I am, of course, arranging the metaphorical material *in* that pattern."[35] Nevertheless, his essays are valuable in that they draw attention to a basic principle of construction which, anticipating *gestalt,* gives full value to the actual unit of construction, the autonomous yet related image or fact.

For, in *gestalt* (which began as a theory of mind as a repudiation of older ideas imported into the philosophy of mind by analogy with atomic physics), "the elementary and irreducible units of experience are articulated and structured, though unitary, wholes akin rather to the modern atom with its internal pattern of structured forces."[36] George Eliot, in **"Notes On Form In Art,"** states as one of the new aesthetic principles she was evolving, that "Form, as an element of human experience, must begin with the perception of separateness . . . & that things must be recognized as separate wholes before they can be recognized as wholes composed of parts, or before the wholes can be regarded as relatively parts of a larger whole." Because of the number of dynamic wholes that can make a unity, "fundamentally, form is unlikeness," and therefore "every difference is form."[37] Darrel Mansell, in an article on George Eliot's conception of form, states that for George Eliot "Form is not outward appearance but 'inward' relations."[38] The concept of symbolic form which George Eliot was working towards is one in which everything is related to everything else without sacrificing its own *quidditas,* the actuality of its present existence.

On a moral level (to show how George Eliot integrates theme, plot, language, and so on, within an encompassing form), we might note that the ideal outlined above entails the concept of self-sacrifice. George Eliot always insisted that self-sacrifice was far more viable if it emanated from a strict self-knowledge, from an integrated personality. Thus, in **Middlemarch,** Mr. Farebrother gives up Mary because he knows that she is in love with Fred and because he realizes his own shortcomings, that he is "only a decent makeshift" (130). By renunciation, he becomes more useful and achieves greater dignity. Similarly, Dorothea, who wishes to sacrifice her life on Casaubon's altar, finds not only that her desire stems from her incomplete personality, her ignorance, but that self-sacrifice is an exercise in self-knowledge involving the giving up of large and grandiose ideas, personal pride and dignity. When she is able to do this, she is able to give herself fully, able to break down the egotism of Rosamund and the reticent pride of Lydgate. George Eliot knew as well as Jung that the "intentional loss" in self-sacrifice is also a gain, "for if you can give yourself it proves that you possess yourself."[39] The *quidditas* of the self which sacrifices itself from a position of strength, not of vague benevolence, is related to the *quidditas* of each part of the plot. Creating a true relation to others through self-sacrifice is only possible by a knowledge of the integral sense of self. The individual unit of the plot, in *gestalt* terminology, is "articulated and structured, though unitary."[40]

II *MIDDLEMARCH*: THE NOVEL ITSELF

(1) *SYSTOLE AND DIASTOLE: THE SCENE AS SYMBOLIC CENTER*

Apart from the exigencies of publishing, there seems to be no organic reason why **Middlemarch** is divided into eight books. What *is* intentional, though, is the principle of construction in each book, for there is always one scene in which issues are summarized and evaluated from the widest possible point of view. This scene is generally a scene bringing together more people than in other scenes, and is the larger movement in the dance of characters, a symbolic center of consciousness. Lydgate, who shares with his creator certain important artistic principles, gives us a metaphor by which to apprehend this device: "there must be a systole and diastole in all enquiry," he says. That is, "a man's mind must be continually expanding and shrinking between the whole human universe and the horizon of an object-glass" (468).

For George Eliot there is no private life that has not been influenced by public life. Each symbolic scene such as we are about to examine is a large beat in the life of the novel, when issues come to the fore in more dramatic or clearer ways. We shall deal only with the first of these scenes, Book 1, Chapter 10, but the principle holds for all the others.[41]

In Chapter 10 we have the point, Jerome Beaty informs us, at which the "Miss Brooke" portion of the novel ends, and where the main "Middlemarch" characters are introduced. The reason why George Eliot decided to fuse the earlier story which she had had in mind for some time, with the other story is that they have points in common, and George Eliot's syncretic imagination saw them as essentially parts of the same story. Both are about "high ideals which come to nothing or little more than nothing; in both cases an unwise and unhappy marriage plays a part in obstructing the realization of these ideals."[42] Moreover, the time element and scene of the two stories are similar. As the two stories are really one story, even the characters seem to be part of one character, parts of an ideal whole which exists in the narrator's consciousness (a point to be taken up again later).

Chapter 10 focusses initially on Will, but only to dismiss him in short space. To balance this introduction, Lydgate makes a brief first appearance at the end of the chapter, and is meant to contrast favorably with the ephemeral Will. Apart from Fred, these two are the only young men in the novel, and some readers as the navel appeared in serial form saw possibilities of a romance between Lydgate and Dorothea. But George Eliot had a more subtle effect in mind, and at this point carefully keeps Dorothea and Lydgate apart (though they seem to have met because Lydgate makes the fatuous judgment on page 69 that she is "a little too in earnest"). The Dorothea story is beginning to look further than Middlemarch. Will the exotic has already left the small stifling community to find his way in an area no "more precise than the entire area of Europe" (61), and we next see him in Rome, where he meets Dorothea. In Chapter 10 we begin to sense a kinship between Dorothea and Will, for Will's world of "possibilities" (61) contrasts strongly with Casaubon's "small taper of learned theory exploring the tossed ruins of the world" (61). Dorothea's dissatisfaction in this chapter is caused by Casaubon's insensitive remark that she had better take Celia with her, in order to give Casaubon more time for his serious work; the implication is that Dorothea cannot share his *esoterica*. Estrangement is already in the air.

Most of the men in the novel (except, perhaps, Will) are ignorant about the nature of women. This fact is used as a symbol of moral decay in the town and in the nation as a whole, for it traverses society from the local squire, Mr. Brooke, to "the Lydgate's of Northumberland" (69). It pervades the run-of-the-mill moral judgments of such men as Chichely who prefers what he regards as a truly feminine woman, not Dorothea but Rosamund; someone with "a little filigree," "something of the coquette" (68). Lydgate will become the scapegoat for sharing such ideas. He will attain a kind of tragic dignity by seeing beyond the mask when it is too late, and having to make the best of it.

In this chapter, the "second-line characters," Vincys, Bulstrodes, and so on, anchor us firmly in the prosaic "medium" which Dorothea is trying to escape, which Will evades, and which Lydgate, ironically sharing so much with them, has come to try and improve. This party "before Reform had done its notable part" (65), symbolizes the sheer bulk and weight of the reality facing Dorothea, emphasizes that any reform which might come to Middlemarch will be dreadfully slow in succeeding.[43] This dumpy reality, the same which is testing Dorothea who tries to crusade for improved housing while her uncle runs the worst estate in the district, will test Lydgate and his brittle self-possession. Lydgate does not know how to deal with Middlemarch, and the scene is a masterly way of bringing the main characters together in order for us to see them in the context of their invidious environment.

(II) The Scene as Symbolic Embodiment

Another vigorous ingredient of the symbolic form of *Middlemarch* is those scenes which George Eliot had always used, scenes which might be called symbolic embodiments, since they imbue naturalistic incidents with thematic or symbolic will to stature. In *Adam Bede,* for instance, Hetty before the mirror is a crude emblematic version of this principle, while in *Daniel Deronda* the first scene at the gambling casino symbolizes in beautifully controlled tones the abrogation of will and abandonment to chance which is Daniel's fate until he embraces the Zionist cause. The drifting of Daniel on the Thames is another embodiment of the same idea.

Middlemarch contains many such scenes, and the novel calls attention to the technique since, like *Daniel Deronda,* it opens with such a scene. The richness of Chapter 1 precludes analysis in depth, but the principle is clear. The "plain dressing" (5) of Dorothea is ironic, and a kind of humorous desperation hangs over her efforts to suppress the "pagan sensuous" (7) strain to her character. The discussion with Celia about their mother's jewels symbolizes this dichotomy. "How very beautiful these gems are!" she exclaims, and then rationalizes her instinctive delight with, "It is strange how deeply colours seem to penetrate one, like scent. I suppose that is the reason why gems are used as spiritual emblems in the Revelation of St. John. They look like fragments of heaven" (10). She attempts to "merge" the sermon's sensuous pleasure "in her mystic religious joy." For Dorothea, spiritual emblem and physical fact never quite coincide, however. The marriage to Casaubon is meant to satisfy the spiritual, but at the expense of the physical. Will, like one of the "little fountains of pure colour" (10), is always associated with the play of light, and is meant to suggest that Dorothea at the end of the novel is well on the way to integrating the dual aspects of her personality, "sensuous force controlled by spiritual passion" (141).

Dorothea's honeymoon in Rome is another example of symbolic embodiment. All the verbal imagery of ruin and decay which have been associated with Casaubon in the early part of the novel finds physical expression in the Eternal City, city of "stupendous fragmentariness" (143). Rome corresponds to Dorothea's spiritual confusion as she discovers more about the man she has married; both city and husband are "broken revelations" (143). Rome undermines her "principles" with its "deep impression" (143), and its confusing sensuousness. "All this vast wreck of ambitious ideals" shocks her out of her English complacency, for she is "tumbled among incongruities" (144). In addition, Rome symbolizes the ruin in Casaubon's personality, where "the large vistas and wide fresh air" which Dorothea had hoped to discover in it "were replaced by anterooms and winding passages which seemed to lead nowhere" (145). Dorothea has to drive out to the Campagna "where she could feel alone with the earth and sky, away from the oppressive masquerade of ages" (143). Correspondingly, it is to Will she turns for freshness of response and open sympathy.

The last example of this sort to be examined differs from the previous two, in that it is what might be termed "symbolic parody": "It is a narrow mind which cannot look at a subject from various points of view" (49). Parody, including the narrator's self-parody, Mr. Brooke's parody of reform and his obsession with his documents which parallels Casaubon's method of compilation, and so on, is a larger element in *Middlemarch* than in any of the other novels. Chapter 23 consists entirely of a parody of one of the strands of the main action. On the narrative level, the purpose of the scene at the horse fair which Fred attends with Bambridge and Horrocks is clear. Fred trusts to his "luck" in having things turn out well, fashioning events "according to desire" (173). He feels that the universe will accommodate itself to his wishes, a characteristic attitude George Eliot regards as peculiarly egoistic. When his venture into horse-dealing turns out badly, Mr. Garth has to pay the penalty for trusting him, and a climax thus comes about in Fred's relations with Mary. On the symbolic level, the fact that Fred was sold a vicious animal which the owner had claimed was a docile beast parodies part of the larger Lydgate/Rosamund plot. The clue is in the sentence describing the horse's viciousness: "There was no more redress for this than for the discovery of bad temper after marriage—which of course old companions were aware of before the ceremony" (177). Fred egoistically chooses a horse by trusting to his "luck"; Lydgate chooses a wife, trusting to his knowledge of women. Just how much he has learned from experience with the fair sex we are meant to gauge from the Laure incident. Lydgate believes, conventionally and vulgarly, that women are for decoration. His choice of Fred's sister is rendered ludicrous when we see Rosamund and the vicious horse superimposed to form one image. One would have expected a reformer and humanitarian not to trust to appearances, and to have enquired closer into the qualities of his mate before marriage. But Lydgate has "spots of commonness" (111). In George Eliot's non-tragic world, these are equivalent to the tragic flaw.

With such scenes in mind, we should pause before agreeing wholeheartedly with Peter K. Garrett's contention that the "staple scene" in George Eliot does "not display a notable concentration of meaning."[44]

(III) "THE EXPANDING SYMBOL"

Some parts of *Middlemarch* are consciously symbolic, such as the well-known passage on page 578. Dorothea has come to the realization that she loves Will and that Lydgate has a strong claim on her aid and sympathy. She regards both men as "objects of her rescue" (577), and "'What should I do—how should I act now . . . ?'":

> It had taken long for her to come to that question, and there was light piercing into the room. She opened her curtains, and looked out towards the bit of road that lay

in view, with fields beyond, outside the entrance-gates. On the road there was a man with a bundle on his back and a woman carrying her baby; in the field she could see figures moving—perhaps the shepherd with his dog. Far off in the bending sky was the pearly light; and she felt the largeness of the world and the manifold wakings of men to labour and endurance. She was part of that involuntary, palpitating life, and could neither look out on it from her luxurious shelter as a mere spectator, nor hide her eyes in selfish complaining.

The passage seems to draw some of its power from memories of the Eden myth and one would not want to be much more specific. Yet the details of the man and the woman seem to refer to specific intentions. One could make analogies, and say Lydgate is the burdened man, but the method does not really work. The symbols are to be understood as expanding into the general consciousness we have of the novel at this point. Details point to the climactic moment. The fact that Dorothea looks out of the window and beyond the gates of her house is an involuntary altruistic gesture. Bundle and baby are the way of the world she is about to be inducted into. The "bending" sky is not only an accurate description, but suggests vastness, and, taking up the suggestion of the burdened man, extends the burden to an overarching principle of labor. Dorothea is about to leave Middlemarch and her "luxurious shelter."

The second kind of expanding symbol is easier to follow. In George Eliot there is generally a relationship between the natural detail and a psychic event or situation. The symbolic relationship is less emphasized in *Middlemarch* than the earlier novels, and does not expand or dilate as it does, for example, in *The Mill on the Floss* or *Adam Bede*. Landscape in *Middlemarch* is strangely muted, and effective mostly as delicate analogy. Thus, when Dorothea visits Casaubon for the first time, it was autumn and "a sparse remnant of yellow leaves" (54) was falling in the Lowick estate. Again, when she realizes what Lydgate's married life is, and that she might help, her insight is set against "the bright green buds which stood in relief against the dark evergreen" (557). In the juxtaposition, promise and tragedy are gently hinted. Finally, when Dorothea returns from her honeymoon, it is mid-January, and snow is falling. Generally, however, this device of nature as symbol is used sparingly. The scene in *Middlemarch* is not the arena of nature, so much as a "mental estate" (207). The point is well made by Quentin Anderson, that what George Eliot surveys "might be called a landscape of opinion, for it is not the natural landscape that is dominant here." The interest is not in "things seen but things felt and believed."[45]

The third kind of expanding symbol is subtler, less immediately apprehensible; a significance of tone, a certainty of nuance. Symbolic use of water in *Middlemarch* depends more on the sharpness of the unconscious mind for its effect than on conscious appreciation. In the novel, water or streams of water slowly come to symbolize sensibility. This verbal symbol does not acquire a physical manifestation as it does for example in **The Mill on the Floss** or **Daniel Deronda** (where Grandcourt drowns in his own egoism). Such phrases as "the living stream of fellowship" (4), "the stream of feeling" (46), and the "open-channels" of Dorothea's "ardent character" (565) indicate the symbolic area George Eliot is cultivating. The symbol is pervasive and seldom stressed. For example, when Dorothea is about to marry Casaubon, she thinks of his mind as an "ungauged reservoir" (17), or as "a lake compared to my little pool" (18). She finds, however, that her marriage in fact cuts her off from the great sea of sensibility. She finds that she is "exploring an enclosed basin" (145) where Casaubon's soul is "fluttering in the swampy ground" (206).

The symbol is also used ironically in the case of Lydgate, who, when his work is going well, exists "in that agreeable after-glow of excitement when thought lapses from examination of a specific object into a suffusive sense of its connections with all the rest of our existence—seems, as it were, to throw itself on its back after vigorous swimming and float with the repose of unexhausted strength" (122). This sense of connectedness, this unity of being which Lydgate possesses briefly, is soon to be dissipated in the division he creates between life and work. Further irony is provided by the dwindling of Lydgate's element from "I have the sea to swim in" (128) to practising at a Spa "bath" (128).

The final expanding symbol is a location. The library at Lowick is initially simply a place where Dorothea sets about learning from Casaubon the Latin, Greek, and Hebrew she craved. Throughout, the library functions as charged background, keeping before us Dorothea's heroic desire for book-learning which will substitute for a "coherent social faith" (3). Gradually, as Dorothea substitutes fellow-feeling for book-knowledge, the library accretes other values.

Dorothea receives Lydgate in the library, the first time she has been there since Casaubon's sickness. The shutters are closed, "but there was enough light to read by from the narrow upper panes of the windows" (212). Even in absence, Casaubon's presence is felt, since "narrow" is one of the epithets habitually associated with him. We are reminded that it is through her suffering in her marriage that Dorothea is beginning to understand others. It is in his library, the "caticom" (353) as Tantripp calls it that the process of rebirth begins for Dorothea, and Lydgate begins to have his eyes opened, for "women just like Dorothea had not entered into his traditions" (213). "For years after Lydgate remembered the impression produced in him" by Dorothea's involuntary appeal for help (214).

This scene with Lydgate also prepares for the scene when Dorothea meets Will in the library. The chink of light that is enough "to read by" anticipates the metaphoric "lunette" which, symbolizing Will, "opened in the wall" of Dorothea's "prison" (265). Lydgate in the first scene allows Dorothea to open her soul to him, while Will in the second gives her "a glimpse of the sunny air" (265). The library then becomes an ironic setting because of its association of staleness and aridity. In addition, the meeting between the two takes place against a rising storm, which seems to herald ominously the growing involvement of Dorothea and Will, or, like the storm in "The Eve of St. Agnes," symbolizes the hostile world outside. When Dorothea makes a motion of revolt, however, beginning to allow her dissatisfaction with Casaubon to rise to the surface by acknowledging that great thoughts seem to have worn him out, the rain seems to stop soon after. Fairer weather is ahead as Dorothea begins to see truly. The influence or hold of the library seems likewise to be loosened, its restrictions giving way to freedom.

The movement from darkness into light is continued in Chapter 48. Dorothea meets Casaubon in "that close library" (352), but he walks into "Yew-Tree Walk" where he expects Dorothea to come and tell him her decision about his proposition. Dorothea never gets the chance, however, to tell him that she will "bind herself" to him, immuring herself, effectively barring herself from the sunny presence, for Casaubon is found dead in the summerhouse. After this death, "the air is milder" (394), and the library loses some more of its malignity, although "the dead hand" continues to exert an influence through the will. When Dorothea returns to Lowick after her sojourn with her uncle, however, the room she stops in longest is the library; but, in the June sun, "the shutters were all open . . . and the morning gazed calmly into the library" (392). She seals and closes the "Synoptical Tabulation" which Casaubon had left and writes within the envelope "I could not submit my soul to yours" (393). The morning that shone on the rows of notebooks is likened to the sun shining on megaliths, "the mute memorial of a forgotten faith" (393), and that is precisely what the library now represents for Dorothea. The sun which shines so brightly is also Will, who is soon after shown, not into the library, but into the neutral drawing-room with its "two tall mirrors and tables with nothing on them" (394), and an open window. A new start seems possible. This "little room," in the words of the Donne poem George Eliot uses as a motto for Chapter 83, the last chapter but three in the novel, has a chance to become "an everywhere" for their "walking souls" (589).

The next time Will and Dorothea meet is in Mr. Brooke's library (Chapter 62). The context is not ominous with the weight of books but lightened by Will's presence. This second parting is in auspicious circumstances, with clear weather. Moreover, the play of irony over the whole scene is welcome release from the heavy serious atmosphere pervading the library at Lowick. But the dead hand is not so easily evaded, and the meeting in Chapter 83 takes place in the Lowick library again; and again there is a storm in the background. Their declaration of love is thus set against the forces of the past and the "wild stupidity of the elements."[46] Will is entering into "the thick of a struggle" (611), and both he and Dorothea are about to enter the adult world, "the drear outer world" (594). The influence of the library is compromised by love. The world, however, is waiting for the fray which will not be spectacular, but part of a whole series of "unhistoric" acts (613).

(IV) The Symbolic Act and Gesture

In the Prelude to **Middlemarch,** the narrator remarks ironically on the "inconvenient indefiniteness" (3) with which the Supreme Power has fashioned the natures of women. Their variety prevents then from being treated with "scientific certitude" (4). Despite scientific investigation, "the indefiniteness remains, and the limits of variation are really much wider than anyone would imagine from the sameness of women's coiffeur" (4). The same is true of the variations George Eliot plays on certain ordinary gestures and acts to heighten the *armoniche.* By such means she enriches the truly poetic texture of the novel.

In the wealth of gestures, even the smallest act becomes symbolic in its context, and summarizes the whole thrust of a character or situation at that particular time. Quentin Anderson suggests that, after the loss of God, George Eliot, aided by her reading in Comte, saw human behavior "as a set of symbolic gestures expressive of individual needs and desires."[47] Only in **Middlemarch,** however, is this symbolic technique used so delicately and expressively. In exemplification of this argument, Hilda Hulme writes copiously on such a simple detail as the act of Dorothea in looking out of a window: Dorothea, "instead of setting down with her usual diligent interest to some occupation, simply leaned her elbow on an open book and looked out of the window at the great cedar silvered with the damp" (35). Miss Hulme points out that the mention of the cedar is a later manuscript addition referring to Dorothea's emotional situation, since Casaubon is a Biblical scholar and the cedar has Biblical associations. Dorothea is looking at the new opportunity of life with Casaubon, and the idealism of her virgin judgment is suggested by the word "silvered." ("Damp" is, of course, another word with Casaubonian links.) One cannot know, says Miss Hulme, whether Dorothea shares Celia's notion that learning may come from mere physical contact (symbolized by the elbow on the open book): "Yet in a novel where physical posture and physical movement so often represent mental state and emotional change, it is hard to know what limits the author would have us set to our readiness in picking up such significances."[48]

A simpler example of the same technique is the occasion when old Featherstone, sick in bed, is visited by his repulsive relatives. He starts to rub "the gold knob of his stick" (78), a gesture we translate into emotional terms, since all his power and the brutal games he plays with it depend on his wealth. All his belligerent triumph is expressed by this unconscious gesture. Mary Garth ('Dove' in the original), supplies him with soothing syrup, and it is Mary who is the only character Featherstone cannot buy. It is this very gold-knobbed stick that he hurls at Mary in frustration when she refuses to obey his machinations and accept a bribe.

Gestures as well as acts and objects can be ideas "wrought back to the directness of sense" (157). Similarly, a gesture can make a narrative point concretely. When Rosamund asks Lydgate to fasten up her hair, "he swept up the soft festoons of plaits and fastened in the tall comb" (426). The husbandly act seems surprisingly degrading. The way the comb is described as "tall" makes the action complete and creates a sense of Rosamund inviolate in her pristine ego. Lydgate is Heracles among the women, his masculinity debilitated, ("to such uses do men come"), ensnared in the physical charms of his wife with her Lamia-like "long neck" (426). Again, before the marriage, Rosamund had dropped the "chain" (222), she was knitting when Lydgate had come to put an end to the flirtation. He "instantaneously stooped to pick up the chain" (222), and, on the way up, seeing the first natural look of distress he had ever seen on Rosamund's face, is as truly captured as if the chain he had retrieved were made of steel. The fact that Lydgate picked it up symbolizes his own responsibility for his fate. This symbol depends as much as anything on a pun. Later, the pun changes to metaphor when we learn that for Lydgate, Rosamund is "another weight of chain to drag" (543).

Sometimes, one is not sure of the exact significance of a gesture which nevertheless strikes us as moving or mysterious. For example, when Mr. Brooke returns from Lowick one day, he has a commission from Casaubon; to deliver the marriage proposal. Dorothea, we are told, sits by the fire as Mr. Brooke begins his preamble, and has just been reading a pamphlet on the early church which Casaubon has sent: "She threw off her mantle and bonnet, and sat down opposite to him, enjoying the glow, but lifting up her beautiful hands for a screen. They were not thin hands, or small hands, but powerful, feminine, material hands. She seemed to be holding them up in propiation for her passionate desire to know and to think, which in the unfriendly mediums of Tipton and Fresshit had issued in crying and red eyelids" (28). That which protects Dorothea is her essential femininity which makes for "a special moral influence."[49] In time to come it will be most needed. Presumably, she is lifting these hands to Casaubon's flame, but, as we see, he is unable to appreciate what she is, because of his vulgar idea that Dorothea is a reward for his celibacy, and because of his jealous pride and fear of being found out. Thus there is irony inherent in this gesture. Casaubon is never associated with light or heat, always with damp or dark. The "ardent" Dorothea is herself more a source of life-giving heat than the man she is lifting her hands to. But it will be noticed that she holds her hands up as a screen, which suggests that George Eliot wished us to note some cross-current of negative thought in the gesture which Dorothea herself is unaware of. Only the reader wiser after the event realizes that the gesture is not a wholly positive commitment. We know, for example, that Dorothea's flame is "fed from within" (3), that Casaubon acknowledges, "I feed too much on the inward sources" (13), and that Will's smile is "a gush of inward light" (152).

(v) Character as Symbol

Finally, one ought not to overlook the role played in the symbolic action by a cast of characters who are so intimately related by blood or theme that, as Mark Schorer puts it, "the major characterizations depend on a single value, or perhaps we should say, a single contrast: the quality and kind of social idealism as opposed to self-absorption."[50] The way Mr. Schorer phrases the fact, however, does not distinguish the characters in *Middlemarch* from those in the early novels: the issues in all of them can be resolved into such a division. What distinguishes *Middlemarch* is the "sense of expanding life"[51] in its characters; how they all seem splittings-off from an archetypal stock, symbolizations of a larger consciousness, "reflected light of correspondence" (18), "irradiations."[52] In many cases, the characters seem to be composed all of the same flesh, an aboriginal tissue.

Freud, in *The Interpretation of Dreams,* talks about the way in which the dream-image of a person can be created by "identification" of a number of disparate elements. Such identification "consists in giving representation in the dream-content to only one or more persons who are related by some common feature." The other way in which the dream-image works is by "composition," that is, "when persons are combined, there are already present in the dream-image features which are characteristic of, but not common to, the persons in question, so that a new unity, a composite person, appears as the result of the union of these features." The two ways do not seem vitally different, and what happens in each is that the ego is given "multiple representation" in the dream. "By means of several such identifications an extraordinary amount of thought material may be condensed."[53] Without wishing in any way to sound as if I were psychoanalysing George Eliot, I think it is possible to see a similarity between the dream

structure Freud describes here with its composite symbol for the ego, and the curious way in which the characters of *Middlemarch* interact with each other, autonomously, yet within the overarching consciousness of the narrator, the "collective mind,"[54] the "ego" who creates them all and is a part of them.

From George Eliot's conscious point of view, the narrator's aim is to show "the stealthy convergence of human lots" in which we see "a slow preparation of effects from one life on another" (70). Even "inconsistency" and, with the Raffles plot in mind, coincidence are part of the "living myriad" (380), where each and all are related, as George Eliot put it in *Adam Bede,* "in my mind."[55] Thus, it is curious that many of the characters in *Middlemarch* are orphans (Celia, Dorothea, Will, Bulstrode, Lydgate), and that there is not one "interloper" (554), but two, Bulstrode and Lydgate. To stress that her main characters are orphans means that George Eliot can symbolize man's existential situation in more dramatic fashion. Orphans in the universe, men have to turn to other men; "to mercy, pity, peace, and love / All pray in their distress" (556).

In an 1861 letter to Sara Sophia Hennell, George Eliot expressed the desire for "a temple besides the outdoor temple—a place where human beings do not ramble apart, but *meet* with a common impulse."[56] From her "quarry" for *Middlemarch,* we can see how George Eliot attempted to meet this need in her novel, with her lists of character inter-connections under the rubric, "Relations to be developed."[57] In the novel's multiform connective tissue, all parts linked by the symbol of reform, each character possesses something of each of the others. They are "various small mirrors" (62) reflecting each other, and "one life."

Dorothea and Will are kept in conjunction down to the smallest verbal unit, Will's "inner light" (152) complementing Dorothea's "inward fire" (10). To find Casaubon and Bulstrode linked in this way however is somewhat of a surprise, since on the narrative level they have virtually no connection. Nevertheless, we find that Casaubon has the desire for Dorothea to "irradiate the gloom which fatigue was apt to hang over him" (46), and then we learn that Bulstrode kept "a kind of moral lantern" (91) over the lives of Middlemarchers. Casaubon wants Dorothea to be a diversion, something of an amusement not to be taken overseriously after he has been wandering around in mental gloom with "his taper" (147). Bulstrode is a false light to his people, driven by that religious egoism which George Eliot had condemned in her essay on the poet Young. Casaubon's pride, egoism, and blindness are equal to Bulstrode's, and both men are essentially of the same kind. Each uses people to feed his own selfish needs.

Will enjoys "the very miscellaneousness of Rome," because it makes "the mind flexible with constant comparison" (157). Such a mind is needed to read *Middlemarch* adequately, and one despairs of ever picking up all the structural *nuances*. The most abstruse comparisons, almost bizarre comparisons, result from placing the candle of our attention to the scratches of events on the pier-glass (194-95). Just one example, and this section must be concluded. George Eliot had difficulty in connecting the story of Fred and his troubles with the other important plots. Yet she clearly intended Fred as a kind of foil to Will. Both are unsteady, go through a period of trial and apprenticeship for the hand of the woman they love, and finally marry her. George Eliot intends us to keep the comparison constantly in mind, and summarizes the theme: "to Will, a creature who cared little for what are called the solid things of life and greatly for its subtler influences, to have within him such a feeling as he had towards Dorothea, was like the inheritance of a fortune" (344). Will had been disinherited because of his mother's imprudent marriage. Similarly, Fred's chances of inheriting old Featherstone's fortune had been lost, and he sets about making his own fortune with the help of Mary and Caleb.

(VI) FORM: SOME CONCLUSIONS

By the time George Eliot wrote *Middlemarch,* Darrel Mansell says: "The diversity which her kind of fiction can include is only limited by what she herself thinks she is able to find together in a wholeness in her own mind." Hence, "The more varied the relations she can present in her fiction, the higher the degree of form she can attain if she is successful in binding everything together in a wholeness." As Mr. Brooke sagaciously points out, "Life isn't cast into a mould—not cut out by rule and line, and that sort of thing" (30). George Eliot intends to refract life in all its multiplicity; but, since the human mind will no more accept an artistic chaos any more than a "moral chaos" (80), a tension is created in the novel between refraction and selection. Resolution depends not on "explicit relations" (the kind found more frequently in the earlier novels), but on "obscure implicit ones."[58] The structure thus approaches multiplicity and verges on inconsequence (as James hinted). But the symbolic action provides a complicated and unifying dance of motifs. George Eliot's own metaphor of the web to describe the structure of society and the structure of the novel is slightly misleading as a definition of the aesthetic principle because it evokes, in fact, a structure "cut out by rule and line." The metaphor of the connective thread (153) is better, but the critic is safer if he duplicates the methods of Lydgate's enquiry, as he looks for "new connections and hitherto hidden facts of structure" (110). George Eliot may be "enamoured of arduous invention" (122), but her tri-

umph is that the result appears completely spontaneous. In Caleb Garth's words describing something well-made, "Things hang together" (297).

Middlemarch also enacts in its structure a truth it preaches. "Our good depends on the quality and breadth of the emotion" (345), she writes; a phrase which sounds as though it could have come from **"Notes On Form In Art."** George Eliot's perfect reader will force himself, like Dorothea after her interview with Ladislaw, "to dwell on every detail and its possible meaning" (577). Signs, however, "are small measurable things, but interpretations are illimitable" (18). That is one barrier to a perfect reading. Another is that all of us, attempting to describe a "sign" "get our thoughts tangled in metaphors, and act fatally on the strength of them" (63). Fully to understand how the concept of symbolic action works in *Middlemarch* we must pay strict attention to the individual detail and then evaluate its "quality and breadth." Details mean more than themselves. In symbolic action, a structure vibrates with significance.

If, as I said earlier, George Eliot was writing beyond the capacities of contemporary critical acumen, and their critical vocabulary was inadequate to deal with *Middlemarch,* today, when *Middlemarch* is at last appreciated as the masterpiece it is, we might have such a vocabulary. Unfortunately, however, even on the question of plot there is widespread disagreement, not to say confusion. The followers of Northrop Frye, for example, regard the novel as a long poem, and attempt to see "the whole design of the work as a unity. It is now a simultaneous pattern radiating out from a center, not a narrative moving in time."[59] Neo-Aristotelian critics, on the other hand, following the lead of R. S. Crane, while not denying that plot is no simple matter, prefer not to give undue emphasis to what Norman Friedman calls "the images"[60] (which, in fiction, can be characters). Mr. Friedman finds unfortunate "the failure of many critics today to take seriously, on a material level, the various unifying principles which may shape in a novel action and the way it is handled."[61] The trouble is that we have "no commonly accepted body of terms, principles, and distinctions for grasping satisfactorily the literal action of a novel as it functions in the whole of which it is a palpable part."[62] In this essay, I have attempted to reconcile both schools of criticism, by stressing the fact that literal and symbolic are not exclusive; that the "literal action" *can* possess the qualities of a long poem. In my discussion on *Middlemarch* I have tried to show, in fact, that George Eliot's style transmutes the literal plot, which nevertheless exists fully in its own right. Mr. Friedman demonstrates a looseness of critical vocabulary when he bluntly opposes "the facts of the case" to "symbolic interpretation,"[63] and "what happens in the literal action" to "a critic searching for subtleties."[64] Apart from anything else, who is to say that the "subtleties" a sensitive critic finds are, in fact, not there?

One has to ask oneself if there is any *real* insurmountable difference between the neo-Aristotelian critic and the symbolic critic. When, for instance, we note in *Middlemarch* the "meticulously counterpointed"[65] stories of Lydgate and Dorothea, each an orphan with a Continental education, each well-born but disregarding rank, each a reformer, are we falsifying our reaction to say that literal plot pattern becomes symbolic of some ideal George Eliot had in mind? How else can we suggest that the double pattern is more than mere coincidence? Again, when we note the Aristotelian *peripeteia,* as the roles of Dorothea and Lydgate are reversed, he becoming the patient, and she the doctor; when we see this inversion of roles repeated in various ways with other characters, with Will and Bulstrode, for instance, we need a terminology which will *distinguish* literal or traditional plot from the way George Eliot uses it in *Middlemarch.* There is a sense, even, in which plot turns out to be what Walter Naumann terms a "pseudo-structure": "George Eliot has an incredibly easy effortless manner, the manner of the spinner of tales who passes from one chapter to the next, from one object to another even when remote, without the slightest difficulty."[66] Such a technique, he claims, does not use plot as structure; the novel works because of its slow-moving "orchestrated" themes. Or again, along similar lines, Richard S. Lyons has remarked, in an intensive study of only one chapter of *Middlemarch,* that at a certain point, "plot and character become inseparable, for plot becomes the growth in consciousness by which character is defined."[67] Clearly, then, plot is no simple matter. And by now, it should be obvious that the symbolic approach to plot and texture is not a game of symbol-hunting. Since in *Middlemarch* there is a complicated "correspondence of one plot with another. They are not tenuously related parts, but different versions of the same story,"[68] it is not stretching the concept of symbolic action to call each plot a symbolic representation of the other, and all four symbolic of an overall consciousness.

Mr. Friedman himself gives us a clue to the full meaning of a form which becomes symbolic, while retaining the appearance of a plot-outline. He asks, "What, then, is a symbol? An image alive with an idea; a fact saturated in value."[69] The surface or "superficial" approach is then a vital part of any critical evaluation which stresses symbolism, since we must emphasize "the dependence of symbol on particular sensation and feeling."[70] Of course, we run the risk of hardening a scene or gesture when we abstract it from its field of expressive meaning, but so we do when we abstract the plot element. The critic's job, however, is made slightly easier in George Eliot's case because of the happy tendency of places and people "quietly and easily" to "gather emotional value and meaning, become charged with natural piety,"[71] when "a given poet's preoccupation with certain settings, situations, and characters will be seen, when viewed in the perspective of his total achievement to act as a symbolic key to his ultimate vision in life, just as his recurrent metaphors, when systematically inspected, will do."[72]

Without wanting to claim that *everything* in *Middlemarch* is symbolic (i. e., not itself), I would like to insist that everything is part of a symbolic action, for "there are *practical* acts, and there are symbolic acts," and "the symbolic act is the dancing of an attitude."[73] Symbolic acts are "representative acts"[74] which only receive their full and most potent force from other acts. George Eliot's symbolic method in *Middlemarch* does more than "reinforce and lend emotional values to other kinds of meaning,"[75] a critical judgment that has become commonplace though none the less popular. Symbolic imagery, in fact, is only part of the total effect which includes plot, character, and so on, and transmutes them into something rich and strange. This totality is so rich, in fact, that one comes away from the novel with a feeling of dangerous frustration; "dangerous" because frustration leads to dogmatism, and the discoveries one had set out to "whisper" freeze into assertions, lose their elastic tentativeness, and thus distort. One retains a sense of the tough delicacy of *Middlemarch* by not shouting; by being satisfied with thoughts and observations which provide, in Frost's definition of poetry, "a temporary stay against confusion."[76]

Notes

1. Ludwig Andreas Feuerbach, *The Essence of Christianity,* trans. Marian Evans (London, 1854), p. 46.

2. Henry James, *The Galaxy,* 15 (1873), 424-25.

3. John Blackwood to George Eliot, 24 April 1868, in *The George Eliot Letters,* ed. Gordon S. Haight (New Haven, 1954), IV, 243.

4. *The Galaxy,* p. 428.

5. Many of the leading journals found themselves baffled by the book, or praised it for the wrong reasons. See, for example, *The Spectator* (2 December 1871), 1458-60; *Atheneum* (2 December 1871), 713-14; *Quarterly Review,* 134 (April, 1873), 336-69; *The Times* (7 March 1873). Frederic Harrison might seem to be George Eliot's perfect reader from the evidence of a letter he wrote in 1866 (*Letters* [*The George Eliot Letters*], IV, 284-85), in which he discusses *Felix Holt* in terms of a poem.

6. Calvin Bedient, "*Middlemarch*: Touching Down," *Hudson Review,* 22 (1969), 71.

7. For a brief and cogent introduction to the topic of organic unity, see Richard Stang, *The Theory of the Novel in England, 1850-1870* (London, 1959), pp. 134-35.

8. 24 July 1871, *Letters,* V, 168.

9. 8 August 1863, *Letters,* IV, 97.

10. Ursula Brumm, "Symbolism and the Novel," *Partisan Review,* 25 (Summer, 1958), 329.

11. "Symbolism and the Novel," p. 330.

12. "Symbolism and the Novel," p. 331.

13. 15 August 1866, *Letters,* IV, 301.

14. Henry James, *Partial Portraits* (London, 1899), p. 51.

15. August 1866, *Letters,* IV, 301.

16. "Symbolism and the Novel," p. 333.

17. "History by Indirection: the Era of Reform in *Middlemarch,*" *Victorian Studies,* 1 (September, 1957), 173-79.

18. George Eliot, *Middlemarch,* ed. Gordon S. Haight (Cambridge, Mass., 1956), p. 612. Throughout, all references are to this edition.

19. Thomas Carlyle, *Sartor Resartus* (London, 1940), p. 54.

20. José Ortega y Gasset, "The Nature of the Novel," *Hudson Review,* 10 (Spring, 1957), 28.

21. Ortega y Gasset, "The Nature of the Novel," p. 30.

22. "Art always aims at the representation of Reality, i. e., of Truth; and no departure from truth is permissible, except such as inevitably lies in the nature of the medium itself. Realism is thus the basis of all Art, and its antithesis is not Idealism but Falsism." From "Realism and Idealism," in *The Literary Criticism of George Henry Lewes,* ed. Alice Kaminsky (Lincoln, Nebraska, 1964), p. 87.

23. Lewes, in *Principles of Success in Literature,* writes that Imagination is "simply the power of forming images," and "to imagine—to form an image—we must have the numerous relations of things present to the mind" (Kaminsky, pp. 14-15).

24. In "George Eliot and the Unified Sensibility," *PMLA,* 79 (1964), 130-36, N. N. Feltes suggests that George Eliot obtained this ideal from Lewes' pioneer work *The Problems of Life and Mind.*

25. *The Philosophy of Literary Form* (Louisiana State, 1941), pp. 26-28.

26. "The Nature of the Novel," p. 28.

27. *Philosophy of Literary Form,* p. 10.

28. *Rhythm in the Novel* (Toronto, 1950).

29. "The Nature of the Novel," p. 30.

30. George Eliot to Anthony Trollope, 23 October 1863, *Letters,* IV, 110.

31. George Eliot to Mrs. Alfred Taylor, 30 July 1863, *Letters,* IV, 95.

32. George Eliot to Sara Sophia Hennell, 15 September 1864, *Letters,* IV, 103.

33. George Eliot, "The Progress of the Intellect," in *The Essays of George Eliot,* ed. Thomas Pinney (London, 1963), p. 28.

34. "Fiction and the Matrix of Analogy," *Kenyon Review,* 11 (Autumn, 1949), 550.

35. "The Structure of the Novel," in *Middlemarch: Critical Approaches to the Novel,* ed. Barbara Hardy (Oxford, 1967), p. 20.

36. Harold Osborne, "Artistic Unity and Gestalt," *The Philosophical Quarterly,* 14 (July, 1956), 215.

37. "Notes On Form In Art," in *Essays* [*The Essays of George Eliot*], pp. 432-33.

38. "George Eliot's Conception of Form," *SEL* [*Studies in English Literature, 1500-1900*], 5 (1965), 653.

39. C. G. Jung, "Transformational Symbolism in the Mass," in *Pagan and Christian Mysteries,* ed. Joseph Campbell (New York, 1933), p. 131.

40. Osborne, "Artistic Unity and Gestalt," p. 215.

41. Other examples of such scenes are Chapter 18 in Book 2, Chapter 25 in Book 4, Chapter 32 in Book 3, Chapter 51 in Book 5, and Chapters 60 and 63. For a more complete, though different list of what he calls "conglomerate" scenes, see Neil D. Isaacs, "*Middlemarch*: Crescendo of Obligatory Drama," *NCF* [*Nineteenth-Century Fiction*], 18 (June, 1963), 21-34.

42. Jerome Beaty, *Middlemarch from Notebook to Novel* (Urbana, 1960), p. 9.

43. J. W. Beach, *The Twentieth-Century Novel* (New York, 1932), pp. 129-30, discusses what he calls these "second-line characters."

44. *Scene and Symbol from George Eliot to James Joyce* (New Haven, 1969), p. 15.

45. "George Eliot in *Middlemarch,*" in *From Dickens to Hardy,* ed. Boris Ford (Harmondsworth, 1960), p. 280.

46. Jean Giraudoux, *Tiger at the Gates,* trans. Christopher Fry (New York, 1955), p. 1.

47. "George Eliot in *Middlemarch,*" p. 289.

48. Hilda Hulme, "The Language of the Novel," in *Middlemarch: Critical Approaches to the Novel,* p. 90.

49. George Eliot to Emily Davies, 8 August 1868, *Letters,* IV, 468.

50. "The Structure of the Novel," p. 13.

51. Barbara Hardy, *The Novels of George Eliot,* p. 93.

52. Brown, *Rhythm in the Novel,* p. 27, is the source of this term.

53. *The Interpretation of Dreams,* trans. A. A. Brill (New York, 1950), pp. 306-08.

54. J. Hillis Miller, in *The Form of Victorian Fiction* (Notre Dame, 1968), p. 81, writes that the characteristic work of George Eliot, Dickens, Meredith, Trollope, Thackeray, "comes into existence" when the novelist "chooses to play the role not of a first person narrator who is an actor in the drama, and not even the role of an anonymous storyteller who may be identified with an individual consciousness, but in the role of a *collective mind*" (my italics).

55. *Adam Bede,* ed. Gordon S. Haight (New York, 1960), p. 178.

56. 18 September 1861, *Letters,* III, 452.

57. Anna Theresa Kitchel, *Quarry for Middlemarch* (Berkeley, 1950), p. 45.

58. "George Eliot's Conception of Form," pp. 656-58.

59. Northrop Frye, "Literary Criticism," in *The Aims and Methods of Scholarship in Modern Languages and Literatures,* ed. James Thorp (New York, 1963), pp. 63-65.

60. "Imagery: From Sensation to Symbol," *Journal of Aesthetics and Art Criticism,* 12 (September, 1953), 31.

61. "Criticism and the Novel," *Antioch Review,* 18 (1958), 344.

62. "Criticism and the Novel," p. 345.

63. "Criticism and the Novel," p. 347.

64. "Criticism and the Novel," p. 370.

65. U. C. Knoepflmacher, *Religious Humanism and the Victorian Novel* (Princeton, 1965), p. 76.

66. "The Architecture of George Eliot's Novels," *Modern Language Quarterly,* 9 (1948), 38.

67. "The Method of *Middlemarch,*" *NCF,* 21 (June, 1966), 38.

68. Barbara Hardy, *The Novels of George Eliot,* p. 99.

69. "Imagery: From Sensation to Symbol," p. 40.

70. Barbara Hardy, "The Surface of the Novel," in *Middlemarch: Critical Approaches to the Novel,* p. 152.

71. Jerome Thale, *The Novels of George Eliot* (New York, 1959), p. 158.

72. Friedman, "Imagery: From Sensation to Symbol," p. 31.

73. Burke, *The Philosophy of Literary Form,* p. 10.

74. Burke, *The Philosophy of Literary Form,* p. 25.

75. Thale, *The Novels of George Eliot,* p. 158.

76. Mention of poetry reminds me of Charles Olsen's revolutionary program for "Projective Verse," one of the prescriptions for which concerns "the Kinetics of the thing." That is, "the poem must, at all points, be a high-energy construct and, at all points an energy discharge." Stressing "FIELD COMPOSITION," Olsen comes to the conclusion (not unlike the conclusion Darrel Mansell comes to about *Middlemarch*), that "FORM IS NEVER MORE THAN AN EXTENSION OF CONTENT." In other words, form is anything the poem will hold within its field of force. In these essential aesthetic points, *Middlemarch* anticipates an important aesthetic movement of twentieth-century American poetry! See "Projective Verse," in *The New American Poetry,* ed. Donald M. Allen (New York, 1960), pp. 386-97.

U. C. Knoepflmacher (essay date June 1975)

SOURCE: Knoepflmacher, U. C. "*Middlemarch*: An Avuncular View." *Nineteenth-Century Fiction* 30, no. 1 (June 1975): 53-81.

[*In the following essay, Knoepflmacher explores the symbolic importance of uncle figures in* Middlemarch. *According to Knoepflmacher, the book's male characters—all "uncles" in one way or another—serve as surrogates for an absent patriarch, a role they are ill-equipped to fill. Their failure to provide Dorothea with intellectual, moral, or imaginative guidance represents a broader disintegration of familial and social relationships in the nineteenth century. In the end, only the narrator, as "the novel's prime builder of relations and prime restorer of order," has the power to safeguard traditional ideals of kinship and societal bonds.*]

Etymological Note: The word "uncle" is derived from "*auunculus*"—a mother's brother—a word that stems from the combination of "*auus*" (an ancestor, especially a maternal grandfather) and *"unculus"* (a diminutive). An uncle or *avunculus* thus is a substitute for the ancestral parent, a lesser father figure. Thus, for instance, when the Fool in *Lear* calls the King "nuncle" ("an uncle") he is calling attention to the diminished power of a father and king who has parted with his crown, a symbol of authority as well as of wit.

In the prelude to *Middlemarch,* the reader is immediately invited to take a look at Saint Theresa of Avila as a prototype for the yet unnamed Dorothea. But the incident which the narrator selects for us is not taken from the Spanish saint's adult life: it is taken neither from Theresa's accounts of her mystical revelations nor from her writings about conventual reform. Instead, the allusion is to a "child-pilgrimage" undertaken by a highly imaginative seven-year-old girl and by her still smaller brother. Toddling out from "rugged Avila," Theresa and Rodrigo are propelled by a desire to seek martyrdom, to be beheaded by infidels such as those encountered by the impressionable child in the Saints' Lives owned by her parents. Fortunately, Theresa's precocious fancies are checked: "domestic reality met them in the shape of uncles, and turned them back from their great resolve."[1]

Like Maggie Tulliver's flight to become a gypsy queen, the event is given a mock-epic treatment. Yet to Theresa of Avila herself, who records the incident in her *Vida* or autobiography, it helps to dramatize her confident belief that will and self are subordinated to God's design. Even a "domestic reality in the shape of uncles" is to Theresa an integral part of the providential order shaped by her heavenly Father. Looking back at her childhood, Theresa may well have been convinced that the uncle who appeared at the gate of the town to stop her and her brother was nothing less than an agent for a Divine Providence. By restoring the girl to her father's house, this uncle (it was her father's brother, Don Francisco Alvarez de Cepeda) was instrumental in preserving her for a more epic task, the "great resolve"—to use George Eliot's words—that was still to come.[2]

The author of *Middlemarch* can no longer believe in the sacramental universe that still existed for a sixteenth-century mystic—a universe in which any action, no matter how small, could be seen as part of a larger plan. In the novel's "Finale," the narrator insists that "a new Theresa will hardly have the opportunity of reforming a conventual life, any more than a new Antigone will spend her heroic piety all for the sake of a brother's burial: the medium in which their ardent deeds took shape is for ever gone." The epos found by a Theresa rescued by a firm uncle, or, in a different age of belief, found by an Antigone who defied her own firm uncle in the name of "sisterly piety" and a "reverence for the Gods,"[3] belongs, as far as George Eliot is concerned, to a world animated by poetic systems of belief no longer available to a nineteenth-century agnostic.

And yet, in *Middlemarch,* George Eliot, like Theresa, wants her readers to perceive a higher order of interrelations; although her fictional universe is a replica of a godless world, she hopes to reanimate that world with essence and meaning. Fielding, a century before, could still pretend to imitate the motions of a world ruled by some deistic providence. For George Eliot such a pretense has become impossible. It is no coincidence that in the first paragraph of her opening chapter, she should call attention to the separation between inner essence and outward form that exists in her world. Nor is it a coincidence, I think, that this long opening paragraph, which begins by contrasting Miss Brooke's beauty to her outward attire, should end with a reference to Dorothea's uncle, guardian, and provider, Arthur Brooke.

The uncle of Dorothea and Celia bears little resemblance to a Squire Allworthy or Matthew Bramble in eighteenth-century fiction. The "domestic reality in the shape of uncles" that he epitomizes is, by way of contrast, rather grim. He shares this new reality with Mr. Casaubon (who is consistently mistaken for Will Ladislaw's uncle), with Peter Featherstone (the uncle of Fred and Rosamond Vincy as well as of Mary Garth), with Bulstrode (Fred and Rosamond's *other* uncle and also Ladislaw's surrogate grandfather), and with Sir Godwin Lydgate (the uncle of the physician to whom Rosamond applies for financial help). All of these figures in one way or another pervert the traditional role of father substitute, provider, and agent for justice assigned to the uncle or *avunculus* in an ordered universe.

George Eliot, curiously enough, singles out Mr. Brooke as the prime "nuncle" of her novel. To be sure, she makes it clear from the outset that he shares the parsimoniousness of the others. He is a poor landlord, who fails to provide his tenants with the minimal comforts demanded for them by Dorothea. For all his "benevolent intentions," he spends—we are told—"as little money as possible to carry them out"—a trait that most certainly does link him to Casaubon, Featherstone, Bulstrode, and Sir Godwin (ch. 1). Yet whereas these other uncles deliberately harm younger relatives by denying or withdrawing favors, Mr. Brooke is not really indicted for miserliness or vindictiveness towards his two nieces. Whereas money is to Casaubon or Featherstone or Bulstrode a means of exerting power over others, Mr. Brooke is not power-hungry: it is vanity rather than a desire to control others that leads this uncle to seek power as a liberal member of Parliament. Unlike the others, Mr. Brooke does mean well; he is a benevolist, a latter-day version of the good Squire Allworthy. Quite genuinely concerned about the welfare of his two nieces and vaguely concerned about the welfare of the land, he also becomes the patron of the same Ladislaw who refuses to be dependent on either Casaubon's or Bulstrode's money. Why, then, does George Eliot single out this bumbling, yet quite amiable and well-meaning, paternalist as an object of some of her sharpest irony?

It is Mr. Brooke's failure to provide for nourishment of a different sort which, I think, lends him his importance. As we shall soon see, George Eliot actually holds Mr. Brooke responsible for Dorothea's plight. Totally incapable of perceiving any pattern or design in human events, he fails to provide the hungry imagination of his older niece with that large vision of relations which she, like the niece of the good Don Francisco Alvarez de Cepeda, so desperately needs and desires in order to live in an intelligible universe. As impotent in rescuing a poacher from a death sentence as he is in rescuing Dorothea from her self-willed martyrdom as Casaubon's wife, Mr. Brooke lacks authority. Undisciplined, he has no consistent code such as that possessed by Creon, that other uncle whose sense of justice, though excessively self-righteous and unduly punitive, at least provided a niece with a martyrdom that was truly heroic. Mr. Brooke cannot furnish his niece with the mental and emotional provisions she requires. Mired in a confusing present, he forces Dorothea to turn to Casaubon as her provider and thus causes her to become mired in a dead and destructive past.

Mr. Brooke's depleted imagination thus is crucial to George Eliot's aims. This inadequate substitute for a father helps the novelist to dramatize the orphaned condition of superior nineteenth-century minds who can no longer count on the security of an earthly *avus* or ancestor nor on the security of an infinite *"I AM"* for a sense of identity and relation. Mr. Brooke's surrogate daughter, like the novel's two male orphans—Lydgate and Ladislaw, needs larger props than those which the slovenly "domestic reality" of Tipton Grange can provide. The master of the Grange cannot fuse object and subject, form and essence, the real and the ideal. He remains a caricature of the paternal provider, a figure of absurdity. And it is precisely his absurdity that George Eliot wants to seize upon, because it is that absurdity and dislocation, as much as the lovelessness of the novel's other uncles, that the narrator of *Middlemarch*—Mr. Brooke's avuncular antitype—sets out to counter with all might.

* * *

We can now look at the opening paragraph of the novel's first chapter—a paragraph that concludes with a reference to the "bachelor uncle and guardian" of the Brooke sisters. The paragraph relies on a series of contrasts. There is a discrepancy between Dorothea's Madonna-like plain garments and the more ostentatious "provincial fashion" of the times; there is a discrepancy also between the local opinions about Dorothea and those held about Celia, who, though dressed in an attire

that differs only slightly from her sister's, is felt by observers to possess "more common-sense." The discrepancy which separates these sisters from the daughters of country-hucksters thus leads to a sense of the discrepancies between themselves. What seems complementary, is not. The effect of the paragraph's progression is to isolate Dorothea. She can no more be incapsulated by the petty provincial world her sister readily accepts than "a fine quotation from the Bible,—or from one of our elder poets" can be made to fit into "a paragraph of to-day's newspaper." Essence and container, ideally one and the same, remain at odds. Seemingly balanced with its equal attention to past and present, Dorothea and Celia, the protrusions of drapery and Pascal's *Pensées,* the paragraph only manages to disengage what is unique and exceptional from all that is common and ordinary.

As we progress further in the paragraph, we discover that it is Dorothea's religiosity, her concern with "the destinies of mankind," that sets her apart. Indeed, the narrator's detached and ironic tone seems to shift as soon as the "eccentric agitation" that separates Dorothea from others is more closely examined: "she was enamoured of intensity and greatness, and rash in embracing whatever seemed to her to have those aspects; likely to seek martyrdom, to make retractations, and then to incur martyrdom after all in a quarter where she had not sought it." The reader by now has no difficulty in identifying Dorothea with one of those "later-born Theresas . . . helped by no coherent social faith and order" alluded to in the novel's Prelude. The paragraph has forced us into a sense of dislocation akin to that of Dorothea herself. Although it ends with homely facts—the ages of the two sisters and the details of their inconsistent education—these facts cannot account for the differences between them and hence only accentuate our uneasiness over a heroine who seems incapable of anchoring her undefined but "lofty conception of the world" in the parish of Tipton.

Our mounting uneasiness about the elder Miss Brooke is checked by the paragraph's final allusion to a "bachelor uncle and guardian" of whose existence we had not been apprised. This uncle's apparent willingness to "remedy the disadvantages" of the two sisters' "orphaned condition"—particularly of the orphaned condition of the elder of the two—somehow seems vaguely reassuring. It has hardly been a year, after all, since the girls have come to live with their guardian at Tipton Grange. The effects of their education—an education grounded on "plans at once narrow and promiscuous"—cannot yet have worn off. Dorothea's continued exposure to a benevolent yet firm and discriminating guardian should permit her to make the proper adjustments, to enable her "to reconcile the anxieties" set off by the incongruities the first paragraph has described. The precedents of fictional convention encourage the reader's hopefulness. Benefactors living in country houses are, after all, noted for their ability to restore and replenish. We think of Squire Allworthy reinstalling his nephew Tom Jones in Paradise Hall; we recall the avuncular Mr. Knightley who becomes both father and husband to the impulsive Emma Woodhouse. Less than two decades before **Middlemarch,** Charles Dickens had still fallen back on the stereotype of the kind country guardian: John Jarndyce in *Bleak House* offers shelter to Esther Summerson as well as to Ada and Richard, his orphaned wards; it is through his benevolence that Esther, at least, can come to terms with the shifting world from which she seemed so irrevocably sundered.[4]

Ideally, then, the first Middlemarcher to which the reader is introduced may turn out to be a firm guide and a gentle helper. We want to know more about the "bachelor uncle and guardian" mentioned at the end of the first paragraph. And George Eliot obliges us. She does not return to Dorothea's "discontent with the actual conditions of her life" (ch. 5) until she has fully satisfied our curiosity. The second paragraph of the novel is exclusively devoted to the person of Mr. Arthur Brooke. The ironic vignette shatters our expectations rather quickly:

> It was hardly a year since they had come to live at Tipton Grange with their uncle, a man nearly sixty, of acquiescent temper, miscellaneous opinions, and uncertain vote. He had travelled in his younger years, and was held in this part of the county to have contracted a too rambling habit of mind. Mr Brooke's conclusions were as difficult to predict as the weather: it was only safe to say that he would act with benevolent intentions, and that he would spend as little money as possible in carrying them out. For the most glutinously indefinite minds enclose some hard grains of habit; and a man has been seen lax about all his own interests except the retention of his snuff-box, concerning which he was watchful, suspicious, and greedy of clutch.
>
> (ch. 1)

The portrait seems to be a burlesque of all those benevolist Allworthys sheltering orphans in a deistic universe. We are disturbed—but not by Mr. Brooke's age nor by his stinginess, since we are soon told that "if Dorothea married and had a son, that son would inherit Mr Brooke's estate, presumably worth about three thousand a-year" (ch. 1). What disturbs us is that "glutinous" character, those miscellaneous opinions, that uncertain vote. Instead of the guide we have expected, Mr. Brooke decidedly seems Dorothea's inferior: "In Mr Brooke the hereditary strain of Puritan energy was clearly in abeyance; but in his niece Dorothea it glowed alike through faults and virtues, turning sometimes into impatience of her uncle's talk or his way of 'letting things be' on his estate." Far from restraining Dorothea's dissatisfaction or from soothing our uneasiness over her dissatisfaction, Mr. Brooke seems to belong to the same reality that has made her and us so dissatis-

fied. He cannot reconcile us to discrepancy because he is himself a discrepancy—as much at odds with Dorothea as a paragraph of today's prose is at odds with a fine quotation from yesterday's poetry.

We take some comfort from the fact that the "rambling habit of mind" ascribed to Mr. Brooke is, after all, not directly attributed to him by the narrator, but rather by those same provincial minds who have already looked askance at Dorothea's enthusiasm. There is some comfort, too, in the notion that Dorothea's "impatience of her uncle's talk" may be unjustified, a product of her own intolerance. Such comforts, however, are small. Moreover, they are short-lived. We are forced to *listen* to Mr. Brooke's voice in the opening paragraph of chapter two. It is the first male voice we overhear in **Middlemarch** and its cadence only confirms the accuracy of the narrator's earlier description:

> "Sir Humphry Davy?" said Mr Brooke, over the soup, in his easy smiling way, taking up Sir James Chettam's remark that he was studying Davy's Agricultural Chemistry. "Well, now, Sir Humphry Davy: I dined with him years ago at Cartwright's, and Wordsworth was there too—the poet Wordsworth, you know. Now there was something singular. I was at Cambridge when Wordsworth was there, and I never met him—and I dined with him twenty years afterwards at Cartwright's. There's an oddity in things, now. But Davy was there: he was a poet too. Or, as I may say, Wordsworth was poet one, and Davy was poet two. That was true in every sense, you know."
>
> (ch. 2)

Only a trite coincidence, as subject to chance as fads in female fashion or news items in "a paragraph of today's newspaper," permits Mr. Brooke to yoke Wordsworth to Sir Humphry Davy. By accidentally meeting the two men at the same table, he can relate them to each other and to himself. Remembering Sir Humphry Davy's interest in poetry, he converts the scientist into a "poet too" as well as "poet two." The pun itself is indicative of the strained fashion in which his mind attempts to impose some order on a reality that would otherwise remain intractable, furnishing no "similitude in dissimilitude."[5] To Mr. Brooke there will always be an "oddity in things, *now*"—in the succession of odd and random "nows" his mind forever fails to process. Seizing on an analogy (Wordsworth and Davy as fellow poets), he tries to confer a further semblance of order through subordination by ranking them as "one" and "two." His mind rests satisfied. He has created order out of chaos.

Mr. Brooke's order, however, is spurious and mechanical. This "amiable host" who recalls a bygone dinner for Sir James and the Rev. Mr. Casaubon, his current dinner guests, remains totally oblivious to the mental and emotional starvation of his elder niece. His feeble attempt to yoke Wordsworth the subjective poet to Sir Humphry Davy the objective scientist is an affront, a mockery of the more serious mental structures desired, not only by Dorothea, but also by all those characters in the novel who yearn for more meaningful relations between subject and object than his mind can ever presume to establish. His speech, moreover, also parodies the efforts of the syncretic narrator of the novel—and of the novelist who stands behind that narrator. Only the novelist can integrate feeling and knowledge into the larger vision of relations aspired by a Casaubon or Lydgate, on the one hand, and a Dorothea or Ladislaw, on the other.

By making us aware of her omnipresent intelligence, George Eliot can cause the reader to perceive links undetected by Mr. Brooke. If the conversationalist who tries to order events over "his soup, in his easy smiling way," falls short of a judicious Allworthy, he seems even punier when compared to the narrator who insists that the task of connecting and "unravelling certain human lots" has become infinitely more difficult for minds no longer living in the ordered eighteenth century enjoyed by Allworthy's creator, a Fielding who could bring "his arm-chair to the proscenium and chat with us in all the lusty ease of his fine English" (ch. 15). The genial uncle as guide and interpreter is gone. No Mr. Great-heart can conduct dispossessed pilgrims to a Heavenly Jerusalem in a world that has become a chance-ridden Vanity Fair. No Mr. Knightley's voice can return us to "English verdure, English culture, English comfort."[6] Though he has traveled far more widely on his expeditions than did Matthew Bramble, Mr. Brooke has gained no self-synthesis. As dilettante and dabbler, he even lacks a hobbyhorse, some eccentric obsession that would at least give him the charm of an Uncle Toby. As we shall later see, there is only a short step from this ineffectual county magistrate to Sir Hugo Mallinger in *Daniel Deronda*—a benevolent uncle who now heads an entire society bereft of vision and purpose.

Mr. Brooke's opening speech thus becomes symptomatic of more than an elderly bachelor's "too rambling habits of mind." By yoking Sir Humphry Davy and William Wordsworth so arbitrarily, without reflecting on their actual historical relation and without the imaginative skill of interpreting the significance of that relation, Mr. Brooke exhibits a plight common to other nineteenth-century minds. As a creature of that century, he is forced to fall back on the resourcefulness of his synthetic powers to find meanings and correspondences once guaranteed by religion but lacking in the rational systems of the Enlightenment. At the very beginning of the nineteenth century, in his Preface to the 1800 edition of *Lyrical Ballads,* Wordsworth had tried to describe that "more than usual organic sensibility" required by those concerned with the weaving and interweaving of reality into new structures of meaning.[7] Since, for Wordsworth, the imagination is a form of knowledge, he detects little difference between the pursuits of the Poet and those followed by the "Man of Science, the Chemist and Mathematician." Both are connectors, both derive an intense psychological pleasure from seeing the general in the particular: "However painful may be the objects with which the Anatomist's knowledge is concerned, he feels that his knowledge is pleasure."[8] Rather than discrete activities, poetry and science have a common denominator in the psyche's delight in order.[9]

Would the disordered mind of Mr. Brooke recollect that Wordsworth and Sir Humphry Davy became friends after the latter agreed to proofread this selfsame 1800 edition of *Lyrical Ballads*? Probably not.[10] But the narrator of *Middlemarch,* who possesses that unusual organic sensibility that Mr. Brooke lacks and whose erudition makes him equally familiar with the history of English science as with the history of English literature, presumably not only knows this fact, but also would know that the physician who owed his rapid fame, not to his medical work, but to his electrochemical researches, was a prodigy who took charge of the Pneumatic Institution at Bristol at the age of twenty (Dorothea's age) in 1798, the same year in which Wordsworth and Coleridge published the first edition of their work. Nor would the history-conscious narrator have forgotten that Sir Humphry Davy died at Geneva—the seat of Dorothea's nonscientific education—in May of 1829, a few months before the conversation at Mr. Brooke's dinner table takes place.

Such facts, however poignant, still belong to the same order as a chance meeting at Cartwright's. And facts (as Mr. Casaubon so painfully knows) remain capricious and meaningless unless lighted up by the imagination. For the novelist who will later contrast Lydgate the anatomist to Ladislaw the poet and relate both men to Dorothea, the modes of Sir Humphry Davy and William Wordsworth obviously carry a relevance which even a more alert Mr. Brooke could not aspire to penetrate. To her, as to the Romantic poets before her, science and poetry are alternates that stem from the same mental impulse, the same need to gratify our yearning for relation and order.[11]

Wordsworth's allusion to Chemist and Anatomist in his Preface may well have been intended as a complimentary reference to the "poet two" who kindly volunteered to proofread his galleys. Lord Byron, too, in *Don Juan,* had made use of the figure of Sir Humphry as a comment on his own creative efforts to restore meaning to a far more chaotic universe than that perceived by the sober mind of William Wordsworth.[12] As interested as Wordsworth and Byron had been in the fusion of knowledge and feeling, George Eliot uses Mr. Brooke's careless reference to call attention to one of the key concerns of her novel. To those for whom "words are things,"[13] there is an obvious significance in Mr. Brooke's unenlightening reference to the inventor of the coal miner's lamp and to the poet most concerned with the lamp of the imagination. But the narrator, so helpful on other occasions, refrains from pointing out this significance for us. In chapter two, George Eliot deliberately frustrates our imagination; she wants us to be wholly dependent on Mr. Brooke as our avuncular guide. Our dependence encourages us to empathize with Dorothea's own frustration. We share her increasing annoyance over her uncle's garrulous ramblings: "Dorothea felt a little more uneasy than usual. In the beginning of dinner, the party being small and the room still, these motes from the mass of a magistrate's mind fell too noticeably. She wondered how a man like Mr Casaubon would support such triviality. His manners, she thought, were very dignified."

Like Dorothea, we are being deflected from Mr. Brooke to Mr. Casaubon. We have abandoned all hopes that Dorothea's uncle may act as a substitute for the father she needs. We remember her desire to engage in a marriage "where your husband was a sort of father, and could teach you even Hebrew, if you wish." Reminded also of her "venerating expectation" about Casaubon, who is "noted in the county as a man of profound learning" and "of wealth enough to give lustre to his piety," the reader finds Dorothea's obvious attraction to the newcomer's dignified manners rather encouraging (ch. 1). Mr. Brooke's lack of dignity thus helps increase our own expectations. Is Mr. Casaubon the teacher and guardian Dorothea really needs? Is he not an *avunculus,* too? Or, dare we hope, if Mr. Casaubon should become *avunculus* one, can Mr. Brooke be relegated to *avunculus* two?

But George Eliot does not allow us to reflect on such pleasant possibilities for too long. Mr. Brooke's voice obtrudes itself again. Dorothea has been addressed by Sir James Chettam, yet it is her uncle who interposes and announces, "I went into science a great deal myself at one time." When he finishes, Dorothea finally gets a chance to answer Sir James's question. But her uncle rudely puts her down and indulges in an even more rambling parade of unintegrated ideas and associations:

> "Young ladies don't understand political economy, you know," said Mr Brooke, smiling towards Mr Casaubon. "I remember when we were all reading Adam Smith. *There* is a book, now. I took in all the new ideas at one time—human perfectibility, now. But some say, history moves in circles; and that may be very well argued; I have argued it myself. The fact is, human reason may carry you a little too far—over the hedge, in fact. It carried me a good way at one time; but I saw it would not do. I pulled up; I pulled up in time. But not too hard. I have always been in favour of a little theory:

we must have Thought; else we shall be landed back in the dark ages. But talking of books, there is Southey's 'Peninsular War.' I am reading that of a morning. You know Southey?"[14]

Mr. Casaubon's polite reply catches Dorothea's eager attention. Like his manners, his speech is dignified—but the dignity we and she sense seems stronger because it is in apposition to her uncle's babble. The narrator intervenes to make that point: "This was the first time that Mr Casaubon had spoken at any length. He delivered himself with precision, as if he had been called upon to make a public statement; and the balanced sing-song neatness of his speech, occasionally corresponded to by a movement of his head, was the more conspicuous from its contrast with good Mr Brooke's scrappy slovenliness."

"My mind," says Mr. Casaubon in the speech that so fascinates Dorothea, "is something like the ghost of an ancient, wandering about the world and trying mentally to construct it as it used to be, in spite of ruin and confusing changes." The words are stately, melancholic. To the reader who hears Mr. Casaubon speak for the first time, the aim itself seems noble—not at all unlike, in fact, that of the novelist who is eager to reconstruct a meaningful world of relations for a "later-born Theresa." Dorothea, at any rate, impetuously declares Mr. Casaubon to be the most interesting man she has ever seen. Her starved imagination gratefully seizes on Mr. Casaubon's words and makes them her own: "To reconstruct a past world, doubtless with a view to the highest purposes of truth—what a work to be in any way present at, to assist in, though only as a lamp-holder!"

The conversation that began with a reference to the inventor of the coal miner's lamp has led Dorothea's own invention to revere the lantern of a man she likens to Milton, Wordsworth's predecessor in the egotistical sublime. It is evident at the beginning of chapter two that Dorothea will never share Sir James's enthusiasm for Davy's experimentations in the electrical germination of seeds and plants; by the end of the chapter, however, she has shifted into an overenthusiastic awe for the man who, unlike her uncle, does not seem to depreciate her understanding but shields her by saying: "We must not inquire too curiously into motives. . . . We must keep the germinating grain away from the light" (ch. 2). It is Celia, not Dorothea, who will partake of Sir James's vegetative world of Freshitt. Dorothea hopes for a higher light to emanate from Lowick. When Mr. Brooke brings her religious pamphlets, and, as it turns out, an accompanying letter from Mr. Casaubon, she feels as if "an electric stream went through [her], thrilling her from despair into expectation" (ch. 4).

Dorothea's unbridled fancy converts a sterile scholar, associated with catacombs and darkness, into a light-bringer and light-giver. Her inexperience and her impetuosity are much to blame: Dorothea receives but what she gives—a feeble reflection of the light she has bestowed. But George Eliot blames Mr. Brooke's unenlightenment far more than an innocent girl's belief in a light that never was. Had Dorothea's parents been replaced by a more suitable guardian than this unimaginative paternal uncle, she would not have been forced to animate the scholar who complained about living "too much with the dead" and whom Sir James considers "no better than a mummy" (ch. 6). Mr. Brooke inverts the role of St. Theresa's uncle: instead of preventing an unnecessary martyrdom, he facilitates it. He is fully responsible for the hair shirt that awaits his niece. Blind and ineffectual, this poor substitute for a father turns Dorothea over to a figure who also subverts the traditional role of guide and mentor—but who subverts it far more deliberately and far, far more destructively.

* * *

Unsuspecting and unaware, Mr. Brooke is shocked by Dorothea's choice of a suitor:

> Well, but Casaubon, now. There is no hurry—I mean for you. It's true, every year will tell upon him. He is over five-and-forty, you know. I should say a good seven-and-twenty years older than you. To be sure,—if you like learning and standing, and that sort of thing, we can't have everything.

(ch. 4)

But when Dorothea proves firm, Mr. Brooke backs off. He can think of no other objections than Casaubon's age and is disarmed by his niece's determination not to have "a husband very near my own age" but rather "a husband who is above me in judgment and in all knowledge." Incapable of any further remonstrance, Mr. Brooke soon reconciles himself by "thinking that it was perhaps better for her to be early married to so sober a fellow as Casaubon" (ch. 7). Although the narrator pokes fun at Mr. Brooke's projections on an uncertain future, the reader may be disposed to agree with his rationalization at this point of the novel. When compared to Mr. Brooke at least, Casaubon's sobriety seems desirable.

Though no instructive archangel, Casaubon does not suffer from Mr. Brooke's "too rambling habits of mind." He possesses a ruling passion and Mr. Brooke's facile belittlement of all such obsessions as "hobbies" only helps to confer, once again, some dignity to Casaubon. To Mr. Brooke, Dorothea's plans for cottages and Casaubon's plans for future research are equally meaningless: "Hobbies are apt to run away with us, you know; it doesn't do to be run away with. We must keep the reins. I have never let myself be run away with; I always pulled up. That is what I tell Ladislaw. He and I are alike, you know: he likes to go into everything" (ch.

39). Compared to Mr. Brooke's tendency to go into everything, Mr. Casaubon's monomaniacal devotion to the task "of making his Key to all Mythologies unimpeachable" almost seems appealing (ch. 29). Mr. Brooke cannot even sort out his personal experiences—his "documents," he tells Casaubon, "want arranging"; Casaubon, who can at least arrange his documents "in pigeonholes partly," is far more single-minded (ch. 2).

But it is precisely this single-mindedness—the egotism that he shares with both Nicholas Bulstrode and Peter Featherstone—that causes Mr. Casaubon to pervert the role of the nourishing *avunculus* in far more dangerous ways than Mr. Brooke. Dorothea's uncle, as we have seen, lacks self-consciousness: he is as oblivious of his effect on others as he is of their mark on him. Mr. Casaubon, however, is hyperconscious: he cannot be "liberated from a small hungry shivering self" that remains ever-suspicious and self-protective (ch. 29). Dorothea's uncle is thoughtless, quite capable of hurting others through involuntary carelessness and imprudence; Dorothea's husband, however, is unfeeling, quite deliberately willing to cause pain in order to protect himself from exposure. Mr. Casaubon thus is closer to the Bulstrode who kills another human being to escape detection than he is to the injudicious Mr. Brooke who cannot prevent a "sheep-stealer" from getting hanged or a niece from getting hurt (ch. 4).

The girl who had hoped to be a helpmate to Casaubon by reading Latin and Greek aloud to him, as "Milton's daughters did to their father" (ch. 7), finds her bond to this egotistical father-husband to be far crueler than her former bond to her father-uncle. Dorothea's ties to Mr. Brooke could be dissolved upon her marriage; her ties to Mr. Casaubon threaten to extend even beyond his death. The birth granted to Celia at Freshitt is denied to Dorothea upon her return to Lowick after her Roman honeymoon. The city of visible history to which Casaubon brought Dorothea, only mocks her earlier desire for "a binding theory which could bring her own life and doctrine into strict connection with that amazing past" (ch. 10). Rome acts as an emblem for Casaubon's inadequate rationalism—his persistence in finding revealed truths through that human reason which, according to Mr. Brooke, is needed in small doses lest we land "back in the dark ages." Incapable of energizing mind through feeling, to have his "consciousness rapturously transformed into the vividness of a thought, the ardour of a passion, the energy of an action" (ch. 29), Mr. Casaubon can no more bring meaning than Mr. Brooke.

Unlike Mr. Brooke, however, Casaubon wants to condemn Dorothea to meaninglessness. Selfishly, the dying man demands that she devote her future life to the Key to all Mythologies: "And now she pictured to herself the days, and months, and years which she must spend in sorting what might be called shattered mummies, and fragments of a tradition which was itself a mosaic wrought from crushed ruins—sorting them as food for a theory which was already withered in the birth like an elfin child" (ch. 48). Having given her nothing, Casaubon nonetheless demands that Dorothea sacrifice herself as a funeral offering. Small wonder that the narrator should liken this young wife to Santa Barbara, a daughter immured in a tower and then tortured by her pagan father, or that epigraphs from Chaucer's "Physician's Tale" and Dante's *Purgatorio* should link Dorothea's plight with that of other children sacrificed by unfeeling fathers.

Yet it is through his relationship to Will Ladislaw that Mr. Casaubon best illustrates his inversion of the role of provider. When Sir James tries to remonstrate with Mr. Cadwallader about Mr. Casaubon's eligibility as a husband, the clergyman assures him that Mr. Casaubon *does* have a heart:

> He is very good to his poor relations: pensions several of the women, and is educating a young fellow at a good deal of expense. Casaubon acts up to his sense of justice. His mother's sister made a bad match—a Pole, I think—lost herself—at any rate was disowned by her family. If it had not been for that, Casaubon would not have had so much money by half. I believe he went himself to find out his cousins, and see what he could do for them. Every man would not ring so well as that, if you tried his metal. *You* would, Chettam; but not every man.

(ch. 8)

The picture painted by Mr. Cadwallader is that of a generous *avunculus*. Yet, as the novel progresses, we see that Casaubon increasingly projects on Will Ladislaw the hatred and resentment he has previously directed only at rival scholars. Like these scholars, Will calls attention to Mr. Casaubon's inadequacies—inadequacies Casaubon has tried to hide from Dorothea just as he has locked an adverse review of one of his "Parerga" in a "small drawer" of his desk (ch. 29). To Casaubon, Will's crime is twofold: the young man has made Dorothea doubt the worth of the Key to all Mythologies and, moreover, he has managed to make her happy by imparting to her "the enjoyment he got out of the very miscellaneousness of Rome, which made the mind flexible with constant comparison" (ch. 22). This flexibility of mind—which makes Ladislaw attractive to Dorothea and endears him to Mr. Brooke—causes Casaubon's deepest distrust. He brands Will as a sciolist, a dilettante; but the true cause of his resentment lies elsewhere. Will has been able to provide Dorothea with meaning; Casaubon has not. Accordingly, he decides to withdraw his provisions from his relative and also from Dorothea should she choose to marry his rival after his death.

Casaubon's jealousy causes him to impute to Ladislaw the very same materialism he is himself so guilty of. He reasons:

> This man has gained Dorothea's ear: he has fascinated her attention; he has evidently tried to impress her mind with the notion that he has claims beyond anything I have done for him. If I die—and he is waiting here on the watch for that—he will persuade her to marry him. That would be calamity for her and success for him. *She* would not think it calamity: he would make her believe anything; she has a tendency to immoderate attachment which she inwardly reproaches me for not responding to, and already her mind is occupied with his fortunes.

(ch. 42)

Casaubon conceals from himself that Ladislaw is entitled to a share of his money—more so, in fact, than Dorothea. Under the guise of protecting his future widow, Casaubon only tries to protect his own wounded ego. The codicil to his will, however, only helps to make public his pettiness and jealousy.

The codicil, of course, links Mr. Casaubon to another uncle who hopes to thwart others from beyond the grave: Peter Featherstone. Similarly, Casaubon's self-defensiveness, his eagerness to remove a threatening rival who might call attention to his inadequacies as well as to some past injustice, links him to Nicholas Bulstrode. The three men are yoked in other ways: the Bulstrode who kills Raffles at Featherstone's former house, Stone Court, in order to protect his hidden past also tries to give money to the same person Casaubon wants to bar from inheriting his fortunes, Will Ladislaw. Before we look at these other two harmful uncles, however, as well as at Sir Godwin Lydgate, we must probe deeper into Mr. Casaubon's relationship to Will and Dorothea.

When Ladislaw follows the Casaubons back to England after meeting them in Rome, he arouses his older relative's displeasure upon deciding to remain in the neighborhood as Mr. Brooke's guest and employee. Frigidly, Casaubon asks Will to turn down Mr. Brooke's proposal: "That I have some claim to the exercise of a veto here, would not, I believe, be denied by any reasonable person cognisant of the relations between us: relations which, though thrown into the past by your recent procedure, are not thereby annulled in their character of determining antecedents" (ch. 37). The convoluted sentence only underscores Mr. Casaubon's inadequate understanding of "relation" and kinship. What, exactly, is and what, exactly, ought to be the relationship between the two men? When Will decides to stay, the Middlemarchers conclude that his "relationship" to Mr. Casaubon cannot serve as "an advantageous introduction" to the community: "if it was rumoured that young Ladislaw was Mr Casaubon's nephew or cousin, it was also rumoured that 'Mr Casaubon would have nothing to do with him'" (ch. 46).

The defamation Ladislaw later suffers at the hands of the Middlemarchers thus is caused by Mr. Casaubon's initial denial of kinship, a denial of kinship which again links Mr. Casaubon to figures like Featherstone and Bulstrode. Ladislaw is denied a social identity by the closest member of his family, a second cousin repeatedly mistaken for his uncle. It is Dorothea's own uncle who first makes the mistake which becomes a motif when repeated by several other characters:[15]

> "What is your nephew going to do with himself, Casaubon?" said Mr Brooke, as they went on.
>
> "My cousin, you mean—not my nephew."
>
> "Yes, yes, cousin. But in the way of a career you know."
>
> "The answer to that question is painfully doubtful. On leaving Rugby he declined to go to an English university, where I would have gladly placed him, and chose what I must consider the anomalous course of studying at Heidelberg. And now he wants to go abroad again, without any special object, save the vague purpose of what he calls culture."
>
> (ch. 9)

When Will, led to Rome by "culture," meets the Casaubons there, his friend Naumann compounds Mr. Brooke's mistake by thinking that "the sallow *Geistlicher*" who has left Dorothea near the reclining Ariadne "was her father" (ch. 19). Ladislaw corrects Naumann by explaining that the clergyman is Dorothea's husband and that, moreover, the older man happens to be his cousin. Naumann professes disbelief: "What, the *Geistlicher*? He looks more like an uncle—a more useful sort of relation." Irritated, Ladislaw sharply retorts: "He is not my uncle. I tell you he is my second cousin."

The young man's irritation recalls Casaubon's own, but it is caused by quite different feelings of resentment. Naumann's stereotype of the uncle as a munificent giver galls Will because it reminds him that Casaubon, though not an uncle, has indeed financed his education. His past dependence on Casaubon stings him since, like Naumann, he has come to consider "Mrs Second-Cousin the most perfect young Madonna" he has ever seen. Naumann's trained artistic eye detects a true tragic correlative for the young woman he calls "a sort of Christian Antigone." Ladislaw's dilemma, however, he finds to be amusing: "I see, I see. You are jealous. No man must presume to think that he can paint your ideal. This is serious, my friend! Your great-aunt! 'Der Neffe als Onkel' in a tragic sense—*ungeheuer*!" Ladislaw does not appreciate Naumann's heavy-handed joke. To the German, the situation of "Der Neffe als Onkel"—the Nephew as Uncle—is comical. To the Ladislaw who lost his family rights when his grandmother—Casaubon's Aunt Julia—eloped with a foreigner, the situation only acts as reminder of his disinherited condition.

He has no claim, no social identity which would allow him to entertain expectations such as those which permit Fred or Rosamond Vincy to regard an uncle as "a useful sort of relation" indeed.

To a Marian Evans who was disowned and denied membership in her family by Robert Evans's patrilineal successor, the plight of Aunt Julia and the resulting disenfranchisement of Will Ladislaw carry a deep personal significance. This personal meaning alone would help account for George Eliot's interest in the variables involved in the relationship that social anthropologists call the "avunculate"—a relationship which is not limited to that between uncles and nephews but also includes the relation between parent and child, husband and wife, and, significantly enough, brother and sister.[16] *Middlemarch* is, among other things, an investigation into the roots of kinship. And Dorothea, the novelist's deputy, begins to look into the codifications of kinship. She fixes her gaze on the portrait of Aunt Julia and begins to probe into a past less dead than that lighted by Mr. Casaubon's dim taper:

> What a wrong, to cut off the girl from the family protection and inheritance only because she had chosen a man who was poor! . . . Here was a daughter whose child—even according to the ordinary aping of aristocratic institutions by people who are no more aristocratic than retired grocers, and who have no more land to "keep together" than a lawn and a paddock—would have a prior claim. Was inheritance a question of liking or of responsibility? All the energy of Dorothea's nature went on the side of responsibility—the fulfillment of claims founded on our own deeds, such as marriage and parentage.
>
> (ch. 37)

Dorothea does not yet know at this point of the novel that she will eventually emulate this female *avus,* whose delicate face seems "so like a living face she knew." But she will renounce the Casaubon wealth of her own accord, and not be punished by a harsh, male prohibition. Moreover, she will become herself an *avunculus* when she replaces Bulstrode as Lydgate's financial provider and begs the young doctor "to grant her the position of being his helper in this small matter, the favour being entirely to her who had so little that was plainly marked out for her to do with her superfluous money" (ch. 76). At this point of the novel, however, Dorothea feels it incumbent upon her to prompt Mr. Casaubon to restore to Will Ladislaw the privileges that are rightfully his. Her efforts are checked first by her husband's increasing jealousy and then by the vindictive codicil of his last will. The destructive *avunculus* seems to have triumphed. Will cannot confess his love for her lest such a confession be misinterpreted as fortune-hunting. She, in turn, cannot offer him the money she feels he is entitled to. She can at best offer Will "that beautiful miniature of your grandmother" (ch. 54). But the gesture only acts as a reminder of the wealth and status that seem to separate them. Will professes to be uninterested in this "family memorial" (ch. 54). Only after Dorothea has become Lydgate's provider, can she escape the clutch of Mr. Casaubon's dead hand. It is within her power to have her and Will's life "maimed by petty accidents." Finally, she understands her kinship with Aunt Julia: "We could live quite well on my own fortune" (ch. 83).

Their fortune—or providence—must suffice. Fittingly, Mr. Brooke the provider now becomes the bearer of what he calls the "sad news." It is he who first informs an angry Sir James of the "ungentlemanly" codicil in Casaubon's will—only to get blamed for that codicil: according to Sir James, the names of Dorothea and this "young fellow" would not have been coupled had not Mr. Brooke retained Ladislaw. Now that he knows that Dorothea and Ladislaw are coupled in a more permanent fashion, Mr. Brooke is even less eager to evoke Sir James's wrath: "you've no notion what it is, you know. And, Chettam, it will annoy you uncommonly—but you see, you have not been able to hinder it any more than I have. There's something singular in things: they come round, you know."

* * *

Neither Mr. Brooke, then, nor Mr. Casaubon can "hinder" the happier things which manage to "come round" for Dorothea and Will. The effects which the other obstructionist uncles in **Middlemarch** have on their younger kin are, however, far more mixed. To complete our avuncular view of the novel we must, however briefly, also look at Nicholas Bulstrode, Sir Godwin Lydgate, and Peter Featherstone as figures who complement George Eliot's survey of the structures of kinship.

In the beginning of the novel, Mr. Bulstrode's *affidavit* is required to clear his nephew's reputation in the eyes of Peter Featherstone; by the end of the novel, long after Fred's expectations have been dashed by Featherstone's last will, Bulstrode sullies the reputation of his nephew-in-law, Tertius Lydgate. Dorothea tries to counter Bulstrode's action. She advances Lydgate the thousand pounds he needs to repay the banker; she acts as a Madonna as well as a kind aunt when she clears Lydgate in the eyes of Rosamond, only to have Ladislaw's name cleared in her own eyes by Miss Noble, Mr. Farebrother's maiden aunt. But this feminine intervention cannot repair the damage done to Lydgate by his association with his wife's uncle.

Bulstrode, like Casaubon, disguises self-protection as avuncular manifestations of rectitude. He offers money to Will Ladislaw, not to make amends for appropriating the fortune that rightfully should have belonged to an-

other disenfranchised female, Ladislaw's mother, but to circumvent a disclosure by Raffles. He likewise professes to offer money to Lydgate because "Mrs Bulstrode is anxious for her niece, and I myself should grieve at a calamitous change in your position" (ch. 70). Ladislaw rejects the money; Lydgate accepts it, overjoyed. Uncritically Lydgate also accepts the banker's explanation of this complete reversal of the stand taken only a day before; then, Bulstrode had coldly advised the doctor not to involve "yourself in further obligations" and counseled him "you should simply become a bankrupt" (ch. 67). The words are bitterly ironic. By incurring this further obligation, Lydgate has become Bulstrode's associate. He must pay for a kinship the older man never felt. Although he can restore the money with Dorothea's loan and thus avoid financial bankruptcy, he has now become a moral bankrupt.

Both Lydgate and Bulstrode are exiled from Middlemarch. The commonness of their fates is attributable to those "spots of commonness" that yoked the ambitious young doctor not only to Rosamond's uncle but to Rosamond herself. George Eliot skillfully relates Lydgate's dependence on Bulstrode to Rosamond's genteel aspirations and to her application for money to his own uncle, Sir Godwin Lydgate. Ashamed of her maternal grandfather, an innkeeper, Rosamond finds that Lydgate's aristocratic connections in the North make him more attractive than any Middlemarcher. When the couple's style of living exceeds their income, Rosamond is convinced that "Sir Godwin, who had chucked her under the chin, and pronounced her to be like the celebrated beauty, Mrs Croly, who had made a conquest of him in 1790, would be touched by any appeal from her, and would find it pleasant for her sake to behave as he ought to do towards his nephew" (ch. 64). Rosamond is quickly disabused. In a social system that can deny the rights of consanguineous kinship to Aunt Julia, Sir Godwin is hardly bound to be moved by more sentimental considerations. He ignores Rosamond and writes to Lydgate instead, accusing his nephew of impropriety and deviousness: "Don't set your wife to write to me when you have anything to ask. It is a roundabout wheedling sort of thing which I should not have credited you with. I never choose to write to a woman on matters of business. As to my supplying you with a thousand pounds, or only half that sum, I can do nothing of the sort." If Sir Godwin resembles Mr. Brooke in his contempt for the understanding of young ladies, he also resembles Mr. Bulstrode in his cruel and detached advice: "Your money would have held out for that, and there would have been a surer ladder before you. Your uncle Charles has had a grudge against you for not going into his profession, but not I. I have always wished you well, but you must consider yourself on your own legs entirely now.—Your affectionate uncle, GODWIN LYDGATE" (ch. 65).

Rosamond's brother Fred is thwarted when he, too, expects a boon from that useful relation, an uncle. But unlike Rosamond, this "long-legged" brother does eventually manage to walk off unscathed (ch. 35). Though disappointed by Peter Featherstone's testament, Fred finds freedom through his financial loss. He overhears a discussion concerning "Mr Casaubon's strange mention of Mr Ladislaw in a codicil to his will" (ch. 59), yet, chastened by the will that has affected his own life, he remains uninterested in this gossip, knowing little and caring less about Ladislaw and Mrs. Casaubon. Still, by escaping the clutch of a vindictive relative's desire to affect the future, and by rejecting the allurements of money and status, Fred becomes Dorothea's closest counterpart.

Like Dorothea, Fred must renounce his initial identity. In the opening chapters of the book, he is a caricature of the aspiring nephew. Confident of "his prospect of getting Featherstone's land," Fred tries to endear himself to the hard old man (ch. 12). Yet Stone Court is impenetrable, as immune to feeling as that other seat of false expectations, Lowick. Bleak and desolate, Stone Court is the grimmest emblem of the breakdown of kinship portrayed in *Middlemarch.* The Christian Carnivora who crowd the room in which Featherstone's testament is read have just as eagerly pressed around the dying man—"peeping, and counting and casting up" (ch. 33). His vindictiveness is as justified as theirs. He wants them to go hungry; they expect to feed on his carrion simply because, as Mrs. Waule ruefully complains, they are "his own lawful family—brothers and sisters and nephews and nieces" (ch. 35). There is no feeling attached to relationship, no bond other than the reciprocity of contempt. The hatred of Featherstone is reborn when Mrs. Waule inveighs against the uncle who has chosen to cheat "lawful" relatives by leaving all to his unlawful son, the batrachian Joshua Rigg. Yet even this legacy is meaningless. It is no act of restitution such as Matthew Bramble's eager willingness to recognize Humphry Clinker as an extension of his own identity. The choice of heir has been capricious; no acknowledgment of responsibility is involved.

Just as Casaubon, that other flinty man without a heart, tries to force Dorothea into devoting a lifetime to the hoard to be opened by his Key to all Mythologies, so does Featherstone try to make Mary the instrument of his will by thrusting his key at her and asking her to unlock his "iron chest" (ch. 33). Casaubon tries to control Dorothea's future by making her his heiress; Featherstone tries to control the future of his dependents by bribing Mary; "Look here! take the money—the notes and gold—look here—take it—you shall have it all." This Peter who bears the name of that apostle who denied Christ and yet founded a living church dies as a

monstrous caricature of the providing father, with "his right hand clasping the keys, and his left hand lying on the heap of notes and gold" (ch. 33).

Mary thinks that her action may well have prevented Fred from being the beneficiary of this old man's vindictiveness. She tells Fred: "I do believe you are better without the money" (ch. 35). She is correct. By renouncing the dead world of Stone Court, Fred can partake of a different parental identity, be nurtured by the same father that has made Mary so strong. Caleb Garth is a true *avunculus* to Fred: though mild and timid in "reproving," he is also a "ruler" who can, when he chooses, be "absolute." Stone Court, however, is soon visited by another perversion of the nourishing father substitute. John Raffles, "very florid and hairy," tries to insinuate himself into the good graces of Featherstone's bastard son. He wants to feed off Joshua Rigg just as Featherstone's relatives had tried to feed off the miser; like these relatives, Raffles claims the bond of "lawful" relationship: "Come now, Josh . . . here is your poor mother going into the vale of years, and you could afford something handsome now to make her comfortable." But this new father meets with repulsion: "The more you want me to do a thing, the more reason I shall have for never doing it. Do you think I mean to forget your kicking me when I was a lad, and eating all the best victual away from me and my mother? Do you think I forget your always coming home to sell and pocket everything, and going off again leaving us in the lurch? I should be glad to see you whipped at the cart-tail. My mother was a fool to you; she'd no right to give me a father-in-law, and she's been punished for it" (ch. 41).

Raffles will die at Stone Court, like Peter Featherstone. By killing his nemesis there, Bulstrode only completes the circle. His action is the novel's supreme denial of human relation, but it is appropriately set in relief by all those other figures to whom kinship is either a matter of indifference or of self-interest.

* * *

We are now ready to dwell on at least a few of the implications of this "avuncular view" of *Middlemarch.* Why are uncles so much more prominent than fathers in this novel? And why are the various uncles of *Middlemarch* so uniformly destructive? George Eliot had not always regarded the uncle with such a jaundiced eye. Her first full-length novel closed with a domestic picture that includes little Addy riding on the shoulders of a doting Seth Bede: "to walk by Dinah's side, and be tyrannised over by Dinah's and Adam's children, was Uncle Seth's earthly happiness."[17] Yet George Eliot, toward the end of her career, continues the emphasis of *Middlemarch* in *Daniel Deronda*: the uncles of Gwendolen and Daniel, Mr. Gascoigne and Sir Hugo

Mallinger, are weak and overly optimistic rationalists who cannot alleviate the deprivations suffered by their wards. Dissatisfied by his "indulgent and cheerful" guardian, Daniel becomes doubtful about their actual relationship. He suspects that the man "whom he called uncle was really his father"[18] and that he therefore is socially disenfranchised, and subject—like Joshua Rigg—to the whims of one not legally responsible for him. Deronda's suspicions prove unfounded. But once he is provided with his true identity, he disengages himself not only from Sir Hugo but also from the social reality represented by Sir Hugo's real nephew. Featherstone's Stone Court has become the world of Grandcourt, a world which Daniel can reject far more radically than Dorothea or Fred.

The implications of the patterns I have traced are both social and psychological. The George Eliot who found the writings of the Victorian anthropologist Edward Tylor so "worth studying" and "edifying,"[19] conducts in *Middlemarch* an investigation into the social forms of kinship. Her investigation lends credibility to the view still upheld today by those who argue that a "kinship system does not exist in the objective ties of descent or consanguinity" but exists rather in "human consciousness" as a symbolic "system of representation."[20] *Middlemarch,* that novel of relations, is also a work about the imaginative act of relating. To describe this act, George Eliot deliberately resorted to the symbolic representations of the *avunculate,* a set of relationships which, in Lévi-Strauss's words, make up "the most elementary form of kinship," or, "properly speaking, *the unit of kinship.*"[21] As mentioned before, the avuncular relationship is not limited to uncle and nephew, but involves three other types of relationships as well; moreover, as Lévi-Strauss explains, the attitudes of kinship involved are also four: mutuality, reciprocity, rights, and obligations.

More important for our purposes, however, is Lévi-Strauss's observation that "the avuncular relationship re-emerges unmistakably and tends to become reinforced" each time a societal system "reaches a crisis" (p. 47). The George Eliot who would, in her next novel, send Daniel Deronda away from England to found a new Canaan, had diagnosed the crisis of her times in *Middlemarch.* That crisis, borne out by her own personal experiences, seemed to involve an erosion of the kinship traditionally assured by human institutions. The paternalism of church and state had waned long ago; only the family, that Victorian bulwark of identity, seemed able to guarantee cohesion and kinship. To counter disintegration, the popular culture of the mid-nineteenth century had revived the figure of the kind uncle. The proliferation of children's books with titles like *Tales Uncle Told* (1865) or *My Uncle's Tales and Stories* (1877) coincided with the emergence of other popular avuncular types such as the American "Uncle Sam," who, by 1860, was no longer regarded as a caricature of vulgar democracy but as benign, white-bearded, paternal provider.[22] Nor was this sentimental stereotype at all limited to the male gender. Periodical publications such as *Aunt Judy's Magazine, Aunt Kate's Almanac,* and *Aunt Mai's Annual* undoubtedly owed their popularity to this new trend; Charlotte Yonge chose to instruct her little readers in Aunt Charlotte's Stories of English and Biblical and French and Classical History while in America Louisa May Alcott added successive volumes to her *Aunt Jo's Scrapbook* (1872-1882). The avuncular self could, to be sure, produce an occasional masterpiece such as Lewis Carroll's *Alice in Wonderland* (1865) or *Through the Looking Glass* (published in 1871, the same year in which the first installment of *Middlemarch* appeared). To less discerning writers, however, the *avunculus* as character and as persona often became little more than an outlet for the ever-increasing hunger for relations and relationship.

Middlemarch stems from this selfsame hunger. As I have tried to suggest, George Eliot guards herself against the sentimental exaggerations of so many of her contemporaries by undercutting the avuncular stereotype in two distinct ways: through Mr. Brooke, she reminds us that benevolent intentions are not enough; through the other uncle figures—Casaubon, Bulstrode, Sir Godwin, Featherstone, even Raffles—she examines the perversions of a social structure of relationships based on male power and male prerogative. If Mr. Brooke is used to expose the shortcomings of a liberal sympathy devoid of intellect or purpose, the other uncles illustrate the decay into rapaciousness and brutality of patrilineal values that had originated out of the human need for protection, support, and tenderness. To offset this bleak panorama, George Eliot tries to create two positive avuncular characters. The first of these is feminine—a Dorothea Brooke who, unlike a Romola or a Janet Dempster, is not condemned to care for the children of others but rather allowed to become the nucleus of her own family. The second of these figures is masculine—a Caleb Garth who possesses the sense of purpose absent in Mr. Brooke together with the feelings of tenderness lacking in the novel's other uncles. Dorothea extends her help to Lydgate; Caleb manages to re-educate Fred. Both characters contribute to "the growing good of the world" through actions of no great name. Yet while Dorothea must leave the community of Middlemarch, Caleb is allowed to stay there. Together with Mary and his new son, this patriarch replenishes the land neglected by Mr. Brooke, Featherstone, and Bulstrode.

Deep personal implications underlie these wish fulfillments: the Dorothea who imitates Aunt Julia by accepting the role of outcast resembles George Eliot; Caleb Garth, on the other hand, is a softer and desexualized version of the same father whom Marian Evans had first portrayed as the severe and punitive Adam Bede. The masculine Adam is the titular hero of the novel that bears his name; Caleb, however, belongs to a far more complex fiction in which George Eliot manages to parcel out her identity among a greater number of important characters. Thus robbed of prominence, the droll father of Mary Garth cannot really offset the cumulative effect of the novel's many destructive uncles. Although George Eliot invests him with power and authority at the end of the novel, she invests a far greater power and a much more commanding authority in the figure of her narrator, the novel's prime builder of relations and prime restorer of order.

Yearning after stronger units of kinship, George Eliot nonetheless was driven to embody that ideal, not through the relations formed by her characters, but through the verbal consciousness of her narrator, the male or female owner of the voice that immediately catches our attention in the opening lines of the novel's Prelude. That voice possesses authority: it belongs to one who can extract meaning out of "the history of man," one who well knows how that "mysterious mixture" behaves under Time's varying experiments. And yet this same sober narrator is also able "to smile with some gentleness" at the thought of the little girl and her still smaller brother toddling out of Avila. Serious yet tender, authoritative yet tolerant, the figure who addresses us in **Middlemarch** is the entity we consider, according to Lévi-Strauss, as "a male mother," a true *avunculus.*[23]

The narrator of **Middlemarch,** then, is that genuine avuncular figure that Mr. Brooke—and so many nineteenth-century minds like his—no longer can be. Whereas Mr. Brooke dabbles incessantly in the particulars of history, arts, politics, without the ability to integrate these discrete activities, the novel's narrator is forever fusing contrary modes of beholding life into a new and integrated reality. Able to construct meaning out of the dead landscapes beheld by lesser imaginations, the narrator can also address the reader in the soothing tones employed by a kind and understanding uncle or aunt. The novel that begins by looking for epic correlatives ends with a reassurance that "things are not so ill with you and me as they might have been" ("Finale"). Like *Paradise Lost,* **Middlemarch** is an epic effort at justification and persuasion. Yet through the "domestic reality" created by her narrator's concern with shapes that are not necessarily grandiose, George Eliot managed to humanize and domesticate Milton's epic voice. It is no derogation but rather a tribute to her warmer, maternal imagination that we can think of this, her finest justification of man's kinship to man, not only as a new *Paradise Lost,* but also as "The Very Best Tale that Aunt Marian told."

Notes

1. George Eliot, *Middlemarch,* ed. Gordon S. Haight, Riverside ed. (Boston: Houghton, 1956), Prelude, p. 3. Further references to this edition are given in the text.

2. See Santa Teresa de Jesús, *Libro de la Vida,* in *Obras Completas,* 3 vols. (Madrid: Editorial Católica, 1951), I, 597-98 (ch. 1, para. 5). The details of the story are not given by Theresa herself but are found in the *Procesos* published after her death. The title of chapter one is "Which Tells How the Lord Began to Awaken this Soul in its Childhood toward Virtuous Things and Of the Help of Parents to Achieve that End." Theresa ends the chapter by alluding to the loss she incurred when her mother died when she was but twelve years old; Dorothea and Celia have been educated on "plans at once narrow and promiscuous" since they "were about twelve years old and had lost their parents" (*Middlemarch,* ch. 1). Theresa credits another paternal uncle, Don Pedro Sanchez de Cepeda, a widower who at a later age became a monk, with returning her to a sense of God's dispensation (*Vida,* I, 605-6 [ch. 3, para. 41]). Saint Theresa's *Life* had been newly edited in 1870 by David Lewis; George Eliot's interest in Spanish subjects, however, dates back to her work for *The Spanish Gypsy* (published in 1868).

3. "The Antigone and Its Moral," *Leader,* 7 (29 March 1856), 306; reprinted in *Essays of George Eliot,* ed. Thomas Pinney (London: Routledge, 1963), p. 263. Dorothea is first called a "Christian Antigone" by the painter Naumann in chapter 19 of the novel.

4. Still, John Jarndyce's benevolence is strangely qualified: although to Esther he seems an agent for that "Providence" she detects in her life, he cannot really counter the fortuitousness of the order represented by Chancery by protecting Richard Carstone from its destructiveness. In *Great Expectations,* Dickens undermines even further the stereotype of the benevolent guardian he had himself played in *Uncle John*: Pip comes to regret the nurture he receives from Magwitch or "Provis" almost as much as Estella regrets her upbringing at Satis House.

5. William Wordsworth, Preface to the 1800 edition of *Lyrical Ballads,* in *Wordsworth: Poetical Works,* ed. Thomas Hutchinson, rev. Ernest de Selincourt (London: Oxford Univ. Press, 1966), p. 740.

6. Jane Austen, *Emma,* ed. Lionel Trilling, Riverside ed. (Boston: Houghton, 1957), Bk. III, ch. 6, p. 282.

7. Wordsworth, Preface, p. 735.

8. Ibid., p. 738.

9. For Wordsworth, "Poetry is the breath and finer spirit of all knowledge; it is the impassioned expression which is in the countenance of all Science" (ibid., p. 738). The poet communicates with a wider audience. As a man speaking to man, he can share with others the search for order and truth which the man of science "cherishes and loves" in solitude. Yet, in a prophetic forward look, Wordsworth asserts in 1800 what would become a mandate, seventy years later, for a "philosophic" novelist living in a post-Darwinian world: "If the time should ever come when what is now called science . . . shall be ready to put on, as it were, a form of flesh and blood, the Poet will lend his divine spirit to aid this transfiguration, and will welcome the Being thus produced, as a dear and genuine inmate of the household of man."

10. Still, if Mr. Brooke overheard the two men speak to each other at Cartwright's, he might well have heard them allude to the origins of their friendship. Wordsworth's first letter to Sir Humphry Davy was written on 29 July 1800; Davy had been previously approached by Coleridge for help in correcting both the manuscript and the proof sheets of *Lyrical Ballads*. As a result of this collaboration, Davy became one of Wordsworth's closer friends. He visited Grasmere in 1804, stayed at Dove Cottage in 1805 (giving Dorothy a medical checkup after a too strenuous horse ride), and had portions of *The Recluse* read to him on 27 October 1805. See *Letters of William and Dorothy Wordsworth*, ed. E. de Selincourt, rev. Chester L. Shaver (Oxford: Clarendon, 1967), pp. 289-90 et passim.

11. See the epigraph at the head of chapter 1 of *Daniel Deronda*, ed. F. R. Leavis, Harper Torchbook (New York: Harper, 1960), p. 1: "Even Science, the strict measurer, is obliged to start with a make-believe unit, and must fix on a point in the stars' unceasing journey when his sidereal clock shall pretend that time is at Nought. His less accurate grandmother Poetry has always been understood to start in the middle; but on reflection it appears that her proceeding is not very different from his; since Science, too, reckons backwards as well as forwards, divides his unit into billions, and with his clock-finger at Nought really sets off *in medias res.*"

12. Mocking this "patent age of inventions," the narrator of *Don Juan* refers to "Sir Humphry Davy's lantern, by which coals / Are safely mined for in the mode he mentions" (*Don Juan*, ed. Leslie A. Marchand, Riverside ed. [Boston: Houghton, 1958], 1:132, p. 39). The allusion to the lantern and to the light it brings to coal miners evokes

that other "mode" of invention used by the poet who wants to illuminate what is otherwise dark and cheerless.

13. Cf. *Don Juan*, III:88, p. 130: "words are things, and a small drop of ink, / Falling like dew, upon a thought, produces / That which makes thousands, perhaps millions, think."

14. In *The English Cyclopaedia: A New Dictionary of Universal Knowledge: Biography*, conducted by Charles Knight, 25 vols. (London: Bradbury and Evans, 1854-72), a work that George Eliot consulted for biographical details of the lives of many of the historical figures mentioned in *Middlemarch*, the novelist would have found a description of Robert Southey that seems rather applicable to her characterization of Mr. Brooke: "He had little subtlety of intellect, and he took rather a passionate than a reasoning view of any subject that greatly interested him. Much of his political and economical speculation is now regarded as altogether wrong-headed, even by the most ardent of his admirers. But there can be no question that he was thoroughly honest and earnest in whatever opinions he at any time professed" (V, 615).

15. See chapter 34:

> "A very pretty sprig," said Mrs Cadwallader, dryly. "What is your nephew to be, Mr Casaubon?"
>
> "Pardon me, he is not my nephew. He is my cousin."

16. See Claude Lévi-Strauss, *Structural Anthropology*, trans. Claire Jacobson and Brooke Grundfest Schoepf (Garden City: Doubleday, 1967), pp. 39-40.

17. *Adam Bede*, ed. John Paterson, Riverside ed. (Boston: Houghton, 1968), "Epilogue," p. 447.

18. *Daniel Deronda*, ch. 16, p. 123.

19. *The George Eliot Letters*, ed. Gordon S. Haight, 7 vols. (New Haven: Yale Univ. Press, 1954-1955), V, 288; VI, 90.

20. Lévi-Strauss, p. 49.

21. Ibid., p. 43.

22. According to *The Oxford Companion to American Literature*, ed. James D. Hart, 4th ed. (New York: Oxford Univ. Press, 1965), the figure of Uncle Sam gradually replaced the homespun philosopher Major Jack Downing or "Uncle Josh Downing" in the popular imagination, so that by 1860 it entered the dictionary without any "opprobrious connotation."

23. Lévi-Strauss, p. 39.

Henry Alley (essay date summer 1979)

SOURCE: Alley, Henry. "The Subterranean Intellectual of *Middlemarch*." *Midwest Quarterly* 20, no. 4 (summer 1979): 347-61.

[*In the following essay, Alley concentrates on the intellectual pursuits of the novel's main characters, documenting the various ways in which their accomplishments fall short of their ambitions. Alley asserts that, in spite of Eliot's frequently ironical portrayal of her characters' failures, their scholarly endeavors still represent valid, and vital, contributions to the intellectual climate of their times.*]

Middlemarch, like its successor, **Daniel Deronda,** creates a world of subterranean intellectuals, people who, with varying degrees of commitment, carry on projects of minor or limited study. While Casaubon, the most prominent example, struggles to find the key to all mythologies, Lydgate travels in pursuit of the primitive tissue, Farebrother widens his bemused advances in natural history, Mrs. Garth sustains her small peripatetic school in her kitchen—her daughter, Mary, living on to write "a little book for her boys, called *Stories of Great Men, taken from Plutarch*" (Finale, 890)—and Mr. Brooke, more euphoric than all of them, floats airily from one literary reflection to another. Surrounding this community of underground scholars is the grand world of immortalized thinkers and discoverers, the world of Vesalius, Aquinas, and Milton, which the omniscient narrator is careful to introduce via allusion. How one responds to Lydgate when he is placed side by side with Vesalius or to Casaubon when the figure of Aquinas is continually conjured, or—to make the comparison a bit more complicated—to Caleb Garth when his household says he is like Cincinnatus, has a great deal of bearing on our total reaction to this vast novel.

In his article, "The Intellectual Background of the Novel: Casaubon and Lydgate," W. J. Harvey concludes that "while the irony of Casaubon is that he is in ignorance of the real work already done by German scholars in the near-past, the irony of Lydgate is that he is just too soon for the real work to be done, again by German scholars, in the near future" (p. 36). This article, so central to one's understanding of exactly what Lydgate and Casaubon are after, raises even further questions as to the nature of the irony governing the lives of these intellectuals, as well as all the Middlemarch intellectuals in the novel. Is there a universal irony, a program of total frustration implied by the mock-heroic comparison of Casaubon to Aquinas? The answer would seem to be that there is not, as Harvey would suggest at the end of his essay when he says that "George Eliot does not wish us to think of Lydgate's endeavours as futile in the same way as Casaubon's." I would add that if one moves through a spectrum of character, from Casaubon to Mrs. Garth (with Brooke, Lydgate, and Farebrother as transitional figures), one may move from clear failure to clear fulfillment.

First off, the critic must try to discover the standard which determines the success or failure. If Dorothea's life escapes irony because, as the Finale says, "the growing good of the world is partly dependent on unhistoric acts," then what of the rest of her fellow sufferers? The standard, it would seem, is clearly not a worldly one; although Casaubon and Lydgate anguish over the disparity between themselves and their famous predecessors, Eliot is less concerned with the difference than the compromise which must ensue, once the difference has been perceived. Vesalius, Milton, and Aquinas are not there to ironize all the Middlemarch endeavors but to press the reader toward the subtler method of judgment which the finale will ultimately articulate. If a character can use his or her sense of failure as a means of communication, then, ironically, involvement in a truly historical process is made possible; as Dorothea says, nearly at the exact center of the novel, "we are part of the divine power against evil—widening the skirts of light and making the struggle with darkness narrower" (XXXIX, 427).

Set against this standard, Casaubon's failure is the worst, since his academic life is a mere metaphor for his total moral decline. Casaubon is a failure as a man first, as a scholar second. The narrator, particularly in the early sections in Rome, is careful to point out that Casaubon, even in the midst of intellectual disaster, could have made a success of his marriage, had his nature not been narrower, "if he would have held her hands between his and listened with the delight of tenderness and understanding to all the little histories which made up her experience, and would have given her the same sort of intimacy in return, so that the past life of each could be included in their mutual knowledge and affection . . ." (XX, 230). The point is not so much that Casaubon is a "complete anachronism, lost in the labyrinth of an exploded pseudo-science" as that he is a complete moral coward when the awareness of his lostness arrives; convinced of his own futility, he is driven inward toward his own self-deluded and desperate search for minor immortality, rather than outward toward Dorothea's pity and tenderness. Part of the binding force of mutual knowledge and affection could have been the awareness of failure and weakness, as is certainly true in the case of the Garths, and later in the case of Fred and Mary Vincy.

Once Casaubon has missed this opportunity and Dorothea's consciousness of his failure begins outstripping his own, his degeneration accelerates, moving quite quickly from jealousy to abhorrence of pity to the cardinal sin in Eliot's universe, the equation of fame with greatness. The attempt to bind Dorothea to a life of "sorting what might be called shattered mummies" (XLVIII, 519) tells us more about Casaubon's moral decision than it does about hers. If the "growing good of the world is partly dependent on unhistoric acts" and the reduction of our ills "is half owing to the number who lived faithfully a hidden life, and rest in unvisited tombs," then Casaubon enters the last circle of the damned, through his disbelief in the invisible goodness, in his attempt to create a visible tomb which others would surely visit: "But he had come at last to create a trust for himself out of Dorothea's nature: she could do what she resolved to do: and he willingly imagined her toiling under fetters of a promise to erect a tomb with his name upon it. (Not that Mr. Casaubon called the future volumes a tomb; he called them the Key to all Mythologies.)" (L, 535). Ironically, Dorothea, as the potential choric figure, could have preserved her husband's memory—as she does, in a sense, preserve Lydgate's—had he abandoned his obsession with intellectual immortality. In the end, however, his post-mortem attempts to manipulate the living and resurrect his name (as represented also by the codicil to his will) actually serve to cover it with ignominy; Casaubon's ghost is slain by his own dead hand.

Mr. Brooke, who, particularly during the earlier sections of the novel, offers relief from the darker story of Casaubon, also participates in a polite scholarship befitting his class and undergoes, just after Casaubon's death, a kind of intellectual disaster. An important difference, however, resides in Brooke's willingness to admit defeat, and in his own comic way, to compromise. Although he shares Casaubon's muddleheadedness, along with his pedantry, and above all his inability to bring his intellectual life into the world of action, his comic resiliency saves him from moral failure. Just as Casaubon's quotation of "Who with repentance is not satisfied, is not of heaven nor earth" (XXI, 242) during an understated marital crisis forecasts his final descent, so Brooke's "I assure you it was rather comic: Fielding would have made something of it—or Scott, now— might have worked it up" (XXXIX, 428) forecasts his good-humored resignation when he proves unable to offer "the forces of his mind honestly to the nation" (XLIX, 528).

As an "intellect," Brooke occupies himself mainly with the stitching together of random ideas taken from literature and history, a process which culminates in his support for moral reform in general and the Reform Bill in particular. Taken together, Chapters 39 and 51 form a relentless comedy, whereby his lack of moral reform on his own land is driven home with such force that he is first driven from his own property and then from his own lofty oration. Further, the illogic of his jump from "ideas" to action is dramatized by the intellectual diffusion which overcomes him, the moment he must address someone else, whether it be Dagley or the crowd:

This was a bold figure of speech, but not exactly the right thing: for, unhappily, the pat opening had slipped away—even couplets from Pope may be but "fallings from us, vanishings", when fear clutches us, and a glass of sherry is hurrying like smoke among our ideas. Ladislaw, who stood at the window behind the speaker, thought, "It's all up now."

(LI, 547)

Eliot, in a sense, turns the allusions in on Brooke at this moment, since the passage, complete with literary quotation, imitates the drift of Brooke's cluttered mind. As in the case of Casaubon, a fragmentation of intellectual purpose spells disaster, but because we are in a comic universe, the nightmare images of dim anterooms and "the dark river-brink" of Acheron change into the Punch-voiced effigy of Brooke himself. Consistent with his unconscious hypocrisy, he proves unable to "see himself," and thus when the crowd laughs at his own caricature, he laughs with them. When the voice ultimately calls for the Bill, Brooke is placed in the rather painful position shared by Mrs. Arrowpoint, who, in *Daniel Deronda,* is forced to live up to her own words, which have been stylishly and safely developed within a basement intellect.

The laughter, however, is soon over, and what strikes the reader the moment the humiliated Brooke enters the committee room is not his silliness but his indestructible good humor. His compromise, in the face of defeat, takes two forms, one minor and one major. The first is altogether expected, his bowing out of the race. The second, however, involves his surprising willingness to follow the progress or retrogression of political reform at a humble distance and to defer, where his own land is concerned, to those of better judgment— Caleb Garth and Sir James. Thus in the finale, Brooke and his anthropomorphic pen are presented in a wholly sympathetic light, the pen not representing, as it did in the past, Brooke's lack of intellectual control but, rather, his total defiance of a custom which exiles two people he loves, Dorothea and Will. In the end, Brooke participates in "the growing good" of the world, because, with the failure of his ideas, his benevolent nature—the wellspring of his muddled good intentions—reasserts itself.

When one turns to the final three characters, Lydgate, Farebrother, and Mrs. Garth—those who achieve some active good both consistent and inconsistent with their studied principles—one must first look at their external failures. Lydgate ends up marrying an egoist and gradually looses hold of his original scientific pursuit; Farebrother's interest in natural history hardly advances beyond the pickled animals in his study; and Mrs. Garth's peripatetic school is only a further reminder to her neighbors that she had been a teacher once and had had to make her own way. Their willingness, however, to create a compromise—or in Mrs. Garth's case, sustain a coexistence—once their academic pursuits recede from them is largely responsible for their growth in character and, together with Dorothea's "sacrifice," instrumental in building the "network" of good which laces the novel. Intellectual failure or loss becomes the chief catalyst to moral fulfillment.

Lydgate is never entirely fulfilled, either morally or intellectually, yet critics have tended to overemphasize the irony of his life, accepting too readily Lydgate's final view of himself as the correct one. Within the body of the novel itself, Lydgate moves from a "benevolently contemptuous" conceit (XV, 179) to "that twice-blessed mercy [which] was always with Lydgate in his work at the Hospital or in private houses, serving better than any opiate to quiet and sustain him under anxieties and his sense of mental degeneracy" (LXVI, 720). That he believes in his steady intellectual decline cannot be denied, but this fact, taken in the context of the larger vision of the novel, acquires only secondary importance, especially when one sees Lydgate more and more entering the role of the compassionate healer.

One may look at him in relation to one man alone, Farebrother, in order to see the change. In Chapter 17, which subtly contrasts them, Lydgate is presented as having strong reservations about a man who does not share his fixity of purpose or high sense of vocational commitment; he is reading Farebrother's life the way he will later read his own. Yet, ironically, as the chapters progress, Lydgate proves able to achieve the wider view only in relation to his friend's life and work, not to his own. Once he has come to reflect on his mistake of voting for Tyke over and against Farebrother—as well as to reflect on his own struggles to obtain medical reform in Middlemarch—Lydgate advances to a clear perception of Farebrother's true worth, to the point that he intercedes on his friend's behalf.

> "Instead of telling you anything about Mr. Tyke," he said, "I should like to speak of another man—Mr. Farebrother, the Vicar of St. Botolph's. His living is a poor one, and gives him a stinted provision for himself and his family. His mother, aunt, and sister all live with him, and depend upon him. I believe he has never married because of them. I never heard such good preaching as his—such plain, easy eloquence. He would have done to preach at St. Paul's after old Latimer. His talk is just as good about all subjects: original, simple, clear. I think him a remarkable fellow; he ought to have done more than he has done."
>
> "Why has he not done more?" said Dorothea, interested now in all who had slipped below their own intention.
>
> "That's a hard question," said Lydgate. "I find myself that it's uncommonly difficult to make the right thing work: there are so many strings pulling at once."
>
> (L, 536-537)

Lydgate, in rejecting the rigid standard of judgment of his earlier days, can now achieve some active good. Be-

cause of this conversation, Farebrother is given the Lowick living two chapters later. Lydgate's reference to his own failure is crucial, since in Eliot sympathy is possible only through a keen recollection of one's own losses. The "many strings pulling at once" anticipate the channels of the finale, and in this instance, Lydgate is speaking to the right person, since Dorothea, eleven chapters earlier, has also anticipated the wider standard of the final pages.

The perception of Lydgate's true worth, then, over and beyond his intellectual failure, must rest with Dorothea, in a manner parallel to Lydgate's perception of Farebrother's innermost talents. In the midst of the Bulstrode scandal, coupled with the collapse of his marriage, Lydgate is snatched back from total dishonor and self-hatred by Dorothea's belief in him. In Chapter 76, perhaps the most important in the novel, the narrator says, "The presence of a noble nature, generous in its wishes, ardent in its charity, changes the lights for us: we begin to see things again in their larger, quieter masses, and to believe that we too can be seen and judged in the wholeness of our character" (819). This is the charge which Eliot brings to bear upon the reader: we cannot allow ourselves to share Lydgate's narrow view of himself, as a man who began with great intellectual dreams and ended up paralyzed. Rather, the wholeness of his character testifies to his active participation in achievements which are not ironized. Dorothea can save Lydgate's memory in a way she cannot her former husband's, because in the face of intellectual loss, he has become concerned with the saving of others rather than the immortalization of his achievements. When he says, "Yet you have made a great difference in my courage by believing in me" (825), we are forced to think of him not as a man who started in pursuit of the primitive tissue and concluded with a treatise on gout but as a man who, facing up to the pressure of external circumstances as well as his misguided decisions, rose to tragic dignity.

As has been suggested, Farebrother escapes tragedy, because he does not have as far to travel in his moral education, and because others have seen to recognizing his value—his simplicity of speech and his sureness of touch with the common people. In contrast to Lydgate, Farebrother has undergone his "failure" by the time the novel begins, so that he is perceived as a consistently humble and compassionate man, who has only a self-amused struggle of feeding "a weakness or two lest they should get clamorous" (XVII, 202) to undergo. If he had a calling in the field of natural history, it is surely gone by the time Lydgate meets him. This fact does a great deal to explain why, in Chapter 17, Farebrother is so understanding toward their mutual friend Trawley and Lydgate is so harsh. Farebrother knows "what it is to want spiritual tobacco" (202), whereas Lydgate has never tried out his intellectual endeavors—at least to the point that he could understand why someone could fail. Farebrother is keenly aware of this problem, and tries to give him a warning cast in simple scriptural terms:

> Your scheme is a good deal more difficult to carry out than the Pythagorean community, though. You have not only got the old Adam in yourself against you, but you have got all those descendants of the original Adam who form the society around you. You see, I have paid twelve or thirteen years more than you for my knowledge of difficulties.
>
> (203)

Since this warning, as well as others, goes unheeded, Lydgate must be the one to repeat Trawley's example.

As a subterranean intellectual, Farebrother stands in contrast to his friend—and indeed to Casaubon and Brooke as well—by being the first to reconcile his basement studies with the "upperworld"—the realm of social relationships. It is very important that, symbolically speaking, Farebrother can move smoothly and comfortable from his mother's drawing room to his study and back again, as distinct from Casaubon, whose mind often goes "too deep during the day to be able to get to the surface again" (XX, 231-232). The success of Farebrother's transition can be explained in a variety of ways: the relative smallness of his intellectual commitment, his perception of his own limitations, and, above all, the significance he assigns to his want of "spiritual tobacco." Unlike Casaubon and Lydgate, who are driven toward desperation once their intellectual failings have become apparent, Farebrother uses his "study" as a fixed and self-satiric symbol of what he cannot achieve, how far he cannot go.

Ironically, then, he travels a great deal further, both vocationally and spiritually. As has already been seen, he does not find it difficult to unite his deep scriptural learning with the world of action; he knows which *exempla* apply and which do not. In participating in the invisible channels of good in the novel, he imitates Lydgate—and goes beyond him, by sacrificing himself so that Fred Vincy's self-respect can survive. Characteristically and symbolically, during the middle stages of his intercessions with Mary, he leaves the couple alone in his study so that they can speak freely, transforming his place of cogitation into a theater for self-denial. Because of the Vicar's efforts, Fred Vincy's courtship—and therefore his vocation—are saved, and, ironically, by renouncing himself, Farebrother seals his commitment to the clerical profession, where one's own desires must come second. Although earlier in the novel, he is led to dismiss Prodicus's story of Herculean virtue as a "pretty tale" (XVIII, 218)—by way of excusing Lydgate's vote against him—Farebrother, through his magnanimous intervention, rises to "a very good imitation of heroism" himself (LXVI, 729).

Like Farebrother, Mrs. Garth closes the gap between the worlds of learning and activity, but in her case the closure is more complete: what could be more direct than firing out questions on Roman history while doing the baking? There is little, if any, of the mock-heroic here, since the juxtaposition of Roman agrarian virtue and the lives of the Garths points to continuity rather than difference. Like the Farebrother household, the family lives amidst a lovingly heaped accumulation of past and present, which becomes a metaphor for the ease with which the wisdom of the past, both personal and historical, is infused into their daily existence. It is the opposite side of the coin of Casaubon, whose researches take him further and further into anterooms and the tombs of "shattered mummies," where daylight has been banished; the Garths live in a vital coexistence where Livy may be discussed or Walter Scott read aloud over and above the clatter of dishes or the sound of children's voices.

One cannot say, however, that as a subterranean intellectual Mrs. Garth has reached a compromise. There is little of the subterranean in her life—which is exactly the point: it is only through the errors of others that the spheres of activity and learning are falsely polarized; from her point of view, it is "good for them to see that she could make an excellent lather while she corrected their blunders 'without looking',—that a woman with her sleeves tucked up above her elbows might know all about the Subjunctive Mood or the Torrid Zone . . ." (XXIV, 275). Thus she undergoes a transition that is even smoother than Farebrother's; there is not even the small separation between drawing room and study: all occurs in her kitchen. To Ben's question concerning the relevancy of grammar, she has an immediate and simple answer; the concept of a useless or cloistered education does not exist for her, anymore than a concept of "failure" or "compromise" exists in the aftermath of her past teaching life.

Thus, unlike Casaubon and Brooke, Mrs. Garth does not find it difficult to live up to the virtue extolled in her favorite *exempla*. When Fred Vincy interrupts the Roman history lesson with news that the Garth family is going to be even harder pressed, she asserts the rare quality of *gravitas*, so cherished in the remote early republic: "Like the eccentric woman she was, she was at present absorbed in considering what was to be done, and did not fancy that the end could be better achieved by bitter remarks or explosions" (XXIV, 281). Just as there is no division between learning and the workaday world, so there is no hypocritical division between word and deed.

Eliot's use of literary allusion in this episode is very telling, especially in light of these consistencies. In the Casaubon and Brooke sections, the mock-heroism is rampant, but as the gap between intellectual and practical activity narrows, along with the diminishing sense of intellectual failure, so does the potential for mockery. Casaubon, for all the special pleading the narrator offers, is laughed at when placed alongside the shade of Aquinas. When, however, Mrs. Garth is indirectly compared to a Roman matron, or Caleb Garth directly called Cincinnatus, there is no laughter, because there is no disparity. As a quick historical check will show, Mr. Garth, for his part, is like the historical personage in at least three ways: his devoted love of the land, associated with strength of purpose, his intense hatred of petty talk, and his strong belief that one should leave a task if it cannot be completed on one's own terms. Thus when, in a later chapter, Mrs. Garth says, "Here is an honour to your father, children . . . He is asked to take a post again by those who dismissed him long ago," the parallel is nearly exact, since Cincinnatus was called back as well, thus showing "That he did his work well, so that they feel the want of him" (XL, 437).

Such continuities, as represented by Mrs. Garth and, by extension, her husband, belong to an even larger one—that of past and present—and through all of them we may return to the universal perspective of the final. At the conclusion we find that both Fred and Mary live to produce works of minor research and scholarship, Fred's being the *Cultivation of Green Crops and the Economy of Cattle-Feeding,* consistent with what he learned from his father-in-law, and Mary's being *Stories of Great Men, taken from Plutarch,* consistent with what she learned from her mother. Even the life of intellect in the case of the Garths is cyclical: belonging to the links between generations rather than the rise and fall of individual endeavor. The products of Fred and Mary Vincy's studies form a direct contrast to Casaubon, who struggled to create a neatly self-contained achievement, with his name brightly labeled on the outside. Thus, taken together, the Garth chapters develop the most clearly romantic pattern in the novel, culminating in communal celebration and forming the affirmative note that the novel proper ends on, since they are the most consistently aware of the "fine issues" that can result though they are "not widely visible."

As a group, all the subterranean intellectuals in *Middlemarch* (with perhaps the exception of Casaubon) take part in the growing good of the world and constitute the nucleus of a theme, reasserted with widening emphasis, that to fail to achieve universal acclaim is not to fail at all. Those who begin furthest from this fact suffer the bitterest anguish; those who start with it as a given achieve the greatest fulfillment. In between we find Dorothea, who, approaching the roar on the other side of silence and driven by a "keen memory of her own life" (LXXVI, 823), achieves that finely tuned consciousness which perceives "that element of tragedy which lies in the very fact of frequency" and even heroism in efforts that are at best only partially fulfilled and

at worst ironically undermined. In light of this recognition—Dorothea's, the narrator's, and finally the reader's—all intellectual quests, no matter how laughable or minute, are saved from irony.

Bibliography

Bradley, Anthony G. "Family as Pastoral: The Garths in *Middlemarch." Ariel,* 6, No. 4 (October 1975), 41-51.

Eliot, George, *Middlemarch.* 1872. Ed. W. J. Harvey. New York: Penguin, 1965.

Harvey, W. J., *The Art of George Eliot.* London: Chatto and Windus, 1961.

Harvey, W. J., "The Intellectual Background of the Novel: Casaubon and Lydgate." *"Middlemarch": Critical Approaches to the Novel.* Ed. Barbara Hardy. London: Athlone Press, 1967. 25-37.

Kenny Marotta (essay date winter 1982)

SOURCE: Marotta, Kenny. "*Middlemarch*: The 'Home Epic.'" *Genre* 15, no. 4 (winter 1982): 403-20.

[*In the following essay, Marotta evaluates Eliot's attitude toward personal ambition in* Middlemarch. *Marotta argues that renunciation, rather than achievement, represents the heroic ideal in the novel.*]

How ambitious is the author of *Middlemarch*? Does George Eliot aspire to epic grandeur in this novel? Her narrator often appears to reject the epic as a model for her work. In the "Prelude," we are told that for modern women who share the "ideal, passionate nature" of Saint Theresa—women like Dorothea Brooke, whom we meet in the novel's first chapter—no "epic life" of "far-resonant action" is possible as it was action for that saint, who "found her epos in the reform of a religious order."[1] The other major plot of *Middlemarch,* the story of the loves of Fred and Rosamond Vincy, is introduced by an epigraph which speaks of mimetic comedy:

> But deeds and language such as men do use,
> And persons such as comedy would choose,
> When she would show an image of the times,
> And sport with human follies, not with crimes.
>
> (Ch. 11, p. 69)

The epigraph to a later chapter continuing the story of Rosamond asserts: "Let the high Muse chant loves Olympian: / We are but mortals, and must sing of man" (Ch. 27, p. 194). Yet several critics have found an epic strain in the novel despite such disclaimers.[2] The disclaimers themselves illustrate the narrator's persistent consciousness of the world of epic action, even though she might consider modern man exiled from that world:

she compares and contrasts her characters to the heroes of history, literature, and myth; the characters themselves take such heroism as their ideal. In the novel's "Finale," the narrator speaks of marriage, the most significant act of most of the characters, and the only significant action of the heroine, Dorothea, as "the beginning of the home epic" ("Finale," p. 608). The oxymoron "home epic," combining domesticity with grandeur, suggests the uneasy relation of this novel to the epic genre. In what ways does any of Eliot's characters escape the traditional limits of the home, and does Eliot escape the traditional limits of the novel?

In the most important discussion of ambition in *Middlemarch,* Alan Mintz locates the originality of George Eliot in her use of the idea of vocation as a subject and source of values in the novel. While novels traditionally focused on love and espoused the value of selflessness, *Middlemarch* focuses on work and suggests the value of that selfish ambition which is necessary to heroic accomplishment. This new "ethos of vocation" may have had one source, Mintz suggests, in Eliot's reading in epic and medieval romance.[3] Yet while *Middlemarch* puts forth the claims of egoistic ambition, Mintz argues, it finally affirms the traditional novelistic virtues of altruism. According to this argument, the novel's inconsistency is evident in the portrayal of Dorothea, whose heroic aspirations are presented sympathetically by the narrator, but whose actual accomplishments—her submission to her unworthy husband, her effort to rescue Lydgate's reputation and his marriage—we are asked to admire for their very renunciation of selfish ambition.[4] The other characters whom we admire—the Garths, Mr. Farebrother—also preserve their integrity only by diminishing their ambition.

Yet both the narrator and the characters themselves persist in describing the renunciatory actions of Dorothea, the Garths, and Mr. Farebrother in the language of heroism. Mr. Garth's children compare him to Cincinnatus, Mr. Farebrother thinks of his renunciation of Mary Garth as "a very good imitation of heroism" (Ch. 66, p. 496), Dorothea is compared by the narrator and other characters to Saint Theresa, Antigone, the Virgin Mary. Dorothea herself defends one of her renunciatory acts—her defense of Lydgate's reputation—in the context of glory, complaining that "People glorify all sorts of bravery except the bravery they might show on behalf of their nearest neighbours" (Ch. 72, p. 538). Joseph Wiesenfarth has argued that Eliot is seeking to re-define heroism, to show that the old heroic types are re-born in characters who display the virtues Mintz calls novelistic: integrity, sympathy, a realistic sense of their place in history.[5] But in such a re-definition, the element of heroic ambition has disappeared—as it has not in the minds of Dorothea, of Mrs. Garth who schools her children by the example of Roman heroes, of Mary Garth who similarly maintains a high standard by writing "for

her boys" a volume of "Stories of Great Men, taken from Plutarch" ("Finale," p. 608), or of the narrator, who still speaks of Theresa and Antigone in the novel's "Finale." For the more uncompromising characters of *Middlemarch* make renunciation the vehicle of their epic ambition.

Eliot's focus on epic ambition may be partly obscured by elements of what appears to be a traditionally novelistic polemic against romance. The story of Lydgate and Rosamond, in particular, seems to call forth a conventionally novelistic judgment. We might call their unhappy marriage the punishment deserved by their egoism, which finds expression in dreams cast in the mold of a specifically literary romance. Lydgate and Rosamond see themselves as hero and heroine of such a romance, he of properly high background, she of magical powers appropriately subdued to his demands, the two of them undergoing the necessary trials of endurance, their reward to be "ideal happiness (of the kind known in the Arabian Nights, in which you are invited to step from the labour and discord of the street into a paradise where everything is given to you and nothing claimed)" (Ch. 36, p. 257).[6] Blinded by this romantic illusion, Rosamond believes that Lydgate's aristocratic blood and her charm are sufficient to assure them the income necessary to maintain her desired standard of living, while Lydgate believes that his good taste and his wife's apparent submissiveness can create the home life he desires, an idyllic retreat which will not interfere with the conduct of his career as surgeon and medical researcher. Both are mistaken: Lydgate's social gracelessness thwarts Rosamond's ambition, and Rosamond's extravagance and lack of sympathy thwarts Lydgate's. Both characters fail to penetrate these flattering illusions, to try to understand the other's desires and capacities.

To demonstrate the folly of these egoistic romantic illusions, and the contrary novelistic wisdom of sympathy and accommodation, may have been Eliot's original intent in devising the story of Lydgate and Rosamond, which, as we know, was conceived independently of the story of Dorothea.[7] If we think of the configuration of *Middlemarch* without Dorothea's plot, the anti-romantic moral seems clear. The affairs of two couples are juxtaposed: Rosamond and Lydgate, on the one hand, and Rosamond's brother Fred and his sweetheart Mary Garth, on the other. Rosamond helps Lydgate fail at his chosen vocation, while Mary helps Fred choose and succeed at his. Both men are tempted away from realistic reliance on their own work to dependence upon untrustworthy men who seem to offer an easy fulfillment of their desires. But while Lydgate, tacitly encouraged by the extravagant Rosamond, becomes increasingly dependent upon the banker Bulstrode—thus accelerating the decline in his own reputation when Bulstrode is publicly humiliated by the airing of his shady past—

Fred, whom Mary has never encouraged in his dependence on an inheritance from his wealthy uncle Featherstone, is disappointed by Featherstone's will and forced to become more self-reliant. The stories of the two couples are also juxtaposed by the presence of Farebrother as advisor to each. Farebrother's counsel of accommodation, of realistic evaluation of one's own talents and the power of others to help or hinder those talents, is proudly ignored by Lydgate, but accepted by Fred.

Whatever Eliot's original intention, the heroic context provided by the novel's language—a context which may have been introduced along with the merging of Dorothea's story with the Vincys'—leads us to think about Lydgate and the other characters in terms not simply novelistic. We find ourselves not so much criticizing their ambitions as observing the inescapability of ambition and nothing the ways in which it can succeed or, more often, fail. When Lydgate regrets the fate of his original ambition he criticizes less his uncompromising folly than his lack of will: "Lydgate was aware that his concessions to Rosamond were often little more than the lapse of slackening resolution" (Ch. 58, p. 428). From the start, Lydgate's tendency to compromise is presented as a weakness rather than a wise realism. Although he aspires to "everlasting fame" as a "great originator," Lydgate chooses not to take the most direct road to such greatness (Ch. 15, pp. 108, 109). Rather, he comes to Middlemarch to "keep away from the range of London intrigues, jealousies, and social truckling, and win celebrity, however slowly, as Jenner had done, by the independent value of his work" (Ch. 15, p. 108). In explaining to Farebrother his motives for this self-reliance, Lydgate betrays the fears that motivate his compromise: "In the country, people have less pretension to knowledge, and are less of companions, but for that reason they affect one's *amour-propre* less: one makes less bad blood, and can follow one's own course more quietly" (Ch. 17, p. 129). The delicacy of Lydgate's *amour-propre*, which motivates his choise of pastoral quietness over direct confrontation of his rivals, will defeat his highest ambitions.

Rosamond is more successful in achieving her more modest ambition: to rise a little higher in society, and ultimately to leave Middlemarch. But while her greater success depends upon her firmer determination not to compromise, Rosamond is as ignorant as Lydgate of the centrality of ambition to her life. Even in her period of greatest frustration she never gives up the model of romance, only contemplating her own perfection and imagining that other men might have been—might still be—able to provide her the romance Lydgate does not. Lydgate, too, can never give up his belief in this model: Rosamond can always make him feel like a brute when he expresses his frustration. Although they do not realize it, the discontent of Lydgate and Rosamond, like their behavior towards each other, stems not so much from the frustration of romantic expectations as from the thwarting of ambition.

Unlike Lydgate and Rosamond, Dorothea rejects the model of romance in her own life. But while novelists traditionally reject this model for its untruth, Dorothea rejects it for its insignificance. The "Prelude" distinguishes romance from the larger epic: "Theresa's passionate, ideal nature demanded an epic life: what were many volumed romances of chivalry and the social conquests of a brilliant girl to her?" ("Prelude," p. 3). Dorothea, like Theresa, spurns romance: her "notions about marriage took their colour entirely from an exalted enthusiasm about the ends of life, an enthusiasm which was lit chiefly by its own fire, and included neither the niceties of the *trousseau,* the pattern of the plate, nor even the honours and sweet joys of the blooming matron" (Ch. 3, p. 20). In her disregard for the conventionally feminine concerns which are essential to Rosamond's romance, Dorothea regards Casaubon as a guide who will lead her along the "grandest past," and help her "to bring her own life and doctrine into strict connection with [the] amazing past, and give the remotest sources of knowledge some bearing on her actions" (Ch. 3, p. 21, Ch. 10, p. 63). She is to join with him in purposes whose tenor in "unsuited . . . to the commoner order of minds," to "help him in his life's labour"—but with the understanding that that labour was "something greater, which she could serve in devoutly for its own sake" (Ch. 5, p. 311, Ch. 48, p. 351). For "she had not reached that point of renunciation at which she would have been satisfied with having a wise husband: she wished, poor child, to be wise herself" (Ch. 7, p. 47).

Dorothea's franker recognition of the ambitious motivation of her marriage enables her to see her disappointment more clearly than Rosamond or Lydgate see theirs. At Will Ladislaw's first suggestion that Casaubon's project is worthless, both superfluous and carried out on false principles, she embraces Will's view; soon she also judges her husband as wrong in refusing to offer his impoverished cousin Will more financial help. When her first efforts to enlighten her husband are rebuffed, she chooses to act no further, resigning herself to "hopelessness that she could influence Mr. Casaubon's action," attempting neither to improve nor to expedite her husband's work but instead "to check her weariness and impatience over this questionable riddle-guessing" (Ch. 39, p. 286; Ch. 48, p. 351). In this passivity, as in her original decision to fulfill her ambition only at second hand, as helper to another's project, Dorothea would appear to be eschewing epic action. But her high standard, and her confidence in the judgments she makes by that standard, never wavers; and by refusing to seek any accommodation between her ideas and her husband's, Dorothea preserves herself from implication in his failure, remaining instead his silent critic. As Will sees, she has moved "into the remoteness of pure pity and loyalty towards her husband"; as Casaubon sees, she acts with "a self-approved effort of forbearance" (Ch. 37, p. 269, Ch. 42, p. 307). About both Will and Casaubon's "Key to All Mythologies," Dorothea's attitude is a conviction "that she was in the right and her husband in the wrong, but that she was helpless" (Ch. 48, p. 348).

In *Middlemarch,* such renunciation of action is the only outlet for conscious ambition. The would-be hero must become the critic of unworthy action, rather than himself an actor. Unlike the traditional epic hero who needs a war in which to prove himself, the renouncing hero can engage in this competition even at his own hearth; the case of Rosamond and Lydgate shows that such contests of ambition are enacted even in marriages conceived romantically. Such competition is the form battle takes in the home epic.

Marriage thus plays a different part in the home epic from the part it would play in the traditional novel. As Lydgate's failure might in a more conventional novel have led us to blame the romantic folly of his ambition, so his blighted marriage and near-cuckolding by his wife might have dramatized the difficulty of achieving romantic fulfillment in marriage, of making the necessary compromises between individual desire and social convention. But *Middlemarch* treats marriage not as the realm of compromise between individual and society, but as the arena for that struggle of ambitions which proves one's epic worthiness. This emphasis appears, for instance, in the contrast between Dorothea's avowedly epic marriage and Rosamond's avowedly romantic marriage. The unattached Will Ladislaw takes on the role of potentially adulterous lover in both marriages. The characters themselves are conscious of the parallel: Rosamond first gets the idea of winning extra-marital admiration from Will by observing his admiration for the married Dorothea; Dorothea, troubled by Will's private visits to Rosamond, remembers that he makes similar visits to herself. And Casaubon imputes romantic motives to Will, just as Rosamond does. But Will believes that Rosamond and Dorothea offer him two distinct models for action. Dorothea, whom Will suspects of a critical attitude towards him the first time they meet, becomes for him a judge; he admires the high standard of renunciation she maintains by submission to Casaubon, and he fears offending her by falling below that standard himself.[8] And Dorothea is in fact proud to consider Will's behavior towards her as beyond reproach. Rosamond, on the other hand, happily contemplates the prospect of a romance with Will—a romance whose unoriginality she is ignorant of: "At that time young ladies in the country, even when educated at Mrs. Lemon's, read little French literature later than Racine. . . . Still, vanity with a woman's whole mind

and day to work in, can construct abundantly on slight hints" (Ch. 43, p. 319). Will can imagine himself participating in Rosamond's projected romance, becoming "enslaved by this helpless woman" (Ch. 78, p. 571). But he finds this yielding to adultery a disheartening relinquishment of ambition—"insipid misdoing and shabby achievement" such as Lydgate has fallen into (Ch. 79, p. 574). It is less the misdeed that troubles him than the insipidity, the shabbiness of the achievement of adultery. He finally chooses his more original and ambitious relationship with Dorothea over the trite relationship with Rosamond.

The language Dorothea and Will use in describing their final rapprochement shows that, for them, their marriage is as heroically original as their earlier platonic relationship was. Having, in the course of a visit to Rosamond, discovered Will in a compromising position with that lady, Dorothea is angry at his decline from the heroic standard. This decline makes her believe that the admiration he has shown her is not noble but a "cheap regard," that he has spoken "lip-born words to her who had nothing paltry to give in exchange" (Ch. 80, p. 576). But Dorothea decides that the way for her to avoid a like paltriness would be to persist in her earlier intention of assuring Rosamond of her husband's innocence of Bulstrode's scandals, asking herself, "what sort of crisis might not this be in three lives whose contact with hers laid an obligation on her as if they had been suppliants bearing the sacred branch?" (Ch. 80, p. 577). Dorothea returns to Rosamond with this consciousness of divinity, and rouses Will to compete with her in holding to that standard. He wants to marry her in the face of the financial loss she will incur as a consequence of Casaubon's will, refusing to be "maimed by petty accidents" as he imagined being maimed by entering into Rosamond's romance—and as Lydgate, in his compromise with Rosamond, has consented to lead the life of "men who have lost their limbs" (Ch. 83, p. 594, Ch. 82, p. 588, Ch. 64, p. 477).

The marriage they achieve, founded on epic ambition rather than romantic dreams, holds the same promise of struggle as Dorothea's marriage to Casaubon. Even before their marriage, Will's admiration for Dorothea is "accompanied with a chilling sense of remoteness. A man is seldom ashamed of feeling that he cannot love a woman so well when he sees a certain greatness in her: nature having intended greatness for men" (Ch. 39, p. 285). Also like Casaubon, Will tends to imagine a world of critics around him; such criticism will presumably become more focussed once, after his marriage, he gives up the dilettantism by which he has avoided any specific "shabby achievement," and settles into a political career.[9] Dorothea's remoteness is not likely to be diminished by her position as helper in this political career. Although the advantage of this position is that her life is filled with "a beneficent activity which she had not the doubtful pains of discovering and marking out for herself," her confidence in her own judgment, which we have no reason to believe has been dissipated, in conjunction with her tangential relation to Will's career, his fear of criticism and his distrust of her greatness, may well produce another marriage in which Dorothea maintains a detached, privately pitying or critical stance to the ambition her husband enacts, and becomes for that husband an embodiment of the critical audience which preys on his mind ("Finale," p. 610).

Renunciation like Dorothea's is enacted by all of the novel's admirable characters. Mary refuses to consider Farebrother as a suitor, preferring the less promising Fred, and she refuses to help Featherstone alter his will, although that alteration might enrich her sweetheart; Caleb Garth rejects Bulstrode's job after learning of Bulstrode's scandalous past; Will Ladislaw also rejects money offered by Bulstrode, in compensation for the inheritance Bulstrode kept from Will's mother, as well as the variety of jobs he temporarily undertakes. All these characters prefer the position of critic which depends upon these renunciations: Mary's refusal to help Featherstone enables her to school him, as her choice of husbands gives her one she can instruct; Caleb's and Will's refusals of Bulstrode's money enables them to sermonize him about his ungentlemanliness; and Will's turning away from various fields of endeavor enables him to criticize more persistent workers in those fields. Will even considers the conventional epic hero's work of founding a society, a "settlement on a new plan in the Far West" (Ch. 82, p. 587).[10] But such a plan would demand accepting the money from Bulstrode which Will has already once renounced; Will does not follow through. For Will, the better course is to refuse to be "stained" or "blemished" by accepting Bulstrode's money, as Caleb refuses to be "hurt" and Mary to be "soiled" by any action other than renunciation.

This ideal of purity in renunciation, if heroic, is yet distinct from the active heroism of an Achilles, or of the historical conquerors Cyrus, Alexander, and Caesar, to whom the narrator alludes. But that very history is what makes renunciation the only form of epic conquest available to these characters. The ambitious man aspires, as Lydgate aspires, to be a "great originator" and win "everlasting fame." Such achievement depends on the possession of great talent; but the novel's language blames failure less on insufficiency of talent than on the historical position of its characters. For modern man, originality is difficult and perhaps impossible: the most he can do is to maintain the critical standard of originality without committing himself to actions likely to prove unoriginal. The narrator makes clear the futility of her characters' efforts at originality by her superior wisdom. Not only does she foreknow the mistakenness of Lydgate's medical hypotheses, but she knows historical and literary precedents beyond her characters' ken.

Having read Herodotus, which Dorothea is still learning to read in Chapter 48, the narrator can compare Dorothea to the unfortunate Io (Ch. 11, p. 71). Knowing the scandalous French literature which has been kept from Rosamond, the narrator can remark on the tradition behind the post-marital romantic intrigue Rosamond thought she had invented.

The threat of all these precedents is most troubling to the character who seeks to enact an epic ambition more traditional than any of those to which the characters aspire: Casaubon, who hopes to produce in his Key to All Mythologies an explanation of all myths as corruptions of Biblical revelation. The narrator, like Dorothea, frequently compares Casaubon to Milton, who also undertook to explain the origins of things, including the myths of various cultures. The narrator notes ominously, however, that Casaubon's project fails to match Milton's boast: while Milton's song pursued "things unattempted yet in prose or rhyme," Casaubon's undertaking "indeed had been attempted before" (Ch. 3, p. 17). But Casaubon does share Milton's singleness of purpose. Unlike any of the other characters, Casaubon has devoted thirty years to this grand project, refusing to compromise, for he wishes his work to be "unimpeachable." And this project engages more directly than any of the other characters' goals the faith, hope, and risks of ambition: for in the view of characters and narrator alike, writing is the medium for immortality, the undying memorial to great original acts. In the "Prelude," the narrator reminds us that men are saved from oblivion by "sacred poets." Books can immortalize men because, unlike men, they do not die, and so can become the "drifted relics of all time" (Ch. 13, p. 91). Even children are spoken of as the "copies" of their parents which preoccupied Elizabethan sonneteers, eager for their subjects' immortality (Ch. 29, p. 205, Ch. 41, p. 203). Not only the learned narrator but also the provincial characters of this novel read or imagine becoming the subjects of memoirs, histories, eulogies. Casaubon's own thoughts about his writing focus exclusively on its recognition by others as original and potentially immortal work: he concerns himself less with the validity of his views than with the rivals he is refuting, the audience whom he fears will deny his achievement, and the power of his work to become a memorial—what Dorothea thinks of as "a tomb with his name upon it" (Ch. 50, p. 362). The grandeur of his hope conflicts, however, with his realistic lack of confidence in his ability to achieve originality. Consequently, in his daily confrontation with his ambition, he becomes obsessed with death, long before Lydgate's diagnosis of his fatal illness. As he says during his first recorded speech in the novel, "I live too much with the dead" (Ch. 2, p. 13).

This preoccupation with death is the fate of ambitious men who did not, like the "great historian" Henry Fielding, have the "happiness to be dead a hundred and twenty years ago" (Ch. 15, p. 104). For those who would be great in this late age must preoccupy themselves with the difficulty of confronting a past which threatens with its "dead hand" to snuff out their efforts at originality. Casaubon, sorting "shattered mummies," lost among "the tombs of the past," is thwarted by his imagined ideal audience, which exerts the "vaporous pressure of Tartarean shades" (Ch. 48, p. 351, Ch. 42, p. 308, Ch. 10, p. 63). Bulstrode, whose path in life has been "widened" by the deaths of wealthy benefactors, and who enjoys a "sort of vampire's feast in the sense of mastery," is similarly haunted by a dead past that invades and overwhelms the present (Ch. 61, p. 452, Ch. 16, p. 115). Lydgate's contest with the heroes of the past whom he emulates (Vesalius, Jenner, Bichat) also depends on a path widened by death: his reliance on autopsies appalls not only Mrs. Dollop, but Rosamond, who refuses to "dote on skeletons, and body-snatchers," and believes his experiments show a "morbid vampire's taste" (Ch. 45, p. 336, Ch. 64, p. 484). The ambitious man is a vampire, seeking to prolong an unnatural life by feeding on the corpses of the past—and murdering if necessary to provide his sustenance.

The somewhat lurid images which Eliot associates with ambition not only reveal the desperation of ambitious men in the modern world, but again show how the apparent renunciation of ambition in marriage can be an expression of ambition. For the marriage struggle is similarly to the death. Rosamond, whom her husband likens to the basil plant that feeds on murdered men's brains, incurs a miscarriage, feels rewarded by Lydgate's death, believes Dorothea is lucky to have found in Casaubon a husband both wealthy and likely to die soon, and presumably feels just as lucky in finding for her second husband a man who is both wealthy and elderly.[11] Contemplating Rosamond's potential murderousness, which reminds him of the actress Laure, who actually murdered her husband, Lydgate distinguishes both women from Dorothea. But the distinction attests only to Dorothea's higher ambition: as Lydgate contemplates Dorothea's uniqueness among women, he finds that his memory of her has the same effect on him as "the enkindling conceptions of dead and sceptered genius" (Ch. 58, p. 433). Rosamond desires the easy social position of a well-off widow; Dorothea's ambition is to be numbered among the immortals. Rosamond waits with relative passivity for events to bring about her more modest goal. Dorothea's unworthy husband is dead within two years of the wedding. Dorothea acquiesces in Will's criticism of her husband, which the narrator suggests is a form of murder; and, though she fears the effect of agitation on his illness, proceeds to risk his agitation.[12] Dorothea's fitness for a place in the pantheon of the dead is attested to by Will as well as by Lydgate, as he declares, "I would rather touch her hand if it were dead, than I would touch any other woman's

living" (Ch. 78, p. 571). And Dorothea succeeds in exerting the power of the "dead hand" over Will as over Casaubon. Will is able, however, to continue longer in the competition to which Dorothea challenges him: "if he could have written out in immortal syllables the effect she wrought within him, he might have boasted after the example of old Drayton, that—

'Queens hereafter might be glad to live
Upon the alms of her superfluous praise.'"

(Ch. 47, p. 344)

Dorothea's uniqueness challenges Will's ambition as it challenged Lydgate's, but it also reveals the limits of his originality, his inability to write immortal poetry, and the likelihood that such poetry, if he produced it, would only imitate Drayton, who has forestalled Will's originality.

We know that George Eliot shared the anxieties about ambition which she reveals in her characters. Ruby Redinger made these anxieties central to her study of Eliot's life and work.[13] In the period of *Middlemarch*'s composition (1869-72), this anxiety becomes particularly associated with immortality. The notebooks Eliot kept in preparation for *Middlemarch* record her interest in literary immortality and instances of its failure, in the incalculability of consequences, and in the ideas of great men which proved to be erroneous.[14] Poems composed in 1869, such as **"The Legend of Jubal"** and **"Armgart,"** treat the tragedy of the loss of fame. Eliot discusses these issues most extensively, however, in the late essays collected in *Impressions of Theophrastus Such* (1879) and the posthumously published *Leaves from a Notebook.*

These essays, most of them focusing on literary ambition, harshly criticize those who fail in worthiness for immortality. Vorticella, the author of a trivial book on the Channel Islands, exhibits in that work an "uneasy vanity" unjustified by any but commonplace ability.[15] The modern age is cluttered with a mass of such unjustifiable literary productions, the result of "uneasy ambition."[16] The **"Too Ready Writer,"** an "importunate hawker of undesirable superfluities," "obtrudes his ill-considered work where place ought to have been left to better men"; he has nothing original to contribute but the flavor of his personality, like "the too cheap and insistent nutmeg," to the substantial matter already provided by the "great writer."[17] These essays criticize not only the unjustifiable pretensions of ambitious writers, but also the more modest productions of less ambitious men, whose confessedly unoriginal conversation "has no deep hunger to excuse it," who become "indistinguishable from the ordinary run of moneyed and money-getting men," who lack "appetite."[18]

Despite this harshness towards failure or minor accomplishment, the essays also vividly imagine the anxiety that accompanies ambitious effort. "Great and precious origination must always be comparatively rare," and the world is full of critics cruelly eager to demonstrate failure in originality, to show that "something apparently much the same as what [the writer] has said in some connection not clearly ascertained had been said by somebody else."[19] The fate of Proteus Merman, who gives up a Protean, Will Ladislaw-like dilettantishness to concentrate on a single, Casaubon-like project—a treatise on "the possible connection of certain symbolic monuments common to widely scattered races"—bears out all of Casaubon's fears.[20] His book is received with cruel, unjust criticism—it main idea eventually becoming generally received, but long after any possibility that the now permanently embittered Merman will be credited with it.

The fictional character Theophrastus Such, to whom these essays are attributed, resolves the conflict between his own high standard of achievement and his lack of confidence that he can succeed (the one work he has published, a modest humorous romance, has been a failure) by apparently renouncing ambition. He claims to eschew subjection to "self-importance," to reject the "consolations of egoism," which he characteristically describes in terms of literary immortality: "Examining the world in order to find consolation is very much like looking carefully over the pages of a great book in order to find our own name, if not in the text, at least in a laudatory note." He becomes self-abnegating in conversation, allowing his acquaintances to "tell me unreservedly of their triumphs and their piques; explain their purposes at length, and reassure me with cheerfulness as to their chances of success," etc. But in this way he only conceals the ambition for triumph he shares with his acquaintances, for "My conversational reticence about myself turned into garrulousness on paper." His writing—these essays—remains concealed, unpublished: we are to believe that they are published posthumously by one of Theophrastus's friends. But the high standards of criticism these essays maintain reveal the persistence of Theophrastus's ambition, as does his very renunciation of a possibly unworthy publication.[21]

Theophrastus himself points out how ambition can be expressed by apparent renunciation of ambition. As he writes in "A Man Surprised at His Originality,"

> Accustomed to observe what we think an unwarrantable conceit exhibiting itself in ridiculous pretensions and forwardness to play the lion's part, in obvious self-complacency and loud peremptoriness, we are not on the alert to detect the egoistic claims of a more exorbitant kind, often hidden under an apparent neutrality or an acquiescence in being put out of the question.[22]

The character to whom these words refer, Lentulus, is apparently "nobody's rival," but constantly implies a critical attitude of superiority to other writers about whom he speaks with reserve. Lentulus chooses to express his ambition in this way because of a justified fear of his possible unoriginality.

> Your audibly arrogant man exposes himself to tests; in attempting to make an impression on others, he may possibly (not always) be made to feel his own lack of definiteness; and the demand for definiteness is to all of us a needful check on vague depreciation of what others do, and vague ecstatic trust in our own superior ability.[23]

Theophrastus's essays can help us locate the epic ambition in the avowedly unambitious *Middlemarch.* A publishing novelist, Eliot is more willing than Lentulus to risk definiteness; more willing to be tested than the fictional Theophrastus, who does not want to hear his friend's opinion of the value of his writing, and who therefore, like Casaubon and Featherstone in their wills, seeks to exert the influence of the dead hand only posthumously. But *Middlemarch* presents itself as a modest achievement, at most only a "home epic," its narrator a critic of epic ambitions rather than the ambitious singer of epic achievement. Yet Eliot herself teaches us to see through such modesty. In renouncing the subject of the conventional epic, Eliot still demonstrates an epic ambition; and, as Dorothea achieves two original marriages, so Eliot achieves an epic originality within the genre of the novel.

In discussing Lydgate's ambition, Eliot presents what Alan Mintz argues is her own credo:

> Many men have been praised as vividly imaginative on the strength of their profuseness in indifferent drawing or cheap narration:—reports of very poor talk going on in distant orbs; or portraits of Lucifer coming down on his bad errands as a large ugly man with bat's wings and spurts of phosphorescence; or exaggerations of wantonness that seem to reflect life in a diseased dream. . . . [But Lydgate] wanted to pierce the obscurity of those minute processes which prepare human misery and joy, those invisible thoroughfares which are the first lurking-places of anguish, mania, and crime, that delicate poise and transition which determine the growth of happy or unhappy consciousness.
>
> (Ch. 16, p. 122)

Certainly *Middlemarch* offers this study of the minute and delicate rather than the Miltonic sublime. By spurning the supernatural subject matter of Milton's work, Eliot seems to be including him in the criticism she always saves for those who dwell on otherworldly things, usually for self-serving purposes. Yet her words also call up Milton's achievement as a standard of comparison for Lydgate's exploration—and, analogically, her own—with minute psychological processes.

Eliot invokes the same standard in *The Spanish Gypsy* (1868), her major published work immediately preceding *Middlemarch,* far more epic in appearance than that novel is, and yet also apparently eschewing that model. A long verse narrative about the effort to found a homeland for the gypsies, **The Spanish Gypsy** repeatedly implies an epic context for its characters' acts and its author's achievement. One of the characters, the poet Juan, anticipates the journey to Africa, where the homeland is to be: "I shall grow epic, like the Florentine, / And sing the founding of our infant state, / Sing the Zincalo's Carthage."[24] As we might expect, the characters who most confidently embrace this cause are defeated: Zarca, the leader, frank in his aspiration for immortality, is killed; Don Silva, who at first is one of the soldiers seeking to make Spain "the modern Cyrus," but then embraces the gypsy's plan out of love for Zarca's daughter Fedalma, is "maimed" by his rejection of his Spanish heritage, and lives in undying remorse for his betrayal. Fedalma, who takes up her father's quest, is described like him in heroic terms, precisely the terms applied to Dorothea: she is like a goddess, like the Virgin Mary. Yet she earns these honors only by renunciation: her task is a sorrow to her, since it demands that she renounce her love for Silva, and since she knows that, unlike Zarca, she has no chance of succeeding in her mission. Apparently rejecting not only Christian consolation but Miltonic epic grandeur as well, she tells Silva, "We may not make this world a paradise / By walking it together hand in hand."[25] Like Fedalma, Eliot invokes epic as a critical standard, while rejecting epic ambition herself. Yet the language of the poem persists in honoring Fedalma as an epic heroine, and therefore implicitly makes epic claims for itself.

Eliot's sensitivity to the disguises of ambition enables her to see the epic struggles that take place at the domestic hearth, and the uncompromising will of an apparently renunciatory character like Dorothea. Eliot is an innovator not only in introducing the ethos of vocation into the novel, but in focusing on marriage as a covert competition, a struggle for mastery, rather than as a community which images the larger society with which individuals must achieve some accommodation. Eliot's study of the battle of marriage in **Middlemarch** prepares the way for the intenser struggle, also to the death, between Grandcourt and Gwendolen Harleth in **Daniel Deronda.** This study will be the most subtle and powerful in all of Eliot's novels—and more successful as home epic than Daniel's story is as a traditional epic of the hero setting out to found a society.

The mixed success of **Daniel Deronda** is more characteristic of Eliot's novels. Throughout Eliot's career, renunciation is presented as the only reliable expression of ambition; but **Middlemarch** is her only work in which the narrator so frankly raises the epic context and so consistently, like her heroine, renounces epic ambition. The completeness of the renunciation allows Eliot to mock Dorothea's prenuptial eagerness for active martyrdom as she cannot mock the same eagerness in her

other heroes and heroines. Eliot's mockery is employed not in the name of realism, as Calvin Bedient asserts, but of epic ambition. It is by an epic standard that Eliot's characters and her work are to be judged. In the novel's "Finale," having made the claim that her work is a "home epic," the narrator quickly withdraws even this qualified term, urging that her work is minor, that Dorothea has failed to win fame, and that this failure is not even particularly significant: she might have written of "far sadder sacrifices" than Dorothea's. Yet the allusion to the *Cyropedia* with which the final paragraph opens suggests that Dorothea's sacrifice is in some ways as significant as Cyrus's conquest of Babylon: "Her full nature, like that river of which Cyrus broke the strength, spent itself in channels which had no great name on the earth" ("Finale," p. 613). The heroic analogy is to a defeat rather than a victory; Dorothea is not Cyrus, but the river the Babylonians mistakenly saw as their defense. Yet the analogy suggests another parallel: who broke Dorothea's strength, who made her so memorable, so challenging a figure of heroic renunciation, but the conqueror George Eliot?

Notes

1. *Middlemarch,* ed. Gordon S. Haight (Boston: Houghton Mifflin, 1956), "Prelude," p. 3. Further references to chapter and page number in this edition will appear in the text.

2. Critics who find an epic element in *Middlemarch* include Harold Fisch, "*Daniel Deronda* or *Gwendolen Harleth?*", *Nineteenth-Century Fiction,* 19 (1965), 351; U. C. Knoepflmacher, "*Middlemarch:* Affirmation through Compromise," in *Laughter and Despair: Readings in Ten Novels of the Victorian Era* (Berkeley: University of California Press [1971]), p. 178; Joseph Weisenfarth, *George Eliot's Mythmaking* (Heidelberg: Winter, 1977), p. 186; and Felicia Bonaparte, *The Triptych and the Cross: The Central Myths of George Eliot's Poetic Imagination* (New York: New York University Press, 1979), p. 19. In the course of her treatment of *Romola,* Bonaparte asserts that the epic is an "indispensable current in [*Middlemarch*'s] theme," although "the epic does not dominate the novel." Knoepflmacher, Fisch, and Weisenfarth agree that the novel is an epic achievement, but that none of its characters rises to such epic action. I will argue rather that renunciation is the vehicle for the epic ambition of novelist and characters alike.

3. *George Eliot and the Novel of Vocation* (Cambridge, Mass.: Harvard University Press, 1978), p. 69.

4. Mintz, pp. 114-15.

5. Weisenfarth, p. 209.

6. V. Ch. 16, p. 123, Ch. 36, p. 258, Ch. 31, p. 219.

7. For discussion of the novel's composition, see Jerome Beaty, *Middlemarch from Notebook to Novel: A Study of George Eliot's Creative Method,* Illinois Studies in Language and Literature, 47 (Urbana: University of Illinois Press, 1960); and Stanton Millet, "The Union of 'Miss Brooke' and 'Middlemarch': A Study of the Manuscript," *JEGP* [*Journal of English and Germanic Philology*], 79 (1980), 32-57.

8. V. Ch. 22, p. 162, Ch. 47, p. 344, Ch. 37, pp. 265, 270. Ch. 43, p. 318.

9. V. Ch. 47, p. 344, Ch. 60, p. 441. Will's similarity to Casaubon is also noted by Kathleen Blake, "*Middlemarch* and the Woman Question," *Nineteenth-Century Fiction,* 31 (1976), 308, and by Laura Comer Emery, *George Eliot's Creative Conflict: The Other Side of Silence* (Berkeley: University of California Press, 1976), who suggests that Will's idealization of Dorothea is defensive, pp. 188-92. Blake also notes the element of ambition in Dorothea's choice of Will: Dorothea needs him "for the testament he gives her of her own power," p. 301. For a persuasive treatment of the heroic aspect of Will's dilettantism, see George Levine, "The Hero as Dilettante: *Middlemarch* and *Nostromo,*" in *George Eliot: Centenary Essays and an Unpublished Fragment,* ed. Anne Smith (Totowa, N. J.: Barnes and Noble, 1980), especially p. 165.

10. Dorothea also considers founding "a little colony," but decides not to, Ch. 55, p. 401.

11. V. Ch. 31, p. 216, "Finale," p. 610.

12. V. Ch. 21, p. 154, Ch. 37, p. 274.

13. Ruby V. Redinger, *George Eliot: The Emergent Self* (New York: Alfred A. Knopf, 1975).

14. John Clark Pratt and Victor A. Neufeldt, in their introduction to *George Eliot's Middlemarch Notebooks: A Transcription* (Berkeley: University of California Press, 1979), note these interests of Eliot's, pp. xxix, xxxvii, xliv. The notebooks' quotations from Sir Thomas Browne's *Pseudodoxia Epidemica* may express the same interest in Browne's own erroneous notions, for Eliot's 1865 essay, "The Influence of Rationalism," discusses Browne's belief in witches; see *Essays of George Eliot,* ed. Thomas Pinney (New York: Columbia University Press, 1963), pp. 401-02.

15. "Diseases of Small Authorship," in *Impressions of Theophrastus Such and Miscellaneous Essays* (New York: Harper and Brothers, 1910), p. 161.

16. "Authorship," in *Leaves from a Notebook,* rpt. in *Essays,* ed. Pinney, p. 438.

17. "The Too Ready Writer," in *Impressions,* p. 145.

18. "A Too Deferential Man," "A Half-Breed," "A Political Molecule," in *Impressions,* pp. 69, 101, 81.

19. "Value in Originality," "Judgments on Authors," in *Essays,* pp. 448, 442.

20. "How We Encourage Research," in *Impressions,* p. 36.

21. "Looking Inward," in *Impressions,* pp. 10, 12, 13. G. Robert Stange suggests that the essay form itself is an ironically unambitious one, in "The Voices of the Essayist," *Nineteenth-Century Fiction,* 35 (1980), 323. Stange's is the only considerable treatment of *The Impressions of Theophrastus Such.*

22. "A Man Surprised at His Originality," in *Impressions,* p. 51.

23. "A Man Surprised," p. 58.

24. *The Spanish Gypsy,* Book III, in *Poems* (New York: Harper and Brothers, 1910), I, p. 211.

25. *The Spanish Gypsy,* Book III, in *Poems,* I, 239.

Ellin Ringler (essay date spring 1983)

SOURCE: Ringler, Ellin. "*Middlemarch*: A Feminist Perspective." *Studies in the Novel* 15, no. 1 (spring 1983): 55-61.

[*In the following essay, Ringler surveys various feminist attitudes toward the character of Dorothea Brooke. Ringler asserts that, while Dorothea's genius is stifled by the male-dominated social and intellectual climate of Victorian England, she still manages to achieve a private superiority over the novel's male characters by virtue of her "nobility of character and moral intelligence." Ringler concludes that the work should trouble feminists not because Dorothea fails to earn recognition in the public sphere but because Eliot ultimately idealizes her renunciation of outward ambition.*]

In almost every respect, George Eliot occupies a profoundly uneasy position among feminist literary critics. Virginia Woolf gave voice to that uneasiness as early as 1919, when she contrasted the fates of Eliot's heroines (which end in "tragedy, or in a compromise that is even more melancholy"[1]) with the "story of George Eliot herself" for whom the confrontation of her "feminine aspirations with the real world of men" had a triumphant issue, "whatever it may have been for her creations."

Certainly, much of Eliot's own "story" supports this claim for her personal triumph as a woman. She was accorded a veneration by her contemporaries—men and women alike—unequalled by that of any other woman writer in nineteenth-century England. Neither Jane Austen nor the Brontës, for example, managed to escape condescension to the fact of their womanhood as fully as she did. Her credentials as a feminist are less clear. She did support the cause of women's education, donating £50 to the founding of Girton College. Her 1855 essay on Margaret Fuller and Mary Wollstonecraft [**"Margaret Fuller and Mary Wollstonecraft"**] liberally quotes both feminists, and sympathetically reviews their respective works: *Woman in the Nineteenth Century* (1855) and *A Vindication of the Rights of Woman* (1792).[2] In 1856, Eliot helped to circulate her friend Barbara Bodichon's petition demanding a married woman's right to her own earnings, because she believed this right would have a salutary effect on "the position and character of women."[3] Finally, whatever one may say about the ultimate destinies of her heroines, George Eliot's sensitivity to feminist concerns seems evident in her creation of such figures as Dinah Morris, Maggie Tulliver, Dorothea Brooke, and Gwendolen Harleth.

Yet, Eliot's ambivalence about the Woman Question is inescapable. We know that she was at best indifferent, at worst hostile, to the cause of women's suffrage. Acknowledging that other women were extraordinarily attracted to George Eliot, Gordon Haight observes that, though she "sympathized with women . . . the friendship and intimacy of men was more to her." She simply had no place in her emotions for the lesbian passion of Edith Simcox, whom she told bluntly that "she had never all her life cared very much for women."[4] Eliot's essay, **"Silly Novels by Lady Novelists,"** has become, of course, a classic indictment of the literary endeavors of uneducated women. Although Eliot affirms in the piece that "women can produce novels not only fine, but among the finest," what are we to make of the peculiar limitations she sets for the works of women? Even the most educated woman "does not write books to confound philosophers" but to "delight them," novels that "have a precious specialty, lying apart from masculine aptitudes and experiences."[5]

Evidently, Eliot's own female contemporaries felt as uneasy about her as many twentieth-century feminists do. Elaine Showalter indicates in *A Literature of Their Own* that they "never faltered in their praise of her books, but they felt excluded from, envious of, her world. Her very superiority depressed them." Eliot was to them "reserved, inaccessible, opaque" and "violated the values of sisterly communion in the female subculture by avoiding close friendships with other women writers."[6]

These mixed reactions to her person among Eliot's female peers, as well as the contradictions evident in her biography, are, not surprisingly, echoed in recent feminist criticism of her greatest novel. *Middlemarch,* ap-

parently, shares the same equivocal position vis à vis the Woman Question that is occupied by the author herself. A survey of fifteen fairly representative feminist critiques of *Middlemarch,* published between 1972 and 1978, reveals only two that view it as a profoundly feminist work; the other thirteen reactions range from vehement condemnation of Eliot's betrayal of feminism in *Middlemarch* to the judgment that she was an "uncertain feminist"[7] with "a complex ambivalence toward the contemporary lot of women."[8]

The arguments that *Middlemarch* fails as a feminist work swirl naturally and almost without exception about the figure of Dorothea Brooke; and the stridency of tone pervading the criticism of Eliot's heroine is frequently startling. For example, in her highly praised book, *Literary Women,* Ellen Moers writes: "Dorothea Brooke . . . is good for nothing *but* to be admired. An arrogant, selfish, spoiled rich beauty, she does little but harm in the novel. Ignorant in the extreme and mentally idle, . . . Dorothea has little of interest to say, but a magnificent voice to say it in. . . . She also has what must be the most stunning wardrobe in Victorian fiction."[9] Lest this attack seem to be merely the dyspeptic outburst of one disgruntled feminist, consider Anthea Zeman's comment on Eliot's heroine: "We are asked to believe in the importance of a girl who seldom succeeds in doing anything of the remotest practical use," who is blighted by "physical and social myopia," and whose history is "uninspiring."[10] Patricia Beer's equally strong censure of Dorothea Brooke touches upon a complaint hinted at by Virginia Woolf and echoed by many feminists since. Claiming that Eliot condescends to Dorothea, Beer writes: "What is fatally hampering to George Eliot's heroines is not society, not even provincial society, but their own lack of creativity, which includes creative intellectual powers. . . . George Eliot herself triumphed over greater handicaps than any of her women characters are faced with."[11] This unflattering comparison between George Eliot and her own heroines, to the detriment, in particular, of Dorothea Brooke, is taken up by several other recent feminist critics such as Lee Edwards, Marlene Springer, Ellen Moers, and it is certainly implied in Virginia Woolf's earlier contrast between Eliot's "triumphs" and the "melancholy compromise" she created for her heroines. These critical observations may be summarized by a rhetorical question: Why, when Eliot herself was able to defy social tradition and achieve her own epic life, did she relentlessly consign Dorothea to the unmitigated mediocrity of a conventional marriage to Will Ladislaw?

Even the defenders of Eliot's feminism, like Kathleen Blake and Patricia Spacks, agree that Dorothea's is a constricted and disappointing lot, which Blake justifies by appealing to the old chestnut, Eliot's "realism." "George Eliot," writes the critic, "does not show her heroine summoned to sweet ascent, but surely to supply such satisfactory summons would be to endanger realism."[12] An extension of this defense, which is at least questionable, is offered by Zelda Austen, who tells us that "realistically, Dorothea is far more representative than George Eliot."[13] Other critics sympathetic to Eliot's feminist insights attribute her limitation of Dorothea's destiny to a "complicated pessimism,"[14] or label it the "complete embodiment of sound, conservative"[15] mid-Victorianism.

Whatever the label, at the heart of this controversy about Eliot's feminist consciousness in *Middlemarch* is what critics have come to refer to as the "Saint-Theresa Syndrome,"[16] the terms of which are laid out by Eliot herself in the novel's "Prelude." This phenomenon describes the especially female fate, as Eliot would have it, of desiring an epic life but finding no outlet for achievement apart from the socially limiting role of "common womanhood,"[17] i.e., marriage. For, no matter what attitude they take, the recent feminists admit that Eliot has raised a perplexing issue about feminine destiny in *Middlemarch.* A great deal, it would seem, is expected of Dorothea Brooke, but, and here the critics differ as to degree, far less is realized.

Of course, all its significant characters—men as well as women—experience a constriction of their expectations. However, as Patricia Spacks points out, the men "have more 'public' resources (Casaubon can publish, or project publishing; Lydgate can achieve, or project achieving, medical discoveries); women, it seems, develop more significant 'private' ones." In actual fact, Spacks herself and many other critics have observed that the male characters of *Middlemarch* are singularly ineffective in achieving any of their "public projections" on their own. "Only when taken in hand by a good woman can they succeed,"[18] she writes.

Indeed, when one looks closely at Dorothea's relations with the major male figures of *Middlemarch,* one sees that she is neither useless nor without creative mental power, however "stunning" her wardrobe. In fact, she comes to exert a significant influence over the men she is close to, but on a private, psychological level, rather than a public, social one. The hourglass pattern of Dorothea's encounters with Casaubon, Lydgate, and Will Ladislaw is carefully delineated by Eliot. Always, her heroine begins as suppliant in these relationships; always these men's social roles, their very positions as males, are superior to hers. Yet, in every case, though she submits to social convention (perhaps, *because* she does) Dorothea's psychological strength prevails, and she emerges more powerful than the men.

For example, although she turns to Casaubon as to a teacher, the "guide who will take her along the grandest path," he becomes, as circumstances and her perceptions change, a shallow and pitiful soul who must look to his young wife for help. Her decision to comply with her ailing husband's selfish and constricting demand that she complete his scholarly treatise should he die enlarges Dorothea's nature; she reveals herself to be Casaubon's moral superior in every way. But Dorothea's psychological growth is purchased at the expense of her social independence. Believing it to be a "grand path," Eliot's heroine enters the narrow labyrinth of marriage to Casaubon and is spiritually transformed from a child to a woman, from dependent to protector. Still, she remains as socially limited as she is psychologically strong.

U. C. Knoepflmacher has traced in detail the intricate counterpoint between the fates of Dorothea and Tertius Lydgate.[19] An early meeting between the two pictures Dorothea turning to the socially promising young physician for help with Casaubon. "Oh, you are a wise man, are you not? You know all about life and death. Advise me," she begs (p. 214). By the end of the novel, when Dorothea hears Lydgate's confession about his involvement with the Bulstrode scandal and offers him her faith and help, a significant transformation has taken place. Knoepflmacher concludes his analysis of the role reversals of these characters with, "Dorothea has become the healer; Lydgate the patient."[20]

During their first encounters in Rome, Dorothea confesses her ignorance of painting and poetry to Will Ladislaw; and he willingly plays the role of instructor. But Eliot soon makes it evident that Ladislaw requires Dorothea's steadiness and depth of character to focus his own comparatively flighty nature. "It is undeniable that but for the desire to be where Dorothea was, and perhaps the want of knowing what else to do" (p. 318), Will would have flagrantly dispersed his energies. The fact that Eliot reverses the roles here so early may be one reason why there is such controversy about Will's fitness to be cast as Dorothea's second husband; he is, as one critic remarks, "a slight figure beside her."[21] Again though, we are reminded that Dorothea's final influence is moral and spiritual—private, rather than public. It is, after all, Will who (with Dorothea's "wifely help") eventually becomes "an ardent public man" (pp. 610-11).

There is a broad irony involved in the fact that Dorothea consistently turns to the men in *Middlemarch* for guidance and is just as consistently disappointed. An extension of the irony is that, not only must she "learn without a teacher,"[22] she must become a teacher herself. The same, it appears, may be said of the other women in the novel. For a variety of reasons, neither Rosamond, nor Mary Garth—not even the "imperfectly taught" Mrs. Bulstrode—can ultimately depend upon her consort for strength; and each, in the end, significantly directs her husband's course for better or worse. Each develops, in spite of her apparent social submission to the male, an impressive personal dominance.

What should attract twentieth-century feminists to *Middlemarch* is Eliot's portrait of that dominance: her impulse, as strong as that of the most ardent believer in women's liberation, to imagine a heroine whose nobility of character and moral intelligence are entirely persuasive. And, however much she may have preferred the friendship of men in her own life, Eliot does not demonstrate much respect for them in her novel. Every one of her major male characters, Casaubon, Lydgate, Will Ladislaw, Fred Vincy, Nicholas Bulstrode, displays a virulent and weakening form of "moral stupidity" (p. 156). One might add that this is also true of most of the minor masculine figures in the novel. They are guilty of egotism, self-deception, greed, hypocrisy, or what the author calls "spots of commonness." With that insight, too, some feminists might very well agree.

Finally, what should draw them to the novel are Eliot's many thoughtful protests against the limitations of education and opportunity imposed upon her female characters by the "imperfect social state" (p. 612) in which they struggle. The web of connections she has carefully traced in *Middlemarch* is, as the author often acknowledges, significantly ruptured because the public roles of women are in no way commensurate with their personal force. It is when Eliot offers to mend the rupture, with rationalizations about the "good" perpetrated by "unhistoric acts" and the efficacy of "hidden lives," that feminists must demur. The disjunctures between male and female social power illustrated throughout the novel simply cannot be adequately patched by those weak threads.

It would appear, then, that the feminists' uneasiness about *Middlemarch* is justified, but not because Dorothea Brooke never gains the public stature achieved by George Eliot herself. To introduce that external comparison between an author and her heroine is, I would suggest, to commit a serious aesthetic and historical fallacy. No, what should make us uneasy is the sense that Eliot seems, at the very last, to shrink from the implications of her own novel. The imbalance between male and female strength and the unjust channeling of women's "full natures" in *Middlemarch* finally demand more from the narrator than sad resignation or phrases about "incalculably diffusive" effects (p. 613). We would prefer, instead, a healthy anger. That cleansing emotion seems far truer to the disheartening spectacle of women's "spiritual grandeur ill-matched with meanness of opportunity" (p. 3), which Eliot has so convincingly traced in *Middlemarch.*

Notes

1. Virginia Woolf, "George Eliot," *The Common Reader* (New York: Harvest Books, 1953), p. 176.

2. *Essays of George Eliot,* ed. Thomas Pinney (New York: Columbia Univ. Press, 1963), pp. 199-206.

3. Francoise Basch, *Relative Creatures: Victorian Women in Society and the Novel* (New York: Schocken Books, 1974), p. 95.

4. Gordon S. Haight, *George Eliot: A Biography* (New York and Oxford: Oxford Univ. Press, 1968), pp. 493, 495, 535.

5. Pinney, pp. 210, 324, 317.

6. Elaine Showalter, *A Literature of Their Own* (Princeton: Princeton Univ. Press, 1977), p. 107.

7. Laurence Lerner, "Dorothea and the Theresa-Complex," *Middlemarch, a Casebook,* ed. Patrick Swinden (New York: Macmillan, 1972), p. 243.

8. "Angels and Other Women in Victorian Literature," *What Manner of Woman,* ed. Marlene Springer (New York: New York Univ. Press, 1977), p. 142.

9. Ellen Moers, *Literary Women* (New York: Doubleday, 1977), pp. 295-96.

10. Anthea Zeman, *Presumptuous Girls* (London: Weidenfeld and Nicolson, 1977), p. 60.

11. Patricia Beer, *Reader, I Married Him* (New York: Harper and Row, 1974), p. 181.

12. Kathleen Blake, "*Middlemarch* and the Woman Question," *Nineteenth-Century Fiction,* 31 (Dec. 1976), 310.

13. Zelda Austen, "Why Feminist Critics Are Angry with George Eliot," *College English,* 37 (Feb. 1976), 552.

14. Patricia Meyers Spacks, *The Female Imagination* (New York: Knopf, 1972), p. 307.

15. Lloyd Fernando, *"New Women" in the Late Victorian Novel* (New York: Knopf, 1972), p. 307.

16. See, e.g., Blake, p. 288 and Lerner, pp. 225-47.

17. George Eliot, *Middlemarch,* ed. G. S. Haight (Boston: Houghton Mifflin, 1956), p. 3.

18. Spacks, p. 300.

19. U. C. Knoepflmacher, *Religious Humanism and the Victorian Novel* (Princeton: Princeton Univ. Press, 1965), pp. 75-96.

20. Knoepflmacher, p. 94.

21. Blake, p. 308.

22. Beer, p. 212.

John Kucich (essay date winter 1985)

SOURCE: Kucich, John. "Repression and Dialectical Inwardness in *Middlemarch*." *Mosaic: A Journal for the Interdisciplinary Study of Literature* 18, no. 1 (winter 1985): 45-63.

[*In the following essay, Kucich examines the tension between Dorothea's personal ambition and her sense of obligation to the community. Kucich contends that Dor-*

othea's selflessness, rather than embodying an altruistic ideal, in fact symbolizes a painful repression of desire, one all-too prevalent in Victorian society.]

At the end of **Middlemarch,** Dorothea Brooke seems to discover the principles that permit an ideal communion between her desires and the world. Resolving to overlook her own disappointed love for Will, and to mediate unselfishly between Lydgate and Rosamond, Dorothea finds that "the objects of her rescue were not to be sought out by her fancy: they were chosen for her."[1] Far from diminishing her capacity for love, however, the compulsoriness of her duty only enlarges Dorothea emotionally—she feels "a part of . . . involuntary, palpitating life." Her ego-less union with others also seems to ratify her more private love for Will, as the broken dam of her feeling opens possibilities for their reconciliation, and their marriage.

Dorothea's transformation is, perhaps, Eliot's most famous expression of passionate individualism vitalized by impersonal feeling, by what she called "wider sympathy." Appropriately, readers have looked to the ending of **Middlemarch** to focus many of their disagreements about nineteenth-century syntheses of the personal and the social: disagreements about whether these tenuous syntheses really diffuse social commitment;[2] whether, on the contrary, they socialize and repress emotional life;[3] or whether they do successfully unite romantic self-expression with interdependence—a crucial stage in the doctrine of melioration Eliot derived from Spinoza, from French and German Idealists, and from Herbert Spencer.

Regardless of how Dorothea's resolution is interpreted, however, most readers accept the terms of this nineteenth-century conflict as they are given, and often merely repeat them by arguing one of these three readings. That is, George Eliot is seen as struggling, through Dorothea, with the essentially antagonistic relationship between two different kinds of desire: one private and romantic, the other altruistic, impersonal and implicitly collective. Eliot's apparent attempt to resolve this opposition, though perhaps the most psychologically and philosophically discursive in nineteenth-century fiction, is, after all, widely-grounded in the preoccupations of the period's novelists. Dickens' thematic oscillations between personal guilt or violence and communal sentimentality, the Brontës' between rage and dependence, and even Thackeray's between ambition and irony, all express divided nineteenth-century loyalties to two kinds of desire, selfish and selfless. But the nineteenth century is partly responsible for teaching us to regard these forms of desire as antithetical, and in conflict. We must be suspicious of the apparent naturalness, as well as the static simplicity, of this general cultural ambivalence.

There are, in fact, distinct advantages to be had by representing desire in this way, as divided against itself in a conflict that might never be adequately resolved. For this familiar impasse in Victorian fiction also works to produce a general conception of desire as self-conflict. That is to say, the opposition of two coherent and self-consistent forms of desire that appears to split novels like **Middlemarch** actually conceals a unilateral representation of desire as labyrinthine in its inward irresolvability. The divisive claims of desire in these novels seem to reflect a real, inevitable conflict between private and public needs, and they idealize self-conflict as evidence of a conscientious concern for accommodating the self to the external world. The convoluted, conflictual impulses of Victorian protagonists, however, in which the clash between private and public needs is reconceived as an infinite debate between expressive and repressive energies, often come to obscure any connection to problems of internal or external completion. They suffuse these problems instead with an introspective texture of hesitation, qualification and doubt in which self-conflict comes to seem the very origin and limit of all desire—personal or impersonal—and the only field in which desire's intensity can be expressed. The play of conflicting forces within self-consciousness comes to seem an autonomous dynamic, a secret, personal struggle that is much more central to identity, especially in its limitlessness, than the public/private antagonism it rarely manages to mediate successfully anyway.

This unstated conception of desire as essentially, vitally self-conflictual is useful to Victorian bourgeois culture primarily because it values the internal suspension and circulation of emotional energy. It diminishes desire's vulnerability to otherness in both social and personal relations, at the same time that it deceptively presents conscientiousness as its chief context. For through this narrative ordering of desire, public life is not simply absorbed into private life—even within the private, intimacy with others is replaced by a more pure and unlimited self-reflexivity. While this internalization of conflict may be disguised in the strained adjustments between romantic indulgence and altruism made by the works themselves—as in the ending of **Middlemarch**—we can locate it in the enclosed, unified relationship of self-expression to repression that saturates both these kinds of desire and defines them as complementary forms of a conflictual but dynamic inwardness.

This dynamic inwardness, and its partial dependence on repression, is usefully clarified by the recent work of Michel Foucault, whose theory of Victorian sexual repression parallels the more ethical terminology of novelists like George Eliot. Foucault argues that sexual desire and repression are not at all contrary forces in Victorian culture, but that they cooperate in a strategy whose sole function is to introvert the search for knowledge and gratification and to structure it within an "in-finitized" subjectivity. In *The History of Sexuality,* he argues that Victorian culture actually enshrined sexual passion as the cherished and mercurial "secret" of identity by veiling it in repression—a strategy that bases identity in self-relation and self-conflict rather than in the forms of an individual's relationship to others: "let us not isolate the restrictions, reticences, evasions, or silences which [Victorian sexuality] may have manifested, in order to refer them to some constitutive taboo, psychical repression or death instinct. What was formed was . . . an affirmation of self."[4] According to Foucault, repression reinforces sexual desire and names it as the internal origin of identity in two key ways: by mystifying it and by enjoining individuals to seek out and define the dangerous, primal "truth" of the sexuality buried within themselves. Increasing self-conflict through repression only increases an absorption with seemingly bottomless and unmediated internal conditions, seen as the "meaning" of an individual existence: "what was involved was not an asceticism, in any case not a renunciation or a disqualification of the flesh, but on the contrary an intensification, a problematization of health and its operational terms: it was a question of techniques for maximizing life" (pp. 122-23). In short, the intensity of the Victorian conjunction of desire and repression works outside the questions of "fulfillment" that it makes endlessly problematic by heightening interiority at the expense of relationship—a displacement with ominous implications for Victorian theories of social melioration that hope to produce melioration out of the self-conflicts of individual actors.

Foucault's analysis of Victorian repression is very narrowly focused on the sexual and it is, perhaps, excessively concerned with "power" as the ultimate end of human desire. But his notion that forms of self-negation became a widespread Victorian strategy for heightening interiority (a notion that has been supported by a number of recent cultural studies),[5] rather than simply reflecting a conflict between self and society, has broad implications for the study of Victorian fiction generally and of George Eliot in particular. For self-negation obviously dominates the wider regions of emotional and ethical life in Victorian fiction. The psychological and philosophical discursiveness of George Eliot's attempted resolutions of antithetical desire, as opposed to the more discontinuous juxtapositions of self and society in other Victorian novelists, makes her work a particularly good starting point for an analysis of self-conflict as a reigning form of subjectivity. And by placing the ambiguous resolutions of *Middlemarch* in this context, we can see very clearly how desire might be represented as self-conflict on the two parallel—not oppositional—levels of personal and impersonal impulse.

On the one hand, Eliot's romantic narrative ultimately undermines the quest for union implicit in all romance, turning the progress of Will and Dorothea's love into a counterpointing, mutual refinement of interiority through repression. On the other, as much as *Middlemarch* seeks social improvement, it also demonstrates George Eliot's deep-seated, contradictory conviction that "wider sympathy" can best be sustained by a certain tension within personality, and that its exercise depends on a careful insulation of identity from the influence of otherness, even in altruistic action. Dorothea's altruism actually appears to contain its own inversion, a fundamental reversal of impulses to confront others, while her love for Will reflects and enhances this conflictual inwardness through its associations with more conventional images of intense, constricted feeling. In both public and private spheres, Eliot shifts the drama of her characters' desires away from the field of relationship to others, and instead focuses it in a more dynamic framework, one that thrives on the confrontation of forces solely within the self. In effect, the charged, climactic places in her novels become those in which emotional conflicts within certain characters privately sustain the passion denied to them by Eliot's public world. The deepest tragedy of Eliot's work lies here, in the ideology of self-reflexiveness infecting and distorting what she clearly intended as progressive social theory and as a general escape from the cell of egotism. Eliot's abstract ethical pronouncements, of course, often imagine a stronger, more dialectical relation between self and world than she is able to project through characters like Dorothea.[6] But while the novels hardly abandon this concern with otherness, they always distort it through a characteristically Victorian discourse of productive self-conflict.

The concept of a cooperation between love and altruism, as covert means of heightening interiority through self-relation, can be aligned with Eliot's own language more accurately if we refer to the philosophical origins of her ideas about desire. The model for self-conflict in *Middlemarch* is best understood as a Hegelian one: Eliot's characters are self-divided by impulses that complete each other dialectically. That is, they combine within themselves impulses that seem to exclude and contradict each other, as "personal" and "impersonal" (or "positive" and "negative") versions of the self. But these oppositional energies eventually form a dialectic that enlarges selfhood in relation to itself, and in isolation from the inconclusive and fragmentary world of others. It is a common tendency to assimilate this kind of inner conflict to Freudian theory, which sees repression as the internalization of social constraints—the frustration of any movement of desire outward toward objects in the world. But repression in *Middlemarch* is more usefully placed in relation to its philosophical sources: in Eliot's novel, personal and impersonal energies form a passionate inward world, a world in which the need to engage "otherness" is fulfilled through internal mediations. It is only by examining this dialectic of Hegelian inwardness that we can better understand the identity of love and altruism in *Middlemarch* as a basic cooperation between desire and its own negation.[7]

To call this strategy of internal opposition "Hegelian" is not to identify Hegel as its direct source, but only to isolate one particular thread in the neo-Romantic subjectivism Eliot inherited, mostly from Strauss and Feuerbach.[8] In *The Essence of Christianity,* which Eliot translated in 1854 with great enthusiasm, the internal opposition of an impersonal "human nature" to individual will is the key to Feuerbach's entire system. As Feuerbach describes the dynamic, man encounters others chiefly as the instruments through which he recognizes a dualism within himself, a tension between what he calls "subjective" and "objective" energies within his own being: "Man is nothing without an object. . . . But the object to which a subject essentially, necessarily relates, is nothing else than this subject's own, but objective nature. . . . The power of the object over him is therefore the power of his own nature. Thus the power of the object of feeling is feeling itself."[9] In this way, by using external objects as vehicles for self-recognition, "feeling" permits the self to expand by dividing it internally: "Feeling is thy own inward power, but at the same time a power distinct from thee, and independent of thee; it is in thee, above thee: it is itself that which constitutes the objective in thee—thy own being which impresses thee as another being" (pp. 10-11). This displacement of external powers into an inward dialectic is usually ignored by readers of Feuerbach's Religion of Humanity, but it is dangerous to regard his notion of fraternity as a fundamental orientation to others, as "selflessness." Ultimately, Feuerbach defines religion itself as a dialectical self-relation: "Religion, at least the Christian, is the relation of man to himself, or more correctly to his own nature (i.e., his subjective nature); but a relation to it, viewed as a nature apart from his own" (pp. 13-14). Karl Marx's attack on Feuerbach begins precisely at this point, with his contempt for the idealism—and the solipsism—of such self-relation, which he finds to be an avoidance of otherness in history common to Hegel, Feuerbach and German philosophy generally.[10]

Before examining the role of *Middlemarch*'s inward dialectic in either the social or the romance plots, it is necessary first to see why an internalization of the power of "otherness" becomes inevitable in the novel. Eliot's difficulty imagining a satisfactory form of external relationship is, of course, the presupposition of *Middlemarch*: the Preface to the novel begins by idealizing a kind of desire that tests itself against others in such a way as to bracket that desire as an impossibility. St. Theresa's "epic" desire is a confrontation between her "ideal, passionate nature" and an oppositional social world: as a child, she is turned back from martyrdom by "domestic reality . . . in the shape of uncles"; ultimately, she achieves satisfaction of her passion in the "reform of a religious order." Whatever else is contained in St. Theresa's passion—a nostalgia for lost origins, for faith—it is, in a very powerful way, a quest for relationship to others.

Yet this is a more complicated form of relationship than it initially appears. St. Theresa's passion assumes that a profoundly satisfying engagement of opposing energies can be found in a confrontation between the self and forces external to it. She acts assertively, assaulting and then reforming the world. But she is also filled by an energy whose source lies beyond her: Theresa can engage the world in the first place only because she is "helped by a coherent social faith," because her heart "beat to a national idea." This dialectical movement—an assertion of the self against the force of others, and a transpersonal union with it—is implicit in Theresa's achievement of a place in her world. Without this opposition, her desire would not be able to form itself even internally: modern Theresas find that "their ardour alternated between a vague ideal and the common yearning of womanhood." Theresa's passion manages to satisfy in social terms what might be called a paradox of all desire: self-expression at its highest pitch seeks to burst the constraints of its own egotism and to be united with its negation, with a power that is not self. And society, representing that power for Theresa, is able to order desire and to make it visible by clearly defining the difference between personal and impersonal energies.

George Eliot's warning in the Preface, however, seems to be that desires based in a need for this kind of dynamic relatedness are no longer possible: the world has become too confused a place to be confronted directly, its coherence reduced to "tangled circumstances," its diffused energies producing only "inconsistency and formlessness." The modern-day Theresa is compared to a "cygnet . . . among the ducklings in the brown pond," who can never find "fellowship with its own oary-footed kind." On the simplest level, the Preface tells us that the contemporary world defeats desire; but one cause for that defeat is a loss of the social differentiation necessary to produce any kind of tension between desire and otherness. The concentrated external powers against which desire can form and project itself have disappeared. As the novel develops, we see clearly that the relatedness necessary to desire is frustrated by the inconsistent authority of figures like Mr. Brooke, Sir James—or Parliament;[11] by the obfuscations of gossip; and, in general, by the "movement and mixture" of "old provincial society" (ch. 11). Eliot seems to have understood, too, that no private vision by itself can reconstitute the necessary oppositional force of St. Theresa's world.

Clearly, however, it is not just the "movement and mixture" of the social world that is too unstable to become a foil for desire. The word "mixture," in fact, is one of the most frequently-used words in **Middlemarch,** and it applies to personalities as well as to social conditions. In the first sentence of the book, man himself is called a "mysterious mixture." And the narrator often reflects that disorder and confusion have a source within personality: "There are many wonderful mixtures in the world which are all alike called love" (ch. 31), she muses, when considering Rosamond's thorny aspirations. Mr. Brooke is "an odd mixture of obstinacy and changeableness" (ch. 38). In a telling passage, the narrator notes that the "few personages or families that stood with rocky firmness amid all this fluctuation, were slowly presenting new aspects in spite of solidity, and altering with the double change of self and beholder" (ch. 11). Without the social coherence against which they might define themselves, characters display an inner confusion that appears to be innate. Mr. Brooke's instability is not explicitly made to reflect flaws in society; neither is Bulstrode's hypocritical blending of business and religion, or Lydgate's divided interest in both science and beautiful women. Fragmentation is a central theme in **Middlemarch,** the root of its many frustrated passions. But the novel does not locate the source of fragmentation only in the "meanness of opportunity" inherent in the world, as the Preface would have us believe. Instead, it involves us in a kind of "double change" of characters and context, in which diffusion becomes a universal state. The struggle for relatedness is lost on two fronts: neither self nor world are homogeneous enough to form an opposition, to define the limits separating and, potentially, energizing them.

At the same time, however, the novel seems absorbed in a subtle counter study, in a reevaluation of the problem of psychological "mixtures." For rather than simply garbling relationships, the mixtures within Eliot's characters tend to become a source of promise. In fact, it is the favored characters in **Middlemarch** who most concentrate mixedness within themselves, and who seem more interesting because of it. From the outset, for example, such mixtures heighten Dorothea's attractiveness. Chapter 1 begins by telling us that Dorothea "had that kind of beauty which seems to be thrown into relief by poor dress," and that she has "the impressiveness of a fine quotation from the Bible . . . in a paragraph of today's newspaper." Frequently, the narrator dwells on Dorothea's contradictions in this flattering way. More importantly, several characters seem drawn to Dorothea because of the conflicts within her personality. Lydgate finds in her "the piquancy of an unusual combination" (ch. 10). Naumann, struck by the contrast between Dorothea's beauty and her "Quakerish grey drapery," calls her "antique form animated by Christian sentiment—a sort of Christian Antigone—sensuous force controlled by spiritual passion." (ch. 19) Will at first finds her cold and critical, yet with a strikingly beautiful voice that was like "the voice of a soul that had once lived in an Aeolian harp." Fascinated, he calls her "one of Nature's inconsistencies" (ch. 9).

Dorothea is not alone in being alluring by reason of her multiplicity. Mr. Farebrother, for example, described as "a mixture of the shrewd and mild" (ch. 16), intrigues Lydgate, who finds him "exceptionally fine" and compares his personality to "those southern landscapes which seem divided between natural grandeur and social slovenliness" (ch. 18). Mary Garth's very integrity lies in her contradictions: she had not "that perfect good sense and good principle which are usually recommended to the less fortunate girl, as if they were to be obtained in quantities ready mixed"; instead, "her shrewdness had a streak of satiric bitterness continually renewed and never carried utterly out of sight, except by a strong current of gratitude" toward those who treat her well (ch. 12). Her father, too, mixes "business" and religion in a rustic way that earns general approval. But it is Will Ladislaw who openly promotes the virtues of internal multiplicity. Speaking enthusiastically of Rome's "miscellaneousness," Will claims that it "made the mind flexible with constant comparison" (ch. 22). And Will's esthetic, early in the novel, glorifies this love of multiplicity: "if I could pick my enjoyment to pieces I should find it made up of many different threads," he tells Dorothea in their discussion about art; interestingly, this is also his reason for giving up painting: "It is too one-sided a life," he claims, "I should not like to get into [that] way of looking at the world entirely from the studio point of view" (ch. 21). Will's quest for flexibility may make him a dilettante, but it is also the source of his charm.[12]

No doubt there is some kind of symbolic drama, some bifurcation, at work in the novel's treatment of mixedness. That Will, with his acute and appealing self-contradictions, should reside and work with the absurdly irresolute Mr. Brooke through much of the novel, pinpoints the need for a hierarchy. Though all personalities in **Middlemarch** are mixed in one way or another, certain compounds are more attractive than others—they promise not confusion but vital sparks. As Mr. Farebrother observes of Will's hybridized genealogy: "some sorts of dirt seem to clarify" (ch. 71). Through Eliot's lovers, two crucial standards for a hierarchy of mixtures suggest themselves. First, Dorothea and Will are divided internally by impulses that come to seem diametrically opposed. Instead of balancing public and private energies, they balance psychological forces that directly deny each other, but that also seem to promise a dynamic cooperation—the dynamic of Hegelian internal mediation. Second, the nature of these impulses is transformed in such a way as to conserve Will's and Dorothea's autonomy, despite the mixedness of their personalities and despite their gestures toward public action. In sum, Dorothea and Will escape the enervating diffusion of their society not by becoming whole themselves, or by achieving interdependence, but through a generative conflict of internal impulses that is protected from the entropy of the outside world. Their mixed personalities are both heightened and circumscribed at the same time.

To see more clearly how this process works, it is worth looking at Dorothea first, and outlining her particular self-division in some detail. Putting it simply, the essential contradiction in Dorothea might be said to lie between two kinds of passion—one appetitive and sensuous, the other self-renouncing and ascetic. Though some form of this conflict is obvious to all readers of **Middlemarch,** many describe the second passion simply as the force of Freudian repression, or as a sublimation of self-actualizing desires.[13] Certainly, renunciation is the source of Dorothea's "self-repression" (ch. 50), when she binds herself to Casaubon's wishes instead of defying them, as she sometimes wants to. However, in Eliot's imagination this ascetic self-denial has the unmistakable force of a passion in its own right. It is not conceived as an internalization of social constraints or as displaced energy—no matter what its occasional effects—so much as a desire for ecstatic union with an energy that originates beyond the self. Self-denial in Dorothea corresponds roughly to St. Theresa's eroticized surrender to greater authority than herself, her ability to "reconcile self-despair with the rapturous consciousness of life beyond self" (Preface). In Naumann's terms, Dorothea expresses both "sensuous force" and "spiritual passion" (ch. 19). And through this analogy to religious passion, self-denial is conceived as a need to internalize essentially impersonal energy, energy that—despite its private origins—overcomes isolation and egotism by negating the self. For Dorothea, the force of the impersonal, public energy available to St. Theresa is replaced by a private self-denial, an inward form of energy whose source is nevertheless felt to be non-personal.

This privately-motivated renunciation is initially what makes Dorothea seem priggish: Celia chides her because she "likes giving up" (ch. 2), with no apparent purpose in mind. But in Hegelian terms, Eliot is attempting to conceive self-denial as the force of a negative power within subjectivity.[14] St. Theresa's wish for union with the external world becomes for Dorothea the search for a purely inward impersonality, what Hegel often describes as the mind's ability to imagine and to dwell within its own death.[15] Though inspired initially by religion, Dorothea's passion for self-immolation is an impulse that has broken free of external contexts: her mind is "theoretic," we are told, and "she was enamored of intensity and greatness, and rash in embracing whatever seemed to her to have those aspects; likely to seek martyrdom, to make retractions, and then to in-

cur martyrdom after all in a quarter where she had not sought it" (ch. 1).

Dorothea's isolation, early in the novel, further stresses the personal, abstract and unshaped character of this passion for martyrdom. And, ultimately, her need for a pure self-negation, which has no necessary connection either to social constraints or to altruistic action, is what generates the contrapuntal tension within Dorothea's private crisis of passion with Will. What had once been the "inconsistency" of an imbalance becomes a dynamic mixture: at the end of her night of anguish, in which renunciation of Will has climaxed as a sacramental "grief" we are told that "she felt as if her soul had been liberated from its terrible conflict: she was no longer wrestling with her grief, but could sit down with it as a lasting companion and make it a sharer in her thoughts" (ch. 80). Dorothea's emotional development climaxes not in the singleness of her desires, but in a potent kind of doubleness.

Even though most readers have found Will an inadequate lover for Dorothea, the two characters' desires mirror each other exactly. Independently, Dorothea and Will both experience love as self-contradiction, as the same opposition of sensuous yearning and passionate asceticism we found first in Dorothea. The prohibition Casaubon places over them is only the distractingly official imposition of a conflict that is essential to their love at all its stages. Long before Casaubon's interdiction, Will reveals that his passion for Dorothea is inherently double, thriving both in a desire to possess and in a desire to renounce. The narrator tells us: "there were plenty of contradictions in [Will's] imaginative demands. It was beautiful to see how Dorothea's eyes turned with wifely anxiety and beseeching to Mr. Casaubon: she would have lost some of her halo if she had been without that duteous preoccupation; and yet at the next moment the husband's sandy absorption of such nectar was too intolerable; and Will's longing to say damaging things about him was perhaps not the less tormenting because he felt the strongest reasons for restraining it" (ch. 22).

Will's strong reasons for restraint are partly just good manners and prudence; but the passage also links them with his desire to preserve Dorothea's devotion to Casaubon, which Will can appreciate only through renunciation of his own desires. Later, the narrator tells us explicitly that Will does not wish for Casaubon's death, does not imagine himself as Casaubon's successor with Dorothea: "it was not only that he was unwilling to entertain thoughts which could be accused of baseness . . . there were yet other reasons. Will, as we know, could not bear the thought of any flaw appearing in his crystal: he was at once exasperated and delighted by the calm freedom with which Dorothea looked at him and spoke to him, and there was something so exquisite in thinking of her just as she was, that he could not long for a change which must somehow change her." This admiration for Dorothea's perfect autonomy inspires Will to devote himself to Dorothea without thought for his own satisfaction. Yet the narrator is quick to tell us: "he was not without contradictoriness and rebellion even towards his own resolve. . . . [for] notwithstanding his sacrifice of dignity for Dorothea's sake, he could hardly ever see her. Whereupon, not being able to contradict these unpleasant facts, he contradicted his own strongest bias and said, 'I am a fool'" (ch. 47).

For Will, one passion feeds the other: his yearning compelling him to renounce, renunciation in turn flaming his desire, even as the very object of it. And although Casaubon's codicil makes this self-conflict in Will seem to be the result of mere circumstances and social constraints, it is crucial to see it operating here as an essential doubleness within Will's original attraction to Dorothea. Self-conflict is the structure of love in **Middlemarch,** not an impediment to it. This doubleness makes Will's and Dorothea's later encounters simply an elaboration of an inherent paradox of desire, with Will nearly torn apart by the violence of his internal division, by "the stormy fluctuations of his feelings." Love is forbidden to him, he tells Dorothea, not "merely by being out of my reach, but forbidden me, even if it were within my reach, by my own pride and honor—by everything I respect myself for." Will's own passion for ascetic purity divides him inwardly: "Indeed, he felt that he was contradicting himself and offending against his self-approval in speaking to her so plainly; but still—it could not be fairly called wooing a woman to tell her that he would never woo her. It must be admitted to be a ghostly kind of wooing" (ch. 62). But the phrase "ghostly wooing" perfectly combines two passions: the spiritual with the sensuous.

The general dissatisfaction with Will as a strong match for Dorothea has its source here: Will is essentially at war with himself, and for that reason incapable of any undivided, consequential action. We are never meant to find Will an active resolver of Dorothea's doubleness, a potent Shelley fulfilling Dorothea's mistaken quest for a Miltonic guide. Rather, Will and Dorothea are meant to be recognized as twins, both undergoing an inward transformation that enlarges their territory of self-knowledge. In love, for both characters, the power of external influence is deliberately minimized. Eliot's favorable attitude toward Will does not derive simply from his "feminine" qualities, as some feminists have argued, if these qualities are seen to lie only in his dispossession and his non-competitive compassion.[16] Will's capacity for self-negation mirrors Dorothea's more closely in its expansive internal power than in any affiliation with victimage or with maternal nurturance.

While a number of recent feminist works have argued persuasively that female repression in Victorian culture often became a strategy of authority and power,[17] this productive aspect of repression is so firmly grounded in the general nineteenth-century heightening of interiority that a slightly eccentric relation seems to exist between gender difference and repressive self-conflict. As Nancy Armstrong has argued persuasively, the authority Victorian woman derived from her privileged claims to inwardness was very deeply rooted in a cross-sexual ambivalance about public and private life.[18] In effect, the nineteenth-century discourse of self-conflict tended to represent the emotional organization of men and women as the same, even as it argued that a different experience of and response to self-conflict was natural to each sex.

In George Eliot's case, Dorothea does demonstrate a fullness of command in self-conflict that Will cannot attain (though Daniel Deronda will attain it later), which implies the Victorian woman's more meditative and passive relationship to self-conflictual inwardness. Not as bitter as Will, Dorothea finds their division from each other, as well as the division within herself, to be actually a kind of wholeness; if Will is sensitive to the tension in their self-divided love, Dorothea is sensitive to this tension as a kind of emotional envelopment: "in the months since their parting Dorothea had felt a delicious though sad repose in their relation to each other, as one which was inwardly whole and without blemish. She had an active force of antagonism within her, when the antagonism turned on the defense either of plans or persons that she believed in; and the wrongs which she felt that Will had received from her husband . . . only gave the more tenacity to her affection and admiring judgement." These "wrongs," it goes without saying, are the suspicions that Will is encouraging Dorothea's love; and yet denying those suspicions only increases her affection. Or again, Dorothea is conscious of "a deeper relation between them which must always remain in consecrated secrecy. But her silence shrouded her resistant emotion into a more thorough glow" (ch. 77). Dorothea may articulate the experience of their love as more of a unity than Will, but the internal opposition for her is the same as his: negations of feeling give rise to passion, which becomes the passion to affirm negated feeling. One movement facilitates the other.

It is significant that Dorothea first feels love for Will only when she discovers Casaubon's codicil prohibiting their marriage. Her "sudden strange yearning of heart towards Will Ladislaw" occurs at precisely the moment that she becomes aware of "unfitting conditions" (ch. 50). This moment, in a curiously circular way, is repeated when, at the end of the novel, she discovers her love for Will through his supposed betrayal: "Oh, I did love him," Dorothea moans only when it seems to be too late, and the narrator tells us: "she discovered her passion to herself in the unshrinking utterance of despair" (ch. 80). During their separation, too, Dorothea often finds that the intensity of her renunciation of love is precisely what allows her inwardly to exercise her own passion. At one point we are told: "Their young delight in speaking to each other . . . was forever ended, and become a treasure of the past. For this very reason she dwelt on it without inward check. That unique happiness too was dead, and in its shadowed silent chamber she might vent the passionate grief which she herself wondered at" (ch. 55). And immediately following separation: "They were parted all the same, but—Dorothea drew a deep breath and felt her strength return—she could think of him unrestrainedly. . . . The joy was not the less—perhaps it was the more complete just then—because of the irrevocable parting" (ch. 62).

It is impossible to read these passages only as rationalizations of an internalized constraint, or as untransformed romantic idealizations of absence and negativity. While romantic conventions commonly posit impeded consummation as the highest pitch of desire, Eliot's more Victorian use of these conventions refines them by radically diminishing the influence of the object over the lover, never attempting to mystify the inaccessibility of the object. She also emphasizes the internal origin of refusal, as a non-conventional or "organic" double of desire that insulates it from all external mediation, rather than locating refusal in social obstacles or expectations, which are deliberately trivialized. Dorothea's sense of wholeness within contradiction, her ability to let the force of her emotions flow in two directions at once, implies that two quite separate and contradictory passions have created a world within her in the form of an endless inner conflict. This world formed by the self remains permanently unstable, which explains why it can have a history, just as Will's and Dorothea's love has a history as it swings between the two poles of its expression; yet its unstable dynamism depends on its never being interrupted by external demands. And as we will see, that radical protection from others keeps personal history from contributing effectively to social history.[19]

What we have, finally, within both characters is a kind of oppositional relationship that is, in some sense, self-sufficient. Significantly, the content of verbal exchanges between Dorothea and Will comes to seem much less important than their ability to catalyze within each other an intensification of internal conflict. For this reason, too, Eliot extends their separation, preserving emotional contradiction through what many readers have complained is an artificial device. Having Dorothea misunderstand Will's reference to "what I care more for than I can ever care for anything else" (ch. 62) allows Eliot to prolong the separation they seem to require, while also ensuring that their divided passion will continue, since Dorothea then corrects herself and recognizes

Will's love just minutes after it is too late. And, unwilling to resolve their inward drama even at the end, the narrative almost completely abandons Will and Dorothea after they escape the paradoxes of their "ghostly wooing."

Yet "escape" is too strong a word: nothing alters this balance of oppositions, or creates a different kind of love—rather, Dorothea's self-negation is preserved even in marriage, though it is shifted slightly: at the heart of her acceptance of Will is Dorothea's conviction that marrying him abolishes her desires for an epic life. The terms may be different here, but Dorothea and Will's marriage is presented in a deliberately vague way as both a personal triumph and as a loss. And the resigned sense of limitation in their marriage can thus be understood as Eliot's attempt to preserve some trace of the inward conflict necessary to her characters' passions.

Ironically, while George Eliot may not have believed that her characters' sole source of satisfaction lay in their affections,[20] despite herself she often conceived their marital choices in this way as the medium for an inward balance—a cooperation of assertion with self-denial—and could only leave characters like Dorothea disengaged from the world, self-reflexive.[21] Eliot's failure, within such marriages, to consider action as the scene in which self meets world is precisely what has earned her the charge that she is reactionary. We should note here, too, that self-division is a climactic experience for many of Eliot's lovers. The best example, perhaps, is Maggie Tulliver, who divides her love among three men, feeling each passion to be both pure and impure, legitimate and affirmed only through its denial. But other characters in her fiction—Adam Bede, Dinah Morris, Gwendolen Harleth—end by enduring an exacerbation of contrary motions within themselves, what Eliot called an "antagonism between valid claims" in her essay on Antigone (p. 264), a figure to whom Dorothea is compared several times.

The second criterion for differentiating the hierarchy of mixtures in **Middlemarch** is just as crucial: the balance Dorothea and Will achieve between appetite and renunciation protects their autonomy from the dangerous mixedness of the external world. Will calls their invisible love "a world apart" (ch. 82). In **Middlemarch,** the crucial problem with either appetite or renunciation alone is that each threatens to enslave the self in dependence on others. It is not so much that passion violates a social taboo, and self-negation a personal one; the danger for Eliot in both is that they compromise the autonomy of the self, and in that way ultimately seem to stifle desire. For all Eliot's interest in interdependence, her narrative logic betrays a counter-desire: any excess of feeling in **Middlemarch,** unchecked by an internal balance such as Will's and Dorothea's, runs the risk of consuming the self through relationship to others. For Eliot, this dread is an obsessive one, and a cursory sketch of its extension in **Middlemarch** can suggest how dominant it is for her characters.

On the one hand, characters who too easily gratify their own appetites place themselves unwittingly at the mercy of others. Lydgate and Rosamond are perhaps the best examples here. What begins for both as the gratification of a secret wish—for Lydgate, the "fitful swerving of passion to which he was prone" (ch. 15), for Rosamond, her aspiration for "prestige" and social refinement— ends in a double imprisonment. Lydgate falls under the "yoke" (ch. 71) of Rosamond's selfishness and suffers her "feminine dictation" (ch. 64). Rosamond herself finds that, rather than having achieved refinement, she has been ensnared by Lydgate's failures. Later, Lydgate's decision to accept money from Bulstrode nearly ruins him through association with the banker. Bulstrode himself is another, more dramatic example of this loss of autonomy through appetite: having given in to his greed, Bulstrode is pathetically ensnared by Raffles. On the other hand, a complete denial of self-will brings about enslavement just as surely. Fred Vincy's reliance on his Uncle Featherstone renders him absurdly powerless and vulnerable, especially when Featherstone capriciously cuts Fred out of his will. With even purer intentions, Caleb Garth entrusts his money to Fred, only to lose it through Fred's carelessness. But the most important example here is Dorothea herself: abnegating her own will before Casaubon leaves her an emotional prisoner and forces upon her a debilitating self-repression. In all of these cases, the surrender of self to others proves disastrous.

In contrast, the figures in the pastoral plot—which is relatively ahistorical, outside the possibility of progress and, therefore, the need for effective social relationship—achieve an uncomplicated kind of autonomy. Mary Garth has a nearly religious terror of involving herself in Featherstone's will and his money. She is extremely wary not to promise herself away to an unreliable Fred; she is also adamant that, for the sake of his own integrity, Fred does not submit himself to conscription in the clergy and to his father's demands. Mr. Farebrother's "duty" toward Mary and Fred, his refusal to play the rival, while it seems to deny him personal satisfactions, also stresses the reformation of the Rector's will and his assertion of his own independence, since it coincides with his escape from financial entanglements and indebtedness: "his was one of those natures in which conscience gets the more active when the yoke of life ceases to gall them" (ch. 52). Ultimately, however, Will stresses the need for autonomy more emphatically than anyone else: by dissolving his dependence on Casaubon, by refusing dependence on Bulstrode, by proving his independence from Dorothea's own fortune.

In this context, it is helpful to remember that Eliot's novels are replete with warnings about the dangers of dependence on others. Gwendolen Harleth, Arthur Donnithorne, Godfrey Cass, Maggie Tulliver—all suffer excruciating torment from the power they have allowed others to gain over them. Autonomy, in Eliot's world, is a prerequisite for any kind of fruitful action. Even in her ethical formulations of interdependence, Eliot sees autonomy as the necessary position of strength from which one can then fulfill selfless interests. Though her thoughts on sympathetic interdependence are complex, she borrows from Spinoza a central emphasis on self-possession.[22] This remark in an essay attacking doctrinaire evangelicalism is typical: "If the soothing or the succor be given because another being wishes or approves it, the deed ceases to be one of benevolence, and becomes one of deference, of obedience, of self-interest, or vanity" (p. 187). And at the same time, her most enthusiastic expressions of connection to the world often turn on relatively autonomous acts of perception and knowledge, rather than on action, as when Lydgate exclaims, "A man's mind must be continually expanding and shrinking between the whole human horizon and the horizon of an object-glass" (ch. 63). As a result, many readers have been bothered by Eliot's dominantly condescending and ironic attitude toward the visible communities of her novels.[23] If the world has any force of its own in her novels, it is primarily a predatory, entrapping one. No wonder, then, that for Eliot self-renunciation becomes an internal act, not an interdependent one.

Fully aware of the idiosyncratic inwardness Eliot develops within private relations, we can now pursue Dorothea's vision of impersonal desire and altruism to make several important, complementary qualifications. For one thing, Dorothea's altruism preserves within it an unmistakable reserve, a protection of her own autonomy against the widespread dangers of dependency. The obligations she has taken on are indefinite, non-coercive: her duty is toward "involuntary, palpitating life" (ch. 80), not toward some specific person or principle. In particular, by resolving to mediate between Rosamond and Lydgate, Dorothea has not by any means entered into a mutually-determining relationship with them.[24] It is a certain excess of generosity that Dorothea extends here, not a surrender of self to enlarging, external powers.

Earlier, that kind of generosity had been conveyed in an image of melancholy self-sufficiency: "she adhered to her declaration that she would never be married again, and in the long valley of her life, which looked so flat and empty of way-marks, guidance would come as she walked along the road, and saw her fellow-passengers by the way" (ch. 77). And it had been "superfluous money" that she gave to Lydgate. Now, the very rhetoric of Dorothea's benevolence stresses her distance from other characters. She imagines Lydgate, Rosamond and Will all as "suppliants bearing the sacred branch" to her, while Dorothea herself has "the perfect Right," making "a throne within her." She expects to "save" Rosamond; the three of them are "objects of her rescue" (ch. 80). And when she goes to Rosamond, her presence is hardly self-abnegating. Lydgate realizes "that he was rather a blundering husband to be dependent for his wife's trust in him on the influence of another woman." Rosamond feels "something like bashful timidity before a superior, in the presence of [Dorothea's] self-forgetful ardour" (ch. 81). Whatever Dorothea's generosity, her actions here do nothing to make us feel that she has opened herself to others, in the kind of trusting receptivity she displayed—almost fatally—by marrying Casaubon. If anything, her actions confirm the essential difference of Dorothea, and the private convolutions of her desire.

Dorothea's difference rests finally in the degree of emotional intensity her self-conflict produces. Even when Dorothea and Rosamond embrace, weeping together, the origin of feeling is largely an inward conflict between willing sympathy and suppressed rebellion: "Dorothea, completely swayed by the feeling that she was uttering, forgot everything but that she was speaking from out the heart of her own trial to Rosamond's." Or again: "She was too much preoccupied with her own anxiety to be aware that Rosamond was trembling too." The emphasis on Dorothea's "trial" and "anxiety" here places the origin of her actions firmly within an internal conflict between impulses to affirm and to negate herself. For while it would be reductive to call Dorothea's impulses egoistic,[25] her emotional energy comes from internal conflict, and not from an uncomplicated and consistent form of generosity. In this scene we see Dorothea struggling mainly with her own divisive emotions. When Rosamond suddenly bursts into tears of remorse, "poor Dorothea was feeling a great wave of her own sorrow returning over her—her thought being drawn to the possible share that Will Ladislaw might have in Rosamond's mental tumult. She was beginning to fear that she should not be able to suppress herself enough to the end of this meeting, and while her hand was still resting on Rosamond's lap, though the hand underneath it was withdrawn, she was struggling against her own rising sobs." Later, battling herself, she feels "as if she were being inwardly grappled" (ch. 81).

The emotional intensity of Dorothea's altruism comes entirely from this inward conflict, not from a homogeneous and unqualified sympathy. It is only this tortured conflict between two competing impulses that distinguishes Dorothea's generosity here from her earlier, blander projects to house the peasantry—certainly, it is difficult to see any important difference in the results of either impulse. In her final, most direct confrontation with herself, Dorothea experiences a purely Feuerbachian moment, discovering the meeting ground between her own individual desire and an impersonal internal impulse, her "own being which impresses [her] as another being."

But most importantly, Dorothea's motives here do not originate in any interactive relationship to the objects of her altruism. Her self-renunciation finally has only an ephemeral relation to Rosamond, Lydgate and the outside world; it has a much more profound and permanent relation to her own self-reflexive passion for Will, to that "possible share that Will Ladislaw might have" in this drama. At this point, private desire and "wider sympathy" merge as interrelated forms of self-conflict. And it is because of this conjunction that Dorothea's generosity cannot be seen as a victory of one side of her nature over the other. Dorothea's renunciation, we must remember, begins not as a denial of selfishness, but as a renunciation of her love for Will. And this passionate renunciation, as we have seen, is paradoxically and inextricably related to Dorothea's very capacity to feel love. Her ability to overcome her disappointment over Will, and to rouse herself to act in spite of it, serves in this way only as the necessary prelude to her giving way to that opposing passion when she and Will meet later. We are never forgetful, during Dorothea's triumph over love, that Will's betrayal had been a misunderstanding, and that there remains the chance of a reconciliation. We are also aware that Dorothea has not ceased to feel passion for Will; rather, she has proved only that such passion does not consume her, that it does not threaten her autonomy, and that it is balanced and heightened by a self-negating passion. Dramatically, Dorothea's altruistic scenes work to counterpoint the coming love scene, and must be evaluated as only one half of this inward context.

The passion of renunciation continues to be a foil for the passion of love, continues to permit and to intensify it. Thus it is that when Rosamond reveals Will's innocence, "the revulsion of feeling in Dorothea was too strong to be called joy. It was a tumult in which the terrible strain of the night and morning made a resistant pain" (ch. 81). Dorothea's feeling for Will climaxes here in isolation, in a "tumult" of mutually resisting and mutually augmenting emotions. And the afterglow of Dorothea's "resistant pain" is carried over to the crucial love scene itself, which is composed almost entirely of affirmations that they are both still capable of separation. "Since I must go away," Will says, "since we must always be divided—you may think of me as one on the brink of the grave. . . . It is impossible for us ever to belong to each other." Dorothea answers: "Don't be sorry . . . I would rather share all the trouble of our parting" (ch. 83). And at that very moment, they kiss for the first time.

In Dorothea's vision of communion with the world, her passion for ascetic self-denial is complexly woven into a fabric of desire that depends also on its opposite, on self-expression. This endlessly self-conflictual model of desire is identical in both the private world of romance and the public world of "wider sympathy." Such desire is based finally not on a wish for union with others in either sphere, but in the cultivation of internally sensitized limits, and Dorothea's effect, both on the world and on Will, remains tangential to the structure of that desire. Social melioration, in particular, to whatever extent it does occur—since Dorothea's effect on both Lydgate and Rosamond, at least, is hardly as profound as she imagines—may be dependent on human desire, but not as the distinct object of it. In this sense, melioration becomes a purely abstract faith that, for Eliot, has somehow come to seem sufficient to justify the insulated play of self-assertion and self-denial that Victorian culture cherished as a safe haven for desire.

Notes

1. George Eliot, *Middlemarch,* ed. Gordon S. Haight (Boston, 1956), ch. 80. All further references will be to this edition and quotations will be identified by chapter.

2. See Raymond Williams, *The Country and the City* (New York, 1973), esp. pp. 165-81; and Terry Eagleton, *Criticism and Ideology: A Study in Marxist Literary Theory* (London, 1978), esp. pp. 110-29.

3. The most strident of these is Calvin Bedient, *Architects of the Self: George Eliot, D. H. Lawrence, and E. M. Forster* (Berkeley, 1972). The general trend of modern criticism to fault Eliot for her Victorian "repressiveness" is especially strong among feminist critics. For a summary, see Zelda Austen, "Why Feminist Critics are Angry with George Eliot," *College English,* 37 (1976), 549-61. In particular, Sandra M. Gilbert and Susan Gubar, *The Madwoman in the Attic: The Woman Writer and the Nineteenth-Century Literary Imagination* (New Haven, 1979), though they have some respect for the "feminine" virtues animating George Eliot's repressiveness, describe such repression primarily as an avoidance (p. 513).

4. Michel Foucault, *The History of Sexuality,* trans. Robert Hurley (New York, 1978), p. 123. For a compelling description of the historical replacement of social relations by internal ones as the locus of "truth" in the modern Western world, see Richard Sennett and Michel Foucault, "Sexuality and Solitude," *London Review of Books,* Vol. 3, no. 9 (May 21, 1981), 3-7. A similar argument is made by Leo Bersani, *A Future for Astyanax: Character and Desire in Literature* (Boston, 1976).

5. See, e.g., Bruce Haley, *The Healthy Body and Victorian Culture* (Cambridge, Mass., 1978); Carl N.

Degler, *At Odds: Women and the Family in America from the Revolution to the Present* (New York, 1980); Nina Auerbach, *Woman and the Demon: The Life of a Victorian Myth* (Cambridge, Mass., 1982), pp. 249-97.

6. In "The Antigone and Its Moral," for instance, she describes a "struggle between elemental tendencies and established laws by which the outer life of man is gradually and painfully being brought into harmony with his inner needs." *The Essays of George Eliot* (hereafter referred to as *Essays*), ed. Thomas Pinney (London, 1963), p. 264.

7. Eliot's use of Hegelian subjectivism is only one path Victorian novelists could employ to make "repression" the means toward a passionate inward world. See my essay "Repression and Representation: Dickens' General Economy," *Nineteenth-Century Fiction,* 38 (1983), 62-77.

8. As pointed out by Sara M. Putzell, "'An Antagonism of Valid Claims': The Dynamics of *The Mill on the Floss,*" *Studies in the Novel,* 7 (1975), 227-44, Eliot never directly mentions Hegel, but she did work with German and French post-Hegelians who wrote out of the Hegelian dialectic.

9. Ludwig Feuerbach, *The Essence of Christianity,* trans. Marian Evans (London, 1854), pp. 4-5.

10. See "The German Ideology," in *The Marx-Engels Reader,* ed. Robert C. Tucker (New York, 1972), esp. pp. 118-19.

11. U. C. Knoepflmacher, *"Middlemarch*: An Avuncular View," *Nineteenth-Century Fiction,* 30 (1975), 53-81, has an excellent discussion of the "hunger for relation and relationship" that is frustrated by *Middlemarch*'s weak authority figures.

12. J. M. S. Tompkins, "A Plea for Ancient Lights," in *"Middlemarch": Critical Approaches to the Novel,* ed. Barbara Hardy (London, 1967), pp. 178-79, provides a good defense of Will on the grounds of his amiable "discrepancies."

13. This description is made both by critics and sympathizers. There are, however, numerous defenses of "moral restraint" in Eliot as an undisplaced, unmediated passion. One of the most compelling is still Joan Bennett, *George Eliot: Her Mind and Her Art* (Cambridge, 1948). But for a more complex view, see Knoepflmacher, *Religious Humanism and the Victorian Novel* (Princeton, 1965).

14. Perhaps Hegel's clearest formulation of the concept of internal mediation, as a generative self-negation, is to be found in *The Phenomenology of Mind,* trans. J. B. Baille (1910; New York, 1967) esp. pp. 80-81.

15. This self-antithesis is most prominent in Hegel's master-slave dialectic. But it is also crucial to his

general discussion of the "labour of the negative" within consciousness. See *The Phenomenology of Mind,* p. 93.

16. Gilbert and Gubar make this argument, pp. 528-29.

17. See esp. Auerbach; Degler; Elizabeth Janeway, "On the Power of the Weak," *Signs,* 1 (1975), 103-09; and Judith Lowder Newton, *Women, Power, and Subversion: Social Strategies in British Fiction, 1778-1860* (Athens, Ga., 1981).

18. Nancy Armstrong, "The Rise of Feminine Authority in the Novel," *Novel,* 15 (1982), 127-45.

19. Discussions of Hegelian dialectics in Eliot tend to focus on her efforts to put individuality and history into relation, without noting how the novels disrupt the actual interchanges between self and others. See, for example, Putzell, esp. pp. 236-41. A refreshing exception is Linda Bamber, "Self-Defeating Politics in George Eliot's *Felix Holt,*" *Victorian Studies,* 18 (1975), 419-35.

20. For a good summary of Eliot's attitudes toward the values of work and vocational choice as an alternative to narcissism, see Alan Mintz, *George Eliot & the Novel of Vocation* (Cambridge, Mass., 1978).

21. Derek Oldfield's excellent linguistic analysis parallels my argument. See "The Language of the Novel: The Character of Dorothea," in *"Middlemarch": Critical Approaches,* esp. p. 80.

22. For a good discussion of Eliot's relation to Spinoza and his conception of egotism as necessary to self-sacrifice, see Rosemary D. Ashton, "The Intellectual 'Medium' of *Middlemarch*" *Review of English Studies,* 30 (1979), 154-68. For other sources for Eliot's justification of some degree of egotism, see George Levine, "Determinism and Responsibility in the Works of George Eliot," *PMLA,* 77 (1962), 268-79.

23. See Williams, for example, or Mintz, who, despite his claim that Eliot idealized social commitment, observes that the idea of "community" in the novels is always handled ironically (p. 99).

24. Michael York Mason, *"Middlemarch* and Science: Problems of Life and Mind," *Review of English Studies,* 22 (1971), 151-69, argues that Dorothea never fully recognizes Rosamond because of her own anxiety. See also J. Hillis Miller's argument that Dorothea's ethical action—especially in the case of Lydgate and Rosamond—depends on ignorance; Miller, Barbara Hardy, and Richard Poirier, *"Middlemarch,* Chapter 85: Three Commentaries," *Nineteenth-Century Fiction,* 35 (1980), 432-53.

25. This claim has, however, been made by Mason, p. 168.

Jeanie G. Thomas (essay date spring 1987)

SOURCE: Thomas, Jeanie G. "An Inconvenient Indefiniteness: George Eliot, *Middlemarch,* and Feminism." *University of Toronto Quarterly* 56, no. 3 (spring 1987): 392-415.

[*In the following essay, Thomas considers Eliot's attitude toward feminist issues in* Middlemarch. *While conceding that Eliot's views on women's rights are essentially conservative, Thomas maintains that she remains a vital voice for reform, primarily through the complexity and scope of her social vision.*]

In **Middlemarch,** during one of those tender and tense conversations of farewell between Dorothea and Will that take place after Casaubon's death, George Eliot lets her heroine confess, "'I used to despise women a little for not shaping their lives more, and doing better things.'" Dorothea admits that she has learned to think differently, having experienced "'the unexpected way in which trouble comes, and ties our hands, and makes us silent when we long to speak.'"[1] Some of George Eliot's deepest insights about life are expressed through Dorothea's evolving understanding of limitation. But they are misconstrued by many modern feminist critics who, echoing Dorothea's original bias, despise George Eliot for not allowing her character to shape her life more and do better things. It is this breach between George Eliot and many of her feminist readers that I wish to address, in order to make a gesture towards healing it. For I believe that George Eliot's feminist credentials are strong, and that the considerable amount of conflict between her and her critics stems not from any significant difference of opinion about women's constrained lives or the numerous forces that maintain them, but rather from a different understanding of the processes of change. George Eliot's perspective, let me say from the outset, is conservative, but she is no less committed thereby to a fuller life for women, as well as men, than are her current feminist detractors, whose cause she has supposedly betrayed.

Although for the most part an Eliot defender, Ellin Ringler sums up the feminist complaint against **Middlemarch** with the question, 'why, when Eliot herself was able to defy social tradition and achieve her own epic life, did she relentlessly consign Dorothea to the unmitigated mediocrity of a conventional marriage to Will Ladislaw?'[2] Clearly, for feminists, this is not only, or even primarily, a literary matter. The stakes are deeply personal. Hungry for models of achievement, looking to literature, as Carolyn Heilbrun does, 'for the proclamation of the possibilities of life,'[3] these disgruntled critics are the temperamental heirs of Dorothea Brooke herself, for Dorothea also sought what her immediate world did not offer and longed for a guide who would light her spiritual and intellectual way. Just as

Dorothea's desire for transcendence caused her to imagine 'a living Bossuet' and 'a modern Augustine' (p 18) in the poor Casaubon, so, Lee Edwards tells us in her classic statement of feminist expectation, she and many women once looked to *Middlemarch* to deliver 'a world whose shadowy existence we have long suspected, but whose reality has been perpetually denied.' Critic and character alike come to realize that they have drastically misread their subject. But where Dorothea's developing experience leads her to a more complex, less reductive understanding of many things, including her own desire for fulfilment, Edwards summarily rejects the once 'sacred text,' *Middlemarch,* when she discovers that 'what I had seen as revolution was in fact reaction.'[4]

Edwards's political language takes us to the heart of the controversy between George Eliot and her feminist critics. For this novelist's sensibility is not a reforming one, if by 'reforming' we mean something like her critics' often categoric rejection of the way things are, and a correspondingly aggressive effort either to secure specific change or to envision an ideal world. But a commitment to reform may wear different guises, and what is not revolution is not automatically reaction. No stranger to pressure to involve herself actively in her contemporary women's movement, George Eliot in 1878 explained her abstention from open advocacy of particular measures in deference to the strengths and weaknesses of her own sensibility. 'I thought you understood,' she wrote to her friend, Mrs Peter Taylor,

> that I have grave reasons for not speaking on certain public topics. No request from the best friend in the world—even from my own husband—ought to induce me to speak when I judge it my duty to be silent. If I had taken a contrary decision, I should not have remained silent till now. My function is that of the *aesthetic,* not the doctrinal teacher—the rousing of the nobler emotions, which make mankind desire the social right, not the prescribing of special measures, concerning which the artistic mind, however strongly moved by social sympathy, is often not the best judge. It is one thing to feel keenly for one's fellow-beings; another to say, 'This step, and this alone, will be the best to take for the removal of particular calamities.'[5]

Her defence of the artistic mind explicitly identifies the evocation of feeling—'the rousing of the nobler emotions, which make mankind desire the social right'—as her personal contribution to what she had a few years earlier described in *Middlemarch* as 'the growing good of the world' (p 613). It also recalls implicitly her contemplative disposition to see and to ponder the complexities of any situation and her dramatist's inclination to encompass and tolerate the authentic force of opposing claims. These temperamental resources, apparently

so different from those of many of her critics, ought not to disqualify George Eliot from sisterhood. While she is not a political reformer, in the sense defined above, I think there can be no doubt that she is profoundly feminist—in her insight into the restrictions on women's development and the complex social and psychological dynamics that maintain those restrictions, and in her feeling for the human waste and suffering often thereby engendered. But her philosophic and dramatic sensibility admittedly couple that feminism with what emerges as a deep conservatism, nurtured by her appreciation of the tangled web of which any issue is but a strand and her experienced awareness that all change bears mixed and unpredictable results.

Feminist, conservative—this is surely not an impossible linkage; nor need the pairing derive from unresolved neurotic conflict within the novelist herself, although some critics seem to require this patronizing explanation.[6] In fact, George Eliot's perspective embraces these two apparent extremes, and her understanding is thereby larger, more inclusive than her critics want to allow. Her knowledge of the female personality in all its variety and her sympathy with its sundry capitulations to the powerful imperatives of social life are as canny as any modern-day feminist's. But although *Middlemarch* begins with the story of 'Miss Brooke,' that individual female focus quickly disperses. Feminists want it to be Dorothea's novel, but, in fact, for all our interest in Dorothea's fate, *Middlemarch* makes no claim to be a sacred text for a new feminist ideology. Instead, it offers itself as the history of a community, evolving slowly, reluctantly, usually unconsciously, and of the various people—women and men alike—whose growth requires that they abdicate youthful romance and accept the limits life imposes. This sobering process affects a conventional woman like Rosamond Vincy as well as an exceptional one like Dorothea Brooke, and it chastens the aspiring men, such as Lydgate, Ladislaw, Casaubon, and Bulstrode, as painfully as it does the nineteenth-century Saint Theresas.

This enlargement of focus need not exclude a feminist interpretation, for it does not result in any diminishment of insight into women's constricted lives. But in designating *Middlemarch* the history of a community rather than a woman's story, George Eliot urges us to regard Dorothea's life as a version (in a particular time and place, with its peculiar female details) of an ancient theme—the gap between aspiration and fulfilment that began with the inhabitants of Eden. No complacent observer, George Eliot never belittles individual pain, female or male, nor is she in any way indifferent to the hunger for a fuller life. But she also acknowledges the complex, entangling processes of history, society, and psychology, and is therefore more tolerant than are many of her critics of the slow and unpredictable dynamics of change. To insist, as Anais Nin does, that liberation for women 'means the power to transcend obstacles . . . educational, religious, racial, and cultural,'[7] to expect, as Edwards, Heilbrun, and others seem to have done, that the *Middlemarch* cygnet should find 'the living stream in fellowship with its own oary-footed kind' (p 4), is to evade the rigour and the richness of George Eliot's comprehensive vision.

But let me for the moment follow tradition and begin where the novel and many feminists do, with Dorothea. To illuminate George Eliot's feminist understanding of the difficulties experienced by a woman of Dorothea's aspirations, emanating both from her own inner promptings and from the pressures of her immediate social environment, I want to follow one small but representative movement of the novel and attend closely to the subtle yet potent interactions portrayed there between the individual and the community consciousness. Chapter 48 has focused claustrophobically on the private pain of the Casaubon marriage, and on Dorothea's struggle to decide whether she can say yes to her ailing husband's wish that she complete his scholarly work. In the last paragraph of the chapter, she is hysterical after his death. Stunned by its suddenness in the midst of her emotional turmoil, she feels guilty about hesitating to give her promise and desperate after the fact to have been an agent of good to her husband, to have made her last act to him one of mercy.

Then, abruptly, opening chapter 49, we hear the voices of Dorothea's male relatives, of decent Sir James Chettam and amiable Mr Brooke, discussing the surprise codicil to Casaubon's will which forbids Dorothea's marriage to Will Ladislaw, on penalty of disinheritance. George Eliot skips over the funeral, indeed omits any of the details of the time from Casaubon's death to the reading of the will, leaves out any recounting of the feelings during this time of the person most intimately affected, Dorothea. Instead, we move swiftly into the public domain, that county world of relatives, in-laws, and friends, whose practical viewpoints, while they chafe uncomfortably against our sense of Dorothea's finely tuned sensitivity, also bring us welcome relief from the terrible choices faced by Dorothea and Casaubon, and from the tragic intensity of their hapless marriage. The whiff is comic, as Sir James and Brooke bandy their differing opinions, each guided by his own quirky interests, each conditioned, in his fashion, by his life and code as a gentleman. Two men who care for Dorothea talk of her, expressing concern for her welfare, all the while betraying the primary allegiances of class and self-interest. Without any capacity to imagine her delicate complexity of feeling about either her dead husband or Will Ladislaw, the protective Sir James is anxious to keep the fact of the codicil from her, even to engineer Ladislaw's swift exit from Middlemarch. It is

all honourably intentioned, but, as is made plain by Sir James's indignant query, '"You admit, I hope, that I have a right to speak about what concerns the dignity of my wife's sister?"' (p 355), his chivalrous motives are inextricably bound up with his own sense of honour and with his guardianship of his family, involving protection of its unblemished name and of the women attached to it. This chapter, intervening as it does between the death of Casaubon in chapter 48 and the satisfaction in chapter 50 of the reader's impatient desire to see how Dorothea will fare in its aftermath, reminds us that Casaubon's death is a public event as well as a private one, and that Dorothea's life as a widow must be lived not just in fidelity to her private feelings but in uneasy adjustment to the imperatives and interference of her immediate community.

The constant demands of that adjustment create the drama of the next chapter. Finally, we see Dorothea, safely recuperating with the Chettams at Freshitt, as she takes the first tentative steps towards making sense of the new condition of her life, towards trying to discover continuity between her marriage and her widowhood. Whatever its repressive constraints, marriage has made her a wife, and she has discovered a personal definition in the unexpected demands of that role. Now, although she inherits expanded financial resources, she is again without focus, with a need once more to find a meaningful channel for her energies. Some feminists complain of Dorothea's failure to blaze a new, triumphant trail for herself, but this chapter, among many, shows how difficult and elusive a course it is that Dorothea must mark out for herself through a moral terrain where the only guideposts are either the conventional opinions of friends and family or the hesitating, unprecedented, original instincts of her own mind and heart.

Her first effort to get on with her life, by considering 'what she ought to do as the owner of Lowick Manor with the patronage of the living attached to it' (p 357), illustrates the complexities of Dorothea's situation. Characteristically, she seeks out action for the good. The responsibility of choosing a successor to her husband's clerical living offers an opportunity to enhance the spiritual lives of the villagers through her choice; it also provides one posthumous chance to fulfil her husband's wishes—if he has left any written instructions to guide her in the administration of his properties. It thereby presents a much-needed occasion for establishing continuity between the past and the future through the agency of her own action and values. But, in the skittish but kindly opposition of her uncle, who assures her there are no such instructions, '"nothing about the rectory, my dear—nothing. . . . Nothing in the will"' (p 358), and who encourages her to take up enthusiastically her assigned role as aunt to Celia's baby, as well as in the complacent assurances of her sister that '"I never did like him, and James never did. . . . If he has been taken away, that is a mercy, and you ought to be grateful'" (p 360), we sense Dorothea's utter isolation. In no other voice than hers is there any indication of grief at Casaubon's death, any suggestion of a sense of loss, however ambivalent, or of pain. Although George Eliot does not explicitly describe Dorothea's feelings until the middle of the chapter, throughout the early pages she makes clear her emotional vulnerability and her susceptibility to intimidation by the caring pressure of those close to her. Her 'lip quivered,' she 'sank back in her chair,' she speaks 'quite meekly,' and she 'was almost ready now to think Celia wiser than herself' (p 358). And yet, she is able to state, simply and deliberately, '"I wish to exert myself,"' knowing that, habitually for her, action in a good cause is the way to restore confidence and a sense of identity.

However difficult in this instance, the need to draw on personal resources in opposition to her family's opposition is, in fact, a familiar challenge. What shatters totally her sense of moving in a recognizable world is Celia's revelation of the codicil and its contents. At that moment, the narrator tells us, Dorothea

> might have compared her experience . . . to the vague, alarmed consciousness that her life was taking on a new form, that she was undergoing a metamorphosis in which memory would not adjust itself to the stirring of new organs. Everything was changing its aspect. . . . Her world was in a state of convulsive change. . . .
>
> (P 359)

Celia chatters on, documenting the various opinions of the community: '"James . . . says it is abominable, and not like a gentleman"'; '"Mrs Cadwallader said you might as well marry an Italian with white mice!"'; and, in her own satisfied matron's opinion, '"Mr Casaubon was spiteful. . . . *We* should not grieve, should we, baby?"' (pp 359-60). In the midst of Celia's instructions about what should be her sister's proper reaction, Dorothea is experiencing the possibility of a radical disjunction between her present and past—the sudden and shocking realization that her husband has perceived her and her most tender efforts in a light which cheapens them—and is grappling with the consequent necessity to understand anew her most private, authentic experience. Even her relation to Will Ladislaw, which had seemed so pure and innocent, now, suddenly, is reflected back to her in the sullied light of her husband's consciousness and the vulgar interpretation of the world.

At this moment, for Dorothea to act independently to restore self-confidence and a sense of perspective, in the midst of active family opposition and the confusion of her own psyche, would require a superhuman act of will. She does rouse herself to ask Lydgate for help in choosing a new rector of Lowick, but even this 'effort was too much for her; she broke off and burst into sobs'

(p 360). What she needs is someone to hear and minister to her, to supply the support for her efforts that she cannot sustain for herself. This aid comes in the person of Dr Lydgate, the physician with no interest but his patient's welfare, who can act on his professional insight that Dorothea is suffering from 'the strain and conflict of self-repression' and most needs '"perfect freedom"' (pp 360-1). George Eliot knows that sometimes in our lives the right person is there, offering what we need. In this instance, Lydgate moves Dorothea over the threshold of Freshitt protectiveness and helps her achieve some privacy in which to seek the personal understanding she needs to get on with her life.

In the remainder of the chapter, Dorothea tries, in three different ways, to restore this semblance of wholeness for herself. Each effort embodies George Eliot's feminist knowledge of the inadequacy of the options available to women who want to direct their own lives, and of the complex (I think we must also say compensating) grasp of limitations these women acquire in the process. Dorothea's first decision to return to Lowick, to seek some personal message from her husband, some sign which will soften his terrible, last, vindictive act towards her, is prompted again by the need to discover some thread of continuity, this time between her feelings towards him during their marriage and those she must bear with her for the rest of her life. But, in looking to Casaubon as a healer, as she had once turned to him as a guide to wisdom, she is inevitably disappointed and left to her own as yet undiscovered resources:

> she locked up again the desks and drawers—all empty of personal words for her—empty of any sign that in her husband's lonely brooding his heart had gone out to her in excuse or explanation; and she went back to Freshitt with the sense that around his last hard demand and his last injurious assertion of his power, the silence was unbroken.
>
> (P 362)

Her feelings of revulsion towards Casaubon, the uncharacteristic movement of her mind to judge him rather than to pity, the sense of disgust at a memory changing its aspects, becoming a cruel mockery of what she had believed while her husband lived, all these are hers to face alone, with no sweetening aid from the dead. Impotent in life, the author of the 'Key to All Mythologies' cannot bless the efforts of his young wife to reconcile the contradictory fragments of their marriage. The pieces remain ragged and the story incomplete, awaiting whatever acceptance of the incomprehensible Dorothea will be able to achieve for herself.

From this abortive effort to restore the wholeness of the past, 'Dorothea tried now to turn her thoughts towards immediate duties' (p 362). With this decision, which leads to a consultation with Lydgate regarding the Lowick living, we feel with relief that what is vital in Dorothea has not been permanently stifled, and we have reason to hope that in Lydgate she has an interested, perhaps a sympathetic, listener, who may help her, as her husband could not, to find channels of effort and usefulness. But Lydgate, no different from any other man in the novel in this regard, never indicates any empathy for Dorothea's hunger for achievement, even though his own idealism and ambition parallel hers closely. He finds her marriage situation interesting, and he will learn to revere her capacity for trust and commitment to healing, but in her role as a wealthy woman, it is mainly her power to help him pursue his own professional goals that engages him, not her personal, urgent sense of aspiration. So, when Lydgate suggests Farebrother to Dorothea as a worthy successor to the Lowick living, he sees here 'a possibility of making amends for the casting-vote he had once given with an ill-satisfied conscience' (p 362), just as he had earlier solicited her attention and commitment of funds to the fever hospital primarily to gain support for his own idealistic plans. Dorothea's channels for action are those of the rich patron, dispensing favour, able to use her power judiciously and for the good, but still efforts far short of the grand work she hoped to discover for herself. She can decide who will have the Lowick living, she can pledge two hundred a year to the hospital, but it is Farebrother who will actually give pastoral care and be compensated financially for it, as it is Lydgate who will garner the tangible and spiritual compensations of his medical project.

Apparently insignificant details earlier in the chapter now resonate disturbingly. In response to Dorothea's initial declaration that she wishes to exert herself, her ineffectual uncle skirts the issue with his own declaration of vocation, "'I have no end of work now—it's a crisis—a political crisis, you know'" (p 358). In the same breath he directs Dorothea's attention to Celia's "'little man,'" who when he grows up undoubtedly will be granted opportunities for whatever work he wants to do, however much he may resemble his conventional father and windy uncle more than his splendid aunt. As a woman, Dorothea is expected to find her happiness in making an adoring audience for the 'little man,' or to be gratified making the careers, by means of her wealth and moral support, of the big men who people her life.

And so, at the close of the chapter, when the narrator tells us that the 'picture of Ladislaw lingered in her mind and disputed the ground with that question of the Lowick living' (p 364), we should not be surprised or angry. Just as one of Dorothea's responses to Celia's announcement about the codicil had been 'a sudden strange yearning of heart towards Will Ladislaw' (p 360), so now, into the hungry space denied nourishment by both her husband's silence and her own responsible but incompletely satisfying efforts on behalf of Lydgate

and Farebrother, there moves her image of Will, and with it comes memories of mutual appreciation and her passionate defence of him against his detractors. Although objectionable to many feminists,[8] this conventional movement of Dorothea's mind—towards the man who gratifies her emotional needs—actually clinches the argument for George Eliot as a feminist. Dorothea yearns for significant work to do, and Lydgate helps her to put her money and her power of ownership to good use. But, lacking the structured opportunities to discover a vocation, which men inherit with their sex, Dorothea's energy endures, diffuse and unchannelled, but still charged, waiting for the opportunity to release itself, if not in active vocation, then in passionate devotion to a human being, most likely a man, who touches her heart and taps her idealism. It may be a too-familiar story, this cleaving of the woman's heart to the man who seems to satisfy the quest for a purpose in life. But in the careful, detailed narration of Dorothea's movement towards that choice, George Eliot exposes and critically ponders the inner and outer forces that conspire to confound a woman's public aspirations and to steer her towards a private conclusion which is at once a disappointing compromise and a sort of fulfilment, and through both an index to the complex dynamics of female experience in the world.

Surely we are meant to be disappointed by this transfer of Dorothea's idealistic energy from the larger world to the lesser man, at the same time that we are allowed to appreciate its inevitability. The 'growing good of the world' may be 'partly dependent on [the] unhistoric acts' of those who 'lived faithfully a hidden life' (p 613), but this quiet acknowledgment of the 'Finale' does not annul the fact that the world and the subdued individual are poorer than they might have been if the individual talent had been less impeded, more nurtured by the world. Ringler laments that in these last sentences, George Eliot 'seems . . . to shrink from the implications of her own novel,' as she attempts feebly to 'mend the rupture' she has portrayed between 'the public roles of women' and 'their personal force.' She wishes Eliot had expressed 'a healthy anger,' and concurs that, in the last analysis, 'the feminists' uneasiness about ***Middlemarch*** is justified.'[9] My own experience of the novel does not culminate in anger on Dorothea's behalf; instead, I feel regret, intensely so, followed by difficult acceptance. And it is this complex feeling which I believe George Eliot intends us to tolerate and value, in place of total satisfaction of our desires or anger at their frustration. To achieve it, we need to pay the sort of close attention I have been attempting here to her sophisticated portrayal, in chapter 50 and throughout the novel, of the 'dim lights and tangled circumstance' (p 3) that always hinder our course through the world. But we also need to appreciate the shadowy illumination thrown by George Eliot's own wise lights on the unpredictable, incalculable, subtle processes of social change to which Dorothea, after all, through the 'not ideally beautiful' (p 612) acts of her life does in fact contribute.

The progress of Dorothea's education, formal and informal, helps us to achieve this poised response. It is abundantly clear that, despite her own and our aspirations for her, nothing in Dorothea's life experience prepares her to take up any ardent public career. Deprived of an education that might illuminate and develop her own interests and talents as well as help her choose how to use those in active service to the world, her efforts to educate herself belatedly (both under Casaubon's reluctant tutelage and later on her own) are pathetic, as piecemeal as was her girl's semblance of an education, and hopelessly isolated from the larger culture. Instead of expanding her sense of the scope of public action and strengthening her confidence in her own knowledge and judgment, her nibblings at Latin and Greek and the geography of Asia Minor leave her depressed about the arduous, slow process of learning, and less sure than ever about worldly affairs. As a result, she grows increasingly dependent on the men in her life, especially Sir James, for guidance on matters that seem to her to belong firmly to the 'provinces of masculine knowledge' (p 47). For example, she would prefer not to have the power residing in the Lowick living (p 375), and she quietly accepts her brother-in-law's negative advice about purchasing land in Yorkshire to build a model colony (p 560). But while her knowledge of and involvement in worldly action remain tentative and faltering, resulting in her deference to the surer mastery of men, her confidence in herself as a judge of people and an actor on their behalf matures, becoming an authentic source of personal motivation. Born of her growing insight into Casaubon's frightened centre of self, developed through the private struggle to understand and accept the contradictions of her marriage revealed by her husband's death, strengthened through her defence of Will Ladislaw in the face of opposition, Dorothea's trust in her own heart's knowledge finally expresses itself in powerful action when, in the aftermath of the Raffles affair, she intercedes on Lydgate's behalf, in open defiance of her male advisors.

George Eliot wants us to acknowledge this sort of private effort as a *bona fide* influence for good in the world, but Patricia Stubbs speaks for many feminists when she deplores the limited arena of action that Dorothea shares with so many other women in the English novel. They are

> firmly place[d] . . . in a private domestic world where emotions and personal relationship are at once the focus of moral value and the core of women's experience.
>
> Women in fiction are still 'Pamela's daughters' and are likely to remain so until they are defined through their contacts with the 'outer' as well as their 'inner' world.[10]

From evidence both within and apart from *Middlemarch,* it seems clear to me that George Eliot knows this, every bit as much as Stubbs does, and that her consignment of Dorothea's influence to this private domestic sphere is neither complacent nor reactionary. In 1870, while she was drafting the novel, she confided to her friend, Mrs Robert Lytton:

> We women are always in danger of living too exclusively in the affections; and though our affections are perhaps the best gifts we have, we ought also to have our share of the more independent life—some joy in things for their own sake. It is piteous to see the helplessness of some sweet women when their affections are disappointed—because all their teaching has been, that they can only delight in study of any kind for the sake of a personal love. They have never contemplated an independent delight in ideas as an experience which they could confess without being laughed at. Yet surely women need this sort of defence against passionate affliction even more than men.
>
> (v, 107)

Years before, in her 1855 essay on Mary Wollstonecraft and Margaret Fuller ["**Margaret Fuller and Mary Wollstonecraft**"], George Eliot had quoted supportively the latter's plea for an equality of opportunity for women as well as men to be whatever it is in them to be:

> If you ask me what offices they (women) may fill, I reply—any. I do not care what case you put; let them be sea-captains if you will. I do not doubt there are women well fitted for such an office, and, if so, I should be as glad as to welcome the Maid of Saragossa, or the Maid of Missolonghi, or the Suliote heroine, or Emily Plater. I think women need, especially at this juncture, a much greater range of occupation than they have, to rouse their latent powers . . . [George Eliot's ellipsis]. In families that I know, some little girls like to saw wood, others to use carpenter's tools. When these tastes are indulged, cheerfulness and good-humour are promoted. When they are forbidden, because "such things are not proper for girls," they grow sullen and mischievous. Fourier had observed these wants of women, as no one can fail to do who watches the desires of little girls, or knows the *ennui* that haunts grown women. . . . I have no doubt, however, that a large proportion of women would give themselves to the same employments as now, because there are circumstances that must lead them. Mothers will delight to make the nest soft and warm. Nature would take care of that; no need to clip the wings of any bird that wants to soar and sing, or finds in itself the strength of pinion for a migratory flight unusual to its kind. The difference would be that *all* need not be constrained to employments for which *some* are unfit.[11]

In that same essay, George Eliot commented on the heavy price 'men pay . . . for their reluctance to encourage self-help and independent resources in women.' Anticipating the creation of Rosamond Vincy Lydgate fifteen years later, she warned that 'the precious meridian years of many a man of genius have to be spent in the toil of routine, that an "establishment" may be kept up for a woman who can understand none of his secret yearnings, who is fit for nothing but to sit in her drawing-room like a doll-Madonna in her shrine.'[12] And in Edward Casaubon's assurances to his fiancée that '"the great charm of your sex is its capability of an ardent self-sacrificing affection"' (p 37), George Eliot conveys her open-eyed awareness of the exploitation of women's finer feelings often induced by the marriage relationship.

As aware, then, as any modern-day feminist of the terrible price often paid by both sexes for perpetuating their traditional relationship, where George Eliot parts company is in her tolerance of the slow evolution of human things, her understanding that 'there is a perpetual action and reaction between individuals and institutions; we must try and mend both by little and little—the only way in which human things can be mended.'[13] At this juncture the 'woman question' merges with that of the human condition. In their important feminist analysis, *The Madwoman in the Attic,* Sandra Gilbert and Susan Gubar see a contradiction in the fact that 'both *The Mill on the Floss* and *Middlemarch* announce themselves as sociological studies of provincial life, though they were originally conceived and still come across as portraits of female destiny.'[14] But the title-page's declaration of *Middlemarch* as a 'study of provincial life' deserves to be taken more seriously by those considering *Middlemarch* and the 'woman question,' for George Eliot's complex, guardedly hopeful assessment of human progress as 'a perpetual action and reaction between individuals and institutions' is expressed through the lives of all the Middlemarchers, not just through Dorothea's. The narrator early on has described this operation:

> Old provincial society had its share of this subtle movement: had not only its striking downfalls, its brilliant young professional dandies who ended by living up an entry with a drab and six children for their establishment, but also those less marked vicissitudes which are constantly shifting the boundaries of social intercourse, and begetting new consciousness of interdependence. Some slipped a little downward, some got higher footing: people denied aspirates, gained wealth, and fastidious gentlemen stood for boroughs; some were caught in political currents, some in ecclesiastical, and perhaps found themselves surprisingly grouped in consequence; while a few personages or families that stood with rocky firmness amid all this fluctuation, were slowly presenting new aspects in spite of solidity, and altering with the double change of self and beholder. Municipal town and rural parish gradually made fresh threads of connection—gradually, as the old stocking gave way to the savings-bank, and the worship of the solar guinea became extinct; while squires and baronets, and even lords who had once lived blamelessly afar from the civic mind, gathered the faultiness of closer acquaintanceship. Settlers, too, came from distant counties,

some with an alarming novelty of skill, others with an offensive advantage of cunning. In fact, much the same sort of movement and mixture went on in old England as we find in older Herodotus.

> (Pp 70-1)

Middlemarch begins, and ends, with Dorothea, but it is not her story alone, and in the narrator's description of old provincial society we recognize, among others, Fred Vincy, his sister Rosamond, Mr Brooke, Will Ladislaw, Casaubon, the Chettams, the Cadwalladers, Tertius Lydgate, and Nicholas Bulstrode. Dorothea's life indubitably demonstrates the liability which in the 'Prelude' George Eliot has specified as peculiarly female—to alternate 'between a vague ideal and the common yearning of womanhood' (p 3), a pattern creative of lives which in their erratic search for direction may fairly be described as 'blundering.' But, in fact, the lives of most of the Middlemarchers, male and female, are blundering. Men usually have the advantage, and it is no small one, of opportunity of vocation and support for its pursuit. We should remember, however, that the early life of Will Ladislaw alternates between a vague vocational ideal and a yearning for Dorothea, and that Fred Vincy's life threatens to be quite shapeless unless Mary and Caleb Garth take him in hand to provide a vocation and a reason for steadiness in it. To be sure, these two late bloomers, once they have discovered work to do, pursue it successfully and with contentment, but most of the men in the novel—those aspiring ones who do in fact early discover their vocation and have the financial means and social support to follow a chosen course—are guaranteed no safe survival or glorious fulfilment. For Lydgate, Casaubon, Bulstrode—all now or once youthful idealists and aspirants—the passage of life unfolds the awful experience of failure or the tortuous twistings of the mind to evade acknowledgment of what is failure nonetheless. Surely they are not rare exceptions—in the novel, or in the lives of those of us who read *Middlemarch.*

Indeed, in light of the strong feminist dissatisfaction with George Eliot's portrayal of women, it is fascinating to consider Richard Poirier's complaint that 'George Eliot so contrives things that "discontent" rather than the glamour of heroic failure, gradually emerges as the destiny of all the men in the novel,' a conclusion in which the critic thinks he detects 'the accents of feminist revenge.'[15] Jerome Thale also voices disappointment, though of a milder sort, with George Eliot's endings: 'Having seen the largeness of spirit of the characters and the magnitude of their errors, we expect that they should either attain a large fulfilment or else be left as failures.'[16] The critics' dissatisfaction finally cuts across gender lines and comes to lodge with George Eliot's non-heroic view of life, as it envelops both men and women. A century ago, Abba Gould Woolson registered the same grievance as Poirier and Thale:

it is not merely that George Eliot's novels end unhappily, but that never, save in one instance, is the ruin brought about after the grand, heroic, stormy fashion which readers love. . . . George Eliot's heroines do not die; they do not plunge wildly into sin, suffer stout martyrdom, or surrender proudly to fate. They simply fail, and live on.[17]

Today, Lee Edwards remarks upon the same thing in **Middlemarch,** and confesses that she is 'alternately angered, puzzled, and finally depressed' on account of the novel's failure to fulfil its opening chapters' 'promise of a new spiritual incarnation, possibly even an entirely new creation.'[18]

But from page one, there has been no effort to fool us, to raise heroic expectations which will be slyly snatched beyond our aspiring grasp. On the contrary, in the 'Prelude,' George Eliot has explicitly warned us that her novel is not to be a story of heroic fulfilment, that a modern-day Saint Theresa will be 'foundress of nothing' (p 4), and shortly after, in Lydgate's introduction to us, she has honestly spelled out the disheartening possibilities:

> in the multitude of middle-aged men who go about their vocations in a daily course determined for them much in the same way as the tie of their cravats, there is always a good number who once meant to shape their own deeds and alter the world a little. The story of their coming to be shapen after the average and fit to be packed by the gross, is hardly ever told even in their consciousness; for perhaps their ardour in generous unpaid toil cooled as imperceptibly as the ardour of other youthful loves, till one day their earlier self walked like a ghost in its old home and made the new furniture ghastly. Nothing in the world more subtle than the process of their gradual change!
>
> (P 107)

Nothing in the world more subtle. Or familiar. Has any of us lived some years in the world without some experience of this imperceptible process of disenchantment? Has any of our young dreams escaped erosion by circumstances which we can only partially, if at all, identify or hold responsible? I ask these questions because of my difficulty in grasping the feminist urgency about female success stories, or in understanding the male critic's demand for the glamour of heroic failure. I sympathize with the yearning, the 'young dream of wonders that he might do' (p 372) that we all share with Will Ladislaw, born of our own memories of early aspiration and promise. But the anger many readers feel at George Eliot's refusal to satisfy that dream eludes me, not, I think, because my own memories are any hazier than theirs, but because their demand seems grounded in a stubborn desire for literature that contradicts what our lives confirm, what time has yielded as essential knowledge.

For all George Eliot's efforts to lead us elsewhere, beyond illusion, these disappointed critics seem trapped in the fantasy of literary form to which George Eliot so often partly attributes the naïve expectations of her characters. When Rosamond imagines herself a romantic heroine (p 219); when Will Ladislaw chooses a personal model in the young hero of chivalric romance (p 344); when Dorothea idealizes the married lives of Milton and Hooker (p 7) or Lydgate compares the prospects of his own career to those of Bichat and Vesalius (pp 109-10, 335)—biographical variations on the literary model; when Bulstrode convinces himself that he plays a lead role in God's drama (pp 451-2)—they are all getting the prospects of their own lives confused with romantic or heroic metaphors. It is a dangerous process to which George Eliot suspects that her readers are no less vulnerable, and from which she deliberately undertakes to disengage us. From the outset, the narrator explicitly alerts us to delusive literary conventions—in the contrast she points to in the 'Prelude' between the wide 'limits of variation' in actual female lives and the sameness of the way those lives are portrayed in 'the favourite love-stories in prose and verse' (p 4). Somewhat later, introducing Lydgate, she laments the 'excess of poetry or of stupidity' which results in our infatuation with the romance of the sexes and our dullness to that other 'passion' which 'must be wooed with industrious thought and patient renunciation of small desires.' Never tiring of 'telling over and over again how a man comes to fall in love with a woman and be wedded to her, or else be fatally parted from her' (p 107), we want the grand gesture, the spectacular finish, whether of success of failure, and we have no taste for 'the story of their coming to be shapen after the average and fit to be packed by the gross.' Much farther on in Lydgate's history, when he is well on his way towards that bulk state of professional nondistinction, George Eliot again raises the issue of our conventional literary expectations, in order to induce a less consoling but truer identification:

> Some gentlemen have made an amazing figure in literature by general discontent with the universe as a trap of dullness into which their great souls have fallen by mistake; but the sense of a stupendous self and an insignificant world may have its consolations. Lydgate's discontent was much harder to bear: it was the sense that there was a grand existence in thought and effective action lying around him, while his self was being narrowed into the miserable isolation of egoistic fears, and vulgar anxieties for events that might allay such fears.
>
> (P 473)

Lydgate's discontent is not only 'harder to bear' than that of the 'amazing figure in literature,' but also closer to us and hence, the narrator suggests, more likely to be neglected and devalued. The common ground, where all but a few of us actually live our lives, yields strenuous, uneasy knowledge. By clinging to heroic standards of success or failure, we deny ourselves this more complex, and truer, understanding.

And even those few who do achieve what history acknowledges as fame do not in fact escape the liabilities of being human. This fundamental truth is illustrated no more poignantly than by George Eliot's own life—which so many feminists and others idealize as the model she should have duplicated in her novels.[19] A reading of her letters or of one of the numerous biographies leaves one less with the impression of an epic life, mimicking the sweep of literary narrative, than with a sense of the ongoing modest heroism life requires of each of us, consisting, in her own words, of 'the daily conquests of our private demons, not in the slaying of world-notorious dragons' (VI, 126). Her hypersensitivity to criticism—that self-distrust and 'morbid diffidence'[20] which made writing as much pain as pleasure to her and caused Lewes to exercise a vigilant censorship over public reactions to her novels; her chronic poor health; the social dislocation caused by her liaison with Lewes, and the broken relationship with her family which was only patched the year before her death with her marriage to John Cross; her parental responsibilities to Lewes's children and the harrowing experience of Thornie's illness and death from tuberculosis of the spine; her increasing sense thereafter of 'a permanently closer companionship with death' (V, 70)—these well-known facts of her personal life surely throw its epic character into question and establish the more common ties that bind her to all her less gifted readers. Wary as she was of literary biography, finding it 'odious that as soon as a man is dead his desk is raked, and every insignificant memorandum which he never meant for the public, is printed for the gossiping amusement of people too idle to re-read his books' (VI, 23), she perhaps would have approved the sympathetic identification made possible by publication of her own biographical materials. For in *Middlemarch* she deliberately sets out to counter the seductiveness of biographical overview with the reminder that each of 'those Shining Ones' who holds an honoured place in the history books 'had his little local personal history sprinkled with small temptations and sordid cares, which made the retarding friction of his course towards final companionship with the immortals' (p 109). It is knowledge that even a fellow novelist may need to be reminded of, if Henry James is a fair example. On the day the young American writer was finally to meet the great English one, he records that she greeted him 'in no small flutter,' for Thornie had just arrived home gravely ill. James was 'infinitely moved . . . to see so great a celebrity quite humanly and familiarly agitated.'[21]

To be sure, something in many of us hungers for a grand fulfilment, a glorious achievement. George Eliot knows well this hunger and shares it with us; otherwise, she could not have portrayed it so sympathetically in *Middlemarch.* But she has deliberately disappointed us, not only to provoke our consideration and valuation of non-heroic lives like our own,[22] but to deepen our understanding and develop our tolerance of the entangled losses and gains by which the world apparently evolves. Ringler is mistaken when she attributes George Eliot's ameliorative statements at the end of the novel to a failure in courage, a timidity in facing up to the implications of her own work. All of *Middlemarch* leads to its temperate conclusions. Lydgate's medical talent is sacrificed, but in the terrible demands of intimacy with Rosamond he grows as a human being, and if his sensitivity is still riddled with assumptions of male superiority, his awareness of women is nonetheless deepened and his understanding of responsibility enlarged. His wife, whose selfish will wins out, also changes. Rosamond's young fantasies of her queenly rule over enchanted, adoring slaves yield to a reduced expectation of marriage and a chastened sense of her power to attract and hold men. Our image of the satisfied matron, victorious over her husband's rebellion, may not easily inspire confidence about the world's moral progress; still, Rosamond in her way has learned more than she originally knew. Nicholas Bulstrode's financial, social, and would-be spiritual ascendancy over his Middlemarch neighbours is reversed violently by the Raffles scandal, but in the darkening field of their life together his wife's emotional and moral resources are forced to grow, and strengths that might forever have been dormant, unknown even to her, flower in the shadowed light. Mary Garth chooses Fred Vincy over Camden Farebrother and thereby makes the quiet success of one human being. In so doing, she forsakes her opportunity for happiness in marriage to a man more her moral and emotional equal, as well as the chances for wider social influence as the wife of the Vicar. Mary explains her attachment to Fred in terms that stress continuity with their shared past—'"It has taken such deep root in me—my gratitude to him for always loving me best, and minding so much if I hurt myself, from the time when we were very little. I cannot imagine any new feeling coming to make that weaker"' (p 380)—but, unconsciously or not, she also chooses the match where her power is most direct. She mothers Fred, and he loves it, while in the Farebrother household she would join three other women, already established, to whose traditional power structure she would have to adapt. Considering her two alternatives—marriage to Fred or marriage to Farebrother—the personal and social variations are numerous and unpredictable. For either choice will make the individuals and the community somewhat different from what they would otherwise have been, thereby altering subtly the forces of action and reaction.

Dorothea's life forms part of this kaleidoscopic pattern. She, unlike Mary, breaks with family and tradition when she marries Will Ladislaw. The choice to marry, however conventional, if the very fact of marriage is taken as all-defining, is also the protest that it is within her power to make against the existing structure of things. That she is torn between her love and loyalty to Will and her regard for the opinion of her family and friends is clear in her thinking as her coach passes Will, leaving Middlemarch on foot to seek his fortune:

> 'I only wish I had known before [that he loves her]—I wish he knew [that she loves him]—then we could be quite happy in thinking of each other, though we are for ever parted. And if I could but have given him the money, and made things easier for him!'—were the longings that came back the most persistently. And yet, so heavily did the world weigh on her in spite of her independent energy, that with this idea of Will as in need of such help and at a disadvantage with the world, there came always the vision of that unfittingness of any closer relation between them which lay in the opinion of every one connected with her. She felt to the full all the imperativeness of the motives which urged Will's conduct. How could he dream of her defying the barrier that her husband had placed between them?—how could she ever say to herself that she would defy it?
>
> (Pp 465-6)

But, finally, impelled by her love for Will, she does in fact defy that barrier. In this defining and strengthening of the emotional core of her experience, which feminists object to as the reactionary culmination of her search for identity, in the traditional womanly affirmation of the needs of the heart, Dorothea in fact denies the primacy of the values that her family and society live by. Most feminists resent the conclusion that 'Dorothea could have liked nothing better, since wrongs existed, than that her husband should be in the thick of a struggle against them, and that she should give him wifely help' (p 611). But through her personal choice, she does make a political difference, and it is this kind of modest, indirect, incalculable influence that, in George Eliot's view, slowly transforms the world.

Dorothea had once tried directly to change her small part of it by convincing Casaubon to share his estate with his younger cousin. That effort to make moral right prevail over legal custom and landed power must fail, of course, for it depends on the agreement of her husband, whose own values are rigidly conservative, defensively committed to the comfortable condition of things as they are. But she is free to defy social opinion and choose love over money on her own behalf, and in a small way she thereby alters the dynamics of power. Sir James had wanted to buy Will a post in the colonies, to get him out of Middlemarch and away from Dorothea. Mr Brooke had offered letters of introduction, thereby through patronage to help him on with a career, and had expressed regret that he and Chettam had no borough at their disposal to give Ladislaw, since, in Brooke's establishment opinion, Will would never get elected on his own. In marrying Will, Dorothea accepts exile from Middlemarch and its traditional ways of doing things and thereby opens a door to different possibilities, wherein Will can be 'returned to Parlia-

ment by a constituency who paid his expenses' (p 611). George Eliot's presentation of Will's career in politics is complicated and mottled, embodying no simple judgment of its value. But whatever George Eliot's long-term assessment of the democratic movement, it seems clear that she thinks Dorothea makes a modest contribution to it—through the only avenue open to her.

Through these hazy, ambiguous movements of personal and social life does the world change. We know from her letters how sceptical George Eliot was about political reformers' optimistic faith in particular measures.[23] *Middlemarch*—set on the eve of the First Reform Bill and written three years after the passage of the Second—assumes extended manhood suffrage and implicitly expresses (through its dramatization of the faulty thinking and limited grasp of things on the part of those already enfranchised) George Eliot's mixed apprehension of resulting benefits and liabilities. The 'woman question' is not the political issue in the foreground of the contemporary scene of *Middlemarch.* But it is nonetheless one of the novel's great concerns. For all her fidelity to her own aesthetic sensibility, we may, I believe, assume that George Eliot expects that the 'woman question' will one day move forward in the political consciousness, and anticipates that legislative action taken on its behalf will be as liable to good and ill, advancement and hazard, as any act conceived by human beings.

Her views about the movement towards sexual equality are consistent with her guarded assessment of democratic developments, for her desire for progress is always inseparable from her desire to protect evolved values. From the early essay on Fuller and Wollstonecraft, in which she speaks of 'the folly of absolute definitions of woman's nature and absolute demarcations of woman's mission,'[24] to the admission in 1869 that 'I know very little about what is specially good for women—only a few things that I feel sure are good for human nature generally' (v, 58), to the quiet mockery in the 'Prelude' to *Middlemarch* of those who would treat 'the social lot of women . . . with scientific certitude' (p 4), she leaves as an open question, defying exact measure, the relationship between equality of opportunity and what she calls 'the preparation that lies in woman's peculiar constitution for a special moral influence' (IV, 468). Admittedly perplexed by so vast and complicated an issue, she often ponders the physiological differences between men and women which she surmises are 'deep roots of psychological development' (IV, 468). Reflecting that, 'as a fact of mere zoological evolution, woman seems to me to have the worse share in existence,' she counters that 'for that very reason I would the more contend that in the moral evolution we have "an art which does mend nature"' (IV, 364), and urges that we cannot 'afford to part with that exquisite type of gentleness, tenderness, possible maternity suffusing a woman's being with affectionateness, which makes what we mean by the feminine character' (IV, 468). Taken together with George Eliot's consistent commitment to 'an equivalence of advantages for two sexes, as to education and the possibilities of free development' (IV, 364), her statements about the differences between men and women based on physiology constitute no crude 'biology is destiny' argument. Instead, they are some of the complex fragments of the large human picture she contemplated, whose imperfect illumination led her to confess, 'there is no subject on which I am more inclined to hold my peace and learn, than on the "Women Question"' (V, 58).

Dorothea's marriage to Will Ladislaw should be viewed against this acknowledgment of fitful illumination. Their union is not just a realistic conclusion to the tale of limitations and modest fulfilment that George Eliot traces in the lives of all her characters, nor is it simply the one avenue of rebellion available to Dorothea. It is also an ending true to George Eliot's confession of her inadequate knowledge and consequent patience on the 'Women Question,' for it insists on withholding any resolution of the 'indefiniteness' (p 3) of woman's nature announced in the 'Prelude.' Clearly, Dorothea has the capacity for and inclination towards grand work in the world. Given a good education and another moment in history, she might well have lived an admirable public life. But her nature is also seeded with profound emotional resources—maternal, nurturing ones—which sensitize her to the people near her and impel her to seek the satisfactions of intimacy. Here, in the richness of Dorothea's mixed psychological endowment, George Eliot does give voice to her concern that equality of opportunity not be won at the expense of the sympathetic attentiveness to other human beings which she thinks may be the special evolutionary strength of women. Here she does express a thoughtful caution.

Surely her point of view is not obsolete, even among today's feminists. For many of us perceive the same difficulty she did—how to achieve vocational opportunities and access to power for ourselves and other women without sacrificing the attentiveness to others and disposition to nurture which may have evolved from the constrained conditions of women's lives, whether imposed by biology or society. In fact, after a period of what Helen Longino calls 'remedial masculinity' (wherein 'differences between women and men are minimized and such as remain seen as impediments to be shed by women'),[25] some theorists of female psychology are beginning to reidentify women's capacities for caring as a legitimate core of female identity. Concomitantly, they are redefining standards of human maturity and exposing the inadequacy of any account of human development which equates adulthood with male patterns of experience and ignores the possibility of a different truth for women. Freud may have been baffled by women's failure to develop along the vectors of individuation normally followed by men, leading him and later theorists, such as Erik Erikson and Lawrence Kohlberg, to suggest that women are deficient in their maturation.[26] The research of current feminist theorists, such as Nancy Chodorow and Carol Gilligan, reveals two different patterns of development, male and female, neither superior to the other, 'whose complementarity is the discovery of maturity.'[27] In thus reinstating the legitimacy of the female perspective, these feminists hope to revise a conception of adulthood that, in Gilligan's words, 'is itself out of balance, favoring the separateness of the individual self over connection to others, and leaning more toward an autonomous life of work than toward the interdependence of love and care.'[28]

As we have seen, in George Eliot's case, such concerns, as they manifest themselves in the history of Dorothea Brooke, have often been undervalued, even dismissed as reactionary. In fact, they do not betray a defensive attachment to outworn values or, I think, the novelist's guilt over her own deviations from the conventional female life. Instead, they reflect a carefully pondered commitment to preserving and extending the web of connections between human beings, men and women, while evolving more spacious roles for both sexes. Neither revolutionary nor reactionary, George Eliot's long social vision steers a difficult middle way. It encompasses an understanding of why that enriched condition is not yet possible, to the sad detriment of men and women living now and wanting more; it simultaneously embraces a sense of how that desirable goal may yet slowly be realized, albeit in a form unknown and unforeseeable. There is hope in this vision, but not such as fuels revolutionary action. Instead, by investing our lives with complex knowledge, George Eliot's feminism helps us to come to terms with the present, enabling us to live in it with courage, perhaps even with a measure of grace.

Notes

This article will form a chapter in *Reading 'Middlemarch': Reclaiming the Middle Distance,* a monograph by Jeanie Thomas, forthcoming from UMI Research Press, Ann Arbor, Michigan.

1. George Eliot, *Middlemarch,* ed Gordon S. Haight, Riverside edition (Boston: Houghton Mifflin Co 1956), p 397. Subsequent *Middlemarch* references are to this edition and will be noted parenthetically in the text.

2. '*Middlemarch*: A Feminist Perspective,' *Studies in the Novel,* 15 (Spring 1983), 57. In her essay, Ringler provides an up-to-date summary of the objections of George Eliot's discontented feminist critics, who include Patricia Beer, *Reader, I Married*

Him: A Study of the Women Characters of Jane Austen, Charlotte Brontë, Elizabeth Gaskell, and George Eliot (New York: Barnes and Noble 1974); Lee R. Edwards, 'Women, Energy, and *Middlemarch,*' in *Woman: An Issue,* ed Lee R. Edwards, Mary Heath, and Lisa Baskin (Boston: Little, Brown, and Co 1972), pp 223-38; Sandra M. Gilbert and Susan Gubar, *The Madwoman in the Attic: The Woman Writer and the Nineteenth-Century Literary Imagination* (New Haven and London: Yale University Press 1979); Carolyn G. Heilbrun, 'Marriage Perceived: English Literature 1873-1941,' in *What Manner of Woman: Essays on English and American Life and Literature,* ed Marlene Springer (New York: New York University Press 1977), pp 160-83, and *Reinventing Womanhood* (New York: W. W. Norton and Co 1979); Jean E. Kennard, *Victims of Convention* (Hamden, Conn: Archon Books 1978); Kate Millett, *Sexual Politics* (Garden City, NY: Doubleday 1970); Ellen Moers, *Literary Women* (Garden City, NY: Doubleday 1976); Marlene Springer, 'Angels and Other Women in Victorian Literature,' in *What Manner of Woman,* pp 124-59; Patricia Stubbs, *Women and Fiction: Feminism and the Novel 1880-1920* (Sussex: Harvester; New York: Barnes and Noble 1979); and Anthea Zeman, *Presumptuous Girls: Women and Their World in the Serious Woman's Novel* (London: Weidenfeld and Nicolson 1977). Zelda Austen, Kathleen Blake, and Ruth Yeazell are the novelist's most articulate defenders amongst feminists. See Austen, 'Why Feminist Critics Are Angry with George Eliot,' *College English,* 37 (1976), 549-61; and Yeazell, 'Fictional Heroines and Feminist Critics,' *Novel,* 8 (1974), 29-38. Blake's fine essay, '*Middlemarch*: Vocation, Love and the Woman Question,' in her *Love and the Woman Question in Victorian Literature: The Art of Self-Postponement* (Sussex: Harvester; New Jersey: Barnes and Noble 1983), pp 26-55, has been an important stimulus to my own complementary ideas.

3. Heilbrun, *Reinventing Womanhood,* p 34.

4. Edwards, pp 232, 224.

5. *The George Eliot Letters,* ed Gordon S. Haight, 9 vols (New Haven: Yale University Press 1954-78), VII, 44. All further references are to this edition and appear parenthetically in the text.

6. For example, Gilbert and Gubar argue that 'Eliot's punishment of her heroines, her frequent bouts of illness, her own censorious avuncular tone, and her masculine pseudonym all suggest the depth of her need to evade identification with her own sex' (p 466). They also refer to her 'guilt about creativity' (p 452). Similarly, Calvin Bedient, in *Architects of the Self: George Eliot, D. H.*

Lawrence, and E. M. Forster (Berkeley, Los Angeles, London: University of California Press 1972), assures us that George Eliot wrote 'out of unexamined guilt, paying in her fiction a debt that she had incurred by her own independent life' (p 38).

7. 'Notes on Feminism,' in *Woman: An Issue,* p 27.

8. See, for example, Jennifer Gribble, *The Lady of Shalott in the Victorian Novel* (London: Macmillan 1983), pp 118-19; and Edwards, p 235.

9. Ringler, p 59.

10. Stubbs, pp x, xv.

11. 'Margaret Fuller and Mary Wollstonecraft,' *Leader,* 6 (1855), 988-9, rpt in *Essays of George Eliot,* ed Thomas Pinney (London: Routledge and Kegan Paul 1963), pp 203-4.

12. Eliot, *Essays,* pp 204-5.

13. Eliot, *Essays,* p 205.

14. Gilbert and Gubar, p 491.

15. Barbara Hardy, J. Hillis Miller, and Richard Poirier, '*Middlemarch,* Chapter 85: Three Commentaries,' *Nineteenth-Century Fiction,* 35 (1980), 452.

16. *The Novels of George Eliot* (New York and London: Columbia University Press 1959), p 146.

17. *George Eliot and Her Heroines: A Study* (New York: Harper and Brothers 1886), pp 104-6.

18. Edwards, pp 238, 232.

19. See, for example, Beer, p 181; Edwards, pp 235-6; Millett, p 139; Heilbrun, 'Marriage Perceived,' in *What Manner of Woman,* p 165; Bedient, p 50.

20. The phrase is Gordon Haight's, in *George Eliot: A Biography* (New York and Oxford: Oxford University Press 1968), p 366.

21. *The Middle Years* (New York: Charles Scribner's Sons 1917), p 65.

22. See Felicia Bonaparte's interesting discussion of this subject, in *Will and Destiny: Morality and Tragedy in George Eliot's Novels* (New York: New York University Press 1975), pp 160-80, especially pp 167-9.

23. See, for example, her letter to Charles Bray, 19 December 1868 (*Letters,* IV, 496).

24. Eliot, *Essays,* p 203.

25. 'An Education with Which to Build the Future,' *Mills Quarterly,* 66 (November 1983), 8-9.

26. See the discussions of the ideas of these and other theorists in Carol Gilligan, *In a Different Voice:*

Psychological Theory and Women's Development (Cambridge, Mass, and London: Harvard University Press 1982), pp 6-23, 151-74.

27. Chodorow, *The Reproduction of Mothering: Psychoanalysis and the Sociology of Gender* (Berkeley, Los Angeles, and London: University of California Press 1978). The quotation is from Gilligan, p 165.

28. Gilligan, p 17. Chodorow's psychoanalytically oriented studies locate the source of gender differences in family structure. She shows how women's primary parenting to children of both sexes may account for the very different ways that young boys and girls resolve their oedipal conflicts and establish their primary identities: 'From their oedipus complex and its resolution, women's endopsychic object-world becomes a more complex relational constellation than men's, and women remain preoccupied with ongoing relational issues (both preoedipal mother-child issues and the oedipal triangles) in a way that men do not. Men's endopsychic object-world tends to be more fixed and simpler, and the masculine heritage of the oedipus complex is that relational issues tend to be more repressed. Masculine personality, then, comes to be defined more in terms of denial of relation and connection (and denial of femininity), whereas feminine personality comes to include a fundamental definition of self in relationship. Thus, relational abilities and preoccupations have been extended in women's development and curtailed in men's' (p 169). Gilligan explores the different ways that men and women, so oriented to the world from early childhood, perceive and resolve situations involving moral conflict, and she envisions a more inclusive experience for both sexes that might result from a less male-biased valuation of the two perspectives: 'In women's development, the absolute of care, defined initially as not hurting others, becomes complicated through a recognition of the need for personal integrity. This recognition gives rise to the claim for equality embodied in the concept of rights, which changes the understanding of relationships and transforms the definition of care. For men, the absolutes of truth and fairness, defined by the concepts of equality and reciprocity, are called into question by experiences that demonstrate the existence of differences between other and self. Then the awareness of multiple truths leads to a relativizing of equality in the direction of equity and gives rise to an ethic of generosity and care. For both sexes the existence of two contexts for moral decision makes judgment by definition contextually relative and leads to a new understanding of responsibility and choice' (p 166). Gilligan documents the efforts of some adult men and women

to achieve this more comprehensive sense of things, while Chodorow suggests that, as men come to share more primary parenting responsibilities, the identity formations of early childhood may be modified to allow children of both sexes to experience a healthier balance between autonomy and intimacy.

Laura Mooneyham (essay date summer 1991)

SOURCE: Mooneyham, Laura. "Closure and Escape: The Questionable Comedy of George Eliot's *Middlemarch*." *Genre* 24, no. 2 (summer 1991): 137-53.

[*In the following essay, Mooneyham analyzes Eliot's narrative strategy in* Middlemarch. *In Mooneyham's reading, Eliot's use of formal fictional techniques to structure the novel contrasts with the themes of discontinuity and open-endedness that dominate the work.*]

> Oh dear, yes, the novel tells a story.
>
> (Forster, *Aspects of the Novel* 28)

> The most fruitful direct approach to fiction is through the focus on romance elements, the romance being the generator of form.
>
> (Levine, "Realism Reconsidered" 343)

I. *Middlemarch* and the Fear of Form

Readers have been puzzled about the generic status of George Eliot's **Middlemarch** since its first publication. This puzzlement was surely shared by its author, who seems to write in the comic mode for most of the novel but who in its Finale suggests that the happiness achieved by her heroine should be greeted as a somber and ambiguous victory. In part, this generic tangle follows from Eliot's own ambivalent attitude toward the conventions of fictional form. She quite rightly recognized that the indeterminacies of life are distorted by fictions which shape and contain them, yet in **Middlemarch** she found her plots following the conventional lines of comedy nonetheless. The comic mode, in fact, most does justice to Eliot's overarching vision of identity gained and accommodations with the world won. And yet the comic mode is challenged and compromised by Eliot's own radical unease about the formal requirements of narrative.

Early in **Adam Bede,** the narrator confesses her contempt for "that order of minds that pant after the ideal" (189). That order of mind is, of course, that of her readership, who finds in George Eliot's novels its expectations raised and its sympathies touched towards desirable ends; these wishes and sympathies are the creation of plots which promise either to fulfill or frustrate those desires. George Eliot had, it seems, a firm distrust of plots which too thoroughly keep their generic promises, which adhere too closely to the comic or tragic mode. She feared the too-easy dollops of earned retribution or reward we term poetic justice; *her* definition of the term, from her essay **"The Morality of *Wilhelm Meister,"*** makes her scorn plain. "Poetic justice," claims Eliot, is a "scheme"

> by which rewards and punishments are distributed according to those notions of justice on which the novel-writer would have recommended that the world should be governed if he had been consulted at the creation.
>
> (145)[1]

That readers and authors alike fall too readily into such over-easy conventions of judgment is, further, a fault of that "God-like omniscience" Roland Barthes has identified with the past tense historical employed by the great realist novels of the nineteenth century (30). In *Middlemarch,* Eliot herself mocks that too-easy historicism which the past tense confers. The accretion of cause upon effect is, for her, "incalculable," and she wishes us to muse on how life is distorted by the hindsight of those too ready to read by the syntax of conventional patterns. Early in *Middlemarch,* she muses:

> What elegant historian would neglect a striking opportunity for pointing out that his heroes did not foresee the history of the world, or even of their own actions?—for example, that Henry of Navarre, when a Protestant baby, little thought of being a Catholic monarch; or that Alfred the Great, when he measured his laborious nights with burning candles, had no idea of future gentlemen measuring their idle days with watches. Here is a mine of truth, which however vigorously it may be worked, is likely to outlast our coal.
>
> (54)

As C. Comstock notes, this passage "not only mocks our supercilious hindsight, but [also] our attempts to establish causal relations in general" (46); such attempts in fiction we call "plots." Even the metaphors of mine and coal shift our certainty about the linear design—down and back—of our historical (and narrative) understanding. Eliot sees herself as the "historian" of fictional lives, the form of which comes from the form of life. That form Eliot herself defined in **"Notes on Form and Art (1868)"**: "fundamentally, form is unlikeness . . . and . . . every difference is form" (432-3).

J. Hillis Miller sees Eliot's use of form as "inorganic, acentered and discontinuous":

> Against the notion of a work of art which is an organic unity and against the notion that a human life gradually reveals its destined meaning, George Eliot opposes the concepts of a text made of differences and of human lives which have no unitary meaning, for whom 'every limit is a beginning as well as an ending.'
>
> (468)

The quotation Miller includes above comes from the Finale of *Middlemarch* (677) in which Eliot attempts to open and extend those closed plot lines of the novel proper. Here we follow after-histories of all the major characters of the novel, Bulstrode excepted, forward some thirty-five years into the putative present. It is the Finale which protests against a cessation of interest in characters merely because the conventional curve of their plots has brought them to the stasis, the pause which stands for the end, of marriage:

> Who can quit young lives after being so long in company with them, and not desire to know what befell them in their after-years. . . . Marriage, which has been the bourne of so many narratives, is still a great beginning, as it was to Adam and Eve, who kept their honeymoon in Eden, but who had their first little one among the thorns and thistles of the wilderness.
>
> (677)

Eliot in essence protests against the practice of concluding a narrative at all. In a letter she wrote, "some of the fault lies in the very nature of a conclusion, which is at best a negation." Conclusions negate, as Helen Gardner has commented, by employing "an arbitrary act of will [that of the novelist]" to abolish the further "movement of time [and] the continuity of human lives" (39). A similar disservice to the real experience of human time is rendered by beginning a fiction; George Eliot notes at the start of *Daniel Deronda* that "Man can do nothing without the make-believe of a beginning" (3). Eliot thus seems uncomfortable with her own practice of beginning and ending her fictions; as she wrote in a letter, "Beginnings are always troublesome, and conclusions are the weak point of most authors" (qtd. by Gardner 39). Henry James agreed, at least as far as Eliot was concerned, calling her conclusions "signally weak" (*Felix Holt* 39). *Middlemarch* in particular James claims is "unconscious of the influence of a plan," and, complaining of its formlessness, he asks, "If we write novels so, how shall we write history?" ("On *Middlemarch*" ["George Eliot's *Middlemarch*"] 87). The very diffuseness of plot James faults becomes for a deconstructionist like Miller a planned exposure on Eliot's part of the "metaphysical system of history" (471), a demystification of illusory beliefs in origins, centers, goals—either in fiction or in history. What *Middlemarch* deconstructs, Miller asserts, are the parallel assumptions that fiction and history are teleological. But is this indeed *Middlemarch,* a novel wholly bent on subverting structure in the service of depicting more fully the random directions of life? Is the replacement of which Miller speaks, of "the concepts of origin, end and continuity . . . by the categories of repetition, of difference, of discontinuity, of openness," as thorough as he intimates?[2] We may find that though Eliot surely doubts the purposive movement of history, it does not follow that she finds such movement entirely dispensable in fiction.

In *Middlemarch,* Eliot's formalism—chief antagonist to discontinuity and openness—is apparent on many fronts. The novel is meticulously designed into its constituent parts of volumes, books and chapters. All eight books are titled; many, such as "The Dead Hand" (Book V) and "Sunset and Sunrise" (Book VIII), give clear signals about the development of plot. I would argue, in fact, that these book titles augment the reader's sense of the novel's comic form. "The Dead Hand," for instance, refers to the lingering powers of the two dead *senex* figures, Casaubon and Featherstone, to block the happy ending for the two sets of lovers whose stories end happily—Will and Dorothea on the one hand and Fred and Mary on the other. Unlike the books, the chapters are untitled, yet each is numbered and has an epigram, many composed by Eliot herself. Each epigram creates possibilities for ironic resonance with the contents of the chapter and prepares the reader for likely developments in plot. For example, chapter twelve is tagged at its start with the following from Chaucer: "He had more tow on his distaffe / Than Gerveis knew" (84). This "tow on his distaffe" refers us to the growing and parallel weights of influence exercised on Lydgate by Rosamond and on Fred Vincy by Mary Garth, influence which sets both these respective plots in motion and influence which this chapter begins to detail by setting all four characters at Stone Court one fine morning.

Everywhere is evidence of design. The plots are carefully set in parallel directions, as Lydgate and Dorothea both set out in ardent pursuit of the root meanings of things and find themselves harnessed in restrictive marriages. Lydgate's search for the key to organic tissue parallels Casaubon's search for the Key to All Mythologies. The three love stories weave and interweave. All the characters of *Middlemarch,* in fact, are roped together by various strands, as the dominant image of the web makes plain. Plot and imagery support each other, as Mark Schorer has shown in his analysis of *Middlemarch*'s figurative language. Schorer demonstrates that the novel is dominated by totalizing metaphors of unification and progress, of "shaping and making, of structure and creative purpose" (555). Most important to the comic mode to which Eliot uncomfortably adheres is the language of expectation, taking form most frequently, as Schorer notes, in the phrase "to look forward," a phrase which "appears on nearly every page of *Middlemarch*" (555). Our looking forward, so to speak, is rewarded by movements in the plot which accord with our sense of justice and with our desires. Bulstrode the hypocrite is exposed, punished and expelled. The two men who block the happiness of the lovers, Casaubon and Featherstone, first die, and when that act alone proves insufficient to create the happy endings, have their posthumous tyrannies overruled or rendered void. After much suffering and delay, the two pairs of lovers marry. And yet, and yet. . . . Where in this vision of a unified and clearly developed plot is there

room for the tragic end of Lydgate? Even more essentially, where is there room for the "martyrdom" proposed for our heroine in the Preface and her "sad" "sacrifice" of the Finale? Where is the sense of a redeemed society so central to the comic mode? If *Middlemarch* indeed participates in the comic mode, it does so in an equivocal fashion.

Now because the novel as a genre is essentially founded on irony, all great novels of the nineteenth century to some extent eschew the conventional modes of comedy and tragedy. The impulse towards realism which is at the heart of the novelistic experience necessitates ironic modifications of either mode. As James Kincaid has noted, Victorian narrative as a whole demonstrated a remarkable facility both to "use and deny formal patterns." The exemplary comedy he notes in this regard is Butler's *The Way of All Flesh,* but his comments apply with equal validity to Eliot's strategy in *Middlemarch*:

> Are the disasters real or not? We receive some protection from the comic form of the action, but the [ironic] narrator does his best to rip that protection from us, thus exposing the artificiality of the comic form the novel is at the same time exploiting.
>
> (2)

This critique of comic conventions, however, surfaces most prominently in *Middlemarch* in Eliot's treatment of the incipient romances between the two mismatches of the novel, those of Lydgate/Rosamond and Casaubon/Dorothea. For such disastrous unions, the narrator has sympathy but no illusions: "has any one pinched into its pilulous smallness the cobweb of prematrimonial acquaintanceship?" (19). When, on the other hand, the curve of plot moves towards the fulfillment of the lovers who indeed belong together, irony is replaced almost entirely by pathos. Derision aimed at generic conventionality is wholly absent at the climax of Dorothea and Will's love story:

> 'Oh, I cannot bear it—my heart will break,' said Dorothea, starting from her seat, the flood of her young passion bearing down all the obstructions which had kept her silent—the great tears rising and falling in an instant: 'I don't mind about poverty—I hate my wealth.'
>
> In an instant Will was close to her and had his arms round her, but she drew back and held his away gently so that she might go on speaking, her large tear-filled eyes looking at his very simply, while she said in a sobbing childlike way, 'We could live quite well on my own fortune—it is too much—seven hundred a-year—I want so little—no new clothes—and I will learn what everything costs.'
>
> (663)

Later reflection on the part of the reader that £700 was not the income of those in poverty and that Dorothea is still her uncle's heir may allow some degree of ironic perspective on this scene. Nonetheless, the pathos of this romantic climax—enhanced as it is by the emphasis on tears, emotion and childishness—contains Dorothea and Will's love story within the bounds of romance rather than irony.

Are the generic promises of *Middlemarch* then delivered upon? Each mode is, after all, a syntax by which we learn the shape of particular narratives. If *Middlemarch* not only mixes its generic signals, most particularly in the contrast between Dorothea's happy fate and Lydgate's bitter one, it also, as we have seen, expresses covert and overt dissatisfaction with the conventional shaping strategies of fiction. As David Daiches has suggested, "*Middlemarch* is twisted at more than one point and especially at its conclusion, into a shape that is not the true shape of the vision of life that is presented" (139). Daiches here complains of the *over-determined* shape of the plot, complains that Eliot has misshapen into conventional structures the haphazardnesses of her characters' lives. He makes, in fact, a criticism exactly opposite to that of Henry James. Such contrary but heart-felt criticism demonstrates, if nothing else, the root problem of Eliot's ambiguous attitude towards form and her equally ambiguous employment of the same.

II. Beginnings and Ends

Generic dissonance in *Middlemarch* sounds most aharmonically in the novel's Finale, and it is here we might start to discover to what extent a genuine comedic shape determines the novel as a whole. The novel proper ends, not with the union of Will and Dorothea, but with that of Fred and Mary. As Marianne Torgovnick has revealed in her study of the closural properties of *Middlemarch,* the novel if left thus closed would break off in the direction of a happy futurity:

> Fred almost in a whisper said—
>
> 'When we were first engaged, with the umbrella-ring, Mary, you used to—'
>
> The spirit of joy began to laugh more decidedly in Mary's eyes, but the fatal Ben came running to the door with Brownie yapping behind them, and bouncing against them, said—
>
> 'Fred and Mary! are you ever coming in?—or may I eat your cake?'
>
> (673)

Cake, children, dogs, proposed kisses: here is the sentimental circle of achieved happiness, plain and unchallenged. "If Eliot authentically wanted a sense of 'new beginnings' at the end of *Middlemarch,*" Torgovnick writes, "she should have ended it here, with Fred and Mary, Will and Dorothea about to marry, and Lydgate and Rosamond entering a new stage in their marriage"

(24). But Eliot instead moves to the Finale, which would extend the sense of comic tranquility through the years if not for its inclusion of the news of Lydgate's death at fifty after a life of only partly reconciled bitterness and some puzzling last comments regarding Dorothea's "sacrifice." The Finale, after all, has recorded in its next-to-last paragraphs Dorothea's reconciliation with her family, a reconciliation which erases that sense of expulsion and alienation which had marred the comic sense of the close (so far as it had been worked through the last chapter).

Comedies require a sense of accommodation, a sense of the social world, even if only a small part of that world, remade in concord and peace.[3] This the Finale achieves, especially by its emphasis on the harmony of the next generation:

> It became an understood thing that Mr and Mrs Ladislaw should pay at least two visits during the year to the Grange, and there came gradually a small row of cousins at Freshitt who enjoyed playing with the two cousins visiting Tipton as much as if the blood of these cousins had been less dubiously mixed.
>
> (681-2)

Mary and Fred are likewise left in harmony; indeed the Finale expends the majority of its pages in describing the successful marriage of the Vincys. They have had three boys; Fred has become a thriving businessman and farmer; and, finally, by moving into the doleful Stone Court, the Vincys redeem its history and transform it into a charmed domestic space. The sense of comedy is not injured by such an extension into time for two reasons: first, because what is documented is the very stability through time a comic close promises, and, second, because what we find out of the Vincys' after-history corresponds with a comforting exactitude with what our best wishes for them would be:

> On inquiry it might possibly be found that Fred and Mary still inhabit Stone Court—that the creeping plants still cast the foam of their blossoms over the fine stone-wall into the field where the walnut-trees stand in stately row—and that on sunny days the two lovers who were first engaged with the umbrella-ring may be seen in white-haired placidity at the open window.
>
> (679)

This pastoral tableau signals the achievement of the desired aim of the comedy: the happy, stable, free space.

To find the disharmonies of the Finale, we must look to the final words accorded to Dorothea:

> Many who knew her, thought it a pity that so substantive and rare a creature should have been absorbed into the life of another, and be only known in a certain circle as wife and mother. But no one stated exactly what else that was in her power she ought rather to

have done—not even Sir James Chettam, who went no further than the negative prescription that she ought not to have married Will Ladislaw.

(680)

A new Theresa will hardly have the opportunity of reforming a conventual life, any more than a new Antigone will spend her heroic piety in daring all for the sake of a brother's burial: the medium in which their ardent deeds took shape is for ever gone. But we insignificant people with our daily words and acts are preparing the lives of many Dorotheas whose story we know. . . . [T]he effect of her being on those around her was incalculably diffusive: for the growing good of the world is partly dependent on unhistoric acts; and that things are not so ill with you and me as they might have been, is half owing to the number who lived faithfully a hidden life, and rest in unvisited tombs.

(682)

What exactly is the nature of Dorothea's "sacrifice"? And why the muted and sad reference to the "unvisited tombs" of those like Dorothea who find no epic destiny beyond love, a happy life, and a vocation of charity and good works among her neighbors? The answer lies in the Prelude, which sets up the novel's theme as that of a superlative woman's tragic inability to find an epic life. This false prophecy continues in the first chapter of *Middlemarch* in which Dorothea is characterized as one who is "likely to seek martyrdom, to make retractions, and then to incur martyrdom after all in a quarter where she had not sought it" (8). But how to characterize Dorothea's martyrdom except as the passing phenomenon of her marriage to Casaubon? Can there be such a thing as a temporary martyr?[4]

Harriet Farwell Adams has explained many of these inconsistencies through an examination of how the Prelude and Finale were composed in relationship to the rest of the novel. The Prelude was part of an early story called **"Miss Brooke"** in which Dorothea presumably made the same initial mistake of marrying Casaubon but was doomed to abide by that mistake instead of being allowed ultimately to accept Will. Incidentally, this aborted possibility struck Henry James with some force: "an ardent young girl *was to have been* the central figure, . . . wasting her ardor and soiling her wings against the meanness of opportunity" (my emphasis; 81). The movement to the comic close he found the novel's chief weakness, in part through repugnance for Will Ladislaw but more, I judge, from a dissatisfaction with the novel's comic direction:

Mr. Casaubon's death befalls about the middle of the story, and from this point to the close our interest in Dorothea is restricted to the question, will she or will [she] not marry Will Ladislaw? The question is relatively trivial and the implied struggle slightly factitious. . . . The dramatic current stagnates; it runs between hero and heroine almost a game of hair-splitting.

(82)

In a sense, James redresses Eliot's errors, as he saw them, by rewriting Dorothea's story as Isabel Archer's in *Portrait of a Lady*; there he beats off the comic impulse with a vengeance and gives Isabel the close he would have preferred for Dorothea. At any rate, in *Middlemarch* as we have it, Eliot refuses to give Dorothea the martyrdom she was initially to have had. As the novel progressed, Eliot found that she no longer wished to consign Dorothea to a future of renunciation, but the Prelude remained essentially as first written. As Jerome Beaty details in his *Middlemarch: From Notebook to Novel*, the original version of Dorothea's story, **"Miss Brooke,"** survives as the first nine-and-a-half chapters of *Middlemarch*, while Lydgate's story, first called **"Middlemarch,"** constitutes chapters 10 through 16 (24-36). The Finale was likewise composed separately from the rest of the novel; it was, moreover, composed in enormous haste. As Adams notes, the Finale was written, mailed to Eliot's publisher John Blackwood, returned in the form of proofs, corrected and mailed again to Blackwood, all in the space of two weeks (9).

That the final paragraphs of the Finale seem at odds with the body of the novel is in part due then to its speedy composition, but also to Eliot's strategy of reconciliation between beginnings and ends. As Barbara Hardy has shown, Eliot's entire novelistic career was marked by a strong aesthetic need to make her entrances and exits correspond to each other ("Relationship of Beginning and End" ["The Relationship of Beginning and End in George Eliot's Fiction"] 7). Both Prelude and Finale are clearly set apart from the rest of the novel and mirror each other, especially in their attention to the theme of epic possibilities thwarted. Adams directs our attention to a letter Eliot wrote to a friend just before the last installment of *Middlemarch* came out: "Expect to be immensely disappointed with the close of '*Middlemarch*.' But look back to the Prelude" (*Letters* [*The George Eliot Letters*] 330; qtd. in Adams 10). Torgovnick claims that the Finale is "completely integrated with the aesthetic, and more important, the thematic shape of the novel" (36). It might be more justly argued that the Finale accords with the Prelude, but not with the whole movement of narrative which divides one from the other. Dorothea is not ultimately a martyr, nor is hers an example of a thwarted life. She has fulfilled her comic mission, to discover her true self and to discard her illusory view of the world; her marriage to Will represents that achievement and the establishment of inner concord and unity. By consigning her heroine as she does to those terminal "unvisited tombs," Eliot does her own creation a disservice.

Yet Eliot's ambivalence must be served, and in this respect, the disrespect the Finale accords the comic close of the narrative proper may be understood as necessary. If what drives our movement through a narrative is the dynamic conglomeration of the various casts of our desire for identity, then theoretically the end of desire is the end of the text.[5] Frye tells us that identity "means a good many things, but all its meanings in romance have some connection with a state of experience in which there is nothing left to write about. It is existence before 'once upon a time' and subsequent to 'and they lived happily ever after'" (*Secular Scripture* 54). Yet if the desires which furnish **Middlemarch** with its energies oppose any final claim for identity as thoroughly as those which affirm identity, then this conflict in narrative desire will incite conflict in the text's end. As Daniel Cottom notes, "Romance is not wrong, as far as Eliot was concerned, but rather is only too right. It represents as a desirable world one that everyone does indeed desire, and that is precisely the problem. Everyone is a figure of Romance—and so Romance is untenable" (361). If Eliot feels impelled to chasten her own romantic expectations—those which call for a comic close—so as not to "fancy our space wider than it is" (**Adam Bede** 100), then she must find a close which expresses her discontent with her own comic creation. And thus the seeming discord of **Middlemarch**—a novel whose "happily ever after" still leaves something which must be written, something which must be left desiring.

III. The Comic Form of *Middlemarch*

Northrop Frye, who understands better than anyone else the form and shape of comedy, has characterized comedy as primarily teleological, concerned with leading alienated lovers past the obstructions posed by parental figures and restrictive society to fulfillment and rebirth. That fulfillment and rebirth are in most cases symbolized by marriage, which in turn symbolizes the establishment of a new and revivified society, even if that society has only two members ("Old and New Comedy" 1-2). Malcolm Bradbury affirms this vision of the comic, while placing it specifically within the terms of fiction:

> There is a basic species of the novel which regards the contingent world of the life in time as reconcilable with that other element in which the novel deals, the life by values; so contingency becomes plot, and life in time is finally teleological; the universe of chance becomes a universe of meaning, and the individual and history unite. This is apt to be a comic genre.
>
> (33)

It is this element of reconciled and accommodated ends which most firmly binds **Middlemarch** to the comic tradition.

In particular, this reconciliation in serious comedy must take place between the self and the world; what must occur is the "resolution of incongruities between the self-image and the way the world goes" (Heilman 58). Such is Dorothea's stance, as she acknowledges to Celia, "It is quite true that I might be a wiser person . . .

and that I might have done something better, if I had been better. But this is what I am going to do. I have promised to marry Mr. Ladislaw; and I am going to marry him" (670). Here is what Robert Heilman describes as the comic emotion of "elation": "the joy at finding an accommodation of things, of knowing more without letting the knowledge become a burden and a justification for sad disillusionment" (48). This elation is most properly tied to the idea of marriage; Dorothea and Will's union is more, after all, than a sign of "a state of good repair in the life force" caused by "a happy pairing of the sexes" (56), as Heilman ironically puts it. Marriage is rather the symbol for the integrated self. Robert Polhemus speaks of marriage as the comic compromise "between self-gratification and social responsibility," as the "potential remedy for the incompleteness of personality in an individualistic age" (89). As a "remedy" for "incompleteness," marriage represents the reconciliation between warring elements in the self. For until the consummation of what Frye terms the Eros quest (2) becomes less of the human obsession than it remains at present, marriage will remain the most useful and pressing metaphor by which the comic understanding of experience may express the achievement by the protagonist of psychic wholeness and social harmony.

The happy marriages accorded to Fred and Mary, Will and Dorothea, present differing examples, then, of Eliot's enduring theme Barbara Hardy identifies, the rescue into love (*Novels* [*The Novels of George Eliot*] 66). Dorothea's rescue is of particular interest in that she must move beyond the clutches of a first marriage to the freedom of her second. She is married, in fact, to a *senex* figure, for Casaubon is nothing if not marked by the most prevalent of *senex* traits: jealousy, miserliness, pedantry, sexual sterility, a tendency towards tyranny, a position *in loco parentis,* and, above all, advanced age. He is paralleled in his function as blocking figure by Mr. Featherstone, whose will denies his avuncular responsibility for Fred Vincy while demolishing Fred's hopes for an easy and early independence. As U. C. Knoepflmacher has shown, **Middlemarch** is fraught with avuncular figures who deny familial obligations. Mr. Brooke is a well-meaning but ultimately irresponsible uncle both to Dorothea and Celia. Mr. Casaubon denies being Will's uncle, thrice reminding those about him that Will is only his second cousin. Once aroused by jealousy, Casaubon cuts thin and then abolishes his former sponsorship of Will. Mr. Bulstrode is an exacting, tyrannous and uncharitable uncle to Fred. And can we forget the impedimentary force discovered by St. Theresa in the Preface as she meets "domestic reality . . . in the shape of uncles" who turn her and her brother back "from their great resolve" (3)? True to the shape of comedy, all the obstructionist uncles—except St. Theresa's—are overcome in the course of the novel, while, true to Eliot's humane vision, none is treated one-dimensionally. We see each as he appears the hero to himself, not merely as he appears the ogre to another.

Other common comic elements in the novel include the social comedy of Dorothea's unseeing ignorance of the matrimonial hopes Sir James directs at her. This situation, incidentally, Eliot borrowed from Jane Austen's *Emma* in which Mr. Elton courts that novel's equally imperceptive heroine, a borrowing which even has Dorothea deride the same expression—"Exactly"—in her unacknowledged lover as does Emma with Mr. Elton, though his is an "Exactly so." *Middlemarch* also includes the low comedy of social inversion; its variant of the universal comic theme of "beggars upon horseback and justices in the stocks" (Gardner 45) is the festival brutality which attends Mr. Brooke's unfortunate attempt at a political speech. Perhaps one of comedy's more stock situations is that of the hypocrite/villain and his public unmasking. Here Bulstrode fills the ancient role, though our comic sense of purgation is mixed with sympathy (the same can be said of our feelings as Shylock or Tartuffe exits). The foundling theme likewise finds a place in Eliot's workings of plot; Will the outsider, the alien, is revealed as the rightful heir of Bulstrode's estate. Will's unmasking, however, does *not* lead directly to his romantic resolution. In fact, the seriousness of Eliot's conception is made most evident by the long period of suffering both Will and Dorothea must undergo after they recognize their errors. In the simpler forms of comedy, the happy solution automatically and directly follows the unmasking of error and/or identity (Cox 71). But in serious comedy, comedies, that is, which are serious about the problem of identity, "the device of recognition and the whole sequence of denouement" becomes elaborated and extended (Jagendork 20). For Will and Dorothea such a delay necessitates that they not only recognize their false sense of self—a negative requirement—but also that they acknowledge what they at heart desire, each other.

One last sign of the comic mode in *Middlemarch* is the general amnesty bestowed as if by grace on the whole company of *dramatis personae*. Better than strict poetic justice is the ameliorated escape offered Bulstrode. Lydgate's fate is less than we were expecting. Even more importantly, the reconciliation Celia effects between her husband and her sister signals the reconstitution of a society, though a relatively narrow one. Nonetheless, somehow there is a wideness to Dorothea's end. As the wife of a Member of Parliament and an "ardent public man," Dorothea has a range of charitable operations wider than it ever was in Lowick or Middlemarch. We remember her confession to Celia in chapter 84: "I have never carried out any plan yet" (669). In London, she works demonstrable good, even if such acts are "incalculably diffusive" (682). The metaphor Eliot employs to describe this spreading out of Dorothea's goodness is

that of a river spent into myriad channels. And the claim that this particular spatial metaphor of widening and spreading is by nature comic rather than ironic leads us to the next stage of our discussion, that of Eliot's creation of comic space.

IV. THE COMIC SPACE OF *MIDDLEMARCH*

The spatial goal of all comic events is to achieve a rehabilitated center, be this the gathering of lovers at a feast, the domestic center of a house or estate, or the pastoral retreat of a reclaimed Eden. The spatial images which dominate *Middlemarch* may be understood as participating both for and against the movement to this comic space; there are the imagery and settings that inhibit and restrain this movement and those which propel it forward.[6] Hardy has written eloquently of the former, that spatial language and description of enclosure and annihilation which stand for Dorothea's entrapment in marriage and the demolition of all her cherished notions of selfhood. Hardy finds, for instance, a recurring symbol in Eliot's fiction of the disenchanted day-lit room (*Novels* 194). When Dorothea returns from her honeymoon she finds her boudoir at Lowick an altered thing.

> The very furniture in the room seemed to have shrunk since she saw it before; the stag in the tapestry looked more like a ghost in his ghostly blue-green world; the volumes of polite literature looked more like immovable imitations of books . . . Each remembered thing in the room was disenchanted, was deadened as an unlit transparency.
>
> (224-6)

What has altered, of course, is not the room but Dorothea herself:

> Her blooming full-pulsed youth stood there in a moral imprisonment which made itself one with the chill, colourless, narrowed landscape, with the shrunken furniture, the never-read books, and the ghostly stag in a pale fantastic world that seemed to be vanishing from the daylight.
>
> (226)

The images which dominate the novel—of labyrinth and maze, swamp and tomb, prison and ruins—all stand for Dorothea's imprisonment both by marriage and by her self-delusions and egotism. The ruins which oppress her so particularly in Rome do so because they represent the threatened dissolution of Dorothea's sense of self; Rome's "stupendous fragmentariness" (158) speaks to Dorothea's feeling of desolation and loss of purpose (Fisher 172-3). What comedy requires, of course, is a language of space which counters such restraints, enclosures, and disintegrations and which can represent the self's victory over its own delusional selfishness. The language of the web which pervades the novel stands as one form of this comic symbology, but webs both connect and entrap. To close a comedy, one must discover places analogous to the comic achievement of harmony and freedom.

Since *where* a novel ends, its final setting is integrally related to *how* it ends—comically, tragically or ambiguously ever after—the end places of a novel have symbolic resonance and stand for the social and psychological status earned by the protagonists. Where the characters end thus symbolizes and helps establish the generic status of their narrative, for comic and tragic ends say vastly different things about the human condition. For this reason, the comic use of place in a novel diverges from the tragic: to end comically is to find a stable place which promises safety but which allows a potential escape. We are never fully boxed in at a comedy's end; such is the realm of tragedy, the box that is the grave.

Where are these safe havens in *Middlemarch*? Where is "one little room, an everywhere," John Donne's secure microcosm for love, which Eliot provides as an epigram for chapter 83 (657)? For Fred and Mary the comic solution of place is conventional. They ultimately live—and own—Stone Court, scene of greed, hypocrisy and sin, and in their habitation exorcise the place, redeem it with their comic experience of unified love. Our last glimpse of them provides us with the required comic spatiality of closure and openness combined; they are securely framed by Stone Court but that security includes a window, a vista. Theirs is the consummate comic space: a room with a view. But such literally-grounded freedom within an enclosure cannot be granted to Will and Dorothea. In fact, one express condition of Dorothea's acceptance of Will as a husband is her giving up all claims to Lowick, Casaubon's estate. This estate, no den of refuge but rather a prison-house, is abandoned, and we know only that Dorothea and Will live in London. This refusal to set Dorothea and Will in an estate demonstrates both their freedom and Eliot's dissatisfaction with the estate as an overtly conventional symbol of comic reward. Like Anne Elliot and Captain Wentworth in Austen's *Persuasion,* another novel in which the concept of the estate is so degraded that undefined placement is the better good, Will and Dorothea create in love alone a moveable island. What they achieve instead is a comic space, a *hortus conclusus* of the mind, a metaphorical rather than a physical placement. For her part, Dorothea has been prepared for the comic resolution by her vision at the window of the ongoingness and expansion of life:

> She opened her curtains, and looked out towards the bit of road that lay in view. . . . On the road there was a man with a bundle on his back and a woman carrying her baby; in the field she could see figures moving— perhaps the shepherd with his dog. Far off in the bending sky was the pearly light; and she felt the largeness

of the world and the manifold wakings of men to labour and endurance. She was part of that involuntary, palpitating life.

(664)

To look out a window is to make the movement from the enclosed self to other.

But such amorphous yearnings towards humankind are insufficient to create comedies; Dorothea must find a particular and private expansion into love. We might notice the spatial language accorded to Dorothea's emotional state *after* the epiphanic scene just quoted and *before* the romantic resolution with Will, when her sense of love is still impersonal: "No—she adhered to her declaration that she would never be married again, and in the long valley of her life, which looked so flat and empty of way-marks, guidance would come as she walked along the road, and saw her fellow-passengers by the way." Dorothea is in error here, blind to the compulsion of personal love. Another window-scene is necessary to desacralize Dorothea's self-set dreary pilgrimage, the scene of the romantic impulse, when watching a storm through the study window allows the lovers to make another movement from enclosed self to other, here not the Other of suffering humankind but the desired Other of human love. This second window scene grounds the movement of expansion and accommodation in the sacred space of shared love. As Will describes it, "all their vision, all their thought of each other, [was] in a world apart, where the sunshine fell on white lilies, where no evil lurked, and no other soul entered" (657). Here is a pastoral of the mind only, an established world, nonetheless, which then frees the lovers from the physical and social narrowness of Middlemarch's provincial society (Middleton 117). *Middlemarch* closes by placing its protagonists in a freely imagined space, yet provides them with the language of Edenic retreat. This is indeed the "country of the mind to be attained only by the force of imagination" Helen Gardner has identified as the bourne of all comic narrations (51). As such, it remains far more impervious to defeat, even by Eliot's own ambivalence about whether, having brought her lovers into the comic round, she can believe in the comic promise of her own creation.

Notes

1. Margaret Kenda uses this quotation to begin her analysis of Eliot's uneasy adherence to the dictates of poetic justice (336); Kenda goes on to remark that "in George Eliot's repeated insistence upon 'moral development' lies the beginning of her capitulation to some form of poetic justice" (339). Such a comment raises the interesting question of what sorts of cohesion, expansion or enrichments of identity Eliot presupposes adhere to her fictional characters as they move forward in

time and what these presupposed developments of identity require of her narrative strategies. A belief in moral development allows for a comic or tragic plot, but not for an absurdist or nihilist one.

2. Miller acknowledges the formal elements of *Middlemarch,* but considers them wholly subverted by the novel's "elaborate deconstruction" of form— and of history: "For those who have eyes to see it, *Middlemarch* is an example of a work of fiction which . . . exposes the metaphysical system of history, reject[ing] historicism with its ideas of progress and of a homogenous time within which that progress unfolds." Miller's Gospel allusion provides a clue that we are witnessing a battle between opposing systems of belief. But *Middlemarch* is no more stalwart in an insistence on repetition and difference than it is on the side of form and convention. The generic pressures of telling a story make what Miller sees happening in *Middlemarch,* "the exploding of the continuum of history," impossible.

3. For amplifications on the vital role social accommodation plays in the close of comedies, see Cox, Heilman, Galligan, and, especially, Frye, in both his *Anatomy of Criticism* and *The Secular Scripture.*

4. Calvin Bedient, in his devastating "*Middlemarch*: Touching Down," identifies the falsities of the Prelude and the Finale as issuing from Eliot's vanity. Bedient argues that since Eliot wishes one thing for Dorothea—for her to be "famously good" (77)—Dorothea's failure makes *Middlemarch* a "prolonged protest of the dissatisfied ego" (76): "What George Eliot resents, what makes her strike out against phantoms, is Dorothea's lack of fame. . . . To be only known in a certain circle! As wife and mother! The pangs, the emptiness, the comparative vulgarity of an unglorious life—it is this George Eliot regrets on Dorothea's behalf. Her pity flows unchecked, and is almost palpable; for in Dorothea she sees her worst fears enacted" (79). Bedient may be too harsh, but surely no comic close is secure if the author hungers after an epic one instead.

5. Peter Brooks' *Reading for the Plot* and D. A. Miller's *Narrative and Its Discontents* both analyze this push of desire as the driving force in narrative, that which impels us from the quiescence of beginning to the quiescence of end. Miller offers a particularly cogent reading of *Middlemarch* from this perspective of narrative desire, though his interest does not lie in the clash between expectations derived from comic structure *per se* and the expectations engendered by the web of plot and language of *Middlemarch* itself.

6. The most extensive reading of George Eliot's language of space may be found in Mann's "Self, Shell and World: George Eliot's Language of Space." Mann identifies the shell as the spatial image which most commonly embodies Eliot's sense of the relation between self and world, since a shell may be understood as a dynamic center which encloses but also expands, "perceptually defined . . . by the equal pressures of internal and external life" (456). She also discusses Eliot's use of such symbols as the horizon, the labyrinth, and the temple, the last of which stands for the idealized space Eliot hopes to gain for her protagonists, a "defined and delimited space [with] some indwelling spirit which provides a center" (469). Such temples in Eliot's fiction are similar to the "rooms with a view" I discuss in the following paragraphs.

Works Cited

Adams, Harriet Farwell. "Prelude and Finale to *Middlemarch.*" *Victorian Newsletter* 68 (1985): 9-11.

Barthes, Roland. *Writing Degree Zero.* Trans. Annette Lavers and Colin Smith. NY: Hill and Wang, 1970.

Beaty, Jerome. Middlemarch *From Notebook to Novel: A Study of George Eliot's Creative Method.* Urbana: U of Illinois P, 1960.

Bedient, Calvin. "*Middlemarch*: Touching Down." *Hudson Review* 22 (1969): 70-89.

Bradbury, Malcolm. *Possibilities: Essays on the State of the Novel.* London: OUP [Oxford UP], 1973.

Brooks, Peter. *Reading for the Plot.* NY: Knopf, 1984.

Comstock, Cathy. *Disruption and Delight in the Nineteenth Century Novel.* Ann Arbor: UMI Research Press, 1988.

Cottom, Daniel. "The Romance of George Eliot's Realism." *Genre* 15 (1982): 357-377.

Cox, Roger L. "The Structure of Comedy." *Thought* 50 (1975): 67-83.

Daiches, David. *The Novel and the Modern World.* Rev. ed. Chicago: U of Chicago P, 1960.

Eliot, George. *Adam Bede.* Ed. Stephen Gill. NY: Penguin, 1967.

———. *Daniel Deronda.* Ed. Barbara Hardy. NY: Penguin, 1967.

———. *The George Eliot Letters.* Ed. Gordon S. Haight. Vol. V. New Haven: Yale UP, 1954.

———. *Middlemarch.* Ed. David Carroll. Oxford: OUP [Oxford UP], 1988.

———. "The Morality of *Wilhelm Meister.*" *The Essays of George Eliot.* Ed. Thomas Pinney. NY: Columbia UP, 1963. 143-47.

———. "Notes on Form and Art (1868)." *The Essays of George Eliot.* Ed. Thomas Pinney. NY: Columbia UP, 1963. 431-6.

Fisher, Philip. *Making Up Society: The Novels of George Eliot.* Pittsburgh: U of Pittsburgh P, 1981.

Frye, Northrup. *The Anatomy of Criticism.* Princeton: Princeton UP, 1957.

———. "Old and New Comedy." *Shakespeare Survey* 22 (1969): 1-5.

———. *The Secular Scripture: A Study of the Structure of Romance.* Cambridge: Harvard UP, 1976.

Galligan, Edward. *The Comic Vision in Literature.* Athens: U of Georgia P, 1984.

Gardner, Helen. "Happy Endings: Literature, Misery, & Joy." *Encounter* 57.2 (1981): 39-51.

Hardy, Barbara. *The Novels of George Eliot.* NY: OUP, 1959.

———. "The Relationship of Beginning and End in George Eliot's Fiction." *Cahiers Victoriens & Edouardiens* 26 (1987): 7-19.

Heilman, Robert Bechtold. *The Ways of the World: Comedy and Society.* Seattle: U of Washington P, 1978.

Jagendork, Zvi. *The Happy End of Comedy.* Newark: U of Delaware, P, 1984.

James, Henry. "Felix Holt." *A Century of George Eliot Criticism.* Ed. Gordon S. Haight. Boston: Heath, 1956.

———. "George Eliot's *Middlemarch.*" *A Century of George Eliot Criticism.* Ed. Gordon S. Haight. Boston: Houghton Mifflin, 1965. 80-87.

Kenda, Margaret Mason. "Poetic Justice and the Ending Trick in the Victorian Novel." *Genre* 8 (1975): 336-51.

Kincaid, James R. "Victorian Narrative Forms and the Explanation of Calamity." *Victorian Newsletter* 53 (1978): 1-4.

Knoepflmacher, U. C. "*Middlemarch*: An Avuncular View." *NCF* [*Nineteenth-Century Fiction*] 30 (1975): 53-81.

Levine, George. "Realism Reconsidered." *Essentials of the Theory of Fiction.* Ed. Michael J. Hoffman and Patrick D. Murphy. Durham: Duke UP, 1988. 336-48.

Mann, Karen. "Self, Shell and World: George Eliot's Language of Space." *Genre* 15 (1982): 447-75.

Middleton, Catherine A. "Roots and Rootlessness: An Exploration of the Concept in the Life and Novels of George Eliot." *Humanistic Geography and Literature: Essays on the Experience of Place.* Ed. Douglas Pocock. London: Croom Helm, 1981. 101-120.

Miller, D. A. *Narrative and its Discontents.* Princeton: Princeton UP, 1981.

Miller, J. Hillis. "Narrative and History." *ELH* 41 (1974): 455-73.

Polhemus, Robert M. *Comic Faith: The Great Tradition from Austen to Joyce.* Chicago: U of Chicago P, 1980.

Schorer, Mark. "Fiction and the Matrix of Analogy." *Kenyon Review* 11 (1980): 539-59.

Torgovnick, Marianna. *Closure in the Novel.* Princeton: Princeton UP, 1981.

John L. Tucker (essay date autumn 1991)

SOURCE: Tucker, John L. "George Eliot's Reflexive Text: Three Tonalities in the Narrative Voice of *Middlemarch.*" *Studies in English Literature, 1500-1900* 31, no. 4 (autumn 1991): 773-91.

[*In the following essay, Tucker examines the relationship between history and fiction in* Middlemarch. *Tucker asserts that Eliot's attitude toward her major themes is complicated by a type of stylistic ambivalence that is at once satirical and earnest, self-effacing and authoritative. The resulting tension reflects the author's broader ambivalence concerning the ability of the novel form to depict human life in a realistic, authentic manner—an ambivalence that is, according to Tucker, the very essence of Eliot's fiction.*]

The reflexiveness of George Eliot's fiction has become one of its chief attractions: modern criticism likes a self-conscious text, a novel that investigates its own authority. No one is scandalized any more by what used to be called George Eliot's "intrusions"; in fact, epigraphs, footnotes, and narrative asides are now thought of as central to her practice rather than as peripheral mannerisms.[1] This revision belongs to a larger movement that is deepening (and complicating) our understanding of nineteenth-century realism. Within this movement, however, there has been sometimes a misleading tendency to describe complexity as if it were incoherence. To take an extreme, but much-cited example, the pier-glass passage in **Middlemarch**—how the scratches on a mirror seem to form concentric circles around any source of reflected light—has been interpreted as a sign that the book itself is fundamentally "unreadable."[2] Variants of this idea are now common in political and in psychological criticism; **Middlemarch** is said to be a novel at war with itself, a text that either misunderstands or disguises its true, "subversive" message.[3] For all their emphasis on textuality, these readings are less interested in the text than in something supposed to be behind it. They reflect, sometimes brilliantly, modern insights about the hidden interconnectedness of language, perception, and privilege, but they do so at the risk of obscuring the nature of pre-modern literature.[4] A characteristic weakness of these readings is a kind of tone-deafness; speaking the modern languages of power and pain, they may not be able to hear that complex tone which is one of the triumphs of *Middlemarch* and finally, perhaps, its subject: tone is the novel's civilized response to what the narrator calls, in a memorable phrase, "the difficulties of civilization."

Awareness of those difficulties makes the novel's tone varied and complex. The religion of humanity turns into satire, punctuated with moments of terror; the narrator looks on amused while the heroine struggles for her life. More confusingly for modern theory, *Middlemarch* laughs at its own epistemological difficulties even while it takes them seriously. This seeming contradiction arises in part from peculiar relations between author and narrator. The shadowy presence of "George Eliot" makes itself felt throughout the novel, but to the extent that it is incarnated in the narrator, that presence suffers limitation and partiality.[5] The result is not disorientation or anomie; the footing is tricky, but the novel finds a balance in self-awareness. We could simplify the novel's mixed tone by calling it ironic wit, and certainly it is a funnier book than modern criticism tends to notice. But George Eliot's narrative devices introduce other frames of mind, too: detachment, a Wordsworthian sense of loss, and fear. None of these outlooks dominates the novel. Each has its characteristic successes and failures, articulated by the overlap and competition of several kinds of discourse, notably comedy, history, and science, which *Middlemarch* wryly understands as its precursors and rivals; their complex relations with George Eliot's fiction are part of the novel's subject.

We can begin by noticing that comedy in *Middlemarch* usually appears in conjunction with other modes. A lot of jokes get told under the cover of scientific talk, for instance; in George Eliot's narrator, the scientist is never very far from the satirist, perhaps because both tend to distance themselves from their targets. But the comic-objective tone does not represent the whole mind of the novel, which is managed in such a way that the narrator's amusement sometimes seems an inadequate response to Dorothea Brooke's "life of mistakes." Chapter 2, for example, contains the masterpiece of urbanity already quoted above: while describing Dorothea's romantic misperception of Casaubon, the narrator comments, "Dorothea's inferences may seem large; but really life could never have gone on at any period but for this liberal allowance of conclusions, which has facilitated marriage under the difficulties of civilization" (22).[6] This pokes fun at Dorothea, but even more at the

dismayed reader, who naturally wishes Dorothea to see Casaubon as he really is. The narrator will have no such interference: start that sort of thing, and nobody would ever get married—you could finish off the race with your altruism. This is the joke of someone with a classical turn of mind, who admires restraint of passion, and all that it enables. His satires display, without radically challenging, the price of social arrangements.

The narrator is a character here, individuated, like all George Eliot characters, by a way of talking. Listen to his sophisticated drawl: "Dorothea's inferences may seem large; but really . . ." The word "large" ironically diminishes Dorothea's error; "but really" asks us not to anguish over necessary misadventures. In his homilies and asides, the narrator often takes this detached tone; his good humor requires it. But at this point in the novel, few readers find themselves so detached; most are apt to agree with Chettam and Will Ladislaw, who describe Dorothea's marriage as "horrible." Moreover, the narrator's urbane humor seems at odds with his own vision of Dorothea as a kind of latter-day Saint Theresa. In the "Prelude" he leads us to think of Dorothea as a swan "raised uneasily among the ducklings," doomed by the conventions of modern English life to be "foundress of nothing," but a potential genius nevertheless. After that introduction, the narrator can never fully revoke Dorothea's status as the Heroine, uniquely endowed, capable of great deeds. And so we may laugh when she embraces her fate in the person of Casaubon, but at the same time we know that she is courting death, and we don't want to follow her. In that reaction we resist the narrator's comic view, and begin to take part in the novel's tension of competing tones.

Sometimes the narrator's own voice betrays that tension, as, for example, whenever he issues one of his mock-apologies for having described "low" people or "common" situations. In these passages the narrator always lets his audience know that he suspects them of hankering after romance and epic, of wishing to escape the salutary contemplation of their own recent history. He points out that readers disturbed by vulgar lives are at liberty to imagine them in more exalted dress. Apologies of this sort are a well worn convention of the novel, which since its beginnings has often sounded defensive about its modern, comic, realistic bias. To this tradition *Middlemarch* adds the Romantic principle that man is more completely understood when looked at in common life than in exceptional circumstances; George Eliot shares the Romantic conviction that only by representing common human nature can literature become a positive moral force, speaking for brotherhood instead of serving as an ornament for the élite. Yet when her narrator suggests an attitude along these lines he also implies that in achieving this new world much of value will be lost from the old. He makes, one feels, an unwilling democrat. He stands at the watershed, looking both ways, and his voice always carries regret. Sometimes he even seems to feel that comedy is a penance borne by a middle-class world incapable of grandeur. This is the attitude of the well-known passage in *The Mill on the Floss,* Book 4, chapter 1, where a memory of the castled Rhine recalls a vanished era of "living religious art and religious enthusiasm . . . the grand historic life of humanity."[7] A similar nostalgia, a wish to reconstitute a kind of epic in "our own vulgar era" is at work in *Middlemarch,* although it runs counter to the narrator's acceptance of "the difficulties of civilization," and is frequently subjected to various deflating ironies. At the end of the novel, in the "Finale," we find the narrator speaking as though bourgeois life could still be thought of as a kind of epic:

> Marriage, which has been the bourne of so many narratives, is still a great beginning, as it was to Adam and Eve, who kept their honeymoon in Eden, but had their first little one among the thorns and thistles of the wilderness. It is still the beginning of the home epic—the gradual conquest or irremediable loss of that complete union which makes the advancing years a climax, and age the harvest of sweet memories in common.
>
> (818)

Traditionally, of course, marriage is a comic theme, the final resolution of disorder. The narrator's intent is to begin where novels usually end—to show what really follows marriage. Thus George Eliot signals her impatience not only with the social inaccuracies of novels, but also with the comic mode itself. She may be said to be inaugurating a new mode—neither epic, because social conditions have changed; nor tragic, because she aims to represent common life; nor comic, because she offers no resolution, nor does she fully share the comic view. The tension of these constituent parts of her enterprise tends to pull the novel's tone in contrary directions.

Another conflict of mode in *Middlemarch* arises from the novel's claim to being a kind of history. The complex ironies of this theme account for some of the density of the novel's celebrated final paragraph, which sums up Dorothea's later life:

> Her finely-touched spirit had still its fine issues, though they were not widely visible. Her full nature, like that river of which Cyrus broke the strength, spent itself in channels which had no great name on the earth. But the effect of her being on those around her was incalculably diffusive: for the growing good of the world is partly dependent on unhistoric acts; and that things are not so ill with you and me as they might have been, is half owing to the number who lived faithfully a hidden life, and rest in unvisited tombs.
>
> (825)

The reference to Cyrus reminds us of Herodotus, whose history is also alluded to in chapter 11. Both references suggest that Western history has focused on the lives of men, ignoring or slighting women. Herodotus wrote of a monarch, a breaker of rivers; George Eliot, on the other hand, has recounted the "unhistoric acts" of a woman whose life was diverted, if not broken. In each case, the protagonist influences and represents the text. In the case of Herodotus, the result is called history, and even if its veracity is now doubted, still it is something known, established. In the case of George Eliot, the result is called a novel, something equivocal and problematic, whose function in the world is as self-contradictory as the life of its heroine. On the one hand, we are offered namelessness, invisibility, dammed-up rivers diverted and broken by male power, anonymous death.[8] On the other hand, Dorothea's spirit is said to have been so "finely-touched" that it bore "fine issues," a progeny dispersed like a rare gas to blend with and invigorate every molecule of air. Fecundity and death: every phrase in this passage pulls both ways. Does "diffusive" mean that Dorothea's life permeated the universe, or merely that it had that potential? If hidden lives diffuse "incalculably," how can their effect be evaluated? The difficulty is compounded by the possibility, suggested by several critics, that Dorothea's "fine issues" are the pages of *Middlemarch,* invisible in her world, but disseminated everywhere in ours.[9] This suggestion opens two complementary senses in which Dorothea's life is "unhistoric." Convention hinders women from doing famous deeds; Dorothea can only be the heroine of a fictional history. Since lives lived in novels are always "hidden" to a degree, and the tombs where they end cannot be visited, how can they contribute to the good of the world?

George Eliot tackles the problem by suggesting that fiction may have more in common with history than is generally supposed.[10] This theme begins at the point where the novel first turns away from Dorothea's story. Chapters 1-10 focus on the landed gentry of Dorothea's circle; then the Middlemarchers come bustling in, and we are invited to see them as examples of an historical process:

> Old provincial society had its share of this subtle movement: had not only its striking downfalls, its brilliant young professional dandies who ended by living up an entry with a drab and six children for their establishment, but also those less marked vicissitudes which are constantly shifting the boundaries of social intercourse, and begetting new consciousness of interdependence.
>
> (93)

Today's tragedies are deflated in the series, "brilliant young professional dandies": in bourgeois life there is no tragedy, only ridiculous economic disgrace. Writers are not poets anymore, but natural historians, scientists interested in "less marked vicissitudes." Their appropriate mode is a kind of comic history, which the narrator insists, tongue in cheek, is no upstart genre:

In fact, much the same sort of movement and mixture went on in old England as we find in older Herodotus, who also, in telling what had been, thought it well to take a woman's lot for his starting-point; though Io, as a maiden apparently beguiled by attractive merchandise, was the reverse of Miss Brooke, and in this respect perhaps bore more resemblance to Rosamond Vincy, who had excellent taste in costume, with that nymph-like figure and pure blondness which give the largest range to choice in the flow and colour of drapery.

(94)

The outrageously easy transition from Herodotus to drapery mocks the decadence of modern life, which, though it has lost the past, has still no other frame of reference. The modern idiom cheapens Io, "beguiled by attractive merchandise," and yet the narrator needs her, and the writer who celebrated her, to lend the novel some authenticity. The wit and irony of the passage do not deny that need—they demonstrate its complexity.

If history has roots in myth, may not fiction call itself history? George Eliot went on to develop this idea in *Daniel Deronda,* where all origins are seen as fictional, and art, science, and personal identity equally require "the make-believe of a beginning." This can be a liberating concept, but *Middlemarch,* which faces the past more than *Daniel Deronda* does, keeps apologizing for not having the scope of its literary ancestors. Herodotus wove the whole fabric of Greek history from a single thread. Even a writer as recent as Henry Fielding could take in more of the world than modern life has time to contemplate:

> A great historian, as he insisted on calling himself, who had the happiness to be dead a hundred and twenty years ago, and so to take his place among the colossi whose huge legs our living pettiness is observed to walk under, glories in his copious remarks and digressions as the least imitable part of his work, and especially in those initial chapters to the successive books of his history, where he seems to bring his armchair to the proscenium, and chat with us in all the lusty ease of his fine English. But Fielding lived when the days were longer (for time, like money, is measured by our needs), when summer afternoons were spacious, and the clock ticked slowly in the winter evenings. We belated historians must not linger after his example; and if we did so, it is probable that our chat would be thin and eager, as if delivered from a camp-stool in a parrot-house. I at least have so much to do in unravelling certain human lots, and seeing how they were woven and interwoven, that all the light I can command must be concentrated on this particular web, and not dispersed over the tempting range of relevancies called the universe.

(138-39)

This is of course a Ciceronic disclaimer—while deprecating his talent for digression, the narrator has actually demonstrated it. He has also managed to appropriate

Fielding's title of historian while distracting us with elaborate modesties about antecedent colossi. But though Fielding has given novelists the right to call their work history, this novel is "belated" history.[11] It must, says the narrator, keep up with the tempo of modern life, too hasty for leisurely digression. In consequence, *Middlemarch* will seem less personal than *Tom Jones,* where in fact Fielding speaks of his digressions as "a kind of mark or stamp, which may hereafter enable a very indifferent reader to distinguish what is true and genuine in this historic kind of writing, from what is false and counterfeit."[12] Fielding claims to have originated "this historic kind of writing"—"historic" meaning both "like history" and "history-making"—and his sense of doing a new thing is partly what confers authority on the enterprise. He speaks of originating as "true and genuine," like making accurate history. Thus in one move Fielding posits the idea that originality is truth, and his fiction true history. *Middlemarch,* its narrator implies, is no less true, but more anonymous. The coinage has been devalued, like so much else in modern life, and a true history must go forth without so much of the author's personality visible upon it.

For George Eliot, history in this age means evolution, slow and subtle, both in society at large and in the growth of individual character. Tracking these developments the narrator of *Middlemarch* sees himself as a kind of natural historian, but the author's attitude towards this scientific stance is more complicated than some modern critics have suggested.[13] In the first place, science does not rule the novel unopposed—it simply represents one of the competing movements in the novel's narrative style. George Eliot does seem to have hoped sometimes that the truths discoverable to fiction would turn out to be laws as elegant and lucid as those governing the physical universe. But several important episodes in *Middlemarch* tend to balance this enthusiasm for the scientific point of view with a sense that science has its own special liabilities.

"Who that cares much to know the history of man," the narrator asks in the first line of the novel, "and how that mysterious mixture behaves under the varying experiments of Time, has not dwelt, at least briefly, on the life of Saint Theresa?" Thus the novel itself is offered us as a kind of experiment, in which we are invited to see "how that mysterious mixture behaves." By implication, the narrator is outside the world of the experiment, a dispassionate observer. Similar language occurs in the opening lines of chapter 40: "In watching effects, if only of an electric battery, it is often necessary to change our place and examine a particular mixture or group at some distance from the point where the movement we are interested in was set up" (389). As we have already observed, the narrator sometimes uses his scientific detachment for satiric purposes. A good many critics have discussed this clinical distance in *Mid-*

dlemarch, but its alienating effect on the clinical observer has not been adequately recognized.[14] In chapter 3, for example, the narrator comments anthropologically on women's hairstyles of the period: "public feeling required the meagerness of nature to be dissimulated by tall barricades of frizzed curls and bows, never surpassed by any great race except the Feejeean" (27). This double satire says that fashion is no index of civilization, and that English provincials might as well have been savages anyway in those days. But the joke boomerangs on the narrator, isolating him in his superiority. Hoping, perhaps, to avoid that kind of isolation, the narrator sometimes makes fun of his own scientific postures, but in his laughter one can hear notes of menace and despair. In chapter 6, for instance, after watching Mrs. Cadwallader on her social rounds, the narrator boasts of his ability to perceive hidden causes of behavior:

> Even with a microscope directed on a water-drop we find ourselves making interpretations which turn out to be rather coarse; for whereas under a weak lens you may see a creature exhibiting an active voracity into which other smaller creatures actively play as if they were so many animated taxpennies, a stronger lens reveals to you certain tiniest hairlets which make vortices for these victims while the swallower waits passively at his receipt of custom. In this way, metaphorically speaking, a strong lens applied to Mrs. Cadwallader's match-making will show a play of minute causes producing what may be called thought and speech vortices to bring her the sort of food she needed.
>
> (58-59)

A "strong lens" may take us beyond "coarse" interpretations of behavior. But at that level of magnification, the universe has shrunk to a water-drop, and humanity has become an affair of hairlets and vortices, where all that matters is food. This is not objective science, but Swiftian satire, and as in Swift, the satire is double-edged. We may need to see the animal in man, but we lose some of our own humanity in the process.[15]

We have looked at passages where the narrator's scientific language has ironic overtones. In the "Prelude," however, an opening itself unstable in tone, the narrator seems ambivalent about science: he both adopts and disavows a scientific approach to his material. Referring to the modern Theresas, doomed to "a life of mistakes," he says:

> Some have felt that these blundering lives are due to the inconvenient indefiniteness with which the Supreme Power has fashioned the natures of women: if there were one level of feminine incompetence as strict as the ability to count three and no more, the social lot of women might be treated with scientific certitude.
>
> (5)

What gets laughed at here is partly the desire for "scientific certitude," which the narrator associates with narrow prejudice, an association the novel goes on to study in the character of Lydgate. It would also seem that the narrator hereby disclaims any pretensions of his own to scientific truth in his study of "the social lot of women."

What sort of enterprise is he engaged in, then? We have been invited to think of the novel as an experiment, to imagine the book as a kind of terrarium, a miniature ecosystem where all the flora and fauna of English provincial life are allowed to flourish. Into this little world a creature from another time and place is released, a modern Saint Theresa.[16] What will happen to her? The "Prelude" ends with this prediction:

> Here and there a cygnet is reared uneasily among the ducklings in the brown pond, and never finds the living stream in fellowship with its own oary-footed kind. Here and there is born a Saint Theresa, foundress of nothing, whose loving heart-beats and sobs after an unattained goodness tremble off and are dispersed among hindrances, instead of centering in some long-recognizable deed.
>
> (5)

Hardly the usual introduction to a novel—a promise of anticlimaxes and missed opportunity. Nor would this seem to be the most effective invitation to the witnessing of an experiment: if we already know the results, why go on? "Experiment," therefore, is only a partial way of describing what the novel is up to. More precisely, the experimental impulse is visibly in conflict here with another, older set of values.

In connection with this theme a curious parallel arises between the narrator and Lydgate, who is not only a scientist but also an investigator of human nature. Sometimes his studies sound like a version of the novel's own project:[17]

> Many men have been praised as vividly imaginative on the strength of their profuseness in indifferent drawing or cheap narration. . . . He for his part had tossed away all cheap inventions where ignorance finds itself able and at ease: he was enamoured of that arduous invention which is the very eye of research . . . he wanted to pierce the obscurity of those minute processes which prepare human misery and joy . . . that delicate poise and transition which determines the growth of happy or unhappy consciousness.
>
> (161-62)

Ironically, Lydgate cannot observe his own "delicate poise and transition." George Eliot can—she makes a detailed anatomy of Lydgate's moral decay, and one of the agents of that decay as she describes it is precisely that coldness of clinical perspective into which the narrator himself seems to fall at times. Perhaps the point is that all experiments have in them an element of cruelty. This theme emerges in chapter 15, where the narrator summarizes Lydgate's history before coming to Middlemarch. The young doctor had been studying in Paris, where among other things he conducted "some galvanic experiments":

> One evening, tired with his experimenting, and not being able to elicit the facts he needed, he left his frogs and rabbits to some repose under their trying and mysterious dispensation of unexplained shocks, and went on to finish his evening at the theatre of the Porte Saint Martin, where there was a melodrama which he had already seen several times; attracted, not by the ingenious work of the collaborating authors, but by an actress whose part it was to stab her lover, mistaking him for the evil-designing duke of the piece.
>
> (148)

Lydgate's experiments parody Providence, also a "trying and mysterious dispensation of unexplained shocks." The narrator's diction is ghoulishly fastidious ("some repose"), suggesting despite the humorous tone a monstrous lack of feeling on Lydgate's part. From his demonic laboratory the sentence magics him to the theater; he goes there "to finish his evening," as though the melodrama and his experiments were two acts in the same grand guignol, as though they satisfied the same impulse. Moreover, the passage invites one to suspect that Lydgate himself is a kind of experimental animal "attracted" by a cruel and deceptive bait that will transform him from master to slave. In that case, who can be the cruel experimenter but George Eliot?

An interesting feature of this little history is the ease with which Lydgate's scientific inquiries blend into his erotic delusion, as though the one prepared the way for the other. Is it simply that science is no guarantee against egoism, or does George Eliot suggest a moral flaw in the scientific outlook itself? An oddly macabre passage in chapter 36 may shed some light on this question. At this point Lydgate and Rosamond are engaged, and spinning the "gossamer web" of "young lovemaking." The narrator is amused at Lydgate's susceptibility, "in spite," as he says, "of experience supposed to be finished off with the drama of Laure." He continues:

> In spite too, of medicine and biology; for the inspection of macerated muscle or of eyes presented in a dish (like Santa Lucia's), and other incidents of scientific inquiry, are observed to be less incompatible with poetic love than a native dulness or a lively addiction to the lowest prose.
>
> (337)

Saint Lucy, it will be remembered, tore out her eyes rather than submit to a pagan lover who had admired them; she is often depicted holding a plate with her eyes on it. There is no evidence, however, that Lydgate is familiar with Christian iconography, nor would a believer associate Saint Lucy's sacrifice with a Petri dish. That grotesque association only occurs to the narrator.

At one level, of course, the narrator is only insisting that a sensitive man should have no trouble keeping his feelings and his intellect in separate compartments. But the violent juxtaposition of images from the legend of Saint Lucy creates another possible reading—that Lydgate's love is as brutal as his science. Lucia's eyes demand a more emotional response than "inspection," and in that light objectivity becomes pathological. Since, as I have pointed out above, the narrator sometimes adopts a similarly clinical view of his subjects, one is led to speculate on the possibly pathological impulse directing his interest, and by extension, George Eliot's as well, for like the scientist, the novelist can be accused of playing God.[18]

In this connection it is important to note that George Eliot frequently treats the theme of science in language full of theological echoes. To be sure, it is a secularizing consciousness that hears these echoes. For the narrator, the only God is Time, the cosmic scientist whose interest in man, if any, is a clinical one. In the narrator's universe, Providence has been replaced by the great Experiment, which may not even have an object. But this secularized world view is as dogmatic as any religion; witness the polemical tone of the novel's opening line: "Who that cares much to know the history of man, and how that mysterious mixture behaves under the varying experiments of Time, has not dwelt, at least briefly, on the life of Saint Theresa?" This practically amounts to a test of the reader's faith: one who has not dwelt "at least briefly" on the life of Theresa is no student of humanity; one who has is, ipso facto, a communicant, sharing the narrator's view—acknowledging, that is, the Experimenter's unconcern, and taking consolation only in the fact that humans have sometimes achieved greatness.

This valuing of human achievements implies a protest against the indifference of the Experimenter. But in the world of the novel, George Eliot herself, as she insists on pointing out, is the Experimenter—not indifferent, surely, but still the source of that "trying and mysterious dispensation of unexplained shocks" which we call, significantly, the novel's plot. The image keeps recurring of the little world in relation to which outside observers have divine or semi-divine status. A striking example occurs at the beginning of chapter 41. Here the narrator introduces an elaborate apology for a certain piece of plot machinery, Bulstrode's letter, which Raffles will casually pick up unburnt from Joshua Rigg's fender and use to wedge his pocket-flask, where it will remain, hidden and mute, until "chance" will bring it to light at the appropriate moment. Now George Eliot might well feel some embarrassment at having stooped to such a hoary old stage-device as this; here is how the narrator justifies it:

> Who shall tell what may be the effect of writing? If it happens to have been cut in stone . . . it may end by

letting us into the secret of usurpations and other scandals gossiped about long empires ago:—this world being apparently a huge whispering-gallery. Such conditions are often minutely represented in our petty lifetimes. As the stone which has been kicked by generations of clowns may come by curious little links of effect under the eyes of a scholar, through whose labours it may at last fix the date of invasions and unlock religions, so a bit of ink and paper which has long been an innocent wrapping or stop-gap may at last be laid open under the one pair of eyes which have knowledge enough to turn it into the opening of a catastrophe. To Uriel watching the progress of planetary history from the Sun, the one result would be just as much of a coincidence as the other.

Having made this rather lofty comparison, I am less uneasy in calling attention to the existence of low people by whose interference, however little we may like it, the course of the world is very much determined. It would be well, certainly, if we could help to reduce their number, and something might be done by not lightly giving occasion to their existence.

(402)

This passage contains some by-now familiar elements: deprecation of "petty" modern life, nostalgia for the aristocratic values of epic and tragedy, and ironic deflation of that lost world as seen by modern science, reading the secrets of the past only to find "scandals gossiped about long empires ago." The whispering-gallery, aimless and cold, mixing the trivial with the lasting, qualifies the optimistic idea of recovery. One also recognizes in the word "catastrophe" the narrator's idea that history and drama overlap, that the real and the imagined are intermingled. But the narrator adds a new and chilling note in the last remarks about reducing the number of "low people." We have noticed other apologies for obtruding "low" figures on the reader's attention, passages that laugh at one of the reasons why people read novels—the bourgeois hunger for a peep at the aristocracy. This time, however, the irony is darker; for a moment, the narrator seems to toy with the idea of eugenics: "something might be done by not lightly giving occasion to their existence." Of course, the reference is to low figures in novels, not in life.[19] At the level of plot, this is a slap at Peter Featherstone, whose bastard son, Joshua Rigg, inherits Featherstone's estate only to sell it. But Rigg, though denominated a "superfluity" by the Middlemarchers, functions in the plot as one of those "curious little links of effect" which bring about a catastrophe, as the chapter goes on to tell. Thus, while Featherstone may have lightly given "occasion" to Rigg's existence, George Eliot has not; she needs him and she is prepared to defend her procedure. At first reading, her comparison of the discovered letter to an archaeological find looks like a confession: she is publicly, theatrically embarrassed by her machinations.[20] But her embarrassment is a pose intended to be seen through: behind it lies a warning, almost a threat. Should the reader complain too much at the fortuitous

intervention of chance, he may tempt the novelist to a more sinister intervention, which would violate "the course of the world." The world of epic is gone; what we have is the whispering gallery, a good image for the novel itself. And though the novelist had better not be too promiscuous in generating minor figures to carry out the plot, she cannot rule out the "chance" interference of "low people." The business of playing God has enough complications already.

Modern criticism is so familiar with this kind of ironic self-consciousness in art that we sometimes underestimate the moral dilemma that it represented in George Eliot's time. The Victorian audience was deeply attracted to the spectacle of a miniature world governed by a visible Creator. Fiction was, in U. C. Knoepflmacher's words, a joint enterprise undertaken by writer and audience "to devise alternate models of reality in which . . . anxieties could be scrutinized and, ideally, be allayed, arrested, or countered."[21] Much of the contemporary criticism recognizes that attraction, more or less explicitly. In January 1873, for example, the *Edinburgh Review* remarked that "George Eliot and George Sand are inspired with a generous pity for their own creations, and whilst they punish are content to do their best to pardon."[22] Especially striking is one reviewer's biblical anguish over the ending of *The Mill on the Floss*:

> It is *not* right to carry on through these three marvellous volumes, and leave us at the last standing by the grave of the brother and sister, ready to lift up an accusatory cry, less to a beneficent deity than to the humanly-invented Arimanes of the universe,—"Why should such things be? Why has Thou made us thus?"[23]

Passages like this one suggest that one of the powers of fiction for Victorian readers was the opportunity of seeing through the eyes of the demiurge, or of holding him in colloquy.

Such an experience, on the other hand, was also potentially sacrilegious; to immerse oneself in a substitute world might be a dereliction of Christian duty. Carlyle, J. S. Mill, and Arnold worried about this possibility, and their fear is also testimony, albeit on the negative side, to the Victorian belief in the power of fiction.[24] It was the mishandling of that power that concerned some Victorian readers. As one critic put it,

> Fiction has . . . the great defect that it encourages both the writer and the reader to treat the most solemn problems of human life as things that are to be started, discussed, and laid aside at pleasure. The conduct of the story always affords an opening to escape from the responsibility of definite thought. It does even more than afford an opening—it forces the mind to escape from reflection into the study of outward life. The subjects started are, therefore, always too large for the manner in which they are handled.[25]

George Eliot's fictions recognize and address this problem through self-consciousness; they take visible responsibility for creating their alternate worlds. They are not only defending themselves: these fictions seek to establish community with the reader on the grounds that his own consciousness is creative, not merely mimetic; that his imagination is, in other words, as fictive as the novel's. This perception should not be confused with modern death-of-God philosophies. George Eliot's novels do not believe in ultimate unintelligibility; they are aware of what some modern critics call the scandal of language, but they do not think of it as a scandal. George Eliot's novels are, as George Levine has said, constructive enterprises.[26] They require that we become aware of the transformative power of words, so that we can take responsibility for our own fictions.

Notes

1. Cf. Michal Peled Ginsburg, "Pseudonym, Epigraphs, and Narrative Voice: *Middlemarch* and the Problem of Authorship," *ELH* 47, 3 (Fall 1980): 542-58; *pace* Robert Alter, *Partial Magic: The Novel as a Self-Conscious Genre* (Berkeley: Univ. of California Press, 1975), p. 220, a surprisingly late description of *Middlemarch* as the kind of "traditional realistic novel" which criticism can only approach in "the indicative mode," unlike self-conscious novels, which "lend themselves to analytic criticism." Some important earlier revisionists: Quentin Anderson, "George Eliot in *Middlemarch*," in Boris Ford, ed., *The Pelican Guide to English Literature*, 7 vols., *From Dickens to Hardy* (London and New York: Penguin Books, 1958, rev. edn., 1966), pp. 274-93; David B. Carroll, "Unity Through Analogy: An Interpretation of *Middlemarch*," *VS* [*Victorian Studies*] 2, 4 (June 1959): 305-16, 305; Barbara Hardy, *The Novels of George Eliot: A Study in Form* (New York: Oxford Univ. Press, 1959, 1963), pp. 155-66; W. J. Harvey, *The Art of George Eliot* (London: Chatto and Windus, 1961), especially chaps. 1 and 3.

2. J. Hillis Miller reaches this conclusion from observing how the novel displays "the irreducible figurative or metaphorical nature of all language": Miller, "Optic and Semiotic in *Middlemarch*," from *The Worlds of Victorian Fiction*, ed. Jerome H. Buckley (Harvard Univ. Press, 1975), rpt. in Harold Bloom, ed., *George Eliot* (New York: Chelsea House, 1986), pp. 109-110.

3. E.g. Sandra M. Gilbert and Susan Gubar, *The Madwoman in the Attic: The Woman Writer and the Nineteenth-Century Literary Imagination* (New Haven and London: Yale Univ. Press, 1979), pp. 69, 525-26; John Kucich, *Repression in Victorian Fiction: Charlotte Brontë, George Eliot, and Charles Dickens* (Berkeley: Univ. of California Press, 1987), p. 116.

4. Cf. Penny Boumelha, "George Eliot and the End of Realism," in Sue Roe, ed., *Women Reading Women's Writing* (New York: St. Martin's Press, 1987), pp. 15-35, esp. 19-26. Boumelha warns against anachronistic and "damagingly author-based" thinking in some feminist studies of George Eliot, but her critique can be applied to any criticism that is not aware of itself as "an *appropriation* of the work . . . rather than a revelation of any pre-existing belief or intention of the author."

5. Cf. Dorothea Barrett, *Vocation and Desire: George Eliot's Heroines* (New York and London: Routledge, 1989), pp. 28-30. Noting that the gender of George Eliot's narrators "is open to endless debate," Barrett thinks Gilbert and Gubar "have most nearly resolved the problem when they claim: 'Doing in a woman's way a traditionally male task of knowing, combining "a man's mind and a woman's heart," Eliot makes such gender-based categories irrelevant . . . this narrator becomes an authentic "we"' (Gilbert and Gubar, p. 523)." Nevertheless, Barrett opts for the female pronoun, partly, she says, "in opposition to the critics who avoid it, one suspects, because they consider George Eliot's narrators too rational to be female." But what if the book were satirizing that "rationality"? Or, more precisely, that *apparent* rationality, for I agree that what's interesting about the narrator is his/her lack of control over the book. What I hear, however, below "the apparently smooth surface" of the narrative, is not Barrett's "anxious rushing back and forth between extremes," but the ironic tone of one who is frequently aware that none of the kinds of discourse he deploys can fully apprehend the experience in front of him. I say "he" and "him" because I suspect that the book makes visible this embarrassment of the narrator as a way of exploring and gently satirizing the public voice that many nineteenth-century readers would have expected from "George Eliot."

6. Page references in this essay are to the Clarendon edition of *Middlemarch*, ed. David Carroll (Oxford: Clarendon Press, 1986).

7. Clarendon edn., ed. Gordon S. Haight (Oxford: Clarendon Press, 1980), p. 238.

8. Cf. Suzanne Graver, *George Eliot and Community: A Study in Social Theory and Fictional Form* (Berkeley: Univ. of California Press, 1984), p. 91; Mary Wilson Carpenter, *George Eliot and the Landscape of Time: Narrative Form and Protestant Apocalyptic History* (Chapel Hill: Univ. of North Carolina Press, 1986), pp. 107-11, 208, notes 12, 14, and 16.

9. J. Hillis Miller, "Narrative and History," *ELH* 41, 3 (Fall 1974): 455-73; Ginsburg, pp. 554 f.

10. Miller, "Narrative and History," pp. 459 f.

11. Cf. U. C. Knoepflmacher, *George Eliot's Early Novels: The Limits of Realism* (Berkeley: Univ. of California Press, 1968), pp. 15-16, 28-34; Michael McKeon, *The Origins of the English Novel, 1600-1740* (Baltimore and London: Johns Hopkins Univ. Press, 1987), pp. 384, 405-409. Knoepflmacher claims that George Eliot "made sure to dissociate herself from his [Fielding's] example." But the passage under consideration articulates connections with Fielding at the same time as it points out differences. Knoepflmacher's reading misses Fielding's ironic self-consciousness about literary authority (McKeon, pp. 384, 405-409), a quality in his writing that George Eliot enjoys and in her own way continues, while recognizing the new distances imposed by an increasingly anonymous culture.

12. Henry Fielding, *The History of Tom Jones, A Foundling,* bk. 9, chap. 1 ("Of Those Who Lawfully May, and of Those Who May Not, Write such Histories as This"), the Wesleyan edition, 2 vols., ed. Fredson Bowers, with an introduction and commentary by Martin C. Battestin (Oxford: Oxford and Wesleyan Univ. Press, 1975), p. 487.

13. Sally Shuttleworth, *George Eliot and Nineteenth-Century Science: The Make-Believe of Beginning* (Cambridge: Cambridge Univ. Press, 1984); George Levine, "The Scientific Texture of *Middlemarch*," from *The Realistic Imagination: English Fiction from Frankenstein to Lady Chatterley* (Chicago: Univ. of Chicago Press, 1981), rpt. in *George Eliot,* ed. Harold Bloom (New York: Chelsea House, 1986), pp. 187-202; Felicia Bonaparte, *Will and Destiny: Morality and Tragedy in George Eliot's Novels* (New York: New York Univ. Press, 1975), esp. chap. 2; Robert A. Greenberg, "Plexuses and Ganglia: Scientific Allusion in *Middlemarch*," *NCF* [*Nineteenth-Century Fiction*] 30, 1 (June 1975): 33-52; Michael York Mason, "*Middlemarch* and Science: Problems of Life and Mind," *RES* [*Review of English Studies*] n.s. 22, 86 (May 1971): 151-69; U. C. Knoepflmacher, *George Eliot's Early Novels,* and "*Middlemarch*: The Balance of Progress," in *Religious Humanism and the Victorian Novel: George Eliot, Walter Pater, and Samuel Butler* (Princeton: Princeton Univ. Press, 1965); and Bernard J. Paris, *Experiments in Life: George Eliot's Quest for Values* (Detroit: Wayne State Univ. Press, 1965).

14. Cf. Graver, pp. 66 f. No doubt George Eliot was influenced by the Comparative Method of Comte, Spencer, and Tönnies, but her art is a good deal more ironic than a summary of its intellectual influences can suggest.

15. Cf. Steven Marcus, "Literature and Social Theory: Starting in with George Eliot," in *Representations: Essays on Literature and Society* (New York: Random House, 1975), pp. 196-200, 206 f.

16. Cf. Bonaparte, p. 80: Dorothea is not a St. Theresa, "but only someone who wishes she had been."

17. Cf. Shuttleworth, pp. 142-46; George Levine, "George Eliot's Hypothesis of Reality," *NCF* 35, 1 (June 1980): 7-15; Levine, "The Scientific Texture of *Middlemarch*." p. 201; John P. McGowan, "The Turn of George Eliot's Realism," *NCF* 35, 2 (September 1980): 174 f.; Alan Mintz, *George Eliot and the Novel of Vocation* (Cambridge, MA: Harvard Univ. Press, 1978), pp. 97-102; Bonaparte, pp. 3-12; Paris, pp. 25-51, 116-26. These critics have assumed, without distinguishing author from narrator, that Lydgate embodies a positive representation of George Eliot's own practice as a novelist.

18. Cf. Hardy, p. 116: "there is no President of the Immortals" sporting with George Eliot's characters.

19. Cf. Alexander Welsh, *George Eliot and Blackmail* (Cambridge, MA and London: Harvard Univ. Press, 1985), pp. 253-56.

20. Cf. Neil D. Isaacs, "*Middlemarch*: Crescendo of Obligatory Drama," *NCF* 18, 1 (June 1963): 21-34, 28-31: George Eliot talks about her characters without ever "giving the impression that she is pulling the strings."

21. U. C. Knoepflmacher, *Laughter and Despair: Readings in Ten Novels of the Victorian Era* (Berkeley and London: Univ. of California Press, 1971), p. xii.

22. Quoted in John Holmstrom and Laurence Lerner, eds., *George Eliot and her Readers: A Selection of Contemporary Reviews* (New York: Barnes and Noble, 1966), p. 106.

23. *Macmillan's Magazine* (April 1861), quoted in Holmstrom and Lerner, pp. 38-41.

24. Graver, p. 10.

25. *Saturday Review* (14 April 1860), quoted in Holmstrom and Lerner, pp. 28 f.

26. Levine, "George Eliot's Hypothesis of Reality," pp. 1-28; Levine, "The Scientific Texture of *Middlemarch*," pp. 187-202.

Carol Siegel (essay date spring 1998)

SOURCE: Siegel, Carol. "'This thing I like my sister may not do': Shakespearean Erotics and a Clash of Wills in *Middlemarch*." *Style* 32, no. 1 (spring 1998): 36-59.

[In the following essay, Siegel analyzes the link between Eliot's feminism and her depictions of sexuality in the novel.]

At my local card shop a little book of romantic pictures is on display for Valentine's Day.[1] The only text is Shakespeare's "Sonnet 116." The pictures are all of heterosexual couples. Apparently it remains difficult for many people to think of the first hundred and twenty-six sonnets as homoerotic, yet it seems equally difficult for readers, other than some scholars in Renaissance studies, to see them as anything other than romantic. And when we read the sonnets addressed directly to the beloved, we may not be able to avoid a sense of voyeuristic eavesdropping. The ordinary response of voyeurs is to imagine themselves within the scene by identifying with one of its participants. Reading "Sonnet 22"'s, "My glass shall not persuade me I am old, / So long as youth and thou are of one date" in the context provided by "Sonnet 18"'s famous assertion, "thy eternal summer shall not fade," the reader may feel most seductively called to identification not with the other reader whom the apostrophe evokes, but with the writer whose love both confers and is immortality. Although George Eliot's *Middlemarch* usually has quite a different effect on readers, because Eliot brings Shakespeare's sonnets into her novel, if only briefly, eavesdropping on their interchange can draw us into other scenes of literary relation, suggesting different, because differently gendered, pleasures, frustrations, and pains in the erotics of authorship.

Like Shakespeare, Eliot changes with the times, for new readings emerge with every new group of readers. In an overview of the reception of *Middlemarch,* Gillian Beer notes that while Eliot's contemporaries recognized the centrality of "feminist issues" to the novel, these issues received almost no attention from "critics of the next 100 years" (148). Then by 1976 Eliot was so regularly castigated by feminist critics that Zelda Austen entitled an article "Why Feminist Critics Are So Angry with George Eliot."[2] Laying out a pattern for much later feminist criticism, Austen and Kathleen Blake, in "*Middlemarch* and the Woman Question," published the same year, defend Eliot both against the charge that her novels inadequately address the feminist questions they raise and, further, that Eliot denies her heroines the same sort of success at transcending gender roles she had enjoyed. Working against the idea that women's fiction should provide liberatory role models, both Austen and Blake praise Eliot for realistically depicting the possibilities open to most nineteenth-century women and for refusing to set up as a model the extraordinary person (herself) at the expense of more compromised and less successful women. While feminist objections to Eliot do continue, defenses on the grounds of realism also continue to appear. According to these defenses, Eliot's tendency to resolve her heroines' life crises with marriage becomes fidelity to the truth of ordinary women's lives. Thus some critics find a model not in the fiction, but through it, and Eliot is remade as an exemplary feminist author.

In the last twenty years, Eliot's novels, her cultural authority, and her egalitarian relationship with George Henry Lewes all figure prominently in the narratives feminist critics have made of the rise of women writers in the nineteenth century. Because of her balanced and deliberately sensible discussions of "love problems" and the common understanding that her own life was defined by both companionate love and respectfully received work, Eliot is perhaps not the first writer who comes to mind when one thinks about the impact on prose style of wildly romantic longings. Nor is focus on the depiction of romantic longing a topic that initially seems compatible with a feminist approach to Eliot. But now that Eliot's place in literature is secured without doubt, perhaps we can acknowledge another Eliot, the one who, at what would seem to have been her last possible moment for romantic abandon, married John Cross, a good-looking admirer twenty years her junior. While Eliot probably had motivations here other than the enjoyment of a charming spouse, this marriage, because of her fame, inevitably contributed to the still ongoing work of transforming the position of woman author from that of ungendered observer to actor in that theater of love which by the very nature of eroticism is never far removed from the theater of cruelty.

If one sees a feminist style in Eliot's transformation of herself as author from ungendered objectivity to passionate erotic engagement, this reinvention of the authorial subject position is of a different sort than usually receives much critical attention. Yet, as Phyllis Rose's comparative biography of Victorian marriages, *Parallel Lives,* pointed out some time ago, Eliot's marriage to Cross belongs to a recurrent pattern in nineteenth-century literary circles among women who had achieved some autonomy. The most notable of these is the passionate union of Elizabeth Barrett and Robert Browning. Even the *Norton Anthology of Literature by Women,* which characteristically downplays any hint of romance in its authors' lives, admits that Browning's "veneration of her work was to change her life" ([Gilbert and Gubar] 258). One is left to speculate that the handsome younger poet's worship of her person did not have an entirely negative effect on Barrett Browning's morale either. Among women who might have been considered past the age of girlish susceptibility to romance were Charlotte Brontë, who, in middle age, married her father's curate, and William Makepeace Thackeray's daughter Anne, who at 40 married a young man just out of university.[3] Allowing Anne fame by association, one might consider each of these stories as potentially redefining the relation between audience and literary luminary. This sort of redefinition emphasizes the erotics of reading, the proximity of intellectual and sexual excitement, by moving from the literary world to the actual world the delightful confusibility of the reader and muse that so often appears textually in the form of an address to the beloved. Such moves are familiar features of male authored texts. But something more worthy of comment occurs when a woman transforms the polite phrase "Reader, I married him," from an address to a third party into a remark on the reader himself. This public assertion of espousal confounds the conventional separation between the subject positions of male, beloved, and reader.

Authors as well as critics have often commented on the masturbatory quality of literature that touches on love. In such literature, as authors explore what excites them and also what disturbs them, they move through intersections of pleasure and pain up to the brink of loss of control, while trying to maintain a grip on the slippery text. Because such experimentation with strong feeling takes place within the closed system of the text, writing about love can be, like masturbation, an experience that allows one the full amount of control attainable while giving in to eroticism. When the reader enters the picture, however, the illusion of authorial control is as thoroughly shattered as is the illusion of sexual control when the masturbatory act has an acknowledged observer. The reader's intervention into the process of textual meaning-making is traditionally understood as a sort of rivalry with the author for control of the text. But just as reader response to a text works against authorial control of signification, so, too, readerly presence disrupts the author's relation to the text as a controllable site of pleasure and turns private excitement into public spectacle. Because each reader literally embodies loss of authorial control, to embrace and even more to espouse one reader is to attempt to enfold him into the text's enactment of the author's erotics. Writing the reader into the erotic/romantic script means turning display into intercourse. For female authors, this process entails remaking oneself from erotic object to erotic subject.

Such maneuvering to enunciate a subject position within the literary text involves issues both of gender politics and of style. Elizabeth Grosz suggests that "neither the author, the reader, nor the content of a text explains how we are able to designate it as feminist." Rather, she claims, "there is a distinctive feminist style of writing" (17). For Grosz, the feminist text is one whose style "render[s] the patriarchal or phallocentric pre-

sumptions governing its contexts and commitments visible" in such a way as to question "the power of these presumptions in the production, reception, and assessment of texts" and to "facilitate the production of new and perhaps unknown, unthought discursive spaces" (22-23). More important than an author's identification as a feminist is a text's "problematiz[ation of] the standard masculinist ways in which the author [conventionally] occupies the position of enunciation" (23). Because the feminism that inheres in such self-stylings is elusive, Grosz urges feminist critics to look carefully for "some trace of the process of production" from which we may read the author's feminism (19). It is in this spirit that I will closely examine two areas of *Middlemarch,* one the depiction of Will Ladislaw, which continues to receive intense critical scrutiny, and the other Eliot's references to Shakespeare's sonnets, references which are frequently dismissed as so slight as to be insignificant.

As his name might suggest, *Middlemarch*'s most complex engagement with Shakespeare's sonnets centers on the characterization of Will. Will is not only Shakespeare's nickname, but a name that recurs in such sonnets as "134," "135," and "136" in apparent reference to both the poet-narrator and the fair youth he loves. If Will Ladislaw is investigated as an intertextual node where the erotics of the sonnets meet those of *Middlemarch* and Eliot defines herself in relation to Shakespeare, a new reading of the novel's troubling conclusion becomes possible, one that comments not so much on what was available to nineteenth-century heroines as on what could be represented by Victorian women novelists.

The critical attention afforded to Will's ultimate failure as a romantic hero is easily explained by the current interest in whether sexuality and the subjectivity from which sexuality comes are textually constructed, and if so, to what extent. One might expect critics concerned with these issues to have a corresponding increasing interest in the places in narratives of romantic love where literary conventions seem to block the fulfillment of a promise of release from the strictures of misogynist binarism. For if texts directly inform our identities, then it would seem that the conventions that shape love narratives toward disappointingly limited resolutions must act upon our lives in somewhat the same ways. Realist novels should be of special interest because their conventions derive from belief in the possibility of accurate representation of social situations and, in turn, they have traditionally been read as authoritative records by many who write history or create accounts of the inner life. Until very recently, many social historians and psychoanalytic theorists have looked to the realist novel for help in achieving a vision of what was possible in the world. As is evident from even a cursory knowledge of the development of psychoanalytic theory, theories that arose in part from generalizations about life as it appears in the realist novel have had far reaching impact on current social practices. For this reason, investigation of the workings of Victorian marriage-plot novels can lead beyond attempts to reconstruct nineteenth-century social history.[4] Readings of marriage plots could well lead to an interrogation of the bases of current concepts of sexuality. Thus the weight of the question that has vexed professional and casual readers of George Eliot's *Middlemarch*: why is marriage to Will Ladislaw not a satisfying solution to the problems of Dorothea Brooke?

While a sense of diminuendo comes to most readers at the end of *Middlemarch,* the majority of critics take the position that we must read the novel's conclusion as happy, within the context of nineteenth-century women's literary conventions. Most critics, like Austen and Blake, begin from the premise that these conventions reflect an actual social situation. Readings that focus on the conventions highlight their ideologically determined limitations. For instance, Rachel Blau DuPlessis sees *Middlemarch*'s conclusion as characteristic of "contradictions" in how Victorian women writers transmit a cultural ideology that demands both heroic individualism and domesticity: "As a gendered subject in the nineteenth century, [Dorothea] has barely any realistic options in work or vocation, so her heroism lies in defining herself as a free agent, freely choosing the romance that nonetheless, in one form or another, is her fate. The female hero turns herself into a heroine; this is her last act as an individual agent" (14). But do the limitations on Dorothea's life come from her being "a gendered subject in the nineteenth century" or from a specific nineteenth-century narrative tradition that is not identical to women's social reality?

Elizabeth Langland argues that although "the limited fates of [Eliot's] heroines have been read as part of her compelling realism," the novels actually offer a version of realism predicated on ignoring the power middle-class women exercised as managers of the domestic sphere (90). In *Middlemarch,* not only is "social life represented only insofar as it confirms the triviality of women's lives," but the adjective most frequently applied to women's domestic experiences is "little" (Langland 98-99). Marriage shrinks Dorothea into relative inconsequence, but only because within the "realism" about domestic life and gender relations that Eliot is helping to create, Dorothea is restricted from acting except to diminish herself. Although Eliot maintains the illusion of free choice in *Middlemarch,* "society emerges as a monolith of oppression rather than as a medium for interactions" (Langland 97). Because the novel is far from monovocal, Dorothea's transformation traverses at least two competing narratives.

Because of the novel's fidelity to the concept of individualism and its reliance on the concept of free agency

to provide its moral grounding, the very choices that mark Dorothea as virtuous cause her to pass from one narrative and its discourse(s) into another. Since to remain virtuous after she becomes a wife means that she must shrink to fit the "little" world of women, Dorothea diminishes into subordination to her man. As she moves from the nineteenth-century capitalist narrative of free individualism to Eliot's particular narrative of domesticity, Dorothea is reconstructed from a subject who makes significant choices in love to a woman who finds her significance as the object of another's love. This journey suggests that a woman's claiming of the subject position in love ironically initiates her entrance into a relation with man in which she is inevitably made the love object. Because she loses subjectivity in relation to a specific man, when readers attempt to recover Dorothea as subject, to examine her "choices" and "acts," they must turn the critical gaze to Will Ladislaw. Consequently, questions about the novel's representation of Dorothea's choice and will, entail questions about her choice of Will.

Will Ladislaw is a disappointing character, and he could hardly be otherwise. In a novel that displaces onto Protestant liberalism the passion of Catholic female mysticism, that places its Saint Theresa in the nineteenth-century English provinces, and replaces the saint's anti-materialism with faith in social work and education (while denying that women can ever be leaders in those fields), Will seems called upon to stand in for God as the love object who confers meaning on the life of his worshipful servant. Of course, he is doomed to seem puny, inadequate in comparison. Still, the depression with which many readers are overwhelmed at the novel's conclusion seems out of proportion to Will's failure to elevate Dorothea's passion to a transcendent level. After all, not only were we told from the beginning that Dorothea is no Saint Theresa, but, furthermore, all experienced readers know they are reading a marriage-plot novel offering emotional, not metaphysical, pleasures. Why then, do many readers feel that the love affair comes down to earth, but also comes down to nothing? The problem seems to be that Will's presence in the narrative promises so much and yields so little.

Will's failure, like his promise, lies in the register of the erotic. The text, like Will himself, offers the home in place of the cloister and erotic love in place of religious devotion. To be satisfying, such a narrative must at the very least suggest that the heroine's experience of love includes moments of passionate transcendence of the ordinary, not the unbroken descent into domestic practicality signaled when Dorothea pulls back from their first embrace to begin prattling about household management (560). This conclusion of chapter 83 disturbingly echoes the long, drawn-out treatment of the failed marriage of the parallel couple Lydgate and Rosamond. Both marriages go from strong physical attraction to boring concern with domestic finance. While Dorothea's interest in such things adds to her characterization as admirably unselfish in contrast to Rosamond, it does little to mitigate the dismal picture of marriage drawn by the preceding 559 pages and does nothing to reassure the reader that true love can lead to legalized erotic pleasure. Marriage is presented simply and, in the case of Will and Dorothea's love scene, concisely as a place where virtuous wives must support husbands' ambitions and worry about the bills.

Yet the novel is not devoid of suggestions of the erotic. If it were, the dilemma caused by Dorothea's first marriage would seem meaningless. Eliot bombards the reader with not very subtle messages that Dorothea's mistake in overvaluing Casaubon's academic research is symptomatic of a completely mistaken, because too exclusively intellectual, notion of marriage. Repeated references to her sensual beauty show us that Dorothea would have been wrong to bestow herself even on a man who was intellectually worthy of her support without also making sure not only that he was physically worthy, but also that his ability to appreciate beauty would do her justice. But the erotic space in which such justice could be done always seems elsewhere, outside the text. No passionate attraction is suggested by the union of Celia and Sir James, for physical proximity and social circumstances dictate their choice of each other. Eliot hints that Dorothea and Casaubon's marriage is not consummated, but in any case it could hardly seem less erotic.

Likewise, the other "love problems" in the text are de-eroticized. For instance, we are told that while Mary Garth feels a stronger attraction to Mr. Farebrother than to Fred, duty and familiarity bind her to the latter. Similarly, Lydgate's relationship with Rosamond has the potential for romance, but that potential remains unrealized. The courtship and early marriage are dramatized through a series of ironic misunderstandings, emphasized in the proposal scene, about what the other expects from marriage. Rosamond, envisioning their honeymoon exclusively as an opportunity to display her new evening gowns to Lydgate's aristocratic relatives, begs that it last more than the one week Lydgate had planned. Lydgate gives in because he "readily understood that she might wish to lengthen the sweet time of their double solitude" (242). "Double solitude" is telling here, of course, for it shows the reader the unlikeliness of their coming together either in the polite or the sexual sense. Not only does this scene reveal Eliot's characteristic view of marriage as an ironic site of miscommunication caused by blind self-absorption, it also places that miscommunication physically in an image of the wife dressing herself at the same moment as the husband would like to see her undress. Here Eliot severs essence and sexuality as Rosamond reveals her "nature" through her lack of interest in revealing her body.

An erotic space in which couples eagerly bare their bodies in mutual passion seems impossible within the locations actually depicted in *Middlemarch,* but our awareness of the erotic as a possibility absent from these specific places creates a sense of bitter irony in scenes like the one between Lydgate and Rosamond. This awareness comes from the text itself, from the places where the erotic inheres not in physically accessible space but in memory and speculation, in half-told stories such as that of Will's grandmother, Julia, and in evocation of other literary texts, such as Shakespeare's sonnets.

Many critics have followed U. C. Knoepflmacher in arguing that reference to sixteenth- and seventeenth-century sonnets plays a notable role in *Middlemarch.* Because specific references to Shakespeare's sonnets figure most prominently in the text, they have received the most attention. The predominant view has been that Eliot uses Shakespeare's sonnets to represent a courtly aesthetic and eroticism irreconcilable with the "prosaic" realities of nineteenth-century English life (Knoepflmacher 54). Otice Sircy sees the question of representation in *Middlemarch* as determined by Eliot's faith in the possibility of making a novel reflect reality and truth. While acknowledging that the journal entries on Shakespeare's sonnets that Eliot made from 1869 to 1872 (the year of *Middlemarch*'s publication) suggest admiration as well as criticism of Shakespeare's style and themes, Sircy argues that ultimately Eliot neither saw the sonnets as "a product of an aesthetic she trusts, nor [as] reflections of a reality with which she can sympathize" (225). But, as Sircy observes, Eliot's criticisms of the sonnets in her journals are qualified by such statements as "Nevertheless, I love the sonnets better & better whenever I return to them. They are tunes that for some indefinable reason suit my frame" (223). One is left to wonder why, if the sonnets are so opposed to Eliot's sense of objective reality and therefore what she feels it is the highest duty of art to reflect, they should not only so strongly influence her mind, but also reverberate within her body.

Marianne Novy claims that though Eliot, in her notebook, dismisses the majority of Shakespeare's sonnets as "artificial products" shaped by an adherence to Petrarchan convention, she objects only to the traditional form and not the specific content of each sonnet (*Engaging* [*Engaging with Shakespeare*] 96). In some instances, as Novy shows, Eliot clearly makes this distinction between the sonnets' subject matter, which she sometimes admires, and their form, which she considers derivative and artificial. But, as Novy herself says, the sonnets Eliot selects, both in her notebook and by allusion in the novel, as the most "tedious" are the ones in which Shakespeare departs from tradition in order to urge the beloved to procreate (*Engaging* 108). In Eliot's treatment of Shakespeare's first seventeen sonnets, as

Sircy and Knoepflmacher argue, the allusions create a contrast between the artificiality Eliot associates with conventional representation of erotic experience and the realism she claims for her own technique.

Rather than a striking innovation of realism, such contrast is one of the oldest motifs in literature. Shakespeare himself uses it in several of the sonnets. For example, in 21, the poet-narrator favorably compares his style with the Petrarchan, exclaiming "O, let me true in love but truly write." In 59, in a less confident mood, he achieves a similar effect by conceding that there may be "nothing new" in literary creation, while he continues to stress his loyalty to the truth of his subject. That Eliot should make similar claims for the accuracy of her mimicry of the real is unsurprising. What is more interesting is that she seems much more ambivalent about the gap between literature and life than many of her critics give her credit for. Yes, Eliot sees Shakespeare as a negative model of falsification and artificiality, but she also often seems to be implicitly comparing her own situation as author to the erotic power of the poet-narrator's subject position.

There is an enabling aspect to Eliot's much remarked identification with Shakespeare. Working from the nineteenth-century understanding of Shakespeare as unusually sympathetic to women, Novy stresses ways Eliot's readings of the plays focus on women's friendship and the active role of women in love affairs ("*Daniel Deronda*" ["*Daniel Deronda* and George Eliot's Female Re-Vision of Shakespeare"] 90-91). She concludes that, "Reading Shakespeare from a woman's viewpoint, emphasizing qualities in him and in his characters that crossed gender boundaries, Eliot reimagined a literary tradition that she could claim as her own" ("*Daniel Deronda*" 104). But what happens when gender boundaries are crossed in this way? Could Eliot have fully enjoyed what she denies Dorothea: the freedom to choose a culturally feminized fate and, having thus chosen, the power to continue to act as a subject? Critics have long remarked that Eliot denies her characters the sort of power that she enjoyed both in her life as an author and with Lewes (let alone with Cross). Authorial power is especially important because it is in Eliot's self-styling as an author that we look for evidence of her text's feminism. If, disguised as an androgynous Shakespeare, Eliot unproblematically experienced transgression of gender norms, it seems rather unfair that Dorothea diminishes into a heroine as the price of acting heroically. But here it seems that Eliot treats her heroine equitably, for she presents Dorothea's final enclosure within Victorian marriage conventions through intertextualization to reflect her author's entrapment by narrative conventions. Dorothea crosses the border into the domestic plot because within the strictures of Eliot's realism that is the only place Eliot's Shakespearean fantasies can lead.

Eliot's letters provide an extratextual clue to one of the forms her Shakespearean fantasies took. Novy claims Eliot's condemnation of Act 2, Scene 4 of *Two Gentlemen of Verona* comes from her rejection of feminine "passivity" ("*Daniel Deronda*" 92). But the scene's climactic transfer of Valentine's affections from Silvia to Proteus also typifies the privileging of male friendship over heterosexual love so characteristic of the sonnets. In the scene, Julia, who loves Proteus, is disguised as a page and stands by as Proteus threatens to rape Silvia, who steadfastly states her preference for his friend Valentine. Valentine intervenes and Proteus quickly apologizes; his apology is accepted by Valentine, who then offers him Silvia. As Novy points out, Eliot wrote of her "disgust" at Valentine's behavior in the scene ("*Daniel Deronda*" 91-92). Yet some scenes in Eliot's work suggest that she could not entirely dismiss the vision of a love like Valentine's for Proteus. This sort of love is eager, almost unconditional. It can be satisfied by any sort of gesture, and it leaps over the lowest acts to meet the beloved. Dorothea's night of inner struggle after surprising Will and Rosamond together typifies the same type of highly romantic representation of love. In ***Middlemarch,*** such depictions of unwavering devotion suggest not only that Eliot retained as a standard an image of poetic love of the sort Shakespeare assigns to male-male love, but that she also used this image as a signpost pointing the way to that elsewhere in which passion, without necessitating the death of the lovers, could finally win out over domesticity and practicality. Some moments in the text point to "Another part of the forest," as clearly as the stage direction for Valentine's love scene. They suggest Eliot's longing for a place outside conventional Victorian heterosexuality, a place where she could wear the "androgynous" not-quite-man disguise her culture demanded of a woman writer, and (like Shakespeare's Julia) could look on at a love scene by which she would be transformed upon entering.

Some of what is entailed in assuming such a disguise is suggested in Judith Butler's theory of gender melancholia, first articulated in *Gender Trouble*. Seeing the construction of gender as performative, Butler says that the performance of gender cannot be completed; instead, it is made up of continually reiterated citations of an ultimately unattainable ideal (57-65). This process of construction is melancholic in that each subject's performance of gender comes from "the renunciation of the possibility of homosexuality" and consequent identification with a lost and/or forbidden love object. According to Butler, heterosexuality is constructed out of the remains of an unacknowledged desire for a same sex object. Thus, "The straight man *becomes* (mimes, cites, appropriates, assumes the status of) the man he 'never' loved and 'never' grieved; the straight woman *becomes* the woman she 'never' loved and 'never' grieved" (*Bodies* [*Bodies That Matter*] 235, 236). "Drag" presentations of one's self as the "opposite" sex are more complicated because in them the "unacknowledged loss" acted out is the loss of the sexual identity forbidden by a culture in which heterosexuality is compulsory. Drag has a conservative element because it "allegorizes some set of melancholic incorporative fantasies that stabilize *gender*"; its performance "is an effort to negotiate cross-gendered identification" without refusing the normative descriptions and exclusions on which gender difference depends (*Bodies* 235).

It is useful to approach Eliot's assumption of a Shakespearean persona in relation to this model for three reasons. First, because Shakespeare's putative "androgynous" sympathy with female characters authorizes her own representation of heroines like Dorothea, Eliot's identification with him as an unusually empathetic genius is deeply invested in maintaining gender difference. As Novy explains, "For Eliot, the idea of sympathy mediated between her culture's ideal of womanhood, associated at its highest with maternity, and her culture's ideal of art, associated at its highest with Shakespeare" (*Engaging* 112). In emulating Shakespeare's sympathy, Eliot's writing gains value because it simultaneously inhabits two spheres that late nineteenth-century culture usually treats as rigidly separated: masculine rationality and feminine emotion. Second, while Eliot's writing gains prestige from its perceived similarity to Shakespeare's in terms of her "sympathy," it is barred from being understood as showing insight into human nature equal to Shakespeare's insight because she lacks his masculine authority to author through naming, limiting, and defining. Within culture, where textuality must remain, Eliot can never hope to accede to the literary father's presumed objectivity. As long as male authorship remains the unmarked norm, a female author is by definition tainted with subjectivity, just as her authorship must be qualified: not writer but woman writer. Consequently, Eliot's identification with Shakespeare will always be inflected by the impossibility of its completion; he will represent what is denied to her. The third reason Butler's theory seems applicable here is that Eliot's performance of a Shakespearean authorship bears traces of a melancholic recognition that the sort of love he represents (both as the figure of ideal authorship and as a figure within his sonnets) is one to which Eliot can never lay claim. Loving man from the position of subject can seem impossible for a woman within a culture founded on heterosexual difference. It follows that her very writing of the "lovely boy" paradoxically places him outside her control.

Possibly because it has become a commonplace of feminist theory to consider it dauntingly difficult, if not utterly impossible, for heterosexual women within patriarchy to envision themselves as lovers rather than love objects, academic feminists have recently started to turn serious attention to the role male homosexuality plays in women's wish-fulfillment narratives of sex and ro-

mantic love. By wish-fulfillment narratives, I mean fantasies written in narrative form. Recovering the traces of these fantasies in nonpornographic literature is part of the project of investigating what happened after the nineteenth-century proliferation of categories of sexuality described by Foucault in *The History of Sexuality*. His genealogy of the discourse of (pathologized) sexualities has begun to be followed by attempts to account for how, in Eve Sedgwick's terms, "the Victorian multiplication of sexual species has today all but boiled down to a single, bare,—and moreover fiercely invidious— dichotomy" (*Tendencies* 117). A major part of gender studies has been the recovery of the sexualities subsumed into binary and totalizing descriptions of homosexuality and heterosexuality. Sedgwick has often articulated the formerly silenced positions that defy this separation. A part of what had been treated as unspeakable found utterance when in the 1987 essay "A Poem is Being Written," Sedgwick publicly denied that her interest in male homosexuality was veiled lesbianism and instead asserted, "In among the many ways I do identify as a woman, the identification as a gay person is firmly a male one, identification 'as' a gay man" (*Tendencies* 209). What might become more visible to us after such a statement is that all the homoeroticism in texts written by women need not be read as lesbian.

Since Sedgwick's landmark essay, both popular and academic culture have relaxed a little, so that on one front women have become so active in publishing erotica about male homosexual relations that collections like *Flesh and the Word 2* feature sections of "gay male" pornography by women. On the academic front, such cultural critics as Constance Penley study ways fanzines express heterosexual women's desires through representation of male homosexuality. Penley claims that by fantasizing about love between men, women can avoid falling into "the usual erotics of dominance and submission found in the typical romance formula"; because women are inclined to see men as potentially equally empowered within society, love can be reimagined in such a context as transcending fixed power relations (490). In other words, while many women may be skeptical about their own ability to function as pure individuals exercising free agency in the world, they can suspend disbelief sufficiently to attribute such erotic freedom to men. And where women may fear that acting to initiate sexual relationships puts them in danger of objectification and domestic entrapment, they tend to imagine male freedom as less easily contained and the subjectivity of men as less easily destroyed. For many women, envisioning love between two men creates a space of identification in which it is possible to imagine acting on desire without being reduced to an object of someone else's desire or to a biological function.

The relevance to ***Middlemarch*** of women's fantasies about love between men can be clarified by looking at

Will's function as an erotic object in the novel. As many critics have noted, Will is depicted in a way consistent with nineteenth-century Western cultural concepts of effeminacy. Feminine allure in the nineteenth century, as today, has as one of its primary signifiers an adorable physical immaturity. Upon our first introduction to him, Will's most outstanding feature, mentioned seven times in two pages of the Norton text, is that he looks "quite young" (51-52). His other distinguishing characteristics are "light-brown curls," which get three mentions, a "slim figure" (51), a "pouting air" (52), and a striking resemblance to his grandmother when she was a girl. When he visits Dorothea during her honeymoon, we hear again that Will has unusually pretty hair, an "exquisite smile," and a "transparent complexion," and although he is "several years" older than Dorothea, "he looked much the younger" (142). "Delicacy" is a word often associated with Will. The sturdier Tertius Lydgate describes Will as "a sort of Daphnis in coat and waistcoat" (343-44). Mrs. Cadwallader finds him "very pretty" (226). As Blake says, "Will is a slight creature," but that is the essence of his charm for Dorothea, who "needs him for the testament he gives her of her own power" (308, 300).

Eliot is not offering a revisionary erotics in which maleness will be associated with exquisite fragility. Rather, her many descriptions of Will play against the standards of masculinity employed by the community of Middlemarch to evoke a parallel world conceived as textual in contrast to the "reality" of Middlemarch. Mr. Brooke's comment that Will "seems to me a kind of Shelley, you know" (248), locates Will's significance in the poetic and thus outside the literally prosaic practicality that defines Middlemarch. Because *Middlemarch*'s verisimilitude is partly created through references to literary texts that Eliot implicitly describes as unrealistic, Will's extravagant sense (reminiscent of "Sonnet 29") that his love for Dorothea "is like the inheritance of a fortune" (325) places him outside the "real world" of *Middlemarch.* The contrast between "real" and "literary" worlds is emphasized by Sir James's abrupt transfer of his affections from Dorothea to Celia because, with "no sonnets to write," he has no interest in a passion that exceeds its return (40). As Sircy comments, the passage does evoke "the unrealistic lament of languishing sonnet lovers" (226). But it does so perhaps not in a way that causes the reader to long for an admirer like Sir James.

The references to sonnets not only heighten the reality effect of the long, mundane passages of detailed description and the accounts of tedious conversations between minor characters, they suggest a cultural context to which *Middlemarch*'s less dramatic and stylish narrative mode may be read as corrective. This corrective, like most disciplinary actions, has its unpleasant and even repulsive aspects, so that at the very moment that

the reader is urged to face reality, unreality figured by Will, shines forth all the more seductively. Sandra Gilbert and Susan Gubar say that "Will is Eliot's radically anti-patriarchal attempt to create an image of masculinity attractive to women" ([*The Madwoman in the Attic*] 529-29). Remarking his feminine characteristics, they compare him to the fantasy male twin in Adrienne Rich's poem "Natural Resources" and claim that on the "quasi-allegorical level of the plot" Dorothea's marriage to him represents her attainment "at last" of "her noble will" (530). In this way Will fulfills a function similar to what David Romàn attributes to the boy actors in adaptations of Shakespearean homoerotic spectacle. "They embody the simultaneous arousal of homoerotic possibility and homoneurotic disavowal" (319). Both effeminized and heterosexual, Will allows one to fantasize about what it would be like to love in a prohibited mode, to take a male as love object, but he is then abjected as less than real. To read the marriage in Gilbert and Gubar's terms means to move it outside the conventions of realism and to afford Will meaning only as a symbol for Dorothea's fantasy of love. Interpreting him this way strengthens his similarity to the fair youth of the sonnets who moves ever deeper away from the world of time and change and into the poet-narrator's imagination, because, as he says, "When I most wink, then do mine eyes best see" ("Sonnet 43").

It is probably safe to assume that Eliot would have followed the usual nineteenth-century interpretive practice and read the love relationship between the poet-narrator of Shakespeare's sonnets and the fair youth as platonic. As Joseph Pequigney shows, from the middle of the eighteenth century on, Shakespeare's commentators "have frequent recourse to a cult of male friendship that enjoyed a certain vogue in the Renaissance when the amicable ideal was more assiduously practiced and consciously esteemed than in later times; but the thing about this friendship that above all appeals to expositors is their conviction that it was free of all traces of eroticism" (30). At the same time, however, Eliot attempts to universalize the emotions expressed in the sonnets through translation of them into Victorian heterosexual terms. Although this response seems a bit bizarre because it involves a double move in which eroticism is denied and then displaced and reasserted, it is typical of commentators on the sonnets, as Pequigney's account demonstrates (67-80) In consulting Pequigney's history of the critical reception of Shakespeare's sonnets, we are in danger of becoming lost in the intricacies of the ongoing critical debate about how the sonnets should be read. It is, therefore, important to note this debate's irrelevance to my immediate concerns here. The relevance of Pequigney's reading of the sonnets readers lies in its unusual attentiveness to areas of strain in their interpretations, as they attempt to imagine what their own cultural situations make almost, but not quite, unimaginable. Seen in this way, Eliot's strangely negative translation of the Sonnet's fair youth into Will as bourgeois husband accords with contemporary Victorian practice.

Nineteenth-century literary allusions to Shakespeare's sonnets often followed the same complex pattern. Richard Dellamora discusses such allusions in Tennyson's *In Memoriam* (1850). For instance, Tennyson directly evokes Shakespeare's sonnets in the lines: "I loved thee, Spirit, and love nor can / The soul of Shakespeare love thee more" ("Lyric 61"). Dellamora also points out that the lyric which follows these lines paraphrases "Sonnet 116," in this case "explicitly subordinat[ing] the marriage of male minds to marriage in the usual sense" (32). But Dellamora observes that "Tennyson in the body of the poem subordinates the domestic sanctities to an engrossing friendship" (41). Thus, in Tennyson, homoeroticism is both made acceptable through its reduction into a metaphor for matrimonial love and recovered as a free space outside domesticity. The possibilities for such double moves of desire through appropriation of what is easily read as Shakespeare's erotic have special implications for a female writer.

More than common practice must have tempted Eliot to respond to the sonnets as she does in *Middlemarch.* The first 126 sonnets offer an ideal model for a woman who wants to love without losing power, because the love between men portrayed in the sonnets takes place in a sort of emotional meritocracy where the lover with the most passion and artistry in its expression can prevail. Although this theme is not always evident on the surface of the poems, it is a major one in the "rival poet" sonnets "78"-"86." Making much of Eliot's comment on "56" and "57" that "[s]ome of the sonnets are painfully abject. He adopts language which might be taken to describe the miserable slavery of oppression wives" (*Notebooks* [*Middlemarch Notebooks*] 211), Novy claims that at the end of the novel "Dorothea acts like an assertive heroine from the comedies rather than like the self-abnegating speaker of the sonnets" (*Engaging* 97). Yet it is not in the comedies that Shakespeare dramatizes the connection, in romantic matters, between writing and power, the same connection that Eliot's writing of Dorothea's relation to Will initially enacts. Could Eliot have found the poet-narrator self-abnegating when he asserted that "So long as men can breathe or eyes can see, / So long lives this, and this gives life to thee" ("Sonnet 18")? When at last the long immortalizing song is cut off, it is not Nature that ends the celebration of the "minion of her pleasure," but the poet, showing in twelve lines that all along he had control ("Sonnet 126"). To return to my initial metaphor of writing the beloved as a sort of public sexual act, the Sonnet's poet-narrator plays with (the images he creates of) his darling before our eyes. Although he sometimes reveals himself swooning in a apparent loss of control, masochistically waiting and enduring, weeping and hop-

ing, in the end he asserts his power. He was never deceived any more than he wanted to be, he said only what he wanted to say, and he concludes the game when it has yielded its last thrill.

As Gregory Bredbeck shows, the sonnets' naturalization of multiple forms of desire encourages an enormous variety of interpretations of their erotics, always a useful situation for the interpreter who wants to authorize prohibited modes of love (171-79). Moreover, the sonnets delineate a space free in some surprising ways from the pejorative gendering of affective modes. As in "I love thee in such sort / As, thou being mine, mine is thy good report" ("Sonnet 36"), they allow receptivity to and containment of another to signify possession and triumph rather than powerless passivity. To hold the beloved in a part of one's self (the mind/the poem) and to identify utterly with him means not self-effacement, but mastery because containment is also equated with artistic representation as a higher form of immortality—as in the following lines—than that conferred by procreation: "My love shall in my verse ever live young" ("Sonnet 19"); "you live in this" ("Sonnet 55"); "Thy gift, thy tables, are within my brain / Full charactered with lasting memory, / Which shall above that idle rank remain / Beyond all date, even to eternity" ("Sonnet 122"). Such beliefs seemingly must contribute to the poet-narrator's "relaxed and urbane" treatment in "Sonnet 20" of erotic attraction to a youth so pretty as to be of near indeterminate gender (Sedgwick, *Between Men* 35). If a universal space for love exists where a pen rather than a penis would convey with such confidence the power to observe beautiful males and one's own reaction to them, then a passionate woman would have no need to despair.

It is not at all beside the point however, that both participants in Shakespeare's love drama are male. As Sedgwick says, "[F]or a man to undergo even a humiliating change in the course of a relationship with a man still feels like preserving or participating in a sum of male power," because the youth "is a very touchstone of maleness; he represents the masculine as pure object" (*Between Men* 45, 44). Within the sonnets there can be no triumphant masculinity except as defined through reference to a subordinated femininity. No matter how important marital relations, their value is explicitly defined by their efficacy in bonding men. Often it seems that the poet-narrator recognizes no higher purpose to marriage than that it allows his beloved youth to "Make thee another self for love of me" ("Sonnet 10"). The utility of women is the foundation on which the transcendent passion of the first 126 sonnets is built. As Sedgwick says, "The sonnets present a male-male love that . . . is set firmly within a structure of institutionalized social relations that are carried out via women: marriage, name, family, loyalty to progenitors and to posterity" (*Between Men* 35). It is within a structure parodically parallel to that of the "procreation sonnets" that Dorothea's attempts take place to love, and by loving to contain, that beautiful object, Will. And not coincidentally, it is also within this structure that Eliot's first attempts to describe him occur.

Eliot evokes the first section of the sonnets when the narrator says that part of Casaubon's motivation to marry Dorothea comes from a desire "to leave behind him that copy of himself which seemed so urgently required of a man—to the sonneteers of the sixteenth century" (192). The novel's parodic treatment of such attitudes, already implicit in the grotesque image of a little Mr. Casaubon, is reinforced by the next sentence: "Times had altered since then, and no sonneteer had insisted on Mr. Casaubon's leaving a copy of himself." Comic development of the idea that procreation is intrinsically good continues to be framed as response to sixteenth-century sonnets when the narrator remarks on the origins of Joshua Rigg: "those who like Peter Featherstone never had a copy of themselves demanded, are the very last to wait for such a request in either prose or verse" (285). While it seems laughably unfair for a Victorian writer to attribute a cultural imperative to procreate exclusively to the sixteenth century, the comedy in the passages seems meant to derive from the ugliness of Casaubon and Featherstone, and so the reader's mind is likely to turn toward a more likely candidate for poetic urging of procreation, the fair young man Will Ladislaw. And it is here that the allusions to Shakespeare gain bitterness.

Eliot's phrasing and imagery closely connect Will and the young man of the sonnets. We are first led to consider Will's beauty Shakespearean by Dorothea's thought that his smile illuminates his features "as if some Ariel were touching them with a new charm" (142). The Shakespearean connection is further developed through Will's narrative association with art objects. In "Sonnet 20," we are told that the young man has "[a] woman's face, with Nature's own hand *painted*," and the sonnet draws on the diction of artistic production to convey a sense of the youth's beauty. He is a painting, an artwork brought to life. Not only is Will Ladislaw introduced to us as a living version of his grandmother's painted picture, Dorothea first falls "a-doting," as Shakespeare puts it, when she takes the miniature of Will's grandmother into her palm and "blend[s] the woman" with the man (378). Taking more from Shakespeare's stock of comparisons, Eliot says, "The first impression on seeing Will was one of sunny brightness" (145). "Shall I compare thee to a summer's day?" ("Sonnet 18").

In contrast, Dorothea physically resembles the dark lady of the sonnets in hair and eye color. Like the dark lady, moreover, Dorothea is compared to the classic ideal of feminine beauty and found more desirable. Will

and his friend Adolf Naumann see her standing next to a statue of Ariadne in Rome "not shamed" by the comparison (131), but rather exciting their intense admiration. Later our attention is drawn to the "striking" contrast between Dorothea's compelling presence and the "infantine blondeness" (298) of Rosamond Vincy, that fashionably artificial "stage Ariadne" (207). Conventional-minded idiots like Mr. Chichely may prefer Rosamond's "filigree" to Dorothea's simplicity (60), but otherwise "every tongue says beauty should look so" ("Sonnet 127"). Over and over, Dorothea is praised for her naturalness, "as rare / As any she belied with false compare" ("Sonnet 130").

Physical darkness is not simply the mark of authenticity in Shakespeare's lady. The lady's darkness is the outward sign of "black . . . deeds" and the supposed duplicitous nature of woman ("Sonnet 131"). While the novel clearly does not take this view of Dorothea, Eliot often shows us that Casaubon does. To Casaubon Dorothea is a near succubus, "darkly feminine," visiting him "in the darkness of the night" to unsettle his thoughts (139, 290). He feels that she has betrayed him with her premarital show of submissive adoration and is tortured by a "suspicion and jealousy" (289), that, if not as "coarse" as that of the poet-narrator in Shakespeare's sonnets, seems more serious in that it clearly hastens his death. Embodying against her inclination his worst fears and frustrations, Dorothea is this unpoetic lover's dark lady. Indeed, the comparison in the sonnets between bright, sunlit masculine beauty and dark, deathly feminine attraction is from the beginning of the novel replicated and located with reference to marriage. Outside marriage the young man shines brightly, inside marriage woman darkens into a demoness.

The structural use of puns on the word "will" to reflect triangulated desires also connects Dorothea and Will with the dark lady and fair youth of the sonnets and reiterates the necessity of understanding that connection through thinking about marriage as a social and legal institution. Sonnets "135" and "136" play most exhaustively with multiple meanings of the word "will," although puns on "will" also appear in "57," "134," and "143." It seems worth noting that the one in "57" begins, "[B]eing your slave, what should I do but tend / Upon the hours and times of your desire," and that when Will decides that he will devote his life to "watch[ing]" over" Dorothea, the way he puts it to himself is that "she would know that she had one slave in the world" (249). The unrestrained punning of sonnets "135" and "136" is not directly echoed in Eliot's phrasing, but rather in our knowledge that the battle of wills that Dorothea and Casaubon fight over Will culminates in the will forbidding Dorothea her will, which is to have Will. To point up the puns, when Dorothea does take her Will, Mr. Brooke breaks the news to Celia and Sir James by saying, "I couldn't help Casaubon's will;

it was a sort of will to make things worse" (562). As Novy demonstrates, the puns create an opposition between Will and will (*Engaging* 109), but whereas in sonnets "135" and "136" the wills/Wills never lose touch with the body, in *Middlemarch* they become disembodied, relocating from the bed to the law office, and from the poem to the document.

Still the fluid playfulness of the sonnets' ocean of wills does not seem completely dried out of the text at this point since, if we look only at this level of intertextuality, it would seem that the novel resolves the conflict over competing modes of sexuality presented in the sonnets by urging, as Lysander does in *A Midsummer Night's Dream,* that the woman should have her will. Critics who wish to read the conclusion of *Middlemarch* as romantically successful can relate it, as Novy does, to Eliot's discussion, in **"Love in the Drama"** of Shakespeare's female characters who "have no more decided characteristic than the frankness with which they avow their love" (255). But one might note that the first examples of female erotic willfulness that Eliot discusses, Juliet and Desdemona, hardly suggest that when woman asserts her desire all will end well. The reader who can take such a moral from *Middlemarch* is dreaming indeed. Like the dark lady whose appearance is characterized as mournful and Dorothea herself who is most often referred to as "grave," the novel is deeply melancholy. Kathryn Stockton attributes this tonal sadness to the way Dorothea's aspirations for "material change," as well as those of other characters in the novel, come up against "the hindrances of domestic reality" (194-95). Once their love travels from their poetic imaginations into the world, Will cannot remain the delightful androgyne whose love inspires and elevates the soul of his admirer "like to the lark at break of day arising" ("Sonnet 29"). More than any other force, the gender roles demanded by the nineteenth-century belief in professional activity constitute a disciplinary power that Dorothea and Will cannot resist.

Will's effeminizing situational likeness to the novel's women is always mitigated by his much greater freedom to choose how to make his living (Beer 172). And as Stockton notes, "[W]hen Will moves into the political mainstream, his character seems to become more masculine" (221). His masculinization is not achieved solely through affect but also through circumstance. He becomes a Victorian patriarch, and Dorothea is reduced in complementarity to a help-meet wife. It is this reduction that sets us up to read as deeply morose Eliot's use of the closing line of "Sonnet 50"—"my grief lies onward and my joy behind"—as the epigraph introducing Chapter 82. The epigraph obviously refers to Will's soon-to-be-resolved conflict over whether to flee from or toward Dorothea, but its meaning is far from exhausted by this surface reading. The quotation also stands as an expression of profound nostalgia for a lost

age in which love seems more realizable than it can be within the novel, where the best that can be expected seems to be to avoid a totally disastrous marriage like the Lydgates'. Will and Dorothea's marriage threatens her life with the dangers of childbirth and breaks "her full nature" into domestic services (578). And this vision of domesticity hard-gained is not least sad in that it is always haunted by another vision, of passionate reciprocity that would enable creativity rather than make it impossible.

My title, "This thing I like my sister may not do," comes from Eliot's sonnet **"Brother and Sister."** Keeping in mind Virginia Woolf's famous discussion of "Shakespeare's sister," one finds that this line expressing the brother's judgment of his sister's abilities might be read as metaphoric of Eliot's sense of her position as a writer in relation to both the literary production of her masculine precursors and to their thematics. For nineteenth-century writers Shakespeare was, as he is for Woolf, *the* precursor, the older brother par excellence. In the intertextual connections between *Middlemarch* and Shakespeare's sonnets, we may read extensive commentary both on the ways Eliot seems to have believed that a Victorian woman's experience of love necessarily differed from a Elizabethan man's and on the ways a Victorian woman novelist's representation of love must differ from his.[5]

Although the first of these commentaries has some sociological value, it is mitigated, as Langland has shown, by the novel's construction of an ideologically consistent narrative through omitting facts about women's social lives. But, while Eliot distorts nineteenth-century women's lives by following the conservative dictum that political action, and indeed any impact on the world, can come to women only through marriage and the indirect influence it provides, she seems more realistic in showing that once Dorothea is married, as Stockton suggests, Will's charming "receptivity" and lack of masculine careerism can only limit her own power to do good (220).[6] Like Hareton in *Wuthering Heights,* Will must be conventionally masculinized according to bourgeois standards in order for his woman to have any effect on the world. That the sort of platonic love that Victorian critics liked to read into the first 126 sonnets is also impossible for Dorothea as a means to action is shown in the comedy of errors that results from her attempt to work with Sir James as a friend. Her "cold" response to him "with the air of a handsome boy [is] in amusing contrast to the solicitous amiability of her admirer" (12).

Paralleling this commentary on the limits within which respectable women could either erotically or platonically love men is an implicit commentary on Shakespeare's Victorian sisters' inability to write about love in the same way an Elizabethan man could. This secondary line of narrative illuminates more about the cultural constraints within which the erotics of nineteenth-century novels took form than it does about the romantic possibilities available to nineteenth-century literary women. The differences in available discursive modes center on the man's opportunity to love another man and to express his love in ways closed to Victorian women writers because of the intersection of aesthetics and morality specific to each era.[7] Shakespeare's poet-narrator directly and indirectly tells us that his erotic love has three uses: to facilitate procreation, to cheer the soul, and to inspire art.[8] The first two of these uses of love he treats as equivalent in value. Making families is important, but no more so than raising one's spirits. Better than either one is making poems. Loving an unfaithful person is depressing, but if you can get good poetry out of it, it seems worth the pain. For, as the narrator stresses after a series of poems castigating his friend for being as deceptive as a cankered rose, it is not only the beloved who receives immortality, but the poet himself. Moreover, the poet's immortalization is of a higher kind. "Sonnet 107"'s defiant claim that "death to me subscribes, / Since, spite of him, I'll live in this poor rhyme" implicitly compares the poet's continuing ability to speak (through his deathless poem) to the stasis the poem confers on the beloved: "And thou in this shall find thy monument." To Victorians like Eliot, reacting against the Romantics, this aesthetic could not be morally acceptable, for it posits art as the highest good and its production as the highest human purpose. Eliot's position as a woman writer, whose gender places her always on the verge of violating the injunctions against selfishness, doubly prohibits valorizing erotic enjoyment of male beauty and charm as an end in itself or as a means to heightened creativity.

Criticizing Eliot as a "morally conservative liberal," Dellamora cites her condemnation of Pater's *Studies in the History of the Renaissance* for a "false conception of life" she deems "poisonous" (18).[9] But disappointing as her judgment here is, its salient feature is its safety. That she already had an admiring helpmeet and would later in her life embrace an attractive and subordinate young man, successfully incorporating his possession within her authorly identity, is nowhere suggested in *Middlemarch.* The events of Eliot's life, her relationship with Lewes and the aspects of her personality that would make possible her marriage to Cross seem outside the margins of legitimate representation. To write of her own experience as a woman would be to undermine her authority as a realist author. In the English tradition intellectual women have often chosen public repudiation of their desires as the easiest road to being taken seriously. Because Eliot, like Mrs. Garth, defines facing up to reality, and the principles one has developed in accordance with it, as resigned acceptance of one's gender role, she is left with only one way to be respected as an honorable realist. Just as Dorothea cannot attain the position of lover without immediately being rewritten by a discourse of gender ideology that makes her into a beloved object, Eliot as a realist and a woman cannot admiringly contemplate Will for long without transferring to him the patriarchal power her authorship threatens to usurp.

More complicated motivations for Eliot's transformation of Will are suggested by Neil Hertz's and Leland Monk's discussions of Eliot's unease with the egotism writing demands. Hertz reads Eliot's development of a moralistic realist aesthetic based on the suppression of self as a "comforting" defense against recognition of the inescapable limits on authorial control (85). It is more emotionally satisfying to fight voluntarily against selfishness than to recognize limits to the self's dominion. Eliot's promulgation of a specifically female ideology of self-repression obviously offered similar benefits. Working from Hertz's reading, Monk explores Eliot's pitiless treatment of characters, like Raffles, who represent what even the novelist cannot control (68, 72). As Monk notes, Raffles is disruptive because his embodiment of chance not only goes against Eliot's "usual realistic mode"; it calls that mode into question (54). Consequently, Eliot's inclusion of Raffles in the novel, as well as her sudden expulsion of him from it, acts as a sort of exorcism of what she cannot fail to be aware of and yet resents. Eliot enacts the same sort of gesture with the disruptively romantic and seductive Will. She plays with the delicious possibility of having her will and then demonstrates to herself and her audience that in enjoying Will we have been had. As Shakespeare puts it: "Mad in pursuit, and in possession so; / Had, having, and in quest to have, extreme; / A bliss in proof, and proved, a very woe"? The narrative's progression is a little like "Sonnet 129"'s in that it seems unavoidable that it should be so.

In *Middlemarch,* the social and cultural structures that govern expressions of heterosexuality push every attempt at escape back into the same disappointing pattern. In this context, Will's failure as a romantic hero is no flaw, but instead serves an important narrative function. It demonstrates the impossibility of translating from the discourse of Renaissance male-to-male relations into the discourse of nineteenth-century heterosexuality a love founded in an aesthetic that includes the presumption that writing is a legitimate means to power. By doing so it reveals how Eliot's expression of her own position as a writer is informed by her era's construction of gender and its consequent delineation of an erotics inseparable from domesticity. As Nancy Armstrong remarks: "Not only does [Eliot] ask us to understand women's history as something outside and essentially different from that of men, but in concluding the novel, she also asks us to acknowledge the fact that human experience is profoundly affected by those whose work takes place in a domain outside the political sphere. What is true for women's history, she implies, holds true for the novelist's craft as well" (43). If we think of the novel as being primarily about work, this similarity between the experience of the wife and that of the woman novelist may be cheering, but when we look at the erotics of *Middlemarch,* the similarity between being a woman writer and being a wife is depressing. Now it highlights not wide and pervasive influence through love, but all encompassing frustration of desire. Writing and gender fold in upon each other maddeningly.

Within this claustrophobic space, Will Ladislaw is a multivalent erotic object who both promises and prohibits to Dorothea the pleasures enjoyed by the poet-narrator of the sonnets and to Eliot the enjoyment of entering language like a lover with power enough to play. Each time the prohibition is enacted, the text shifts from romanticism to cynicism and from critique of Eliot's own culture to denunciation of past modes, as if despair about romantic love (and its representation) were so troubling that the anger aroused must be displaced onto those in the past, like Shakespeare, who led our hopes astray.

Why blame him? Eliot cannot turn against compulsory heterosexuality as Shakespeare does in "Sonnet 129" and elsewhere. For a woman trying to depict satisfying erotic connection with a man, repudiation of heterosexuality would mean defeat. Her real enemy is domesticity, but because she equates acceptance of a narrowly defined domestic role with heroic realism in women (whether they be writers or wives), she cannot repudiate that. She is left no place to insert her anger into the discourses of her own times, and so must transfer it to the sixteenth century, and no object for her annoyance but the one who promised "such a beauteous day." The poet-narrator and his beloved do indeed become one for Eliot, and their union in the character Will becomes the site of her discontent, the point where women's hopes are aroused and then dashed. The act of enclosing this composite figure for eroticism within her narrative becomes the occasion for expression of anger and distaste. It is here, moreover, that we are given a hint of depressing literary conventions as well as cultural developments that will flourish later, as without any overt treatment of homosexuality at all, the novel manages to cast aspersions on homoeroticism. Will's "failure" as a character becomes a sign of difference marking an early departure point in Western culture's journey toward its present jealous demonization of homosexual love.

Notes

1. The book *Only You,* by Richard Kehl, is mostly composed of reproductions of Victorian paintings, but has some additional pages of twentieth-century photographs and illustrations.

2. See Jane Gallop's *Around 1981* for a sympathetic overview of the debate over "prescriptive" feminist criticism (77-118).

3. Rose discusses Anne's marriage and Eliot's approval of it as part of an argument that such unions, although they might shock or disturb the general population, were acceptable to female intellectuals of the time (232).

4. Many metatheorists of the psychoanalytic have commented on nineteenth-century psychologists' treatment of literary texts as interchangeable with case studies. In *Dreams of Authority,* Ronald Thomas gives a particularly interesting account of ways that "narrative forms of fiction provided the explanatory models that led to [Freud's] shift from a physiological to a psychological understanding" of his patients' symptoms (133).

5. Beer argues persuasively that Eliot looked to Shakespeare's sonnets to confirm her own "doubts about the extent to which men and women are different in nature" (13).

6. As Grosz points out, where "the framework of sexual difference" structures meaning, "one lives one's sexual indeterminacy, one's possibilities for being sexed otherwise differently depending on whether one is male or female" (77).

7. This is not to say that lesbian eroticism is missing from *Middlemarch,* simply that there are other sorts of homoeroticism in the text. For discussion of lesbianism in *Middlemarch,* see Kathryn Bond Stockton (193-249).

8. Joseph Pequigney remarks the unusualness of Alexander Schmidt's gloss of "master-mistress" in "Sonnet 20" as "'one loved like a woman, but of the male sex'" (31, 228:n3). As Pequigney shows, the dominant view of the relation between the poet-narrator and the fair youth from the early 1800s to the early 1980s has been much closer to that of chaste ideal friendship propounded in Edmund Malone's 1790 edition of *The Plays and Poems of William Shakespeare* than to Schmidt's homoerotic interpretation.

9. The intensity of Eliot's reaction against Pater might be attributed to the leading role he was then playing in making the "androgynous" male body emblematic of "the highest aesthetic state" and his insistence that male friendship was central to Aestheticism, a vision which leaves no room for the female artist except as contaminating intruder (Morgan 324-25).

Works Cited

Armstrong, Nancy. *Desire and Domestic Fiction: A Political History of the Novel.* New York: Oxford UP, 1987.

Beer, Gillian. *George Eliot.* Cambridge: Harvester, 1986.

Bredbeck, Gregory. *Sodomy and Interpretation: Marlowe to Milton.* Ithaca: Cornell UP, 1991.

Butler, Judith. *Bodies That Matter: On the Discursive Limits of "Sex."* New York: Routledge, 1993.

———. *Gender Trouble: Feminism and the Subversion of Identity.* New York: Routledge, 1990.

Dellamora, Richard. *Masculine Desire: The Sexual Politics of Victorian Aestheticism.* Chapel Hill: U of North Carolina P, 1990.

DuPlessis, Rachel Blau. *Writing Beyond the Ending: Narrative Strategies of Twentieth-Century Women Writers.* Bloomington: Indiana UP, 1985.

Eliot, George. "Love in the Drama." 1855. *A Writer's Notebook, 1854-1879, and Uncollected Writings.* Ed. Joseph Wiesenfarth. Charlottesville: UP of Virginia, 1981: 253-55.

———. *Middlemarch.* 1871-1872. Ed. Bert G. Hornback. New York: Norton, 1977.

———. *Middlemarch Notebooks: A Transcription.* Ed. John Clark Pratt and Victor Neufeldt. Berkeley: U of California P, 1979.

Gallop, Jane. *Around 1981: Academic Feminist Literary Theory.* New York: Routledge, 1992.

Gilbert, Sandra, and Susan Gubar. *The Madwoman in the Attic: The Woman Writer and the Nineteenth-Century Literary Imagination.* New Haven: Yale UP, 1979.

———, ed. "Elizabeth Barrett Browning." *The Norton Anthology of Literature by Women: The Tradition in English.* New York: Norton, 1985. 256-59.

Grosz, Elizabeth. *Space, Time, and Perversion.* New York: Routledge, 1995.

Hertz, Neil. "Recognizing Casaubon." *The End of the Line: Essays on Psychoanalysis and the Sublime.* Ed. Neil Hertz. New York: Columbia UP, 1985: 75-96.

Kehl, Richard. *Only You.* Seattle: Blue Lantern, 1994.

Knoepflmacher, U. C. "Fusing Fact and Myth: The New Reality of *Middlemarch.*" *This Particular Web: Essays on Middlemarch.* Ed. Ian Adam. Toronto: U of Toronto P, 1975. 43-72.

Langland, Elizabeth. "Inventing Reality: The Ideological Commitments of George Eliot's *Middlemarch.*" *Narrative* 2 (1994): 87-111.

Monk, Leland. *Standard Deviations: Chance and the Modern British Novel.* Stanford: Stanford UP, 1993.

Morgan, Thaïs E. "ReImagining Masculinity in Victorian Criticism: Swinburne and Pater." *Victorian Studies* 36 (1993): 315-32.

Novy, Marianne. "*Daniel Deronda* and George Eliot's Female Re-Vision of Shakespeare." *Women's Re-Visions of Shakespeare: On the Responses of Dickinson, Woolf, Rich, H. D., George Eliot, and Others.* Ed. Marianne Novy. Urbana and Chicago: U of Illinois P, 1990: 89-107.

———. *Engaging with Shakespeare: Responses of George Eliot and Other Women Novelists.* Athens: U of Georgia P, 1994.

Pequigney, Joseph. *Such Is My Love: A Study of Shakespeare's Sonnets.* Chicago: U of Chicago P, 1985.

Penley, Constance. "Feminism, Psychoanalysis, Popular Culture" *Cultural Studies.* Ed. Lawrence Grossberg et al. New York: Routledge, 1992. 479-94.

Romàn, David. "Shakespeare Out in Portland: Gus Van Sant's *My Own Private Idaho,* Homoerotics, and Boy Actors." *Genders* 20 (1994): 311-33.

Rose, Phyllis. *Parallel Lives: Five Victorian Marriages.* New York: Knopf, 1984.

Sedgwick, Eve Kosofsky. *Between Men: English Literature and Male Homosocial Desire.* New York: Columbia UP, 1985.

———. *Tendencies.* Durham: Duke UP, 1993.

Sircy, Otice C. "'The Fashion of Sentiment': Allusive Technique and the Sonnets of *Middlemarch.*" *Studies in Philology* 84 (1987): 219-44.

Schmidt, Alexander. *Shakespeare-Lexicon: A Complete Dictionary of All English Words, Phrases and Constructions in the Works of the Poet.* London and Berlin 1874-75.

Stockton, Kathryn Bond. *God Between Their Lips: Desire Between Women in Irigaray, Brontë, and Eliot.* Stanford: Stanford UP, 1994.

Thomas, Ronald R. *Dreams of Authority: Freud and the Fictions of the Unconscious.* Ithaca: Cornell UP, 1990.

Valerie Wainwright (essay date spring 2000)

SOURCE: Wainwright, Valerie. "Anatomizing Excellence: *Middlemarch,* Moral Saints and the Languages of Belief." *English* 49, no. 193 (spring 2000): 1-14.

[*In the following essay, Wainwright discusses aspects of saintliness in Dorothea's character. Wainwright suggests that Dorothea's unwavering faith in the goodness of human beings, in spite of their ethical failings, forms the essence of her "moral greatness."*]

Boldly voicing her disgust with 'fearful, delicate, dainty ladies', Dixon, the heroine's servant in Elizabeth Gaskell's novel *North and South,* suggests that the cult of femininity is to blame for the lack of saints in the modern world (ch. 51). In Dickens' novels saints abound; and males, like Stephen Blackpool of *Hard Times,* attribute saintliness to those females, like Rachel or Sissy, who are capable of acute moral perception and responsiveness to the needs of others.[1] In the Prelude to *Middlemarch* George Eliot identifies Saint Teresa's saintliness with her great act of institutional and spiritual reform, a manifestation of moral excellence apparently inconceivable in the nineteenth century. So how do we recognize a modern saint? What qualities does she possess? And what can act in place of the 'social faith' that according to the narrator of *Middlemarch,* in earlier times spurred the saint to accomplish great good? That Dorothea Brooke is proposed by George Eliot as a likely candidate seems obvious. It is less obvious whether by the end of the novel she can be seen to have reached such glorious heights. In the opinion of one of Dorothea's neighbours, the mordant Mrs Cadwallader, Dorothea suffers from a 'constitutional disease' that makes her obstinate 'in her absurdities' (84-85).[2] Absurd at times she may be, but more significantly, Dorothea misses her vocation 'to make her life greatly effective', and her lack of worldly recognition is generally read as signalling failure.[3]

Nowadays moral excellence is not only difficult to achieve, it is difficult to identify, to understand and even to admire. In what has become a classic on the subject, philosopher Susan Wolf claims there are two types of moral saint—the rational (who sacrifices her own interests to her moral ideal, and who 'feels the sacrifice as such') and the loving (whose happiness is strictly bound up with making others happy)—but finds that both kinds of saint and the saintly life she lives are likely to be unappealing, perhaps even disturbing. It is Wolf's contention that the saint is not someone we would much care for and that the saintly life is at odds with our post romantic ideals of a life of personal fulfilment, a life of many and varied goods. When moral concerns dominate the self will suffer, will in all likelihood lack individuality or authenticity. Saintliness, in Wolf's view, is incompatible with 'roundness' and moral perfectionism is an unsatisfactory ideal given that the saint in pursuing her moral project will necessarily have to sacrifice the non-moral interests and skills that contribute to a richly developed character.[4]

George Eliot's idealist, Dorothea Brooke of Middlemarch, has (initially) much the same goals as Wolf's would-be rational saint as she strives to achieve a higher mode of life and feeling. In common with Wolf, Eliot realizes this commitment is going to give rise to apprehensions. Thus neighbours think of Dorothea as strange or alarming, and even friends find her 'fanatical', while the reader's attitude to Dorothea's fervour cannot but be influenced by an ironic view of her marriage prospects which signifies Eliot's own perplexity. However,

where Wolf's major concern is with lack of *roundness,* what most preoccupies Eliot is *wholeness.* In the young Dorothea Casaubon, Eliot devises a picture of what a moral saint might be like, examines it thoroughly, admires some characteristics, but dismisses it as a flawed moral ideal. In *Middlemarch,* I shall argue, Eliot's vision of 'what it is good to be' involves considerations as to what makes a life cohere. Essential to her concept of virtue is the insight that a good life exhibits a harmony between values and motives; between what one believes in or values most and the reasons that motivate one's behaviour. In other words, built into the foundations of her definition of virtue is the requirement of achieving good in an integrated way.

Of Saints we have high expectations, though what we expect and admire may differ.[5] Eliot's heroine can be seen to meet many of the requirements of conventional notions of saintliness: she strives for self-perfection, responds to pain with fortitude, takes an exceptional interest in the welfare of others, and feels deeply and compassionately for those in distress. Eliot explores the implications of such actions even as she suggests that saintliness involves something extra, a special kind of faith, an enduring capacity for 'perfect' trust. Put in such a way Eliot's views may gain some of the clarity of Wolf's, but any reading of her novel which investigates its moral concerns must sooner or later acknowledge that those critics who claim the novel is confused or contradictory have good reasons for doing so.[6] The roles Eliot attributes to the narrative voice indubitably complicate as they animate her moral discourse. As in *Adam Bede,* Eliot's narrator expounds a didactic rhetoric of the emotions (asserting, for example, that 'our good depends on the quality and breadth of our emotion', 510), while holding a brief for the supreme value of vocation. If we are to be able to distinguish between the novel's conceptions of morality and what looks like morality but is not, and between morality and exceptional goodness or saintliness, it will help, I suggest, to background the passions and desire and take a closer look at the ways in which forms of belief function in the novel.

Dorothea Brooke is endowed with the kind of distinctive character traits that impress as the expressions of a forceful personality; outspoken, impulsive and energetic, fortunately—unlike Eliot's heroes Felix Holt and Daniel Deronda—she is not given to long speeches of an edifying nature. That such a vibrant personality runs great risks of being suppressed and subsumed, becomes ever more apparent as the story of her married life with the scholar Casaubon unfolds. Dorothea's marriage presents her with many an occasion to exercise her finest qualities just as it affords Eliot the opportunity to explore the complexities of influential notions of goodness. The key moral question as to whether Dorothea is to be taken as an exemplar of great virtue becomes compelling the moment the dying Casaubon requests his wife 'to apply herself to do what he should desire' (518) even after his death. This is the moment when the issue has to be faced and the reader must decide whether the motives or reasons which so often have determined Dorothea's behaviour—her great compassion and sense of duty, together with her remarkable powers of endurance—are qualities which make for saintliness. It seems as if Dorothea will comply with her husband's request for her continuing and total dedication to his monumental project after his death, a project in which she no longer believes. But are her reasons for doing so good ones? In her intricate rendering of Dorothea's mental state George Eliot conveys Dorothea's bewilderment and distress. In response to critics who recoil at what they take to be a puritanical morality that condones the repression of the vital self, Jeanie Thomas claims that we are meant to find Dorothea's psychological suffering unacceptable.[7] But I would add that we are also expected to evaluate the ideal of (female) virtue as a nice mix of sympathy and self-suppression, which Dorothea effectively embodies at this time, and by making use of ideas supplied by the novel itself find it fundamentally flawed.

At stake then is a crucial moral question: can the selfless action Dorothea is contemplating doing be judged to be right or ethically desirable? Does it in fact conform to her own idea of what is 'right and best', which, as Casaubon has realized, fires her powers of devotion (517). Significantly, Dorothea asks herself this question but does not answer it:

> Was it right, even to soothe his grief—would it be possible, even if she promised—to work as in a treadmill fruitlessly? . . .
>
> 　　　　　* * *
>
> here was a deep difference between that devotion to the living, and that indefinite promise of devotion to the dead . . . his heart was bound up in his work only: that was the end for which his failing life was to be eked out by hers.
>
> 　　　　　　　　　　(520-21)

During her emotional turmoil, it is the image Dorothea conjures up of herself that comes to assume most relevance. In the finely nuanced portrayal of her mental struggle, one thought becomes dominant, the thought that she cannot inflict pain on her husband: 'she was too weak, too full of dread at the thought of inflicting a keen-edged blow on her husband, to do anything but submit completely . . . she saw clearly enough the whole situation, yet she was fettered, she could not smite the stricken soul that entreated hers'. It is at this much discussed point in the novel that we get the narrator's comment: 'If that were weakness, Dorothea was weak' (521-23).[8] Dorothea's unbounded pity, we are to infer, is debilitating yet to be prized. It brings to mind a previous example of the narrator's admiration for Dorothea's 'resolved submission' to Casaubon, an act energized when 'the noble habit of the soul re-asserts itself' (464). Now, the narrator's rhetoric again seems to assume and convalidate a view of the moral issue in terms associated with the images in which Dorothea in her anguish has come to conceive it: Refusal=defiance=violence=strength. Either, it seems, she must accept the role of (noble) victim, 'doomed to submit', or of aggressor and harm the 'stricken soul'. But so far she is unable to 'resolve' or decide either way.[9]

In delineating her heroine's moral predicament, George Eliot insists on the fact that Dorothea can see the whole situation clearly—that there is no view of marriage duties that impose such an obligation on her to help Casaubon, that all such labours are moreover futile—but what Dorothea does not, apparently cannot, try to see clearly is herself. What she sees is the stark vision of herself as aggressor, smiting Casaubon. And this vision is mesmerizing. All moral meaning, all sense of self, resolves itself into this nightmare image. That self-representation may play a vital role in moral action is acknowledged by philosopher Jonathan Dancy: 'In the most extreme cases, the [moral] dilemma is what it is because it involves the question of what sort of person one will be'.[10] Yet Dorothea's image of herself as assailant is a monstrously distorted one—the product of a conflictual relationship that has given birth to painful fancy and continual fear. Her dilemma thus points up the potential for disaster that inheres in a motivational process in which self-conception or representation becomes the decisive factor.[11]

What has got totally lost as Dorothea's thoughts focus on this vision of herself—what indeed is missing from the text at this point—is something Eliot has already indicated as crucial to her heroine's sense of self: a firm belief in and desire for 'what is perfectly good', the pursuing of which makes life worth living (427). Kierkegaard expresses such an idea in the following terms: 'Eternally speaking, there is only one means and there is only one end: the means and the end are one and the same thing. There is only one end: the genuine Good: and only one means: this, to be willing only to use those means which genuinely are good—but the genuine Good is precisely the end'.[12] In *Middlemarch,* at this moment of crisis, there is no 'reaching forward of [Dorothea's] *whole* consciousness towards *the fullest truth, the least partial good*' which the novel has noted is a defining characteristic of her moral personality (235, emphasis added).[13] For Eliot there is a disharmony between Dorothea's deep rooted belief in and desire to discover 'what is perfectly good' and the reasons, the emotions of fear and pity, which now seem likely to motivate the actions that will have such a critical effect on her life. The moral incoherence which necessarily ensues from such an unresolved conflict is made manifest in the text in the fragmentary speech characterizing Dorothea's breakdown. If we are to assess the alternatives in Eliot's terms then any momentary relief afforded Casaubon by Dorothea's promise must constitute a 'partial good' when set against Dorothea's damaging loss of integrity or wholeness of consciousness.[14] Paradoxically, it seems that Dorothea's great qualities are, in this case, the wrong qualifications for 'saintliness'. Such a martyrdom as Dorothea faces has no meaning, no genuine good can come of it, and George Eliot contrives Casaubon's timely death.[15] If, as Dorothea affirms during her conversation with Will Ladislaw, the poet, however imbued with sensibility he may be, needs to produce poems to qualify as such, so, George Eliot recognizes, does the saint need not only faith, but faith that in shaping her actions is productive of a (great) good.

To claim that in *Middlemarch* beliefs ground the moral personality is to run counter to a strong tradition of criticism that emphasizes the vital role of the passions in Eliot's conception of character.[16] In the words of Quentin Anderson: 'she knew and could show that every idea is attended by a passion; that every thought is a passional act' (247). The readings of K. M. Newton, Barbara Hardy, Paris and Anderson all suggest that the moral thrust to good is a function of some kind of emotion and that it is more often than not inextricably linked to the satisfaction of a personal need, so that the action thus prompted is to be considered fundamentally egoistic in its motivation. To quote Anderson again: 'human behaviour is now seen as a set of symbolic gestures expressive of individual needs and desires' (289). Desire, the emotions, beliefs; in her ambitious imaginative engagement with the phenomenology of motivating states, Eliot attempts to render transparent the complex springs of human action, the promptings of the inner life, developing an elaborate account of motives that is quite novel in her fiction. But what is striking about her understanding of what makes motivation moral are its crucial points of contact with and significant departures from dominant theories. An idea of the development occurring in her thought may be gained by even a brief look at the language of belief found in her earlier historical novel *Romola.* Whereas in *Romola* the narrator emphasizes the saving power of 'energetic belief' in enabling the heroine to find a way out of despair and engage in meaningful acts to aid the suffering, in *Middlemarch* this precise explanatory expression is absent from the text; probably because George Eliot realized that it was not in fact sufficiently explanatory of moral motivation.

From the moment Casaubon prevents further discussion of Dorothea's seemingly inexplicable decision to give up riding by asserting that: 'we must not inquire too curiously into motives . . . they are apt to become feeble

in the utterance . . . we must keep the germinating grain away from the light' (44), the novel directs a strong light on motives. Given that much is made of Dorothea's impetuous generosity of feeling, the role played by principled belief in Eliot's account of moral motivation may appear surprising. In the 'great' Kant's view (as Eliot referred to him) the moral agent's will responds purely to principles, reasons which are understood to be generally applicable.[17] Kant's cognitive theory of motivation in which practical reason and self control are elements of central importance—in so far as they are the distinguishing features of the moral self—has been modified recently in ways that strike resonances when read alongside Eliot's text. In this revisionist view 'moral reasons are purely cognitive states, but they are beliefs which we would not have unless we already had a concern for others. On this account the moral reasons do not require the presence of independent desires in order to motivate, since the independent desires are needed at an earlier stage. The desires are not among one's reasons for acting, though they are necessary for one to have the reasons one has'.[18] Such a re-working of Kant has significant implications as regards our view of the moral agent. If the mental rigour or detachment essential to the practice of the Kantian moral principle has provoked repugnance in critics, the capacity to feel and care for others required by this revised Kantianism must condition favourably our response to the actor. In short it gives us a strong reason to admire.[19]

In Eliot's novel a disposition to care—a ready sensibility to appreciate the needs of others—plays an active part in the moral personality; and the character of Lydgate appears exemplary in this respect. As the novel repeatedly illustrates, Lydgate's capacity to provide the kind of care that comes from caring makes him a good doctor. Eliot's portrayal of Lydgate's mental state at the time he aids the ailing Bulstrode, highlights the importance of his recognition that he is first and foremost 'a Healer', one who brings 'rescue or relief to the sufferer' (783). But her description of exactly how he 'checks' 'resentful hatred' for Bulstrode, and gets into the frame of mind that makes for a moral action links two elements that do not usually go together in accounts of moral agency. Lydgate, as one who has developed a valuable instinct or propensity which is bound up with the duties of a social role that is a determining feature of his identity, belongs in a special category of moral agent. His ability to 'check' his repugnance for Bulstrode is owing to his awareness of 'that *instinct* of the Healer which *thinks* first of bringing relief' (my emphasis). The phrasing of the motivational structure implies then that the thrust to action, of which Lydgate himself is conscious, comes from an instinctive reflex that channels his thoughts in the appropriate direction. Lydgate finds himself automatically thinking of helping. And once he has had the thought the outcome, the action, is inevitable. To recognize the situation for what it is, is to feel bound by it to act, to be motivated to act on this recognition: . . . 'Lydgate felt sure there was not strength enough in him [Bulstrode] to walk away without support. What could he do? He could not see a man sink close to him for want of help. He rose and gave his arm to Bulstrode, and in that way led him out of the room; yet this act, which might have been one of gentle duty and pure compassion, was at this moment unspeakably bitter to him. It seemed as it he were putting his sign-manual to that association of himself with Bulstrode . . . Poor Lydgate, his mind struggling under the terrible clutch of this revelation [that "the town knew of the loan, believed it to be a bribe, and believed he took it as a bribe"] was all the while morally forced to take Mr Bulstrode to the bank . . .' (783-4). Lydgate feels he is 'morally forced' to act. In adding these two words to an account of Lydgate's moral reasoning which already suggests a lack of conviction, George Eliot completes her assessment. Lydgate is a human being acted upon, not a complete initiator of his actions. His motives lack the conviction or firm belief that comes from a choice freely or resolutely made. Kant makes the point that 'if the practice of virtue were to become a habit the subject would suffer loss to that freedom in adopting maxims which distinguishes an action done from duty'. Thus, it is one's duty to confirm or re-affirm resolutely one's duty: 'Virtue can never settle down in peace and quiet with its maxims adopted once and for all but, if it is not rising, is unavoidably sinking'.[20] The novel denies Lydgate the accolades of moral heroism. Lydgate is the only one present at the meeting to act, yet his mechanical response calls into question the appropriateness of any admiration we might feel.

As the novel draws to its close, Dorothea—in a scene to be compared with that of her earlier moral dilemma—also perceives an opportunity to help someone, in this case Lydgate's wife, and must also check strong feelings—this time of anger and scorn—if the crucial moral action is to get underway. Here it is worth noting first that Dorothea doesn't just 'check' her feelings, she 'overcomes' 'the tumult' of emotion, though it must be admitted that the time span is longer. In Eliot's long and complex account, in chapter 80, of the process that ensures Dorothea's movement from her cold bedroom and the solitude of her anguish to a fervent embrace with Rosamond, the emotions or feelings are recognized as vital forces, but forces that must sometimes be mastered. Furthermore, although desire certainly plays a crucial role in the motivational process, Dorothea's desire is no simple inclination or impulsive feeling but is of a special nature: it contains a belief. It is an 'informed' or 'idealized desire',[21] which involves a prior belief in a rational ideal, in this case the standard of 'perfect Right' or Justice as Fairness: thus she 'yearned towards the perfect Right, that it might make a throne

within her and rule her errant will' (846). Dorothea desires that her will might be constrained by the authority of a moral principle of absolute value.[22] The many references to 'all the active thought' that goes into determining what action 'should' be undertaken so that she can fulfil the 'obligation' laid on her by the three lives in contact with her own has further Kantian overtones. But Eliot's revised cognitivism finds room in a crucial parenthesis for the idea that a desire for the well-being of others is a necessary pre-condition for moral motivation. 'For *now* the thoughts came quickly. *It was not in Dorothea's nature . . . to sit in the narrow cell of her calamity, in the besotted misery of a consciousness that only sees another's lot as an accident of its own . . .* She began *now* to live through that yesterday morning deliberately again, forcing herself *to dwell on* every detail and its possible meaning . . . She forced herself *to think* of it as bound up with another woman's life . . .' (845, emphasis added). Thus within the narrative of the dynamics of moral agency which unfolds in the novel's present time—the time 'now'—we find an explicatory parenthesis which refers 'back' to Dorothea's habitual (and admirable) concern for others. Kant distrusts the efficacy of 'certain feelings and propensities', and requires a 'deliberate resolve': 'the capacity and considered resolve to withstand a strong but unjust opponent [impulses of nature or natural inclination] is fortitude (fortitudo) and, with respect to what opposes the moral disposition within us, *VIRTUE*.'[23] Likewise in Eliot's text, Dorothea *deliberately* forces herself to think and then to achieve the 'calm resolve' that will enable her to determine (freely) what to do. Dorothea is capable of this resolve—this calmly deliberate engagement of the will—coming at last to a decision to return to Rosamond that necessitates a great deal of self-control. Though often near to breaking point, it will take her through her emotionally fraught encounter.

Eliot's treatment of motivation might seem to confirm our impression that Dorothea's beliefs and the acts that they instigate are to be taken as evidence of her exceptional moral goodness—her saintliness. However, for a Kantian—and this reading suggests that Eliot underwrote key elements of Kant's moral theory—the capacity to adhere to Kantian moral precepts is proof of morality but no more. It provides a system of action-guiding principles by which all can abide. Those who do so may be virtuous but not necessarily saints.

II

Attitudes to Eliot's characters are inevitably conditioned to a considerable degree by the nature of the beliefs that orient their lives. If Mary Garth earns respect for her belief in the duty of gratitude which informs her loyalty to Fred and her family, the response to Ladislaw's conviction that 'the best piety is to enjoy, when you can' (252) is always likely to be mixed. Of all the varied discourses of belief articulated in *Middlemarch* there is one beginning with the words 'it is fitting' that Eliot finds disquieting and compelling.

Traditionally, the concept of 'what is fitting' involved the perception of an appropriate match between the nature of the person and their circumstances that was taken to correspond to some eternal standard of right or of naturalness. The eighteenth century philosopher Samuel Clarke provides a lucid exposition of key ideas of this theory: there are 'necessary and eternal different relations that different things bear to one another', and a 'consequent fitness or unfitness of the application of different things and different relations one to another . . . these eternal and necessary differences of things make it fit and reasonable for creatures so to act; they cause it to be their duty or lay an obligation upon them. . . .' In Clark's view, determining wherein lies the fitness of things requires the rational agent 'to act in constant conformity to the eternal rules of Justice, Equity, Goodness and Truth' as ''tis very unreasonable and blameworthy in Practice, that any Intelligent Creatures . . . should either negligently suffer themselves to be imposed upon and deceived in Matters of Good and Evil, Right and Wrong, or wilfully and perversely to allow themselves to be over-ruled by absurd Passions, and corrupt or partial Affections, to act contrary to what they know is Fit to be done'.[24]

Always a problematic morality,[25] in *Middlemarch* the ubiquitous discourses of fitness have become emptied of any moral meaning. They are now expressions of convenience, impersonal words masking personal aspirations or desire, and of which they are the rationalization. 'What can the fitness of things mean, if not their fitness to a man's expectations?' (163). The narrator's ironic comment highlights the presumption in Fred Vincy's confident assumption that he will get what he has done nothing to deserve. Fred believes that it is appropriate given that he possesses the tastes and manners of a gentleman that he should inherit the Featherstone fortune. The clergyman-scholar Casaubon believes that there is 'a fitness' or it is fitting that '[Dorothea's] ardent and self-sacrificing affection [should] round and complete the existence of [his] own' (73). Dorothea will make his life 'whole'. This time the irony is missing. Later contemplating his imminent death, Casaubon does not stop to ask himself whether it is reasonable, just or fair, that his young wife continue, as he urges her to do, his arduous and abstruse intellectual labours. Nor do notions of what is fitting prevent him from adding the infamous codicil to his will. Of even greater expectations is the evangelical banker Bulstrode, who, faced with the ruin of his hopes for spiritual and social eminence, believes that 'it would be more fitting for the Divine glory that he should escape dishonour' (740). But presumption is again punished, and Eliot ensures that shame and disgrace, through the medium of a rambling

Raffles, await the man whose original sin is—significantly—a betrayal of 'feminine trustfulness' (666). If in the novel the language of fitness signifies assumptions and opinions—degraded forms of belief—about the *correctness* or appropriateness of relationships or situations, the discourses of trust deal with *goodness*. In *Middlemarch* those capable of trust possess a willingness or readiness to believe in the virtues of others, which is itself virtuous. It is a morality that making for vulnerability requires a kind of inner strength like courage to sustain it.

The capacity to trust is a characteristic of the hard working Caleb Garth, who was 'not distrustful of his fellow men when they had not proved themselves untrustworthy' (264). Though far from well-off, he makes a loan to Fred Vincy. His trust is based on a belief that Fred will be as scrupulous as himself. He is willing to count on Fred's reliability; and his trust is thus, in this instance, specific. When Fred fails to pay back the loan on time and Caleb Garth reveals his doubts about Fred to his daughter—'I'm afraid Fred is not to be trusted, Mary'—his lack of confidence in Fred does nothing to dent the astute Mary's constancy and loyalty, and this despite her vexation voiced when she sees him next that Fred seems 'fit for nothing in the world that is useful' (288-290). Fred may be caring, but he is as yet insufficiently careful: 'Fred means better than he acts, perhaps. But I should think it a pity for anybody's happiness to be wrapped up in him . . . And so should I, father, said Mary . . . Fred has always been very good to me; he is kind-hearted and affectionate, and *not false,* I think, with all his self-indulgence' (290-91, emphasis added). Fred's untrustworthiness is acknowledged with regret; but father and daughter try to see his character whole; his unreliability is perceived as a critical but not fatal flaw of character.

Unreliable, but not 'false', just as there are different types of untrustworthiness so are there different kinds of trust. The 'perfect' trust knows no boundaries: this 'indefinite' or 'over-trust' 'extends beyond the limits of reason' or hard 'external fact' and is accompanied by complete confidence.[26] This trust is invested with good; it is a form of generosity that confers great value on the recipient; it is life-enhancing and empowering. It is the kind of belief that imparts self-esteem for it involves not simply an assumption as to the reliability of the subject so perceived but, more seriously, constitutes an affirmation of his fundamental goodness, his moral worth, his good will; it is a belief that 'you cleave to what you believe to be good'.[27] As a firm belief there is no conditional element in the thought; there is no opening for doubt, no provision for the possibility of failure. At the time he is implicated in the sudden demise of Raffles, Lydgate waits in vain for a sign from Rosamond that she possesses this kind of trust in him: 'If she has any trust in me—*any notion of what I am,* she ought to speak now and say she does not believe I have deserved disgrace' (emphasis added, 814). This is the 'perfect' trust that Dorothea has in Lydgate, Ladislaw, and, at the start of her marriage, in Casaubon. As Eliot's contrast in the attitudes of Dorothea and Rosamond makes clear perfect trust is grounded not in feelings—which are derivative—but in the conviction that one's fundamental beliefs about what is right and good are shared and constitute the grounds for action. For Dorothea, without that conviction 'spiritual emptiness and discontent' (516) ensue.[28]

Whereas Casaubon, set hard against Dorothea's ideals of justice, is unable to live up to her 'perfect' trust, Will Ladislaw, it appears, carelessly destroys her trust in him, and she experiences great misery. In Eliot's plot, the climax of the increasingly intimate relations between Will and Rosamond prepares the trap of circumstances—Dorothea is shown into the wrong room, and is literally closed in by a table—in which she is caught. But there is another 'place' in which Dorothea must not remain entrapped, the Slough of Despond (cited in the epigraph of the previous chapter).[29] It belongs to Dorothea's moral greatness, then, that she is not crushed by despair, nor touched by cynicism. Unlike Lydgate her 'resolution is [not] checked by despairing resentment' (814). Dorothea emerges from her experience of betrayal, still believing in and determined to use her own moral powers, and confident of the capacity of others to preserve their integrity (wholeness of character) and to respond to her goodwill.[30] This is the 'overtrust' that William James, like George Eliot, perceives as central to saintliness: 'We find that error by excess is exemplified in every saintly virtue', James observes (340). 'The saints, existing in this way, may, with their extravagances of human tenderness, be prophetic . . . Treating those whom they met, in spite of the past, in spite of all appearances, as worthy, they have stimulated them to be worthy, miraculously transformed them by their radiant example and by the challenge of their expectation . . . The saints are authors, *auctores,* increasers, of goodness . . . The world is not yet with them, so they often seem in the midst of the world's affairs to be preposterous. Yet they are impregnators of the world, vivifiers and animators of potentialities of goodness which but for them would lie forever dormant. It is not possible to be quite as mean as we naturally are, when they have passed before us. One fire kindles another; and without that over-trust in human worth which they show, the rest of us would lie in spiritual stagnancy' (358).[31] Supreme value has been attached to trust more recently by Aurel Kolnai: 'the attitude of Trust . . . unless it is vitiated by harebrained optimism and dangerous irresponsibility, may be looked upon, not to be sure as a starting point and the very basis, but perhaps as the epitome and culmination of morality'.[32] If James's remarks seem most relevant to the effect Dorothea has on Will and Rosamond, what Kolnai has to say points up

the crucial difference between morality and saintliness, or the moral outlooks of Farebrother and Dorothea. When they both learn of the suspicions that Lydgate may have been bribed by Bulstrode, Farebrother, noted for his selflessness, kindness, and compassion, is pained but has his doubts; he cannot be 'confident' that Lydgate has not fallen below himself. He knows that 'character is not cut in marble' (790). Dorothea's energetic speech emphasizes the fact of her belief: 'You don't believe that Mr Lydgate is guilty of anything base. I will not believe it. Let us find out the truth and clear him' (784-5). At which point the reader may make his assessment of character on the basis of the following inferences—Dorothea believes that it is possible (for Lydgate) to conserve integrity despite strong temptation, whereas Farebrother, who has actually proved in his relations with Fred and Mary, that his own integrity can survive such a trial, is nevertheless not prepared to believe that others are equally capable.[33] Dorothea has no doubts, her great virtue, her 'overtrust', which prompts the risky action that is anathema to the hesitant males who surround her, is an irrepressible expression of her identity, and accordingly the manifestation of the great gap that exists between the saint and the lesser mortals of **Middlemarch.**[34]

Notes

1. On the role of perception in Dickens' conception of virtue see Valerie Wainwright, 'On Goods, Virtues and *Hard Times*', *Dickens Studies Annual,* 26 (1997), pp. 169-186.

2. All references to the novel in the text are taken from the Penguin Edition, Harmondsworth, 1965, reprinted, 1981, ed. W. J. Harvey.

3. For example, Jerome Thale asserts that 'Middlemarch is, specifically, a novel about vocations, and Lydgate and Dorothea fail because they have not taken the measure of the world in which they are to work as medical reformer and as modern St Theresa'; see *The Novels of George Eliot* (New York: Columbia University Press, 1959), p. 144. Barbara Hardy claims that 'Dorothea's strength lies in aspiration, not in action or creation', in 'Public and Private Worlds', *George Eliot's* Middlemarch ed. Harold Bloom (New York: Chelsea House, 1987), p. 45. According to Kathleen Blake, 'Middlemarch shows that not to shape the world is to be shapeless oneself'; see '*Middlemarch* and the Woman Question', in *George Eliot's* Middlemarch, p. 55.

4. Susan Wolf, 'Moral Saints', *Journal of Philosophy,* 79 (1982), pp. 419-39.

5. For views that disagree with Wolf on the nature of the moral saint see R. M. Adams 'Saints', *Journal of Philosophy,* 81 (1984), pp. 392-401; L. Blum

'Moral Examplars: Reflections on Schindler, the Trocmes, and others', in *Moral Perception and Particularity* (Cambridge: CUP [Cambridge University Press] 1994); and Owen Flanagan, 'Prologue: Saints' in *Varieties of Moral Personality: Ethics and Psychological Realism* (Cambridge: Harvard University Press, 1991).

6. For different reasons, this is the viewpoint of Richard Poirier and J. Hillis Miller; see '*Middlemarch*: Chapter 85: Three Commentaries', *Nineteenth-Century Fiction,* 35 (1980), pp. 448-53.

7. See Jeanie Thomas *Reading Middlemarch: Reclaiming the Middle Distance* (Ann Arbor: UMI Research Press, 1987), p. 10. Among readings that view Eliot as a stern moralist prescribing an ethos of duty and self-renunciation see, for example, Walter Allen, *George Eliot* (New York: Macmillan, 1964), p. 95; John Holloway, *The Victorian Sage: Studies in Argument* (London: Macmillan, 1953), p. 126; John Halperin, *Egoism and Self-Discovery in the Victorian Novel: Studies in the Ordeal of Knowledge in the Nineteenth Century* (New York: Burt Franklin, 1974), p. 161; and U. C. Knoepflmacher, *Religious Humanism and the Victorian Novel: George Eliot, Walter Pater and Samuel Butler* (Princeton: Princeton University Press, 1965), p. 84. Calvin Bedient criticises George Eliot's 'puritanical' morality which condones the repression of the vital self. For Bedient, Eliot also proposes the negation of such a position, but unwittingly. See *Architects of the Self: George Eliot, D. H. Lawrence, and E. M. Forster* (Berkeley: California University Press, 1972), pp. 36-44.

8. Susanne Graver argues against the views of Sandra M. Gilbert and Susan Gubar (*The Madwoman in the Attic: The Woman Writer and the Nineteenth-Century Literary Imagination* [New Haven: Yale University Press, 1979]) that there is no tension between the novel's rhetoric and its plot with regard to this episode: 'The doctrine of living for others is examined so thoroughly as to reveal how it miscarries even when one attempts to practice it as an ideal'. See *George Eliot and Community* (Berkeley: California University Press, 1984), p. 206.

9. As Professor Ken Newton has suggested to me, there are parallels between this scene and the scene where Mary Garth is requested by Featherstone to burn one of his wills (Ch. 33). Both women are subjected to the pressure of an unreasonable man. However, Eliot does not examine Mary Garth's motivation in any depth because there is no mental conflict, and her integrity is never under threat at the crucial moment. Significantly, it is only later that she questions 'those

acts of hers which had come *imperatively* and excluded all question in the critical moment' (emphasis added, p. 353).

10. Jonathan Dancy, *Moral Reasons* (Oxford: Blackwell, 1993), p. 124.

11. Elizabeth Ermath discusses the moral implications of George Eliot's representation of the clergyman Farebrother's self-conception in *Realism and Consensus in the English Novel* (Princeton: Princeton University Press, 1984), pp. 235-36. Farebrother alerts Fred to the folly of his ways, thus acting in Fred Vincy's interest rather than his own; as a result, Fred avoids losing Mary's affection, which Farebrother had hoped to win for himself. Ermath comments that 'By recognizing the presence in himself of two distinct motives, Farebrother is able to keep control of himself, literally to maintain his identity'. Clearly, desiring to be true to his best conception of self is a good reason, but the novel seems to suggest that there is a nobler, less fallible, motive involving a belief in something external to the self. This conviction is reserved for Dorothea.

12. Sören Kierkegaard, *Purity of Heart,* trans. D. Steere (London, 1961), p. 177.

13. An article by J. A. Froude on Spinoza published in the Westminster Review of 1855, points up the crucial link that according to Spinoza must exist between conceptions of the good and well-being: 'While we are governed by outward temptations, by the casual pleasures, the fortunes or misfortunes of life, we are but instruments, yielding ourselves to be acted upon as the animal is acted on by its appetites, or the inanimate matter by the laws which bind it—we are slaves . . . So far, on the contrary, as we know clearly what we do, as we understand what we are, and *direct our conduct not by the passing emotion of the moment, but by a grave, clear and constant knowledge of what is really good,* so far we are said to act—we are ourselves the spring of our own activity—we desire the genuine well-being of our entire nature' (emphasis added). George Eliot remarked of this article that although she did not agree with Froude's own views she thought his account of Spinoza's doctrines admirable. The passage is quoted by Hilda M. Hulme, 'Imagery', in *Middlemarch: Critical Approaches to the Novel,* ed. Barbara Hardy (London: Athlone Press, 1967), p. 119.

14. Hence Bernard J. Paris's statement (in *Experiments in Life: George Eliot's Quest for Values,* [Detroit: Wayne State University Press, 1965] p. 248), that Eliot insists 'upon other men as the objective sanction of morality and upon living for

others as its end is the rock, as it were, upon which her religion of humanity is built', fails to do justice to the complexity of Eliot's moral vision as portrayed in this scene.

15. Carol Christ discusses the implications of such 'providential' deaths in 'Aggression and Providential Death in George Eliot's Fiction', *Novel,* 9 (1976), pp. 130-140.

16. Thus M. C. Henberg: 'Motivation, Eliot believes, comes from the feelings alone, and the ethical task is to educate our feelings by imaginative "experiments in life" unflinching projections of the actual likely consequences of our actions'; see 'George Eliot's Moral Realism', *Philosophy and Literature,* 3 (1979), p. 22. Likewise emphasis is given to the role of the emotions in Eliot's fiction in the following works: K. M. Newton, *George Eliot, Romantic Humanist: A Study of the Philosophical Structure of her Novels* (London: Macmillan, 1981); Barbara Hardy, 'Middlemarch and the Passions', in *This Particular Web: Essays on Middlemarch* ed. Ian Adam (Toronto: Toronto University Press, 1975), pp. 3-21; Paris, op. cit; and Q. Anderson, 'George Eliot in Middlemarch', *From Dickens to Hardy,* ed. Boris Ford (Harmondsworth: Penguin, 1958), pp. 274-93.

17. In a letter to her friend Sara Hennell of 19 July 1854, Marian Evans referred to 'the great Kant'; quoted by Rosemary Ashton, in *George Eliot: A Life* (London: Hamish Hamilton, 1996), p. 112. G. H. Lewes and George Eliot continued to acquire books on Kant for their library. Among these were the books on Kant now in Dr Williams Library in London, see *The George Eliot-George Henry Lewes Library: An Annotated Catalogue of their books at Dr Williams Library,* London, ed., William Baker (New York: Garland, 1977).

18. Dancy, op. cit. p. 10; D. Z. Phillips, '*In Search of the Moral Must*: Mrs Foot's Fugitive Thought', *Philosophical Quarterly,* 27 (1977), pp. 140-157.

19. On this dilemma see M. Stocker: 'In so far as one acts from duty one is unable to realize the great goods of love, friendship, affection, fellow-feeling and community'; 'The Schizophrenia of Modern Ethical Theories', *Journal of Philosophy,* 63 (1976), pp. 453-466. Marcia Baron seeks to dispel such doubts in 'On the Alleged Moral Repugnance of Acting from Duty', *Journal of Philosophy,* 81 (1984), pp. 197-219. Baron argues against the view that acting from duty means that the moral agent does not really care about others but simply seeks to meet a minimum requirement, and that it must nurture the wrong attitude to others. Baron argues that a Kantian does not have to be preoccupied with morality rather than people.

20. *The Metaphysics of Morals,* ed. Mary Gregor (Cambridge: CUP, 1991), pp. 209-10. Kant observes that 'the true strength of virtue is a *tranquil mind* with a considered and firm resolution to put the law of virtue into practice. That is the state of *health* in the moral life . . .' (209).

21. For an analysis of the implications of this concept see Michael Smith 'Realism' in *Ethics,* ed. Peter Singer (Oxford: OUP [Oxford University Press], 1994), pp. 170-76.

22. For Kant the concept of duty involves the idea of a reason determining the will by a priori principles; *The Metaphysics of Morals,* ed. Mary Gregor, p. 188.

23. *The Metaphysics of Morals,* p. 186.

24. Quoted by J. L. Mackie, *Hume's Moral Theory* (London: Routledge & Kegan Paul, 1980), p. 15.

25. See L. A. Selby-Bigge, 'Introduction' to *British Moralists; Being selections from writers principally of the eighteenth century* (New York: Dover, 1965), 1. xxxiii-xxxv.

26. According to Elizabeth Ermath, George Eliot is working with a conception of trust that is of minimal value and somehow functions strategically: 'All the novels deal with the politics of trust, that is with those strategies for maintaining at least provisional agreement in a world characterized by misunderstanding and clashes of will'; *Realism and Consensus in the English Novel,* p. 253.

27. The phrase is taken from a letter Marian Evans wrote to her friend Sara Bray, admonishing her for her lack of trust: 'If we differ on the subject of the marriage laws, I at least can believe of you that you cleave to what you believe to be good, and I don't know of anything in the nature of your views that should prevent you from believing the same of me'. The letter is cited by Rosemary Ashton in *George Eliot: A Life,* p. 138.

28. George Eliot makes Dorothea short-sighted, observes that she is hasty in her trust (48), and asks 'what believer sees a disturbing omission or infelicity?' (74). Karen Jones expresses the same idea in 'Trust as an Affective Attitude', *Ethics,* 107 (1996), p. 12. This account of trust emphasizes the importance of feelings of optimism but plays down the significance of belief.

29. Hence this reading contrasts with that of David Carroll, who finds that at this point Dorothea's 'trust in human nature is shattered'. See 'Middlemarch and the externality of fact' in *This Particular Web,* pp. 73-90.

30. Herbert Morris observes that 'We operate with a conception of worth of human beings that leads to

our esteeming more highly those who are not just moral persons but morally wise persons. They have . . . not been crushed by what they have confronted, but have emerged, victorious, capable, despite and because of knowledge [of betrayal] of affirming rather than denying life.' See *On Guilt and Innocence* (Berkeley: California University Press, 1976), p. 161.

31. *The Varieties of Religious Experience: A Study in Human Nature* (London: Longmans, Green & Co, 1920).

32. Aurel Kolnai, 'Forgiveness', *Ethics, Value and Reality,* ed. B. Williams & D. Wiggins (Indianapolis: Hackett, 1978), p. 223.

33. On the question of how we are to read Farebrother's character see also n. 14.

34. Relevant here is L. Lerner's criticism of criticisms of G. Eliot's ethics in 'Dorothea and the Theresa-Complex' in *Middlemarch* ed. P. Swinden (London: Macmillan, 1972), pp. 225-247.

Jessie Givner (essay date spring 2002)

SOURCE: Givner, Jessie. "Industrial History, Preindustrial Literature: George Eliot's *Middlemarch*." *ELH* 69, no. 1 (spring 2002): 223-43.

[*In the following essay, Givner evaluates the tension between fictional abstraction and historical realism in* Middlemarch. *Givner takes issue with the assertion, put forth by such Marxist critics as Terry Eagleton, Georg Lukács, and others, that the language of literature is inherently figurative while the language of history is direct and literal. Through a close analysis of the novel's descriptions of industrialization, Givner concludes that all forms of discourse are essentially figurative and that distinctions between fictional and historical narration are ultimately false.*]

An especially gruesome historical event impresses itself on the minds of several characters in Eliot's **Middlemarch.** The first allusion to that event occurs when Mr. Hackbutt, explaining his reservations about the 1832 Reform Bill, remarks, "I myself should never favour immoderate views—in fact I take my stand with Huskisson."[1] William Huskisson, who opposed reform until it was all but inevitable, is remembered equally well for his horrific death. In 1830, after he had resigned as Secretary of State, he was riding in one of the show trains that marked the beginning of the railway system. When the train stopped, Huskisson stepped down onto the tracks to admire the new machine. The accident is related in one particularly vivid account:

Those inside [the train] stretched their legs discreetly and consulted their watches, wondering how long it would be before the other engine reached them. "I think you had better get in," called the Duke of Wellington to the loiterers outside. Only then did they see the Rocket bearing down on them fast on the other rails. There was not enough room, they suddenly realised, for them to stand safely on the opposite side of the line, and no space either between the two sets of rails . . . The former Secretary of State had already tried to escape the oncoming train by crossing the track. He now ran back in panic and was clutching at one of the doors when the engine caught him and flung him on the rails. Even inside the carriage, Lady Wilton could distinctly hear the crushing of bones, followed by Mrs. Huskisson's piercing shriek.[2]

This accident, compulsively repeated in Eliot's text, is referred to a few chapters later, when Mr. Raffles takes "the new-made railway, observing to his fellow-passengers that he considered it pretty well seasoned now it had done for Huskisson" (379). As Linda Colley notes, the death of Huskisson became a historical set-piece, in part, because of its obvious and facile symbolism: after resisting reform, he was both literally and figuratively flung in front of the fast moving and inevitable engine of change, which symbolized not only the advent of middle-class emancipation, but also the revolution of industrialization, signalled by the new railway system.

The head-on collision between literary and historical character in **Middlemarch** is important, for Eliot criticism has long been divided by divergent interpretive tracks, one which runs along the lines of a kind of Lukácsian march of history, and the other which follows the perhaps slower lines of figurative reading. In Eliot criticism, the political / literary tension manifests itself through the historical / literary distinction, where "history" is frequently substituted for "politics."[3] The polarized critical climate surrounding Eliot's work results, in part, from the fundamental misconception of tropological discourse as wholly incompatible with historical and political discourse. In Eliot's **Middlemarch,** however, historical and political discourse is inescapably tropological. Tropes, in particular, the trope of personification, allow Eliot to create a world in which the terms associated with the literary are *turned* into the terms aligned with the historical and political. Like politics, the term history, in both Victorian texts and in current critical theory, is aligned with action and practice.[4] Because the related tropes of personification and prosopopeia enable a turn from inanimate to animate, from object to subject, and from description to action, those tropes are central to Eliot's historical turn.

In the polarized climate of Eliot criticism, figurative reading tends to emerge as a kind of preindustrial form opposed to the industrial realm of history. Terry Eagleton, for example, argues that Eliot's novel reduces the historical to the literary because "[t]he Reform Bill, the railways, cholera, machine-breaking: these 'real' historical forces do no more than impinge on the novel's margins."[5] The forces of industrial revolution, that is, are "real" history, and those forces are contained and reduced by the text. Distinguishing "between the *text and* the '*real*' *history* to which it alludes" (my emphasis), Eagleton cites Eliot's overarching figure of the web as an exemplary "dehistoricizing" (and therefore depoliticizing) literary structure. In a famous passage in *Middlemarch,* the web appears as a figure for history itself, when the narrator refers to the novel's form of history as "this particular web" (128). Eagleton writes that "the web's symmetry, its 'spatial' dehistoricizing of the social process, its exclusion of levels of contradiction, preserve the essential unity of the organic mode."[6] The metaphor of the web, Eagleton suggests, belongs to a timeless, spatial, rural, organic realm, a realm that he associates with preindustrialism. While Eliot figures history through the metaphor of the web, Eagleton figures figuration itself as a historical period prior to industrialization. Although history, in Eagleton's formulation, becomes the larger structure containing literature, it is ultimately a metaphor itself and thus both contains and is contained by figuration. What does it mean that Eagleton figures figuration itself as preindustrial? The language of Eagleton's own argument points to the fact that he can conceive of history itself only through figurative form, in terms of a referent / figure structure, where industrialism is a figure for the referentiality (the "real" force of history) and preindustrialism is a figure for figurative language itself. Eliot's *Middlemarch* is troubling to Eagleton precisely because it suggests what the language of Eagleton's argument unwittingly implies, that it may be impossible to formulate the historical / literary, political / literary distinctions *except* through tropological discourse.

I cite Eagleton's criticism as exemplary of a resistance to the notion that figures and tropes might operate as historical and political forces. The assumption that tropes and figures are inherently incompatible with historical and political discourse marks not only Eagleton's 1978 reading, but also more recent Eliot criticism. Daniel Cottom, for example, argues that Eliot's novels are part of the "cancellation of history" that is the "essence of liberal intellectual discourse." And figurative language, he suggests, is instrumental to that cancellation, for the "process of constructing metaphor through the repression of social reference was the fable of culture in the Victorian age and generally provided the plot of its novels."[7] Like Eagleton's intervention, Cottom's is based on the assumption that literary discourse is essentially tropological, while historical and political discourse is essentially referential and literal. Eliot criticism is marked by some notable attempts to combine the two seemingly divergent critical modes of literary and historico-political analysis. Yet many of these ear-

nest attempts at reconciliation ultimately give priority to either a social / historical reading or a figurative / literary one and thus reinforce the literary / historical impasse.[8] The failure to get beyond the literary / historical impasse is, in part, a result of the failure to throw into question the assumption that literary discourse is inherently tropological, and historical or political discourse inherently referential.

I.

The train which runs through the center of *Middlemarch* is a quintessential Eliot figure in its tendency to suddenly switch from literal to figurative tracks. Some time after the unsavory Mr. Raffles takes his train, he meets up with Mr. Bulstrode and manages to extort money by threatening to expose the history of Bulstrode's fraudulent business. Referring to the inexorable (figurative) train of events that hurtles Bulstrode toward his public humiliation, Eliot writes that "the train of causes in which he had locked himself went on" (564). Like so many of the characters in *Middlemarch,* Bulstrode has made the mistake of viewing his past as "a dead history, an outworn preparation of the present" (562). Through a prosopopeic turn, Eliot brings his history back to life, so that his memory is "set smarting like a reopened wound," a "still quivering part of himself, bringing shudders and bitter flavours and the tinglings of merited shame" (562). Thus, what Eagleton considers to be one of the unambiguously "'real' historical forces," the railway, is turned into a trope, but a trope that is at once literary and historical.

If we look for Eliot's more explicit remarks on the problem of history, not in her novels, but in her 1856 review essay, **"The Natural History of German Life,"** we once again encounter the trope of the train through which she articulates her particular vision of history. Formulating the relation between concrete and abstract history, she begins her essay with a commentary on the varying degree of "concrete knowledge" that one word represents for two different people:

> The word *railways,* for example, will probably call up, in the mind of a man who is not highly locomotive, the image either of a "Bradshaw," or of the station with which he is most familiar, or of an indefinite length of tram-road; he will alternate between these three images, which represent his stock of concrete acquaintance with railways.[9]

According to Eliot, this non-locomotive man with limited experience of railways will likely view "railways in the abstract" and "may talk of a vast net-work of railways stretching over the globe." But, in the mind of a man who has gained wider experience of the railway through his positions as "a 'navvy,' an engineer, a traveller, a railway director and shareholder," she argues, "the word 'railways' would include all the essential facts in the existence and relations of the *thing*." And, as she sees it, we should look to this latter man "if we want a railway to be made."[10] For the non-locomotive man, then, the word "railway" is understood through literary operations, through a condensation of images and associations. For the man who has actual "experience" with operating the railway, however, the word is understood in terms of the "essential facts" which Eliot views as the foundation of "natural history." What is most significant about Eliot's formulation of historical discourse is that it depends upon a distinction between *describing* and *acting*. The man who has an imagistic, literary understanding of "railway," she suggests, can only describe railways "in the abstract," while the man who understands the "essential facts" can actually *make* the railway. Eliot's distinction between concretion and abstraction, mapped onto her distinction between simply *describing* the railway and actually *making* one, is crucial, for it places her vision of history within a broad tradition that formulates history through a distinction between constative and performative, descriptive and active language.

Eliot's literary / historical, constative / performative mapping suggests an unexpected point of intersection between her notion of the historical novel and the Lukácsian formulation of historical literature through the distinction between narration and description.[11] In his essay, "Narrate or Describe?" Lukács writes that "[w]hen the artistic literature of a period does not provide actions in which typical characters with a richly developed inner life are tested in practice, the public seeks abstract, schematic substitutes." Lukács's claim is followed by his assertion that such abstraction can be avoided if literature relies more on action than description. "The predominance of description," he writes, "is not only a result but also and simultaneously a cause, the cause of a further divorce of literature from epic significance."[12] Like Lukács's cautionary words about literary abstraction, Eliot's essays repudiate literary abstraction as a hindrance to historical realism. Yet there is some ambivalence in Eliot's articulation of the literary / historical relation; her desire for "concrete history" often seems to be at odds with her equally strong desire for a highly figurative history, a history that she describes, in a different context, as "pregnant movements of the past."[13] The figure of pregnancy is worth examination, for it belongs to a personification of temporal, historical movement, a personification that allows her to negotiate the concrete / abstract, action / description, history / literature impasse. Insofar as personification turns an object or thing into a living, moving subject, insofar as it animates the inanimate, it turns description into action. Thus, the figure bridges the two divided realms of Eliot's essay on natural history, the realms of concrete and abstract, constative and performative, literary and historical language.

In her efforts to historicize history, Phillipa Levine points out that, for the Victorians, industrialism was associated with history in such a way that the mechanization of time and measurement became linked to history as a form of measuring time. Indeed, the figuration of history as a self-regulating machine continues in current criticism, from Eagleton's early vision of industrial history to Judith Newton's reference to the "motor of history." Newton, however, is self-conscious about the figuration of history both as a machine and body. As she notes, the figure of pregnancy is persistent in Victorian narratives about history, and, she suggests, the figure is invoked not only to naturalize but also to feminize the narrative of industrial progress. In McCulloch's 1835 article, "Philosophy of Manufacturers," she notes that "qualities dominantly associated with women in nineteenth century representation, such as nature, embodiment, and birth, are also employed at times to familiarize, naturalize, and assign life-giving functions to material and largely machine-based production." At the same time, however, those naturalizing figures of pregnancy and embodiment are eventually displaced by "machines [that] completely outstrip nature in importance as they begin to intervene in history."[14] In Eliot's work, I would argue, we can see a movement that is exactly the opposite of the female embodiment / man-made machine shift which Newton observes in nineteenth-century narratives about history. Eliot's essays and novels literally *turn* not only man-made machines, but also histories, into bodies, and often, into female bodies.

If we return to the figure of the railway in *Middlemarch,* we can see that pregnancy once again serves the prosopopeic function of bringing history to life. At one point in the novel, when Caleb Garth's surveying of land is increasingly in demand, his maxim, "Business breeds," leads into a passage that continues the breeding figure:

> And one form of business that was beginning to breed just then was the construction of railways. A projected line was to run through Lowick parish where the cattle had hitherto grazed in a peace unbroken by astonishment; and thus it happened that the infant struggles of the railway system entered into the affairs of Caleb Garth, and determined the course of this history with regard to two persons who were dear to him.
>
> (502)

The business of the railways is linked, via the figure of breeding, to other forms of business in the novel, most notably to Joshua Riggs's obsession with "breeding coins." We are told that Riggs's one ambition is to have "a money-changer's shop on a much-frequented quay" and "to look sublimely cool as he handled the breeding coins of all nations" (475).

In Eliot's connection between the two figures of breeding, breeding machinery and breeding coins, we can also see a point of divergence between two different measurements of history and money. Unlike Riggs, Caleb Garth is incapable of conceptualizing either business or money because he cannot think figuratively; his mind does not exchange land into monetary value. Nor does it translate labour into the figure of breeding coins:

> he thought very well of all ranks, but he would not himself have liked to be of any rank in which he had not such a close contact with "business" as to get often honourably decorated with marks of dust and mortar . . . he could not manage finance: he knew values well, but, he had no keenness of imagination for monetary results in the shape of profit and loss.
>
> (228)

We are reminded of Caleb Garth's literal, concrete ties to the land much later, when the narrator tells us, "It must be remembered that by 'business' Caleb never meant money transactions, but the skillful application of labour" (475). So incapable is he of imagining financial transactions that Caleb eventually devotes himself entirely to the "kinds of work which he [can] do without handling capital" (229). Caleb's inability to conceive of capital is, in part, an inability to think figuratively. The understanding of money not for what it *is* but for what it represents is, after all, what makes possible a money economy. As Walter Benn Michaels has argued, nineteenth-century naturalism is permeated by an anxiety about the abstract, substitutive, representative value of money and by a concomitant fantasy of money returning to nature (in the form of the natural resource of gold).[15] Although Michaels's argument is about American naturalism, it could just as easily apply to nineteenth-century British naturist discourse and to Eliot's concept of natural history.

The distinction that Michaels makes between the inherent value of "a natural resource like coals or cows" and the representative value of currency is nowhere more apparent than in the nineteenth-century political debates about the railway. If we turn to those political debates, we can see a connection similar to the one that Eliot makes, in her novel, between the increasing circulation of coins (Riggs's "breeding coins") and the expansion of the railway ("the business that was beginning to breed just then"). The recorded minutes of the 1833 House of Commons debate about the Railway Bill, for example, demonstrate that the expansion of the railway is promoted, not because the railway in and of itself has any inherent value (like, for example, the value of a natural resource), but rather because the railway facilitates the exchange of commodities and money. In his testimony before a select committee of the house, a director of the Stockton and Darlington railway explains that the construction of the railway through his own properties has increased commerce between various locations, which in turn has increased rents, and in turn, increased the value of property: "the rent of the prop-erty is increased one-fifth. I let the farm, subject to its being given up on the railroad being made, and I have since received one-fifth additional rent."[16] Such testimony is cited in the report as evidence, not of the railway's intrinsic value, but rather as evidence of its role in the abstract circulation of values, for its role in "the increased speed and cheapness of communication," and for its "saving of the time and money of those who are compelled by business, or induced by pleasure, to travel." When the railway is praised for increasing land value, it is said to increase, not the intrinsic value of the land, but "the *factitious* value which tracts of land immediately surrounding the metropolis and large towns acquire from the proximity of the markets" (50). In other words, the railway has no inherent value but rather acquires value only as part of an abstract, substitutive, representative exchange and circulation of values. Indeed, those in favour of the expansion of the railway (railway directors, engineers, and shareholders) promote the railway as a mode of transportation that will increase not only the national circulation of commodities but also international circulation, thus "rendering [the value of agricultural property] in a great measure independent of local circumstances" (50).[17]

The desire, expressed in Eliot's essays and fiction, to return to a concrete, natural history, exemplified by an experiential understanding of the term "railway," is perhaps a reaction to the increasing expansion of the railway and of commerce as well as to the result of that expansion: the increasingly abstract representation of value. Again and again in *Middlemarch,* a tension emerges between intrinsic and representative value, between literal and figurative value. That tension is apparent when Featherstone, suggesting that Fred Vincy will not inherit his land, upbraids Fred for valuing money over land. "God A'mighty sticks to the land," he tells Fred, "But you take the other side. You like Bulstrode and speckilation better than Featherstone and land" (100). By "speckilation," Featherstone means the abstract values of currency and exchange that are alienated from the intrinsic value of natural resources such as land, cows, and coal. Vincy's protests, that he likes neither Bulstrode nor speculation, have no effect on Featherstone, who eventually leaves his land, Stone Court, to Joshua Riggs. One of the novel's ironies is that Riggs immediately exchanges the land for money, while Fred Vincy ends up actually working on the land under the supervision of Caleb Garth.

The tension between land and money, in *Middlemarch,* is connected, via the railway, to the tension between spatial and temporal, abstract and concrete history. The history of the railway itself intersects both spatially and temporally with the Reform Bill at a point in time where the use value of the land is transformed, by the railway, into exchange value (monetary value), which is in turn transformed into the political value of votes established by the Reform Bill. That temporal intersection between the beginning of the railway system and the appearance of the Reform Bill is made explicit when Eliot writes that, at that time in Middlemarch, "railways were as excitable a topic as the Reform Bill" (502). While the railway coincides with the time period of the Reform Bill, the Bill itself hinges on the commercial valuation of the land. As the arguments between Caleb Garth and the labourers suggest, the railway is controversial because it detracts from the intrinsic value of the land and natural resources at the same time that it increases the commercial traffic through the land, and thus, increases property value for the landholder. Protesting the surveying of land for the railways, one of the labourers, Mr. Solomon, says to Caleb, "Traffic is what they put fo'ard; but it's to do harm to the land and the poor man in the long-run" (502). The Reform Bill is equally controversial because it ties property value to political power: it gives the vote only to those who pay 10 pounds or more in property tax. The "breeding coins" which circulate throughout Eliot's text are thus changed into "the minting of Tory votes" (455).

Not only does the emergent railway system create a new evaluation of land, but it also produces a new evaluation of time, for it speeds business up so that time can be saved.[18] Yet the railway's role in speeding up industrialization also ensures that time is more readily spent. As Phillipa Levine observes, the changing measurement of time, produced in part by the advent of the railway, changed the Victorian concept of history. "The radical alteration in perceptions of time and speed," inaugurated by improved travel and communication, she notes, brought with it a new respect for history as "the intellectual mechanism whereby time could be measured and evaluated."[19] The increasingly easy equation between time and money (as quantities that can be saved and spent), and its impact on the measurement of "history," are the subjects of a much cited passage in *Middlemarch*:

> Fielding lived when the days were longer (for time, like money, is measured by our needs), when summer afternoons were spacious and the clock ticked slowly in the winter evenings. We belated historians must not linger after his example; and if we did so, it is probable that our chat would be thin and eager, as if delivered from a camp-stool in a parrot-house. I at least have so much to do in unravelling certain human lots, and seeing how they were woven and interwoven, that all the light I can command must be concentrated on this particular web, and not dispersed over that tempting range of relevancies called the universe.
>
> (128)

There has been no shortage of critical ink spilled on the subject of Eliot's metaphor of the web, particularly as it relates to the literary and historical. For Eagleton, we have seen, the figure of the web is an example of Eli-

ot's reduction of history to literary form. More recent criticism, however, has read the passage as an affirmation of the reciprocity between historical and literary discourse. Yet the critical assumption remains that figurative and tropological discourse, in this instance, as it is manifested by the metaphor of the web, is intrinsically ahistorical and thus must be shown to be compatible with history or to insert itself in history.[20] The passage, however, has consistently been misread, for the "particular web" is a product of the specifically Victorian conception of history articulated by Levine, a history influenced "by an increasingly quantitative approach to work and leisure governed far more by clocks and public time."[21] According to the narrator, it is because we are no longer in the era of spacious summer afternoons, because the clock is ticking faster, that the "particular web" is the most appropriate form for the novel's historical realism. Even within the strictures of Eagleton's definition of history as the forces of industrialization, Eliot's trope of the web turns out to be intrinsic to history. It is not simply that Eliot's passage on history articulates the particular web as a product of the forces of industrialization, but also that weaving, textile production itself, emerges, in the Victorian era, as a form radically altered by the industrial revolution. The work of weaving moves from the domestic space of the drawing room to the industrial arena of the factories, the cotton mills, flax mills, and woollen mills. For those who would insist on a strict demarcation of literary and historical discourse, the trope of the web is a source of anxiety perhaps because it suggests the way in which textuality and figuration might be inherently historical.

The constellation of figurative, historical, commercial, and industrial (relations) can be seen in those passages in *Middlemarch* where figurative transactions turn out to inhabit commercial and industrial transactions. When Fred Vincy copies "figures" for Farebrother's evaluation of land, the word "figure" itself undergoes an exchange between language and money. Vincy, who has chosen land surveying over "desk-work," is alarmed to discover that his employer, Caleb Garth, expects him to translate the results of his physical labour into letters and numbers. Because he has not been trained in handwriting, he feels "an awkward movement of the heart" when Caleb hands him the pen and says, "Copy me a line or two of that valuation, with the figures at the end" (515). Eliot describes the formation of those figures in detail:

> At that time the opinion existed that it was beneath a gentleman to write legibly, or with a hand in the least suitable to a clerk. Fred wrote the lines demanded in a hand as gentlemanly as that of any viscount or bishop of the day: the vowels were all alike and the consonants only distinguishable as turning up or down, the strokes had a blotted solidity and the letters disdained

to keep the line—in short, it was a manuscript of that venerable kind easy to interpret when you know beforehand what the writer means.

(515)

This passage is characteristic of the close tangle of commercial and textual transaction throughout Eliot's work.[22] In the case of Fred Vincy's handwriting, money emerges as a metaphor for metaphoricity itself via his figures: the word "figures" refers both to his numbers and letters, and those figures in turn represent the monetary value of the land. What is striking about the passage, however, is the ambiguity of the word "figure," as it slides between literal and figurative quantities. When the term is used in one of its most literal senses, to mean numbers, it is nonetheless an abstraction; the literal figures become numbers that abstract, that represent the measurements and value of the land, whose value is in turn converted into a whole network of other values, from that of votes determined by the property tax to the elusive value of reputation that is attached to the landed class.

When the word "figure" refers to Fred's letters, it would seem to convey the most literal (or letteral) sense of the term. Indeed, it is worth noting that the very word "figure" has a contradictory etymological [sic] direction, pointing at once to the opaque form of language and to its oppositional other, transparent content. As the OED [Oxford English Dictionary] tells us, "figure" refers both to the literal or letteral ("a letter of the alphabet, the symbol of a musical note, a mathematical symbol") as well as to the rhetorical and tropological ("any of the various 'forms' of expression, deviating from the normal arrangement or use of words . . . e.g. Aposiopesis, Hyperbole, Metaphor, etc."). It refers at once to the body ("Of a living being: Bodily shape") and to the representation of the bodies and matter ("The image, likeness, or representation *of* something material or immaterial"). In this passage on handwriting, Eliot exploits the contradictory meaning of figure as both literal letters and figurative form, for even Fred's literal letters are given a figurative turn; they are in such a messy handwriting that they become unreadable, "easy to interpret" only "when you know before-hand what the writer means" (515). At the same time that his letters lose their referential meaning, they gain a figurative one through the personification of the unreadable vowels and consonants, as gentlemanly letters that "disdained to keep the line" (515).

Fred Vincy's unreadable figures, written in a hand "as gentlemanly as that of any viscount or bishop" (515), recall an earlier passage in which aristocratic gentility is inscribed in figurative language. After mentioning the unseemly character of Joshua Riggs, the narrator explains that "if any bad habits and ugly consequences are brought into view, the reader may have the relief of regarding them as not more than figuratively ungenteel" (309). Finally, she concludes, the low truth about "petty sums" may be raised "to the level of high commercial transactions by the inexpensive addition of proportional ciphers" (309). The position of figurative language in this instance is part of the narrator's larger meditation on history. In fact, the paragraph begins, not with figures as a means of elevating low sums, but with "[h]istorical parallels" as "the means of elevating a low subject" (309). But such "historical parallels" present a problem, Eliot writes, for "the diligent narrator may lack space, or (what is often the same thing) may not be able to think of them with any degree of particularity" (309).

What is to be done when history is disabled by this lack of space and particularity? According to the narrator, the figurative form of parables offers one solution, "since there never was a true story which could not be told in parables" (309). And these facts, "ennobled by being considered a parable," will then be only "figuratively ungenteel" (309). The problem of history thus emerges once more as part of the problematic relation between the value of literal and figurative language. The ironic tone here further complicates a narrative interlude that is already tangled in the figurative knot of metaphor and money. When read literally, the narrator's remarks might be taken to mean that figuration is unambiguously aligned with money (both old and new). But the ironic turn of the passage suggests that the novel's figurative language is anything but a merely decorative, "genteel" form that clothes the raw material of concrete history. For Eliot, figurative language is neither an erasure of history nor an ennobling outer form but rather the very content of history's form. That historical form appears in Eliot's images of handwriting. How does handwriting escape beyond the bounded lines that would keep it neatly within the bounded lines of concrete, literal history? I will suggest handwriting flows between the literal / figurative, historical / literary borders, in part, as it is exchanged into another word that is a synonym for handwriting, "character."

II.

Eliot's detailed development of character has long been held up as the defining element of her novels' historical realism.[23] For J. Hillis Miller, "the fullness of characterization" in **Middlemarch** makes the novel "perhaps the masterwork of Victorian realism."[24] Indeed, in her letters, Eliot herself stresses the centrality of character to realism. We will see that character is, in fact, one of the most destabilizing forces in her work, an element which exists on the faultline between literature and history and which produces an unpredictable shifting of the very grounds of fiction. That instability arises whenever Eliot's work approaches the problem of the false dichotomy between passive description and active narration. When it is used in its most obvious sense to classify Eliot's work as realist, character refers to a protagonist whose psychological processes are consistent with her actions. Such is the sense of the word implied by Eliot when she writes, in a letter to John Blackwood, "I am unable to alter anything in relation to the delineation or development of character, as my stories always grow out of my psychological conception of the dramatis personae."[25] Much later, in a letter praising the realism of *Middlemarch,* Blackwood writes to Eliot, "In all this life like gallery that you put before us every trait in every character finds an echo or recollection in the reader's mind that tells him how true it is to Nature."[26] I want to turn, at this point, from Eliot's character development (where character refers to an individual protagonist) to the development of the very word, "character," as it shifts in her text through variegated shades of literal and figurative meaning and eventually floats free from its referential moorings.

In *Middlemarch,* character makes its first appearance in the form of Casaubon's literal, decaying history. When Sir James, chirping up about history at a dinner party, asks his guest if he has read Southey's multivolumed history of the Peninsular War, Casaubon cursorily dismisses the subject:

> I have little leisure for such literature now. I have been using up my eyesight on old characters lately; the fact is, I want a reader for my evenings; but I am fastidious in voices, and I cannot endure listening to an imperfect reader. It is a misfortune in some senses: I feed too much on the inward sources; I live too much with the dead.
>
> (13)

The word "character" here points in two directions, referring to the literal typographical characters read by Casaubon and later on dutifully copied by Dorothea, and to the characters (individual subjects) who populate Casaubon's history. But Casaubon himself later becomes a character whom Dorothea reads, first in a very literal sense and then in a more abstract one. Believing that Casaubon will come to understand the debt owed to Ladislaw, Dorothea tells Ladislaw, "The great strength of his character lies here" (339). After Casaubon's death, she recognizes her "subjection" to a husband "whose exorbitant claims for himself had even blinded his scrupulous care for his own character" (450).

Dorothea's subjection is literally inscribed in her copying of characters, and her release from that subjection, accompanied by her own increasingly strong subjectivity, manifests itself in her formation of characters. Several months after Dorothea marries Casaubon and agrees to copy characters for him, one of the many arguments of their marriage produces its emotional after-effects in Casaubon's handwriting:

> Here Mr. Casaubon dipped his pen and made as if he would return to his writing, though his hand trembled so much that the words seemed to be written in an unknown character.
>
> (258)

When Dorothea sits down to write, immediately after their argument, her hand does not tremble but rather produces strong characters, "forming her letters beautifully" (258). The contrast between Casaubon's spidery, unrecognizable characters and Dorothea's strong, beautifully formed ones accompanies their increasingly divergent conceptions of history. As the novel progresses, Casaubon's history becomes a compilation of "old characters," dead letters whose cumulative dead weight ultimately drags him down to his own untimely death. Dorothea eventually loses interest in copying Casaubon's dead historical characters and begins to recognize the limits of that history during her visit to Rome, "the city of visible history, where the past of a whole hemisphere seems moving in funeral procession with strange ancestral images and trophies from afar" (176). When she visits the galleries, basilicas, and palaces, she sees "the dimmer yet eager life gazing and struggling on walls and ceilings," where "all that was living and warm-blooded [seems] sunk in the deep degeneracy of a superstition" (177). Dorothea's recognition of this degenerating history marks the beginning of her release from the dead weight of Casaubon's tomb of history, "The Key to All Mythologies." After Casaubon's death, Dorothea comes to understand history as a fully personified form.

The alienation of Casaubon's typographical characters from the individual characters (historical subjects) to which they refer is conveyed largely through Eliot's prosopopeic turns. Earlier in the novel, Mrs. Cadwallader jokes that someone put a drop of Casaubon's blood "under a magnifying-glass, and it was all semicolons and parentheses" (62). While this prosopopeic joke drains Casaubon of life, it also animates the typographical mark of the semicolon, through the familiar figurative flow of ink into blood.[27] Such passages point to what Neil Hertz, among others, observes is the ease with which characters (in the sense of fictional protagonists) become "texts or clusters of signs." The personifications involved, he notes, "exist somewhere between realistically represented persons and configurations of signs."[28] What I want to suggest here is that personification, in *Middlemarch,* also functions as a middle ground between the two terms that Eliot and her critics find so difficult to reconcile: literature and history. In fact, the word "character" is the site of a whole cluster of personifications that turn on various distinctions between historical and literary representation, from the characters of Farebrother's "Natural History" to the characters (protagonists) of the narrator's meditations on narrative to the characters of Rosamond's frivolous and trivial understanding of history.

A microscopic form of historical character emerges in Farebrother's "Natural History." As the OED tells us, one of the several meanings of character is that used "in *Natural History.* One of the distinguishing features of a species of genus." Interestingly, the double meaning of character as a linguistic sign and as a feature of a natural species is one that Darwin makes use of in his natural history when he writes that we have "no pedigrees or armorial bearings; and we have to discover and trace the many diverging lines of descent in our natural genealogies, by characters of any kind which have long been inherited." As Gillian Beer notes, the term character in this passage shifts from a semiological meaning ("armorial bearings") to a natural historical one.[29] That same instability in the word's meaning can be seen in Eliot's portrayal of Farebrother's collection of species. We first encounter the characters of Farebrother's Natural History when he takes Lydgate into his study to view his collection of meticulously ordered fauna and flora. Explaining his obsession with entymological species to Lydgate, Farebrother tells him:

> You don't know what it is to want spiritual tobacco—bad emendations of old texts, or small items about a variety of *Aphis brassicae,* with the well-known signature of Philomicron, for the *Twaddler's Magazine*; or a learned treatise on the entomology of the Pentateuch, including all the insects not mentioned, but probably met with by the Israelites in their passage through the desert; with a monograph on the Ant.
>
> (157)

The dead characters in his collection of "pickled vermin and drawers full of blue-bottles and moths" (156) don't remain pinned down to their most concrete realm for the duration of the novel but rather float free from their boxed containers and circulate as figurative forms for Eliot's characters (protagonists): Casaubon's soul becomes an injured moth, "fluttering in the swampy ground where it was hatched, thinking of its wings and never flying" (254), and Will Ladislaw cannot resist giving "another good pinch at the moth-wings of poor Mr. Casaubon's glory" (331). At one point, all the characters in the novel shrink into the microscopic form of insects, particularly when gossip spreads through Middlemarch and news is "dispersed as thoughtlessly and effectively as that pollen which the bees carry off (having no idea how powdery they are) when they are buzzing in search of their particular nectar" (546).

In spite of his preoccupation with the minute, concrete characters of his Natural History, Farebrother also concerns himself with more abstract and figurative forms of character, insisting at one point that Dorothea is taking the notion of character (in the sense of reputation) too literally. After Lydgate's reputation has been destroyed by rumours of his collaboration with Bulstrode's fraudulent and homicidal deeds, Dorothea pleads with Mr. Farebrother for a restoration of Lydgate's character.

"[T]here is a man's character to speak for him," she says to Farebrother, who replies, "But my dear Mrs. Casaubon . . . character is not cut in marble—it is something living and changing, and may become diseased as our bodies do" (672). Dorothea picks up his figure, concluding that if character is living, "then it may be restored and healed" (672). This prosopopeic flow of one character into another, from microscopic characters to telescopic ones, from dead characters to living ones, extends beyond **Middlemarch,** so that the novel's characters flow into the characters of Eliot's letters and essays and finally into the character of Eliot herself.[30]

Like Eliot's readers and critics, the characters within **Middlemarch** read each other as representatives of literary, political, and historical traditions. To Dorothea, Casaubon is a personification of history. But to Casaubon, Dorothea represents all that is outside of his historical volumes and all that threatens his identity as an author. We are told that "Dorothea was not only his wife: she was a personification of that shallow world which surrounds the ill-appreciated or desponding author" (184). This reading of one character by another is enabled by the same operation that allows George Eliot to stand in for social communities and great literary traditions: personification. In order for one character to read another as a text, the character reading must herself move beyond the merely textual. She must come to life as a character who is above the text and thus can identify the character she reads as one who is reduced to text. It is this slippery movement between characters that allows Dorothea to bleed into the historical character of Saint Theresa and that allows both those figures to bleed into the character of George Eliot.

Dorothea, Saint Theresa, and George Eliot converge at the end of **Middlemarch** in a final passage which provides no closure to the literature / history problem. The two categories of literature and history are once again joined at the seams of words and deeds. This time, however, the alignment between history and action is broken when the narrator remarks upon Dorothea's "unhistoric acts" (766). After noting that the era which would allow for a "new Theresa" has passed, the narrator goes on to say that "we insignificant people with our daily words and acts are preparing the lives of many Dorotheas" (766). The paragraph concludes with the observation that the good of the world is partly dependent on such "unhistoric acts." This reference to the seventeenth-century nun in the frame of the novel makes a connection not only between Dorothea and Saint Theresa, but also between George Eliot and Saint Theresa. The historical reference framing the novel draws attention to the temporal convergence of Eliot's own act of writing the novel in 1870 with the church's recognition of Saint Theresa's acts. By moving the novel outward to this historical frame, the concluding paragraph locates Eliot's **Middlemarch** in the realm of both historic and unhistoric acts.

Notes

1. George Eliot, *Middlemarch* (London: Bantam, 1985), 326. Hereafter cited parenthetically by page number.

2. Linda Colley, *Britons: Forging The Nation 1701-1837* (New Haven: Yale Univ. Press, 1992), 334-35.

3. Terry Eagleton, for example, argues that the "ideological matrix" of Eliot's work is "set by the increasingly corporate character of Victorian capitalism and its political apparatus." Eliot's fiction, he suggests, reduces history to literature and therefore reduces politics to literature. See Eagleton's *Criticism and Ideology: A Study in Marxist Literary Theory* (London: Verso, 1978), 120. Daniel Cottom similarly aligns the historical and political in his study of George Eliot. Suggesting an incompatibility between Eliot's figurative discourse and historical / political discourse, Cottom asserts that "social forms or institutions do not play a mediating role" in Eliot's plots, because "[h]er resolutions happen only figuratively, or in the minds and emotions of those characters who are brought to an approximation of the figural consciousness of her narrators," *Social Figures: George Eliot, Social History, and Literary Representation* (Minneapolis: Univ. of Minnesota Press, 1987), 28. "[Literature's] reference and meaning," he concludes, "can be determined only in terms of the *historical* and *political* conditions of its existence" (214, my emphases). The definition of history *as* politics also marks nineteenth century texts. Thomas Carlyle, for example, defines history as the memory of "the whole fortunes of one little inward kingdom, and all its politics, foreign, and domestic" ("On History," in *English and Other Critical Essays* [London: J. M. Dent & Sons, 1950], 80).

4. Carlyle, for example, thus defines "History" as "all Action" ("On History," 90). As we have seen, history, in twentieth-century criticism and theory, is persistently aligned with action. Lukács's famous distinction between narration and description rests on the distinction between action and description. The properly *historical* novel, for Lukács, is one of action, for "only in activity do men become interesting to each other." See Georg Lukács's "Narrate or Describe?" in *Writer and Critic and Other Essays,* ed. and trans. Arthur Kahn (London: Merlin Press, 1978), 123. In current critical theory, history is similarly associated with action. Eagleton, for example, associates the "flight from real history" in some forms of literary

theory as synonymous with a flight from "political action." See Eagleton's "Political Criticism," in *Literary Theory: An Introduction* (Minneapolis: The Univ. of Minnesota Press, 1996), 171, 179, 187.

5. Eagleton, *Criticism* [*Criticism and Ideology*], 120.

6. Eagleton, *Criticism,* 120.

7. Cottom, 25, 9.

8. In one of the earliest examinations of Eliot's combination of aesthetics and historicism, Avrom Fleishman describes Eliot's work as an "esthetic equivalent of that strain of historicism which views individual action in the context of the social organism." See Fleishman's *The Historical Novel: Walter Scott to Virginia Woolf* (Baltimore: The Johns Hopkins Univ. Press, 1971), 158. For an early deconstructive reading of the problematic relationship between literature and history in *Middlemarch,* see J. Hillis Miller's "Narrative and History," *ELH* 41 (1974): 455-73. Mark Seltzer's intervention in the literature / history problem is an exception in its combination of what he terms "the apparently incompatible claims of a radical formalism and a radical historicism." See Seltzer, "Statistical Persons," *Diacritics* 17 (1987): 92. Seltzer uses personification in order to illuminate a body-machine complex, arguing that "in the discourse of realism, having a character is precisely to internalize, personify, or embody the social" (86). He thus articulates a close fit between "the at once physical and immaterial act of putting letters and words on paper and the powerfully animating or animistic effects of this act" (91). In his study of modernism, Tony Jackson also tries to reconcile a literary / deconstructive approach with a social / historical one, bringing a psychoanalytic reading together with a Lukácsian historical one. See *The Subject of Modernism: Narrative Alterations in the Fiction of Eliot, Conrad, Woolf, and Joyce* (Ann Arbor: Univ. of Michigan Press, 1994). In her discussion of history and the Victorian novel, Christina Crosby departs from the conventional mapping of literary figures onto commodity fetishism and argues instead that nineteenth-century history itself functioned as a commodity fetish (see "Reading the Gothic Revival: 'History' and *Hints on Household Taste,*" in *Rewriting The Victorians,* ed. Linda Shires [New York: Routledge, 1992], 102). Crosby also expresses her resistance to "'history' as teleology, as totality," in *The Ends of History: Victorians and "The Woman Question"* (New York: Routledge, 1991), 147. As its title suggests, Cottom's *Social Figures* tries to bring together a figurative and social / historical analysis. Cottom, however, aligns Eliot's figurative language with her conservatism and her era-

sure of social history. See Cottom, 25. As Kathryn Stockton notes, Eliot did indeed subscribe to the positivist philosophies with which Cottom quite rightly associates her work. But Stockton disagrees with Cottom's characterization of Eliot as a bourgeois humanist and a "figure of patriarchy" and argues that Cottom himself "repeats a 'bourgeois' masculine move" by overlooking Eliot's own difficult position as a woman writer whose male pseudonym enabled the acceptance and success of her work. As Stockton notes, Barbara Bodichon, who campaigned for women's right to work, was one of Eliot's closest friends and may have been the model for the central character of *Middlemarch,* Dorothea Brook. See Stockton's *God Between Their Lips: Desire Between Women in Irigaray, Brontë, and Eliot* (Stanford: Stanford Univ. Press, 1994), 175, 83. In contrast to Cottom, Bert Hornack views *Middlemarch,* above all, as a social, historical work, "a novel of reform," but, like Cottom, he suggests that an emphasis on figurative language and text is incompatible with an analysis of social history. Deconstructive critics, he comments, have "appropriated *Middlemarch*" in order to read, "not George Eliot's novel but its 'text.'" He goes on to cite approvingly Kerry McSweeney's assertion that such deconstructive criticism "is excessively *engagé* and ideological, too concerned with its own premises, methods, and self-delighting excruciations, and insufficiently disinterested in George Eliot's novel." Hornback, Middlemarch: *A Novel of Reform* (Boston: Twayne Publishers, 1988), 12.

9. Eliot, "The Natural History of German Life," reprinted in *Essays of George Eliot,* ed. Thomas Pinney (New York: Columbia Univ. Press, 1963), 267.

10. Eliot, "Natural History," 267, 267-68.

11. Lukács similarly sets up an opposition between describing and doing, experiencing and observing. In his essay, "Narrate or Describe?" he writes that "[w]hen the artistic literature of a period does not provide actions in which typical characters with a richly developed inner life are tested in practice, the public seeks abstract, schematic substitutes" (124).

12. Lukács, 127.

13. Her reference to "pregnant movements of the past" appears in her remarks under the heading "Historic Imagination," collected in "Leaves from a Note-book," in *Essays of George Eliot,* 447.

14. Judith Newton, "Engendering History for the Middle Class: Sex and Political Economy in the *Edinburgh Review,*" in *Rewriting the Victorians,* 12.

15. Walter Benn Michaels, *The Gold Standard and The Logic of Naturalism: American Literature at The Turn of the Century* (Berkeley: Univ. of California Press, 1987), 146.

16. "Minutes of Evidence before a Select Committee of the House of Commons on the London and Birmingham Railway Bill," *Edinburgh Review* 61 (1834): 47.

17. *Edinburgh Review* 61 (1834): 52 ("increased speed"; "saving"), 50 ("*factitious* value"; "rendering").

18. In his discussion of "railway novels," Nicholas Daly observes that the emergence of the railway system coincides with modernity in general and with a "modernization of the senses" in particular. For the Victorians, Daly notes, the railway "stood as both agent and icon of the acceleration of the pace of everyday life; it annihilated an older experience of time and space, and made new demands on the sensorium of the traveler" ("Railway Novels: Sensation Fiction and The Modernization of The Senses," *ELH* 66 [1999]: 463).

19. Phillipa Levine, *The Amateur and The Professional: Antiquarians, Historians, and Archeologists in Victorian England, 1838-1886* (Cambridge: Cambridge Univ. Press, 1986), 3.

20. Two of the most compelling readings of Eliot's web as both literary and historical can be found in Marc Redfield's *Phantom Formations: Aesthetic Ideology and the Bildungsroman* (Ithaca: Cornell Univ. Press, 1996), and David Ferris's *Theory and The Evasion of History* (Baltimore: The Johns Hopkins Univ. Press, 1993). Ferris, for example, reads the web as an "unbinding bond" between literary and historical discourse. Ultimately, however, he concludes that "[n]ot only is the bind always unbound in this model but history is itself denied as it becomes what never happened" (189-90). Interestingly, Ferris maps the literary / historical distinction onto a constative / performative one, when he writes that "what we call history would be as strange to Cyrus as language would be to an act or an event" (190). As I have been arguing, the prosopopeic and anthropomorphic formulations of history in Eliot's essays and novels are precisely what make such distinctions impossible. In his reading of *Middlemarch,* Redfield argues that the novel opens up the possibility of "aesthetic history" (138). Connecting Eliot's metaphor of the web to Lydgate's histology and thus to the web of bodily tissue, Redfield writes that "[h]istory, inscribing itself within bodies, is itself a body to the extent that the metaphors of web and current convey a promise of telos and form, and to the extent that 'unhistoric acts' can be ab-

sorbed into history just as unperceived sensations or unacknowledged meanings are recorded by the embodied self" (141). Redfield, that is, demonstrates the way "the body tropes the insertion of the self into the larger intentional structure of history" (141). My own intervention owes much to Redfield's analysis, and my reading of the web is intended to suggest the possibility that tropological structure itself is inherently historical.

21. Levine, 3.

22. Neil Hertz traces an interlocking of textual and commercial figures both in Eliot's fictional and non-fictional work. Hertz concludes that Eliot's figures of "unrelieved debt are figures not just for the gestation of her fictions but also for the gerundive time (the time of owing, or of dying) over which their peculiar life-in-debt is extended" ("George Eliot's Life-in-Debt," *Diacritics* 25 [1995]: 70).

23. Catherine Belsey, for example, finds Eliot's characters to be exemplary of the "classic realist text" (*Critical Practice* [New York: Methuen, 1980], 73).

24. Hillis Miller, "Optic and Semiotic in *Middlemarch*," in *The Worlds of Victorian Fiction*, ed. Jerome Buckley (Cambridge: Harvard Univ. Press, 1975), 127.

25. *Selections from George Eliot's Letters*, ed. Gordon S. Haight (New Haven: Yale Univ. Press, 1985), 165.

26. *The George Eliot Letters*, ed. Gordon S. Haight, 7 vols. (New Haven: Yale Univ. Press, 1968), 5:167.

27. Mark Seltzer provides a very detailed analysis of the body-machine complex and its manifestation in the blood-ink pattern of personification. The personification of literal text through the blood-ink relation, he argues, is part of the identification of realist discourse, an identification that "involves the perfect 'fit' between the ontology of writing and the specific material—the historically specific subject-matter—of the social body-machine complex, the perfect 'fit' between the (apparently non-historicizable) ontology of writing and a historically specific biomechanics" (92).

28. Hertz, "Recognizing Casaubon," *Glyph: Textual Studies* 6 (1979): 78.

29. Charles Darwin as quoted from Gillian Beer, *Darwin's Plots: Evolutionary Narrative in Darwin, George Eliot, and Nineteenth-Century Fiction* (London: Routledge, 1983), 63.

30. When Eliot and Lewes were vacationing at Ilfracombe in the summer of 1856, they amassed a collection of microscopic species almost identical in its character(s) to Farebrother's collection of species. In a letter to Charles Bray, Eliot describes her room at Ilfracombe "decked with yellow pie-dishes, a *footpan*, glass jars and phials, all full of zoophytes or molluscs or annelides." The journal Eliot kept during her visit records the various characters collected, their excitement over "the discovery of this little red Mesembryanthemum," and their delight at finding "the pale fawn coloured tentacles of an Anthea Cereus viciously waving like little serpents" (The trip to Ilfracombe is described in *The George Eliot Letters*, 2:252-53). These species of Natural History provide the over-arching metaphor for the review essay that Eliot was writing at the time of the Ilfracombe visit, the "Natural History" review that begins with the concrete and abstract train. In the essay, Eliot structures her argument about the history / literature relation through the relation between natural and metaphorical, concrete and abstract character. What is needed, Eliot argues, is a historical language that conveys its naturalism through literary resonances, a language that grows "in precision, completeness, and unity, as minds grow in clearness, comprehensiveness, and sympathy." Such naturalism, she concludes, should enable an understanding of history on the order of the complexity of Natural History where "your particular society of zoophytes, mollusks, and echinoderms may feel themselves, as the Germans say, at ease in their skin" ("Natural History," 288).

Dwight H. Purdy (essay date autumn 2004)

SOURCE: Purdy, Dwight H. "'The One Poor Word' in *Middlemarch*." *Studies in English Literature, 1500-1900* 44, no. 4 (autumn 2004): 805-21.

[In the following essay, Purdy interprets Eliot's repeated use of the adjective "poor" throughout the novel as an expression of both sympathy and irony toward her characters.]

George Eliot's synthesis of sympathy and irony in *Middlemarch* (1871-72) and the impressive unity of the novel's details—of metaphors, motifs, images, and allusions—have been at the center of George Eliot criticism for many years. Granted, one does not even need deconstruction to sense imperfections in that unity, as Barbara Hardy argued long ago in examining the inadequacies of Will Ladislaw.[1] George Eliot's ethic of sympathy also raises questions about her realism.[2] Nonetheless, extremely minute details vibrate in tremolo for the attentive reader, especially when one keeps in mind that synthesis of sympathy and irony.[3] This essay will treat one very small detail indeed, a single monosyllabic adjective, an adjective that in *Middlemarch* distributes sympathy and irony in roughly equal portions.

The adjective, as my title implies, is the humble "poor," used as a term of commiseration and thus often followed hard by a proper noun. Excluding all other meanings of the term such as "low," "inadequate," or "impoverished," I make out 145 instances of the commiserating "poor" in *Middlemarch.* Its chief recipients, as one would expect, are Dorothea, Rosamond, Lydgate, and Casaubon, with Rosamond (perhaps surprisingly) leading them all, a disposition that I hope to show tells us something about how and why George Eliot mixes irony with sympathy. Rosamond gets the adjective 26 times, Dorothea 22, Casaubon 12, and Lydgate 9. But other instances, especially the first two that set the theme, are worth attending.

With wonderful portentousness for *Middlemarch,* the OED [*Oxford English Dictionary*], to exemplify the commiserating sense of "poor," cites Sir Humphrey Davy with whom the genial Arthur Brooke dined years ago, accompanied by William Wordsworth, as we learn in the first paragraph of the second chapter.[4] In this sense, the term means "so circumstanced so as to excite one's compassion or pity," and the OED adds that "In many parts of England" the word regularly refers to "the dead of whom one knew."[5]

The adjective is one of George Eliot's verbal tics. Laurence Lerner, writing about her *Felix Holt: The Radical* (1866), notes one instance of the rhetorical impact of "poor." To show the unevenness of that novel, he contrasts two brief passages from one chapter concerning Mrs. Transome: the first concerns her relationship with her maid of forty years, Denner; the second deals with the heroine, Esther. The first, spare and direct, Lerner prefers to the second, heavily adjectival, especially the offensive "poor": Esther "kissed [Mrs. Transome's] poor quivering lips and eyelids." The adjective, Lerner says, "is a direct assault on the reader."[6] Even here I suspect the adjective has more meanings than the indictment suggests, as it does throughout George Eliot's fiction. For instance, in chapter 13 of **"Janet's Repentance,"** the final story in *Scenes of Clerical Life* (1858), the adjective is applied to Janet Dempster three times, as the narrator prepares for the climax when her alcoholic husband Mr. Dempster forces her out of the house at midnight. It suggests not only the narrator's compassion and pity but also Janet's state as one among the living dead, a condition created by her abusive husband and her own alcoholism. "Poor Janet" lives "in leaden stupor."[7] The word appears prominently in *Adam Bede* (1859) as the plot moves toward Hetty Sorrel's suffering. Particularly notable is an instance in which George Eliot weds "sympathy" to the adjective. The narrator tells us that sympathy comes from suffering,

such suffering as Adam Bede's in his blasted love for Hetty and his respect for Arthur Donnithorne: "Let us rather be thankful that our sorrow lives in us as an indestructible force, only changing its form, as forces do, and passing from pain into sympathy—the one poor word which includes all our best insight and our best love."[8] Here George Eliot invests "poor" with ennobling irony, related to but transcending the depreciatory sense of the word. To be "poor" in this way is to be rich with feeling, and, as Adam learns, "'feeling's a sort o' knowledge.'"[9] "Poor" passes into metaphor as it does in *The Mill on the Floss.*

Although *The Mill on the Floss* (1860) uses the adjective fewer times than *Middlemarch* (only 45), George Eliot's second novel embeds several senses of the word into the plot, the consequences of Mr. Tulliver's failed lawsuit and Tom's eventual repayment of the debt. At one point, just as Tom sets out to restore the family's money and respectability, the narrator juxtaposes the metaphorical and denotative meanings in a single paragraph. At sixteen, "Poor Tom was not without hopes to take refuge in," reflecting that "[b]oth Mr Glegg and Mr Deane . . . had been very poor once." Tom resolves to imitate his Uncle Deane because "[i]t was intolerable to think of being poor and looked down upon all one's life."[10] George Eliot balances sympathy and judgment here. Young Tom, whatever his faults, deserves our respect for his determination to set things right, yet at the same time he is "poor" in the sense that he acts always in accordance with the worshipful materialism of the "emmet-like Dodsons and Tullivers."[11] No one in the novel is more the victim of that value than Mrs. Tulliver, and perhaps to drive the moral home, she gets the adjective 8 times, equally distributed between the narrator and other characters.[12] For that same reason, the word identifies Tulliver's sister, the desperately impoverished and perfectly named Gritty.[13] Maggie, of course, leads all the rest with 16 instances, though in her case, unlike Tom's, the word often seems a rhetorical reflex action rather than a necessity derived from the plot or the nature of the narrator's analysis. The very last instance is such a case, coming just before brother and sister go down into the raging Floss: "Tom rowed with untired vigour, and with a different speed from poor Maggie's."[14] "Poor Tom" would be more to the point, since his "vigour," so the text implies, sends them to their doom.[15] Granted that reading, "Poor Tom" would neatly address the gender bias foregrounded in the earlier parts of the novel. Indeed, Maggie is anything but "poor" at this moment, if we are to believe her dearest wish to be reunited with the beloved Tom. "Poor Maggie" seems a symptom of the notoriously vexed ending of this novel.

George Eliot, perhaps conscious that "poor" had become reflex, may thus have renounced the word deliberately when she wrote *Felix Holt.* In addition to the example Lerner cites, I know of only two others—"Poor maiden!" applied to Esther and "poor woman" to Mrs. Holt.[16] The word asserts itself again, however, in *Daniel Deronda* (1876). Although I have not conducted a careful scavenger hunt in its pages, I find 124 instances of the commiserating sense of the adjective, 22 of them modifying Gwendolen.[17]

"Poor" is always with us in *Middlemarch,* where it rarely seems a verbal tic. The word encapsulates George Eliot's ethic of sympathy. Advertently or not, two early uses of the commiserating adjective establish the theme of its incremental repetitions. Both come from the mouth of Arthur Brooke. He speaks to Dorothea in a prelude to the news that Casaubon has asked permission to make her an offer. Dorothea has asked him for news of a sheep stealer, and he replies, "'What, poor Bunch?—well, it seems we can't get him off—he is to be hanged.'" When Dorothea responds with a gesture "of reprobation and pity," her uncle adds, "'Hanged, you know . . . Poor Romilly! he would have helped us. I knew Romilly.'"[18] Although Bunch is not yet dead, the idiomatic meaning of "poor" applies to both men, "the dead of whom one knew." It also includes the meaning of Dorothea's gesture, "so circumstanced, as to excite one's compassion or pity." Sir Samuel Romilly (1757-1818), law reformer, Member of Parliament, and author of *Observations on the Criminal Law of England as It Relates to Capital Punishment, and on the Mode in Which It Is Administered* (1810), committed suicide. Juxtaposed with Casaubon's request, these early uses of the epithet augur Casaubon's death and foretell a marriage that becomes for Dorothea, as well as Casaubon, a suicidal hanging. Mr. Brooke innocently corroborates that reading when, in the same conversation with Dorothea, he confesses that he never married because "'I never loved any one well enough to put myself into a noose for them. It *is* a noose, you know'" (p. 41). George Eliot achieves varied effects through Brooke's comic habit of repeating himself. Here she gives the modifier finer subtleties than one expects. Indeed, the word achieves the force of dramatic irony when, immediately after her uncle's noose, Dorothea sanctimoniously declares that "'Marriage is a state of higher duties. I never thought of it as mere personal ease,'" to which the narrator enjoins the epithet to her protagonist, "said poor Dorothea" (p. 41).[19] The modifier emphasizes Dorothea's ignorance of men and marriage and asks us to forgive it and to forgive the religiosity that prevents her from seeing so much.[20]

When the narrator again uses the epithet for Dorothea, she is "sobbing bitterly," suffering the first crisis in her married life and the partial end of her ignorance. The scene asks us to recall her earlier untried idea of marriage. After a few weeks with Casaubon, "her wifely relation . . . was gradually changing . . . from what it had been in her maiden dream" (p. 189). She has begun to sense no hope of intimacy with Casaubon, no means

by which she can assuage her keen desire to be the devoted helpmate. In her husband, she has found "a blank absence of interest or sympathy" (p. 191). The narrator rounds out her analysis with the epithet, "poor": "all her strength was scattered in fits of agitation, of struggle, of despondency, and then again in visions of more complete renunciation, transforming all hard conditions into duty. Poor Dorothea! she was certainly troublesome—to herself chiefly; but this morning for the first time she had been troublesome to Mr Casaubon" (p. 192). The word solicits compassion, although in the context of its sentence, especially the diminishing adjective "troublesome," the epithet suggests ironies in the narrator's point of view. Dorothea has willfully made her own troubles, borne out of her religious but woefully vague and inadequate idea of duty. Experience has certainly proved her correct when she declared that marriage did not entail "mere personal ease," but the duties have proved lower than she can even now understand. If, as Hardy argues, Casaubon's impotence has helped to bring on her sobbing, if Dorothea is coming to grips not only with Casaubon's aridity but with sexual issues she cannot possibly comprehend, then "poor" acquires even more force and stronger ironies.[21] She might read his impotence as her inadequacy. The signification of deficiencies in the epithet would then have a specific referent.

Applied to Dorothea, "poor" in the first half of the novel persistently reminds us of the emotional and intellectual deficiencies rooted in her religiosity. By way of contrast, Dinah Morris's convictions in *Adam Bede* never get this kind of scrutiny because Dinah has none of Dorothea's ignorance. Dinah is not a pampered child of the landed gentry who sits with aristocrats at the assizes. Dinah works, and she works with the poor, and thus never in the novel becomes "poor Dinah." Dorothea's religiosity is not by itself the cause of her woes. It combines with her class status to make her "poor." She is "poor" because she has so little contact with what George Eliot called "reality" or "truthfulness," with the ordinary lives depicted, she says famously in *Adam Bede,* by Dutch painters.[22] "Poor Dorothea" is so because of her wealth. Unlike Dinah, she has no community of fellow believers, and so, for the eleventh time, she is "[p]oor Dorothea" because she "had never found much room in other minds for what she cared most to say" (p. 352). No incident more dramatically reveals her isolation from other minds and the ignorance of her idealism than when, in bed with Casaubon, she asks him to leave half of his estate to Will Ladislaw. His anger baffles her, and she again becomes "[p]oor Dorothea" (p. 367). Her request comes from excusable ignorance of her husband's hostility to Will. But she also knows nothing about Will's history, which becomes clear only as the Bulstrode plot works its slow length along. Feeling may be a sort of knowledge, but, divorced from understanding, feeling only impoverishes Dorothea the more.

In the second half of **Middlemarch,** however, the distance between narrator and character sometimes all but dissolves, and with that distance goes irony. The narrator gives less weight to Dorothea's ignorant idealism and more to her formidable isolation. Then the nuances of the adjective shift to almost unalloyed compassion: "It was another or rather fuller sort of companionship that poor Dorothea was hungering for, and the hunger had grown from the perpetual effort demanded by her married life" (pp. 465-6). It is perhaps too unalloyed, in the manner to which Lerner objects, when the narrator shortly thereafter calls Dorothea "[t]he poor child" (p. 469).[23] Irony disappears when, lamenting another sort of ignorance in Dorothea, not knowing "whether Will Ladislaw was still at Middlemarch," the narrator exclaims, "Poor thing!" (p. 528).

Yet irony returns vigorously when Dorothea offers help to Lydgate. Telling him how money has afflicted her, she speaks with "childlike grave-eyed earnestness" (pp. 754-5). Then the narrator refers explicitly in parenthesis to the fact of Dorothea's limited experience: "(Of lower experience such as plays a great part in the world, poor Mrs Casaubon had a very blurred short-sighted knowledge, little helped by her imagination)" (p. 755). "Mrs Casaubon" and the parenthesis itself reassert distance, and the narrator is at her most severe when she suggests that "poor" includes imaginative deficiencies—a warning to readers to exercise their own powers of imaginative judgment. In the parallel scene with Rosamond, "poor" occurs again. Dorothea tries to engage "lower" experience, warning Rosamond against infidelity. Given her shortsightedness, "poor Dorothea, in her palpitating anxiety, could only seize her language brokenly" (p. 785). Having vainly sought her soul's companionship with Casaubon and, thus far, vainly with Will, what biting irony there is in Dorothea's expressing "pitying fellowship" with the almost soulless Rosamond, who seems small selfishness incarnate.

This reading of one small rhetorical device illustrates two related problems with **Middlemarch**: Dorothea's contradictory characterization and the narrator's inconsistencies, both impossible to reconcile with George Eliot's deliberate—though problematic—efforts to create a patterned web of allusion, metaphor, and image, a problematic web to which dozens of critical studies attest.[24] On the one hand, George Eliot meticulously planned and plotted; on the other, she did not maintain a consistent point of view for her narrator and therefore maintains no consistent idea of Dorothea. Perhaps by default, George Eliot's narrative strategies illustrate Casaubon's futile quest for organic unity in a world made of a baffling mixture of chance and intention.[25]

For every "Poor Dorothea," a "Poor Casaubon." The narrator, absolutely consistent with Casaubon, invests a great deal in the adjective's power to arouse sympathy. Whenever it appears, it comes with a thick array of other rhetorical pleas for compassionate understanding. But, as we will see, the narrator does not get the last "Poor Casaubon," the context of the final references implying an ironic judgment.

George Eliot's apprehensions that the reader might too readily condemn Casaubon figure frequently in critical estimates of him. Alexander Welsh even suggests that Casaubon mirrors George Eliot's anxieties as a writer.[26] The theme of authorship as well as George Eliot's pains to extract sympathy for him dominate the first use of this epithet for Casaubon. The narrator analyzes Casaubon's emotional troubles attending his engagement to Dorothea in that passage on the dangers of metaphor frequently cited to illustrate the narrator's sophisticated ideas about the nature of language:

> Poor Mr Casaubon had imagined that his long studious bachelorhood had stored up for him a compound interest of enjoyment, and that large drafts on his affections would not fail to be honoured; for we all of us, grave or light, get our thoughts entangled in metaphors, and act fatally on the strength of them. And now he was in danger of being saddened by the very conviction that his circumstances were unusually happy: there was nothing external by which he could account for a certain blankness of sensibility which came over him just when his expectant gladness should have been most lively, just when he exchanged the accustomed dulness of his Lowick library for his visits to the Grange. Here was a weary experience in which he was as utterly condemned to loneliness as in the despair which sometimes threatened him while toiling in the morass of authorship without seeming nearer to the goal. And his was that worst loneliness which would shrink from sympathy. He could not but wish that Dorothea should think him not less happy than the world would expect her successful suitor to be; and in relation to his authorship he leaned on her young trust and veneration, [sic] he liked to draw forth her fresh interest in listening, as a means of encouragement to himself: in talking to her he presented all his performance and intention with the reflected confidence of the pedagogue, and rid himself for the time of that chilling ideal audience which crowded his laborious uncreative hours with the vaporous pressure of Tartarean shades.

(p. 84)

The adjective makes a prelude (minor key) to this man of negations, blankness, loneliness, and despair: a portrait of an unsuccessful author as an old man. The narrator begs us to feel for him and with him in the sentence on metaphor ("we all of us"), to empathize with his immense, irremediable loneliness.[27] Almost one of the shades himself in a labyrinthine underworld, "[p]oor Mr Casaubon . . . was lost among small closets and winding stairs" (p. 192). Such loneliness guarantees that Casaubon will suspect Will's feelings for Dorothea, and in another use of the plural pronoun the narrator remarks that "[p]oor Mr Casaubon felt (and must not we, being impartial, feel with him a little?) that no man had juster cause for disgust and suspicion than he" (p. 368). Moreover, "must not we" be aware that Casaubon rightly intuits Will's desire for Dorothea? Two paragraphs later another modifying plea appears at the head of a sentence: "Poor Mr Casaubon was distrustful of everybody's feeling towards him, especially as a husband" (p. 369). As she is not with Dorothea, the narrator consistently uses the modifier to assure sympathy and forestall judgment. Hardy makes a good case for Casaubon's sexual impotence, a notion my last citation might support. Hardy justifies George Eliot's reticence about impotence on the grounds that such reticence fits Dorothea's innocence and Casaubon's struggle not to recognize his own despair.[28] I suspect, too, that an explicit reference to impotence would also affect the quality and degree of the reader's sympathy for Casaubon or even undermine it completely, adding a contemptuous or even risible nuance to "poor." We are less apt to empathize with sexual inadequacy than with a prosperous man's fear of public exposure (Bulstrode), or a young man's stupidity in hoping to make up a debt through horse trading (Fred Vincy). "Poor" in this case encompasses the possibility of impotence without remotely naming it.[29]

George Eliot (or the narrator) is, however, loudly explicit in asking for our sympathy whenever she applies the adjective to Casaubon. When Casaubon becomes convinced that Dorothea has changed from the worshipful "young creature" to "critical wife," he is again "Poor Mr Casaubon!"—the phrase heading a sentence and paragraph, with an exclamation (p. 409). Again the narrator asks us to consider how we ought to identify with "Poor Mr Casaubon." His misery has a "quite ordinary" cause: "Will not a tiny speck very close to our vision blot out the glory of the world?" Casaubon is, after all, "like the rest of us" (p. 409).

All of this pleading, of course, prepares us to be less severe than Sir James and others when we learn of the proviso in Casaubon's will. The emotional rhetoric has had that turn of the plot in view. The narrator hints darkly at the turn in the next instance of the modifier, when Lydgate tells Casaubon of his terminal heart condition. Instead of bethinking himself, as a minister and "believing Christian" ought, of the life to come, we learn that "his acts will give us a clue to" his "bias." He is, like all of us in "what we strive to gratify," determined by "an immediate desire": "And Mr Casaubon's immediate desire was not for divine communion and light divested of earthly conditions; his passionate longings, poor man, clung low and mist-like in shady places" (p. 415). Here is reticence. His bias is to prevent the union of Dorothea with Ladislaw, but instead

of naming the act, the narrator asks us to consider the pressure and quality of his grief (p. 416).

This is the last time that the narrator herself applies the adjective to Casaubon. When we do learn of Casaubon's act, a character utters the phrase; it is Mr. Brooke, who explains the act with either remarkable obtuseness or remarkable generosity: "'Well, you know, Casaubon was a little twisted about Ladislaw . . . Poor Casaubon was a little buried in books—he didn't know the world'" (p. 475). Given all the Tartarean imagery associated with Casaubon, the cliché fits, although I doubt we are to imagine that Brooke knows that. The remaining two uses applied to Casaubon also come from Brooke. A few paragraphs later, Brooke exclaims, "'One of poor Casaubon's freaks!'" (p. 476). Finally, when Brooke looks for an excuse to get out of politics, he has Casaubon's example: "'I have felt uneasy about the chest—it won't do to carry that too far . . . I must pull up. Poor Casaubon was a warning, you know'" (p. 498). In all 3 cases, Brooke uses the word in the same sense as he uses to refer to Romilly, a nice symmetry. Nonetheless, readers such as U. C. Knoepflmacher, who blame Brooke for the marriage, might find that the adjective is weak, like the man,[30] and that it defeats sympathy, although he merely echoes the wholly sympathetic narrator. Brooke has in full the amiability that the narrator values, a trait obviously lacking in other males in the novel—Lydgate, Bulstrode, Casaubon, even Ladislaw. That he is blind to how badly off he leaves his tenants warns us, though, that amiability may be a positive hindrance to one's virtue. To have Brooke make the final "poor" pleas seems at best an ambivalent gesture, a turn toward satire and a reminder not to lose our capacity for moral criticism despite appeals to empathy. Although Casaubon's will eventually leads to what George Eliot conceives as a fortunate loss, to judge from *Felix Holt* and *Daniel Deronda,* the act makes Casaubon into another Peter Featherstone, who, living and dead, uses his will as an instrument of torture.

Lydgate and Rosamond, the other pair of unfortunate lovers, are equally "poor."[31] The epithet underscores the similarities that, for all of their vast differences, the two men and women share. Several readers of *Middlemarch* have noted scenes, images, language, and plot lines linking Casaubon and Lydgate.[32] Parallels between the two wives follow in tandem, despite their enormous personal and moral dissimilarities. The narrator emphasizes their physical attractions, their pampered upbringing, and the willfulness with which each very young woman fixes upon her choice for marriage, neither understanding in the least the man she chooses. In each case, a similar incident brings home to the reader, if not to the character, how poorly Dorothea and Rosamond know their husbands. Rosamond foolishly, and disastrously, goes behind Lydgate's back to ask his uncle for money. Dorothea just as foolishly but openly, in an excruciating scene in bed and in the dark, asks Casaubon to give half his estate to Ladislaw. Both women have the good fortune to go on to happier lives thanks to the death of the first spouse. That these four should be by far the chief "poor" citizens of *Middlemarch* should come, then, as no surprise.

The first instance of the modifier applied to Lydgate and Rosamond embraces them both: "Poor Lydgate! or shall I say, Poor Rosamond! Each lived in a world of which the other knew nothing" (p. 162). As in many of the passages I have cited, the expression gets rhetorical emphasis through sentence structure. Here it heads a paragraph, as it often heads sentences, followed by the exclamation mark. In this passage, the narrator particularly asks us to judge Rosamond with the understanding that she, too, is a victim of what, in the famous final paragraph, delimits Dorothea, "an imperfect social state" (p. 824). Rosamond has nothing "to divert her mind from that ruminating habit, that inward repetition of [a man's] looks, words, and phrases, which makes a large part of the lives of most girls." On the other hand, Lydgate's special appeal to her, "the piquant fact" about him, "was his good birth." Marriage to Lydgate would mean "rising in rank and getting a little nearer to that celestial condition on earth in which she would have nothing to do with vulgar people." Rosamond has a fine nose for "the faintest aroma of rank" (p. 163). She is "poor," then, by virtue of her class-bound soul, which is also shaped by that "imperfect social state."

Lydgate, if he does not make his own bed, is more reprehensibly blind than Rosamond, and George Eliot accordingly restrains the adjective until a "Poor Lydgate!" (again heading a paragraph) marks the nadir of their relationship and his complete capitulation to her selfishness (p. 703). He is again "Poor Lydgate" (and again heading a paragraph) when circumstance forces him to aid the ill Bulstrode at the public meeting of the Hospital Board when the town turns against the banker (p. 718). As Lydgate sinks ever lower into the negativity and loneliness of Casaubon, the adjective follows him (pp. 729, 730, 748). In the final instance, he comes to "a perilous margin" where he "look[s] passively" at his future self, consenting to "insipid misdoing and shabby achievement. Poor Lydgate was inwardly groaning on that margin" (p. 772). The image of the margin recalls Casaubon's Tartarean shore. In a moral sense, he has become "poor" in the idiom, one of "the dead of whom one knew."

Rosamond might too easily be condemned to outer darkness, like Casaubon, and so George Eliot gives her a high degree of particularity and the full benefit of the adjective.[33] In fact, because the narrator foregrounds the word with her, its meanings become a manifest issue:

> Mrs Bulstrode, paying a morning visit to Mrs Plymdale, happened to say that she could not stay longer, because she was going to see poor Rosamond.

> "Why do you say 'poor Rosamond'?" said Mrs Plymdale, a round-eyed sharp little woman, like a tame falcon.

> "She is so pretty, and has been brought up in such thoughtlessness. The mother, you know, had always that levity about her, which makes me anxious for the children."

(p. 288)

Mrs. Plymdale, unhooded, glares balefully at the word "poor" because Rosamond rejected her son, Ned, apparently in favor of Lydgate. Mrs. Bulstrode means "poor" in a religious sense, insufficiently attentive to spiritual matters, clearly true of Rosamond.[34] The rumored engagement to Lydgate surprises Mrs. Bulstrode, and she immediately goes to ask Rosamond about it. Confronted with the question, "[p]oor Rosamond's feelings were very unpleasant," because Lydgate, though acting every bit the suitor, has not proposed (p. 290). Rosamond is "poor" now because, as her Aunt Bulstrode says, "'You have allowed your affections to be engaged without return'" (p. 291), a condition making a mythological analogy appropriate: "Poor Rosamond lost her appetite and felt as forlorn as Ariadne" (p. 293). Lydgate, however, is no Dionysus. Married, she is still to him "'Poor Rosy'" (p. 459). After the miscarriage, she becomes her mother's "'poor thing'" (p. 556). Lydgate commiserates, too, through the adjective, but now the word acquires an aroma of irony. Rosamond lost the baby because she disobeyed Lydgate's advice not to go riding, though she denies that was the cause. Her mild obstinacy empties the adjective of its conventional meanings: "Lydgate could only say, 'Poor, poor darling!'— but he secretly wondered over the terrible tenacity of this mild creature. There was gathering within him an amazed sense of his powerlessness over Rosamond" (p. 571). The context calls attention to the word as merely an empty verbal gesture on Lydgate's part, since it is not her poverty but her power that stuns him. Its emptiness measures the decline of their intimacy. He thinks "secretly," and she acts "secretly" when debt overwhelms them, by asking her father for help and writing to Lydgate's uncle. Her secrecy, selfishness, and avidity for rank reduce her to "poor Rosamond" (p. 587). In her "secret soul," "the poor thing" becomes "utterly aloof" from her husband (p. 636), by which the narrator seems to imply sincere pity for a person who, unlike Casaubon, has no sense whatsoever of her own loneliness, her moral despair. The narrator shares Mrs. Bulstrode's feelings: she subsides "into pity for poor Rosamond" (p. 680).[35] When next the narrator and Lydgate pity Rosamond, the word defines her lack of intelligence or imagination and her moral nullity. The primary meaning also applies. Lydgate tries to reconcile himself to "the makeshifts of poverty," thinking that "two creatures who loved each other . . . might laugh over their shabby furniture." The narrator scuttles his dream, observing, "in poor Rosamond's mind there was not room enough for luxuries to look small in." When Lydgate echoes the narrator—"'Forgive me for this misery, my poor Rosamond! Let us only love one another,'"—the narrator deflates that hope, too, as Rosamond looks at him with "blank despair on her face" (p. 689). The phrase echoes attributes of Casaubon, his "blank absence of interest or sympathy" and "the despair which sometimes threatened him" (pp. 191, 84).

Rosamond's moral state is subtler and more profoundly distressing than mere selfishness. "Poor" applied to her signifies existential despair, the specific quality of which, says Sören Kierkegaard, is precisely being unaware that it is despair. It may not be an exaggeration to say that, given her moral and emotional condition, Rosamond suffers more than the novel's histrionic sufferers, Lydgate and Dorothea. Hers is the suffering of Casaubon, acute because it cannot speak its name, because it does not know itself. She becomes the "poor thing" who feels "as if trouble were . . . some invisible power with an iron grasp that made her soul faint within her" (p. 745). "[P]oor Rosamond," "'poor thing'" descending into "dreamy ennui" and "melancholy" (p. 760), conceives of writing Ladislaw to urge on his visit, assuming that his presence will incite Lydgate to leave Middlemarch. George Eliot's narrator remarks that her illogical thought process gauges her distress. Instead of saving her, it results in Ladislaw's wrath when Dorothea interrupts their dalliance. Will's anger paralyzes Rosamond and foregrounds her loneliness: "The poor thing had no force to fling out any passion in return . . . ; her little world was in ruins, and she felt herself tottering in the midst as a lonely bewildered consciousness" (p. 769). Lydgate's "'poor Rosamond'" is reduced to "hysterical sobbings and cries" (p. 770). When Dorothea comes again, "poor Rosamond's pained confused vision" makes her suspect Dorothea of coming to flaunt her predominance (p. 781). The adjective emphasizes the terrible narrowness and therefore confusion of Rosamond's point of view. By the final, twenty-sixth time we hear the adjective given Rosamond, it has come to stand for a complex web of emotional and moral meanings. The last limns the sad reunion of the lovers and suggests in its imagery of torture the degree of Rosamond's suffering: "Poor Rosamond's vagrant fancy had come back terribly scourged" (p. 789).

Ferreting out this humble adjective may, alas, seem a Casaubon's pursuit. But this one thin thread of the web of **Middlemarch** affects our angle of vision and may even alter it, especially regarding Rosamond. The narrator's particularity about Rosamond, the range of feelings she encourages us to share about her, and the subtlety of those feelings indicate her special relevance to George Eliot's ethic of sympathy. Hardy observes of the ending that George Eliot "modifies the moral depreciation of Rosamond."[36] I would go farther. It requires little of us to sympathize with Dorothea or with Lyd-

gate. Rosamond offers a far greater challenge, the most exacting test of the reader's capacity for sympathy.

Notes

1. Barbara Hardy, "Implication and Incompleteness: George Eliot's *Middlemarch*," in *The Appropriate Form: An Essay on the Novel* (London: Athlone Press, 1964), pp. 105-31.

2. Tony E. Jackson, *The Subject of Modernism: Narrative Alterations in the Fiction of Eliot, Conrad, Woolf, and Joyce* (Ann Arbor: Univ. of Michigan Press, 1994), pp. 41-6.

3. A classic example of such an attentive reader is U. C. Knoepflmacher in his "*Middlemarch*: An Avuncular View," *NCF* [*Nineteenth-Century Fiction*] 30, 1 (June 1975): 53-81.

4. Here, as Knoepflmacher shows, is a detail that vibrates with a vengeance ("*Middlemarch*," pp. 60-4).

5. OED [*Oxford English Dictionary*], 2d edn., s.v. "poor."

6. George Eliot, qtd. in Laurence Lerner, *The Truthtellers: Jane Austen, George Eliot, D. H. Lawrence* (New York: Schoken Books, 1967), p. 240; Lerner, p. 240.

7. George Eliot, "Janet's Repentance," in *Scenes of Clerical Life*, ed. Thomas A. Noble (Oxford: Clarendon Press, 1985), pp. 189-334, 267. See also pp. 268, 269.

8. George Eliot, *Adam Bede*, ed. Carol A. Martin (Oxford: Clarendon Press, 2001), p. 453.

9. George Eliot, *Adam Bede*, p. 473.

10. George Eliot, *The Mill on the Floss*, ed. Gordon S. Haight (Oxford: Clarendon Press, 1980), p. 197.

11. George Eliot, *Mill*, p. 238.

12. George Eliot, *Mill*, pp. 186, 195, 218, 227, 298, and 427.

13. George Eliot, *Mill*, pp. 68, 189-90.

14. George Eliot, *Mill*, p. 458.

15. George Eliot also uses "poor Tom" when she writes to R. H. Hutton about her novel *Romola* (1863): "The psychological causes which prompted me to give such details of Florentine life and history as I have given, are precisely the same as those which determined me in giving the details of English village life in *Silas Marner*, or the 'Dodson' life, out of which were developed the destinies of poor Tom and Maggie" (qtd. in George Levine, "*Romola* as Fable," in *Critical Essays on George Eliot*, ed. Hardy [London: Rout-

ledge and Kegan Paul, 1970], pp. 78-98, 80, and in John Bayley, "The Pastoral of Intellect," in the same collection, pp. 199-213, 200).

16. George Eliot, *Felix Holt, the Radical,* ed. Fred C. Thomson (Oxford: Clarendon Press, 1980), pp. 110, 349.

17. George Eliot, *Daniel Deronda,* ed. Graham Handley (Oxford: Clarendon Press, 1984).

18. George Eliot, *Middlemarch,* ed. David Carroll (Oxford: Clarendon Press, 1986), p. 38. Subsequent references will be to this edition and will appear parenthetically in the text.

19. Although I will use the feminine pronoun for the narrator of *Middlemarch,* for a persuasive argument in favor of using the masculine pronoun, see Catherine Maxwell, "The Brooking of Desire: Dorothea and Deferment in *Middlemarch,*" *YES* [*Yearbook of English Studies*] 26 (1996): 116-26. Maxwell also provides a plausible explanation for the narrator's wavering view of Dorothea.

20. The third use of "poor" early in the novel sets George Eliot's ironic tone for the word. Mrs. Cadwallader refers to "'[p]oor people with four children, like us'" (p. 56). The context heightens the irony. She is talking to Celia about getting Mr. Brooke's cook to teach hers the finer points of pastry. The really poor we meet in the novel, such as "Poor Dagley" (p. 388), Brooke's exasperated tenant whose poverty the narrator conveys through minute details, have more essential worries than Mrs. Cadwallader has.

21. Hardy, *Particularities: Readings in George Eliot* (Athens: Ohio Univ. Press, 1983), pp. 15-36.

22. George Eliot, *Adam Bede,* p. 166. For a recent account of George Eliot's realism and its problems, see Jackson, pp. 43-6. Jackson argues that the realist novel, especially as George Eliot writes it, entails a contradiction between its efforts to show the contingencies and changes of reality and its conventions of omniscience and a neat narrative pattern. Although George Eliot repeatedly urges the reader toward a wide sympathy with her characters because moral life is so problematic, her narrator's omniscient stance never becomes problematized.

23. It is as if the narrator adopts with Dorothea Caleb Garth's tone with Mary, who twice calls Mary "poor child" (pp. 391, 552). Knoepflmacher discusses the resemblance of Mary to Dorothea in "Fusing Fact and Myth: The New Reality of *Middlemarch,*" in *This Particular Web: Essays on Middlemarch,* ed. Ian Adam (Toronto and Buffalo: Univ. of Toronto Press, 1975), pp. 43-72, 65-6.

24. For a recent review of some critics on this narrator's instability, see Linda S. Raphael, *Narrative Skepticism: Moral Agency and Representations of Consciousness in Fiction* (London and Cranbury NJ: Associated Univ. Presses, 2001), pp. 62-3. The classic deconstructing analysis of the issue is J. Hillis Miller's "Optic and Semiotic in 'Middlemarch,'" rprt. in *Modern Critical Views: George Eliot,* ed. Harold Bloom (New York: Chelsea House Publishers, 1986), pp. 99-110.

25. Rosemary Ashton concisely describes the "two-way pull of meaning" in George Eliot's web metaphor and in the construction of the novel as a whole: "The web is organic, connective, infinitely complex, and so a fine metaphor for society and the individual's place in it . . . The web is also, seen in an extension of some of its attributes, airy, light, imaginative, possibly delusive" ("Introduction," in George Eliot, *Middlemarch* [London: Penguin, 1994], pp. vii-xxii, xxi).

26. Alexander Welsh, "The Later Novels," in *The Cambridge Companion to George Eliot,* ed. Levine (Cambridge: Cambridge Univ. Press, 2001), pp. 57-75, 64.

27. In her analysis of loneliness and the instability of the narrator of *Middlemarch,* George Eliot prefigures the great poet of loneliness in modern fiction, Joseph Conrad. Conrad goes farther, of course, with both the narrative technique and the philosophical position. In his *Lord Jim,* the convivial Marlow, always eager to talk to anyone about Master Jim, fears that Jim illustrates a general truth that he delivers in the style of the *Middlemarch* narrator: "It is when we try to grapple with another man's intimate need that we perceive how incomprehensible, wavering, and misty are the beings that share with us the sight of the stars and the warmth of the sun. It is as if loneliness were a hard and absolute condition of existence; the envelope of flesh and blood on which our eyes are fixed melts before the outstretched hand, and there remains only the capricious, unconsolable, and elusive spirit that no eye can follow, no hand can grasp." At the end of Jim's life, "[l]oneliness was closing on him" (Conrad, *"Lord Jim": Authoritative Text, Backgrounds, Sources, Criticism,* ed. Thomas C. Moser, 2d edn. [New York and London: Norton, 1996], pp. 109, 242).

28. Hardy also says that Victorian readers may have been more alert than we are to such themes, that what seems reticence now was not then. She also concedes that "social and literary restraint" play a part, too ("Implication and Incompleteness," p. 120).

29. Richard Ellmann argues against me, claiming that to name Casaubon's sexual problem would make

him too sympathetic and reduce our sense of his culpability ("Dorothea's Husbands," in *George Eliot* [*Modern Critical Views: George Eliot*], ed. Harold Bloom, pp. 65-80, 71). The possible varieties of reader response suggest that we might both be correct.

30. Knoepflmacher, "*Middlemarch.*"

31. Of the other lovers, Fred is never so called, though Mary is twice "poor child" (pp. 391, 552). Will once says, "poor mother," quoting his mother about her mother, and Lydgate to himself calls Will a "poor devil," thinking of Will's infatuation with Dorothea (pp. 609, 429).

32. On those similarities, see, among others, Raphael, pp. 73, 81; Carroll, "*Middlemarch* and the Externality of Fact," in *This Particular Web,* ed. Adam, pp. 73-90, 84-5; Carroll, *George Eliot and the Conflict of Interpretations: A Reading of the Novels* (Cambridge: Cambridge Univ. Press, 1992), pp. 238-40; and Jan B. Gordon, "Origins, *Middlemarch,* Endings: George Eliot's Crisis of the Antecedent," in *George Eliot: Centenary Essays and an Unpublished Fragment,* ed. Anne Smith (Totowa NJ: Barnes and Noble, 1980), pp. 124-35.

33. Allowing for their proportions in the novel, Rosamond gets as much particularity as Dorothea, which leads Welsh to note that Dorothea "seems the invented character" and Rosamond "the real thing" (p. 65).

34. The Sermon on the Mount lurks behind George Eliot's adjective: "Blessed *are* the poor in spirit: for theirs is the kingdom of heaven" (Matthew 5:3 KJV [King James Version]). It is the source, too, for the passage cited above about Casaubon—"Will not a tiny speck very close to our vision blot out the glory of the world" (p. 409)—"Judge not, that ye be not judged . . . And why beholdest thou the mote that is in thy brother's eye; but considerest not the beam that is in thine own eye?" (Matthew 7:1-3 KJV). This text, parallel to George Eliot's both in grammar and language, resonates throughout *Middlemarch*. Nonetheless, it is only a parallel. George Eliot adjusts her biblical texts in revealing ways.

35. The word appears twice at p. 680, both times as indirect discourse from Mrs. Bulstrode. Her use of the term contains some irony, since at about the same time she is pitying "poor Rosamond," her friends are pitying Mrs. Bulstrode—"poor thing," "poor creature" (pp. 733-4); "Poor Mrs Bulstrode" (p. 735); "the poor woman" (p. 737). The repeated technique of indirect discourse heightens the irony.

36. Hardy, "The Ending of *Middlemarch*," in *The Collected Essays of Barbara Hardy, Volume One:*

Narrators and Novelists (Brighton UK: Harvester Press, 1987), pp. 102-8, 104.

Nina Auerbach (essay date 2006)

SOURCE: Auerbach, Nina. "Dorothea's Lost Dog." In Middlemarch *in the Twenty-First Century,* edited by Karen Chase, pp. 87-105. New York: Oxford University Press, 2006.

[*In the following essay, Auerbach undertakes a detailed critique of Dorothea's character. Auerbach refutes popular critical assertions that Dorothea is a saintly, noble figure, arguing on the contrary that she is solipsistic, intellectually lazy, and ultimately ineffectual.*]

Dorothea Brooke has always irritated me; in fact, she makes my flesh creep. My allergy to this saintly, statuesque heroine, whom everyone else seems to adore, should disqualify me as a lover of **Middlemarch,** but I hope it won't: when I first read the novel as a junior in college, its greatness made me shiver, but I shivered at, and with, poor Casaubon, struggling with an intractable book and a hectoring wife, and I do still. After all, Casaubon alone among the novel's characters is doing something he doesn't have to do. He has money, land, and a respectable position. Working on the shapeless Key to All Mythologies is a labor of sheer love. He flays himself on with the grotesque obsession that is another face of faith, while Dorothea glorifies herself by flailing about crying "What can I do?"

I admit to a quirky bias against this floridly self-mortifying girl. She begins the novel by highhandedly rejecting two things I cherish: her dead mother's jewels and Sir James Chettam's offering of "a tiny Maltese puppy" (ch. 3, 28). She is prevailed on to accept some of the jewels, pretending to see them as pieces of Heaven rather than what they are, but she's adamant about the Maltese, claiming grandly that "creatures . . . bred merely as pets" are soulless and parasitic; besides, she adds, she would be "afraid of treading on it; I am rather short-sighted" (ch. 3, 28).

As part-owner of a little Maltese dog and sole owner of a trove of family jewels, more beautiful than valuable, I think Dorothea begins her story by spurning the greatest prize the secular world of Middlemarch holds: the treasure of fellowship. Family jewels are a clasp from the past; they are far from Heaven, but through them, we touch the flesh and spirit of lost ancestors. Dorothea is less attuned to the spirit of her own mother than she is to Casaubon's Aunt Julia, whose miniature morphs romantically into the enticing face of Will Ladislaw, Aunt Julia's grandson who will become Dorothea's second husband (ch. 9, 70; ch 28, 258). Dorothea's ancestral bond is capricious and impersonal, not intimate or tactile.

As for the Maltese, poor Dorothea is rejecting an enchantingly sympathetic friend, one unavailable among Middlemarch humans; even mercurial Will is too self-absorbed to emulate this responsive dog. A Maltese is uncommonly agile and preternaturally attuned to human steps and sounds. No healthy Maltese would let Dorothea, or anyone, tread on it; before the foot reached it, it would bark or skitter out of the way. Dorothea's condescension toward a clever little dog teaches her nothing about the fellowship of marriage. She will continually tread on her less clever and more fragile husband Casaubon, until he wilts. A Maltese sensing her steps and missteps might have helped her self-consciousness evolve into self-awareness.

Of course, according to the rules of courtship, Dorothea has to reject the Maltese: for Sir James, the dog portends a marriage proposal, as does the horse he offers, which she also rejects; in the still-rural world of Middlemarch, animals, not money, are the visible counters of courtship. Still, Dorothea is too myopic to know that Sir James is courting her, and even if she has inklings, she never plays by the rules; mightn't she keep the animals and forfeit the husband? Rejecting the horse seems to me a loss; not only does Dorothea love riding so intensely that she "always looked forward to renouncing it" (10) but a good rider is in perpetual communion with her horse. Riding is not only erotic excitement, though it is that; it throws a skilled rider into constant contact with the body of another, faster and stronger, creature.

Horses, though, can be perilous in George Eliot's novels, as Fred Vincy's disastrous venture into horse-trading shows. Mr. Tulliver in *The Mill on the Floss* and Dunstan Cass in *Silas Marner* gallop off on horses to their doom; in *Daniel Deronda,* Gwendolen Harleth's acceptance of a horse from the sinister Grandcourt is her first step into an evil abyss. It might be prudent to turn down Sir James's horse, but rejecting the dog seems to me a tragic error. For hundreds of pages, I wondered what happened to the Maltese, waiting until page 515 to learn that, as Dorothea had scornfully suggested at the beginning, it has gone to Dorothea's literal-minded sister Celia, now Sir James's wife. Celia is too absorbed in her baby Arthur to notice the dog, but I can only hope that pampered little Arthur will play with it when he is old enough, if Middlemarch characters ever play, and the neglected Maltese will have a friend at last.

Lovers of George Eliot are quick to exonerate Dorothea from dog-hating. Felicia Bonaparte's excellent introduction to the 1997 Oxford World's Classics edition assures us that "Eliot was very fond" of dogs, and so, finally, is Dorothea, for she "owns a St. Bernard named Monk" (xxvi). But Monk is actually, of course, her uncle Mr. Brooke's dog, part of the slovenly milieu of

his estate Tipton Grange; when she marries, Dorothea fortunately makes no attempt to bring Monk to Casaubon's gloomy home at Lowick. When she returns to Tipton, she is too busy suffering to pay attention to Monk: "She leaned her back against the window-frame, and laid her hand on the dog's head; for though, as we know, she was not fond of pets that must be held in the hands or trodden on, she was always attentive to the feelings of dogs, and very polite if she had to decline their advances" (ch. 39, 366). Compare Dorothea's distant noblesse oblige to Mary Garth's easy interchange with her "small black-and-tan terrier," who may be no bigger than the Maltese:

> She took his fore-paws in one hand, and lifted up the forefinger of the other, while the dog wrinkled his brows and looked embarrassed. "Fly, Fly, I am ashamed of you. . . . This is not becoming in a sensible dog; anybody would think you were a silly young gentleman."
>
> (ch. 52, 483)

Mary Garth is no model for Dorothea in great things, for she clings rigidly to the status quo; but her freedom to hold her terrier and share her wit with him exemplifies the fellowship Dorothea longs for. Her rejection of animals is not only a denial of physicality and the body, though it is that; it also withholds the sympathy so needed in Middlemarch, yet so generally absent from it.

No doubt my irritation at Dorothea is subjective, at least as far as jewels and dogs are concerned, but it pervades my reading of the novel and deepens my appreciation of its sometimes duplicitous subtlety. Though *Middlemarch* claims to be spinning an encompassing web in which egoism and secrecy implicate us all, it also seduces us into exonerating Dorothea from selfish humanity by making her as much a monument as the icon of Saint Theresa who presides over the novel's prelude. Both Ladislaw and Lydgate enthrone Dorothea in reverential imagery, enticing the reader to do the same. For most of the novel, Will wants less love from her than benediction:

> The remote worship of a woman throned out of their reach plays a great part in men's lives, but in most cases the worshipper longs for some queenly recognition, some approving sign by which his soul's sovereign may cheer him without descending from her high place. That was precisely what Will wanted.
>
> (ch. 22, 204)

In almost the same imagery, though he claims "a man can make a friend of her," Lydgate disregards friendship for a dream of a woman fixed safely in a high place. After Dorothea has subsidized his hospital and covered his debts, Lydgate rhapsodizes her in a strangely antimaterial hymn:

> This young creature has a heart large enough for the Virgin Mary. She evidently thinks nothing of her own future, and would pledge away half her income at once,

as if she wanted nothing for herself but a chair to sit in from which she can look down with those clear eyes at the poor mortals who pray to her.

(ch. 76, 723)

Verbal pictures of Dorothea enthroned are strewn throughout *Middlemarch,* so that the reader, like the worshipful men around her, perceives less an active character than a charismatic icon. Slyly, George Eliot lures us into reading *Middlemarch* as a Dickens novel, with Dorothea a generic figure of salvation like Florence Dombey, swooping from a self-generated Heaven to redeem weary men. But George Eliot is smarter about people, both sanctified women and sanctifying men, than Dickens is.

For Rosamond Vincy also becomes a picture to Lydgate and Ladislaw. True, she is only a domestic miniature, a nymph tinkling decoratively at her piano, framed, not enthroned, a drawing-room respite from men's important affairs, not a beacon of inspiration. Rosamond, the novel's selfish and trivial apparent antiheroine, who aims to ensnare all men while blessing none, becomes the conduit of male delusion, by implication allowing sanctified Dorothea's overflowing spirituality to appear authentic: Rosamond's steely blond blandness makes her look like the Satanic opposite of good Dorothea. In fact, though, they are similarly locked into the poses that loving men compose, and their wifely performances are similarly, softly, murderous.

"But why all this Dorothea-bashing?" the reader may ask. Surely Dorothea is noble, if thwarted by "the meanness of opportunity" (prelude, 3), with Rosamond, her worldly foil, exemplifying that very meanness. In the tapestry of *Middlemarch,* though, I think Dorothea and Rosamond are more alike than different.[1] My suspicion of Dorothea as heroine is only tangentially related to the familiar feminist complaint against George Eliot, who allegedly blocks Dorothea from doing anything commensurate with her potential grandeur.[2] Rather, I think wily George Eliot created a character who by nature would do nothing but batten, with the best intentions, on those who try to achieve, erecting a lovely idol for deluded readers just as Rosamond is a lovely idol for sentimental men.

My evidence concerns not dogs this time but Dorothea's vulnerable first husband Mr. Casaubon, who pours his diminishing energy into a book that is probably unwritable. Dorothea marries him to exalt herself into becoming his student and research assistant, but almost instantly, she falls into disenchantment with his great work. Because reading and writing are the heart of my life, as they were of George Eliot's, I have always identified with Casaubon. Personal disclosure: I hate people asking dulcetly when my book will be finished, as Dorothea does incessantly. I find Dorothea's well-

intentioned probing particularly grating because she, quite picturesquely, never reads. Pictures of Dorothea dreaming over a book are almost as recurrent, and iconic, as those of Dorothea enthroned: "Celia observed that Dorothea, instead of settling down with her usual diligent interest to some occupation, leaned her elbow on an open book and looked out of the window at the great cedar silvered with the damp" (ch. 5, 44). To Mr. Brooke's patronizing caution "We must not have you getting too learned for a woman, you know," she can honestly reassure him: "There is no fear of that, uncle. . . . When I want to be busy with books, I am often playing truant among my thoughts. I find it is not so easy to be learned as to plan cottages" (ch. 39, 364). In *The Mill on the Floss,* George Eliot's earlier, less well-bred Maggie Tulliver read ferociously, often dangerously, and panted to be learned, but Dorothea, who is closer to Jane Austen's imperious dilettante Emma Woodhouse than she is to Maggie, is wealthy enough to covet the trappings of learning without actually studying—and, like Emma, Dorothea is sufficiently immune from poverty to seek out the poor for the good of her own soul, rather than enduring poverty as Maggie does.

From the beginning to the end of *Middlemarch,* Dorothea expresses her sensibility by not reading:

> Here was a weighty subject which, if she could but lay hold of it, would certainly keep her mind steady. Unhappily her mind slipped off it for a whole hour; and at the end she found herself reading sentences twice over with an intense consciousness of many things, but not of any one thing contained in the text. This was hopeless.

(ch. 83, 756)

It is left to us to decide whether these pictures illustrate her great soul or her Rosamond-like veneer of pseudoculture. Marriage to a scholar, even an amateur one, teaches her only to disdain scholarship as lightly as Rosamond disdains Lydgate's puttering around with corpses. I see no great distance between Rosamond's ignorant dismissal of medicine—"I do not think it is a nice profession, dear" (ch. 45, 430)—and Dorothea's disingenuous dismissal of scholarship: "But it is very difficult to be learned; it seems as if people were worn out on the way to great thoughts, and can never enjoy them because they are too tired" (ch. 37, 341).

George Eliot of all people knew that it is indeed difficult to be learned, and so, I assume, do most readers of this essay. Is it adorable of Dorothea to dream over books instead of reading them, to sigh that great thoughts are tiring, to denigrate Casaubon's life's work primarily on the authority of jealous Will Ladislaw? We all know that Rosamond, like Laure, the homicidal actress who was Lydgate's first love, obliquely murders her husband. If we need proof, we have Lydgate's own despairing diagnosis of his wife as a "basil plant," which he glosses by explaining to her that basil "had flourished wonderfully on a murdered man's brains" (finale, 782). Rosamond is an easy target of satiric censure, but Dorothea may also have a touch of basil. Her offers of help to Casaubon are, as he senses, implicit criticisms, especially once she decides his book is worthless; her later hounding of the dying man to change his will in favor of Ladislaw is as abrasive as the more voracious relatives hounding dying Peter Featherstone about his will. Most devastatingly, her refusal even to try to work on Casaubon's Key to All Mythologies after his death is as consummate a posthumous murder as a spouse can commit, sealing her husband alone forever in the tomb he designed for her in life.

Just as I wish Dorothea had kept the little Maltese, I wish she had done something with the Synoptical Tabulation Casaubon left for her. Instead of reading it, she writes a plaintive justification to the dead: "I could not use it. Do you not see now that I could not submit my soul to yours, by working hopelessly at what I have no belief in?" (ch. 54, 506-7) I would not expect Dorothea to write the entire Key, hard on her though I may seem, but surely, had she studied her husband's notes, she would have found something of some value to extract, if only as a memorial. One thinks prophetically of George Eliot, shattered by the death of George Henry Lewes, diligently preparing for publication the final two volumes of his posthumous *Problems of Life and Mind,* an enterprise as monumental as Casaubon's. True, unlike George Eliot, Dorothea neither loves, trusts, nor depends on Casaubon, but then Dorothea has nothing else to do. One may argue that Lewes was a proven talent, while Casaubon is a deluded pedant, but whose business is it to draw that distinction? Dorothea has no more authority than Rosamond to say her husband's work is valueless; the girl who began by wanting to be learned soon sighs at the very thought of great thoughts. Though she talks a lot about work and vocation, she herself has not worked hard enough to say her husband's work is insufficiently great, or not great at all, or not even good.

* * *

Dorothea and Rosamond are yoked together less by inherent egotism or the human condition than by the conditions of wifehood—an antechamber of the "dim lights and tangled circumstances" *Middlemarch* invokes but never names. Both Dorothea and Rosamond aim to elevate themselves by marrying exceptional men, but as wives, by definition, they are shut out from the sanctuary of male achievement. Casaubon anticipates an ardent acolyte:

> He had formerly observed with approbation her capacity for worshipping the right objects; he now foresaw with sudden terror that this capacity might be replaced

by presumption, this worship by the most exasperating of all criticism,—that which sees vaguely a great many fine ends, and has not the least notion of what it costs to reach them.

> (ch. 20, 188)

Lydgate cherishes similar self-deifying assumptions— "he held it one of the prettiest attitudes of the feminine mind to adore a man's pre-eminence without too precise a knowledge of what it consisted in" (ch. 27, 251)—and he falls into the same lacerating abandonment. But when the great man flounders, what happens to the life of his wife?

Caleb Garth, that model of rectitude and traditionalism, puts it with his usual pithiness: "a woman, let her be as good as she may, has got to put up with the life her husband makes for her" (ch. 25, 242). Caleb makes usable household objects, but if a man is entombed with ancient gods or entangled in medical disputes, he is unlikely to be equipped, emotionally or materially, to make a life for a wife. Since her husband's putative great work is her only life-raft (at the end of the novel, Dorothea and Rosamond cling to each other "as if they had been in a shipwreck" [ch. 81, 749]), a wife must attempt to control that sanctified work in order to have a life at all. Such thralldom does not make for greatness of soul.

The oppressive medium of *Middlemarch,* with its dim lights and tangled circumstances, thwarts men and women alike, but George Eliot is sometimes so scathing about wifehood that she seems to anticipate explicitly feminist imagery like that of John Stuart Mill in *The Subjection of Women,* whose suffocating medium is not, like that of *Middlemarch,* an unchanging cosmic deposit but an artificial environment constructed solely to stunt women:

> What is now called the nature of women is an eminently artificial thing—the result of forced repression in some directions, unnatural stimulation in others . . . a hot-house and stove cultivation has always been carried on of some of the capabilities of their nature, for the benefit of their masters. Then, because certain products of the general vital force sprout luxuriantly and reach a great development in this heated atmosphere and under this active nurture and watering, while other shoots from the same root, which are left outside in the wintery air, with ice purposely heaped all round them, have a stunted growth, and some are burnt off with fire and disappear; men . . . indolently believe that the tree grows of itself in the way they have made it grow, and that it would die if one half of it were not kept in a vapour bath and the other half in snow.

> (Mill, 22-3)

In Mill's *Subjection,* as in *Middlemarch,* wives are the victims and the culprits of unnatural cultivation, not of the thwarted human condition. The end of the *Subjection* is an indictment of wives more explicit, if not more devastating, than anything in *Middlemarch:*

The wife is the auxiliary of the common public opinion. A man who is married to a woman his inferior in intelligence, finds her a perpetual dead weight, a drag, upon every aspiration of his to be better than public opinion requires him to be. It is hardly possible for one who is in these bonds, to attain exalted virtue.

(Mill, 80)

Such partisan language would have been anathema to George Eliot, who aims to draw her characters together, but significantly, her narrator does reserve the word "tragedy" for self-immolated men, especially Casaubon. Dorothea and Rosamond are relegated to postures of melodrama, with the nobility of one balancing the pettiness of the other, though like most melodramatic personifications they are really two facets of a single character, one alarmingly close to Mill's "dead weight."

There is much striving in **Middlemarch,** but little protest: both Dorothea and Rosamond turn against their husbands' work, but neither questions the conditions that stunt her own life. Though most readers remember the women's stories, for me at least, the book lives through its excruciating accounts of Casaubon and Lydgate, the two exemplary husbands who, once they marry, are strangled by their own aspirations. Without commenting on its denunciations, as Dickens would have done, **Middlemarch** seems to provide a scathing account of marriage as an institution. Of course the novel includes salutary exceptions, notably the durable marriage of Mary Garth and Fred Vincy, whose union, the finale implies, is so firmly rooted that it survives like a tree to this day. Mary, of course, has no exalted reforming ambitions; she keeps loving Fred because they were engaged as children with an umbrella-ring, and she fears change (sensibly, perhaps, in this milieu). Moreover, Mary has a constructive father who remakes floundering Fred as a farmer, thus putting him in a position to give Mary a life much like her mother's. Caleb is the only successful patron in **Middlemarch,** no doubt because he represents an older rural England; as in so much British fiction, the land, or what is left of it, saves and preserves.

Obliquely, the novel assures us that marriage does not always lacerate; even Dorothea and Rosamond, rootless compared to Mary Garth, thrive, apparently, in second marriages, though these unions that flourish beyond the ending are as cloudy as David Copperfield's culminating marriage to perfect Agnes after he has exorcised the wrong impulses that were the heart of his story. Most of **Middlemarch** concerns married erosion.

This is not to revive the old dull debate about whether George Eliot was, covertly or inadvertently, a feminist. All nonrural institutions in **Middlemarch,** from the ballot to medicine to the church to Parliament, seem as pointlessly ensnaring as marriage. Moreover, marriage

scarcely discriminates against women. As I find myself repeating endlessly, entangled husbands suffer far more memorably than trapped wives do: we watch Dorothea and Rosamond pose, but, at least if we have tried to achieve anything ourselves, we live with Lydgate and Casaubon. Moreover, **Middlemarch** contains a chorus of wifely voices beyond the trio of Dorothea, Rosamond, and Mary Garth. On the left, there is the radical—and of course, French—motto of the actress Laure, who kills her husband during a performance: "I do not like husbands. I will never have another" (ch. 15, 144). It is tempting, for those of us with a Gothic sensibility, to see Laure as the primitive tissue underlying wifehood in **Middlemarch.** After all, Dorothea and Rosamond also learn to perform wifehood, and as we have seen, they too kill their husbands "accidentally on purpose," as children used to say. But choosing Laure as a paradigm ignores the wife at the other end of the spectrum, Harriet Bulstrode, who, silly in the background throughout most of the story, inspires perhaps the most beautiful passage in the entire Victorian novel.

Harriet Bulstrode's husband Nicholas is not merely a failure but a liar, a criminal, probably—in the oblique manner of **Middlemarch** homicide—a murderer. A wealthy banker and sanctimonious evangelical, he is not a simple Dickensian hypocrite; he believes in his own religiosity, making his exposure late in the novel all the more devastating. Harriet learns his story only as he is about to be forced out of Middlemarch. Though this innocent jolly woman has every justification for leaving him, in an inspired performance of wifehood, she changes her costume as a

> way of expressing to all spectators visible or invisible that she had begun a new life in which she embraced humiliation. She took off all her ornaments and put on a plain black gown, and instead of wearing her much-adorned cap and large bows of hair, she brushed her hair down and put on a plain bonnet-cap, which made her look suddenly like an early Methodist.

(ch. 74, 707)

The truest marriage we see is a marriage of guilt:

> He burst out crying and they cried together, she sitting at his side. They could not yet speak to each other of the shame which she was bearing with him, or of the acts which had brought it down upon them. His confession was silent, and her promise of faithfulness was silent. Open-minded as she was, she nevertheless shrank from the words which would have expressed their mutual consciousness, as she would have shrunk from flakes of fire. She could not say, "How much is only slander and false suspicion?" and he did not say, "I am innocent."

(ch. 74, 707-8)

The novel's only saintly self-renunciation is performed by one of its worldliest characters. To accompany it, George Eliot plays her sublimely simple prose like an organ, for George Eliot, like Dorothea, "likes giving up," reserving her most resonant commentary for moments of penance or loss. Surely, at least at the moment of our reading, Harriet Bulstrode is the paradigm of wifehood, an implicit reproach to her niece Rosamond: as Mrs. Bulstrode is embracing her husband's disgrace, in which Lydgate, along with his many other troubles, is more or less unfairly implicated, Rosamond is withdrawing into self-pitying fantasies about an affair with Will Ladislaw. Harriet Bulstrode even seems a retrospective reproach to Dorothea, who, though penitential garb suits her beauty more than it does blooming Mrs. Bulstrode's, has refused to embrace her husband's Key in the spirit that impels Harriet to embrace her husband's crimes. Surely the old woman exemplifies ideal self-sacrifice to these two young wives.

When we last see her, though, her role as exemplary wife is not so clear. Like the other wives, she has remained ignorant of her husband's actual deeds—here, his crimes—though she suffers for them: Bulstrode shrinks from any confession that might evoke the word "murder." Her renunciation brings neither communion nor solace, simply erosion:

> Set free by [her daughters'] absence from the intolerable necessity of accounting for her grief or of beholding their frightened wonder, she could live unconstrainedly with the sorrow that was every day streaking her hair with whiteness and making her eyelids languid. . . . Bulstrode, sitting opposite to her, ached at the sight of that grief-worn face, which two months before had been bright and blooming. It had aged to keep sad company with his own withered features.
>
> (ch. 85, 773—4)

No one is healed or redeemed. Harriet Bulstrode's glorious gesture of fidelity leads only to a shared decay. No doubt she has given a more sublime performance than that of her actress antitype Laure, with her laconic "I do not like husbands. I will never have another," but is she really an exemplar for the younger wives? Is this withering, blind grief what we want for our blooming Dorothea and Rosamond? Surely it seems a more natural ending to have them thriving in second marriages, even, in Rosamond's case, a worldly one or, in Dorothea's, an obscuring one.

* * *

This perplexity is the web of *Middlemarch.* Rhetorically, this web draws the characters together. The famous experiment with the pier-glass and the candle that opens chapter 27, whereby random scratches on the glass seem to orbit purposefully around the light, illuminates the egoism of all the characters, not just Rosamond's (ch. 27, 248); it may also illuminate the reader's need to make the novel more coherent than it is. The more stirring, because deceptively commonplace,

passage about the ordinariness of tragedy: "If we had a keen vision and feeling for all ordinary human life, it would be like hearing the grass grow and the squirrel's heart beat, and we should die of that roar which lies on the other side of silence" (ch. 20, 182) glosses the Casaubons' honeymoon, but ostensibly—while we read at least—it articulates all of our heartbeats, all of our silent roars. The narrator of *Middlemarch* uses the material world, animal and inorganic, to draw us together in a comprehensive lament, but the stories she tells alienate while they implicate us.

The symphony of wives that composes much of *Middlemarch* scarcely allows us to extract an essence of wifeliness; rather, it confuses noble with mean, renunciation with murder. With the exception of wholesome Mary Garth, whose father remakes her suitor to her specifications, all the wives live more or less the same story, but instead of falling into order on the moral scale, they subvert each other. Dorothea's high-mindedness throws Rosamond's selfishness into relief, but once we see, or sense, that they are judging their husbands in the same way, Dorothea feels less noble and Rosamond's withdrawal becomes comprehensible, though we have been trained not to like her. And what is their precise relation to the distasteful alternatives of Laure's murder or Harriet Bulstrode's self-immolation? We want someone to believe in, even though we are no longer Victorians, but we end up with a snarl of motives and lives.

The characters who enmesh our heroes, most notably seemingly immune Dorothea, are not only wives or even women: toward the end of the novel, Dorothea enters into a tacit competition with the villainous Nicholas Bulstrode as to who can best support needy men. When Raffles the blackmailer arrives to expose Bulstrode, one of whose sins was defrauding Will Ladislaw's mother, Bulstrode offers Will a grand sum as recompense. Will, despite his poverty, grandly rejects the banker's hush money. In the high romance at the end of the novel, wealthy Dorothea promises to marry Will, and to subsidize him as well, even though she must give up Casaubon's fortune and fall back on her own: "We could live quite well on my own fortune—it is too much—seven hundred a-year—I want so little—no new clothes—and I will learn what everything costs" (ch. 83, 762). Will might presumably want new clothes for his career in Parliament, but his participation in any financial transaction is cleansed, even made idealistic and childlike, by the sweetness with which Dorothea holds out her money, apparently redeeming the desperately self-interested calculations of Bulstrode.

In the same manner, Dorothea replaces Bulstrode as Lydgate's patron, rescuing both the New Hospital and the doctor himself, who, though he is drowning in debts, is fatally compromised when he accepts money from

Bulstrode. When Dorothea grandly writes Lydgate a sanctified check, Lydgate, cleansed, can save himself by returning Bulstrode's corrupt gift. Twice, Dorothea consecrates Bulstrode's wicked money, blessing rather than contaminating the men who need it. It may be, though, that Bulstrode's troubling amalgam of religiosity, philanthropy, and wealth rubs off on Dorothea after all. Both try to purify their fortune by giving it away; both involve themselves in Will Ladislaw's ancestry; and most important, they are the only praying (and paying) characters in the novel. Their flaunted piety functions as spiritual distraction from their wealth. Dorothea is certainly an antidote to Bulstrode, in that she defrauds no one but herself; but if we read irreverently, the secretive old man sheds a changed light on the pure young woman because they are doing the same thing: both engage in pious philanthropy. Both pray and pay.

Throughout *Middlemarch,* low characters like Bulstrode illuminate exemplars like Dorothea. At several points, the narrator apologizes, with awkward jocularity, for the inclusion of "low people" in her epic:

> whatever has been or is to be narrated by me about low people, may be ennobled by being considered a parable; so that if any bad habits and ugly consequences are brought into view, the reader may have the relief of regarding them as not more than figuratively ungenteel, and may feel himself virtually in company with persons of some style. Thus while I tell the truth about loobies, my reader's imagination need not be entirely excluded from an occupation with lords; and the petty sums which any bankrupt of high standing would be sorry to retire upon, may be lifted to the level of high commercial transactions by the inexpensive addition of proportional ciphers.

(ch. 35, 320)

In theory lowness is a matter of class and money; ironically, the narrator assures us that the low exist only as parables for the high. This apology sits oddly on an author whose reputation was founded on the glorification of the supposedly low Adam Bede and Maggie Tulliver, but in the better-bred *Middlemarch,* low characters are deprived of moral elevation; they are vulgar opportunists like frog-faced Rigg Featherstone and his still coarser stepfather Raffles. These people are so low that they are exiled from the human condition, for they cannot suffer richly. Neither Rigg Featherstone nor Raffles is included in the narrator's definition of "universal" tragedy; they are too coarse to join the roar that lies on the other side of silence; so, for that matter, are Featherstone himself and his greedy relatives. These last would be more at home in Dickens's *Great Expectations,* whose only authentic sufferer is the charmed sinner who tells the story, than they are in the supposedly comprehensive web of *Middlemarch.* In George Eliot's novel, the low characters lack the entitlement of inner lives, but within its restricted social parameters, "low"

and "high" are resonant words, keys to a complex moral interdependence whereby the low enacts what the high withholds.

On a moral scale, Rosamond and Bulstrode are lower than Dorothea, but as the novel unfolds they also become Dorothea; Rosamond lethally repudiates her husband's mission as Dorothea does, while the murdering Laure and the suicidally self-immolating Harriet Bulstrode oscillate for possession of her struggle to be a perfect wife. Bulstrode himself casts a sickly air of falsity over her piety about her wealth. Will Ladislaw too, another character who seems immune from the dim lights and tangled circumstances that hamstring Middlemarch citizens, has a cluster of low characters who dim his luminosity. Like Will, but more selfishly, Fred Vincy flounders about in search of a vocation, but Fred has the sturdy Garths to pound him into shape, while Will has only his erratic employer, Mr. Brooke, as amorphous a dilettante as he is, and his dream of Dorothea, who is herself, perhaps, a dream. Will's charming incoherence becomes, in Fred, diseased: for a Middlemarch man, a vocation may be doom, but the absence of vocation sows sorrow and disorder. As a directionless outsider, Will is echoed by the novel's most disreputable characters: Rigg Featherstone, another illegitimate son inserted like a walking dissonance into the community, and Raffles, an uncontrolled itinerant like Will and a carrier of secrets—the same secrets Will's ancestry incarnates. Like Will, Raffles refuses to leave Middlemarch, and both topple households—the Bulstrodes, the Casaubons, the Lydgates—by their persistent presence. Will wants to believe that his love story removes him to "a world apart, where the sunshine fell on tall white lilies, where no evil lurked, and no other soul entered" (ch. 82, 755), but if we are reading attentively we know that *Middlemarch* has no such set-off world. Instead of white lilies, there are obnoxious growths that taint the purest lovers. No character is free from contamination by low recapitulations of his disinterested purity.

The characters in *Middlemarch* infect each other so easily, at least as I read the novel, because, like Dickens's characters, they are unamenable to change. The narrator is so famously wise, so penetrating and embracing, that we tend to attribute her versatility to her people. After all, in the words of Mr. Farebrother, the town's natural historian manqué, and of the many appreciative critics who have quoted him since the novel was written: "character is not cut in marble—it is not something solid and unalterable. It is something living and changing, and may become diseased as our bodies do" (ch. 72, 692). This is a wonderful gloss on the novel we think we are reading, but actually, the characters in *Middlemarch* change very little; they simply reveal facets of themselves, in large part through the echoing characters who affect our attitudes almost subliminally. Dorothea ends as she began, with her ardor intact to simultaneously possess and renounce—at the beginning she spurns, then keeps, her mother's jewels; at the end she rejects and retains her fortune. Less radiant characters are more obviously static: Casaubon or Rosamond bruised are Casaubon and Rosamond still.

Lydgate, who receives the most detailed case history in *Middlemarch,* also finds his end in his beginning: his visionary voyages of discovery, his "spots of commonness" (an inherent, not an acquired, disease) that translate into sexist snobbery, his early obsession with an unregenerate husband-murderer, all recapitulate themselves in excruciating detail as his life develops, but he writes no new stories for himself. At the end, as with Casaubon, Lydgate broken is Lydgate still. Fred and Mary pride themselves on their fidelity to what they were, but in fact all the characters end up encased in their beginnings. It is their resistance to change that makes them vulnerable to infection by each other.

The titles of the different books yoke the characters together still more inextricably. The first book, "Miss Brooke," deludes us into thinking Dorothea is an autonomous, free-standing character, but parallel destinies quickly crowd around her. "Old and Young," like the last book, "Sunset and Sunrise," presents a deceptive contrast, for the young characters—Lydgate, Dorothea, Fred, Mary Garth—are in increasing subjection to the old ones, Bulstrode, Casaubon, Featherstone, who drink their youth in "a sort of vampire's feast in the sense of mastery" (ch. 16, 146), as the Middlemarch chorus says of Bulstrode. As the novel continues, the young characters age irreparably, the elegiac tone of the finale making "sunrises and sunsets" indistinguishable. Other books ("Waiting for Death," "The Dead Hand," "The Widow and the Wife") exist less to highlight individual stories than to cast a pall over all stories: through much of "Waiting for Death," young Fred seems closer to death than the desiccated characters who will actually die, while the other young characters live mournful lives; "The Dead Hand" is more potently inhibiting in the living—Bulstrode, Raffles, Mr. Brooke, the deadening medium of Middlemarch itself—than in Featherstone's or Casaubon's ineffectual wills; by the time of "The Widow and the Wife," Lydgate is so financially and morally paralyzed that it is hard to distinguish Rosamond from the literally widowed Dorothea. Death, not any one narrative, is the star of all these books, blanketing all stories not as life's end but as its primary condition. Low or high, the characters are inhibited not only by Middlemarch but by each other's plots.

"Everything is so sad," says callow Rosamond at the end (ch. 81, 750). I think, as she is so often, she is right. Many of us have been assured that, properly understood, at least for the mature reader, *Middlemarch* is not a sad book,[3] but for me at the age of sixty, it seems as sad as it did when I was nineteen. It is a novel about inhibition and entrapment, whose grand heroine Dorothea is bound to the pettiest and most degraded of her fellow-citizens. She scarcely knows these low people, for she lives in a solitary daydream of herself, but they cling to her throughout her story. For me, no "mature" reading could mitigate the diminution that is *Middlemarch,* but its sadness might have been alleviated had a little Maltese puppy been allowed in to clear its heavy air.

Notes

1. My association of Dorothea with Rosamond is not at all original; their kinship was one of the most startling insights of early feminist criticism; see for instance Beer, 188-9, and Gilbert and Gubar, 502-21. For the most part, though, feminists legitimized Rosamond's angry intransigence by endowing it with Dorothea's grandeur. I hope to dim Dorothea's unearned aura of magnificence by exposing the Rosamond within her.

2. Lee R. Edwards has written what still seems to me the most appealing indictment of *Middlemarch,* especially of smug teachers who use Dorothea's destiny to reproach restless female students.

3. Many contributors to Kathleen Blake's revealing collection of essays about the difficulties of teaching *Middlemarch* strain to assure chafing undergraduates that the novel is not depressing but wise and true; see especially Jeanie Thomas, "Middlemarch in the Undergraduate Classroom," which concludes with the tactful hope that students who resent the novel—like Lee R. Edwards, cited above—will "return to Middlemarch later in their lives, when they may be ready to experience it differently" (170). See also Karen Chase's insistence that the ending is not after all sad: "The note of tragic compulsion fades into a note of romantic liberation, the large symphonic amplitude preventing any one tone from becoming final" (88). To me, though, the integrity of *Middlemarch* is its unrepentant sadness.

References

Beer, Patricia. *Reader, I Married Him: A Study of the Women Characters of Jane Austen, Charlotte Brontë, Elizabeth Gaskell and George Eliot.* New York: Barnes and Noble, 1974.

Blake, Kathleen, ed. *Approaches to Teaching Eliot's "Middlemarch."* New York: Modern Language Association, 1990.

Bonaparte, Felicia. Introduction to *Middlemarch,* by George Eliot. Oxford World's Classics. Oxford: Oxford University Press, 1997.

Chase, Karen. *George Eliot: "Middlemarch."* Landmarks of World Literature. Cambridge: Cambridge University Press, 1991.

Edwards, Lee R. "Women, Energy, and *Middlemarch.*" *Massachusetts Review* 13 (1972), 223-38.

[Eliot, George. *Middlemarch.* Oxford: Oxford University Press, 1998.]

Gilbert, Sandra M., and Susan Gubar. *The Madwoman in the Attic: The Woman Writer and the Nineteenth-Century Literary Imagination* (1979). 2nd ed. New Haven: Yale University Press, 2000.

Mill, John Stuart. *The Subjection of Women.* 1869; reprint, Cambridge, Mass: MIT Press, 1970.

FURTHER READING

Criticism

Adams, Harriet Farwell. "Dorothea and 'Miss Brooke' in *Middlemarch.*" *Nineteenth-Century Fiction* 39, no. 1 (June 1984): 69-90.

Examines the evolution of Dorothea's character throughout the process of the novel's composition.

Beaty, Jerome. "On First Looking into George Eliot's *Middlemarch.*" In *The Victorian Experience: The Novelists,* edited by Richard A. Levine, pp. 151-76. Athens: Ohio University Press, 1976.

Discusses the circumstances surrounding the novel's composition, and evaluates the work's impact on twentieth-century moral and intellectual thought.

Bedient, Calvin. "*Middlemarch*: Touching Down." *Hudson Review* 22 (1969): 70-84.

Analyzes the novel's techniques and central themes.

Carroll, David R. "Unity Through Analogy: An Interpretation of *Middlemarch.*" *Victorian Studies: A Journal of the Humanities, Arts and Sciences* 2 (1959): 305-16.

Argues that Dorothea's quest for self-realization reflects Eliot's struggle to express a unifying principle for her narrative.

Clark-Beattie, Rosemary. "*Middlemarch*'s Dialogic Style." *Journal of Narrative Technique* 15, no. 3 (fall 1985): 199-218.

Discusses Eliot's use of multiple narrative voices in the novel.

Fraser, Hilary. "St. Theresa, St. Dorothea, and Miss Brooke in *Middlemarch.*" *Nineteenth-Century Fiction* 40, no. 4 (March 1986): 400-11.

Explores diverse literary, historical, and artistic representations of St. Teresa, examining their influence on the creation of Dorothea Brooke's character.

Hagan, John. "*Middlemarch*: Narrative Unity in the Story of Dorothea Brooke." *Nineteenth-Century Fiction* 16, no. 1 (June 1961): 17-31.

Discusses elements of narrative unity in the novel, analyzing the evolution of Dorothea's character over the course of the work.

Hardy, Barbara. "*Middlemarch*: Public and Private Worlds." *English* 25 (1976): 5-26.

Evaluates the depiction of the individual's relationship to historical forces in the novel.

Hollahan, Eugene. "The Concept of 'Crisis' in *Middlemarch.*" *Nineteenth-Century Fiction* 28, no. 4 (March 1974): 450-57.

Examines the character of Will Ladislaw as an embodiment of thematic unity in the novel.

Hooton, Joy W. "*Middlemarch* and Time." *Southern Review: Literary and Interdisciplinary Essays* 13, no. 1 (November 1980): 188-202.

Discusses representations of temporality in the novel.

Hughes, Linda K. "Constructing Fictions of Authorship in George Eliot's *Middlemarch, 1871-1872.*" *Victorian Periodicals Review* 38, no. 2 (summer 2005): 158-79.

Argues that Eliot's unsympathetic portrayal of Rosamond Vincy reflects her antipathy toward the crass commercialism of the literary marketplace.

Hulme, Hilda M. "*Middlemarch* as Science-Fiction: Notes on Language and Imagery." *Novel: A Forum on Fiction* 2, no. 1 (fall 1968): 36-45.

Evaluates Eliot's attitude toward scientific knowledge in the novel through an analysis of the character of Tertius Lydgate and a discussion of the theories of French physician Xavier Bichat.

Karlin, Daniel. "Having the Whip-Hand in *Middlemarch.*" In *Rereading Victorian Fiction,* edited by Alice Jenkins and Juliet John, pp. 29-43. Basingstoke, England: Macmillan, 1999.

Discusses the relationship between hand imagery and Eliot's authorial presence in the novel.

Langland, Elizabeth. "Inventing Reality: The Ideological Commitments of George Eliot's *Middlemarch.*" *Narrative* 2, no. 2 (May 1994): 87-111.

Explores Eliot's treatment of class and gender roles in the novel.

Maxwell, Catherine. "The Brooking of Desire: Dorothea and Deferment in *Middlemarch*." *Yearbook of English Studies* 26 (1996): 116-26.

Analyzes qualities of ambivalence in Eliot's portrayal of Dorothea's character.

Mitchell, Sherry L. "Saint Teresa and Dorothea Brooke: The Absent Road to Perfection in *Middlemarch*." *Victorian Newsletter* 92 (fall 1997): 32-7.

Discusses the subversive elements in Eliot's associating Dorothea with the historical figure of Saint Teresa.

Moscovici, Claudia. "Allusive Mischaracterization in *Middlemarch*." *Nineteenth-Century Literature* 49, no. 4 (March 1995): 513-31.

Examines the function of allusion in the delineation of the novel's characters.

Nicholes, Joseph. "Vertical Context in *Middlemarch*: George Eliot's Civil War of the Soul." *Nineteenth-Century Literature* 45, no. 2 (September 1990): 144-75.

Analyzes the novel within the context of the reform movement in nineteenth-century England.

Sorensen, Katherine M. "Evangelical Doctrine and George Eliot's Narrator in *Middlemarch*." *Victorian Newsletter* 74 (fall 1988): 18-26.

Discusses the influence of Eliot's Christian upbringing on the novel's religious themes.

Wright, T. R. *George Eliot's* Middlemarch. London: Harvester Wheatsheaf, 1991, 111 p.

Offers an analysis of the novel's central themes through detailed interpretations of the work's characters, plot, and structure.

Additional coverage of Eliot's life and career is contained in the following sources published by Thomson Gale: *British Writers,* **Vol. 5;** *British Writers: The Classics,* **Vols. 1, 2;** *British Writers Retrospective Supplement,* **Vol. 2;** *Concise Dictionary of British Literary Biography,* **Vol. 1832-1890;** *Contemporary Novelists,* **Ed. 7;** *Contemporary Popular Writers*; *Dictionary of Literary Biography,* **Vols. 21, 35, 55;** *DISCovering Authors*; *DISCovering Authors 3.0*; *DISCovering Authors: British Edition*; *DISCovering Authors: Canadian Edition*; *DISCovering Authors Modules: Most-studied Authors* **and** *Novelists*; *Feminism in Literature: A Gale Critical Companion,* **Ed. 1:3;** *Literary Movements for Students,* **Vol. 1;** *Literature and Its Times Supplement,* **Ed. 1:1;** *Literature Resource Center*; *Nineteenth-Century Literature Criticism,* **Vols. 4, 13, 23, 41, 49, 89, 118;** *Novels for Students,* **Vols. 17, 20;** *Poetry Criticism,* **Vol. 20;** *Reference Guide to English Literature,* **Ed. 2;** *Reference Guide to Short Fiction,* **Ed. 2;** *Short Stories for Students,* **Vol. 8;** *Short Story Criticism,* **Vol. 72;** *Twayne's English Authors*; *World Literature and Its Times,* **Vol. 3; and** *World Literature Criticism,* **Vol. 2.**

E. T. A. Hoffmann
1776-1822

(Born Ernst Theodor Wilhelm Hoffmann) German short story writer, novelist, essayist, letter writer, and critic.

The following entry presents an overview of Hoffmann's life and works. For additional discussions of Hoffmann's career, see *NCLC,* Volume 2.

INTRODUCTION

E. T. A. Hoffmann was arguably the most original and influential fiction writer of the German Romantic era. He began his career as a composer, writing nine operas, a symphony, and numerous shorter pieces over the course of a successful music career. By his early thirties, however, he had begun to devote more of his energy to writing prose, publishing his first collection of stories, the landmark *Fantasiestücke in Callot's Manier,* in 1814-15. His fiction eschews traditional narrative techniques and plot devices, focusing instead on exploring the unpredictable, unstable workings of human consciousness. His writings continually blur the line between reality and fantasy, employing dreamlike imagery to depict unsettling psychological states. In many respects, Hoffmann's fiction resembles music; images flow together in lyrical, unexpected ways, and many of his themes are derived from popular opera of the late-eighteenth and early-nineteenth centuries. At the same time, Hoffmann was a fearsome satirist, directing his sharp critical eye at bureaucratic hypocrisy, philistinism, and government ineptitude.

In spite of his prodigious talent, Hoffmann struggled throughout his career to balance the demands of earning a living with his desire to create great art, and his turbulent life circumstances exerted a powerful effect on the style and themes of his writings. A sense of profound division, of irreconcilable conflict between opposing forces of reason and inspiration, nature and science, life and art, lies at the heart of Hoffmann's greatest work. Hoffmann was also one of the preeminent innovators of German prose, infusing his high literary style with vernacular phrasing, legal jargon, and music terminology. Many scholars contend that Hoffmann's fiction presages the surrealist literature of the twentieth century while also forming the cornerstone of the modern horror and fantasy genres. Indeed, Hoffmann's influence on the development of modern literature was pervasive, and his admirers and imitators included Sir Walter Scott, Nikolai Gogol, Edgar Allan Poe, Hans Christian Andersen, Charles Baudelaire, Franz Kafka, and Samuel Beckett, among numerous others.

BIOGRAPHICAL INFORMATION

Ernst Theodor Wilhelm Hoffmann was born in Köningsberg, East Prussia, on January 24, 1776, the youngest child of Christoff Ludwig Hoffmann, a lawyer and civil servant, and Luise Albertine Doerffer Hoffmann. Hoffmann's parents divorced when he was only two years old; his father, who suffered from serious mental illness, was never seen again. For the remainder of his childhood, Hoffmann and his mother lived in the home of his maternal grandmother—a Christian zealot—and her three children. Although these years were marked by intense loneliness and sadness, Hoffmann quickly discovered creative outlets for his grief, primarily under the guidance of his uncle, Otto Wilhelm Doerffer, a dilettante and amateur musician who inspired his nephew to study music. As a young boy, Hoffmann learned to play piano, guitar, and violin and soon began to compose his own short pieces. Hoffmann's passion for music soon spread to other artistic pursuits; in his early teens, he studied drawing and painting and became an avid reader, devouring the works of Cervantes, Shakespeare, and Goethe, as well as contemporary adventure novels.

In spite of his obvious creative talent, Hoffmann was pressured by his family to pursue a legal career, and in 1892 he enrolled in the law program at the University of Königsberg, where he proved an exceptional student. After passing his preliminary legal examination in 1795, he began working as a legal assistant, dedicating his evenings and weekends to painting, composing music, and writing. To supplement his income, he also took part-time work as a music instructor. He soon became romantically involved with one of his students, an older married woman named Dora Hatt, with whom he would remain entangled for the next three years. Hoffmann's affair with Hatt later provided the impetus for his story "Das Majorat" (1816-17; "Rolaudsitten; or, The Deed of Entail," 1826). During this brief period, Hoffmann also completed drafts of two novels, although neither manuscript has survived.

In 1796 Hoffmann received an appointment as a judicial aide in Glogau, a provincial town in Silesia. For the next two years, he lived with distant relatives and became engaged to a cousin, Minna Doerffer. After passing his second round of law exams in 1798, Hoffmann obtained a transfer to the Prussian capital of Berlin. The city proved a fertile environment for the aspiring artist's imagination, and Hoffmann immersed himself in Berlin's vibrant cultural life, attending musical and theatrical events frequently and becoming a regular figure at the city's elite literary salons. Although he devoted a great deal of his time to socializing and carousing, he also remained dedicated to his music, and in 1799 he completed his first opera, *Die Maske*. Inspired by Mozart's *Don Giovanni, Die Maske* confronts questions of madness, evil, and guilt, themes that would later become integral to Hoffmann's major writings.

This happy phase of Hoffmann's life was cut abruptly short in 1800, when he was suddenly transferred to the small town of Posen. Bitter and lonely, Hoffmann began drinking more heavily and broke off his engagement to his cousin. He devoted his free hours to making scathing caricatures of the town's prominent citizens and military officials, which soon earned him a second transfer, this one a permanent assignment to the even more remote town of Plock. There he met Maria Thekla Michaelina Rorer-Tracinska, or Micha, whom he married on July 26, 1802. Although Micha contributed some much-needed stability and loyalty to his troubled existence, Hoffmann remained profoundly depressed during his two years in Plock; his journal writings from the period describe repeated drinking binges, illness, and morbid, self-destructive fantasies.

These bleak days came to an end in 1804, when Hoffmann's childhood friend Theodor Gottlieb von Hippel, a government administrator, helped arrange a transfer to Warsaw. The move to the city provided Hoffmann with the creative spark he needed to resuscitate his music career. During the next two years, he composed several musical pieces, including a symphony, and worked as a conductor for the city orchestra. In Warsaw, Hoffmann changed his middle name from Wilhelm to Amadeus, in homage to Mozart. He also discovered the works of Ludwig Tieck, Clemens Brentano, Novalis, and other contemporary German authors, whose nationalistic themes and idiomatic prose styles would influence Hoffmann's later fiction. In July 1805 Micha gave birth to a daughter, Cäcilia.

Hoffmann's good fortune didn't last; after Napoleon seized Warsaw in 1806, the aspiring composer found himself out of work. That year Hoffmann sent Micha and Cäcilia to live with family in Posen, while he moved to Berlin, hoping to earn a living as a freelance artist. The Prussian capital had been decimated by the Napoleonic wars, however, and bore little resemblance to the vibrant city Hoffmann had known before. At around this time, his life took a tragic turn when Cäcilia, not yet two years old, died unexpectedly. Although

Hoffmann's marriage to Micha survived Cäcilia's death, the couple lived apart for many years, and the details surrounding their relationship remain obscure.

In 1808 a desperate Hoffmann accepted a position as the music director of a theater in Bamberg, in southern Germany. The job never materialized, however, and Hoffmann was once again unemployed. For the next several years, he struggled to earn a living as a music teacher in Bamberg, continuing to compose whenever he could. At around this time, Hoffmann developed an unhealthy infatuation with one of his students, a fourteen-year-old girl named Julia Mark. Although his love was unreciprocated, his passion for the girl later inspired one of his best-known early stories, "Nachricht von den neuesten Schicksalen des Hundes Berganza" (1814).

In spite of the adversity of these years, Hoffmann's experiences in Bamberg were vital to his literary career. He still aspired to earn fame as a composer, but he began to devote more time to writing prose; he primarily wrote essays and music criticism at first, and eventually he wrote stories. In 1809 he published his first significant work—an unorthodox piece of music criticism titled "Ritter Gluck"—in the *Allgemeine musikalische Zeitung,* a renowned Leipzig journal. A mix of musical knowledge, satire, and fantasy, the essay exhibited many of the stylistic and thematic characteristics that would become trademarks of Hoffmann's fiction, in particular the dreamlike structure and the exploration of the link between creative genius and madness. The piece proved popular among the journal's readers, and Hoffmann contributed to the journal regularly for the next six years. One essay, "Beethovens Instrumental-Musik" (1814), was especially influential to later music criticism, particularly in its analysis of the Romantic elements in Beethoven's oeuvre.

Hoffmann remained in Bamberg until 1813, when he left to become the conductor of an opera company in Leipzig and Dresden. Germany's ongoing war with France once again disrupted Hoffmann's career, however, and the position lasted only nine months, forcing him to take an unpaid court appointment in Berlin. Despite these continued hardships, Hoffmann managed during this period to publish his first story collection, *Fantasiestücke in Callot's Manier,* which included some of his more inventive music criticism. The collection also contained what would become Hoffmann's most enduring tale, "Der goldne Topf" ("The Golden Pot," 1821). A novel, *Die Elixiere des Teufels* (1815-16; *The Devil's Elixir,* 1824), followed soon after, while a second story collection, *Nachtstücke,* appeared in 1816-17. All three of these works were published anonymously. In 1816 Hoffmann also composed his most famous opera, *Undine,* which brought him popular and critical acclaim in Berlin.

Almost overnight, Hoffmann became the most popular fiction writer in Germany. Between 1819 and 1822 he published three novellas, an unfinished novel, and a story collection. He also began to enjoy success in the legal profession in Berlin, eventually earning a seat on the Prussian supreme court of appeals. His good fortune was again extremely short-lived. In the aftermath of the Napoleonic wars, Hoffmann received an appointment in 1819 to serve on a government commission charged with investigating crimes against the state. He proved himself a vigorous defender of the accused, a group comprising primarily students and intellectuals; Hoffman's position put him altogether at odds with the city's powerful police administration. Angered by the government's tactics of intimidation and harassment, Hoffmann wrote a ruthless satire of police practices, the novella *Meister Floh* (1822; *Master Flea,* 1826). The work enraged the city's police chief, who brought charges against Hoffmann. With his health worsening, Hoffmann struggled to compose his legal defense in the face of aggressive interrogation. Plagued by the threat of incarceration and suffering from a mysterious nervous ailment that had rendered him paralyzed, Hoffmann died in Berlin on June 25, 1822. A new story collection, *Die letzten Erzählungen von E. T. A. Hoffmann,* appeared posthumously in 1825.

MAJOR WORKS

Hoffmann remains best known for his short stories. In such works as "The Golden Pot," he blends supernatural imagery with scathing social satire to tell the story of Anselmus, a young student who travels freely between two worlds: the mundane reality of his daily life and a fantasy realm populated by evil spirits, talking salamanders, and other exotic creatures. The student's effort to choose between these two realms forms the central theme of the novel. On one hand, his struggle symbolizes the tension between the freedom of creativity and the confining expectations of the social order, represented in the story by the philistinism of the university officials. At the same time, Hoffmann uses the division in Anselmus's psyche to question the dominance of physical reality over the intangible yet powerful and vivid reality of the mind. This blurring of the line between rationality and the imagination recurs throughout Hoffmann's most important stories, notably "Nachricht von den neuesten Schicksalen des Hundes Berganza" (1814), a love story told from the point of view of a talking dog who has read Cervantes; "Der Sandmann" (1816-17; "The Sandman," 1844), in which a young man becomes terrified that a mysterious chemist is trying to poison him; and "Rolaudsitten; or, The Deed of Entail," the story of a doomed encounter between a lawyer and a baroness in a haunted castle, which later inspired Poe's 1839 story "The Fall of the House of Usher." Hoffmann's longer prose works explore similar questions concerning the dualistic nature of human experience. In the novel *The Devil's Elixir,* a tormented monk is forced by Satan into a life of crime so that he might atone for the evil deeds of his ancestors, while the unfinished novel *Lebens-Ansichten des Katers Murr* (1820-22; *The Life and Opinions of Kater Murr,* 1969) employs a dual narrative to draw parallels between the life story of a tormented musician and the memoirs of a cat. *Master Flea,* one of Hoffmann's most scathing satires, uses the metaphor of a magic flea in a harsh indictment of the Prussian police state.

Hoffmann's fiction has also inspired a number of famous musical compositions, including Pytor Tchaikovsky's *Nutcracker Suite* (1892), which was based on Hoffmann's 1816 story "Nußknacker und Mausekönig" ("Nutcracker and Mouse-King"); and Jacques Offenbach's 1881 opera *Les contes d'Hoffmann.*

CRITICAL RECEPTION

At the height of his career, Hoffmann enjoyed widespread popularity among German readers and critics, who praised the suspense and imaginative power of his fiction. Translations of Hoffmann's works began to attract attention in England and the United States shortly after his death. While some critics praised Hoffmann's ability to integrate supernatural motifs into the fabric of ordinary human experience, others found the dreamlike quality of his work disturbing, and more than one reviewer questioned his sanity. Reviews of Hoffmann's work appeared periodically throughout the nineteenth century as new editions of his writings became available in English. These early commentators rarely provided insight into the thematic importance of Hoffmann's works, however, generally focusing only on their sensational aspects. In the early twentieth century, critics began to examine Hoffmann's major themes in more detail. Scholar George Brandes, in his 1902 essay "Romantic Duplication and Psychology," was among the first to delve into Hoffmann's explorations of the ego in his supernatural stories. In 1919 Sigmund Freud published a seminal article on Hoffmann's treatment of the uncanny in his supernatural tales. After World War II, a number of scholars, notably Ronald Taylor and Ursula Lawson, began to focus on the relationship between creativity and madness in Hoffmann's fiction. By the late twentieth century, scholars had begun to analyze the stylistic and structural aspects of Hoffmann's work. Michael T. Jones wrote on the relationship between Hoffmann's use of a double narrative in *The Life and Opinions of Kater Murr* and the work's exploration of psychic duality; Todd Kontje discussed Hoffmann's technique of manipulating social discourse as a means of subverting traditional conceptions of selfhood. In the early twenty-first century, such scholars as Jeanne Riou and Michael Kumbier have begun to pay closer attention to Hoffmann's musical career, examining the connection between music and prose in his major fiction.

PRINCIPAL WORKS

*Fantasiestücke in Callot's Manier. 4 vols. [published anonymously] (short stories) 1814-15; revised edition, 1819

Die Elixiere des Teufels [published anonymously; *The Devil's Elixir*; also published as *The Devil's Elixirs*] (novel) 1815-16

†*Nachtstücke.* 2 vols. [published anonymously] (short stories) 1816-17

‡*Klein Zaches genannt Zinnober* [*Little Zach*, published in *Hoffman's Fairy Tales*; also published as *Little Zaches, Surnamed Zinnober* in *Three Märchen of E. T. A. Hoffman*] (novella) 1819

Die Serapions-Brüder. 4 vols. [*The Serapion Brethren*] (short stories) 1819-21

Lebens-Ansichten des Katers Murr nebst fragmentarischer Biographie des Kapellmeisters Johannes Kreisler in zufälligen Makulaturblättern. 2 vols. [*The Educated Cat*, published in *Nut-Cracker and Mouse-King, and, The Educated Cat*; also published as *The Life and Opinions of Kater Murr: With the Fragmentary Biography of Kapellmeister Johannes Kreisler on Random Sheets of Scrap Paper* in *Selected Writings of E. T. A. Hoffman, Vol. 2: The Novel*] (unfinished novel) 1820-22

Prinzessin Brambilla: Ein Capriccio nach Jacob Callot [*Princesa Brambilla*, published in *Three Märchen of E. T. A. Hoffman*] (novella) 1821

Meister Floh: Ein Mährchen in sieben Abenteuern zweier Freunde [*Master Flea*, published in volume 2 of *Specimens of German Romance, Selected and Translated from Various Authors*] (novella) 1822

§*Die letzten Erzählungen von E. T. A. Hoffmann.* 2 vols. (short stories) 1825

Hoffman's Fairy Tales (fairy tales) 1857

E. T. A. Hoffmann im persönlichen und brieflichen Verkehr: Sein Briefwechsel und die Erinnerungen seiner Bekannten. 4 vols. (letters) 1912

Gesammelte Werke: Neuausgabe. 5 vols. (short stories, novels, and criticism) 1960-65

E. T. A. Hoffmann Briefwechsel. 3 vols. (letters) 1967-69

Selected Writings of E. T. A. Hoffman. 2 vols. (short stories and novel) 1969

Selected Letters of E. T. A. Hoffmann (letters) 1977

*This work includes, in volume 1, "Jacques Callot," "Ritter Gluck," "Kreisleriana Nro. 1-6," and "Don Juan"; in volume 2, "Nachricht von den neuesten Schicksalen des Hundes Berganza" and "Der Magnetiseur"; in volume 3, "Der goldne Topf" ["The Golden Pot"]; and in volume 4, "Die Abenteuer der Silvester-Nacht" and "Kreisleriana."

†This work includes, in volume 1, "Der Sandmann" ["The Sandman"], "Ignaz Denner," "Die Jesuiterkirche in G." ["The Jesuits Church in G-"],

and "Sanctus"; and in volume 2, "Das öde Haus," "Das Majorat" ["Rolaudsitten; or, The Deed of Entail"], "Das Gelübde," and "Das steinerne Herz."

‡This work includes, in volume 1, "Der Einsiedler Serapion," "Rat Krespel" ["The Cremona Violin"], "Die Fermate," "Der Dichter und der Komponist," "Ein Fragment aus dem Leben dreier Freunde," "Der Artushof," "Die Bergwerke zu Falun," and "Nußknacker und Mausekönig" ["Nutcracker and Mouse-King"]; in volume 2, "Der Kampf der Sänger," "Eine Spukgeschichte," "Die Automate," "Doge und Dogaresse," "Alte und neue Kirchenmusik," "Meister Martin der Küfner und seine Gesellen" ["Master Martin and His Workmen"], and "Das fremde Kind" ["The Strange Child: A Fairy Tale"]; in volume 3, "Nachricht aus dem Leben eines bekannten Mannes," "Die Brautwahl," "Der unheimliche Gast," "Das Fräulein von Scuderi" ["Mademoiselle de Scuderi"], "Spielerglück," and "Baron von B."; and in volume 4, "Signor Formica" ["Signor Formica: A Tale, in Which Are Related Some of the Mad Pranks of Salvator Rosa and Don Pasquale Capuzzi"], "Erscheinungen," "Der Zusammenhang der Dinge," and "Die Königsbraut."

§This work includes, in volume 1, "Haimatochare," "Die Marquise de la Pivardiere," "Die Irrungen: Fragment aus dem Leben eines Fantasten," "Die Geheimnisse: Fortsetzung des Fragments aus dem Leben eines Fantasten," "Der Elementargeist" ["The Elementary Spirit"], and "Die Räuber: Abenteuer zweier Freunde auf einem Schlosse in Böhmen"; and in volume 2, "Die Doppeltgänger," "Datura fastuosa" ["The Datura Fastuosa: A Botanical Tale"], "Meister Johannes Wacht," "Des Vetters Eckfenster," and "Die Genesung: Fragment aus einem noch ungedruckten Werke."

CRITICISM

Robert Herndon Fife (essay date 1907)

SOURCE: Fife, Robert Herndon. "Jean Paul Friedrich Richter and E. T. A. Hoffmann." *Publications of the Modern Language Association of America* 22 (n.s. 15), no. 1 (1907): 1-32.

[*In the following excerpts, Fife evaluates Richter's influence on Hoffmann. Fife focuses on Richter's writings concerning the double ego and their impact on Hoffmann's explorations of the Doppelgänger motif. Fife argues that, while Richter examines the internal divisions of his characters with ironic detachment, Hoffmann's descriptions of dual personalities are intimately related to his own experiences and reflect actual conflicts within his psyche.*]

[I]t is more than probable that from the time of his arrival in Bamberg in 1808, Hoffmann had looked forward to a personal connection with Jean Paul [Richter], and not improbable that here, under the shadow of the popular author, he renewed and deepened his acquaintance with Richter's works. The three great romances, *Siebenkäs, Titan,* and the *Flegeljahre,* which in progressive series show an emancipation from those eccentricities of style which mark the earlier romances and idylls, were published in the ten years preceding the battle of Jena, and although not so popular as Richter's earlier and more sentimental romances, nevertheless formed the *ne plus ultra* of a considerable part of cultured Germany. The few followers of the Weimar group, the aristocrats of culture, could make no headway against the broad flood of sentimentality with which Richter swept on the youthful and especially the feminine part of the reading public. The Romanticists in Jena and Berlin, although going their own path, recognized Jean Paul tacitly, or with grudging openness, as one with themselves in many ways.[1] Jean Paul's attitude toward Romanticism at this time is that of one who gives and takes. To the younger *literati,* the Brentanos and Hoffmanns, he was the giver; from the semi-mystical physicians and natural scientists and above all from the philosophers there came to him, however, a constant stream of suggestion.

Of these philosophers, especially Fichte was of importance for Jean Paul's development. From the appearance of the *Wissenschaftslehre* in 1794 Fichte interests and irritates him, and for the next ten years the Fichtean idealism appears in one form or another in Richter's works. While he mocks and scoffs and attempts a refutation in the *Clavis Fichtiana,* in such characters as the leading persons in his three great romances the influence of Fichte is plainly visible.[2] In each of these three romances Richter gives us two sides of his own double personality, the idealist and the realist. This tendency toward the splitting of his own double nature is already visible to some extent in *Hesperus,* and comes sharply into view in *Siebenkäs* and still more sharply in the later romances. The sentimentalist and satirist, with their affirmation and negation of life, to use an expression of Schopenhauer's, reveal themselves in Siebenkäs and Leibgeber, in Albano and Schoppe, in Walt and Vult, even in Theudobach and Katzenberger, as clearly as in Faust and Mephistopheles or *mutatis mutandis* in Don Quixote and Sancho Panza. In all of the greater romances of Jean Paul we have on the one side the sentimental, subjective spirit, with a tendency to soar into the regions reserved for gods and titans; on the other hand, the acid realism of the "Geister, die verneinen," with a dash of *Weltschmerz.*

The same tendency toward the projection of the *ego* in a dual form may be found in Hoffmann's characters. The contrasts which Dr. Ellinger has pointed out in the East Prussian character, depth of feeling, paired with cold and clear intellect, were existent in Hoffmann's and were intensified by the constant struggle which went on between the cold world of fact, as represented by the dry-as-dust briefs and court records of his judicial labors, and the world of music, where his heart lay. But, unlike Richter, Hoffmann had no philosophical speculations in his head. A student at Königsberg in the early nineties, he never seems to have heard one of Kant's lectures, and in his works he refers only once to his great fellow-citizen, and then indirectly.[3] Fichte and Schelling are just barely mentioned, one can hardly say more.[4] The double personality that appears in his works,

especially in *Kater Murr,* is therefore a far more objective projection of himself and his fortunes than we have in the Leibgebers and Albanos and Lindas and Schoppes of Richter, influenced and contaminated as they are by satirical side-strokes at Fichte's idealism. With Hoffmann it is always the contrast of artist and Philistine, and it cannot be too strongly emphasized—a point which most Hoffmann critics seem to have overlooked—that the Philistine is as clearly Hoffmann as the artist is.

The deep cleft in the *ego,* which finds such complete expression in *Kater Murr* in the persons of Kreisler and the cat, reveals itself so far as Kreisler is concerned in the first two volumes of the *Fantasiestücke.* Here Kreisler, the musical genius, stands in hostile attitude toward the whole Philistine world. He is unconsciously the typical ironical *ego* of Romanticism. He stands far above the facts among which he lives, and he moves with mad satire through an unsympathetic world. Music is his sanctum from which every profane foot is banished. It may be true, as Robert Schumann suggests,[5] that a certain odd musical character of Thuringia sat for Kreisler's portrait originally; but Kreisler is Hoffmann himself, satire, grimaces, wild antics and all. It is my purpose now to point out certain characteristics of the Leibgeber-Schoppe-Vult family of pessimists which are reproduced in Kreisler. In the first place, it is not too much to claim that the idea of having one figure run through a series of fantasies as the representative of the author's satire and *Weltschmerz* was caught by Hoffmann from Jean Paul's bizarre figures. Leibgeber in *Siebenkäs* re-appears as Schoppe in *Titan,* just as Kreisler appears as the bearer of Hoffmann's satire among the fantasies of the first volume of the *Fantasiestücke* and among the *Märchen* of the second volume, and again in *Kater Murr* as the hero of the fragmentary romance which alternates with the biography of the Philistine tom-cat. Now, in addition to their personal note or background, a literary original can be shown for nearly all of Hoffmann's stories; it is more than probable, therefore, that the permanent humorous figure, at least in cellular form, owes its origin to Richter.

Schoppe-Leibgeber, for the figures are not to be separated, represents the climax of Jean Paul's *Weltschmerz,* and Schoppe, as found in *Titan,* is the figure that influenced Kreisler most strongly. Thus, a striking peculiarity of Schoppe is his fear of his own second-self, which, as he conceives it, may assume an actual form. The *ego*-fear becomes with him a fixed idea. "Alles kann ich leiden," he tells Albano, "nur nicht den Mich, den reinen, intellektuellen Mich, den Gott der Götter—Wie oft hab' ich nicht schon meinen Namen verändert . . . und wurde jährlich ein Anderer, aber noch setzt mir der reine Ich merkbar nach."[6] The fear grows with Schoppe's growing insanity. He cannot look into a mirror; the sight of his own limbs sets him in chattering terror; occasionally he seizes his own wrist and shouts, "Wen hab' ich da, Mensch?"[7] The satirical hit at Fichte is apparent; but the motive borrowed earnestness and gloom from Schoppe's own horribly earnest realism and in the end Jean Paul feels obliged to compensate for it by the introduction of Schoppe's double, Siebenkäs, from the preceding romance, as an actual basis for Schoppe's fear. The motive re-appears in the *Flegeljahre,* where Vult actually gives the *ego* corporal punishment.[8]

Turning to Hoffmann, we find that the illusion of a double, or second-self, was one of the most persistent dreams that tormented the nervous Geisterseher.[9] How fearfully fertile the "*Doppelgänger* motive" becomes in Hoffmann's works is shown by even a careless reading of the *Elixiere des Teufels* and several of the stories from the *Serapionsbrüder.* With regard to the former, Fouqué's *Zauberring* has been suggested,[10] merely as a literary source: in view of Hoffmann's fondness for Jean Paul, there seems no reason why Schoppe may not have furnished him with an earlier suggestion, to be worked out with the logical realism that makes the *Elixiere des Teufels,* burdened tho it is with the cumbersome romance machinery of the eighteenth century, a most intense bit of reading. In the earlier Kreisler sketches we have no mention of a double; but with the development of Kreisler's character in **Kater Murr** comes the incorporation of this motive. Here Kreisler has also a *Doppelgänger,* the painter Leonhard Ettlinger, who preceded him by some years at the court of Prince Irenaeus. Ettlinger, like Richter's Schoppe, had a fondness for cutting silhouettes,[11] and he, like Schoppe, goes insane. After hearing of his lamentable fortunes, Kreisler is terrified by the fear of meeting him. He fancies that his own reflection in the water is his crazy double, and he makes him a half-insane address. When he sees his image again (we are left in doubt here as to how much of the supernatural Hoffmann means us to accept), he babbles in wild fear to his friend, Meister Abraham, "Erstarrt ist mein Gesang, denn der Ich hat seine weisze kalte Totenhand auf meine Brust gelegt!"[12]

From the first Richter's Schoppe sees himself followed by insanity. He is tormented by dreams,—"Dante und sein Kopf sind Himmel dagegen!",[13] he confesses himself in the ban of a fixed idea, he hears wax figures laughing at him and shoots at them, and he finally comes into a mad-house.[14] We know from Hoffmann's diary and letters that he himself suffered from this common form of neurasthenia, the fear of insanity,[15] and that he sought the company of alienists in Bamberg and Berlin. It is also more than probable that the realism of some of the *Nachtstücke* and stories from the *Serapionsbrüder* and especially of the fearful scenes in the *Elixiere des Teufels* is the result of observations of patients in the insane asylum at Bamberg.[16] In the second volume of the *Fantasiestücke* Kreisler is said to be insane, according to common report.[17] He sees the fearful monster of madness following on his trail, "das bleiche Gespenst mit den rot funkelnden Augen—die krallichten Knochenfäuste aus dem zerrissenen Mantel nach dir ausstreckend—die Strohkrone auf dem kahlen glatten Schädel schüttelnd!"[18] Kreisler signs himself a "verrückter Musikus,"[19] and he promises a cycle, to be known as the "Lichte Stunden eines wahnsinnigen Musikers."[20] When Kreisler reappears six years later in **Kater Murr,** written in fulfilment of a plan long entertained, Hoffmann makes him the hero of a romance which, had it been completed, would certainly have brought him into a mad-house. "Von jeher," says the author, "hatte er die fixe Idee, dasz der Wahnsinn auf ihn lauere."[21] It follows him from the court to the convent, and there "regten sich die finstern Geister, die so oft Macht hatten über ihn und griffen schonungslos mit scharfen Krallen in seine wunde Brust."[22] The third part of **Kater Murr** was never put on paper; but what has already been said, together with the well-known sketch by Hoffmann of Kreisler with a bubble-pipe, dancing in wildly disheveled array, leaves no doubt that the musician, like Richter's Schoppe, would have come to the mad-house.[23]

MINOR MOTIVES COMMON TO BOTH AUTHORS.

In addition to the Kreisler figure and "*Doppelgänger* motive," we have another Richter trait in Hoffmann's **Kater Murr.** We have seen the importance of Jean Paul's *Titan* for the Kreisler figure. The scene of the greater part of the action in *Titan* has a close parallel in **Kater Murr.** It is very natural that Richter should have taken a small German court as the background for his romance and a small German *Residenz* as its stage, for his youth had been passed in close proximity to the duodecimo courts of Thuringia, and manhood years had brought him into relations with the court circles at Weimar, Meiningen and Bayreuth. Hoffmann, however, knew nothing of court life at first hand, had never been in a small *Residenz,* nor come into contact with personages more important than the judicial dignitaries of Berlin or the landed aristocracy of the East Elbian provinces. It does not surprise us, therefore, that the court picture in the *Elixiere des Teufels* has nothing sharp and realistic about it. In **Kater Murr,** however, otherwise strongly reminiscent of *Titan,* we have a *Residenz,* drawn in the same satirical manner as in Jean Paul's romance. Jean Paul's realistic descriptions of Hohenvliesz and Haarhaar[24] have their caricature in Hoffmann's portrayal of the court of Prince Irenaeus, whose land has been mediatized, who nevertheless retains all the pomp and appurtenance of a grand duchy.[25] The nerveless Luigi of *Titan* has a counterpart, again exaggerated, in the idiotic Prince Ignatius, and Jean Paul's Fichtean egotist Roquairol in Hoffmann's demoniacal egotist Hector. As additional evidence of the importance of *Titan* for Hoffmann, it is worth noticing that the hero of one of his early tales, the **"Magnetiseur,"**[26] bears in German form the name of Richter's hero in *Titan*, Albano; and further that the only *bon mot* which Hoffmann quotes in later years from Jean Paul is the one in *Titan* of the princess who found herself in a different condition from her country, "nämlich im gesegneten"[27]—all minor evidence, to be sure, but of weight in showing the persistent impression of Richter's greatest romance on Hoffmann.

Again, one of Richter's queer whims of style may have suggested the peculiar double biography in **Kater Murr.** The biography of the worthy Kater is interrupted by fragments of the Kreisler romance, the author stating in the preface that these fragments were torn from a printed book by the cat and became accidentally mixed with Murr's biography.[28] We think at once of the "Extra-Blätter," "Extra-Gedanken" and "Extra-Silben," and all of those intercalations and appendices with which Jean Paul interrupts the thread of the narrative and gives a serious or satirical excursus on some general subject suggested by the context. Perhaps a still more striking forerunner of this disconnected biography may be found in *Des Feldpredigers Schmelzle Reise nach Flätz mit fortgehenden Noten,* where we have a number of notes printed under each page of the text, characteristic, general remarks of a humorous nature, with absolutely no bearing on the text above. Richter blames the printer for the arrangement, the notes having been written, he says, on separate sheets, and then, through oversight, left out of the final manuscript. The printer sets them up with their proper numbers, to be sure, but absolutely regardless of the text.[29]

In Richter, Hoffmann found a forerunner in enthusiastic interest in the shadow-sides of human consciousness, notably the so-called "animal magnetism," which so much engaged the attention of natural scientists during the first two decades of the nineteenth century.[30] Jean Paul's works abound in references to mesmerists, second-sight, etc.;[31] indeed his enthusiasm regarding hypnotic phenomena and his half mystical utterances about the ethereal or intra-physical body would have done credit to the most radical of the romantic natural philosophers.[32] Hoffmann makes animal magnetism the subject of one of his earlier tales, the **"Magnetiseur,"** and comes back to theme again and again in the *Serapionsbrüder.* Such things were in the air during all of those years; it is, however, noteworthy that in a conversation of the Serapion's Brethren, Cyprian-Hoffmann says, "Dieser Glauben (in animal magnetism) müsse in jedem wahrhaft poetischen Gemüt wohnen, deshalb habe auch Jean Paul solche hochherrliche Worte über den Magnetismus gesprochen, dasz eine ganze Welt voll hämischer Zweifel dagegen nicht aufkomme."[33]

An author of Hoffmann's musical attainments, and one who had made his way into literature thru a musical door, would naturally make some phase of music the theme of much of his work; as a matter of fact, all of the sketches in the first volume of the *Fantasiestücke* treat more or less directly musical themes. Nevertheless, it can be pointed out that even here in one or two points he had a predecessor in Richter. First, in the relief of emotion thru improvisation on a musical instrument, making a "Klavierauszug" of the feelings, as Jean Paul in one place expresses it.[34] In *Hesperus* blind Julius accompanies Emanuel's death by playing the "Lied der Entzückung" on the flute.[35] In *Titan* Albano reproduces his emotions and tells the story of his love for the absent Liane in a fantasie on the piano;[36] and on another occasion he talks with the absent maiden and improvises his love-plaint in tones.[37] Here again we have to do with general romantic motives: the harmony of thought and sound belongs to the best-known canons of romantic art. It is Kreisler again, however, this "Unmensch ohne Zweck und Ruh," who otherwise bears marks of Richter, that carries out the idea in Hoffmann's sketch entitled **"Kreisler musikalisch-politischer Klub,"**[38] doing it of course with an objectivity of style and a technical frame-work that would have been impossible to Jean Paul. Further, the delicate Liane hears at critical moments an inner music. This "Selbstertönen," which comes as a message from the supernatural world, with unspeakable sweetness, is illustrated by Jean Paul, characteristically enough, by a reference to the death of Jacob Böhme.[39] In the first sketch which Hoffmann published at Bamberg, Ritter Gluck hears this inner music. He calls it the "Euphon." It is defined as a chiming which comes with moments of excitement and which may remain for two days at a time.[40]

Not to be forgotten also is Hoffmann's following of Richter in the use of *Ich* as a person, as *nomen commune,* as a substitute for every personal pronoun. These *ich*-fantasies rooted in Jean Paul's studies of Fichte and used originally with satirical force, become a perfect mania with him in *Siebenkäs, Titan,* and the *Flegeljahre,* leading to such expressions as, "Auch schwur sein Ich wie ein Gott seinem Ich, dasz er nur diesen Tag noch bleibe."[41] This mannerism descends to Hoffmann. We meet with it as early as 1797 in a letter to Hippel from Glogau,—"Du sagst, mein Teurer, dasz selbst meine Briefe von der Veränderung zeugen, die mein Ich,—die guten Seiten meines Ichs gewaltsam zerstört hat."[42] As might be expected, examples abound in the great *Doppelgänger* romance, the **Elixiere des Teufels**: "Mein eignes Ich konnte ich nicht erschauen, nicht erfassen;"[43] "Das zweite Ich hatte grimmige Kraft;"[44] etc. Becoming rarer in the *Nachtstücke* and the *Serapionsbrüder,* the mannerism appears again in **Kater Murr** and in the story written in the last year of Hoffmann's life, the **"Doppeltgänger."**

Notes

1. [Alfred] Kerr, *Godwi* [ein Kapitel deutscher Romantik, Berlin: G. Bond:, 1898], S. 64 ff, shows

the cordial appreciation of Jean Paul's ironical tone by the Schlegels, both in the *Athenæum* and their correspondence, and the influence of this tone on Tieck. Cf. [Rudolf] Haym, *Romantische Schule* [: ein Beitrog zur Geschichte des deutschen Geistes, Berlin: Gaetner, 1870], 689, 791, for the difference in the attitude of the Schlegels toward Jean Paul. Such enthusiasm as there is comes from the side of Friedrich; August Wilhelm, as the temperate and somewhat anæmic form-artist, has little sympathy for Jean Paul's "fast gichterische Reizbarkeit der Einbildungskraft."

2. For a general treatment of the intensely interesting subject of Jean Paul's double relation to Fichte, cf. Nerrlich, *Jean Paul* [*Jean Paul. Sein Leben and seine Werke,* Berlin: Weidmann, 1889], 60 ff. Especially in the third volume of *Titan* and in the earlier pages of the *Flegeljahre* the idealistic philosophy is satirized and caricatured.

3. *Kater Murr,* HW. [*E. T. A. Hoffmanns Sämmtliche Werke,* edited by E. Grisebach, Leipzig: Hesse, 1900], x, 110: "mir fiel ein, irgendwo gelesen zu haben, ein jeder müsse so handeln, dasz seine Handelsweise als allgemeines Prinzip gelten könne." The reference is of course to the "categorical imperative," here used with satirical force.

4. Cf. Grisebach's "Verzeichnis," [*Schopenhauer,* Berlin: E. Hofmann, 1905]. A close search has failed to show other instances than those there mentioned.

5. Letter to Hauptmann von Fricken in Asch, Sept., 1834. Schumann, *Jugendbriefe,* 2. Aufl., S. 254.

6. JPW, [*Jean Pauls Sämmtliche Werke,* Berlin: G. Reimer, 1826-38], xxv, 114.

7. JPW., xxv, 136.

8. JPW., xxvii, 139.

9. Tagebuch, Hz. [Hitzig, *Aus Hoffmanns Leben und Nachlasz,* 3 Ausg., Stuttgart, 1839], ii, 43: "Sonderbarer Einfall auf dem Ball vom 6 ten. Ich denke mir mein Ich durch ein Vervielfältigungsglas;—alle Gestalten, die sich um mich herumbewegen, sind Ich's, und ich ärgere mich über ihr Tun und Lassen." Cf. further, Hz., iii, 29, and [Ott.] Klinke, *E. T. A. Hoffmanns Leben und Werke vom Standpunkt eines Irrenarztes* [Braunschweig: R. Sattler, 1902], S. 126 ff.

10. [Georg] Ellinger, [*E. T. A. Hoffmann: Sein Leben und Seine Werke.* Hamburg and Leipzig: L. Voss, 1894,] 119, 120.

11. HW., x, 138.

12. HW., x, 148.

13. JPW., xxv, 24.

14. JPW., xxiv, 18, xxv, 112, etc.

15. Tagebuch, 1810: "Warum denke ich schlafend oder wachend so oft an den Wahnsinn?" Hz., ii, 46. Cf. Klinke, 89, who treats the matter from the standpoint of an alienist.

16. In the *Serapionsbrüder* Cyprian-Hoffmann says: "Ihr alle kennt ja meinen besondren Hang zum Verkehr mit Wahnsinnigen." HW., vi, 28. Dr. Klinke (108-109) shows with what a master hand H. [Hoffmann] sketched into the *Elixiere des Teufels* symptoms which he had observed directly from life: "Aus der Wahrheit und tiefen Wirkung seiner Figuren geht schon hervor, dasz er Geisteskranke direkt beobachtet hat."

17. HW., i, 280: "schon lange galt der arme Johannes allgemein für wahnsinnig."

18. HW., i, 291.

19. HW., i, 288.

20. HW., i, 281. This work was taken up at a later period, but was found in H's papers only in the form of a sketch, reproduced Hz., ii, 115. Cf. letter to Kunz, May 24, 1815. [Karl Friedrich] Kunz [*Aus dem Leben Zweier Dichter (Erinnerungen aus meiem Leben,* i), Leipzig: F. A. Brockhaus, 1836] 162 ff.

21. HW., x, 140.

22. HW., x, 356.

23. Hitzig [Tagebuch] expressly confirms this, although apparently without authority from Hoffmann for his statement (ii, 114). The biographer adds that the "Lichte Stunden eines wahnsinnigen Musikers," cf. above, was to close the work.

24. *Titan,* 2. Jobelperiode, 10. Zykel.

25. HW., x, 37.

26. HW., i, 139 ff.

27. *Prinzessin Bramabilla,* HW., xi, 105.

28. HW., x, 10.

29. JPW., l, p. vii.

30. Cf. the chapter on "Romantische Ärzte" in Ricarda Huch's *Ausbreitung und Verfall der Romantik,* [Leipzig: Haessel, 1902], S. 273 ff. Of contemporaries, Oehlenschläger, *Lebenserinnerungen,* iii, 184, 209, gives an interesting account of mesmeric séances in Berlin and Vienna.

31. As a characteristic instance, cf. the simile of the "Hell-Seherin" in a later work, "Die wenig erwogene Gefahr (1815)," JPW., xlviii, 144. Here and

elsewhere Richter shows an intimate acquaintance with the hypnotic phenomena. Cf. especially the articles from the *Museum,* reprinted in "Mutmaszungen über einige Wunder des organischen Magnetismus," etc. JPW., XLIX, 1 ff.

32. Most strikingly in the articles from the *Museum,* noted above. Richter seems to have undertaken magnetic cures himself. Nerrlich, *Deutsche Nationallit,* Bd. 130, p. lxi ff.

33. HW., VII, 65.

34. JPW., XXI, 202.

35. JPW., X, 48. Jean Paul may have borrowed the motive from Sterne (cf. Czerny [*Sterne, Hippel und Jean Paul.* Berlin, [18]04, S.38 Anm.], 64), altho one thinks involuntarily of Richter's own piano fantasies in the circle of super-sentimental women of the "Erotic Academy" at Schwarzenbach. The anonymous author of the *Nachtwachen des Bonaventura* (1804) has probably the scene from *Hesperus* in mind at the end of the first "Watch," where the nightwatchman sings a passing song beneath the window of the dying freethinker: "Den Sterbenden ist die Musik verschwistert, sie ist der erste süsze Laut vom fernen Jenseits, und die Muse des Gesanges ist die mystische Schwester, die zum Himmel zeigt." Michel's edition, B. [Berlin] 1904, 9.

36. JPW., XXI, 202 ff.

37. "Ihm war bis zur Täuschung als sprech' er mit Lianen, und wenn die Töne immer wie Liebende dasselbe wiederholten vor Innigkeit und Lust; meinte er nicht Lianen, und sagte ihr: wie lieb' ich Dich, O wie lieb' ich Dich?" JPW., XXII, 159.

38. HW., I, 288.

39. JPW., XXII, 231 and note. "Dieses Selbstertönen—wie die Riesenharfe bei verändertem Wetter unberührt anklingt—ist in Migraine und andern Krankheiten der Schwäche häufig; daher im Sterben; z. B. in Jacob Böhme schlug das Leben wie eine Konzertuhr seine Stunde von Harmonien umrungen aus." JPW., XXII, 231, Anm. In the passage of the *Nachtwachen,* above referred to, the author illustrates also by a reference to the "ferne Musik" which accompanied Böhme's death. Cf. above Note; further, Abraham von Franckenberg, "Bericht v. d. Leben und Abschied Jacob Boehmens" in *Des Jacob Boehmen Alle Theosophischen Schriften.* Amsterdam, 1682, 1. Abschnitt, 29; quoted by Michels, 151.

40. HW., I, 16, 18. Kreisler also is filled with an inner music, which rages in wild dissonances at times and which may be calmed into angelic harmonies by the appearance of a congenial person. Cf.

"Brief des Kapellmeisters Kreisler an den Baron Wallborn," HW., I, 285 ff. Klinke, 70 ff., seeks to explain the phenomenon of the "inner music" on psycho-pathological grounds.

41. JPW., XIV, 164. Dozens of similar examples might be cited from *Siebenkäs* and *Titan.*

42. Hz., I, 146.

43. HW., II, 119.

44. HW., II, 265.

Peter Bruning (essay date March 1955)

SOURCE: Bruning, Peter. "E. T. A. Hoffmann and the Philistine." *German Quarterly* 28, no. 2 (March 1955): 111-21.

[*In the following essay, Bruning observes the role of the philistine in Hoffmann's fairy tales. Bruning contends that Hoffmann's antagonism toward the German petty bourgeois was rooted in his ambivalence about his own middle-class origins.*]

Philistines as personages of fiction scarcely appear in Hoffmann's tales of chilling mystery. However, they constantly recur in those of lighter vein into which he wove much of his personal philosophy: the fairy tales, and the works centered around Hoffmann's literary double, Kapellmeister Kreisler. The primary aim of this study is to throw light on this aspect of Hoffmann's creativeness, which seems not to have been adequately covered before.[1]

The philistine, the smug and narrow-minded bourgeois, had been the target of many authors in the romantic period.[2] Fichte wrote a crusty *Naturgeschichte des Philisters* in 1802, and Clemens Brentano was so alarmed by the danger of creeping philistinism to the national culture that, between 1799 and 1806, he detailed, catalogued, and minutely illustrated his charges against the philistine in a satirical treatise. But these and most other attempts at presenting a true-to-life portrait of the philistine had been one sided and did not extend beyond the reaches of journalism and literary polemics. Hoffmann initiated the philistine as a major literary type by breathing life into the tart phrases of his predecessors. The force of his interpretation is largely determined by his singular "Lebensgefühl," the conviction that the artist is lonely in a hostile world, a view which shaped his attitude toward the bourgeoisie. It found literary expression through his ability for keenly realistic observation, which sets him apart from the other romantics.

The chasm between the ideal and the real, the chronic dualism he was prone to, was irrevocable and absolute for Hoffmann. Jean Paul, in an introduction for Hoffmann's *Fantasiestücke in Callots Manier,* showed little taste for this state of mind. He bluntly observes of Hoffmann that an artist could easily "aus Kunstliebe in Menschenhass geraten."[3] Hoffmann's frustration with his social environment was intensified by a change in his personal fortunes. As a musician, he was compelled to hire out a real and sensitive talent to entertain tea circles and to teach middle-class dilettantes—people with whom he had nothing in common, and whom in reality he resented.

The seeds of this resentment were sown early. In *Der Musikfeind,* 1814, Hoffmann describes with autobiographic accuracy the musical evenings he was subjected to as a small boy, events that were repeated with monotonous and almost ritualistic regularity in his parental home in Königsberg. There he was first confronted with the bewildering but sometimes amusing behavior of musical dilettantes, their insensitive and grotesque zeal and their acclamation of complicated musical patterns as they disdained simplicity of form and dismissed it as "Dudeldumdei, das den Verstand nicht beschäftigen könne."[4] As time goes on Hoffmann detests music-making as a means of escaping boredom more and more. On the other hand, music in its noble sense so stirs him that he must rush away and seek solitude. Thus, by a weird paradox, he finds himself an "enemy of music."

The antagonism of the "Musikfeind" was symptomatic of the late romantic turn of mind, but it was intensified in Hoffmann's case by the fact that he, more than any other romanticist, fought the burgher within himself. More or less voluntarily abandoning the relatively secure and respectable civil service to which his legal education commended him—"die Staatskrippe" as he termed it—he temporarily slid into the bohemian life of a poverty-ridden private tutor of piano and voice. Under these circumstances he found himself entirely at the mercy of the well-to-do bourgeoisie from whose ranks he had alienated himself. At best the proud burghers of Bamberg could only tolerate this capricious, cynical, freethinking musician at the periphery of their lives, and then as though he were some kind of half-tamed animal oddity, never to be trusted as a social equal, and to be accepted only as a witty entertainer. This altered social status is, beyond any doubt, largely responsible for Hoffmann's increased hostility toward the burgher in himself, as his own alter ego, and in the world around him. The rebuffs of the Bamberg period found their literary culmination in the early, incongruous tale **"Die Lebensschicksale des Hundes Berganza."** Partly autobiographic, it reflects Hoffmann's idealistic, platonic love for Julia Marc, "das reine Engelsbild," whose marriage of convenience to a wealthy and vulgar merchant had appalled Hoffmann.

"Die Lebensschicksale des Hundes Berganza" vents Hoffmann's pent-up rage over his unhappy love affair.

He introduces his despised rival thinly disguised as Monsieur George, an academician, but other than this it may be assumed that his characterization is faithful to the original. Engaged to Cäcilie, this gentleman arouses the scorn of his fiancé's devoutly aesthetic friends by bursting into the family's tea parties, smugly dispensing trivialities and jocular obscenity. Cäcilie's amorous senses are awakened, none-the-less, by George's cunning tactics, and the wedding ensues. The climax of Hoffmann's outcry of resentment is the rescue of Cäcilie from the clutches of her drunken husband, who is attacked and dragged from the bridal chamber by the enraged dog, Berganza.

To bring the "Menschenhass aus Kunstliebe" of Hoffmann, alias Berganza, into the proper perspective, we must realize the strength of Hoffmann's identification of Julia as the very embodiment of music, the "Ombra Adorata," who is also hauntingly present in later tales. The venomous epithets, devil, debauchee and weakling, applied to M. George are reminiscent of Brentano's *Philisterabhandlung,* which also equated philistinism with a satanic spirit.[5]

"Der goldene Topf," 1814, reveals a better natured and more humorous version of this type that we will call the *smug* philistine. Previously a product of personal ill feelings, he now becomes the inhabitant of a mythical world. Among casual readers of the "Gespensterhoffmann," it is little known that he was preoccupied with such idealistic philosophy as Schelling's theory of the world soul.[6] Here he found, in a scholarly presentation, the idea that nature emerges from the spirit. Fascinating to him was Schelling's concept of the "intellektuale Anschauung," the intuitive knowledge of the absolute in nature, which, according to Schelling, only artists could possess. Schelling's idea that the contradiction between nature and spirit reaches a state of harmony in the process of artistic creation appealed to Hoffmann's innermost being. Rejecting the purely scholarly approach, he turned to Gotthilf Heinrich Schubert, who interpreted Schelling in terms of legends, myths, visions, and mysterious prophecies. For use in his fairy tales, Hoffmann borrowed the theory of the three epochs from Schubert's *Ansichten von der Nachtseite der Naturwissenschaften.*[7]

According to Schubert, the harmony of both the empirical and spiritual worlds, exhibited in a primeval period of the history of mankind, has been turned in our era into a clashing dualism. In the first epoch, the primeval paradise, man still lived "in der ersten heiligen Harmonie mit der Natur, ohne eigenen Willen, erfüllt von dem göttlichen Instinkt der Weissagung und Dichtkunst."[8] Then he awakes to consciousness, "das klare Selbstbewusstsein, die Reflektion,"[9] so that the gift of pure perception inherent in him is destroyed. An identical cosmogony forms the substratum of **"Der goldene Topf"** and *Prinzessin Brambilla.* Hoffmann calls the destructive force "der Gedanke," and any mortal struck by it will blindly flounder about: "losgerissen von der Mutterbrust wankt in irrem Wahn . . . der Mensch heimatlos umher."[10] Such is Hoffmann's somber conception of the philistine of the early part of the second epoch. But the prosaic life the philistine now faces does not seem so grim after all. While the poet can perceive the voices of the exotic past and is filled with gnawing "Sehnsucht,"[11] the philistine lives merrily as the comfort-loving official who regards everything as incomprehensible that bears the mark of dream, inspiration or miracle and dismisses it as nonsense.

The *smug* philistine is man in a primitive form, dominated by his instinct for self-preservation, by greed and lust for power. This complacent and sly creature displays outwardly the undeviating stateliness of a wigged, powdered and frockcoated bureaucrat, properly equipped with snuff box and cane. Hoffmann's talent for the bizarre conveys to him a sense of mystery which at times impresses us as a reversal in the relationship of the real and unreal, so that it is the humdrum life which seems supernatural, while the wondrous visions of the poet become almost tangible reality.

Frequent are such expressions as "das paradiesische Wunderreich," "das Geisterreich Atlantis," "das Leben in der Poesie." For Hoffmann these signify a metaphysical world which remains remarkably constant throughout his life, as is best demonstrated by his aesthetic writings about music, particularly **"Beethovens Instrumentalmusik,"** 1813. His religious beliefs were not based upon Christianity, as were Brentano's, but exclusively upon this "wonderland," which for him was the realm of music. If we may speak of guilt suggested by the "evil" smugness of the philistines in **"Der goldene Topf,"** it is that of the genuine "Musikfeinde," rather than a Christian concept.

This also holds true for the women in the tales who are delineated as philistines. The only critic who has attempted to classify all feminine characters in Hoffmann's work, Ben van Eysselsteijn, confined himself to an outline. In the first group he listed the unscrupulous flirts; in the second, the pale, dreamy maidens; and in the third, woman as the embodiment of music.[12] The designation "unscrupulous flirts" for the first group seems an overstatement. Van Eysselsteijn obviously means the superficial coquettes of middle-class milieus, like Veronika in **"Der goldene Topf,"** Candida in *Klein Zaches* [*Kleine Zaches genannt Zinnober*], Christine in **"Der Artushof,"** and Albertine in **"Die Brautwahl."** Less sharply outlined than the male representatives, they are usually lighthearted and afflicted with sadness only when a new scarf has become stained.

In **"Der goldene Topf"** there are two levels where the polarity between matter and spirit exists: the mythical,

exemplified by the struggle between a dragon and the Geisterfürst Phosphorus, and the real, opposing rationalism and materialism of officialdom to the lofty ideals of the poetic dreamer Anselmus. This young man undergoes a refining process, which lifts him from an ordinary life to an "ever higher reality,"[13] reaching its apex in a fabulous existence of pure poetry: the realm of Atlantis. The philistine environment constitutes a stumbling block for him. The smug bureaucrats, and especially Konrektor Paulmann's flirtatious daughter Veronika, attempt to draw him back into the philistine orbit. In the unfounded conviction that a marriage to Anselmus will give her more social prominence, Veronika attempts to distract him from his ideals, resorting to the assistance of a sorceress who hypnotizes the hero by means of alchemy and magic telepathic mirrors.

The motif of an alliance between the philistine and occult forces was not a novelty at the time Hoffmann wrote **"Der goldene Topf."** Novalis, with whose writings Hoffmann had been preoccupied prior to conceiving **"Der goldene Topf,"** depicts such an alliance in a similar mythical philosophy in Klingsohr's tale of *Eros und Fabel.* But instead of the theory of successive epochs, Novalis evokes the picture of two worlds in a state of chaos which must fuse in order to reach harmony. The enemy of this envisaged harmony is presented allegorically as an evil, brooding clerk, personifying the "petrifizierende und petrifizierte Verstand," as opposed to sacred wisdom. As such he is the precursor of a type which often occurs in Hoffmann's tales, and which might be called the *demonic* philistine.

At first glance this seems a contradiction in terms, but to Hoffmann, who had an aversion to the scholarly mind, scientists, especially those in the natural sciences, were "retailers of nature," repulsive in their fanatic quest for something new which never brought them closer to the essence of nature. Mosch Terpin, in *Klein Zaches genannt Zinnober,* is one of them. His spectacular career as a professor of natural science runs parallel to the sudden introduction of an enlightened regime in his country, the effects of which Hoffmann sums up as stifling regimentation and uniformity in state and public affairs.[14] Education has also been reformed: it is said of Professor Mosch Terpin that the way he lectures on nature is agonizing; a weird sensation of horror grips one as though seeing an insane king fondling a straw puppet he has fashioned instead of embracing the royal bride. These materialists consider God to be nothing but a clever mechanic of the universe. Through their superior technical skills they are enabled to imitate nature to such horrible perfection that the product of their ingenuity confuses people to the point of insanity. Thus the professor of anatomy, Spalanzani, and his friend the "Physikant" Coppelius in **"Der Sandmann"** cause the hypersensitive hero to become infatuated with a robot.

After her clock-work interior is revealed, the young man falls ill of nervous fever and later leaps to his death. A fine psychologist, Hoffmann here leaves the question open as to whether such expert mechanics and rationalistic teachers produce supernatural phenomena, or whether it is all in the minds of certain hypersensitive people who are predestined to fall prey to hallucinations.

Less dangerous but indisputably demonic is Magister Tinte in **"Das fremde Kind."** The grotesque, spiderlike tutor, who incessantly dances about and relishes stuffing his pupils with encyclopedic knowledge, climaxes his activities by changing into a huge, droning fly.

Light is shed on the philistine of a third category, which might be called *"Bildungsphilister."*[15] In Hoffmann's principal work, ***Lebensansichten des Katers Murr nebst fragmentarischer Biographie des Kapellmeisters Johannes Kreisler in zufälligen Makulaturblättern*** [*Kater Murr*], the playful psychological autobiography of the conceited pseudo-poet, Kater Murr, has been contrasted with the tragic love of Kreisler. Each represents a pole in Hoffmann's vision of life. The humdrum life of the mediocre is the negative pole, whereas the hypersensitivity, loneliness, exhilarations and suffering of a genius are the positive pole, the essence of life. Hoffmann had now reached a complete maturity of self-expression and style. By blending human and animal characteristics he summarized successfully in Kater Murr the various philistine traits with which his predecessors had been concerned. The arrogance of the pseudo-intellectual in an enlightened period is coupled with sentimentality and voracity in Kater Murr. Observing himself with minute exactness, without failing to enlighten the reader about his years of indiscretion and experiences with love and error, he depicts his development from tomcat adolescence to maturity.

Murr, fancying himself a great poet and novelist, is stimulated most by his appetite. Conversely, the act of writing is a satisfactory means of abating this appetite and other such mortifications of the flesh as toothache. Contemplation of nature fills him with enthusiasm, for the dove he sights whets his appetite. He is a patriot, true to his fatherland, the attic, for it affords him "manch Mäuslein, manche Wurst oder Speckseite." Even able to turn his voracity into an asset to his dandyism in the presence of applauding ladies, he catches mice with amiable agility or attacks his bowl of milk with dainty licks at the edge. The tomcat philistine knows ways to find the best spot in the attic and explains to everyone how he managed to get the place and what he is going to do to improve his situation. He is selfish, though he always apologizes with effusive diplomacy for not helping his fellow cats. At heart he is a homebody, curled up under the stove with frequent sighs about the hot day. His life of leisure is briefly interrupted by his af-

filiation with the revolutionary "Katzburschentum," resulting in excessive drinking of herring pickle juice, and heroic duelling. Unluckily, he is soon chased back to his stove by the "Spitzphilister."

In the passage about the "Katzburschen" and "Spitzphilister," Hoffmann ventures into the field of politics. On one hand he derides the pathos and cowardice of the "Burschen," who feel superior to the philistines but are really no different, on the other he scoffs at the witch hunt of the reactionary regime, to which the name "Spitzphilister"—a play upon the word "Spitzel," informer—points.

The late romantic tendency toward criticism of society becomes apparent, though Hoffmann's interest in topics of the day should not be overestimated. The amused neutrality shown in *Kater Murr* springs in fact from a complete indifference toward politics, an attitude he stubbornly maintained throughout his life. Above all, Hoffmann was an artist and an individualist, not a social reformer. Not as a liberal politician, but rather from a personal sense of justice he made the famous satirical thrust at the fanatical minister of police von Kamptz in one of his last mythical tales, *Meister Floh.*

The question arises as to why Hoffmann chose an animal as the symbol of philistinism. Apart from artistic motivations and a great affection for his own cat, Hoffmann's concern with mechanical theories of his time influenced this decision to show the philistine as a mechanically drilled animal. Hoffmann's starting point was the question of producing natural sounds through mechanical means. Could the animated tone of the violin be measured by an artificial procedure? Was it possible to disclose psychic impulses by means of technical tricks? Mechanics was still a new field, and it was as much in vogue as is psychoanalysis today. If robots in the guise of human beings could be created by mechanical devices, would it not be possible to train dumb animals, providing them with all external characteristics of the human psyche?

The first step toward the realization of this idea is the ***Nachricht von einem gebildeten jungen Mann,*** 1814, in which the insipidity and snobbishness of high society salons are derided. The central figure, the monkey Milo, is first drilled in social poise by a professor in aesthetics and then poses as an artistic genius. Unlike Kater Murr he is delineated hazily and should be considered the mere mouthpiece of Hoffmann's opinions. And in the portrayal of another *"Bildungsphilister,"* Klein Zaches, the parvenu and clever intriguer of whom no one notices that he is actually a gnarled little monster, Hoffmann touches upon the problem of sham and reality. Klein Zaches, the "stepchild of nature," had a small stature in common with his creator, so that many critics have suggested that Hoffmann consciously incorporated in this creature some of his own individuality, a burgher ego enclosed in a diminutive body.[16]

In Hoffmann's professional career the duplicity of sham and reality took an uncannily concrete form. In Berlin, his residence from 1814 until his death, he was the conscientious, seemingly devoted civil functionary during the day, the bohemian habitué of *Weinstuben* at night. An equal paradox existed in his marital life. It revealed a contented but prosaic domesticity, while his writings showed a vague yearning for the ideal woman. In reality Hoffmann had no wish to have this yearning satisfied, for its fulfillment in this world would have killed both the emotion and the inspiration it gave him. So there existed no desire for a harmonious integration of spirit and matter, of love and sensuousness, so characteristic of another romantic, Novalis. Neither could the mystic part of him be completely reconciled with the spirit of order and exactness to which he unwillingly submitted in spite of having learned, in his parental home, to loathe its stifling effect on ideas.

The wellsprings of Hoffmann's antagonism to the philistine obviously rise from family tensions in his boyhood. The struggle between his stable middle class heritage and his unstable genius created early an inner discord Hoffmann could never overcome. Yet it was the impelling influence of the contemporary romantic ideology which gave definite direction, scope and color to his conception of the philistine. To Kleist, Jean Paul and Tieck he largely owed stylistic skills; Novalis and Schelling influenced his teleological speculations; G. H. Schubert shaped his imagery. To this list of creditors the name of Brentano should be added. It can be assumed that his *Philisterabhandlung* gave Hoffmann the impetus for his philistine characterizations, as it was later Heine's great source of inspiration for the portrayal of the hilarious figures in his *Harzreise*. The keen romantic awareness of a conflict between spirit and matter which pervades these satires is fundamental to "Philisterkritik" in general and has been persistently manifest in German literature up to Mann and Hesse. No wonder that the history of "Philisterkritik" does not come to an end with Hoffmann but can be traced from Heine through Raabe, Fontane and well into the modern period. Hoffmann's role in this process is considerable, though the scope of his philistine conception is necessarily limited by his intellectual horizon, interests and ideals. "Er hatte keinen weltumfassenden Blick aber schöpfte das Wunderbare aus dem Menschen," said Ricarda Huch of Hoffmann,[17] and this seems valid enough when applied to Hoffmann's "Philisterkritik," since its motivations are chiefly individualistic and aesthetic, rather than cultural or social. Hoffmann's poetic interest in "das Wunderbare" of the philistine was rather a *tremendum* than a *fascinosum* for him. Hence he had the delightfully paradoxical and unique idea of conferring on the German petty bourgeois a mysterious or

even satanic quality befitting the negative values this type embodied. It was only in Kater Murr that Hoffmann abandoned the supernatural in favor of a more detached satirical approach to the philistine in his social environment.

Notes

1. Ernst von Schenk enters succinctly into the problem in his book, *E. T. A. Hoffmann, Ein Kampf um das Bild des Menschen,* Berlin, 1939. E. Kohn-Bramstedt deals extensively with German philistinism of the 19th century, but fails to mention E. T. A. Hoffmann. Cf. *Aristocracy and the Middleclasses in Germany, Social types in German Literature,* London, 1937.

2. See, for the erratic history of the word "Philister," F. Kluge, *Wortforschung und Wortgeschichte,* Leipzig, 1912, p. 20.

3. E. T. A. Hoffmann, *Werke,* ed. G. Ellinger, Berlin, 1912, I, 17 (cit. Hoffmann throughout).

4. Hoffmann I, 40.

5. Brentano had charged the philistine with virtually all sins of history, originating with those of Lucifer, the rebel against God. His punishment is "die Gründung der Erde . . . der Satan und in seinen weiteren Ausgeburten die Sünde, der Philister." Cf. *Der Philister vor, in und nach der Geschichte,* Berlin, 1905, p. 6 (cit. Brentano).

6. *Von der Weltseele, eine Hypothese der höheren Physik zur Erklärung des allgemeinen Organismus,* Hamburg, 1798.

7. G. H. Schubert, *Ansichten von der Nachtseite der Naturwissenschaften,* Dresden, 1808, p. 21 (cit. Schubert).

8. Schubert, p. 4. For a detailed and convincing exposé of Schubert's *Ansichten* as a running commentary to "Der goldene Topf" see Hans Dahmen, *E. T. A. Hoffmann's Weltanschauung,* Marburg, 1929, p. 17.

9. Schubert, p. 324.

10. Hoffmann, X, 64.

11. Hoffmann, IV, 171.

12. Ben van Eysselsteijn, *E. T. A. Hoffmann, de verteller der romantiek,* Den Haag, 1941, p. 33.

13. Anselmus does not live in a world which is a mixture of fantastic and prosaic elements, as many critics claim. The fairy tale world of wonders is ever present and *inherent* in forms of every day life. It is Anselmus' task to learn how the various outer shells of reality can be pierced in order that he may see "das Wunderbare."

14. Brentano ascribes this uniformity directly to the philistines "Sie [die Philister] wollen ein Land in ein rein gewürfeltes Damenbrett verwandeln" (Brentano, p. 21). He goes even a step further by questioning their political ethics: "Ueberhaupt ist Staatsklugheit mit Niederträchtigkeit verbunden ein Hauptzug aller Philister" (p. 21).

15. A person who is commonplace in ideas and tastes but claims to be highly cultured. The word was coined by Bettina Brentano in *Ilius Pamphilius und die Ambrosia,* 1848. (*Sämtliche Werke,* ed. W. Oehlke, Berlin, 1920, V, 207.)

16. For a discussion of the point see H. W. Hewett-Thayer, *Hoffmann, Author of the Tales,* Princeton, 1948, p. 233.

17. Ricarda Huch, *Die Romantik,* Leipzig, 1924, II, 206.

Francis J. Nock (essay date January 1962)

SOURCE: Nock, Francis J. "E. T. A. Hoffmann and Nonsense." *German Quarterly* 35, no. 1 (January 1962): 60-70.

[*In the following essay, Nock analyzes the comic elements in Hoffmann's writings. According to Nock, Hoffmann doesn't enjoy the same widespread popularity in his native country as he does in other European nations because his sense of humor, with its emphasis on nonsense and absurdity, is distinctly un-German.*]

In his *E. T. A. Hoffmann als bildender Künstler*[1] Theo Piana implies that no present-day Berliner is acquainted with E. T. A. Hoffmann and adds that he "ist auch im übrigen Deutschland kaum noch bekannt, während er im Ausland noch heute als einer der bedeutendsten Bahnbrecher des deutschen kritischen Realismus gewertet wird." The wealth of editions of Hoffmann's works that has appeared in Germany since these words were written make them seem too strong. Yet there is unquestionably truth in the statement that Germans, on the whole, do not rate Hoffmann the writer as highly as do people from other countries. One reason for this, it seems to me, is that Hoffmann's writings are pervaded with a sense of humor that is not typically German. For the same reason that Noel Coward's *Blithe Spirit* was not a success when translated and performed in Germany[2], Hoffmann's writings have always been derogated to a greater or lesser extent: back of even the wildest flights of humorous fancy it is felt that there must be some rational explanation, or else the work can not be considered truly great literature.

This can be seen, for instance, in the slowness with which the recognition has made its way that ***Kater Murr*** is Hoffmann's masterpiece. One reason for this slow-

ness has been the form of the novel. The comment of (the Glasgow-born) John G. Robertson in his *History of German Literature*[3] exemplifies this well: "A romance more fantastically planned than this could not be imagined . . . The contents of the book, too, are extraordinarily confused . . . The chief features of ***Kater Murr*** are, however, its irony and satire."

While a great deal has been written about Hoffmann and *Humor,* practically nothing has been written about his sense of humor[4], his delight in nonsense and absurdity. Then, too, many who have discussed Hoffmann apparently do not consider him in any way connected with humor or *Humor.* For example, Ricarda Huch, Wilhelm Scherer and Oskar Walzel[5] do not mention this feature at all. Ellinger[6], to whom we owe so much for the revival of interest in Hoffmann, dismisses ***Prinzessin Brambilla*** as one of the "geringwertigsten Leistungen des Dichters" (p. 163) and also calls it "matt und farblos" (p. 180). On page 147 he discusses ***Klein Zaches*** and speaks of the "humoristischen Kraft, die aus diesen Schilderungen spricht," and he admits (p. 151) that in ***Kater Murr*** "frei waltender Humor neben bitterer Ironie" is to be found. Otherwise there is nothing along these lines.

The general trend in the discussion of Hoffmann's *Humor* is to ascribe it to the "merkwürdige Zweiheit seines Wesens. Er war (wie alle Humoristen) Humorist aus Not und wider Willen."[7] Probably the most solemn statements are those by Egli[8], such as:

> So wandelt sich denn für die abgeklärte Weisheit, die Hoffmanns letzte Lebensjahre bestimmt, die Ironie der Gottheit in eine unendliche Güte, die mit zartem Humor auf die menschliche Unzulänglichkeit hinweist, um die ewige Sehnsucht in den Menschenherzen zu erwecken, und der endlich erwachten selbst diese Unzulänglichkeit ertragen und überwinden hilft.

Or this, concerning ***Prinzessin Brambilla***:

> . . . es ist, vom Standpunkt des Dichters aus gesprochen, der das abstrakte Gedankengebäude des Philosophen in anschauliche Gestaltung umzusetzen hat, die Betrachtung der Welt mit den Augen des *Humors,* zu der Held und Heldin des Capriccios sich erheben sollen. Hoffmann selbst hat im "Klein Zaches" sein erstes Werk geschrieben, das aus dem Geist des Humors geboren ist.

(p. 133)

And finally:

> Hoffmanns Begriff des Humors ist mit dem der Tragik aufs innigste verwandt und nur die Ergänzung des tragischen Lebensgefühls in *dem* Sinne, daß erst *er* die Freiheit vollends zum Durchbruch bringt, deren Aufbrechen die tragische Erschütterung einleitet.

(p. 141)

Similar thoughts may be found expressed to a greater or lesser extent in the works of Fritz Martini, Harvey W. Hewett-Thayer, Ernst von Schenck, Arthur Sakheim, and Wolfgang Kayser[9]. Urs Orland von Planta[10] also finds this dichotomy in Hoffmann, who "sein Inneres absichtlich verschleiert und immer eine Maske zur Schau trägt, . . . der scherzt, wenn es ihn schmerzt, und mit seinen Possen und Schwänken die tiefsten Leiden verdeckt." His insistence on the *ridi, Pagliaccio* theme is overdone, for Hoffmann, at least, is not putting up a theatrical front; he must really have enjoyed his flashes of humor[11]. Furthermore von Planta seems a little confused about this dichotomy. In the passage just quoted he speaks of the "tiefsten Leiden," but on page 29 he says of Hoffmann: "Wie die heutigen Existenzialisten gelangt er zu einer Bejahung des Absurden, indem er, ohne das eigentliche Leben zu kennen, aber das Rationale, dem er selbst angehört, als unerquicklich ablehnend, das wahre Sein in der bloßen Umkehrung des Rationalen . . . sucht." Elsewhere (p. 36) he refers to Hoffmann as "ohne wirkliche Seele, von seinem Körper fast losgelöst, von der Natur völlig entfernt."

Nowhere does there seem to be any recognition of Hoffmann's sheer delight in nonsense, in idiocy, in the absurd, a delight that is there per se[12]. This aspect of humor does, of course, frequently tie in with *Humor,* with irony and satire; and, I suppose, if it is so desired, a rational basis can always be found somewhere. It is the same sense of humor that is found in such disparate items as *Blithe Spirit,* the writings of W. S. Gilbert, the old Keystone Comedies, some of the poetry of Christian Morgenstern; it has been one of the bases of American humor for a century or more. It is expressed in play on words, in things and situations "that just can't be," in grotesque exaggeration of what is normally not funny. Above all, it appears in the author's poking fun at himself, even when not for publication[13].

Hewett-Thayer does touch on this at one point (*op. cit.,* p. 237) when he discusses **"Die Königsbraut."** There he says: "The story is indeed a remarkably entertaining and sustained bit of persiflage . . . no touch of the serious, as in the other Märchen, underlies the waggery." Harich, too, sees a glimmering of this. Of the **"Königsbraut"** he can not help seeing—and remarking on— "tiefere Bedeutung," but he admits that the various elements combine "zu einem äußerst reizvollen Gebilde" (*op. cit.,* II, p. 209). In Hoffmann's—published—letter to Johanna Eunike (the third of the **Briefe aus den Bergen**) there is found (*ibid.,* p. 385) "ein leiser schalkiger Humor, der die besuchenden Freunde bis zum letzten Tag erschütterte."

Before looking at Hoffmann's works and analyzing the pertinent passages, it would be well to examine what he has to say himself on the subject of humor. In **Brambilla** [**Prinzessin Brambilla**] he puts in the mouth of Franz Reinhold sentiments which are undoubtedly his own:

> Wahr ist es, immer habt Ihr uns Deutschen vorgeworfen, daß wir von jedem Scherz verlangten, er solle noch etwas anderes bedeuten als eben den Scherz selbst, und ich will Euch recht geben, wiewohl in ganz anderm Sinn, als Ihr es wohl meinen möget. Gott tröste Euch, wenn Ihr uns etwa die Dummheit zutrauen solltet, die Ironie nur allegorisch gelten zu lassen! Ihr wäret dann in großem Irrtum. Recht gut sehen wir ein, daß bei Euch Italienern der reine Scherz als solcher, viel mehr zu Hause scheint als bei uns.[14]

German humor, he goes on, is the language of "ein . . . sichtbar gewordenes Urbild."[15]

Later on (*ibid.,* p. 333) Reinhold further states of German *Humor* that it is

> . . . die wunderbare, aus der tiefsten Anschauung der Natur geborne Kraft des Gedankens, seinen eigenen ironischen Doppeltgänger zu machen, an dessen seltsamlichen Faxen er die seinigen und . . . die Faxen des ganzen Seins hienieden erkennt und sich daran ergötzt.

Hoffmann can be as solemn as any of his critics, in spite of himself!

In **Kater Murr** (**H.** [**E. T. A. Hoffmanns Dichtungen und Schriften**] V, 141) Hoffmann, through Kreisler, denies to the organ builder Liscov that "Humor" which was "jene seltene wunderbare Stimmung des Gemüts, die aus der tieferen Anschauung des Lebens in all seinen Bedingnissen, aus dem Kampf der feindlichsten Prinzipe sich erzeugt." Instead, Liscov's humor was "nur das entscheidende Gefühl des Ungehörigen, gepaart mit dem Talent, es ins Leben zu schaffen, und der Notwendigkeit der eigenen, bizarren Erscheinung." More such discussion is given by "der Braune" in **Seltsame Leiden eines Theaterdirektors** (**H.** XIII, 190).

In the discussions of the Serapionsbrüder, Lothar utters his conviction that women as a rule have no understanding for irony, "aus der sich der tiefste ergötzlichste Humor erzeugt" (*ibid.,* 315). Later on Sylvester objects that the French "Bonmots, ihre Calembours, die sich machen lassen auf den Kauf," are not to be considered social "Witz." To this Cyprian points out that French "Gesellschaftswitz" is based on mutual contempt, and "Dafür haben die Franzosen auch nicht den mindesten Sinn für den Witz, dessen Grundlage der echte Humor ist" (*ibid.,* 438-9). Finally it might be mentioned that on Jan. 27, 1819, Hoffmann sent his friend Hippel a copy of **Klein Zaches** [**Klein Zaches genannt Zinnober**] and a letter, in which he speaks of it. He says of **"Zinnober,"** "das tolle Märchen wird Dir gewiß, ich darf es glauben, manches Lächeln abzwingen. Wenigstens ist es bis jetzt das humoristischte [sic], was ich geschrieben" (**H.** XV, 250).

In *Kater Murr* Hoffmann, in addition to portraying the tragedy of his own life and, by extension, of all artists, manages to satirize thoroughly the philistines of his time, especially the *Duodez* princes and their courts. At the start of the novel he does this, however, in a way that far surpasses the usual bounds of satire and irony. The whole description of the birthday celebration of the *Fürstin* (**H.** V, 20-9) is as wildly absurd as any silent movie comedy, despite the tragic framework in which it is placed. The figure of the *Genius* with the wax candles, accidentally turned upside down and, as it is pulled along above the solemn procession, dripping hot wax on those below; all the subsequent confusion and destruction; the thunderstorm to add a grand climax— all these are vividly narrated. It is one of those scenes which either bring forth explosions of laughter from the reader or leave him relatively untouched. It is, perhaps, anarchistic, but it is delightful and absurd nonsense. *Kater Murr* is filled with this. It is invariably connected with parody or satire, as when Murr is inducted into the *Burschenschaft* (*ibid.,* 302-6), when he duels with his love rival (333-40), and when the funeral oration is held over the corpse of Kater Muzius (402-10).

The whole external structure of *Kater Murr* is based on the whimsical and highly improbable fact that the tomcat's autobiographical scribblings get mixed in with pages from the biography of Johannes Kreisler and that the mixture is then published. But as Hoffmann moves further and further along in his somber narration about Kreisler he finds less and less need for the figure of the tomcat. He adopts the abrupt method of getting rid of him by announcing his death. He does this in language that is as flowery as any introduction to a work of a deceased author (527-8). The whole idea of the demise of Murr was given to him by the death of his own tomcat Murr. On this occasion he sent to his friends the following announcement (**H.** XV, 322):

> In der Nacht vom 29. bis zum 30. November d.J. entschlief, um zu einem besseren Dasein zu erwachen, mein theurer geliebter Zögling der Kater Murr im vierten Jahre seines hoffnungsvollen Lebens. Wer den Verewigten Jüngling kannte, wer ihn wandeln sah auf der Bahn der Tugend und des Rechts, mißt meinen Schmerz und ehrt ihn durch Schweigen.
>
> Berlin d. 1. Decbr: 1821
>
> Hoffmann

It is known that Hoffmann was much attached to his pet, and therefore the absurdity of this essentially nonsensical announcement makes it all the more affecting.

With all its satire and parody *Klein Zaches* indulges in some practically pure nonsense. For example, Hoffmann gives a list of what "überschwengliche Dichter" demand of a young lady (**H.** III, 159-60). Among other things "muß besagtes Fräulein des Dichters Lieder singen nach der Melodie, die ihm (dem Fräulein) selbst aus dem Herzen geströmt." Here, among other things, we have a slight example of Hoffmann's delight in playing with words, his clarifying the ambiguity of "ihm."

The same work has another bit of parodying nonsense in the description (204-7) of the bestowal of the "Orden des grüngefleckten Tigers" on Zaches.

Prinzessin Brambilla has been discussed at great length by most of the writers on Hoffmann. Little touches of nonsense occur in this work which are there, I am sure, simply because Hoffmann had fun writing them. Giglio has seized Giacinta's hand and been stuck by a needle. She reproaches him for his forward behavior. Whereupon: "'Meine Giacinta', sprach Giglio im Schmerz der Liebe und des Nadelstichs, 'Meine Giacinta, laß uns alle Qual der Trennung vergessen!'" (**H.** III, 354-5). In a later situation Celionati refuses to tell the young people a story because the reader of *Prinzessin Brambilla* already knows it, since it was told before (411).

What rapturous poets demand in a young lady is well exemplified by Hoffmann's own character, the Berliner Albertine Voßwinkel, in **"Die Brautwahl"** (**H.** VII, 175). Among her many charms and virtues are: "daß sie mit niedlicher, sauberer Perlschrift Gedichte und Sentenzen, die ihr in Goethes, Jean Pauls und anderer geistreicher Männer und Frauen Schriften vorzüglich wohlgefallen, in ein Büchlein mit einem goldverzierten Maroquindeckel einträgt und das Mir und Mich, Sie und Ihnen niemals verwechselt."

"Die Königsbraut" has already been referred to. The whole story has no ulterior motive. One example of the "waggery" is Ännchens letter to her beloved Amandus (*ibid.,* 254-6). He has written her a letter with a high-flown sonnet, which she admits she does not quite understand. But she bravely writes him a poem:

> Ich lieb' Dich, bist Du mir auch ferne,
> Und wäre gern recht bald deine Frau.
> Der heitre Himmel ist ganz blau,
> Und abends sind golden alle Sterne.
> Drum mußt Du mich stets lieben
> Und mich auch niemals betrüben.
> Ich schick' Dir den virginischen Tabak
> Und wünsche, daß er Dir recht wohl schmecken mag!

Hoffmann's pleasure in word play comes out in her prefacing remarks to this poem: ". . . ich habe auch Verschen gemacht, und sie reimen sich gut. Schreib mir doch, wie das kommt, daß man so gut weiß, was sich reimt, ohne gelehrt zu sein." This same word play Hoffmann perpetrates in *Kater Murr* (**H.** V, 229), where the tomcat comments on the fact that there is no rhyme for *Mensch,* whereas there is for *Kater*; therefore man is "ein ungereimtes Tier," he, on the contrary, is "ein gereimtes."

It would fill too much space to discuss all the places in which Hoffmann lets his fancy go along the lines of absurdity and nonsense. We find them, for example, in *Blandina, Heimatochare, Irrungen, Geheimnisse, Seltsame Leiden eines Theaterdirektors*[16], and in the discussions of the Serapionsbrüder.

These flights of numerous fancy were not, however, purely literary endeavors indulged in for possible effect, but represent something fundamental in Hoffmann's nature. This is attested by the frequency with which he made them in his letters to his friends, and above all by his entries in his diaries. In particular he likes to poke fun at himself and to play with words. The former makes it clear that he thinks rather well of himself, yet is under no illusions that he is one of the world's geniuses. He especially likes to portray himself as a victim of fate, as, indeed, he was.

Again, a complete quoting of all the passages not intended for publication in which Hoffmann gave reins to his delight in this activity would fill too much space. A few examples must suffice. To his friend Hippel he wrote (18.7.96; **H.** XIV, 83): "Du glaubst jetzt meine Ankunft zu lesen mit allen Att- und Pertinenzien." This same parody of German style appears in his diary for 2.10.03 (**H.** XIV, 170) when he writes of a "de- und wehmütigen Brief." This phrase also appears in the "Vorwort des Herausgebers" in *Kater Murr* (**H.** V, 4): "De- und wehmütig muß nun der Herausgeber gestehen . . ." To Hippel he wrote again (1.4.98; **H.** XIV, 124): "Da bin ich hineingeworfen an einen Platz, wo alles an einem seidnen Faden hängt—platzt er, so liegt der Herr Regierungs-Rat *in spe* im Dr . . . k! (Die Damen halten hier den Fächer vor und zischeln sich in die Ohren 'Er ist expressiv—à la Goethe im Goetz.')" Also to Hippel is a letter (14.5.04; *ibid.,* 201) with the footnote: "Der Renegat—eine komische Oper, die der geistvolle Verfasser des Riesen Gargantua [himself] mit unerschöpflicher Laune dichtet und die, wird sie wills Gott im Jahre 1888 vollendet, alles übertreffen wird, was der Stümper Goethe jemals in dieser Art schrieb!—"

On 24.3.14 (**H.** XV, 123) he wrote a long letter to Kunz in Bamberg, which he divides into labeled "Capitel—Segmente." The second of these is "B. Aus meinem Leben (aber bloß Wahrheit ohne Dichtung.)" Kunz was said to have played the part of Kaiser Karl in an amateur theatrical performance. In the same letter Hoffmann wrote: "Sie, mächtigster Kaiser, verehre ich im Staube und sehe Ihre stattliche Figur mit dem Purpur mit Golde gestickt, Kron' auf dem Haupte, Stirne gerunzelt, mit Jovis Augenbrauen, Szepter in der Hand, einherschreiten! Blicke herab, großer Kaiser! auf einen armen Erd-, Stadt-, Haus-, Stuben-, Kammerbürger und Podagristen . . ." (130).

A letter to Franz von Holbein (**H.** XV, 237) starts off: "Vorigen Sonntag, d.h. am 5ᵗ April d.J. am Sonntage *Miserere Dom. Maximus* (Evangel: vom guten Hirten Joh: 10 Neumond nach halb 5 Uhr Nachm. Tageslänge 13 St. 4 Min.) brachte mir . . ." To Graf von Pückler auf Muskau he indulges in the old chestnut (24.1.19; **H.** XV, 247): "Ich schickte den Brief daher nicht ab und glaube aus diesem Grund mit Recht vermuten zu können, daß Sie ihn nicht erhalten haben."

He requested Chamisso (27.1.19; **H.** XV, 251) to borrow some books for him with these words: "Haben Sie die Güte, obige Bücher auf Ihren Namen für mich zu leihen und mir durch den Boten der Bibliothek, den ich dafür königlich belohnen werde, in meine Wohnung . . . zu senden und verhelfen Sie auf diese Weise der Welt zu neuen ergötzlichen Produkten."

In a letter of uncertain date to his close friend Ludwig Devrient (**H.** XV, 256) he assumes "daß die Katzenjammerschwangeren Morgennebel sich verzogen haben werden." Finally, the three *Briefe aus den Bergen,* especially the first and third, are filled with nonsense.

His diaries were certainly not meant for others to read, not even his wife. They are on the whole factual, or filled with despondent utterances. A few times, however, he jokes with himself, as when (6.10.03; **H.** XIV, 176) he bemoans: "Wann werden meine Leiden sich wenden! sagte *Frédéric le grand* auf dem Schlachtfelde—ich *H. le petit* sag' es wenn ich mich erhebe aus den staubigten Akten!" In November 1803 he let his diary lapse, then wrote on 1.1.04 (*ibid.,* 185): "Die Oktober und November-Stücke des nun seit dem 17ᵗ November recht sanft ruhenden Tagebuches . . ." Next month (7.2; *ibid.,* 191) we find: "Abends ging ich mit *Weiß* und *Schwarz* zu Hause—man könnt' dies für ein Bonmot halten—die Leute heißen aber wirklich so!"

Hoffmann drew numerous caricatures of himself, but none is as funny as his self-portrait with the features labeled with letters[17]. Below the picture the letters are explained, "a." being "die Nase," "b. die Stirn." The cheeks are labeled "d," and this is explained as "Dallashsche Beafsteek u Portwein"; "k." is "Ein Rokaermel mit willkührlichen Falten"; "n. fehlt" [and it does]; "p. Und so weiter."

Both in his writings intended for the general public and in his letters and his diaries Hoffmann, as we have seen, betrays a sense of humor that is unusual among his countrymen. To rephrase what was said earlier, he often wrote things "just for the fun of it." This by no means denies the truth of what others have said about Hoffmann and *Humor,* irony, satire, and the grotesque[18]. It is an added element that seems to have passed by unnoticed. It alone does not make a great writer. There are many American writers, for example, who have had it, but not much else, and have therefore fallen by the wayside. However, it is a distinct addition to the equipment of a great writer; and he should not be belittled for it. Rabelais is an outstanding example of a great writer who possessed this element. Thus it is regrettable that it is ignored in Hoffmann and his writings, and that he is known only as the author of such works as **"Der goldene Topf,"** *Die Elixiere des Teufels,* and the many horror tales that he has written.

Notes

1. Berlin, 1954 (*Berlin in der Kunst,* Bd. III), p. 5.

2. My authority for this is H. H. Carwin, the translator of *The Seven Year Itch* and other plays, who told it to me orally and has confirmed this by letter.

3. Edinburgh and London, 1908. First ed., p. 483. In the 2nd ed. (p. 477) the novel is discussed a little more sympathetically.

4. An examination of *Grimms Wörterbuch, Trübners Wörterbuch,* the *Oxford English Dictionary* and *Webster's New International Dictionary* show that "Humor" and "sense of humor" are not identical, even though there is some overlapping. Trübner's statement: "Jetzt bezeichnet H[umor] bereits mehr als bloße Laune, es drückt eine bestimmte Grundstimmung aus, die nicht unterzukriegen ist und auch unter Tränen noch lächelt," certainly fits the various discussions of Hoffmann's *Humor* mentioned in the following. The Oxford and Webster's are in agreement in their definitions of "humor." The Oxford defines: "That quality of action, speech, or writing, which excites amusement; oddity, jocularity, facetiousness, comicality, fun." A second definition really fits our "sense of humor" (which is not listed in the OED [Oxford English Dictionary]): "The faculty of perceiving what is ludicrous or amusing, or of expressing it . . . ; jocose imagination or treatment of a subject." Webster defines "sense of humor" as: "Faculty of perceiving and appreciating the humorous, now esp. in one's own character or actions."

5. Ricarda Huch, *Die Romantik,* II, 13. u. 14. Aufl. (Leipzig, 1931); Wilhelm Scherer, *Geschichte der deutschen Literatur,* 12. Aufl. (Berlin, 1910); Oskar Walzel, *Dia deutsche Literatur von Goethes Tod bis zur Gegenwart,* 5. Aufl. (Berlin, 1929).

6. Georg Ellinger, *E. T. A. Hoffmann: Sein Leben und seine Werke* (Hamburg u. Leipzig, 1894).

7. Walther Harich, *E. T. A. Hoffmann,* I, (Berlin, n.d.), pp. 24-5.

8. Gustav Egli, *E. T. A. Hoffmann: Ewigkeit und Endlichkeit in seinem Werk* (Zürich/Leipzig/Berlin, 1927), p. 106.

9. Fritz Martini, *Deutsche Literaturgeschichte,* 9. Aufl. (Stuttgart, 1958), p. 330; Harvey W. Hewett-Thayer, *Hoffmann: Author of the Tales* (Princeton, 1948), pp. 116, 158, 303; Ernst von Schenck, *E. T. A. Hoffmann: Ein Kampf um das Bild des Menschen* (Berlin, 1939), p. 668; Arthur Sakheim, *E. T. A. Hoffmann* (Leipzig, 1908), pp. 238, 246-7; Wolfgang Kayser, *Das Groteske* (Oldenburg u. Hamburg, 1957), p. 72-81.

10. Urs Orland von Planta, *E. T. A. Hoffmanns Märchen "Das fremde Kind"* (Bern, 1958), p. 45.

11. This will be shown later in the discussion of Hoffmann's diaries and letters.

12. My colleague Mr. Werner Marx, who is a native German, commented, in connection with this paper, that there is no real German equivalent for the English phrase "to have fun." I do not think "sich amüsieren" covers all the meanings, and certainly not that meant when I say, "Hoffmann quite often is just having fun."

13. It is the same sense of humor that led Mozart to write *Die Dorfmusikanten* and Schubert to play his music on a comb.

14. *E. T. A. Hoffmanns Dichtungen und Schriften,* ed. Walther Harich (Weimar, 1924), III, p. 317. Hereafter this edition is cited as "H."

15. This somewhat cryptic statement helps lead into the narration of the allegorical, metaphysical tale of "König Ophioch und die Urdarquelle." Reinhold's complete statement may be of interest. After the passage quoted just above, he continues: "vermöcht ich aber nur Euch recht deutlich zu erklären, welchen Unterschied ich zwischen Euerm und unserm Scherz, oder besser gesagt, zwischen Eurer und unserer Ironie finde.—Nun, wir sprechen eben von den tollen, fratzenhaften Gestalten, wie sie sich auf dem Korso umhertreiben; da kann ich wenigstens so ungefähr ein Gleichnis anknüpfen.—Seh' ich solch einen tollen Kerl durch greuliche Grimassen das Volk zum Lachen reizen, so kommt es mir vor, als spräche ein ihm sichtbar gewordenes Urbild zu ihm, aber er verstände die Worte nicht und ahme, wie es im Leben zu geschehen pflegt, wenn man sich müht, den Sinn fremder, unverständlicher Rede zu fassen, unwillkürlich die Gesten jenes sprechenden Urbildes nach, wiewohl auf übertriebene Weise, der Mühe halber, die es kostet. Unser Scherz ist die

Sprache jenes Urbildes selbst, die aus unserm Innern heraustönt und den Gestus notwendig bedingt durch jenes im Innern liegende Prinzip der Ironie, so wie das in der Tiefe liegende Felsstück den darüber fortströmenden Bach zwingt, auf der Oberfläche kräuselnde Wellen zu schlagen."

16. Another example of word play is the "Brown" director's remark (H. XIII, 155): "Mein Unstern wollte es, daß ich bei meinem kleinen beschränkten Theater einmal zwei Jungfrauen hatte—von Orleans, meine ich nämlich."

17. It is reproduced as frontispiece in vol. VII of Carl Georg Maassen's *E. T. A. Hoffmanns Sämtliche Werke* (München u. Leipzig, 1914). On page 400 Maassen states that it is taken from an etching made from the original by J. B. Sonderland and printed in the third edition of Eduard Hitzig's *E. T. A. Hoffmanns Leben und Nachlaß* (Stuttgart, 1839). According to Hitzig the original belonged to Karl Immermann. This is now lost, but Maassen quotes Immermann's *Memorabilien,* 3. Teil, p. 60 f. (I have checked the quotation), where mention is made of a visit in Bamberg at the home of Kunz. Here Hoffmann was present. ". . . von letzterem empfing ich auch eine interessante Hand-Zeichnung, sein eigenes Gesicht, mit humoristischer Marginalbezeichnung der darin erfindlichen Vorkommenheiten."

18. Cf. also Belcampo's discussion of "Narrheit" in *Die Elixiere,* in which he claims Folly is the true spiritual ruler (Geisterkönigin). Here he also pays tribute to word play by saying, "ein Wortspiel ist ein glühendes Lockeisen in der Hand der Narrheit, womit sie Gedanken krümmt." (H. IV, 297-8)

Robert Mollenauer (essay date summer 1963)

SOURCE: Mollenauer, Robert. "The Three Periods of E. T. A. Hoffmann's Romanticism: An Attempt at a Definition." *Studies in Romanticism* 2, no. 4 (summer 1963): 213-43.

[*In the following essay, Mollenauer evaluates Hoffmann's ideas concerning Romanticism. Describing his theories as "impressionistic," rather than analytical, and lacking in scholarly rigor, Mollenauer argues that Hoffmann's critical writings still represent an important contribution to the development of modern literary thought.*]

Although E. T. A. Hoffmann's reputation as a German Romanticist rests on his ability as a writer of fantastic tales, he is also due consideration as a theorist of Romanticism.[1] Prior to his own first formulations Hoffmann used the Romantic in the general sense that was current in Germany at the end of the eighteenth century. The term itself had existed long before the first Romanticists arrived to champion it. In fact, three distinct strains had established themselves by the end of the eighteenth century: "Da ist der antithetische Begriffskomplex Herders, mit den Stichworten: Mittelalter, gotisch, Rittertum, Liebe, Religion; da ist der von Wielands romantischer Epopöe, der auf ähnlicher Grundlage auf baut und das 'Wunderbare' einbezieht; da ist schliesslich der landschaftlichromanhafte Begriff, der alle literarischen Schichten erfüllt und eigentlich vorherrschend im breiten Publikum war."[2] If the Romantic was not a vague concept, it was at least a cluttered one by the time the Jena group began to organize its forces into a literary movement. Throughout this time and even up to his move to Bamberg in 1808 Hoffmann's references to the Romantic betray every aspect of the historical complex cited above—but no awareness of the critical writings of the Schlegel group.[3] Hoffmann's first attempt at a theory is as much a matter of attitude as of understanding. Indeed, attitude is a better word than theory, for Hoffmann's approach to Romanticism is emotional rather than critical. The whole range of his thinking on this matter is subject to three such periods—or attitudes.

The first phase of Hoffmann's Romanticism began when he was engaged as a critic for the well-known *Allgemeine Musikalische Zeitung.* Hoffmann was first sent two symphonies by Witt to review, and his critical technique was apparently satisfactory, for his next assignment was a review (1810) of Beethoven's *Fifth Symphony* [titled **"Beethoven, C moll-Sinfonie (No. 5)"**]. Hoffmann knew Romanticism to be the aesthetic fashion of the day, and he knew also that it embraced emotional exhilaration; when he came under the spell of the *Fifth,* the Romantic idea coalesced with his own enthusiasm, and Hoffmann found in music the core of Romanticism and his first impulse to champion it:

> Wenn von der Musik als einer selbständigen Kunst die Rede ist, sollte immer nur die Instrumentalmusik gemeint sein, welche, jede Hilfe, jede Beimischung einer andern Kunst verschmähend, das eigentümliche, nur in ihr zu erkennende Wesen der Kunst rein ausspricht. Sie ist die romantischste aller Künste—fast möchte man sagen, allein *rein* romantisch.—Orpheus' Lyra öffnete die Tore des Orkus. Die Musik schliesst dem Menschen ein unbekanntes Reich auf; eine Welt, die nichts gemein hat mit der äussern Sinnenwelt, die ihn umgibt, und in der er alle durch Begriffe bestimmbaren Gefühle zurücklässt, um sich dem Unaussprechlichen hinzugeben.

(XIII, 41)

Here is Hoffmann's first "definition": music is the most Romantic, the only purely Romantic art because it transcends the limitations of mortal sense. As the only purely spiritual form of artistic expression, it is *transcendental*. This fundamental character is never renounced by Hoffmann, even when the definition eventually is extended to many other artistic genres and ideas.

Hoffmann's enthusiasm for music is so unbounded and his unconcern for historicity so pronounced that he does not hesitate to call any great composer Romantic. The review of the *Fifth* also betrays Hoffmann's view that the Romantic fellowship is an exclusive society when he thrusts the three greatest exponents of the Classical period in music under the heading of Romanticism:

> Der romantische Geschmack ist selten, noch seltner das romantische Talent: daher gibt es wohl so wenige, die jene Lyra, welche das wundervolle Reich des Unendlichen aufschliesst, anzuschlagen vermögen. Haydn fasst das Menschliche im menschlichen Leben romantisch auf; er ist kommensurabler für die Mehrzahl. Mozart nimmt das Übermenschliche, das Wunderbare, welches im innern Geiste wohnt, in Anspruch. Beethovens Musik bewegt die Hebel des Schauers, der Furcht, des Entsetzens, des Schmerzes und erweckt jene unendliche Sehnsucht, die das Wesen der Romantik ist.
>
> (XIII, 42)

Clearly this system of classification is not in accord with traditional concepts in musicology; nevertheless for Hoffmann Romanticism, in its highest essence, is nothing other than the best in serious music—the best in serious *instrumental* music.

But Hoffmann's continuing work as a critic for the *Allgemeine Musikalische Zeitung* soon forces an expansion of his narrow doctrine, and this comes first through opera. Because of his esteem for Mozart's operas, Hoffmann is compelled to accept words as ornamentation, at least, for instrumental music; however, Romantic opera, too, is restricted to an intellectual elite. Thus, in a review of Gluck's *Iphigenia in Aulis* (1810), Hoffmann advises aspiring composers, "ältere, energische Werke zu studieren, als ohne dieses Studium der hohen Romantik Mozarts nachzujagen. Nur ein romantisches tiefes Gemüt wird den romantischen tiefen Mozart ganz erkennen . . ." (XIII, 60). Romanticism is a high calling, to be aspired to by few. It would be a still greater travesty to subject the truly Romantic opera to the depicting of scenes in daily life. In a review of Josef Weigl's *Das Waisenhaus* (1810) Hoffmann warns against such a misuse: "Vollends als Gegenstand der Oper, die die menschliche Natur höher potenziert, wo die Sprache Gesang ist . . . und die überhaupt nur in dem wundervollen Reiche der Romantik existiert, ist es gewiss verwerflich, Szenen des gemeinen Lebens zu wählen, die jeder Romantik geradezu entgegenstreben" (XIII, 63). Almost grudgingly Hoffmann concedes that this one music form must deal with life; but, he argues, a Romantic opera must preserve its transcendental purpose.

Throughout the Bamberg years (1808-13) Hoffmann did not waver in his insistence upon the exalted purpose of music. In a review of Gyrowetz' *Der Augenarzt* (1812) Hoffmann goes a step farther in prohibiting the use of Romantic opera not only for ordinary life but in particular for middle-class life: "Was soll aber aus unserer theatralischen Musik werden, wenn auch die *Oper* sich bis zu dem gemeinen Tun und Treiben des beengten bürgerlichen Lebens erniedrigt, das dem Geiste, der sich in das romantische Reich, wo Gesang die Sprache ist, emporschwingen will, die Fittiche lähmt und die Phantasie erdrückt?" (XIII, 105). One sees here a reluctance that the theater should be used for anything but opera. Moreover, Hoffmann's belief at this stage is that words can penetrate the ethereal only when accompanied by music.

The extension of Hoffmann's views on opera to Romantic drama comes with the review of an overture by Beethoven for Collins's play *Coriolan* (1812). However, Hoffmann chides the master because "Beethovens rein romantischer Genius der Collinschen, meistens reflektierenden Poesie nicht ganz befreundet zu sein scheint, und der Komponist dann erst mächtig die Seele ergreifen und ganz für die folgenden Erscheinungen aufregen würde, wenn es ihm gefiele, zu den die Romantik im höchsten Sinn aussprechenden Trauerspielen Shakespeares und Calderons Ouvertüren zu schreiben" (XIII, 88-89). Here words, unaccompanied by music, are first accorded Romantic status; but the favor thus shown drama is due not only to Beethoven. The reference to Shakespeare and Calderón betrays, for the first time in his printed works, the influence of the Jena Romanticists.[4] But again Hoffmann is selective, and here as well he admits nothing but the transcendental. Only that drama which exhibits a purposeful freedom of form, the ability to interweave the supernatural and the physical, is admitted to this closed society.

The new horizons that had been championed by the Jena Romanticists also led Hoffmann to the Gothic ideal. In the beginning of 1813 Hoffmann "compiled" a number of fragmentary utterances dealing with art criticism; in these *Höchst Zerstreute Gedanken* Hoffmann speaks, among other things, of the music of Bach: "Ich sehe in Bachs achtstimmigen Motetten den Kühnen, wundervollen, romantischen Bau des [Strassburger] Münsters mit all den phantastischen Verzierungen, die künstlich zum Ganzen verschlungen, stolz und prächtig in die Lüfte emporsteigen . . ." (I, 56). The similarity found by Hoffmann between the configurations in Bach's music and those of Gothic architecture is not as striking as this new addition to the private Hoffmann Romanticism-complex. The preoccupation of the "official" Romanticists with the Gothic is here paralleled in Hoffmann's own formulations.

With the publication of the first half of the *Phantasiestücke in Callot's Manier* (1814) Hoffmann made his first substantial venture into the literary field, yet this, too, was done in the interest of music. Nearly all of the articles in this collection deal with music and musicians. But though the ***Phantasiestücke [Phantasiestücke in Callot's Manier]*** established Hoffmann's reputation as a writer, he was still unwilling to share with literature the esteem which he bestowed upon music. Hoffmann was so smitten with music and with his own ideas on Romantic art that he republished in the ***Phantasiestücke*** the introductory part of his earlier essay—"Beethoven, C moll-Sinfonie (No. 5)"—as **"Beethovens Instrumental-Musik"** (1813). An examination of a passage from the **"Instrumental-Musik" ["Beethovens Instrumental-Musik"]** reveals that the changes are slight—but significant:

> Sollte, wenn von der Musik als einer selbständigen Kunst die Rede ist, nicht immer nur die Instrumental-Musik gemeint sein, welche, jede Hilfe, jede Beimischung einer andern Kunst (der Poesie) verschmähend, das eigentümliche, nur in ihr zu erkennende Wesen dieser Kunst rein ausspricht?—Sie ist die romantischste aller Künste, beinahe möchte man sagen, allein echt romantisch, denn nur das Unendliche ist ihr Vorwurf.
>
> (I, 48)

This version has added "(der Poesie)" and "denn nur das Unendliche ist ihr Vorwurf," which can only be viewed as renewed determination to restrict the stamp of purity in Romanticism to music. These additions were taken not from the **"C moll-Sinfonie" ["Beethoven, C moll-Sinfonie (No. 5)"]** but instead from ***Gedanken über den hohen Wert der Musik*** (1812), which also was included later in the ***Phantasiestücke***. Furthermore, Hoffmann was so pleased with the statement "sie ist die romantischste aller Künste" from the **"C moll-Sinfonie"** that he used it again in both the ***Gedanken [Höchst Zerstreate Gedanken]*** and the **"Instrumental-Musik."**

Next, through a synthesis of enthusiasm for music and appreciation of the Jena Romanticists, Hoffmann develops a profound personal creed which is to become the keystone of his Romantic doctrine. In the ***Gedanken über den hohen Wert der Musik*** Hoffmann, speaking ironically, allows the questionable position of the artist in society to be demonstrated by the artist's own convictions:

> Sie meinen nämlich, die Kunst liesse dem [sic] Menschen sein höheres Prinzip ahnen und führe ihn aus dem törichten Tun und Treiben des gemeinen Lebens in den Isistempel, wo die Natur in heiligen, nie gehörten und doch verständlichen Lauten mit ihm spräche. Von der Musik hegen diese Wahnsinnigen nun vollends die wunderlichsten Meinungen; sie nennen sie die romantischste aller Künste, da ihr Vorwurf nur das Unendliche sei; die geheimnisvolle, in Tönen ausgesprochene Sanskritta der Natur, die die Brust des Menschen mit unendlicher Sehnsucht erfülle, und nur

in ihr verstehe er das hohe Lied der—Bäume, der Blumen, der Tiere, der Steine, der Gewässer!

(I, 46)

The irony is poignant but not misleading. Into this holy brotherhood only the select few are to be admitted. This body is to be the highest intellectual elite, made up solely of artists—Romantic artists. But even more interesting are the obvious literary undertones. This new concept is a striking mixture of tonal and literary essences, an interweaving of music and *Naturphilosophie*. The literary inspiration for Hoffmann's new religion is Novalis' *Die Lehrlinge zu Sais*. In the review ***Über die Aufführung der Schauspiele des Calderon de la Barca auf dem Theater in Bamberg*** (1812) Hoffmann gives his new religion a name. He states that Calderón's dramas, in the masterful Schlegel translation, created "eine nicht geringe Sensation, wiewohl in ihre tiefe Romantik nur die wenigen eingehen konnten, welche mit wahrhaft poetischem Gemüt sich zu der unsichtbaren Kirche bekennen, die mit göttlicher Gewalt gegen das Gemeine, wie gegen den Erbfeind kämpft und die triumphierende sein und bleiben wird" (xv, 35). Vague, yet thereby appropriate, the emphasis is again on the transcendental—the invisible church. And once more only art of the highest (Romantic) calibre will qualify an artist for membership. In another music review, ***Beethoven, Zwei Trios*** (1813), the influence of Novalis is again seen. Here the religious idea, though determinedly unorthodox, is carried a step farther: "das Tanzstück der Isispriester kann nur ein hochjauchzender Hymnus sein" (xIII, 119). Thus the hierarchy is designated and Novalis is confirmed implicitly as the high priest. This profound and highly personal Romantic faith develops in the music reviews; its application to literature is the next step.

Because the music critic and theoretician of Romanticism became a writer as well, a concession was forced upon Hoffmann which he was unwilling to make earlier—the complete acceptance of the poet in the Romantic fellowship. This happens first in **"Don Juan: Eine fabelhafte Begebenheit, die sich mit einem reisenden Enthusiasten zugetragen"** (1812): "Nur der Dichter versteht den Dichter; nur ein romantisches Gemüt kann eingehen in das Romantische; nur der poetisch exaltierte Geist, der mitten im Tempel die Weihe empfing, das verstehen, was der Geweihte in der Begeisterung ausspricht" (I, 79). Yet even this generosity is not conclusive, for the Don remains an operatic figure for Hoffmann and for the reader. A slightly later essay, **"Der Dichter und der Komponist"** (1813), finally establishes equality between poet and composer. Here Hoffmann re-emphasizes the consecrated nature of his new music-religion in a significant way: "Ja, in jenem fernen Reiche, . . . da sind Dichter und Musiker die innigst verwandten Glieder *einer* Kirche, denn das Geheimnis des Worts und des Tons ist ein und dasselbe, das ihnen die höchste Weihe erschlossen" (v, 119-120).

The promotion of the poet here is not due entirely to Hoffmann's recent venture in the *Phantasiestücke.* He still thinks of himself, at this stage, as a composer. The indulgence shown here toward the writer is, in reality, a result of Hoffmann's collaboration at the time with a well-known Romantic writer: Friedrich de la Motte Fouqué. Hoffmann composed the music and Fouqué provided the lyrics for reworking the latter's *Undine* as an opera. As with Beethoven's *Fifth,* here again an external influence produces a further development in Hoffmann's system of aesthetics.

Love is the final contribution to Hoffmann's Romanticism during the first phase of its development; the deployment of love, arising from Hoffmann's own situation, results in still another addition to the doctrine: insanity. Hoffmann's last review of a composition by Beethoven, *Musik zu Goethes "Egmont"* (1813), is the only publication to this time in which Hoffmann equates love with the Romantic: "Mancher Komponist hätte eine kriegerische, stolz daherschreitende Ouvertüre zum 'Egmont' gesetzt: aber an jene tiefere echt romantische Tendenz des Trauerspiels—kurz, an Egmonts und Clärchens Liebe, hat sich unser sinniger Meister in der Ouvertüre gehalten" (XIII, 147). It must be stressed, though, that this addition is made only because of the particularly spiritual nature of the love depicted in *Egmont.* In **"Don Juan"** and in **"Nachricht von den neuesten Schicksalen des Hundes Berganza,"** both of the *Phantasiestücke* (1814), the frustrated love of the hero is essentially the theme. In neither of these works does Hoffmann refer to love as Romantic. However, his diary at this time is overrun with such references. In one of the better homes in which Hoffmann gave private music lessons in Bamberg he met and fell in love with Julie Mark. The first mention of Julie in Hoffmann's diary is on May 21, 1809, with the simple entry: "Julchen Mark trat zum erste [sic] mal mit der Arie aus 'Sargino'—Gran Dio auf und erhielt Beifall" (**Harich** [*E. T. A. Hoffmann, Dichtungen und Schriften sowie Briefe und Tagebücher*], XIV, 292). Two years later, though, the entry is of a quite different nature: "romaneske Stimmung—Abends in der 'Rose'—stark gepunscht—Das Kthch wird obligat—*o miserere mei domine*" (Feb. 2, 1811, XIV, 326). A hasty glance would suggest that the "romaneske Stimmung" derives entirely from Hoffmann's frequentation of the "Rose"—a favorite drinking place. The similarity between *romanesk* and *romantisch* is obvious. But an unusual code word is found in the obligato indicated. *Kthch* (elsewhere *Ktchn, Ktch,* etc.) is an abbreviation for Kätchen von Heilbronn, the heroine in Kleist's drama of the same name. Kätchen, considered Kleist's ideal of the perfectly loving woman, is Hoffmann's symbol for Julchen Mark. In the diary entry for the next day *romanesk* is replaced with *romantisch*: "bis zum Exzess romant. und kapriziös. Ktchn . . . *De profundis clamamus*" (XIV, 326). The entry a few days later leaves no doubt that *Ktch* was the

source of Hoffmann's exaltation: "*Ktch: plus belle que jamais et moi—amoureux comme quatre vingt diables*" (Feb. 5, 1811, XIV, 326). On Feb. 16, 1811, the most curious entry of all occurs. It is almost a certainty that Hoffmann's wife read no Greek. That she would be unable to read German written with Greek letters seems just as certain, for it is to such a circuitous device that Hoffmann resorts when an especially incriminating entry is to be made: "Abends den Julianen-Tag feierlichst begangen bei Mark—exaltierte Stimmung—διεσε ρομαντιςχε στιμμ8νγ γρειφτ ιμερ μερ 8μ ςιχ 8νδ ιχ φürχτε ες wiςδ 8νheiλ δαρα8ς ενςτεν—Ktch" (XIV, 328). One other diary entry during February is of definite significance: "exotische Streiche im Uebermass. Ktch—Ktch—Ktch!!!! exaltiert bis zum Wahnsinn" (Feb. 25, 1811, XIV, 329). *Exotisch* appears as a synonym for *romantisch*. This in itself is not an expansion of the definition. In fact, the less specific *exotisch* is probably only another indication that Hoffmann feels constrained even more to hide his love for Julchen Mark. But the association of insanity with Romantic (exotic) exuberance is an important addition to Hoffmann's doctrine, and it is significant that it is found first in the letters. In many later works Hoffmann refers to insanity and to a *fixe Idee*. By then insanity is a definite literary concept. At this point, however, it is a symptom of a very real emotional obsession.

The initial phase of Hoffmann's thinking on Romanticism had begun with the formulation of an enthusiastic but narrow concept which nevertheless developed into a markedly expanded and more conventional one. Writing as a music critic, Hoffmann seized upon the intangible nature of instrumental music and called it the truest Romanticism. In time Hoffmann's work as a reviewer for the *Allgemeine Musikalische Zeitung* forced him to apply his view to literary genres and concepts as well. In every instance, musical and literary, the label "Romantic" was granted only to matter of an essentially transcendental nature; the most profound extension of this—*die unsichtbare Kirche*—derived from both musical and literary sources. Hoffmann's critical writing also fostered the author in him, yet the *Phantasiestücke,* which made him known at this time, exude enthusiasm for music. This was the theoretical period, when Hoffmann's *attitude* toward the Romantic as a concept was positive. At this time Hoffmann would readily have called himself a Romanticist. It was also the period in which he reconciled himself to being a writer, and this was a step of deep emotional significance, one which made itself apparent only in the next, the negative, phase of Hoffmann's thinking on Romanticism.

The second stage of Hoffmann's theorizing is characterized by coolness toward the Romantic, and the reasons for this are to be found in the author's letters, some of which date from early in the first, music criticism period. As early as 1795 Hoffmann's letters reveal an almost anguished drive for recognition in any one of the several fields of painting, music, or writing. Here also is seen the decision to rely finally on music as the surest road to fame. With only occasional infidelity Hoffmann remains devoted to music even to the end of the Bamberg period when the last touches are being put on the first edition of the *Phantasiestücke.* Georg Ellinger shows that in July 1812 Hoffmann's determination to gain fame in music is still undaunted: "Zum Musiker bin ich nun einmal geboren . . . das habe ich von meiner frühesten Jugend an in mir gefühlt und mit mir herumgetragen. Nur der mir innewohnende Genius der Musik kann mich aus meiner Misere reissen,—es muss jetzt etwas geschehen, etwas Grosses muss geschaffen werden im Geiste der Bach, Händel, Mozart, Beethoven."[5] In the contract of 1813 drawn up with his friend Kunz for the publication of the *Phantasiestücke* Hoffmann calls himself a *Musik-Direktor* (**Harich,** XIV, 419). Here, too, the name Wilhelm is replaced with Amadeus. But most telling is Hoffmann's determination to publish the *Phantasiestücke* anonymously (XV, 43), even though the two vignettes—drawn by Hoffmann himself—are signed; he calls this a "Versteckspielen" (XV, 54). Yet the letters also bear witness to the author's pleasure in seeing his reviews and stories, and especially the first edition of the *Phantasiestücke,* in print. In fact, a trend may be observed leading from an almost cynical determination to gain fame through music to a cautious pleasure at seeing himself in print. Another letter to Kunz shortly before the publication of the *Phantasiestücke* affirms Hoffmann's new dedication to literature as sincere: "Gott lasse mich nur das Märchen enden, wie es angefangen—ich habe nichts besseres gemacht, das andere ist tot und starr dagegen, und ich meine, dass das *Sich heraufschreiben* zu etwas ordentlichem vielleicht bei mir eintreffen könnte" (September 8, 1813, XV, 65)! The "Märchen"—**"Der goldene Topf"**—was being written for the third volume of the *Phantasiestücke* (1815). However, because Hoffmann had struggled once so desperately for recognition as a composer, the breakthrough in literature did not come without regret and bitterness.

The bitterness reveals itself as a complete reversal of Hoffmann's former attitude, for now irony is developed as a concept to replace Romanticism. A *negative* attitude, then, characterizes the second phase of Hoffmann's thinking on art and it manifests itself first in **"Der goldene Topf"** (1814). Not only is no mention made in the **"Topf"** [**"Der goldene Topf"**] of *Romantik* or *romantisch,* but the closest Hoffmann ever comes to these terms is a curious usage of *das Romanhafte* and later *Romanenstreiche*: "'Ach geehrtester Registrator,' erwiderte der Konrektor Paulmann, 'Sie haben immer so einen Hang zu den *Poeticis* gehabt, und da verfällt man leicht in das Phantastische und Romanhafte'" (I, 185). The conjunction in the phrase "das Phantastische und Romanhafte" functions here as an equal sign. The use of *romanhaft* instead of *romantisch* shifts the emphasis from the generally aesthetic to a narrower concept of purely literary scope; it also diverts attention, on Hoffmann's as well as the reader's part, from the purely Romantic. In another instance of "literary" significance the narrator speaks of Veronika's reliance upon black magic to help her ensnare Anselmus. Her original abhorrence of the supernatural turns almost to fascination and the questionableness of her relationship with the old sorceress appears "nur im Schimmer des Ungewöhnlichen, Romanhaften . . ." (I, 213). Again the equation of *das Romanhafte* with *das Ungewöhnliche* lacks the affirmative tone that is usual with Hoffmann. But Veronika's willingness to resort to devious means to get Anselmus had been preceded by a troubling premonition. In a setting of most proper *Bürgerlichkeit*—her father is reading his *Cicero de Officiis* and Veronika is indulging in daydreams of herself as the wife of Hofrat Anselmus—a painful revelation comes: "'Ach, es ist ja wahr, er liebt mich nicht, und ich werde nimmermehr Frau Hofrätin!' 'Romanenstreiche, Romanenstreiche', schrie der Konrektor Paulmann, nahm Hut und Stock und eilte zornig von dannen" (I, 201)! There is irony against the Philistine here—but also irony of another sort: irony against literature, and specifically against the prose narrative. This also is irony against Hoffmann the writer—the writer who would rather have been a composer.

The avoidance of such a favored term as the Romantic in **"Der goldene Topf"** is an indication of irony toward Romanticism, an indication of a new negative attitude. It must be stressed, though, that such terms as *das Romanhafte* and *Romanenstreiche* are used exclusively from the point of view of the unimaginative "Philistine" mentality, whereas the Romantic poet, Anselmus, ends up in glorious "Atlantis". The use of the Romantic idea in connection with mediocrity is an attitude that, in the context of the whole work, Hoffmann apparently does *not* espouse. For Hoffmann *romanhaft* and *Romanenstreiche* never mean *romantisch.* However, the avoidance of even this last term in connection with Anselmus and the obviously Romantic side of the story is an indication of a negative attitude on Hoffmann's part, and various explanations must be considered. First, accident: still it has been seen that, especially where Romanticism is concerned, Hoffmann is not careless with words. Second, the desire to avoid formerly overworked words in a story to which he admittedly attributed so much importance: this could be the case since a change of heart regarding Romanticism is present in the **"Topf,"** but Hoffmann does *allude* to the Romantic if only through the secondhand and derogatory terms discussed above. Third, the primary association of the term with music: this, perhaps, is the reason sought, but this reason, too, supports the argument for a new ironic attitude toward Romanticism, since Hoffmann's turn to literature was due as much to his failure as a composer as to his success as a writer. Finally, it must be acknowledged that sufficient evidence is not given by Hoffmann himself with respect to the point taken: irony toward Romanticism. The importance of the **"Topf"** to Hoffmann justifies this argument, however, and the same point is made more strongly in another work of the same period: **"Der Magnetiseur."**

Although the Romantic is placed in an unbecoming light in **"Der goldene Topf,"** irony is used in such a way that it is established as a fully developed literary principle. Lindhorst uses irony as a weapon against mediocrity. Thus when Anselmus finally succeeds in making a good copy of the work placed before him, a profound change comes over the Archivarius: "statt der Ironie, die sonst den Mund zusammenpresste, schienen die weichgeformten anmutigen Lippen sich zu öffnen zur weisheitsvollen, ins Gemüt dringenden Rede" (I, 211). Irony is here the painful awareness of the duality of life. Hoffmann further attests to the development of irony as a conscious literary principle in a letter of March 4, 1814, to Kunz: "Ohne Säumnis schicke ich Ihnen in der Anlage das vollendete Märchen mit dem herzlichen Wunsche, dass es Ihnen in seiner durchgehaltenen Ironie Vergnügen gewähren möge!" (xv, 115-116). This "durchgehaltene Ironie" has become now the intermediary between ordinary life and a higher reality. Previously only music would have fulfilled this function, and this would suggest a realization by Hoffmann of failure as a composer. If this ever came, Hoffmann never admitted it. The fact was that with but a few exceptions he simply stopped writing about music in the old way. On the one hand Beethoven withdrew from the public eye from 1812 to 1818. Also, Hoffmann's last review for the *Allgemeine Musikalische Zeitung* was published January 11, 1815. Chief among the reasons must have been Hoffmann's realization that he was neither a Mozart nor a Beethoven but instead a successful author of fantastic tales. Obviously irony was more at home in the latter situation.

However, irony is not the sole doctrine of the middle period, for insanity becomes its partner and, in many instances, its alias. On April 29, 1812, the diary records: "V. M. bei der Mark—das Ding wird merkwürdig und ich trete der wahren Auflösung näher—Göttliche Ironie!—herrlichstes Mittel Verrücktheiten zu bemänteln und zu vertreiben, stehe mir bei!!" (xiv, 358). The comradeship between irony and insanity, which crystallized in the diary, becomes now a major theme in Hoffmann's literary works. The essay *Gedanken über den hohen Wert der Musik* (1812) is an early example of this: "Das überlesend, was ich geschrieben, finde ich den Wahnwitz mancher Musiker sehr treffend geschildert, und mit einem heimlichen Grausen fühle ich mich mit ihnen verwandt. Der Satan raunt mir ins Ohr, dass ihnen manches so redlich Gemeinte wohl gar als heillose Ironie erscheinen könne . . ." (I, 47-48). One senses

again the frustrated musician, and now firmly established is the transition from a veneration of Romanticism in music to the shunning of it as an artistic concept and to the espousal of irony and insanity as comparable literary substitutes. The two works which carry out this transition are **"Der goldene Topf"** and **"Der Magnetiseur."** In the former it is irony, in the latter the mental principle which prevails. In both there is an unmistakable lack of sympathy for the Romantic as an aesthetic criterion.

"Der Magnetiseur" (finished 1813) reveals a new fascination for the psychic—in particular for hypnotism—and here are found the references to the Romantic that are missing in **"Der goldene Topf."** On December 21, 1812, Hoffmann records in his diary his first opportunity to see a *Somnambule*. A letter of July 26, 1813 (xv, 50), reveals that Hoffmann sought to obtain G. H. Schubert's *Ansichten von der Nachtseite der Naturwissenschaft* (1808).[6] Though Hoffmann had finished **"Der Magnetiseur"** before he read Schubert's book, by this time he had acquired such an interest in the psychic that he now expressed the same enthusiasm for the **"Magnetiseur"** that he formerly had for **"Der goldene Topf"**: "Erinnern Sie sich denn nicht, dass ich Ihnen selbst sagte: es würde das Beste im Ganzen werden? . . . es ist, als schlösse ich mir ein wunderbares Reich auf, das, aus meinem Innern hervorgehend und sich gestaltend, mich dem Drange des Äussern entrückte" (letter to Kunz, August 19, 1813, xv, 56). This "wunderbares Reich" is the same invisible church which previously was associated with music. Now the religion is one simply of the psychic, and it is not the artist but the hypnotist in **"Der Magnetiseur"** who holds the key to the invisible church: "Es musste gerade ein Arzt sein, der zuerst von meinem Geheimnisse zur Welt sprach, das eine unsichtbare Kirche wie ihren besten Schatz im stillen aufbewahrte . . ." (I, 169). When Alban, the hypnotist, alludes to the compelling power of the hypnotic principle, he again refers to the established cult: "Diese innigste geistige Verbindung mit dem Weibe, im Seligkeitsgefühl jeden andern, als den höchsten ausgeschrieenen tierischen Genuss himmelhoch überflügelnd, ziemt dem Priester der Isis . . ." (I, 172). Hoffmann's introduction of the invisible church in **"Der Magnetiseur"** is evidence that his concern with psychic phenomena is serious. However, the danger which can result from its misuse is also stressed in the story. The dual role which hypnosis can play can be interpreted in terms of irony. Archivarius Lindhorst had used irony as a devastating weapon against the unimaginative Philistine. In Alban's case irony becomes an attribute of cynicism, a hint that the face behind the mask is distorted: "Alban fasste ihn scharf ins Auge, und mit einem Tone, in dem, des Ernstes unerachtet, eine gewisse höhnende Ironie lag, sprach er: 'Ruhig, Herr Baron! die Kleine ist etwas ungeduldig . . .'" (I, 161). In view of this "höhnende Ironie" it seems strange that Hoffmann would have incorporated in this work so many references to the invisible church. But the misuse to which Alban puts the psychic does not detract from the favor in which Hoffmann still holds this intellectual elite. The psychic, as was music before it, is merely another means to attain this realm, for its reality, too, is spiritual. Hoffmann simply developed a fad of the time into a fruitful and perhaps unique narrative device and at the same time took advantage artistically of the danger of its misuse.

A reference to the Romantic in **"Der Magnetiseur"** brings Hoffmann back to a topic too long neglected. However, nothing significant is added to the doctrine of the Romantic, whereas the concept of the invisible church is measurably enriched. Marie's mention of the Romantic in a letter to a friend explaining the nature of her meeting with Alban, appears to denote simply the fantastic: "Das Besondere ist aber, dass in meinen Träumen und Erscheinungen immer ein schöner ernster Mann im Spiele war, der . . . mir wie der romantische König in der märchenhaften Geisterwelt erschien und allen bösen Zauber löste. . . . Bald kam er mir vor wie der weise Salomo, und dann musste ich auch wieder auf ganz ungereimte Weise an den Sarastro in der Zauberflöte denken, wie ich ihn in der Residenz gesehen" (I, 164-165). Not the fantastic or the dream commands attention here—but rather the projection of Marie's Romantic king into other worlds. Sarastro in Mozart's *Magic Flute* is the Priest of Isis and the setting of the opera is Egypt. Thus Mozart's opera becomes a parallel source for Hoffmann's *Isisreligion*. The veiled reference allows perception only to the musically initiate. But why the analogy to Solomon? Again insight into the *Magic Flute* sheds light on an apparently casual reference. Mozart's opera is considered to reflect the ideas of Freemasonry, which, according to some traditions, goes back even to Solomon, and thereby yet another dimension is added to the invisible church. The obscurity of the analogy is purposeful. Perhaps there is even a tinge of irony in Hoffmann's use of the long avoided *romantisch*—as camouflage for a more important maneuver. At any rate, the structure of the invisible church is expanded significantly in **"Der Magnetiseur"**; but, even though this comes under the guise of the Romantic, the prevailing tone is one of irony and negation, for the outcome is tragic.

Irony is also the underlying theme of **Die Elixiere des Teufels** (1814-16), Hoffmann's only extant completed novel (his early work, **Cornaro,** was completed, but was not published and the MS has not been found); here it is awareness of right and wrong, of the duality of life. When the novice Medardus first tries to hide from Prior Leonardus his baser drives, Leonardus betrays his better understanding of the youth "mit einem gewissen ironischen Lächeln . . ." (II, 33). On the other hand, irony can be the sign of inner corruption. When Medardus

recognized among certain paintings a portrait of Aurelie, an innocent girl for whom he had an overwhelming but ignoble desire, he was still able to discuss it "mit einem besondern Glanz des Ausdrucks, der nur der Reflex der höhnenden Ironie war . . ." (II, 97). The novel ends with a reference to the mental debility that had befallen the colorful Peter Schönfeld: "des Peters Licht sei im Dampf der Narrheit verlöscht, in die sich in seinem Innern die Ironie des Lebens umgestaltet" (II, 275-276). The final words of the *Elixiere [Die Elixiere des Teufels]* thereby see the basis of life to be irony. This apparently is the fundamental dilemma of existence for Hoffmann at this stage. As a "philosophy of life" irony receives its fullest development in the *Elixiere* and in the framework of *Die Serapionsbrüder*—the section dealing with the "divine madness" of the hermit Serapion. As with so many of Hoffmann's ideas, however, the formulation is so superficial, so completely unelaborated, that it often seems naive—and acceptance of it is just as often a matter of emotional response.[7]

References to the Romantic are numerous in the *Elixiere,* and in some instances they are clearly ironic, while others betray a return to Hoffmann's earliest ideas on Romanticism. Medardus' wanderings brought him into aristocratic circles, and his chance to command the attention of a dignified audience in one instance was not passed up: "und es waren Andeutungen aus meinem eigenen Leben, die ich unter der Hüller romantischer Dichtung auf anziehende Weise vorzutragen wusste" (II, 131). Here Romantic means second-rate, and behind the cynicism one sees Hoffmann the author. In yet another instance a serious analogy is put in the mouth of a fool, Peter Schönfeld, when he offers his services as a barber to Medardus. Schönfeld's method is to examine first his subject's carriage and manner, and "dann werde ich sagen, ob Sie sich mehr zum Antiken oder zum Romantischen, zum Heroischen, Grossen, Erhabenen, zum Naiven, zum Idyllischen, zum Spöttischen, zum Humoristischen hinneigen . . ." (II, 89). Hoffmann is playing here with the antithetic concept of the late eighteenth century, with Herder's formulation of the Romantic as the modern (really, the Middle Ages) and as opposed to Classical antiquity. Herder's *Begriffskomplex* is called upon in still another passage where Medardus discusses architecture: "Es ist mit einem Wort der seltene Sinn für das Romantische, der den gotischen Baumeister leiten muss, da hier von dem Schulgerechten, an das er sich bei der antiken Form halten kann, nicht die Rede ist" (II, 120). It might be argued here that Hoffmann is pointing again to the transcendental ideal expressed in Gothic architecture. It seems, though, that he is simply using the Romantic in its earliest sense. This opinion receives further support from another example that recalls the early meaning of the term. With a touch of humor Hoffmann allows the narrator some uneasiness, "wenn er [italienische] Namen erdenken soll da, woschon wirkliche, und zwar schön und romantisch tönende, vorhanden sind, wie es hier der Fall war" (II, 218). Here, perhaps, is a reflection of Wieland's contribution to the historical complex: *das Heterogene*. Only one more allusion is necessary to make the recall of the traditional eighteenth-century development complete. This, too, is supplied by Medardus in a description of his trip through a certain mountainous region: "Die anmutige Jahreszeit sowie die herrliche romantische Gegend bestimmten mich, den Weg zu Fusse zu machen" (II, 159-160). Here finally the association of Romantic with the *Wild-Landschaftliche*. That Hoffmann's return to his own earliest understanding of the Romantic is a conscious effort is borne out by the continuing description of the mountainous landscape. It is almost a copy of the impressions that were recorded in a letter of October 15, 1798 (XIV, 133-138), to Hoffmann's friend Hippel.

The emphasis on an ironic view of life and the return of the Romantic to a traditional role in the *Elixiere* affirm a continuing coolness on Hoffmann's part toward the Romantic, yet once again the position of the invisible church is strengthened. Eventually Medardus reaches Rome where he finds conditions about the pope in a sordid state. He has taken on his robe again and, because of honest penitence, is regarded by the people almost as a saint. When the pope offers him an audience Medardus seizes the opportunity to remonstrate with the Church leader for his waywardness: "Nicht von dieser Welt ist Euer Reich, und doch seid Ihr berufen zu herrschen über alle Reiche dieser Erde, die Glieder der unsichtbaren Kirche sammelnd unter der Fahne des Herrn" (II, 237)! This is the closest Hoffmann ever comes to an orthodox religious orientation in his work.[8] Though this obviously does not violate the transcendental ideal of the invisible church, its exclusively artistic nature is affronted. Hoffmann's action here is too purposeful for this to be only a casual development. The principal lesson which Medardus learns in his wanderings is that individual desires must yield to the service of one's fellow man. Furthermore, the monastery from which Medardus originally ventured never ceased in its surveillance of his movements. *Die Elixiere des Teufels* is a *Bildungsroman*. It is, in my opinion, Hoffmann's attempt to match Goethe's *Wilhelm Meisters Lehrjahre*. Its openly social tendency also makes it Hoffmann's most "unRomantic" work.

But Hoffmann's bitterest assault on Romanticism is contained in the self-mockery of a play he never completed—*Prinzessin Blandina: ein romantisches Spiel in drei Aufzügen* (May 1814). Done in obvious emulation of Gozzi and of Tieck's *Der gestiefelte Kater,* the dramatic irony in *Blandina* [*Prinzessin Blandina*] reveals Hoffmann's own lack of self-assurance, for he not only left the work a fragment, but withdrew it as well from the final volume of the *Phantasiestücke* before

the second edition came out. To Kunz he wrote: "Hätte ich gewusst, dass der Teil so unverhältnismässig stark werden würde, so hätte ich die Blandina, als mein schwächstes Produkt nicht eingeschoben . . ." (May 24, 1815, xv, 182). The poet in the play, when asked to explain his function, brings ridicule on himself and upon the Romantic: "So ging auch mir das Dichterleben auf. | Mein Aug' erfasst' das ferne Geisterreich, | Romant'schen Putz geb' ich dem, was ich sehe" (xv, 79). Irony is also directed against the musician when, to the command to light a torch, the musician's servant replies from off stage: "Gleich!—Doch wenn Sie gütigst erlauben, gnädiger Held, so tue ich es hier oben. Es nimmt sich besser aus, eine recht malerische romantische Beleuchtung so aus der Ferne von oben herab" (xv, 83). The reason for this self-irony on Hoffmann's part and for the fragmentary state in which the drama remains is hinted at in the diary. The entry of March 14, 1814, two months before work began on *Blandina,* shows that the old fury of self-doubt was back: "doch werde ich eine gewisse Unruhe des Geistes nicht los, die mich recht sehr quält und vorzüglich meine dichterischen Arbeiten sehr erschwert. . . . Es fehlt mir zuweilen an Mut, und dann verzweifle ich an mir selbst" (xv, 119). A few years later the disappointment of *Blandina* was heightened further (and its failure thereby reaffirmed) by a conversation held with Clemens Brentano. These remarks were set down in a letter of January 1816, which was never sent, although Müller assumes that the contents were transmitted personally: "In der *Prinzessin Blandine* [sic] hat mir Vieles sehr gefallen, die Ironie des aus dem Stück Fallens allein schien mir sich überlebt zu haben; ich halte es für frühere Arbeit. Ich fühle überhaupt, dass Sie ein grosses Talent für's Drama haben müssten, wenn das Gaukeln anfangen dürfte, Sie zu langweilen."[9] Hoffmann had written *Blandina* a year and a half earlier, but it was by no means early work. Except for *Der Preis,* a comedy written in 1803 and since lost, this was Hoffmann's only attempt at pure drama. It was also one of his few attempts at verse, another discipline whose intransigence vexed Hoffmann. The third volume of *Die Serapionsbrüder* (1820) puts a seemingly casual remark in the mouth of Cyprian, one of the frame-characters: "seltsam ist es aber doch, dass Schriftsteller, die lebending erzählen, die Charakter und Situation gut zu halten wissen, oft an dem Dramatischen gänzlich scheitern" (VII, 186). Cyprian is often considered, in addition to Theodor, one of Hoffmann's literary alter egos.

In most of the novellas which appear between the writing of *Prinzessin Blandina* and *Kater Murr*—from 1814 to 1819—the Romantic plays an oddly narrow role. In virtually every instance of its appearance *romantisch* is used to represent love as a self-forgetful and misleading passion. Even in the somber **"Das Majorat"** of the *Nachtstücke* Hoffmann equates the Romantic manner with adolescent infatuation: "Diese romantische, ja wohl ritterliche Liebe, wie sie mir aufging in schlafloser Nacht, spannte mich dermassen, dass ich kindisch genug war, mich selbst auf pathetische Weise zu haranguieren und zuletzt sehr kläglich zu seufzen: 'Seraphine, ach Seraphine'" (III, 179)! Here Romantic signifies the excessive. Also, in each such example from this period the love-smitten hero is a representative of the bourgeoisie. Hoffmann always snipes at the bourgeois, but as a contrast to this mundane love a new concept now establishes itself in his writing: *Künstlerliebe.*

Bourgeois love and *Künstlerliebe* both figure in **Kater Murr** (1819/21), yet the middle-class sort is called Romantic while the artist's love is veiled with irony. Murr, the tomcat, is a parody of the unflinching devotion of the bourgeois to becoming *gebildet.* Part of such cultural accomplishment is assured by being so recklessly in love that artistic inspiration results. Yet the paths of such love are too often beset with frustration and Murr is compelled to lament, "Welch ein feindliches Schicksal, . . . der himmlisch-romantischen Liebe halber werde ich in die Gosse geworfen, und das häusliche Glück verhilft mir zu nichts anderm als zu grässlichen Prügeln" (IX, 182). The capacity to experience "himmlisch-romantische Liebe" seems unquestionably to betray hidden genius. Still the true Romanticist is also subject to melancholy, and noble thoughts require solitude: "Eine gewisse Schwermut, wie sie oft junge Romantiker befällt, wenn sie den Entwicklungskampf der grossen erhabenen Gedanken in ihrem Innern bestehen, trieb mich in die Einsamkeit" (IX, 67). The very title "Romanticist" has become here the possession of the bourgeois. This is the bitterest irony on Hoffmann's part. It is significant also that only in connection with love does Kreisler refer to the Romantic and then always with ironic sarcasm. When his friend the abbot warns him that he will not find happiness in earthly love and suggests that he take up the priesthood, the reaction is immediate: "Da begann aber auf Kreislers Antlitz jenes seltsame Muskelspiel, das den Geist der Ironie zu verkünden pflegte . . ." (IX, 246). Bitterly indignant, Kreisler assures the abbot that he could win any "rotwangichte Professors- . . . blau- oder braunäugichte Hofratstocher . . ." or, for that matter, "ich könnte mich auch versteigen in das höhere Romantische, eine Idylle beginnen und der glauen [sic] Pachterstochter mein Herz offerieren und meine Hand, wenn sie eben Ziegenkäse bereitet . . ." (IX, 247). But the one word that really hurts is "Entsagung" (IX, 246). This is the essence of the abbot's counsel for Kreisler, yet, unlike Wilhelm Meister, this is a lesson that Kreisler is never allowed to learn. **Kater Murr** never went beyond Volume II (1821), and Hoffmann never returned to this most important of his several alter egos. *Künstlerliebe*—for Kreisler as for Hoffmann—had to mean unrequited love. Perhaps this is one reason for the fragmentary state of **Kater Murr.**

Still, the Romantic appears in **Kater Murr** in one sense that is positive, and, though the predominant emphasis in **Murr** is on the ironic, the affirmative tone in this instance is important. During a walk in a park laid out after the English model, Julia (the name is significant) tries to calm the anxiety of the Princess concerning the uncultivated remoteness of the place, but then Julia, too, confesses, "Aber sonst muss ich dir gestehen, dass mir irgendein kleines Abenteuer hier in dem einsamen romantischen Walde recht hübsch, recht anmutig bedünken möchte" (IX, 62). As in the *Elixiere,* Hoffmann reverts here to an early usage of the Romantic: a usage which is not original with him and which is essentially nonaesthetic. Here only is the Romantic a positive concept in **Kater Murr.** It is also noteworthy that this reference does not come from Kreisler.

The Serapion-tale **"Die Brautwahl"** (1819) continues the treatment of the relationship between *Künstlerliebe* and Romanticism, but a softening of the stand against Romanticism is now apparent. Here the goldsmith Leonhard "saves" the young artist, Edmund, from the embroilment of marriage and affiliation with practical bourgeois circles by compelling him to continue his art studies in Italy. The figure of Leonhard is a fascinating combination of Hoffmann's concept of the white magician (e.g., Lindhorst) and the timeless figure of Ahasverus, the Wandering Jew. When questioned once by the suspicious but well-meaning heroine of the tale about his background, Leonhard acknowledges that many hold him to be the goldsmith Leonhard Turnhäuser who stood in such high favor at the court of the Elector Johann George in 1580. But such accusations come only from the worst sort: "Geben mich nun solche Leute, die man Romantiker oder Phantasten zu nennen pflegt, für jenen Turnhäuser, mithin für einen gespenstischen Mann aus, so kannst du dir denken, welchen Verdruss ich von den soliden, aufgeklärten Leuten, die als tüchtige Bürger und Geschäftsmänner den Teufel was nach Romantik und Poesie fragen, auszustehen habe" (VII, 77). The attitude revealed in this contrast, where Romanticists are considered eccentrics and yet are also viewed apart from the self-satisfied bourgeoisie, is not one of bitterness. The irony here is directed exclusively against the prosaic middle class, and fantasy and the Romantic are praised indirectly.

The end of the second phase of Hoffmann's thinking on Romanticism thus reveals a seeming lack of interest in the value of it as a concept, a lack of interest which is not apparent in **"Der goldene Topf"** and **"Der Magnetiseur"** at the beginning of the period, when irony is seized upon as a substitute for Romanticism. During this period the Romantic retains its fundamental transcendental nature, but its association with music is purposely avoided. Hoffmann's willingness to see Romanticism derided suggests self-irony, and this leads also into his development of insanity as the irony inherent in the duality of life. Toward Romanticism, then, this phase has shown a negative attitude (this was the period which witnessed Hoffmann's failure as a dramatist). Yet irony became eventually not only a recourse but a useful demon as well. To Tieck's admonishing concerning the extravagances of his literary style, Hoffmann replied in a letter of August 19, 1820: "Ach!—nur zu sehr fühle ich das, was Sie mir über die Tendenz, über die ganze (hin und her wohl verfehlte) Art meiner schriftstellerischen Versuche sagen" (xv, 306). Accompanying this admission of malaise is no indication of a willingness to change. Hoffmann finally mastered the disharmony in his soul not by nullifying it—but by putting it to work. When his friend Hitzig recommended Scott's *Guy Mannering* as a model to emulate for a saner style Hoffmann wrote in reply: "Ein ganz treffliches—treffliches Buch, in der grössten Einfachheit reges lebendiges Leben und kräftige Wahrheit!—Aber! fern von mir liegt dieser Geist, und ich würde sehr übel tun, eine Ruhe erkünsteln zu wollen, die mir, wenigstens zur Zeit noch, durchaus gar nicht gegeben ist" (between July and November 1820, xv, 307-308). Essentially, however, irony did not just replace Romanticism for Hoffmann in this second period—it *became* Romanticism for him, because it, too, was a means to the transcendental. And with the change in name came a change in attitude from positive to negative.

With the addition to irony of a new concept—humor—the *Seltsame Leiden eines Theaterdirektors* (1818) initiates the third and final stage of Hoffmann's use of the Romantic as an aesthetic idea. This comes under the pretext of a discussion by two directors of the problems of the theater, and, when the subject of comedy is raised, an interesting synthesis is made: "Wer mag denn die Ironie wegleugnen, die tief in der menschlichen Natur liegt, ja die eben die menschliche Natur in ihrem innersten Wesen bedingt und aus der mit dem tiefsten Ernst der Scherz, der Witz, die Schalkheit herausstrahlen" (IV, 56). The association of irony with humor is an indication that the bitterness reflected in earlier appearances of irony is no longer present. In a reference to the fragmentary "Märchen von den drei Pomeranzen" by Gozzi, one of the directors explains why he considers his troupe highly qualified: "Ich meines Teils glaube nun, dass in jetziger Zeit solche echt romantische Dramen, wie ich eins hier in Händen habe, von keiner andern Gesellschaft als eben der meinigen in solcher Ründe, in solch hoher Vortrefflichkeit dargestellt werden können" (IV, 95). In this reference to a Romantic drama the irony is not missing, for the actors of this director are puppets. Yet the fact that *Seltsame Leiden* [*Seltsame Leiden eines Theaterdirektors*] is a very long essay on the theater—a discipline in which Hoffmann failed—is further evidence of the amelioration in Hoffmann's ironic attitude. Humor now becomes the companion of irony and is, even more than irony, to be considered the keystone of the last period of Hoffmann's aesthetics.

The purposefulness of Hoffmann's development of humor as an artistic tenet is attested to when he also associates humor with the invisible church. In 1820 Hoffmann published *Prinzessin Brambilla,* a long narrative about actors and the theater, which is sketched against the background of carnival time in Italy. During a discussion of art the mysterious Master Celionati relates a *Märchen* that is a fascinating fusion of allegory and myth. This fiction is praised by the Germans who find the humor in it to be a link between the German and the Italian temperament: "aber hab' ich Euch recht verstanden, so ist die Urdarquelle, womit die Bewohner des Landes Urdargarten beglückt wurden, nichts anders, als was wir Deutschen Humor nennen, die wunderbare, aus der tiefsten Anschauung der Natur geborne Kraft des Gedankens, seinen eignen ironischen Doppeltgänger zu machen . . . Doch in der Tat, Meister Celionati, durch Euern Mythos habt Ihr gezeigt, dass Ihr Euch noch auf andern Spass versteht als auf den Eures Karnevals; ich rechne Euch von nun an zur unsichtbaren Kirche . . ." (x, 65). Into the artistic work Hoffmann interpolates here a new spirit. The ironic nature of life is reaffirmed, but the disparity is emphasized as humorous, and this is confirmed by the admission of the humorist Celionati to the invisible church.

Now for the first time since the early music reviews, Hoffmann returns to an affirmative view of Romanticism, and, in consideration of his earlier disappointment in the theater, it is striking that this stand is taken first with drama. In fact, the strong emphasis on drama which initiates this period begins with the *Seltsame Leiden* and with the bizarre theater in *Prinzessin Brambilla,* "wo Ironie gilt und echter Humor" (x, 126). In the framework of the *Serapionsbrüder* Hoffmann takes issue extensively with apparent violations of the Romantic manner by the major Romantic dramatist of the time—Zacharias Werner: "Das 'Kreuz an der Ostsee', ein Stück, dessen Romantik sich nur zu oft ins Abenteuerliche, in geschmacklose Bizarrerie verirrt, dessen szenische Einrichtung wirklich, wie es bei den gigantischen Schöpfungen Shakespeares oft nur den Schein hat, allen unbesiegbaren Bedingnissen der Bühnendarstellungen spottet" (VIII, 98). In his concern for the misuse of Romanticism Hoffmann reveals, first, a reawakened regard for the term itself and, second, the assurance that Romanticism is still for him fantasy—but true fantasy, not "geschmacklose Bizarrerie." Throughout the frame-discussion it is Werner's *Hypermystik* that is held up to ridicule. And Hoffmann's ironic humor is no less apparent when Werner is made an honorary member in the Serapion brotherhood: "nur zu, werter Zacharias—geniere dich nicht, wir lieben dich, verschlossener Ironiker!—Ha! Freunde!—Serapionsbrüder!—Die Gläser zur

Hand, wir wollen ihn aufnehmen zum Ehrenmitglied unsers Serapionsklubs, auf die Brüderschaft anstossen, und für keinen Frevel wird es der Humorist achten, wenn ich vor seinem Bildnis eine Libation vornehme, was weniges [sic] Punsch mit zierlicher Andacht auf meinen blank gewichsten Pariser Stiefel vergiessend" (VIII, 103). It is done, after all, because of Werner's own irony and humor.

Elsewhere in the *Serapionsbrüder*—through drama and music—a reaffirmation of Romanticism is to be found. In the framework Hoffmann lets another of his alter egos, Theodor, take issue with a contemporary dramatist who endeavors to write Romantic drama, while interspersing song with "as little artificiality" as possible: "Das merkwürdigste traurigste Beispiel davon gibt das sogenannte romantische Schauspiel 'Deodata', ein kurioser Wechselbalg, an dem ein wackrer Komponist nicht gute Musik hätte verschwenden sollen" (VII, 123). Here, once again, is the old preference for the ethereal language of music over the spoken word. The earlier recognition of opera as even more Romantic than drama is voiced again in the Serapion frame, in part at least, when Vinzenz comments, "rührt bloss davon her, weil der Wohlselige . . . etwelche Poesie nicht sonderlich verspüren liess und in dem romantischen Gebiet der Oper nicht Steg und Weg zu finden wusste" (VIII, 87). Having returned to opera, it was only a step to instrumental music. This, too, came when Hoffmann reintroduced in the second volume of the *Serapionsbrüder* the early essay of 1814, **"Alte und neue Kirchenmusik,"** with its enthusiastic espousal of Romanticism.

Yet the really strong feelings about Romanticism, as they existed in the Bamberg years, were unlocked when Hoffmann functioned once again as a music critic. In a review entitled *Nachträgliche Bemerkungen über Spontinis Oper "Olympia"* (1821) the old formulations are found again: "Mozart brach neue Bahnen und wurde der unnachahmliche Schöpfer der romantischen Oper" (XIV, 113). Nothing is new here; this arbitrary evaluation has been seen before. But the sentence which immediately precedes the one above is revealing: "Glühende Phantasie, tiefer, sinniger Humor, überschwengliche Fülle der Gedanken bestimmten dem Shakespeare der Musik den Weg, den er zu wandeln hatte." The humor in Mozart is specifically referred to. The pioneer review, **"Beethoven, C moll-Sinfonie (No. 5),"** had referred frequently to Mozart's fantasy, and it especially stressed the evocation of the demonic in Mozart's work. The fullness which humor gives to Mozart's music, though Hoffmann might have been aware of this earlier, is a recent addition to the evaluation of Mozart. Here, too, is a happy blend of Hoffmann's earliest and his latest understanding of Romanticism. In this review Hoffmann praises a relative newcomer, Gasparo Luigi Spontini, as the equal of Mozart—an appraisal not upheld by time. In particular Hoffmann is overjoyed, "dass er für

uns Opern komponieren wird, die zugleich der unsichtbaren Kirche angehören werden, deren Glieder, von dem himmlischen Feuer der Kunst durchglüht, nichts wollen als das Wahrhaftige in der reinsten Integrität" (XIV, 119). Here the highest achievement in Hoffmann's Romanticism is acknowledged for a mediocre talent; at another place in the article Hoffmann speaks of the "heiliger Isistempel der Kunst" (XIV, 115). Yet these remarks have still another significance: this is the last time Hoffmann ever writes about music—it is also his last reference to the invisible church.

Indeed, after this last flurry of "positive" Romanticism, Hoffmann seems consciously to avoid the term Romantic. His works after this never again betray even the softened irony of **Blandina** or the conscious humor of **Brambilla** [*Prinzessin Brambilla*]. The irony which is so firmly established in Hoffmann's writing with **"Der goldene Topf"** now reflects only distance. In April 1822 Hoffmann published **Meister Floh,** which he also fashioned in his favorite form of the *Märchen*. Here again Hoffmann returned to jibes against the popular novel style of the time. As argued previously, references to the *romanhaft* are not necessarily references to Romanticism. But *romanhaft* is a reflection of the Romantic in its original sense, and the point of interest here is that Hoffmann has resorted again to the novelistic when he might have labeled a thing Romantic. Just such a passage in **Meister Floh** is the following: "Da es ferner in einer romanhaften Historie keinem Gebüsch an rauschenden Blättern, seufzenden, lispelnden Abendlüften, murmelnden Quellen, geschwätzigen Bächen u. s. w. fehlen darf, so ist zu denken, dass Peregrinus das alles an seinem Zufluchtsorte fand" (X, 214-215). The qualification established by *romanhaft* here is too vague. It signifies the highly emotional, though in particular it refers to the narrative art. And the derogatory intention is unmistakable. That such is intended is further substantiated in yet another place: "Wenigen Dank würde aber gegenwärtiger Referent des tollsten, wunderlichsten aller Märchen einernten, wenn er, sich steif und fest an dem Paradeschritt der daherstolzierenden Romanisten haltend, nicht unterlassen könnte, hier die jedem regelrechten Roman höchst nötige Langeweile sattsam zu erregen" (X, 252). Here the disparity between the novel and the *Märchen* is as pointed as if Hoffmann had designated the former negative and the latter positive. Irony against art becomes, in this instance again, self-irony as well.

However, the final irony of **Meister Floh** lay not with Hoffmann. The published version was not the same as the original, for the original had been too apparent an attack on an important Prussian official, and Hoffmann was forced to change his text and prepare a sworn statement to defend himself against a charge of slander. Hoffmann argued that the *Märchen* as such was a form which mythologized time and thereby was incapable of contemporaneity. With regard to his artistic intention Hoffmann's defense follows still another familiar pattern: "Ich bitte . . . den Gesichtspunkt nicht aus dem Auge zu lassen, dass hier nicht von einem satirischen Werke, dessen Vorwurf Welthändel und Ereignisse der Zeit sind, sondern von der fantastischen Geburt eines humoristischen Schriftstellers, der die Gebilde des wirklichen Lebens nur in der Abstraktion des Humors wie in einem Spiegel auffassend reflectiert, die Rede ist" (**Harich,** xv, 345). Bearing in mind that this document was dictated from the sickbed, the bitter irony behind Hoffmann's humor is tragically apparent.

In comparison with the theoretical tendency so apparent in all of Hoffmann's earlier writings, his last works are strikingly devoid of any doctrinology. The words *Ironie* and *Humor* almost never present themselves in the final literary product. Hoffmann now reveals a return to the world instead of a flight from it through fantasy. In the *Elixiere* the adjective Romantic was used, in one instance at least, in its original sense to describe a natural and picturesque landscape. This had not been done by Hoffmann since his earliest writings. Now in **"Meister Johannes Wacht"** (finished June 1822 and his last completed work) the same usage occurs again: "Mitten in dem schönen Garten war ein sehr geräumiger Pavillon gelegen, . . . aus dessen jedem Fenster man einer andern romantischen Aussicht genoss" (xii, 125). To the best of my knowledge this is the last time Hoffmann uses the term Romantic. Its various meanings have gone through a full circle of development and come finally to rest on the original meaning that Romanticism conveyed for Hoffmann. It is dangerous to argue that this one instance is conclusive evidence of a full evolution. Yet Hoffmann never used the term casually. Midway in his literary career he turned away from Romanticism. To take its place came irony and then humor. But even though the tone of his late works is often ironic, Hoffmann eventually no longer refers directly to irony and humor as aesthetic principles. His not doing so is unusual, for, from his earliest writings on, Hoffmann professes and adheres to some dogma. The new attitude of Hoffmann's Romanticism, however, is hardly a dogma. On the contrary, it would seem that he simply returned the Romantic to its original meaning for him and concentrated on writing for writing's sake.

In Hoffmann's last works a new interest is evident which suggests a replacement altogether for former theorizing. The last two completed stories—**"Des Vetters Eckfenster"** and **"Meister Johannes Wacht"**—reveal a keen observation of society at every level. To the time of his death Hoffmann worked on another story that would surely have become one of his most important works: *Der Feind* (xii, 180-216), an arresting character study of Albrecht Dürer. In this fragment Hoffmann begins with a development for the introduction of his main character that is unusually purposeful. This is done in part through the secondary characters, but even more it is the careful description of sixteenth-century Nürnberg and its citizenry which enhances the figure of Dürer. When the Serapion-story **"Der Kampf der Sänger"** is held up for comparison, one sees immediate parallels in the use of historical figures, the background of *Meistergesang,* and the importance of art and demonic influences. Perhaps in *Der Feind* art would have been venerated as a healing force, dispelling the emotional problems that are beginning to situate themselves in the fragment. But in *Der Feind,* as in **"Eckfenster"** [**"Des Vetters Eckfenster"**] and **"Wacht"** [**"Meister Johannes Wacht"**], it is precisely the care with which Hoffmann describes the social situation that reveals a new trend. The former preoccupation with aesthetics appears to be no longer necessary. That is why a reference in **"Meister Johannes Wacht"** to a pretty landscape as Romantic no longer commands special interest. Hoffmann had apparently turned in his last works from the transcendental and the abstract to life itself.

In summary, then, it must be admitted that Hoffmann's definition of Romanticism is loaded with emotional but not always with aesthetic content. Hoffmann's Romanticism is not a well-elaborated system by which various art forms are evaluated—that would involve a rational procedure—but rather it is the art forms themselves which are accepted at face value, and the standard of Romanticism turns out to be merely a shifting personal attitude, an emotional response to art. This would explain the more frequent appearance of the adjective *romantisch* as compared to the noun *Romantik.* In the first stage of its development as an aesthetic idea Romanticism was for Hoffmann first music, and then to this art discipline others were eventually added. But even these were emotional values, for in each of the several art forms Hoffmann sought the exaltation that is unlocked by inspiration. In its succeeding stages Romanticism became for Hoffmann purely an attitude—first irony and then humor. The concepts thus seized upon were themselves shallow generalizations for a relatively uncomplicated if consistent philosophy of life. This philosophy was—for the artist, to be sure—that life was a constant struggle between artistic longing and the frustrations of everyday existence. Furthermore, this philosophy and its terminology never progresses from the emotional to the intellectual. In fact, the stages of Hoffmann's shifting philosophy derived largely from his own emotional experience, and they were shaped further by the successive aesthetic stimuli that he stumbled upon. Hoffmann became a Romanticist as much because this was the literary fashion of the time as because his love for music met head on with Beethoven's *Fifth Symphony,* which he, disregarding the classification even of his own time, called Romantic. However, he did restrict the Romantic to the artistic, to the psychic, and even to the spiritual and abstract, and these being essentially products of the mind it can be said he thereby approached a unified definition: Romanticism is the transcendental.

The cluttered nature of Hoffmann's prose style is usually explained away as a reflection of the espousal of music that is characteristic in German Romanticism. But Hoffmann was not simply a writer-composer who ran words together as if they were musical notes, even though this is the view that has prevailed in so many histories of the movement and in general works on Hoffmann. In Richard E. Benz's history of German Romanticism Hoffmann is evaluated as just such an inspired and compulsive author-composer: "Hoffmann ist der Dichter sozusagen ohne Worte oder trotz der Worte; nichts ist bei ihm bis in den Wohllaut der Silbe notwendig geformt, eine beliebige gehäufte Rede ist zusammengerafftes Gewand für einen tieferen Dichter-Sinn."[10] The same stand is taken by Richard von Schaukal, yet here an apologetic tone is more apparent: "Hoffmanns Stil . . . ist von einem innern musikalischen Gesetz bewegt, das kontrapunktisch, nicht grammatisch die Worte aneinanderreiht, weshalb das oft seltsam Klischeeartige der Hoffmannschen Ausdrucksweise zur Beurteilung seiner Schriftstellerpersönlichkeit nicht ins Gewicht fällt. Bei ihm sind die Worte nicht so sehr intellektuell zu begreifende Zeichen für Mitzuteilendes, als vielmehr konventionelle Notenschrift, deren Musik hinter ihnen tönt."[11] But the "seltsam Klischeeartige" must be taken into account when evaluating the character of the man as a writer, because Hoffmann does use specific terms and ideas purposefully in his literary and critical works, and the aesthetic values thus established reveal method and critical development. If Hoffmann's prose style is not equally purposeful and direct—as is truly the case—that is a fault and must be acknowledged as such. And it is a fault to the discredit of Hoffmann as an aesthetician, for it betrays a basic irrationalism on his part.

Specifically, it is with regard to his function as a critic that Hoffmann's irrationalism renders dubious a contribution on his part to Romantic theory. In fact, his influence has been greater as a critic of music than of literature. His contribution to music criticism is acknowledged by the compendious *Grove's Dictionary of Music and Musicians,* while no reference whatever is made to an influence on literary theory: "Hoffmann was also a music critic of great acumen and deep insight. . . . Hoffmann's essays on Beethoven's instrumental music—far in advance of the period—are of great interest even today."[12] However, *Baker's Biographical Dictionary of Musicians* cites Hoffmann's influence on the evolution of German composition as well as on literature: "As a writer of fantastic tales, he made a profound impression on his period, and influenced the entire Romantic school of literature; indirectly, he was also a formative factor in the evolution of the German school of composition."[13] Thus Hoffmann influenced literature—but as a writer. His creative imagination in fic-

tion and not technical or formal accomplishment—whether in art or criticism—was the source of this influence. It is apparent also that Hoffmann failed to see (or refused to acknowledge) the purposefulness in Beethoven's apparent freedom of form. Despite Hoffmann, Beethoven was a Classical composer even in his late works, and so was Hoffmann except when he wrote *about* music. Paul Greef's recent evaluation of Hoffmann's over-all position in music states that Hoffmann's affinity to Beethoven was of such a dual nature: "Hoffmann ist im Grunde klassisch orientiert. Das beweist . . . seine Verwurzelung in Haydn, Mozart und Beethoven. Romantisch ist er da, wo er diese Musik der Klassiker deutet—romantisch also vornehmlich da, wo er als Dichter spricht."[14] The purely technical parts of the music reviews—in particular the Beethoven reviews—may still be of value today, but in the introductory parts where Hoffmann discusses the nature of music (i.e., the passages which were reintroduced in the **Phantasiestücke**), of art in general, and where his particular view of Romanticism is first shaped, Hoffmann too often shows unquestioning enthusiasm. In such places a more critical attitude is desirable; Hoffmann, however, in the opinion of René Wellek simply lacked the intellectual faculty that was necessary to be a good critic: "While the actual poetic achievement of the earlier romantics, with the exception of Novalis, seems small today, the newer generation has far greater works of art to its credit: Brentano and Arnim, Kleist and E. T. A. Hoffmann created genuine worlds of imagination. But they suffer from a lack of self-criticism, from a fundamental lack of form which prevents them from ranking with the greatest writers. Their anti-intellectualism came back at them with a vengeance."[15] It is explainable then, that Hoffmann did not make a noticeable contribution to Romantic theory in literature. For one thing, this might have been because the later Romanticists were valued as artists whereas their theoretical writings were more or less neglected (Heine and especially Eichendorff wrote extensively on the history of Romanticism). Hoffmann, too, tried hard to be a formulator of Romantic theory, and, had he been less in love with music, the disappointments out of which his narrow views grew might not have resulted in the intellectual escapism that art became for him. His last works, to be sure, present an essentially unaesthetic view of Romanticism.

In the last analysis, the reason for neglect of Hoffmann as a theorist of Romanticism lies with Hoffmann himself. As Paul Sucher, a French critic, explains, Hoffmann's approach to art is a modern one: "Il fut avant tout un tempérament: c'est par la sensation qu'il vaut, par le vif et profond sentiment qu'il eut du merveilleux, et sa fidélité, sa sincérité absolue dans la traduction de son émotion. . . . Hoffmann fut, sinon 'le plus grand artiste de la littérature allemande' (Reichel), comme le veulent ses admirateurs contemporains, au moins un très grand artiste, sincère et habile, un impressionniste, et par là véritablement un moderne."[16] His manner was not expository but impressionistic, and on that basis alone his standing as a critic is due a favorable word. By no means could he be considered a precursor of the modern school of Impressionism in literary criticism (other Romanticists such as Wackenroder and Novalis—even Lessing—would have to be accounted for in German literature alone), but he certainly anticipated this method, if only superficially. Only when he refers to the invisible church does Hoffmann move from the impressionistic to the symbolic. True, the reality behind the symbol is indefinite, but this concept is the one "concrete" idea to which Hoffmann consistently reverts when his feelings about a subject approach exaltation. It is regrettable that this idea was not further developed. However, it is because impressionism resists communication, as a rational system, that Hoffmann fails as a theoretician, even though this impressionism is the rewarding quality in his narrative works.

Notes

1. Citations from Hoffmann's narrative and critical writings will be from *E. T. A. Hoffmanns Werke in fünfzehn Teilen,* ed. Georg Ellinger (Berlin, 1912); referred to in this paper as *Werke* or by volume and page number alone. The succinct "Lebensbild" of *Werke* (I, vii-cxxvii), with few exceptions adequate even today, is the source of general biographical information here. The edition *E. T. A. Hoffmann, Dichtungen und Schriften sowie Briefe und Tagebücher: Gesamtausgabe in fünfzehn Bänden,* ed. Walther Harich (Weimar, 1924), has been used for references to Hoffmann's letters and diaries (lacking in *Werke*); references will be by volume and page number alone.

2. Richard Ullmann und Helene Gotthard, *Geschichte des Begriffes 'Romantisch' in Deutschland: Vom ersten Aufkommen des Wortes bis ins dritte Jahrzehnt des neunzehnten Jahrhunderts,* in *Germanische Studien,* Heft 50 (Berlin, 1927), p. 121.

3. This comes first in the diary (Harich): on Jan. 12, 1811, Hoffmann writes, "viel in Schlegels dramatischen Vorles. gelesen—Ich will die wichtigsten Definit. aus dem Werke *ad usum* ausziehn" (XIV, 323) and on Apr. 17, 1812, "im Novalis gelesen und sehr erbaut worden (Studium der Naturphilosophie—Schelling)" (XIV, 351).

4. Hoffmann knew the theoretical and artistic works of the other German Romanticists only superficially, and his knowledge of world literature was equally limited. Jean F. A. Ricci, in his book *E. T. A. Hoffmann: l'homme et l'oeuvre* (Paris, 1947), points out this limitation and reveals also that, in other respects, Hoffmann's taste was not always the best. Apart from the literature in popular de-

mand at the time "il ne reste à l'actif des influences subies par Hoffmann que quelques grands noms de la littérature universelle, Rousseau, Goethe, les romantiques allemands, Shakespeare, Gozzi, Calderon, Cervantès et, en outre, des ouvrages techniques" (p. 520).

5. *E. T. A. Hoffmann: Sein Leben und seine Werke* (Hamburg, 1894), p. 68; a statement made to Kunz even after Hoffmann had lost his position in the Bamberg theater due to Holbein's withdrawal from its leadership.

6. Again Ricci, in showing Hoffmann's preference of occult arts to a sound philosophic system, makes clear the significance of Hoffmann's reading taste: "Outre les idées qu'il a puisées dans l'air du temps, il doit bien plus, par exemple, à un vulgarisateur comme G. H. Schubert qu'à un philosophe authentique comme Schelling. Ce qui importe donc, c'est non la doctrine de la philosophie romantique allemande, mais plutôt les notions sommaires, simplifiées, peu exactes parfois que Hoffmann avait à ce sujet" (p. 520). In an allusion to Schubert in "Das Sanctus" (1816), on the other hand, Hoffmann was capable of extreme sarcastic irony: "er wird gleich auf seinem Steckenpferde sitzen und gestreckten Galopps in die Welt der Ahnungen, Träume, psychischen Einflüsse, Sympathien, Idiosynkrasien u. s. w. hineinreiten, bis er auf der Station des Magnetismus absitzt und ein Frühstück nimmt" (III, 125).

7. In support of this argument for naïveté in Hoffmann's irony as a philosophy of life see Richard von Schaukal, *E. T. A. Hoffmann: Sein Werk aus seinem Leben* (Zürich, 1923): "Denn Hoffmann, der Ironiker, der Menschenverächter, der Zyniker, war, als das er sich selbst so gerne darstellt, ein Enthusiast, das ist ein naiver, inniger Mensch, ein Mensch, dem nichts fremder war als 'Literatur' und nichts näher als das Wunder des Lebens" (p. 113).

8. George C. Schoolfield, in *The Figure of the Musician in German Literature,* in *University of North Carolina Studies in the Germanic Languages and Literatures,* No. 19 (Chapel Hill, 1956), delineates clearly the extent of Hoffmann's religion: "Hoffmann's attitude toward the Catholic Church may well be identified with the author's attitude toward religious music, since the writer's association with Lutheranism had no influence upon his musical thought . . . his church music was composed exclusively for Catholic use. Yet he never became a Catholic nor does he allow his Kreisler . . . to do so" (p. 26). And also "Kreisler realizes that he must return to life in order to save music from those who would misuse it. The service of the Church through music is a noble mission, to be

sure, but the true musician has made music his religion" (p. 27).

9. This revealing document is not included by Harich; see *E. T. A. Hoffmann in persönlichen und brieflichen Verkehr: Sein Briefwechsel und die Erinnerungen seiner Bekannten,* ed. Hans von Müller (Berlin, 1912), II, 255.

10. *Die deutsche Romantik: Geschichte einer geistigen Bewegung* (Leipzig, 1937), p. 336.

11. *Hoffmann,* p. 127.

12. 5th ed., ed. Eric Blom (London, 1954), s.v. "Hoffmann."

13. 5th ed., ed. Nicolas Slonimsky (New York, 1958), s.v. "Hoffmann."

14. *E. T. A. Hoffmann als Musiker und Musikschriftsteller* (Köln, 1948), pp. 257-258.

15. *A History of Modern Criticism: 1750-1950, II. The Romantic Age* (New Haven, 1955), p. 291.

16. *Les Sources du Merveilleux chez E. T. A. Hoffmann* (Paris, 1912), p. 230.

Kenneth Negus (essay date 1965)

SOURCE: Negus, Kenneth. "The Underworld." In *E. T. A. Hoffmann's Other World: The Romantic Author and His "New Mythology,"* pp. 95-117. Philadelphia: University of Pennsylvania Press, 1965.

[*In the following essay, Negus investigates the evil figures in Hoffmann's* Nachtstücke *tales.*]

The figures emerging from the black chaos in several of Hoffmann's tales are many and various. Beginning primarily as variations on Satan, they are then transformed into many types representing the forces of darkness and destruction. The all-embracing symbol for this realm is the night. This is reflected in the very title of the key work of this phase, *Nachtstücke.*

Hoffmann experimented with various forms of his underworld. Consequently there were varying degrees of success in creating the appropriate means of expression. He himself recognized this unevenness in *Nachtstücke* when he wrote in his letter of March 8, 1818, to Kunz: "Im zweiten Theil der Nachtstücke empfehle ich Ihnen das Majorat und das Gelübde; das öde Haus taugt nichts und das steinerne Herz ist so—so!"

The first two stories in the collection—**"Der Sandmann"** (1815) and **"Ignaz Denner"** (1814-1816)—actually belong more to the earlier "satanic" phase of Hoffmann's writings than the others, and were therefore

discussed in detail in the previous chapter. Associated with these satanic figures there is, of course, an "underworld." In the first, the symbolic night atmosphere is the backdrop for the activities of a practitioner of black magic, who evokes tormenting anxieties in children, creates the beautiful, but deceptive figure of superhuman beauty (Olimpia), and drives Nathanael to madness. At the same time, it is an exploration of the abyss of a mind which creates for itself such fearsome creatures and situations. In **"Ignaz Denner,"** the underworld is a sinister forest, in which thieves and murderers have their refuge and base of operation, and infect others with brutality and baseness. In both cases the underworld night atmosphere clearly exists in actuality, and therefore is not in itself mythical; it is, however, pervaded with a power derived from a satanic concept, and is therefore strongly suggestive of a myth.

In **"Die Jesuiterkirche in G."** Hoffmann greatly extended his exploration of that part of the underworld involving mainly the artist, in this case Berthold, a painter who in his absolute devotion to his art is on the verge of criminal insanity. (A discussion of this artistic aspect of the story appears in Chapter III.) There is a strong demonic element in Berthold's art. This comes up in connection with the nature myth, which apparently also includes a threatening underworld: "Die ganze Natur, ihm sonst freundlich lächelnd, ward ihm zum bedrohlichen Ungeheuer, und ihre Stimme, die sonst in des Abendwindes Säuseln, in dem Plätschern des Baches, in dem Rauschen des Gebüsches mit süssem Wort ihn begrüsste, verkündete ihm nun Untergang und Verderben." ([*E. T. A. Hoffmanns Werke in fünfzehn Teilen,* Berlin, 1927,] III, 114. [All further citations are from this edition.]) One might expect Hoffmann to portray these "threatening monsters" in some concrete form or other, but this would probably have tended to shift the center of attention from the artist figure per se. Thus in **"Die Jesuiterkirche in G.,"** he did not develop any further a demonic world of nature in landscapes, just as he had left a *Märchen* landscape-myth in embryonic form.

"Das Sanctus," the final story of the first volume of *Nachtstücke,* adds but little to Hoffmann's underworld. The tale provides a capriccio-like ending to this otherwise bleak collection; for an extreme tone of irony, even buffoonery, is created by the narrators and audience in the *Rahmen.* The bearing of **"Das Sanctus"** on the night and underworld symbolism lies in its preoccupation with mental illness—a mild kind, to be sure: a psychological block preventing a singer from performing. The source of this aspect of the "Nachtseite" of life is clearly G. H. von Schubert's *Ansichten von der Nachtseite der Naturwissenschaften* and similar works. One of the comments of the doctor to the narrator abounds with typical terms from Schubert: "'O,' rief der Doktor lachend, 'o, nur Geduld, er wird gleich auf seinem Steckenpferde sitzen und gestreckten Galopps in die Welt der Ahnungen, Träume, psychischen Einflüsse, Sympathien, Idiosynkrasien u. s. w. hineinreiten, bis er auf der Station des Magnetismus absitzt und ein Früh-stück nimmt.'" (III, 125.) It is obvious that the area of the underworld discussed is not especially fearsome in this case, nor even to be taken seriously. Even the deep earnestness of the inner story of Zulema, the Moorish convert to Christianity, is attenuated by its remoteness in time and place from the narrative present, and by the buffoonery of the dialogue surrounding it.

Such a mechanism of irony could not operate, however, in **"Das öde Haus,"** the first story in the second volume of *Nachtstücke.* Something is definitely lacking that might possibly have resolved the dilemma of the two mutually incompatible realities presented in this story. Irony could not be the solution here, however, for Theodor, the narrator and hero, is too desperate to laugh in his vain search for deeper forces underlying every-day life—which are embodied in myth in other tales of Hoffmann. Thus the story is, in a sense, incomplete; this might have been what Hoffmann sensed about it when he called it "worthless." One might be inclined to agree with him, were it not for certain aspects of it, making it important in the development of his demonic tales. Few stories by him are so weak as a whole but so interesting in individual parts.

The desolate house stands at the center of attention as an appropriate symbol of wearisome emptiness and de-cay that cries out for identity and vitality. Theodor feels this intensely as he walks by it, for he can identify it with his own need for something to deepen and nurture his insights into his own everyday life. Theodor is ab-solutely opposed to "prosaic" solutions to important problems. This word "prosaic" recurs several times in the story; then he attaches it as attributive to a "demon" plaguing him with rational explanations for the myster-ies that he wants to see (III, 142 f.).

Thus when he sees the portrait of a beautiful woman—an ideal feminine figure—in the window, he endows it with a life stemming from his most desperate need for some spiritual regeneration. The way is paved thereby for a breakthrough of a myth embodying the transcendent powers for which he seems to be yearning. Another Anselmus is in the making.

Nothing of the kind comes about, however. The remain-der of the story is a confused jumble of explanations, counter-explanations, mysteries, and frustrations. As in **"Der Sandmann,"** great suspicion is cast on the hero's sanity. Here he even goes to a psychiatrist! Unlike the story of Nathanael, however, there is no tragic resolu-tion of the problem. Theodor is *not* necessarily insane. After all, even the psychiatrist sees the image of the ideal beloved in the "magic mirror." Moreover, if The-

odor is insane, then he has a chance of entering into long-distant spiritual rapport with various strange be-ings by means of the occult powers with which the mentally ill are believed to be endowed. This associa-tion is supported by the neurotic Edwine, who is the re-alization of Theodor's image of the ideal beloved, and is somehow shown to be in communication with the powers controlling the mysteries in the tale.

Then we have the "rational" explanation for it all in a background story of the previous generation. Jealousy, adultery, child-stealing, and revenge make up a fitting backdrop for the ominous "desolate house." Behind it all, in turn, stands a mysterious old woman and her gypsy band, who somehow exert sinister, occult influ-ence on events.

The story is left dangling with the question as to just how and why Theodor became involved in all this. Yet it is not at all "worthless," for it is a milestone in Hoff-mann's career. We can see in it certain old and new motifs used in a significant manner. The ideal beloved is now mentally debilitated, but her illness has to do with a mysterious power affecting her lover. (This an-ticipates Hedwiga in the Kreisler novel in *Kater Murr.*) A nomadic group (cp. **"Ignaz Denner"**) is associated therewith, as later in *Kater Murr* and **"Die Doppelt-gänger."** The problem of humdrum existence—"the prosaic"—finds here a new setting, and its solution seems even more difficult than in **"Der goldne Topf."**

Finally, the story shows Hoffmann's new awareness of some scarcely surmountable difficulties in penetrating through the empty external phenomena of our world and lives, and into a mythical essence. We are, as one of his characters states, blind moles searching along dark paths, with manifestations of the world above lead-ing us eventually to the light (III, 155 f.). But the way is hard, and Hoffmann's indications as to which path to follow are—like this story—inconclusive. It can be madness to seek anything beyond "the prosaic"—yet he must. This dilemma is at its worst in **"Das öde Haus."**

The inconclusiveness of this story is more than com-pensated for by the following tale, **"Das Majorat,"** the masterwork of the collection and one of Hoffmann's greatest achievements as a writer. Hoffmann himself recommended it highly in his letter to Kunz (p. 95 [March 8, 1818]), and singled it out as the best in a let-ter to his friend, Hippel (Dec. 15, 1817). It is pervaded with the symbolic atmosphere of the night as none of the others, with the possible exception of **"Ignaz Den-ner."** It is night when Theodor and his great-uncle V. arrive at the old castle. It is night when Theodor, while reading Schiller's *Der Geisterseher,* hears Daniel's ghost for the first time. And it is night when in a remote past, the man-servant, Daniel, murders his master by pushing him through a door into an abyss. As in **"Ignaz**

Denner" and *Die Elixiere des Teufels* this night is all the more sinister for its setting in a German forest, where wolves can suddenly appear and attack people, as when Theodor was hunting. Other sinister figures seem to come alive from the pictures and statues of the dimly-lit castle at night. Thus a typical Hoffmannesque underworld is indicated.

This ghostly background, however, does not comprise a myth. There are not even any devils inhabiting the night surrounding the locale of R . . . sitten. Only human beings participate in these stories. Even the ghost is motivated by a common personal feeling: that of guilt, and not by universal forces causing him to act according to the laws of some "other world," divorced from immediate concerns.

Even the "other world of music" loses here its former stature. Formerly when a musician sat at a piano singing with a beautiful young lady, he was transported with her into ethereal realms where they experienced a few moments of eternity. Here, when Theodor has such a love affair with the young wife of the baron of the manor at R . . . sitten, his wise and severely candid uncle V. convincingly portrays him as a foolish adolescent, engaging in hopelessly "romantic" nonsense that could have disastrous consequences (III, 192).

In **"Das Majorat"** there is a previously unknown concern for some of the fundamental problems of everyday life: for family, legal and social matters of the type which were Hoffmann's concern only in his daily work as a lawyer. Associated with this is the obvious warmth and nearness felt toward the main characters, with their human nature perfectly envisioned and portrayed. This is especially true of Theodor's uncle—cantankerous, clever, witty, yet loving and pious—one of Hoffmann's finest character studies. In few works by Hoffmann does an individual human character stand out in such sharp relief and warm vitality.

Also essential problems of human interrelationships are central to the plot, particularly those concerning different generations. In the confrontation of Theodor and V. we see a very young man—inexperienced, "romantically" inclined, and extremely foolish—put in sharp contrast with an elderly and wise old gentleman who can view things with well-informed sobriety. This theme of conflict of generations is then given many variations in the background story, told by V. to Theodor, concerning the history of the family at R . . . sitten, going back to 1760.

The historical aspect implicit here is unusual for Hoffmann, yet it is quite close to the surface, as I attempted to demonstrate in a detailed study of the matter.[1] This amounts to a commentary by Hoffmann on the generation of the last third of the eighteenth century, seen from the quite different circumstances of 1817.

There is no coherent myth embodied in the atmosphere of the *Nachtstücke.* Fragments of myth are present in occasional figures of speech alluding to Satan; in the resemblance of the background to a mythical underworld (the night and the abyss); in certain figures common to other myths, such as that of the master and apprentice; in gold, associated with an evil underworld (the family's treasure store); and in the dark forest of the German fairy tale. But these things do not constitute a myth. Not until the writing of the **"Bergwerke zu Falun"** did Hoffmann create a coherent nocturnal myth of the underground. The mythical motifs in **"Das Majorat"** embody an overall symbolism whereby a human situation is deepened through suggestions of a myth. Because of their strongly allegorical nature we may call such themes mythical emblems.

A central figure in this night symbolism is Daniel peering over the edge of an abyss, where formerly stood a tower suggesting the might of a dynasty. Out of these dark depths emerges a story of past crime, horror, hatred, guilt—all of which asserts itself once more in the present, then dies forever in ruins. This all happens on earth in dead-earnest actuality, but points beyond itself to fundamental truths like those in a myth. Thus the essence of life is not absent here, as in Hoffmann's usual everyday world, but manifests itself in common experience. In a sense, parts of Hoffmann's personal mythology here take on actuality, and in so doing are no longer myth, but life with a profundity made visible with myth emblems.

The remainder of the *Nachtstücke,* the two stories, **"Das Gelübde"** and **"Das steinerne Herz,"** have little relevancy here. **"Das Gelübde"** is a *Nachtstück* only in the figurative sense of G. H. von Schubert: it deals with psychological aberrations, mixed with a mysterious telepathic power—all part of the "nocturnal side of nature." **"Das steinerne Herz"** provides a *capriccio* as the final work in Volume Two, like the frame of **"Das Sanctus"** in Volume One. It also repeats some themes related to the other world of the past, as represented in **"Das Majorat."** Otherwise, **"Das steinerne Herz"** belongs to the *Nachtstücke* for negative reasons: it exorcises the demons of the night with light-hearted persiflage.

The *Nachtstücke* comprise an amorphous collection. The exploration of the demonic nocturnal underworld involved false starts and blind alleys, especially in the second volume. In the first volume, however, **"Der Sandmann," "Ignaz Denner"** and **"Die Jesuiterkirche in G."** make full use of a symbolic night in which various kinds of demons obtrude into human life. This spell is gradually broken. This is anticipated by the painful buffoonery in the frame of **"Das Sanctus."** Then, as was demonstrated, **"Das öde Haus"** ends in frustrating dilemma and mystification. **"Das Majorat,"** although one of Hoffmann's greatest accomplishments, takes a totally new direction, out of myth into realistic symbolism and warm-hearted humanity. **"Das Gelübde"** utilizes a *psychological* "night" symbolism. **"Das steinerne Herz"** puts the finishing touches to the exorcising of the demons. Thus something new was needed in the materials and techniques of portraying an underworld. Two main trends followed: Hoffmann either explored new areas, or he displaced mythical underworlds into common experience. Thus the *Nachtstücke* contain a tangle of successes and failures in the progress of Hoffmann's career as a writer. Even the failures were not vain efforts, for there is a clear line of development from the *Nachtstücke* into two major works of the time which follows the actual *Nachtstücke* collection (completed in the fall of 1817). These are **"Das Fräulein von Scuderi"** and **"Die Bergwerke zu Falun,"** both written the following year.

"Das Fräulein von Scuderi" appears in the *Serapionsbrüder,* and thus is followed by a critical discussion of the work on the part of the "brothers." The immediate reaction is that the story is truly "Serapiontic," "weil sie, auf geschichtlichen Grund gebaut, doch hinaufsteige ins Phantastische" (VII, 185). Thus the trend of **"Das Majorat"** is continued here; for it is a story rooted in actual experience, yet has certain fantastic adjuncts. Where **"Das Fräulein von Scuderi"** "rises into the fantastic," it is a dark night, thus making it a true "Nachtstück." The very first scene, where Olivier attempts to gain entrance to give the jewels to Fräulein von Scuderi, takes place during a night pervaded with fear for the unleashed violence of criminals. Later Olivier under the cover of night tells the whole fearful story of Cardillac's life and heinous crimes. The central figure in this night atmosphere, Cardillac himself, comes out only at night to regain possession of his magnificent works of the jeweler's art by murdering his clients. The night is simultaneously an appropriate background and the symbolic essence of this greedy and murderous part of his schizophrenic personality. As in **"Der Sandmann"** and **"Ignaz Denner,"** there is a connection with Satan, the king of the night, although this complicity is not emphasized and can be regarded as merely metaphorical.[2] It is Hoffmann's night symbolism that reaches here a height of intensity and complexity; the satanic is only suggested.

The foundation for it is laid with masterful artistry in the section following the opening scene. Here Hoffmann only seems to be telling history, describing a crime wave in Paris. What he actually does is proceed from the general to the particular, from the overall picture to the focus, first by telling of the series of poisonings, then of the nocturnal murders by stiletto, supposedly committed by a band of robbers. The particular kind of poison and poisonings in the first case is symbolically significant: it is a "devilish" concoction that can cause death by mere inhalation, leaving no symptoms of poisoning behind. When these poisonings become more and more widespread, there is a sense that the very air is deadly. This intangible aura is made more concrete, but still omni-present, by the rumors of a large band of murderous thieves circulating through the streets of Paris at night. Here again a fearsome underworld is painted with mysterious, frightening creatures emerging out of the blackness to destroy life and creativity. This mythical emblem is proved, of course, to be unsubstantiated in reality, since Cardillac committed these crimes; but the effect of this image of an underworld remains engraved on the mind as background for the Cardillac story.

Thus Cardillac is already characterized before we meet him: his role in the story is to form a focus for the poison and violence of the night. The intensity of this focal symbolism is Hoffmann's consummate artistic achievement in the work. The pitch-black side of Cardillac's character is portrayed with highly pregnant details of great originality. The prenatal influence from his mother, deriving from a sinful obsession with a jewelled necklace and its handsome owner, is a combination of G. H. Schubert's "nocturnal" mumbo-jumbo and Hoffmann's own association of jewels, metals, and other subterranean products with evil and the underworld. Cardillac's art of goldsmithing thus takes on a symbolic superstructure. His obsession with his work leads him into an artist's exclusive scheme of values and behavior in absolute opposition to those of his society, as with Berthold in the **"Jesuiterkirche in G."** With this art are also associated other stone and metal objects (of "underworld" origin), such as the "Stein der Weisen" sought by Glaser and Exili in the story, leading to the discovery of the dangerous poison (VII, 134). By the sharp contrast with Cardillac's virtuous "day" identity, his evil nocturnal self is intensified.

The day symbolism of the story, however, is far less rich than that of the night. Yet it is not nearly so colorless as it often is in Hoffmann's tales. The creature standing in opposition to the evil night-wanderer is the magnificent Mlle. de Scuderi herself, standing by her two young protégés, Madelon and Olivier. Olivier is in a somewhat neutral zone as a non-demonic goldsmith (although he is the apprentice of Cardillac), and is the ally of Mlle. de Scuderi. Madelon, however, (as we are repeatedly assured by the author) is a heavenly creature: unfortunately, her earthly being is far less interesting except as a mere role-filler in the story. She does not represent a mythical upper world, such as that in **"Der goldne Topf"**: this realm is totally absent here. Nor is she convincing as a portrayal of a loving and feminine humanity, as is Klara in **"Der Sandmann."**

What opposes the realm of darkness is not the usual mythical world of light and creativity, but rather a fundamental humanity suffering under the violence and delusions brought about by a pestilence of evil in the atmosphere of the time. This all-pervading destructive spirit has managed to penetrate everywhere (even the police is dominated by it: VII, 137: 27), *except into the sanctum of Frl. von Scuderi's conscience.* This moral absolute enabling her to judge others intuitively is severely challenged, causing a Kleistian "Verwirrung des Gefühls" (VII, 157: 40), but she eventually regains her inner composure, along with the accompanying infallible power that opposes the forces of darkness. When appearances are absolutely against Olivier's innocence, her last hope is expressed in the simple words "be human" (VII, 157: 32 and 160: 26).

This is far removed from the resolution of the battle of light and darkness in **"Der goldne Topf."** The difference is highly significant and characteristic for Hoffmann's development as an author from 1813 to 1818. Now Hoffmann's concern is far more for the fundamentally human as it manifests itself in living persons, rather than for transcendent forces influencing human life from without, from a primeval and metaphysical distance. We have already observed the beginnings of this shift in emphasis in **"Der Sandmann"** (Klara) and **"Das Majorat"** (Grossonkel V . . .); even higher manifestations of Hoffmann's humanity appear later in *Kater Murr* (Meister Abraham). This new center for his art is greatly advanced in the character of Frl. von Scuderi, whose prime importance is brought to the fore by the very title of the story, and eventually, by her successful manipulation of events as the instrument of this pivotal point of view.[3]

The power of the story stems from the interaction of absolutes in Cardillac and Fräulein von Scuderi. This confrontation is beautifully—although ironically—expressed by the "betrothal" of Cardillac and Fräulein von Scuderi. A symbolic marriage is suggested toward the beginning of the story when the jewels given her by Cardillac are discussed (VII, 148). The "marriage" is complete when she adorns herself with Cardillac's jewelry. She also wears mourning clothes when she pleads Olivier's case before the king. The deep irony of the situation lies in their diametric opposition to one another, as does the similar juxtaposition of Lindhorst and Liese in **"Der goldne Topf."** Here, however, the conflict is not between two myths, but between life (intensified by young love), and a symbolic figure and atmosphere originating in an underworld myth. But the myth is on the verge of losing its identity by its incorporation into life.

"Die Bergwerke zu Falun" is the companion piece of **"Das Fräulein von Scuderi."** These stories—both written toward the end of 1818—comprise a part of the same phase of Hoffmann's writings in that they are more sharply dualistic than at any other point in his life. The two worlds of light and darkness, and their reflections in the double personalities of Cardillac and Elis Fröbom, contrast more severely with each other than such elements in previous works. The areas of conflict are a sympathetically viewed world of actuality (the Olivier-Madelon and Elis-Ulla relationship) and a mysterious dark realm nearby from which destructive figures emerge (the Parisian night inhabited by murderers, and the sinister and dangerous mine of Falun). The symbolic materials of both dark underworlds are the same: stone and metal.

"Die Bergwerke zu Falun" does not have a pivotal character of such magnificent humanity as Fräulein von Scuderi. In this respect the **"Bergwerke"** is obviously a lesser accomplishment. In the Falun atmosphere, however, Hoffmann creates a more extensive and concrete demonic background, which is perhaps a greater accomplishment than the deadly Paris atmosphere. The success of the former stems from the underworld myth that Hoffmann injected into the mine at Falun. Rather than a miasmic night inhabited by murderous thieves, the underworld here has a fully developed and concrete structure. For the first time, Hoffmann is successful in creating a type of "landscape" myth. We have seen indications thereof in **"Die Jesuiterkirche in G."** (see page 78). Also about the same time as when he wrote **"Die Bergwerke,"** he made a similar attempt at such a myth in **"Der unheimliche Gast"** (e.g., Angelika's dream: VII, 103f.). These other two works probably could not be successful in this respect because their abode was a conventional Romantic nature landscape, where Hoffmann was not at home. Even the natural phenomena in **"Die Bergwerke"** were not directly observed. He made a thorough study of books about Falun (in Sweden) and mining, resulting in the use of many terms unknown to the average reader—even of his day—because they were technical or restricted to a knowledge of the Swedish language and geography, thus removing the story somewhat from the common experience of his average readers.

The emergence of the myth of the story is carefully prepared for and motivated. Elis Fröbom, like Anselmus in **"Der goldne Topf,"** is isolated from society. Elis, however, isolates himself by choice. Besides being a "Neriker"—a member of a melancholy clan of the Swedish nation—he has also lost his parents and two brothers. The most recent bereavement—his mother's death—leaves an empty place in his life that apparently can be filled only by another woman. When Elis has an opportunity to make such an acquaintance near the beginning of the story, however, he rejects it. We are shown the connection between the mother and the girl by the "ostindisches Tuch"—intended for the mother—that he gives the girl upon parting.

With the jubilation of his fellow-sailors and the girls within hearing, he falls into despair, and wishes for death. This utterance evokes the figure of the sinister old miner Torbern out of nowhere. This is the point where the myth breaks through into actuality—although Elis and the reader cannot know that Torbern is from another world until later. There is, however, a suggestion of a Faustian pact—making Torbern a Satan-like figure—in the promise to Elis that, if he becomes a miner, he will be able to see ". . . in dem wunderbaren Gestein die Abspieglung dessen . . . was oben über den Wolken verborgen" (V, 203). Torbern's world emerges gradually throughout the sequence of events that follows: Elis' becoming a miner, his betrothal to Ulla, his growing obsession with the depths, and his ultimate destruction by the cave-in at the mine.

After Torbern verbally introduces Elis to the fascinating glitter of underworld metals, Elis has a highly significant dream. Here typical themes of his old way of life, the sea, and of his future role as a miner, merge into a weird landscape in which the water and clouds of a scene at sea become stone; and beneath the surface of the crystalline water magnificent metallic flowers are blossoming amidst beautiful mermaids. Elis unwittingly commits himself to the underworld forever when he impulsively flings himself into this "sea," and comes face-to-face with the queen of this realm; but Elis still can look upward and see a beautiful creature of the "surface"—who, as is later learned, is Ulla. Again the connection between the mother and the other feminine figures is made when his mother's voice comes from above. The mixture of bliss and horror in Elis' reaction to all this typifies his subsequent internal conflict between the influence of the world of the surface and the lower depths.

Before the lower world appears to him in actuality as a concrete entity, it takes on the old form already familiar to us: that of a black, empty abyss. When Elis first sees the huge open pit of the mine (V, 207), its similarity to other underworld scenes in Hoffmann is striking: not only does it have the usual blackness, but also the frightening figures—for the stones seem to form animal and human images. The typical description of the mine as an "Abgrund" recurs several more times in the story. This time, however, Hoffmann goes far beyond such a vague portrayal, and step-by-step penetrates into an underworld that is concrete and visible.

After Elis becomes a miner, the myth breaks through again with the sudden, inexplicable appearance of Torbern deep in the mine. The purpose of his appearance seems to be to warn Elis that he is being unfaithful to the underworld because of his love for Ulla, and that the "Metallfürst"—a new figure—might take revenge. Thus a masculine figure—a counterpart to Elis' dead father—gives further rounding out of the meaning of the myth for Elis' personal psychology.

As Elis becomes more obsessed with the underworld, he begins to see the metallic plants and beautiful maidens of his dream in the mine itself. He is interrupted by Pehrson Dahlsjö, who has pursued Elis into the mine, and finds him "*wie erstarrt* stehend, das Gesicht gedrückt in das kalte Gestein" (italics mine). Here Elis is beginning to take on the characteristics of the lower depths. Finally, just before his death, the mine seems to promise the revelation of superhuman truths, in fulfillment of Torbern's promise at the beginning that Elis would find a transcendent wisdom in the mine. Elis believes that he will find "den kirschrot funkelnden Almandin" on which his and Ulla's "Lebenstafel" is engraved. This knowledge, far beyond the normal range of human beings, offers the resolution of Elis' conflict, for both temporal and eternal things merge here. There is tragic irony in this, however, for Elis meets his death when he descends into the mine.

Thus the final goal of the underworld and its forces is clearly death. Hoffmann is nowhere else so clear about this. In retrospect, Torbern is discovered to be a kind of angel of death, for he has appeared as a result of Elis' uttering the desire to die. The inexorable sequence leading to the end of the story has an inner necessity growing out of a melancholy man's subconscious but definite desire to escape the bright, sensual world of the surface, thinking he can delve into dark recesses of the mind for greater satisfactions, but failing tragically. The symbolic mine is really a realm of the dead with its beautiful but rigid forms anticipating in a ghastly, hidden symbolism the *rigor mortis* of those who succumb to it. His statuesque form witnessed 50 years later is the final, perhaps somewhat melodramatic touch.

This work is the culmination of Hoffmann's underworld symbolism. Although such realms appear before and after the writing of the **"Bergwerke zu Falun,"** none takes on such an intense focus and circumscribed locale as the mine at Falun. This is the result of a long development, in which the underworld was constantly scrutinized, remolded and enlarged. It began with the "Reich der Träume" in **"Ritter Gluck"**; then Hoffmann remolded it into the lower depths of a primeval world in **"Der goldne Topf"**; then he varied and relocated it in such stories as **"Ignaz Denner," "Die Jesuiterkirche in G.," "Der unheimliche Gast"** and **"Das Fräulein von Scuderi."** Finally, its serious artistic possibilities as a central realm are largely exhausted by **"Die Bergwerke zu Falun."**

Now Hoffmann can jest about the underworld as he did with Satan (**"Nachricht aus dem Leben eines bekannten Mannes"**) after there were no more horrors to write about him. He did just this in the charming fantasy (often neglected by Hoffmann scholars), **"Die Königsbraut,"** written at the beginning of 1821, about two years after **"Die Bergwerke zu Falun."** Hoffmann's imaginary underworld, once portrayed in dead earnest, now gives rise to the purest delight that reading

Hoffmann can afford. It is remarkable how the same basic plot and many motifs common to the **"Bergwerke zu Falun"** could be transformed into such a good-natured parody on the underworld. Here, as with Elis Fröbom, underworld figures emerge into the lives of human beings and attempt to dominate them. In **"Die Königsbraut,"** however, not only do the "demons" fail, but the characters and action are superbly designed to dispel humorously the spooks of Hoffmann's murky Hades. The central figure, Anna von Zabelthau (rather pretty, but on the plump side) has problems that could be serious. These stem from her bungling recluse father and her fine-frenzied poetic lover. She is, however, a much too simply motivated creature of the earth's surface—a farm girl who wants to get married—to cause us the concern that Elis Fröbom's tortured problems arouse. The father, Dapsul von Zabelthau, is a typical Hoffmannesque "master figure," possessing occult knowledge and powers, but his peccadillos ("Ich fresse erschrecklich!") and frequent bungling at critical moments make him a travesty of such characters as Torbern or Archivarius Lindhorst. The lover, Amandus von Nebelstern, is the self-styled voice of a "higher world," a poet who writes pompous gibberish and inanities that are worth reading only as unconscious self-parody.

Then there is the "underworld" itself. This is *not* primarily the realm of stones and metals—although some of these motifs occur (e.g., VIII, 213:7ff.)—but another realm that was anticipated eight years before in **"Der goldne Topf."** It will be remembered that the witch-figure Liese was the offspring of a black dragon feather and a beet root, and that when conquered in the tenth *Vigilie* she was transformed into the latter. Now, in **"Die Königsbraut,"** Hoffmann expands on this symbolism and creates a whole new sub-kingdom of the underworld, consisting of all varieties of personified bulbous vegetables, ruled over by a gnome, the Vegetable King Daucus Carota I, *alias* Baron Porphyrio von Ockerodastes genannt Corduanspitz. This realm of the underworld, one might suppose, is less deadly than that of Torbern's, simply because it is less subterranean.

Anna von Zabelthau has a slight obsession with these vegetables, which might be compared with Elis' fascination for the mine. This, it seems, makes her more susceptible to the designs of Daucus Carota to marry her than she otherwise might be. Perhaps this is Hoffmann's answer to the question of why Proserpina, goddess of vegetable fertility, should become the queen of Pluto's underworld! In any case, she, like Fröbom, is gradually dominated more and more by subterranean forces until she temporarily acquires their physical characteristics: her head becomes enlarged and she turns yellow, apparently turning into a demi-carrot. (The parallel with Fröbom would be his stone-like rigidity when fetched from the mine by Dahlsjö.) Likewise her father must suffer the indignity of being transformed for a time into a mushroom: he does not quite make the grade to be absorbed into this subcutaneous level of the underworld.

Only once is this good fun interrupted, and then there is some rather frightening grotesquery. This occurs when Dapsul sets aside the spell that causes Daucus Carota and his subjects to appear so affluent and elegant, and, with some whimsical mumbo-jumbo, shows Anna these creatures in their true form: as the epitome of ugliness, wriggling about in a puddle, in "einem farblosen, ekelhaften Schlamm" (VIII, 214 f.). This point of the story approaches the fearsomeness of other areas of Hoffman's underworld, and Anna's reaction contains the same horror that we have seen in other characters when peering into an underworld abyss. This horror does not last long, however, for we are soon led to the grotesque humor of Anna's feminine vanity when she sees her physical appeal seriously damaged by her new carrot-like appearance.

The resolution of the story dispels any seriousness that might possibly remain. This occurs with the conquest of the demons by the "higher forces" manifested in Amandus von Nebelstern's "poetry," which causes Daucus Carota such a terrible stomach-ache that he loses all his power, then shrinks into his original vegetable form, and Anna's and her father's normal appearances are restored. Thus a further parody is added here: that of the "higher world" of poetry, portrayed seriously (at the end at least) in **"Der goldne Topf."**

The "cosmos" in this story again consists of a high, middle and lower realm, but the story differs essentially from **"Der goldne Topf"**: instead of ending up, like Anselmus, in the upper reaches of eternal beauty, Anna and Amandus finish their lives together in the amicable, unpoetic world that it was in the first place—a world that Hoffmann came to love more and more toward the end of his life.

This did not prevent him from reworking certain materials of his personal mythology, this time drawing heavily on traditional myths. We have already pointed out the similarity of this story to the myth of Pluto and Proserpina. In addition, Hoffmann drew heavily on a favorite book, *Graf von Gabalis oder die verborgenen Wissenschaften,* for the doctrine of the "elemental spirits," which Dapsul summarizes in the text: "Erfahre . . . dass die tiefe Erde, die Luft, das Wasser, das Feuer erfüllt ist mit geistigen Wesen höherer und doch wieder beschränkterer Natur als die Menschen . . . Gnomen, Salamander, Sylphen und Undinen." (VIII, 191.) Hoffmann had made use of "Elementargeister" before. Archivarius Lindhorst was, "in reality," a salamander. The opera, **Undine,** has a water-sprite as heroine. And, of course, the tale **"Der Elementargeist"** also has a creature of this category, a salamander. All the traditional mythical sources added together, however, do not constitute Hoffmann's entire mythology, but are merely some of the vocabulary words of his poetic language. Again, as in **"Der goldne Topf,"** we have pieces of myths drawn from "sources"; but they are incorporated into Hoffmann's personal mythical cosmos: a meaningful, triadically structured universe, with ambiguous blendings of the three realms.

Finally it should be pointed out that in **"Die Königsbraut"** Hoffmann succeeded to a limited degree in creating another mythical landscape—one that endows nature with a metaphysical depth by using fantastic images. Its subtitle is, after all, "ein nach der Natur entworfenes Märchen." Yet the demonic trend of **"Die Bergwerke zu Falun"** is still present in it, for the author takes us briefly to the edge of the abyss of the underworld and, for a brief moment, among the fiendish demons themselves. Hoffmann created no fully-formed and consistent myth of a bright, sunny landscape, with one possible and magnificent exception: **"Das fremde Kind."**

In **"Die Königsbraut,"** Hoffmann seems to have exhausted the possibilities of his underworld. After its writings, he did not methodically explore any more areas of it, although its emblems are still utilized as they had been in **"Das Fräulein von Scuderi."** Few writers since Dante had explored an underworld so thoroughly as Hoffmann.

Notes

1. "The Allusions to Schiller's *Der Geisterseher* in E. T. A. Hoffmann's 'Das Majorat:' Meaning and Background," *German Quarterly,* XXXII (1959), 341-355.

2. Cf. VII, 139: 41ff.; also the frequent figures of speech throughout the story using the word "Teufel," "teuflisch," etc.

3. For an interpretation that places positive emphasis on Cardillac rather than Frl. von Scuderi, see Marianne Thalmann's "E. T. A. Hoffmanns 'Fräulein von Scuderi'," *Monatshefte für deutschen Unterricht,* XLI (1949), 107-116. Professor Thalmann's argument is evolved out of Cardillac's majesty as a demonic master-figure and absolutely dedicated artist. Fräulein von Scuderi is seen merely as the "Detektiv auf der Suche nach dem wahren Mörder," and her investigation activity as "ein sehr damenhaftes Abhören von Konfessionen, die ihrer altjüngferlichen Sanftmut zufliegen." I consider this description an unjustified and unnecessary minimization of this grand lady's character. Cardillac's majesty need not be purchased at the expense of the "Fräulein," for they are in totally different categories. There is no reason why we should not allow her gentle, yet powerful humanity and unerring conscience to stand side-by-side with the artist's magnificent demonry in a disturbing, but beautiful dissonance that can be resolved only by Cardillac's "Künstlermärtyrertum." Professor Thalmann portrays Cardillac with a sensitivity and power that is indeed rare among Hoffmann scholars, and I believe her portrayal, in itself, perfectly accurate. But one should not overlook the evergrowing realistic humanism that is present in Frl. von Scuderi and other characters of Hoffmann's later works, culminating in the synthesis of artistic mastery and humanity in Meister Abraham.

James M. McGlathery (essay date summer 1966)

SOURCE: McGlathery, James M. "The Suicide Motif in E. T. A. Hoffmann's 'Der Goldne Topf.'" *Monatshefte* 58, no. 2 (summer 1966): 115-23.

[*In the following essay, McGlathery speculates on the nature of Anselmus's death in "Der goldne Topf." Drawing from Hoffmann's descriptions of suicide fantasies in his journal writings, McGlathery contends that Anselmus, who suffers from similar phantasmagorical visions, actively courts death in order to discover proof of his own immortality.*]

Since E. T. A. Hoffmann's letters indicate that he cherished **"Der goldne Topf"** as his masterpiece,[1] his interpreters have dwelt at length on this enigmatic tale, and at least two detailed studies of it have appeared in the past fifteen years.[2] The story is interpreted as though it were a *Bildungsroman* in fairy-tale form, for Anselmus' weird adventures obviously concern his initiation into poetically conceived truths about man and the universe.[3] Thus it is surprising that the interpreters ignore the problem of Anselmus' mortal end, because prior to Thomas Mann's *Zauberberg* the death of the hero in a *Bildungsroman* was unacceptable. Keller's Grüner Heinrich originally died of melancholy remorse, but in the revised version a conventional ending was substituted. Even Mann, like Hoffmann, left the hero's death a matter of conjecture. In **"Der goldne Topf"** Anselmus quits the confines of mortal life, but whether he dies or how he dies goes unsaid. It is surprising that the possibility of Anselmus' suicide has not been advanced, because on one occasion he almost puts an end to his life involuntarily and on another he begs for death as an escape from phantasmagorical torture. To be sure, the eventual suicide, if it occurs, is glossed over deliberately. It appears, however, that Hoffmann left the circumstances of Anselmus' death unclear for personal, as well as for aesthetic reasons.

Not until the publication of Hoffmann's diaries in 1915, more than a century after **"Der goldne Topf"** (1814) first appeared, did it become known that Hoffmann had experienced suicide fantasies in connection with his romantic interest in his young Bamberg music pupil, Julia Marc. That **"Der goldne Topf"** is a poetic retelling of these experiences is suggested by the date of the denouement. The fourth of February is one of the two dates in Hoffmann's diary for 1812 on which he refers to the *Liebestod* fantasies (3 February is the other).[4] The significance of the date seems emphasized by the fact that no other simple calendar date is mentioned in **"Der goldne Topf."** Ascension Day, on which the story opens, and the autumnal equinox, during which Liese produces the mirror, are both celestially determined dates with obvious symbolic import. Furthermore, Hoffmann calls attention to 4 February through his manipulation of chronology. Anselmus is freed from the glass bottle and is united with Serpentina in October, but the narration is arranged in such a way that his arrival in Atlantis seems to be postponed until sometime after 4 February. This is only an illusion, of course, because the events of the apotheosis are divorced from historical chronology. The pretended reason for the delay is that the author is unable to envision Anselmus' apotheosis until Archivarius Lindhorst invites him over for a drink of his magic punch.

It could be argued that the date of the denouement was chosen because Hoffmann wished to name his bourgeois heroine Veronika and 4 February is her saint's day. But Hoffmann chose the name Anselmus because Julia Marc was born on Saint Anselmus' day, and yet he did not assign the date a function in the story. In each case the name was chosen because of the significance of the date. Indeed, it may be that a subsequent association of 4 February with the legend of Saint Veronica did give rise to a curious passage in **"Der goldne Topf."** The legendary Veronica was a pious woman who gave her handkerchief to Christ as he bore the cross to the Crucifixion. Hoffmann's Veronika, too, seems to be moved with compassionate awareness of Anselmus' suffering and sacrifice. When she accepts Heerbrand's marriage proposal (on 4 February) she asks him to carry out a ritual for her which, unknown to Heerbrand, amounts to a sentimental farewell to Anselmus (240.7).[5] The fragments of a magic mirror which has enabled her to communicate with him until the moment of his death are to be dropped from the Elbe river bridge at midnight. Thus Veronika apparently believes together with the "Kreuzschüler und Praktikanten" that Anselmus was standing on the bridge prior to his death and was not imprisoned in a glass bottle on a shelf in Lindhorst's library, as Anselmus believes (233.14).

Anselmus' suicide seems presaged by two related incidents involving the river, both of which occur early in the story. Anselmus fancies that he sees Serpentina, the metaphysical heroine in the tale, swimming in the river (it is really the reflection of a fireworks display cel-

ebrating Ascension Day), and without thinking for a moment of the danger he starts to plunge into the water. In a famous literary borrowing Heine uses the situation (in "Seegespenst") as a humorous, self-ironic example of the perils involved in romantic daydreaming. Unlike Heine, Hoffmann portrays Anselmus' lapse of common sense as being magically motivated. A short time earlier, at sunset, Anselmus had indeed seen Serpentina plunge from the river bank into the water. It could be said that Anselmus is following her example as though hypnotically and that Lindhorst has introduced a suicide urge into Anselmus' subconscious mind. The moment of Anselmus' death—his release from the crystal bottle—would seem to be prefigured by the shattering of the crystal bells "im schneidenden Mißton" when Lindhorst thunders out to his daughters the command: "Hei-hei-Her u-u-u nter-Her u-u-u nter!" (181.42)

One of the incongruities which has been ignored by interpreters of **"Der goldne Topf"** concerns Liese's prophecy of a "fall into the crystal," whereas Anselmus does not suffer a physical fall, but rather is enveloped by a crystalline mass. Liese claims nonetheless that her prophecy has come true. There are then two explanations: either Liese does not mean to specify that Anselmus must fall into the crystal, but only that he is to meet a tragic fate in the crystal bottle, or she is talking not so much about the imprisonment in the crystal bottle as about its consequence for Anselmus—his fall or plunge into the waters of the Elbe. The second possibility would seem the most likely, especially because her triumphant words to the imprisoned Anselmus ("Nun dein Fall ins Kristall," 233.42) may be interpreted as referring not to the present moment, but to the immediate future. Furthermore, there is some evidence for a symbolic association of the river with "the crystal." If Anselmus actually did commit suicide, then his body would be lying at the bottom of the frozen river when the story ends. In the last vigil, the author overhears the brooks in Atlantis tell Anselmus that his "image" dwells within their crystalline waters (244.11). Thus, both from the natural and the supernatural perspective the prophecy comes true: Anselmus' body lies under the ice of the Elbe, while his soul abides in the waters of heaven (cf. the crystalline river of life, Rev. [Revelations] 22:1-2). Finally, Anselmus' grave does seem marked for posterity, because Veronika apparently regards a cross which stands on the bridge as his grave marker. If this is the case, then it is symbolically important that the river is not frozen over at this one spot, because Anselmus' romantic faith has dissolved the crystalline boundary between life and the beyond. In the moment of his death he hears for the last time the crystal bells which had been so much a part of his dream of paradise. The harmonious sounding of the bells becomes so powerful that it shatters the crystal bottle, and Anselmus is released. In Atlantis the crystal has turned to water.

Supernatural elements predominate in **"Der goldne Topf,"** but Anselmus' victory over death is rather obviously the joker in Hoffmann's poetic double-dealing. Except for the apotheosis, the hero's adventures might be interpreted as poetically conceived projections of his inner visions. This impression is reinforced when, after the hero's death, the author injects himself into the story to carry forward poor Anselmus' last great vision. Be this as it may, one point nevertheless is clear: Anselmus' salvation can be nothing short of an act of divine grace. This is underscored by the fact that in each of the three mythological tales which constitute Lindhorst's prophecy to Anselmus a miracle is required to bring about the happy ending. The blossoming of the lily on the barren hillock (189.16), the metamorphosis of the flowers of the valley (190.21), and the incarnation of the salamander (222.27) all are miracles. In each instance, as in the case of Anselmus' salvation, the act of grace is regenerative. A degeneration originating in despair is reversed by a miraculous revival or rebirth.

Hoffmann of course did not believe in miracles, but he did believe in the almost miraculous reversal of despair. The melancholy depression which tormented him during the Julia crisis gave way to the birth of a poetic idea which secured him the artistic renown which he so sorely needed. His hopeless infatuation with a pubescent girl twenty years his junior had increased his persistent fear that he was losing his mind. The diaries indicate that the adoption of an ironic view of his despairing passion saved him.[6] Throughout the tales which he subsequently wrote, but most candidly in *Prinzessin Brambilla* (1819),[7] Hoffmann attributes to this self-ironic mirroring of romantic despair the healing powers of divine grace. It is this idea to which he undoubtedly alludes in the interpretive digression which he singled out to Kunz[8] as the key to **"Der goldne Topf."** In this passage Hoffmann says that the tale is supposed to lift the veil of Isis so that the reader may discover how she teases mankind (194.12). Thus, we may suppose that behind the sublime seriousness of Anselmus' longing lies an ironic truth about mankind: although the operations of the psyche are predicated on a belief in immortal fulfillment, nature confronts us with compelling evidence that we shall never transcend our mortal lot. In creating man with this dual, paradoxical awareness, nature has been at the same time kind and cruel. Anselmus misses the point of his own experiences, because he lacks Hoffmann's philosophical irony. Unfortunately for Anselmus, it is Serpentina, not Isis who is revealed to him.

Hoffmann's tales abound with Christian themes and saintly lore, and he occasionally indulges in piquant blasphemy. A major case in point is Anselmus' romantic martyrdom, which is not merely saintly, but also Christ-like. It may be said that the association of the Crucifixion with the suicide of a gullible young student

is the tour de force in Hoffmann's mingling of the miraculous with the everyday[9] and of the sublime with the ridiculous. Anselmus' heretical faith exposes him to ridicule, he is beset by temptations which cause him to stray, but finally he gains everlasting life through repentance. However, of the martyrs only Christ is reported to have ascended bodily to heaven. Although Anselmus is imprisoned in a bottle, not nailed to a cross, echoes of the Crucifixion persist. Anselmus is ridiculed and is tempted to escape from his suffering passion, Liese tempts him to blaspheme Serpentina, in his agony he cries out to Serpentina to end his torment, and he makes an attempt to convert his fellow prisoners (who, however, feel no need of salvation because their philistine hearts are not troubled). Furthermore, Anselmus' crucifixion and ascension, which form the climax and the denouement of the plot, are telescoped symbolically in the prophetic opening of the story. Anselmus overturns Liese's basket of apples, that is, he symbolically triumphs over the flesh, at three o'clock in the afternoon (the popularly accepted hour for the end of Christ's Passion), and the date is Ascension Day. Another scene which prefigures the climax—the hallucinatory adventure at Lindhorst's door—begins at the stroke of noon. The awesome final hours of the Passion begin at noon, and, as if to reinforce the association, Anselmus' phantasmagorical torture is heralded by the striking of the bell atop the "Church of the Cross." Finally, the imprisonment itself also begins at noon and, like the beginning of Christ's last three hours, it is accompanied by a black thunderstorm.

Imagery from the Fall of Man plays as ironic and complex a role in **"Der goldne Topf"** as that from the Crucifixion. Hoffmann sets tempter and temptation in opposition to one another; the snake and the apple become sworn enemies. The result is that Anselmus is given no choice between absolute good or evil, since damnation—a "fall" into the crystal—awaits him at either turn. When Anselmus chooses marital bliss, he is punished with imprisonment. When he tries to escape insanity by reaching out for eternal fulfillment, he is punished with death. Ultimately, however, it is neither Lindhorst nor Liese who judges him, but Isis, the goddess whose wisdom consists in her awareness of the irony of human life.

Serpentina's dual role as tempter and redeemer is prefigured by an ambiguity in the snake imagery of the Bible. The topos of the satanic snake exists alongside a prefigurative association of Christ with the bronze snake image which Moses fashions at God's command (John 3:14-16; Num. [Numbers] 21:6-9). John's allusion stresses Christ's mission as Redeemer, for the snake image in the Old Testament was a sign of God's reconciliation after he had visited a plague of fiery poisonous snakes on the Israelites. This ambiguity in the Biblical snake imagery enabled Hoffmann to give symbolic form to the idea that romantic longing is at once the curse and the blessing of mankind.

A plague of snakes is visited on Anselmus as a preliminary to his imprisonment in the glass bottle. The palm trees in Lindhorst's library are transformed into gigantic fiery serpents which wind themselves around Anselmus and then are transformed into a fiery crystalline mass (cf. Rev. 15:2) which hardens to form the bottle. In the Old Testament God releases the afflicted when they turn their eyes to the snake image, and Anselmus is released from his torment when he renews his faith in Serpentina. But the price of salvation is Anselmus' suicide, as Liese predicted. She tried to warn Anselmus when she appeared in Lindhorst's doorknocker, and she did succeed in terrifying him. But the ill-starred Anselmus accidentally grasped the bellrope instead of the doorpost for support and thereby seemingly defied Liese's warning. She thereupon gave him a taste of what was in store for him if he pursued his present course. Liese transformed the bellrope into a snake with fiery fangs which wound itself around Anselmus. Although in this prophetic phantasmagoria Anselmus begged for death, he paradoxically refuses to believe that he is courting death when he later seeks release from the crystal bottle. This time he is blinded by faith and by despair, by the glaringly reflective walls of the bottle and by the glaring surface of the Elbe. He apparently remembers that death cheated him before, and therefore he is possessed by the fixed idea that death would not bring him release now. He would awake the next morning in the crystal bottle, just as he awoke the morning after Liese had given him a preview of his eventual torment and suicide.

A major source of humor in **"Der goldne Topf"** is the identification of philistinism with satanism in the figure of Liese. Philistinism, like the Biblical apple with which it is associated symbolically (204.30, 234.3), offers the temptation of a clear knowledge of good and evil—bourgeois happiness and romantic transport, respectively—and implicitly advocates the substitution of erotic gratification for spiritual fulfillment. Liese, one of many satanic agents loose in the world, subverts romantic faith by peddling false promises of salvation. The story about Liese's father which is told to Anselmus leaves no doubt that Liese is descended from the satanic dragon in the Apocalypse. The dragon is defeated in combat by Phosphorus (by the angel Michael in the Bible, Rev. 12:7), he is bound and exiled to the infernal regions (Rev. 20:1-3), but his work is carried on by numerous offspring (Rev. 12:17), among them Liese. Liese's mission to kill Serpentina is prefigured by the Biblical dragon's unsuccessful attempt to devour the Holy Child (Rev. 12:4). She claims to be trying to save Anselmus by offering him bourgeois happiness, but at the point where she has won him as a disciple, he is sacrificed to madness and suicide. Veronika's reward

for discipleship is little better. Not only does she fail to win Anselmus; at our last glimpse of her she appears as little more than a display window mannequin smiling mechanically at passers-by who pay tribute to the ideality of her newly won bourgeois elegance.

Undoubtedly, it is the subtle and complex use of Biblical topoi and archetypes which explains why **"Der goldne Topf"** succeeds in the matter of artistic form and economy, while Hoffmann's later fairy tales lack this characteristic of the literary masterpiece. But Hoffmann's technique of parodying novelistic genres also deserves attention. Anselmus is cast at once in the roles of the Wertherian and the *Bildungsroman* hero, yet he plays opposite a bourgeois heroine who belongs to the living-space of the Gothic novel. To confuse matters further, his mentor, Lindhorst, is both the wise philosopher of the *Bildungsroman* and an elemental spirit masquerading as the clairvoyant charlatan familiar to the tradition of the conspiratorial novel. Liese, while functioning as Lindhorst's conspiratorial rival, is identified also with the sentimental and the Gothic novel in her roles as the nanny who tells fairy tales and as the fortuneteller who variously prophesies misfortune or foretells the romantic happy ending.

Anselmus' obscured role as a Wertherian hero conflicts with his apparent role as the philosophical apprentice of the *Bildungsroman*. Anselmus' fate, like Werther's, is pretty well sealed from the outset and is put off only by a transitory belief that domestic bliss is the temporal equivalent of paradise. Anselmus' romantic longing is positive, whereas Werther's *Weltschmerz* is largely pessimistic, but the melancholy of the heroes is similar in its origins, and the symptoms in each case are manifest from the beginning. Like Werther, Anselmus does not progress, but vacillates between faith and despair until the issue is forced. In **"Der goldne Topf"** this characteristic of the plot remains partly obscured, because Anselmus at least goes through the motions of the *Bildungsroman* apprentice. Like Novalis' Ofterdingen and Goethe's Meister, he is exposed to profound truths in stories which he hears or in manuscripts which he reads. Significantly, however, Hoffmann spares his hero the philosophical discussions and broadening travel experiences which ordinarily make up a good part of the apprentice's education. The reason is clear: Anselmus would find it all a bore. Intellectual curiosity is so lacking in him that he makes no attempt to understand the deeper philosophical meaning of the mythological stories. Instead, Lindhorst shrewdly tempts Anselmus with his most passionate interest—beautiful girls. Here again Hoffmann departs from both the tradition and the spirit of the *Bildungsroman,* since Anselmus' erotic involvement with Serpentina violates the decorum observed between Wilhelm and Natalie and between Heinrich and Mathilde. In endowing his heroine with seductive charms, Hoffmann returns to the tradition of the conspiratorial novel.[10] He deliberately ignores the refinement of the love relationship introduced by the authors of the *Bildungsroman,* because his hero's experience of life is subconscious and elemental, not moral or philosophical. Finally, and most importantly, Anselmus' ambiguous fate—his poetic apotheosis, but factual suicide—suggests that his aesthetic education fills him with revulsion at his mortal lot, not with a newly found belief in the goodness of man and the harmony of the universe. His apprenticeship results in anything but a rededication to man and to society. It is as though Werther, not Wilhelm Meister, had been the hero of Goethe's *Bildungsroman.* Intellectual cultivation and broad experience of life play no role in **"Der goldne Topf,"** for these things are of no help to a young man who is possessed by the positive counterpart of *Weltschmerz*—metaphysical longing.

If Hoffmann seems out to demonstrate the limitations of the *Bildungsroman* apprenticeship for coping with the problems of the human subconscious, he also seems intent on laying bare the deeply spiritual origin of *Weltschmerz,* which Goethe's plot somewhat obscures. Goethe leaves the way open to a sentimental interpretation of the denouement, for Lotte's rejection of Werther remains at least the immediate cause of his suicide. Hoffmann goes out of his way to avoid this ambiguity. In doing so, he rejects two of Goethe's chief novelistic refinements. Anselmus is once more the semi-ridiculous romantic daydreamer, and the fairy tale ending of the sentimental novel is restored. Recognizing that Goethe's handicap lies in an apparent glorification of suicide, Hoffmann rejects the expedient of overmotivation in favor of obscuring the suicide from all readers except those who refuse to be put off by poetic embellishments.

Veronika does not suffer tragically, for her nightmarish experiences lack the metaphysical dimension of Anselmus' romantic urge. Her adventures are outgrowths of her reading of Gothic romances (212.35). Although it is Aurelie in Hoffmann's ***Elixiere des Teufels*** who is identified specifically as a reader of Matthew Gregory Lewis' Gothic classic, *The Monk,*[11] Veronika is associated at least indirectly with Lewis' heroines, since the magic mirror which Liese produces for her finds its model in *The Monk.*[12] Veronika prefers to confine her contacts with the supernatural realm to the witching hour, whereas Anselmus finds himself pursued by phantasmagorical experiences in broad daylight, particularly at high noon. Anselmus lacks Veronika's strong sense of literary convention, and furthermore, unlike Werther, he apparently has had little exposure to romantic literature. The sudden entrance of poetic visions into his extremely pedestrian life stuns him into a fateful suspension of disbelief.

Lindhorst and Serpentina promise Anselmus eternal bliss, yet Atlantis is identified not as Heaven, but rather as the realm of the elemental spirits. According to occult teachings, elemental spirits are pitiable creatures, in so far as they long for eternal life, but lack an immortal soul.[13] They court human beings, because only through marriage to them can they enter heaven. Thus, Hoffmann appears to have written a cruelly humorous tale about the halt leading the blind. The elemental spirits have usurped the role of the angels as messengers of paradise, and this results in a paradoxical absurdity. An elemental spirit who believes in his immortality cuts a ridiculous figure, but a human being who seeks proof of his immortality by accepting the claim of elemental spirits to eternal life is that much more ridiculous. We know from Hoffmann's letters that the golden pot originally was a jeweled chamber pot with which the hero was to be rewarded for his gullibility.[14] In the final version the pot became simply an objet d'art. Hoffmann even considered changing the title of the story, since the golden pot was no longer central to the plot, but he became convinced that the title should stand anyway.[15] Although his motive in this remains unclear, it should be remembered that at one prominent place in Hoffmann's works the bodily function in question receives symbolic importance as giving the lie to the hero's belief in his immortality.[16] And indeed, Hoffmann, as a disciple of Isis, must have looked upon Anselmus' "Leben in der Poesie" as simply the bewitching dream of eternal bliss which haunts all men, in one form or another, and which haunts even elemental spirits, according to occult lore.

Notes

1. Letter to Kunz, March 4, 1814, *E. T. A. Hoffmann im persönlichen und brieflichen Verkehr,* ed. Hans von Müller (Berlin, 1912), II, p. 195. (Hereafter abbreviated "*Bw.*"). Also letter to Hippel, Aug. 30, 1816, *Bw.,* I, p. 263.

2. Robert Mühlher, "Liebestod und Spiegelmythe in E. T. A. Hoffmanns Märchen 'Der goldne Topf,'" in Mühlher, *Dichtung der Krise* (Vienna, 1951), pp. 41-95, and Kenneth G. Negus, "E. T. A. Hoffmann's 'Der goldne Topf.' Its Romantic Myth," *GR* [*Germanic Review*] XXXIV (1959), 262-275.

3. Marianne Thalmann documented Hoffmann's obvious indebtedness to the *Bildungsroman* in *Der Trivialroman des 18. Jahrhunderts und der romantische Roman* (Berlin, 1923).

4. *E. T. A. Hoffmanns Tagebücher und literarische Entwürfe,* ed. Hans von Müller (Berlin, 1915), I, p. 108. (Hereafter abbreviated "*Tb.*").

5. All references to page and line of the text refer to *E. T. A. Hoffmanns Werke,* ed. Georg Ellinger, 2nd ed. (Berlin, 1927), Vol. I.

6. *Tb.,* (1812) Jan. 19, p. 103; April 27, p. 126; April 29, p. 127.

7. *Werke,* ed. Ellinger, X, p. 64, line 42 ff.

8. *Bw.,* II, p. 190 (Jan. 16, 1814).

9. Letter to Kunz, March 4, 1814, *Bw.,* II, p. 195.

10. Cf. Thalmann, *Der Trivialroman,* for a useful study of elements common to the *Bildungsroman* and to its precursor, the conspiratorial novel.

11. *Werke,* ed. Ellinger, II, p. 192, line 22 ff.

12. *Ambrosio; or the Monk.* A Romance. 4th ed. (London, 1798), II, p. 265:

   'Though you shunned my presence, all your proceedings were known to me; nay, I was constantly with you in some degree, thanks to this most precious gift!'

   With these words she drew from beneath her habit a mirror of polished steel, the borders of which were marked with various strange and unknown characters.

   '. . . On pronouncing certain words, the person appears in it on whom the observer's thoughts are bent. . . .'

13. Paul Sucher, *Les sources du merveilleux chez E. T. A. Hoffmann* (Paris, 1912) documents Hoffmann's knowledge of occult sciences. At the time that he was writing "Der goldne Topf," Hoffmann was composing his opera *Undine,* for which Fouqué himself prepared a libretto version of his popular story. At this early stage in his literary career, then, Hoffmann was greatly intrigued by the occult lore about marriages between human beings and elemental spirits.

14. Letter to Kunz, Aug. 19, 1813, *Bw.,* II, p. 154.

15. Letter to Kunz, Jan. 16, 1814, *Bw.,* II, p. 191.

16. Johannes Kreisler in *Kater Murr, Werke,* ed. Ellinger, IX, p. 220, line 25 ff.

Maria M. Tatar (essay date fall 1975)

SOURCE: Tatar, Maria M. "Mesmerism, Madness, and Death in E. T. A. Hoffmann's 'Der goldne Topf.'" *Studies in Romanticism* 14, no. 4 (fall 1975): 365-89.

[In the following essay, Tatar explores the relationship between mesmerism and poetic inspiration in Hoffmann's "Der goldne Topf."]

Heinrich Heine once advised literary critics to abandon their efforts at interpreting E. T. A. Hoffmann's works; the task of dissecting these tales, he felt, should be delegated exclusively to physicians. In his view, Hoffmann, like Novalis, had made the unfortunate error of confounding disease with poetry.[1] Surely Heine never entertained the hope that physicians would take this statement to heart, nor did he seriously propose that critics turn to medical treatises for their studies of Hoffmann's tales. Yet literary scholars of our own age have not hesitated to document Hoffmann's acquaintance with contemporary medical literature and to draw upon such sources in order to shed light on **"Der Magnetiseur," "Der unheimliche Gast," "Das Gelübde,"** and other stories in which mesmerist trances and related mental states play a significant role in the development of plot.[2]

In Hoffmann's day there existed a vast literature on mesmerism; as early as 1797, F. A. Murhard could cite nearly seven hundred titles in his bibliography on the subject.[3] The theories advanced by the German physician Franz Anton Mesmer (1734-1815) first gained currency in prerevolutionary Paris, where they became the topic of heated debate at academies, in salons, and on the streets.[4] To the many subtle fluids sent swirling into the atmosphere by eighteenth-century scientists, Mesmer had added an ethereal magnetic fluid which he viewed as the elixir of life. Illness, he maintained, resulted from an obstacle placed in the fluid's path through the human body. In order to remove such obstacles, Mesmer allegedly "magnetized" his patients by first passing his hands over the "poles" of their bodies and by then projecting the fluid emanating from his own eyes into those of the patients. The procedure almost invariably induced a so-called crisis (which took the form of convulsions) or a hypnotic trance. Mesmer's ability to cure Parisians of diseases ranging from gout to ennui rested largely on the use of what psychoanalysis now identifies as abreaction and hypnotic suggestion. In the early nineteenth century, however, mesmerism and animal magnetism were used synonymously to designate hypnotism alone.

Although Mesmer's influence and the enormous interest that his theories inspired died with the Ancien Régime in France, the year 1789 marked only the birth of a mesmerist age in Germany. Mesmer's ideas captured the popular imagination and quickly penetrated the literary world. Jean Paul used mesmerism to cure toothaches and extolled the virtues of magnetic phenomena in his "Muthmassungen über einige Wunder des organischen Magnetismus." Fichte kept a diary on animal magnetism in which he recorded observations made at Dr. Wolfart's clinic in Berlin and entered notes on Mesmer's publications. Goethe introduced several episodes dealing with this fashionable topic into *Die Wahlverwandtschaften.* Even Schiller, according to Caroline von Wolzogen, expressed mild enthusiasm for magnetic cures. Countless allusions to magnetic operations and to mesmerist theories appear in Romantic literature, perhaps most notably in the works of Kleist and Hoffmann.[5]

Hoffmann's principal sources of information about the medical and philosophical foundations of mesmerism included David Ferdinand Koreff, Adalbert Friedrich Marcus, and Gotthilf Heinrich Schubert—all three of whom managed to preserve untarnished reputations as physicians in spite of their endorsement of mesmerist doctrines. Koreff, who served as the model for Vinzenz of the *Serapionsbund,* supplied Hoffmann with first-hand information about his own patients and those of Mesmer's dwindling band of disciples in France. Dr. Marcus gave Hoffmann a guided tour of the sanatorium in which he performed mesmerist cures. After this visit Hoffmann noted in his diary: "Zum erstenmahl im Hospital eine Sonnambule [*sic*] gesehen—Zweifel!"[6] Finally, Schubert introduced Hoffmann to the "Nachtseite der Naturwissenschaft" and shaped his views on the broader implications of mesmeric control and hypnotic trances. It was Schubert who suggested to Hoffmann the connections linking mesmerist trances to poetic inspiration, the lucid intervals of madmen, and visionary moments preceding death.

Because Hoffmann frequently indulges in lengthy digressions on mesmerism and generally takes pains to document his sources for these ideas within the framework of his narrative, it is easy to miss his less explicit allusions to the subject. In **"Der goldne Topf,"** for example, Hoffmann borrows from the lexicon of mesmerism to describe the electrifying events that take place in the first two chapters, or "vigils" of his tale. He also explores those states of consciousness which Schubert associated with the mesmerist trance. At times, Anselmus's behavior bears an arresting resemblance to that of a mesmerist medium. In the eyes of respected bourgeois citizens, however, his conduct is unmistakably pathological: both Heerbrand and Paulmann insist that Anselmus has lost his wits. Yet the narrator regards him as a divinely inspired artist, and Lindhorst assures the narrator that Anselmus's happiness in Atlantis constitutes nothing less than "das Leben in der Poesie." Hoffmann's *Märchen* thus confronts the reader with a variety of ostensibly conflicting interpretations not only of the hero's fate, but also of his psychic disposition. The elusive quality of **"Der goldne Topf"** stems in part from certain words, phrases, and metaphors that Hoffmann uses to depict the mental state of his hero. To a great extent this vocabulary derives from nineteenth-century psychology, and for this reason a study of Hoffmann's allusions to contemporary views on mesmerism and madness can enlarge our understanding of his work.

I

The first vigil of **"Der goldne Topf"** reveals Anselmus's predisposition to mesmerist control. After inadvertently upsetting an applecart, Anselmus is obliged to compensate its irate proprietress for damages. He feels compelled to escape from the crowd that has witnessed his humiliation and somewhat reluctantly resolves to forego the Ascension Day festivities. Brooding over his misfortune in the shade of an elder tree near the Elbe, he indulges in an extensive reverie about the sublime delights of the local celebration. Strange melodies and whispers issuing from the tree distract him from his thoughts and rivet his attention upon the deep blue eyes of a snake entwined in its branches. The serpentine movements in the tree, the steady gaze of the seductive eyes, and the melodic rustling of leaves all seem to have a mesmerizing effect on Anselmus, just as the visionary experience that follows in the wake of these events closely resembles the hallucinations of mesmerist mediums.

The description of the landscape, suggestive of the classical *locus amoenus,* echoes the setting for a mesmerist scene in Kleist's *Käthchen von Heilbronn,* but more importantly it anticipates the backdrop of an episode in Hoffmann's **"Der unheimliche Gast."** Angelika, the heroine of Hoffmann's story, is haunted by a recurring precognitive dream in which she feels drawn to a mysterious tree, "dem Holunder ähnlich." In its branches she perceives a pair of human eyes gazing intently at her:

> . . . die Augen [standen] dicht vor mir, und eine schneeweisse Hand wurde sichtbar, die Kreise um mich her beschrieb. Und immer enger und enger wurden die Kreise und umspannen mich mit Feuerfaden, dass ich zuletzt in dem dichten Gespinst mich nicht regen und bewegen konnte. Und dabei war es, als erfasse nun der furchtbare Blick der entsetzlichen Augen mein innerstes Wesen und bemächtige sich meines ganzen Seins.[7]

The reader later learns that Graf S——i, a disciple of the Marquis de Puységur (one of Mesmer's most eminent pupils in France), controls Angelika's thoughts by means of magnetic influence. Although there is nothing demonic about the eyes that peer out at Anselmus, the striking similarities between the first scene of **"Der goldne Topf"** and this passage from **"Der unheimliche Gast"** indicate that Anselmus, like Angelika, is subject to a potent hypnotic force. Furthermore, the passage cited here demonstrates that Hoffmann was well-versed in magnetic practices. Mesmerists revered trees as ideal repositories of the magnetic fluid with which they bathed the universe. In Mesmer's day it was in fact not unusual to observe large groups of people tied together around a magnetized tree. Whenever his elegant Parisian clinic was filled to capacity, Mesmer would regularly magnetize a tree for the benefit of his patients. In Bayonne, Puységur mesmerized a tree on the village green and, with full support from local officials, sent ailing peasants to absorb its salubrious emanations.

The serpentine mesmerist of **"Der goldne Topf"** seems, however, to possess electrical rather than magnetic properties. When Serpentina extends her body out of the tree toward Anselmus, she jolts him with an "elektrischer Schlag" (I, 183). Sitting next to Serpentina, Anselmus imbides the "elektrische Wärme ihres Körpers" (I, 227). He marvels at "die schlanken in tausend Funken blitzenden Leiber" (I, 201) of Serpentina and her sisters. If we recall that Galvani conducted his experiments on animal electricity at the same time that Mesmer was using animal magnetism to cure his patients in France, it is not surprising to find that a character in **Kater Murr** speaks of an "elektrisches Fluidum" (III, 424) in connection with animal magnetism. Electricity and magnetism were both regarded as universally diffused and incomparably subtle fluids that penetrate and surround all matter. Mesmer's own magnetic apparatus closely resembled the Leyden jars and electrical machines designed by eighteenth-century scientists to produce electrical effects on a grand scale. And electricity, like magnetism, was considered the essence of the life force—a magical power that promised to restore health by renewing the harmony between man and nature.[8]

Serpentina appears to have inherited her salutary electrical properties from her maternal grandfather Phosphorus. The myth narrated by Lindhorst in the third vigil contains the history of Serpentina's ancestors, Phosphorus and his consort the *Feuerlilie*. When the lily first encountered Phosphorus, she was inflamed with love for him and implored him to remain with her. He, however, warned that

> die Sehnsucht, die jetzt dein ganzes Wesen wohltätig erwärmt, wird in hundert Strahlen zerspaltet, dich quälen und martern, denn der Sinn wird die Sinne gebären, und die höchste Wonne, die der Funke entzündet, den ich in dich hineinwerfe, ist der hoffnungslose Schmerz, in dem du untergehst, um aufs neue fremdartig emporzukeimen.—Dieser Funke ist der Gedanke!

> (I, 192-93)

Sparks also fly when Anselmus meets Serpentina. The spark that this bewitching green snake casts into Anselmus also kindles thought, and thought, as Anselmus himself observes, represents Serpentina's love. Gazing at Serpentina, he experiences "ein nie gekanntes Gefühl der höchsten Seligkeit und des tiefsten Schmerzes" (I, 183). Whenever Anselmus's thoughts dwell on Serpentina, the narrator introduces a new variation of the oxymoron "wonnevoller Schmerz" to render the intensity of Anselmus's emotions. Schubert, one of Hoffmann's mentors in psychological matters, held that this combination of feelings is most likely to surface when the so-called cerebral system of nerves, which serves as the seat of consciousness, yields control to the ganglionic system of nerves, which governs involuntary behavior and unconscious mental processes.[9] The dream, the mesmerist trance, intoxication, and madness exemplify states in which the activity of the cerebral system is in-hibited and the sensations of "Wonne" and "Schmerz" are especially intensified. Schubert also argued that such mental states are characterized by a heightening of cognitive powers.[10] It is, of course, through Serpentina's influence that Anselmus attains cognition—"die Erkenntnis des heiligen Einklangs aller Wesen" (I, 254).

Electrical sparks sent forth by mesmerizing gazes kindle Anselmus's longing for Serpentina, just as electrical energy fires the passions of other figures in Hoffmann's tales. At a performance of Mozart's *Don Juan*, the narrator of the **Fantasiestücke** divines the presence of a woman who fixes "den durchdringenden Blick ihres seelenvollen Auges" (I, 70) on him. Her deep blue eyes emit sparks and flashes of light that ignite his imagination and transport him into a mental state which he describes as "eine Art Somnambulismus." That evening he returns to his box at the opera with the hope of meeting the enigmatic Donna Anna once again. "Ein warmer elektrischer Hauch" (I, 78) discloses her presence. The narrator concludes his story by apostrophizing a distant spiritual realm that he now hopes to enter. It is a world "wo ein unaussprechlicher, himmlischer Schmerz, wie die unsäglichste Freude, der entzückten Seele alles auf Erden Verheissene über alle Massen erfüllt!" (I, 78).

"Das öde Haus" outlines a strikingly similar situation. Theodor, the narrator, is captivated by a woman whom he surreptitiously observes through a magical looking-glass. He finally resolves to rid himself of the obsession with her image by discarding the mirror, but precisely at that moment he perceives the reflection of her celestial eyes: ". . . ja ihr Blick war auf mich gerichtet und strahlte bis ins Herz hinein. Jenes Grausen, das mich plötzlich ergriffen, liess von mir ab und gab Raum dem wonnigen Schmerz süsser Sehnsucht, die mich mit elektrischer Wärme durchglüht" (I, 471).

In a suggestive study of language and style in Hoffmann's works, Helmut Müller isolates and analyzes phrases that Hoffmann repeatedly used to punctuate the transition from a world of everyday reality to the realm of the poetic imagination.[11] The imagery of these recurring expressions, or *Konflikt-Formel* as Müller calls them, forms a consistent and coherent pattern. Whenever sparks fly, eyes flash, or electricity pulses through the atmosphere, we know that the hero is about to enter a strange and marvelous fairy-tale world—in **"Der goldne Topf"** a magical kingdom harboring enchanting serpents, loquacious plants, and temperamental salamanders. It is a realm which radiates heat, sheds light, and casts reflections. On the other hand, images of coldness and rigidity signal either a return to the prosaic life of bourgeois society or, as I will later discuss in detail, exposure to the demonic potential of "das ferne Geisterreich." The sensation of chilly water coursing through the veins often precipitates the hero's rude awakening. He feels as if he has been doused with ice water and freezes with terror. His limbs stiffen to become as life-less and inflexible as those of a statue.

The repeated occurrence of such phrases as "wie vom Blitz getroffen" and "zur Bildsäule erstarrt"—Müller speaks of "manische Wiederholung"—borders on the compulsive, and literary critics have not hesitated to attack what they consider the hackneyed element in Hoffmann's style. Yet these expressions are not arbitrarily inserted into the text merely to evoke an emotional response to the hero's dilemma; in many instances the language of these phrases is inextricably bound up with contemporary psychological explanations for the consciousness of a character. The electrical metaphors, for example, are deliberately invoked whenever the hero enters the realm of poetic imagination in order to suggest connections between visionary experience and the mental activity of the mesmerist medium.

II

In view of Anselmus's constant exposure to radical extremes in temperature, it is hardly surprising that he develops a feverishly active imagination and begins to fear for his own sanity (I, 234-35).[12] Beneath the elder tree he is introduced to the wonders of Atlantis and, for a brief moment, senses a mystical union with nature. When a harsh voice calling from the distance awakens him from his trance, the snakes abruptly slither off toward the river and Anselmus, left alone on the banks, vainly implores them to return. He does not come to his senses until he hears the voice of a puzzled onlooker commenting on his imprudent behavior. Whenever Anselmus enters the realm of poetic imagination, ordinary people suspect that he is "nicht recht bei Trost," "wahnwitzig," or "toll." But a far more dreadful form of madness menaces him whenever he elects to embrace the sanity of the bourgeois world. By repudiating the existence of Lindhorst's poetic realm, he invokes the "Wahnsinn des innern Entsetzens" (I, 237) and senses "das dumpfe Brausen des Wahnsinns" (I, 240). For Hoffmann, these two versions of madness—one divine, the other demonic—represent a benign and a perilous form of consciousness. The mental state defined as insanity by the bourgeois world figures as a means of cognition, a vehicle for transcending the limitations of the empirical world, while the second far more terrifying form of madness, serves as a punishment for deviation from the path leading to cognition.

Madness as a source of poetic inspiration can be traced back to Plato. In the *Phaedrus,* Socrates identifies four types of divine madness, one of them being that of men possessed by the Muses. Artists who surrender themselves entirely to the divine afflatus and who become wisely passive and receptive vessels of such an influence are especially vulnerable to this form of madness. Like spiritual mediums, they achieve their finest results by yielding to impalpable forces. But as Berganza, the canine interlocutor of the *Fantasiestücke,* recognizes, bourgeois society feels nothing but contempt for these artists:

> In gewissem Sinn ist jeder nur irgend exzentrische Kopf wahnsinnig, und scheint es desto mehr zu sein, je eifriger er sich bemüht, das äussere matte tote Leben durch seine inneren glühenden Erscheinungen zu entzünden. Jeden, der einer grossen heiligen Idee, die nur der höheren göttlichen Natur eigen, Glück, Wohlstand, ja selbst das Leben opfert, schilt gewiss *der,* dessen höchste Bemühungen im Leben sich endlich dahin konzentrieren, besser zu essen und zu trinken, und keine Schulden zu haben, wahnsinnig.

(I, 98)

Hoffmann's views on madness are informed not only by a Platonic tradition that became infused with fresh meaning through its affinity with mesmerist doctrines, but also by a current of thought issuing from contemporary psychological theories. In order to underscore the pathological traits of his artists and ultimately to show that poetic inspiration corresponds to the bourgeois concept of insanity, Hoffmann draws on terminology used by nineteenth-century physicians to define madness. New developments in mental therapy comprised the principal topic of his conversations with Dr. Marcus, director of an asylum near Bamberg. It was undoubtedly on Marcus's recommendation that Hoffmann read Philippe Pinel's pioneering *Traité médico-philosophique sur l'aliénation mentale, ou la manie* and later its German counterpart, Johann Christian Reil's *Rhapsodieen über die Anwendung der psychischen Curmethode auf Geisteszerrüttungen.* Hoffmann's tales are filled with allusions to Reil's ideas, and industrious editors have not failed to draw the obvious parallels in their exhaustive commentaries on Hoffmann's works.[13]

Before examining connections between the *Rhapsodieen* and **"Der goldne Topf,"** it might prove instructive to sketch briefly Reil's biography and to call attention to the work that earned him a solid reputation in both medical and literary circles.[14] Reil launched his career as a physician in Halle, where he held a post as professor of therapeutics at the university and maintained an extensive private practice. The stature of his patients bears witness to his success: both Goethe and Wilhelm Grimm sought his advice in medical matters. In order to establish psychology as a legitimate and independent discipline, Reil helped to found an institute devoted to that branch of study in Berlin. His zealous efforts to promote clinical psychology and institutional reform of mental asylums continued until his death in 1813. His *Rhapsodieen,* more significant as a document recording contemporary psychological views and attempts at social reform than as an innovative treatise, argues for a more tolerant and humane attitude toward the mentally ill. The bulk of Reil's study consists of a descriptive summary of mental aberrations and a detailed program for treating patients.

In his *Rhapsodieen,* Reil divides demented behavior into two categories: *Vertiefung* and *Zerstreuung.* His description of *Vertiefung* concisely formulates what a witness of Anselmus's curious behavior beneath the elder tree might observe:

> In der Vertiefung geht die ganze Kraft der Seele vorwärts in der Meditation, daher sie die Aussendinge nicht beachtet und an äusserer Besonnenheit Mangel leidet. Eben so verhält es sich im fixen Wahnsinn, in dem cataleptischen Hinstarren der Seele auf ein Object, in der Entzückung und im fieberhaften Irrereden. Der Kranke nimmt entweder gar nichts von allen dem wahr, was um ihm [sic] herum vorgeht, oder er nimmt die äusseren Gegenstände falsch wahr, und unterscheidet sie nicht genau von den Phantomen, die seine Phantasie ausheckt.[15]

A person who allows his imagination free reign is particularly susceptible to the perils of *Zerstreuung:* "er lässt gerne seiner Einbildungskraft den Zügel schiessen, belustigt sich mit ihren Geschöpfen, hängt sich mit Wärme an dieselben und wünscht ihnen Objektivität. Allein die Besonnenheit weist ihn aus diesem Feenlande in seine natürlichen Verhältnisse zurück" (*Rhapsodieen* [*Rhapsodien über die Anwendung der psychischen Curmethode auf Geisteszerrüttungen*], p. 104).

The key word in these passages is *Besonnenheit.* According to Reil, *Besonnenheit* and *Aufmerksamkeit* constitute the two attributes which a physician must restore to his patient in order to effect a cure. Reil's description of unbridled imagination corresponds closely to Hoffmann's portrayal of Anselmus's febrile imagination. Anselmus repeatedly translates the prosaic events of an everyday world into poetic wonders. At first he is not certain that his subjective perceptions accord with empirical reality, and he attempts to find a rational explanation for his visionary experience. He attributes the voices he hears, for example, to the sound of "der Abendwind, der heute mit ordentlich verständlichen Worten flüstert" (I, 183); the emeralds sparkling in the elder tree may simply be an optical illusion caused by "die Abendsonne, die so in dem Holunderbusch spielt" (I, 183). The air of ambiguity surrounding all of his fantastic visions is made eminently clear by the narrator's use of "es war, als" or "es schien, als" before each descriptive statement.[16] Only after Anselmus is jolted by a force resembling an electrical shock and sees Serpentina's eyes gazing at him does he discard all rational explanations—and the narrator likewise abandons the subjunctive mood. Emeralds now drop from the tree's branches and surround Anselmus; the elder, the wind, and the rays of the sun all speak to him. As Anselmus becomes increasingly entranced by Serpentina's eyes, the activity of nature mounts to an overwhelming crescendo:

> Und immer inniger und inniger versunken in den Blick des herrlichen Augenpaars, wurde heisser die Sehnsucht, glühender das Verlangen. Da regte und bewegte sich alles, wie zum frohen Leben erwacht. Blumen und Blüten dufteten um ihn her, und ihr Duft war wie herrlicher Gesang von tausend Flötenstimmen und was sie gesungen, trugen im Widerhall die goldenen vorüberfliehenden Abendwolken in ferne Lande.

> (I, 183-84)

Anselmus comes to his senses when a woman who has witnessed his desperate attempt to conjure up the visionary experience once again voices her doubts about his sanity. The narrator informs us: "dem Anselmus war es so, als würde er aus einem tiefen Traum gerüttelt oder gar mit eiskaltem Wasser begossen, um ja recht jähling zu erwachen" (I, 185). Reil links demented behavior to dreams—in fact, he defines madness as a waking dream: "Im Wahnsinn träumt die Seele ohne dass der Körper schläft" (*Rhapsodieen,* p. 96). In the dream, as in moments of madness, the vividness of images produced by the unconscious mind rivals reality.

Reil's techniques for restoring *Besonnenheit* to his patients are not always as humane as one would hope. He endorses a Dutch psychologist's suggestion that the best remedy for seizures and fits of madness consists of dunking the patient in cold water (*Rhapsodieen,* p. 192).[17] As soon as Anselmus receives a metaphorical cold shower, he begins to recover the faculty of *Besonnenheit* and banishes the fairy-tale realm of imagination from his mind: "Nun sah er erst wieder deutlich, wo er war, und *besann sich,* wie ein sonderbarer Spuk ihn geneckt und gar dazu getrieben habe, ganz allein für sich selbst in laute Worte auszubrechen" (I, 185; my emphasis). As Anselmus flees from the baffled couple standing by the river, he dismisses his experience under the elder tree as a moment of folly. "Alles was er Wunderbares gesehen, war ihm rein aus dem Gedächtnis geschwunden, und er *besann sich* nur, dass er unter dem Holunderbaum allerlei tolles Zeug ganz laut geschwatzt . . ." (I, 185; my emphasis).

Anselmus succeeds in convincing himself that his vision was generated by an overactive imagination and accepts Konrektor Paulmann's invitation to a boat ride. While gazing from the boat at reflections of fireworks in the river, he catches a glimpse of golden snakes swimming in the current: "Alles was er unter dem Holunderbaum Seltsames geschaut, trat wieder lebendig in Sinn und Gedanken, und aufs neue ergriff ihn die unaussprechliche Sehnsucht, das glühende Verlangen, welches dort seine Brust in krampfhaft schmerzvollem Entzücken erschüttert" (I, 186). This statement is prefaced by phrases which indicate that Anselmus is again passing through the incipient stages of a hypnotic trance. Deeply engrossed in thought, he perceives crackling sparks and flames playing on the surface of the water. The swaying motion of the boat also seems to lull him into a semi-conscious state. In his definition of imagination, Reil gives an account of the inner workings of Anselmus's mind:

> Die Imagination erneuert diejenigen Vorstellungen ohne Gegenwart ihrer Objekte wieder, die ehemals durch die Sinne und das Gemeingefühl hervorgebracht sind. Sie reproducirt sie in ihrer vorigen Gestalt, mit dem Bewusstseyn, dass sie schon ehemals dagewesen sind, oder setzt aus dem Vorrath vorhandner Ideen neue Gruppen und Züge in der mannigfaltigsten Ordnung zusammen.[18]

The deranged mind assembles images of such intensity "dass der Kranke dieselben von realen Objekten nicht unterscheidet und aus der wirklichen Welt in ein Feenland seiner eignen Träumereien versetzt wird" (*Rhapsodieen*, p. 277). Hoffmann, it should be noted in passing, repeatedly uses variations of the term "Feenland" to define Serpentina's world. The narrator of **"Der goldne Topf"** urges the reader to try to recognize the familiar figures of ordinary life in the realm which the spirit reveals in the dream. Such a "Feenreich" (I, 232) or "feenhaftes Reich" (I, 197) is, as Reil suggests, the sphere of poetic imagination.

Anselmus's eccentric behavior bears the earmark of a clinical case of madness; the narrator's account of his condition corresponds to the symptoms of madness that Reil outlines in the *Rhapsodieen*. Knowledge of the *Rhapsodieen* undoubtedly influenced Hoffmann's views on the pathology of abnormal minds. But in one crucial matter, Reil and Hoffmann radically diverge in their opinions. Reil was above all concerned with social reform of mental institutions. Madness interested him primarily as a medical and social problem, and the desire to cure the deranged mind motivated him to write on this subject. Even when he asserts that the madhouse constitutes a microcosm of bourgeois society, he aims principally to divest his audience of its intolerant attitude toward madness rather than to remind his readers of their own aberrations. Reil was by no means unaware of the connections between madness and poetic inspiration, but he does little more than mention this matter in passing. For Hoffmann, on the other hand, the true romantic artist generally behaves in a manner consonant with the bourgeois concept of madness.

Hoffmann does not however reject Reil's therapy. Just as Celionati tries to cure Giglio Fava's "chronic dualism" in *Prinzessin Brambilla,* so Lindhorst assumes the role of psychic healer and rigidly adheres to Reil's directives in performing his own version of a cure on Anselmus. He aims largely to protect Anselmus from the fatal form of demonic madness threatening the budding poet whenever his thoughts turn from Serpentina to Veronika. At the same time, he seeks to cultivate in Anselmus a form of divine madness that may appear to

the bourgeois world as insanity, but which in fact corresponds to a creative form of artistic consciousness. Like Reil, Lindhorst strives to endow his patient with the faculty of *Besonnenheit,* though his interpretation of the term deviates considerably from Reil's definition and is closer to that of another figure in Hoffmann's tales. The eccentric musician Johannes Kreisler argues that *Besonnenheit,* an innate characteristic of the finest composers, is nurtured by the diligent study of music. Beethoven, whose *Besonnenheit* is matched only by the serene control exercised by Haydn and Mozart, composed his finest works by interposing aesthetic distance between his own consciousness and a spiritual realm of musical sounds. The structure of Beethoven's works reveals

> die wunderbarsten Bilder, in denen Freude und Schmerz, Wehmut und Wonne neben- und ineinander hervortreten. Seltsame Gestalten beginnen einen luftigen Tanz, indem sie bald zu einem Lichtpunkt verschweben, bald funkelnd und blitzend auseinanderfahren, und sich in mannigfachen Gruppen jagen und verfolgen. . . .
>
> (I, 47)

Serpentina awakens Anselmus's poetic talent, but Lindhorst disciplines this talent by subjecting him to the painstaking task of copying manuscripts. In the sparkling prism of Lindhorst's ring and in Lindhorst's library, Anselmus discerns the same kinds of images that Kreisler finds in Beethoven's music. Although he does not yet possess Beethoven's serene command over a spiritual kingdom of art, under Lindhorst's tutelage he begins to approach this artistic ideal.

Lindhorst is endowed with the very traits that Reil feels a physician must possess in order to be effective. Reil underscores the value of an impressive gait, built, and voice and attaches special importance to a steady and penetrating gaze. The physician must inspire fear and respect in his patient. These are the very aspects of Lindhorst's personality which impress Anselmus: "er konnte dem Archivarius Lindhorst kaum in die starren ernsten Augen sehen, ohne innerlich auf eine ihm selbst unbegreifliche Weise zu erbeben. Zumal hatte die rauhe, aber sonderbar metallartig tönende Stimme des Archivarius Lindhorst für ihn etwas geheimnisvoll Eindringendes, dass er Mark und Bein erzittern fühlte" (I, 195). By means of "den stechenden Blick der funkelnden Augen" (I, 202), he creates an appropriately awe-inspiring effect. According to Reil, it is imperative that the patient have full confidence in his physician. "Er glaubt alsdenn anfangs auf Auctorität; und dies bahnt den Weg zum Glauben aus Überzeugung" (*Rhapsodieen*, p. 214). It is, of course, through his love for Serpentina and belief (*Glaube*) in the world of Atlantis that Anselmus secures Serpentina as his bride and receives the lily as her dowry.

Lindhorst's literary predecessor is the emissary, a stock figure of the *Bundesroman*. In a comprehensive study of the League Novel, Marianne Thalmann defines the emissary as the deputy of a mysterious league or lodge and identifies his most salient characteristics.[19] Generally of foreign origin, he possesses superhuman powers, a penetrating gaze, and the ability to change his appearance. It is his duty to guide the novice to the attainment of an ideal. Should the hero falter or waver in the pursuit of this ideal, the emissary stands by to admonish him for his vacillation—just as he is prepared to reward him for loyalty and perseverance. Like the hero of the League Novel, Anselmus serves a term of apprenticeship before he gains admission to Atlantis. When Anselmus appears in Lindhorst's chambers to copy his manuscripts (the archives of Lindhorst's "order"), he is told: "Indem du hier arbeitest, überstehst du deine Lehrzeit; Glauben und Erkenntnis führen dich zum nahen Ziele, wenn du festhältst an dem, was du beginnen musstest" (I, 217). Thalmann also observes that the emissary and the mesmerist physician, a type that makes a frequent appearance in Hoffmann's stories, share many traits. Lindhorst himself appears to be a curious combination of mesmerist, emissary, magician, and astute psychologist.

By returning now to Reil, we can examine the methods that Lindhorst uses to help Anselmus attain "Besonnenheit." Reil begins his description of a psychic cure by positing a patient "der in einem hohen Grade faselt oder kataleptisch und unverwandt auf einen Gegenstand hinstarrt und daher der Besonnenheit und alles Bewusstseyns äusserer Nothwendigkeit beraubt ist" (*Rhapsodieen*, p. 224). He then divides all psychic remedies into three groups. The first category includes physical stimuli—massaging the body's "poles" for a magnetic cure or administering electrical charges for shock therapy—which can induce a pleasurable or painful physical sensation. The second classification comprises objects which affect the senses, especially sight, sound, and touch: "Wir halten nur ein Object vor und rechnen auf die eigenmächtigen Erregungen, die durch die Anschauung desselben in der Seele geweckt werden, auf den Übergang der Anschauung zur Einbildungskraft, dem Gefühls- und dem Begehrungsvermögen" (*Rhapsodieen*, p. 199). When Anselmus lies under the elder tree, he hears melodic tones and whispers. These sounds blend with the perfumed breezes and mellifluous odors of a synesthetic vision triggered by the perception of Serpentina's eyes—a sight that evokes both pleasure and pain and awakens in Anselmus an ineffable yearning. This reverie succeeds in producing exactly what the doctor prescribes: "die Erregung der Imagination, der Leidenschaften und des Begehrungsvermögens" (*Rhapsodieen*, p. 180). Finally, the third group of psychic remedies at the physician's disposal includes "Zeichen und Symbole und besonders Sparche

und Schrift, die bloss dadurch wirken, dass sie die Vehikel sind, durch welche unsere Vorstellungen, Phantasieen, Begriffe und Urtheile, als äussere Potenzen, auf den Kranken übergetragen werden" (*Rhapsodieen*, pp. 211-12). In this case it is actually Heerbrand who contrives the idea of employing Anselmus to copy Lindhorst's exotic manuscripts. Heerbrand, Veronika, and Paulmann all agree that Anselmus's behavior is somewhat eccentric and that his condition dictates some kind of distraction.

The first afternoon that Anselmus works in Lindhorst's library, he hears Serpentina's voice encouraging him and pledging him her aid. After proving his merits in that first trial, Anselmus is ushered into Lindhorst's blue chamber. But he is rather alarmed by the strange hieroglyphs which Lindhorst now expects him to reproduce. Serpentina visits him here as well and provides a second installment to the myth narrated by Lindhorst in the third vigil. Her story corresponds to the text of the mysterious manuscript which she inspires Anselmus to duplicate. Lindhorst's manuscript functions as the vehicle which conveys to Anselmus the wonders of Atlantis. Once the manuscript has been copied, Anselmus deciphers its hieroglyphs and comprehends its meaning. With Lindhorst as his spiritual mentor, he attains a form of divine madness in which he recognizes the harmony of nature. Lindhorst encounters some difficulties in guiding his protégé to this goal, but he ultimately succeeds by following the precepts outlined in Reil's *Rhapsodieen*.

Lindhorst uses the strategies mapped out by Reil in order to capture and hold Anselmus's attention. Reil's cure consists of two major phases. During the first stage the patient is expected to remain relatively passive; he is acted upon by stimuli devised by the physician. Later, however, the patient is obliged to fall back upon his own resources. "Er darí jetzt nicht mehr blosser passiver Zuschauer bleiben, sondern muss handelndes Subject werden" (*Rhapsodieen*, p. 237). This can easily be accomplished by exposing the patient to a dangerous situation that will stimulate his imagination, excite his passions, and compel him to devise a means of escape. "[Die Gefahren] müssen den Kranken weder verwirrt noch muthlos machen, sondern ihm Hoffnung zu Rettung anbieten und durch dieselbe seine Vermögen in Thätigkeit setzen" (*Rhapsodieen*, p. 238). Anselmus plays the agonist for this scenario in the tenth vigil when he struggles to liberate himself from his crystalline prison. Liese tempts him with visions of domestic bliss, but he staunchly defies her blandishments and marshals his forces: "er stiess mit Gewalt, als sollten Nerven und Adern zerspringen, gegen das Kristall—ein schneidender Klang fuhr durch das Zimmer und der Archivarius stand in der Tür" (I, 243). Though Anselmus is not released from confinement until Lindhorst has conquered Liese, he has at least been instrumental in bringing Lindhorst to the rescue. In this last trial he has actively struggled against the forces of evil and, in recognition of his faith and love, he receives Serpentina as his bride.

The evidence of Reil's influence on Hoffmann, though striking, is not entirely incontrovertible. Before discussing the implications of the parallels between the views of the psychologist and those of the poet, it is perhaps appropriate to insert a cautionary note. In the preface to *Prinzessin Brambilla,* Hoffmann responded to a tedious review of *Klein Zaches genannt Zinnober.* The pedantic author of this review had ruthlessly dissected his tale and painstakingly traced every possible allusion to a source. With characteristically dry wit, Hoffmann recorded his delight in discovering this review—without it he could never have tracked down and read his own sources. In the case of Reil's *Rhapsodieen* we can at least be assured that Hoffmann read this work. He mentions Reil by name; he cites case histories from the *Rhapsodieen*; and he even adopts Reil's diction to describe states of consciousness which appear abnormal to the bourgeois world.

III

All of Hoffmann's characters who are blessed with a poetic spirit are beset by the "chronic dualism" that afflicts Anselmus. Their inner sensory faculties constantly produce such appealing images that external reality appears bland and dull by contrast. Totally unequipped to cope with the exigencies of daily life, these artists are equally incapable of transcending its demands. Only a select few, like Anselmus, manage to escape their bourgeois environment and to dwell in a purely aesthetic realm of the spirit. For Lindhorst and the narrator, Anselmus's life in Atlantis constitutes "das Leben in der Poesie." Heerbrand however takes a quite different view and asserts that Anselmus has gone mad. In the months that intervene between the disastrous party at Paulmann's home and Veronika's name day, Anselmus does not make a single appearance in Dresden; the narrator casually mentions that Anselmus has simply disappeared. Readers of Hoffmann's works are accustomed to search for—and inevitably to find—an elaborate rational explanation for each supernatural event. But an alternative explanation for Anselmus's poetic life in Atlantis appears to be conspicuously absent from the narrative. In a provocative essay on **"Der goldne Topf,"** James M. McGlathery argues that Anselmus's suicide could account for his otherwise puzzling disappearance from Dresden.[20] By diving into the icy depths of the Elbe, Anselmus fulfills once again Liese's prophecy, "bald dein Fall ins Kristall," for *Kristall* can refer both to the glass jar in Lindhorst's library and to the partially frozen waters of the Elbe.[21] As the first two vigils

demonstrate, Serpentina's natural habitat is the river, and Anselmus nearly plunges into the water several times in order to prevent her departure. When Anselmus is ostensibly imprisoned in the glass jar, he is, according to the consensus of five other students, actually standing on a bridge gazing into the Elbe. Lindhorst liberates Anselmus from his prison, and "das Glas, welches den Anselmus umschlossen, zersprang und er stürzte in die Arme der holden lieblichen Serpentina" (I, 245). This evidence suggests that Veronika's decision to cast the mementos of her brief flirtation with Anselmus into the Elbe is not entirely without meaning. She delivers them to Heerbrand and instructs him to throw them into the river "von der Elbbrücke, und zwar von da, wo das Kreuz steht" (I, 249). McGlathery marshals persuasive evidence for Anselmus's suicide, but he fails to mention the most obvious and perhaps the most compelling argument for asserting that Anselmus finds death in Atlantis: in order to reach the submerged mythical realm of Atlantis, Anselmus would have to take the plunge and swim through the crystalline depths of the waters. At the moment of his death, then, the vision of Atlantis is bestowed upon him.

Liese's prophetic utterance appears therefore to anticipate both the imprisonment in the glass jar and the descent into the waters of the Elbe. But Anselmus's suffocating experience in the constricting space of the *Kristallflasche* contrasts sharply with the sensation of release generated by the shattering of the glass, the subsequent ejection into the *Kristall* of the Elbe, and arrival in the kingdom of Atlantis. In order to understand fully the nature of the substance in which Anselmus becomes entrapped, we must turn to two other tales in which *Kristall* figures as a medium of confinement.

In **"Die Bergwerke zu Falun,"** Elis Fröbom's dream evokes an association between oceanic depths and *Kristall*:

> Es war ihm, als schwämme er in einem schönen Schiff mit vollen Segeln auf dem spiegelblanken Meer, und über ihm wölbe sich ein dunkler Wolkenhimmel. Doch wie er nun in die Wellen hinabschaute, erkannte er bald, dass das, was er für das Meer gehalten, eine feste durchsichtig funkelnde Masse war, in deren Schimmer das ganze Schiff auf wunderbare Weise zerfloss, so dass er auf dem Kristallboden stand, und über sich ein Gewölbe von schwarz flimmerndem Gestein erblickte.
>
> (II, 177-78)

Beneath this surface Elis sees myriads of virginal nymphs whose hearts sprout metallic plants and flowers. Just as Anselmus feels "ein nie gekanntes Gefühl, er wusste selbst nicht, ob Wonne, ob Schmerz" (I, 187) and tries to jump ship when he sees the snakes gliding along in the waves, so Elis is seized by an "unbeschreibliches Gefühl von Schmerz und Wollust" (II, 178) at the sight of these maidens and desperately tries to penetrate the crystalline surface. Elis later learns that such a vision of unfathomed depths augurs death, and soon after this experience he descends into the depths of a mine in Falun to fetch a sparkling stone which, as he reports to Ulla Dahlsjö, portrays "wie unser Inneres verwachsen ist mit dem wunderbaren Gezweige das aus dem Herzen der Königin im Mittelpunkt der Erde emporkeimt" (II, 194). He does not return from this excursion into an underground realm similar to the submarine world of his dream, but is trapped in the mine and buried alive. In **"Die Bergwerke zu Falun,"** the nether world of *Kristall* is associated with a fall from grace; it is a demonic realm which preserves the body alone, keeping it in an eternal state of suspended animation.

Both the *Kristallflasche* and the crystalline sphere of the "Bergwerke" represent constricting spaces which compel Anselmus and Elis to remain in agonizing limbo.[22] But Elis is never released from his underground entrapment, and the subterranean pit finally becomes his grave. Because he failed to perceive the true nature of the underground realm and confused it with a celestial paradise, he is punished with paralysis and petrifaction. Berthold, the eccentric painter of Hoffmann's **"Jesuiterkirche in G.,"** asserts that in striving to comprehend nature's divine sublimity, the artist must remain on his guard, for "es ist eine Klippe—ein schmaler Strich, auf dem man steht—der Abgrund ist offen!—über ihm schwebt der kühne Segler und ein teuflischer Trug lässt ihn unten—unten *das* erblicken, was er oben über den Sternen erschauen wollte!" (I, 419). Anselmus, on the other hand, only briefly confounds the bliss of Atlantis with the delights of Dresden, and he is ultimately liberated from his glass prison to bask in the blazing splendor of Atlantis, a world diametrically opposed to the frigid bleakness of *Kristall.*

In *Prinzessin Brambilla, Kristall* also figures as a medium of confinement. The moment of redemption for King Ophioch and Queen Liris in the myth narrated by Celionati does not occur until "ein Prisma von schimmerndem Kristall" (IV, 255) melts to serve as the source for a bright, placid lake. As in the *Märchen* told by Klingsohr in Novalis's *Heinrich von Ofterdingen,* the thawing of ice signals the end of a long, cold season and the advent not only of spring, but of a new era.

Ice and fire, emblematic of the terrors and delights of "das ferne Geisterreich," represent opposite ends of the spectrum in Hoffmann's aesthetics. Paralysis, coldness, and rigidity are hallmarks of a zone that imprisons the spirit; luminosity and warmth pertain to the radiant brilliance of Atlantis. The radical extremes of temperature in these two realms correspond to the difference between two artistic modes that Lothar, a member of the *Serapionsbund,* tries to define:

> Woher kommt es denn, dass so manches Dichterwerk das keinesweges schlecht zu nennen, wenn von Form und Auserbeitung die Rede, doch so ganz wirkungslos

> bleibt vie ein verbleichtes Bild, dass wir nicht davon hingerissen werden, dass die Pracht der Worte nur dazu dient den inneren Frost, der uns durchgleitet, zu vermehren. Woher kommt es anders, als dass der Dichter nicht das wirklich schaute wovon er spricht, dass die Tat, die Begebenheit vor seinen geistigen Augen . . . ihn nicht begeisterte, entzündete, so dass nur die inneren Flammen ausströmen durften in feurigen Worten.

(II, 54)

Kristall, however, often appears to blend properties that are normally attributed to fire and ice. In the crystal jar, Anselmus is physically paralyzed by the painful constraints of everyday life, and at the same time he is literally blinded by the glaring light radiating from a poetic sphere. Imprisonment in crystal thus allows him to sense both the chilling gloom of one world and the blazing splendor of the other, but leaves him an alien in both worlds. The narrator enjoins his reader to empathize with Anselmus's predicament by entering the glass jar for a few moments: "Du bist von *blendendem* Glanze dicht umflossen, alle Gegenstände rings umher erscheinen dir von *strahlenden* Regenbogenfarben erleuchtet und umgeben . . ." (I, 239-40; my emphasis). The italicized words anticipate the diction used by the narrator to introduce his own vision of Atlantis: "blendende Strahlen schiessen durch den Duft . . . immer blendender häuft sich Strahl auf Strahl, bis in hellem Sonnenglanze sich der unabsehbare Hain aufschliesst, in dem ich den Anselmus erblicke" (I, 253). A fine mist initially obscures the narrator's vision of Atlantis, but is then dispersed by rays of light that increase in intensity and finally modulate into a bright sunshine that allows him to *see* Anselmus in Atlantis.

Through love for Serpentina and steadfast faith in the world she inhabits, Anselmus's spirit breaks free from its corporeal prison and enters Atlantis. For Anselmus the moment of liberation, the sudden passage from blindness to insight, coincides with the appearance of a coruscating flash of lightning that strikes him to the quick and brings his martyrdom to an end by releasing a radically polarized self. His body seems to remain trapped in the waters of the Elbe, but his soul soars into an empyrean realm of art. Dresden becomes the locus of paralysis, rigidity, and death, whereas the aesthetic world of Atlantis takes on all the warmth and vividness ordinarily associated with life.[23]

Shortly before Anselmus is released from his glass prison, he hears crystal bells sounding a magnificent triad. Serpentina and her siblings are no doubt responsible for the musical accompaniment, for the sound of *Kristallglocken* and *Kristallklänge* and the light of *Kristallstrahlen* constantly attend them and betray their presence. In their serpentine form, they too remain enchanted and await liberation. Serpentina fortifies Anselmus with celestial music and gleaming rays of light. He strains to understand each syllable of her magical language as it resonates within him and illuminates his spirit. At the same time he basks in and absorbs the electrical heat which her body radiates, unaware that this sensation of "elektrische Wärme," as a character in **"Das Majorat"** asserts, indicates that death is imminent.[24] Serpentina's scintillating qualities anticipate the lambent brilliance of Atlantis: rays of light, glowing flowers, and sparkling diamonds transform Atlantis into a world of pellucid clarity.

Since Phosphorus rules over this dazzling paradise, it is not surprising to find that luminosity figures as the most impressive quality of Atlantis. In his *Ansichten von der Nachtseite der Naturwissenschaft,* Schubert devotes several pages to a discussion of the element phosphorus and points out that it possesses lethal properties—decaying organic matter, for example, emits a phosphorescent glow.[25] He connects the action of phosphorus with the inner illumination and heightening of cognitive powers in both the magnetic trance and the lucid moments preceding death. Wherever this substance appears, Schubert finds

> die Thätigkeit des Lebens erhöht, und in einem höheren Maas [*sic*] das Leben selber zerstört. . . . Auf die letzte Weise bewirken die Gifte, von der Verwandschaft [*sic*] des Phosphors, und der Blitz, auf gleiche Weise als ein zu hoher Grad von Leidenschaften eine augenblickliche Vernichtung des organischen Lebens, und bey vielen Wesen fällt der Moment wo das thierische oder vegetabilische Leben am mächtigsten erhöht ist, der Moment der Begattung, mit dem des Todes zusammen.[26]

The blossoming of a flower, that moment in which a plant attains the zenith of its existence and transcends its vegetable nature, coincides with a diminishing degree of biological vigor and the approach of death. In the human sphere, moments of ecstatic rapture and intense lucidity also foreshadow the imminence of death. When Serpentina brings the lily (in full bloom) to Anselmus, she tells him: "Ach, Geliebter! die Lilie hat ihren Kelch erschlossen—das Höchste ist erfüllt, gibt es denn eine Seligkeit, die der unsrigen gleicht?" (I, 254). Anselmus finds fulfillment for his yearning in the love and knowledge bequeathed to him in Atlantis. But we cannot fail to hear, in the background, strains of a mystical *Liebestod,* not unlike the *Pflanzentod* described in **Meister Floh.** In that story, Peregrinus Tyss learned that fulfillment bears within it the seeds of physical destruction. "Das Mysterium ist erschlossen," he declares after Georg Pepusch and Dörtje Elwerdink have mysteriously disappeared. "Der höchste Augenblick alles erfüllten Sehnens war auch der Augenblick [des] Todes" (IV, 813).

Hoffmann did not hesitate to express his personal conviction that visionary insight can be attained only at the moment of death. When he received the distressing news of Julia Marc's divorce and learned of her distracted state, he asked Dr. Speyer to tell Julia

dass das Engelsbild aller Herzensgüte, aller Himmelsanmuth wahrhaft weiblichen Sinns, kindlicher Tugend, das mir aufstralte in jener Unglückszeit acherontischer Finsterniss, mich nicht verlasssen kan beim letzten Hauch des Lebens, ja dass dann erst die entfesselte Psyche jenes Wesen das ihre Sehnsucht war, ihre Hoffnung und ihr Trost, recht erschauen wird, im wahrhaftigen Seyn![27]

IV

The climactic recognition scene of the last vigil, in which past revelations of the unconscious mind are suddenly experienced on a conscious level, crowns Anselmus's bliss. The soul celebrates its joyful union with nature in Atlantis. For a view of the opposite end of the spectrum we must return to the first vigil in which Anselmus's thoughts still cling tenaciously to the "Glückseligkeit des Linkischen Paradieses" (I, 180), to a bourgeois paradise replete with raucous music, potent spirits, and smartly attired maidens. The fundamental tension between these two worlds, the inner vision of Atlantis and the conventional reality of Dresden, sets the plot of **"Der goldne Topf"** in motion. And the plot itself traces Anselmus's development through a series of stages—the trance, madness or poetic inspiration, and death. When Anselmus lies beneath the elder tree, his attention is deflected, for the first time, from a bourgeois paradise to a magical realm of nature. During his trancelike state, he discovers a poetic world of the unconscious mind and senses its harmonious fusion with external nature.

Once he has been introduced to the marvels of this fairy-tale kingdom, he becomes painfully aware of the ultimate poverty of bourgeois existence and finds radical contradictions between the sphere of consciousness and the unconscious. Through discovery of the unconscious, Anselmus begins his apprenticeship as poet, but he also begins to break his ties with the bourgeois world. The thrilling passion he feels whenever his attention turns to Serpentina may be regarded either as a form of divine inspiration or as a mundane form of madness; the perspective of the observer determines the nature of the condition. By drawing on the vocabulary of contemporary psychology to describe Anselmus's frame of mind, Hoffmann ultimately demonstrates that the bourgeois conception of madness is identical with celestial inspiration. The poetic quality of this inspiration emerges most clearly in the eighth vigil when Anselmus transcribes the legend of Atlantis. The composition is unanticipated, involuntary, and spontaneous; it requires no exertion on his part; Anselmus is in a state of ecstatic rapture during the entire process; and the finished product is so unfamiliar and strange to him that he feels as if it were written by another hand. This description follows the classical pattern of composition by poetic inspiration, perhaps the oldest and most venerable form of poetic invention.[28] In the twelfth vigil, the narrator of **"Der goldne Topf"** also attains this exalted state and writes down his vision of Atlantis under similar circumstances.

But revelations of dreams and of the unconscious, as Hoffmann stresses in **"Ritter Gluck,"** remain distinct from true cognition. In an engaging study of the myth of Atlantis, Robert Mühlher suggests that the following passage from *Prinzessin Brambilla* succinctly formulates the main pattern of development that emerges in **"Der goldne Topf"** and demonstrates how Anselmus moves from the realm of dreams to cognition:[29]

> Der Gedanke zerstört die Anschauung und losgerissen von der Mutter Brust wankt in irrem Wahn, in blinder Betäubtheit der Mensch heimatlos umher, bis des Gedankens eignes Spiegelbild dem Gedanken selbst die Erkenntnis schafft, dass er *ist* und dass er in dem tiefsten reichsten Schacht, den ihm die mütterliche Königin geöffnet, als Herrscher gebietet, muss er auch als Vassal gehorchen.

(IV, 257)

The surface of the "goldne Topf," polished by rays of diamonds, mirrors the magical landscape of Atlantis. Like the *Kristall* of the "stream of consciousness" in Atlantis, it brings to Anselmus reflection in both the literal and figurative senses of the word. For Mühlher, the moment of cognition coincides with Anselmus's perception of this surface, for it both preserves and casts back to Anselmus not only his own image, but also that of the thought inspired in him through Serpentina.

The myth of Atlantis is in many respects a poetic version of Schelling's *Ideen zu einer Philosophie der Natur* (1797). According to Schelling, nature evolves through a complex series of interactions between higher and lower forces in which the Absolute objectifies itself in nature. The human organism represents the culmination of this development, for in the human mind nature returns to itself as subjectivity in the world of representation. Thought, however, brings discord and strife into the original perception of harmony in nature by introducing a split between the subjective and objective. But paradoxically it is thought alone (in the form of philosophical reflection) that can reunite the divided elements and restore the identity of nature and spirit. In Hoffmann's tale, the spark that kindles thought in Anselmus produces anguish and despair, but it is also through thought, in the form of Serpentina's love, and "reflection" that Anselmus attains the highest level of consciousness, "die Erkenntnis des heiligen Einklangs aller Wesen."

In order to dwell permanently in the kingdom of Atlantis, Anselmus severs all connections with the bourgeois world and retreats into an aesthetic realm of the spirit. The contradictions between the two worlds are clearly never resolved, for until the very end the narrator per-

sists in applying the technique of doubling. Marriages are celebrated almost simultaneously in Dresden and in Atlantis; Heerbrand and Anselmus find fulfillment in two radically different spheres. Heerbrand, according to the dictates of the *Volksmärchen*, lives happily ever after in Dresden, but for Anselmus, whose spirit is released from its earthly dwelling, fulfillment coincides with death. The narrator, suspended between these two possibilities, is doomed to remain in a state of inner strife, constantly aware of the rift between the everyday world and the supernatural paradise of Atlantis. A resolution of tensions between these two worlds can be achieved only after Lindhorst has married off his two other daughters. In a final masterstroke of irony the narrator suggests that his own poetic composition may well cast into his reader's breast a spark that will kindle longing for the green snake, allow him to see the kingdom of Atlantis, and perhaps even to celebrate his own marriage with Lindhorst's daughter. It is thus the work of art which may bring salvation to the salamander.

Notes

1. Heinrich Heine, *Sämtliche Werke,* ed. Ernst Elster (Leipzig: Bibliographisches Institut, n.d.), v, 302.

2. See especially Paul Sucher, *Les Sources du merveilleux chez E. T. A. Hoffmann* (Paris: Félix Alcan, 1912); Hans Dahmen, *E. T. A. Hoffmanns Weltanschauung* (Marburg: N. G. Elwert, 1929); and Hans-Georg Werner, *E. T. A. Hoffmann: Darstellung und Deutung der Wirklichkeit im dichterischen Werk* (Weimar: Arion, 1962), pp. 84-109.

3. For a discussion of Murhard's bibliography, see Eugen Sierke, *Schwärmer und Schwindler zu Ende des achtzehnten Jahrhunderts* (Leipzig: S. Hirzel, 1874), p. 121.

4. For a lucid account of Mesmer's ideas and the mesmerist movement in France, see Robert Darnton, *Mesmerism and the End of the Enlightenment in France* (Cambridge, Mass.: Harvard U. Press, 1968).

5. Jean Paul, *Sämtliche Werke,* ed. Preussische Akademie der Wissenschaften, Section 1, xvi (Weimar: Hermann Böhlaus Nachfolger, 1938), 9-43; Johann Gottlieb Fichte, *Nachgelassene Werke,* ed. J. H. Fichte (Bonn: Adolph Marcus, 1835), iii, 295-344; Caroline von Wolzogen, *Schillers Leben* (Stuttgart: J. G. Cotta, 1851), p. 238.

6. E. T. A. Hoffmann, *Tagebücher,* ed. Friedrich Schnapp (Munich: Winkler, 1971), p. 186.

7. E. T. A. Hoffmann, *Die Serapions-Brüder,* ed. Walter Müller-Seidel and Wulf Segebrecht (Munich: Winkler, 1963), p. 619. Subsequent references to Hoffmann's works will be cited from

this edition of the collected works. Since the publisher did not assign numbers to the volumes, I have arranged them in the following order. Volume I refers to the *Fantasie- und Nachtstücke,* ed. Walter Müller-Seidel and Wolfgang Kron, 1960; volume II to *Die Serapions-Brüder*; volume III to *Die Elixiere des Teufels, Lebens-Ansichten des Katers Murr,* ed. Walter Müller-Seidel and Wolfgang Kron, 1961; and volume IV to the *Späte Werke,* ed. Walter Müller-Seidel and Wulf Segebrecht, 1965.

8. For an informative discussion of electrical therapy in Hoffmann's day, see Philip C. Ritterbush, *Overtures to Biology: The Speculations of Eighteenth-Century Naturalists* (New Haven: Yale U. Press, 1964), pp. 43-56.

9. G. H. Schubert, *Die Symbolik des Traumes* (Bamberg: C. F. Kunz, 1814), pp. 148-49. Although the publication date of Schubert's study indicates that it did not appear until after Hoffmann had completed the final draft of "Der goldne Topf," persuasive arguments for Hoffmann's knowledge of *Die Symbolik des Traumes* prior to its official date of publication can be found in Hans Dahmen's study of Schubert's influence on Hoffmann. See "E. Th. A. Hoffmann und G. H. Schubert," *Literaturwissenschaftliches Jahrbuch der Görres-Gesellschaft,* 1 (1926), 62-111.

10. Schubert, *Symbolik,* p. 151.

11. Helmut Müller, *Untersuchungen zum Problem der Formelhaftigkeit bei E. T. A. Hoffmann* (Bern: Paul Haupt, 1964).

12. In a veiled reference to "Der goldne Topf," Balzac called attention to this aspect of Anselmus's psychic disposition. The trilogy, *Histoire des Treize,* contains the following passage: "Une bien belle chose est le métier d'espion. . . . Mais il faut se résigner à bouillir de colère, à rugir d'impatience, à se glacer les pieds dans la boue, à transir et brûler, à dévorer de fausses espérances. Il faut aller, sur la foi d'une indication, vers un but ignoré, manquer son coup, pester, s'improviser à soi-même des élégies, des dithyrambes, s'exclamer niaisement devant un passant inoffensif qui vous admire; puis renverser des bonnes femmes et leurs paniers de pommes, courir, se reposer, rester devant une croisée, faire mille suppositions" (Honoré de Balzac, *La Comédie humaine,* ed. Marcel Bouteron, v [Paris: Gallimard, 1952], p. 36).

13. Kater Murr posits his definition of delirium on the authority of Reil and other physicians who wrote on the subject of sleep and dreams (III, 525). In "Das öde Haus," a friend disturbed by Theodor's compulsive behavior discreetly leaves a copy of

Reil's "Buch über Geisteszerrüttungen" (I, 474) at Theodor's home. Cyprian's story of Serapion contains several references to case histories of abnormal behavior cited in Reil's *Rhapsodieen* (II, 22-23). Other allusions to Reil's works are documented in the *Personenregister* of E. T. A. Hoffmann's *Werke,* ed. Georg Ellinger (Leipzig: Bong, n.d. [1927]), XV, 87.

14. For more detailed biographical information on Reil, see Max Neuburger, *Johann Christian Reil: Gedenkrede* (Stuttgart: Ferdinand Enke, 1913) and Sir Aubrey Lewis, "J. C. Reil: Innovator and Battler," *Journal of the History of the Behavioral Sciences,* 1 (1965), 178-90. A complete bibliography of Reil's works, along with several articles on his contributions to medical knowledge, appears in the proceedings of the "Reil-Feier" held in Halle on Feb. 25, 1959: "Johann Christian Reil: 1759-1813," *Nova Acta Leopoldina,* 22 (1960), 1-159.

15. Johann Christian Reil, *Rhapsodieen über die Anwendung der psychischen Curmethode auf Geisteszerrüttungen* (1803; rpt. Amsterdam: E. J. Bonset, 1968), pp. 64-65. Citations from Reil's work will refer to this reprint of the first edition. I quote *verbatim et literatim* and use *sic* sparingly.

16. Tzvetan Todorov's definition of the fantastic is based on this type of ambiguity. See *The Fantastic: A Structural Approach to a Literary Genre,* trans. Richard Howard (Ithaca, New York: Cornell U. Press, 1975), pp. 24-40.

17. Kater Murr is actually cured of his madness by this method. An unappreciative witness of his nocturnal serenades pours a bucket of ice water on him, and a few days later he recuperates from his foolish infatuation.

18. Johann Christian Reil, *Über die Erkenntnis und Cur der Fieber* (Halle: Curtsche Buchhandlung, 1802), IV, 278.

19. Marianne Thalmann, *Der Trivialroman des 18. Jahrhunderts und der romantische Roman. Ein Beitrag zur Entwicklungsgeschichte der Geheimbundmystik* (Berlin: Emil Ebering, 1923).

20. "The Suicide Motif in E. T. A. Hoffmann's 'Der goldne Topf,'" *Monatshefte,* 58 (1966), 115-23.

21. Hoffmann consistently uses the neuter form of the noun "Kristall" (cut glass and crystalware) rather than the generic term "der Kristall" not only in "Der goldne Topf" but in other stories as well.

22. Lothar Pikulik makes this point. See "Anselmus in der Flasche: Kontrast und Illusion in E. T. A. Hoffmanns 'Der goldne Topf,'" *Der Euphorion,* 63 (1969), 341-70. I have also profited from Peter von Matt's discussion of "Die Bergwerke zu

Falun" (*Die Augen der Automaten: E. T. A. Hoffmanns Imaginationslehre als Prinzip seiner Erzählkunst* [Tübingen: Max Niemeyer, 1971], pp. 117-60).

23. For the painter Reinhold in "Meister Martin der Küfner und seine Gesselen," a similar reversal occurs. Reinhold's infatuation with Rosa, Martin's charming daughter, sharply diminishes once he completes her portrait. Putting the finishing touches on the painting, he is suddenly seized by the odd sensation that his portrait embodies the Rosa he loves, while Martin's daughter is a mere imitation of his life-like portrait. He gives up his apprenticeship as cooper and hastily departs for Italy, an aesthetic paradise that he calls the "Heimat aller Kunst."

24. The uncle of the narrator announces that "ein ganz besonderes Wohlsein, wie ich es seit vielen Jahren nicht gefühlt, durchdringt mich mit gleichsam elektrischer Wärme. Ich glaube, das verkündet mir einen baldigen Tod" (I, 527).

25. G. H. Schubert, *Ansichten von der Nachtseite der Naturwissenschaft* (Dresden: Arnoldsche Buchhandlung, 1808), pp. 357-60.

26. Schubert, *Ansichten*, pp. 358-59.

27. *E. T. A. Hoffmanns Briefwechsel,* ed. Hans von Müller and Friedrich Schnapp (Munich: Winkler, 1968), II, 249. The deviations from modern orthography are Hoffmann's.

28. I follow here Meyer Abrams's discussion of poetic inspiration. See *The Mirror and the Lamp: Romantic Theory and the Critical Tradition* (New York: Oxford U. Press, 1953), p. 189.

29. Robert Mühlher, "Liebestod und Spiegelmythe in E. T. A. Hoffmanns Märchen 'Der goldne Topf,'" *Zeitschrift für deutsche Philologie,* 67 (1942), 21-56.

Hermann F. Weiss (essay date May 1976)

SOURCE: Weiss, Hermann F. "'The Labyrinth of Crime': A Reinterpretation of E. T. A. Hoffmann's 'Das Fräulein von Scuderi.'" *Germanic Review* 51, no. 3 (May 1976): 181-89.

[*In the following essay, Weiss discusses the social and political context of Hoffmann's "Das Fräulein von Scuderi." According to Weiss, Hoffmann's exploration of the effects of criminal behavior on the community reveals the underlying fragility of social institutions in general.*]

Interpretations of Hoffmann's suspenseful story **"Das Fräulein von Scuderi"** have, in general, focused on one or both of the principal characters[1] without fully investigating the richly detailed social, political, and cultural context in which Hoffmann places them. However, such features of this narrative as its subtitle, the lengthy account of the crimes terrorizing Paris, as well as the descriptions of life at the court of Louis XIV suggest that the author is interested in analyzing the societal processes in which Mlle. de Scudéry and Cardillac, together with the numerous other figures in the story, become intimately involved. In this paper I will first show how skillfully Hoffmann explores the various factors leading to a grave national crisis, particularly the disruptive effects of a stunning increase in criminal behavior as well as the questionable reactions of the political and cultural leadership to this disintegration of the social fabric. Subsequently I will discuss how a few brave and determined individuals, prominently among them Mlle. de Scudéry, help to resolve this crisis.

After Hoffmann has confronted the reader with the fear and distrust prevailing in Paris by means of his dramatic opening, he circumstantially traces the menacing rise in crime and the corresponding deterioration of interpersonal relationships and social institutions. The purpose of the historical materials which he adapted from Voltaire's *Siècle de Louis XIV,* Pitaval, and other sources[2] is by no means limited to providing the reader with background information or to evoking a certain mood; on the contrary, they help to support the theme of a civilization in crisis. It is Hoffmann's aim to analyze the roles played by dissimulation, distrust, and violence in the ever intensifying waves of terror which pose a grave threat to the stability of French society. While Exili undermines the master-apprentice relationship, Godin de Sainte Croix brings dishonor and finally death to the family of his mistress, the Marquise de Brinvillier. Since the Marquise and Godin put on a show of piety and concern for others, the authorities are, for a long time, unable to penetrate the "undurchdringliche Schleier" (654) covering up the crimes of this vicious couple. The all-pervasive themes of deceit and the subversion of relationships reach a first culmination-point in Desgrais' capture of the murderess. Disguised as a priest he simulates an erotic interest in the Marquise who is hiding in a nunnery. During the second and more devastating wave of murders the number of victims is much greater and therefore the level of fear and suspicion rises markedly. Valuable human bonds—"Verwandtschaft-Liebe-Freundschaft"—are undermined even more extensively than before: "Das grausamste Mißtrauen trennte die heiligsten Bande" (655). As the authorities gradually seem to gain the upper hand, a third wave of terror strikes the frightened city which is even more difficult to investigate. The public's sense of helplessness intensifies further and expresses itself in the idea that the new series of murders is the work of spirits or even the devil.

Already in his exposition Hoffmann's concern with man's loss of control over his life reveals itself. Baptiste is forcibly driven from a wedding by an impulse which he fails to understand, and all the criminals are governed by obsessions which they cannot resist. Thus the Marquise de Brinvillier degenerates into an "Ungeheuer" that is increasingly ruled by the "unwiderstehliche Leidenschaft" (654) of killing indiscriminately for pleasure. No figure in **"Das Fräulein von Scuderi"** embodies the loss of control and the deception plaguing this society more poignantly than Cardillac who, like the other criminals before him, poses a serious threat both to those closely associated with him as well as to the public at large. Like Mme. de Brinvillier he appears "das Muster aller Frömmigkeit und Tugend" (702) and therefore the detection of his crimes is likewise all the more difficult. Whereas we learn relatively little about the motivations of the other criminals, Hoffmann traces Cardillac's obsession back to an event during his mother's pregnancy, but since he associates the other criminals with Cardillac, he may be suggesting that in some way their lives were also shaped by events beyond their control. In addition, they seem to pave the way for Cardillac's crimes. By falling prey to their various destructive impulses they create a climate of violence and dissimulation which is likely to breed further crimes. It is in this context, which is characterized by a wide-spread collapse of moral restraints, that Cardillac's criminality unfolds fully.

J. M. Ellis' ingenious attempt to elucidate the latent meaning of Cardillac's explanation of his criminality overlooks the fact that prenatal influences had been much discussed in late eighteenth century medical and psychological literature.[3] That such influences were real enough to Hoffmann is corroborated by a hitherto ignored entry in a notebook from his last years which is based on a newspaper report:

> Eine im ersten Monath schwangere Frau sieht einen Harlekin auf dem Seile tanzen, als das Zuschauergerüst bricht und sie herabstürzend hängen bleibt—Ganz glücklich und beschwerdelos komt sie nach neun Monathen mit einem Foetus nieder, dessen weiße pergamentartige Haut blutrothe Streifen hat—(Harlekinsjacke) . . .
>
> (V, 903)

Hoffmann is clearly interested in this incident because it, too, illustrates the "wunderbaren Einfluß solch lebhaften, willenlosen Eindrucks von außen her auf das Kind" (691). Hoffmann's contemporaries, then, would in all likelihood have agreed with Cardillac's pessimistic assessment of his life as essentially predetermined by fate—a theme which was of great concern to Hoffmann and other German romantics.[4] Hoffmann demonstrates in **"Das Fräulein von Scuderi"** how fate, through its destructive influence on an individual, can

negatively affect an entire social system. Like Christian and many other figures in romantic fiction Cardillac is propelled by an inner voice, "die Stimme des Satans" (694), which he can only temporarily resist. At those times his conscience reestablishes itself, "eine tief innere Stimme, sehr verschieden von der, welche Blutopfer verlangt wie ein gefräßiges Raubtier" (697).

Cardillac's unsuccessful inner struggle differentiates him to some extent from the other criminals and assures him of some understanding on our part. However, I cannot agree with M. Thalmann who, superimposing the artist-philistine dichotomy on this story, glorifies Cardillac as the supreme artist who is beyond good and evil.[5] It seems to me that Hoffmann, rather than depicting Olivier and Mlle. de Scudéry as philistines, emphasizes their innate moral strength. To be sure, the figure of Cardillac constitutes a variation upon one of Hoffmann's dominant themes, the artist as outsider, but I think that in **"Das Fräulein von Scuderi"** it forms only part of a comprehensive investigation into the crisis of a society. While in **"Meister Martin und seine Gesellen"** (1818) Hoffmann pictures a relatively stable community, he also explores the opposite possibility in such narratives as **"Das Fräulein von Scuderi,"** *Klein Zaches,* and **"Doge und Dogaresse,"** all written within a few years of each other.[6] In these stories Hoffmann focuses on the disintegration of social systems and on attempts to stabilize them, as well as on the role of individuals, institutions, and social groups in these processes.

How are we to evaluate the reactions of the political and cultural establishment to the growing disorder around them? Because of their power and their intellectual qualifications they could be expected to provide leadership in the struggle against the disruption within their society. On the whole, however, they do not fulfill this important stabilizing function. Hoffmann seems to suggest that the sophisticated culture at the court of Louis XIV remains too much centered on itself. Its detachment from the grave social upheavals becomes painfully apparent in the scene in which the frenetic competitiveness of her fellow-writers prevents Mlle. de Scudéry, who only gradually removes herself from this circle, from returning the jewelry to Cardillac:

> Kaum hatte la Chappelle die Szene eines Trauerspiels geendet, und schlau versichert, daß er nun wohl Racine zu schlagen gedenke, als dieser selbst eintrat, und ihn mit irgendeines Königs pathetischer Rede zu Boden Schlug, bis Boileau seine Leuchtkugeln in den schwarzen tragischen Himmel steigen ließ. . . .
>
> (672)

As if to point out the absurdity and artificiality of such self-centered brilliance, Hoffmann almost immediately afterwards describes the tumultuous scene before Cardillac's house in which the viciousness of the mob and of the representatives of authority contrasts sharply with the humane concern of Mlle. de Scudéry. Rather than involving themselves in social issues, these artists and intellectuals make strenuous efforts to appeal to each other's sophisticated tastes and is rather symptomatic for the preoccupation of this group with itself that Mlle. de Scudéry wants to present to Racine a ring embellished with the emblems of art. The selfishness of these artists, as opposed to that of a Cardillac, is not enforced by fate, but is the outcome of a profitable social arrangement. Its glamorous appearance cannot belie the fact that it, too, has negative implications for society. The artists at court are eminently involved in enhancing the power of the king and, in turn, they derive prestige from his grandeur. Rather than functioning as critical mediators between the populace and Louis XIV, they distract him as well as each other from the mounting problems of the nation.

The king's esthetic sensibilities, his predilection for the beautiful and the witty, shield him from the harsh realities of his disordered country. The delegation of judicial power to a special court may in itself be justifiable, but instead of involving himself in the continuous supervision of justice in an increasingly lawless society, Louis XIV is only too willing to be the arbiter of the competitions of his literary protégés. Rather than abolishing or at least modifying the excesses of the *Chambre ardente,* he merely indulges in feelings of shock at the horrors perpetrated by it. The superficiality of these sentiments is proved by the fact that he would easily have been swayed by the poem advocating more stringent measures, had it not been for Mlle. de Scudéry's witty response. The king is so impressed by its pithy form as opposed to the long-winded tirades of the poem that he neglects to analyze the moral implications of her chivalrous sentiment. Typically both the poem as well as the rebuttal fail to express sympathy for the sufferings of the people at large and exclusively focus on various aspects of the life at court. For example, in addition to playfully obscuring social tensions, the poem depicts the king as a heroic redeemer and concludes with a panegyric to him. The repeatedly mentioned graceful smiles and gestures at court as well as the aura of admiration and flattery surrounding the king seem designed to keep life within this privileged setting as harmonious as possible and to ward off tensions encroaching on it from the outside.

In their lobbying efforts, the members of the court have to appeal to the king's esthetic interests. Mlle. de Scudéry is the only figure who learns to use this method responsibly. If it had not been for her carefully calculated performance before Louis XIV, which is based on her striking dress and jewels, her awe-inspiring presence, and above all her magnificent story-telling, Olivier may have had to die. It is only now that the king feels impelled to have Olivier investigated independent of *Chambre ardente* and to halt the further spread of injustice. Previously he had simply shared la Regnie's negative view of Olivier and rashly and angrily discouraged dissenting views, an attitude which, as d'Andilly suggests, may be a politically motivated act of scapegoating: "Der König wird nimmer einen Verbrecher *der* Art begnadigen, der bitterste Vorwurf des gefährdeten Volkes würde ihn treffen" (700).

In addition to hindering the fair administration of justice, Louis XIV also displays a questionable approach to his royal prerogative of pardon. D'Andilly, one of the few characters of integrity in this story, defines the royal pardon as an ultimate corrective to the rationally arrived-at decisions of the law courts and he emphasizes that the king's mercy derives from his "inneres Gefühl" (703). However, the inner conviction and discretion necessary for the proper exercise of pardon is marred by the king's personal preoccupations. For example, when the *Chambre ardente* kills guilty and innocent alike, his power of pardon remains unused. Also, Madelon's beauty as well as her resemblance to La Vallière, the king's former mistress, are regarded as having a decisive influence on his ruling in the Brusson case. The narrator speculates that Louis XIV may have been in danger, "das strenge Recht der Schönheit aufzuopfern" (706).

In view of the failure of the political and cultural leadership to re-establish the rule of law and to help create an atmosphere of trust it is not surprising that a lack of moral fibre is also revealed lower down in the social pyramid. Several times Hoffmann shows the fickleness and irrationality of the city folk and their distorted view of justice. At first they, like Louis XIV, accept la Regnie's suspicions against Olivier uncritically and their attempt to lynch him resembles the actions of the *Chambre ardente* in that it, too, tries to cope violently and impatiently with a baffling and vicious reality. Once Miossens' statement becomes known, the mob again acts violently, this time against le Regnie, which disturbs public order even further. Hoffmann's critical view of this reversal becomes apparent in the following sardonic remark: "Nun erst erinnerten sich die Nachbarsleute seines tugendhaften Wandels, der großen Liebe zu Madelon, der Treue, der Ergebenheit mit Leib und Seele, die er zu dem alten Goldschmied gehegt" (706).

The perversion of justice and the danger of a general dehumanization of society become particularly visible in the machinations of the *Chambre ardente*. Much like the criminals that they try to eliminate from the body politic, Desgrais and la Regnie become the victims of their own obsessions. In the absence of strict controls by the court, a "blinder Eifer" (656) transforms these agents of justice into criminal inquisitors, which destabilizes the society further. Rather than allaying the hatred and suspicion racking the country, they themselves personify these negative attitudes and, as a result, intensify them in others. It is typical of the general collapse of values that the protectors of the people become their enemies and that from their habitually distrustful point of view, angelic Madelon may be just as guilty as the seemingly pious Mme. de Brinvillier. Like this murderess they enjoy tormenting others. Inevitably the loss of confidence in the supposed protectors encourages vigilantism, an extreme deviation from the proper course of justice. Miossens clandestinely takes the law into his own hands because, as he points out, recourse to the legal system might have endangered him just as it did the Duke of Luxembourg.

A conscientious and well-esteemed judge and lawyer,[7] Hoffmann was concerned about possible perversions of justice such as the ones which occurred in Prussia around the time our story was published (1819). As a member of the *Immediat-Untersuchungs-Kommission* he repeatedly opposes the harsh measures taken by the Prussian government against political dissidents[8] and he satirized the misuse of the judicial system for political repression in *Meister Floh*.[9] Hoffmann's scrupulous attitude towards his profession and the law, which also underlies the narrative discussed here, is aptly defined in the following protest against the government's high-handed approach to the Jahn case:

> Wir bemerken hierbei eherbietigst, daß wir demgemäß unseren Standpunkt nicht verkennen und uns frei von jeder ungeziemenden Anmaßung fühlen, wenn wir diejenige Pflicht, nämlich: jedermann ohne Ansehen der Person und Unterschied des Standes nach Vorschrift der Gesetze und nach unserer besten Kenntnis und Überzeugung unparteiische und rücksichtslose Justiz zu administrieren, welche wir als die heiligste in unserem Amtseide beschworen haben, mit der strengsten Gewissenhaftigkeit, mit der unerschütterlichsten Treue zu erfüllen streben und auf der Überzeugung beharren, daß nur Se. Majestät der König unmittelbar die Macht haben, aus höheren Staatsgründen den Gang des Rechts zu hemen.
>
> (iv, 900)

As if to demonstrate the precariousness and unpredictability of historical developments, **"Das Fräulein von Scuderi"** explicates in much detail how, because of their respective obsessions, as well as their lack of moral standards and commitment to others, a wide variety of groups and individuals can undermine a civilization as great and seemingly stable as the one which arose under Louis XIV. However, the story also holds out the hope that the efforts of a few dedicated individuals can eventually avert a complete societal breakdown. Hoffmann ingeniously adopts features of the detective story in order to adequately convey the intricacy of these processes and the difficulty of reestablishing communication and truth within this endangered na-

tion.[10] Even these few characters are in danger of losing their orientation in what Olivier despairingly calls the "Labyrinth des Verbrechens" (694). Olivier cannot help loving the angelic Madelon, but unfortunately this also makes him an accomplice to the crimes of her demonic father, a dilemma which almost drives him into suicide. Mlle. de Scudéry is deeply shocked by the realization that appearances can no longer be trusted. When her innermost convictions appear to be overturned, she swoons[11] and loses her will to live: "So bitter noch nie vom innern Gefühl getäuscht, auf den Tod angepackt von der höllischen Macht auf Erden, an deren Dasein sie nicht geglaubt, verzweifelte die Scudéri an aller Wahrheit" (680). For a while she falls prey to la Regnie's suspicious approach to others and even accuses Madelon of being an accomplice to murder.

However, even before Mlle, de Scudéry receives confirmation through Olivier's confession, her basic trust and virtuousness reassert themselves. Both Olivier and Mlle. de Scudéry possess the inner strength and goodness necessary to overcome their shocking confrontations with a deceptive and chaotic reality. As opposed to Cardillac, Louis XIV, and the other individuals and groups discussed above, they alone are capable of making sacrifices in order to assist others and thus they help to reintroduce humaneness to their troubled society. Unlike Mme. de Maintenon, whose principle it is to shield Louis XIV from unpleasant news,[12] Mlle. de Scudéry courageously confronts him and in contrast to the king and his henchmen she displays the patience and faith in man's capacity for goodness which allows her to counteract the general confusion of appearance and reality. While Cardillac cannot but create only for himself, destroying others in the process, Mlle. de Scudéry learns to use her artistic talents to help others.

Hoffmann attaches considerable importance to the fact that such activism does not come naturally to the elderly authoress. Even though she has been charitable in the past, she only hesitantly involves herself in these ominous events which seem to call for more than a conventional act of charity. Initially we see Mlle. de Scudéry playing her accustomed role as a member of the cultural elite at the court. As such she improvises her concise response to the long-winded poem on the plight of courtly lovers and writes the piece about herself as the goldsmith's bride. To be sure, she painfully realizes that "Worte, halb im Scherz hingeworfen" (662) unexpectedly have detrimental consequences and she is also vaguely aware of the menace emanating from Cardillac: "Und nun hat selbst Cardillacs Betragen, ich muß es gestehen, für mich etwas sonderbar Ängstliches und Unheimliches" (669). But she remains out of touch with the ugly realities outside her group and fails to explore such dark inklings further. In fact, initially she always tries to take refuge in her accustomed posture of dignity and gracefulness. Thus she speaks to Cardillac "anmutig scherzend" (668) and after his departure she is only too happy to be drawn "in den sprudelnden Strom tausend lustiger Einfälle" (669) by Mme. de Maintenon whose unusual outburst of playful humor likewise represents a defensive reaction against Cardillac's disturbing intrusion into this insulated circle. Similarly her parodistic poem on the goldsmith's bride could be seen as an attempt to render the uncanny harmless by laughing it off because she writes it "alle Schauer unheimlicher Ahnung besiegend" (670). One also wonders why she allows herself to attend to the literary extravaganzas of her colleagues and other business at court rather than returning the jewelry to Cardillac as soon as possible. Once more she seems to seek the protection of her role at court but again a darker knowledge haunts her, this time in the guise of a guilt-ridden dream:

> es war ihr, als habe sie leichtsinnig, ja strafwürdig versäumt, die Hand hülfreich zu erfassen, die der Unglückliche, in den Abgrund versinkend, nach ihr emporgestreckt, ja als sei es an ihr gewesen, irgendeinem verderblichen Ereignis, einem heillosen Verbrechen zu steuern.

(672)

Finally, however, the mob scene before Cardillac's house rudely forces her out of her customary existence as an accomplice to the self-centered court-culture. At first she is "halb entseelt vor Schreck und furchtbarer Ahnung" (672), that is to say, she is stunned by both this atmosphere of violence and mystery and her hitherto suppressed awareness of it. But soon her humaneness asserts itself and, having rescued Madelon, she involves herself fully in Olivier's case. By using nonviolent means she is able to extricate herself from the "wunderbare Verschlingungen" (682) as she calls the confusing and labrinthine reality she is confronted with, and she creates a valuable model for others by breaking away from the vicious circle of terror and counterterror. Mlle. de Scudéry begins to experience states of mind which the almost anxiously controlled court culture seems to make no allowance for, namely deep emotions in the quest for truth and the intense disorientation discussed above. She learns from d'Andilly that emotions have to be harnessed in the pursuit of justice and that well-planned lobbying efforts are essential in the restoration of public order. While the tragic world of Cardillac, whom Hoffmann repeatedly associates with animals of prey, remains alien to Mlle. de Scudéry, the dignified representative of virtue, her contact with this world nevertheless broadens her outlook. Under the pressure of events even her creativity increases, as evidenced by her splendid performance before the king, but she remains a minor writer. Whereas Hoffmann admires Cardillac's genius and distrusts his character, he values her personality more than her artistic gifts; that is to say, a true reconciliation between life and art does not take place in this story.

In spite of Mlle. de Scudéry's eventual success and the assurance that Madelon and Olivier will have a secure existence, the reader is left with an uneasy awareness of the frailty of the individual as well as of man's social institutions. After all, how could Mlle. de Scudéry have carried out her redemptive mission if Miossens' vigilantism had not occurred? Also, the tragic end of Olivier's parents and the slaughter of many innocent people raises the question whether society can ever reach a high degree of stability if, as Hoffmann points out, "die ewige Macht des Himmels" (654) does not always intervene against the forces of evil.

Notes

1. See, for example, J. M. Ellis, "E. T. A. Hoffmann's 'Das Fräulein von Scuderi,'" *MLR* [*Modern Language Review*], 64, 1969, 340-350. This stimulating paper also contains a concise survey of research on this story.

2. For an extensive discussion of the sources, see *E. T. A. Hoffmanns Sämtliche Werke,* ed. C. G. von Maassen [München und Leipzig: G. Müller, 1908-28], vol. vii, pp. XXXIV-XLV and 360-385. Quotations from Hoffmann's works are from the edition by Walter Müller-Seidel, Friedrich Schnapp, et al., 5 vols. (München: Winkler, 1960-65). "Das Fräulein von Scuderi" is contained in the vol. entitled *Die Serapionsbrüder* (vol. iii).

3. Cf. *Sämtliche Werke,* ed. von Maassen, vii, 379f.

4. For a discussion of the role of fate in other works of Hoffmann, see, for example, Horst Daemmrich, *The Shattered Self. E. T. A. Hoffmann's Tragic Vision* (Detroit: Wayne State UP, 1973).

5. "E. T. A. Hoffmanns 'Fräulein von Scuderi,'" *Monatshefte* 41, 1949, 107-116.

6. Cf. Jürgen Walter, "E. T. A. Hoffmanns Märchen *Klein Zaches genannt Zinnober.* Versuch einer sozialgeschichtlichen Interpretation," *Mitteilungen der E. T. A. Hoffmann-Gesellschaft,* 19, 1973, 27-44. Walter places this story in the social and political context of Prussia after the Napoleonic Wars.

7. See Wulf Segebrecht, "E. T. A. Hoffmanns Auffassung vom Richteramt und Dichterberuf," *JDSG* [*Jahrbuch der Deutschen Schiller-Gesellschaft*], 11, 1967, 62-138.

8. Cf. E. T. A. Hoffmann, *Juristische Arbeiten,* ed. Friedrich Schnapp (München: Winkler, 1973).

9. In his defense of *Meister Floh* against the censors he points out "daß jeder Schriftsteller von seinem Metier nicht abläßt, sondern sich an Schilderungen daraus ergötzt," and that he has accordingly exposed "zwei der größten criminalistischen Miß-

griffe" (iv, 910) in this story. This idea can, of course, also be applied to the integration of legal matters into "Das Fräulein von Scuderi."

10. For a more detailed discussion of the similarities between this story and the detective story, see Rainer Schönhaar, *Novelle und Kriminalschema. Ein Strukturmodell deutscher Erzählkunst um 1800* (Bad Homburg: Gehlen, 1969), pp. 18ff, 127ff.

11. Lothar Köhn rightly notes that Mlle. de Scudéry's breakdown resembles one of the central conflicts in Kleist's work (*Vieldeutige Welt. Studien zur Struktur der Erzählungen E. T. A. Hoffmanns und zur Entwicklung seines Werkes,* Tübingen, Niemeyer, 1966, p. 158). Ellis briefly compares Cardillac and Kohlhaas (p. 346).

12. In spite of her religious principles, Mme. de Maintenon is shown to be preoccupied with herself. Her jealousy of Valliere and Madelon prevents this proud woman from assisting her friend, Mlle. de Scudéry, in her efforts on behalf of the young couple.

Ronald Taylor (essay date October 1976)

SOURCE: Taylor, Ronald. "Music and Mystery: Thoughts on the Unity of the Work of E. T. A. Hoffmann." *Journal of English and Germanic Philology* 75, no. 4 (October 1976): 477-91.

[*In the following essay, delivered as a lecture in February 1976 and revised for publication, Taylor underscores the relationship between Hoffmann's unconventional ideas concerning music and qualities of irrationality and fantasy in his literary works. Taylor argues that creativity and madness are inextricably linked in Hoffmann's writings.*]

It is a worrying, but hardly surprising, consequence of versatility in a creative mind that critical attention should focus on one facet of this versatility or another, and thus be open to the danger of mistaking the part for the whole, or—to change the metaphor—that we should allow our attraction to one aspect of our subject's personality to produce a distorted or fragmented image of that personality as a whole. Consciously or unconsciously, we are always liable, I suspect, to be searching for unitary principles (beyond the obvious biographical principle, and the not-always-so-obvious psychological one) under which to subsume the individual moments of our own experience and the individual actions of others. For such principles, if they exist, would have both explanatory and predictive power, enabling us to give a comprehensive account of the situations we observe, and to foresee the ways in which these situations can develop. When, therefore, we confront a personality active in a variety of fields, we may find ourselves concentrating into one of those fields all the attributes that we allege to constitute the essence of that personality, explicitly or implicitly detracting from the importance of the other fields.

So it has been with E. T. A. Hoffmann, whose bicentennial birth date is being celebrated this year. The nineteenth century recognised two Hoffmanns—linked personalities but not necessarily equally accessible. The one was the Hoffmann of biographical legend, the bizarre mimic and raconteur, smothered in the alcoholic haze that enveloped the writers, artists, and other dubious elements carousing into the small hours at Lutter and Wegener's wine-cellar in Berlin. The other personality was the Hoffmann of the **"Tales,"** who had established himself with the publication of the four slim volumes of *Fantasiestücke in Callots Manier* in 1814 and 1815, and had acquired for himself entrepreneurial status in the exploitation of a mysterious area of irrational, frightening, and destructive human forces.

This latter identity is the Hoffmann that was uppermost in the minds of nineteenth-century readers, and it is still, I suppose, what Edgar Allan Poe was to call *Tales of the Grotesque and Arabesque* that first come to mind when Hoffmann's name is mentioned. Opinions were sharply divided over the value of these works and the influence they exerted. Hebbel considered that most of them, with the particular exception of *Die Elixiere des Teufels,* were passé, but at the same time admitted, with the critical approval of the realist, "Hoffmann gehört mit zu meinen Jugendbekannten und es ist recht gut, daß er mich früh berührte; ich erinnere mich sehr wohl, daß ich von ihm zuerst auf das Leben, als die einzige Quelle echter Poesie, hingewiesen wurde. . . . Ich liebte Hoffmann sehr, ich liebe ihn noch und die Lectüre der Elixire giebt mir die Hoffnung, daß ich ihn ewig werde lieben können. Wie Viele, die mir einst Speise gaben, liegen jetzt schon völlig ausgekernt hinter mir!"[1]

Richard Wagner, whose later ideas—on opera, on Beethoven, and on the ethos of music—owed a great deal to Hoffmann, and who drew subject matter from his tales, wrote: "Leidenschaftlich unterhielt man sich oft über die Hoffmannschen Erzählungen, welche damals noch ziemlich neu und von großem Eindruck waren. Ich erhielt von hier an durch mein erstes, zunächst nur oberflächliches Bekanntwerden mit diesem Phantastiker eine Anregung, welche sich längere Jahre hindurch bis zur exzentrischen Aufgeregtheit steigerte, und mich durch die sonderbarste Anschauungsweise der Welt beherrschte."[2] In the same year (1827) to which Wagner's remarks refer, Carlyle published a translation of **"Der goldne Topf,"** with the first significant appraisal in English of Hoffmann's intentions and achievements.

Sir Walter Scott, on the other hand, struck an extravagantly antagonistic pose. "[Hoffmann's stories]," he thundered, "are not the visions of a poetical mind, they have scarcely even the seeming authenticity which the hallucinations of lunacy convey to the patient; they are the feverish dreams of a lightheaded patient, to which, though they may sometimes excite by their peculiarity, or surprise by their oddity, we never seem disposed to yield more than momentary attention. In fact, the inspirations of Hoffmann so often resemble the ideas produced by the immoderate use of opium, that we cannot help considering his case as one requiring the assistance of medicine rather than of criticism."[3]

Goethe, following Scott's lead, then asked in rhetorical and somewhat querulous tones: "Welcher treue, für Nationalbildung besorgte Theilnehmer hat nicht mit Trauer gesehen, daß die krankhaften Werke des leidenden Mannes lange Jahre in Deutschland wirksam gewesen und solche Verirrungen als bedeutend-fördernde Neuigkeiten gesunden Gemüthern eingeimpft worden."[4] What "sickness" Hoffmann was "suffering" from, and what kind of "aberrations" his works represented, Goethe does not diagnose, but the imagery immediately recalls his equation of Classicism with health and Romanticism with morbidity.

A different kind of opposition to Hoffmann's influence came from Eichendorff, whose Catholicism was deeply offended by the disturbing, destructive, sometimes diabolical forces that prised open the minds of Kapellmeister Kreisler, of Anselmus, Nathanael, Medardus, Cardillac and other unbalanced, not to say schizophrenic, creatures: ". . . seine gedichteten, friedlichen Zustände sind fühlbar nur *gemacht,* fast Alles endigt mit einer schrillenden Dissonanz." And so, going to the heart of the matter: "Sein Mangel war daher weniger ein literarischer, als ein ethischer, und es ist keineswegs zufällig, daß die ganz unmoralische sogenannte Romantik in Frankreich ihn fast ausschließlich als ihren deutschen Vorfechter anerkennt."[5]

It is not my purpose here to chronicle the fluctuating fortunes of Hoffmann's stories in the nineteenth and twentieth centuries. His influence is a commonplace of literary and aesthetic history, from Baudelaire and Edgar Allan Poe to Wagner and Busoni, from Nerval to Dostoevsky, Gogol, and Chekhov. But although it was known that he had also written music, and that by assembling various items of the **"Kreisleriana"** and other works, one could produce the outlines of an aesthetic of music, it was not until 1900 or so that people began to look seriously at this sphere of his activity.

On the one side, Peters in Leipzig published a piano score of Hoffmann's opera *Undine,* edited by Hans Pfitzner. No less a figure than Carl Maria von Weber had called this opera "eines der geistvollsten [Werke],

die uns die neuere Zeit geschenkt hat." But it was to be more than a hundred years before it was publicly performed again. (As an ironical Chance would have it, when the Schauspielhaus on the Gendarmenmarkt in Berlin—now Platz der Akademie, as the tourist guides will tell you—was burnt down during a sequence of successful performances of *Undine,* it was with the premiere of Weber's *Freischütz* that Schinkel's rebuilt Schauspielhaus was inaugurated four years later, in 1821.)

On the other side, attention was also beginning to be paid to Hoffmann's views on the nature of music, on the inner significance of the message of Palestrina, Bach, Mozart, and Beethoven, and on the relationship between the artist and society. Oswald Spengler cast him as a prototype in his account of the progressive musicalisation of European culture in the eighteenth and nineteenth centuries: "Es gab damals, vor allem im Deutschland des 18. Jahrhunderts, eine wirkliche Kultur der Musik, die das ganze Leben durchdrang und erfüllte, deren Typus Hoffmann's Kapellmeister Kreisler wurde und von der uns kaum die Erinnerung geblieben ist."[6]

It is only proper, to be sure, that a representative selection of Hoffmann's musical compositions should be published and performed; and a twelve-volume set of *Ausgewählte musikalische Werke* is now in process of publication (Schott). After all, right down to 1813, only nine years before his death—the nine years during which he produced all but a handful of his literary sketches and stories—he was convinced that it was as a composer that he was destined to make his mark in the world; not counting works which we know he wrote but which have not survived, we have today no fewer than eighty-five compositions to consider, among them six full-scale operas. To complete this bibliographical interlude, there are four commercially available recordings of Hoffmann's music; only one piece, however, a Harp Quintet in C minor, is also accessible in published form. The bicentennial celebrations of the E. T. A. Hoffmann-Gesellschaft in Bamberg in June 1976 also made generous provision for musical performances.

But over the last fifty years or so Hoffmann's compositions have been receiving more attention, it seems to me, than they can really bear. Perhaps it is a case of overcompensation for previous neglect. At all events, having reflected the activity of musicologists whose field of vision may have been rather narrower than the nature of Hoffmann's complex personality properly demands, this critical attention has tended to have a divisive effect, leaving us with a literary Hoffmann, whom we had known for a long time and could take for granted, and a musical Hoffmann, who was in process of being discovered.

So we return to the situation that I described at the beginning: a fragmentation of vision, fluctuating and apparently unconnected canons of judgment, or the dangers of a one-sided interpretation that comes from taking the part for the whole. Leaving aside his actual musical compositions, which, whatever their innate value, really do have to be discussed in their own terms and within the history of music, we then have, on the one hand, Hoffmann the writer on music, the man for whom music represented the deepest of human experiences, emotions, and desires, the man who sought to uncover the sources of the mysterious power of music, and, on the other hand, Hoffmann the explorer of psychological aberration, of the violence attendant upon delusion, schizophrenia, and other paranoiac conditions, Hoffmann the master of the bizarre and the grotesque, of terror and suspense.

As I warned myself at the beginning, one is constantly tempted, in one's determined efforts to make a coherent picture out of what one observes, to claim to see a unity that is not really there. But I think that in Hoffmann there *is* a unity, of which these two realms are an expression, and I should like to suggest where it resides—where, in other words, we may find what links **"Don Juan"** and **"Der Sandmann,"** the **"Kreisleriana"** and *Die Elixiere des Teufels,* Hoffmann the musician and Hoffmann the storyteller.

As a matter of plain biographical fact, we should not forget that Hoffmann's activity as a writer grew immediately out of his activity and experience as a musician, above all during his five years as Kapellmeister and theatrical producer in Bamberg. He had arrived there, in 1808, in a state of excitement and elation, convinced that at long last he was about to prove to the world his worth as composer, conductor, and artistic director. What he found were conventions and artistic standards that were beneath contempt, and a public that aroused in him a mixture of scorn and rage: hence the mockery, the savage irony, the inveterate recourse to the bizarre and the grotesque whenever his subject matter led him to draw on his experiences of these Bamberg years. By the time he left, his disillusion was complete; the year spent as music director and conductor with the opera company of Joseph Seconda in Leipzig and Dresden only taught him the same lesson, and with the bankruptcy of the company he could no longer escape the harsh reality that it would not, after all, be as a musician that posterity would remember him. As he wrote to his friend Hippel from Berlin in 1814: "Es ist in meinem Leben etwas recht Charakteristisches, daß immer *das* geschieht was ich gar nicht erwartete, sey es nun Böses oder Gutes, und daß ich stets *das* zu thun gezwungen werde, was meinem eigentlichen tieferen Prinzip widerstrebt."[7]

But throughout these years, the first years of his literary career, everything he wrote was either about music or a situation dominated by music, or an expression of his response to a musical experience. Not until 1813, the year when he left Bamberg, do we find his first work that is not the product of a musical impulse—the story **"Der Magnetiseur."** A few months later came **"Der goldne Topf,"** then *Die Elixiere des Teufels* and many familiar works that contain no musical recollections at all. With the massive exception of *Kater Murr,* music became less and less important to him as a source of inspiration for his fiction; he seems to have composed nothing later than 1815, the year after leaving the opera troupe, and his occasional reviews of contemporary compositions—by Spontini, for instance, and Weber's *Freischütz*—are all that remain of his once burning concern with the aesthetics of music and the meaning of musical greatness.

Yet the moment of transition, the fulcrum that bears the weight both of Hoffmann's conception of music and of the world of mystery and psychological extremity in which his characters live, is already present in his very first story, **"Ritter Gluck."** As he sits with the deranged genius who has made himself the reincarnation of the great composer who had died ten years before, Hoffmann watches his strange companion work himself into a frenzy as he describes how the wild power of musical inspiration surges through him: "Ha, wie ist es möglich, die tausenderlei Arten, wie man zum Komponieren kommt, auch nur anzudeuten!—Es ist eine breite Heerstraße, da tummeln sich alle herum, und jauchzen und schreien: wir sind Geweihte! wir sind am Ziel!—Durchs elfenbeinerne Thor kommt man ins Reich der Träume: wenige sehen das Thor einmal, noch wenigere gehen durch!—Abenteuerlich sieht es hier aus. Tolle Gestalten schweben hin und her, aber sie haben Charakter—eine mehr wie die andere. Sie lassen sich auf der Heerstraße nicht sehen: nur hinter dem elfenbeinernen Thor sind sie zu finden."[8] "Geweiht"—self-dedication to art as to religion, with music as a religious rite; "das Reich der Träume"—the dream-world in which the Romantics found revealed the higher truths and realities of our existence; "tolle Gestalten"—the fantastic creatures whose purposeful irrationality was to make them the special vehicles of their creator's message: such are the symbolic terms that I would ask you to keep in mind as we follow the trail of Hoffmann's thought.

So, turning over the blank pages of the score of *Armide* on the piano before him, "Gluck" confides to his ever more mystified guest: "Alles dieses, mein Herr, habe ich geschrieben, als ich aus dem Reich der Träume kam. Aber ich verriet Unheiligen das Heilige, und eine eiskalte Hand faßte in dies glühende Herz! Es brach nicht; da wurde ich verdammt, zu wandeln unter den Unheiligen, wie ein abgeschiedener Geist—gestaltlos, damit mich niemand kenne, bis mich die Sonnenblume wieder emporhebt zu dem Ewigen" (I, 20, in Grisebach's edition [of *Sämmtliche Werke*], Leipzig [1900]).

Again the world of dreams, the fear of being without individuality and therefore without purpose, however irrational, and again the creation of art as the celebration of a sacred ritual; here with the characteristic Hoffmannesque overtone that art is for an élite of initiates, not for the Philistine masses. Like the demented nobleman who lives as a hermit under the delusion that he is the monk Serapion, the mad "Gluck" has driven a wedge between the life of the body and the life of the spirit, forcing them further and further apart until the gap becomes unbridgeable. A servant of art, he has become a stranger to life.

Of all the arts, music is the furthest removed from material reality. It obeys a private inner logic that owes nothing to the public logic of demonstrable experiences; it is not representative of objects or ideas, like literature, painting, and sculpture, nor is its *raison d'être* functional, like architecture. From one point of view it creates and lives in its own world of unreality, a world governed by arbitrary values and beset with the dangers that attend a condition of isolation. Yet at the same time, it is to this very detachment that music owes its supreme quality of immediacy as a mode of communication and understanding. For since it is not burdened with association, or restricted by the pressure of relativity and qualification, it extends—indeed, it *is*—a direct experience of pure, timeless reality, which the representational arts, employing the finite forms and language of human sense perception and human thought, can never offer. Music, said Schelling, "ist diejenige Kunst, die am meisten das Körperliche abstreift, indem sie *reine* Bewegung selbst als solche, von dem Gegenstand abgezogen, vorstellt und von unsichtbaren, fast geistigen Flügeln getragen wird."[9]

This is what lies behind the most explicit and most precise expression of the Romantic conception of a cosmos ordered by, and thus to be understood through, music—namely Schopenhauer's *Die Welt als Wille und Vorstellung*: ". . . da unsere Welt nichts Anderes ist, als die Erscheinung der Ideen in der Vielheit . . . so ist die Musik, da sie die Ideen übergeht, auch von der erscheinenden Welt ganz unabhängig, ignorirt sie schlechthin, könnte gewissermaßen, auch wenn die Welt gar nicht wäre, doch bestehn: was von den andern Künsten sich nicht sagen läßt. Die Musik ist nämlich eine so *unmittelbare* Objektivation und Abbild des ganzen *Willens,* wie die Welt selbst es ist, ja wie die Ideen es sind, deren vervielfältigte Erscheinung die Welt der einzelnen Dinge ausmacht. Die Musik ist also keineswegs, gleich den andern Künsten, das Abbild der Ideen; sondern *Abbild des Willens selbst,* dessen Objektität auch die Ideen sind: deshalb eben ist die Wirkung der Musik so sehr viel mächtiger und eindringlicher, als die der andern Künste: denn diese reden nur vom Schatten, sie aber vom Wesen."[10]

Thus the supremacy of music is seen to lie in its very unreality, that is, in its immediacy and absoluteness—which many might consider a very "real" unreality. Indeed, music has virtually become the unknowable *Ding an sich.* The realms of *noumena* and *phenomena* have coalesced, the Kantian dualism has been overcome. In Schopenhauer's words: "Man könnte demnach die Welt ebenso wohl verkörperte Musik, als verkörperten Willen nennen."[11]

Die Welt als Wille und Vorstellung was published in 1818. Four years earlier, after Theodor had read his story **"Die Automate"** to the assembled company of Hoffmann's "Serapionsbrüder," Ludwig observed: "Kann denn die Musik, die in unserm Innern wohnt, eine andere sein als die, welche in der Natur wie ein tiefes, nur dem höhern Sinn erforschliches Geheimnis verborgen?" (VII, 96). And in the discussion **"Über alte und neue Kirchenmusik"** Cyprian declares: "Keine Kunst, glaube ich, geht so ganz und gar aus der inneren Vergeistigung des Menschen hervor, keine Kunst bedarf nur einzig rein geistiger ätherischer Mittel, als die Musik. Die Ahnung des Höchsten und Heiligsten, der geistigen Macht, die den Lebensfunken in der ganzen Natur entzündet, spricht sich hörbar aus im Ton und so wird Musik, Gesang, der Ausdruck der höchsten Fülle des Daseins—Schöpferlob!" (VII, 153). Hence it is the musician—like Wackenroder's Joseph Berglinger in the *Herzensergießungen* and Hoffmann's Johannes Kreisler—who holds in his hand the key to the meaning of God, of man, of life.

And when the focus shifts from the speculative, aesthetic plane to the characterisation of a particular piece of music or the work of a particular composer, the language remains the same: "Beethovens Musik bewegt die Hebel der Furcht, des Schauers, des Entsetzens, des Schmerzes, und erweckt eben jene unendliche Sehnsucht, welche das Wesen der Romantik ist:" (I,39). Thus Hoffmann in **"Beethovens Instrumentalmusik."** And in identical terms Schopenhauer, in *Zur Metaphysik der Musik*: ". . . So zeigt uns eine Beethoven'sche Symphonie die größte Verwirrung, welcher doch die vollkommenste Ordnung zum Grunde liegt, den heftigsten Kampf, der sich im nächsten Augenblick zur schönsten Eintracht gestaltet; es ist *rerum concordia discors*, ein treues und vollkommenes Abbild des Wesens der Welt, . . . Zugleich nun aber sprechen aus dieser Symphonie alle menschlichen Leidenschaften und Affekte: die Freude, die Trauer, die Liebe, der Haß, der Schrecken, die Hoffnung usw. in zahllosen Nüancen, jedoch alle gleichsam nur *in abstracto* und ohne alle Besonderung: es ist ihre bloße Form, ohne den Stoff, wie eine bloße Geisterwelt, ohne Materie."[12]

For Hoffmann, as for Schopenhauer, the world—the true, Romantic world—was indeed "embodied music," and the primacy of the creative act raised the composer to a position of supreme knowledge and power, establishing a relationship between ego and the world around it which was a relationship between monarch and subject, between ruler and ruled. This is the philosophical point of association between art and transcendental idealism, as well as the foundation of the argument that would see in music the supreme manifestation of the forces of German Romanticism. As Nietzsche was to put it, at the other end of the century: "Ich fürchte, ich bin zu sehr Musiker, um nicht Romantiker zu sein."

What I have tried to advance so far is an account of the nature of music in the terms which Hoffmann used or recognised, dwelling on such moments as its unreality and absoluteness, its irrationality and quasi-religious power, its claim to lift us into the realms of understanding in which we experience a revelation of ultimate values and verities, and a power to convert this understanding into artistic creativity. But these are also the terms, it seems to me—or, at least, some of the terms—in which one can properly speak of the Hoffmann who made the paranoic, the demonic, the satanic his special province: the portrayal of minds under stress, men for whom madness, however one defines it, has become the only possible, the only tolerable state of mind, because it alone guarantees the conditions in which creative artistic power can manifest itself.

Again it is in Hoffmann's works themselves that we find our point of departure, the explicit contiguity of the two worlds of art and madness. It is relevant to recall *en passant* that Hoffmann had a penchant for casting himself in the role of the ostensibly disinterested editor of his stories, not as their direct author, a technique which allowed him to strike a detached, ironic pose while presenting situations expressive of his profoundest convictions and insights. The fictional distance between himself and his subject matter that he thus creates, serves, I think, as in most such cases, to intensify the committed meaning of that subject matter rather than to cast doubts upon it. As Friedrich Schlegel said of *Wilhelm Meisters Lehrjahre*: "Man lasse sich also dadurch, daß der Dichter selbst die Personen und die Begebenheiten so leicht und launig zu nehmen, des Helden fast nie ohne Ironie zu erwähnen und auf sein Meisterwerk selbst von der Höhe seines Geistes herabzulächeln scheint, nicht täuschen, als sei es ihm nicht der heiligste Ernst."[13]

The deranged musician calling himself Gluck had visions and intuitions denied to the denizens of the "sane" world around him. Seven years later, in the preamble to the second set of **"Kreisleriana,"** Hoffmann makes the relationship between madness and insight explicit in the title of a proposed collection of sketches—"ein Cyklus des Rein-Geistigen in der Kunst", as he described it—which was to have been called *Lichte Stunden eines wahnsinnigen Musikers.* The musician, of course, was

Hoffmann's *alter ego,* Johannes Kreisler, but although the *Lichte Stunden* were never written, the conception of revelation through that state of unbalance which is inseparable from, and, indeed, a normal condition for, artistic creativity and understanding, still dominates Hoffmann's mind. As a state of heightened awareness it fills the mind of the autobiographical "reisender Enthusiast" whom Hoffmann presents as the author of the *Fantasiestücke in Callots Manier.* In *Die Elixiere des Teufels,* the irony with which Pietro Belcampo had tried to protect himself from the world had also turned to insanity: "Des Peters Licht [ist] im Dampf der Narrheit verlöscht, in die sich in seinem Innern die Ironie des Lebens umgestaltet" (II, 281). And as a conception of revelation, it reached its climax in *Kater Murr,* that most extraordinary and disturbing of Hoffmann's works, in which unrequited love and the mockery that the artist has to suffer at the hands of a Philistine society (experiences that hounded Hoffmann throughout his life) drive the ironically tragic figure of Kreisler to acts of uncontrollable despair and savagery, destroying the true art that burns within him. "Wilder, unbesonnener Mensch," cries Meister Abraham, ". . . wann wird endlich der verwüstende Brand in deiner Brust zur reinen Naphtaflamme werden, genährt von dem tiefsten Sinn für die Kunst, für alles Herrliche und Schöne, der in dir wohnt!" (x, 22).

Likewise the "reisender Enthusiast" in the wonderful little story **"Don Juan"** gives an idiosyncratic account of Mozart's *Don Giovanni,* in which Donna Anna, like the Enthusiast and his creator, is cast as a prisoner of the "zauberischer Wahnsinn sehnender Liebe." Her mission, which she tragically fails to accomplish, is to redeem Don Juan by her love, as the Enthusiast dreams of his redemption by the singer who is playing the role of Donna Anna in the performance he is watching, as Kreisler longs for release from his torment through the love of Julia Benzon, and as Hoffmann himself yearned for redemption through the love of Julia Marc.

Anselmus, too, in his own way, shows that living for the values of love and true art entails breaking one's links with the bourgeois world and sacrificing notions of prosperity, social esteem, and other conventional virtues. The outcome of the conflict in Anselmus between the sweet, faithful, respectable Veronica and the alluring, demonic Serpentina can never be in real doubt; nor, in their different ways, can Kreisler, or Nathanael in **"Der Sandmann,"** or Cardillac in **"Das Fräulein von Scuderi,"** or Medardus in *Die Elixiere des Teufels* resist the demonic power that drives them to their terrifyingly rational acts of irrationality. "Ja, ich Hochbeglückter habe das Höchste erkannt," cries Anselmus in his moment of highest bliss: "—ich muß dich lieben ewiglich, o Serpentina;—nimmer verbleichen die goldnen Strahlen der Lilie, denn wie Glaube und Liebe ist ewig die Erkenntnis" (I, 251). But the victorious ideal, realised on the distant isle of Atlantis, claims as its due the renunciation of earthly joy and success. Like the kingdom of Heaven, Atlantis is not of this world.

A step closer toward utter domination by the demon of madness leads us into that sphere in which Hoffmann explored the relationship between men and machines, between the pulsating, organic world of vital human expression and the sinister, soulless manifestations of a creative will that emanates from the dark, mysterious realms of life. Such are the machines that surround Professor X in **"Die Automate,"** the toys made by Onkel Drosselmeier in *Nußknacker und Mausekönig,* and the mechanical doll Olimpia in **"Der Sandmann."** Olimpia is endowed by the Devil with the perverse power to command the holiest of human emotions, as though she were a creature of flesh and blood, and then to drive her victim out of his mind. Kreisler too, in that extraordinary fragment **"Kreislers musikalisch-poetischer Klub,"** is gripped by satanic visions as he sits at his piano in the darkened room, modulating wildly from one key to another and uttering mad cries as he sees the form of the Devil bearing down upon him. Music, madness, the demons of mystery, surrender to an uncontrollable inspiration which issues from the lord of the underworld: all these combine as Kreisler is pursued by visions of hell and shrieks: "Es ist der Wahnsinn. . . . Laß ab von mir!—ich will artig sein! ich will glauben, der Teufel sei ein *Galanthuomo* von den feinsten Sitten!—*hony soit qui mal y pense*" (I, 291). And so he raves on, until his faithful friend among the embarrassed onlookers lights the lamps in the pitch-black room and breaks the morbid spell.

This Kreisler, the Kreisler also of the correspondence with Baron Wallborn and of **"Kreislers Lehrbrief,"** both written within the same few months—this Kreisler now disappears from the scene until the first of the "Makulaturblätter" of *Kater Murr,* four years later. In his place come other artist figures: the young poet Anselmus in **"Der goldne Topf,"** whose soul becomes the battleground for the struggle between the poetic and the prosaic forces in life; the painter Berthold in **"Die Jesuiterkirche in G.,"** who loses his power to paint, is driven by despair almost to the point of murdering his wife and child, and finally kills himself. And in **"Der Artushof,"** another painter, the man who believes himself to be the reincarnation of one Gottfried Berklinger, sits in front of a blank canvas and describes in rapt detail the features of his painting called 'Paradise Regained,' just as his spiritual forebear who believed himself to be Gluck had played the overture to *Armide* from a sheaf of blank pages.

These artist figures, no less than Kreisler, embody the concept of art as a consuming mystery alien to the world of common reality, and the artist as a man possessed, sometimes to the point of murder or suicide. But the most diabolical, perverse manifestation of artistic obsession in the whole of Hoffmann's work is surely the figure of Cardillac in **"Das Fräulein von Scuderi."** On the one hand he consorts with the most respected members of society as one of the great craftsmen of his day; on the other, he is a homicidal maniac who murders not for gain but because, supreme artist that he is, he cannot endure the thought that the products of his inspired hands should stay in the possession of the contemptible Philistines who commissioned them. He is the Platonic murderer, the perverted idealist, with the idealist's frightening singlemindedness; he is as conscious of his motives as he is of his crimes, and his demand is absolute. Equally absolute is the dominion exerted over his whole being by what he calls his 'evil star': dark, demonic forces that impel him to act as he does, forces whose control of his mind and body he dispassionately and fatalistically accepts, and which come (most perverse of all ironies) in the divine name of art. Seen in this light, his behaviour has a pathological abstractness about it that makes formal issues of moral or legal responsibility seem irrelevant. And, hardly noticing it, we find ourselves using the same vocabulary (absoluteness, abstractness, remoteness from the formal affairs of human society and from the tradition of representationalism) as in our analysis of the power of music. "Musik ist dämonisches Gebiet," said Thomas Mann. Well, the author of *Doktor Faustus* ought to know.

Also the tool of a destructive purpose, a man obsessed and conditioned by an evil past which he could not control but whose consequences he is made to suffer and ultimately atone for, is Medardus in *Die Elixiere des Teufels.* Medardus is neither musician nor painter, nor have the values of art any role to play in this Doppelgänger story to end all Doppelgänger stories. Moreover, through the interplay of the conscious and the unconscious, which forms the framework over which the complex web of actions and relationships is woven, there emerges an ethical, even Christian message of atonement for sin and redemption through transfigured love which is unique in Hoffmann's work. Yet in describing the novel to his friend and publisher Kunz, he still had recourse to musical terminology: ". . . [Der Roman] fängt . . . mit einem *Grave sostenuto* an—mein Held wird im Kloster zur heiligen Linde in Ostpreussen geboren, seine Geburt sühnt den verbrecherischen Vater—Joseph und das Christenkind erscheinen *pp*—dann tritt ein *Andante sost. e piano* ein—das Leben im Kloster, wo er eingekleidet wird—aus dem Kloster tritt er in die bunt-bunteste Welt—hier hebt ein *Allegro forte* an."[14]

Hoffmann takes it no further in his letter, but his use of such terms to characterize actions and moods cannot but call to mind that terrifying evening at the "musikalisch-poetischer Klub" when Kreisler's fevered imagination conjured up a sequence of scenes and figures released by the qualities and associations of the various keys through which he passed during his frenzied improvisation at the keyboard.

So, as we escape from the satanic worlds of Cardillac and Medardus, Trabacchio and Ignaz Denner, of Coppelius and Dapertutto, we find ourselves back—appropriately, inevitably—in the company of Hoffmann's "wahnsinniger Musiker," the deranged visionary whose outbursts threaten no one but himself. "Endlich gestand er mir," says his creator and master, driving his musical imagery to its utmost limits, "wie er seinen Tod beschlossen und sich im nächsten Walde mit einer übermäßigen Quinte erdolchen werde" (I, 280). The production of an augmented fifth as a murder weapon, and a verdict of "Death by Music," raise interesting possibilities.

Kreisler's ultimate fate, like his origins—which only Meister Abraham seems to know—remains a mystery. The third part of **Kater Murr,** which would have resolved the mystery, was never started. For a moment it had looked as though he might find peace in the monastery, composing music *ad majorem Dei gloriam,* but figures from the past and realities of the world beyond the cloister quickly close in upon him. At the end of the second volume, brought to an abrupt end by the tragic demise of the feline genius to whom we owe the preservation of the Kreisler story, we leave our Kapellmeister reading a letter from Meister Abraham, summoning him back immediately to the residence at Sieghartsweiler. Did he go? Did he watch as his beloved Julia became the wife of the imbecilic Ignaz? Did he slump into a state of despair and self-pity, or, as he had been seen to do ten years earlier, in his *Musikalische Leiden,* did he seek consolation in playing the Goldberg Variations to a company of kindred spirits? Or was his end perhaps like that of Berthold in **"Die Jesuiterkirche"** [**"Die Jesuiterkirche in G."**], who experienced a last, desperate burst of creative energy, then fell into a state of insanity and suddenly vanished; a few days later his hat and stick were found near the river: ". . . glauben wir alle, er habe sich freiwillig den Tod gegeben"? (III, 114).

What we choose to call "uncompleted" works of art may sometimes need to be more closely defined. Are Michelangelo's *infiniti* really "incomplete," and in what sense is Schubert's Symphony No. 8 in B minor really "unfinished"? Speculation about the outcome of **Kater Murr,** like any attempt to complete the apparently uncompleted, is a delightful pursuit, because it requires a maximum of imagination with but a minimum of self-discipline. The critical student of literature, however, can only criticise and study what is actually there—though sometimes it may seem that what he is talking about is not there at all, and that he has invented something in order to be able to talk about it.

But there is a great deal really 'there' in E. T. A. Hoffmann—far more than I have even hinted at in these remarks to honour the bicentennial of his birth in the city of Simon Dach and Heinrich Albert, of Hamann, and of Kant. And Hoffmann himself, for all his fantasies of a life devoted to music, had his roots firmly set in reality. Already at nineteen he wrote to Hippel: "Sieh nur, unser Uebel ist entgegengesetzt, Du hattest zu viel Fantasie, ich habe zu viel Wirklichkeit."[15] But it was a reality which embraced the unreal, which found the transcendental, the ideal, the mysterious, the irrational to be as demonstrably and heuristically real as the causal, the time-bound, the mundane, and which knew that the antinomies were inseparable. Such a reality weighs heavily on the mind, and for Hoffmann's heroes the burden is often too great. But that, it seems to me, is what his stories of music and of mystery are all about.

Notes

1. Diary, 9 January 1842. In: Friedrich Hebbel, *Sämtliche Werke,* hrsg. R. M. Werner (Berlin, 1901-1907), 2. Abt., II, 135-36.

2. Richard Wagner, *Mein Leben,* hrsg. Martin Gregor-Dellin (München, 1963), p. 26.

3. Sir Walter Scott, "On the Supernatural in Fictitious Composition . . . ," in *Foreign Quarterly Review,* I (Edinburgh, July 1827), 97.

4. Goethe, *Werke* ("Sophienausgabe"; Weimar, 1887-1919), XLII, pt. 2, 88.

5. Joseph von Eichendorff, *Sämtliche Werke,* hist.-krit. Ausg., hrsg. Wilhelm Kosch, u.a., IX (Regensburg, 1970), 454-55.

6. Oswald Spengler, *Der Untergang des Abendlandes* (München, 1922-23), I, 383.

7. Hoffmann, *Briefwechsel,* hrsg. Friedrich Schnapp (München, 1967-69), II, 26.

8. Hoffmann, *Sämtliche Werke,* hrsg. Eduard Grisebach (Leipzig, 1900), I, 14. Further references also are to this edition and are given in parentheses in the text.

9. Schelling, *Sämmtliche Werke* (Stuttgart, 1859), 1. Abt., 5, 502.

10. Schopenhauer, *Sämtliche Werke,* II (Wiesbaden, 1972), 304.

11. Schopenhauer, *Sämtliche Werke,* II, 310.

12. Schopenhauer, *Sämtliche Werke,* III (Wiesbaden, 1972), 514.

13. Friedrich Schlegel, *Kritische Schriften,* hrsg. Wolfdietrich Rasch (München, 1956), p. 270.

14. Letter to Kunz, 24 March 1814. *Briefwechsel,* I, 454.

15. Letter to Hippel, 1 May 1795. *Briefwechsel,* I, 62.

Charles E. Passage (essay date October 1976)

SOURCE: Passage, Charles E. "E. T. A. Hoffmann's *The Devil's Elixirs*: A Flawed Masterpiece." *Journal of English and Germanic Philology* 75, no. 4 (October 1976): 531-45.

[*In the following essay, Passage offers a close reading of the novel, focusing on the work's complex structure, its diverse literary influences, and its psychological and religious themes.*]

When Napoleon dissolved the Prussian government late in 1806, our author, who had as yet written no literary works, found himself without a job, indeed without a country. After months of hand-to-mouth existence, sometimes knowing actual hunger, he advertised in a newspaper for employment as a practical musician and as a man familiar with all aspects of the theater. About his musical training there was no question: he was an accomplished instrumentalist and director, as well as a published composer. But his qualifications for dramatic direction were more nearly an earnest wish than a fact. When at last the south-German city of Bamberg offered him the music directorship of its theater, he accepted with alacrity, rejoicing that he was now to live by art.

The four and a half years in Bamberg, 1808-1813, brought him a full share of frustrations, but they also furnished vivid experiences that he would later put to literary use. Julia Marc, his very young vocal student with the ethereal soprano voice, became the model for Aurelia, the heroine of the present novel [*The Devil's Elixirs*]. A visit to a nearby Capuchin monastery provided him with authentic details for his monk Medardus. From the court physician, Dr. Markus, he learned a good deal about the new theories of psychiatry and psychiatric therapy. Life at court taught him much that he would never have learned in Prussian government offices. The Roman Catholic ambience of Bamberg quite fascinated the nominally Lutheran author-to-be.

Meanwhile the literary artist in him was emerging. Amid circumstances unknown, and probably just after arrival in Bamberg in September 1808, he wrote the fine short story, "**Ritter Gluck,**" the very first of the *Tales of Hoffmann.* He was just past his thirty-third birthday when it appeared in a music magazine early in 1809. Reception was enthusiastic, and from various quarters there came encouragement to write more stories.

Cautiously he experimented further with literature, tending at first to stick close to themes about music and musicians, since he still regarded music as his proper art and literature as a side line. In March of 1813, just before leaving Bamberg, he entered into a contract with his friend, creditor, and admirer, Karl Friedrich Kunz, the Bamberg wine merchant and publisher. Published

stories were to be gathered up, new stories were to be composed, and Kunz would bring out a two-volume collection under the title of *Fantasiestücke in Callots Manier,* that is, imaginative tales suggestive of the engravings by the seventeenth-century French artist, Jacques Callot.

Through the year 1813, when he was not dodging Napoleon's retreating armies and the Russian armies pursuing them, Hoffmann supported himself as an orchestra conductor in the east-German cities of Dresden and Leipzig. The two slim volumes of the *Fantasiestücke* were published at Easter of 1814, and such was their immediate success that a third volume was brought out in the autumn of 1814 and a fourth volume in the spring of 1815. On 4 March 1814, in Leipzig, he finished copying out the last pages of Volume III for the printer, and on the very same day he began work on his novel, *The Devil's Elixirs (Die Elixiere des Teufels).* He was then two months past his thirty-eighth birthday.

For five weeks he wrote steadily at the novel, which must have long been in formation in his mind. Headlong composition matched the headlong pace of the story, until, on 23 April, Part I was completed. Then came a pause. Kunz was informed of the project and he seems to have declined to publish the book. More than a year went by before work was resumed, with other compositions, both literary and musical, under way and completed in the interim. From the slower pace of Part II of the novel, and from other aesthetic considerations, some critics have inferred a revision of the original scenario, but that point is moot.

In any case, Part II of the novel was composed in the late spring and the summer of 1815, by which time Hoffmann had moved to Berlin and had re-entered the Prussian judiciary. Wearing the prescribed uniform of the civil service, he now spent regular hours on the board of the supreme court (*Kammergericht*), and official letters are still extant commending his punctilious performance of his duties. At the same time he was the highly successful author of the *Fantasiestücke.* His full-length opera *Undine,* in composition since 1812, was finished. Its delayed première was finally given in Berlin in August of 1816. (One of its rare revivals was staged at Wuppertal in April of 1970.) New tales were coming into being one after another. The reading public could not get enough of them.

But meanwhile, *The Devil's Elixirs* was making slow progress. After rejection by a second publisher, it was accepted by the Berlin firm of Duncker & Humblot, who brought it out in two volumes, the first in 1815, the second in 1816. Reception was cool, then and later. For a century it remained the least read of all the *Tales of Hoffmann.* As a saint's legend and as a "fate" story, it flouted established norms; its realistic touches seemed raw and harsh; its vivid psychological insights passed for unbelievable; Medardus as a scallywag with a conscience seemed absurd; the ending might be inspirational but it was too slow in reaching that stage; its lightning-stroke revelations of various passions came with disconcerting abruptness. Nothing seemed right about the book. It was ahead of its time.

Not until the early twentieth century did **The Devil's Elixirs** come to be appreciated, and with the passing decades of the twentieth century its solid worth has grown more securely established. It is one of those flawed masterpieces in which the flaws are almost as interesting as its sure strokes.

* * *

The structure of **The Devil's Elixirs** is rather more complex than might be expected of an essentially one-man story narrated in first person. Not only is there recourse to the device of a lengthy purloined letter in order to establish the true nature of Aurelia, but the conclusion of the hero's life, indispensable to the overall plan, has to be entrusted to a certain Father Spiridion as epiloguist. There are three time planes: first, the autobiography of the monk Medardus, constituting the story proper; second, the genealogical account of his own family as read by Medardus in the course of his adventures; and third, the explanatory Foreword by "the Editor" (Hoffmann), which sets the total novel within a frame tale and removes it to a bygone era. Such manipulation of time planes was a process dear to the hearts of the German Romantic writers and not least dear to Hoffmann. Finally, there is, wholly unconnected with the rest of the novel, that extended anecdote read from manuscript by the court physician for the entertainment of the Prince's guests in the fourth sub-section of Part I.

Such detachable insets were common enough in eighteenth-century English novels, several German Romanticists overdid the practice, and Goethe, in the last stages of his career, overburdened his sequel to *Wilhelm Meister* with such insets. In fact, it was Goethe's opinion that such "retarding motifs" were intrinsic to the novel form. Of the court physician's tale about Mr. Ewson and Dr. Green we may charitably say that it is not over-long and that it serves to create suspense in the main story. Its facile humor is not unwelcome in a book so predominantly somber as **The Devil's Elixirs.**

* * *

Our awareness of Hoffmann's literary sources enhances the originality displayed in this book. The direct and immediate source is identified by Aurelia in that purloined letter as *Der Mönch,* "a novel translated from the English" (by Fr. von Oertel, 3 vols., Leipzig, 1797). The original was that lurid shocker which Coleridge, in

his review of 1797, termed "the offspring of no common genius," entitled *Ambrosio, or The Monk* and commonly remembered as simply *The Monk*. Its author, Matthew Gregory Lewis, was nineteen when he wrote it, twenty-one when it made him famous overnight in 1796—not 1795 as usually stated—and it earned for him the nickname of "Monk Lewis." At age seventeen (1792) he had learned German during a stay in Weimar, where he met Goethe, and a year later he had won limited fame by published translations from Schiller, but his highest success was attained with *The Monk,* which went through five editions in the four years, 1796-1800. Two "Gothic" dramas also had success in 1797 and 1802, yet he renounced writing in 1808. After a stay with Shelley and Byron in Italy in 1816, he died on a return voyage from Jamaica, of yellow fever, and was buried at sea in May of 1817.

The hero of Lewis' "romance" was a foundling discovered at the door of a Capuchin monastery in Madrid. The monks christened him Ambrosio, fostered his precocious bent for study, accepted him as fellow monk, and finally chose him for their abbot. At age thirty he emerges from his monastery walls to preach in the cathedral. His "noble port and commanding presence" impress everyone, his mighty oratory astounds them all. Grandees load him with gifts, their wives will have no other confessor, he is considered a saint. In his heart, however, he is consumed with pride and ambition. Within the monastery there appears (Ch. 2) a tender youth and novice monk named Rosario, who presently reveals that he is a girl named Matilda: love for Ambrosio induced her to this elaborate deception. Ambrosio is charmed, his charm soon becomes raging passion, and Chapter 2 ends with their sexual union.

For three chapters the narrative turns to other subjects; then, in Chapter 6, we learn that Ambrosio has wearied of Matilda and that he sometimes undertakes harsh penances for his sins, only to abandon those penances almost at once. Then it is that a young noblewoman called Antonia comes to implore his spiritual assistance for her gravely ill mother, Elvira. With Ambrosio it is love at first sight, yet he ultimately causes the death of the mother and seduces the daughter by force. Crime follows crime, until at last the monk is brought (Ch. 12) before the Inquisition. Faced with death by torture, he buys rescue from Satan at the price of his soul.

Satan does rescue him, carrying him from the dungeon off through the air, but as they pass over the peaks of the Sierra Morena he hurls him down and impales him on a spiky crag, much as Pallas Athena impaled Ajax, son of Oileus, in lines 44 and 45 of the first *Aeneid*. Here we suspect a schoolboy's unconscious recall on Lewis' part. The sinner's lingering and grisly death from devouring vermin was deleted from all editions of the novel after the first, so that most readers have the impression that he perished instantly. Before dropping him, however, Satan reveals that "that Antonia whom you violated, was your sister! that Elvira whom you murdered, gave you birth!" What is more, Matilda was not human: she was "a subordinate but crafty spirit" who, at Satan's behest, came out of hell, adopted the features of the Virgin in Ambrosio's favorite painting, and initiated the ruination of the monk's soul.

"Spanish" Ambrosio, Capuchin monk and fervent pulpit-orator, false saint and crafty sinner, lustful, violent, murderous, and incestuous unawares, is patently the model for Hoffmann's Medardus, German-born but of Italian origins, who recapitulates all those sins, but with opposite outcome, for Medardus contends against evil and wins his way to ultimate salvation and genuine sainthood. Ambrosio's alliance with the devilwitch out of hell is transferred, however, to Medardus' sinning ancestor, Francesko the painter, five generations before.

Hoffmann's over-all transformation of his source material from sinister to benign recalls also Chapter 3 of *The Monk*, which reports an adventure unconnected with Ambrosio. Don Raymon's traveling chaise breaks down—not accidentally—on a forest road near Strasbourg and the gentleman is guided to genial folk in a remote dwelling. The geniality is sham. These people are cutthroats who lure travelers to their deaths and rob them; the house shows bloodstains and the grounds are a graveyard. Only the surly wife is honest, and at her warning Don Raymon escapes. In our German novel Medardus' postilion makes an innocent error on a stormy night, the forest ranger and his family are wholesome folk, and the episode brings Medardus to an entirely different adventure.

These specifics from Lewis' English novel were blended in Hoffmann's imagination with more generalized impressions from Calderón's Spanish drama, *Devotion to the Cross* (*La Devoción de la cruz*). In 1811 Hoffmann had produced this play of 1634 on the Bamberg stage, using the recent German translation by August Wilhelm Schlegel, and in 1812 he had published an essay on methods of staging this and two other plays of Calderón as translated by Schlegel.

In the three-act *Devotion to the Cross* the destinies of the principal characters depend on previous family events, which are revealed piecemeal to the audience. Some twenty years before, a certain nobleman, doubting his pregnant wife's fidelity, took her to an isolated spot where there was a cross, intending to kill her there. Instead, he abandoned her. At the foot of the cross she bore a pair of twins. The boy she was obliged to leave behind, but with the infant girl in her arms she staggered home to her husband, who forgave her. The boy

was named Eusebio by the shepherds who rescued him, and he grows up to fall in love with Julia, his twin sister. On the chests of each of them there is the imprint of a cross.

As the play opens, Eusebio mortally wounds Julia's brother Lisardo, who has ventured to defend his sister's honor against a would-be seducer. Julia conceals Eusebio from her angry father and enables him to escape. Between Acts I and II the lovers are secretly married, but Act II reveals Eusebio as captain of a band of robbers and Julia as confined to a convent. When Eusebio discovers the imprint of a cross on her body he leaves her, but without explaining his reason for doing so. In male clothing Julia escapes from the convent, murdering certain persons in the process, seeks out Eusebio, and declares her identity. During a battle between robbers and peasants Eusebio falls to his death from a high cliff and is found at the foot of the very cross before which he was born. There Julia and her father come upon him, and when Julia confesses everything, her outraged father is about to slay her. She throws her arms around the cross, as her mother had once done, but this time the cross is mysteriously taken up into the skies, with the desperate girl clinging to it.

Sometimes termed a "fate drama," *Devotion to the Cross* is rather a mystical parable about the unfathomable powers of the Cross, and the primary characters are "examples" demonstrating how the Higher Will may resolve the most extreme of human complications. In Hoffmann's novel we readily discern a parallel mysteriousness of "fate," the motif of the Cross-imprint, which now marks the throats of Medardus and his half-brother Viktorin, and the extension of family involvements, including incestuous love.

Tentatively, then, Medardus may be defined as a blend of the unredeemable Ambrosio with the seemingly redeemed Eusebio, while Aurelia stands parallel on the one hand to the pallid figure of Antonia, who in *The Monk* is little more than a pathetic victim, and on the other hand to the sainted sinner Julia in *Devotion to the Cross*. With regard to Aurelia, but not to Medardus, a third important influence derives from Kleist's *Das Käthchen von Heilbronn* (1808-10), which Hoffmann produced on the Bamberg stage in 1811, just as he produced Calderón's *Devotion to the Cross* and Shakespeare's *Romeo and Juliet* (using the new Schlegel translation, not Goethe's "adaptation"), but the borrowed matter from *Das Käthchen von Heilbronn* may be more appropriately discussed in a later section of the present essay. Those three plays were, moreover, Hoffmann's favorite stage works, as he remarks in a letter dating from the Bamberg period, but if Aurelia bears resemblance to all three heroines: Käthchen, Julia, and Juliet, we may plausibly conjecture that he tended to see all three of them as having the features of Julia Marc, his *ombra adorata* of the Bamberg years.

* * *

The visitation of sins of fathers upon unborn generations has ever been a troublesome article of faith, and in its specialized form in the present work it is more than a little troublesome. We are asked to believe that the sin of Francesko the painter five generations ago has "infected" his descendants and will continue to "infect" them until his line is extinct. It is the function of Medardus, and to some degree of Aurelia as well, to end the sinning line and bring the old painter's weary ghost to rest. Thus the story-within-a-story is akin to the old legend of the Wandering Jew and to such future works as Charles Maturin's *Melmoth the Wanderer* (1820) and *Der fliegende Holländer* (Heine's anecdote, 1834; Wagner's opera, 1843). An analogous idea underlies the *Romanzen vom Rosenkranz,* that poem sequence at which Clemens Brentano worked off and on from 1802 until his death in 1834, without completing or publishing it. We suggest that there is a qualitative disparity between the theme of the ghost's "salvation" and the theme of the false saint's sinning his way to true sainthood; the second, we feel, is humanly valid in any era, whereas the first is fanciful—"mere literature"—and the book suffers by the combination.

The elaborate account of Medardus' ancestry, which the author presents piecemeal, is a suspense device, and not an ineffective one. Taken as a unit, it betokens the coexistence of "two worlds"—in this case historical past and living present—and the old painter's lugubrious role effects that "interpenetration of two worlds" which constitutes a characteristic feature of Hoffmann's fiction. In **"Der goldne Topf,"** that long *Märchen* that the author finished copying out on the very day when he began **The Devil's Elixirs,** and in his future long *Märchen* of **Klein Zaches, Prinzessin Brambilla,** and **Meister Floh,** the "other world" is represented, not by ancestors of living characters, but by deathless spirits of immemorial antiquity.

Serious authors are often troubled by the problem of having their work dwindle to relative insignificance as the mere record of events and characters isolated in past time, and serious authors have had recourse to various expedients to "rescue" their work from the limitations of time, to "universalize" and to "eternalize" their creations. Hoffmann's device of coexistent worlds, one past and one present, was his way of arriving at "the cosmic." In the present instance, his expansion of time involves a family ghost striving through three centuries to accomplish the expiation of his sin; in the four long *Märchen* Hoffmann more happily took his cue from *A Midsummer Night's Dream,* where mortal humans and immortal fairies meet on a single plane.

From the moralist's point of view, the old painter's sin was fornication; that his partner was a female devil out of hell in temporary human guise was a grotesque detail borrowed from *The Monk* and prudently relegated by the author to an era that was distant from his main characters as it was distant from his readers. From Hoffmann's point of view, however, the real sin of the old painter was a desecration of Holy Art.

All the German *Romantiker* were agreed on the high seriousness of Art. Some, like Tieck and Wackenroder, held that Art was holy, but in support of that claim they usually spoke only of religious art. Hoffmann, steeped as he was in music, carried the principle further. To him, a secular masterpiece by Mozart was also "holy," in a way that his fellow-*Romantiker* might have found disturbing, and more than any of them he lived by the principle of Art's sacredness. He was the specialized type of "the aesthetic man," and in his makeup "the moral man" and "the religious man," though by no means excluded, were subordinate. (We use these terms after the fashion of Eduard Spranger, the speculative philosopher of the 1920's.)

Hence, the essential difficulty with **The Devil's Elixirs** may, in our opinion, be described as "the aesthetic man's" not wholly successful attempt to write a novel in terms of moral and religious values. Nowhere is this point so clearly evidenced as by the old painter's "sin" of desecrating Holy Art; and on that "sin" all the rest of the book is made to depend. If the moralist reader defines Francesko's "sin" as merely fornication, three centuries of haunting and five generations of misguided lives become an implausible and downright absurd consequence.

But if lust and self-will caused Francesko to desecrate Art in the first place, his descendants are lustful and self-willed without being much concerned with Art. They are a shadowy and uninteresting lot, primarily because the main story left so little space to tell about them. Their penchant for brother-sister incest is a "horror detail" common to many Romantic works. About it there is nothing confessional in this case: Hoffmann had no sister—as Brentano and Chateaubriand did. Moreover, these sinning ancestors of Medardus are Italians: to Hoffmann as to his fellow Germans, Italy was that ambiguous realm of beauty and of horror, the land of Raphael and of the Borgias. And these ancestors are aristocrats. One needs to redraw the genealogical table from Walther Harich's 1920 version to include the "German maiden" who was Aurelia's grandmother and "the poor girl," apparently also German, who was Medardus' mother, both unnamed. These two tiny details are not without significance. To put it frankly, the impetus that enables the good strain in these dual natures to prevail over the evil strain, comes, it would seem, from an infusion of German blood.

Over these fictitious ancestors Hoffmann cast a very thin veil of verisimilitude. Francesko's career of wantonness began after the death of his master, Leonardo da Vinci, who died in 1519. *That* Leonardo, supreme master in his own right and surrogate "father-in-Art" to Francesko, then "prefigures" Prior Leonardus in the latter's surrogate fatherhood of Medardus. Five successive generations must, therefore, fit into the approximately 250 years from 1520 to, say, 1770. (Insurance actuaries might lift eyebrows at this.)

The family founder, sea-hero Camillo, "Prince of P.," died fighting against Algerian pirates in the service of the Republic of Genoa. Vaguely he reflects Andrea Doria, *doge* of Genoa, who fought Algerian pirates in 1541 and 1550 but survived those expeditions. Vaguely too, Francesko the painter, who initiated a sensual new style in art, may reflect either or both of the two painters Caravaggio, one of whom died in 1543, the other in 1610. The rest of the chronicle resembles any number of scandal-ridden families in Europe. It may be worth mentioning that nineteenth-century aristocrats still dwelt nostalgically over that encyclopedia of aristocratic scandal, the *Mémoires* of the Duc de Saint-Simon, so that readers of 1816 might rather relish a genealogical account like the one in the present novel.

In making Francesko a painter and in allowing painting (in this novel) to stand for all the arts, Hoffmann was again following a literary vogue. In 1816, painter-heroes were still *de facto* sympathetic, just as disorder in studios was still picturesque. Before mid-century, readers would weary of them and would regard their studios as merely slovenly. In other tales of his, Hoffmann has musician heroes, a poet or two, an actor, even a master goldsmith, as well as a few heroes not dedicated to one of the arts. Significantly, however, he was himself also a painter. Hewett-Thayer's *Hoffmann: Author of the Tales* (1948) reproduces twelve of his surviving pieces, which reveal a considerable talent, though something short of pictorial genius. Among lost items there was a group picture of Julia Marc together with her sister Minna and her brother Maurice, painted by Hoffmann in the autumn of 1809. It is reported that he easily completed the figures of the sister and brother but that he reworked the face of Julia ten times. Thus Francesko's difficulty in painting the face of his St. Rosalia, especially the eyes, recapitulates an actual experience of the author's. Most likely to startle the modern reader in **The Devil's Elixirs** is its vivid and accurate portrayal of abnormal mental states. Such knowledge is widely mistaken to be of the twentieth century only and dependent on Freud, whereas in fact German Romanticism was characterized by extensive theorizing about what we would now term psychology and psychiatry. Any summary of those complex and varying theories would exceed space available here and would lie beyond the present writer's competence, but, borrowing terms from one of those theorists and quickly generalizing them, we may state certain basic concepts.

There was postulated a "sidereal self," or "star self," analogous to the Christian soul, within the human body or "Adamitic self." Inhibited, not so much by "flesh" as by the constrictions of the conscious mind, this "sidereal self" was normally mute, undetected even. Hypnosis might enable it to speak in its own right. All abnormal states were manifestations of it: madness, ecstasy, dreams, catatonia, schizophrenia, intuition and prophecy, "visions" and "inspirations," even physical disease. Existing outside of time, it might "see" the past or foresee the future, sometimes without being able to distinguish either "sight" from the present moment. Its capabilities were well nigh infinite, and it had enormous power to compel the "Adamitic self" to "impossible" feats of strength or endurance. Speculation tended to shade these concepts off, in different directions, into religion, into science, and into the ever mysterious matter of artistic creation.

Madness, some thought, was itself a type of dream state, and Medardus, in the first stage of his Italian journey, is mad and confined to a madhouse. From Belcampo he hears a description of the prolonged catatonia from which he has recently revived. The ghastly hallucinations that beset him during his weeks of self-inflicted "penitential exercises" are rather more literary in nature and may derive from painting, such as from the canvases of Hieronymus Bosch, but earlier in the novel his dreaming mind—his "sidereal self"—sensed his mother's death, far away, at the moment when that event occurred. In prison, his dreaming mind foresaw the same murderous Dominican conclave that he was later to behold in reality. Which is to say he foreknew that experience without being able to locate it in time (the future) or space (in or near Rome).

One important instance of such dream-knowledge comes from an immediate literary source, hence at second remove from the Romantic theorists. Toward the close of the opening subsection of the novel, Medardus relates the episode of the beautiful woman who came to him as he was sitting in the confessional and declared her passionate love for him; that was in the monastery church in "B." and before he fled "into the world." In Part II, Aurelia (in that purloined letter) reports the same story. So it was she who came to Medardus' confessional—but *her* episode occurred in a church of the *Residenz* and long before Medardus arrived there in secular garb. The two accounts, which are related with identical details, even to the wording, cannot be identified as a single realistic encounter, nor should we strain our imaginations to an incredible parallelism of coincidence. Rather, we are to understand that their two "sidereal selves," in mystical affinity, left their corporeal bodies to meet in a place which was neither the monastery church in "B." nor a church in the *Residenz,* but in a church outside of earthly time and space. Both accounts are told as actualities, which they cannot be; but they are not dream fantasies either. One, and only one, meeting occurred, and it was "real" to their "essential" selves while being quite "impossible" to their human bodies.

Patently, the motif is borrowed from Kleist's *Das Käthchen von Heilbronn.* In that play (ii, 9) it is narrated how the hero lay ill with fever in his home castle on St. Sylvester's night (New Year's Eve) and how, during an interval when he seemed like dead, his spirit (*Geist*) was in Heilbronn encountering Käthchen, of whose very existence he was then unaware; Käthchen tells him his own dream as being an experience of *hers* on that same St. Sylvester's night (iv, 2). Both foresaw *and pre-experienced* the same future event simultaneously while their physical persons were miles apart.

That dream encounter was, however, "pure," as the Medardus-Aurelia encounter was not. Medardus' covert lust is abundantly clear, but in that purloined letter Aurelia reveals her own impure sexuality. At age three or four, she writes to the Abbess, "the seed had already been sown which for so long flourished rampant and disastrously in my heart." At that tender age, namely, she was witness of her mother's guilty passion before that painting of a richly clad man—who proves to have been Medardus' deceased father "Francesko"—and herself conceived a passion for the man in the picture.

She "forgot" the picture then; she "forgot" it after a second viewing about ten years later; but in her adolescence (at the age of puberty) she recalled it suddenly, vividly, and totally in a "dream-state," that is, in a waking moment when her "sidereal self," or, as we would say, "her subconscious," assumed abrupt, momentary control of her conscious mind. In that instant of devastating recall, the man in the picture said to her, "You are in love with me, Aurelia," and then it was that she realized the man was not richly clad, as in his portrait, but was wearing the garb of the Capuchin Order. Her "subconscious" had "updated" the costume, indeed "updated" the generation, without her ever having seen or heard of the living Medardus, and the "sidereal self" of Medardus had "projected itself" to *her* through the medium of "a portrait come to life."

A few lines further in the letter she recounts how she chanced upon the copy of *The Monk* "in her brother's room" and how she took it away, read it, and learned from it about "wicked love." The book itself is a corruptive influence, in fact, one of a series of corruptive influences. It informs her, in some "impossible" way, about Medardus. In some "impossible" way it was "sent" by Medardus. Moreover, her presence in her brother's room suggests a subconscious incestuous connection with Hermogen. Her entire adolescence, the letter goes on to report, was a troubled period of tomboyish ways, of moods of near-hysterical mirth alternating with moods of brooding withdrawal. Such awareness on Hoffmann's part of "adolescent psychology" is far in advance of Rousseau and anticipatory of such Dostoevskian figures as Netochka Nezvanova, or even Kolya Krasotkin.

In a word, Aurelia is the feminine counterpart of Medardus, prone like him to evil from the start, corrupted by book and picture, obsessed with the dream-image of the Capuchin monk to the point where she goes, in spirit (though to her it seemed in reality), to his confessional and declares her passion for him.

One source for Hoffmann's psychological information was Gotthilf Heinrich Schubert's *Symbolik des Traumes,* which was published in Bamberg in 1814 and which he read in the interval between composition of Part I and Part II of his novel. He also knew J. C. Reil's *Rhapsodien über die Anwendung der psychischen Curmethode auf Geisteszerrüttungen* (1803) and C. A. F. Kluge's *Versuch einer Darstellung des animalischen Magnetismus* [i.e., hypnosis] *als Heilmittel* (1811), as well as similar books from abroad. Hypnosis had first been widely used in therapy by the renowned Franz Anton Mesmer, who died in 1815 when he was in his eighties. In addition, Hoffmann was personally acquainted with two of the new "practicing theorists." In Bamberg he had associated with Dr. Markus, physician to the Prince-Bishop of Bamberg, director of the St. Getreu asylum for the insane, and uncle of Julia Marc; the portrait of him that Hoffmann painted is still to be seen in the Bamberg Municipal Library. In Berlin he was associating with Dr. Koreff, physician to Prussian Chancellor Hardenberg, professor at the University of Berlin, a member of the real-life club of "The Serapion Brethren," and represented as the moody Vinzenz in the fictionalized version of that club in the frame tale of *Die Serapionsbrüder.*

As symbols for the twofold self, "sidereal" and "Adamitic," any twofold things from real life might serve literary purposes: one's shadow or mirror-image, a painted portrait or a statue that came alive, a ventriloquist and his dummy or an automaton and its magician operator, identical twins or even non-identical twins, or any two persons not akin but so resembling each other as to pass for "doubles." A superstition to the effect that meeting one's double signified approaching death is alluded to by Medardus, but nothing comes of the matter.

Hoffmann exploited several of the motifs in the above inventory, but it was the motif of the "double" that he developed most elaborately, and precisely in *The Devil's Elixirs.* Later writers would vary the theme: Poe, in *William Wilson,* where the "other" William Wilson is objectified conscience; Stevenson, in *The Strange Case of Dr. Jekyll and Mr. Hyde,* where the brutish "Mr. Hyde" is the suppressed aspect of Dr. Jekyll's "normal self"; Conrad, in *The Secret Sharer,* where the other "man" is the ship captain's guilty past, objectified.

In these stories there is, regularly, one body; the antithetical "half" of the divided personality is depicted as if it were a separate person. The evil "Mr. Hyde" within the good Dr. Jekyll is "released" by drinking a certain chemical potion, but there is only one body. The final scene of *William Wilson* reveals that "the other man" is "represented" by the hero's mirror-image. The more complex *Secret Sharer* works on two levels: realistically, the captain manages to hoodwink the visiting officer from the *Sephora,* his former ship, into believing he is not, despite the resemblance, the murderer who escaped from the *Sephora* by swimming away, so that the visiting officer leaves without denouncing him; symbolically, the captain's guilty past, allegedly as a second body, comes swimming to the present ship, where he remains hidden until, by a desperately dangerous sailing manoeuvre of the captain's, "he" is dropped off at sea near a large island. It is left for the reader to identify the visiting officer with the swimming fugitive, the knower of the secret with the secret itself, personified.

But in *The Devil's Elixirs* there are two bodies, Medardus and Viktorin, sons of one father but different mothers. Through Part I the two half-brothers pass through symmetrically alternating episodes. While Medardus is planning to escape from monkhood to a secular existence, Viktorin is planning to conceal his secular personality in a bogus monkhood. The two meet at the Devil's Chasm and exchange their lives and their garbs. While Medardus travels, Viktorin wanders the forests. While Medardus is at Baron von F.'s castle, where he commits murder and almost commits rape, Viktorin is in the forest ranger's house, where he unsuccessfully attempts murder and rape. At the forester's the two meet but do *not* re-exchange lives and garbs. While Medardus is at court in the *Residenz,* Viktorin is in the *Residenz* madhouse. On Medardus' wedding day the two meet once more; they "escape" together, and in the forest Viktorin effects by force the re-exchange of lives and garbs.

As Part II begins, Medardus is in the Italian madhouse, clothed, thanks to Belcampo, in his original Capuchin habit. We would now expect Viktorin, who is in court dress, to be at court for as long a period as Medardus remains in the madhouse, but no such claim is made and we are left wondering about Viktorin's whereabouts. Perhaps we are to understand that his return to the monastery in "B." and his confession of sins there are "simultaneous" with Medardus' confession of sins to the Prior of the Capuchin motherhouse in Rome. But then Viktorin feigned death and vanished, so that Medardus' Roman adventures are left without symmetrical parallel in Viktorin's life.

For a moment we wonder whether there *are* two bodies after all. Can Medardus' turn to the good signify that

"the Viktorin side of him" is suppressed and no longer exists? The idea is untenable. Medardus cannot very well murder Aurelia before a churchful of people without being apprehended; moreover, his subsequent blessedness would in that case be impossible. There must be two bodies, as we understood all along, but with such interpenetration of personalities as to elude rational explanation. As half-*brothers,* they have the mysterious affinities of identical twins, but as *half*-brothers they embody the Good-Evil dichotomy which marks their whole family line.

Unique among the characters of this novel is Medardus' "second double," Peter Schönfeld, who prefers the Italian translation of his name, Pietro Belcampo. Like Medardus, he is half German, half Italian; both are "mad," in specialized senses of that word; both journey through the world, both end up in the Capuchin monastery at "B.," Medardus as a monk, Belcampo as lay brother Peter. The two are "companions through life," even if they seem to be only intermittently so. They represent an interesting variation on the companion pairs, Don Quixote and Sancho Panza, Don Giovanni and Leporello.

If Belcampo is not exactly blood-brother to Shakespeare's clowns, he may fairly be said to be their first cousin. He babbles "nonsense" like Feste, he reasons like Touchstone, he speaks the bitter truth like King Lear's Fool. Like them, he moves easily among the "real" characters without being quite real himself and without the author's attempting to account realistically for his presence or actions. As a barber, he "transforms" people (and how Thomas Mann was to transform that transformation scene in *Der Tod in Venedig* just short of a century later, in 1911!). As the rescuer of Medardus, first from the mercantile city, then from death in the forest, he serves a utilitarian story-function, but both rescues are mysterious and, in a sense, "impossible."

Not only does Belcampo talk "nonsense," he *is* Nonsense personified. He is almost an allegory of that freesoaring artistic imagination that releases the spirit from the handcuffs and shackles of "rationality" and dullness. As the begetter of spontaneous laughter, like a clown with a small child, he finds his proper niche in Rome as a puppeteer, a one-man side show, dealing in the pure comedy of the zany, old Italian *commedia dell' arte.* Medardus, upon witnessing his antics, bursts out in long disaccustomed, spontaneous, childlike laughter—as we never dreamed him capable of. To Hoffmann, such pure comedy represented the pinnacle of Art, it is true, yet the episode comes oddly in a book that purports to deal with a somber religious theme.

The verbal antics of Belcampo are no less extravagant in their innocent truth than Medardus' less-than-innocent antics of behavior. In some of the exchanges between these two we tend to hear the mad Don Quixote conversing with the mad Cardenio in the Sierra Morena, and then we feel that the novel has passed its self-imposed religious limits to raise the wholly different question of: What is reality?

Michael T. Jones (essay date spring 1977)

SOURCE: Jones, Michael T. "Hoffmann and the Problem of Social Reality: A Study of *Kater Murr.*" *Monatshefte* 69, no. 1 (spring 1977): 45-57.

[*In the following essay, Jones examines Hoffmann's use of a double narrative in* Lebens-Ansichten des Katers Murr. *According to Jones, the novel's technique reflects Hoffmann's underlying belief that the artistic imagination is ultimately irreconcilable with predominant social institutions.*]

E. T. A. Hoffmann's *Lebensansichten des Katers Murr* is known superficially to Germanists as a unique and humorous experiment in novelistic form, containing a double narrative and told from the perspective of a lively and endearing cat. Critics who have dealt with the novel, however, have concerned themselves primarily with the figure of Johannes Kreisler, and condescending commentary on the largely unknown Murr section—usually regarding the parallel structures of the two narratives—has often seemed perfunctory. The cat's autobiography presents a difficult problem indeed to tradition-minded scholars who approach Hoffmann's novel nourished on German Classicism and Romanticism as insuperable models of literary creation, for Murr's immersion in and perversion of various aspects of this tradition are occasions for inexhaustible humor and satire. The difficulty is already unmistakable in Murr's preface, in which he appeals in the language of *Empfindsamkeit* to the responses of kindred spirits and beautiful souls as consolation for the cold rebuffs of insensitive reviewers. Hoffmann's *magnum opus* varies widely from—indeed parodies—the *Bildungsroman* scheme of a dreamy-eyed Franz Sternbald wandering through an idyllic German landscape, chasing a "schöne Unbekannte" on his way to a mythical, paradisaic Italy. Here, Nürnberg and Rome are replaced by Göniönesmühl and Sieghartsweiler, and idealization of geographic localities which were previously mere ciphers is abandoned in favor of savage satire of isolated German provincial reality.

Faced with such departure from romantic tradition, Hoffmann scholarship has in general contented itself with long journeys into the labyrinths of plot and character, into the "buntscheckige Welttändelei"[1] of his multi-faceted world. As the foundation of this world, it has uncritically accepted Hoffmann's own view of an irreparable, unbridgable dualism between the "higher realm" of art and a bourgeois existence essentially hostile to art and to those who devote themselves to it. From this unhistorical perspective, interpretations of *Kater Murr,* if they do not exhaust themselves in plot summaries,[2] usually center on the artist figure and his encounters with an unfavorable environment, on the situation of "the" artist in "the" world. Peter von Matt, for example, describes the dichotomy as follows: "Für Hoffmann gibt es keine Analogie mehr zwischen Natur- und Kunstprodukt,—nicht weil er das künstlerische Tun gegenüber der fraglosen Vollendung alles Gewachsenen als nichtig empfände, sondern umgekehrt: auf Grund einer scharfen Verneinung alles Natürlichen im Sinne des Vegetativ-Organischen. Nur im Innern des Einzelnen befindet sich das Absolute, das Göttliche. . . ."[3] The critic borrows imagery from Romanticism to refer ostensibly to nature but actually to the social world rejected by Hoffmann: "das Vegetativ-Organische" is a vague, hypothetical construct of the early nineteenth century which is not only—correctly enough—attributed to Hoffmann but also *uncritically accepted* by the critic himself, who ignores the essential insight of the social sciences into the dialectical tension between productive individual subjectivity and socio-cultural lifeworld; it is a static, mechanistic, ahistorical category which he hypostatizes and reifies.

In contrast to simple acceptance of romantic and neoromantic conceptions of art as somehow necessary, inevitable, even mystical and of a higher ontological order, Hans Mayer, in an influential essay, first interpreted the radical dualism of Hoffmann's world as an "Ausdruck ungelöster deutscher Gesellschaftsverhältnisse."[4] Building on this foundation, Charles Hayes recognizes in a recent essay the primarily social nature of the conflicts portrayed in Hoffmann's work and asserts that the reality seen as universal by Hoffmann is actually bourgeois reality.[5] Most recently, Diana Stone Peters has endeavored to show by means of his metaphor of the heavenly ladder that Hoffmann conceived of art as firmly rooted in everyday life, that the dualistic opposition of artist and philistine actually involves mutual interaction and relativization, that the fact that Hoffmann "examines the artist as well as the philistine from a critical point of view reveals the essentially constructive and conciliatory intention of his satire."[6] While accepting the centrality of the problematic relationship of art and social reality in Hoffmann's work, the following reading of *Kater Murr,* with greater emphasis than is customary on Murr's role as foil for Kreisler, will take issue with Peters' thesis of conciliation and will rather be concerned to show Hoffmann's increasing awareness of the hopeless omnipresence of social sanctions and strictures and of the deceptive nature of the haven apparently offered by the "other realm" of art.

I

A mechanistic Marxist analysis of class determination of ideology cannot do justice to Hoffmann, since Peters is certainly correct that Hoffmann directs his satire specifically against the philistine, who can be found among either bourgeoisie or nobility, so that "court and bourgeoisie can be treated as one entity".[7] Refinement of traditional Marxist categories is available in the theoretical treatise of Peter L. Berger and Thomas Luckmann, who delineate a general phenomenological theory of the sociology of knowledge which emphasizes knowledge of everyday, routinized life.[8] Knowledge consists of common-sense definitions of reality; these include institutionalized, socially-patterned modes of behavior, activity, feeling, or experience. Such social constructs—in our context, for example, knowledge of what constitutes appropriate sexual or occupational roles—are experienced as external, objective, given, and autonomous; the internalization of these social expectations and standards constitutes their "reification" (*Verdinglichung*), which is defined as the "apprehension of human phenomena as if they were things, that is, in non-human or possibly super-human terms."[9] In actual fact, however, the institutions of society, as well as the processes of legitimation which support them, are historical products of the activity of men. Berger and Luckmann's philosophical anthropology of the self recognizes man's primordial capacity for externalization of his own potentiality, which can be congealed and objectified in products. These products are not only economic in nature but also include the patterns of the socio-cultural life-world. Thus, the fundamental dialectic of social life is that social institutions and meaning systems (including intellectual products), while humanly produced, yet obtain massive objective facticity. They may exert a compelling force which can transcend their class origins.

In his somewhat reluctant conversation with the Geheimrat, Kreisler reveals the massiveness of the socially-produced meaning system which he confronts from earliest childhood. "So ist es auch gewiß, daß es nicht Erziehungszwang, nicht besonderer Eigensinn des Schicksals, nein, daß es der gewöhnlichste Lauf der Dinge war, der mich fortschob, so daß ich unwillkürlich dort hinkam, wo ich eben nicht hin wollte" (381). The ominous phrase "der gewöhnlichste Lauf der Dinge" designates the pervasive social reality with which Johannes comes into conflict in his youthful choice—or lack of choice—of a future vocation. Despite the family's extensive and apparently rather successful musical activity, its most respected member succeeded in life by rejecting the musical proclivities of the family and beginning a career as *Beamter,* in which he made rapid progress and thus became the family's model of achievement. Under the influence of the formulative force of "primary socialization" occurring during child-

hood, young Johannes naturally desired to emulate his successful relative and therefore rejected the musical career for which he was obviously suited: "Daß die Kunst, welche mein Inneres erfüllte, mein eigentliches Streben, die wahre einzige Tendenz meines Lebens sein dürfe, fiel mir um so weniger ein, als ich gewohnt war, von Musik, Malerei, Poesie, nicht anders reden zu hören, als von ganz angenehmen Dingen, die zur Erheiterung und Belustigung dienen könnten" (382). Even a musically active family uncritically accepts the socially normative view of art as merely a pleasant pastime but as certainly no way to get ahead on the social scale, and this is, after all, one's goal in life. Documented in great detail in the **"Kreisleriana"** is the misery of providing music for people who consider it either as part of the education of daughters from better families or as a pleasant background for card games, as part, in other words, of what "one does." Kreisler cannot accept such degradation of the art he loves and flees it again and again.

Such social norms, although humanly produced, attain not only normative but also cognitive status, so that they are experienced as eternal, objective givens which, although "known," must be constantly reaffirmed. The process of legitimation ascribes cognitive dignity to objectivated norms, thereby justifying the existing institutional order. Accepted norms of social behavior and their legitimation are a recurrent theme of *Kater Murr* and are always the object of satire. These "konventionelle(n) Verhältnisse, wie sie nun einmal bestehen" (351), as Benzon calls them, are unmercifully ridiculed in the description of Irenäus' pseudo-court. Although the actual business of governing the minute area had been taken over by the duke, Irenäus, as heir to a small fortune, insists despite his true status as a private citizen on playing prince in a royal court. Hoffmann never tires of poking fun at everyday life in the Irenäus court: the competition among scheming advisers for the ear of the prince, his excessive concern with matters of royal dignity, his fear of assassination, his playing political games with the marriages of his children, his princely fear of conspiracy among rebellious vassals, and finally his insistence on the use of French for festive occasions. This creates problems for the rather obese Hofmarschall: "'Erzeigen Sie,' sprach Meister Abraham, 'erzeigen Sie mir die Güte, beste Exzellenz, und beobachten Sie sich selbst. Hat Ihnen der Himmel nicht ein schönes volltönendes Stimmorgan verliehen, und wenn Ihnen das Französische ankommt, da beginnen Sie plötzlich zu zischen, zu lispeln, zu schnarren, und dabei verzerren sich Dero angenehme Gesichtszüge ganz erschrecklich, und selbst der hübsche, feste, ernste Anstand, dessen Dieselben sonst mächtig, wird verstört durch allerlei seltsame Konvulsionen'" (349). The novel is a veritable treasure-house of such gems. Behind the biting humor, of course, lies Hoffmann's contempt for the political system of small, territorial courts and their endless pomposity and intrigues.

The process of legitimation of socially-accepted norms of behavior is far from foolproof; there always exists the possibility of rebellion, and with the position of choir master begins Kreisler's rebellion. To hinder the possibility of rejection of social norms, conceptual mechanisms for the maintenance of universes of meaning can be called into play when the ruling reality definition is threatened. Since the rise in economic significance of the middle class had not been accompanied by corresponding political influence, the new "bourgeois" values had assumed a distinctly "escapist" appearance. In his cultural history of the phenomenon of melancholy, Wolf Lepenies has analyzed the values codified in *Werther*—love of nature and "freedom," lonely "Schwärmen," inwardness, depth of feeling etc.—as manifestations of "bourgeois escapism"; however, they were labeled in the "Eigenschaftspsychologie" of the late eighteenth century as "melancholy" in accordance with an old tradition.[10] Such values were experienced as threatening as soon as their attraction began to spread to larger groups: "In that case . . ., the deviant version congeals into a reality in its own right, which, by its existence within the society, challenges the reality status of the symbolic universe as originally constituted. The group that has objectivated this deviant reality becomes the carrier of an alternative definition of reality."[11] The passage in which Kreisler relates of his conflicts with the institutional order in his position as choir master is an example of such deviance in choosing among competing reality definitions. The danger for society of such deviance is not altered by the vague, amorphous, undefined character of the alternative: indeed, because of its obscurity and formlessness, it may be perceived as even more attractive and thus more threatening.

Information regarding this previous conflict is revealed in Johannes' conversation with Benzon. Although they had been intimate friends in the past and she had encouraged him to continue his musical endeavors (397), he now finds his friend greatly changed. Having attempted to describe his inner unrest and deep depression, for which there exists only the remedy of music, he only meets with her rebuke: ". . . immer habe ich gedacht, daß die Musik auf Sie zu stark, mithin verderblich wirke . . ." (356). Benzon, having established herself as an important personage in Sieghartshof and now plotting courtly intrigues to further her own ends, has obviously "copped out" to a social system she had previously disdained. Kreisler reacts in the characteristic manner: ". . . indem er, so ernst und tiefbewegt er zuvor gesprochen, plötzlich den besonderen Ton der Ironie wieder aufnahm, der ihm eigen . . ." (356). Irony is a defense mechanism he employs when confronted

with lack of comprehension in the philistine world, and ironic is his tone as he continues his account of life as a choir director. Having suffered repeated indignities, he at last has learned to respect the "Verhältnisse, wie sie nun einmal bestehen," or so he says, and is ready to admit how artists really should live, that it cannot be otherwise: "Ja Verehrte, Sie glauben nicht, was ich während meiner Kapellmeisterschaft profitiert, vorzüglich aber die schöne Überzeugung, wie gut es ist, wenn Künstler förmlich in Dienst treten, der Teufel und seine Großmutter könnte es sonst mit dem stolzen übermütigen Volke aushalten. Laßt den braven Komponisten Kapellmeister oder Musikdirektor werden, den Dichter Hofpoet, den Maler Hofporträtisten, den Bildhauer Hofporträtmeißler und Ihr habt bald keine unnütze Fantasten mehr im Lande, vielmehr lauter nützliche Bürger von guter Erziehung und milden Sitten" (357). Such terms as "Erziehung" and "Sitte," as well as "Ordnung" and "Verhältnisse," signify throughout the novel ruling social norms and values which, having achieved cognitive status, are beyond any possible doubt. Kreisler's obvious contempt for the artist who sells himself out to some prince and becomes a "nützlicher Bürger" solidifies his own position as a social outsider, for only in a recognized and paid position does he become a recognized and accepted member of the social structure. The conflict finds its inevitable culmination in the mutual rejection of court and musician when Kreisler refuses to succumb to the pressures put upon him: ". . . da ich mich schon durch einen geheimen Ostrazismus verbannt sah . . .", Kreisler—echoes of Werther—". . . lief hinaus ins Freie, unaufhaltsam fort, immer weiter fort!" (358).

These brief remarks on some aspects of Kreisler's life can serve to illuminate both his subjective state as advocate of a deviant reality definition and his resulting objective position as an unsuccessfully socialized individual, as an outsider in the social structure. From this perspective, Abraham's angry question to Benzon shows profound insight: ". . . was habt ihr alle gegen diesen Johannes, was hat er euch Böses getan? . . . wißt ihr's nicht?—Nun so will ich es euch sagen.—Seht, der Kreisler, trägt nicht eure Farben, er versteht nicht eure Redensarten . . . Er will die Ewigkeit der Verträge die ihr über die Gestaltung des Lebens geschlossen, nicht anerkennen . . ." (499). Unable to accept as eternal these social "contracts," Kreisler's tenuous position is analogous to that of the intellectual as described by Berger and Luckmann: because of his social marginality and lack of theoretical integration, he appears as a "counter-expert" in reality definition. (Abraham: ". . . ja er meint, daß ein arger Wahn, von dem ihr befangen, euch gar nicht das eigentliche Leben erschauen lasse . . ."). Although he has vague notions of an alternative plan for society, it conflicts with institutional order and thus vegetates in an institutional vacuum. For a musician in Hoffmann's Germany, the only existing institutional niche is that of choir director, and that experience had been a disastrous one indeed. In dealing with such a deviant, society must categorize him, must label him in some fashion according to a recognizable and pre-defined type; as a result of such typification, any contrary self-identification will lack all social plausibility. Thus Kreisler becomes known as a "melancholic" in the tradition of the Jacques of *As You Like It,* an identification which he also subjectively accepts (353). The essentially social nature of this category—in contrast to a notion of melancholy as a fixed essence or *Wesen*—must be emphasized.

The function in Kreisler's life of vocational role expectation has been discussed, but the second example—sexual norms and challenges to them—occupy the center of attention after his arrival at Sieghartshof. During his meeting with Hedwiga and Julia in the park, Hedwiga is disturbed by her improper erotic feelings. She also fears Kreisler's irony and disdain for her royal person and for the order she accepts as natural. By contrast, Julia is pure, innocent, unsuspecting, and passive. As a girl of bourgeois birth (as far as anyone knows), her attraction for Kreisler can assume somewhat more suitable social form and is certainly clear enough. For the widow Benzon, instructed fully as to what has transpired in the park, he represents a definite threat. His deviant conduct "challenges societal reality as such, putting into question its taken-for-granted cognitive and normative operating procedures."[12] The danger is that Kreisler may not recognize as valid the accepted "cognitive and normative operating procedures" regarding the right of a parent to choose the mate of a child and may run away with Julia. This threat to accepted social norms and its concomitant implication that the prevalent, ruling conceptual universe is less than inevitable—this is the answer to Abraham's question. In the constellation of *Kater Murr,* even the problem of romantic love, despite its apparent individuality, is basically a social one, to say nothing of marriage. Social sanctions permeate all human relationships, are omnipresent, cannot be avoided or fled.

This principle is brought home most forcefully later in the novel. Kreisler, forced to flee, seeks asylum for a time in the protective arms of cloister and church, an alternative with at first seems attractive: "Kreisler konnte nicht anders als dies zugeben und überdies versichern, daß die Abtei sich ihm aufgetan wie ein Asyl, in das er geflüchtet . . ." (539). But Hoffmann's description of the abbot, with whom this conversation occurs, is already cause for suspicion; he is described as a "Zögling der Propaganda in Rom.—Selbst gar nicht geneigt, den Ansprüchen des Lebens zu entsagen, insofern sie mit geistlicher Sitte und Ordnung verträglich . . ." (535). Those insidious demons "Stand," "Sitte," and "Ordnung" have not been left behind at all in this superficially protective haven for the surrender of life to art. The abbot's goal in this exchange has indeed little to do with art: Benzon has enlisted his aid in removing Johannes from Sieghartshof to the cloister, so that she can proceed unhindered to marry Julia off to Ignaz. So the abbot speaks eloquently enough of the "wirres Treiben" of the world and of the higher existence for which Johannes was born; Benzon has tutored him well as to how Johannes can be most deeply touched and which means of persuasion should best be employed. Johannes is momentarily deceived. He agrees yet admits his distrust of "Entsagung," a point the abbot seizes upon to his misfortune, for the exhortation of sexual abstinence causes the reversal now familiar: "Da begann aber auf Kreislers Antlitz jenes seltsame Muskelspiel, das den Geist der Ironie zu verkünden pflegte, der seiner mächtig worden" (542). In the speech that follows, Kreisler, as a reaction to the abbot's mention of social sanctions which could ruin him, pours out his bitterness at the games played and power struggles fought around the phenomenon of romantic love and marriage: the pretty speeches and downcast eyes of the lovelies, the fathers' eagerness to shed their daughters on such respectable persons as an "Exkapellmeister," alternative possibilities of romantic idylls with the daughter of a butcher or a miller. He expresses his deep resentment at a social system which accomplishes the total perversion of romantic love and employs marriageable daughters as pawns. In *Kater Murr,* beginnings of possibly genuine, authentic romantic relationships are smothered by the ever-scheming Benzon, just as the romance of Chiara and Abraham is thwarted by the prince, always, that is, by means of an all-powerful system of social sanctions. Thus, when Peters asserts that Kreisler leaves the monastery when he "fully realizes the dangers of creation in 'splendid isolation'"[13] in order to "compose in a manner which directly effects his fellow man's communion with God,"[14] she misinterprets the passage and misses the point. It is rather when the abbot at last shows himself to be an agent of the machinations of courtly intrigue that Kreisler understands that the temptation of the superficially safe retreat of a life spent in a cloister and in dedication to art is nothing more than a trick, a trap to eliminate him for evil ends. It has become clear in this central scene of the Kreisler narrative that there is no haven, no refuge from the brutal world of Irenäus and Benzon, that the vision of bourgeois escapism even into the realm of art is a cruel delusion, a form of quiescent passivity which only reinforces the despised social order.

By means of the socially distributed knowledge of accepted, routinized, and habitualized roles regarding vocational endeavor and sexual behavior, some of the prime points of conflict with society in Kreisler's life have been summarized which resulted in his unsuccessful social integration and consequent typification as a bizarre, unconventional, melancholic individual. But the title hero and his relationship to the whole can no longer be ignored.

II

Hoffmann's critics have, understandably enough, been somewhat unwilling to consider the force and function of the devastating satire so unconsciously offered by the irrepressible Murr. Understandably, because Hoffmann is not only content to parody the literary genre begun by *Wilhelm Meister*; but rather, as Herbert Singer has remarked in a fine essay, ". . . er unternimmt nichts Geringeres, als das Gesamtphänomen von Kultur und Gesellschaft der glanzvollsten Epoche der deutschen Geistesgeschichte, der Goethezeit, planvoll zu negieren und zu zerstören."[15] To destroy everything, in other words, dear to the hearts of tradition-minded critics. Whereas the Enlightenment receives a few sideswipes, the harder blows are saved for "Empfindsamkeit" and "Geniekult." Neither is Romanticism itself spared: Singer notes that Murr once actually refers to himself as a "Romantiker" and that particularly Murr's poems must be considered "Parodien romantischer Poesie."[16] Murr's poetic theory is clear enough in its "justification" of Romantic poetic practice: "Verse sollen in dem in Prosa geschriebenen Buche das leisten was der Speck in der Wurst, nämlich hin und wieder in kleinen Stückchen eingestreut . . ." (638). And in another splendid passage, Murr offers the results of his linguistic studies: "Vorzüglich faßte ich den Charakter der Sprache auf, und bewies, daß da Sprache überhaupt nur symbolische Darstellung des Naturprinzips in der Gestaltung des Lauts sei, mithin es nur *eine* Sprache geben könne, auch das Kätzische und Hündische in der besondern Formung des Pudelischen, Zweige eines Baums wären, von höherem Geist inspirierte Kater und Pudel sich daher verstünden. Um meinen Satz ganz ins klare zu stellen, führte ich mehrere Beispiele aus beiden Sprachen an und machte auf die gleichen Stammwurzeln aufmerksam, von: Bau—Bau—Mau—Miau—Blaf—blaf—Auvau—Korr—Kurr—Ptsi—Pschrzi u.s.w." (348). A more marvelous rendition of the Romantic philosophy of and preoccupation with language can scarcely be imagined.

But even in the midst of his smiles, the reader is justified in becoming somewhat puzzled. What is the function of such satire of the ideal of *Bildung* and of an entire intellectual tradition? Singer quotes Jean Paul—that the task of humor is to reveal "Thorheit und eine tolle Welt"—and adds: "Die 'tolle Welt' ist aber die, welche die unsterblichen Meisterwerke deutscher Dichtung und Musik ermöglicht hat und in die hineingeboren zu sein ein Dichter und Musiker wie Hoffmann, so sollten wir glauben, als höchstes Glück empfinden müßte."[17] Then why not? Although Singer does not pose it (and this is a major weakness of his essay), the question seems unavoidable and leads once again directly to the problem of social reality.

Murr's first moments of consciousness reveal already his decisive trait: ". . . ich machte die erste Erfahrung von moralischer Ursache und Wirkung und eben ein moralischer Instinkt trieb mich an, die Krallen ebenso schnell wieder einzuziehen, als ich sie hervorgeschleudert" (305). This action earns Murr the name "Samtpfötchen." Of course, moral instinct is not at work here at all but rather Murr's first experiences with the sanctions and authority of society—his "primary socialization," to which he readily acquiesces. Subsequently, the point is made more clearly when Murr describes his education: Abraham had left him complete freedom to educate himself as long as he continued to bow to "gewisse Normalprinzipien" (320), without which no society would be possible. Natural language and behavior ("natürliche Artigkeit") are stressed in contrast to stiff, formal courtly convention. Despite his "freedom," Murr cannot avoid the occasional sting of Abraham's birch rod; often forced to renounce his natural instincts, he comes, theoretically at least, to reject them because they "[entstehen] aus einer gewissen abnormen Stimmung des Gemüts." (321). Only Murr's instinctual inclination toward "higher culture" prevents his running away. Higher culture consists of acquiescence to conventional social sanctions and of the "Drang nach den Wissenschaften und Künsten" (321) personified by Murr. Hayes has seen in this passage a critical view of the typical education of a German *Bildungsbürger*,[18] and Singer formulates concisely: "Murr ist jederzeit bereit und bestrebt, sich mit allen seinen Talenten in den Dienst der 'herrschenden Macht' zu stellen. Die oberste Richtschnur seines Verhaltens ist die Anpassung an die Gesellschaft."[19]

The key aspect of Murr's characterization is precisely "Anpassung." Such a category is a good deal more discomforting for traditional criticism than "philistine," the notion borrowed from Muzius to describe ahistorically an "ideal type" of "Spießbürger" insensitive to art. ("Philistine" carries with it, as did "melancholic," connotations of a particular fixed essence, eternal and unchanging.) Murr shares the stage in his autobiography with other figures who are manifestations of other kinds of accommodation to the exigencies of the middle-class world: Hoffmann offers in the Murr sections a number of contrasts which illustrate various developments and possibilities of the middle class. Whereas the bourgeoisie is, with the problematic exceptions of Kreisler and Abraham, virtually absent in the Kreisler story, it is to be found in Murr in all its "buntscheckige Welttändelei"; yet such figures as Muzius and Ponto have received little critical comment.

The character of Murr is a splendid parody of the dilettante artist and the pedantic scholar. The first book he reads is Knigge—a marvelous touch on Hoffmann's part—, and he finds in this Emily Post of the German bourgeoisie important insights for cats who want to succeed in human society. Meanwhile, his diverse literary efforts are crowned with a tragedy; Knigge and high tragedy, social convention and pedantry, and self-glorification are fused in the character of this unforgettable cat. With his first painful experiences of the outside world, however, Murr begins to realize that there is much of the world he does not yet understand. Thus, he is susceptible to the elucidations of his friend Muzius concerning the nature of the philistine, the first of Hoffmann's several contrasts. Muzius' solution is the "Burschentum," and he explains ". . . daß der Katzbursch offen, ehrlich, uneigenützig, herzhaft, stets bereit dem Freunde zu helfen" (503). Murr joins the fraternity amid great rejoicing, but the further course of events reveals the hollowness of these values, their status as "bürgerliche Klischees."[20] Neither the institution of "Burschentum" itself nor its subsequent persecution and illegality—a clear contemporary reference—finds any favor with Hoffmann, and both alternatives of the contrast prove fallacious.

Hoffmann takes much greater pains, particularly in volume two of *Kater Murr,* to develop a second false contrast personified by the poodle Ponto. Ponto demonstrates his worldly *savoir faire* in the episode with the little girl and the sausage, then goes to great length to prove his worldly wisdom with a long narrative of the friends Walter and Formosus, calculated to unmask realistically the true sentiments behind their public display of affection. His views gain in plausibility for Murr with his account of a life of indolence and ease under the Baron von Wipp. Murr objects to such "Knechterei" and insists upon his own "Freiheitssinn" (615) but to no avail; Ponto's jesting, condescending reply indicates sympathy for his ignorant, theoretically radical, freedom-loving friend and sounds remarkably like Benzon: ". . . du redest, guter Murr, wie du es verstehst, oder vielmehr wie es dir deine gänzliche Unerfahrenheit in den höheren Verhältnissen des Lebens erscheinen läßt . . ." (615). After expending considerable meditative effort on the matter, Murr surrenders at last to Ponto's version of high society and agrees to accompany the poodle to sweet Badine, center of the finer canine social world. His preparations for the adventure are splendid details which, through the explicit mention of French, provide a parallel to Sieghartshof: "Ich putzte mich heraus so gut ich es vermochte, las noch etwas im Knigge und durchlief auch ein paar ganz neue Lustspiele von Picard um nötigenfalls auch mich im Französischen geübt zu zeigen . . ." (642). Despite the instructions from Knigge, Murr behaves most ungallantly, but more interesting than his adventures is his theoretical self-justification. Torn between Ponto's elegance and frivolity and his own philosophical and moral principles, Murr struggles to convince himself once more that his view is correct: "Mit aller Gewalt wollte ich mich selbst überreden, daß ich bei meiner wissenschaftlichen Bildung, bei meinem Ernst in allem Tun und Treiben auf einer viel höheren Stufe stehe als der unwissende Ponto, der nur hier und da etwas von den Wissenschaften auf-

geschnappt. Ein gewisses gar nicht zu unterdrückendes Gefühl sagte mir aber ganz unverhohlen, daß Ponto überall mich in den Schatten stellen würde; ich fühlte mich gedrungen einen vornehmern Stand anzuerkennen und den Pudel Ponto zu diesem Stande zu rechnen" (638-639).

We have now arrived at a crucial point for an understanding of the entire novel. For the third contrast, and not a false one, developed by Hoffmann is the most important of all: the polar opposition throughout the entire work of Johannes Kreisler and Murr, who functions in the novel as his continual foil. Many details delineate their opposing views and opinions. As a man familiar with the true nature of art, for example, Kreisler composes from inner necessity and often suffers for it, whereas Murr sees only its utilitarian and therapeutic value—it creates a warm inner feeling which can overcome all human suffering, even hunger and toothaches (597). Yet such details come into focus only when the question of contrasting attitudes toward social reality—far from any reifying typifications concerning "the" artist or "the" philistine—is at last squarely faced. In the preceding elucidations, Kreisler was interpreted as a deviant, an outsider, as a proponent of an alternate reality definition which, in revealing the less than inevitable status of the ruling conceptual universe, is perceived as threatening and thereby evokes repressive measures of legitimation. Murr, in the passage just quoted, is wrestling with precisely the same problem, with the undeniable incongruence of two world views whose conflicting claims about goals, values, and the nature of man cannot be reconciled. Kreisler held to his views and consequently was chased from pillar to post, from court to cloister and back again, stigmatized as deviant by an uncomprehending world. How does friend Murr deal with this, the fundamental problem of the novel?

Murr rationalizes:

> Der gute Ton besteht aber so wie der gute Geschmack in der Unterlassung alles Ungehörigen. Nun meine ich ferner, daß der Unmut, der sich aus dem widersprechenden Gefühl der Überlegenheit und der ungehörigen Erscheinung bildet, den in dieser sozialen Welt unerfahrenen Dichter oder Philosophen hindert, das Ganze zu erkennen und darüber zu schweben. Es ist nötig, daß er in dem Augenblick seine innere geistige Überlegenheit nicht zu hoch anschlage und unterläßt er dies, so wird er auch die sogenannte höhere gesellschaftliche Kultur, die auf nichts anders hinausläuft als auf das Bemühen, alle Ecken, Spitzen wegzuhobeln, alle Physiognomien zu einer einzigen zu gestalten die eben deshalb aufhört eine zu sein, nicht zu hoch anschlagen. Dann wird er, verlassen von jenem Unmut, unbefangen, das innerste Wesen dieser Kultur und die armseligen Prämissen, worauf sie beruhet, leicht erkennen und schon durch die Erkenntnis sich einbürgern in die seltsame Welt, welche eben diese Kultur als unerläßlich fordert.

(639-640)

Singer's comment is pertinent: "Was Murr hier fordert und zu leisten bereit ist, ist nichts weniger als die Kapitulation des Geistes vor der Gesellschaft."[21] Capitulation, resignation, eventual integration, and theoretical justification by the intelligentsia of the "armseligen Prämissen" of a social reality apprehended as irrational, cruel, destructive, and evil on the one hand, resistance and rebellion against this reality sustained by romantic and even utopian visions of genuine art and a better mankind on the other: this is the alternative posed by *Kater Murr*. The obscurantist profundity of German Idealism is satirized in the character of Murr, who, crawling back under his oven to his scholarship and pedantry while rationalizing a system concerned with the "Bemühen, alle Ecken, Spitzen wegzuhobeln," epitomizes the social impotence of the German intelligentsia.

III

In contrast to an impression of Hoffmann's "artist's increasing tendency to recognize the necessity of living in the social world and the inefficacy of creating in splendid isolation,"[22] which is essentially what Murr does, *Kater Murr* reveals the absolute irreconcilability of the two realms, not only in its content but also in its form. In the simultaneity and polar opposition of the two narratives, the sympathy of the author is clearly with Kreisler, and negative aspects of the artist figure are missing; his irony or "melancholy" is socially determined and an understandable defense mechanism against the world. Foregoing analysis has shown Hoffmann's deadly serious intention of portraying the incongruity between the compensatory, overblown sentiments of German philosophy and poetry and the prevailing conditions of social misery in post-Napoleonic Germany. In this late, most extensive portrait of "Kleinstaaterei," Hoffmann, hardly conciliatory, recognizes more clearly than before that social norms and sanctions had pervaded and corrupted every aspect of life, including his beloved music. Creation in splendid isolation offers a kind of "inner emigration" rejected by Kreisler and by Hoffmann. "Necessity of living in the social world" indeed: there is no escape from it.

The point is brought home even more forcefully diachronically than synchronically: the episode of the birthday party, which occurs after Johannes' departure from the monastery and therefore chronologically occurs last, is narrated first and only understood by the reader when he has reached the end. Kreisler is simply left stranded in no-man's-land. (It is useless to speculate on the novel's continuation.) Along with double narration, then, *circularity* of narration in *Kater Murr* is Hoffmann's contribution in form which reinforces the impression of futility and hopelessness in the face of a system here subjected to the most pointed social satire of German Romanticism.

Notes

1. E. T. A. Hoffmann, *Elixiere des Teufels* and *Lebensansichten des Katers Murr,* ed. Walter Müller-Seidel (Darmstadt, 1971). All page references to *Kater Murr* are to this edition; quote p. 541.

2. Such is unfortunately the case with Robert S. Rosen, *E. T. A. Hoffmanns "Kater Murr": Aufbauformen und Erzählsituation* (Bonn, 1970).

3. Peter von Matt, *Die Augen des Automaten. E. T. A. Hoffmanns Imaginationslehre als Prinzip seiner Erzählkunst* (Tübingen, 1971), p. 38. Matt offers a convincing analysis of the role of Meister Abraham in the novel, a problem with which this essay does not deal; but his interpretation suffers from his neglect of Murr, who receives only one condescending footnote (p. 111).

4. Hans Mayer, "Die Wirklichkeit E. T. A. Hoffmanns," *Von Lessing bis Thomas Mann* (Pfullingen, 1959), p. 211.

5. Charles Hayes, "Phantasie und Wirklichkeit im Werke E. T. A. Hoffmanns, mit einer Interpretation der Erzählung 'Der Sandmann'," in *Ideologiekritische Studien zur Literatur: Essays I,* Volkmar Sander, ed. (Frankfurt, 1970), p. 184.

6. Diana Stone Peters, "E. T. A. Hoffmann: The Conciliatory Satirist," *Monatshefte,* 66 (1974), 56.

7. Peters, p. 58.

8. Peter L. Berger and Thomas Luckmann, *The Social Construction of Reality. A Treatise in the Sociology of Knowledge* (Garden City, N.Y., 1967).

9. Berger and Luckmann, p. 89.

10. Wolf Lepenies, *Melancholie und Gesellschaft* (Frankfurt, 1972), pp. 76-114.

11. Berger and Luckmann, pp. 106-107.

12. Berger and Luckmann, p. 113.

13. Peters, p. 57.

14. Peters, p. 58.

15. Herbert Singer, "Hoffmann: *Kater Murr,*" in *Der Deutsche Roman I,* Benno von Wiese, ed. (Düsseldorf, 1963), p. 305.

16. Singer, p. 307.

17. Singer, p. 306.

18. Hayes, pp. 212ff.

19. Singer, p. 308.

20. Singer, p. 308.

21. Singer, p. 309.

22. Peters, p. 72.

David E. Wellbery (essay date winter 1980)

SOURCE: Wellbery, David E. "E. T. A. Hoffmann and Romantic Hermeneutics: An Interpretation of Hoffmann's 'Don Juan.'" *Studies in Romanticism* 19, no. 4 (winter 1980): 455-73.

[*In the following essay, Wellbery analyzes Hoffmann's narrative technique in "Don Juan." According to Wellbery, structural complexity and an ambiguous portrayal of states of fantasy and madness introduce an underlying element of uncertainty to the story.*]

By Romantic hermeneutics I mean a set of terms and values recurring in a number of texts of the late eighteenth and early nineteenth centuries and having to do with the status and interpretation of artistic works. Briefly stated, Romantic hermeneutics is a model of understanding as the re-cognition of the sponsoring spiritual source of a work, a re-cognition made possible by the presence of this same spiritual source in the interpreter. This conception underlies Schleiermacher's celebrated contribution to hermeneutic theory, but its provenance reaches beyond Romanticism proper to the young Goethe and Herder.[1] The theoretical model elaborated by Schleiermacher is itself a function of developments within the literary system of the late eighteenth and early nineteenth centuries. A basic aspect of this system is the emergence of originality as a central norm in the evaluation of texts. Artistic works are no longer produced and received in terms of a code to which, within prescribed limits of variation, they conform, but rather are viewed as unique expressions of a specific individuality. Where this is the case, the problem of how to understand such works in the absence of binding conventions and canons of interpretation is bound to arise, and Romantic hermeneutics represents an attempt to master this problem.[2] Reflection on the possibility and conditions of adequate understanding is not, however, restricted to the theoretical texts of the period. Rather, it is a recurrent component of the literary works themselves, Faust's remarks to Wagner being only the most famous example.[3] At such points, the literary work often problematizes its own communicative status; indeed, certain works draw much of their energy from precisely such a self-critical dimension. Hoffmann's neglected **"Don Juan"** seems to me an exemplary text in this regard.[4]

Since the appearance of Hans Mayer's essay on Hoffmann in 1959, much attention has been devoted to the ambiguities and problems of reliability that arise from Hoffmann's manipulation of narrative perspective.[5] The results of this line of research are inevitably formulated within an epistemological framework involving subjects (Hoffmann, the narrator, the reader), acts of presenting and knowing, and a world or reality more or less perfectly apprehended. This framework is then taken to define the overall purport of Hoffmann's work, which is seen as exhibiting a world-view characterized by cognitive uncertainties and multiple interpretive possibilities. There is, needless to say, much that is valid and valuable in all this, but what has been overlooked is that the epistemological issues emerging as the results of inquiry are themselves engendered by the line of questioning adopted at the outset. That line of questioning focuses almost exclusively on the level of the text which the structural-semiotic theory of narrative terms discourse and which has to do with such procedures as arrangement, emphasis, ellipsis, and perspectivization— procedures particularly apt for the production of epistemological ambiguities.[6] To what degree this attention to the discourse level of Hoffmann's texts represented an unnecessary restriction of research became clear with the publication of Peter von Matt's Hoffmann book in 1971.[7] The thematic approach employed by von Matt allowed for the consideration of various levels of Hoffmann's narratives and shifted the focus of inquiry away from epistemological issues toward more general questions of artistic production and the theory of the imagination. This reorientation in turn brought Hoffmann's critical position as regards the Romantic movement clearly into view.

It is this critical position that interests me here. By examining Hoffmann's relationship to that model of understanding I call Romantic hermeneutics, I hope to make clear how his texts situate themselves vis-à-vis a certain cultural construct that commanded widespread authority during his time. This does not mean that I am using Hoffmann's tale as a document in the history of ideas. The problem of understanding is not merely a thematic element in **"Don Juan,"** not just a matter of stated opinion; rather, it determines the narrative structure of the text at all levels. If **"Don Juan"** problematizes Romantic hermeneutics, it does so as the complex textual system that it is. For this reason, my discussion will follow the pattern of a structural analysis, moving across various narrative levels in an effort to show how each, in interrelation with the others, contributes to the overall significance of the text.

The story level (the *fabula*, the level of the narrated events) is so thin as regards physical actions that, in the words of one commentator, "almost nothing happens."[8] No doubt this is why the text has so often been misread as a serious, non-fictional discussion of Mozart's *Don Giovanni* framed by a fiction which has no intrinsic significance. In any case, from the perspective of a structural analysis, the lack of what might be termed anecdotal interest is itself interesting in at least three respects.

First of all, the reduced importance of the anecdote signals a displacement of the action or drama (in an extended sense) from a primarily physical plane of execution to a cognitive plane. The cognitive status of the events narrated (e.g., seeing, knowing, believing,—Hoffmann's works reveal a proliferation of intensional contexts) does not preclude an organization according to a narrative logic. Indeed, I shall argue subsequently that Hoffmann's text exhibits a quite deliberate narrativization or emplotment of such cognitive events, that it dramatizes interpretive processes. For the present, it will suffice to say, not that "nothing happens," but that what does happen takes place on other than a physical plane.

Second remark: While the primary story narrated in the text (that of the narrator's night at the opera) is poor in anecdotal interest, a second story is told within the first one and this second story is quite rich in physical actions. This second-order story is, of course, the tale of Don Juan. The narrative status of the sequence of events surrounding the Spaniard's career is complex and ambiguous. In part, the story is told to the narrator by the opera performance he views in the course of the primary story; it is as if the narrator had met someone who recounted the story of the Spaniard to him. In this regard, the *fabula* of *Don Giovanni* is entirely autonomous within the text of **"Don Juan"** and inhabits its own "diegetic level."[9] In part, however, the story is produced by the narrator himself. This is especially the case in the interpretive section of the text, where the narrator writes of events that, as anyone familiar with the Mozart/DaPonte *Don Giovanni* knows, cannot be inferred from the opera. In this way, the Spaniard's exploits become the contents of cognitive events taking place within the primary story, thereby relinquishing their claim to a separate and autonomous diegetic level. This blending, or rendering ambiguous, of diegetic levels is, as can be seen very clearly regarding the figure "Donna Anna," one of the central textual strategies involved in Hoffmann's narrative, and I shall have occasion to return to it. At this point, I merely want to remark that **"Don Juan"** does indeed relate a second-order story which—however vague its status—is replete with extroverted actions such as rape, murder, attempted revenge, escape, and attack by demonic hordes. In other words, the second-order story compensates grandiosely, melodramatically, for the non-dramatic nature of the primary story. In this regard as well, it is not entirely accurate to say of **"Don Juan"** that "nothing happens."

Finally, it should be noted that the lack of anecdotal interest characteristic of the narrated events corresponds to an aesthetic value enunciated within the text. In his interpretation of the opera, the narrator rejects the anecdotal level as superficial and seeks to penetrate beyond this surface to a deeper significance that lies in the music and that, at the same time, has to do with the hidden relationships among the characters. This interpretive

strategy, with its opposition of depth and surface, and its gesture of disclosing an occult meaning, is itself related to the values of Romantic hermeneutics.

Let us consider now the primary story level in terms of its broadest articulations. The story is divisible into two symmetrical halves, the first being the narrator's experience of the opera performance, the second his writing of an interpretation of that experience in a document addressed to a certain "Theodor." (The entire text of **"Don Juan,"** except perhaps for the title and subtitle, pretends to be that document. One element of the story, then, is the production of the text that relates the story.) The symmetry of these two sections is thoroughly and carefully established. Each takes place in three scenes, the first and most briefly treated of which is the narrator's hotel room. Although the hotel room is abandoned after the third sentence of the second section, it serves there exactly the same function as in the first: it is the faintly satanic space from which the narrator is summoned.[10] In the first instance, the musical sounds emanating from the theater invite the narrator out of his room; in the second, the imagined voice of the text's addressee Theodor calls him. The second and weightiest scene of each section is the "Fremdenloge" of the theater to which the narrator has direct access from his hotel room. It is here that he views the opera and experiences the marvelous visitation of Donna Anna in the first section, interprets the opera and senses Donna Anna's liminal presence in the second. The third scene is the hotel dining room, where the traveling enthusiast (the term applied to the narrator in the subtitle by the apparent editor of the text) is exposed to the banal chatter of the other opera-goers. The special isolation of this scene ("als Nachtrag") in the second section is required by the narrated event preceding it: the visionary apotheosis which concludes the previous scene with a series of ecstatic appeals does not allow for a narrative transition of the sort employed in the first section but demands instead a break in the narrative that is manifested on the level of the text as well.

The symmetrical disposition of the scenes foregrounds the fact that the narrative consists of two equivalent action sequences. In each, the narrator is summoned, has a visionary or otherwise ecstatic experience involving the opera, in particular Donna Anna, and falls back into the philistine environs of the dining room. Whenever values or elements are deployed in such a mirror-like manner, a comparative reading in terms of similarities and differences is encouraged. Here, for example, the elements "music" and "Theodor" appear as functionally equivalent and such equivalence poses the question of their sameness on other than a functional level. Could they, despite their apparent differences in denotation, connote the same value? The mirror structure likewise correlates the experience of Donna Anna as physically present and the experience of her as physically absent as regards the second scene. It is this opposition which lends special emphasis to the problem of interpretation: because the story sets an act of vision (object present) and an act of interpretive writing (object absent) as positionally equivalent, it draws attention to the relationship in which these two activities stand.

This hermeneutic problem enters the story structure in another respect. The text refers to two types of event, those related as experienced by the narrator and those related as presupposed but not actually experienced by him. This epistemological distinction inevitably emerges from the structure of personal narration, but in Hoffmann's text it is functionalized in a significant way. There are only two events that are explicitly mentioned by the narrator but of which he has, or could have, no experiential knowledge: the first, chronologically anterior to the events experienced and narrated, is Mozart's creation of the opera; the second, chronologically posterior even to the writing of the text, is Theodor's act of reading and understanding. Since *Don Giovanni,* like the document which **"Don Juan"** fictionally is, is a text, then we can say that the two epistemologically inaccessible events the text posits lie at the extreme ends of a communication chain: Mozart (sender)—*Don Giovanni* (message)—narrator (receiver/sender)—**"Don Juan"** (message)—Theodor (receiver). The ultimate sender and the ultimate receiver postulated by the text remain outside the text in the sense of outside the narrator's purview. In this way, the text is epistemologically cut off from its ultimate origin (Mozart's act of creation) and its ultimate end, the *telos* of the written text (Theodor's act of comprehension). The story structure thus enacts the problem of how it is possible to understand and to communicate to another what the truly originary meaning of an artwork is, "wie es der große Meister in seinem Gemüt empfing und dachte!" (p. 68).

The problem of how to appropriate the creative intuition at its radically subjective point of origin—the problem implicitly posed by the story structure of **"Don Juan"**—is the problem that Romantic hermeneutics set out to solve, and much in Hoffmann's narrative mobilizes the commonplaces of the standard Romantic solution. Thus, in a gesture of self-justification, the narrator claims for himself and Mozart the "congeniality" that, in Romantic hermeneutics, guarantees the possibility of understanding: "Nur der Dichter versteht den Dichter; nur ein romantisches Gemüt kann eingehen in das Romantische; nur der poetisch exaltierte Geist, der mitten im Tempel die Weihe empfing, das verstehen, was der Geweihte in der Begeisterung ausspricht" (p. 74). The general proposition stated here has its equivalent in other texts of the period. Faust's "Erquickung hast du nicht gewonnen, / Wenn sie dir nicht aus eigner Seele quillt,"[11] draws essentially the same stipulation. Tieck's brief poem "Erkennen" employs a nearly identical terminology and an identical rhetoric of exclusivity to

make the same point.[12] The important fact to keep in mind regarding Hoffmann's text, however, is that, unlike Tieck's, it limits the force of the assertion, undermines slightly its credibility, by presenting it as the utterance of one of the characters, in this case the narrator. Hoffmann's use of the Romantic commonplace has some of the critical force of citation in general: it displays the statement as an object to be reflected upon. This is often the case in Hoffmann. Faced, for example, with a locution such as, "ich weiss, dass auch *dir* das wunderbare, romantische Reich aufgegangen" (p. 71), the reader must recognize that this "Reich" is not the aim or object of the work, something to be evoked, but rather a citation and is thereby deformed vis-à-vis its direct usage.[13]

"Don Juan" problematizes Romantic hermeneutics in a much more thorough-going and complex way than that of quasi-quotation. In fact, the narrated action surrounding the encounter with Donna Anna is a *mis en scène* of the problem of artistic understanding, a dramatization of its internal dynamics. To show how this is accomplished, I have to consider first an important value opposition that informs the text at the level of the narrated message, an opposition which the text makes use of in order to classify aspects of the characters and action it narrates. Only when the presiding values of the text are made explicit can the connotative levels of the narrative be described.

I shall begin with a second guarantee of access to Mozart's creative act: "Hier am deutschen Orte italienisch? . . . ich werde alle Rezitative, alles so hören, wie es der große Meister in seinem Gemüt empfing und dachte!" (p. 68). This statement encodes an opposition between the German and Italian languages in terms of their proximity to the creative act. Italian allows for complete, undistorted comprehension, whereas German introduces a semantic loss or establishes a barrier between sender (Mozart) and receiver (the narrator). Subsequent passages reinforce and ramify this opposition: "indem ich das, was sie sagte, deutsch hinschreiben will, finde ich jedes Wort steif und matt, jede Phrase ungelenk, das auszudrücken, was sie leicht und mit Anmut toskanisch sagte" (p. 71). This is a variant of the Romantic myth (cliché) of a naive or natural language, a language unspoiled by civilization, poetic and creative. Whenever one of the speakers of this language is heard, either the message itself is only faintly understood or much of its affective force as well as its grace and charm is lost in translation. Recall, for example, the epoch's two most famous speakers of "Naive," Goethe's Mignon and Wordsworth's solitary reaper.[14]

The opposition between naive and civilized languages, between Italian and German in the case at hand, is homological with several other oppositional pairs: south and north, passion and reason, poetry and prose, all of which are commonplace in European literature after Rousseau. Because the Romantic stereotype inevitably presents its naive speakers as singing, if possible with primitive instrumental accompaniment, the opposition naive / civilized can likewise be translated into the pair music / language. Thus, when Friedrich Schlegel sets out to classify the various characters of *Wilhelm Meisters Lehrjahre* in terms of art forms, he quite properly encodes Mignon, Sperata and Augustino—"die heilige Familie der Naturpoesie"—as "Musik."[15] This aspect of the Romantic code is decisive for the text of "Don Juan" where the homological relation between Italian and German on the one hand, music and language on the other, allows for the allegorization of musical communication.

The term Italian (represented in the text either as "Italienisch" or "Toskanisch") functions on two levels at once. On the level of the represented action it is the language spoken by the actress who plays Donna Anna, the language of the libretto and of the performance which the traveling enthusiast witnesses. On this level, Italian is something that can be spoken and understood and which can convey messages with the clarity and definiteness of ordinary linguistic communication. On a second, allegorical level, Italian is not a language at all but rather music, and as such is set in opposition to all language. On this allegorical plane, German is likewise not one of several languages, but language in general. In the visitation scene, then, the conceptually impossible occurs: music, the antithesis of language, is "spoken" in such a way that it conveys a fully articulate message; allegorically, the narrator and Donna Anna are "speaking music."

This allegorical significance is carefully built up in the first paragraph of the visitation scene. Already the reader has learned that performance of the opera in Italian guarantees access to Mozart's creative intuition. The first fact that is established about Donna Anna is that she speaks "in dem reinsten Toskanisch" (p. 71)—the superlative emphasizes what the noun means: language as pure music—and that she can converse with the narrator only in this language, a stipulation not unlike the earlier quoted "Nur der Dichter versteht den Dichter . . ." Immediately following this intensification of the term Italian, the shift to the allegorical level is accomplished: "Wie Gesang lauteten die süßen Worte" (p. 71). The preparatory paragraph then concludes with the assertion that the conversation that takes place between the two cannot be adequately translated into German (read: language).

In the conversation between the narrator and Donna Anna the full significance of the term music is unfolded. First of all, what Donna Anna says allows the narrator to understand the opera as never before, to see clearly into "die Tiefen des Meisterwerks" (p. 71). This is en-

tirely in accord with the narrator's hermeneutic principle that in interpreting the opera one must understand the music and ignore the text ("in der Musik, ohne alle Rücksicht auf den Text," p. 77). Secondly, Donna Anna herself is identified with music: "Sie sagte, ihr ganzes Leben sei Musik . . ." (p. 71), and music, for her, provides an understanding of her own internality such as language cannot afford: "und oft glaube sie manches im Innern geheimnisvoll Verschlossene, was keine Worte aussprächen, singend zu begreifen" (p. 71). Donna Anna, then, not only "speaks in music" to the narrator, she is music itself, and as such she provides access to the truth of Mozart's masterpiece and to an internality of spirit otherwise not to be grasped. As an embodiment of music, Donna Anna represents a privileged hermeneutic medium in and through which the internal source of artistic creation can be known.

The narrator is capable of understanding Donna Anna because, apparently, he too knows intimately the effect of music: "du verstehst mich, denn ich weiss, dass auch *dir* das wunderbare, romantische Reich aufgegangen, wo die himmlischen Zauber der Töne wohnen!" (p. 71). This mutual understanding shared by the initiates to the Romantic realm points to a profound identity between them:

> Ging nicht der zauberische Wahnsinn ewig sehnender Liebe in der Rolle der *** in deiner neuesten Oper aus deinem Innern hervor?—Ich habe dich verstanden: dein Gemüt hat sich im Gesange mir aufgeschlossen!—Ja (hier nannte sie meinen Vornamen), ich habe *dich* gesungen, so wie deine Melodien *ich* sind.
>
> (pp. 71-72)

The passage establishes a set of equivalences that can be related to the notion of con-geniality at the basis of Romantic hermeneutics. Donna Anna has sung the female role in an opera by the narrator just as she now sings the lead in a Mozart opera. Singing this role, she understands the "Gemüt" of the narrator, the internality ("Innern") which is the subjective source of artistic creation. This understanding must be taken emphatically, as identification: singing the role, she sings the narrator ("ich habe *dich* gesungen"), and in so doing she coincides with his music ("so wie deine Melodien *ich* sind"). By implication, the same process of identification takes place in terms of Mozart. The passage allegorizes the disclosure through music of a common stratum of identity, a single self, uniting the otherwise isolate individuals Mozart, Donna Anna, and the narrator.[16]

The equivalence of subject and object hinted at here, whereby the object (Donna Anna as music and as role) is the subject's own creative activity and inner self objectified, is a common constellation in Hoffmann. An example from his **"Berganza" ["Nachricht von den Neusten Schicksalen des Hundes Berganza"]** relies on the same pronominal underlining as the above-quoted passage: "Das Mädchen sang so vortrefflich, dass ich es wohl merkte, wie der Kapellmeister Johannes Kreisler nur *sie* gemeint hatte, wenn er von der geheimnisvollen zauberischen Wirkung des Tons der Sängerin sprach, deren Gesang in seinen Werken lebe, oder sie vielmehr dichte."[17] It is an equivalence which, while functional already in certain early texts of Goethe's, is at the center especially of Jena Romanticism.[18] In the beautiful, the Romantics sought the adequate objectification and representation of the animating, synthetic, productive force which the transcendental subject was conceived as, that is, the universal structure of subjectivity subtending all particular, empirical identities.[19] For example, Friedrich Schlegel, at the outset of his "Gespräch über die Poesie":

> Alle Gemüter, die sie lieben, befreundet und bindet Poesie mit unauflöslichen Banden. Mögen sie sonst im eignen Leben das Verschiedenste suchen, einer gänzlich verachten, was der andre am heiligsten hält, sich verkennen, nicht vernehmen, ewig fremd bleiben, in dieser Region sind sie dennoch durch höhere Zauberkraft einig und in Frieden.[20]

In Hoffmann, access to this "region" is provided, preeminently, by music.

Now it is essential to keep in mind that this allegory of music as a privileged hermeneutic medium disclosing a spiritual commonality and therefore a kind of self-recognition between sender and receiver is not all that the text offers us. The allegory of musical communication does not saturate the textual system but is only one component within that system, and as such its privileged status is undermined. This becomes especially clear if we consider the level of character.

Character in Hoffmann's texts is an extremely labile structure, as the visitation scene just discussed illustrates. There, the ambiguity on the level of character derives from the ambiguity of diegetic levels. That is, it is impossible to say whether the name Donna Anna refers to a character in the *Don Giovanni* story (the role) or to a character in the story of the narrator's experience (the actress). The fact that the actress lay backstage "in Ohnmacht" (p. 78) during the time when the conversation between her and the narrator took place together with the narrator's remark that he experienced this conversation in a state similar to "Somnambulism" (p. 71) only confound further this confusion of characters. For, if the conversation was a direct communication of spirits, as these two references to the code of occultism suggest, was it as role or as actress that the spirit appeared to the narrator? The text deliberately leaves this ambiguity unresolved: the thrust of the scene is to allude to a level of identity beneath the differences among individual characters, in the words of the narrator, ". . . die geheimen Beziehungen . . . , die mich so

innig mit ihr verbanden, daß sie selbst bei ihrer Erscheinung auf dem Theater nicht hatte von mir weichen können" (p. 71).

The same lability of character which here produces a positively evaluated identification can also lead to a doubling which threatens the integrity of an individual personality. Such is the case wherever the famous Hoffmannian *Doppelgänger* appears, and he appears in this text in the figure of Don Juan. Why else, in a text that so emphasizes the use of Italian, refer to Mozart's Don Giovanni by his Spanish name if not to indicate a certain duplicity, or doubling, of the character? And why else, in a text where the narrator is the central figure, select the title **"Don Juan"** if not to indicate an affinity between the Spaniard and the writer-protagonist? Don Juan is, quite simply, the narrator's double; the narrator is Don Juan.

Everything, of course, depends on clarifying the nature of the equivalence between the two characters. The first sense in which the two are the same is that several allusions attribute to them the same predicates. Don Juan, as the narrator's interpretation emphasizes, is pursued by Satan. Apparently the narrator too has his troubles with the arch fiend: "Sollte der allezeit geschäftige Satan mich im Rausche—? Nein!" (p. 67). The "Nein!" anticipates, or echoes, the Spaniard's famous "No!" The so-called champagne aria "Fin ch'an dal vino," in which Don Juan expresses "sein inneres, zerrissenes Wessen" (p. 70), likewise links him to the narrator, evidently a restless voluptuary himself: "ich hatte mittags an der Wirtstafel Champagner getrunken!" (p. 67). Finally, the actor who plays Don Juan (again the confusion of diegetic levels) is said to reveal occasionally "etwas vom Mephistopheles" (p. 68) in his physiognomy. The allusion to Goethe's *Faust* is then picked up in the narrator's account of his hotel room ("Es war mir so eng, so schwül in dem dumpfen Gemach!" p. 73), recalling Gretchen's intuition that Mephistopheles has been in her room.

These shared predicates have no finality in themselves. Rather, their function is to signal the reader that the narrator and Don Juan are also identical at the actantial level, that is, that each fills the same role within the identical action sequence. Thus, the narrator's story appears as the recapitulation of Don Juan's story or—to put it another way—the primary diegetic level is modeled after the secondary diegetic level. The decisive point of convergence between the two is, of course, that both the narrator and Don Juan stand in important relations to Donna Anna. The Don Juan-Donna Anna story is an extroverted, melodramatic version of the story involving the narrator and Donna Anna. What in the visitation scene initially appeared as the unproblematic disclosure of a spiritual commonality through music is in fact a component within an essentially violent and tragic situation. In this way, the equivalence between the narrator and Don Juan which is posed by the textual system serves to problematize the Romantic hermeneutic model.

The actantial identity between Don Juan and the narrator lies in the fact that both violate Donna Anna. In the case of Don Juan, this violation is his rape of the lady, an event strongly marked in Hoffmann's text since it so manifestly goes beyond the evidence of the libretto. Even in the melodramatic tale of the Spaniard's exploits, however, this event carries an internal, spiritual significance. Donna Anna's function vis-à-vis Don Juan is to reveal to him—precisely as she does to the narrator in the visitation scene—an essential and divine aspect of himself: "Wie, wenn Donna Anna vom Himmel dazu bestimmt gewesen wäre, den Juan in der Liebe, die ihn durch des Satans Künste verdarb, die ihm inwohnende göttliche Natur erkennen zu lassen, und ihn der Verzweiflung seines nichtigen Strebens zu entreißen?" (p. 77). By raping Donna Anna, Don Juan violates what is really an aspect of his own identity. His misapprehension of the chance at "Erkennen," at essential self-recognition, that Donna Anna provides him derives from the fundamental error of his existence, his expectation of earthly fulfillment: "In Don Juans Gemüt kam durch des Erbefeindes List der Gedanke, daß durch die Liebe, durch den Genuß des Weibes, schon auf Erden das erfüllt werden könne, was bloß als himmlische Verheißung in unserer Brust wohnt, und eben jene unendliche Sehnsucht ist, die uns mit dem Überirdischen in unmittelbaren Rapport setzt" (p. 75). Rape is not merely physical aggression in this text; it is the reduction of the spiritual to the physical, of the transcendent to the immanent earthly realm.

This form of reduction likewise occurs in the narrator's response to the actress and to the music which she embodies. Following the visitation scene, the narrator asserts that the music has an entirely new effect on him: "Es war, als ginge eine lang verheißene Erfüllung der schönsten Träume aus einer andern Welt wirklich in das Leben ein . . ." (p. 72). The claim of fulfillment exactly repeats Don Juan's erroneous belief that "schon auf Erden das erfüllt werden könne, was bloss als himmlische Verheißung in unserer Brust wohnt. . . ." And, as the passage continues, the metaphorics of fire and drunkenness that are linked to Don Juan throughout the text likewise characterize the narrator's experience: "In Donna Annas Szene fühlte ich mich von einem sanften, warmen Hauch, der über mich hinwegglitt, in trunkener Wollust erbeben; unwillkürlich schlossen sich meine Augen, und ein glühender Kuß schien auf meinen Lippen zu brennen: aber der Kuß war ein wie von ewig dürstender Sehnsucht lang ausgehaltener Ton" (p. 72). During this scene in the opera's second act—so we learn from the "Nachtrag"—the actress playing Donna Anna suffered "Nervenzufälle" (p. 78), symptoms of a traumatic response to the narrator's eroticized attitude toward her.

What in the Don Juan story is a reduction of the spiritual to the physical is, in the case of the narrator, the reduction of music to language. With its superimposition of the modified opera plot upon the narrator's experience, the text constitutes a dramatization of the problem of artistic representation and understanding: the attempt to bring the animating spiritual source of the work, its music, into the representational order of language inevitably distorts and violates that source. Language stands to music as Don Juan's erotic fetishization of the body stands to the spirit. Thus, at the very moment the narrator believes himself in possession of the spiritual source of the opera and experiences "eine lang verheißene Erfüllung" he in fact has violated that spiritual source in a manner analogous to Don Juan's rape of Donna Anna. The impulse of Romantic hermeneutics toward a reappropriation of the creative intuition is thus exhibited as a tragic impulse insofar as it violates the very thing it sought to know in its purity.

The equivalence of erotic desire with linguistic representation, or with representation in general, is common to several of Hoffmann's texts and leads to the nerve of his poetics. In **"Der Goldene Topf,"** the narrator, as he tries to describe Anselmus' experience, finds himself incapable of finishing his narrative: ". . . als hielten mir recht tückische Geister . . . ein glänzend poliertes Metall vor. . . ."[21] This false mirroring of the artistic vision in language echoes an earlier passage where Anselmus' erotic error, his choice of the real Veronika over the ideal Serpentina, is explained in terms of the same image. Indeed, it seems axiomatic for Hoffmann's prose that whenever an artist claims the full presence of his artistic ideal, whenever he believes the transcendent source of his art to be actually embodied in a worldly representation, he is horribly in error. His artistic production becomes an obsessive, erotically charged idolatry often resulting in violence. Such is the law that governs the destiny of Medardus in **Die Elixiere des Teufels** and that finds its most definitive discursive explication in Kreisler's remarks on his double Ettlinger in **Kater Murr.**[22] In the early prose, the theme takes the form of a critique of language: because it specifies, because it evokes empirical experience, because in its very nature it is material, language is inadequate to the pure self-presence of the creative source afforded by music.[23] We can say, then, that Don Juan's erotic obsession mirrors the literalism of a representational aesthetics which claims the inspirational source can be adequately embodied in a material work. It is against such an aesthetics—and against the hermeneutics it is allied with—that Hoffmann's text, in its very structure, issues its protest. Artistic communication is dramatized as the conflictual interplay of two opposed elements (the text speaks of "der beiden im Kampf begriffenen Naturen," p. 77). Whether we name these music and language, creative source and dissimulating representation, soul and body, or, quasi-mythologically, Donna Anna and Don Juan, seems to me of little import: the essential point is that the work is constituted as their perpetual antagonism and dissonance. For Hoffmann, the work exhibits a conflict between representation and the non-representable as such, a conflict which Nietzsche—his eye on Wagner rather than Mozart—later recasts with Apollo and Dionysius.

My implicit claim in the foregoing is that the rape of Donna Anna is not merely a speculation on the part of Hoffmann, an idle addendum to the libretto text, but rather a functional element within the significant construct that **"Don Juan"** is. The rape is there as a narrative element because of its relation to the problem of artistic violation. The same thing can be said of the other noticeable emendation of the libretto, the assertion that Donna Anna will die within a year ("Sie wird dieses Jahr nicht überstehen" p. 77). The significance of this death emerges from the narrator's commentary, which correlates it with the death of Don Juan: "Sie fühlt, nur Don Juans Untergang kann der, von tödlichen Martern beängsteten Seele Ruhe verschaffen; aber diese Ruhe ist ihr eigner irdischer Untergang" (p. 77). Like every Hoffmannian *Doppelgänger*, Don Juan must be killed off in order to release the hero, in this case the narrator, from the violent actions the double carries out in his name. Donna Anna's salvation or "Ruhe" is the security of the narrator's creative self, and the association of her salvation with her death indicates that the creative source is free only when released from the bodily representation which makes it into an object of desire, an idol instead of an ideal. Only when the literalism of representation is renounced, when the specifying nature of language is overcome and the Don Juan within the narrator is annihilated, can the drama of artistic communication reach a stabile resolution.

This moment of renunciation can be located within the drama of the traveling enthusiast's experience. The text, as just mentioned, states that Don Juan's death is the precondition of Donna Anna's death and salvation. As we learn from the "Nachtrag," the actress who represents Donna Anna dies precisely at two A.M. What has made this death possible? Within the text, just before it is said that the clock strikes two, the narrator quotes a line from Donna Anna's final aria, a line which, as he emphasizes, expresses her internal state. It is the only citation from the opera which is set off from the body of the text, a typographical index of its significance:

Forse un giorno il cielo ancora sentirà pietà di me!

(p. 78)

It is a statement of acceptance and piety, a statement which places the fate of the speaker in the hands of a higher power. In other words, it is exactly the sort of statement which Don Juan, confronted by imminent damnation, refuses to make. By quoting the line, the narrator has at once renounced the Don Juanian element within himself and guaranteed the security of the creative source, Donna Anna. As soon as the words are spoken the clock strikes two and the singer expires, released from the corporeal appearance that made her representable, an object of desire. In her physical absence (in the radical sense of separation from the body), she is more truly herself than in the bodily presence in which she appeared to the narrator in the visitation scene. With the renunciation of representation and the death of the actress, the final apotheosis occurs, free this time of any tinge of "trunkener Wollust." The "lang verheißene Erfüllung" (the key phrase linking the narrator and Don Juan) is situated outside the earthly, experiential realm. The vision is carefully held in the optative, not confident assertion but prayer-like appeal: "Schließe dich auf, du fernes, unbekanntes Geisterreich—du Dschinnistan voller Herrlichkeit, wo ein unaussprechlicher, himmlischer Schmerz, wie die unsäglichste Freude, der entzückten Seele alles auf Erden Verheißene über alle Maßen erfüllt!" (p. 78). Here too the experience of the traveling enthusiast recapitulates the modified opera plot. The salvation of Donna Anna, the inviolate security of the creative source, is ultimately assured by the narrator's renunciation of language as eros. Only in its essential non-presence, in its difference from all representation, is the animating movement that here carries the names music and Donna Anna truly itself. The text remains faithful to its Idea by refusing to represent that Idea other than as that which is essentially absent from the order of representation.

The absence of the Idea is likewise the absence of the subject in its full identity and self-understanding. This becomes clear when we consider the relationship between the narrator and the fictional addressee Theodor. The latter, though absent from the represented action, functions in a more complex way than the "you" implied in every first person discourse. His imagined voice summons the narrator to the empty theater at the opening of the second section, a fact which correlates him with music and with Donna Anna whose voice is also heard by the narrator. The correlation with Donna Anna is especially marked since Theodor's voice pronounces the narrator's name ("Du sprachst deutlich meinen Namen aus," p. 73), an action performed also by the actress during the visitation scene. Both Theodor and Donna Anna, then, possess knowledge that relates to the narrator's identity, knowledge to which the reader is given no access. Finally, a "Postskript des reisenden Enthusiasten" which is attached to **"Die Abenteuer der Sylvester-Nacht"** names the addressee of the "Tagebuche" as "mein lieber Theodor Amadäus Hoffmann," whom we as readers know to be the "author" of the pages before us.[24] This collection of references indicates that the text's addressee is identical with the creative source represented by Donna Anna, by music, and by Mozart, whose middle name Hoffmann adopted as his own.[25] The self writes in order to reach its own center, which, however, cannot gain full presence within the text but must remain forever postponed like the irreducibly future act of comprehension on the part of the addressee Theodor. The text is the fragmentation of the subject, not its adequate objectification.

What I have here called Romantic hermeneutics is part of a larger set of values regarding the nature and function of art and literature. In my view, this cultural complex can be described in terms of four key terms: authorship (the genial subject is the sponsoring source of the work), totality (the work is an organized whole, complete unto itself, its organic structure adequately expressing the structure of the subject), spirituality (the production and reception of the work play themselves out in a region that is essentially imaginative and are oriented toward and actualize an Idea that is a spiritual product, if not the spirit itself), and legitimacy (the work embodies a vision or knowledge that is intersubjectively universalizable, that is binding for mankind). These values, which in various degrees are normative in the texts of both Romantic and classical writers as traditionally classified in German scholarship, represent a specific institutionalization of art: the bourgeois humanism of what Heine termed the "Kunstperiode." My argument here is that **"Don Juan,"** along with Hoffmann's other narratives, can be conceived as a practice of writing that disrupts that system of norms and subverts its authority. Such writing is a complex activity of cultural labor requiring analysis in terms of various levels and relations. Here I have concentrated on the construction of the *fabula,* the system of connotations carried by the terms music and language, allegorization, the manipulation of diegetic levels, and the construction of character to show that **"Don Juan"** dramatizes the entire artistic situation—production, product, reception—as a conflict between music and language or Idea and representation. This conflict is resolved in **"Don Juan"** through resignation and pious waiting; in other texts, it is transformed through irony into a second-order aesthetic play. Such agonistic or ironic foregrounding of conflict relates to the art-religion of bourgeois humanism as a fierce iconoclasm to aesthetic idolatry.

As regards the other levels of Hoffmann's texts, I can only suggest here how they can be viewed in terms of this complex of values. On the level of discourse, the interplay between editor and narrator or narrator/hero, so common in Hoffmann's narratives, troubles the value of authorship. The texts one holds before one are traces left in a state of relative dispersion by their author (e.g., Kreisler's jottings on the back of pieces of sheet music) and later compiled by an editor. They do not pretend to

be the products of a sovereign act such as the mythical "in seinem Gemüt empfing und dachte" attributed to Mozart. Furthermore, this assemblage of traces (the self does not come to paper in a totalized fashion) is a decidedly material activity and the moment of materiality likewise interferes with the authority of the sponsoring subject. Thus manuscripts in Hoffmann often suffer a destiny that changes their nature from that intended by their author. Examples of this are meaning changes produced in printing or deletions and additions performed by another writer (Kater Murr!). Inevitably, attention is drawn to the material, textual, manufactured status of the object before one (the level of the text itself is actualized), a status which removes the text from the control of a single authorial source. Perhaps this loss of authorial sovereignty is also related to the fact that the text is a commodity made for the market; that, at least, is one of the implications of **"Das Fräulein von Scuderi."** On the thematic level, I would especially emphasize Hoffmann's interest in the mechanical—the automaton, Meister Abraham's contraptions in *Kater Murr*—which always competes with the spiritual in his texts. In part, it is a question here of the machinery of representation, a group of hackneyed tricks and devices that are mobilized to produce illusions. By making their functioning obvious (as in the case of the clock striking two in **"Don Juan"**), Hoffmann exposes them as illusion machines (cf. "Der vollkommenste Machinist"). I suspect a similar effect can be attributed to Hoffmann's often cliché-riddled, formulaic style: a phrase like "du fernes, unbekanntes Geisterreich"—especially when it prompts an appositional "du Dschinnistan voller Herrlichkeit"—marks its own stereotypic quality even as it names the supreme value of the text. Finally, the uncertainty provoked by Hoffmann's use of the fantastic undermines the legitimacy of the work by placing it in the shadow of possible madness.

Notes

1. On Schleiermacher, see Hans-Georg Gadamer, *Wahrheit und Methode,* 2. Auflage (Tübingen: J. C. B. Mohr [Paul Siebeck], 1965), p. 177: "Der genialen Produktion entspricht auf der Seite der Hermeneutik, dass es der Divination bedarf, des unmittelbaren Erratens, das letzten Endes eine Art Kongenialität voraussetzt. Wenn nun aber die Granzen zwischen der kunstlosen und kunstvollen, der mechanischen und der genialischen Produktion fließend sind, sofern sich immer eine Individualität zum Ausdruck bringt und darin immer ein Moment der regelfreien Genialität wirksam ist—wie in den Kindern, die in eine Sprache hineinwachsen—, so folgt daraus, dass auch der letzte Grund alles Verstehens immer ein divinatorischer Akt der Kongenialität sein muss, dessen Möglichkeit auf einer vorgängigen Verbundenheit aller Individualitäten beruht." Goethe's early theoretical writings ought to be looked at in view of

their implicit hermeneutics. See, for instance, "Zum Schäkespears Tag": "Wir ehren heute das Andencken des grössten Wandrers, und thun uns dadurch selbst eine Ehre an. Von Verdiensten die wir zu schätzen wissen, haben wir den Keim in uns" (*Der junge Goethe,* hrsg. von Hanna Fisher-Lamberg, neu bearbeitete Ausgabe in fünf Bänden [Berlin: Walter De Gruyter, 1963-73], II, 83); or "Von deutscher Baukunst": "Deinem Unterricht dank ich's, Genius, dass mirs nicht mehr schwindelt an deinen Tiefen, dass in meine Seele ein Tropfen sich senkt, der Wonneruh des Geistes, der auf solch eine Schöpfung herabschauen, und gottgleich sprechen kann, es ist gut!" (ibid., III, 105).

2. Here I follow Marianne Wünsch, *Der Strukturwandel in der Lyrik Goethes* (Stuttgart: Kohlhammer, 1975), esp. pp. 58-63. Michel Foucault (*The Order of Things* [New York: Random House/Vintage Books, 1973], esp. pp. 280-300) has also shown the systematic place of the hermeneutic-philological disciplines in "modern thought."

3. *Faust* I, ll. 575-79.

4. Hoffmann's "Don Juan" was first published in 1813 in the *Allgemeine Musikalische Zeitung* edited in Leipzig by Johann Friedrich Rochlitz. In 1814 it was republished in the collection *Fantasiestücke in Callots Manier.* Here I have used the edition: E. T. A. Hoffmann, *Fantasie- und Nachtstücke,* hrsg. von Walter Müller-Seidel (München: Winkler, 1967), to which page references are given parenthetically.

5. Hans Mayer, "Die Wirklichkeit E. T. A. Hoffmanns," in his *Von Lessing bis Thomas Mann* (Pfüllingen: Neske, 1959), pp. 198-246. The most important studies of Hoffmann's use of narrative perspective and the ambiguous world that results from it are: Lothar Köhn, *Vieldeutige Welt. Studien zur Struktur der Erzählungen E. T. A. Hoffmanns und zur Entwicklung seines Werkes* (Tübingen: Niemeyer, 1971); Wolfgang Preisendanz, "Eines matt geschliffenen Spiegels dunkler Widerschein. E. T. A. Hoffmanns Erzählkunst," in *Festschrift für Jost Trier zum 70. Geburtstag,* hrsg, von William Foerste und Karl Heinz Borck (Köln: Böhlau, 1964), pp. 411-29; Preisendanz, *Humor als dichterische Einbildungskraft* (München: Fink, 1963), esp. pp. 47-117, 290-307.

6. On the structural-semiotic theory of narrative, see Roland Barthes, "Introduction à l'analyse structurale des récits," *Communications,* 8 (1966), 1-27; Rolf Kloepfer, "Zum Problem des 'narrativen Kode,'" *LiLi. Zeitschrift für Literaturwissenschaft und Linguistik,* VII (1977), 69-90; Umberto Eco, "Introduction: The Role of the Reader," in his *The Role of the Reader* (Bloomington and Lon-

don: Indiana U. Press, 1979), pp. 3-46. The most thorough discussion of the discourse level of narrative remains Gerard Genette's "Discours du récit," in his *Figures III* (Paris: Seuil, 1972), pp. 65-273.

7. Peter von Matt, *Die Augen des Automaten. E. T. A. Hoffmanns Imaginationslehre als Prinzip seiner Erzählkunst* (Tübingen: Niemeyer, 1971).

8. Leo Weinstein, "Hoffmann's Romantic Interpretation of Don Juan," in his *The Metamorphoses of Don Juan* (New York: AMS Press, 1967), p. 66.

9. On the problem of diegetic levels, cf. Genette, "Discours du récit," pp. 238-51. Diegetic levels are levels of fictionality. In normal narratives, every event accounted for as part of a story is at a level immediately superior to that on which the narrational act producing that story is situated.

10. The connotation "satanic" is established explicitly in the first section ("sollte der allezeit geschäftige Satan," p. 67) and by an allusion to *Faust* I, 2753, in the second section ("Es war mir so eng, so schwül in dem dumpfen Gemach!" p. 73).

11. *Faust* I, ll. 568-69.

12. The text of Tieck's poem is worth quoting:

> Keiner, der nicht schon zum Weihefest gelassen,
> Kann den Sinn der dunkeln Kunst erfassen,
> Keinem sprechen diese Geistertöne,
> Keiner sieht den Glanze der schönsten Schöne,
> Dem im innern Herzen nicht das Siegel brennt,
> Welches ihn als Eingeweihten nennt,
> Jene Flamme, die der Töne Geist erkennt.

(Ludwig Tieck, *Gedichte. Zweiter Teil,* facsimile of the edition 1821-23 [Heidelberg: Verlag Lambert Schneider, 1967], p. 30.)

13. Cf. Michail Bachtin, "Typen des Prosaworts," in his *Literatur und Karneval,* trans. Alexander Kaempfe (München: Hanser, 1969), pp. 107-31.

14. Goethe's text is exemplary: "Melodie und Ausdruck gefielen unserm Freunde besonders, ob er gleich die Worte nicht alle verstehen konnte. Er ließ sich die Strophen wiederholen und erklären, schrieb sie auf und übersetzte sie ins Deutsche. Aber die Originalität der Wendungen konnte er nur von ferne nachahmen. Die kindliche Unschuld des Ausdrucks verschwand, indem die gebrochene Sprache übereinstimmend und das Unzusammenhängende verbunden ward." *Goethes Werke,* hrsg. von Erich Trunz, 9. Auflage (München: Beck, 1977), VII, 145-46.

15. Friedrich Schlegel, *Schriften zur Literatur,* hrsg. von Wolfdietrich Rasch (München: Hanser, 1970), p. 278.

16. This identity of "Mozart" and the narrator has likewise been noted by Hélène Cixous, though without connecting it to other aspects of the text ("The Character of 'Character,'" *New Literary History,* v [1974], 398).

17. *Fantasie- und Nachtstücke,* p. 101.

18. Cf. Goethe's "Nach Falconet und über Falconet": "Nimm ietzo das *Haften* an *Einer* Form, unter *allen* Lichtern, so wird dir dieses Ding immer lebendiger, wahrer, runder, es wird endlich du selbst werden" (*Der junge Goethe,* v, 356). See also "Des Künstlers Erdewallen": "Wo mein Pinsel dich berührt bis du mein / Du bist ich bist mehr als ich ich bin dein / Uranfängliche Schönheit Königinn der Welt!" (*Der junge Goethe,* IV, 231).

19. Here I follow Philippe Lacoue-Labarthe and Jean-Luc Nancy, *L'Absolu littéraire. Theorie de la litterature du romantisme allemand* (Paris: Seuil, 1978), esp. pp. 11-22, 43-52.

20. *Schriften zur Literatur,* p. 279.

21. *Fantasie- und Nachtstücke,* pp. 250-51.

22. The relationship of "Don Juan" to this artistic problematic has been pointed out by Peter von Matt, *Die Augen des Automaten,* p. 106.

23. See, for instance, *Fantasie- und Nachtstücke,* pp. 41-43, 48, 81, 314, 326. Two passages seem especially close to the problematics of "Don Juan": "Die Ahnungen des höchsten Wesens, welche die heiligen Töne in des Menschen Brust entzünden, sind das höchste Wesen selbst, welches in der Musik verständlich von dem überschwenglich herrlichen Reiche des Glaubens und der Liebe redet. Die Worte, die sich dem Gesange beigesellen, sind nur zufällig, und enthalten auch meistens nur bildliche Andeutungen, wie z.B. in der Missa" (*Fantasie- und Nachtstücke,* p. 315). From the Beethoven essay: "Es sucht das tiefe Gemüt für die Ahnungen der Freudigkeit, die herrlicher und schöner als hier in der beengten Welt, aus einem unbekannten Lande herübergekommen, ein inneres, wonnevolles Leben in der Brust entzündet, einen höheren Ausdruck, als ihn geringe Worte, *die nur der befangenen irdischen Lust* eigen, gewähren können" (*Fantasie- und Nachtstücke,* p. 48, my emphasis).

24. *Fantasie- und Nachtstücke,* p. 283.

25. On the "you" or addressee as a higher "I," see the following remarkable passage from Fr. Schlegel: "Wenn wir uns beim Nachdenken nicht leugnen können, dass alles in uns ist, so können wir uns das Gefühl der Beschränktheit . . . nicht anders erklären, als indem wir annehmen, dass wir nur ein Stück von uns selbst sind. Dies führte

geradeswegs zu einem Glauben an ein Du, nicht als ein (wie im Leben) dem Ich Entgegengesetztes, Ähnliches . . . , sondern überhaupt als ein Gegen-Ich, und hiermit verbindet sich denn notwending der Glaube an ein Ur-Ich." Quoted in Walter Benjamin, *Gesammelte Schriften,* I, I, hrsg. von Rolf Tiedemann und Hermann Schweppenhäuser (Frankfurt a.M.: Suhrkamp, 1974), 34-35 (from *Der Begriff der Kunstkritik in der deutschen Romantik*).

Todd Kontje (essay date summer 1985)

SOURCE: Kontje, Todd. "Biography in Triplicate: E. T. A. Hoffmann's 'Die Abenteuer der Silvester-Nacht.'" *German Quarterly* 58, no. 3 (summer 1985): 348-60.

[*In the following essay, Kontje explores the figure of the tragic artist in Hoffmann's "Die Abenteuer der Silvester-Nacht," discussing its thematic relationship to the author's failed romance with the musician Julia Marc. Drawing from the theories of Mikhail Bakhtin and Roland Barthes, Kontje argues that Hoffmann manipulates existing literary and social discourses in order to undermine traditional representations of the creative self.*]

I

In his introduction to the six-volume edition of E. T. A. Hoffmann's works published by the Aufbau Verlag, Hans Mayer discusses Hoffmann's love for Julia Marc under the heading "Die Liebestragödie als gesellschaftliche Erfahrung."[1] In Bamberg, writes Mayer, Hoffmann experienced both the pure worlds of Julia and music, and the shallow, hostile world of the Philistines, which eventually destroyed her and the world of beauty she represented: "Alle Erfahrung mit Kunst und Künsten, alle Sehnsucht nach Reinheit, körperlicher wie geistiger Schönheit fand sich in der Bamberger Umwelt. Die Umwelt zerstörte das Schöne und das schöne Menschentum." Out of this personal experience of the clash between the aesthetic realm and the mundane world which enclosed it, concludes Mayer, was to arise the central theme of Hoffmann's major poetic works, "das Verhältnis von Künstlertum und kunstfeindlicher Gesellschaft."[2]

Hoffmann's love for Julia Marc becomes thus a key moment in Mayer's understanding of the relationship between the artist and the bourgeoisie within Hoffmann's oeuvre. It is an interpretation which has found frequent echoes among other critics of Hoffmann's life and works. As Wulf Segebrecht writes, "Julia war für Hoffmann von Anfang an ein literarisiertes Erlebnis. . . . In diesem Erlebnis und in seiner Bewältigung durch die Darstellung sammelten und klärten sich die Fragen nach Kunst und Leben, nach Autobiographie und Dichtung, nach der Menschlichkeit in der Kunst und der Unmenschlichkeit in der falschen Kunsterkenntnis, nach Phantasie und Wirklichkeit, nach Begeisterung und Phlegma—das ganze Fragenarsenal des Dualismus bei E. T. A. Hoffmann fand in Julia oder bildete sich in Julia die Figur, in der es sich selbst kunstgemäß darstellbar machen ließ."[3]

In this understanding of Hoffmann's work, then, we have on the one hand the aesthetic realm in all its purity, an ideal world of plenitude and harmony inspired by the beloved, and on the other the crassly material world of the Philistine which engulfs and destroys it. The opening incident of **"Die Abenteuer der Silvester-Nacht,"** for example, seems to be structured on just such a clash between the artistic sensibility of the Travelling Enthusiast and the stifling atmosphere of the party he attends at the home of a Justizrat in Berlin. Furthermore, Hoffmann's use of the name "Julia" for the Enthusiast's former beloved suggests the biographical parallel to Hoffmann's own life, a parallel which is further encouraged by the appearance of his name in the Enthusiast's postscript to the work.[4] We have then in **"Die Abenteuer der Silvester-Nacht"** one of the key texts in which we can examine Hoffmann's fictional representation of the social conflict experienced in his relationship with Julia Marc.[5]

This analysis is divided into two major sections. In the first I follow the Travelling Enthusiast's perspective on the events which take place in the course of the work. Beginning with a close examination of his unexpected encounter with Julia, I note both the presence of the paradigm identified by Mayer of the Romantic artist in society, but also its insufficiency for either the complete understanding of this opening scene or of the events which follow. As the story continues we see the Enthusiast move gradually from a concern with his alienation from the rest of society to a disconcerting discovery that the plot of his life closely resembles that of two fictional characters he encounters that evening. The result is a confusion of the seemingly clear distinction between the self and the other, between poetry and reality by the end of the work.

Hoffmann's fictional account of his personal experience with Julia Marc thus results only incidentally in the dualistically structured conflict between the artist and society, and primarily in the triplication of his own biography in a series of closely parallel plots. In the second section of this essay I therefore seek to elucidate the type of poetics suggested by the structure of Hoffmann's text, both as it contrasts with the work of the early Romantics, in particular Novalis, and as it continues the tradition of the comic or "polyphonic" novel in both Germany and Europe. Mikhail Bakhtin's study of "Discourse in the Novel" provides a useful vocabulary for discussing Hoffmann's poetics, particularly because it permits increased attention to the formal aspects of the literary text without avoiding the question of their sociological import.[6] In conclusion, I suggest that Hoffmann offers an implicit critique of the early Romantic faith in the sovereignty of the individual's creative imagination, stressing instead how much of one's seemingly unique self is a product of the various intersubjective codes within which one is inscribed. The artist becomes less the possessor of an authentic voice which produces pristine aesthetic worlds than the playful manipulator of these various discourses.

II

"Die Abenteuer der Silvester-Nacht" begins with the Enthusiast's lament about his increased sense of social alienation during the holiday season. "Du weißt es ja, daß diese Zeit, Weihnachten und Neujahr, die euch allen in solch heller herrlicher Freudigkeit aufgeht, mich immer aus friedlicher Klause hinauswirft auf ein wogendes tosendes Meer."[7] The celebration of the year's end, with its implicit promise of new growth in the spring, is transformed into a grim reminder of the inevitability of death for the Enthusiast. "Immer mehr und mehr Blüten fallen jedes Jahr verwelkt herab, ihr Keim erlosch auf ewig, keine Frühlingssonne entzündet neues Leben in den verdorrten Ästen" (p. 257). Whereas the average individual is comforted by the impersonal rhythm of the seasons, the Enthusiast transforms the natural world into a metaphor for his sense of isolation and mortality.

When the Travelling Enthusiast first glimpses Julia that evening, however, he is transported by his love for her into an aesthetic realm which promises a moment of fulfillment and duration in the midst of personal and natural loss. "*Sie* war es—*sie* selbst, die ich seit Jahren nicht gesehen, die seligsten Momente des Lebens blitzten in *einem* mächtigen zündenden Strahl durch mein Innres—kein tötender Verlust mehr—vernichtet der Gedanke des Scheidens!" (pp. 257-58). Again towards the end of the scene, the Enthusiast exclaims "'Nun lasse ich dich nimmer, deine Liebe ist der Funke, der in mir glüht, höheres Leben in Kunst und Poesie entzündend—ohne dich—ohne deine Liebe alles tot und starr—aber bist du denn nicht auch gekommen, damit du mein bleibest immerdar?'" (p. 260). In these brief moments, then, the Enthusiast seems to be granted access to a higher realm of personal fulfillment and artistic inspiration through his love for Julia.

As the first person narrative of this section is structured, however, the promise of this moment is denied even before it is described. It was all a trick, the Enthusiast tells us, a malicious incident staged by the devil to remind him that he is forever forbidden access to the beloved and the realm of aesthetic plenitude she inspires.

Thus the poetic rapture experienced by the Enthusiast at the party is placed in an ironic light at the outset of the story, an irony which is confirmed as Julia snubs her former lover and reveals that she is in fact married to one of the Philistines the Enthusiast detests. "eine tölpische, spinnenbeinichte Figur mit herausstehenden Froschaugen" (p. 260). While the broad social satire implied by this characterization of Julia's husband seems obvious enough,[8] the scene also suggests a criticism of the Romantic artist. A society which has no room for the artist's transcendent visions is certainly lamentable, but at the same time, an artist so detached from his surroundings can easily be rendered ridiculous in his encounter with a reality he fails to perceive. One is reminded of another such figure in Nathanael in **"Der Sandmann,"** who deliriously falls in love with a wooden puppet.[9] Instead of demonstrating the superiority of the Romantic artist over the bourgeoisie, the Enthusiast's encounter with Julia results in the mutual ironization of both extremes.

If the customary understanding of the place of the Romantic artist in society reaches this impasse in the opening pages of **"Die Abenteuer der Silvester-Nacht,"** we are naturally led to ask what sort of aesthetic concerns will emerge as the tale continues. A clue of the direction the work will take is already suggested by another aspect of the Enthusiast's encounter with Julia in the opening scene of the work. Whereas the Enthusiast invokes an unattainable aesthetic ideal which is the antithesis of his actual situation, there is another aspect of his encounter with Julia which directly undermines the distinction between the aesthetic ideal and reality. When he first sees her, she seems strangely unfamiliar: "Ihre ganze Gestalt hat ewas Fremdartiges angenommen, sie schien mir größer, herausgeformter in fast üppiger Schönheit, als sonst" (p. 258). Yet the very novelty of Julia's current appearance awakens dim memories of a previous encounter with someone else for the Enthusiast: "sie war beinahe anzusehen, wie die Jungfrauen auf den Gemälden von Mieris—und doch auch wieder war es mir, als hab' ich irgendwo deutlich mit hellen Augen das Wesen gesehen, in das Julie verwandelt" (p. 259).

The most striking aspect of the Enthusiast's attempt to identify this foreign, yet familiar Julia is that he makes no distinction between his memory of her or someone like her, and the likeness of a woman he has seen in a painting by Mieris. Thus while the distinction between the aesthetic ideal and reality is emphasized in the overall context of this opening scene, the direct encounter with Julia leads the Enthusiast to conflate his memory of individuals with his memory of works of art. Our attention thus shifts from a concentration on the external conflict between the artistic individual and bourgeois society to a consideration of the way in which the Enthusiast's perception of reality is complicated by his memory of previous aesthetic experiences.

Having made this observation at the critical moment of poetic rapture inspired by the sight of Julia, we find that this tendency extends to include a wide variety of similar quotes and allusions in the Enthusiast's perception of the events on this New Year's Eve. The entire experience, as he tells us at the start of the story, is a sort of festive morality play ("ein ganz besonderes Feststück" [p. 257]) staged by the devil to remind the Enthusiast of his social alienation and mortality. A later allusion to the devil in this scene is introduced by a reference to a character in Tieck's *Oktavian*.[10] When the Enthusiast recoils from Julia for the first time he likens her to the basilisk of Classical mythology, while he is later to identify the music which inspires him as "das Andante aus Mozarts sublimer Es-dur-Sinfonie" (p. 260). Even his thirst for an English beer causes the Enthusiast to recall the literary precedent of Shakespeare's Prince Hal, while his initial characterization of Schlemihl as a man who looks "vornehm und unzufrieden" is an implicit reference to the appearance of Goethe's Faust in Auerbach's Keller.[11]

The Enthusiast lives his life, that is, as a series of quotes from works of fiction he has read, paintings he has seen, music he has heard. In the opening section of the work this tendency is enough to set him off from the rest of the guests at the party, resulting in the mutual ironization described above. There is a gradual change as the story progresses, however, which begins when the Enthusiast meets two unusual companions in the pub, Erasmus Spikher and Peter Schlemihl. From the Enthusiast's point of view, these two figures are as real as the geographical details of the Berlin environment in which he meets them. In terms of the contexts from which they are taken, however, their status varies greatly. Schlemihl occupies a position which straddles the realms of fiction and reality: he is of course a character from another work of fiction, and with his lost shadow and seven-league boots he clearly makes no claim to being drawn from the real world. On the other hand, he is the creation of Hoffmann's friend Chamisso and a part of the contemporary literary scene of Berlin. Spikher, in turn, with his lost reflection and changing forms, is a creation of Hoffmann's imagination, yet also indirectly linked to the Berlin milieu through his constant implicit reference to Chamisso's creation.

We have then a realistically portrayed character in one work of fiction who tends to view reality in terms of quoted art works coming into contact with two characters who are taken from other considerably more "marvelous" tales.[12] Whereas in the opening section it was possible to understand the party at the Justizrat's home as the basis of a reality which the Enthusiast shared but was unable to perceive, leading to a clash between the two modes of perception, here three objectively different planes of reality meet in a moment of rare harmony: "In dem Maskenspiel des irdischen Lebens sieht oft der innere Geist mit leuchtenden Augen aus der Larve heraus, das Verwandte erkennend, und so mag es geschehen sein, daß wir drei absonderliche Menschen im Keller uns auch so angeschaut und erkannt hatten" (p. 263). When the Enthusiast joyfully recognizes Peter Schlemihl at the end of the section, having typically likened him to a painting by Rubens after originally having identified him as Faust, we have the successful convergence of the Enthusiast's perception of reality in terms of works of art with a figure who really is what the Enthusiast perceives.

Yet this harmonious blend of reality and fiction is disrupted by the Enthusiast's unwitting use of language which involves shifts between the literal and the figurative meanings of given phrases. This occurs first with his comments on Schlemihl's use of the idiomatic phrase "'Das hat auch seinen Haken'" (p. 264) = "'There's a problem there as well.'" The Enthusiast picks up the same word, but literalizes the metaphor: "'Ach Gott,' fiel ich ein, 'wie viel Haken hat der Teufel überall für uns eingeschlagen, in Zimmerwänden, Lauben, Rosenhecken, woran vorbeistreifend wir etwas von unserm teuern Selbst hängen lassen. Es scheint, Verehrte! als ob uns allen auf diese Weise schon etwas abhanden gekommen, wiewohl mir diese Nacht vorzüglich Hut und Mantel fehlte. Beides hängt an einem Haken in des Justizrats Vorzimmer, wie Sie wissen!'" (p. 264). Yet what for the Enthusiast is a harmless play on words functions as a dangerous allusion to the conditions of Spikher and Schlemihl, as both suffer from the actual loss of part of themselves. They thus react with unexpected defensiveness: "Der Kleine schaute mich recht häßlich mit seinem alten Gesichte an, sprang aber gleich auf einen Stuhl und zog das Tuch fester über den Spiegel, während der Große sorgfältig die Lichter putzte" (p. 264). When the conversation resumes with some difficulty in a few minutes, the same process occurs in reverse, as the Enthusiast's figurative use of the phrase "'wie aus dem Spiegel gestohlen'" (p. 264) is literalized by Spikher by applying it to his own condition. These sudden shifts in the value of the signifiers used by the three disparate figures in the text trigger the dispersal of the group (literally), and the disruption of the brief moment of harmony between the various levels of the text (figuratively).

As the story continues, however, we find that the Enthusiast not only is to encounter Erasmus Spikher by surprise in his room that night, but that Spikher's identity is remarkably close to his own. The parallel begins to be suggested in the third section of the work, entitled "Erscheinungen." While the Enthusiast envisions Julia in the mirror, Spikher dreams of Giulietta; then while the Enthusiast dreams, Spikher writes the story of his life, which turns out to parallel closely both Schlemihl's story and the Enthusiast's experience at the start of the work. The Enthusiast's dream, for its part, consists of a series of cross-readings between the lives of the three figures, in which again their identity is suggested.

In the dream the Enthusiast returns to the party at the home of the Justizrat, but this time his own experience is interpenetrated with the lives of the two characters he met in the bar. For the second time Julia is identified with a reference to paintings of the seventeenth century, the "Warnungstafeln von Breughel, von Callot oder von Rembrandt'" (p. 267), but in this case the allusion serves to link her to her demonic counterpart Giulietta, who will appear in Spikher's subsequent narrative. Julia is thus identified with Giulietta, the beautiful virgin painted by Rubens or Mieris with the seductress painted by Breughel, Callot, or Rembrandt, the heavenly angel with an emissary of the devil, and finally, in the eyes of Schlemihl, she is "Mina, die den Raskal geheiratet" (p. 268). While Schlemihl is thus reading Julia in terms of his own story, the Justizrat sees the Enthusiast as Schlemihl: "'Stellen Sie sich doch nur auf Ihre lieben Füße, denn schon lange bemerke ich, daß Sie in den Lüften über Stühle und Tische wegschreiten'" (p. 268). At the same time, Julia addresses the Enthusiast in words which could only properly be spoken by Giulietta to Spikher, assuring him that she still has his reflection. The moment of spiritual unity which the three experienced in the pub has been intensified in this "'lebhafter Traum'" (p. 268); the Enthusiast's life becomes interchangeable with the fictions of Schlemihl and Spikher.

In the wake of the confusion wrought by the Enthusiast's dream, the narrative of Spikher seems quite straightforward. As a French biographer of Hoffmann noted, it is told in the language of popular fiction: "elle se passe dans l'atmosphère des livres populaires, avec le diable, une belle sorcière, le pacte à signer avec du sang."[13] The most direct stylistic echo of "des Kleinen wundersame Geschichte" (p. 268) is of course "Peter Schlemihl's wundersame Geschichte." Yet Hoffmann also plays on what has become a Romantic cliché, the journey from "die nördliche Heimat [Germany] . . . nach dem schönen warmen Welschland" (p. 269). There is a note of parody in this formulation, and indeed Erasmus Spikher is not the typical young man in search of love and adventure, but an already married "Familienvater" whose doting wife manages to express her concern for his "schöne Reisemütze" amidst her tears at his departure. The Italy which Spikher visits is also less realistic than the popular image of a land filled with "liebliche Donnas," scheming villains, and singing German bachelors on holiday: "Ist ja doch Italien das Land der Liebe" (p. 269).

Spikher's story thus forms a striking stylistic contrast to the ecstatic first-person narrative of the Enthusiast. If the final section of **"Die Abenteuer der Silvester-Nacht"** parodies a hackneyed Romantic convention, the

Enthusiast represents an example of extreme Romantic subjectivity, to the point of an implicit critique, as noted above. However, there are close parallels between the two passages, and in turn to the story of Peter Schlemihl. Like Spikher, the Enthusiast has accepted a glass of intoxicating wine from Julia/Giulietta who for the third time is likened to a painting by Mieris or Rubens. The devil seems to offer him Julia, yet as it turns out she is married to another man, just as Schlemihl's Mina marries Raskal. In Spikher's case this motif is varied, as he is prevented from fulfilling his love for Giulietta by his refusal to murder his own wife and child. All three are left to wander alone, having lost reflection, shadow, or in the case of the Enthusiast, his coat.

The Enthusiast reappears briefly after Spikher's story in the postscript to **"Die Abenteuer der Silvester-Nacht."** By this time he is not only uncertain as to Julia's identity, but also of his own. "—Was schaut denn dort aus jenem Spiegel heraus?—Bin ich es auch wirklich? O Julie—Giulietta—Himmelsbild—Höllengeist—Entzücken und Qual—Sehnsucht und Verzweiflung" (p. 283). The process we have traced through the course of the story is now complete: what begins with the depiction of an aesthetic ideal which cannot be realized within the antagonistic bourgeois world gradually shifts to focus on the Enthusiast's confusion of actual events with various aesthetic experiences in his perception of reality. The distinction between subjective and objective reality completely collapses in the final phase of the story. The Enthusiast, who has consistently shown a tendency to perceive reality in aesthetic terms, now becomes a reader of his own fictionalized biography. What begins as an encounter between the self and the other leads to an acute identity crisis precipitated by the alarming realization that the self *is* the other.

III

Seen in the context of German literary history, the experiences of the Travelling Enthusiast reflect Hoffmann's break with the aesthetics of the early Romantics. In Novalis' *Heinrich von Ofterdingen,* for example, poetry is granted a privileged, almost sacred status, and Heinrich's instruction about the nature of the poet by Klingsohr sounds much like the initiation of the novice into a mystic religion.[14] The Enthusiast begins his evening citing this understanding of poetry and the poet when he first glimpses Julia, but as the evening progresses, as we have seen, he moves into a disturbing world where fictional characters shake his sense of identity. The result is a different understanding of the relationship between art and reality which is summarized in the editor's preface to **"Die Abenteuer der Silvester-Nacht."**

The Enthusiast is introduced as an individual who barely separates his inner from his outer life. This personal idiosyncrasy is then made into a principle for the effect which the editor hopes the work will have on its readers: "Aber eben, weil du, günstiger Leser! diese Grenze nicht deutlich wahrnimmst, lockt der Geisterseher dich vielleicht herüber, und unversehens befindest du dich in dem fremden Zauberreiche, dessen seltsame Gestalten recht in dein äußeres Leben treten und mit dir auf du und du umgehen wollen, wie alte Bekannte" (p. 256). The logic of this passage can be summarized as follows. On the one hand, it relies on a series of binary oppositions: between the "inner" and the "outer," between the reader's reality and the "fremden Zauberreiche" of poetry. On the other hand, poetry itself is not defined as a transcendent, autonomous realm, but rather as a world where poetic creations and actual experience exist without contradiction. Thus the second half of the binary opposition is defined in a way which erases the boundary which initially establishes its identity. The result is to thrust the work of art into a direct engagement with its surrounding reality. The concluding pages of this essay will therefore specify the nature of this engagement as it relates to both the production and reception of **"Die Abenteuer der Silvester-Nacht."**

We began by noting the obvious parallel between Hoffmann's love for Julia Marc in Bamberg and the Enthusiast's encounter with a former lover named Julia in Berlin. The setting of the story in Berlin complicates the biographical parallel, for we know that Hoffmann never actually saw Julia Marc after she left Bamberg in December, 1812.[15] In the meantime Adelbert von Chamisso had completed his "Peter Schlemihl," a work which Hoffmann greeted with great enthusiasm.[16] Finally, a third link to Hoffmann's biography is suggested in the postscript to this work, as we learn that the "du" addressed throughout the work is none other than Theodor Amadäus Hoffmann! This technique is directly taken over from the first-person narrative of Peter Schlemihl, who repeatedly identifies his reader as Adelbert von Chamisso.[17] In the case of **"Die Abenteuer der Silvester-Nacht"** this technique takes on added significance, because we know that Hoffmann actually began work on the story on January 1st, 1815, in Berlin.[18] Thus while the Enthusiast sits down to read Spikher's story on New Year's Day within the fictional world of **"Die Abenteuer der Silvester-Nacht,"** Hoffmann is beginning to write the tale in which this act of reading takes place. And just as the Enthusiast realizes that there is a close similarity between his own life and the biography of the man he reads, Hoffmann constructs a narrative in which he becomes the direct addressee of his own fictional character. In a sense, then, the text becomes Hoffmann's mirror image, as he writes about himself writing, just as within the text the Enthusiast reads about himself in the lives of Spikher and Schlemihl.

Thus Hoffmann's personal experience, his reading experience, and the act of writing itself are all implicitly present within the fictional world of **"Die Abenteuer der Silvester-Nacht."** The result of this combination can be described as follows: the Hoffmann who found himself alienated from a society in which his beloved Julia Marc was married to the rich businessman Graepel from Hamburg writes a story about a fictional character who also loses his beloved Julia to another man. The plot of *this* story in turn looks very much like that of a fairy tale he has written about a man without a reflection who is separated from both his wife and his lover, which further looks like a story which his good friend Chamisso has just written about a man who loses his shadow and as a result his Mina. In other words, the gradual fragmentation of the self which occurs to the Enthusiast in terms of reading reality mirrors the changing image of Hoffmann's self as he is engaged in the act of transforming autobiography to fiction.[19]

The point of these comments is not to "deconstruct" Hoffmann's work, but to show how the image of the self which emerges is a construct of a variety of different idioms. Here the work of Mikhail Bakhtin is suggestive. "For the novelist," he writes, "there is no world outside his socio-heteroglot perception—and there is no language outside the heteroglot intentions that stratify that world."[20] Thus "language, for the individual consciousness, lies on the borderline between oneself and the other. The word in language is half someone else's."[21] From this perspective the private *Zerrissenheit* of the Romantic artist is the result of the plurality of public discourses which constitute his individuality. Instead of producing a pure aesthetic world which opposes the mundane reality of the bourgeoisie, the artist differs from the Philistine only in his greater awareness of their mutual implication within the same order of social discourse. Thus Hoffmann is typical of the novelistic tradition in which the "author does not speak in a given language (from which he distances himself to a greater or lesser degree), but he speaks, as it were, *through* language, a language that has somehow more or less materialized, become objectivized, that he merely ventriloquates."[22]

This understanding of Hoffmann's role as the author of **"Die Abenteuer der Silvester-Nacht"** is directly related to the sort of reading his text demands. Here again a contrast with Novalis is instructive. Like the Travelling Enthusiast, Heinrich von Ofterdingen encounters a narrative which is a mysterious account of his own life.[23] Although Heinrich is unable to read the language in which the work is written, he clearly recognizes his own image in the manuscript's illuminations, and senses that it mystically reveals the events of his future. Its function within the work, therefore, is to strengthen Heinrich's growing awareness of his own future destiny as a poet. The effect of the Enthusiast's reading of Spikher's narrative is directly opposed to the sort of reading portrayed in Novalis' work. By replacing the

prophetic medieval manuscript with a work of popular fiction contemporary to the Enthusiast's Berlin setting, Hoffmann creates a situation in which reading does not strengthen his hero's sense of identity by revealing his future calling, but instead only serves to complicate his already fractured sense of identity in the present.

Thus the identity crisis precipitated by the act of reading portrayed within **"Die Abenteuer der Silvester-Nacht"** is directly related to the temporal structure of the work as a whole. Instead of a direct linear progression through a series of events, we have a series of repetitions of the same basic plot to the point where it becomes impossible to tell what is original and what is a quote, what an event and what a memory. Time is at once stopped in its forward motion and in a sense "thickened," as the events in the lives of the various characters reverberate with reference to one another. For this reason it is significant that the work takes place on New Year's Eve, the point in the year when our awareness of time is most acute. The result is a circularly structured text which demands the sort of rereading which Roland Barthes describes in *S/Z*: "it contests the claim which would have us believe that the first reading is a primary, naive, phenomenal reading which we will only afterwards have to 'explicate,' to intellectualize (as if there were a beginning of reading, as if everything were not already read: there is no *first* reading. . . .[24] In this way Hoffmann's text urges us to undertake "an operation contrary to the commercial and ideological habits of our society, which would have us 'throw away' the story once it has been consumed ('devoured'), so that we can then move on to another story, buy another book. . . ."[25]

Barthes' statements suggest that the poetics of a work such as **"Die Abenteuer der Silvester-Nacht"** can be cause for affirmation as well as the reflection of a lament. The contrast with Novalis defines Hoffmann's work negatively, as we see a loss in the authority of the poet's voice, and a subsequent decline in the formerly privileged status of the literary text and the reading experience. The desperate tonality of the Enthusiast's postscript is indicative of that aspect of Hoffmann's works which caused Heinrich Heine to speak of them as "nichts anders als ein entsetzlicher Angstschrei in zwanzig Bänden."[26] However, the very loss of the early Romantic ideal allows for the liberating possibility of a particular sort of humor in Hoffmann's text. We have in fact seen that some of the most obvious sources of humor in **"Die Abenteuer der Silvester-Nacht"** are the satirical portraits of such figures as the guests of the Justizrat, Julia's husband, Spikher's wife, and the Enthusiast himself. Yet there is also a subtler type of humor evidenced in the sudden shifts between the literal and figurative meanings of such phrases as "das hat auch seinen Haken," and "wie aus dem Spiegel gestohlen." The fluctuations in the meanings of these phrases in the second section of the story are typical of larger patterns within the text as a whole, as the various stories cross back and forth between each other, as in the encounter with fictional characters in a Berlin pub, in the Enthusiast's dream, or when Signor Dapertutto tells Spikher to get back into the parchment where he belongs (p. 272). If Hoffmann demonstrates that the self is bound up in a variety of social idioms, he does so by "tricking" language, by violating the integrity of any given discourse.[27] In this sense the dissolution of the self implied by the triplication of Hoffmann's biography in **"Die Abenteuer der Silvester-Nacht"** becomes the source of its ongoing life in the text. In the place of a work which leads its reader through a series of events to a harmonious conclusion, this story ends on a note of extreme discord which suggests that nothing is over and that we must therefore begin again.

Notes

1. Hans Mayer, "Die Wirklichkeit E. T. A. Hoffmanns: Ein Versuch," in Hoffmann, *Poetische Werke* (Berlin: Aufbau, 1958), I, xxvii. Reprinted in Hans Mayer, *Von Lessing bis Thomas Mann: Wandlungen der bürgerlichen Literatur in Deutschland* (Pfullingen: Neske, 1959), pp. 198-246; also in *Romantikforschung seit 1945,* ed. Klaus Peter (Königstein: Athenäum/Hain/Scriptor/Hanstein, 1980), pp. 116-44.

2. Mayer, I, xxix.

3. Wulf Segebrecht, *Autobiographie und Dichtung: Eine Studie zum Werk E. T. A. Hoffmanns* (Stuttgart: Metzler, 1967), pp. 107-08.

4. Hoffmann spells the name both "Julia" and "Julie" within this story and also in *Kater Murr.* For the sake of consistency I use the former variant throughout this essay.

5. Mayer mentions "Die Abenteuer der Silvester-Nacht" only in passing in this regard (xxvii), and what little has been written on the work is primarily psychoanalytic in its concerns. Thus Jean Giraud, the author of the only extensive article on the work, focuses on "les difficultés psychologiques et morales de l'amour spirituel" which he feels are thematized in the text. "E. T. A. Hoffmann: 'Die Abenteuer der Silvester-Nach': Le double visage," *Recherches Germaniques,* 1 (1971), 121. Elizabeth MacAndrew sees in the various levels of the plot the image of "a subject expressed in shifting images of mental instability." *The Gothic Tradition in Fiction* (New York: Columbia University Press, 1979), p. 217. Similarly, Theodor Ziolkowski has recently spoken of Spikher and Schlemihl as characters who suffer "an der Zerrissenheit des romantischen Helden, wobei der verlorene Schatten bzw. das verlorene

Spiegelbild ihre schizophrene Angst zeichenhaft exemplifiziert." "Figuren auf Pump: Zur Fiktionalität des sprachlichen Kunstwerks," in *Jahrbuch für Internationale Germanistik,* Reihe A, Band 8, 1 (1980), 170. My concern in this essay will be to shift our attention back to Mayer's sociological concerns, yet to do so in a way that counters the common dualistic understanding of Hoffmann and the Philistines by focusing on the problem of writing as it is thematized in the work. In doing so, I am in full agreement with David Wellbery's assertion that Hoffmann's "writing is a complex activity of cultural labor requiring analysis in terms of various levels and relations." "E. T. A. Hoffmann and Romantic Hermeneutics: An Interpretation of Hoffmann's 'Don Juan,'" in *Studies in Romanticism,* 19 (1980), 472.

6. Mikhail Bakhtin, "Discourse in the Novel," in *The Dialogic Imagination: Four Essays,* ed. Michael Holquist, trans. Caryl Emerson and Michael Holquist (Austin: University of Texas Press, 1981), pp. 259-422. I am also indebted to some of Roland Barthes' comments about the nature of reading in his *S/Z: An Essay,* trans. Richard Miller (New York: Hill and Wang, 1974).

7. E. T. A. Hoffmann, "Die Abenteuer der Silvester-Nacht," in *Fantasie- und Nachtstücke,* ed. Wolfgang Kron, afterword Walter Müller-Seidel (München: Winkler, 1976), p. 256. Hereafter cited in the text.

8. Hans Mayer points out that Hoffmann's treatment of his contemporary society is generally sarcastic, but does not include the equally ironic presentation of many artist figures in Hoffmann's works (I, xviii).

9. Jochen Schmidt has recently focused on Hoffmann's critique of the extreme subjectivity of the early Romantics with particular reference to "Der Sandmann" in "Die Krise der romantischen Subjektivität: E. Th. A. Hoffmanns Künstlernovelle 'Der Sandmann' in historischer Perspektive," in *Literaturwissenschaft und Geistesgeschichte: Festschrift für Richard Brinkmann* (Tübingen: Niemeyer, 1981), pp. 348-70.

10. Ludwig Tieck, *Kaiser Oktavianus* (1804), part II, act 4. In Ludwig Tieck, *Schriften* (Berlin: Reimer, 1828), I, 348.

11. "Sie scheinen mir aus einem edlen Haus, / Sie sehen stolz und unzufrieden aus." Goethe, *Werkausgabe* (Frankfurt: Insel, 1977), III, 65.

12. I use the term "marvelous" in the sense defined by Tzvetan Todorov, in which "new laws of nature must be entertained to account for the phenomena" of a particular literary work. In *The Fantas-*

tic: A Structural Approach to a Literary Genre, trans. Richard Howard (Ithaca, New York: Cornell University Press, 1975), p. 41.

13. Jean-F.-A. Ricci, *E. T. A. Hoffmann: L'homme et L'oeuvre* (Paris: José Corti, 1947), p. 371.

14. See chapters seven and eight of *Heinrich von Ofterdingen,* in Novalis, *Schriften* (Stuttgart: Kohlhammer, 1960), I, 279-90.

15. See Gabrielle Wittkop-Ménardeau, *E. T. A. Hoffmann: in Selbstzeugnissen und Bilddokumenten* (Hamburg: Rowohlt, 1966), p. 82.

16. "Nie werde ich die Stunde vergessen, in welcher ich es *Hoffmann* zuerst vorlas. Außer sich vor Vergnügen und Spannung, hing er an meinen Lippen, bis ich vollendet hatte; nicht erwarten konnte er, die persönliche Bekanntschaft des Dichters zu machen, und, sonst jeder Nachahmung so abhold, widerstand er doch der Versuchung nicht, die Idee des verlornen Schattens in seiner Erzählung: 'Die Abenteuer der Silvesternacht', durch das verlorne Spiegelbild des Erasmus Spikher, ziemlich unglücklich zu variieren." Eduard Hitzig to F. de la Motte Fouqué, from Berlin in January 1827. Quoted from *Peter Schlemihls wundersame Geschichte,* Reclams Universal-Bibliothek, 93 (Stuttgart: Reclam, 1976), pp. 8-9. References to Chamisso's work are cited from this readily available edition.

17. On pages 20, 35, 53, 54, 65, 70, and 76 of the Reclam edition. The first mention of Chamisso as Schlemihl's reader is the most remarkable, as he is seen in his study surrounded by books, but, as Schlemihl notes, "du rührtest dich aber nicht, du holtest auch nicht Atem, du warst tot."

18. See the entries in E. T. A. Hoffmann, *Tagebücher* (München: Winkler, 1971), pp. 258-59.

19. David Wellbery reaches a similar conclusion in his recent study of "Don Juan," namely that the "text is the fragmentation of the subject, not its adequate objectification." Wellbery, "'Don Juan,'" p. 472.

20. Bakhtin, p. 330.

21. Bakhtin, p. 293.

22. Bakhtin, p. 299.

23. In chapter five, in Novalis, *Schriften* I, 264-66. A similarly mystic reading experience is contained in "Das Märchen von Hyazinth und Rosenblüte," *Schriften* I, 93.

24. Barthes, p. 16.

25. Barthes, pp. 15-16.

26. Heinrich Heine, *Die romantische Schule: Kritische Ausgabe,* Reclams Universal-Bibliothek, 1831, ed. Helga Weidmann (Stuttgart: Reclam, 1976), p. 96.

27. "Cette tricherie salutaire, cette esquive, ce leurre magnifique, qui permet d'entendre la langue horspouvoir, dans la splendeur d'une révolution permanente du langage, je l'appelle pour ma part: *littérature.*" Roland Barthes, *Lecon* (Paris: Seuil, 1978), p. 16.

Lee B. Jennings (essay date May 1986)

SOURCE: Jennings, Lee B. "Blood of the Android: A Post-Freudian Perspective on Hoffmann's 'Sandmann.'" *Seminar: A Journal of Germanic Studies* 22, no. 2 (May 1986): 95-111.

[*In the following essay, Jennings considers the tension between reality and imaginative vision in Hoffmann's "Der Sandmann." Jennings identifies several levels of vision in the story, ranging from the subjective perceptions of personal experience to the ambiguous, almost incommunicable manifestations of a transcendental reality. According to Jennings, the constant interplay between interior and exterior realms in the story blurs traditional distinctions between ordinary life and the supernatural.*]

Hoffmann's **'Der Sandmann'** is above all an essay on vision—on reality-perception, imagination, and the interplay between the two. Hoffmann, as author-narrator in his lengthy interpolation about his difficulties in writing the story, calls attention to a common problem: communicating colorful inner experience in terms that will not render it prosaic and rob it of its color.[1] Though Hoffmann stresses the common nature of the experience, it is one that comes to the fore in Romantic thought. Indeed, Hoffmann seems to have created a test-case for Romantic subjectivism here, an exploration of the question: Can the inner vision be communicated, and does it convey information about reality? The question is complex, since Hoffmann conceives 'reality' broadly. It is unlikely that he is always being ironic (a currently much-abused claim) when he speculates about other worlds.[2] The inner vision, in his view, may thus convey information about a hyperreality, a timeless and archetypal realm of more essential existence à la G. H. Schubert, a realm whose empirical validation may be difficult. The theme of vision impinges on two related ones: supernaturalism and insanity. The vision may be merely private, idiosyncratic, and devoid of informational content; it may be a true perception of another reality, but incommunicable, or communicable only in symbolic terms; and it may be a different way of perceiving the present reality, with gradations between these possibilities.

Hoffmann subjects the theme of reality-perception to a severe test in **'Der Sandmann.'** His protagonist, Nathanael, unlike many poetically sensitive heroes of his other tales, is a practising poet. He is also, however, a borderline psychotic, subject to violent outbreaks. These are not rationalized in the popular fashion but are described with surprising psychological realism as being apparently senseless but suggestive of hidden conflicts. The story reads something like a case history, and as a result it has attracted considerable attention on the part of psychoanalytical interpreters from Freud on.

It might seem that psychological interpretations are pre-empted, or even rendered futile, by the widely accepted view of a basic ambiguity or parallelism of reality-modes in this and other of Hoffmann's works, a view principally expounded by Preisendanz.[3] The sandman-ridden Nathanael, he feels, should not be entirely dismissed as a solipsistic fantast (though he *can* be understood that way), since there are enough indications that his visions represent some mythic verity. It is not thereby implied that Hoffmann is indifferent to the issue of 'natural versus supernatural,' nor that he is engaging in non-committal intellectual play and mystification. It is precisely Preisendanz's point that for Hoffmann and the Romantics the physical world is incommensurable, 'reality' being only a construct of the perceiving and interpreting mind, and that their works are organized around this concept. One might say that, in this view, the dark side of Kant emerges in Romantic thought.

Yet it is instructive to put aside momentarily this onto-logically problematic approach, which, profound as it is, tends not to lead us further, and to consider the psychological interpretations in some detail. These, at least until recent times, presuppose an unequivocal 'reality' and are concerned primarily with Nathanael's striking failure to adapt to it. The assumption is that Hoffmann, a psychological realist, intuitively conveys information about the unconscious levels of human motivation, whether or not he intended to do so. Even if we reject this premise, something may be gained by provisionally pursuing it, since it is in this area that the most provocative and intriguing insights emerge. **'Der Sandmann'** invites interpretation because it seems to contain symbolically encoded information, not only about the parochial dilemma of the 'Romantic artist' but also about more basic issues: the interrelation between love, creativity, and psychic wholeness, the cognition of reality, the notion of personal identity, and the dependence of mind upon body. These factors are peculiarly and surprisingly interwoven, and we need the help of both metaphysics and depth-psychology to arrive at an underlying pattern (the goal of all research). Such a pattern may lie in Hoffmann's implied conception of cosmic eros, defying strict philosophical and psychological categorization because it has the nature of a universal principle operating through the individual unconscious.

Freud, in his essay *Das Unheimliche,* credits Hoffmann with pre-psychoanalytical insight and attempts to uncover the causes which might underlie the behavior of a person such as Nathanael, while accounting for the exemplary air of uncanniness about the story. Assuming that the uncanny is that which is overtly strange but covertly familiar, he finds the answer in Nathanael's childhood traumas, in Oedipus complex and castration fear; in terms now familiar, he establishes blinding as a symbolic displacement of castration, the Sandman/Coppelius/Coppola as the punishing father, and Olimpia as Nathanael's father-pleasing feminine aspect, an object of narcissistic love and an impediment in the way of his more mature love for Clara.[4] While the uninitiated may boggle (as Freud expects) at the immediate equation of eyes with testicles, it is less easy to dismiss the role of repressed and distorted childhood trauma in the work and the function of Olimpia as a projection of Nathanael's own psyche, a regressive substitute for the flesh-and-blood fiancée.

Others have followed in Freud's footsteps. McGlathery, drawing upon recent studies of Hoffmann's narrative perspectives, has evolved a consistent scheme of interpretation whereby the fantastic events not only of **'Der Sandmann'** but in all of Hoffmann's tales are hallucinatory projections of the characters, resulting mainly from sexual anxiety.[5] Mahlendorf, accepting Freud's basic thesis, concentrates on Nathanael's post-pubertal development, concluding that he attempts to gain mastery over unresolved unconscious conflicts through his poetry but is thwarted by Clara's failure to understand and support him in this struggle.[6]

Weber, following Lacan, reinterprets Freud's concept of 'castration,' understanding it as the common onset of individual self-awareness and, in its later reverberations, as the continuing struggle of the thinking subject to preserve its precarious integrity, while yet longing for the wholeness of infancy which this self-awareness necessarily precludes. The ambiguity and uncanniness of the tale, he claims, has little to do with the 'reality' of the events described, which rather represent reactivations of this basic insecurity and thus pose insoluble problems. It is the enigma of 'castration' in this sense which Nathanael seeks to probe with his spyglass, and he presumably finds his dilemma disconcertingly exemplified in Clara.[7]

Largely Lacanian in conception also, and likewise unsettling in its equivocation of 'normal' reality-perception, is Lehmann's thought-provoking discourse, in which Hoffmann's tale is seen as an allegory on the role of vision, symbol, and language in forming and maintaining personal identity. Nathanael is seen as wavering between prelinguistic body-oriented existence and stereotyped, automatonlike social identity. (Peculiarly compelling in its way is Lehmann's analysis of Hoffmann's drawing of Nathanael spying on Coppelius and his father, viewed as a kind of hermaphroditic primal scene.)[8]

Von Matt has provided what might be described as a quasi-psychological approach to this and other works of Hoffmann. Olimpia is, in his view, a *teraphim,* i.e. an artifact, usually of human form, which serves to concentrate and activate the artistic imagination of Hoffmann's protagonists. In order to attain full, untroubled creativity, they must recognize the role which projection has played in animating the object. This occurs, however, only in utopian settings such as 'Atlantis.' Nathanael patently fails to learn his lesson, and the incipient recognition that not only Olimpia, but also Clara, is essentially a projection from within himself is too much for his mind to bear. It is, after all, Clara that Nathanael glimpses through the telescope just before his final attack of madness.[9] While von Matt's view has much in common with the psychoanalytical speculations about projection and narcissistic love, he regards the self-recognition process, like pre-Freudian writers, as a peculiarity of the artistic temperament, not as a common psychological phenomenon, removing it somewhat from our more intimate concerns.

None of these approaches would seem to conflict seriously with the traditional philosophical-aesthetic view of Hoffmann as a tormented idealist nor with the more recent image of him as a determinedly ambiguous master of the literary narrative, and a composite reading, which we may take as a point of departure, is rather easily constructed. The importance of early trauma is impressed upon us by Hoffmann himself, and it can hardly be denied that Olimpia, as Nathanael sees her, is a product of his own fantasy, and fair proof of a less-than-normal love relationship—unless, of course, Hoffmann means to suggest that *all* love is of this nature, which would again place him in close company with Freud. Nathanael's propensity for fantasy is no doubt a prominent feature of the artistic temperament, though not exclusive to it, and the narcissistic behavior seen by Freud as neurosis may have been slightly closer to the prevailing norm, at least in some quarters, during that era. This is not to say that Hoffmann entirely condones such behavior, even in himself. Indeed, the spectacle of a young poet, apostrophizing, à la Novalis, a mechanical woman seems clearly to constitute a reductio ad absurdum or parody of the Romantic movement, or at least of some of its excesses.[10] Neither is the madness of his hero flattering to the Romantic cause, but, given

Hoffmann's fascination with insanity, we are on less firm ground here. The solipsism with which Nathanael views Olimpia as perfect audience and love-object can easily be read parodistically, whether one denounces Nathanael, praises the 'ideal' he is pursuing, or blames the society which does not provide him with fulfillment.[11] But, strangely, his more strictly psychotic belief that he is persecuted by an evil fate is more difficult to regard as parody, or, indeed, to explain away.[12] Hoffmann, as author-narrator, distances himself most directly from his hero by pronouncing the ultimate author's anathema on his verse: it is boring ('Nathanaels Dichtungen waren in der Tat sehr langweilig,' 347).

Although the popular but uneasy alliance between Freudianism and Marxism seems not to have penetrated into the mainstream of Hoffmann-research as yet, the sociological approaches to his work dovetail nicely with the psychological ones and may be mentioned as their necessary concomitants. Generally speaking, the sociological interpreter says that Hoffmann, though politically naive, rather accidentally produces many telling criticisms of the bourgeoisie, the class responsible for disenfranchising the artist because of its intransigently prosaic attitude. (The assumption is that a proper society would immediately grasp great art and clasp the artist to its bosom.) To the extent that Hoffmann actually subscribes to the primacy of art and supernatural influences, he further demonstrates the central thesis, becoming the victim forced to withdraw into a fantasy world by his heartless contemporaries.[13] The implication is that Hoffmann's true calling was direct social criticism (as opposed to indirect cultural comment), whether he himself thought so or not. Thus, Hayes complains that Hoffmann introduces fantasy as an end in itself, shamelessly flaunting the neurosis of the whole Romantic period. He praises the imaginary because it does not exist, the incomprehensible because it cannot be understood, and mysterious 'truths' because they are inaccessible to ordinary people; failing to sight the true enemy, he caricatures prosaic types only toward the greater glory of the ostensibly superior (but in fact miserable) artist. The watershed for schools of thought about **'Der Sandmann'** seems to be the evaluation of Clara's character. For Hayes, she is cut from the same cloth as those tea-swilling fops who, after Olimpia's unmasking, suspect their fiancées of being automatons. She is a *Bürgermädchen* par excellence, a member of that class which has willingly transformed itself into automatons. This, claims Hayes, accounts for her parallel with Olimpia; she is also an automaton, as Nathanael once states, and as he finally fully recognizes when he sees her through the telescope (now become an instrument of clarity rather than obfuscation). Nathanael's anxiety is nothing but dread at the prospect of a bourgeois marriage. As for Coppelius, he has simply disguised himself as the Italian peddler Coppola to escape the law, and, in disgrace again, resumes his true identity as he leaves the city at the end of the narrative (though Hoffmann tells us that he had just arrived).[14]

Lying somewhere between Mahlendorf's and Hayes's views is the non-doctrinaire argument of Ellis, based on intricacies of the narrative process, that there is an actual conspiracy against Nathanael on the part of Coppelius (= Coppola) and Spalanzani, aggravated by Clara's increasingly domineering, self-centered, and uncomprehending attitude toward him. Like Hayes, Ellis ranks Clara with the conformist robots elsewhere satirized. He points out that the assumption that Coppola is Coppelius (which he sees as decisive) does much to corroborate Nathanael's alleged delusions.[15] This makes either conspiracy or supernatural influence more likely, however, and since the point is crucial we must pursue it further.

The flaw in the conspiracy theory is that the experimenters have no motive for wishing Nathanael's downfall, and his interest in Olimpia is of only peripheral benefit to them. They succeed in fooling the whole town even without, or perhaps in spite of, Nathanael's help, and this seems to have been their predominant intent. More probable, but again bordering on the hostile-fate theory, is the idea of a long-standing, irrational grudge on Coppelius' part, perhaps because he knows that Nathanael justly holds him responsible for the death of his father (and, in the first version, the death of his sister also), or because of an old hatred for the meddling child who seemed to be prying into his secrets. This is borne out by his words at the tower in the original version (see below), in which he repeats the imprecation 'kleine Bestie' from the earlier scene and refers to Nathanael's supposed curiosity about manufacturing eyes (a secret he seems anxious to protect).

It is the usual fate of the paraliterary schools of interpretation that their findings remain privy to their own adherents. Both the psychological and the sociological approaches lend valuable perspective to the work by probing the grey area of the author's semi-intentionalities and by clearing away some of the dead wood of older, neo-Kantian (or, as McGlathery calls it, 'neo-Platonic') Hoffmann-literature. Both, however, do some injustice to an overt intentionality of the author, his suggestion of supernatural influence; and both neglect some symbolic references that do not happen to fall into their respective areas of concern, especially those having to do with eyes and the automaton. It is these that point the way toward a new evaluation of the work, but in order to arrive at it, we must dissect out, as it were, the anti-supernatural bias that has tended to inhibit receptiveness toward symbolisms transcending the personal sphere. This cannot be done, however, without reexamining the decisive junctures of the narrative.

The question of the supernatural is rather too easily dismissed by saying that Hoffmann leaves the question open. An equivocality of outlook on the author's part is not necessarily implied by this commonplace device for heightening the effect of wonder and eeriness (prototype: Henry James's *The Turn of the Screw*). It may be that Hoffmann meant to baffle the reader, creating a web of ambiguity. Probably he turned the screw too far in places, creating only confusion instead of mystery. But in such a work, attempting to unravel the strands of real and more or less imaginary events is part of the agreement between author and reader. In the end, the very writing of supernatural fiction presupposes a certain open-mindedness toward the unexplained.

Hoffmann seems to have taken pains to leave the reality-question in doubt here. The revisions undertaken after the first manuscript version seem aimed at toning down the implication of demonic influence, an implication that his readers no doubt would have uncritically seized upon. In the printed version, Coppelius no longer strokes the eyes of Nathanael's younger sister, shortly after which she goes blind and dies; the narrator no longer intervenes to state that Coppelius and Coppola are no doubt one and the same person; and Coppelius' remarks at the end, below the tower, are less incriminating. Spalanzani still refers to 'Coppola' as 'Coppelius' just after the quarrel between them, however,[16] and the figure beneath the tower is clearly identified as Coppelius, and there can be little doubt that they are indeed identical. But though Hoffmann may have toned down the demonic effect, he is careful not to rule it out entirely. It remains unclear why Coppelius is so intent on pursuing Nathanael and why his telescope functions so miraculously in Nathanael's hands; either it is indeed magical, or 'Coppola' (whoever he is) is preternaturally able to foresee the effect an ordinary telescope will have on the impressionable Nathanael— one would, after all, expect such an instrument to help dispel his illusion that the distant Olimpia is a live girl. Further, Coppelius' appearance below the tower (especially if he is *not* Coppola) is extremely coincidental, and in both versions his remarks imply some superior knowledge of the course of events.[17]

To say that the reality-question is irrelevant seems to fence off important areas of author-intent and reception. In a pedestrian sense, it is indeed irrelevant what is 'real' in a made-up story. When the story is manifestly designed to explore the borderlands of empirical reality, however, the question becomes central in our response, and the psychological aspects of perception and cognition must be dealt with. Then we seem to do better justice to the author's enterprise by provisionally suspending our rationalistic disbelief than by persisting in it.

To the modern mind, the psychological (or socio-psychological) interpretation appears to preclude any serious contemplation of the supernatural. If Nathanael is suffering delusions, or, to be more precise, if the author intends us to think that he is, then his interpretation of the facts is discounted from the outset. For the sociological critics, moreover, alternate perceptions of reality are ideologically precluded in any case. The mutual exclusion of 'reality' and 'fantasy,' as noted, may have been less binding for Hoffmann.

Clara, whose opinion is valued precisely by those who grasp life with 'profound clarity' ('die das Leben in klarer Tiefe aufgefaßt,' 345—surely one of Hoffmann's least ironic turns of phrase) makes just this point about alternate perspectives in her often-quoted attempt to wean Nathanael away from his obsessive and depressed state of mind. She does not deny that there are evil and ruinous cosmic principles, but she states that they must operate through the individual mind, becoming a part of it. It is this very factor, she says (here quoting her brother Lothar), that may cause us to project parts of ourselves into random external occurrences. Her advice is not to deny the existence of supernatural forces, but to recognize them and learn to displace them with firm life-goals (340-341).[18] In our day, this might appear as extremely artful psychotherapy; Hoffmann, only too prone to think that the Devil sets snares for us, probably meant it seriously. The supernatural, for Clara, exerts itself just at the bounds of the individual unconscious and merges with it. The fantast and the paranoiac may be justified in some way as interpreters of reality.

The question remains as to why Clara, intuitively perceptive as her letter shows her to be, is denounced by Nathanael as an automaton, why she seems to be equated with the 'Holzpüppchen' Olimpia in Nathanael's crazed fantasies, and why the sight of her precipitates his final crisis. She actually has little in common with the crass social robots elsewhere satirized, whom she also scorns. Her serenity, the narrator suggests, is not that of suppressed spontaneity and superficiality, but that of integrity and depth.[19] One problem here is the multiplicity of the automaton symbol. Far from being a mere representation of standardized behavior or a symbol of determinism (this is usually reserved for the stringed puppet or marionette), the automaton aroused an existential dread in Hoffmann's generation somewhat analogous to the fascination with thinking computers or androids in our own time. Insofar as **'Der Sandmann'** explores the potential impact of technological discovery, it can in fact be regarded as science fiction. The robots of the time, crude as they now seem, aroused doubts as to the primacy and uniqueness of human life and intelligence. The mad 'Serapion' asks, in defense of his delusions: 'Ja was hört, was sieht, was fühlt in uns?—vielleicht die toten Maschinen die wir Auge—Ohr—Hand etc. nennen und nicht der Geist?'[20] The automaton calls attention to the 'dead machine' which the physical body in fact is, and it arouses new confusion as to what it is (perhaps electricity?) that en-

livens it. Even *Geist* is no guarantee of integrated self-awareness and volition, since even a madman may possess it. What animates Hoffmann's automatons is the eye. He seems to hint that these contrivances contain actual human eyes as their sole organic component. Thus it may not be merely malicious teasing when Coppelius, surrounded by eyeless masks, threatens to appropriate the eyes of the spying child Nathanael.[21] To be sure, it is difficult to accept Nathanael's further contention, in recalling the scene, that Coppelius unscrewed his arms and legs and temporarily reattached them in other places, a contention Nathanael himself seems to repudiate a page later.[22] Still, we must doubt that the child Nathanael could have invented Coppelius' remark about the Creator, reflecting grudging professional admiration: The Old Man knew his business, there is no other way the parts will fit together.[23] Whatever oedipal trauma the scene may reflect, there is an existential trauma also. The young Nathanael, perhaps suffering the physical trauma of dislocated joints, becomes painfully aware that the physical body is indeed a 'dead machine'—we are all automatons.

Freud has called attention to the indeed puzzling detail that Spalanzani seems to say the eyes have been stolen from Nathanael. Though we assume that 'Coppola' had tried to repossess the eyes, his contribution to the project, shortly before this (perhaps having some other use for them), as it develops they are the only part of Olimpia that has *not* been stolen. Hoffmann seems to have labored over the passage. The manuscript version reads:

> Coppelius—Coppelius—mein bestes Automat hat er mir geraubt—zwanzig Jahr daran gearbeitet—Leib und Leben daran gesetzt—[die Augen—die Augen—er hat sie ge . . . *durchstrichen*] aber das Räderwerk—Gang—Sprache—Gesang—mein mein.—Die Augen die Augen—er—er—Dir gestohlen[24]

(Cf. the pertinent section in the more coherent but perhaps 'normalized' printed version: 'Das Räderwerk—Sprache—Gang—mein—die Augen—die Augen dir gestohlen,' 359.)

In both versions, Spalanzani begins to contrast 'Coppola's' paltry contribution with his own but breaks off or suppresses his train of thought, perhaps not wishing to reveal the precise manner in which the eyes were provided. Perhaps he meant to say (depending on punctuation and printer's caprice) that now all this (the entire Olimpia figure) has been stolen from Nathanael, who has come to have a kind of proprietary interest in the creation, or that Coppelius had just previously removed the eyes, intending to make off with them, thus performing a kind of potential and indirect tort upon Nathanael. Or perhaps the pronoun *dir* is not to be taken quite literally, and he means to hint that the eyes are not clever artifacts but were *stolen,* i.e. from human bodies, notwithstanding 'Coppola's' earlier claim 'Ich habe die Augen gemacht' (358).

Nathanael's psychotic episode upon seeing the eyeless, inorganic Olimpia and upon being bombarded with apparently organic eyeballs is rather easily accounted for on a combination of psychoanalytical and existential grounds. Olimpia has become part of his ego, and giving her up would mean losing his sense of self, which is already none too steadfast.[25] At the same time, he is reminded that we can all be dismembered into lifeless (or soulless) clockwork.

It is indeed Nathanael's quest for a sense of self, and for the spark of vitality, two intermingled goals, that seem to inform his fantasies, which, not accidentally, revolve about the motif of disembodied eyes. The epic poem he composes in an evident attempt to come to terms with the sandman-principle in his life has to be taken as a fair account of his fantasy's content. Nathanael, in whose imagination the sandman-figure, curiously, has begun to recede, attempts to revive it by writing the poem, on the theme of Coppelius' possible dire intervention in his relationship with Clara. In it, Coppelius touches Clara's eyes just as Nathanael is being married to her; her eyes fly like bloody sparks into his bosom, and Coppelius casts him into a circle of fire that is compared to a hurricane stirring up gigantesque waves. In the midst of the fire-storm, he hears Clara calling out to him that she still has her eyes—the ones that bombarded him were 'glowing sparks of his own heart's blood.' The storm recedes into the abyss, and he looks into Clara's eyes, but it is the 'kindly' gaze of Death that he sees there (347-48).

Certain aspects of the fantasy have been overlooked in the search for psychoanalytical or philosophical-aesthetic keys to it. One is the obvious resemblance of the flying eyeballs to the 'sparks' of soul-substance routinely exchanged between Hoffmann's characters at the moment of first passionate love.[26] Another is the symbolic equation of fire with vital force or, in the broader understanding of the term, libido. This is the welling-up of psycho-physical energy which Hoffmann refers to as 'ignition' (*Entzündung*) and which leads to the dangerous but gratifying condition of 'exaltation,' in which reality may easily take on a different cast. Finally, though von Matt notes that Clara seems to possess two sets of eyes in the passage,[27] the two different symbolic connotations of these have been largely ignored.

Nathanael's fantasy can be taken as a drastic commentary on passionate love, as it occurs in the 'poetic' types who, for Hoffmann, are the ones that experience existence fully. He is under no illusion as to the subjective nature of passion, and much of his writing explores the enigma that what seems more than real may not be reciprocated, i.e. empirically confirmed. The spark may not oscillate between like but opposite poles. To speak of 'narcissism' and 'projection' here on the basis of an unquestioned consensus of the empirical is to abnormalize what Hoffmann still regards as lying within the broad and mysterious range of the normal.

In the fantasy, Nathanael, enflamed by passion (however one-sided) has taken leave of ordinary finite circumstances to become one with the vortex of cosmic energy, or eros. Giving himself over to it, he falls prey also to anti-eros, the principle of decay and chaos embodied by Coppelius, whose outstanding function is corrupting and spoiling ('ein häßlicher gespenstischer Unhold, der überall, wo er einschreitet, Jammer—Not—zeitliches, ewiges Verderben bringt,' 335). Depression and despair is the price of vitality. There is no *telos,* no orderly structure in this eros-universe, which whirls blindly from the void to points unknown. The puzzling contradiction in the fantasy-poem is resolved if we assume that Nathanael now becomes aware of another universe, or a polar antithesis of the dualistic one he inhabits. It is the world of eternal stasis and structure, that of the Platonic-Kantian 'ideal.' This must be the 'kindly death' he sees in Clara's eyes, the death that precedes life and stands apart from time. 'Coppola's' telescope is an imagination-enhancer, not necessarily a distorter of reality.[28] Looking at Olimpia's eyes, he sees, at first, an aqueous moonglow, then animated, flaming glances, a portent of the oceanic fire-storm. The effect has set in already upon the sight of 'Coppola's' displayed spectacles: '. . . und immer wilder sprangen flammende Blicke durcheinander und schossen ihre blutrote Strahlen in Nathanaels Brust' (351). It is, of course, paradoxical that a flow of life-energy should be associated with inorganic objects. We must assume here a deep-seated kinship of all physical things (as we should now say, of matter and energy), such as Elis Fröbom glimpses in the mines of Falun. Thus, in Hoffmann's world, inanimate phenomena may become animated (inspirited), but a transphenomenal realm need not therefore be posited. Focusing on Clara at the end, Nathanael may apprehend not life and soul, but eternal order he is forced to abandon to gain these elusive entities, in a non-theological equivalent of eternal damnation.

What is said about Clara's eyes earlier in the story seems to bear this out, while helping to explain the evident awe in which Hoffmann holds his character. Poeticizing fantasts see in her eyes a lake by Ruisdael, in which is reflected 'des wolkenlosen Himmels reines Azur, Wald- und Blumenflur, der reichen Landschaft ganzes buntes, heitres Leben,' or they apprehend 'wunderbare himmlische Gesänge und Klänge, [. . .] die in unser Innerstes dringen, daß da alles wach und rege wird.' The impression is thus one of animation, but an animation descending from the ethereal spheres of order and serenity, not that of the inner flame. Clara, like Hoffmann, holds effusive fantasts ('Nebler und Schwebler') in contempt and mocks them for believing their fleeting figments ('verfließende Schattengebilde') are concrete and possess life. It is for this reason that the fantasts consider her cold and prosaic, as opposed to those who see life in its 'clear depth' (345). It might be said that while she incorporates a cosmic order, she scorns attempts to translate it into finite terms and to draw life from it. The 'clear depth' of the ultimate harmony (as it seems to Nathanael) may be intuited, but it may not enkindle the flame of vitality.[29]

Nathanael, caught again in the maelstrom, finally sees her as a 'Holzpüppchen,' a physical machine like himself (and thus, in a sense, like Olimpia), who, for all her posturing, cannot convince him of an informing ethereal spirit. One might say that he has opted for *Seele* instead of *Geist*—'soul' in its archaic sense of a unit of evanescent vitality, as symbolized by fish, butterfly, bee, bird, flame, and spark. Like modern man, he is unable to conceive of an existence apart from the body and its warming humors. No doubt valid psychological and social reasons can be found for Nathanael's reluctance to enter into a union with Clara. Beyond these, however, he cannot comply with her attempt to subdue the dark side of his nature, without which the flame of vitality and creativity cannot exist. The possibility of a channeling of libidinous drive in the service of the ego, which is closer to what Clara actually recommends and which might have furthered a more harmonious experiencing of the cosmos also, is foreign to him. The cold, clear eyes of *Geist* convey no sense of individuality and life. It is only the eyes of blood and fire, the soul-substance seeming to oscillate between living beings, that can animate the 'dead machine.' To be sure, the oscillation may be illusory, but the fire of eros is not. Deprived of reciprocation, it may consume the psyche. It is the flame of his own soul that Nathanael first sees in Olimpia's eyes, the enfueling of blind nature. In Clara's eyes he glimpses an order and clarity denied to him, the missing eyes of nature. The machine can be animated, but it cannot be given real sight, Olimpia to the contrary. Perhaps Olimpia's eyes, after enkindling Nathanael's vital forces, did promise a union of *Geist* and *Seele*. If her eyes are those of a cadaver, it is possible that, like Clara's in the vision, they revealed something of a realm beyond finite reality. If they are mechanical, their abstract perfection may have mocked the clear vision we cannot attain to. The actual automaton, like the computer, may be imbued with a cold, selfless spirit, mocking the human machine with its poorly incorporated and poorly controlled animating fluid. Clara simulates an unearthly, passionless perfection. She is like an automaton, in the more awe-inspiring sense, in this. Yet she is only an animated machine—an automaton in the derogatory, despairing sense—like the rest of us. Nathanael, to be sure, calls her an automaton because she cannot, or will not, share in his vision and seems prosaic to him at that time. But the other connotations of the term may resonate here, as they undoubtedly do in his crazed outcry of 'Holzpüppchen.'

Nathanael's vision may be subjective, but it is no less valid in its grasp of an archetypal reality. He is a child of the infinite, roseate 'nature' of Feuerbach—but with the dark side of chaos added. He is Hoffmann in moments of despair—not torn between 'Heaven' and 'Hell' or between the 'real' and the 'ideal,' but buffeted about in a world of plurality out of contact with its unity. His lament is the failure of the timeless Ideal to interact with the chaotic but fulfilling existence of the body and of nature, a world that has its own heavenly and hellish aspects. This is a problem of the post-Kantian age as well, and one not merely shared by poets and artists,[30] so that the charge of Hoffmann's non-involvement with the issues of the day may have to be reexamined. His 'poets' are not always quaint fantasts; they are sometimes seers who envision a world robbed of its ultimate justification.

Notes

1. E. T. A. Hoffmann, *Fantasie- und Nachtstücke,* ed. Walter Müller-Seidel and Wolfgang Kron (München: Winkler, [1960]), pp. 343-4. References hereafter given in parenthetical page numbers.

2. See Kenneth Negus' remarks in a review in *Seminar,* 19 (1983), 298: 'One need only to consider the opening of "Beethovens Instrumental-Musik," or the end of "Der goldne Topf," or the passages on the *serapiontisches Prinzip* to determine that, *at times,* Hoffmann was a most ardent idealist. To suggest otherwise is preposterous.' Of the more recent treatments that do not dispute, or in some way discount, a serious transcendentalism on Hoffmann's part, while avoiding the older clichés, see especially Diana Stone Peters, 'The Dream As Bridge in the Works of E. T. A. Hoffmann,' *Oxford German Studies,* 8 (1973), 60-85, and Klaus Heinisch, *Deutsche Romantik: Interpretationen* (Paderborn, 1966), 134-53 ('Die Bergwerke zu Falun') and 171-81 ('Das Majorat').

3. Wolfgang Preisendanz, 'Eines matt geschliffenen Spiegels dunkler Widerschein,' *Festschrift für Jost Trier zum 70. Geburtstag,* ed. William Foerste and Karl Heinz Borck (Köln, 1964), pp. 411-29. See also Walter Müller-Seidel, epilogues to the *Fantasie- und Nachtstücke* (749-70) and to *Die Serapions-Brüder,* ed. with Wulf Segebrecht (München, [1963]), pp. 999-1026,

4. Sigmund Freud, 'Das Unheimliche,' *Studienausgabe in zehn Bänden,* ed. Alexander Mitscherlich et al. (Frankfurt, 1969-72), IV, 241-74. Ingrid Aichinger, 'E. T. A. Hoffmanns Novelle "Der Sand-

mann" und die Interpretation Sigmund Freuds,' *Zeitschrift für deutsche Philologie*, 95 (1976), 113-32, adds little to the interpretation but makes a plea for the compatibility of psychoanalytical and other literary approaches.

5. James M. McGlathery, *Mysticism and Sexuality: The Tales of E. T. A. Hoffmann*, Pt. 1: *Hoffmann and His Sources* (Bern, 1981), esp. pp. 172-3. Pt. 2, *Interpretations of the Tales* (1985), has since appeared. Nathanael, McGlathery argues here with persuasive consistency, is plagued by guilty prenuptial sexual desires, which, both to him and to the 'enthusiast' narrator, must appear as 'an inversion or perversion of transcendental longing.' Olimpia is a surrogate for Clara, the telescope a device for surreptitious ogling, the ubiquitous eyes a medium for lascivious gleams. Parental intercourse is transformed, in Nathanael's mind, into alchemistic experiments. Attention is called to the quasi-incestuous nature of the Nathanael-Clara relationship (pp. 57-9). Of McGlathery's previous publications along this line see especially 'Bald dein Fall—ins Ehebett? A New Reading of E. T. A. Hoffmann's "Goldne Topf,"' *Germanic Review*, 53 (1978), 106-14.

6. Ursula Mahlendorf, 'E. T. A. Hoffmann's "The Sandman": The Fictional Psycho-Biography of a Romantic Poet,' *American Imago*, 32 (1975), 217-39. Reprinted (translated) in *Psychoanalyse und das Unheimliche*, ed. Claire Kahane (Bonn, 1981), pp. 200-27.

7. Samuel M. Weber, 'Das Unheimliche als dichterische Struktur: Freud, Hoffmann, Villiers de l'Isle-Adam,' *Psychoanalyse und das Unheimliche*, pp. 122-47. First printed as 'The Sideshow, Or: Remarks on a Canny Moment,' *Modern Language Notes*, 88 (1973), 1102-33.

8. Hans-Thies Lehmann, 'Exkurs über E. T. A. Hoffmanns "Sandmann": Eine text-theoretische Lektüre,' *Romantische Utopie/Utopische Romantik*, ed. Gisela Dischner and Richard Faber (Hildesheim, 1979), pp. 301-23.

9. Peter von Matt, *Die Augen der Automaten: E. T. A. Hoffmanns Imaginationslehre als Prinzip seiner Erzählkunst* (Tübingen, 1971). Cf. also Horst S. Daemmrich, *The Shattered Self: E. T. A. Hoffmann's Tragic Vision* (Detroit, 1973), pp. 47-51, where 'clear' and 'broken' eyes and the fiery circle are related to the disintegration of Nathanael's personality in a failed self-realization.

10. Cf. especially Silvio Vietta, 'Romantikparodie und Realitätsbegriff im Erzählwerk E. T. A. Hoffmanns,' *Zeitschrift für deutsche Philologie*, 100 (1981), 575-91, and Lothar Köhn, *Vieldeutige Welt: Studien zur Struktur der Erzählungen E. T. A. Hoffmanns und zur Entwicklung seines Werkes* (Tübingen, 1966).

11. Raimund Belgardt, 'Der Künstler und die Puppe: Zur Interpretation von Hoffmanns "Der Sandmann,"' *German Quarterly*, 42 (1969), 686-700, combines all of these positions.

12. Ernst Fedor Hoffmann, 'Zu E. T. A. Hoffmanns "Sandmann,"' *Monatshefte*, 54 (1962), 244-52, comments: 'Wohl bleibt es offen, ob nicht Nathanael in seinem abnormalen Geisteszustand vielleicht tiefer blickt als seine Mitmenschen' (p. 249).

13. Cf. Hans-Georg Werner, *E. T. A. Hoffmann: Darstellung und Deutung der Wirklichkeit im dichterischen Werk* (Weimar, 1962).

14. Charles Hayes, 'Phantasie und Wirklichkeit im Werke E. T. A. Hoffmanns, mit einer Interpretation der Erzählung "Der Sandmann,"' *Ideologiekritische Studien zur Literatur: Essays* I, ed. Klaus Peter *et al.* (Frankfurt, 1972), 171-214, esp. 179, 185, 189-96.

15. John M. Ellis, 'Clara, Nathanael and the Narrator: Interpreting Hoffmann's "Der Sandmann,"' *German Quarterly*, 54 (1981), 1-18.

16. To say that Nathanael only *imagined* that Spalanzani said 'Coppelius' is to overburden the concept of narrative perspective.

17. The first manuscript version is printed in Hoffmann's *Sämtliche Werke*, ed. Carl Georg von Maassen, Vol. 3 (1912), pp. 354-86, esp. 359-60, 384-5. The variants are discussed especially by S. S. Prawer, 'Hoffmann's Uncanny Guest: a Reading of "Der Sandmann,"' *German Life & Letters*, 18 (1965), 297-308, Ernst Fedor Hoffmann, and Köhn, pp. 91-108. In the printed version, Coppelius says in the tower scene: 'Ha ha—Wartet nur, der kommt schon herunter von selbst'; in the manuscript: 'Ey ey—kleine Bestie—willst Augen machen lernen—wirf mir Dein Holzpüppchen zu!' (Maassen, p. 385). It might seem that Coppelius has entered Nathanael's fantasy-world here, but it can be argued that he heard Nathanael ranting about a 'Holzpüppchen' and saw him attempting to throw Clara from the tower, and drew remarkably astute conclusions (cf. Köhn, pp. 102-3). The fact that Nathanael describes Coppelius in white clothing as resembling a red-faced, coal-eyed snowman in the manuscript version (Maassen, pp. 356-7) casts little light on the demonism problem, since, in its grotesqueness, the image is at once demonic and ludicrous, as is, indeed, Coppelius in general, according to Michael Steig, 'Defining the Grotesque: An Attempt At Synthesis,' *Journal of Aesthetics and Art Criticism*, 29 (1970), 253-60.

18. '. . . gibt es eine solche Macht, so muß sie in uns sich, wie wir selbst gestalten, ja unser selbst werden; denn nur *so* glauben wir an sie und räumen ihr den Platz ein, dessen sie bedarf, um jenes geheime Werk zu vollbringen. Haben wir festern, durch das heitre Leben gestärkten, Sinn genug, um fremdes feindliches Einwirken als solches stets zu erkennen und den Weg, in den uns Neigung und Beruf geschoben, ruhigen Schrittes zu verfolgen, so geht wohl jene unheimliche Macht unter in dem vergeblichen Ringen nach der Gestaltung, die unser eignes Spiegelbild sein sollte. Es ist auch gewiß, [. . .] daß die dunkle physische [—psychische? see Kron's note, 794] Macht, haben wir uns durch uns selbst ihr hingegeben, oft fremde Gestalten, die die Außenwelt uns in den Weg wirft, in unser Inneres hineinzieht, so, daß wir selbst nur den Geist entzünden, der, wie wir in wunderlicher Täuschung glauben, aus jener Gestalt spricht. Es ist das Phantom unseres eigenen Ichs, dessen innige Verwandtschaft und dessen tiefe Einwirkung auf unser Gemüt uns in die Hölle wirft, oder in den Himmel verzückt.' Clara's apparent belief in the dark powers is noted by Wolfgang Kayser, *Das Groteske: Seine Gestaltung in Malerei und Dichtung* (Oldenburg, 1957), p. 80.

19. 'Heiter,' 'unbefangen,' 'gemütvoll,' 'verständig' (345) are not the attributes of a shrew. The truculence which some interpreters find in Clara seems poorly substantiated. Her complaints about the morbidity of Nathanael's verse (not about its visionary quality) are brought forth with reasonable good humor and circumspection. It is Nathanael who is defensive and irritable.

20. *Serapions-Brüder,* p. 26. Cited, disparagingly, by Hayes, p. 183.

21. 'Nun haben wir Augen—Augen—ein schön Paar Kinderaugen' (336).

22. The passage has attracted surprisingly little attention. Cf. Silvio Vietta's review of Peter Gendolla, *Die lebenden Maschinen,* in *Mitteilungen der E. T. A. Hoffmann-Gesellschaft,* 28 (1982), 89.

23. ''s steht doch überall nicht recht! 's gut so wie es war!—Der Alte hat's verstanden' (336).

24. Maassen, p. 359.

25. Mahlendorf, p. 233.

26. The phenomenon is related to Mesmer's doctrines by Maria M. Tatar, *Spellbound: Studies on Mesmerism and Literature* (Princeton, 1978), pp. 121-51. On fire and heat, see also Susan Brantly, 'A Thermographic Reading of E. T. A. Hoffmann's "Der Sandman,"' *German Quarterly,* 55 (1982), 324-35, and Lee B. Jennings, 'The Role of Alco-

hol in Hoffmann's Mythic Tales,' *Fairy Tales As Ways of Knowing,* ed. Michael M. Metzger and Katharina Mommsen (Bern, 1981), pp. 182-94.

27. Von Matt, p. 81.

28. Cf. Yvonne Jill Kathleen Holbeche, *Optical Motifs in the Works of E. T. A. Hoffmann* (Göppingen, 1975), pp. 88-105 (stresses Nathanael's mental collapse).

29. Clara has 'die lebenskräftige Fantasie des heitern unbefangenen, kindischen Kindes.' This would seem to be a non-visual, non-cerebral type of fantasy expressed through action. Nathanael's reading of the message in her eyes may be mistaken, like that of the poetasters. She possesses a mental integration which he lacks and cannot understand, which seems remote and illusory.

30. Cf. Ellis, p. 3, who complains that art should enlighten us about general problems, not merely those of artists. Though Hoffmann sometimes encourages the parochial view, critical preconceptions have no doubt played a role in it (patriotic Neo-Kantianism, fin-de-siècle aestheticism, and the recent *littérateur* approach).

Liane Bryson (essay date summer 1999)

SOURCE: Bryson, Liane. "Romantic Science: Hoffmann's Use of the Natural Sciences in 'Der goldne Topf.'" *Monatshefte* 91, no. 2 (summer 1999): 241-55.

[*In the following essay, Bryson analyzes the influence of scientist G. H. Schubert's theories of mesmerism on Hoffmann's story "Der goldne Topf." Bryson identifies numerous parallels between Anselmus's progressively trancelike existence and Schubert's ideas concerning magnetic sleep.*]

In a letter to his friend and publisher, Carl Friedrich Kunz, E. T. A. Hoffmann (1776-1822) outlined plans for a new story that would continue the ideas and themes presented in **"Der Magnetiseur,"** which he had just completed. The new work, he said, would be in the form of a fairy tale, but unlike the fairy tales of "*Scheherazade* and *Thousand and One Nights*. . . . [t]he whole is intended to become fairylike and wonderful, yet it is to enter boldly into ordinary everyday existence and capture its characters."[1] He continued by giving a brief sketch of his plans for the story:

> Denken Sie dabey nicht, Bester! an Scheherazade und Tausend und Eine Nacht . . . Feenhaft und wunderbar aber keck ins gewöhnliche alltägliche Leben tretend und sei[ne] Gestalten ergreifend soll das Ganze werden. So z.B. ist der Geheime Archivarius Lindhorst, ein ungemeiner, arger Zauberer, dessen drey Töchter, in

grünem Gold glänzende Schlänglein in Krystallen aufbewahrt werden; aber am H. DreyfaltigkeitsTage dürfen sie sich drey Stunden lang im HollunderBusch an Ampels Garten sonnen, wo alle Kaffee und Biergäste vorübergehn—aber der Jüngling, der im Fest[t]agsRock sei[ne] Buttersemmel im Schatten des Busches verzehren wollte ans morgende Collegium denkend, wird in unendliche, wahnsinnige Liebe verstrickt, für eine der grünen—er wird aufgeboten—getraut—bekomt zur MitGift einen goldnen Nachttopf mit Juwelen besetzt—als er das erstemal hineinpißt verwandelt er sich in einen MeerKater u.s.w.²

The fairy tale Hoffmann described was, of course, **"Der goldne Topf."** However, the final form of this story differs radically from the version he outlined. Rather than writing another cautionary tale about an evil magician manipulating others to his own malign purposes, a counterpart to Alban in **"Der Magnetiseur,"** Hoffmann converted this tale into a representation of mesmerism or animal magnetism as a predominantly positive force, capable of elevating an individual to a higher level of existence. Although vulnerable to evil uses, as evidenced in descriptions of the Rauerin's influence, it is magnetism in the service of a higher purpose that prevails in **"Der goldne Topf."**³

Why did Hoffmann make these changes, and what sources did he draw upon to reformulate his thinking? This article examines two texts, G. H. Schubert's (1780-1860) *Ansichten von der Nachtseite der Naturwissenschaft* (1808) and C. A. F. Kluge's (1782-1844) *Versuch einer Darstellung des animalischen Magnetismus als Heilmittel* (1811), that apparently changed Hoffmann's perspective on mesmerism and determined the nature of the final version of **"Der goldne Topf."** Schubert's book drastically altered Hoffmann's conception of animal magnetism and mesmeric influence from that presented in **"Der Magnetiseur,"** and made it necessary for him to rework **"Der goldne Topf."** Kluge's treatise presents a description of six stages of what he termed "magnetic sleep." These stages underlie the narrative structure of Hoffmann's text and are used to define Anselmus' progress toward the higher level of existence envisioned by Schubert, an existence described by Hoffmann as ". . . das Leben in der Poesie, der sich der heilige Einklang aller Wesen als tiefstes Geheimnis der Natur offenbaret" (338).

Hoffmann was familiar with both the therapeutic and spiritualistic applications of mesmerism, and this knowledge informed both **"Der Magnetiseur"** and **"Der goldne Topf."**⁴ He was personally acquainted with several physicians who were practicing mesmerists. Dr. Adalbert F. Marcus (1754-1816) in Bamberg experimented in mesmerism, and Hoffmann reported attending a mesmeric therapy session at his clinic. Notations in his diary about this experience reflect Hoffmann's initial doubts about magnetism.⁵ Hoffmann sent a draft

of **"Der Magnetiseur"** to Dr. Friedrich Speyer (1782-1839), another physician who used mesmerism, and asked him to judge his treatment of medical matters in the manuscript.⁶ Dr. David (after 1816 Johann) Ferdinand Koreff (1783-1851), a physician and poet in Berlin as well as a leader of the mesmerist movement in Germany, was a close friend; he and Hoffmann were members of a group who referred to themselves as the Serapion Brotherhood, and he later served as the model for Vinzenz in **Die Serapionsbrüder.**⁷ It has also been claimed that Dr. Carl Friedrich Gustav Kluge, who was the physician for the Seconda troupe in Leipzig, was the author of the treatise on animal magnetism mentioned above, but this does not hold up under scrutiny.⁸

I

The theory of animal magnetism was initially developed by Franz Anton Mesmer (1734-1815) in his doctoral thesis, *Dissertatio Physico-medica de Planetarum Influxu,* at the University of Vienna,⁹ and later promoted as a therapeutic procedure in his medical practice in Paris. He proposed that an invisible magnetic fluid permeated the universe, infusing both matter and spirit with its vital force. Sicknesses, both physical and psychical, resulted from obstacles to the flow of this fluid through the body, which could be removed by "magnetizing" the patients. Initially iron magnets were passed over the "poles" of the body to correct the flow of the magnetic fluid. As he refined his techniques, Mesmer determined that the physician himself could infuse magnetic fluid into the body of the sick person. This development evolved into "magnetic passes," sweeping movements of the hands to direct the magnetic fluid to the diseased parts of the patient's body, while projecting the fluid from the magnetizer's eyes into those of the patient. This procedure generally produced a "crisis"—convulsions followed by a trance, after which the patient awoke, apparently cured of his disease. Over time, Mesmer and his disciples developed methods for transmitting the magnetic fluid by "magnetizing" inanimate objects, a practice which was elaborated by Mesmer's disciple, the Marquis de Puységur (1751-1825), who treated peasants on his estate by having them grasp ropes suspended from the branches of magnetized trees. The description of Serpentina and her sisters hanging from the branches of the elder tree in the first Vigil alludes to this procedure.

Mesmer's medical practice in Paris flourished from 1778 until the Revolution in 1789. The success of Mesmer's clinics led to the widespread dissemination of his theory and adoption of his treatment techniques, and mesmerist associations, the "Societies of Universal Harmony," were formed as the official organs for teaching the principles of animal magnetism. However, Mesmer's theories were not universally popular. He was attacked and ridiculed by opponents, the medical establishment in Paris moved to suppress Mesmer's clinics, and royal commissions were appointed to investigate the legitimacy of his claims. These challenges, combined with the civil disruption following the French Revolution, spelled the end of Mesmer's activities in Paris. After his departure the mesmerist movement broke into factions, with competing schools espousing different views, and the application of magnetism as a medical therapy declined. Mesmer spent the rest of his life as a country physician near Lake Constance, apparently unaware of the furor created by the revival of Mesmerism at the turn of the century.[10]

In both France and Germany, however, Mesmer's influence continued into the nineteenth century. The "magnetic fluid" that Mesmer had conceived of as a cure for physical illnesses was reconceptualized as a force that could expand one's consciousness, create a "sixth sense," or allow the soul to roam through other worlds while the body remained fixed on earth. In France, Puységur shifted the focus of mesmeric influence to the role of the magnetizer, who was supposedly able to force his will upon others and induce a trance-like state of "magnetic somnambulism" in his patients. The Chevalier de Barbarin, influential in the French *Sociétés de l'Harmonie,* believed that the faith of the patient and the power of the will of the magnetizer were the means by which healing would be achieved. In his view God was the highest magnetizer and, in the magnetized state, patients' souls achieved an intimacy with God. This spiritual side of Mesmerism was also developed in Germany, where an emphasis on spiritualism, somnambulism, and clairvoyance aroused widespread interest among the Romantics. Leaders of the spiritualist movement, such as Justinus Kerner, claimed that paranormal phenomena—clairvoyance and precognition—occurred in the trance state, and that patients were communicating with the spirit world in mesmeric ecstasy.[11] As a belief system Mesmerism was used to explain the interrelatedness of the universe and its parts in a greater cosmic whole, a unified World Spirit. It offered a force common to all nature, a unifying system that could explain "the fantastic, the mysterious, the occult," and provided a link between the natural sciences and the speculations of the German *Naturphilosophen,* such as Schelling and his student, G. H. Schubert.[12]

II

It is clear that Hoffmann was aware of Schubert's book during the period in which he was writing **"Der Magnetiseur."**[13] In a letter to Kunz on 20 July 1813, he alludes to the title of the book in describing his plans for this work:

> Der Aufsatz, welcher nach meiner ersten Idee nur eine flüchtige, aber pittoreske Ansicht des Träumens geben sollte, ist mir unter den Händen zu einer ziemlich aus-

gesponnenen Novelle gewachsen, die in die vielbesprochene Lehre vom Magnetismus tief einschneidet, und eine, so viel ich weiß, noch nicht behandelte Seite desselben (die Nachtseite) enthalten soll.

> (*Tagebücher* [*E. T. A. Hoffmann Tagebücher*] 400)

He also is assumed to refer to the book in the text of **"Der Magnetiseur."** In a letter to Theobald, Alban writes:

> Du weißt auf welche wunderbare Weise ich mir einen Schatz geheimer Kenntnisse gesammelt. Nie hast Du das Buch lesen mögen, unerachtet es Dich überrascht haben würde, wie noch in keinem der physikalischen Lehrbücher solche herrliche Kombinationen mancher Naturkräfte und ihrer Wirkung so wie hier entwickelt sind.

> (227)[14]

However, an examination of Hoffmann's diary entries and correspondence indicates that he could not have read Schubert's text before completing **"Der Magnetiseur."** He first asked Kunz to order a copy of the book for him in a letter of 26 July 1813,[15] and delivery of the book is noted in his correspondence as "Mitte August 1813."[16] In his diary, Hoffmann noted finishing **"Der Magnetiseur"** on 16 August;[17] a copy of the final section was sent to Kunz on 19 August, along with the letter outlining his early ideas for **"Der goldne Topf."**

From these records it is clear that Hoffmann had not read Schubert's book at the time that he wrote **"Der Magnetiseur."** His allusions to the book, in the novella and in his correspondence, reflect his *assumptions* about what Schubert might have meant by the "nocturnal side of natural science," rather than a knowledge of the text. From his own use of the term it is clear that he considered the "nocturnal side" to refer to the occult applications of science (i.e., the "black arts"), a view that was compatible with the concerns and doubts that he himself entertained concerning the potential misuses of mesmeric influence, and which informed **"Der Magnetiseur."**[18]

What Schubert meant by the term *"Nachtseite"* was, however, quite different. For Schubert, it referred to those phenomena of nature that had not been officially recognized by the natural sciences as worthy of examination and, in particular, those forces that had been relegated to the domains of faith and belief in miracles (*Wunderglaube*).[19] By examining these phenomena, he argued, it became possible to demonstrate how all of nature derives from a single source, a sense of unity that has been lost because of man's attempts to investigate and control nature. According to Schubert, the harmony and sense of oneness with nature that had once existed, but was lost, continues to be the ultimate goal of mankind. In special moments of clairvoyance this harmony can be revealed to man, rekindling a longing to return to it. Those phenomena, such as animal magnetism, which belong to the "Nachtseite der Naturwissenschaften" are considered by Schubert tools to prepare for the beginnings of the new era, which he terms "der Anfang der neueren Zeit," a time when mankind will again become receptive to regaining the original state of harmony.[20]

Alban's theory of magnetism, outlined in his letter to Theobald in **"Der Magnetiseur,"** is congruent with Schubert's conception of man's relationship to nature as a dynamic system constructed of two forces, or principles. The superior principle is a force that drives man to re-experience the ecstasy of attaining the unity of all in nature. The subordinate principle derives from the superior, but deflects man away from unity and toward less exalted pleasures. It misuses natural forces for self-aggrandizement and power, or promotes scientific endeavors that separate, rather than unify, experience.

Alban's use of his mesmeric abilities to achieve such power and control over others has been considered to represent Hoffmann's awareness of Schubert's subordinate principle.[21] However, this similarity is coincidental; such binary conceptions of mesmeric influence were commonly held during Hoffmann's era, and need not be ascribed to Schubert's ideas. Hoffmann's letters and diaries suggest that his treatment of mesmerism in **"Der Magnetiseur"** is not uniquely attributable to Schubert. In **"Der Magnetiseur"** Hoffmann examined several distinct conceptions of mesmerism, personified in the characters of Ottmar, Theobald, and Alban. Ottmar, who hopes for the cure of his sister, represents the therapeutic application of mesmerism; Theobald, who uses magnetism to achieve a sense of unity with God, represents a spiritual, theosophical school; and Alban represents the materialistic school. It is Theobald who most closely personifies what Schubert would identify as the superior principle. Hoffmann's subordination of Theobald to the domination of Alban is thus inconsistent with Schubert's characterization of the two principles. For Hoffmann, depiction of the superior principle as triumphant over the subordinate was not achieved until **"Der goldne Topf,"** because he based his development of **"Der Magnetiseur"** on indirect, rather than direct, knowledge of Schubert's treatise.

In **"Der goldne Topf,"** begun three months after receiving Schubert's text, Hoffmann borrows liberally and literally from *Ansichten*.[22] A wide range of story elements, from character names to ancillary details, derives directly from Schubert. The character of Phosphorous, central to the mythology of the third and eighth Vigils, is prefigured by Schubert's recounting of an ancient myth in which Phosphorous was revered as a symbol of the simultaneity of love and death; the name "Serpentina" is a derivative of Proserpina, whom Schubert defined as a feminine embodiment of Phosphorous; Hoff-

mann's Atlantis mirrors Schubert's conception of this mythical city as the home of the "Urvolk," from a time when man lived in harmony with nature; the fire lily of the tale derives from Schubert's account of the fire lily of Kamchatka, and the lily serves as a symbol of harmonious fulfillment in both texts. Even such minor details as the palm trees in the Archivarius' library may be attributed to Schubert, who viewed palm trees as the highest form of plant life.

Of central interest to the present study is the manner in which **"Der goldne Topf"** structures the relationship between Archivarius Lindhorst and the Rauerin, whose antagonism parallels Schubert's conception of the conflict between the superior and subordinate principles. This conflict is not a battle between two opposing forces, but between two manifestations of the same force, striving toward different ends. The magnetic power of Archivarius Lindhorst and Serpentina, like Schubert's superior principle, seeks to return Anselmus to the bliss of harmony and unity with nature, represented by the land of Atlantis. Anselmus is drawn to their influence through an awareness that he is incomplete in this world and can ultimately attain fulfillment through acceptance of their power. Their influence can only be exerted on those who have "ein kindliches poetisches Gemüt," and depends upon the trust and faith of the subject, conceptualized by Schubert as *Wunderglaube*.[23] This concept is represented in Hoffmann's text by Serpentina's exhortations to ". . . glaube—glaube—glaube an uns" (*Fantasiestücke* 247) and "Halte treu—treu—an mir, bald bist du am Ziel!" (306), as well as by the Archivarius' instructions to Anselmus that "Glaube und Erkenntnis führen Dich zu zum nahen Ziele . . ." (287). Schubert viewed magnetism as a means for attaining this ultimate sense of unity, and emphasized the need for trust in this force.[24]

The influence of the Rauerin is almost equal in power to that of Archivarius Lindhorst. However, like Schubert's subordinate principle, her power has one limitation: she can only divert Anselmus from striving toward the higher goal by offering a lesser form of bliss, a secular fulfillment—a desire for and satisfaction with worldly achievements. She lures Anselmus momentarily with the attractions of marriage to Veronica and the position of court councillor but, because he remains true to Serpentina, Anselmus is able to maintain his desire for the more exalted goal. The Rauerin's powers are more fully realized in her influence over Veronica, who is already motivated toward the lesser pleasures of success in a material world. Ultimately, however, even Veronica is able to resist her influence, an ability that Maria never had with Alban. Unlike **"Der Magnetiseur,"** the subordinate force is clearly lesser in influence here, in accordance with Schubert's conceptualization.

Schubert's conception of poetry and the poetic individual is also evinced in **"Der goldne Topf."** Although Anselmus is said to possess a poetic nature, he is not a poet in the usual sense of the word. That is, he does not engage in the production of poetry but rather in its reproduction. His task is to copy manuscripts for the Archivarius, and even these efforts are achieved only through the powers of magnetism. For example, in the sixth Vigil, when Anselmus copies the manuscript pages, Hoffmann writes "ja es war, als stünden schon wie in blasser Schrift die Zeichen auf dem Pergament, und er dürfe sie nur mit geübter Hand schwarz überziehen" (286).

At the end of the eighth Vigil Anselmus perceives that "die Kopie des geheimnisvollen Manuskripts war glücklich beendigt," without being aware of having done any work (306). The narrator subsequently has a similar experience when, after visiting the Archivarius and undergoing a mesmeric induction of his own, he reports: ". . . daß ich sie . . . auf dem Papier, das auf dem violetten Tische lag, recht sauber und augenscheinlich von mir selbst aufgeschrieben fand (337)." Each of these passages draws on Schubert's view of the original function of poetry. He considers the poet as an individual with a higher calling, one who does not feel at home with worldly existence.[25] Accordingly, in the introductory Vigil Anselmus is clearly represented as one who does not fit in, who bemoans his persistent mishaps and considers himself born unlucky. The purpose of the poet, according to Schubert, is to prepare mankind for a return to unity with nature. However, because poets are human, and therefore imperfect, they are incapable of poeticizing perfection independently. Instead, they must surrender themselves to a greater power, which expresses itself through them. That is, poets are not viewed as active creators of texts, but as vessels through which a higher power speaks, just as Anselmus and the narrator complete their writing only by surrendering themselves to the higher power of magnetism.

Hoffmann signals his intention to explore the theme of transcendence, of moving beyond the mundane world to a higher, more exalted level of existence, in two allusive references at the very beginning of **"Der goldne Topf."** The text begins: "Am Himmelfahrtstage nachmittags um drei Uhr rannte ein junger Mensch in Dresden durchs schwarze Tor . . . (237)." The choice of Ascension Day as a temporal locus for this tale is noteworthy for, as mentioned earlier, Hoffmann had initially conceived of the story beginning on Trinity Sunday. This change provides a deliberate allusion to the Biblical account of Christ's ascension into heaven, which prefigures Anselmus's transition into the bliss of life in Atlantis. The use of the Black Gate, a real gate into the city of Dresden, at the same time references Kluge's treatise on animal magnetism, *Versuch einer Darstellung des animalischen Magnetismus als Heilmittel.* In this text Kluge defines six stages of mesmeric trance, on a continuum between rational consciousness and the Schubertian unity with nature.[26] At the third of these stages "an individual stands on the border of two different worlds, by the dark gate at the crossing to a higher, better existence."[27] Thus, at the very outset of this story Hoffmann has compressed two separate allusions, combining his two major themes in the text—transcendence and animal magnetism.

Hoffmann's descriptions of the mesmeric experiences that transform Anselmus from a poor, unlucky student, to one able to live in "in höchster Seligkeit immerdar" (337) are an examination of Kluge's description of the levels of magnetic sleep. Anselmus's experiences with Serpentina and Archivarius Lindhorst are structured as a series of mesmeric inductions, with each instance representing an advance in Kluge's stages, from an initial half-sleep to his highest levels of somnambulism and clairvoyance. The more malign magnetic influences of the apple woman/Frau Rauerin interrupt Anselmus's progression through these stages. Unlike the gentle, seductive influence of Serpentina or the enthralling power of the Archivarius, the Rauerin exerts her influence by inducing mesmeric crises—abrupt, painful, and overwhelming.[28] As a personification of Schubert's subordinate principle, she can only function to divert Anselmus away from his progress toward the increasingly more exalted levels of consciousness, and lure him back to reality. The development of Anselmus's character through these experiences reflects Hoffmann's careful reading of both Schubert and Kluge.

The first stage of magnetic sleep, according to Kluge, is a state of wakefulness in which the senses are not disturbed but the mind is receptive to other thoughts, including what appear to be minor instances of clairvoyance.[29] These characteristics may be seen in Registrar Heerbrand's statement in **"Der goldne Topf"**:

> Sollte man denn nicht auch wachend in einen gewissen träumerischen Zustand versinken können? So ist mir in der Tat selbst einmal nachmittags . . . die Lage eines verlornen Aktenstücks wie durch Inspiration eingefallen, und nur noch gestern tanzte auf gleiche Weise eine herrliche große lateinische Frakturschrift vor meinen hellen offenen Augen umher.
>
> (248)

The blurred line between the normal waking state and this first stage of magnetic sleep is emphasized by ascribing this passage to Heerbrand rather than to Anselmus. The failure of rational man to appreciate the distinction between these states is noted in Dean Paulmann's explanation of Heerbrand's experiences as ". . . und da verfällt man leicht in das Fantastische und Romanhafte" (248).

Anselmus's experiences under the elder tree represent Kluge's second stage, or half sleep. In this passage Hoffmann introduces many of the metaphors he employs to signify trance states. The crystal bells that signal the advent of a trance refer to the practice, begun by Mesmer, of using music, particularly the glass harmonica, as an aid to the induction process. The effect of Serpentina's gaze on Anselmus, described as traveling through him "wie ein elektrischer Schlag" (242), reflects the conflation of magnetism and electricity common in the natural sciences of the day.[30] Later, after Anselmus has been temporarily brought out of this trance by hugging the elder tree,[31] he is once again induced into a magnetized state by gazing at the reflection of fireworks upon the water while on the boat crossing the Elbe, an experience he describes to Dean Paulmann as dreaming with open eyes, a phrasing that parallels Kluge's description of the half-sleep stage.

At the third stage of mesmerism Kluge states that "one steps out of the connection with the outer world and transits into the inner darkness."[32] Anselmus's description of his sensations after the Archivarius has caused him to look into the ring (itself a form of trance induction employed by Mesmer) clearly situates him at this third stage: ". . . denn ich sehe und fühle nun wohl, daß alle die fremden Gestalten aus einer fernen wundervollen Welt, die ich sonst nur in ganz besondern merkwürdigen Träumen schaute, jetzt in mein waches reges Leben geschritten sind und ihr Spiel mit mir treiben" (268). He has gained skills beyond his normal capabilities and these heightened abilities are maintained in everyday discourse. From this point on in the text Anselmus may be considered to be continuously in an ever deepening trance state, interrupted only by the incursions of the Rauerin who, as a representative of the subordinate principle, seeks to deflect him from his progress toward the sixth and highest stage of mesmeric trance.

In the fourth stage, called "simple somnambulism" by Kluge, senses are further enhanced, previously unimagined powers are attained, and expressive abilities are heightened.[33] Anselmus may be seen to attain this stage in the sixth Vigil. His heightened powers are manifested as he begins to copy the manuscripts: He hears Serpentina calling to him, "und so wie er voll innern Entzückens die Töne vernahm, wurden ihm immer verständlicher die unbekannten Zeichen—er durfte kaum mehr hineinblicken in das Original" (286).

Anselmus's somnambulism is heightened further in the eighth Vigil, which is characterized in terms drawn from Kluge's description of the fifth stage. At this stage intellectual capacities are elevated and one is in possession of a more refined language, more liberal and profound thinking and a quicker and sharper ability of judgment.[34] Anselmus's induction into this intensified somnambulistic state is accompanied by music, pleasant fragrances, and the crystal tones that had characterized his earlier experiences. Serpentina appears to him in the form of a lovely maiden, relates an extended account of the myth introduced in the third Vigil, and tells him of their future life in Atlantis. Anselmus appears to awaken as if from a deep dream and discovers not only that the manuscripts have been copied completely without his consciousness, but also that he is now able to see that they are nothing other than the story that Serpentina has just told him. In fact, he is not awake but in a somnambulistic state, as may be seen at the beginning of the next Vigil, in which it is noted that "Alles das Seltsame und Wondervolle, welches dem Studenten Anselmus täglich begegnet war, hatte ihn ganz dem gewöhnlichen Leben entrückt (308)."

Anselmus's progress through increasingly higher levels of magnetic sleep is repeatedly interrupted by Frau Rauerin's conspiracy with Veronica. Initially, it appears that this battle has been won by the Rauerin, just as Alban held sway in **"Der Magnetiseur."** Anselmus continues to be attracted to the pleasures promised by the mundane world and to derogate his prior experiences:

> . . . indem er an Veronika dachte, fühlte er sich recht von einem behaglichen Gefühl durchdrungen. "Ihr allein," sprach er zu sich selbst, "habe ich es zu verdanken, daß ich von meinen albernen Grillen zurückgekommen bin. . . . Aber so wie ich Hofrat worden, heirate ich ohne weiteres die Mademoiselle Paulmann und bin glücklich."
>
> (314-15)

The power of the Rauerin has imposed itself. Anselmus has been diverted from longing for the higher goals promised by the Archivarius and Serpentina, and toward lesser satisfactions. Anselmus's loss of faith in the Archivarius recapitulates man's downfall in Schubert's *Naturphilosophie*. According to Schubert, the unity of man and nature ended when man turned away from the superior principle and gave himself over to a subordinate principle of nature which suppressed the noble in man and dragged him down into idolatry.[35]

In this uncertain condition Anselmus returns to the Archivarius the next day to continue his work. However, his loss of faith also means a loss of the powers gained through the Archivarius's magnetic influence. He can no longer copy the manuscripts, as he had been doing with such skill, and in his irritation he spills ink on the original. In response to this the Archivarius lashes out at Anselmus, inducing a mesmeric crisis that is described in terms which parallel those used to describe the crisis induced by the Rauerin in the second Vigil:

> Die goldnen Stämme der Palmbäume wurden zu Riesenschlangen, die ihre *gräßlichen* Häupter in schneidendem Metallklange zusammenstießen und mit den geschuppten Leibern den Anselmus umwanden . . . und nun sprühten ihre aufgesperrten Rachen Feuer-Katarakte auf den Anselmus, und es war, als verdichteten sich die Feuerströme um seinen Körper und würden zur festen eiskalten Masse.
>
> (316)

Ultimately Anselmus finds himself encased in a crystal bottle on a shelf in Archivarius Lindhorst's library, unable to move, just as the apple woman had predicted at the beginning of the story.

This section of the text appears to violate the relationship established between Anselmus and the Archivarius. However, from the viewpoint of Schubert's philosophy, this episode is critical to Anselmus's progress. His failure, engendered by doubt, may cause his upward movement to be checked temporarily, but it is essential to his ultimate development, for it is only through experiencing the barriers presented by such failings that one becomes conscious of separation from the ideal and renews a sense of longing for that state.[36]

Anselmus's experiences are anticipated by a parallel account of the salamander's punishment in Serpentina's myth. The salamander, failing to heed the warnings of the Prince of the Spirits, inadvertently kills the green snake that he loves and, in his despair, destroys the garden planted by Phosphorous's mother in Atlantis. The Prince of Spirits angrily extinguishes this fire and imprisons him, but then takes pity upon him and alters his punishment, announcing that he will regain his powers only by enduring a period of longing and awareness of loss, which will coincide with the time when man becomes separated from nature.

The salamander's punishment clarifies the connection between Anselmus's imprisonment in the glass bottle and Schubert's conception of man's return to unity with nature.[37] Only through a renewal of faith can one be redeemed; punishment may be necessary to achieve an awareness of how far one has veered from that course. Anselmus's cognizance of his personal failures may be seen in his reaction to the comments of his fellow prisoners:

> Sie wissen nicht, was Freiheit und Leben in Glauben und Liebe ist, deshalb spüren sie nicht den Druck des Gefängnisses, in das sie der Salamander bannte ihrer Torheit, ihres gemeinen Sinnes wegen, aber ich Unglücklicher werde vergehen in Schmach und Elend, wenn Sie, die ich so unaussprechlich liebe, mich nicht rettet.
>
> (319)

The Archivarius and Rauerin renew their struggle for Anselmus in a battle that recreates the conflict between Phosphorous and the dragon in the mythology of the third Vigil and provides an allegorical account of what Schubert foresaw as the outcome of competition between the superior and subordinate principles. This battle reaches its climax in the tenth Vigil. The moral power of Schubert's superior principle is combined with the greater magnetic powers of the Archivarius and the magic of the salamander as the Rauerin is defeated and regresses to her more primitive form—a

beet. The ultimately victorious Archivarius alludes to Schubert in his statement to Anselmus: "Anselmus, . . . nicht du, sondern nur ein feindliches Prinzip, das zerstörend in dein Inneres zu dringen und dich mit dir selbst zu entzweien trachtete, war schuld an deinem Unglauben" (323).

Anselmus's renewed loyalty in turn allows him to be released from the glass jar as "Ein Blitz zuckte durch das Innere des Anselmus, der herrliche Dreiklang der Krystallglocken ertönte stärker und mächtiger als er ihn je vernommen . . ." (324). It is at precisely this point that Anselmus enters into Kluge's sixth and highest stage of somnambulism, the "stage of general clarity."[38] At this stage an individual is said to achieve a heightened state of consciousness:

> . . . the [individual] steps outside of himself and into a higher connection with all of nature . . . the [individual] is removed from all mundane, worldly matters and is elevated to higher and more noble sentiments; supreme calmness, innocence, and purity which emanate from his being make him appear as if transfigured, and a spirit speaks through him as if in a refined tongue.[39]

Hoffmann's depiction of Anselmus in Atlantis mirrors this description in virtually every aspect, as the narrator recounts after observing him in Atlantis.[40] In each regard Anselmus is described in terms consistent with having attained the highest stage of somnambulism, and he has achieved, as Schubert anticipated, a knowledge of the sacred harmony of all beings.

The final version of **"Der goldne Topf"** represents Hoffmann's fullest and most informed use of the natural sciences of his day, or at least of the scientific writings compatible with a romantic sensibility. The theory of animal magnetism presented in this tale differs markedly from the view Hoffmann had advanced only a few months earlier, in **"Der Magnetiseur."** Where the earlier text had been preponderantly negative, describing the tragic results of misusing magnetic powers for personal aggrandizement, **"Der goldne Topf"** represents magnetism as a tool for achieving a higher level of existence, defined in the text as a "life in poetry." The primary influence in this shift was Schubert's *Ansichten von der Nachtseite der Naturwissenschaft,* a philosophical discussion of the primeval state of unity with nature, how mankind became separated from that harmonious state, and how it could be regained. While it has long been assumed that Hoffmann was familiar with Schubert's text when he wrote **"Der Magnetisur,"** his correspondence reveals that he did not actually read the work until the time period between writing these two tales. Hoffmann's reformulation of the relative power of malign and beneficent uses of animal magnetism was informed by Schubert's discussion of the dynamic relationship between the superior and subordinate principles—the forces for and against regaining unity with nature—a conception that defined the conflict between the Archivarius and the Rauerin. Furthermore, the description of Anselmus's progress toward Atlantis may be understood as an ever increasing trance induction, informed by the descriptions of the stages of magnetic sleep presented by Kluge. Ultimately, the golden pot, in which Anselmus can see his own reflection with arms outstretched toward himself, beckons him to Atlantis or, as Schubert would state it, calls him back to a lost and longed for state of harmony.

Notes

1. *Selected Letters of E. T. A. Hoffmann,* ed. and trans. Johanna C. Sahalin (Chicago: U of Chicago P, 1977) 203.

2. *E. T. A. Hoffmanns Briefwechsel,* ed. Friedrich Schnapp (München: Winkler, 1971) 408.

3. The terms "mesmerism" and "animal magnetism" are no longer in use, having been largely replaced by the modern concept of "hypnosis." However, as the latter term did not exist in Hoffmann's day and the two former terms were both in common usage at that time, they will be employed essentially interchangeably for historical verisimilitude.

4. See Maria M. Tatar, "Mesmerism, Madness, and Death in E. T. A. Hoffmann's 'Der goldne Topf,'" *Studies in Romanticism* 14 (1975): 365-90; Maria M. Tatar, *Spellbound: Studies on Mesmerism and Literature* (Princeton: Princeton UP, 1978); *Die deutsche literarische Romantik und die Wissenschaften,* ed. Nicholas Saul (München: Iudicium 1991); Friedhelm Auhuber, *In einem fernen dunklen Spiegel. E. T. A. Hoffmanns Poetisierung der Medizin* (Opladen: Westdeutscher Verlag, 1986); Georg Reuchlein, *Bürgerliche Gesellschaft, Psychiatrie und Literatur. Zur Entwicklung der Wahnsinnsthematik in der deutschen Literatur des späten 18. und frühen 19. Jahrhunderts* (München: Wilhelm Fink, 1986); Wulf Segebrecht, "Krankheit und Gesellschaft. Zu E. T. A. Hoffmanns Rezeption der Bamberger Medizin," *Romantik in Deutschland. Ein interdisziplinäres Symposium,* Sonderband der *Deutschen Vierteljahrsschrift für Literaturwissenschaft und Geistesgeschichte,* ed. Richard Brinkmann (Stuttgart: Metzler, 1987) 267-90.

5. Hoffmann's entry in his diary for 21 December 1812 reads "zum erstenmahl im Hospital eine Somnambule gesehen—Zweifel!" (*E. T. A. Hoffmann Tagebücher,* ed. Friedrich Schnapp (München: Winkler, 1971) 186.

6. In a letter of 13 July 1812 to Speyer, Hoffmann wrote: "Dem Kunz lege ich ein Briefchen nebst Manuskript bey. Es ist die erste Abtheilung einer Erzählung, betitelt: Der Magnetisirer. Wie ich auch glaube wird Ihnen dieser Aufsatz nicht uninteressant seyn, da er eine noch unberührte neue Seite des Magnetismus entwickeln soll; wenn Sie wollen, so lesen Sie das Manuskript" (*Briefwechsel* 398). A letter of 20 July 1813 to Kunz asked, "Speyer mag den Magnetiseur vor dem Druck lesen, damit er beurtheile, ob ich in medizinischer Hinsicht gehörige Consequenz beobachtet" (*Briefwechsel* 401).

7. Robert Darnton, *Mesmerism and the End of the Enlightenment in France* (Cambridge: Harvard UP, 1968) 149; (Segebrecht 275).

8. The similarity in first and last names has been a source of confusion for some time. Hewett-Thayer argues that the two men were the same, as Hoffmann had described a Dr. Kluge (the theater physician) in admiring tones as a clever, perceptive man who treated illness from a psychological perspective; Harvey W. Hewett-Thayer, *Hoffmann: Author of the Tales* (1948: reprint ed. New York: Octagon, 1971) 168-69. Maassen, however, questions this identification, based on the satiric manner in which Hoffmann depicted a character, ostensibly based on the theater physician, in *Seltsame Leiden* (IV, 281). A biographical entry in August Hirsch, ed., *Biographisches Lexikon der hervorragenden Ärzte vor 1880,* vol. 3 (München, Berlin: Urban & Schwarzenberg, 1962) 522-23, which identifies Carl Alexander Ferdinand Kluge (1782-1844) as the author of the treatise on animal magnetism, does not note that he ever lived in Leipzig. Furthermore, Carl Friedrich Gustav Kluge, the theater physician, is noted as b. 1774, d. 1830. Thus the conjecture may be laid to rest; the two men are not the same. In any case, Kluge's treatise was well known and respected (it was translated into four other languages within six years of its initial publication), and was certainly available to Hoffmann, in Kunz's library (Hewett-Thayer 168) and most likely from his mesmerist-physician acquaintances as well. See Segebrecht 268.

9. *Physico-medical Inquiry Concerning the Influence of the Planets.* In later years he referred to his dissertation as *The Influence of the Planets on the Human Body.* In his dissertation he referred to the magnetic fluid as a form of "animal gravitation," and only later came to use the term "animal magnetism." Vincent Buranelli, *The Wizard from Vienna* (London: Peter Owen, 1975) 36.

10. Darnton 42.

11. Tartar, *Spellbound* 128.

12. Darnton 51.

13. According to his diaries, Hoffmann began work on 19 May 1813 (*Tagebücher* 206); he mailed the

last part of the story along with a letter to Kunz in Bamberg on 19 August 1813 (*Tagebücher* 408). The diary entries are a more reliable source of information regarding the actual beginning and completion of work on any project than Hoffmann's letters, which consistently assure his correspondent (principally Kunz) that a work is begun or is written in rough form several months before a beginning is noted in the diaries.

14. According to Maassen, the book referred to here is Schubert's *Ansichten.*

15. *Briefwechsel* 403.

16. Ibid. 407.

17. *Tagebücher* 218.

18. Kohlenbach, who assumes that Hoffmann was familiar with *Ansichten* when writing "Der Magnetiseur," attempts to account for this conflict by stating that Hoffmann wanted to poeticize "die Nachtseite der Nachtseite." See Margarete Kohlenbach, "Ansichten von der Nachtseite der Romantik. Zur Bedeutung des animalischen Magnetismus bei E. T. A. Hoffmann," (in Saul, 220).

19. "Wir werden nämlich in diesen Abendstunden, jene Nachtseite der Naturwissenschaft, welche bisher öfters außer Acht gelassen worden, mit nicht geringerem Ernst als andre allgemeiner anerkannte Gegenstände betrachten, und von verschiedenen jener Gegenstände die man zu dem Gebiet des sogenannten Wunderglaubens gezählt hat, handeln." Gotthilf Heinrich Schubert, *Ansichten von der Nachtseite der Naturwissenschaft* (1808; Darmstadt: Wissenschaftliche Buchgesellschaft, 1967) 2. Translations from this work are mine.

20. Schubert 12. Schubert's appellation for this period provides a more convincing explanation for the subtitle to Hoffmann's fairy tale ("Ein Märchen aus der neuen Zeit") than the suggestion that it represented a desire to locate "Der goldne Topf" in modern times in order to differentiate it from the more common conception of fairy tales as either ancient legends or "Oriental bombast," as argued by others (see Karl Ochsner, *E. T. A. Hoffmann als Dichter des Unbewußten. Ein Beitrag zur Geistesgeschichte der Romantik* (1936; Ann Arbor: University Microfilms, 1982) 97; Gisela Vitt-Maucher, *E. T. A. Hoffmanns Märchenschaffen. Kaleidoskop der Verfremdung in seinen sieben Märchen* (Chapel Hill: U of North Carolina P, 1989) 40.

21. Kohlenbach 215.

22. According to the diary entries, Hoffmann began work on "Der goldne Topf" on 26 November 1813

(*Tagebücher* 237) and completed it on 5 March 1814 (*Tagebücher* 248).

23. Schubert 305.

24. In discussing magnetism Schubert said, "Wir vertrauen uns seiner Führung an, und siehe auf einfachem Wege, führt uns derselbe zu der erhabenen Quelle des Lichts und der Wärme." Schubert 16.

25. Schubert 308.

26. Auhuber notes that Hoffmann was familiar with a number of texts on mesmerism, but most particularly with the work of Kluge. Auhuber 10.

27. ". . . steht der Mensch hier an der Grenze zweier verschiedener Welten, an der dunklen Pforte zum Übergang in ein höheres, besseres Seyn." Quoted in Reuchlein, 232.

28. The crisis event was a critical component of the therapeutic procedure as originally conceived by Mesmer. Later, Puységur and Barbarin in the mesmerist "Societies of Universal Harmony," and the German spiritualist schools of mesmerism rejected the need for a crisis state, emphasizing instead the exertion of the therapist's will over the patient. Reuchlein 32.

29. Ochsner 44; Reuchlein 231.

30. Schubert, for example, proposed that electricity is a complementary, weaker force, which derives from the magnetic fluid. Schubert 312. Kohlenbach notes that Mesmer had debated whether to conceptualize the force underlying his therapy as "electricity" or "magnetism." Kohlenbach 215.

31. This action alludes to a practice introduced by Puységur, who brought his patients out of a somnambulistic trance by instructing them to encircle the trunk of a magnetized tree. Darnton 142.

32. "Weicht die ganze Sinnlichkeit zurück, so tritt der Mensch aus der Verbindung mit der Aussenwelt und geht zu innern Dunkelheit über." Quoted in Reuchlein, 233.

33. Reuchlein 232.

34. Ibid.

35. Schubert 100.

36. Ibid. 68-69.

37. Vitt-Maucher has also noted the parallel between the fate of the salamander and Anselmus, referring to this as an expression of a recurrent theme of redemption without end. Vitt-Maucher 30-34.

38. Reuchlein 232.

39. Ibid.

40. Hoffmann indicates that the narrator is able to see Anselmus only because he also has been magnetized by drinking a goblet of flaming arrack into which the Archivarius has climbed. This fanciful description of magnetic infusion alludes to Mesmer's practice of inducing a trance by giving patients magnetized water to drink.

David Darby (essay date June 2003)

SOURCE: Darby, David. "The Unfettered Eye: Glimpsing Modernity from E. T. A. Hoffmann's Corner Window." *Deutsche Vierteljahrs Schrift für Literaturwissenschaft und Geistesgeschichte* 77, no. 2 (June 2003): 274-94.

[*In the following essay, Darby examines Hoffmann's depiction of urban life in the story "Des Vetters Eckfenster." Darby argues that Hoffmann's use of multiple stylistic modes in his portrayal of Berlin lends the story its decidedly modern quality.*]

E. T. A. Hoffmann's late story **"Des Vetters Eckfenster"** (1822) has since the mid-1980s ridden something of a new wave of critical attention.[1] Its place is reserved in most recent studies on the literary representation of Berlin, and it functions (primarily in German-language scholarship) at the very least as an early reference point in studies of city writing in general, all of which is quite clearly due to the boom in scholarly interest in the writings of Walter Benjamin, who in several essays and notes makes brief mention of the literary-historical importance of the story's depiction of an urban landscape. I too aim in my reading of Hoffmann's story to address questions surrounding the aesthetic perception and literary representation of the city in the early nineteenth century. My project is far more specific than Benjamin's, since it focuses on the representation of one city in one story written before its rapid and wholesale process of industrial modernization. In discussing **"Des Vetters Eckfenster"** I propose to concentrate, at first sight somewhat perversely, on the figure of the younger visitor in the story, whose own views are dismissed by the Vetter of the story's title as utterly worthless and are subsequently radically suppressed within the narrative of Hoffmann's story, not to mention in the ensuing scholarship on the text. Benjamin's comments are central here, since they seem fleetingly to point toward the possibility of a quite different evaluation of the visitor's function in the story, without appearing to consider its implications. My essay takes Benjamin's discussion as its starting point and posits that the apparently quite passive figure of the visitor plays a far more important role in the story than is generally recognized, and that he offers, in contrast to his aging Vetter, a tentative glimpse of new aesthetic possibilities, a new vision of the landscape of the protomodern city. In doing so, I propose an alternative reading of Hoffmann's story pivoting on the vision of the younger visitor, in whose voice the first-person narration of the story is after all conducted.

While Benjamin's concise and somewhat careless comments on **"Des Vetters Eckfenster"** might earlier have received the briefest acknowledgment, they now routinely merit—as they do in the present essay—far more than a passing footnote.[2] His most expansive commentary is made in the broader context of his sprawling essay *Charles Baudelaire. Ein Lyriker im Zeitalter des Hochkapitalismus.*[3] Two passages are relevant (I, 551-552 and 627-629), the specific context of both being a discussion of Edgar Allan Poe's story *The Man of the Crowd,* first published in 1840.[4] Benjamin's immediate concern is with the characteristic literary figures who spectate on modern—or, depending on geographical and historical circumstance, protomodern—city life, from Berlin's "Eckensteher Nante", through the Parisian flaneur, to Poe's man of the crowd in London (I, 627-628). Berlin, Paris, London: three cities at different stages of the process of modernization with their three representative fictional observers in three correspondingly different relationships to the life of the streets. These range from the Vetter's and his visitor's static, external spectatorship "wie in einer Rangloge" (I, 551); through the strolling at leisure of the Parisian flaneur; and finally to the movements of the narrating figure in Poe's story, who leaves the interior of a London coffee house and walks all night, "angezogen von dem Magneten der Masse" (I, 551), among the moving crowds of the modern city. For Benjamin, Hoffmann's story "stellt wohl einen der frühesten Versuche dar, das Straßenbild einer größeren Stadt aufzufassen" (I, 628), and, by virtue not only of its date of composition but also of the relative backwardness of the city in which it is set, it represents an urban environment whose modernization has just barely begun. Two assertions by Benjamin are of particular importance in this context. The first suggests that the "Primizien der Kunst zu schauen",[5] in which the Vetter undertakes to initiate his visitor, consist "in der Fähigkeit, sich an lebenden Bildern zu erfreuen, wie ihnen das Biedermeier auch sonst nachgeht" (I, 628-629). The second argues that, unlike Poe's, Hoffmann's depiction of urban landscape and life is inevitably and fatally compromised by its reliance upon aesthetic norms and social realities that unambiguously antedate the modern age (I, 629).

It is clear from the recent scholarship, however, that Benjamin seriously underestimates the complexities and contradictions of Hoffmann's story. There is for instance some disagreement among commentators regarding the precise historical classification of the theory of aesthetic perception propounded by the elder Vetter, a question to which my essay will return in due course.

Of more immediate interest is another of Benjamin's simplifications, which recent scholars have shown much less inclination to challenge. That is to say: Benjamin slides all too easily from assumptions about the Vetter's project to assumptions about Hoffmann's, and subsequent commentators have largely followed this practice. In a radio broadcast he even states: "Der Vetter ist Hoffmann, das Fenster ist das Eck-Fenster seiner Wohnung, das auf den Gendarmenmarkt hinausging [. . .] Der gelähmte Hoffmann sitzt in einem Lehnstuhl, blickt hinunter auf den Wochenmarkt und weist seinem Vetter, der bei ihm zu Besuch ist, an, wie man aus Kleidung, Tempo, Gebärde der Marktweiber und ihrer Kundinnen vieles aufspüren, noch mehr aber ausspinnen und aussinnen könne" (VII, 92). Even while taking a more cautious position with regard to the Vetter's relationship to Hoffmann, commentary on this story has tended to identify the Vetter's practiced art of seeing relatively uncritically with Hoffmann's, so that **"Des Vetters Eck-fenster"** comes occasionally to be read as a kind of straightforward poetic testament composed by Hoffmann a few weeks before his death.[6] And that is peculiar, if only in view of the fact that the story is placed as a first-person narrative in the mouth of another figure whose attitude to both the Vetter and the Vetter's "Kunst zu schauen" is by no means unambiguously positive. The conflation of the positions—and occasionally the persons—of Hoffmann and of the Vetter has in the course of time effectively squeezed the narrating figure out of the discussion.

Benjamin's role in this process is however not quite so simple. While for him the older Vetter's failure to grasp the scene outside the window as a single entity is synonymous with Hoffmann's, it is important to note that Benjamin, unlike many of those writing in his wake, is unwilling to effect the complete eclipse of the figure and perspective of the visitor in Hoffmann's story. Accompanying Benjamin's brief commentary in the essay on Baudelaire is a footnote comparing the play of colour and light in the visitor's initial vision of the Gendarmenmarkt with a passage written some years later by Gogol in which a village fair is described in terms of flickering abstract patterns.[7] Benjamin speculates, presumably suggesting that this was too new a phenomenon to be grasped in 1822: "Vielleicht hat der tägliche Anblick einer bewegten Menge einmal ein Schauspiel dargestellt, dem sich das Auge erst adaptieren mußte" (I, 628n). Benjamin's note proceeds to suggest a further analogy between the visitor's vision and a more modern mode of representation that was to evolve only later in the nineteenth century, as exemplified in what he refers to as a painting of Chartres Cathedral by Claude Monet: "Das Verfahren der impressionistischen Malerei, das Bild im Tumult der Farbflecken einzuheimsen, wäre dann ein Reflex von Erfahrungen, die dem Auge eines Großstädters geläufig geworden sind".[8] The implications of this remarkable analogy are then simply never pursued. In noting this idea and simultaneously relegating it to a footnote, Benjamin both directs attention to and suppresses the visitor's vision in a way that happens to be entirely consistent with the process enacted in Hoffmann's story. There the vision is described by the visitor and then devalued and systematically overwritten by the older Vetter's codification of an archaic—and equally anachronistic—vision based explicitly on the premodern representational models of Jacques Callot (1592-1635), William Hogarth (1697-1764), and Daniel Nikolaus Chodowiecki (1726-1801). Benjamin's purpose is to establish the modernity of the title figure in Poe's *The Man of the Crowd,* and he exploits **"Des Vetters Eckfenster"**—or rather the dominant vision therein, namely that of the older Vetter—principally as a hastily deployed premodern foil against which that modernity is supposed to be easily visible. The footnote then confuses the issue, and one is left with the impression that the analogy suggested between the vision of the younger visitor and impressionist painting was, on the one hand, too interesting for Benjamin to completely ignore but, on the other hand, given the objectives of his larger discussion of Poe and Baudelaire, too inconvenient to pursue.

The suppression of the young visitor's vision, which is effected as part of the apparently authoritative pedagogic process enacted in **"Des Vetters Eckfenster,"** has nevertheless come to determine a reading stance that has dominated interpretative commentary on the story. The figure of the young visitor is seen for the most part as simply a receptacle for the wisdom of the elder Vetter and a willing learner who brings to the lesson, in his teacher's cited words, "nicht das kleinste Fünkchen von Schriftstellertalent", not even the very first prerequisite: "ein Auge, welches wirklich schaut" (600). This being so, the visitor's initial description of the Gendarmenmarkt is treated as little more than a naive sketch, a sketch to be quickly discarded or erased and redrawn under the patient and practiced guidance of the teacher.[9] However, if Walter Benjamin is right in the half-concealed comparison he draws between the visitor's initial vision of the square from the Vetter's window and impressionist painting, then the judgment of artistic incompetence for which it is summarily condemned is immediately thrown into doubt. This in turn must raise questions about the authority of the aesthetic arbiter, the sick and unproductive older Vetter. These two concerns—the young visitor's vision and the authority of its judge—will preoccupy the following sections of my essay.

The crucial, often cited, and little-discussed passage describing the visitor's impression of the Gendarmenmarkt, seen from above on market day from the perspective of the Vetter's window, reads in full thus: "Der ganze Markt schien eine einzige, dichtzusammengedrängte Volksmasse, so daß man glauben mußte, ein dazwischengeworfener Apfel könne niemals zur Erde gelangen. Die verschiedensten Farben glänzten im Sonnenschein und zwar in ganz kleinen Flecken; auf mich machte dies den Eindruck eines großen, vom Winde bewegten, hin und her wogenden Tulpenbeets, und ich mußte mir gestehen, daß der Anblick zwar rechtartig, aber auf die Länge ermüdend sei, ja wohl gar aufgereizten Personen einen kleinen Schwindel verursachen könne der dem nicht unangenehmen Delirieren des nahenden Traums gliche [. . .]" (599). There are several things here that tend to be ignored or glossed over in the existing literature on Hoffmann's story. First, this description of a compressed "Volksmasse" precedes the descriptions of artificially isolated individuals or small groups of figures that are visualized under the direction of the older Vetter and that attract Benjamin's attention and eventual dismissal as aesthetically inadequate to the task of depicting the human landscape of the early nineteenth-century city. Thus, when Benjamin guesses at the place of Hoffmann's 1822 story in the prehistory of modern urban writing and then concentrates in the body of his text not on this vision but on the dominant vision of the older Vetter, he skews that prehistory in his haste to direct his attention toward more unambiguously modern writing. He is clearly right in emphasizing that the geographical and historical circumstances of Poe's *The Man of the Crowd* render it more important to the canon of early city writing than Hoffmann's story could possibly be, but he is wrong to simplify the questions of aesthetics and representational style raised by Hoffmann to the extent that he does.

Second, it is clear from Hoffmann's description of the sensual "Eindruck" experienced by the younger visitor looking out from the older Vetter's window that the description's anticipation of impressionist representational techniques is neither implicit nor tentative but rather, in all but its exact name, quite explicit.[10] Furthermore, in making its analogy between the market square and a bed of tulips waving in the wind, the visitor's description draws on the imaginary of garden landscapes in a way that supports the discussion of his vision in the context of impressionist painting. There is, it should be emphasized, no contradiction in art-historical terms implicit in the application of such an analogy to the representation of a modern, urban landscape. Benjamin's invocation, proceeding from the brief description of this scene, of Monet's work invites the observation that impressionist styles and techniques lent themselves later in the nineteenth century as readily to the representation of nonurban scenes as to that of urban landscapes. While gardens and rural landscapes may predominate in Monet's œuvre, one cannot overlook the importance to the impressionist canon of his 1877 series of paintings of scenes in and around the Gare Saint-Lazare, an emblematically ultramodern location of crucial significance within the urban, dynamic, industrial world.[11] Even more pertinent points of thematic and stylistic

comparison are found in four paintings by Monet depicting more or less densely crowded Paris streets, each viewed from an upper-storey window or balcony. These are the two paintings *Le Boulevard des Capucines* (1873), the painting *La Rue Montorgeuil, fête du 30 juin 1878* (1878), and the painting *La Rue Saint-Denis, fête du 30 juin 1878* (1878).[12]

Third, this is explicitly a vision of a world in motion, and in this respect too the analogy to impressionist painting remains valid. In the case of gardens, railway stations, or city streets the analogy is clear (the movement deriving from natural or man-made forces), but it holds true even with regard to the example of Rouen Cathedral in which the substance and permanence of the edifice itself are dissolved in the fluidity of the coloured light and the consciousness of the ephemerality of visual experience. The young visitor's aesthetic envisioning of a world in flux, in contrast to the static Biedermeier quality of the Vetter's imaginings, is in Baudelaire's sense essentially modern, to the extent that modernity is described as "le transitoire, le fugitif, le contingent, la moitié de l'art, dont l'autre moitié est l'éternel et l'immutable".[13] Media capable of depicting actual motifs and scenes in motion would of course be developed later in the nineteenth and twentieth centuries, and colour would be incorporated into those media in due course, but the simulation of the fascinating *impression* of movement began decades in advance of such mimetic technologies. That fascination is already present in Hoffmann's young visitor, and its pleasure is inseparable from the dizziness that may be induced by the new and unaccustomed experience of movement captured in the fragment of a description that he offers as he looks out across the Gendarmenmarkt. Crucial here is the sensual overload to which the young visitor more or less voluntarily surrenders in order to achieve the pleasure of this delirium: as in the liminal space between waking and dreaming, the subject's rational capacity to process experience is simply overwhelmed by the flow of sensual data. Though Benjamin does not register the importance of this in his comments on Hoffmann's story, the suggestion that the young visitor's momentary and celebratory encounter with this state of sensual and intellectual overload anticipates aspects of the aesthetic experience of modernity could hardly be clearer.[14]

Fourth, and last, neither the visitor's nor the older Vetter's view from the upstairs window constitutes the story's first glimpse of the crowd in the Gendarmenmarkt. The story begins with an expository passage, narrated in the voice of the visitor, providing some background information on the ailing Vetter. That is followed by the beginning of the narrative of the events of the market day in question: "Es war gerade Markttag, als ich, mich durch das Volksgewühl durchdrängend, die Straße hinabkam, wo man schon aus weiter Ferne meines Vetters

Eckfenster erblickt" (598). The narrative thus begins with the visitor immersed in the crowd that he and the Vetter later describe from a position in the latter's rooms "ziemlich hoch" above the square (598). Unlike the Vetter, who, too ill to leave his rooms, is capable of only a physically and intellectually distanced observation of the human activity below, regulated by his strictly determined artistic principles, the visitor at least begins the story as, very literally, a man of the crowd. I do not of course mean to suggest that he is a thoroughly modern man in the sense of the anonymous and shadowy urban figure, "the type and the genius of deep crime"[15] at the centre of Poe's story or even in the sense of Poe's narrator who is drawn as an observer into the nocturnal life of the city and who is of particular interest to Benjamin. Nevertheless, it is clear that, unlike his housebound Vetter, the visitor in Hoffmann's story is able to move in, through, and out of the crowd comfortably and more or less freely. And this ability, not to mention the question of will, marks him as radically better experienced and equipped to understand and function in the proto-modern world than his aged, invalid relative.

This necessarily raises a question about the older Vetter's teaching. His authority is accepted by Benjamin and remains by and large unquestioned in recent scholarship on Hoffmann's story, and there are a number of likely reasons why this is so. First of all, as discussed earlier, his "Primizien der Kunst zu schauen" quickly and completely eclipse the visitor's own proto-impressionist view of the scene in the course of the narrative. The relationship of teacher and pupil that is established within the fiction, along with the effusive gratitude of the latter for the former's wisdom, seems to offer quite unambiguous evidence of the teacher's authority. In the scholarship there is, furthermore, substantial importance attached to the precise autobiographical elements that went into Hoffmann's depiction of the older Vetter. These similarities—such as the common location of Hoffmann's and the Vetter's rooms, their occupation as writers, their shared interest in specific visual artists, the circumstances of their laming and painful chronic illnesses, and even their appearance and clothing[16]—are direct, clear, and incontrovertible. But the step from the recording of these resemblances to the explicit or implicit identification of the theoretical position of the Vetter with that of Hoffmann most definitely does invite question.[17] For one thing, if **"Des Vetters Eckfenster"** is to be read as Hoffmann's poetic testament, it must be observed that the scholarship has not yet offered a final consensus on its definitive interpretation. There is a unanimous sense of the importance of the story, but opinions vary as to the thrust of the Vetter's "Primizien": do they derive from Enlightenment principles, are they his final artistic statement on the subject of the "Serapiontisches Prinzip", or do they represent, as is periodically suggested, a first step toward the literature of nineteenth-century realism?

The most balanced answers to this question suggest a complex interweaving of stylistic elements in the teaching and aesthetic practice of Hoffmann's Vetter, and such answers are capable of accommodating a variety of the positions taken in the scholarship on **"Des Vetters Eckfenster."** A general explanation is necessary here. First, the compositional principles that determine the Vetter's way of seeing—the fixing of the eye, the isolation within a scene of an individual figure or of a group of figures—derive from the practices of the Vetter's stated models: Chodowiecki and Hogarth in particular, but also in some respects Callot too.[18] In this context the influence of G. C. Lichtenberg's work on Hogarth, emphasizing the importance of precise physiognomic or pathognomic observation and the application of detective-like reason to what is observed, and of Johann Caspar Lavater's *Physiognomische Fragmente* (1775-1778) is frequently drawn into the discussion.[19] Second, the Serapiontic interaction of the outer and inner worlds clearly provides the model both for the Vetter's "Kunst zu schauen" and for his poetic practice in generating the stories he tells about the figures in the Gendarmenmarkt. Brüggemann draws attention in particular to the following two passages in the *Serapions-Brüder,* which together anticipate the teachings of the Vetter:

> Jeder prüfe wohl, ob er auch wirklich das geschaut, was er zu verkünden unternommen, ehe er es wagt laut damit zu werden. Wenigstens strebe jeder recht ernstlich darnach, das Bild, das ihm im Innern aufgegangen, recht zu erfassen mit allen seinen Gestalten, Farben, Lichten und Schatten, und dann, wenn er sich recht entzündet davon fühlt, die Darstellung ins Äußere Leben [zu] tragen.[20]

> Woher kommt es anders, als daß der Dichter nicht das wirklich schaute wovon er spricht, daß die Tat, die Begebenheit vor seinen geistigen Augen sich darstellend mit aller Lust, mit allem Entsetzen, mit allem Jubel, mit allen Schauern, ihn nicht begeisterte, entzündete, so daß nur die inneren Flammen ausströmen durften in feurigen Worten [. . .].[21]

Third, the historically specific socio-economic realism of some of the Vetter's stories lies, on the one hand, in the vivid description of the circumstances of the figures in the Vetter's stories and, on the other, in the musings of the Vetter to his visitor on the organization and order of social and economic life in the years after the Liberation.[22] This dimension of the text is, according to Oesterle, not without political implications with regard to life under the Carlsbad Decrees.[23]

If **"Des Vetters Eckfenster"** is looked at this way, the reading of the story as a kind of poetic testament remains tenable, but, given the complexity of the conflicting aesthetic frameworks in which it is composed and the problems faced by the Vetter as a writer within Hoffmann's story, a sense of ambiguity and of irony (such, for example, as McGlathery notes in this respect) is never far from those who have undertaken its interpretation.[24] Hoffmann's achievement can thus be understood in this story to lie in part in the stylistic balancing act, as these three artistic directions both complement and conflict with each other in the teaching and practice of the older Vetter. But to the same extent that a creative synthesis can be perceived in Hoffmann's work, it is tempting to see the paralysis of the Vetter as a writer, who was previously successful and productive within the aesthetic of his generation but whose writings are now of little interest to the younger visitor, as resulting from a creative impasse precipitated by the collision of his enlightenment-driven vision, his Serapiontic narrative practice, and the development of a new post-Napoleonic social context. This reading must remain tentative but, since the narrative, despite its rather cryptic phrasing, suggests that the Vetter's inability to write derives from a recent disjuncture between fantasy ("d[er] rasch[e] Rädergang der Fantasie [. . .] der in seinem Innern fortarbeitete" [597]) and writing practice, it is reasonable to speculate on this kind of interpretation. The visitor explains: "So kam es, daß er mir allelei anmutige Geschichten erzählte, die er, des mannigfachen Wehs, das er duldete, unerachtet, ersonnen. Aber den Weg, den der Gedanke verfolgen mußte, um auf dem Papiere gestaltet zu erscheinen, hatte der böse Dämon der Krankheit versperrt. Sowie mein Vetter etwas aufschreiben wollte, versagten ihm nicht allein die Finger den Dienst, sondern der Gedanke selbst war verstoben und verflogen" (597). Important here is the distortion of the biographical material: unlike his fictional Vetter, Hoffmann continued, despite his difficulties, to accept commissions and to produce literary texts virtually up until his death. With their author physically unable to write with a pen, these late texts, **"Des Vetters Eckfenster"** included, were dictated. In his own writing Hoffmann thus overcomes the kind of disjuncture on which the literary production of his fictional Vetter founders, but the resultant text is of an aesthetic complexity that the Vetter's literary production—"gut [. . .] und ergötzlich" as it supposedly was (597) and oriented on eighteenth-century formal-aesthetic models—never approaches.

Walter Benjamin's assessment of the story's depiction of the crowd in terms of a series of twelve discretely depicted Biedermeier "Genrebilder" justifies itself only by radically ignoring the ironic distance between E. T. A. Hoffmann and his fictional Vetter. The continued application of such models to the representation of human crowds in the nineteenth century, as a modern, industrial economic and social order began to develop in Germany in the decades following the Congress of Vienna, has the potential only of nostalgic anachronism.

As Benjamin emphasizes, such a modern reordering has no place in the scene as viewed by the Vetter, its limits defined by the neoclassical order and symmetry of Berlin's Gendarmenmarkt.[25] The Vetter's composite vision of "die mannigfachste Szenerie des bürgerlichen Lebens" (600) and of "das anmutige Bild der Wohlbehaglichkeit und des sittlichen Friedens" (620) dominates the story, and in the Biedermeier tradition the maintenance of such a vision of society was absolutely contingent on the suppression of any more modern "Anblick eines scheckichten, sinnverwirrenden Gewühls des in bedeutungsloser Tätigkeit bewegten Volks" (600).[26] Further supporting the view of the Vetter's reactionary, anachronistic conception of society is Hermann Korte's demonstration that the order and self-regulation of the commercial activity depicted in the view from the Vetter's window are informed by the principles of eighteenth-century cameralism,[27] which, in contrast to nineteenth-century bourgeois capitalism, was associated with "das Aufklärungsprojekt eines allgemeinen Fortschritts humaner Sittlichkeit" such as the Vetter perceives as he summarizes the developments he has witnessed in the marketplace over several years (620-621).[28]

The segmentation and narrative framing of landscape and population that characterizes the Vetter's imaginative work represents a larger compositional strategy, and it is at odds with the first-person narrator's conception of "das ganze Panorama des grandiosen Platzes" (598). These words are curious, since, however wide-angled it may be, the view from the Vetter's corner window simply cannot be fully panoramic. Oesterle argues that both the framing of the view from the window and its internal subdivision into a series of discrete images in the eye of the Vetter are consistent with eighteenth-century, chaos-resistant traditions of landscape representation, which stand in radical contrast with the impulse of romantic landscape art.[29] Thomas Eicher, reading **"Des Vetters Eckfenster"** in relation to the panoramic mural paintings that became popular attractions in European cities at the end of the eighteenth century and into the nineteenth century, nevertheless proposes an analogy between the structural principles of the Vetter's vision of the Gendarmenmarkt and the technique of painting and the activity of viewing such paintings.[30] According to Eicher, the effect achieved by the use of the Vetter's aesthetic strategies is that of a not completely successful impression of totality.[31] The tenability of the analogy hinges on an understanding of the production and visual reception, segment by segment, of the panoramic image by painters and viewers. The partial failure of the impression of totality is, I propose, consistent with Oesterle's understanding of the Vetter's technique. Each of the images the Vetter generates, in part assisted by the visitor, is internally coherent and convincing in its verisimilitude. Collectively, however, while the images interrelate harmoniously in their suggestion of social order, they remain isolated from one another, and the eye remains for the most part unable to move freely among them as it might if it were viewing a true panorama. That is to say: even though the Vetter occasionally gives an indication of the spatial organization of the scene as a whole (for example: "Ehe wir uns noch von der Theaterwand abwenden, laß uns noch einen Blick auf die dicke gemütliche Frau mit vor Gesundheit strotzenden Wangen werfen [. . .]" [603], and also the water pumps in the square give some sense of orientation [604, 609, 612]), there emerges no comprehensive network of spatial interrelations that is capable of binding a whole "Panorama"—or even a majority of its segments—together coherently.[32]

Beyond his characterization as a spectator of life, the Vetter is of course also a storyteller, though not the authoritative teller of his own story. Rather, the information we have about the older Vetter is first imparted in the text by the young visitor in whose voice the complex narrative is conducted, and it is only later corroborated in the direct quotation of statements accredited to the Vetter himself. This would not be particularly worthy of note, were it not for the fact that this visitor is no more neutral and devoid of judgment as a narrating voice than he is unperceptive and unexpressive in his vision and description of the Gendarmenmarkt. Indeed, as suggested above, he expresses his own distinct lack of enthusiasm for his Vetter's writings, despite their apparent popularity among "[d]ie Leute" (597). It gives him, he adds, more pleasure to listen to his older relative than to read him, and, given the older Vetter's inability to put word on paper, his "unbesiegbarer Hang zur Schriftstellerei" comes to be little more than a residual curse (597). Such a narrative configuration must necessarily complicate any assumptions about the visitor's role as the older Vetter's—and thus, by association, as Hoffmann's—literary heir.[33]

Even before that, however, the transparency of the autobiographical elements in the composition of the Vetter is compromised, and they become just one frame of reference within which this figure can be viewed. In the very first sentence of the first-person narrator's discourse the Vetter becomes the subject of a complex intertextual framing in his comparison of his present situation with that of Paul Scarron (1610-1660), whose work *Le Roman comique* (1649-1657) is best known for its representation of the customs and manners of the baroque age. This effects a first relativization of the reading of the Vetter's situation as an autobiographical projection of Hoffmann himself. This relativization is further complicated by the critical consensus that the source of the image of Scarron—as well as the structural model for Hoffmann's story composed around twelve figures or groups of figures—is itself quasi-fictional. It is to be found in two short pieces by Karl Friedrich Kretschmann of 1798 and 1799: *Scarron am Fenster* and *Scarron abermals am Fenster*.[34] The third

relativization of the autobiographical value of the figure of the Vetter lies in the suggestion of the importance to Hoffmann of the engraving of Scarron at his window by Chodowiecki, whose illustration accompanied Kretschmann's work.[35] As a consequence of this complex framing, therefore, the biographical data that informs the figure of the Vetter is heavily and to some extent (by means of the initial comparison with Scarron) explicitly fictionalized: the autobiographical elements of the Vetter initially seem clear, but they are ultimately perceived through the complex lens of a visual representation of an imaginative account of the situation of a real seventeenth-century French writer.

Complicating the relationship between the visitor and the Vetter is the fact that it is by no means clear that the former is, at the opening of the story, on his way to visit his housebound relative. This uncertainty in turn raises doubts about his attitude as a more or less willing and receptive listener to the latter's teaching. In addition to the visitor's disinterest in his earlier writing, we learn that at some point—"eines Tages" (597)—in the past the older Vetter has stopped receiving any visitors whatsoever, having people chased away from the door by his invalid helper who performs this duty "murrend und keifend [. . .] wie ein beißiger Haushund" (598). As he walks across the Gendarmenmarkt, the visitor is more than a little astonished to see his relative up at the window, and it seems probable that the Vetter is not watching for him, since his attention has to be attracted by the young man down below in the crowd (598). Adding to the evidence of the young visitor's surprise and the older Vetter's not seeking him out in the crowd (when his vision of the occupants of the square is otherwise so clear and reliable), there is no indication that this is anything other than an unexpected visit: "'Ei', rief mir der Vetter entgegen, als ich in das Kabinett trat, 'ei kommst du endlich, Vetter; weißt du wohl, daß ich rechte Sehnsucht nach dir empfunden?'" (599). While he is surprised at the state of affairs, pleased at his relative's improved condition, and flattered by the latter's welcoming compliment (599), there is nothing to suggest—given his previously stated lack of enthusiasm for the literary production of the older Vetter—that the visitor is doing anything more than humoring his ailing relative. Listening and playing his role in the game-like invention of stories directed by the older Vetter certainly amuses the visitor, but the success of their work as a "dialogisch verschwisterte Einheit"[36] is predicated not so much on his passivity and receptiveness as on his willingness to suppress his own protomodern, "panoramic" vision of the scene while the older figure energetically preaches the principles that inform his archaically determined "Kunst zu schauen". The visitor's sole apparent concern, however emotionally sincere and affectionate, is with the physical and psychic condition of his ailing relative. When the story ends with the close of the market and the sudden relapse of the older Vetter into pain, the silent lament "Armer Vetter!" (620), addressed away from the figure to whom it refers, contains no more clear hint of a personal attachment as a grateful pupil than does the opening of the frame narrative, and there is no sentiment expressed in that frame narrative other than straightforward sympathy. In summary, what precious little is revealed to the reader about the visitor in the course of the first-person narration contains no clear suggestion of either an intellectual engagement with the older relative's ideas or a significant process of learning.[37] If those ideas really do contain Hoffmann's final poetic testament, they fall on apparently indifferent ears, however well entertained the visitor may be by the picturesque stories the Vetter invents about the figures on the Gendarmenmarkt.

An understanding of the Vetter's young visitor as belonging in this sense to the new age dawning in Germany following the Liberation invites the question of the extent to which he can be identified as an early representative of the nineteenth-century tradition of the urban flaneur *à la* Baudelaire. At ease in his anonymity among the urban crowds, the walking man in **"Des Vetters Eckfenster"** is first seen moving through the city without any indication of a destination or purpose (though also, it must be said, without any explicit indication that he does not have one) and clearly has time on his hands to observe his human environment at leisure. If his self-characterization lacks the degree of passion that Baudelaire ascribes to the perfect flaneur, there is enough in the attitude of the visitor in Hoffmann's story toward the crowded urban space to suggest a family resemblance, reaching across generations, to the Parisian ideal. Baudelaire writes in 1859-1860: "Pour le parfait flâneur, pour l'observateur passionné, c'est une immense jouissance que d'élire domicile dans le nombre, dans l'ondoyant, dans le mouvement, dans le fugitif et l'infini. Être hors de chez soi, et pourtant se sentir partout chez soi; voir le monde, être au centre du monde et rester caché au monde, tels sont quelques-uns des moindres plaisirs de ces esprits indépendants, passionnés, impartiaux, que la langue ne peut que maladroitement définir. L'observateur est un *prince* qui jouit partout de son incognito".[38] And in a conception that recalls the visitor's vision of the Gendarmenmarkt in Hoffmann's story, Baudelaire's ideal observer (actually the painter Constantin Guys) is subsequently compared, "à un miroir aussi immense que cette foule; à un kaléidoscope doué de conscience, qui, à chacun de ses mouvements, représente la vie multiple et la grâce mouvante de tous les éléments de la vie" (552).[39]

While this family resemblance is relatively obvious, it cannot of course be forgotten that the invalid Vetter represents a still earlier generation of aesthetic thought and practice vis-à-vis the urban landscape. There seems however to be a rupture in this family, a radical generation gap between the figures in Hoffmann's story. The

older Vetter seems, as a consequence of an epochal disjuncture that antedates his crippling illness, to have lost all orientation in his relationship to the emerging post-Napoleonic world. The "Blumenmädchen" story at the very centre of Hoffmann's text (606-608) tells of his earlier catastrophic attempt to function at leisure in the environment that he now only observes from above. His utter failure to interact in any normally socialized way with the flower girl in the market place precedes not just his alienated and permanent withdrawal to his rooms but also his subsequent illness and inability to write. No strolling prince of anonymity, it is indeed his very act of revealing his identity to the flower girl that precipitates the crisis.

It is therefore highly surprising to find in Benjamin's *Passagen-Werk* an implicit connection, bypassing intermediate generations, between the Vetter, the supposed mouthpiece of Hoffmann's poetic testament, and the flaneur tradition. There he writes: "E. Th. A. Hoffmann als Typ des Flaneurs; **'Des Vetters Eckfenster'** ist dessen Testament" (V, 536). Admittedly this passage alludes to Hoffmann's own predilection for walking and people-watching in the city, but its explicit reference to the testament value of the **"Eckfenster"** story clearly implicates the older Vetter. The revised version of this passage that subsequently appears in Benjamin's Baudelaire essay neutralizes the connection and, in describing Hoffmann as "nach seiner Veranlagung von der Familie der Poe und der Baudelaire" (I, 551-552) has eliminated the Vetter altogether from the genealogy of the flaneur tradition. The *Passagen-Werk* version seems to hint at an indecision on Benjamin's part about the two central figures of Hoffmann's story: his initial comment would make more sense if it pertained to the visitor, who walks in his world with an eye unfettered by premodern aesthetic principles. Once again, as in his footnote addressing the young visitor's vision from the window, there is the suggestion of a more complex relationship between the functions of the two protagonists that Benjamin, in his haste to proceed to other matters, seems to sense but that is then suppressed in the body of his work on Poe and Baudelaire.

This suppression, as suggested earlier, begins not with Benjamin but in the narrative structure of Hoffmann's story itself. The frame narrative that encompasses the actual conversation between the two relatives begins and ends on notes that, despite the visitor's sympathetic attitude toward the Vetter, only emphasize the radical difference in circumstance between these two figures. In the narrated dialogue in the central section of Hoffmann's story, the suppression of the visitor's way of seeing is paralleled by the almost total suppression of his narrating voice. The word "almost" is important here. The long central section of **"Des Vetters Eckfenster"** is presented in the form of tagged direct discourse and is generally read as simulating an enlightenment dialogue in which the visitor assumes an established role, either with the intention of learning something or simply in order to be a good companion. Either way, the voice of the narrating character remains primary and dominant, subordinating that of the third-person figure whose story is being told. The dialogue tags "*Ich*" and "*Vetter*" are minimal, but they sustain our awareness that, as readers of the story told in his voice, we enjoy a privileged relationship with the young visitor, with whom we, as it were, merely visit the rooms of the older relative. This view of the text reveals the immediacy of the Vetter's voice in the dialogue as illusory. What this embedded dialogue suppresses most effectively, as the young visitor amiably allows himself some time to listen to the stories of his sick relative for whom the visitor's main virtue is that he is "ein munterer Geist [. . .] und amüsable" (599), is the voice addressed away from the Vetter and toward the reader. That voice retains its dominance from beginning to end in the story, and, however amiable and cheerful it may be, it consistently withholds any suggestion of accepting the aesthetic principles and practices of the Vetter. The telling of the Vetter's story is throughout contingent on the visitor's mediation, and the latter's tone of benignly ironic scepticism must necessarily be taken into account in any estimation of the testament value of the Vetter's principles.

The constellation of the first-person narrative undermines the older figure's authority in a further, more comprehensive way. Hoffmann's story presents to the reader the fictional illusion of reading a story written by the younger Vetter. Thus, this visitor, the modest harbinger of a new, nineteenth-century vision of the world and benignly dismissive of a previous generation's literary production, is presented as having succeeded with apparent ease and leisure in writing a story, the very thing that "der arme Vetter der Aufklärung", terminally locked in archaic, enlightenment-oriented modes of intellectual and aesthetic activity, can simply no longer do.[40] The purported act of learning that takes place in **"Des Vetters Eckfenster"** can then only be an illusion created for the benefit of the sick, older relative. The more immediate implication of the first-person frame narration is the justification of the younger, more dynamic, and more productive figure's attitude of patience and sympathetic amusement vis-à-vis the literary principles of his moribund, unproductive, and irretrievably alienated older Vetter. Anticipated here is Matthew Arnold's concept of the adequacy of an author to his age, and indeed Arnold's exemplary case of the inadequate writer, the poet-philosopher Lucretius, reveals noteworthy parallels to the situation of the Vetter. Arnold writes in his essay "On the Modern Element in Literature":

[H]ow can a man adequately interpret the activity of his age when he is not in sympathy with it? Think of the varied, the abundant, the wide spectacle of the Ro-

man life of his day; think of its fulness of occupation, its energy of effort. From these Lucretius withdraws himself, and bids his disciples to withdraw themselves; he bids them to leave the business of the world, and to apply themselves "*naturam cognoscere rerum*—to learn the nature of things [. . .]". With stern effort, with gloomy despair, he seems to rivet his eyes on the elementary reality, the naked framework of the world, because the world in its fulness and movement is too exciting for his decomposed brain.[41]

In Hoffmann's story the incontestable proof of authority lies in productivity, and that productivity is rooted in new aesthetic principles and practices that represent an adequate and contemporary response to the emerging world of the nineteenth century.

There is a danger here of overstating the case for what I originally described as a somewhat perverse line of enquiry. The finality of my reading of **"Des Vetters Eckfenster"** is limited by the provisionality of any assumptions that can be made about the young visitor, whose identity—despite the sound of his voice in the text, despite the central role he plays in the events of Hoffmann's story, and despite the suggestion of an active aesthetic intellect—remains by and large shadowy. The combination of intellectual distance with an unequivocally benign nature makes for a narrative situation haunted by ironic indeterminacy, whereby neither the archaic aesthetic practice of the Vetter nor the hint of a new vision imparted by the visitor is endowed with anything approaching final authority. It would be as unjustifiable to identify the ideas of the first-person narrator with those of Hoffmann as it would be to describe the Vetter as a mouthpiece for the unmediated views of the text's real author. There can be no doubt that all the positions represented by the Vetter are crucial within the development of Hoffmann's whole œuvre, but those ideas do not constitute a static aesthetic theory and practice. Even given the identification of the aesthetic practices of the Vetter as archaic, one is still left with the problem of reconciling a number of diverse elements: seventeenth- and eighteenth-century visual models, an understanding of society oriented on enlightenment ideas, and a romantic, Serapiontic imagination. Rather than presenting a definitive testament, the older Vetter's discourse represents a dynamic intermingling of aesthetic directions, all of which have played decisive roles in determining the course of Hoffmann's literary development.[42]

The significance of the visitor within this interpretation lies in seeing these artistic directions within a broader dynamic continuum of aesthetic thought and practice. It is here that the irony of Hoffmann's testament comes most clearly to the fore. To whatever extent the Vetter's ideas represent those espoused in the various parts of Hoffmann's work, there is an awareness in the story, beyond the symbolic decrepitude of the Vetter (however autobiographically motivated it may be), of their loss of artistic currency. The apparently well-educated younger visitor has, as noted earlier, other tastes but registers that his older relative's books still enjoy a popular audience (597). The *Blumenmädchen* in the Gendarmenmarkt, the other reader to be found in the story and thus by default the representative of this popular audience, can, for all her enthusiasm about the book by the Vetter that she is seen reading, say nothing more aesthetically perceptive than that it is "ein gar schnackisches Buch" (607). The sudden comic-painful puncturing of the Vetter's anachronistic illusion about the flower-girl's identity as the idealized romantic reader—characterized by an attitude of awe vis-à-vis the sublime genius of the poet (608) and just waiting to be transported "in die phantastische Welt meiner [i.e., the *Vetter*'s] Träumereien" (607)—is evidence not just of his total misreading of his contemporary social environment but also of the decay of a world view that has defined his identity, his literary practice, and his relationship with the rest of humanity.[43] There is a sense in **"Des Vetters Eckfenster"** that the world has moved on, and the tumultuous political, cultural, and social developments during and in the immediate wake of the Napoleonic age are ushering in a new world to which other eyes and other still nascent artistic responses will be more adequate. The crucial difference between Hoffmann's discourse and that of the Vetter lies in the story's subtle suggestion of another, coming vision of the world, a future to which the Vetter, his eyes bound by an adherence to defunct artistic and imaginative principles, is completely blind. Kremer writes: "Im Zentrum dieser Erzählung steht ein letzter, aber schon nicht mehr gelingender Überblick eines sterbenden Romantikers aus dem poetischen Oberstübchen auf die Niederungen eines Markets und einer Menschenmenge, die die Romantik nachhaltig erschüttern werden".[44] The young visitor, as he prepares to leave the upstairs rooms of his relative and return to the street, may indeed be the Vetter's or even Hoffmann's imagined heir, but not in the sense of his being heir to any specific aesthetic tradition. On the contrary: his inheritance is a dynamic, postromantic future, its manifestation the uncertainly and fleetingly glimpsed new world of nineteenth-century modernity.

Notes

1. Reviewing the work of earlier scholars, Stadler concludes: "Die Anzahl dieser Interpreten ist jedoch—im Vergleich zur hohen Wertschätzung der Erzählung—überraschend klein" (Ulrich Stadler, "Die Aussicht als Einblick. Zu E. T. A. Hoffmann's später Erzählung 'Des Vetters Eckfenster'", *ZfdP* [*Zeitschrifte für deutsche Philologie*] 105 [1986], 498-515, here: 499n4). For a concise, recent summary of the scholarship on this story see Detlef Kremer, *E. T. A. Hoffmann. Erzählungen und Romane*, Klassiker-Lektüren 1, Berlin 1999, 183-186.

2. For example, in its chapter devoted to Hoffmann's story, Riha's 1970 study of city writing acknowledges and cites Benjamin merely in a footnote (Karl Riha, *Die Beschreibung der "Großen Stadt". Zur Entstehung des Großstadtmotivs in der deutschen Literatur [ca. 1750-ca. 1850],* Frankfurter Beiträge zur Germanistik 11, Bad Homburg v.d.H. 1970, 137). By contrast, by the mid-1980s Benjamin's comments have assumed a far more prominent position in the literature; see for example Heinz Brüggemann, *"Aber schickt keinen Poeten nach London!" Großstadt und literarische Wahrnehmung im 18. und 19. Jahrhundert. Texte und Interpretationen,* Reinbek 1985, 173-174; Stadler (note 1), 504-505; Günter Oesterle, "E. T. A. Hoffmann: 'Des Vetters Eckfenster.' Zur Historisierung ästhetischer Wahrnehmung oder Der kalkulierte romantische Rückgriff auf Sehmuster der Aufklärung", *DU* [*Der Deutschunterricht: Beiträge zu Seiner Praxis und Wissenschaftlichen Grundlegung.*] 39/1 (1987), 84-110, here: 84 and 94; Hermann Korte, "Der ökonomische Automat. E. T. A. Hoffmanns späte Erzählung 'Des Vetters Eckfenster'", *Text und Kritik. Sonderband E. T. A. Hoffmann,* ed. Heinz Ludwig Arnold, München 1992, 125-137, here: 126; Detlef Kremer, *E. T. A. Hoffmann zur Einführung,* Hamburg 1998, 172-174; and Kremer, *E. T. A. Hoffmann. Erzählungen und Romane* (note 1), 195-197.

3. Walter Benjamin, *Gesammelte Schriften,* 7 vols. (excl. supplements), ed. Rolf Tiedemann, Hermann Schweppenhäuser, et al., Frankfurt a.M. 1972-1989, here: I, 509-690. The carelessness lies in such superficial errors as Benjamin's allusion to the *Vetter*'s "Operngucker" (I, 551) or "Opernglas" (I, 628); on this point, see also Kremer (note 2), 172; and Kremer (note 1), 195.

4. There are also several notations pertinent to "Des Vetters Eckfenster" in the *Passagen-Werk* (V, 536, 564 and 565), some of whose content is incorporated in the essay on Baudelaire; the story is also discussed briefly at the conclusion of Benjamin's radio talk on Hoffmann, presented in 1930 under the title "Das dämonische Berlin" (VII, 86-92).

5. E. T. A. Hoffmann, *Des Vetters Eckfenster, Späte Werke,* München 1965, 595-622, here: 600.

6. See for example Schirmer's characterization of the story as "ein[e] Art Vermächtnis . . . [ein] poetisch-poetologisch[es] Testament—und zugleich [. . .] ein[] Dokument unverdrossener künstlerischer Selbstbehauptung" (Andreas Schirmer, "E. T. A. Hoffmann. 'Des Vetters Eckfenster'", *Deutsche Erzählprosa der frühen Restaurationszeit. Studien zu ausgewählten Texten,* ed. Bernd Leistner, Untersuchungen zur deutschen Literaturgeschichte 75, Tübingen 1995, 66-86, here:

85) or McGlathery's discussion of "Des Vetters Eckfenster" as "the piece that may be considered Hoffmann's last will and testament in poetic matters" (James M. McGlathery, *E. T. A. Hoffmann,* Twayne's World Author Series 868, New York 1997, 146).

7. The reference is presumably to the crowd description in the story *The Fair at Sorochintsy* (1831), which states that "everything is bright, gaudy, discordant, flitting in groups, shifting to and fro before your eyes" (Nikolai Gogol, *The Fair at Sorochintsy, The Complete Tales of Nikolai Gogol,* 2 vols, trans. Constante Garnett, rev. and ed. Leonard J. Kent, Chicago 1985, I, 8-33, here: 12).

8. Benjamin is presumably referring to Monet's two series of paintings of Rouen Cathedral dating from 1892 and 1893 (Daniel Wildenstein, *Claude Monet: Biographie et catalogue raisonnée,* 3 vols., Lausanne 1974-1979, pl. 1319-1329 and 1345-1361).

9. Stadler for instance declares that, in resorting to natural imagery, the visitor's attempt to describe the urban scene "scheitert kläglich", and that what he learns from his older Vetter is "eine Wahrnehmungsweise [. . .] die spezifisch dem Phänomen der Großstadt angemessen ist und sich diesem Phänomen auch verdankt" (Stadler [note 1], 503-504).

10. Commentators after Benjamin occasionally touch on the impressionist quality of the visitor's vision, though without exploring any of its implications. Oesterle, for instance, simply raises the possibility of seeing it as an impressionist image (Oesterle [note 2], 85); Lethen refers to "ein[] impressionistisch[es] Gesamtbild" (Helmut Lethen, "Eckfenster der Moderne. Wahrnehmungsexperimente bei Musil und E. T. A. Hoffmann", *Robert Musils "Kakanien"—Subjekt und Geschichte. Festschrift für Karl Dinklage zum 80. Geburtstag,* ed. Josef Strutz, Musil-Studien 15, München 1987, 195-229, here: 219); and Eicher mentions that the vision is "wie ein impressionistisches Gemälde mit ungeheuren Ausmaßen" (Thomas Eicher, "'Mit einem Blick das ganze Panorama des grandiosen Platzes': Panoramatische Strukturen in 'Des Vetters Eckfenster' von E. T. A. Hoffmann", *Poetica* 25 [1993], 360-377, here: 363-364). None of these commentators makes explicit reference to Benjamin's footnote.

11. Wildenstein (note 8), pl.438-448.

12. Wildenstein (note 8), pl.292-293 and 469-470.

13. Baudelaire, "Le Peintre de la vie moderne", *Œuvres complètes,* ed. Marcel A. Ruff, Paris 1968, 546-565, here: 553. "By 'modernity' I mean the ephemeral, the fugitive, the contingent, the half of art whose other half is the eternal and the immutable" (Baudelaire, "The Painter of Modern Life", *"The Painter of Modern Life" and Other Essays,* trans. and ed. Jonathan Mayne, London 1964, 1-40, here: 13).

14. See for instance Benjamin's observations on the effect of cinematic experience in the second version of his essay *Das Kunstwerk im Zeitalter seiner technischen Reproduzierbarkeit,* where he discusses how the rational capacity of modern cinema audiences is simply overwhelmed by the surfeit of ever-changing images on the screen: "Man vergleiche die Leinwand, auf der der Film abrollt, mit der Leinwand, auf der sich das Gemälde befinder. Das Bild auf der einen verändert sich, das Bild auf der anderen nicht. Das letztere lädt den Betrachter zur Kontemplation ein; vor ihm kann er sich seinem Assoziationsablauf überlassen. Vor der Filmaufnahme kann er das nicht. Kaum hat er sie ins Auge gefaßt, so hat sie sich schon verändert. Sie kann nicht fixiert werden. Der Assoziationsablauf dessen, der sie betrachtet, wird sofort durch ihre Veränderung unterbrochen" (VII, 379n16). Especially noteworthy here is the idea of the impossibility of the fixing of images in the viewer's consciousness: the first principle prescribed by the Vetter in Hoffmann's story is that of "das Fixieren des Blicks" (600).

15. Edgar Allan Poe, *The Man of the Crowd, The Complete Works of Edgar Allan Poe,* ed. James A. Harrison, 17 vols., New York 1902, IV, 134-145, here: 145.

16. Schirmer (note 6), 73.

17. McGlathery, for example, states that this story "was inspired by Hoffmann's desire to inform the Berlin public of his condition, and how he was bearing up under it, and also to make a final statement, if only ironically and indirectly, of his intentions as an author" (James M. McGlathery, *Mysticism and Sexuality. E. T. A. Hoffmann,* 2 vols., Las Vegas, New York, Bern 1981-1985, II [*Interpretation of the Tales,* Berner Beiträge zur deutschen Sprache und Literatur 5], 157). Stadler writes of it as an "erschütterndes autobiographisches Dokument" (Stadler [note 1], 499).

18. See for instance Brüggemann (note 2), 180-181; Oesterle (note 2), 93-97; Korte (note 2), 135-136; and Hans-Georg von Arburg, "Der Physiognomiker als Detektiv und Schauspieldirektor. Johann Ludwig Christian Hakens *Blicke aus meines Onkels Dachfenster in's Menschenherz* (1802)", *E. T. A. Hoffmann Jahrbuch* 4 (1996), 54-68, here: 59-60.

19. With regard to Lichtenberg, see especially Linde Katritzky, "Punschgesellschaft und Gemüsemarkt

in Lichtenbergs Hogarth-Kommentaren und bei E. T. A. Hoffmann", *Jahrbuch der Jean-Paul-Gesellschaft* 22 (1987), 155-171, here: 163-171; also Riha (note 2), 139-40; Stadler (note 1), 507; Oesterle (note 2), 86-87; Bernhard Dieterle, *Erzählte Bilder. Zum narrativen Umgang mit Gemälden.* Artefakt, Schriften zur Soziosemiotik und Komparatistik 3, Marburg 1988, 107-108; and Arburg (note 18), 59; with regard to Lavater, see Oesterle (note 2), 106; Arburg (note 18), 59-61; and Kremer (note 1), 182-183.

20. E. T. A. Hoffmann, *Die Serapions-Brüder,* Darmstadt 1967, 55.

21. Hoffmann, *Serapions-Brüder* (note 20), 54.

22. With regard to the tension between the Serapiontic and realist elements in the text, see for example Riha (note 2), 141; Brüggemann (note 2), 178-179; Stadler (note 1), 500-501 and 508; Lethen (note 10), 218-219; Dieterle (note 19), 108; Klaus Deterding, *Die Poetik der inneren und äußeren Welt bei E. T. A. Hoffmann. Zur Konstitution des Poetischen in den Werken und Selbstzeugnissen,* Berliner Beiträge zur neueren deutschen Literaturgeschichte 15, Frankfurt a.M. 1991, 189, 191-192 and 206; and Schirmer (note 6), 76-80.

23. Oesterle sees in the representation of a harmoniously structured, self-regulating, pluralist social and economic order an implicit pleading of the case "gegen die sich polizeistaatlicher Maßnahmen bedienende Restauration und für die Fortsetzung der preußischen Reformpolitik Steins und Hardenbergs" (Oesterle [note 2], 104). Kremer, on the other hand, characterizes this thematic realism as superficial (Kremer [note 1], 194).

24. McGlathery (note 17), 157.

25. This problem is discussed incisively by Oesterle (note 2), who projects various reasons for Hoffmann's reliance on archaic artistic models, including the political one outlined above.

26. Lethen discusses this "Parzellierung" in terms of a reactionary "Pazifizierung" (223). He continues: "Während die Rahmenschau im Zeitalter der Aufklärung gerade im Segment sich einer vernünftigen Allgemeinheit vergewissern wollte, hat sich im 19. Jahrhundert der Verdacht eingenistet, daß jenseits des bröckeligen Tellerrands der Sinneinheit, der 'Schauder der Allgewalt der Natur' unbehelligt weiter besteht" (Lethen [note 10], 223-224).

27. Korte (note 2), 134.

28. Kremer (note 1), 194.

29. Oesterle writes of the eighteenth-century artist: "Er segmentiert die Unendlichkeit der Landschaft durch perspektivierende Ausschnitte in überschaubare Kleinheiten; diese Aufstückelung in einzelne Bildchen gewährt im 18. Jahrhundert nicht nur ästhetisches Vergnügen, sondern dient zur Vergewisserung einer faktisch nachvollziehbaren Theodizee. Der Schauder vor der Allgewalt der Natur gelangt auf vernünftige Bahnen, indem die Wahrnehmung sinnverwirrender Unendlichkeit rationalisiert wird. Chaotischer Unübersichtlichkeit ist mit der rechten 'Kunst zu sehen' vernünftig beizukommen" (Oesterle [note 2], 94).

30. Eicher discusses how by the early nineteenth century the term "panorama" broadened its field of denotation and was applied in general to landscape "Landschaftsbilder wie -ansichten [. . .] aber auch—in metaphorischer Bedeutung—etwa Zeitschriften, historische und geographische Darstellungen sprachlicher Art" (Eicher [note 10], 361).

31. Eicher (note 10), 361; see also Stadler (note 1), 509.

32. In contrast to these readings, some commentators have perceived in Hoffmann's text an anticipation of more modern modes of representation. Klaus Deterding, for instance, sees a passage in "Des Vetters Eckfenster" as functioning "[w]ie eine Reihung photographischer Momentaufnahmen" and attempts to distinguish between "[d]er Photographen- und der Malerblick" (Deterding [note 22], 194-195). His distinction is neither fully explained nor fully convincing, but it is significant that the sentences characterized as photographic are among those spoken by the visitor very early in the Vetter's lesson in seeing and so cannot logically be associated with the Vetter's own representational practice of segmentation. In a different vein, Stadler goes so far as to propose an association of the structure of Hoffmann's text "mit Kunstkonzeptionen des zwanzigsten Jahrhunderts [. . .] die der Montage als einschneidendem Prinzip der Rekonstruktion und Konstruktion von Wirklichkeit verpflichtet sind" (Stadler [note 1], 515). This suggestion, offered at the end of Stadler's essay and not fully explored, seems—given not only the competing arguments of Oesterle and Eicher but also the formal and stylistic remoteness of this text from later texts that experiment with modernist montage techniques—unlikely to stand close examination.

33. Schirmer, for example, writes of the visitor's assuming the role of "ein nachwachsender Kollege" vis-à-vis his Vetter (Schirmer [note 6], 76); his subsequent assertion demonstrates even less caution: "Hoffmann unternahm es damit, sich im Angesicht seines bevorstehenden Todes einen Erben zu imaginieren, den er berichten lassen konnte,

wie er sich, ein Ablebender, sah bzw. zu sehen wünschte. Er erfand sich einen durch ihn zum Schriftsteller herangezogenen jungen Mann, der seiner—und sein Vermächtnis bewahrend—angedenkt" (79).

34. On this point, see Stadler (note 1), esp. 502-506. A second, fictional source has been identified by Hans-Georg von Arburg (note 18) in Johann Ludwig Christian Haken's *Blicke aus meines Onkels Dachfenster in's Menschenherz. Ein Beytrag zur Pathognomik* (1802).

35. See Oesterle (note 2), 88-89 and 92; and Schirmer: "Ausdrücklich bezieht sich die Hoffmannsche Notiz auf den Stich, und es war demnach eindeutig zuallererst die Bildvorlage, die anregend auf ihn wirkte" (Schirmer [note 6], 69).

36. Eicher (note 10), 365.

37. This runs counter to Katritzky's discussion of visitor as the "Doppelgänger des Vetters . . . sein zweites Ich" (Katritzky [note 19], 168-169), in which the status of the visitor's comments goes unquestioned: "Seine Charakterisierung ist ausgespart, aber seine Bemerkungen zeigen, daß er ein Mann von der Art des alten Vetters ist [. . .]" (168).

38. Charles Baudelaire, "Le Peintre" (note 13), 552. "For the perfect *flâneur,* for the passionate observer, it is an immense joy to set up house in the heart of the multitude, amid the ebb and flow of movement, in the midst of the fugitive and infinite. To be away from home and yet to feel oneself everywhere at home; to see the world, to be at the centre of the world, and yet to remain hidden from the world—such are a few of the slightest pleasures of those independent, passionate, impartial natures which the tongue can but clumsily define. The spectator is a prince who everywhere rejoices in his incognito" (Baudelaire, "The Painter" [note 13], 9).

39. Baudelaire, "Le Peintre" (note 13), 52. "[W]e might liken him to a mirror as vast as the crowd itself; or to a kaleidoscope gifted with consciousness, responding to each one of its movements and reproducing the multiplicity of life and the flickering grace of all the elements of life" (Baudelaire, "The Painter" [note 13], 9).

40. Korte (note 2), 136.

41. Matthew Arnold, "On the Modern Element in Literature", *Essays in Criticism. Third Series,* Boston 1910, 35-83, here: 73-74.

42. With regard specifically to the significance of Callot, Hogarth, and Chodowiecki within Romantic aesthetic thought and to their representative value with regard to three main directions within Hoffmann's literary work, Oesterle writes: "Die literarische Selbstverständigung mit Hilfe kunstgeschichtlicher Schul- und Richtungsbestimmung ist in der Romantik schon vor Hoffmann üblich. So hat z.B. Jean Paul in seiner *Vorschule der Ästhetik* die Romane der Weltliteratur in die italienische, deutsche und niederländische Schule eingeteilt. Das ist auf E. T. A. Hoffmanns Erzählung übertragbar, die sich damit poetologisch lesen läßt: Der Engländer Hogarth zählt in der deutschen Kunstkritik wegen seiner Drastik zum niederländischen Stil, der Berliner Radierer Chodowiecki vertritt die dämpfende, harmonisierende deutsche Variante, die die Karikatur zum Genre mäßigt, der 1635 verstorbene französische Kupferstecher Callot endlich kann für die komisch phantastische Seite der italienische Schule stehen. Lavater führt diese Stillagen u.a. in seinen *Physiognomischen Fragmenten* als wichtige Orientierungshilfe auf [. . .]" (Oesterle [note 2], 105-106).

43. Stadler argues that the alienation of the Vetter is connected to the commodification of art: "Die geradezu erschreckende Ahnungslosigkeit der Blumenverkäuferin gegenüber den Bedingungen künstlerischer Produktion beleuchtet grell die scheinbar bis zur Funktionslosigkeit verschärfte Isolation des Schriftstellers. Dessen Arbeitsprodukt verrät keinerlei Spuren mehr—weder von der Arbeit noch vom Arbeiter. Damit widerfährt dem Dichter das gleiche Schicksal wie allen übrigen Warenproduzenten—des Gendarmenmarkts wie aller übrigen Märkte. Die Waren- und Geldzirkulation deckt die entscheidenden Vermittlungen zu, macht sie unsichtbar" (Stadler [note 1], 512). This phenomenon is of course of central interest to Walter Benjamin with regard to art in the modern age. See also Korte (note 2), 135-136; Schirmer (note 6), 81-82; and Kremer (note 2), 175.

44. Kremer (note 1), 181.

Birgit Röder (essay date 2003)

SOURCE: Röder, Birgit. "'Der Artushof.'" In *A Study of the Major Novellas of E. T. A. Hoffmann,* pp. 105-25. Rochester, N.Y.: Camden House, 2003.

[In the following essay, Röder concentrates on Hoffmann's portrait of the painter Traugott in "Der Artushof." Röder probes various tensions at play in the work: between artist and philistine, reality and ideal, and male and female societal roles. By forcing Traugott to confront the impossibility of achieving his creative vision, Röder asserts, Hoffmann lends him greater power as an artist, one who still strives to create important work while recognizing that his ideal exists solely within the realm of his imagination.]

Of all Hoffmann's novellas that focus on the artist figure, **"Der Artushof"** (1816) is perhaps the most neglected. Critics, if they do not ignore it altogether, usually dismiss it as a peripheral work. Its apparent simplicity, together with what appears to be a conventional happy ending, may make it appear untypical of Hoffmann's oeuvre. The fact is, however, that **"Der Artushof"** raises many of the same fundamental aesthetic questions to be found in the other novellas: the motivation of the artist, his relationship to a metaphysical realm of transcendent ideas, and his role in society.

In the mid-1950s Joachim Rosteutscher wrote a biographically-oriented interpretation of Hoffmann's work, emphasizing what he saw as the crucial importance of the so-called "Julia-episode" for Hoffmann's work as a whole, suggesting that just as Hoffmann could not believe that his beloved idol Julia could marry Herr Graepel, so too Traugott cannot believe that Felizitas will marry a local civil servant from the court.[1] The "Julia-Episode" also plays a central role in Fritz J. Raddatz's book *Männerängste in der Literatur.* However, as might be expected of a study of such breadth, Raddatz's treatment of Hoffmann's oeuvre is inevitably very general, and his conclusions are, at best, highly speculative, not least when he suggests that Hoffmann's belief in the irreconcilability of art and femininity can be traced back to his deep-rooted fear of women.[2]

In the 1990s Marianne Kesting and Bernhard Dieterle have attempted to decipher the significance of the paintings in the novella. Whereas Kesting arrives at the rather dubious conclusion that "Es besteht, jeder Art Feminismus zum Trotz, eine Solidarität der beiden Männer [E. T. A. Hoffmann und Edgar Allan Poe] in ihrer Auffassung der Frau als vollendete Dienerin und Puppe,"[3] Dieterle concentrates on the formal dimension of the novella and concludes: "Überhaupt erweisen sich die Bilder des Artushofes als bestimmend für Traugotts Berufung zum Künstler,"[4] a conclusion which, although undoubtedly correct, resolves few of the interpretive puzzles posed by the work. Gunther Pix presents a more detailed analysis of the novella and is especially concerned with demonstrating the parallels with certain other stories, notably **"Der goldne Topf"** and **"Die Fermate."** In spite of his insightful comments on the relationship of this story to Hoffmann's work as a whole, certain key issues—notably the relationship between woman and the Ideal—are only touched upon.[5] Claudia Liebrand, Lothar Pikulik, and Peter von Matt devote a great deal of attention to the ending of the story.[6] But whereas Lothar Pikulik regards the end of the story as embodying a "happy end," Claudia Liebrand sees it as a "Taschenspielertrick" (139), as an unsatisfactory compromise since Traugott does not marry his ideal but rather a "Verdopplung" (148). For his part,

Peter von Matt draws attention to Hoffmann's narrative technique in transforming the Ideal that is embodied in the female figure into a "glückliche Philisterin" (404).

NARRATIVE STRUCTURE AND SETTING

In **"Der Artushof,"** the narrator speaks more directly to the reader than in any other comparable story such as **"Der Sandmann"** and **"Die Jesuiterkirche in G."** The novella opens with a typical *captatio benevolentiae*: "Gewiß hast du, günstiger Leser! schon recht viel von der alten merkwürdigen Handelsstadt Danzig gehört" (*SW* [*Sämmtliche Werke*] III, 145). This is followed by over a page of detailed description of the city, in the course of which the narrator, assuming the reader to be familiar with it, reminds him of its main attraction, the Artushof: "dann besuchtest du, günstiger Leser, der du in Danzig warst, den Artushof wohl am liebsten" (145). In this opening passage, the narrator does essentially two things: first, he arouses the reader's support for the well-educated and enthusiastic artist, Traugott; second, he tries to seduce the reader into believing that his own opinions do not differ fundamentally from those of the narrator. The description of the setting gives way almost imperceptibly to a description of the action: "Dir, günstiger Leser! war so etwas erlaubt, aber nicht dem jungen Kaufherrn Traugott" (146). Far from prompting the reader to adopt a position of critical detachment, the *captatio benevolentiae* appeals to him for his sympathetic understanding and plunges him into the discussion about art.

The story is set partly in the well-known Artushof of Danzig,[7] and partly in Italy, two centers of artistic excellence. The Artushof may be a building in which business and trade are conducted, but the narrator goes to great lengths to emphasize its artistic merits, describing in detail the murals, the ornamental stucco, and right in the middle, the awesome marble relief depicting the king, a relief that, carved in the style of the Northern School, includes images of "Miliz aus alter reichsstädtischer Zeit," "Ehrsame Bürgermeister," "Hellebardierer," and "lustige Soldatenmusik" (cf. *SW* III, 145). The traders from all over the world, who meet to do business in this magnificent chamber, have scant regard for the masterpieces which surround them. In the story, strong contrasts are drawn between the mercantile city of Danzig, and the cities of Rome and Naples, which are set in a land where art and beauty are revered. It comes, therefore, as no surprise to discover that it is in Italy, among a group of like-minded artists, that Traugott feels most at home. And it is to this country—a country to which Hoffmann was strongly attracted—that he returns at the end of the novella.

> Italien hatte im Weltbild dieses Dichters [Hoffmann] einen priviligierten Platz. Kein anderes europäisches Land außerhalb Deutschlands ist so oft Lebenshintergr-

und seiner Erzählfiguren [. . .] Seine [Phantasie-Italiens] Funktion in der dichterischen Welt Hoffmanns wurde durch Bedürfnisse und Erfahrungen, die der unmittelbaren nord-, mittel- und ostdeutschen Lebenswelt Hoffmanns zugehörten, strukturiert.[8]

But it is not only geographical location that is highly significant in this story. Hoffmann also makes a point with at least two of the names he uses: Traugott, with its obvious religious connotations, anticipates a positive ending to the story, and the name Felizitas makes an ironic reference to the domestic happiness of marriage to a bourgeois philistine.

THE PHILISTINES

In his description of Traugott's employer and would-be father-in-law Herr Elias Roos, the narrator caricatures a typical member of this philistine society. Herr Roos's business is the be-all and end-all of his life; he is continually anxious that a missed opportunity or a financial miscalculation could place him at a disadvantage. He is particularly worried by his prospective son-in-law's apparent lack of maturity and business acumen, and his hysterical outburst when Traugott forgets to send the letter of advice is so exaggerated as to be comic:

> da schlug Herr Elias Roos die Fäuste über den Kopf zusammen, stampfte [. . .] mit dem rechten Fuße und schrie, daß es im Saale schallte: "Herr Gott! [. . .] Dumme Kinderstreiche!—Verehrter Traugott—korrupter Schwiegersohn—unkluger Associé."
>
> (*SW* III, 147)

Moreover, his absurd fits of despair—"Zehntausend Mark, [. . .] Zehntausend Mark" (*SW* III, 147), he wails,—calls to mind other well known misers such as Ben Jonson's Volpone or Molière's Harpagon. Likewise, when the threat of imminent disaster is averted by the simplest means—it turns out that a courier will take the letter of advice to its destination—his sense of relief and his effusive expressions of gratitude are no less ridiculous: "'Unvergleichlichster Mann!' rief Herr Elias mit vollem Sonnenschein im Blick" (147). Thus the reader is left with a wonderfully vivid impression of this ludicrous, diminutive, though immaculately dressed man in "leberfarbenen Rocke, Weste und Hose mit goldbesponnenen Knöpfen" (148), who tugs at his wig in moments of extreme agitation (148, 160) and who lives in a world where all that matters are shares, profit-margins, and interest rates.

Herr Roos despises those who cannot manage their money. He cannot understand why the Old Painter, who appears at the beginning of the novella, has no sense of the fluctuations of the stock-market and little interest in increasing his personal capital: "Wissen Sie denn, ob mir in diesem Augenblick solch einfältig Papier nicht ganz unnütz, bares Geld aber höchst nötig ist?" (*SW* III,

154). He takes a contemptuous view of the elderly man's management of his financial affairs, exclaiming: "Dumme Bestie, verkauft jetzt das Papier, und bekommt in acht Tagen wenigstens 10 Prozent mehr" (155), for in his view the only sign of respectability and resourcefulness is the ability to increase one's wealth.

When confronted with the ups and downs of life, Herr Roos is far from helpless; he has an infallible remedy for the anguish and frustration the artist feels when he fails to capture the Ideal (a state of mind that, in Traugott's case, he completely misdiagnoses as an attack of jealousy): "Herr Elias Roos riet dem Traugott eine Brunnen- oder Molkenkur an" (160). This comic little incident highlights Herr Roos's lack of imagination, as well as the extent to which he is trapped within the confines of his bourgeois existence, an existence in which the only reality is that of material objects. His treatment of his daughter is no less grotesque than his treatment of Traugott, for example, when he scolds her—quite unreasonably—for what is nothing more than a simple misunderstanding: "Christina—abscheuliche Person, mißratene Tochter" (161). Poor Herr Roos is easily thrown, and it is typical of his approach to life that he always seeks the simplest—and usually most inappropriate—explanations to problems: "Der Schwiegersohn ist ein melancholischer Mensch und in der Eifersucht türkisch gesinnt. [. . .] Man gehe hinein und tröste den Bräutigam" (161).

When Traugott announces that his on-off wedding to Christina will never take place and departs for Italy, the ever opportunistic Elias Roos is mightily relieved to see the back of him, and welcomes his new putative son-in-law (and heir to the family firm), the bookkeeper. As far as Roos is concerned, what might have been seen as a calamitous turn of events is simply a non-event: one man has simply been replaced by another: "Herr Elias fügte sich in alles und versicherte herzlich froh im Comptoir einmal übers andere, daß er Gott danke, den aberwitzigen Traugott los zu sein" (*SW* III, 164). Since he lacks any appreciation of an individual's uniqueness, he believes that given sufficient financial resources, it is always possible to find a replacement.

Herr Roos is not the only philistine Traugott comes across; Hoffmann's cutting irony also exposes Herr Roos's dinner-guests for the philistines they are. When they are introduced as "Herrn Elias Roos' Freunde, d. h. mit ihm in starkem Geldverkehr" (*SW* III, 149), we are left in no doubt as to the nature of this friendship. Herr Roos can be such a buffoon that there are moments when he seems almost endearing, unlike the pseudo-connoisseurs, the uncle and his nephew, who, outwardly more fashionable, have apparently cultivated an appreciation of artistic matters: "Sie [. . .] tragen sich ganz englisch, führen einen Mahagoni-Stiefelknecht aus London mit sich, haben viel Kunstsinn und sind überhaupt feine, ganz gebildete Leute" (149). Furthermore, the uncle has a sizeable art collection of his own, but it is not just as a connoisseur of art that he wants to cut a dash. Even the complexities of contemporary philosophy seem to pose him few problems, and in his capacity as "Professor *physices*" (150), he avails himself of his own jargon to offer an absurd parody of Hegelian metaphysics, claiming that: "der Weltgeist habe als wackrer Experimentalist irgendwo eine tüchtige Elektrisiermaschine gebaut, und von ihr aus liefen gar geheimnisvolle Drähte durchs Leben" (150). Here Hoffmann pokes fun at this Professor who owns a considerable quantity of paintings, and has the requisite "good taste" to go with them, but who clearly lacks any genuine appreciation or understanding of art. Although he would like to give the appearance of being a well-educated man with an informed interest in the arts and humanities, he is little more than a complacent philistine with an overinflated ego. Not only does he lack any understanding of what is involved in a genuine commitment to art, but he treats Traugott with utter contempt when he defends the paintings and carvings that the Uncle has dismissed as tasteless and grotesque:

> aber der Onkel sagte mit recht hämischer Miene: "Ich behaupte es noch einmal, daß ich nicht begreife, wie Sie Kaufmann sein wollen, und sich nicht lieber der Kunst ganz zugewandt haben."
>
> (*SW* III, 150)

Filled with disgust for the older man, Traugott continues the discussion about art with the nephew, who seems, at first, to be more sympathetic to the artistic life and to acknowledge Traugott's ability: "wie beneide ich Sie um Ihr schönes Talent" (*SW* III, 151), he says to him. When Traugott questions him further, the nephew explains that he has delved "tiefer in das eigentliche Wesen der Sache" (151) and as a result has become, as he likes to think, "gelehrt und tiefsinnig" (151). This prompts him to put forward his own insights into the nature of art: "Sie werden mir recht geben, daß die Kunst Blumen in unser Leben flicht—Erheiterung, Erholung vom ernsten Geschäft, das ist der schöne Zweck alles Strebens in der Kunst" (151). Like his uncle, the nephew is also exposed as a philistine; he regards art simply as something decorative and relaxing. But that is as far as he goes because he recognizes that a whole-hearted commitment to art involves risk and can result in discomfort and even disaster, which he sees in purely financial terms. As an out-and-out materialist he maintains: "Sie werden mir doch zugeben, daß man im Leben leben muß, wozu es der bedrängte Künstler von Profession beinahe niemals bringt" (151). Recognizing that genuine artists constantly have to live with artistic and philosophical dilemmas, he opts for art that is essentially pleasant and anodyne. Carried away by the sound of his own voice, the nephew babbles on, making it obvious to both Traugott and the reader that

by "living," the nephew means nothing more than "keine Schulden, sondern viel Geld haben, gut Essen und Trinken, eine schöne Frau und auch wohl artige Kinder, die nie einen Talgfleck ins Sonntagsröckchen bringen" (152). Thus even though the uncle thinks artistic connoisseurship will bring him status, his nephew, still regarding himself as an art lover, avoids all works of art that are personally challenging, an attitude that attributes a purely decorative and trivial function to art.

Like the anonymous nephew and uncle, the bookkeeper, who shares their philistine outlook, is also never referred to by name. He offers no opinions on art or philosophy since, like Herr Roos, he is interested only in the firm and in Christina (which in effect amounts to the same thing). He cannot be described as an unscrupulous character, however, for his total passivity together with the almost automatic manner in which he steps into the role vacated by Traugott, suggests a man whose personality is far too limited for him to contemplate anything as demanding as a disreputable deed.

THE WOMEN

Just as the male philistines, of whom Hoffmann is so bitingly critical, are typical of certain sections of nineteenth-century bourgeois society, so too Christina typifies bourgeois, feminine domesticity. She is her father's daughter in every way, especially in her rigidly utilitarian outlook on life. She has but one aim, the domestic bliss of bourgeois marriage. Her attractive demeanor is not the outward sign of an inner happiness but rather the certain knowledge that a marriage contract is not far off; she possesses "Augen, aus denen es recht hübsch jedermann anlächelt: Nun heirate ich bald" (*SW* III, 149). Nor does she love Traugott for any personal qualities, but simply on account of his eligibility: "[. . .] daß Christinchen den Traugott deshalb ungemein lieb hat, weil er sie heiratet" (149). She is prepared to play her part in the business of finding a husband, and she has the one attribute that potential suitors in her society value above all else: she is the only child of a wealthy businessman. In addition, she is a thrifty house-keeper and an excellent cook: "niemals ist ihr eine Mandeltorte mißraten, und die Buttersauce verdickt sich jedesmal gehörig, weil sie niemals links, sondern immer rechts im Kreise mit dem Löffel rührt" (149). Furthermore, there is nothing, it seems, that can disrupt her pedestrian daily routine: "sollten etwa aus des Nachbars brennenden Hause die Flammen in ihr Zimmer schlagen, so wird sie nur noch geschwinde den Kanarienvogel füttern und die neue Wäsche verschließen" (149).[9] With no little irony, the narrator describes her as the very embodiment of a perfect wife, a domestic robot devoid of imagination and initiative.

Christina is not simply of limited intelligence; she is also heartless, as we see when her father sends her to console her fiancé:

[sie] begab sich auf ihr Zimmer, um sich nur ein wenig umzukleiden, die Wäsche herauszugeben, mit der Köchin das Nötige wegen des Sonntagsbraten zu verabreden und sich nebenher einige Stadtneuigkeiten erzählen zu lassen, dann wollte sie gleich sehen, was dem Bräutigam denn eigentlich fehle.

(*SW* III, 162)

She is equally unfeeling when Traugott tells her that nothing will come of their proposed marriage:

"Es ist auch gar nicht vonnöten," sagte Christina sehr ruhig, "Sie gefallen mir so nicht sonderlich seit einiger Zeit, und gewisse Leute werden es ganz anders zu schätzen wissen, wenn sie mich, die hübsche, reiche Mamsell Christina Roos, heimführen können als Braut."

(*SW* III, 163-64)

This is not the cry of a rejected lover, but the cold and calculated response of a woman who knows that, in the bookkeeper, she has a ready-made replacement for her fiancé waiting in the wings. In this way, Hoffmann's irony leaves us in doubt about the hollowness of a conventional relationship that defines a couple as a social unit of husband and wife and in which neither is considered as an individual. Traugott, who is not prepared to enter into such a relationship is soon replaced, and as a result Christina, her father, and of course, the bookkeeper get what they have always wanted: an uncomplicated life of bourgeois bliss.

Just as the uncle and his nephew fail to grasp the true essence of art because they approach it in terms of convenient pre-packaged categories, so too Herr Roos, Christina, and the accountant betray the notion of Romantic love by attempting to construct a relationship that fits in with the prevailing values of their bourgeois world. The fact that both groups are unambiguously aligned with the philistines can be explained by their inability to regard any sphere of human activity as an end in itself and their reluctance to empathize with anything or anybody that threatens to disrupt the order and simplicity of their world. The reader may smile at these bourgeois clowns, but should not lose sight of the fact that their ignorance and philistinism cause Traugott considerable suffering.

In the attempt to escape his uncomfortable predicament, Traugott repeatedly seeks refuge in the world of art, and it is there that he discovers love not once, but twice: first, in the person of Felizitas, and then, in the person of Dorina. But before he can arrive at true personal fulfillment, he has to undergo a long and painful process of self-discovery because his first feelings of love cause him considerable problems. As is so often the case in a Hoffmann novella, the portrait of a female figure prompts the male artist to equate the real woman depicted in the painting with the Ideal itself.[10] What is distinctive about this particular novella is its undercurrent

of homo-eroticism. Already thrown into turmoil by the image of the young man "der in seiner Lockenfülle und zierlich bunter Tracht beinahe weiblich anzusehen war" (*SW* III, 146), Traugott feels he has been struck by lightning when the young man in question stands before him: "dieser war [. . .] der zarte wunderschöne Jüngling und lächelte ihn an wie mit unbeschreiblicher Liebe" (146). When we are told how this "young man" looked at Traugott "wie bittend, mit Tränen im Auge" (154), casting his eyes downward in embarrassment as he does so, the reader can be in little doubt that this "young man" is in fact a young girl—even though Traugott, naïve and innocent as he is, appears to be incapable of recognizing this. Even when he/she leads him into a neighboring room and he gazes at a painting in which "eine wunderliebliche Jungfrau in altdeutscher Tracht, aber ganz das Gesicht des Jünglings" (158) is portrayed whose "dunkle Augen voll Sehnsucht auf Traugott herabblickten" (158), and whose "süße Lippen halb geöffnet liebliche Worte zu flüstern schienen" (158), Traugott still does not suspect anything, but accepts the "youth's" explanation that this is a portrait of his unhappy sister Felizitas and reflects that he would have liked to have embraced the "boy" "als sei er die geliebte Felizitas" (160).

Traugott falls prey to the illusion that the girl in the picture represents the ideal for which he strives and is the very embodiment of his artistic and love-crazed yearning: "Ach sie ist es ja, die Geliebte meiner Seele, die ich so lange im Herzen trug, die ich nur in Ahnungen erkannte!—wo—wo ist sie!" (*SW* III, 158). Although the "young man" tells Traugott that his "sister" is gone and that he will never see her again, after months of deepest longing, he does in fact succeed in catching a glimpse of her when he turns up unexpectedly at the house of the Old Painter, Berklinger: "Sie war es, sie selbst!—'Felizitas!' schrie Traugott voll Entzücken auf, niederstürzen wollte er vor dem geliebten Himmelsbilde" (160).[11] Of course, there is no time for explanations; a knife-wielding Berklinger throws Traugott out of the house, and by the following day, the artist and his "son" have left the house and disappeared without trace. Traugott never pauses to consider whether this woman with whom he is so in love actually loves him! Confident that she does love him, he throws himself down on his bed and groans: "'Du liebst mich, ach, ich weiß es ja!—In dem Schmerz, der so tötend meine Brust durchbohrt, fühle ich es, daß du mich liebst'" (160).

Here the way in which Traugott, the male artist (and lover), projects his idealized vision onto a particular woman and simply assumes that she cannot but return his feelings of love and admiration proves to be particularly problematic. For by putting himself in thrall to her apparent perfection, he raises her to a metaphorical level, which in turn robs her of her personality. What seems at first sight to be a manifestation of the divine is in fact nothing more than a woman stripped of everything that makes her a unique individual in her own right.[12] That is to say, the male artist is concerned not with a real woman, but rather with the possibility of embodying his artistic striving in objective form.[13]

Inevitably, Traugott's idealized image of Felizitas collapses, though through the use of irony, Hoffmann presents this traumatic event in a manner that avoids tragedy. After considerable anguish, Traugott succeeds in finding Felizitas once again, although by searching for her, he risks jeopardizing his love for a real woman— Dorina—in Italy. But just as the "young boy" ceases to be, once "transformed" into Felizitas, so too Felizitas has ceased to be, as it were, in her new capacity as the wife of Hofrat Mathesius—"Frau Kriminalrätin" (*SW* III, 168)—and prolific producer of children; as we are told, "sie hat diverse Kinder in Kurs gesetzt" (168) There are obvious parallels with Christine and Felizitas: like Christine, Felizitas simply exchanges one fiancé (Brandstetter) for another (Mathesius), embarking on an existence of pure bourgeois domesticity. Both Christine and Felizitas end up with an utterly utilitarian outlook on life that excludes any continuing involvement with art. With Christine this is not surprising as she is the daughter of a merchant and businessman, but Felizitas is the daughter of an artist and herself interested in painting and drawing, thus her transformation is all the more shocking. Both are referred to as "Mamsell" by the local citizens; again Hoffmann's use of irony prevents Felizitas's transformation into the Frau Kriminalrätin from being regarded in a tragic light. Thus the story ends on a happy note. Although Traugott's idealized image of Felizitas is indeed shattered, this is a necessary precondition if he is to free himself from illusion and develop as an individual.

Felizitas is not the only female who attracts Traugott's interest: Dorina too exercises a profound influence on him. Needless to say, when they first meet, Traugott hopes and believes that the woman before him is Felizitas: "'Sie ist es!' rief Traugott" (*SW* III, 165). However, he soon realizes this mistake, even though Dorina does bear a remarkable resemblance to his ideal Felizitas: "Sie hatte die Züge der Felizitas, sie war es aber nicht" (165). And although he is bitterly disappointed for a few moments: "Wie mit tausend Dolchen durchbohrte die bittre Täuschung des armen Traugotts wunde Brust" (165), he recognizes that "außer Felizitas kein Mädchen so ihn im Innersten aufgeregt hatte als Dorina" (165). It is not long before a close relationship develops between the two of them: "Dorina [. . .] ließ deutlich ihre Neigung zu dem jungen deutschen Maler merken. Traugott erwiderte das herzlich" (165). Unaware of how used he has become to seeing her on a regular basis, he is quite vexed when her father insists that if there is to be no prospect of marriage, then for the sake of his daughter's reputation, he will not permit the two to have any further contact.

Traugott's heart is torn in two, and he is unable to choose between the fantasy figure, with whom he believes himself to be in love, and the real and wholly admirable Dorina: "Felizitas stand ihm wieder lebhaft vor Augen, und doch war es ihm, als könne er von Dorina nicht lassen" (*SW* III, 166). Although he already senses that his quest for Felizitas will be in vain, he finds it impossible to shake off her image: "Felizitas stellte sich ihm dar als ein geistig Bild, das er nie verlieren, nie gewinnen könne" (166). At the same time, he cherishes a vision of Dorina as "sein liebes Weib," a vision that fills him with both "süße Schauer" (166) and guilt at the thought of this act of "Verrat an seiner ersten Liebe" (166). He seeks a way out of this impasse by taking flight, and for the second time, he is run out of town by a furious father. When he walks out on Christina to pursue Felizitas, he turns his back on the mundane reality of Herr Roos's household in his quest for the Ideal; when he abandons Dorina, he flees from reality and from the real love of a real woman, which, when contrasted with his metaphysical notion of love, strikes him as profane.

He maintains that he must be true to his "first love," Felizitas, but she is in fact no more his "first love" than Christina was. He never felt any genuine love for Christina, but merely believed that he must conform to the expectations of bourgeois society. In Felizitas's case, he never acknowledged her as an individual in her own right, but saw her only as an allegorical embodiment of love and art; in short, he was not in love with her, but with his own idealized notion of love itself. Up to this point Traugott has never loved a woman for her own qualities, and when he tears himself away from Dorina, he is not aware of how genuinely in love with her he is: "Der Abschied von Dorina zerriß ihm das Herz, aber er wand sich gewaltsam los aus den süßen Banden" (*SW* III, 166). Only when he can free himself from his vision of Felizitas does he recognize that he has awoken "aus einem Traum" (169) and that he must hurry back to Dorina, his true love. But it appears that Dorina has been informed about the existence of Felizitas and her influence on Traugott: "Matuszewski erklärte in wenigen Worten dem Mädchen alles" (165). She recognizes that she must give her beloved free rein, so that having overcome his illusory feelings for Felizitas, he can devote himself to her and her alone: "Sie [Dorina] erwartet Dich stündlich, denn fest steht es in ihrer Seele, daß Du sie nimmer lassen könntest" (169).

THE ARTISTS

Master Berklinger and the "young boy" remain mysterious figures throughout the novella. Traugott first notices them in a painting in the Artushof, where he is working on Herr Roos's business affairs; when his gaze comes to rest on the two figures, he is suddenly filled with a feeling of "seltsamer unbegreiflicher Wehmut" (*SW* III, 146). The "wundersame Jüngling" awakens "süße Ahnungen" in him—he turns out, of course, to be both a girl and the embodiment of his Ideal—but the old man, "ein ernster beinahe düsterer Mann mit schwarzem krausen Barte"—fills him with an "inneren Schauer" (146). Although Traugott and the reader eventually discover the true nature of the "young boy," the Old Painter remains shrouded in mystery to the end of the story. Like a character in a Gothic Novel, he appears as a relic from a past age. He claims to be the German painter Godofredus Berklinger (cf. 155)—a man who died more than 200 years before the painting in the Artushof was completed—which would mean that he had been born sometime in the seventeenth century. The paintings he shows Traugott are indeed painted in the style of the best known Dutch artists (cf. *SW* III, 158), all of which would fit with the alleged chronology of his life were it not for the fact that the old man claims to have known King Arthur! The bookkeeper says that he reminds him of a figure in a painting in St. Johannis church that dates back to about fourteen hundred (cf. 155), which again would fit in with the kind of clothing—the "altteutsche Tracht"—that the old man and the "young boy" wear. We never learn the truth about the old man's real origins; Traugott believes that he must be "von einem besonderen Wahnwitz befangen" (156), but the matter is never explained.

It is equally impossible for Traugott and the reader to get to the bottom of the curious relationship between the Old Painter and his "young boy" or, more correctly, his daughter. We are bound to ask why Berklinger should go to such lengths to ensure that no one comes near her, or why he disappears with her once Traugott has confessed his feelings of love. Is it simply paternal jealousy? His reaction when he discovers her with Traugott suggests that his own existence is in some way dependent upon her: "Verruchter!—Bösewicht ohnegleichen! [. . .] das war deine Liebe zur Kunst?—Morden willst du mich!" (*SW* III, 160).[14] And of course he does die when Felizitas agrees to marry; it has been foretold that "sowie seine Tochter einen Liebesbund schlösse, er eines schmählichen Todes sterben müsse" (163), but we never learn anything more about this prophecy. In his dying moments, the mysterious and gloomy artist who has devoted himself almost exclusively to art and painting is presented in a completely different and ironic light. Initially he had struck Traugott as a terrifying and sublime figure, but in his death he is undignified and almost comic: "er fiel mit einem dumpfen Schrei nieder und war mausetot [*sic*]. Er soll sehr häßlich ausgesehen haben—ganz blau und blutig, weil ihm, man weiß nicht wie, eine Pulsader gesprungen war" (168). By the end of the novella, two transformations have taken place: Felizitas, the beautiful and artistic virgin, who needs to be rescued from the clutches of her father, ends up as a fecund bourgeois wife, and the Old Painter, once so powerful, talented, and mysterious, simply shrivels away once his daughter breaks free of him. Thus the couple who enter the story with such mystery, leave it as farcical figures.

We should not forget, however, that it was Berklinger who influenced Traugott's development as an artist and who prompted him to cultivate this side of his personality. Felizitas may have been Traugott's muse, but it was the Old Painter who recognized his passion for art and gave him the courage to abandon the world of business and commerce for a life of personal fulfillment as an artist. When Traugott draws some figures, the old man walks up behind him and encourages him: "Gut—recht gut!—so lieb ich's, das kann was werden!" (*SW* III, 146). This leads Traugott, who never felt committed to a life of commerce, to give some serious thought to becoming a painter: "Kann ich denn nicht, statt meines unseligen Treibens, ein tüchtiger Maler werden?" (152). And when he shows his interest in the Berklinger's pictures, the latter invites him to his house, saying:

> Ihr seid in der Tat etwas verwegen, daß Ihr schon jetzt darnach trachtet, in das innerste Heiligtum einzutreten, ehe noch Eure Lehrjahre begonnen haben. [. . .] Mag es sein! Ist Euer Blick noch zu blöde zum Schauen, so werdet Ihr wenigsten ahnen!
>
> (*SW* III, 156)

He recognizes Traugott's potential and is prepared to help him, explaining that: "Meine Bilder sollen nicht *bedeuten*, sie sollen *sein*" (156).[15] And although Traugott is taken aback by the ecstatic manner in which the old man interprets his pictures, he recognizes the inner passion of an artist wholly committed to his work and says: "Ich spüre großen unwiderstehlichen Trieb zur Kunst in mir, und bitte Euch gar dringend [. . .] mich zu Eurem fleißigen Schüler anzunehmen" (*SW* III, 158-59). Berklinger takes him on, with the result that Traugott "in der Kunst gar große Fortschritte machte" (159): a vital contribution to the young man's artistic development and one that should not be overlooked.

The other artist figures in the novella belong to the group in Rome, which Traugott comes across when searching for Felizitas. For the first time in his life he feels accepted by a group of like-minded people, so much so in fact that he stays longer in Rome than he had originally planned:

> In Rom nahmen ihn die deutschen Künstler auf in den Kreis ihrer Studien, und so geschah es, daß er dort länger verweilte, als es die Sehnsucht, Felizitas wiederzufinden [. . .] zuzulassen schien.
>
> (*SW* III, 164)

There Matuszewski—another figure who has been converted to the world of art and painting—takes an interest in Traugott's case and turns out to be a true friend.

He tells him that the girl whose portrait he continually paints has been seen in Rome, and he initiates some inquiries that lead to Traugott and Dorina, who of course closely resembles Felizitas, making each other's acquaintance. Although it is not long before Traugott takes off once again in search of his fantasy image of Felizitas, Matuszewski is intelligent enough to realize that it is Dorina who is destined to be Traugott's eventual partner, and he tries to help the two of them find happiness by reminding Traugott of her—"Dorina ist hübscher und anmutiger als je, nur bleich vor Sehnsucht nach Dir [. . .] wann sehen wir Dich wieder?" (*SW* III, 169)—all of which helps bring about the happy ending.

In the end Traugott returns both to the land of art and to his beloved Dorina, but he does so via a long and circuitous route. When we first meet him, he is a melancholy young man, who would rather paint and draw than dedicate himself to his career in commerce, but who accepts his fate even if it causes him "Not und Verdruß" (*SW* III, 146). On more than one occasion, the narrator refers to him using the epithet "gedankenlos" (146, 147), and his insecurity and lack of self-confidence are emphasized when the narrator refer to his "Bestürzung" and "Beschämung." Despite these failings, the introverted young man grows in confidence as the novella unfolds and develops a great passion for art: "da stand es ganz fest in Traugotts Seele, daß er etwas viel Herrlicheres gemacht habe als einen Avisobrief" (148). It soon becomes clear that his sometimes wayward behavior is due to the fact that he feels ill at ease in the world of business and finance, a world with which his fiancée is inextricably bound up, and is convinced that no one really understands him. When Herr Roos looks at Traugott's drawing and makes a snide comment about the bleak prospects for the majority of artists, Traugott rebels for the first time and defends what he is doing: "Gebärden sich Ew. Edlen nur nicht so absonderlich, sonst schreib ich Ihnen in meinem ganzen Leben keinen Avisobrief mehr" (148). However, at this stage of his development, he does not persist with this first attempt to take on the world of bourgeois philistinism.

Only when he comes up against Herr Roos's friends—the uncle and the nephew who pretend to be connoisseurs of art but who are in fact pseudo-intellectual philistines—does he feel moved to mount a more sustained defense, and, in so doing, discovers that "die Schüchternheit, die sonst seine Zunge band [. . .] war verschwunden" (*SW* III, 150). He defends art as an activity practiced purely for its own sake and attacks their view that the function of artistic works is to provide human beings with a sense of "Behaglichkeit" (151). Although he finds the views of both "unbeschreiblich albern" (151), they do force him to think more deeply about the nature of art and its purpose. Their superficial conversation prompts Traugott to reflect upon the role of art in his own life, and he embarks on a process of critical reflection that in the first instance prompts him to exclaim: "Was führe ich doch [. . .] für ein erbärmlich schlechtes Leben! [. . .] Wozu alles Sinnen, alles Schreiben? [. . .] Damit sich nur die Goldstücke im Kasten mehren" (152). This bleak appraisal of his own life contrasts unfavorably with his vision of a fulfilled life as an artist, a vision which is, however, both naïve and illusory:

> Wie mag doch solch ein Künstler und Bildner fröhlich hinausziehn und hoch emporgerichteten Hauptes all die erquicklichen Frühlingsstrahlen einatmen, die die innere Welt voll herrlicher Bilder entzündet, so daß sie aufgeht im regen lustigen Leben.
>
> (*SW* III, 152)

In his frustration with his unsatisfying life, Traugott imagines the life of an artist to be all happiness and success. In this he is sadly mistaken for as his own experiences and those of the artists he meets will confirm, this is anything but the case. Indeed, the higher the artist aims, the more crushing his disappointment is likely to be. In his youthful naïveté, Traugott fails to take account of that aspect of artistic creativity that is bound up with danger and disappointment, and he has little or no idea of the destructive power of art. Although he is, to begin with, overcome by the "tiefsten wehmütigsten Sehnsucht" (*SW* III, 153), feelings which strike him as sweet and enticing, it is only a matter of time before these change into agony and pain.

It is with this in mind that the narrator addresses the reader directly, warning him of the pitfalls of the Romantic artist's desire to capture the Ideal:

> Glaubst du nicht, lieber Leser! daß das was aus dem höheren Reich der Liebe in unsre Brust hinabgekommen, sich uns zuerst offenbaren müsse in hoffnungslosem Schmerz?—Das sind die Zweifel, die in des Künstlers Gemüt stürmen.—Er schaut das Ideal und fühlt die Ohnmacht es zu erfassen, es entflieht, meint er, unwiederbringlich.—Aber dann kommt ihm wieder ein göttlicher Mut, er kämpft und ringt, und die Verzweiflung löst sich auf in süßes Sehnen, das ihn stärkt und antreibt, immer nachzustreben der Geliebten, die er immer näher und näher erblickt, ohne sie jemals zu erreichen.
>
> (*SW* III, 153)

At this point, we are reminded of the eternal cycle of blazing hope followed by unremitting despair that is the lot of all who dedicate themselves to art, but we are also alerted to the close connection between love and art, whereby the beloved comes to stand for the Ideal that the artist so longs to capture in his work. It is, of course, only a small step from here to the cult of the earthly muse and to the idealization of femininity, and it is not long before Traugott takes this step. Almost immediately he is overcome by melancholy and hopelessness when he realizes that his fiancée, Christina, is the woman apparently destined to satisfy his artistic yearning, and he views his prospective marriage to her as "der traurige Abschied von allen schönen Hoffnungen und Träumen" (*SW* III, 154).

This is Traugott's frame of mind when he again meets Berklinger, who addresses him as an artist, rekindles his enthusiasm for a "herrliche, grünende, blühende Künstlerzeit" (*SW* III, 156), shows him his own paintings, and in a state of ecstatic rapture, interprets them for him. The naïve Traugott fails to see that there is something almost tragic about the way the Old Painter implores his pictures to reveal their secret to him: "wirf ab den Isisschleier [. . .] Ich will dein Herz schauen—das ist der Stein der Weisen, vor dem sich das Geheimnis offenbart [. . .] tritt heraus!—tritt her!" (157). In his exalted condition, the Old Painter attempts to discover the essential nature of art and longing, "the artist's stone," but this proves to be beyond him, and he collapses "wie vom Blitze getroffen" (157). Traugott does not recognize this as the climax of a life that has been devoted to art for many years and that has always striven to get ever closer to the Ideal, but believes that the old man has simply suffered an attack of madness. As a result of his exposure to the pictures and the ecstatic performance of the Old Painter, he rediscovers his enthusiasm for art. This prompts him to ask the "young man" to show him some other paintings and explain them to him, all of which results in his developing a "tiefer Sinn" and being filled with an "ergreifende Lebenskraft" (158).

In this heightened mood, Traugott catches sight of the portrait of Felizitas. Suddenly the contemplation of this hybrid object that is part art, part woman, renders him conscious of his own desire to capture the Ideal. We should, of course, remember that it is not a real woman, but an image of a woman that prompts him to channel his creative energy towards a concrete—although as yet imprecisely defined—goal; as the "young man" explains, his sister is dead, and Traugott will never set eyes upon her: "Traugott hätte nun in der Kunst ein wahres helles Sonnenleben geführt, wenn die glühende Liebe zur schönen Felizitas, die er oft in wunderbaren Träumen sah, ihm nicht die Brust zerrissen hätte" (*SW* III, 159). But as chance would have it, a little later Traugott does see her, and it is at this point that the real, living woman is subjected to a process of artistic idealization. That is to say, his concept of the Ideal— the idealized image of Felizitas he cherishes in his imagination—becomes detached from the painted image and is now projected on a real woman in the real world.

However, the Old Painter suddenly departs with his daughter, and Traugott cannot discover their whereabouts; so distraught that he is on the point of abandoning his artistic calling, a reaction that underlines once again the intimate connection between art and love, since in his eyes being abandoned by Felizitas is tantamount to being abandoned by art:

> Ach [. . .] bittre, bittre Täuschung war mein Beruf zur Kunst; Felizitas war das Trugbild, das mich verlockte zu glauben an dem, das nirgends lebte als in der wahnwitzigen Fantasie eines Fieberkranken.
>
> (*SW* III, 162)

Although Traugott is correct, at least as far as Felizitas is concerned, he is wrong to conclude that just because he no longer has his idealized image of her before him his artistic striving has been rendered meaningless. Traugott returns to work for Herr Roos—a move that flies in the face of his true calling—and for a while seems to have settled his differences with Christina. It is only a matter of time, however, before he learns that Berklinger and his daughter are to be found in Sorrento.[16] With rekindled hopes, he sets off once more in search of Felizitas: "Ihr nach in das Land der Kunst" (*SW* III, 163). His idealized image of her returns immediately and, with it, his enthusiasm for art. But there is an obvious ambiguity in his ecstatic exclamation; the expression "Land der Kunst" does not simply refer to Italy, but at the same time tells the reader that Traugott's ultimate destination is the metaphysical realm of the Ideal.

It is not long before Traugott's initial sense of despair at the apparent impossibility of ever capturing the Ideal in art manifests itself as a state of wistful, but positive, longing. Once in Rome, Traugott stays there longer than originally planned and does not rush off at the first possible opportunity to Sorrento. The nature of his artistic striving has changed: "milder war diese Sehnsucht geworden, sie gestaltete sich im Innern, wie ein wonnevoller Traum, dessen duftiger Schimmer sein ganzes Leben umfloß" (*SW* III, 164). As the narrator has already hinted, the pendulum of artistic striving oscillates between the poles of "wehmütiger Schmerz" and "selige Ahnung." This wistful longing is an unending source of artistic inspiration, since "jede weibliche Gestalt, die er mit wackrer Kunstfertigkeit zu schaffen wußte, hatte die Züge der holden Felizitas" (164). Even after he has abandoned Dorina to go off in search of Felizitas, it is his quest for the Ideal, his recognition that what really matters is not reaching the goal but the striving towards it that inspires his art once again. His enquiries in Naples and Sorrento may be fruitless, but he retains his positive state of mind, and his art benefits as a result; as we are told, Traugott remains "endlich in Neapel, und so wie er wieder die Kunst fleißiger trieb, ging auch die Sehnsucht nach Felizitas linder und milder in seiner Brust auf" (*SW* III, 166). He regrets leaving Dorina, but it is always the idealized—though distant— Felizitas who inspires him to create: "Beim Malen dachte er niemals an Dorina, wohl aber an Felizitas, die blieb stets sein Ideal" (167). Here the text underlines two points: it is important for the artist to distance himself to a degree from the Ideal, and it is the striving for the Ideal—rather than the realization of the Ideal—that is the driving force behind artistic creativity. Thus Traugott is an exemplar of the Romantics' emphasis on "Werden" rather than "Sein."

Herr Roos's death calls Traugott back to Danzig and the Artushof, and it is here, where his adventure started, that he discovers the true significance of Felizitas and Sorrento. In a matter of seconds the Ideal with which he had been preoccupied for years is not only destroyed but rendered comic and grotesque—and he reacts accordingly: "Dieser Ausgang seines Abenteuers erfüllte ihn mit Grauen und Entsetzen" (*SW* III, 168). He runs to the Karlsberg and sees for himself what has become of his Ideal Felizitas, now the wife of Kriminalrat Mathesius: "Er schaute hinein in den Sorrent, die Tränen stürzten ihm aus den Augen" (168). Both horrified and filled with despair, Traugott can, nevertheless, recognize that the demise of his Ideal can be blamed neither on Felizitas nor on a cruel twist of fate.[17] He recognizes that what has happened is a direct consequence of his tendency to cherish an illusion: "vermessen wähnte ich das, was vom alten Meister geschaffen, wunderbar zum Leben erwacht, auf mich zutrat, sei meinesgleichen und ich könne es herabziehen in die klägliche Existenz des irdischen Augenblicks" (169). He now sees that by its very nature, the Ideal cannot exist outside the transcendent metaphysical world wherein its origins lie. As Friedrich Schlegel notes: "Ironie ist klares Bewußtsein der ewigen Agilität, des unendlich vollen Chaos."[18] Traugott recognizes that the artist's longing is never static but always dynamic, and that art is not a fixed state but rather a process of development; it is a process of gradual approximation to an Ideal, but one which can never actually be completed.

This newfound insight into the nature of artistic creativity transforms Traugott from a naïve, wistful young man into a mature, wise artist. Far from making him distraught, it prompts him to recognize the endless possibilities that have now opened up before him. Felizitas—"Frau Kriminalrätin"—may no longer be the embodiment of his ideal, but was she ever such, and does this matter any more? Although he must not abandon his quest for the Ideal, he must accept that the Ideal can only exists in the realm of ideas and not in this world. He does not abandon Felizitas as his ideal, but comes to see that she has a purely symbolic function: "Nein, nein, Felizitas, nie habe ich dich verloren, du bleibst mein immerdar, denn du selbst bist ja die schaffende Kunst, die in mir lebt" (*SW* III, 169). That is to say, Felizitas symbolizes the very essence of art itself; she remains the Ideal that every artist must pursue. This unfulfilled striving can cause much pain and tragedy, but

without it the artist lacks the driving force that is essential if he is to create a work of art: "Glaubt er [der Mensch] aber sein Ziel erreicht zu haben, dann erlahmt auch die Schöpfungskraft."[19] Traugott shows that he too recognizes that there is a positive side to this endless process of artistic striving when he remarks, "was klagt das Kind über heillosen Schmerz, das in die Flamme greift, statt sich zu laben an Licht und Wärme" (*SW* III, 168-69). Artists, and human beings generally, are trapped within the constraints of their temporal existence and must expire ("verbrennen") when they attempt to go beyond the limits of that existence. Yet as tragic as this insight may seem, it does not mean that it is impossible to get closer to the Ideal ("Flamme"). Although it is a dangerous undertaking, it is one that is beneficial for humanity and that spreads "Licht und Wärme." In short, the fact that it is not possible ever to capture the Ideal perfectly in this world does not mean—as Traugott now recognizes—that the artist's quest is pointless.

Accordingly, when Traugott returns to Dorina, he does not compromise his artistic integrity; by not idealizing her, he allows her to develop a personality of her own, with the result that she can become a suitable, equal partner for him: "morgen reise ich nach Rom, wo mich eine geliebte Braut sehnlichst erwartet" (*SW* III, 168-69). This "geliebte Braut" will be an altogether different kind of wife from Christina and Felizitas, both of whom, once married, turn out to be bourgeois housewives. We may assume that Traugott continues as an artist since he never suggests that he will abandon his calling. He is a figure whose journey towards self-development ends in fulfillment. Never losing sight of the Romantic Ideal, he recognizes that the pursuit of the unattainable Ideal—and a gradual approximation to it—lie at the very heart the artistic process. By the end of the novella, we see Traugott as an artist who has triumphed and who has discovered his own way: "Verbindet die Extreme, so habt ihr die wahre Mitte."[20] But far from being static, this middle path, as Traugott has grasped, is dynamic and ever changing, and will provide him with the impetus vital to his future life as an artist and lover.

Notes

1. Joachim Rosteutscher, *Das ästhetische Idol im Werke von Winckelmann, Novalis, Hoffmann, Goethe, George und Rilke* (Bern: Francke, 1956), 136.

2. Although the novella "Der Artushof" is not referred to explicitly, the author claims that whenever Hoffman discusses "das Unerreichbare" and "das Unerfüllbare," what is at stake is always his relationship with Julia. See Fritz J. Raddatz, *Männerängste in der Literatur: Frau oder Kunst* (Hamburg: Carlsen, 1993), 109-11.

3. Marianne Kesting, "Das lebendige Portrait," *Athenäum* 3 (1993): 27-54 (54).

4. Bernard Dieterle, *Erzählte Bilder: Zum narrativen Umgang mit Gemälden* (Marburg: Hitzeroth, 1988), 62.

5. Gunther Pix, "Der Variationskünstler E. T. A. Hoffmann und seine Erzählung 'Der Artushof,'" *MHG* [*Mitteilungen der E. T. A. Hoffmann-Gesellschaft*] 35 (1989): 4-20.

6. See Claudia Liebrand, *Aporie des Kunstmythos: Die Texte E. T. A. Hoffmanns* (Freiburg: Rombach, 1996); Lothar Pikulik, *E. T. A. Hoffmann als Erzähler: Ein Kommentar zu den "Serapions-brüdern"* (Göttingen: Vandenhoeck & Ruprecht, 1987); and Peter von Matt, "Die gemalte Geliebte: Zur Problematik von Einbildungskraft und Selbsterkenntnis im erzählenden Werk E. T. A. Hoffmanns," *GRM* [*Germanisch-Romanische Monatsschrift*] 21 (1971): 395-412.

7. Hoffmann's letters show that he was very familiar with the Artushof. Commenting on the story, he notes that "Das Ganze dreht sich um ein wunderbares Bild im Artushoff." See *Briefwechsel II,* 45 (12 March 1815).

8. See Hans-Georg Werner, "Hoffmanns Phantasie-Italien," [*E. T. A.*] *Hoffmann Jb* [*Jahrbuch*] 1 (1992/93): 133-42 (142).

9. There is a parallel here with the figure of Clara in "Der Sandmann," who, we are told, "drohe das Haus den Einsturz, noch vor schneller Flucht ganz geschwind einen falschen Kniff in der Fenstergardine glattstreichen würde" (*SW* I, 339). However, it is clear that Clara is considerably more intelligent than Christina.

10. Cf. the picture of Rosalie in *Die Elixiere des Teufels* and the unfinished picture that Berthold completes shortly before his death in "Die Jesuiterkirche in G."

11. The name of the painter, Berklinger, in Hoffmann's story calls to mind another artist figure, the composer Berglinger in Wackenroder and Tieck's *Herzensergießungen eines kunstliebenden Klosterbruders.*

12. Hoffmann repeatedly reminds the reader of the catastrophic consequences of such a commodification or categorization of a feminine ideal. In "Rat Krespel" the Councilor's disappointment drives him to throw his wife out of the window, then leave her altogether, whilst in "Die Jesuiterkirche in G.," Berthold's wife, Angiola T., disappears in mysterious circumstances, and we are led to believe that she may even have been murdered. Both men have shaped these women into an idealized image in accordance with their personal wishes and have to pay the price—or rather the women pay the price for their "failure" to live up to the unrealistic ideals of their husbands.

13. Commenting on the scene in which Traugott encounters Felizitas for the first time, Peter von Matt notes: "Die Reduktion der entscheidenen Begegnung auf einen einzigen jähen Moment ist nicht zuletzt deshalb von Bedeutung, weil sie zeigt, wie sehr es hier um einen reinen Erkenntnisakt des Helden und nicht um personales Zusammenfinden geht." See Peter von Matt, "Die gemalte Geliebte," 399.

14. Just as Rat Krespel seeks to prolong his daughter's life by shielding her from any contact with the outside world, so too the life of the Old Painter seems to depend on his daughter not becoming involved with any male admirer.

15. The Old Painter's attempt to go beyond the search for meaning in his paintings shows that he is not content to embrace the Romantics' theories of allegory and symbol, but that he is striving instead for a new concept of art in which art simply is, that is to say, a form of art in which signifier and signified coincide, i.e. coincidence of Ideal and real.

16. Ironically, it turns out that the place that they have gone to is the Brandstetter's country cottage at the foot of the Karlsberg—a secret location that is apparently known to all and sundry, just as everyone knows that the mysterious "young boy" is in fact Felizitas in disguise. In his naïveté, Traugott failed to notice any of this, a fact that makes his desperate efforts to discover Felizitas's whereabouts all the more ridiculous.

17. In this respect he is quite different from Berthold in "Die Jesuiterkirche in G.," since the latter blames his ideal—his wife, Angiola T.—for having disappointed him when, after their marriage, she turns out to be nothing more than a real woman, an obvious truth that Berthold has deliberately ignored.

18. *KA* II, 263, §69.

19. See Pix, 17.

20. *KA* II, 263, §74.

Abbreviations

In the text, the following abbreviations for primary sources are used. In each case the abbreviation is followed by the volume number, page number and line/paragraph number (when appropriate):

SW Hoffmann, E. T. A. *Sämtliche Werke.* Ed. Walter Müller-Seidel. 5 vols. Munich: Winkler, 1960-65.

All quotations are taken from the edition published by the Wissenschaftliche Buchgesellschaft, Darmstadt, which is identical to that cited above. In accordance with current practice I have adopted the following system when referring to individual volumes in the above edition:

—*Fantasie- und Nachtstücke* [= I]

—*Die Elixiere des Teufels. Lebensansichten des Kater-Murr* [= II]

—*Die Serapionsbrüder* [= III]

—*Späte Werke* [= IV]

—*Schriften zur Musik* [= Va]

—*Nachlese* [= Vb]

Briefwechsel E. T. A. Hoffmanns Briefwechsel. Ed. Friedrich Schnapp. 3 vols. Munich: Winkler, 1967.

KA Schlegel, Friedrich. *Kritische Ausgabe.* Ed. Ernst Behler with the collaboration of Jean-Jaques Anstett, Hans Eichner, et al. 35 vols. Paderborn: Schöningh, 1958.

William Kumbier (essay date summer 2004)

SOURCE: Kumbier, William. "Composed Composers: Subjectivity in E. T. A. Hoffmann's 'Rat Krespel.'" *Studies in Romanticism* 43, no. 2 (summer 2004): 231-55.

[*In the following essay, Kumbier considers the relationship between music and desire in Hoffmann's "Rat Krespel."*]

1

A romantic *idée fixe* that E. T. A. Hoffmann affirms repeatedly throughout his astute and often forward-looking music criticism is that music characteristically opens avenues into the sublime. This is especially the case when the music in question is that of an accomplished composer, one capable of commanding all the musical ideas, elements and forces at his disposal, say, the Mozart of *Don Giovanni* or the Beethoven of the Opus 70 trios and, crucially, the Fifth Symphony. Witness the fourth article of the first part of Hoffmann's famous collection of music related writings known as **"Kreisleriana," "Beethoven's Instrumental Music,"** which adapts Hoffmann's landmark review of Beethoven's Fifth.[1] There Hoffmann develops his claim that "Beethoven's music sets in motion the machinery of awe, of fear, of terror, of pain, and awakens that infinite yearning which is the essence of romanticism."[2] Hoffmann's diction—"awe," "fear," "terror," "pain," "infinite yearning"—immediately thrusts Beethoven's

music into the topos of the sublime, a place that would have been commonplace to his early nineteenth-century readers.[3] Hoffmann goes on to argue that while in outward appearance Beethoven's music may seem uncontrolled, unorganized, however abounding in wealth of ideas and "vigour of imagination" [*reichen, lebendigen Phantasie*], that is only because one has not grasped the "inner coherence" [*der innere tiefe Zusammenhang*] that characterizes every Beethoven composition. For Hoffmann, Beethoven is preeminently the composer who displays the touchstone quality of *Besonnenheit*, which Charlton [in **"Beethoven's Instrumental Music"**] translates as "rational awareness" but which, of course, can also mean assurance or, with richer implications, self-possession. In his compositions, Beethoven separates his "controlling self" [*sein Ich*] from the "inner realm of sounds" and rules it in "absolute authority" (98). Beethoven's mastery induces in the hearer a state that Hoffmann describes, again, in terms customarily associated with the musical sublime: ". . . Beethoven's instrumental music unveils before us the realm of the mighty and the immeasurable. Here shining rays of light shoot through the darkness of night and we become aware of giant shadows swaying back and forth, moving ever closer around us and destroying us but not the pain of infinite yearning, in which every desire, leaping up in sounds of exultation, sinks back and disappears. Only in this pain, in which love, hope, and joy are consumed without being destroyed, which threatens to burst our hearts with a full-chorused cry of all the passions, do we live on as ecstatic visionaries" (97).

Especially crucial here are the notions that music can comprehend and even consume the listening subject and subjective emotions without destroying them—it can annihilate the subject but not the pain of infinite desire—and that the music transforms the listener into an "ecstatic" visionary, by definition one who sees himself or herself as part of the vision. The articulation and activation of the musical score's texture animates a spirit-realm that seizes and absorbs the listener, subsuming the listener's subjectivity in its transcendent play: ". . . within this artful edifice there is a restless alternation of the most marvelous images, in which joy and pain, melancholy and ecstasy, appear beside and within each other. Strange shapes begin a merry dance, now converging into a single point of light, now flying apart like glittering sparks, now chasing each other in infinitely varied clusters. And in the midst of this spirit realm that has been revealed, the enraptured soul perceives an unknown language and understands all the most mysterious presentiments that hold it in thrall" (102). The phenomenological signals of the onset of the synaesthetic musical sublime—musical sounds spur dancing shapes, converging lights, flying sparks—echo those marking the advent of transcendent or supernatural experience for the protagonists in Hoffmann's tales (e.g., the watersnake fireworks of **"The Golden Pot,"**

Nathanael's "circle of fire" in **"The Sandman"**) and thus may not seem surprising. More remarkable is Hoffmann's further notion, a condition of music's realizing the character and effects he evokes here, namely, that the "true artist" who performs music like Beethoven's "disdains to let his own personality intervene in any way; all his endeavors are spent in quickening to vivid life, in a thousand shining colours, all the sublime effects and images the *composer's magical authority* enclosed within his work, so that they encircle us in bright rings of light, inflaming our imaginings, our innermost soul, and bear us speeding on the wing into the far-off spirit realm of music" (103; my emphasis). Tension, animation, passion and exhilaration all arise from the composition and in the listener, but they are all at the composer's—and in this case also the performing artist's—command.

Thus, easily visible through the scrim of Hoffmann's near mythic description of Beethoven's powers shines the spectre—again, familiar to readers of Hoffmann's tales—of the artist-as-sorcerer, magician, Mesmerist: Herr Drosselmeyer of **"Nutcracker and Mouse King,"** Archivist Lindhorst of **"The Golden Pot,"** or even Berklinger of **"The Artushof."** One implication, therefore, of the similarity of Hoffmann's hypostasized Beethoven and the later, masterful enchanter figures of the tales is that here the composer is imagined as invulnerable to the tensions, uncertainties, illusions and mediations of subjectivity: Hoffmann's analysis of the force of Beethoven's music acknowledges tension, but only as one element among others sounding in the music and arising within the listening subject; the composer himself comprehends it. If the place of the listener before the self-possessed compositions of Beethoven is that of the "ecstatic visionary," yearning to be caught up in the composer's musical vision yet only too well aware that he or she falls farther from that ideal even as he or she surrenders to it, as the music asserts its hold or "thrall," the composer's domain is fantasized as that of the transcendent demiurge. Moreover, just as the figure of Beethoven parallels that of the consummate, though sometimes also diabolic and always ambivalent masters of the tales, so the entranced but torn, enraptured but ruptured listening subject finds its counterparts in Hoffmann's familiar divided protagonists (e.g., Nathanael in **"The Sandman,"** Elis Fröbom in **"The Mines at Falun,"** or Anselmus in **"The Golden Pot"**), who always yearn for the transcendent, occasionally appear to realize it, but more often fall grotesquely far from it.

Hoffmann's **"Rat Krespel"** offers an intriguing variation on this characteristic opposition between the sorcerer-artist and the apprentice-subject. It is a tale with at least *two* subjects, double protagonists, both of them artists: the musician-narrator, Theodor, and his "subject," the eccentric Krespel, a councilor and amateur violinist. Unlike other tales by Hoffmann in which the distinction between artist and apprentice, master and novice subject seems more clear cut, **"Rat Krespel"** presents a complex narrative in which neither protagonist can be said exclusively to be the subject, whether "subject" is understood to imply being *either* firmly in control of or decisively subject to the forces activated in the representations the tale opens: the tale subtly negotiates a dialectic between subjectivity and forces that both express and mediate it. In other words, **"Rat Krespel"** presents the reader with a scenario that foregrounds the question of whether its artist-subjects will control or be controlled by those forces or, in other words, a situation in which artistic self-possession always risks *dispossession,* where the composer is always at risk of being composed as a figure in the story he is at pains to tell.

2

"Rat Krespel," though originally published in the *Frauentaschenbuch für das Jahr 1818* in the autumn of 1817, was later nested by Hoffmann as the second, untitled story in the first 1819 volume of *Die Serapions-Brüder,* where Hoffmann eventually was to publish many of his stories and miscellaneous writings in four volumes that appeared through 1821.[4] The framing device of this collection is a conversation, extended over several meetings, among four friends—Lothar, Theodor, Ottmar and Cyprian—who decide to share stories and who name their association after a character in the first story told (by Cyprian), the (arguably) mad hermit, Serapion. Theodor relates the untitled story usually known as **"Rat Krespel"** (but which has been variously titled in English as **"Councillor Krespel,"** **"Antonia's Song,"** or **"The Cremona Violin"**), he says, "to effect a smooth transition from insanity through spleen to completely healthy rationality." Theodor had argued that Ottmar had gone "too far" in his "distaste for every expression of feeling which takes any rather peculiar or unusual form."[5] Theodor wants, instead, to distinguish from the insane person those persons who are more properly labeled sensitive or susceptible: "The incongruity which the susceptible [*reizbare*] person feels between his inner self and the outer world [*des inner Gemüts mit dem aussern Leben*] drives him to exceptional grimaces, which calm faces, over whom pain has as little power as pleasure, can't grasp, and are only annoyed with."[6] Theodor then introduces his account of Krespel to elaborate this distinction.

Since point of view is always a determining issue in Hoffmann's tales, it is essential to point out that Krespel's story is told exclusively from Theodor's perspective; he narrates it but also involves himself as a participant in the events related. Theodor includes, as significant portions of his narration, anecdotes about Krespel offered to him by a Professor M. and an extended account from Krespel himself, whose uninterrupted narrative, as recounted by the narrator, makes up the last third of the tale and in fact closes with the tale's close. Though critics disagree as to the extent of the narrator's reliability, the narrator certainly is not impartial: his growing desire for Antonia and specifically his longing to hear her sing to a great extent motivate the tale's action and directly provoke Krespel's autobiographical account.[7] The narrator should be seen as a persona distinct from Theodor, even though Theodor is telling the story to the Serapion brothers, and, of course, from Hoffmann himself, though he unabashedly shares one of Hoffmann's names and some of Hoffmann's enthusiasms, especially for music. Before he begins the tale, in fact, Theodor warns his listeners that he is afraid he is going to have to talk a lot about music and that he therefore risks opening himself to the criticism that he himself had made in regard to the story of Serapion, namely, that he will fantastically embellish his subject and interject too much of himself. Critically, he insists this will not be the case. These qualifying remarks warrant at least provisional distinction between the subjects of his tale.

Nevertheless, throughout the range of modes and perspectives by which we receive Krespel's complicated story, in all registers of the tale, key questions persist: to what extent do the subjectivities articulated through the narrative's characters—notably Krespel, Antonia and the narrator—find free expression of their desire? To what extent does that expression, once actualized, turn on them and impair their freedom, subverting the subjectivity it was supposed to voice? How free are the characters to engage in the play that Hoffmann envisions as a possibility for both musical and narrative structurings without losing themselves in it, without themselves becoming subject to it? As the characters perform—singing, fiddling, reciting, composing—in what sense can they be seen, to echo Hegel on Shakespeare's characters, as "free artists of themselves" rather than merely as instruments or puppets? If the characters' subjectivity ultimately is constructed—or, in terms more appropriate to this tale and to Hoffmann generally, "composed"—to what extent are the subjects composers of their own subjectivity?

3

"Rat Krespel" revolves around the eccentric Krespel, a skilled lawyer and diplomat who is also an amateur musician and enthusiast for violins; or, more precisely, for collecting, constructing and dismantling violins. Mystery surrounds Krespel, especially regarding his relationship with Antonia, a young woman who resides in his house and whose singing voice is legendary among the townspeople, though only a few of them have actually heard her sing, and then only once; the narrator never has. As Gabriele Brandstetter points out, the mythic reputation of Antonia's song has spread only

through narrative accounts, through *Erzählung* rather than through song itself.[8] The narrator attempts to penetrate the circle of Krespel's household, getting to know him and Antonia, and grows infatuated with her voice as he dreams it to be, but is expelled from Krespel's house when his attempts to elicit Antonia's song begin to unnerve Krespel. The narrator then decides to leave H.

Two years later, the narrator happens to return, only to find that Antonia has died. He confronts and threatens Krespel, who responds with his own story, in which he reveals that Antonia was his daughter by a celebrated Italian singer, Angela. Krespel had been estranged from Angela since the time when, during one of his transports of violin playing, his violin bow had brushed inadvertently and rather roughly against the then-pregnant Angela, who responded by shattering the violin. He, in turn, hurled her out the window (which fortunately proved to have been only five feet off the ground). Years later, Angela died from a chill caught in the theater, on the night before Antonia's intended marriage to the composer, B., and Krespel became Antonia's guardian. When Krespel learned that an "organic defect" in Antonia's chest both produced and was aggravated by her enchanting singing, he became obsessively protective of her, expelling her accompanist/fiancé, B., from his house and virtually compelling Antonia to give up singing. His vigilance, however, appears to have been of no avail: Antonia and B. were reunited one night, Krespel claims, in a rapturous, nocturnal fantasy duet that Krespel was powerless to stop, and Antonia died. So, at any rate, runs Krespel's account.

As is typical for Hoffmann, the story unfolds much more indirectly than this brief summary suggests. Notably, it begins in a past *medias res,* with the narrator's account of an episode that was transpiring at the time the narrator first arrived in H. This is the strange, almost carnivalesque construction of Krespel's house, which he is erecting entirely according to his own pleasure. I will postpone a reading of this episode, however, and begin with the narrator's account of his first meeting with Krespel, which takes place at Professor M.'s house on the Tuesday following the festival of Krespel's housewarming. Here are the narrator's first impressions of Krespel:

> His movements were so stiff and awkward that he looked as if he would bump into or damage something at any moment. But he didn't, and it was soon obvious that he wouldn't, for the mistress of the house did not bother to turn a shade paler when he stumbled around the table set with beautiful cups or maneuvered in front of a great full-length mirror, or seized a vase of exquisitely painted porcelain and swung it around in the air as if to let the colors flash [*als ob er die Farben spielen lassen wolle*]. In fact, before lunch Krespel scrutinized everything in the Professor's room most minutely. He

even climbed up on one of the upholstered chairs to remove a picture from the wall and then rehung it, while chattering incessantly and with great emphasis. Occasionally—it was especially noticeable at lunch—he jumped from one subject to another; then, unable to abandon some particular idea, he returned to it over and over again, got himself completely enmeshed in it, and could not disentangle his thoughts until some fresh idea caught him [*konnte sich nicht wieder finden, bis ihn etwas anders erfasste*]. Sometimes his voice was harsh and screeching, sometimes it was slow and singsong; but never was it in harmony with what he was talking about.

(171; 33-34)

From this remarkable description, Krespel's behavior appears to manifest opposing tendencies in tension. It is not only strange but deeply conflicted, profoundly paradoxical: he moves erratically, almost spastically around Professor M.'s house, yet does not crash into or break anything. In the flurry of his broad, ungainly gestures he is able to reposition a picture precisely, without a break in his "chatter." His voice is capable of a great range of expression, alternating between the "harsh and screeching" and the "slow and singsong," the "musical," but at any given moment the quality of his voice does not match his topic. Krespel does not appear to control even his own thoughts: the subjects that come to his mind seize him, control him; he loses himself in the twists and turns of one idea and cannot find himself until he is extracted from the maze by the grip of another idea, pinballing from one cluster of lights and bumpers to the next. He appears to be subject to the play of ideas just as an overwhelmed listener might be to the play of ideas in a musical composition he or she cannot comprehend, as one theme or motif succeeds another. When he speaks, he sounds like an instrument—perhaps a violin—that can screech or sing subject to the performer's skill but cannot modulate itself. In any case his behavior—constricted, even tortured—seems far from autonomous.

Yet even more striking than the grotesquerie of this exaggerated, incongruous behavior is what follows. After expressly requesting the paws of the roast hare that the party had just consumed, Krespel pares "every particle of flesh from the bones" and proceeds to awe and delight the children by fashioning "all kinds of little boxes and dishes and balls out of the bones" by turning them on a tiny steel pocket lathe "with incredible skill and speed" (171; 34); a precise, minutely articulated business that jars with his apparent lack of gross motor skills.

As the reader learns more about Krespel, the sphere of Krespel's puzzling, contradictory behavior that seems strangest is his preoccupation with violins. As the narrator learns from Professor M., Krespel has "his own mad way of constructing violins" (172; 35). In the professor's words: "When Krespel has made a violin, he plays it himself with great power and exquisite expression, for an hour or two, then he hangs it up with the rest and never touches it again, nor does he allow anyone else to touch it. If a violin by any of the eminent old masters is on the market, the Councillor buys it, at any price asked, but, as with his own violins, he plays it only once, then takes it apart in order to examine its inner structure [*innere Struktur*], and if he thinks that he has not found what he has been looking for, he flings the pieces into a large chest which is already full of dismantled violins [*zerlegter Violinen*]" (172; 35). Intriguingly, Krespel's absorption with violins involves construction and deconstruction almost equally but surprisingly, whether it is a question of a violin he has made or one made by another master, almost no playing: a violin he has played once is either retired, hung with the "family" of at least 30 other violins in his cabinet, or immediately autopsied.

The one exception to this rule is the violin which we learn Krespel has "crowned with a wreath of flowers . . . a queen over the others," which he cannot convince himself to cut open (175; 37). His reluctance is due mainly to the affinity that Antonia feels with the instrument. When the narrator is first shown this violin, Krespel informs him that Antonia enjoys hearing it [*"Antonia hört es gern—gar gern"*]; much later in the tale, when Krespel tells his own story, we learn that Antonia not only has a strange sympathy with the violin but that she is virtually symbiotic with it: clearly, it figures her subjectivity. When Krespel first played the violin for her, Antonia reportedly exclaimed, "Why that is me—I am singing again!" According to Krespel, the violin's "silvery, bell-like tones" have something uniquely wonderful about them; they seem to have been engendered in a human breast (187; 50). Antonia, who, Krespel says, could not sing if she wished to live, since the act of singing apparently consumed her lungs, used to sing vicariously through the violin as Krespel played her most beautiful songs. The substitution of the violin's voice for hers, at least according to Krespel, brought "a great serenity and happiness" into her life (187; 50).

Yet once Antonia appears to have forsworn marriage and devoted herself to her father, helping him "take old violins apart and put new ones together" and assuring him that she "will not sing anymore" but will live just for him, she becomes as dependent on Krespel as the violin is on him. Though, like many of Hoffmann's female characters, Antonia's independence is never pronounced, when she surrenders her voice to the violin's her subjectivity is compromised and she becomes much more a passive object—an instrument Krespel chooses to animate or not—than an autonomous subject. While Antonia was still alive Krespel had told the narrator that the violin, which he calls "this dead thing [*dies tote*

Ding]," gets its life and voice from him—actually, he says he himself first gave it life and voice, as if he were the creator God—and, though apparently inanimate and dumb, the violin acts as if it were animated: it speaks often by itself to him in a wonderful way, like a somnambulist who reveals her inner visions, imparting them in words [*sie selbstättig ihre innere Anschauung in Worten verkündet*] (175; 38). The violin's paradoxically inanimate but animated nature, the irrational, impossible coincidence of autonomy and dependency that Krespel says the violin displays, corresponds to the inevitable frustration of Antonia's situation in Krespel's household. As long as she wants to live, she must not sing with her own voice but through the violin's, which is at her father's command; she may possess the subjectivity of her inner vision but she can express that subjectivity only by being dispossessed of it through the power of her hypnotist/father.

Thus, the music that she and Krespel produce is a scene of suppression as much as or more than expression. Her "expression" through the violin's voice fantasizes the freedom of a subjectivity that really cannot be realized as long as its articulation depends on Krespel. The "voicing," or what Brigitte Pruitti has called the *Bestimm-barkeit* of Antonia through the violin, ensures the existence of his fantasized "Antonia," founded on the suppression of the "real" Antonia's desire.[9] The consequence of this *Bestimm-barkeit* for Antonia is that she can only exist as an element of the paternal imagination, as the phantasm "Antonia"; her own voice must remain silenced, since the articulation of her own desire would mean the death of the fantasized "Antonia" for Krespel (Pruitti ["Kunstgeheimnis und Interpretation in E. T. A. Hoffmanns Erzählung 'Rat Krespel'"] 41). Pruitti holds that the condition of Antonia's existence is that she must appear as if entranced, for only as entranced subject [*scheintote Somnambule*], entirely dependent on the father's artistic will and not on the voice of her own desire, can the phantasm "Antonia" continue to live for the father. Brandstetter, too, highlights the identity of Antonia's voice and the violin's; in the *Substitutionsstruktur* of the narrative, the violin not only substitutes for Antonia's voice, it embodies and produces the absent voice (20). Yet Brandstetter also notes Krespel's comparison of himself playing the violin to a "hypnotist [*Magnetiseur*] who so affects his somnambulist that she verbally reveals what she is able to see within herself" (Hoffmann ["**Rat Krespel**"] 175; 38). That comparison suggests not only the power over the subject inherent in the Mesmerist metaphor but also a less obvious, double dispossession: the subject "speaks" for herself but only through the medium of the hypnotist, while the hypnotist, apparently in control, is also subject to what the hypnotized subject reveals of her inner vision.[10] While the hypnotist image suggests a certain power that Krespel has over Antonia, it also suggests a certain impotence of the manipulator who cannot, like a virtuoso performer, fully command his instrument, since he is confronted with the self-sufficiency, the autonomy of the subject's inner vision (Brandstetter ["Die Stimme und das Instrument Mesmerismus als Poetik in E. T. A. Hoffmanns 'Rat Krespel'"] 21). Thus, Krespel's violin playing stimulates a complex play of power and impotence, control and freedom. The "impotence of the manipulator" to which Brandstetter refers ultimately will resonate in Krespel's self-confessed impotence (also described as *Ohnmacht*) before his final vision of the transported Antonia in her death duet with B. Therefore, while it is possible and suggestive to understand the sounding of Antonia's voice through the mediation of Krespel's playing in Lacanian terms, as the passage of the subject into the Symbolic (the Name of the Father, the Law), the dynamics of Krespel's violin play also risks his autonomy and subjectivity along with, obviously, Antonia's. Though supernatural phenomena like the violin's animation and ventriloquistic power always have an indeterminate ontological status in Hoffmann's writing, it is certainly possible that the fantasy of Antonia's fulfilling expression is also or even mainly Krespel's own: having all but stifled her, he hears what he wants to hear.

The uncanny identity established between Antonia and the figure of the violin is most strongly suggested by the fact that Krespel apparently imagines Antonia's physiology and the violin's structure as homologous. Starting with Professor M.'s account of Krespel's preoccupation with dismantling violins, we are made aware that Krespel takes apart violins in search of something, but we are not told what. On one of his early visits the narrator finds Krespel in an "especially good mood" because he had found the soundpost (*Stimmstock*) in an old Cremona violin he was dismantling "was so fixed that it was about half a line more oblique [*schräger*] than was customary" (176; 39). Though it is not at all certain that this unusually positioned soundpost was really the grail of his compulsive deconstruction, the discovery clearly elates him. We later learn that Krespel attributes Antonia's tragic condition to what the doctor identifies as an "organic defect [*organischer Fehler*]" in her chest, "from which her voice derives its wonderful power and its strange . . . divine timbre," but which also will cause her early death, precisely through her exerting it to sing (185: 48). If Krespel perceives Antonia as somehow consubstantial with a violin, and if he believes that the incomparable beauty of her song stems, as the doctor says, from an organic flaw, it may be that Krespel's indefatigable dissection of violins is motivated by a search for a defect in the "heart" of the instrument comparable to the one in Antonia's breast; intriguingly, he may think he has found it in the soundpost, which in French is called the violin's "soul" [*âme*].

In the world of this story, already marked by its displacement of the subject into the figure of the violin, to the extent that Antonia is so fully identified with an instrument that she begs her father not to "cut open" but to "spare" that one and play it, it is not surprising that Krespel might, through a kind of sympathetic magic, be attempting to "cure" Antonia by operating on a violin, her analogic double. In his imagination, Antonia and the violin that figures her may well have become one, though the violin could also be regarded as a fetish that Krespel obsessively fingers to contain and control the "real" Antonia. Krespel is quick to buy the doctor's explanation for Antonia's flushed cheeks, perhaps because it allows him to ignore other possible explanations, not the least telling of which might be that her cheeks register her erotic attraction to B, which Krespel clearly wants to deny (Brandstetter 27). Moreover, Krespel tells the narrator that he had already suspected that the violin had "something peculiar about its inner structure," and, much later, he reports that when Antonia died the "soundpost of that violin broke with a resounding crack and the soundboard shattered to pieces. That faithful instrument could only live with her and through her; it lies beside her in the coffin; it has been buried with her" (179; 42). And, after Antonia is buried, Krespel exclaims that he will "never again construct a violin, or play one" (180; 42).

Yet we are told that Krespel's probing of violins began long before he learned of Antonia's condition. At least, that is implied by the detail that, though Krespel says he was tempted to renew his relations with Angela and see his daughter, he held back out of apprehension for what he might do in Angela's presence (since he had already not been able to restrain himself from hurling her out the window) and remained "at home among his dismembered violins" (184; 47). At the same time, at the outset of his own story, Krespel says that even before he met Angela ("about twenty years ago") he possessed an "all-consuming passion for hunting out and buying the best violins" and expressly that he "had not at that time begun to make violins himself, nor consequently had he begun to take them apart" (182; 44). Thus, though it is impossible to pinpoint exactly when, it appears that the construction and deconstruction of—distinct from Krespel's enthusiasm for—violins began at some time after the break with Angela, and well before he knew of Antonia's "organic defect."

Until that decisive quarrel, Krespel had used his fiddling as an extension or instrument of his subjective desire, to woo Angela: ". . . despite his uncouthness, he succeeded, primarily by his bold and most expressive violin playing, in winning her entirely for himself" (182; 45). In a sense, the violin spoke for Krespel, as it would later for Antonia; it is his mediator, his go-between. Yet, more importantly, Krespel's violin playing at this point is also unreflective, self-absorbing—unmediated self-expression. The violin opens up the realm of the Imaginary, in the special Lacanian as well

as the general sense of the word: it exists somewhere between Krespel's subjectivity and what will consequently be realized as Other, figured first through Angela and later through Antonia. Following one of his tumultuous fights with Angela, Krespel fled to her country house, "trying to forget the suffering the day had brought by improvising [*fantasierend*; i.e., fantasizing] on his Cremona violin" (182; 45) When Angela arrived and attempted to make up, "playing the affectionate wife," Krespel remained "lost in the world of his music [*in die Welt seiner Akkorde verstiegen*]," oblivious to Angela, and "continued playing until the walls resounded. . . ." It is then that Krespel happened to touch Angela "a little too urgently with his arm and the bow," provoking her to snatch and smash his violin, and him, consequently, to the violence of flinging her out the window.

Although the violin is portrayed as the fantastic bridge that links Angela and Krespel, couching Krespel's playing in the context of romantic desire, the scene shakes almost farcically with sexual overtones. In the course of a few sentences, Krespel's musical wooing falls first into self-absorption, a sort of musical masturbation, then, however inadvertently, into a sort of musical rape, aggravated and darkened further by the fact that Angela makes it clear some time before the quarrel reaches its climax that she is pregnant (183; 45). This moment marks the point in Krespel's history, if not in the unfolding of the tale, when music loses any trace of innocence it may have held, and the violin stops being merely a violin and becomes irrevocably the figure in the tale that will concentrate and focus the subject's mediation by music—whether the subject is understood to be Krespel, Antonia (later in the story) or their desires; more precisely, it marks the splitting off or alienation of the subject from desire. For it is this moment that triggers Krespel's obsessive fiddling with fiddles and, at least from this point until Antonia's death, his fetishistic engagement with violins, which can be read as metonymic for both him and Antonia and which clearly subverts human engagement. It substitutes for and subverts human interaction, or, rather, interrupts it, acting as a sort of prophylactic, warding off the danger that threatens, first, if Angela and Krespel should again get too close—Krespel prefers working with his violins to renewing intimacy with his wife—and later, if Antonia should sing (an activity always presented in the story as sexualized, an activation of desire, during which her cheeks always redden). Instead, the violin will sing for her, or Krespel will allow the violin to suppress her voice and he will be supremely concerned with preventing her singing duets that are romantic in all senses, whether with her fiancé, B., or with the narrator (who has enjoyed an erotic dream of her singing an adagio he imagines that he has composed! 174; 37).

The striking resemblance of Antonia to Angela implies the incestuous communication of Krespel's desire from mother to daughter, but one which is blocked by the figure of the violin.[11] The "family" of violins suspended in Krespel's closet, we know once we have heard this story, objectifies the suspension of desire that characterizes, that both figures and disfigures, Krespel's "family romance": the suspended violin family looms as both a projection and an alienation of his desire for the females in the family. All the violins, as Angela in a sense was and Antonia will be, are stifled after they have been allowed full voice only once, probably because of what Krespel has experienced as the human consequences of abandoning oneself to unmediated, expressive playing.

Perhaps the most ironic dimension of the tale's figuring of sexual desire through the violin is that Krespel's obsession with violins for all purposes but playing them presumably begins with Antonia's gestation (by the time she is born he already has accumulated a heap of violin debris); estranged from his wife, Krespel initiates a simulacrum of conception and creation, as if exhibiting what Joy Dworkin has called "womb envy," so prevalent in Hoffmann's tales.[12] Hoffmann's artist-protagonists fantasize the creative process through an implied appropriation of female reproductive power: they "labor" to deliver the fruit of their conception. Obviously, unlike human procreation, Krespel's enterprise cannot fructify: at best it can produce "dead, dumb things" that depend on him for life and voice, automata like the "Antonia" violin he treasures. Moreover, his conception remains impossible, stillborn at best, because it involves as much deconstruction as construction: for every new violin Krespel "fathers," several more are acquired, cut open, probed and tossed onto his bin of scrap parts. His violin work is as self-consuming as Antonia's singing; the difference is that it is not "real": it is self-consumption carried out on a figurative level, by displacements and substitutions for the real that keep it "safe." Yet precisely because the activity replaces human subjectivity with something else, because it involves, in fact, the suppression of subjectivity, it must remain a compulsive and not a truly generative activity in which the subject can freely engage.

4

In short, if **"Rat Krespel"** were to go no further than this, or, specifically, if we were given no more than the narrator's account of his first stay in H. (up until the time he is expelled from Krespel's house) and the information we can glean from Krespel's own account as filtered through the narrator, we could view Krespel simply as one more in the long line of Hoffmann characters—magicians, sorcerers, alchemists, professors, painters, composers and assorted evil geniuses—who are more or less successful in their attempts to play God, the devil or some other creating and controlling demiurge and who, as characters, seem in themselves two-dimensional, even if sometimes conflicted, figures not subject to the deeper tensions of some of Hoffmann's protagonists (Nathanael, Anselmus or Elis Fröbom, for instance).[13] The reasons for seeing Krespel in this way would seem even stronger when one remembers the metaphysical reach and richness that music, the realm to which Krespel seeks various means of access, has for many of the German romantics, preeminently Hoffmann. Yet at a crucial turn in the story, Krespel is explicit about the folly of his own fantasizing a godlike role for himself; he blames his agony on his having "made a nightshirt for myself in which I wanted to look like Fate or like God" (180; 42-43), and just before he begins telling his own story, he implies that the narrator incorrectly (madly) imagines that Krespel is "God the father" merely because the narrator considers himself to be "God the son" (181; 44). So the story, though it expressly raises the possibility of reading Krespel as frustrated artificer or demiurge or as blindly misconstruing the "real" through the figural and symbolic, also questions that reading. In addition, though the story seems to close with Antonia's death—"tot" is literally the last word in the text—it opens up a possibility for reading both Krespel and the tale beyond that death and the conflicted family romance it ends.

To see this, it is crucial to note aspects of Krespel that the narrator experiences when he arrives in H. for the *second* time, after Antonia's death and apart from Krespel's own account of his history. First, the narrator is extremely disturbed, alarmed at what he perceives as the grotesque impropriety of Krespel's behavior at Antonia's funeral and immediately thereafter. As he is escorted home by two mourners, Krespel makes "all kinds of strange leaps and turns [*allerlei seltsame Sprünge*]" (179; 41), as if trying to escape, the mourning ribbon fluttering from his tricorner hat, a violin bow dangling from his sword belt in place of a sword. After Krespel informs the narrator that Antonia and "her" violin have been buried, the narrator states that "it was truly horrible to see him [Krespel] hopping about on one foot, the crepe (he was still wearing his hat) flapping about the room and against the violins hanging on the walls [the violins that also were draped in crepe]; indeed, I could not repress a loud shriek when the crepe hit me during one of his wild turns. It seemed to me that he wanted to envelop me and drag me down into the black pit [*Abgrund*] of madness" (179; 42). Krespel's apparently manic behavior peaks when he takes the violin bow from his belt, raises it in both hands over his head and splinters it: "Then he cried with a loud laugh, 'Now you imagine that the staff has been broken over me [i.e., as it would be over a person condemned to death in a German court], don't you, my son? But it's not so. Now I am free, free. I am free! I will no longer make violins—no more violins—hurrah! No more violins!'

This he sang to a hideously mirthful tune, again jumping about on one foot" (179-80; 42).

This behavior convinces the narrator that Krespel is insane, but Professor M. offers an intriguing counterexplanation: "There are men . . . from whom nature or some peculiar destiny has removed the cover beneath which we hide our own madness. They are like thin-skinned insects whose visible play of muscles [*Muskelspiel*] seem to make them deformed, though, in fact, everything soon returns to its normal shape again. Everything which remains thought within us becomes action in Krespel. Krespel expresses bitter scorn in mad gestures and irrational leaps [*Hasensprüngen*], even as does the spirit which is embodied in all earthly activity. This is his lightning rod [*Blitzableiter*]. What comes from the earth, he returns to the earth, but he knows how to preserve the divine. And so I believe that his inner consciousness is well, despite the apparent madness which springs to the surface" (180; 43).

There are several salient points to the professor's reading of Krespel. First, it suggests that Krespel responds in an unmediated way to the "spirit which is embedded in all earthly activity." That spirit's play is reproduced, represented directly in the play of Krespel's "mad gestures" and "leaps." His capacity to do that is described as his "lightning rod," a remarkable label given the popularity that persisted in the popular natural science of Hoffmann's time of using conductors to tap and channel the electrical force in lightning for physical health and rejuvenation, a practice derived from figures like Mesmer, Galvani and Ritter.[14] Krespel is in immediate touch, though apparently not voluntarily, with the force that informs the world and, unlike most humans, simply is unable to mask how that force affects him. The "play of muscles" it galvanizes is visible to all. Though he is an instrument that channels and reproduces the play of those forces, and to that extent mediates them, he does so with remarkable transparency and fidelity, as if their manifestation in him were virtually unmediated.

Another remarkable detail in the professor's analysis is the implicit comparison of Krespel not only to an insect—most likely a grasshopper—but also to a rabbit: the irrational leaps his emotions provoke are called *Hasensprüngen,* "hare's leaps." If Krespel, like Antonia, previously was construed as a violin, here he is figured as a hare, which recalls his earlier association with that creature through his having turned a hare's bones into children's playthings on his lathe. In fact, apart from constructing his own house and making his own clothes, fabricating toys seems to be the only activity that engages Krespel as much as his violin business. When the narrator revisits him after hearing the professor's analysis, he finds Krespel "calmly smiling, making toys" (181; 43), once again producing them by turning them on a lathe, from an unnamed material. The curious aspect of that activity, what at once links it with but also distinguishes it from Krespel's violin work, is its *enlistment of internal structure to structure something new, to turn it inside out and into something else.* Krespel reanimates the hare's skeleton into objects actualized by play, like balls and tops. Remarkably, the bones he most desires for this purpose are those of the hare's paws; that is, those bones closest to touching the earth as the hare leaps. So Krespel in a sense conducts the spirit of play through these bones and into the toys he turns, much as "what comes from the earth," as Professor M. says, is channeled through Krespel. His toys realize their defining form only after something "in" the material has been externalized, even released, from the substance. This drawing out, shaping and directing of internal structure, though like Krespel's violin work in that it is preoccupied with what lay inside, beneath the surface, differs from it in its object and by the fact that it appears to be disinterested. Krespel obviously conceives his violin work passionately, as a matter of life and death; we have already seen how it is overdetermined by its associations with subjectivity and desire. His probing of a violin's inner structure, though always of grave import, is also always frustrated, producing instruments that do not sound and fragments of them. Krespel's dismantling of violins also is radically dissociated from his construction of them, and, as observed earlier, both activities absurdly are kept separate from violin playing (except in the case of the "Antonia" violin) in that they displace rather than display his spirit. By contrast, the toys embody and activate a spirit of play that derives from him and from the material through his articulation of it, but, crucially, they are of no particular consequence to him; he gives them away to children, releasing them as soon as they leave his lathe. This play is both childlike and distinctly asexual.

Krespel's toys, which admittedly may arrest the reader's attention only in passing, are not the only outlets for his playful expression, however. The narrator, in fact, chooses to open the tales with an extended, exuberant account of Krespel's constructing a house "according to his own desire." The construction procedures are stunning in many respects: he does not consult an architect, he does not draw a formal plan—he claims there "was no need for a plan and that everything would turn out very well without one"—and he has the house built without windows and doors because he wants to knock out the doors and windows later, after the walls have been fully erected. The whole construction scene overflows with merriment; the builders laugh continually and the onlookers cheer loudly whenever stones fly out and a window appears "where it was least expected." The construction blooms spontaneously and the "comic aspect of the whole project . . . kept everyone in good humor" (170; 32). The house turns out much better than anyone had expected it would and, significantly, its main distinctive feature is that it is not what it appears to be: when completed, the house presented "a most unusual appearance from the outside" but its "interior arrangements aroused a very special feeling of ease." It requires little stretching of the imagination to see the house, like his other fabrications, as an extension of and a figure for Krespel himself (he comically, stubbornly refuses to leave the house until the housewarming is held). The house springs fully from his imagination, like Berklinger's painting in Hoffmann's **"Der Artushof"** or as Hoffmann's Kreisler imagines Mozart created the overture to *Don Giovanni*: already conceived and thought through, it only has to be transcribed so that it can be played. Like Krespel's toys, the house seems a direct expression of the designer's spirit. Krespel marks the completion of the house with a carnivalesque housewarming, most surprising in that Krespel admits into the house those who might have been expected to be kept outside, those who had a hand in the construction, and shuts out those whom he might have been expected to invite: other friends, acquaintances, townspeople. At that moment, the figure of the house is fully "playful;" that is, fully activated as a scene of play.

Krespel's most distinctive "creation," however, is the story he spins out to the narrator after the narrator has directly accused him of murdering Antonia and threatened him with legal action and the "retribution of the Eternal." Perhaps the most telling aspect of that story is not what it discloses to the narrator and the reader about Krespel's past life, his marriage and his relationship with Antonia, or what it fails to disclose or deliberately glosses over or masks: the story's really distinguishing feature is its *context*. Krespel relates the story only after the narrator's threats and as a response to what he sees as the narrator's outrageous presumption: ". . . how dare you presume to force your way into the life of another person to uncover hidden facts that are unknown to you and must remain so? She [Antonia] is dead now and the secret is revealed" (181; 44). In other words, Krespel is free to divulge his "secrets" to the narrator because Antonia has died; somehow her death enables the disclosure that could not have been made to the narrator earlier. The story that Krespel will tell is introduced, therefore, as a counter to the history the narrator has so far constructed from what he has seen and heard of Krespel as an external observer; it will be Krespel's story told from the "inside" rather than from an accumulation of externally observed details; it will turn Krespel inside out, express him, tell what "really" happened to him, Angela, Antonia and B. Moving into Krespel's story is analogous to moving into Krespel's house, and should induce a comparable re-evaluation of the whole structure.

Krespel's story intriguingly revisits scenes and episodes previously encountered, this time in a different key or register, from a new perspective (and one that, not sur-prisingly, evokes more sympathy for its protagonist). The only evening, for example, when Antonia was heard to sing and which culminated in B.'s expulsion from the house, is described again, this time from the inside, from Krespel's point of view. Krespel's earlier comment to the narrator that Antonia enjoys hearing him play the "queen" of his violins is filled out into the drama of Antonia's and Krespel's discovery of the violin's amazing, sympathetic, ventriloquistic power, and Antonia's equally amazing willingness to surrender herself and her voice to her father's wishes, in a fantasy of compliance with his will. Finally, the story aims to unlock the mystery of—and justify—Krespel's virtual sequestering of Antonia, his violent rebuff of anyone who shows too much interest in her singing, and her death. The power of the story over the narrator is such that once Krespel has finished, the narrator leaves, "deeply moved and ashamed" (181; 44).

Aside from the question of whether Krespel's story should be received by the narrator or the reader as the truth, despite the open question of whether the fact of the story's placement in the tale as the "last word" means we should trust its revelations, another key question remains: what is it that enables Krespel to tell the story now that he could not tell before? What frees his expression? One possible answer lies in how Krespel relates the episode of Antonia's "swan song," her fatal love duet with B. Krespel describes this climactic event as follows:

> One night . . . it seemed to Krespel that he heard someone playing the piano in the next room, and soon he distinctly recognized that it was B., who was improvising in his usual style. He was about to rise, but it was as if there were a heavy weight upon him, he could not so much as stir. Then he heard Antonia's voice singing softly and delicately until it grew into a shattering fortissimo. The wonderful sounds became the moving song which B. had once composed for her in the devotional style of the old masters. Krespel said that the state in which he found himself was incomprehensible, for an appalling fear was combined with a rapture he had never before experienced.
>
> Suddenly he was overwhelmed by a dazzling lucidity [*eine blendende Klarheit*], and he saw B. and Antonia embracing and gazing at each other rapturously. The notes of the song and the accompaniment of the piano continued, although Antonia was not visibly singing nor B. playing. The councilor fell into a profound unconsciousness [*in eine Art dumpfer Ohnmacht*] in which the vision and the music vanished. When he awoke, the terrible anxiety of his dream still possessed him. He rushed into Antonia's room. She lay on the sofa with her eyes shut, her hands devoutly folded, as if she were asleep and dreaming of heavenly bliss and joy. But she was dead.

(187-88; 50-51)

This scene is striking in several respects. Most obviously, it presents a love-death fulfillment of the desire that Krespel has shown himself as devoted to suppressing: Antonia is reunited with her lover in rapturous song, the unrestrained expression of which, as Krespel has said and as the reader suspects, must lead to her death. The scene appears to thwart Krespel's desire once and for all, a not surprising fate for an overprotective father. Somewhat more surprising, however, is the character of the music as Krespel describes it. The low, soft [*leise*], breathed [*hingehauchten*] tones of the song rise, climbing higher and higher to a "shattering [*schmetternde*] fortissimo" and then become the wonderful sounds of the deeply moving [*tief ergreifende*] song that B. had composed. Over the course of the sentence that describes the song's movement and developing character, in fact, the tones *literally become the subject,* gradually figuring themselves (through the reflexive *gestalten sich*) into B.'s composition. Indeed, the music is so fully realized that at its most intensely animated moment, the sounds of the song and the accompanying piano persist without human agents, *without Antonia's visibly singing or B.'s touching the fortepiano.* In this passing instant, in other words, the music is imagined, represented as autonomous, taking on a life of its own, apart from the auditor as well as from both performer and composer. The power of this musical vision is such that it stuns Krespel into an unconsciousness or impotence (depending on how one translates *Ohnmacht*) in which the vision and the music vanish.

The dream vision Krespel represents himself as experiencing has all the hallmarks of an encounter with the sublime; at least, it evokes Edmund Burke's sublime as translated into musical terms by Hoffmann's contemporary, C. F. Michaelis.[15] The music arouses and clashes radically opposed emotions, appalling fear [*entsetzliche Angst*] and a rapture Krespel has never before felt. The "peak" of bliss—figured by Antonia's steadily rising notes—collapse into impotence, in a brilliant oscillation between the poles of erotic charge and discharge, and the implied disparity between extremes widens even more in the falling off from the vision's liveliness to Antonia's lifelessness, the final blow that strikes the listener, and also forces the prospect that the vision is as much fantasy as fulfillment. The music embodies the prepossessing, uncanny clarity of *enargeia,* the rhetorical trope by which a skilled speaker brings an absent subject palpably before the audience's eyes and ears, making it appear like a hologram before them, with a clarity [*Klarheit*] that is ultimately deceptive, or, in this instance, blinding, and that effectively overexposes the vision. The music captivates the listener: Krespel is drawn out by it but it also paralyzes him. The sounds seem to express his deepest subjectivity but in a remarkably alienated way. As Birrell describes it, "Krespel's dreaming psyche itself becomes a kind of instrument or resonating chamber, on which the ecstasy of Antonia's final ascent and emancipation from earthly existence is played. Like an instrument, Krespel feels himself held down and passive; the sounds he hears do

not issue from Antonia's motionless lips, but from his own soul, which registers the passion of her release by producing musical tones."[16] This description is accurate, provided one notes that the "passion" and "ecstasy" in play here only seem to be Antonia's: Krespel imputes to her what originates in him, and though he may between the lines portray himself as an instrument, as Antonia was once his instrument, he retains authority over his story.

Indeed, what is more remarkable than Krespel's vision, whether or not he has it and whether or not it is "real," is the fact that he *presents* himself as having had it, that he presents himself as audience, positioning himself before the sublimity of it so as not to be threatened by it but so that it can be viewed, as Kant would say, "from a safe place." One might say that through this vision he composes himself, makes himself a subject in a composition that is controlled, despite the lack of composure Krespel as subject of the story displays. It is important to remember that it is the narrator, not Krespel, whose threatening anger compels Krespel to tell the story in the first place, after the narrator has arrived at Krespel's house to find him not in mourning or remorseful but "calmly smiling, making toys." In response to the narrator's increasing agitation, Krespel only fixes his eyes on him "serenely." The jarring, discordant agony of Krespel's grief of a few days before has subsided and he is now "composed," or, to recall Hoffmann's critique of Beethoven, he displays a remarkable self-possession, *Besonnenheit,* which contrasts starkly with the narrator's lack of composure.

Like the self-possessed, disinterested artist that Hoffmann envisioned in his writing on Beethoven, Krespel also separates himself from his story. On one hand, he presents himself as a protagonist whose desires ultimately are subject to the play of the transcendent music performed by Antonia and B.; on the other hand, as he relates the story to the narrator, he is presented by Hoffmann through the narrator as a subject who is thoroughly at peace with himself, composed. Even though there persists the important, legitimate question of the extent of Krespel's own awareness of what he accomplishes by telling the story, there is no doubt that the "revelations" of his account, which he prefaces by symbolically throwing open a window in his house and leaning out over the casement, signal the tale's most decisive narrative turn. That Hoffmann turns the tale in this way suggests that the play of the verbal text and the subject's relation to that text may be figured through the play of a musical text and the listener's participation in it. Both texts are conceived of as eliciting the subject's desire, involving it in their play, but also as straining and transforming it: the text itself becomes an instrument for grappling with and finally incapacitating the subject's desire, discharging or defusing it into an abstract "inexpressible longing." This textual play is thus imagined as distinct from the unsuccessful, frustrated figural strategy Krespel is presented as having resorted to in order to manage his desire for Angela and Antonia.

Moreover, again recalling Hoffmann's assessment of Beethoven's music, both the verbal text and the musical text's play are presented as, in turn, subject to the control, the "absolute mastery" of the storyteller or composer. Over the course of **"Rat Krespel,"** subjects are at once dispossessed of their freedom, in the sense that they are revealed to be subject to a more comprehensive, controlling text, to a more encompassing story, the compass of a greater subjectivity's reach and play: the narrator's efforts to "master" Krespel, to penetrate his mystery, are circumscribed by Krespel's narrative, which not only outflanks the narrator but also controls and shapes what we know of Angela, Antonia, B. and, crucially, Krespel himself as conflicted protagonist. The narrator's earlier understanding of Krespel and Antonia, after we learn Krespel's side of the story, is revealed to have been incomplete and in part fundamentally wrong (much like an insensitive or incompetent critic's misapprehension of a Beethoven symphony). Yet that narrative itself, in turn, is framed as part of, complementary to, the narrator's larger, more distant, retrospective and reasoned account—an account framed considerably after the "events" of the tale have transpired—in which he more than once seems to see himself, with some ironic detachment, as a passionate (younger) hero with limited but growing awareness.

The narrator's account also artfully balances the evocation of musical and verbal play in Krespel's final vision with the account of Krespel's whimsical home improvements that open the tale, effectively surrounding the figures of desire in the "heart" of the story with figures of play. As [La Vern] Rippley observes, the metaphors of the house and specifically that of the German toy *Abdeckhäuschen* (*Pyramidhäuschen* or *Zusammensteckhäuschen*), a series of wooden houses within houses, analogous to Russian *matryoshka* dolls, inform and exemplify the story's recessive structure: surrounding and enclosing each house is another.[17] Like most of Hoffmann's tales, **"Rat Krespel"** is characterized by perpetual unfolding, the opening of one narrative register into another: the "problem of externalizing," as Rippley calls it, of realizing and then transmuting an inner vision, becomes a compulsion. "Outside" the theory, all that the narrator says and all the figures he presents are hypostasized by Theodor to the Serapion brothers, with Theodor's assurance that he "will not put too much of himself in his story." He promises that the story will take his audience from madness and insanity to "healthy reason," which, after all, may be very close to the "rational awareness" of the master composer. Though the word *Besonnenheit* etymologically has no relation to *Sonne* [sun], one might

speculate that Hoffmann forces a connection, leading the reader from the obscurities of Krespel's life as it is first perceived to the enlightenment provided by his more self-possessed narrators. The blinding light of Krespel's vision of Antonia, which assures that the Krespel transfixed before the vision glaringly lacks *Besonnenheit,* is transmuted into the illumination of his narrative. This is not to forget, of course, that Theodor himself, along with the other Serapions, can say or do only what Hoffmann allows him to do.

Through the story's concentric yet recursive filterings—by Krespel, by the narrator, by Theodor, by Hoffmann—desire, which on first reading might appear such a powerful determining force in the tale, as Krespel struggles with his love for his wife and his daughter, or as the narrator's passion drives him from one "revelation" of the "truth" about Krespel to the next, is drained of its potency, subsumed into and replaced by an ironic (i.e., reflexive) play presented as the incomparable, impersonal performance of masterful musical and verbal texts. The subject's particular desire, though not negated by this play, is absorbed by it and dissolved into the general ocean of what Hoffmann variously calls, when speaking of sublime musical texts, "inexpressible longing," "infinite yearning," "ineffable yearning," or even an "unknown language." Krespel's violin as instrument of desire, serenading Angela, gives way to violence, or violins as both victims of tortured obsession and as ventriloquists, dislocating the voice, which in turn lift the veil to a nonviolent but really superhuman music that needs no violins and indeed no players.

5

How one ultimately regards the status of subjectivity in this tale, which delights in presenting and representing, figuring and reconfiguring its characters through its perpetual drive from mimesis to metamimesis, displacing them farther and farther from their particular passions, depends to a great extent on how much subjectivity can flex itself in the ever more encompassing, imaginative textual play to which the story gradually opens. **"Rat Krespel"** implies that this subjectivity is compromised in crucial ways, at least if one understands it to include a hypostasized, unimpeded actualization or realization of desire. First, as masterful and composed as Krespel's narrative and its sublime vision may be, it remains predicated on a radical mediation if not utter suppression of subjectivity, the collapse of himself as desiring subject into impotence and the reduction of his beloved Antonia to a corpse. As Pruitti suggests in her probing study of the story, which reads the tale as raising fundamental questions about the possibility of representation, the death of Antonia is the birth of the author, the liberation and differentiation of the writing subject's own creativity from the creativity or creation associated with the female (through both Angela and Antonia); the tale stages the release of the writing subject from the feminine-maternal creation that threatens his own creativity, or, it recounts the history of the author/subject's finding his own voice through artistic representation (Pruitti 42-43). The death of the desiring subject, Antonia, ensures the persistence of Krespel's ideal "Antonia," Antonia as he wants and wants his audience to see her, but also his authority, an actualization of his subjectivity that apparently cannot find its voice without the stifling of another subjectivity. Like Shakespeare's Prospero—another famously overprotective father!—Krespel unquestionably liberates forces when he breaks the "staff" of his art (i.e., his violin bow) at Antonia's funeral, but, where Prospero vows he will "abjure" his "rough magic" and "drown" his book—as well as release his daughter, Miranda, alive to her living lover—and thereby at least appear to abandon some measure of control, it is precisely at the moment when Krespel destroys the articulating instrument of his (old) violin art that he begins to exercise the (new) art and mastery of the storyteller.

Even so, the extent to which Krespel has shaped his story rather than it him remains an open question, for, as is frequently the case in Hoffmann's ingenious tales, whenever one—character, narrator or reader—chooses to open oneself to the entrancing play of the "hieroglyph figures" of the verbal text or musical score, the risk is not slight; it includes, notably, the risk of losing oneself there. The human subject fully involved in **"Rat Krespel"**'s world enters a space very much like one Hoffmann evoked when recounting his "entrance" into Beethoven's Opus 70 trios: Hoffmann says he is ". . . like someone wandering along the labyrinthine pathways of some fantastic park, hedged in by all kinds of rare trees, shrubs, and exotic flowers, and becoming more and more deeply absorbed . . . still unable to extricate myself from the extraordinary twists and turns of your [Beethoven's] trios. The enchanting siren-voices of your music, sparkling with colour and variety, draw me deeper and deeper into its spell" (Charlton [**"Beethoven's Instrumental Music"**] 100). Indeed, as Margotton observes, a darker side of music is always at hand in **"Rat Krespel,"** and the sublime "siren voices" of that tale can lure the musician-subject away from the human: the sublime music of the soul becomes a demonic sorcery that severs the musician from human reality (281). Referring to the legend of the Pied Piper, which Hoffmann's contemporary, Tieck, among others, invoked, Margotton points to the demonic charm of a music that possesses souls and leads them far from the world. Krespel's imagined subjection to the ravishing power of Antonia's song may have compromised his composure more than he suspects, and Hoffmann, himself the composer of symphonies, chamber music and operas in the wake of Beethoven's masterpieces, must have anxiously sensed that the composer himself always risks being composed.

Notes

1. The discussion here of Hoffmann's appraisal of Beethoven closely recapitulates that in my "*Besonnenheit,* Ekphrasis and the Disappearing Subject in E. T. A. Hoffmann's 'Die Fermate,'" *Criticism* 43/3 (Summer 2001): 325-29.

2. E. T. A. Hoffmann, "Beethoven's Instrumental Music," *E. T. A. Hoffmann's Musical Writings,* ed. and trans. David Charlton (Cambridge: Cambridge UP, 1989) 98. Subsequently cited as Charlton. Quotations from the original German refer to the edition of "Kreisleriana" found in E. T. A. Hoffmann, *Fantasie- und Nachtstücke,* ed. Walter Müller-Seidel and Wolfgang Kron (Munich: Winkler-Verlag, 1960).

3. For key texts on the sublime and on the sublime in relation to music in the late eighteenth and early nineteenth century, see *Music and Aesthetics in the Eighteenth and Early-Nineteenth Centuries,* ed. Peter Le Huray and James Day (Cambridge: Cambridge UP, 1981), especially the excerpts from Burke, Kant and C. F. Michaelis. For two studies on the sublime specifically in relation to music, see my "Rhetoric in Haydn's *Applausus,*" *Haydn Yearbook* 18 (1993): 213-66, and James Webster, "The *Creation,* Haydn's Late Vocal Music, and the Musical Sublime," *Haydn and His World,* ed. Elaine Sisman (Princeton: Princeton UP, 1998) 57-102.

4. References to the German text of "Rat Krespel" are to E. T. A. Hoffmann, *Die Serapions-Brüder,* ed. Walter Müller-Seidel and Wulf Segebrecht (Munich: Winkler-Verlag, 1963). English translations are quoted from *Selected Writings of E. T. A. Hoffmann, Volume 1: The Tales,* ed. and trans. Leonard J. Kent and Elizabeth C. Knight (Chicago: U of Chicago P, 1969). Page citations in parentheses give the English text page reference first, then the German.

5. E. T. A. Hoffmann, *The Serapion Brethren,* trans. Alexander Ewing (London: George Bell and Sons, 1886) 23. Subsequently cited as Ewing.

6. Translation adapted from Ewing 31.

7. For contrasting views on the narrator's reliability, see John M. Ellis, *Narration in the German Novelle: Theory and Interpretation* (Cambridge: Cambridge UP, 1974) 94-112, and William Crisman, "E. T. A. Hoffmann's 'Einsiedler Serapion' and 'Rat Krespel' as Models of Reading," *JEGP* [*Journal of English and Germanic Philology*] 85 (1986): 50-69. Ellis argues that "Theodor is not an omniscient narrator who gives us the ultimate truth about the facts and values of the story" (96) and that the "whole tone of . . .

[Theodor's] narrative makes it impossible to view him as an objective and reliable narrator" (100). Crisman, by contrast, stresses both the implied, constructive identity established between narrator and reader (60-61), the humanity of the narrator, but also his "distance" from his "irrational" younger self (68).

8. Gabriele Brandstetter, "Die Stimme und das Instrument Mesmerismus als Poetik in E. T. A. Hoffmanns 'Rat Krespel,'" *Jacques Offenbachs Hoffmanns Erzählungen: Konzeption, Rezeption, Dokumentation,* ed. Gabriele Brandstetter (Laaber: Laaber-Verlag, 1987) 49.

9. Brigitte Pruitti, "Kunstgeheimnis und Interpretation in E. T. A. Hoffmanns Erzählung 'Rat Krespel,'" *Seminar* 28/1 (February 1992): 33-43.

10. Brandstetter also convincingly argues that a (suppressed) missing term in the relation violin-:violinist::somnabulist:hypnotist is the musical instrument much in vogue during Hoffmann's time, the glass harmonica, from which sound is elicited by the performer's passing his hands over moistened glass bottle rims without touching them, somewhat in the manner of a hypnotist's "passes." Brandstetter provides the intriguing detail that Franz Anton Mesmer, from whom Mesmerism takes its name, was one of the first to own a glass harmonica, which had been perfected by Benjamin Franklin in 1761.

11. Brandstetter argues that Krespel seeks to have with Antonia what he could not have had with her mother, Angela: "Die Tochter tritt als Geliebte an die Stelle der Mutter, nicht als Wiederholung, sondern als Erfüllung jener gescheiterten Liebe, die zwischen Krespel und Angela lediglich präfiguriert war. Das verknüpfende Zeichen der erotischen Identifikation von Mutter und Tochter ist die Stimme" (28). The initial "A" not only links the two women in name; the sound "ah" is also the ideal *Gesangsvokal* (28).

12. Joy Dworkin, Professor of English, Missouri Southern State University, personal communication. Pruitti also sees Krespel's tale ultimately as defining itself against feminine, maternal creation (40-41).

13. Jean-Charles Margotton, "Musique et folie: Le Conseillor Krespel de Hoffmann," *E. T. A. Hoffmann et la musique,* ed. Alain Montaindon, *Actes du Colloque Internationale de Clermont-Ferrard* (Berne: Peter Lang, 1987) 269-82. Margotton calls Krespel a "demiurge grotesque" (280).

14. On connections between Hoffmann and Mesmer, see Brandstetter, esp. 21-23, and Maria M. Tatar, *Spellbound: Studies on Mesmerism and Literature* (Princeton: Princeton UP, 1978), esp. 121-51. On Mesmer, Galvani, Ritter and Romantic natural science generally, see Walter D. Wetzels, "Aspects of Natural Science in German Romanticism," *SiR* [*Studies in Romanticism*] 10 (1971): 44-59.

15. See note 3, above.

16. Gordon Birrell, "Instruments and Infidels: The Metaphysics of Music in E. T. A. Hoffmanns 'Rat Krespel,'" *Literature and the Occult: Essays in Comparative Literature,* ed. Frank Luanne (Arlington: U of Texas at Arlington P, 1977) 71.

17. La Vern J. Rippley, "The House as Metaphor in E. T. A. Hoffmann's 'Rat Krespel,'" *Papers on Language and Literature* 7 (1971): 52-60.

Jeanne Riou (essay date 2004)

SOURCE: Riou, Jeanne. "Music and Non-Verbal Reason in E. T. A. Hoffmann." In *Music and Literature in German Romanticism,* edited by Siobhán Donovan and Robin Elliott, pp. 43-55. Rochester, N.Y.: Camden House, 2004.

[*In the following essay, Riou studies the ways in which Hoffmann's ideas concerning the aesthetic power of music informed his writings. Riou argues that Hoffmann's reliance on a nonverbal art form as a primary source of inspiration lends his works their irrational, transcendental qualities.*]

In the following, attention will be focused on issues of Romantic musical aesthetics in E. T. A. Hoffmann. Music is a libidinally driven and dangerous experience in Hoffmann, holding the promise of transcendence in the Romantic sense, which is partially a protest against the rationalizations of modern life. Hoffmann's outsider-protagonists, through their pursuit of artistic transcendence, often sacrifice their ability to function as rational beings. While the disruption of rational identity is a feature of almost all Romantic writing, it is intensified in Hoffmann and takes on a psychological character that is absent in, for instance, Novalis. The radicalized form of transcendence—the violent and self-destructive nature of madness in Hoffmann-protagonists such as Medardus, Ettlinger, or Nathanael—leaves no doubt that in Hoffmann's works the Romantic tendency to undermine identity as a transitional phase in coming to a fuller understanding of human experience is turned into something with more disturbing consequences.

This contribution will argue that parallel to the Romantic motif of art leading to madness is the narration of an aesthetic subjectivity that is not so much irrational as governed by sensations that are inadmissible in a strictly rational sense, because they are not capable of being translated into either verbal reasoning or visible messages. By this, I refer to auditory sensations and, more specifically, the experience of music, which seems, in the instance of Kreisler, to be far from irrational in itself. Kreisler does not hover on the verges of sanity simply because he is a composer, but because something about composition pushes him towards a sense of longing that draws him into conflict with his mercenary environment.

It should be noted at the outset, however, that Hoffmann is one of the least theoretically motivated of the Romantic authors and would have had little interest in using music to challenge the framework of Enlightenment reason. Nevertheless, his work narrates subjectivity in a way that is primarily acoustic, and this does have implications for how the borders of the rational/irrational are conceived. Hoffmann's comments on transcendence in his musical writings cannot be taken literally. These writings lack conceptual stringency, and in his contributions to the *Allgemeine Musikalische Zeitung* (The General Music Newspaper) from 1808 onwards, Hoffmann is not always an authoritative commentator. However, it is possible to find in his literary renditions of musical experience some clarification of his thoughts about music. In this essay I discuss Hoffmann's ironic use of musical transcendence and examine the utopian dimension of musical performance. This is followed by a discussion of the rationality of art and how Adorno treats its utopian potential. The final section, returning to Romantic hermeneutics, examines the idea of music as non-verbal reason.

ENTERTAINMENT VERSUS UTOPIA: HOFFMANN'S
JOHANNES KREISLER AND THE HAZARDS OF
COMPOSITION

Johannes Kreisler's *Gedanken über den hohen Wert der Musik* (*Reflections on the High Value of Music*, 1815) from the **"Kreisleriana"** (Kreisler Papers, 1812-20) begins with a damningly ironic account of how music lessons are essential to good taste in society's better circles. Art, Kreisler comments, is purely about entertainment.[1] It offers us distraction from the serious demands of life. In the case of reading, care has to be taken to avoid "fantastic" literature, where imagination has the unwanted effect that the reader might actually have to think about what he or she is reading. Paintings are harmless, since as soon as the beholder realizes what a painting represents, he or she has lost all interest. Music, Kreisler concludes, is nevertheless the most harmless of all art forms, since, providing it is fairly simple, people can carry on conversations while listening (*FN* [*Fantasie- und Nachtstücke*], 36). Later, Kreisler refers to Romantic art, and how its pursuit of a "higher principle" seems so abhorrent to the mercenary world around it (*FN*, 39).

The **"Kreisleriana"** end on a characteristic note of dual identity. Writing his own ironic apprentice's certificate, Kreisler claims that the musician is always surrounded by both melody and harmony. Furthermore, what inspires composition are impulses from other sensual channels: colors, odors, rays—all of which "appear" to the musician as notes (*FN*, 326). Referring to Ritter's *Fragmente aus dem Nachlaß eines jungen Physikers* (Fragments taken from the Literary Estate of a Young Physicist, 1810), Kreisler describes music as an inner seeing:

> So wie, nach dem Ausspruch eines geistreichen Physikers, Hören ein Sehen von innen ist, so wird dem Musiker das Sehen ein Hören von innen, nämlich zum innersten Bewußtsein der Musik, die mit seinem Geiste gleichmäßig vibrierend aus allem ertönt, was sein Auge erfaßt. So würden die plötzlichen Anregungen des Musikers, das Entstehen der Melodien im Innern, das bewußtlose oder vielmehr in Worten nicht darzulegende Erkennen und Auffassen der geheimen Musik der Natur als Prinzip des Lebens oder alles Wirkens in demselben sein.
>
> <div style="text-align:right">(<i>FN</i>, 326)[2]</div>

The last part of the quotation deals with the concept of the secret music of nature, which is seen as an allegory for life. Ritter asks whether there could possibly be such a thing as a thought or an idea without its particular medium and sign.[3] He defines music as a type of composite medium and sees language as an individuation of music that necessarily relates to music.[4] These thoughts echo Schlegel's reflections on the idea of art as formal continuum,[5] which in turn are influenced by Lessing's *Laokoon* (1766).

Hoffmann's figure of Johannes Kreisler should, therefore, not be taken as the type of artist whose work transcends all matter. His work and artistic subjectivity are inherently shifting between the different media of experience. Johannes Kreisler's problem is one of expression and representation. He embodies the eighteenth-century musical debate on the merits of melody or harmony: Rameau, Carl Philipp Emanuel Bach, or Rousseau. Although Hoffmann in his musical essay, **"Alte und neue Kirchenmusik"** ("Ancient and Modern Church Music," 1814), claims that the musical voice is the ultimate triumph of expression over the ambivalence of construction, this is not borne out by the experience of Johannes Kreisler in the novel *Lebens-Ansichten des Katers Murr* (*The Life and Opinions of the Tomcat Murr*, 1819-21). On a theoretical level, Hoffmann may write of the operatic voice and its promise of transcendence, but there is no escaping the problem that this cannot bypass society. In other words, the alienation described by Jean-Jacques Rousseau in his *Discours sur l'Origine de l'Inégalité parmi les Hommes* (*Second Discourse on Inequality*, 1755) which was to have such a profound influence on the latter half of the eighteenth century, from Herder to Schiller to the Romantics, is a theme not surprisingly echoed by Hoffmann. If music awakens a longing for the archaic or for something that has been lost in the process of civilization, the question is: what status may we ascribe to this? Is music, therefore, a private experience, solipsistic in its essence, transcendent of time itself, and a disavowal of modernity?

Kater Murr** [Lebens-Ansichten des Katers Murr]*, Hoffmann's second novel, is a parody of bourgeois identity.[6] In line with the caricature of musical taste in ***Gedanken über den hohen Wert der Musik, his novel shows the artist (Kreisler) to be at odds with society. He is an emblem of artistry, which is ambivalent in the bourgeois world. The Kreisler of ***Kater Murr*** can find neither total expression nor the pure sound to which he aspires. The closest he comes is the momentary promise of transcendence when he hears Julia singing. This turns into an erotic fixation. It is ironic that Julia becomes the object of physical desire, as Kreisler and Julia embody different types of expression: Julia represents unmediated expression, as opposed to Kreisler, who must accommodate himself within the rules of composition. This is made clear in the first meeting between the two. In this early incident Kreisler throws away his guitar in despair because he cannot tune it. Julia, unperturbed by the idiosyncrasies of tuning, picks up the guitar and begins to sing:

> Julia konnte es nicht unterlassen, sie schlug einen Akkord auf dem zierlichen Instrument an, und erschrak beinahe über den mächtigen vollen Klang, der aus dem kleinen Dinge heraustönte. "O herrlich—herrlich," rief sie aus und spielte weiter. Da sie aber gewohnt, nur ihren Gesang mit der Gitarre zu begleiten, so konnte es nicht fehlen, daß sie bald unwillkürlich zu singen begann, indem sie weiter fortwandelte.[7]

The contrast between Kreisler and Julia is one that underlies all of Hoffmann's writing. Singers like Julia, Antonie in **"Rat Krespel"** (**"Councillor Krespel,"** 1816), or Donna Anna in **"Don Juan"** (1812) always represent direct, immediate emotion. By contrast to the male composer or musician who has to struggle with the principles of composition, the female singer embodies music as something that is not only pre-reflexive, but defies all need for a reflexive consciousness. As the embodiment of a pure sound, Julia, unlike Kreisler, is able to express her innermost self. The criterion for her spontaneous expression is that she should be outside language. Like so many of Hoffmann's heroines, she is given an arsenal of sighs and gentle sounds to match her particular mood. Meister Abraham, filling Kreisler in on the details of the celebrations on the night of the storm, does not fail to observe Julia's reaction:

> Sowie Pauken und Trompeten schwiegen, fiel Julien unter duftenden Nachtviolen versteckte aufbrechende Rosenknospe in den Schoß, und wie strömender Hauch

des Nachtwindes schwammen die Töne deines tief ins Herz dringenden Liedes herüber: Mi lagnèro tacendo della mia sorte amara.—Julie war erschrocken, als aber das Lied, das ich, ich sag es damit du über die Art des Vortrags etwa nicht in bange Zweifel gerätst, von unsern vier vortrefflichen Bassetthornisten ganz in der Ferne spielen ließ—begann; entfloh ein leichtes Ach ihren Lippen. [. . .]

*(**KM** [**Die Elixiere des Teufels: Lebens-Ansichten des Katers Murr**], 313)*

Here Meister Abraham tells how Julia responds with a sigh, "Ach," to the performance of Kreisler's song by distant basset horn players.

"Ach" is the most important word in the female vocabulary. As Friedrich Kittler comments, "Ach" places the female protagonist at the pre-reflexive origin of the Romantic imagination.[8] It echoes a lost unity of consciousness that preempts intellectual reflection. "Ach," Julia again later sighs on seeing Kreisler in conversation with her mother, Benzon:

> "Verehrteste," begann Kreisler, aber in dem Augenblick öffnete sich die Türe und Julia trat hinein. Als sie den Kapellmeister gewahrte, verklärte ihr holdes Antlitz ein süßes Lächeln, und ein leises: Ach! hauchte von ihren Lippen.
>
> *(**KM**, 359)*

Hoffmann's reader, seeing the two engaged in a conversation of dubious integrity, is guided towards apprehending Julia as the intruder, the beholder rather than participant, the utopian outsider who has no words for her discomfort with the untruths of conversation. Removed from language, Julia is allowed to appear as a musical ideal, a pure "interior" in a world of linguistic compromise and feigned "exterior." However, on closer examination it turns out that Julia's subjectivity is not an interior in a compact, independent sense, but a transmitter, something that exudes sound, whether this is uttered as the semi-linguistic "ach" or sung.

Another form of transmitter is the Romantic symbol of the Aeolian harp. In ***Kater Murr*** a variation of this Romantic instrument is used to describe Meister Abraham's longing for the lost Chiara:

> Da schwankte die Glaskugel hin und her und ein melodischer Ton ließ sich vernehmen wie wenn Windeshauch leise hinstreift über die Seiten der Harfe. Aber bald wurde der Ton zu Worten.
>
> *(**KM**, 620)*

On one level this is a metaphor for the Romantic imagination. In the context of Hoffmann's reflection on this in his poetic works, there is, perhaps, a further distinction to be made. Klaus-Dieter Dobat argues that Novalis treats music as a container for a poetic idea, whereas for Hoffmann, musical form is itself the transcendent force.[9] According to Dobat, Novalis's aesthetics imply that musical transcendence relies on the translation into language of the sensations it evokes. In the above example Hoffmann allows Abraham to imagine the musical notes becoming words. What then happens, however, is that the medium does not transcend itself. These words remain medium rather than discarding their materiality. They are not made transparent. Meister Abraham does, of course, interpret the words that ensue from the notes, but in so doing he constructs rather than deciphers a meaning. Abraham himself, therefore, is a clear identity only between music and its transition into language, between language and its interpretation. The ultimate interpretation would rest on his becoming reunited with Chiara, but this does not take place: as in the case of Abraham's constructions for the princess's birthday celebrations, meaning slips away from intention, so that Abraham's mechanical construction of musical instruments and the effects of this become an allegory of Romantic artistry.

Returning to the musical protagonist: Kreisler's dilemma is not to deliver a new and transcendent composition, but to know whether any composition can affect its listener in such a way that he or she transcends a certain predictability of musical composition. As well as expressing Hoffmann's personal frustration and setting out as an ideal what he as a composer did not achieve, this representation of music is made to symbolize a utopian yearning. Kreisler's desire for expression is Romantic, in that the perfect music he almost hears runs parallel to the symbolic relationship with Julia, which is mainly enacted in his imagination. That this depends on a certain level of unfulfillment comes as no surprise to the reader of Romanticism; what is nevertheless uncertain is the status of the attempt to transcend the terms of modern individuality. In the aftermath of Descartes and in the tradition of Scientific Rationalism, the individual is defined by its capacity for cognitive reasoning. Identity is linked to rational understanding and communication takes place between discrete, unconnected intelligences. Kreisler's Romantic aesthetics, and here they represent Hoffmann's, try to capture something different: the merging of feeling and reflection in the experience of music.

Kreisler's need to compose is utopian because it hopes to bring about a unity of consciousness that stretches the terms of European discourse on subjectivity. Clearly, whatever Kreisler *may* compose is not capable of answering the reasons from Descartes onwards for conceiving of individual consciousness as an end in itself. Nevertheless, taking Kreisler's unachieved composition as Hoffmann's rendition of Romantic utopianism, it seems to hold the promise of transcendence and thereby to challenge more philosophical definitions of individual

identity.—What if music, even if it destabilizes a rational thought process only momentarily, were to do so repeatedly?

In several cases throughout E. T. A. Hoffmann's literary work, musical performance brings the protagonist to the brink of transcending the solitariness of experience. Herein lies the essence of Hoffmann's musical utopianism, but if it were to be explained in epistemological terms rather than observed as a one-time literary production, it would be difficult to account for this type of experience other than as an instance of personal faith or private madness. In particular, the fictional composer Kreisler is struggling for a form of connection that is impossible; try as he may to achieve this through music, it is not quite attainable. The question therefore arises: does this imply that what can be shown in literature and therefore imagined can be summarily dismissed as "just imagined"?

That human experience is fundamentally solitary is one of the central premises of modern aesthetics, from Cartesian rationalism to German Idealism. Within this paradigm, art is a form of communication, but also a longing to cross the boundaries between two monadic existences. The writings of Hölderlin, Novalis, Schelling, and Friedrich Schlegel all set themselves the goal of providing a corrective to the isolationism of subject philosophy. In conceptions of the Absolute—an imaginative ideal of poetry and a level of consciousness beyond philosophical reflection—these writers endeavored to conceptualize aesthetic subjectivity as a less solitary way of being.[10] While this would be the subject of a separate study and cannot be dealt with adequately here, it is important to point out that the Romantic invention of a "new mythology" should not be misunderstood as a regressive and reactionary call for the mystical dissolution of consciousness and a return to a pre-modern view of existence. Nor can it be identified with the simplifications and monumentalism of Wagner in the second half of the nineteenth century. Andrew Bowie succinctly identifies Schelling's conception of the Absolute as an artistic ideal that motivates the practice of art and holds aesthetic subjectivity to be an immanent engagement with the Other:

> Schelling insists that art is the unity of conscious and unconscious activity, as part of the attempt to make philosophy confront aspects of self-consciousness which philosophers like Kant can only put into a realm to which philosophy has no access. Schelling is convinced that these aspects are accessible, and faces the philosophical consequences of showing how this is the case.[11]

Bowie then argues that the consequences of Schelling's position are that art can articulate thoughts that may be inaccessible to philosophy, and that this influences Theodor Adorno in the twentieth century, even though Adorno insists that artistic expression has to remain incommensurate with public and political expression if it is not to be used as an instrument of oppression.[12] But the consequences of this are, according to Bowie, that Adorno in *Ästhetische Theorie* (1970) conceives of art as a negative relation to what is, and beyond that (since there can be no reconciliation of the individual and the general that is not oppressive) insists that art has to forfeit the epistemological and experiential utopian quality that Schelling had foreseen for it.[13]

The question of how art can be utopian has always been controversial, from Plato's charge in his *Republic* that art subverts rational truth to Adorno's distrust of any modern aesthetics that are not distinguished in a negative dialectical relationship to what is, and to poststructuralism, in which utopian tendencies are dismissed as ideological and totalizing. Adorno's *Ästhetische Theorie,* implicitly responding to the philosophy of Hegel, provides a melancholy account of the utopian potential of art. Art is, in Adorno's view, capable of embodying protest, since it formally withstands antagonisms that have to be repressed in the historical construction of reality.[14] The work of art can resist reality by refusing the universalism of product-based capitalist exchange. Where Hegel chooses to construe the present as a moment in the dialectical progress towards the Ideal, Adorno points to the work of art as something that discredits such premises by showing the very things that they have had to repress. Art's negativity provides its critical potential, its resistance to the ontological claims of a status quo as, for instance, any stage of capitalism. Likewise, Adorno's conception of time as music seems to be influenced by the idea of rhythm and the repetition of selected themes as a negation of empirical time.[15] Music, although thoroughly conceived in time, can also develop from a concentrated displacement of thematic development.[16] In other words, musical themes can awaken expectations in the listener that are then not fulfilled, with the result that the listener has an awareness of the contingency of historical reality. Adorno explains: "Drängt eine Musik die Zeit zusammen, faltet ein Bild Räume ineinander, so konkretisiert sich die Möglichkeit, es könnte auch anders sein."[17] In his contention that art encompasses possibilities beyond the repressions of conscious knowledge, Adorno does, as Bowie contends, show the influence of Schelling. But overall, Adorno's conception of art as utopian possibility has to be linked to the negation of what is. The moment it lays claim to a better reality, art, for Adorno, falls into the trap of positing an idea of the "best possible of all worlds" (Leibniz), and what had started out as an artistic rendering of something that is possible is frozen into a retrospective justification of ethical stagnation. In other words, ethics has failed in Leibnizian terms, since the "best possible of all worlds" is a lame justification

of historical developments that lets reason off the hook by pointing to a divine source. This is seen to be the case most notably in Hegel, who in *Phänomenologie des Geistes* (*Phenomenology of Spirit,* 1810), regards history as the unfolding of stages of dialectical imbalances on the inevitable course of rational perfection. Art, as far as Adorno is concerned, has to be able to nullify the circular arguments of an ethical practice that has its roots in ideas that do not account for what they have repressed in arriving at their respective representations.

SOUND AS PERCEPTION

In his book, *Aesthetics and Subjectivity from Kant to Nietzsche,* Andrew Bowie discusses Hegel's dismissal of music as "feeling" (rather than concept) in relation to Hoffmann's essay on Beethoven's Fifth Symphony ["**Beethoven, C moll-Sinfonie (No. 5)**"], in which Hoffmann refers to music as the "unsayable" ("das Unsagbare"):[18]

> For Hegel the truth of music is eminently sayable in the form of philosophy. As we saw, in discussing the signifier "I," Hegel maintained that the "*Unsayable,* emotion, feeling is not the most excellent, the most true, but rather the most insignificant, most untrue." For Hoffmann music can articulate the "unsayable," which is *not* representable by concepts or verbal language.[19]

Turning to Novalis, Bowie notes that Novalis understands rhythm in language to be the enabling analogous factor that establishes a continuum that is often mistaken for a cognitive, logical continuum:

> Rhythm, like language, is a form of meaningful differentiality; a beat becomes itself by its relation to the other beats, in an analogous way to the way in which the I of reflection is dependent upon the not-I, the signifier on the other signifiers. Rhythm is a form of reflection.[20]

Bowie sees a connection between Schleiermacher's hermeneutics and Hoffmann's essay on Beethoven's Fifth Symphony. For Schleiermacher, as Bowie has argued in an earlier chapter, the link between music and language is not arbitrary: both show a sequential organization and are therefore linked at an irreducible point of self-consciousness.[21] According to Bowie, Hoffmann "makes music into the means of access to other aspects of self-consciousness because of the way he sees the limitations of conceptual thinking."[22] The question arises, however, as to the purpose of whatever access this may be. Whether the emphasis is on articulation or on the ultimate limits of self-knowledge, art is conceived of here in relation to individuality. In this view of subjectivity, perception is as much defined by "feeling" in the Romantic sense as it is by rational understanding. It is also capable of being more ethically accountable than a form of rationality that is limited to the concept, as is that of Kant and Hegel.

In effect, Bowie's analysis takes issue with deconstruction's rejection of the metaphysics of presence by pointing to alternatives of self-consciousness in German Romanticism. While this is a subtle argument, it nevertheless decouples Romantic subjectivity from the historical and cultural matrix within which, as Michel Foucault shows, the object of knowledge is produced. German Romanticism, including E. T. A. Hoffmann, is a part of this matrix; it can be read in Bowie's sense as the enhancement of thinking of the self. This partially leads in the direction of Adorno, who emphasized music in particular as the zenith of aesthetic autonomy. Romanticism could be read in the context of aesthetic autonomy, albeit departing then from Adorno, as a means of preserving subjectivity. This seems to me to be the thrust of Bowie's defense of Romanticism against Hegel.

Bearing this in mind, it is far from inconceivable that Hoffmann, despite his lack of interest in philosophy, should have understood that music as a form of expression may be a different but no less viable source of individual and cultural identity. Hoffmann's musical transcendence is based on a physical process that has a complex but not subordinate relationship to verbal expression. The fact that there is no direct philosophical explanation for such a phenomenon does not mean—as Bowie's interpretation of Novalis's reading of Fichte shows—that philosophy is uninformed by many types of non-verbal expression.

Hoffmann's first published work, **"Ritter Gluck"** (**"Chevalier Gluck,"** 1809), shows how sound is intrinsic to identity without being transmitted into linguistic reason. The ghostly appearance of the composer Gluck and his trance-like immersion in music links the question of identity to the form of expression. Hoffmann's tale opens with a vivid and detailed description of a late autumn Sunday afternoon in Berlin. The scene is set by the even pacing of the narrative; all sections of society are represented, and the narrator's eye calmly takes in the people passing by. The reader is introduced to this "slice of life" as the narrator lists off the passers-by: "Elegants, Bürger mit der Hausfrau und den lieben Kleinen in Sonntagskleidern, Geistliche, Jüdinnen, Referendare, Freudenmädchen, Professoren, Tänzer, Offiziere" (*FN,* 14). At first the picture is silent, but as some of the passers-by sit down at a café, they are brought to life. The first addition of sound to the picture is localized. As the people begin to talk and argue at their tables, we become aware of sound as a separate dimension to the pictures in which they had first been presented. As soon as this has been established, sound dominates the narrative in the form of an untuned harp, two discordant violins, a flute, and a bassoon. The narrator walks on until he finds a seat out of earshot of the "cacophony" (*FN,* 14). The sound has been banished, allowing pictures once again to predominate: "Immer

bunter und bunter wogt die Masse der Spaziergänger bei mir vorüber, aber nichts stört mich, nichts kann meine phantastische Gesellschaft vescheuchen" (*FN,* 14). With this proclamation we are introduced at an early stage to the tension between interior and exterior, profane reality and the Romantic transcendent imagination. The narrator is at pains to point out his imaginative autonomy. No sooner is this established than it is once again curtailed by the intrusion of badly played music: "Die kreischende Oberstimme der Violine und Flöte und des Fagotts schnarrenden Grundbaß allein höre ich [. . .]" (*FN,* 14). Already there is no reconciliation. Both the narrator's imagination and his sensory experience focus on one thing at a time. Sound and vision do not peacefully coexist, but stamp each other out. In this instance it is the bassoon that drowns out the other noises. The whole business leads to physical pain. From the moment the narrator reports of this physical pain, he has already uttered what will be one of the constant themes of Hoffmann's literary writing: the inadequacy of language to recapture any experience in its underlying form.

The failure of language is only one angle; ironically it draws attention to other ways of showing intelligence, and these ways are innately physical, such as when the narrator's ear is "pierced" by what it hears (*FN,* 14). Whether good or bad, music is actively felt in Hoffmann rather than passively imported. The narrator in **"Ritter Gluck"** also complains of a burning pain. Both the piercing sound and the burning pain are scarcely what might be termed original metaphors. Like so many other figures in Hoffmann's writing, the narrator of **"Ritter Gluck,"** with his punctured eardrums and strange burning sensations, is neither rational nor irrational, neither articulate nor inarticulate.

Central to **"Ritter Gluck"** is the empty page from which the ghostly composer conducts his final performance: it is unclear whether the ghostly composer does not require a score because he is already in the realm of transcendence, or whether we should simply read this as an allegory of all music in performance. Hoffmann seems to imply that all performance rests on harmony and on the designation of notes within a constructed system. Instead of transcendence—or perhaps, as a different way of looking at transcendence—we are left with the unique aesthetic moment: the physical experience of music as a reality that exists in time, not despite it. Gluck, the composer who has returned from the dead to conduct a final performance in Berlin, reads from an empty page. This is in one sense a parody of Rousseau's utopia of original music at the pre-reflexive origin of society. Hoffmann, the writer and composer, is more than aware, as indeed is Rousseau, of the physical reality of the interval. Gluck's presence oddly testifies to the singularity of performance. In a way, performance itself is transcendence. Therefore, though it might hint at utopia, it is characterized by its instantaneous nature. What music is Gluck reading?

From one minute to the next, experience is structured by time. Each interval in frequency between notes implies that nothing is really simultaneous. Simultaneity, carrying this idea a step further, is a manner of expression for a fundamentally incommunicable sensation. The fact that Gluck, a ghost who has cheated on his mortal time-span, is reading invisible notes, could be read as Hoffmann's distortion of time, a reduction of all bodily reality to an atemporal comic utopia. What could instead be concluded, however, is that Gluck's performance stands for the uniqueness of time, not its obliteration; while the notes he reads are invisible, they are nevertheless there, therefore time itself is not transcended. On the contrary, Gluck's rendition of the composition alerts his dumb-struck listener to the singularity of performance. Gluck need not be viewed as a symbol of radical aesthetic autonomy—the solipsistic internal consciousness of a bourgeois performer. He may be seen instead as an altogether more optimistic symbol of the power of performance to outdo the petrification of bourgeois form. If Ritter Gluck, the dead composer, returns to perform for a somewhat smug narrator who is clearly au fait with the contemporary art world, the very singularity of his performance transcends not time itself, but the claim to ownership of art by virtue of its written notation. In other words, though many may read Gluck's invisible notation, possession of the textual product is not the same as the transformation of this product in performance. In relating the language of transcendence to musical performance, E. T. A. Hoffmann differs from other Romantic writers. Although music is as dependent on the medium as a literary text on signification (which inspires the Romantic metaphor of the hieroglyphic for a hermeneutic process) Hoffmann relies on a more psychologically dramatic cliché of music without medium. The genial composer Ritter Gluck surpasses any interpretation of musical notation among his contemporaries by reading from an empty sheet, but that is not to say that the notes are not there. Hoffmann's novella leaves many uncomfortable questions and ultimately allows music to show a transgression of boundaries (Gluck is a ghost) and an *apparent* transcendence of medium; since it is the performance itself which grips, the implication is that the notation, in the manner of all hermeneutic explanation of the world, offers no certainties.

In conclusion, it would seem that Hoffmann understood that expression and desire were not contained in an idealized identity or an absolute textual basis. Romantic transcendence and its path through ambivalence in many ways preempts the psychoanalytic re-thinking of rationality, but also adverts to the less popular and less well understood role of sound in how thought and feeling intertwine. Hoffmann gives this a particular twist in the haunting, music-related themes of his novels and novellas.

Notes

1. E. T. A. Hoffmann, *Fantasie- und Nachtstücke,* ed. Walter Müller-Seidel., rev. ed. (Munich: Winkler Verlag, 1993), 36: "Es ist nicht zu leugnen, daß in neuerer Zeit, dem Himmel sei's gedankt! der Geschmack an der Musik sich immer mehr verbreitet, so daß es jetzt gewissermaßen zur guten Erziehung gehört, die Kinder auch Musik lehren zu lassen, weshalb man denn in jedem Hause, das nur irgend etwas bedeuten will, ein Klavier, wenigstens eine Guitarre findet." Subsequent references to this edition of the *Fantasiestücke* are cited in the text using the abbreviation *FN.*

2. Müller-Seidel's commentary to the *Fantasiestücke* quotes Ritter, noting that Ellinger originally traced the quotation. Johann Wilhelm Ritter, *Fragmente aus dem Nachlaß eines jungen Physikers,* ed. Arthur Henkel, 2 vols. in one (1810; facsimile reprint, Heidelberg: Lambert Schneider, 1969), 224: "Das Hören ist ein Sehen von innen, das innerstinnerste Bewußtsein" (cf. *FN,* 794).

3. Ritter, *Fragmente,* 224.

4. Ibid., 236.

5. Particularly in his "Rede über die Mythologie" within *Gespräch über die Poesie* (1800).

6. See Martin Swales, "'Die Reproduktionskraft der Eidexen.' Überlegungen zum selbstreflexiven Charakter der *Lebens-Ansichten des Katers Murr,*" *E. T. A. Hoffmann-Jahrbuch* 1 (1993): 48-58.

7. *Die Elixiere des Teufels: Lebens-Ansichten des Katers Murr,* ed. Walter Müller-Seidel, rev. ed. (Munich: Winkler Verlag, 1993), 341. Subsequent references are cited in the text using the abbreviation *KM.*

8. See Kittler's analysis of Serpentina as a pre-discursive origin of the subject in Hoffmann's "Der goldne Topf": Friedrich A. Kittler, *Aufschreibesysteme 1800-1900* (Munich: Fink, 1985), 93.

9. Klaus-Dieter Dobat, *Musik als romantische Illusion: Eine Untersuchung zur Bedeutung der Musikvorstellung E. T. A. Hoffmanns für sein literarisches Werk* (Tübingen: Niemeyer, 1984), 62: "Die musikalische Form gilt nicht mehr als beliebige äußere Hülle für eine poetische Idee, die Form ist insofern selbst 'Geist,' als sie entsprechend der Aussageintention gestaltet und geprägt ist."

10. The most comprehensive analysis of Romantic aesthetics and philosophy has been carried out by Manfred Frank, *Einführung in die frühromantische Ästhetik* (Frankfurt a. M.: Suhrkamp, 1989), *Die Unhintergehbarkeit von Individualität* (Frankfurt a. M.: Suhrkamp, 1986), and *Der kommende Gott: Vorlesungen über die neue Mythologie* (Frankfurt a. M.: Suhrkamp, 1982).

11. Andrew Bowie, *Aesthetics and Subjectivity from Kant to Nietzsche* (Manchester: Manchester UP, 1990), 97.

12. Ibid.

13. Ibid.: "Art ends up retreating into autonomy in order to resist such a false reconciliation. [. . .]"

14. Theodor Adorno, *Ästhetische Theorie* (Frankfurt a. M.: Suhrkamp, 1970), 28.

15. Ibid., 207.

16. Ibid. Adorno mentions Schönberg here, holding Schönberg's notion of music as a "Geschichte der Themen" to be an implicit answer to an empiricist notion of the musical progression of an idea. Although the passage is not entirely clear, it would seem that Adorno reads Schönberg as an answer to the notion of time in Idealist aesthetics of the Absolute, whereby aesthetic time can involve a suspension of empirical time, but does so, as far as Adorno is concerned, with a utopian promise that cannot be fulfilled, and fails to realize that it cannot be fulfilled.

17. Ibid., 208.

18. E. T. A. Hoffmann, *Schriften zur Musik: Nachlese*, ed. Friedrich Schnapp (Munich: Winkler, 1963), 34.

19. Bowie, *Aesthetics and Subjectivity*, 184.

20. Ibid., 79.

21. Ibid., 173.

22. Ibid., 184.

FURTHER READING

Biographies

Hewett-Thayer, Harvey W. *Hoffmann: Author of the Tales*. Princeton, N.J.: Princeton University Press, 1948, 416 p.

Presents a detailed overview of Hoffmann's life and career, while offering an in-depth critique of Hoffmann's major writings.

McGlathery, James M. *E. T. A. Hoffmann*. New York: Twayne, 1997, 195 p.

Outlines the biographical and historical context of Hoffmann's literary career.

Criticism

Bresnick, Adam. "Prosopoetic Compulsion: Reading the Uncanny in Freud and Hoffmann." *Germanic Review* 71, no. 2 (spring 1996): 114-32.

Compares representations of the uncanny in the works of Hoffmann and Freud.

Englestein, Stefani. "Reproductive Machines in E. T. A. Hoffmann." In *Body Dialectics in the Age of Goethe*, edited by Marianne Henn and Holder A. Pausche, pp. 169-93. Amsterdam: Rodopi, 2003.

Examines the relationship between gender, sexuality, and science in Hoffmann's "Der Sandmann."

Falkenberg, Marc. *Rethinking the Uncanny in Hoffman and Tieck*. Oxford: Peter Lang, 2005, 258 p.

Discusses Freud's evaluation of the uncanny elements in Hoffmann's "Der Sandmann," while analyzing the relationship between uncertainty and the uncanny in Hoffmann's conception of Romanticism.

Gruener, Gustav. "Notes on the Influence of E. T. A. Hoffmann upon Edgar Allan Poe." *PMLA* 9, no. 1 (1904): 1-25.

Compares elements of the fantastic and the grotesque in the stories of the two authors, arguing that Hoffmann's influence on Poe's work is unmistakable.

Holbeche, Yvonne. "The Relationship of the Artist to Power: E. T. A. Hoffmann's 'Das Fraulein von Scuderi.'" *Seminar: A Journal of Germanic Studies* 16 (1980): 1-11.

Examines the social and political context of the story, focusing on Hoffmann's explorations of the relationship between the artist and power.

Jennings, Lee B. "Hoffmann's Hauntings: Notes toward a Parapsychological Approach to Literature." *Journal of English and Germanic Philology* 75 (1976): 559-67.

Analyzes elements of the supernatural in Hoffmann's works.

Kamla, Thomas A. "E. T. A. Hoffmann's 'Der Sandmann': The Narcissistic Poet as Romantic Solipsist." *Germanic Review* 63, no. 2 (spring 1988): 94-102.

Discusses the narcissistic qualities of the story's protagonist, examining Hoffmann's attitudes toward subjectivity within the context of German Romantic idealism.

Kolb, Jocelyne. "E. T. A. Hoffmann's 'Kreisleriana': A la recherche d'une forme perdue." *Monatshefte* 69 (1977): 34-44.

Argues that Hoffmann's "Kreisleriana" stories, in spite of their seemingly fragmentary quality, actually adhere to a formal structure, one reminiscent of a musical composition.

Nock, Francis J. "E. T. A. Hoffmann and Shakespeare." *Journal of English and Germanic Philology* 53 (1954): 369-82.

Evaluates the influence of Shakespeare on Hoffmann's later writings.

————. "Notes on E. T. A. Hoffmann's Linguistic Usage." *Journal of English and Germanic Philology* 55 (1956): 588-603.

Analyzes linguistic innovations in Hoffmann's work, focusing on his use of the vernacular, legal terminology, and German idioms.

Peters, Diana S. "The Dream as Bridge in the Works of E. T. A. Hoffmann." *Oxford German Studies* 8 (1973): 60-85.

Identifies three functions of dreams in Hoffmann's writings: as a source of artistic inspiration, as a window into a character's inner life, and as a metaphor for the creative process.

Praet, Danny. "Kabbala Ioculariter Denudata: E. T. A. Hoffmann's Ironical Use of Rosicrucianism, Alchemy and Esoteric Philosophy as Narrative Substructures in 'Die Irrungen' and 'Die Geheimnisse.'" *Deutsche Vierteljahrsschrift für Literaturwissenschaft und Geistesgeschichte* 79, no. 2 (June 2005): 253-85.

Analyzes Hoffmann's ironic treatment of self-transformation in his later works, while evaluating the influence of the Kabbala, Rosicrucianism, and other esoteric systems of thought on his narrative strategies.

Robertson, Ritchie. "Shakespearean Comedy and Romantic Psychology in Hoffmann's *Kater Murr.*" *Studies in Romanticism* 24, no. 2 (summer 1985): 201-22.

Discusses the influence of Shakespeare on Hoffmann's depictions of the novel's characters.

Röder, Birgit. *A Study of the Major Novellas of E. T. A. Hoffmann.* Rochester, N.Y.: Camden House, 2003, 193 p.

Provides in-depth textual analyses of Hoffmann's shorter works of fiction.

Schmidt, Ricarda. "E. T. A. Hoffmann's 'Der Sandmann': An Early Example of Ecriture féminine? Critique of Trends in Feminist Literary Criticism." *Women in German Yearbook: Feminist Studies in German Literature and Culture* 4 (1988): 21-45.

Provides a feminist reading of Hoffmann's tale.

Tatar, Maria M. "E. T. A. Hoffmann's 'Der Sandmann': Reflection and Romantic Irony." *Modern Language Notes* 95, no. 3 (spring 1980): 585-608.

Examines Hoffmann's confusion of imaginary and real elements in the story as a deliberate narrative strategy.

Additional coverage of Hoffmann's life and career is contained in the following sources published by Thomson Gale: *Concise Dictionary of World Literary Biography*, Vol. 2; *Dictionary of Literary Biography*, Vol. 90; *European Writers*, Vol. 5; *Gothic Literature: A Gale Critical Companion*, Ed. 1:2; *Literature Resource Center*; *Nineteenth-Century Literature Criticism*, Vol. 2; *Reference Guide to Short Fiction*, Ed. 2; *Reference Guide to World Literature*, Eds. 2, 3; *Short Story Criticism*, Vols. 13, 92; *Something about the Author*, Vol. 27; *Supernatural Fiction Writers*, Vol. 1; and *Writers for Children.*

Thomas Bangs Thorpe
1815-1878

(Born Thomas Bangs Thorp) American sketch writer, short story writer, historian, biographer, and novelist.

The following entry presents an overview of Thorpe's life and works.

INTRODUCTION

Many scholars regard Thomas Bangs Thorpe as among the most influential of the American frontier humorists. Although a Northerner by birth, Thorpe moved to Louisiana as a young man, attracted by the rugged beauty and idiosyncratic way of life associated with the American wilderness. Thorpe's experiences living in the South inspired a range of stories, sketches, and essays, and at the peak of his career, he was among the most popular and prolific magazine writers in the country. He achieved his greatest fame with his 1841 short story "The Big Bear of Arkansas," a fantastical tale about a hunter obsessed with his killing of a legendary bear. Along with A. B. Longstreet, George Washington Harris, Joseph Glover Baldwin, and Johnson Jones Hooper, Thorpe played a vital role in mythologizing the Southwestern wilderness for urban readers while helping to define the genre of the tall tale in American literature. Although Thorpe has been the subject of several valuable critical studies over the years, on the whole his work has attracted relatively little scholarly attention. His influence on the development of Southern fiction writing in America is unquestionable, however, and his work has attracted a range of notable admirers, including William Faulkner, who cited Thorpe's "The Big Bear of Arkansas" as an influence on his own short novel *The Bear.*

BIOGRAPHICAL INFORMATION

Thomas Bangs Thorpe (born Thorp) was born in Westfield, Massachusetts, on March 1, 1815, the son of Thomas Thorp, a Methodist circuit preacher, and Rebecca Farnham. When Thorpe was a small child, his family moved frequently, living for brief spans in Middletown and New Haven, Connecticut, before settling in New York City in 1818. Shortly after their arrival in New York, however, Thorpe's father died of tuberculosis. Left to raise their three children alone, Thorpe's mother moved the family to Albany, where they lived with Thorpe's maternal grandparents. In Albany, Thorpe—inspired by the works of the Dutch masters, the city's Dutch heritage, and the natural beauty of the Hudson River Valley—first discovered his passion for painting.

In 1827 Thorpe returned with his family to New York City, where he completed his high school education. There he also became close friends with Charles Loring Elliot, the future portrait painter. The two friends studied with the artist John Quidor, who introduced Thorpe to the works of Washington Irving. Irving's writings inspired Thorpe's first exhibited painting while also influencing the satirical elements in his later prose. In 1834 Thorpe, intent on becoming a painter, enrolled at Wesleyan University. At college Thorpe befriended a number of students from Louisiana, whose stories about life on the frontier convinced him to seek artistic inspiration in the South. He dropped out of school in 1836 and traveled to Louisiana, arriving in Baton Rouge in September 1837. A year later he moved to New Orleans, hoping to find work as a portrait painter. His prospects as a professional artist never materialized, however, and Thorpe decided to try his hand at writing humorous sketches. In 1838 Thorpe married Anne Maria Hinckley, with whom he had three children.

Thorpe soon became a regular contributor to William T. Porter's popular *Spirit of the Times,* which published his first story, "Tom Owen, the Bee-Hunter," in July 1839. In January 1840 Thorpe traveled to New York City, where he established close relationships with Porter and *Knickerbocker Magazine* editor Lewis Gaylord Clark. Over the next three years, he published more than thirty stories and sketches in the two magazines. Thorpe's impressions of the Southwest, though hyperbolic and satirical, provided audiences in the North with a valuable glimpse into the natural beauty and unique character of frontier society. "The Big Bear of Arkansas" appeared in *Spirit of the Times* in March 1841. The story later provided the title for Porter's seminal anthology of American humor, *"The Big Bear of Arkansas," and Other Sketches* (1845).

In June 1843 Thorpe joined the editorial staff of the *Concordia Intelligencer* in Vidalia, Louisiana. During his stint at the *Intelligencer,* Thorpe published his acclaimed "Letters from the Far West," a series of satirical dispatches concerning the hunting exploits of a wealthy Scotsman traveling in the American West. In November 1845 Thorpe moved to New Orleans to become editor of the *Daily Commercial Times.* Over the next two years, he worked at a variety of papers in New Orleans and Baton Rouge, while continuing to publish sketches and stories in New York magazines. Thorpe's first collection of stories, *The Mysteries of the Backwoods,* appeared in 1846. With the onset of the Mexican-American War in April 1846, Thorpe traveled to Texas, where he reported from battlefields along the Rio Grande. Thorpe's dispatches from the front lines formed the basis of two journalistic histories of the conflict: *Our Army on the Rio Grande* (1846) and *Our Army at Monterey* (1847). Thorpe's informal biography of General Zachary Taylor, *The Taylor Anecdote Book,* followed in 1848.

In 1848 Thorpe again settled in Baton Rouge, where he continued to paint and publish pieces in local newspapers. He also became involved in Whig politics and launched an unsuccessful bid to become superintendent of schools in 1852. For a brief period in the mid-1850s, Thorpe became a regular contributor to *Harper's New Monthly Magazine,* publishing numerous articles describing Southern culture. During this time he also produced another collection of sketches, *The Hive of "The Bee-Hunter"* (1854). The stories from *The Mysteries of the Backwoods* were republished in this book as were several previously uncollected magazine pieces, including a revised version of "The Big Bear of Arkansas." Also in 1854 Thorpe published his first novel, *The Master's House,* in which he addressed the issue of slavery.

In the fall of 1854, Thorpe relocated his family to New York; his wife died a year later. Thorpe married Jane Fosdick in 1857. At around this time, he became an editor for *Frank Leslie's Illustrated Newspaper,* and in early 1859 he bought a partial share of *Spirit of the Times,* although Porter was no longer the magazine's editor. Throughout these years he continued to write and paint, occasionally exhibiting his work in the city, while also working briefly as a lawyer. During the Civil War, Thorpe became a staunch supporter of the Northern cause, participating in army recruiting efforts and serving two years as a colonel during the Union military occupation of New Orleans. While in New Orleans, he once again became involved in politics, running unsuccessfully as a Republican candidate to the Louisiana state legislature.

In October 1864 Thorpe returned to New York City, where he rededicated himself to his painting. Following the death of Charles Loring Elliot, he published a short pamphlet, *Reminiscences of C. L. Elliott* (1868). In 1869 Thorpe began working for the New York custom-house, where he held various positions until his death. Throughout his later years, he continued to write for magazines, contributing articles to *Harper's, Appleton's Journal,* and *Baldwin's Monthly.* Thorpe died in New York on September 20, 1878.

MAJOR WORKS

To most scholars, Thorpe's most significant achievement remains his 1841 short story "The Big Bear of Arkansas." The narrative revolves around Jim Doggett, a rowdy, larger-than-life backwoodsman traveling by steamboat along the Mississippi River. Doggett regales his fellow passengers with the story of how he killed the "creation bear," a fabled creature that once roamed the Arkansas wilderness. Thorpe's story is notable for its use of a frame narrative in which a refined authorial voice sets the stage for the rowdy colloquialisms of Doggett. Doggett is impressive as much for his physical strength as for his outrageous storytelling; over the course of the story, he paints a vivid portrait of Arkansas, a mythical place populated by giant turkeys and killer mosquitoes, while his chronicle of the bear hunt unfolds in the manner of an epic quest narrative. Rich in biblical symbolism, the story is often interpreted in allegorical terms: many scholars regard Doggett's killing of the bear as a metaphor for the demise of the American wilderness. Thorpe's use of the vernacular is also significant in that it helped popularize an unsophisticated, dialogue-driven narrative style that would become prevalent in later nineteenth-century fiction.

Thorpe's first published story, "Tom Owen, the Bee-Hunter," is also an important example of a type of fictional prose new to the era, one exhibiting the formal, high literary style found in the works of Washington Irving while simultaneously foreshadowing the more realistic, demotic techniques of writers like George Washington Harris and Mark Twain. The story's popularity helped bolster sales of William Porter's *Spirit of the Times* at a critical moment in its history, establishing a readership for a range of other young American humorists. Thorpe published two story collections in his lifetime: *The Mysteries of the Backwoods* and *The Hive of "The Bee-Hunter."* While never collected, Thorpe's "Letters from the Far West," which parody the real-life hunting trip of Sir William Drummond Stewart, remain representative works of American frontier satire.

Although not as influential as his sketches and stories, Thorpe's 1854 novel, *The Master's House,* is noteworthy for its insights into the slavery debate. Written in response to Harriet Beecher Stowe's *Uncle Tom's Cabin,* Thorpe's novel draws from both the Northern and Southern perspectives to express the author's profound ambivalence toward the conflict between the two regions. Though little read today, Thorpe's books on the Mexican-American War, *Our Army on the Rio Grande* and *Our Army at Monterey,* are considered by some scholars to be among the earliest examples of war reporting by an American author. The books include portraits of General Zachary Taylor and other officers, as well as army reports, obituaries, and diverse statistics, and provide a valuable historical record of the war.

CRITICAL RECEPTION

With the publication of William T. Porter's 1845 anthology *"The Big Bear of Arkansas," and Other Sketches,* Thorpe earned a reputation as one of America's most accomplished humorists. Although his first story collection was a commercial failure, his second collection, *The Hive of "The Bee-Hunter,"* earned critical acclaim and contained his most representative work. During Thorpe's lifetime, his stories maintained steady popularity among magazine readers, and his best pieces were frequently anthologized. In the twentieth century a handful of scholars, notably Milton Rickels, Eugene Current-Garcia, and Walter Blair, offered important reassessments of Thorpe's influence on the development of the American short story. Rickels's 1962 critical biography *Thomas Bangs Thorpe: Humorist of the Old Southwest* is particularly noteworthy and provides an exhaustive overview of the author's body of work. Such scholars as Katherine G. Simoneaux and Leo Lemay have analyzed Thorpe's use of symbolism in the short story "The Big Bear of Arkansas." Mark Keller, among others, has discussed Thorpe's influence on the development of frontier literature. Daniel F. Littlefield Jr. and Robert J. Higgs have reviewed Thorpe's stories to assess his attitude toward the wilderness and natural beauty. David Estes has investigated Thorpe's use of folk motifs in his short fiction, while both Estes and Leland H. Cox Jr. have written in-depth critiques of Thorpe's satirical writings.

PRINCIPAL WORKS

"Tom Owen, the Bee-Hunter" [published in the *Spirit of the Times*] (short story) (1839)

"The Big Bear of Arkansas" [published in the *Spirit of the Times*] (short story) (1841)

"Letters from the Far West" [published in the *Concordia Intelligencer*] (sketches) 1843-44

The Mysteries of the Backwoods; or, Sketches of the Southwest: Including Character, Scenery, and Rural Sports (short stories and sketches) 1846

Our Army on the Rio Grande (history) 1846

Our Army at Monterey (history) 1847

The Taylor Anecdote Book (biography) 1848

The Hive of "The Bee-Hunter," A Repository of Sketches (short stories and sketches) 1854

The Master's House; A Tale of Southern Life (novel) 1854

Reminiscences of C. L. Elliott (biography) 1868

CRITICISM

Walter Blair (essay date summer 1943)

SOURCE: Blair, Walter. "The Technique of 'The Big Bear of Arkansas.'" *Southwest Review* 28, no. 4 (summer 1943): 426-35.

[*In the following essay, Blair offers a close reading of Thorpe's 1841 story "The Big Bear of Arkansas." Blair pays particular attention to Thorpe's use of a framed narrative to structure the story.*]

I

The fine artistry of the fiction of Poe, Hawthorne and Melville in pre-Civil War days has been analyzed by various critics. They have not, however, noted with comparable care the merits of some of the admirable humorous fiction written by more obscure authors active during the same period. The following comments on T. B. Thorpe's **"The Big Bear of Arkansas"** (1841)[1], long considered a masterpiece of Southwestern humor[2], may suggest something about its artistic structure.

This is a story within a story. In other words, it employs a method similar to the one whereby Chaucer, Boccaccio and many who followed them introduced a narrator and his audience, and then quoted the words of the narrator. Thorpe describes a group on a Mississippi steamboat, and then brings onto the scene Jim Doggett, the yarnspinner, and has Jim tell of his contest with the Big Bear.

A notable thing about Thorpe's handling of this form is the way he sets off various worlds involved in the story by identifying various groups and various scenes with these contrasting worlds. Furthermore, such contrasts become vital to the achievements of the narrative.

The opening paragraphs, which introduce Doggett's audience, depict a crowd which is composed of "men of all creeds and characters"—the rich Southern planter and the poor Yankee pedlar, "the Northern merchant and the Southern jockey—a venerable bishop, and a desperate gambler—the land speculator, and the honest farmer," and so forth. Such violent contrasts are emphasized in all the details about this "heterogeneous" crowd. And when Jim Doggett enters the social hall where this group is gathered, another disparity appears: he stands out from all of them.

Jim's monologue begins at the end of the second paragraph, and Jim, like Thorpe, suggests a contrast. "Perhaps," he begins, "gentlemen . . . perhaps you have been in New Orleans often; I never made *the first visit before,* and I don't intend to make another in a crow's life. I am thrown away in that ar place, and useless, that ar a fact. Some of the gentlemen thar called me *green*—well, perhaps I am, *but I arn't so at home*; and if I ain't off my trail much, the heads of them perlite chaps themselves wern't so much the hardest; for according to my notion, they were real *know-nothings,* green as pumpkin-vine—couldn't, in farming, I'll bet, raise a crop of turnips; and as for shooting, they'd miss a barn if the door was swinging. . . ."

Jim recognizes a difference between his audience and himself, and an even greater contrast between himself and the "perlite" New Orleans dudes. He has had trouble, he indicates, even talking to the New Orleans men. When they talk about "game," they do not mean "Arkansaw poker and high-low-jack" but fowl and wild animals, which Jim habitually calls "meat." Moreover, New Orleans game is "chippenbirds and shite-pokes"—"trash" that the people of Arkansas do not bother with. Jim mentions that the smallest bird he will shoot in his home state has to weigh at least forty pounds.

Arkansas, he goes on, is "the creation state, the finishing-up country. . . . Then its airs—just breathe them, and they will make you snort like a horse." A Hoosier mildly suggests that the mosquitos are a flaw. Jim admits that these are enormous, then defends them in a way which underlines the differentiation which he has begun to make between Arkansas and the rest of the world: Natives are as impervious as alligators to the gallinippers, and the only case of injury resulting from them that he knows about was to a Yankee. "But the way they used that fellow up!" exclaims Doggett, "first they punched him until he swelled up and busted; then he sup-per-a-ted, as the doctor called it . . . ; then he took the ager . . . ; and finally he took a steamboat and left the country." This setting apart of Arkansas from the rest of the world is summarized a few paragraphs later, when Jim quotes the remarks Squire Jones made after marrying an Arkansas couple: "Marriage according to law is a civil contract of divine origin; it's common to all countries as well as Arkansas. . . ."

II

Jim, however, is eventually going to tell a story with a setting and with characters even more splendid than those provided by Arkansas. As he attacks the Hoosier's remarks about mosquitos, Doggett mentions details in the scenery of his state in the order of their size. Not only are the mosquitos of the state large; "her varmints are large, her trees are large, her rivers are large." After that mounting scale, he comes to the bears of the creation state, and shortly he is suggesting that they differ not only from bears anywhere else but also from

bears of any other time: "I read in history that varmints have their fat season and their lean season. That is not the case in Arkansaw, feeding as they do upon the *spontenacious* productions of the sile, they have one continued fat season the year round." It is when a "foreigner" asks, "Whereabouts are these bears so abundant?" that the story-teller gets to a specific mention of the greatest district in this marvelous country of Arkansas—"Shirt-tail Bend" on the Forks of Cypress—Jim's own place.

Shirt-tail Bend is at first described as "one of the prettiest places on old Mississippi," but a few sentences later such mild terms are dropped, and "the government ain't got another such piece to dispose of." Three months after planting, beets there may be mistaken for cedar stumps and potato hills for Indian mounds. "Planting in Arkansaw," says Jim, "is dangerous." Shirt-tail Bend is fittingly inhabited by Doggett, "the best bar hunter in the district;" his gun, "a perfect epidemic among bar;" his dog Bowie-knife, "acknowledged to be ahead of all other dogs in the universe," and an abundance of gigantic bears.

All this (half of the whole piece) is preparatory to the story of the bear hunt itself. It is at this point that two paragraphs of narrative interrupt Jim's talk. Here the scene is switched from the Forks of Cypress back to the social hall of the steamboat. Here several sceptics dispute with Jim about the existence of such a place as Cypress Forks, "particularly . . . a 'live Sucker' from Illinois, who has the daring to say that our Arkansas friend's stories 'smell rather tall'." And one of the passengers says that, though he is no sportsman himself, he would like to hear Jim tell about a particular bear hunt.

Responding to the request for a bear story, Jim first mentions two ordinary bear hunts—ordinary, that is, for the Forks of Cypress—and then has an inspiration: "Stranger . . . in bar hunts *I am numerous,* and which particular one . . . I shall tell, puzzles me. There was the old she devil I shot at the Hurricane last fall—then there was the old hog thief that I popped over at the Bloody Crossing, and then—Yes, I have it! I will give you an idea of a hunt, in which the greatest bar was killed that ever lived, *none* excepted. . . ."

This is the Big Bear, who eludes the peerless Jim, his epidemic gun, and his incomparable dog, for two or three long years. As a rule, Jim mentions, a story of a Doggett bear hunt "is told in two sentences—a bar is started, and he is killed." "Once I met with a match though," he continues, "and I will tell you about it; for a common hunt would not be worth relating." In the account which follows, detail after detail shows this varmint eluding and outwitting Jim.

Meanwhile, the size of the bear has been noticed. Jim's first evidence is the claw marks he makes on a sassafras tree—marks which, experience has taught Jim, show "the length of the bar to an inch." This beast's marks are "about eight inches above any in the forest that I knew of. Says I, 'them marks is a hoax, or it indicates the d——t bar that was ever grown.' In fact, stranger, I couldn't believe it was real, and I went on. Again I saw the same marks, at the same height, and *I knew the thing lived.* That conviction came home to my soul like an earthquake."

Some details about hunting the bear, and about Jim's wasting away in flesh because of his frustration, come in before the size of the bear is mentioned again. This time, the creature is "a little larger than a horse." Next the preparations for the final hunt and the start of the hunt are described. During this hunt, when Jim sights the huge beast, he "looms up like a *black mist,* he seems so large." And when Jim shoots, the varmint *"walks through the fence* like a falling tree would through a cobweb." Thus, like beets and potatoes at Cypress Forks, the Big Bear grows at a terrifying rate.

The bear has reached his maximum size but not his maximum power. Earlier, telling how he pined away because the bear eluded him, Jim has mentioned briefly something quite disconcerting: "I would see that bar in everything I did; *he hunted me,* and that, too, like a devil, which I began to think he was." As bullets bounce off of the beast's head, the wonder grows; and when the bear unaccountably disappears in a lake and a she bear replaces him, says the hunter, "It made me more than ever convinced that I was hunting the devil himself."

Such weird thoughts are preparatory for the way, after growing to the size of a black mist, the Big Bear becomes a supernatural being. Doggett's last words about the monster are: "Strangers, I never liked the way I hunted, and *missed him.* There is something curious about it, I could never understand—and I never was satisfied at his giving in so easy at last. Perhaps, he had just heard of my preparations to hunt him the next day, so he just come in, like Capt. Scott's coon, to save his wind to grunt with in dying; but that ain't likely. My private opinion is, that that bar was an *unhuntable bar, and died when his time come."*

Thus the biggest bear in Shirt-tail Bend, which has the biggest bears in Arkansas, a state which itself is greater than any other country—such a bear in the end is slain not by bullets but by an inscrutable fate. And clearly everything in the narrative from the first sentence to this point is preparatory for this climax.

III

Noteworthy is the way the language used by Thorpe helps mark off the worlds of the story from one another. When Thorpe wrote, the language of literature or business differed much more from the vernacular language than it does now, and he effectively used contrasts in diction.

The first sentence in the story goes: "A steamboat on the Mississippi frequently, in making her regular trips, carries between places varying from one to two thousand miles apart; and as these boats advertise to land passengers and freight at 'all intermediate Landings,' the heterogeneous character of the passengers on one of these up-country boats can scarcely be imagined by one who has never seen it with his own eyes." The language of this sentence is factual, unimaginative—almost of the sort used in a steamboat advertisement such as the one quoted. In its structure, it is stilted, literary. The next sentence is similarly factual, even pedantic or literary in words and order; it ends with a figure of speech which is slightly more imaginative but trite and bookish: "Starting from New Orleans in one of these boats, you will find yourself associated with men from every state in the Union, and from every portion of the globe; and a man of observation need not lack for amusement or instruction in such a crowd, if he will but trouble to read the great book of character so favourably opened before him."

Next, about halfway in the first paragraph, as he begins to particularize this "book of character," Thorpe employs more informal diction—words closer to the vernacular—when he speaks of "the wealthy Southern planter, the pedlar of tinware from New England," a jockey, a land speculator, and the like. The list continues with a series of figurative nicknames bestowed in common speech (but not in dictionaries) on men of various states—"Wolverines, Suckers, Hoosiers, Buckeyes, and Corn-crackers, beside a 'plentiful sprinkling' of the half-horse and half-alligator species of men, who are peculiar to 'old Mississippi.' . . ." Thus in the second half of the paragraph, the progress in diction is similar to that in the first half: the change from the factual to the imaginative in the "elegant" prose is paralleled by a movement from the moderately informal diction to the commonplaces of vernacular speech in which the imaginative figures more and more. A few phrases at the end of the paragraph return to the stilted style of the beginning.

Something like the same movement in diction occurs in the second paragraph: there is a trend from stiff, unimaginative literary prose to more informal, more imaginative vernacular language. Here, it may be mentioned, the vernacular commonplaces start a good deal earlier—in a phrase in the first sentence. But throughout the paragraph, vernacular phrases occur more and more frequently until, at the end, there is a solid passage of oral (as opposed to bookish) speech. Moreover, the vernacular language progresses from various phrases which were widely used in the talk of the folk in 1841 to some very original phrases—from "horse," "screamer," "lightning is slow" (all commonplaces in frontier boasts), to such a phrase as "they'd miss a barn if the door was swinging, and that, too, with the best rifle in the country." Not only does the language become more picturesque, more inventive; it also becomes less grammatical, and its rhythms change to approximate those of ordinary talk.

As the story moves on from this point, there are infrequent interruptions in more formal language after various paragraphs in the vernacular; but after a while these (with the exception of two paragraphs) cease, and the vernacular only is used. With the exceptions noted, vulgar speech is employed almost to the end of the tale. At the conclusion, two paragraphs of literary language occur.

The appropriateness of such a handling of diction is indicated when one considers what is happening in the narrative while these changes in the language take place. The diction of the opening paragraphs appropriately sets off the civilized world, represented by elegant speech, from the Arkansas world, represented by Jim's vernacular. The gradations in the language, from the factual and formal to the highly imaginative, occur simultaneously with the shift of the story from commonplace New Orleans to the heterogeneous world of the steamboat then to the uniquely wondrous state of Arkansas.

After Arkansas has been described, and Jim has first mentioned Shirt-tail Bend, two paragraphs of relatively stilted prose offer a contrast to the flow of Doggett's salty chatter. They tell of the scepticism of the social hall group concerning Jim's claims about Cypress Forks. Hence, in something like the way the opening paragraphs of the story help emphasize a contrast between the rest of the world and Arkansas, these paragraphs help set off Shirt-tail Bend and its inhabitants. The final paragraphs of "literary prose," as will be indicated, also serve a purpose for which their style is appropriate. Thus Thorpe uses language, from beginning to end, in ways admirably adapted to help with the movement of his story.

IV

Three points about this narrative, in addition to those which I have noted, occur to me as possibly worth mentioning. The first has to do with a happening which occurs in Jim's yarn immediately after Doggett has fired and the Big Bear has *walked through the fence* like a falling tree would through a cobweb." At this thrilling moment, says Jim, "I started after, but was tripped up by my inexpressibles, which either from habit, or the excitement of the moment, were about my heels. . . ."

The spectacle of Jim, at the great moment of his conflict with the supernatural bear, losing his pants is a notable achievement in the way of wild incongruity.[3] For the most splendid of the great bear hunters of the earth,

at such a moment, to be tripped up by his "inexpressibles" is a calamity without a shred of dignity or, in some senses, appropriateness. And if, as the context makes possible, this is an act of malignant Fate, even Fate loses its dignity and splendor by using a low comedy expedient. It would be hard to conceive of a more complete descent from imaginative grandeur.

The second point has to do with the characterization of Doggett and its relationship to the narrative as a whole. The uniqueness of Jim's appearance and of his diction ties him up with the unique world of Cypress Forks and helps to contrast that world with the heterogeneous steamboat world. His way of emphasizing words, commented on by Thorpe and indicated by italicization, makes possible the stressing of important details in the story he tells—often details developing the patterns of increasing size which I have been tracing.

Other characteristics—Jim's good nature, his naive superstition, and his great talent for narration—motivate one of the most amusing developments in the narrative. This change may be traced by contrasting Jim's attitude at the beginning and at the end of his yarn.

When he starts, Doggett is jocose, humorous; his eyes sparkle as he flings in comic comments and playfully imagines details which are wildly improbable. For instance, he invents details about Cypress Forks with gusto, showing his expectation that they will arouse raucous laughter. But as he gets on with his story, there are fewer and fewer evidences of his being amused by his narrative. At the end of his yarn, says Thorpe, "our hero sat some moments with his audience in grave silence; I saw there was a mystery to him connected with the bear whose death he had just related, that had evidently made a strong impression on his mind. It was evident that there was some superstitious awe connected with the affair. . . ."

The picture is of a man who tells a beautiful lie—such a beautiful one that he convinces not only his audience but also himself. Fantastic Cypress Forks, which Jim has created out of sheer air, becomes a reality for him. By the soaring of his own eloquence, paradoxically enough, Jim is pulled into a confusion of the real and the imagined.

The final point has to do with Thorpe's conclusion, which, with the return to literary rather than vernacular language, comes down to earth and stays there but which sends Jim back to the world apart from ours that Doggett has been describing. Jim, so Thorpe remarks, is the first to break the silence following his tale: he makes the suggestion, generally adopted, that everybody liquor up before going to bed. Then comes this concluding paragraph:

"Long before day, I was put ashore at my place of destination, and I can only follow with the reader, in imagination, our Arkansas friend, in his adventures at the 'Forks of Cypress' on the Mississippi."

Notes

1. The story, first published in *The Spirit of the Times*, XL, 37 (March 27, 1841), has recently been reprinted in *Tall Tales of the Southwest,* ed. Franklin J. Meine (New York, 1930); *Native American Humor (1800-1900),* ed. Walter Blair (New York, 1937), and *Ring-Tailed Roarers,* ed. V. L. O. Chittick (Caldwell, Idaho, 1941).

2. Introducing the story to his subscribers in 1841, William T. Porter, the editor of *The Spirit* and a great connoisseur of current humor, told his readers "on no account" to miss it, since it was "the best sketch of backwoods life, that we have seen in a long time." In a short time the tale was widely known, and when Porter published an anthology in 1845 he called it *"The Big Bear of Arkansas" and Other Sketches.* . . . In his introduction to this volume, the editor mentioned that Thorpe's "sketches of the men and manners of the valley of the Mississippi . . . have been read and admired wherever our language is spoken." Thereafter the story was frequently anthologized during the nineteenth century, and it was known, by name at least, to many down to the present day. Recent scholars of American humor such as Miss Constance Rourke and Messrs. Franklin J. Meine, V. L. O. Chittick and Bernard DeVoto have recognized the yarn as one of the best and most influential of its time.

3. It seems to me rather typical of American humor thus to anchor the soaringly imaginative to earth with vulgar, realistic, homely details. Thus Crockett, after telling how he liberated the sun, frozen at daybreak, gave mundane details about the bear steaks he ate for breakfast. Thus Snow White, in the Disney picture, ended a poetic day in the forest by meeting the sweaty Seven Dwarfs, the most ingratiating of whom was named Dopey.

Milton Rickels (essay date 1962)

SOURCE: Rickels, Milton. "The Big Bear of Arkansas" and "The Far West Letters." In *Thomas Bangs Thorpe: Humorist of the Old Southwest,* pp. 49-61; 74-90. Baton Rouge: Louisiana State University Press, 1962.

[*In the following excerpts, Rickels analyzes Thorpe's narrative technique in "The Big Bear of Arkansas," while discussing the story's significance within the context of American frontier humor. Rickels also evaluates Thorpe's satirical letters of the early 1840s.*]

Thorpe's best known and easily his finest piece of writing was produced directly from his love of hunting and storytelling, and from his knowledge of the frontier characters of the Old Southwest whom he met on the hunting trips with the planters and on the steamboats of the Mississippi. His story **"The Big Bear of Arkansas"** appeared on the front page of the *Spirit* on March 27, 1841. It represents the most notable achievement of the time in reproducing the character of the American frontiersmen. The tale recounts the hunt of a gigantic bear by Arkansas' greatest bear hunter, and as the sketch was praised and reprinted, it became so well known that Bernard DeVoto has called the body of literature which followed it the Big Bear School of Southern humorists. No other one of the tall tales of the Old Southwest achieved its complexity of structure and richness of content.

Thorpe's story uses the device of the framework, the tale within a tale, which was already old when Chaucer and Boccaccio used it. The reproduction of oral anecdotes lends itself naturally to this sort of treatment, and it became a frequent device in Southwestern humor, which drew heavily on popular lore for its material. Furthermore, the framework is a realistic device, for the art of the oral narrative flourished vigorously in the West and Southwest. Travelers on boats and in stagecoaches, soldiers, hunters around their campfires, politicians, lawyers, and judges all told stories for their own amusement, and they cherished those tales which reproduced the excitement of the chase with color and the vernacular with fidelity. Storytelling is an art which could be shared by the illiterate folk and by well-educated professional men. That it is an art still cherished needs no documentation.

The place and circumstances of the narrator when he heard the tale are significant in establishing the point of view; consequently the framework description characterizes the storyteller and is interesting for the stage it sets. As the framework is used in **"The Big Bear of Arkansas,"** it serves to separate the world of the observer—an intelligent, traveled, well-educated man—from the rest of the audience and, more important, from the world of the Arkansas frontiersman, Jim Doggett.[1]

The first paragraph describes the kinds of people a traveler met in the 1830's and 1840's on upcountry Mississippi River steamboats. The narrator wrote that he had frequently found himself in such a crowd (as indeed Thorpe had). The opening is a conventional literary introduction to the setting. The second paragraph introduces the specific circumstances of the tale and the principal character, a backwoodsman who called himself the "Big Bar of Arkansaw." He is first heard by the passengers in the cabin as he shouts frontier boasts from the bar, a noise he keeps up for some time.

As might have been expected, this continued interruption attracted the attention of every one in the cabin, all conversation dropped, and in the midst of this surprise the "Big Bar" walked into the cabin, took a chair, put his feet on the stove, and looking back over his shoulder, passed the general and familiar salute of "Strangers, how are you?" He then expressed himself as much at home as if he had been at "the Forks of Cypress," and "Perhaps a little more so." Some of the company at this familiarity looked a little angry, and some astonished; but in a moment every face was wreathed in a smile. There was something about the intruder that won the heart on sight. He appeared to be a man enjoying perfect health and contentment; his eyes were as sparkling as diamonds, and good-natured to simplicity. Then his perfect confidence in himself was irresistibly droll.

The Big Bear's talk and actions begin the creation of his character and his world for the reader, while the passengers' reactions to him and the author's comment in the last sentence serve to maintain the separation of the two areas of experience. Thorpe's tale is not merely the telling of an exciting anecdote or the recording of a bit of folklore, although it includes these. It is a literary creation to present an American type, and the experiences of that type, to a literate public.

The contrast between the two worlds is further emphasized when Jim Doggett himself relates some of his experiences in New Orleans. "Some of the gentlemen thar called me *green*—well, perhaps I am, said I, *but I arn't so at home.*" After a few such speeches the reader is ready for the character who is not quite at home in the city—but who remains unabashed in such a condition. He is a citizen whose function lies in a wholly different area.

Doggett continues telling about his experiences in the city until one of his comments about Arkansas turkeys calls forth an exclamation from his audience, and the incredulity expressed at his exaggeration causes him to begin a description of his native state. A Hoosier among the listeners objects to the mosquitoes, and the Big Bear defends them. "But mosquitoes is natur, and I never find fault with her. If they ar large, Arkansaw is large, and a small mosquito would be of no more use in Arkansaw than preaching in a canebrake."

The next comment concerns bears, and the chorus of the audience is increased. ". . . a timid little man near me inquired if the bear in Arkansaw ever attacked the settlers in numbers." The frontiersman answers that they do not, "But the way they squander about in pairs and single ones is edifying." However, he is not ready to talk of bears yet—until he has told of his gun and his dog, Bowie-knife.

> . . . and then that dog—whew! why the fellow thinks that the world is full of bar, he finds them so easy. It's lucky he don't talk as well as think; for with his natural modesty, if he should suddenly learn how much he

is acknowledged to be ahead of all other dogs in the universe, he would be astonished to death in two minutes. Stranger, the dog knows a bar's way as well as a horse-jockey knows a woman's.

This last simile is a brilliant example of Thorpe's genius in capturing the subtle flavor of the American vernacular, with its astonishing imaginative freedom and its sometimes cynical humor. The simile is also proper to the structure of the sketch, for it serves not only to compliment Bowie-knife, but to hint revealingly at Jim Doggett's store of practical worldly wisdom. Throughout the tale the Arkansawyer's easy flow of talk is notable for its abundance and the variety of its figures of speech.

The Big Bear continues to ramble on about Arkansas animals, the fertility of Arkansas soil, and the generosity of the American government in giving it away, all in the tradition of frontier tall talk. Finally the author reintroduces himself in his own character of the quietly observant bystander:

> In this manner the evening was spent; but conscious that my association with so singular a personage would probably end before morning, I asked him if he would not give me a description of some particular bear hunt; adding that I took a great interest in such things, though I was no sportsman. The desire seemed to please him, and he squared himself round towards me, saying, that he could give me an idea of a bar hunt that was never beat in this world, or in any other. His manner was so singular that half of his story consisted in his excellent way of telling it, the great peculiarity of which was, the happy manner he had of emphasizing the prominent parts of his conversation. As near as I can recollect, I have italicized them, and given the story in his own words.

Again the framework of the tale is introduced, the narrator further characterized, and the climactic episode of the tale begun. All the points of view have been fully established, and the character of Jim Doggett concretely and dramatically presented. Almost one-half of the sketch builds toward the final and most important episode.

After some consideration, the Arkansas pioneer decides which of his many hunts he will tell about:

> . . . Yes, I have it! I will give you an idea of a hunt, in which the greatest bar was killed that ever lived, *none excepted*; about an old fellow that I hunted, more or less, for two or three years; and if that ain't a particular bar hunt, I ain't got one to tell. But in the first place, stranger, let me say, I am pleased with you, because you ain't ashamed to gain information by asking, and listening, and that's what I say to Countess's pups every day when I'm home; and I have got great hopes for them ar pups, because they are continually nosing about. . . .

In this exchange of personalities, the polite interest of the narrator is answered with the easy condescension of the frontiersman. Although each man is conscious of the difference of the other's world, they can exchange compliments on the basis of a democratic equality, for each is a citizen of consequence in his own place.

The Arkansawyer opens his story by explaining that he had learned from an old pioneer how to tell the size of a bear by the height of the marks the animal made biting the trunks of trees. He became adept at taking the measure of his bears before seeing them. Then one day he discovered the highest marks he had ever seen:

> Says I, "them marks is a hoax, or it indicates the d——t bar that was ever grown." In fact, stranger, I couldn't believe it was real, and I went on. Again I saw the same marks, at the same height, and *I knew the thing lived.* That conviction came home to my soul like an earthquake.

The hunter vows to kill the bear; the bear begins to eat his hogs; and at the first chase outruns horse and dogs, an impossibility for ordinary bears. "I would see that bar in everything I did," says the hunter, beginning to waste away from the fever of the never-ending chase; "he hunted me, and that, too, like a devil, which I began to think he was." Thus unobtrusively Thorpe introduces Doggett's feeling for the bear as a supernatural creature, a force of evil, but the hearers pay no attention to the frontiersman's casual and ambiguous comment.

The indefatigable hunter continues his pursuit of the great animal which troubles his spirit and wastes his homestead until one day with his pack he comes face to face with the creature. The bear is so ferocious that the dogs will not close with him, the hunter's gun snaps, and finally the animal escapes from the pack into a nearby lake where he swims out to an island. He is chased back into the water, and Bowie-knife goes after him. They sink, struggling together, and the dog comes up alone. With a grapevine for a rope the hunter fishes the carcass out—only to discover that it is not the old creature at all, but a smaller she-bear. "The way things got mixed up on the island was unaccountably curious," mused the Arkansawyer, "and thinking of it made me more than ever convinced that I was hunting the devil himself."

His neighbors begin to jest, and the frontiersman feels near defeat, but he prepares for a final hunt. "It was too much and I determined to catch that bar, go to Texas, or die." The day before the expedition is ready, the bear pays a greatly unexpected visit to the homestead. He catches Doggett in the brush at his morning defecation, but the prudent Doggett always carries his gun and has his dog along on such expeditions. The squatting frontiersman describes the approaching bear's size as the animal climbs over a rail fence: "He loomed up like a *black mist,* he seemed so large and he walked right toward me. I raised myself, took deliberate aim, and fired.

Instantly the varmint wheeled, gave a yell, and *walked through the fence* like a falling tree would through a cob-web." The hunter starts after him, but is tripped up by his "inexpressibles," as trousers were called in polite society. By the time he gathers himself together he hears "the old varmint groaning in a thicket nearby, like a thousand sinners," and he reaches him only to find the bear already dead.

Jim Doggett is delighted with the size of the creature and describes eloquently his immense skin. But he is not satisfied with the way he hunted and missed the animal, and with the way the bear gave in at last. "Perhaps he had heard of my preparations to hunt him the next day, so he just come in, like Capt. Scott's coon, to save his wind to grunt with in dying; but that ain't likely. My private opinion is, that that bar was an *unhuntable bar, and died when his time come.*" Jim Doggett's tale is ended, and the narrator completes the story in two paragraphs in his own person, closing the framework. He observes that somehow the death of the bear was troubling and even mysterious to Doggett. The author adds, "It was also evident that there was some superstitious awe connected with the affair,—a feeling common with all 'children of the wood' when they meet with anything out of their everyday experience." The narrator's comment repeats what Doggett has already revealed dramatically in the story itself through his repeated references to the bear as a devil and through the inexplicable disappearance of the animal on the island. Concretely the hunter reveals the powerful hold the bear had on the imagination of the folk, and more important, through this symbol Thorpe dramatizes the fearfully harsh oppositions of nature on the American frontier.

The language of the story is one of Thorpe's most praiseworthy accomplishments, truly notable for an age which looked upon the prose of Washington Irving as its highest literary achievement. The literary language of the time, as it is used by Cooper, Irving, and a host of lesser figures, is generally distinct from speech—its sentences long, its metaphors restrained and often traditional, its rhythms carefully constructed, and its vocabulary formal. Even Cooper's backwoods characters use an elevated diction. Obviously Thorpe accepted the idea of a literary language as proper under most circumstances, although he used an easier informality even in some of his *Knickerbocker* articles, and the opening and closing paragraphs of the **"Big Bear"** [**"The Big Bear of Arkansas"**] are done in the conventional style. This stiff, formal, literary prose escapes mediocrity in Thorpe's sketch because it is proper to the person of the narrator observing the frontiersman; it serves to contrast not merely the backgrounds of the traveling gentleman and the frontiersman, but more importantly, their characters and attitudes.

Even within the literary convention, Thorpe achieves a more concrete and direct style when he begins to describe the immediate scene. He had a good eye for the significant in whatever he described and a good ear for the spoken language. With only the rudimentary beginnings of a tradition in which to work, he picked up the vernacular terms used for the citizens from the different parts of the country, and in describing his audience he notes Wolvereens, Suckers, Hoosiers, Buckeyes, and Corn-Crackers, as well as the half-horse, half-alligator men of the old Mississippi. In describing the action of his protagonist he achieves a graphic terseness that is vivid and concrete. "In the midst of this surprise the Big Bear walked into the cabin, took a chair, put his feet on the stove, and looking back over his shoulder, passed the general and familiar salute of 'Strangers, how are you?'" Place names such as Hurricane, Bloody Crossing, and Shirttail Bend, Thorpe took from various locations in Arkansas and Louisiana and rearranged them to suit the circumstances of his tale. These, too, reveal the realism and poetry of the American folk imagination, and Thorpe at once recognized the possibility of their use, not only to lend verisimilitude to the language, but also to characterize the frontiersman.

Once he begins reproducing the speech of his main character, Thorpe does his best work. He avoids the extreme of trying to reproduce phonetically the pronunciation of his protagonist but depends more on rhythm, vocabulary, and imagery for his effects of realism. The frontiersman's language is always appropriate to him: its malapropisms are partly innocent and partly contrived; its descriptions racy, vivid, and highly imaginative.

Thorpe's sense of the comic is as sure as his touch with the language. Generally the humor of the piece is not physical. Except for the unusual scatological situation, it does not depend on bodily discomfort, the torture of animals, or the collapse of furniture. On the contrary, it is a humor of character. The interest of the tale lies in the person of the Big Bear of Arkansas, who is representative of the frontier type and who is in no sense ridiculous. He is amusing because his language is coarse and direct when that of polite society is refined to abstract generalities. His life is sufficiently adventurous, but in recounting his experiences, he exaggerates. He is boastful when polite society is modest. He is self-reliant—an individualist—at ease with himself even though he is quite aware that he deviates from the accepted pattern of proprieties and timidities. He is constructing his character on a new pattern. In his individualism there is a touch of the romantic concept of the natural man: the narrator sees him finally as a child of the woods. Thus he is presented at three levels. First, he is seen as the butt of the jokes of the cynical and ignorant New Orleans city cheats. Second, he is seen as the narrator's child of nature. And most elaborately, all points of view, including his own, combine to show him as the American frontiersman in action.

Jim Doggett, whether he ever existed or not, is a far more believable character than the real Davy Crockett of the *Sketches and Eccentricities*. The character of Crockett is a folk creation; it only begins with the real Davy. He is one of the demigods of the frontier. Doggett is not a folk creation. He is a character realistically and formally constructed for the literate and sophisticated audience of the New York *Spirit of the Times*. Doggett is one of the folk, and consequently, through his character the folk element enters the tale—he himself is the hunter larger than life, owning a dog of astonishing abilities, and pursuing a fabulous animal through the Western forests.[2] The pursuit of the fabulous beast, an ancient motif in folklore, is appropriate, not only because it was frequently heard in the tales of the American backwoods, but also because it serves as a symbol of the powerful malignant forces of nature which the frontiersman had to face daily. The Arkansawyer states baldly the pioneer's alternatives in his struggle. "I determined to catch that bar, go to Texas, or die." Thus it is through Thorpe's skillful literary development of the elements of humor, folk fantasies, realism, and local color that he achieves dramatic unity and a complex richness of characterization in the presentation of the Western frontiersman.[3]

In all the body of frontier literature, **"The Big Bear of Arkansas"** is the masterpiece of its kind, created from Thorpe's habits of close observation, his interest in the literary convention of the American frontiersman, and his opportunity to observe at first hand the actual farmer and hunter of the Old Southwest. He was aware of the search for the American character and of the belief that the conditions of the frontier would bring forth that character. He knew the work of Cooper and Irving, both of whom had written of the frontier's pathfinders and hunters in the romantic mode. Upon this conventional background of the educated man, a second tradition had been imposed through his work for William Trotter Porter's *Spirit of the Times*. Before Thorpe knew Porter's paper, he had read the Crockett books, and from his acquaintance with the *Spirit* he became aware of the vigor and variety of the new frontier literature based on the realism of personal observation, on humor, and on the use of local color. His years in Louisiana had given him the opportunity for personal observation, the material of that color. He knew the backwoods of the Felicianas. On his sporting trips with the planters he met the hunters of the country beyond the Mississippi, and on trips aboard the steamers of the great river he met the heterogeneous crowds of adventurers who were opening the western lands.

His own best sketch was written for the *Spirit* and thus immediately in the realistic and humorous tradition, but it was done against the background of the romantic quest, so that his story is primarily a character study and a symbolic representation of life on the frontier. The Big Bear emerges not as a rogue, nor as an object of satire, but as a strongly marked individual, humorous because he has chosen a mode of address to life that is comic, self-reliant because he has met the conditions of his existence, easy and frank because he is free and independent, and withal a little heroic. . . .

[I]n the summer of 1843 Thorpe left Vidalia for a tour through the western Louisiana prairies.[4] Thorpe's account of his trip, largely political, began appearing shortly, and then, to lighten the tone of the [*Concordia*] *Intelligencer,* he conceived the idea of a series of letters burlesquing Field's reports, purporting to be from a member of Sir William's party and yet playing on his own journey. He wrote, in a not very consistent Irish dialect, from the venerable comic point of view of the man whose every effort to be like his fellows is solemn, sincere, and abortive—his heroism degenerates into farce, his prudence into baldest cowardice, and his sentiment into the ridiculous.

Because he was writing for the male audience of a country newspaper of the Southwest, Thorpe was free to make fun of the standard literary treatment of the adventurous life in the Far West. This he could do with precision because he knew the conventions well himself and had exploited in his *Knickerbocker* essays the genteel public's interest in the area and had satisfied its demand for pathos and sentiment. During the course of the dozen letters printed between the summer of 1843 and the early spring of 1844 he burlesqued the extravagant adventures of hunting in the wilderness and satirized several fashions of the time: the joys of outdoor life, the fabulous animals of the backwoodsmen, the noble savage, and the curio collecting of nature lovers and explorers.[5] He captioned his reports **"Letters from the Far West"** and signed them "P. O. F.," initials he never explained.

The first letter solemnly describes the Crow Indians, comments on certain philological questions, notes the difficulties of traveling, and recounts anecdotes about various members of the expedition, including Audubon, who was, in fact, a member of the party for a while. He offered also an etymology of the sort dear to the traveler in strange lands: "The name 'Yellow Stone' is a corruption of the Indian title 'Yalhoo Stunn,' literally, 'the running water with green pebbles.' I got this information from a trapper who had resided several years above the Falls of St. Anthony on the Upper Missouri."[6]

In his second letter Thorpe begins his report of the Noble Savage: "We have had a great many savages with us one time or another, but most of them are more than half civilized, as they will get drunk and steal as quick as any white man I ever saw."[7] In the same letter

Thorpe also described the Indian from his burlesque point of view of the romantic explorer, this time seeing the savage for the first time:

> He was short and thick set, and smelt strongly of rancid bear's oil, which he used as we do cologne. . . . I took to him naturally; there was something that pleased me in his eye and the grateful expression of his face as I gave him a drink out of my canteen; I asked him if he had ever been in war? At the question he started back, placed himself in a most elegant attitude, a perfect representation of a corpulent Apollo, then tracing the sun's course with his finger through the heavens, he turned his face full towards me, uttered a guttural "ugh!" took a plug of tobacco out of my hand, stuck it in the folds of his blanket, and quietly walked out of my tent. . . . I never saw a more noble and beautiful exhibition of savage life.

The canteen which the Indian accepted with such happy alacrity was full of liquor, a wilderness custom the other letters refer to frequently. The fat warrior, whose name was Tar-pot-wan-ja, forthwith attached himself to Thorpe's imaginary expedition as official Noble Savage. For his services he and his squaw were fed, transported about the country, and, no doubt, entertained during the whole course of the adventure.

In a later letter the matter of the Indians was summed up in a sentence. The group was sitting around the campfire drinking, the customary nightly recreation, and the explorers began a series of toasts. The little Irishman's toast was to the wild Far West and its inhabitants: "The Indian hunting grounds—like the Indians themselves, more interesting in ladies' books than any where else."[8]

Thorpe included in his letters many burlesques of the tall tale. One of these described how the noble carcass of a mighty buffalo was attacked by a vulture and two wolves, which, in their rapacity, pushed the corpse about so that it rolled down a bank, killing the bird and pinning the two wolves to the ground with its horns. To complete the poetic justice of the fantasy, the two wolves bit each other's eyes out.

In the same letter another equally absurd tale was told of a buffalo which caught his hind foot behind his horn just as he was shot. As the hunters skinned him, the foot was dislodged, striking an Indian in the head and driving his scalp lock out his mouth. Needless to say, this killed the hunter instantly.

Both of the tales are so fantastic that they are merely ridiculous, and, like many similar pieces being printed in the newspapers of the time, quite lacking in point. The sketches satirize the tall tale neatly, revealing how the form could (and frequently did) degenerate into the telling of grotesque and absurd lies. Idle hunters spinning yarns around campfires did not always create symbolic and profound revelations of the folk mind.

An account of the correspondent's continued effort to kill a buffalo goes on through many of the letters. Early in the series one of the fabulous and mysterious animals of the great American wilderness was introduced. Crafty and evil bears with the intelligence of men, swift and beautiful white steeds, mermaids and mermen occur in the humorous literature of the 1840's, and on Sir William's expedition the little Irishman had his mind stuffed with tales of a mysterious one-horned buffalo. One morning, while out hunting, he thought he saw the mythical creature. He lay down, said his prayers, and prepared to die. Soon he felt the beast's single great horn thrusting him in the side, but hearing a human voice, he opened his eyes to see Sir William poking him in the ribs with the muzzle of his gun in preliminary diagnosis of his difficulty. "'A gude mornin' to you, mon,' said he."[9]

The incident of the one-horned buffalo and other references to a Scotch fiddle are made in such an enigmatic manner that one is led to suspect that either the matters were a private joke or that they had some bawdy significance. But whatever other meaning the great one-horned buffalo might have had, on the surface he made material for a little jest at the fabulous folk creations of the American frontier.

Often Thorpe satirized quite directly Field's reports. Field's letter in the *Picayune,* July 30, 1843, reported happily that he wrote sitting at a fire of "famous Buffalo chips." He added that he had secured "but a few curious things in the way of flower, mineral, vegetable or petrifaction, but in notes of incident my journal is rich as cream."

Thorpe, who had himself hunted buffalo in north Texas, was amused at Field's solemn interest in the staggeringly commonplace Buffalo chip. The mania for collecting things, too, was a commonplace with frontier travelers. Sometimes the relics accumulated were valuable, as was George Catlin's collection, but more often they were conversation pieces with a dismally mnemonic function. So Thorpe had his imaginary little Irishman duplicate Field's experience:

> I have got a real Indian tomahawk, that has been much used, as its appearance indicates. The history of the weapon is singular, as it once belonged to an old hunter by the name of "Collins," who seems to have originally come from "Hartford, Ct.," as he has cut his name on the side. I also have a very fine "Buffalo chip," which I had taken great care of, but having got my coat wet, it has injured it very much, and I shall have to look around for another specimen.[10]

Although here, as elsewhere, Thorpe was directly and specifically satirizing Field's letters, he usually had his imaginary correspondent choose typical samples of innocent (what a later time was to call "tenderfoot") conduct.

Throughout the letters Thorpe made much of the inconveniences and difficulties of outdoor life, the uncomfortable qualities of skin clothing, and scoffed at the idea that hunting expeditions were great fun:

> The other night we sat out all night in the rain, as our baggage took the wrong fork, which is a greater mistake in the prairies, than taking a wrong tooth brush at a hotel. It would have done you good to see us enjoying ourselves out here, sitting Indian fashion, in a ring, soaked through and smoking all over, like rotten straw stirred up in a cold morning.[11]

Thorpe also satirized the American male's addiction to practical jokes by having "P. O. F." complain that he had been killed so often in fun that it would be a relief to be killed in earnest. This almost happened when a half breed who had joined the group lassoed and almost strangled "P. O. F." just to show his skill. "For the fifteenth time since I have been out here," he wrote, "I saw there was no use in being offended at merely being killed, if it was done in fun, so I joined the laugh."[12]

All of the events were told from the point of view of one who was eager to experience such difficulties in the belief that he was enjoying himself and seeing true Life and Nature. The attitude of explorers and innocent adventurers was not the only one burlesqued. Silly tall tales and interminable and difficult hunts were characteristic pleasures of many of the frontier settlers themselves. Altogether, the letters offer comments of a realist with a quick eye for the comic. Thorpe's bogus reports satirized with neatness and precision several prominent aspects of the literary attitude toward the frontier, as well as frontier adventuring and sports.

Notes

1. For this insight and others I am indebted to Walter Blair, "The Technique of 'The Big Bear of Arkansas,'" *Southwest Review,* XXVIII (Summer, 1943), 426-35.

2. Richard Dorson, in "The Identification of Folklore in American Literature," *Journal of American Folklore,* LXX (January-March, 1957), 1-8, says that Doggett's story is no folk tale because it is not to be found elsewhere in collections of American tales. He says, probably rightly, that it is a "literary invention," which does not mean, of course, that Thorpe could not have heard it pretty much as he wrote it. It does, moreover, have folk elements in it. For discussions of folklore in the Southwestern humorists see also Louis J. Budd, "Gentlemanly Humorists of the Old South," *Southern Folklore Quarterly,* XVII (September, 1953), 232-40; James H. Penrod, "The Folk Mind in Early Southwestern Humor," *Tennessee Folklore Society Bulletin,* XVIII (June, 1952), 49-54, and "Folk Motifs in Old Southwestern Humor," *South-*

ern Folklore Quarterly, XIX (March, 1955), 117-24. On bear fights as folklore, W. W. Lawrence sensibly remarks, "The frequency of . . . bear fights in general, should make us cautious about drawing conclusions too confidently." "Some Disputed Questions in *Beowulf* Criticism," *Publications of Modern Language Association,* XXIV (1909), 237.

3. See Daniel G. Hoffman, *Paul Bunyan, Last of the Frontier Demigods* (Philadelphia, 1952), 67.

4. New Orleans *Picayune,* August 2, 1843.

5. Only two of these letters are available in extant copies of the *Concordia Intelligencer,* one in the November 25 and one in the December 30, 1843, issues. All quotations from them are from the *Spirit* [*Spirit of the Times*]. The first letter was printed in the *Spirit,* XIII (August 25, 1843), 303.

6. *Ibid.*

7. *Spirit,* XIII (September 9, 1843), 333.

8. *Ibid.* (November 18, 1843), 445.

9. *Ibid.* (October 14, 1843), 392.

10. *Ibid.* (October 21, 1843), 405.

11. *Ibid.*

12. *Ibid.* (January 27, 1844), 569.

Barrie Hayne (essay date summer 1968)

SOURCE: Hayne, Barrie. "Yankee in the Patriarchy: T. B. Thorpe's Reply to *Uncle Tom's Cabin.*" *American Quarterly* 20, no. 2, pt. 1 (summer 1968): 180-95.

[*In the following essay, Hayne evaluates Thorpe's 1854 novel* The Master's House *as a critique of* Uncle Tom's Cabin. *Hayne asserts that Thorpe's response to Stowe's novel represents a far more thoughtful, and resonant, analysis than other reactions from the period, notably in its willingness to examine the slavery question from both the Northern and Southern points of view. Thorpe's ambivalence toward the issue of slavery, according to Hayne, derived from his experiences as a Northerner living in Louisiana.*]

When *Uncle Tom's Cabin* began to appear in the *National Era* in June 1851, it was only twenty years since the dispute between Jackson and Calhoun had begun to realign the forces of union against those of states' rights, a conflict quiescent since the heyday of Jefferson and the compact of states theory. It was the first year of the decade which had opened with the Compromise of 1850 and the Fugitive Slave Law and which would also see the Kansas-Nebraska Act and the Dred Scott decision.

More than narrowly sectional feelings were liable to be hurt by Mrs. Stowe's novel, therefore, and rebuttals came, predictably, not only from the South, but from the North as well. Of the sixteen works which sought to refute the assertions of *Uncle Tom's Cabin* in the years 1852-54, six were written by Northerners, six by native Southerners, one of whom had been living in the North for twenty years, and three by Northerners who had become Southerners by adoption.[1] None of these works would rival the sale and circulation of *Uncle Tom's Cabin,* though two of them, W. L. G. Smith's *Life at the South* and Mrs. Eastman's *Aunt Phillis's Cabin,* had by normal standards very large sales.[2]

There were two principal reasons for the replies—regional sensitivity and national concern. The Southerners who replied to Mrs. Stowe were primarily concerned with defending the southern institutions which she had attacked; the Northerners defended those institutions only as a secondary matter, their primary aim being the preservation of the union which Mrs. Stowe's divisive words had seemed to endanger. The author of *Buckingham Hall,* who had traveled in the South, and beyond the Kentucky which was Mrs. Stowe's sole acquaintance with the region, represents that characteristically northern aim in rebutting her:

> to contribute his *mite* in endeavoring to allay the great agitation on the Slavery Question between the North and South, which threatens to dissolve our glorious Union; and as that talented authoress, Mrs. Stowe, in 'Uncle Tom's Cabin', has increased that agitation, the author hopes to modify it somewhat, by representing the Planter and Slave in a more favorable light.
>
> (*BH* [*"Uncle Tom's Cabin" Contrasted with Buckingham Hall, the Planter's Home*], "Prefatorial")

The northern replies therefore generally lacked the feelings of suppressed guilt which characterized the southern replies, and which it had been one of Mrs. Stowe's primary aims to elicit ("the book has a direct tendency to do what it was written for,—to awaken conscience in the slaveholding States and lead to emancipation").[3] One of these early replies, however, does seem to be motivated by both considerations; it is not only an attempt to allay agitation but also the chivalric answer to a challenge. That reply, too involved with the southern point of view to be free of those guilt feelings, yet seeking with northern high-mindedness to represent planter and slave more favorably, is Thomas B. Thorpe's ***The Master's House.*** Written by a Northerner who had lived fifteen years in the South, it demonstrates, as its fellows in their tractarian simple-mindedness do not, a will to see both sides of the question or, more accurately, a conditioned inability to see only one side.

It must never, of course, be forgotten how elusive a target *Uncle Tom's Cabin* presented to its contemporary detractors. "The novel," as Edmund Wilson has remarked, "is by no means an indictment drawn up by New England against the South. . . . The author, if anything, leans over backwards in trying to make it plain that the New Englanders are as much to blame as the South and to exhibit the Southerners in a more favorable light."[4] Mrs. Stowe's indictment of southern slaveholding had already with studious objectivity conceded most of the possible defenses, without diminishing at all her passionate attack on slavery as an institution. Her attack on slavery is uncompromising; her sympathy for the South, and especially for the planter class, is considerable. Augustine St. Clare, apart from his Byronic disillusion, and Shelby, apart from his more mundane financial irresponsibility, are of the same stuff as the model masters in the proslavery fiction. None of the apologists' masters, indeed, is as admirable as Shelby's son, Mas'r George, who presumably grew up to be Edward Clayton, the crusading slaveholder of *Dred*.[5] For Mrs. Stowe, as for the apologists, slavery is indeed an aristocratic institution, with the slave at the mercy of his master. The replies show that mercy as never strained; Mrs. Stowe fears the situation when it is absent or nonexistent. The happiness of the slaves on Shelby's plantation is no less than it is on Courtenay's in *The Cabin and Parlor,* but in Mrs. Stowe's vision the specter of separation hovers in the background. When financial difficulty comes to Shelby, he sells Tom away from his family; when financial ruin comes to the Courtenays they sell to neighbors who refuse to separate slave families, and the slaves in fact live under better conditions than the erstwhile masters.

The principal basis of the proslavery argument was, of course, the patriarchal and protective nature of the institution.[6] The planter's life is regulated by the principle of *noblesse oblige*: his slaves are children to be fed, to be clothed, to be instructed in the Christian religion. The Negro's is an inferior culture ("They are the most improvident race in the world, and must have a superior mind to guide them," *NS* [*The North and South*], p. 226), and will survive only so long as it serves the aristocratic culture which sustains it:

> Such too, the fate the negro must deplore,
> If slavery guard his subject race no more,
> If by weak friends or vicious counsels led
> To change his blessings for the hireling's bread.

> (*HS* [*The Hireling and the Slave, Chicora, and Other Poems*], p. 68)

By presenting the institution of slavery as patriarchal and aristocratic, the replies sought to deny those charges which Mrs. Stowe would later accept as her three central ones: "first, the *cruel treatment* of the slaves; second, *the separation of families*; and, third, their *want of religious instruction*."[7] Slaves are never cruelly treated in these novels; a George Harris would not be perversely prevented from following the trade of his choice, nor would a Legree long be tolerated as a master of slaves.[8] Slaves are never separated from their families; it is a point of honor amongst the planters, when one of their number is reduced to selling his slaves, that the Negro families be preserved intact.[9] Slaves are never in want of religious instruction; though the deep superstitious vein in the Negro temperament causes his religious feelings, "if not properly directed, [to] become superstitious and fanatical,"[10] nonetheless the "attention paid by planters to the religious instruction of their negroes yearly increases; the benefit is felt mutually by master and slave."[11]

The paternalism of plantation life in the apologies is impaired only by the disagreeable but necessary presence of the overseer. While there are few bad native southern masters in these novels—slaveholders native to the North are quite another matter[12]—there are but two good overseers, the man who loyally remains behind to guard Peyton's plantation against slave insurrection in Mrs. Hale's *Liberia,* and Mr. Gravity in *Life at the South,* two novels written by Northerners. The southern writers recognize the evils inherent in the delegation of duties—"the worst feature in slavery" one character calls the overseer (*APC* [*Aunt Phillis's Cabin*], p. 96)—but offer no alternative; nor indeed do they seem to advocate reform. As the district attorney prosecutes the overseer Toadvine in *The Master's House,* however, Thorpe's inability to shrug off the problem as a disagreeable necessity is apparent, just as his confidence in procuring any change in the system seems minimal: "'The peculiar character of our institutions requires that the master should necessarily delegate a great deal of power to his confidential agent—the overseer; but that authority is to be exerted wisely, and, except in extreme cases, violence is not to be used. . . . Unless, gentlemen, we protect our slaves . . . from the death-dealing influences of irresponsible white men, society among us will rapidly degenerate into barbarism. . . .'" (*MH* [*The Master's House*], p. 311).

While Mrs. Stowe's Legree is a slaveholder, and not the subordinate overseer of the dramatized versions of *Uncle Tom's Cabin,* he could have appeared centrally in the proslavery novels only as an overseer. By making her villain a Northerner, Mrs. Stowe had already minimized her attack on the southern planter class, and at the same time defused the argument, so common in the replies, that the only bad masters are converted Yankees. Had she made Legree the overseer into which the folk imagination, with subconscious disinterest, has since transformed him,[13] there would have been, here as elsewhere, little point at issue between her and her critics. Indeed, she had already foreshadowed the transformation, by making him *both* planter and overseer: "'I don't keep none o' yer cussed overseers; I does my own overseeing; and I tell you things *is* seen to. . . . I'm none o' yer gentleman planters, with lily fingers, to slop round and be cheated by some old cuss of an overseer!'" (*UTC* [*Uncle Tom's Cabin*], p. 347).

Thorpe's view of the overseer is characteristically dual. On the one hand his Toadvine is a drunken brute, but on the other it is impossible not to hear the tones of conviction in the speech of the defense counsel—as well as the prosecution—at the trial of that same Toadvine: "while the master is treading, with dainty steps, his marble halls, the faithful overseer is winding his devious way through interminable swamps . . . while the master sees his negroes fat, sleek, happy, and idle, the overseer beholds them as the necessary objects of strict discipline, and *is forced* to make them do their work" (*MH*, pp. 315-16, underlining added).

Worse even than the overseer in these novels, though more of a dispensable evil, since sale of slaves is rarely resorted to, is the slave trader. Again Mrs. Stowe anticipates, presenting Haley as less than humane in her very opening chapter, but the proslavery novelists denigrate the class still further. Donald Montrose feels his house "polluted" by the presence of a trader—a "human tiger" (*L and L* [*The Lofty and the Lowly*], II, 34); yet his attitude is different only in degree from Mrs. Shelby's, when she discovers who the "low-bred fellow" under her roof was (*UTC*, p. 36). Uncle Wardloe has "never known one . . . that was not a devil black as hell" (*FFBS* [*Frank Freeman's Barber Shop*], p. 76). When a trader appears at the sale of Mr. Courtenay's slaves, he is hustled away by the neighbors before he can do any harm (*CP* [*The Cabin and the Parlor*], p. 51). Yet all but one of these novels completely ignores the question which Mrs. Stowe had posed: "But who, sir, makes the trader? Who is most to blame? The enlightened, cultivated, intelligent man, who supports the system of which the trader is the inevitable result, or the poor trader himself?" (*UTC*, p. 137). Major Dixon, the trader of **The Master's House,** is allowed by Thorpe to see himself as "a scapegoat for the sins of the buyer" (*MH*, p. 50), and the characterization of this attitude as "a kind of monomania" does not altogether hide Thorpe's recognition of its justice.

Of all these early replies to Mrs. Stowe, the one which might be allowed to stand as representative of simple-minded rebuttal is J. Thornton Randolph's *The Cabin and Parlor.* Hidden behind the unmistakably southern pseudonym is Charles Peterson, a Northerner, the Philadelphia editor of *Graham's Magazine* in Poe's time, and later, for forty-five years, of *Peterson's Magazine,* the long-lived competitor with *Godey's Lady's Book* for the American middlebrow reading audience. Peterson's novel is the more convenient representative of its class by reason of its being the only reply which Mrs. Stowe, apparently, deemed worthy of direct counterstatement.[14] In *The Cabin and Parlor* one finds exemplified the argument that the slave who becomes the hireling suffers and even perishes outside his paternal custody[15]—Charles and Cora flee north where Charles, unemployed, dies of want, leaving Cora only too glad to beg her mistress' forgiveness "if I have to beg my way back to her, walkin' all the road" (*CP,* p. 303). This, of course, she is not called upon to do.

At the center of *The Cabin and Parlor* is a reversal of roles; to emphasize the more onerous slavery of the master, Peterson diagrams the downward course of the slaveholders against the upward rise of the former slaves. As its title and subtitle (*Slaves and Masters*) might suggest, Peterson's novel juxtaposes life in the big house, when hard times have come a-knocking, with life in the Negro cabins. The plot follows the fortunes of Isabel Courtenay and her mother, dispossessed of their plantation by the improvidence of the late Mr. Courtenay. As they sink further and further into poverty, they are kept alive only by the provisions surreptitiously left at their door by their former slave, Uncle Peter, who has been purchased by a kindly master and who continues in much the same comfortable life as he led under the Courtenays. Of all the replies, too, *The Cabin and Parlor* is most obviously an "answer" to Mrs. Stowe, and offers to *Uncle Tom's Cabin* a number of parallels intended to correct Mrs. Stowe's exaggerated departures from verisimilitude. Mr. Courtenay is an aristocratic weakling like St. Clare, but his irresponsibility affects only his blood family, not his slaves. His hypochondriacal wife is a Marie whose passivity does not give way to destructive spite against the Negroes after her husband's death. The noble Isabel is a grown-up Eva, who, in the most ironic reversal of all, almost perishes in a snowstorm, a scene obviously intended to recall Eliza's unforgettable escape across the Ohio. There are no Legrees in *The Cabin and Parlor,* but Peter is a Tom, unmartyred because here the white folks are the martyrs, and he is quite as ingenious as his model in seeing the mercy of God in every misfortune. Not only do the Negroes Charles and Cora suffer unceasingly in the North, beginning with the necessity of Charles' taking a residential job, which prevents husband and wife from meeting more than once a month. Isabel's brother himself is driven north by the loss of the plantation and dies of deprivation in that harsh environment. White families, that is to say, can be broken up by circumstances not of their making, but never the black families, for Charles and Cora are runaways, and the slave families who stayed with the Courtenays remain intact. Finally, like all the replies which have their setting in the South, *The Cabin and Parlor* rests its case firmly on southern benevolent paternalism. The novel opens with a ball in the southern mansion, a scene festooned with such vocabulary as "courtly," "noble," "ancient," "elegant." All cruelty is relegated to the hut of the overseer and the caravan of the trader, and as the scene shifts above and below the Mason-Dixon line, the Yankee is bidden to set his own house in order.

A Southerner of the early 1850s, therefore, asked to put into the hands of a detractor of slavery a single novel of defense, might well have selected *The Cabin and Parlor*. He would have been unwise to entrust his case to what remains the most interesting of all the replies, and the most nearly artistic. Unwise, because the ambivalence of *The Master's House* has, not surprisingly, left open the question whether it is indeed a refutation of Mrs. Stowe's charges or a weightier corroboration of them. Mrs. Stowe's novel ends on a note of hope, with George Harris going to a new life in Liberia, and Tom going on to Glory, a black Christ whose martyrdom may yet bring his race to redemption. The white folks are unscathed, their social structure unshaken. Only, really, in Uncle Tom's cabin is the grief of parting and bereavement felt. In Thorpe's novel, however, the murder of the slave destroys the master's house itself, and puts into hazard the white society which has Mildmay as its center.

Of the sixteen replies in the two years which followed *Uncle Tom's Cabin*, no less than eight bear titles which play, with varying degrees of ironic subtlety, upon one or other of Mrs. Stowe's own titles. *Uncle Robin in his Cabin in Virginia and Tom Without One in Boston* announces its line of rebuttal in unequivocal terms: the gap between southern paternalism and northern hypocrisy. "Uncle Tom's Cabin" is offset, too, by "Buckingham Hall" or by "Frank Freeman's Barber Shop"; "Life among the Lowly" has its imbalance corrected in "The Lofty and the Lowly." *The Cabin and Parlor* seeks to contrast the life of the slave, leisured and carefree, with that of his master, onerous and deprived. But only in the title of *The Master's House* is there more than a gratuitous sneer or a felicitous word play. Here the focus is effectively shifted from the slave hut to the big house, and the master shown to be a principal victim of the slavery system. Several of these novels—and Mrs. Stowe had satirically anticipated the plea in Marie St. Clare—present the master or mistress as the greater slave than the Negro. But only Thorpe—with Mrs. Stowe once more a qualified exception—presents with any persuasiveness the master as a tormented figure, uneasy in his responsibility yet convinced of its propriety.

The task that Thorpe sets himself in *The Master's House* is finally more difficult not only than the other apologists' but than Mrs. Stowe's itself. She sympathizes with the South, yet her northernness enables her to attack intellectually its peculiar institution. He sympathizes with the South as a partially acculturated Southerner, yet is unable to extricate his intellect from his sympathies. What in her is objectivity becomes ambivalence in him. In his mind there is conflict between emotion and principle; in hers there is none. A further reason for Thorpe's ambivalence is that in his mind, as not in the other apologists', southern honor comes into conflict with national interest. He is enough of a Northerner to see that the outright assertion of southern sovereignty, if not the perpetuation of southern slavery, would dissolve the union.

Thorpe was born in Westfield, Massachusetts, in 1815. After exhibiting a precocious talent for painting, and having received "as good an education as the New York schools of his boyhood afforded," he went on to Wesleyan College in 1834. Like his hero Graham Mildmay, Thorpe was called upon to deliver the commencement address—in his first term. This early promise did not, however, come to full fruition, and he left Wesleyan in 1836, because of ill-health or indolence,[16] and having made several southern friends in his two years of college, he first toured the South, and then settled in Louisiana. It was in this region, drawing on local lore, that he wrote the stories which keep his name marginally in literary history. **"The Big Bear of Arkansas"** deserves to live, as it has, longer than anything else he wrote.

The life of this Whig writer-painter-politician is consistent throughout in its dedication to nationalism over regionalism. When the Mexican War, that barometer of manifest destiny versus Little America, broke out, Thorpe was on the side of expansionism, and as Colonel Thorpe was the bearer of dispatches between General Gaines and General Taylor. Here his news stories from the front made him what the New York *Times* at his death called "the first correspondent who penned his descriptions on the battlefield."[17] Two books came out of the war, and out of his experiences came as well his great admiration for Zachary Taylor, whose presidential ambitions Thorpe's writings first furthered, and whom Thorpe, more directly, supported in a series of speeches in the campaign of 1848. His persuasiveness on the platform was noted, and some of the credit for Taylor's victory given to him. Though an article published in the very month of Taylor's death predicts for Thorpe the role of some kind of super patriot-politician-litterateur,[18] he was disappointed if he hoped for any substantial political reward from his patron, and that patron's early death compounded his disappointment. Running for State Superintendent of Education in 1852, he went down with the rest of the Whig ticket to overwhelming defeat. The picture of the quintessential Whig of his day,[19] with overriding national loyalties, yet after so many years in the South considerable sectional sympathies as well, is rounded out by his espousal of the platform of the xenophobic Know-Nothings in 1855, and by his loyalty to the Union during the Civil War, when he was staff officer to General Benjamin Franklin Butler. Leaving the South in 1853, he never returned to it.

In the early 1850s, however, he dreaded the dissolution of the Union, yet hoped for the preservation within it of the integrity of the South, with its patriarchal master-slave system. As Mildmay puts it, and Mildmay is the nearest thing to Thorpe's *raisonneur* in **The Master's House**, even though the identity of *raison* in the novel is all too often doubtful:

> I desire to cut the South loose from its dependence, not only upon the North, but upon every thing but its inexhaustible resources. But this glorious result must be reached not by agitation, or popular speeches, but by harsh self-sacrificing industry. . . . I have no desire to separate the Union, but I am willing to do all I can to render the South commercially free; let us make ourselves independent; and I am willing to leave the cementing together of this Great Republic to the strong bonds of mutual interest,—to say nothing of being by nature and historical associations really one people, members of the same family.
>
> (*MH*, pp. 284-85)

The Master's House begins in the North, but not in the industrialized North, "the land of steady habits" (*LAS* [*Life At The South*], p. 75) of W. L. G. Smith's two-edged sneer. Thorpe's first chapter introduces the reader to the New England town of Malden, deliberately invested with a southern aura: "Until recently, Malden retained quite a rural appearance, and presented a charming mixture of tasteful cottages, ornamented with choice shrubbery, and a few grand old mansions, half hidden away among elms more than a century old." As he describes the house of his heroine Annie Hastings, he appeals to the common American ancestry which should, like the essential similarity of their institutions, unite North and South, but simultaneously he expresses his doubt in the stability of the present: "an old, yet noble looking house . . . seems to stand out from among the more pretentious residences by which it is surrounded, as would John Hancock in his rich but quaint costume, if suddenly thrust into a group of modern gentlemen" (*MH*, pp. 13-14).

Thorpe's oscillating loyalties are apparent as he assigns to the Hastings family all the rigidities of New England puritanism, which is nonetheless "well calculated to command profound respect" (*MH*, p. 14), and the ambivalence continues as he introduces his young southern hero Graham Mildmay who, possessing "what is not uncommon to youth from his section of country, but yet not characteristic, was of rather a serious temperament" (*MH*, p. 16). The defensiveness is there of one who knows well the reputation for frivolity of the southern patrician, and who partially assents to the justice of the reputation.

The very opening chapter, too, draws the line between Roundhead and Cavalier—the elder Hastings are roundheads, ascetic and self-satisfied, Reynolds Calhoun is a cavalier, gifted yet indolent. Mildmay represents the two in equilibrium: the moderation that his name suggests[20] casts him as moderator between two very different cultural norms: "He . . . seemed to happily com-bine industrious habits with the cultivated manners and easy bearing, so peculiar to the youth of the South. There was a sense of innate worth, and pecuniary ability about Mildmay, that so frequently distinguishes the highly educated planter from the mere business man . . ." (*MH*, p. 17). An Augustine St. Clare who can keep accounts, and a Yankee who is also a gentleman. Calhoun is a wastrel, who sees New England only as a contrast to the South, the Hastings may well be abolitionists, and are at best narrow New Englanders, whereas Mildmay refuses to "make mental distinctions between the people of this great republic" (*MH*, p. 20). And already turning with a pleasantry from the specter of division raised, Thorpe uses his comic Louisianian Marigny to unite North and South in his own characteristic way ("'it is after all . . . the beautiful and good girls of this same sterile New England, who make us feel our homes are the same, whether North or South, and I say, may Heaven bless them all!'"—*MH*, p. 20), and then allows Calhoun in similar vein to project wittily the conquest of South by North in the number of southern husbands conquered by northern brides.

This first chapter of **The Master's House,** therefore, puts the reader in possession of Thorpe's methods and aims. His hero will be the perfect southern Whig, jealously conservative of the traditions of the South, and yet anxious for the preservation of the Union. In looking at the possibility of national dissolution, Thorpe will blink his eyes, comically as here, or evasively as later. Over all, will hang a nostalgia for the past in which Americans, working in co-operation, whether in Massachusetts (John Hancock) or in Virginia ("the leader of our revolution," a slaveholder, *MH*, p. 27), have brought the nation to the threshold of national greatness. This glorious past is now in constant tension with a present in which the American's seeming inability to think in national terms may deny him that greatness.

As the novel proceeds, the two-year probation period imposed upon Mildmay by Annie being taken up with the movement of his slaves from the ancestral home in North Carolina to a new plantation in Louisiana, the sketchy figure of Reynolds Calhoun gives place to that of Mr. Moreton, the older and more intractable Southerner who is Mildmay's new neighbor. Annie and Graham are married, and settle at "Heritage Place." In Mildmay's absence his brutal overseer murders his favorite Negro, but is saved by Mildmay from a lynch mob of planters seeking to exact punishment primarily for "the reckless destruction of our property" (*MH*, p. 225). Mildmay insists that the law take its course, which it does—in the acquittal of the overseer. Moreton now runs for the legislature, is defeated by an illiterate piney woods yokel, and in a misunderstanding challenges Mildmay to a duel. Mildmay reluctantly fights, and kills his opponent. Annie's death shortly thereafter is but one more microcosmic indication of the moribundity of the planter's world and the collapse of law and order—after the venal jury, the defeat and death of Moreton, and the obliteration of his grave by the slave teams, to be followed by the social eminence of "General" Dixon, the brutal slave trader turned plantation owner. The darkness of a starless night which enshrouds the grieving Mildmay at novel's end is the final and effective symbol of chaos.

The first article of Thorpe's defense, therefore, is the plea of "I have seen." As in several of the other replies, *Uncle Robin, The Planter's Northern Bride, Buckingham Hall,* the central character has brought back with him a northern wife. Since to see is to be convinced of the virtues of the slavery system, these northern brides are quickly acculturated, for attacks on the system can be made only by those, like Mrs. Stowe, who have barely been south of Cincinnati. *Aunt Phillis's Cabin* is subtitled "Southern Life as it is," and the prefaces of these novels ring with assertions that here is the true picture—"the faithful transcript of the Daguerreotypist"—of southern slavery rather than "the distorted picture of an interested painter," and that it was the intention of "Mrs. Stowe and her stripe" "to deceive those who are as ignorant as themselves, and perhaps as reckless of truth" (*AF* [Antifanaticism], Preface). The pseudonym of the author of one of these novels—"Vidi"—might have stood for all. Thorpe has seen, but is somewhat less convinced than his fellow apologists of the virtues of the peculiar institution. When the master falls, then the patriarchal system must fall with him; it is characteristic that only in *The Master's House* is such a fall contemplated.

It can hardly be said that the remaining articles of Thorpe's defense are very tellingly argued for the southern cause. It is as though he were presenting the case for the South, and simultaneously acting as prosecutor. Whereas one might expect the Fugitive Slave Law to be the center of universal approval in the proslavery response, that law is looked at with characteristically mixed feelings in *The Master's House.* It has put money into the pockets of monsters like Dixon, who keeps a scrapbook of clippings about escapees, and who pursues them into the North to sell them back into slavery. Even for Mildmay it is an evil law, for escaped slaves are not worth pursuing, and the law itself can only further divide North and South.

Whereas the other replies accuse the abolitionists of hypocrisy ("'if they could have raised sugar and cotton . . . they'd have had a Fugitive Slave Law before this,'" *APC,* p. 92), and tend to see all Northerners as abolitionists, Mildmay is to be found deprecating abolitionism, but deprecating no less the similar extremism of Moreton's elitist philosophy ("'The idea of men being free and equal is a humbug.'"). But he defends the North against Moreton's intemperate attacks—the defense of "I have seen" works both ways for this transplanted Northerner—by pointing out that of all the Northerners he knew at school, only two were abolitionists, and that both are now living in the South as ardent pro-slavery secessionists. These "mere time-servers" are "as heartless and unprincipled and dangerous in their new vocation, as they were in their old" (*MH,* p. 150); again Thorpe's appeal is for moderation, though it is the moderation of inaction: "'if we would happily live in the South, we must not look so deeply and darkly upon the things around us;' . . . Mr. Moreton's thoughts launched again into the current of life, allowing the present only to occupy his mind; the future he carefully excluded" (*MH,* p. 152).

Whereas these apologies assert relentlessly the disadvantages of the Negro in the North over the advantages of the protected slave, Thorpe presents in the interpolated story of Charles Broadnax a Negro who escapes to the North to make good: "In six months he learned to read quite fluently, and soon arranging his varied experience, it was found he had naturally a strong and well-balanced mind, and *unlike most of his race,* he was frugal, and took pleasure in saving money" (*MH,* pp. 62-63, underlining added). Even here, the southern stereotype almost swamps the northern open-mindedness.

Whereas the South is presented in most of the replies as the land of health ("warm climates produce warm hearts," *BH,* p. 133), as distinct from the "frigid regions of the North," (*AF,* Preface), Thorpe presents the North as fruitful, burgeoning, and the South as the graveyard of Annie Mildmay's health ("The enervating character of the climate, however, had its effect upon her constitution . . ." *MH,* p. 114). Even subliminally, the moribundity of one world is opposed to the vitality of the other.

Whereas the other replies, meeting one of Mrs. Stowe's principal grounds of concern, assert that slave families never are separated, "except in rare cases, or where the slave has been guilty of some misdemeanor . . . for which, in the North, he would have been imprisoned, perhaps for life" (*CP,* pp. 39-40), Thorpe recognizes that the avarice of the slaveholder—though more usually that of the trader—may dictate the separation of families, but blames the parvenus like Speers rather than the old aristocracy like Mildmay for countenancing such separation.

In the matter of religion, finally, the apologists' defense is twofold: they begin by denying Mrs. Stowe's charge that the slaves were taught no Christianity, and end by entering the teachings of Christ as support for the perpetuation of slavery.[21] On the first point, though in "Cotton and its Cultivation" he does testify to widespread religious teaching on the plantations, Thorpe barely mentions it in *The Master's House*; it is simply another of Mrs. Moreton's slavish duties as mistress of the manor. On the second point, however, *The Master's House* contains the most lengthy and persuasive exposition of the Biblical defense of slavery in the replies (*MH,* p. 202). The reader's momentary assent may be won, until he learns that it is this very sermon which returns the temporarily contrite Dixon to his brutal calling. The church has failed to shoulder its responsibility of inveighing against the evil of the slave system, is Thorpe's point: the church in which the predatory Mr. Goshawk gives his sermon "was the resting place of domestic animals, and never of any philanthropic use" (*MH,* p. 186).

It is a general breakdown which is projected at the end of *The Master's House,* a failure of all the great institutions of the state—the church, the law, the elected legislature, all have fallen out of the hands of the cavalier class in the South, and into the hands of the poor whites. Though it *is* the present which obsessively occupies Thorpe's mind, he is not altogether successful in carefully excluding the future from his novel. What he hopes for is a strong southern region, within the Union, where slavery would be preserved, treated "purely as a local and domestic institution," and where the destinies of the region would be in the benign hands of the landed classes. What he fears is the inflexibility of the South, its unwillingness to compromise. If the salvation of the Union depends upon the Whig party, that Whig party could quell the southern element, but in that act both might be destroyed. The duel between Moreton and Mildmay is a microcosmic Civil War in which both southern pride and supraregional moderation come to grief.

After Thorpe had anatomized his own personal *Zerrissenheit,* and his country's, in *The Master's House,* he deliberately ignored both in giving his sanction to *A Voice to America*[22] in the following year, 1855. This hysterically xenophobic piece of work embodies the platform of the so-called American Party, the "Know-Nothings." One looks in it in vain for equation of "the present crisis in the United States" with the slavery question, or even with the conflict between North and South, for the "present crisis" is merely vaguely postulated, and then blamed upon foreigners and Catholics. *A Voice to America* is the *reductio ad absurdum* of the confusion in Thorpe's mind which appears in *The Master's House.* Committed by the dictates of reason to the preservation of the Union, but joined by ties of congeniality and sympathy to the southern cause, Thorpe found himself, in these few years before the Civil War, torn by a conflict which could not be resolved. The only way in which such a conflict could even be presented was in the confusing ambivalence of *The Master's House,* and in the chaotic social breakdown with which the novel ends.

It is the tense ambiguity and confusion in *The Master's House* which reminds us, for the only time in these proslavery novels, that by 1854 the Civil War was virtually inevitable. Thorpe alone allows his reader to glimpse the decade of drift behind his words. In doing so, of course, he foregoes any chance of making his novel an effective or persuasive reply—even to such an impartially equivocal indictment of the South as *Uncle Tom's Cabin* is. Whereas the other replies pour on the balm of an idealized evocation of southern life, Thorpe is prepared, almost in spite of himself, to probe the wound. The tone of some of the replies to *Uncle Tom's Cabin* is conciliatory, while others fulminate, but only in the disequilibrium of *The Master's House* does one have much of an inkling that a great internecine struggle would rend the nation and sweep away the institution if not the aftermath of slavery within a decade after these novels were written.

Notes

1. The sixteen works, which will hereafter be cited under the initials shown, were:

Martha Haines Butt, *Antifanaticism: A Tale of the South* (Philadelphia, 1853) (*AF*). [Southerner]

Lucien B. Chase, *English Serfdom and American Slavery: or, Ourselves—as Others See Us* (New York, 1854). [transplanted Northerner]

Robert Criswell, *"Uncle Tom's Cabin" contrasted with Buckingham Hall, the Planter's Home: or, A Fair View of Both Sides of the Slavery Question* (New York, 1852) (*BH*). [Northerner]

Mary H. Eastman, *Aunt Phillis's Cabin: or, Southern Life As It Is* (Philadelphia, 1852) (*APC*). [Southerner]

William J. Grayson, *The Hireling and the Slave, Chicora, and Other Poems* (Charleston, 1856) (*HS*). [Southerner]

Sarah J. Hale ("edited by"), *Liberia: or Mr. Peyton's Experiments* (New York, 1853) (*L*). [Northerner]

Baynard R. Hall, *Frank Freeman's Barber Shop: A Tale* (Rochester, N. Y., 1853) (*FFBS*). [Northerner]

Caroline Lee Hentz, *The Planter's Northern Bride: A Novel* (2 vols.; Philadelphia, 1854) (*PNB*). [transplanted Northerner]

Mary E. Herndon, *Louise Elton: or, Things Seen and Heard* (Philadelphia, 1853). [Southerner]

Logan, *Pseud.* (Thomas Bangs Thorpe), *The Master's House: or, Scenes Descriptive of Southern Life* (New York, 1854) (*MH*). [transplanted Northerner]

Maria J. McIntosh, *The Lofty and the Lowly: or, Good in All and None All-Good* (2 vols.; New York, 1853) (*L and L*). [Southerner]

John W. Page, *Uncle Robin In his Cabin in Virginia, and Tom Without One in Boston* (Richmond, 1853) (*UR*). [Southerner]

Caroline Rush, *The North and South: or, Slavery and Its Contrasts* (Philadelphia, 1852) (*NS*). [Northerner]

J. Thornton Randolph, *Pseud.* (Charles Jacobs Peterson), *The Cabin and Parlor: or, Slaves and Masters* (Philadelphia, 1852) (*CP*). [Northerner]

William L. G. Smith, *Life At The South: or, "Uncle Tom's Cabin" As It Is. Being Narratives, Scenes, and Incidents in the Real "Life of the Lowly"* (Buffalo, 1852) (*LAS*). [Northerner]

Vidi, *Pseud., Mr. Frank, The Underground Mail-Agent* (Philadelphia, 1853). [region unknown]

The edition of *Uncle Tom's Cabin* cited is that edited by Kenneth S. Lynn in the John Harvard Library (Cambridge, 1962) (*UTC*).

Not included in the present canvass is a work which not only goes beyond being a mere "reply," but also may be only incidentally addressed to Mrs. Stowe—William Gilmore Simms' *Woodcraft*. Simms himself, in what may have been an ex post facto judgment, suggests it was a reply to *Uncle Tom's Cabin* (see *The Letters of William Gilmore Simms*, edited by M. C. S. Oliphant, A. T. Odell, and T. C. D. Eaves [Columbia, S. C., 1952-56], III, pp. 222-23).

Two previous discussions of the replies to *Uncle Tom's Cabin* are Francis Pendleton Gaines, *The Southern Plantation: A Study in the Development and the Accuracy of a Tradition* (New York, 1925) and Jeanette Reid Tandy, "Pro-Slavery Propaganda in American Fiction of the Fifties," *South Atlantic Quarterly,* XXI, 1 (Jan. 1922), 41-50, and XXI, 2 (Apr. 1922), 170-78.

2. See S. Austin Allibone, *A Critical Dictionary of English Literature* (Philadelphia, 1870), I, 539; "The sale of the former work [*APC*] reached 18,000 copies in a few weeks"; and II, 2164: [*LAS*] "Sale in America, 15,000 in 15 days." See also Gaines, *The Southern Plantation*, p. 46.

3. Letter to the Earl of Shaftesbury, quoted Charles E. Stowe, *The Life of Harriet Beecher Stowe* (New York, 1890), p. 172.

4. Edmund Wilson, *Patriotic Gore* (New York, 1962), pp. 6-7.

5. The slavery fiction of the 1850s discloses a triad of disillusioned masters in Augustine St. Clare,

Edward Clayton and Graham Mildmay of *The Master's House*. Each believes that the sole justification of slavery is its protective character (*Dred: A Tale of the Great Dismal Swamp, Writings of Harriet Beecher Stowe* [Cambridge, 1896], III, 379; *MH*, p. 27). Each believes that "the land groans under it [slavery]; and, bad as it is for the slave, it is worse, if anything, for the master" (*UTC*, p. 237). St. Clare dies violently; Clayton frees his slaves; only Thorpe's Mildmay confronts the coming *dies irae* which Mrs. Stowe's creatures are permitted to avoid.

6. Mrs. Stowe herself refers to slavery as the "patriarchal institution," in a letter to Gamaliel Bailey, the founder-editor of the *National Era*. See Forrest Wilson, *Crusader in Crinoline: The Life of Harriet Beecher Stowe* (New York, 1941), p. 259. The patriarchal character of plantation life, while pervasively implicit in these novels, is the explicit subject of Mildmay's valedictory address at his northern college (*MH*, p. 19).

7. H. B. Stowe, *A Key to Uncle Tom's Cabin* (Boston, 1853), p. 67. Mrs. Stowe is quoting from an unfavorable review "which has been quite valuable to the author, as summing up, in a clear, concise and intelligible form, the principal objections which may be urged to *Uncle Tom's Cabin*." See also, for a much fuller account of the heads on which slavery was attacked outside the South, Gaines, *The Southern Plantation*, pp. 231-35.

8. Public opinion, in these novels, brands the bad master (*PNB*, I, 204).

9. When Mildmay inadvertently buys a slave whose husband is owned by another master, he arranges for the reunion of the couple, even if it means selling at a loss (*MH*, p. 172). See also *AF*, "Preface," *L and L*, II, 36, *CP*, pp. 39-40, *UR*, pp. 39-40 and *APC*, p. 44: "'It [separation] is the worst feature in slavery . . . but such a circumstance is very uncommon. . . . [The master whose sale separated mother and daughter] was a notoriously bad man, and after this wicked act was held in utter abhorrence in the neighborhood.'" See also, for a criticism of Mrs. Stowe's sentimental lack of realism in making so much of the separation of families, E. J. Stearns, *Notes on Uncle Tom's Cabin* (Philadelphia, 1853), p. 147.

10. Mrs. Stowe herself accepts this stereotype (*UTC,* p. 405).

11. T. B. Thorpe, "Cotton and its Cultivation," *Harper's New Monthly Magazine,* VIII, xlvi (Mar. 1854), 461. See also *UR*, p. 28; *L*, pp. 44-45.

12. The Northerner—a fortiori the abolitionist—who turns slaveholder is the epitome of cruelty to his

slaves in these novels, like Preble (*UR,* p. 5) and Harding (*BH,* p. 131). "'I mistrust the sincerity of all men,'" says Mildmay, "'who, owning no negroes themselves, are violent in defense of our peculiar institutions.'" (*MH,* p. 151).

Of course Mrs. Stowe had already presented, in Miss Ophelia, the aversion of the Northerner for the Negro, despite his *distant* concern for that Negro's welfare (*UTC,* p. 184).

13. For an account of the dramatized versions of *Uncle Tom's Cabin,* see J. C. Furnas, *Goodbye to Uncle Tom* (New York, 1956), pp. 259-84. The antislavery quality of these shows was less important than their catering to sentimental public taste, and the placing of full blame upon Legree for the cruelties of slavery rather than upon the cavalier-master surely testifies to the persistence in the American mind of that image. See William R. Taylor, *Cavalier and Yankee* (New York, 1961). The British productions, suggestively, removed St. Clare altogether, leaving Legree as the sole representative of the master class.

14. *A Key to Uncle Tom's Cabin,* p. 133.

15. Abolitionist hypocrisy, climate, the competitive job market, all work to the detriment of the Negro in these novels. Many examples might be cited; the best is perhaps that of Tom in *Uncle Robin.* He dies in squalor, comforted only by a *Southern* samaritan, who wraps him in a blanket against the cold—"a monument to Northern philanthropy, entwined in the drapery of Southern barbarity" (*UR,* p. 253).

16. See Milton Rickels, *Thomas Bangs Thorpe, Humorist of the Old Southwest* (Louisiana, 1962), pp. 24-25; also Kenneth S. Lynn, *Mark Twain and Southwestern Humor* (Boston, 1959), p. 89: "his Yankee soul had been stirred by the gaudy vision of an aristocratic South."

17. New York *Times,* Sept. 20, 1878.

18. *Spirit of the Times,* July 27, 1850.

19. That appellation, of course, belongs more properly to Henry Clay; it seems appropriate that one of the northern replies—*Buckingham Hall*—hails the author of the Compromise, lately dead; *Life at the South,* too, is dedicated to the memory of "Henry Clay, the advocate of the American Colonization Society."

20. Names are obviously of the first importance in *The Master's House,* and reflect particularly Thorpe's dual attitude toward the South, from the intractable Southerner Calhoun (the proponent of nullification himself) to Colonel Lee, the FFV who turns out to be the son of a tavern-keeper.

21. For the Biblical defense, see, esp. *The Pro-Slavery Argument, as maintained by the most distinguished writers of the Southern States . . . Chancellor Harper, Governor Hammond, Dr. Simms, and Professor Dew* (Philadelphia, 1853).

22. (New York, 1855). Already Thorpe is abandoning the moderation of *The Master's House,* and moving as well away from his southern sympathies: "Above all things, *sectionalism* is to be frowned upon as the worst enemy known to the republic. . . . They who cherish it with the hope thereby of raising their individual fortunes, will certainly be classed with the Arnolds and Iscariots of our race. . . . We must earnestly determine to be nothing but AMERICANS" (pp. 378-80).

It seems probable that Thorpe had little to do with the writing of *A Voice to America,* but merely lent his name to the manifesto (See Rickels, *Thomas Bangs Thorpe,* p. 257).

J. A. Leo Lemay (essay date November 1975)

SOURCE: Lemay, J. A. Leo. "The Text, Tradition, and Themes of 'The Big Bear of Arkansas.'" *American Literature* 47, no. 3 (November 1975): 321-42.

[*In the following essay, Lemay examines narrative strategies and major themes in Thorpe's "The Big Bear of Arkansas." Lemay pays particular attention to the story's complex symbolism, notably its use of biblical imagery. In Lemay's view, the story represents Thorpe's elegiac commentary on the conquest of the wilderness by the inexorable encroachment of Christian civilization.*]

The classic story, as well as the most frequently anthologized one, of the humor of the Old Southwest is Thomas Bangs Thorpe's **"The Big Bear of Arkansas."**[1] It first appeared in William T. Porter's sporting magazine, the *Spirit of the Times,* XI (March 27, 1841), 43-44. When Porter reprinted it in what became a popular anthology of humorous stories, he recognized its dominant stature and entitled the collection *"The Big Bear of Arkansas" and Other Sketches* (Philadelphia, 1845). Unfortunately, Porter revised the text of Thorpe's story, evidently with an eye to making it less colloquial—and thus, perhaps, supposedly more suitable for a general audience.[2] When Thorpe himself published the story in his anthology *The Hive of "The Bee-Hunter"* (New York, 1854), pp. 72-93, he evidently used an edition of Porter's anthology as his copy-text, for he followed Porter's changes in numerous accidentals and in all three of Porter's substantives.[3] And Thorpe revised his earlier text. The only previous comparison of the texts of **"The Big Bear of Arkansas"** that I have seen prefers the text as found in *The Hive* (1854) to that of the *Spirit* (1841) because the *Hive* contains Thorpe's "last" revisions. But even the scholars[4] who prefer the later text admit that the later version "changed some dialect words into their standard forms," including "the self-conscious substitution of 'bear' for 'bar.'" Thorpe, I believe, revised his story with an eye to a different audience. Originally, he wrote for the masculine, sporting magazine audience who read the *Spirit of the Times*. When he published *The Hive of "The Bee-Hunter"* thirteen years later, he was attempting to reach a more general and genteel audience. The successful editor William T. Porter had shown the way. In general, what Thorpe did to the text of **"The Big Bear of Arkansas"** in revising it could justly be compared to a pedantic school-marm's corrections of Mark Twain's colloquial prose.

I believe that the best text of **"The Big Bear of Arkansas"** is that of the *Spirit of the Times*.[5]

The urbane narrator of **"The Big Bear of Arkansas"** opens the story by portraying the various characters found on that melting pot of the old frontier, a Mississippi River steamboat, specifically mentioning the Yankee pedlar ("the pedlar of tin-ware from New England"), the aristocratic Southern plantation owner, the gamut of types from the comparatively new states ("Wolvereens, Suckers, Hoosiers, Buckeyes and Corncrackers"), and the English sportsman. Although the archetypal ideas of the ship of fools and of the ship as microcosm are clearly suggested, Thorpe does not draw the expected moral on the universality of the types of mankind nor does he comment on the omnipresence of fools and gulls. Instead, he celebrates a unique and heroic type of man found only in America, "the half-horse and half-alligator species of men, who are peculiar to 'old Mississippi.'" Thus the reversal of the reader's expectations (created by the archetypal setting) emphasizes the distinctness of the peculiarly American hero. The speaker's ambivalent feeling toward this unique American character is immediately revealed when he patronizingly comments that this "species . . . appear[s] to gain a livelihood simply by going up and down the river." Despite the speaker's condescension, the story will show the superiority of the loquacious gamecock of the wilderness not only to the "cynical-looking Hoosier," the "timid little man," the English sportsman, and especially to the urbane narrator (all of whom are bested or insulted by Jim Doggett), but also to the unnamed people "from every state in the union, and from every portion of the world." Thorpe makes the gamecock of the wilderness immediately dominate the crowd on board the boat. Moreover, Doggett is referred to in the story as "our hero," and though the tone of these references may be mocking, the authorial voice behind the supercilious persona is not.[6]

After the introductory paragraph, the narrator tells of the trip up the Mississippi from New Orleans during which he encountered Doggett, who gained the attention of the steamboat crowd with a "loud Indian whoop," a "loud" cock "Crowing," and a shout proclaiming his identity as "the big Bar of Arkansaw" (p. 43b2). The early anecdotes told by Doggett exaggerate the abundance and fertility of the land. Such exaggerations were characteristic of the earliest American promotion tracts. By the early seventeenth century, the anti-American literature commonly burlesqued these "lubberland" motifs, and so later promotion tracts, like Nathaniel Morton's *New English Canaan* (1636), John Hammond's *Leah and Rachel* (1656), and George Alsop's *A Character of the Province of Maryland* (1666), mocked the tradition within the promotion tracts themselves. Burlesques of the tracts (whether published separately or within the tracts themselves) are thereafter a common motif of American literature. And much of the material and humor of Thorpe's story is directly descended from this tradition.[7] No doubt he was most immediately mocking the common promotional literature of his own day (the newspapers were full of it), but contrary to the usual statements about the beginnings of the Old Southwestern school of humor,[8] Thorpe was using a vital tradition of American humor that had been continually popular since the mid-seventeenth century.

In the first anecdote of his monologue, Doggett tells how he replied to the ribbing of the New Orleans inhabitants about his ignorance of the term *game*: "Strangers, if you'd asked me *how we got our meat* in Arkansaw, I'd a told you at once, and given you a list of varmints that would make a caravan, beginning with the bar, and ending off with the cat" (p. 43b2). From emphasizing the plenty and variety of the animals of wilderness Arkansas, Doggett switches to ridiculing the puny game shot by the New Orleans dwellers, sparrows and green herons ("chippen-birds and shite-pokes"). To clench the insult, he tells a specific incident—the first of the tall tales of the story. Doggett claims that he "never did shoot at but one" bird, "and I'd never forgiven myself for that, had it weighed less than forty pounds." This detail is one of several that continues the colonial traditions. The forty-pound wild turkey was a commonplace of seventeenth and eighteenth-century promotion tracts; indeed, only the more restrained writers specified forty pounds, and frequently the colonial authors said that the wild turkeys reached fifty pounds or more, or said that hundreds of them were encountered at a time.[9] But Thorpe, in his outrageous use of specific detail, surpasses the colonial authors as well as the folk who put on the greenhorns by repeating these claims in the eighteenth and nineteenth centuries. After punningly saying of his forty-pound turkey, "Wasn't it a whopper," Doggett claims, "when he fell out of the tree, after I shot him, on striking the ground he bust open behind, and the way the pound gobs of tallow rolled out of the opening was perfectly beautiful" (p. 43b4).[10]

After a brief encomium on Arkansas ("the creation State, the finishing up country; a State where the sile runs down to the centre of the 'arth, and government gives you a title to every inch of it," p. 43b6), the game-cock is taunted about the mosquitoes and replies with a mock-encomium on their "enormous" size, punningly conceding that they are too forward and "do push themselves in somewhat troublesome" (p. 43b8). From the beginning of American colonization, the promotion writers had been replying to English objections concerning American mosquitoes. In an early example of New England dry humor, William Bradford answered the perennial complaint: "They are too delicate and unfit to begin new plantations and colonies, that cannot endure the biting of a mosquito. We would wish such to keep at home till at least they be mosquito-proof."[11] Like Bradford, the Arkansan claims that natives are bothered less than others by mosquitoes; in addition, he implies that mosquitoes actually are useful to the natives of Arkansas in ridding them of such true pests as Yankees. Jim Doggett's reply uses a favorite American technique—it exaggerates the problem and boasts about it, a strategy employed in America's earliest extant folk song, "New England's Annoyances,"[12] which answers the anti-promotion tract satires about early America.

Continuing the celebration of the abundance and fertility of the wilderness, Doggett tells "how numerous bear were in his 'diggins,'" where he represented them to be "about as plenty as blackberries and a little plentifuler" (p. 43b9). From their abundance, Doggett turns to their size. Echoing two Biblical passages (Numbers 13:20 and Ecclesiastes 3:1), Doggett says that he "read in history that varmints have their fat season and their lean season," but in Arkansas (which is thus implicitly compared to another Canaan, as presented in Numbers 13, a "fat land" that "floweth with milk and honey") bears "have one continued fat season the year round" (p. 43c3). Doggett's most striking anecdote of the fertility of Arkansas concerns crops: a "fellow who had stopped at my place, with an idea of buying me out" mistakes beets for cedar stumps and potatoes for Indian mounds (p. 43c7).[13] This is an especially splendid example of the common boast of the large size of American plants, a tradition which also stems from the colonial promotion tracts, where America was portrayed as a cornucopia and where, like the ancient classical idea of heaven, harvests of the extraordinarily large crops were made three times a year.[14] And Doggett immediately tops his outrageous tall tale with a paradox: "the sile is too rich, and *planting in Arkansaw is dangerous.*" He explains: "I had a good-sized sow killed in that same bottom land. The old thief stole an ear of corn, and took it

down where she slept at night to eat; well, she left a grain or two on the ground, and lay down on them; before morning the corn shot up, and the percussion killed her dead" (p. 43c7). This tall tale may reflect an oral anecdote or may be Thorpe's original creation, but the outrageous put-on was commonly used by colonial Americans in replying to the English writers who satirized the promotion tracts. Its continuation in the literature and oral culture of the nineteenth century descended, in part, from the replies to the satires on colonial promotion tracts.

These anecdotes of the abundance and fertility of Arkansas symbolically portray Arkansas as Eden, as the "creation State" (p. 43b6). This view of America also descends from the promotion tracts. And in the colonial promotion tracts, as in **"The Big Bear of Arkansas,"** a tension develops between a celebration of the wilderness as Eden and the portrayal of the future of America, when it will be a land of farms and of cities—in effect, a land like the one the emigrants are invited to leave.[15] So too, in Thorpe's story, even before the central anecdote of the big bear is told, conflict exists. Not only are there mosquitoes in paradise (although the tone of the passage assures the reader that this is really no problem), but the stuff of paradise, the game, is hunted, killed, and eaten; and the inhabitant of the paradisical world of Arkansas is primarily a hunter, a killer, a violator of nature.[16] Doggett's first anecdote, contrasting the rural/primitive idea of killing for food with the urban/modern idea of killing for pleasure or "game," presents a version of the sacramental attitude toward nature. But reverence for nature is dropped as Doggett boasts of his fabulous ability as a hunter, and especially as a killer of bears. Although Doggett twice directly brags about his union with nature ("But mosquitoes is natur, and I never find fault with her," p. 43b8; and "natur intended Arkansaw for a hunting ground, and I go according to natur," p. 43c7), he is in fact the ultimate violator of nature, a man whose primary function is to kill.

Several scholars have commented on the big bear as a version of the magical fabulous beast of folklore.[17] Although tempted by such by-paths as the role of Doggett as the Accursed Hunter or the significance of a grapevine being used as a life-line, I will confine myself here to the central issue of the nature and functions of the bear as a spirit. Since we are dealing with symbols rather than with an allegory, we cannot expect to find a perfect consistency in the implications of the story, but I believe that the dominant symbols clearly imply several themes. The bear is, as I will show, inextricably linked with Christian, as well as with folkloristic, concepts. When Doggett begins the story of the big bear, he immediately hints that it is a story of the supernatural, for it "was never beat in this world, or in any other." And he has prepared the reader for this extraordinary history by concluding his earlier bear anecdote with "much onlikelier things have happened" (p. 43c5). When Doggett first sees the claw marks of the big bear on the trees "about eight inches above any in the forests that I knew of" (p. 44a2), he "couldn't believe it was real." Only after he sees the marks elsewhere does he concede, *"I knew the thing lived."* Since he is the greatest bear hunter of the district, which, according to Doggett, is a reputation "much harder to earn than to be reckoned first man in Congress" (p. 43c10), he immediately views the existence of the great bear as a personal challenge: "here is something a purpose for me—that bar is mine, or I give up the hunting business" (p. 44a2). And the bear seems to reciprocate the feeling, for the bear's initial action is to kill Doggett's hog, thus challenging him. When Doggett first chases the bear, "the dogs run him over eighteen miles, and broke down, [and] my horse gave out." He expresses his wonder: "Before this adventure, such things were unknown to me as possible." How the bear could do it "was past my understanding" (p. 44a3). After hunting the bear for "two or three years" (p. 43c10), Doggett directly identifies the bear with the devil: "I would see that bar in every thing I did,—*he hunted me,* and that too, like a devil, which I began to think he was" (p. 44a3).

When shot by Bill, a greenhorn hunting companion of Doggett, "in the centre of his forehead" (p. 44a3), the immortal bear (which, like other fabulous beasts, can be killed only by a shot in a certain place—in his case, in "his side, just back of his foreleg," p. 44a3)[18] became angry, and with his left paw "brushed out" a pup that attacked him "so totally . . . that he entirely disappeared." The angered spirit-bear is punningly described as "in a wrath"; and a wraith, of course, is a spirit. Doggett's marvelous gun (which "if not watched closely . . . will go off as quick on a warm scent as my dog Bowie-knife will," p. 43b11) mysteriously snaps[19] and the great hunter finds himself inexplicably without another cap. The bear flees to a magical "little island in the lake" (the magic island is a common retreat in folklore and mythology, and was used in at least one tall tale by a colonial Pennsylvania frontiersman),[20] and after Doggett, who has found the caps in the lining of his coat, shoots him in the one "correct" place, the big bear mysteriously changes into another bear. Doggett sums up the episode: "the way matters got mixed on that island was onaccountably curious, and thinking of it made me more than ever convinced that I was hunting the devil himself" (p. 44a3). The actual killing, suitably, takes place on a Sunday morning (we're told that it's the "morning previous to the great day of my hunting expedition," which is to begin "on Monday morning"), the bear unexpectedly appearing while Doggett is defecating. "He loomed up like a *black mist*" and after being shot "*walked through the fence* like a falling tree would through a cobweb," and spent his dying struggle "groaning in a thicket near by, like a thousand sinners."

(This thicket may recall Doggett's earlier coupling of a thicket and religion: "a small mosquito would be of no more use in Arkansaw than preaching in a cane-brake," p. 43b8). After telling of the bear's enormous size, Doggett moralizes to his steamboat audience: "It was in fact a creation bar, and if it had lived in Sampson's time, and had met him, in a fair fight, it would have licked him in the twickling of a dice-box" (p. 44b1). Doggett also remarks on the magical prowess of the bear, muses on "something curious about" his earlier missing the bear, and gives his "private opinion . . . that the bar was an *unhuntable bar, and died when his time come.*" At the end of Doggett's monologue, the narrator further comments on the "mystery" and "superstitious awe connected with" the bear, and superciliously says that such feelings are "common with all 'children of the wood,'"[21] when they meet with anything out of their every day experience"—but we learn that all of the diverse hearers aboard the Mississippi steamboat evidently share the feeling (including the narrator), for Doggett is the first to break the silence that follows his narrative (p. 44b2).

Clearly, the big bear is a spirit. Doggett several times identifies him as a devil (his epithets for the bear include "the old black rascal"), and on occasion the imagery links him with aspects of nature. The magical suggestions establish the bear as an enemy spirit of modern man and further identify him as the spirit of nature, and sometimes as the symbol of the undefiled Eden, the "creation bar" (p. 44b1). The falling tree metaphor used to describe his death is especially suitable, for the cutting down of the trees of the American wilderness had been viewed as the primary symbol of the destruction of the wilderness and as the end of the American paradise since at least the early eighteenth century.[22] The bear's role as the devil, together with the religious imagery, may also suggest that the institution of religion (which is, of course, a chief mark of civilization and a natural concomitant of the destruction of the wilderness) will replace the paganism of nature. In addition to those aspects of the bear as a personification of the wild and savage that modern, fallen man must oppose, there is another reason for the supernatural qualities of the bear, a reason which may have functioned in such epics as *Beowulf,* but which is, comparatively, lacking from such twentieth-century versions of the archetype as Faulkner's "The Bear."[23] The greatness of the bear measures the greatness of his opponent: As the bear becomes a devil, Doggett assumes heroic proportions and becomes a god. If, as Doggett says, the big bear could have defeated Samson, then Doggett is more heroic than Samson (and, by implication, other heroic figures of past ages), for "our hero" has defeated the big bear. But, of course, the tone generally, and the humorous situation of Doggett—caught with his pants down— undercut the heroic tendency of the story. But one may also see in this scatological note a disgust for the act of slaughter, a disgust with the necessary end of the wilderness, and, by implication, a disgust with the nature of man who is necessarily opposed to nature, as well as a regret for the fall of man, symbolized by the killing of the bear, which marks the end of the reign of the Eden-like wilderness of the Old Southwest. No doubt, as Doggett says, the bear died when his time had come—not because of some abstract idea of fate but because Arkansas has passed its wilderness state. Herein lies the significance of Doggett's account of his own history as a hunter: "you see when I and some more first settled in our region, we were drivin to hunting naturally; we soon liked it, and after that we found it an easy matter to make the thing our business" (p. 43c10); for the account implies that the hunting "state" of civilization is past in Arkansas. The hunters are being superseded by the farmers, as the heroic stage of civilization is being superseded by the agricultural;[24] and the farmers include such greenhorns as Bill, who shoots the bear in the center of the forehead, and the "fellow" who wanted to buy Doggett's land for a farm. With the advent of the farmers and greenhorns, the wilderness is passing, the game is becoming scarcer, and the situation of Doggett's camp on the Mississippi (that the river has already swallowed up part of Doggett's land is one more symbolic statement of the inexorable processes of the stage theory of civilization) is becoming like that of the New Orleans dwellers down the river, who have only chippen-birds and shite-pokes as "game."[25]

As the name adopted by Jim Doggett proclaims, he is a double of the big bear whom he hunts and kills. The second paragraph of the story introduces Doggett with the shout "Hurra for the big Bar of Arkansaw" (p. 43b2), and the narrator henceforth calls him the "big Bar" or "the man of Arkansaw" (p. 43c3), whereas it is only incidentally that we learn that his name is actually Jim Doggett (p. 43c1). For the narrator as for his audience, this gamecock of the wilderness remains the "big bar of Arkansaw" (p. 43c8), a fact emphasized by the title of the story, which refers primarily to Doggett and only secondarily to the fabulous bear that he finally kills. In addition to the name, other elements indicate the double motif. One is the reversal of roles: the bear hunts the hunter: "I would see that bar in every thing I did, *he hunted me*" (p. 44a3).[26] In the same paragraph, Doggett tells of loving the bear: "But, wasn't he a beauty, though? I loved him like a brother." In addition to suggesting an Edenic unity and love between man and nature, the brother relationship is one of the commonest clues to the literary double. The imagery too identifies Doggett with the "big bar": after telling of killing the mysterious substitute "she bar" instead of the "old critter," Doggett says that he "grew cross as a bar with two cubs and a sore tail" (p. 44a3). There are also several kinds of sympathetic identification of Doggett and the bear. Just as Doggett said that when he hunted bears, he wore the fat off them (p. 43c3), so too when

he missed the big bear (who is in turn hunting him), the failure "took hold of my vitals, and I wasted away . . . it reduced me in flesh faster than an ager" (p. 44a3). Another similarity between the two is established by their identical reactions to the shooting of the bear by the greenhorn. The bear goes into a "rage . . . in fact, that bar was in a *wrath all over*" (p. 44a3). Correspondingly, Doggett's "wrath was up." And Doggett, who finally succeeds in killing the bear, tells us several times that the effort to kill the bear is killing him: "the thing was killing me" (p. 44a3; although the "thing" here refers to his unsuccessful hunt, we may recall that earlier "the thing" refers to the bear, p. 44a2). So Doggett vows "to catch that bar, go to Texas, or die" (p. 44a3).

There can be no doubt that the big bear is a double for Jim Doggett, and that in killing the big bear, Doggett symbolically slays himself. The double motif also, paradoxically, stresses the Edenic motif, suggesting that the hunter and the bear, like the lion and the lamb, can lie down together. In this context, the killing symbolically repeats the Cain-Abel archetype, confirming both the evil nature of man and the justice of his eviction from Eden. Perhaps I should also point out that the minor doubles also suggest an Edenic situation, where man exists in a complete unity with nature and with all around him. Doggett's dog, suitably named "Bowie-knife," is also a double for the gamecock. Not only does the patronymic Doggett assert this connection, but the dog's prowess as a hunter mirrors Doggett's skill (and Doggett's rifle, a "perfect epidemic among bar," p. 43b11, is another, and still more minor, double). Even more obviously the dog is identified as a double for Jim Doggett's knife (and the knife is thus, at two removes, a double for Doggett). The identifications are most explicit and most ambiguous in the passage where Doggett tells of the dog's fight with the wounded bear in the water: "I stripped off my coat, drew my knife, and intended to have taken a part with Bowie-knife myself [i.e., with his dog and using his knife] when the bar rose to the surface" (p. 44a3). In these series of doubles,[27] as in Doggett's shooting the bear while defecating, we have an obvious humorous spoof of the serious themes of the story, as well as a further pointing up of the themes.

I have already remarked that the death of the bear symbolizes the death of the wilderness, and I should also note that this must necessarily spell out the end of the species of man that inhabits it—the gamecock of the wilderness. Thus the story (like Thorpe's collection *The Mysteries of the Backwoods*) is basically an elegiac tribute to a fast-disappearing type, the gamecock of the wilderness. The English sportsman who has come to America to hunt is going, so the narrator thinks, to "the foot of the Rocky Mountains" (p. 7); i.e., the wilderness has moved on past the Mississippi and past the Old Southwest and was then to be found in Texas and in the area of present-day Denver. A substratum of comment also suggests that bears are becoming scarce along the Mississippi. After all, we have been told that Doggett's gun is "a perfect epidemic among bar" (p. 43b11). And just before this, Doggett has assured the "timid little man" that bears "grow thin in our parts" (although this refers primarily to bears becoming slender because of their running from the sound of Doggett's gun, it also means that they are growing scarcer). The disappearance of the wilderness is implied in other ways. Doggett tells his steamboat audience that in Arkansas, "government gives you a title to every inch" of the soil (p. 43b6), but he also acknowledges that "the government ain't got another such a piece to dispose of" (p. 43c7). Even the setting emphasizes the end of the wilderness. The river, which becomes in *Huckleberry Finn* a symbol of nature, is accurately viewed in **"The Big Bear of Arkansas"** as the highway, the carrier of civilization. Suitably, the river symbolically destroys the wilderness: it makes a "cut off" in Doggett's property. The "cut off," ironically, is called a "great improvement." (Thorpe's attitude was directly expressed in the following year, when he has Mike Fink, the last of the Mississippi riverboatmen—a species then becoming extinct because of the advent of the steamboat—say "He could not help noticing with sorrow the desecrating hand of Improvement.")[28] Thoreau, slightly later, viewed the railroad and its "cut off" as the destructive symbol of industrial civilization, but Thorpe represented it by a steamboat, suitably named *The Invincible*. The imagery used to describe the familiarity of Doggett's dogs with the trail of the big bear, "as plain to the pack as a turnpike-road," is also ironic, for the roads will come, of course, as soon as the hunters have killed the bears and the farmers have replaced the frontiersmen. The setting and its implications supply the most convincing evidence of the elegiac theme, for Doggett himself tells of his necessary demise in urban America: "I am thrown away in that ar place, and useless, that ar a fact" (p. 43b2). Walter Blair has pointed out that Thorpe "set off various worlds involved in the story by identifying various groups and various scenes with these contrasting worlds."[29] But of course, there are primarily only two worlds in the story: that of the narrator, an urbane, bookish type, who is going to learn from "the great book of character so favorably opened before him" (p. 43b1), and of Doggett, the gamecock of the wilderness, who learns from the old hunter and from Countess's pups and from nature itself. And so, as every reader feels without analyzing the story, there lurks, beneath the delightful humor, a lament for the disappearance of a species of American who represents, like the big bear, a more heroic state of mankind, and an Edenic condition. And we must recognize the irony that though the lesson is there in Doggett's story and in his character

and in the disappearance of the wilderness, the urbane narrator, who prides himself on the "instruction" to be found in his situation, actually learns nothing.

The story thus mocks the pretensions of the urbane persona, whose language is stereotyped ("a man of observation need not lack for amusement or instruction in such a crowd, if he will take the trouble to read the great book of character so favorably opened before him," p. 43b1) and whose condescension is mocked by the "savage." Jim Doggett tells the narrator that he is "pleased with" him, "because you ain't ashamed to gain information by asking, and listening, and that's what I say to Countess's pups every day when I'm home—and I have got great hopes for them ar pups, because they are continually *nosing* about, and though they stick it sometimes in the wrong place, they gain experience anyhow, and may learn something useful to boot" (p. 43c10). Not only do Doggett's attitude and words mock the narrator of the story, but the implied scatological motif anticipates the conclusion of Doggett's monologue, thus subtly pointing up the two main cyclic structures contained with the cycle of the framework.

A recurring motif in the story concerns ignorance and knowledge, pride and humility. Doggett begins by narrating his war of wits with the New Orleans city slickers who called him "green" (p. 43b2), but who were in fact *"real know-nothings."*[30] Thorpe bests the New Orleans wits by his frontier accomplishments (which are "thrown away in that ar place, and useless," p. 43b2), and by his superior attitude toward hunting, which is not a "game," but a necessity and a livelihood. At the beginning of the story of the archetypal bear hunt, Doggett pays his dubious scatological compliment to the narrator, and then tells us about his first accomplishment in bear lore: he learned the size of a bear before killing it by its scratch marks on a tree. "Well, stranger, just one month from that time I killed a bar, and told its exact length before. I measured it by those very marks—and when I did that I swelled up considerable—I've been a prouder man ever since." Because of his knowledge and ability, Doggett becomes proud. "So I went on, larning something every day, until I was reckoned a buster, and allowed to be decidedly the best bar hunter in my district; and that is a reputation as much harder to earn than to be reckoned first man in Congress, as an iron ram rod is harder than a toad-stool." Then Doggett tells of his prowess, pride, and certainty on bear hunts. This attitude continues until he hunts the big bear—and the big bear teaches him humility. Not only does it baffle Doggett's bear-knowledge ("How he did it, I never could understand," p. 44a3), but Doggett even comes to doubt that he was the agent that killed the bear ("There is something curious about it, I could never understand,—and I never was satisfied at his giving in so *easy at last*," p. 44b1). The story is, on one level, about pride and humility, ignorance and knowledge. A little knowledge makes Doggett proud—but true knowledge makes him humble. And our supercilious narrator, who pays lip service to "the great book of character" open before him in the steamboat *Invincible,* is mocked by Thorpe when he has Doggett imply that, like Countess's pups, the narrator will not recognize that his assumption of his own superiority and knowledge is false, even when his nose is pushed into it. And the careful reader may even realize that the narrator's first comment on the "half-horse half-alligator species" is a microcosm of his attitudes and of Thorpe's burlesque of these condescending attitudes throughout the piece, for when the narrator characterizes the type as one "who appear[s] to gain a livelihood simply by going up and down the river," the narrator scorns the indolence of the "species"; but in fact we have here the first hint of the Edenic motifs that will characterize the story.

Several suggestions in the story identify Jim Doggett with two celebrated folkloristic heroes of the American imagination. The more obvious is the Davy Crockett or the great hunter/frontiersman type. Crockett had been killed at the Alamo just five years before Thorpe's story appeared, and the various newspaper anecdotes, almanacs, biographies and supposed autobiographies about him establish his great popularity as a folk hero. Although any story of a humorous, tale-telling frontiersman published in the 1830's or 1840's might well suggest Crockett, several elements in the story seem particularly to refer to him. Doggett says of his fame as "the best bar hunter in my district" that it "is a reputation as much harder to earn than to be reckoned first man in Congress, as an iron ram-rod is harder than a toad-stool" (p. 43c10). Crockett, of course, was the best known bear hunter in America, and the conjunction of politics and bear-hunting unmistakably points to him. We may even see in the "iron ram-rod" image a reference to Crockett's political archenemy, Old Hickory. Second, Doggett's vow "to catch that bar, go to Texas, or die" recalls Crockett's rebuke to the voters who did not send him back to Congress ("You may all go to hell and I will go to Texas"), and it may allude to the famous battle in which he died.[31] Third, as Kenneth S. Lynn has remarked, the name *Jim Doggett* itself may echo *Davy Crockett.*[32] And finally, several details of Thorpe's story seem to echo Crockett's popular autobiography, *A Narrative of the Life of David Crockett* (1834).[33] The other well-known American folklore hero with whom Doggett is allied is the Mike Fink or flatboatman/fighter type. Doggett's characterization as a member of "the half-horse and half-alligator species of man" and as "peculiar to old Mississippi" (p. 43b1) points to this identification rather than to the hunter-frontiersman type. The elegiac message (though not the

tone) of the story, the replacement of the flatboats by steamboats (again, the name *The Invincible* is suitable, for the Mike Fink stories almost invariably lament the passing of the preindustrial age, and the flatboatman's muscle has been replaced by the steamboat's boiler in a motif that anticipates John Henry's heroic defeat), and the fact that in July of the following year (1842), Thorpe published an account of Mike Fink in the *Spirit of the Times*—all suggest that Doggett is a combination of the vanishing flatboatman as well as the vanishing frontiersman.[34] The name *Doggett* may also allude to the well-known folk song about Tom Doggett, for just as Jim Doggett foolishly kills his means of survival, the game of Arkansaw, so Tom Doggett in the song kills his lean milk cow.[35]

The allusions in the story shed light upon the major themes and reinforce their significance. There are primarily two kinds of allusions—to religion and to popular frontier folklore. The religious references include two to the Bible (to the fat and lean seasons of history, p. 44c3, and to Samson, p. 44b1) and several to modern Christianity (preaching, the minister performing marriage, and the bear dying like a "thousand sinners," pp. 43b8, 43c1, and 44b1). The popular folklore motifs of nineteenth-century American humor are found throughout the story. In addition to the implied references to Davy Crockett and to Mike Fink, there is a direct reference to the famous marksman Captain Martin Scott,[36] which Doggett uses as a facetious explanation of the mysterious death of the big bear: "Perhaps, he had heard of my preparations to hunt him the next day, so he jist come in, like Capt. Scott's coon, to save his wind to grunt with in dying; but that ain't likely" (p. 44b1). Taken together, these two dominant kinds of allusions imply a comparative mythology. The traditional Christian and Biblical allusions are clearly less vital than the folk references. The authorial stance implies that the American frontier folklore could be the basis for a modern vital mythology which should replace the inherited system ("of no more use . . . than preaching in a canebrake," p. 43b8). Christianity is associated with civilization and the decaying state of modern man—whereas a true vitality exists in the modern mythology of popular culture and especially in nature and in its primary mandala, the big bear. But, ironically (and, in the terms of the values within this fictive world, tragically), the story describes the death of the big bear, the end of the vital religion of nature, and the triumph of civilization and of Christianity, all of which leaves modern man a diminished thing. It is especially ironic that the only vital Christian myth—in terms of the fictive and symbolic world of the story—is the Cain-Abel myth.

Although **"The Big Bear of Arkansas"** is undeniably a classic of the Old Southwestern frontier and although it is solidly within the traditions of American humor, its tone is elegiac and tragic. The power it reveals, as the numerous commentators who have called it *classic, great,* and *archetypal* testify, is basically derived from the use of traditional symbols and mythic archetypes operating within an intellectually complex fictive world: the intellectual views that permeate the authorial voice are a compound of the stage theory of mankind, a comparative mythology, and a Romantic primitivism. The outrageous comedy finally implies that life is a meaningless jest, that the symbolic and thematic world of **"The Big Bear of Arkansas"** is really the ship of fools implied by the archetypal setting of the framework— but it also celebrates the *joie de vivre* of that jest, a *joie de vivre* diminishing as the next stage of culture supersedes the heroic, primitive stage when man existed in a near unity with nature. The Christian religion that is coming to the Old Southwest is a pale shadow of the vibrancy of the pagan mandalas present in the personage of the big bear. But these primitive truths are being conquered and killed. Man will no longer exist in the state of unity and love with the environment that was possible in the Edenic wilderness. And though we, no doubt like T. B. Thorpe, can view these changes with mixed feelings and without fully believing what they imply about the past and the present, we also recognize the truth of Thorpe's portrayal of modern man, caught with his pants down, in the unthinking act of being human, and of destroying, in the natural process of living, the ecology that supports life. Although this reading may seem to reflect too strongly our modern attitudes toward ecology, population, and the wilderness, not only is it symbolically present in **"The Big Bear of Arkansas,"** but Thorpe also directly presents these attitudes in his other works. And the lament for the passing of the wilderness has been a constant in American literature since at least Robert Beverley's *History of Virginia* (1708). Thematically, Thorpe's **"Big Bear of Arkansas"** has numerous eighteenth and early nineteenth-century American predecessors. Doggett seems to emerge triumphant from his quest, but he has really, like Ahab, died in the process, and has symbolically killed himself. The repeated scatological motif emphasizes the bitterness of the final joke: mankind, in going about its unthinking unforesightful natural processes of devouring its natural resources, of creating ever more people ("Marriage according to law is a civil contract of divine origin, it's common to all countries as well as Arkansaw, and people take to it as naturally as Jim Doggett's Bowie-knife takes to bar," p. 43c1), and of befouling the earth with its waste—mankind is like Doggett, caught with its pants down, and the symbolic death of Doggett is only the type of its own doom. The ultimate irony is that the lesson will not be learned by modern man, who will only, like the urbane and self-satisfied narrator, take out of his pocket the latest paper, and perhaps "more critically than usual" examine "its contents" (p. 43b2). Thorpe's bitter classic of American

humor says that the urbane narrator (i.e., proud modern man) will recognize the truth only when, like Countess's pups, his nose is thrust in it.

Notes

1. Epithets such as "classic," "archetypal," and "greatest" are usually used to describe the position of this story in the tradition of the Old Southwestern school of humor. See, for example, Hugh Holman, in the anthology *Southern Writing 1585-1920* (New York, 1970), pp. 432 and 476; or Daniel Boorstin, *The Americans: The National Experience* (New York, 1965), p. 335. Guides to the scholarship on Thorpe are Milton Rickels's notice "Thomas Bangs Thorpe," in Louis D. Rubin, Jr., ed., *A Bibliographical Guide to the Study of Southern Literature* (Baton Rouge, La., 1969), pp. 308-309; and Charles E. Davis and Martha B. Hudson, "Humor of the Old Southwest: A Checklist of Criticism," *Mississippi Quarterly,* XXVII (Spring, 1974), 198-199. Rickels's biography *Thomas Bangs Thorpe: Humorist of the Old Southwest* (Baton Rouge, La., 1962) is the major study. For a brief sketch and estimate of Thorpe see Franklin J. Meine's account in the *Dictionary of American Biography* [New York, 1973-]. Perhaps the most telling single phrase concerning this story's importance is found in the subtitle of Norris W. Yates's book, *William T. Porter and the* Spirit of the Times: *A Study of the Big Bear School of Humor* (Baton Rouge, La., 1957). Walter Blair calls the story "the most widely praised and reprinted comic narrative *The Spirit* ever published," "'A Man's Voice, Speaking': A Continuum in American Humor," in Harry Levin, ed., *Veins of Humor* (Cambridge, Mass., 1972), p. 199.

   The story has been reprinted in nearly every anthology devoted to American humor or specifically to Southwestern humor. All of the standard modern anthologies include it: Franklin J. Meine, *Tall Tales of the Southwest* (New York, 1930), pp. 9-21; Walter Blair, *Native American Humor (1800-1900)* (New York, 1937; repr., San Francisco, 1960), pp. 337-348; V. L. O. Chittick, *Ring-Tailed Roarers* (Caldwell, Idaho, 1941), pp. 87-100; Kenneth S. Lynn, *The Comic Tradition in America* (New York, 1958), pp. 110-123; Brom Weber, *An Anthology of American Humor* (New York, 1962), pp. 246-255; and Hennig Cohen and William B. Dillingham, *Humor of the Old Southwest* (Boston, 1964), pp. 268-278—as well as most of the large anthologies of American literature which do not take the major-writers approach.

2. Porter separated rambling sentences (thus losing part of the mock-oral, monologue effect), frequently added punctuation (with the same unfortu-

nate result), capitalized the "b" in "big" when referring to the Arkansan as the "Big Bar" (thus, regrettably, more clearly distinguishing between the man and the bear), capitalized other proper nouns (e.g., "hoosier" becomes "Hoosier"—thus losing some of the appearance of colloquialness, and perhaps of illiteracy), and he even made three substantive changes in the text: *Spirit,* p. 43b4.2, "he" becomes "it" in Porter, p. 17.10; *Spirit,* p. 44a3.31, "coming" becomes "he came" in Porter, p. 27.5; and *Spirit,* p. 44a3.31, "then he walked" becomes "then walked" in Porter, p. 27.13. Because of the large amount of type in each page of the *Spirit of the Times,* my references to the *Spirit* are to page, column (a, b, *or* c), and paragraph—and, in the case of comparative textual references, line—the counting of the paragraphs beginning anew with each column (the first indented paragraph in each column, except for the opening paragraph of the story, will be counted as paragraph two). Thus the first reference to the *Spirit,* p. 43b4.2, is to p. 43, column 2(b), the fourth paragraph, line 2.

I have used a xerox of the microfilm edition of the *Spirit* in the University of California, Los Angeles, library (American Culture series 2, reel 624); the UCLA Special Collections copy (call no. PN6157 Z5P83b) of *"The Big Bear of Arkansas" and Other Sketches* (1845); (I also collated the first edition with the Huntington Library copy of the Philadelphia: Cary & Hart, 1847 edition, accession no. 265000, and found the two texts of "The Big Bear" identical); and I used the Huntington Library copy, accession no. 124808, of *The Hive of "The Bee-Hunter"* (New York: Appleton, 1854).

3. Thorpe continued the pernicious practice that Porter had begun of breaking up the long paragraphs (perhaps partially to make the story take up more space), added quotation marks wherever possible (thus making the monologue within the frame seem to be less of a mock-oral story), and "corrected" many of his dialect spellings to standard forms. He revised the syntax in several places to make the word order smoother, and in some cases changed the diction to more "correct" (though less colloquial and vital) forms (e.g., "all conversation dropped," *Spirit,* p. 43b2.21-22, became "all conversation ceased," *Hive,* p. 74.15). Most of Thorpe's changes make the text more formal (surprisingly, in a few cases he changed standard spelling into dialect forms), though in one or two cases the loss in colloquialness may be offset by a gain in clarity.

4. Francis Lee Utley, Lynn Z. Bloom, and Arthur F. Kinney, eds., *Bear, Man, and God: Eight Approaches to William Faulkner's "The Bear"* (New York, 1971), pp. 148-149.

5. One substantive revision, however, sheds light on the earlier text, and one seems an improvement. Thorpe substituted "pre-emption" (*Hive,* p. 81.15) for "land" (*Spirit,* p. 43c7.14), thus using a new colloquial term for a homestead; and I agree with the scholars who have earlier considered the texts of "The Big Bear of Arkansas" that this is an improvement. And Thorpe changed the name of the games "chickens and roulette" (*Spirit,* 43b2.42) to "checkers and roulette" (*Hive,* p. 75.19). It may be that Thorpe was originally creating a transferred pun, i.e., that he meant us to realize that "chickens" was dialect for "checkers" and that he was punning on the idea of chickening out in roulette. But I must confess that I never did know what the game "chickens" was until I saw it called "checkers" in the *Hive* version. The printing in the *Spirit* of "chickens" may have been simply a typo for "chickers" (perhaps caused by the compositor's mistaking Thorpe's manuscript "r" for an "n").

6. It is beyond the scope of this essay to trace the developing attitudes toward the American frontiersman. Part of the context is supplied by Henry Nash Smith, *Virgin Land: The American West as Symbol and Myth* (Cambridge, Mass., 1950), and by Richard Slotkin, *Regeneration Through Violence: The Mythology of the American Frontier, 1600-1860* (Middletown, Conn., 1973). For some suggestive comments on the heroic stature of the frontiersman and of America's comic gods, see two articles by Richard Dorson, "America's Comic Demigods," *American Scholar,* X (Autumn, 1941), 389-401; and "Davy Crockett and the Heroic Age," *Southern Folklore Quarterly, VI* (June, 1942), 95-102. In "Thomas Bangs Thorpe and the Literature of the Ante-Bellum Southwestern Frontier," *Louisiana Historical Quarterly,* XXXIX (April, 1956), 199-222, esp. p. 207, n. 29, Eugene Current-Garcia claims that Thorpe's anthology *The Mysteries of the Backwoods* (Philadelphia, 1846) failed commercially because, rather than collecting humorous pieces, it nostalgically portrayed the Old Southwestern frontier as a fast-disappearing Eden. As I shall attempt to show below, this same attitude supplies the thematic basis of Thorpe's humorous, but bitter, masterpiece.

7. The most popular English folksong of the seventeenth century concerning America satirized the promotion-tract portrayals of America. Typical lines are: "There Milk from Springs, like Rivers, flows, / And Honey upon hawthorn grows; / Hemp, Wool, and Flax, there grows on trees, / The mould is fat, and cutts like Cheese; / All fruits

and herbs growes in the fields, / Tobacco it good plenty yields." This song, often untitled, is conveniently available in Charles H. Firth, ed., *An American Garland: Being a Collection of Ballads Relating to America 1563-1759* (Oxford, 1915), pp. 27-30, under the title "A proper Newe Ballett called The Summons to Newe England." For the reactions in one typical colony to such satires, see my *Men of Letters in Colonial Maryland* (Knoxville, Tenn., 1972), especially the discussion of George Alsop's *A Character of the Province of Maryland* (London, 1666) and Ebenezer Cook's *The Sot-Weed Factor* (London, 1708). Nineteenth-century satires of emigrants' expectations continued this tradition: see "Oleana" in Theodore C. Blegan and Martin B. Ruud, *Norwegian Emigrant Songs and Ballads* (Minneapolis, 1936), pp. 192-198; "Amerikavison" in Robert L. Wright, *Swedish Emigrant Ballads* (Lincoln, Neb., 1965), pp. 37-39; and "Can you ride in a cart," *Colonial Magazine and Commercial-Maritime Journal,* VIII (May-June, 1842), 82—quoted in W. S. Shepperson, *British Emigration to North America: Projects and Opinions in the Early Victorian Period* (Oxford, 1957), p. 254.

8. See, for example, Philip D. Jordan, "Humor of the Backwoods, 1820-1840," *Mississippi Valley Historical Review,* XXV (June, 1938), 25-38, especially pp. 25-26.

9. "The Summons to Newe England," cited in n. 7, says, "There flights of Fowl do cloud the light, / Great Turkies of sixty pound in weight, / As Big as Estriges . . . ," Firth, p. 28. The Jesuit promotion writer for Lord Baltimore, Andrew White, in *A Relation of Maryland* (London, 1635), claimed that Maryland contained "wild Turkeys in great abundance, whereof many weigh 50. pounds, and upwards" (p. 23). A skeptical early American scientist, the Rev. John Clayton, published a piece on American birds in the *Philosophical Transactions* of the Royal Society of London in the late seventeenth century which shows that he had heard oral anecdotes about large turkeys: "there be wild Turkeys extreme large. They talk of Turkeys that have been killed that have weighed betwixt fifty and Sixty pound weight. The largest that ever I saw weighed something better than 38 pound." Edmund Berkeley and Dorothy Smith Berkeley, *The Reverend John Clayton* (Charlottesville, Va., 1965), p. 97. Thomas Morton claims that "Turkeys . . . hath bin killed that have weighed forty eight pound a peece," *New English Canaan* ([Amsterdam,] 1637), p. 69. Charles Francis Adams, in his edition of Morton (Boston, 1883), p. 192, notes a number of additional seventeenth-century exaggerations of the size of turkeys.

10. Baughman, motif X1265(ba), cites Vance Randolph, *We Always Lie to Strangers: Tall Tales from the Ozarks* (New York, 1951), p. 98; but Randolph is, indirectly, quoting Thorpe's "Big Bear of Arkansas."

11. Samuel E. Morison, ed., William Bradford, *Of Plymouth Plantation* (New York, 1952), p. 144. Cf. Lemay, *Men of Letters,* p. 234. Other examples of this motif may be found in John White, *The Planters Plea* (London, 1630), repr. in the *Proceedings of the Massachusetts Historical Society,* LXIII (1928-1929), 388; Francis Higginson, *New Englands Plantation* (London, 1630), p. 42; and [Edward Johnson], *Good News from New England* (London, 1648), p. 8. For one later use, see Mark Twain, *Life on the Mississippi* ([Boston,] 1883), chapter 34 ("Tough Yarns").

12. A version of "New England's Annoyances" is conveniently available in Harrison T. Meserole, *Seventeenth-Century American Poetry* (New York, 1972), pp. 503-505.

13. Lies about beets are Baughman's motif X1433 and about potatoes are X1435. Baughman's motif X1435.1(b), about potatoes being mistaken for Indian mounds, citing B. A. Botkin's *Treasury of American Folklore* (New York, 1944), p. 598, ultimately derives from "The Big Bear" by Thorpe. For a classical analogue of a turnip "weighing over 40 pounds," see the Loeb edition of Pliny, *Natural History,* tr. H. Rackham (Cambridge, Mass., 1950), V, 271 (book XVIII, xxxiv, 128). For English jestbook analogues on the extraordinary size of cabbages, see £222 in Anthony Copley, *Wits, Fits, and Fancies* (London, 1614), reprinted in Paul M. Zall, ed., *A Nest of Ninnies and Other English Jestbooks of the Seventeenth Century* (Lincoln, Neb., 1970), p. 6 (I am indebted to my friend Paul Zall for this example); and £120 in John Wardroper, *Jest Upon Jest* (London, 1970), p. 103.

14. In the first Maryland promotion tract, Andrew White, *A Declaration of the Lord Baltimore's Plantation in Mary-land* (London, 1633), claimed that corn "is very plentiful in each of three Harvests in the same year, yeelding in greatest penurie two hundred for one, in ordinary yeares five or six hundred; and in the better, fifteen or sixteen hundred for one." Hesiod in *Works and Days* describes the Elysian fields as a place where harvests are made three times a year. *Hesiod: The Homeric Hymns and Homerica,* tr. Hugh G. Evelyn White (Cambridge, Mass., Loeb Library, 1959), p. 15. Anecdotes about fertility are also a common subject of English jestbooks. See the "great dispute betwixt *Jockey* a *Scotchman,* and Jenkin a *Welch man* . . . about the fruitfullnesse

of their Countries," £61 in John Ashton, ed., *Humor, Wit & Satire of the Seventeenth Century* (1883; repr. New York, 1968), p. 180. For references to the cornucopia theme in early Maryland literature (which is, of course, typical of the promotion literature of other colonies), see my *Men of Letters,* pp. 13, 19, 54, 119, 156, 167, and 177.

15. These implicit tensions of the promotion tracts are made explicit by George Alsop in *A Character of the Province of Maryland* (London, 1666), as well as by such eighteenth-century authors who reflect the promotion tract traditions as Robert Beverley, Richard Lewis, and Ebenezer Cook.

16. Kenneth Lynn, *Mark Twain and Southwestern Humor* (Boston, 1959), pp. 92-93, points out the combination of "urbane confidence and intense uneasiness" in Thorpe's story; and Katherine G. Simoneaux, "Symbolism in Thorpe's 'The Big Bear of Arkansas,'" *Arkansas Historical Quarterly,* XXV, (Fall, 1966), 240-247, argues that Doggett's Arkansas is "the lost Eden" and "a Garden of Paradise."

17. In "Folklore in Literature: A Symposium," *Journal of American Folklore,* LXX (Jan.-March, 1957), Richard M. Dorson, p. 7, Carvel Collins, p. 9, and especially Daniel G. Hoffman, p. 20, comment on the bear's mana. See also Dorson's *American Folklore* (Chicago, 1959), p. 60; Rickels, *Thomas Bangs Thorpe,* pp. 58-60; Simoneaux, p. 244; and John Q. Anderson, ed., *With the Bark On: Popular Humor of the Old South* (Nashville, Tenn., 1967), pp. 80-82. The archetypal background of bears as supernatural mandalas is studied in Richard Bernheimer, *Wild Men in the Middle Ages* (Cambridge, Mass., 1952), *passim,* but especially pp. 53-60; see also Louise G. Clubb, "The Tragicomic Bear," *Comparative Literature Studies,* IX (1972), 17-30; and Beryl Rowland, *Animals with Human Faces: A Guide to Animal Symbolism* (Knoxville, Tenn., 1973), pp. 31-35.

Richard Slotkin, in *Regeneration through Violence,* pp. 480-484, believes that the scene with the bear in the crotch of a tree, surrounded by baying hounds, presents an image "of the hanging god of primitive mythology and, by extension, of the crucifixion" (p. 481). He argues that the sequence in the penultimate climax recapitulates a fire-hunt myth, representing "a quest into the unconscious for the vision of an anima" (p. 482). Quoting excerpts does his intelligent interpretation injustice—and, of course, his interpretation supports the thesis of his book. Slotkin's analysis is the most detailed criticism of "The Big Bear" made from a mythic-archetypal point of view. One of my few radical disagreements with Slotkin is that he evidently presumes that Thorpe is to be identified with the city-slicker narrator ("the hunter's narrative is framed by Thorpe's account of his meeting with the teller on a steamboat," p. 481).

18. One thinks of Achilles, the werewolf, the vampire—and especially of other bear stories. In "A Bear Hunt in Vermont" (1833), the one vulnerable place to shoot the spirit-bear is "just under the off ear": see Richard M. Dorson, *Jonathan Draws the Long Bow* (Cambridge, Mass., 1946), p. 116.

19. This motif also occurs in "A Bear Hunt in Vermont" (1833). Dorson, *Jonathan,* p. 116. Similarly, in Faulkner's "The Bear," Walter Ewell fires and inexplicably misses the bear, even though in "The Old People," we are told that Ewell never misses.

20. See the tale recorded in John W. Jordan, ed., "Journal of James Kenny, 1761-1763," *Pennsylvania Magazine of History and Biography,* XXXVII (1913), 180-181.

21. The allusion is to the common ballad (and chapbook story) of the two orphans who are abandoned in the woods by their cruel uncle. Nature acts as the agent of the uncle and kills the children. Ironically, in Thorpe's story the "children of the wood" are frontiersmen—those best able to deal with the wilderness.

22. Richard Lewis, in "Food for Critics" (c. 1730), Ebenezer Cook, in *Sotweed Redivivus* (1730), and James Sterling, in "Verses occasioned by the Success of the British Arms in the Year 1759" (1760)—all used the cutting down of the tree as a symbol of the passing of Edenic America. For the continuation of this motif, see especially James Fenimore Cooper in chapters two and seven of *The Prairie* (1827). Cf. Mike Fink's sentiments in Thorpe's "The Disgraced Scalp-Lock, or Incidents on the Western Waters," conveniently available in Walter Blair and Franklin J. Meine, *Half Horse Half Alligator: The Growth of the Mike Fink Legend* (Chicago, 1956), p. 71.

23. For some notes on the relationship between Thorpe's story and Faulkner's "The Bear," see William Van O'Connor, "The Wilderness Theme in Faulkner's 'The Bear,'" reprinted (from *Accent,* XIII, Winter, 1953, 12-20) in Frederick J. Hoffman and Olga W. Vickery, eds., *William Faulkner: Three Decades of Criticism* (New York, 1960), p. 326, n. 5; Carvel Collins, "Faulkner and Certain Earlier Southern Fiction," *College English,* XVI (Nov., 1954), 96-97; and Troi Tyner, "The Function of the Bear Ritual in Faulkner's *Go Down, Moses,*" *Journal of the Ohio Folklore Society,* III (1968), 19-40.

24. The stage theory of civilization was one of the dominant ideas of the nineteenth century, and was responsible, in my opinion, for the fundamental attitudes towards the wilderness and civilization from the mid-eighteenth to the early twentieth centuries. Most of the major books (e.g., by Roy Harvey Pearce, Henry Nash Smith, Leo Marx, and Richard Slotkin) on American attitudes toward the wilderness touch upon the stage theory.

25. Cf. Simoneaux, p. 247.

26. Simoneaux, pp. 245-246, also makes this point.

27. A number of other minor points strengthen the double motif: Doggett tells his audience that bears (like men) "squander about in pairs and single ones," p. 43b11; the big bear eats the same food as Doggett, hogs, p. 44a2; and the big bear/"she bar" uses the same log to flee from the island that Doggett used to swim there, p. 44a3.

28. Simoneaux, p. 242, comments: "As its name *Invincible* implies, the steamboat is the carrier of civilization which will inevitably be victorious over the frontier." For the Mike Fink lament, see Blair and Meine, *Half Horse Half Alligator,* p. 71.

29. Walter Blair, "The Technique of 'The Big Bear of Arkansas,'" *Southwest Review,* XXVIII (Summer, 1943) 426-435, especially p. 427.

30. Since the Know Nothing party was not formed until approximately 1852, Thorpe could not have been alluding to it, though he was later associated with the party. Rickels, *Thorpe,* pp. 193-194.

31. James A. Shackford, *David Crockett: The Men and The Legend* (Chapel Hill, N.C., 1956), p. 212.

32. Lynn, p. 92.

33. I cite from the convenient edition of Hamlin Garland, ed., *The Autobiography of David Crockett* (New York, 1923). Chapters 12, 14, and 15 of *A Narrative of the Life of David Crockett, of the State of Tennessee* ([n.p.,] 1834) establish Crockett's fame as "the bear hunter" (p. 108), celebrated for killing "one hundred and five bears . . . in less than one year" (p. 125). Doggett's saying that the bears in Arkansas have "one continued fat season the year round" (p. 43c3) may echo Crockett on bears staying mysteriously fat through the winter (p. 116), and Doggett's saying "fat! it's an enemy to speed" (p. 43c3) may echo Crockett on fat bears being "easily taken, for a fat bear can't run fast or long" (p. 113). Doggett's mastery of bear lore (p. 43c10) may remind us of Crockett's boasting of his knowledge of bears (pp. 117, 120) and of his fame as a bear hunter (pp. 50, 108, 125). Doggett also, like Crockett (p. 113), hunts bears for his neighbors. Doggett's central anecdote about hunting "the bar" may echo Crockett's chapter 12, wherein he describes hunting and killing the "biggest bear that ever was seen in America" (p. 106); like Doggett's mysterious "bar," Crockett's too is almost supernatural, for Crockett's dogs kept "barking up the wrong tree": "They served me in this way three or four times, until I was so infernal mad . . ." (p. 106). Another of Crockett's main anecdotes, in which the bear was treed "in a large, forked poplar, and it was setting in the fork," may have suggested to Thorpe *the* bar's "sitting quietly in the crotch of a tree" (p. 44a3). So too, Thorpe's big bear dying "like a falling tree" (p. 44a3) may have been suggested by Crockett's bear falling down out of a tree upon being shot "like some great log had fell" (p. 118).

Like other stories of the humor of the Old Southwest, Crockett's *Narrative* uses some metaphors (busting his boiler) and clichés (getting wrathy) that are also found in Thorpe's "The Big Bear of Arkansas." It is probably pushing the evidence too far to suggest that Crockett's talk of making his "crap" (i.e., planting his crop) in the wilderness might have inspired the climax and the bitterness of Thorpe's story.

34. Reprinting the Mike Fink stories, Blair and Meine, *Half Horse Half Alligator,* say of Thorpe's "The Disgraced Scalp-Lock" that "It endows Mike with a romantic love of nature and a nostalgia which are hardly in character with his known or even his legendary character," p. 68.

35. See *The Country-man's Lamentation for the Death of his Cow* (London, c. 1670-80), Wing C 6554, conveniently available in Thomas Evans, ed., *Old Ballads* (London, 1810), I, 268; and in William Chappell, ed., *The Roxburghe Ballads* (Hertford, 1875-80), III, 600-603.

36. On Captain Martin Scott's coon, see Thomas D. Clark's *The Rampaging Frontier* (Bloomington, Ind., 1964), p. 206, where an anecdote is attributed to Thomas C. Haliburton in the *Spirit of the Times,* VIII (March 17, 1838), 40; and see the two anecdotes in B. A. Botkin, ed., *A Treasury of New England Folklore* (New York, 1947), p. 239, where the sources are given as Frederick Marryat, *A Diary in America* (Philadelphia, 1839), II, 37-38, and the *Vermont Historical Gazetteer* (Burlington, Vt., 1867), I, 177-178. Jules Zanger's edition of Marryat's *Diary in America* (Bloomington, Ind., 1960), contains some anecdotes of Captain Scott on pp. 237-242; and Sydney Jackman's edition (New York, 1962), p. 267, contains the famous mock-derivation of "gone coon." I might also note that the "pedlar of tin ware from New England," p. 43b1, was a well-known humorous type of the

Yankee pedlar: see the series "Travels of a Tin Pedlar" in the (Boston) *New England Galaxy* for 1827-1828.

Walter Blair and Hamlin Hill (essay date 1978)

SOURCE: Blair, Walter, and Hamlin Hill. "'The Big Bear of Arkansas.'" In *America's Humor: From Poor Richard to Doonesbury*, pp. 200-12. New York: Oxford University Press, 1978.

[*In the following excerpts, Blair and Hill present a close reading of Thorpe's story. The authors contend that the story represents an early, and widely influential, classic of American humor.*]

Fred Shaw, late professor of English in the University of Miami, in mid-summer 1954 got word that he was to show William Faulkner around Miami during a stopover between planes. Shaw and a graduate student met America's greatest living novelist and at once escorted him to the nearest air-conditioned bar. The student mentioned that he was writing a dissertation about a relationship not yet much explored—between Faulkner and antebellum Southwestern humor. Faulkner spoke of his great admiration for such humor and in particular

> paid a fine compliment to Thomas Bangs Thorpe's **"The Big Bear of Arkansas."** The student said he thought he could detect similarities between that story and Faulkner's "The Bear." Faulkner looked surprised. Then: "That's a fine story. A writer is afraid of a story like that. He's afraid he'll try to rewrite it. A writer has to learn when to run from a story."

Faulkner's reaction to talk about resemblances was a typical writer's response, and no doubt he was unconscious of any. Just the same, the likenesses between his short story and Thorpe's are impressive.

Important as an influence, **"The Big Bear"** [**"The Big Bear of Arkansas"**] also merits praise as a classic. On its first appearance in 1841, William T. Porter, knowledgeable editor of one of the leading outlets for such a story, warned readers "on no account" to miss "the best sketch of backwoods life, that we have seen in a long while." Porter printed the story in both *The Spirit of the Times* and a second periodical he edited, and in 1845 featured it in a collection of his favorites—*"The Big Bear of Arkansas" and Other Sketches*. Meanwhile, the piece had been reprinted in sporting magazines and newspapers throughout the United States and Europe. And thereafter, down to the present, it would be published and called a masterpiece again and again.

The subtitle of Porter's anthology, itself a landmark in American humor, suggested an important appeal of Thorpe's story and others like it: "Illustrative of Characters and Incidents in the South and the Southwest." Porter's introduction praised "a new order of literary talent" for blazing "novel and original" trails by writing "in a masterly style . . . valuable and interesting reminiscences of the pioneers." The new breed, Porter said, were men "who live at home at ease" in the midst of the life which they portray. Porter borrowed his epigraph from Dogberry: "This is your charge; you shall comprehend all vagrom men." Like the vagrom men about whom they wrote authentically, Porter said, his writers had "exteriors 'like the rugged Russian bear,'" were "gifted with . . . good sense and knowledge of the world," "fond of whiskey," and loved telling stories.

To the rough exterior, the description fit Thorpe: "a poor little fellow with an awful face," a friend called him, looking "like an embodiment, in semi-human form, of a thick fog on the Mississippi, at half past three in the morning to a man who has just lost his last dollar at poker." The friend perhaps exaggerated, but even portraits—usually flattering—show that Thorpe was short and pudgy, with a big flat nose, auburn hair, and a sour phiz; he resembled a pug dog with russet sideburns.

But his attractive personality helped him comprehend vagrom men, as did his knowledge of the world. The friend went on to say that Thorpe's "grave and saturnine countenance quite belies a kind and playful spirit that seems to live in light and loveliness beneath the madness and gloom of his character." And at twenty-five, when he wrote his masterpiece, Thorpe had had varied experiences. Though born a Yankee, he had lived during most of his childhood and youth in Albany and New York City. In Manhattan he studied painting under a pupil of John Wesley Jarvis, John Quidor; and starting in his teens, Thorpe exhibited—and even sold—paintings. More important for his writing, from the time he was an adolescent, he sat in on story-telling sessions of artistic Bohemians—Gilbert Stuart, Henry Inman, the ubiquitous Jarvis, and others. During more than fifty years, every now and then he praised in print this group, particularly the three men mentioned—their mimicry, their "fluency in speech, their happy manner of description and story-telling." As late as 1872 he recalled the feat of one artist: "Ingham was only remarkable for telling one story, and that one only at the regular meetings of the National Academy. And this story, for a long period of time, was absolutely told every twelve months with mathematical precision as to circumstance, manner, and words."

For a couple of years (1834-1836), Thorpe went to Wesleyan University in Connecticut. Then bad health, invitations by fellow students from the South who liked him, and chances for portrait commissions led him to move to Louisiana. By 1841, he had married, settled down in Feliciana Parish on the Mississippi River, and launched a career as both painter and writer.

In addition to the oral stories of Jarvis and his pals, he knew Irving's writings "by heart." (Like his teacher, Quidor, he had painted illustrations for Irving's comic narratives.) He had read sketches and books by and about Davy Crockett, sermons by critics urging his countrymen to create a national literature, and guesses that the frontier might produce The American Character. He had seen at first hand life in New Orleans, aboard riverboats, and on riverside farms and plantations. Thanks to the hospitality and breezy ways of his neighbors, he was hunting, getting sozzled, and swapping stories with Feliciana planters, and between jollifications, painting portraits of his friends, their wives, and their daughters. On a recent visit to New York, he had called on a couple of editors, sold one a painting, and got orders from both for magazine pieces. He had placed writings with *Knickerbocker Magazine* and *Spirit of the Times.* **"The Big Bear of Arkansas"** first appeared in the March 27, 1841 issue of the *Spirit.*

In this piece, the high point of a long and prolific career, young Thorpe discovered new possibilities for a vernacular style, comic characterization, and imaginative invention. A look at it may suggest why, for all its brevity and its look of artlessness, it caused scholars to dub a whole group of great humorists "The Big Bear School."

Like units in Boccaccio's *Decameron* and Chaucer's *Canterbury Tales,* **"The Big Bear of Arkansas"** is a story within a story. It has two narrators, a writer who tells about the gathering of an audience aboard a riverboat, and an oral narrator who unfolds an enclosed tale about a bear hunt.

The first sentence is: "A steamboat on the Mississippi frequently, in making her regular trips, carries between places varying from one to two thousand miles apart; and as these boats advertise to land passengers and freight at 'all intermediate landings,' the heterogeneous character of the passengers on one of these up-country boats can scarcely be imagined by one who has never seen it with his own eyes." The language—even for a day when most writings were quite formal—is stilted and unimaginative: its lightest touch is a drab quotation from an advertisement. The ponderous tone, the big words, and the sentence construction show up the first narrator as a bit stuffy. So does his next sentence, also highfalutin, its sole figure of speech (here italicized) smelling of the lamp: "Starting from New Orleans in one of these boats, you will find yourself associated with men from every state in the Union, and every portion of the globe; and a man of observation need not lack for amusement or instruction in such a crowd, if he will take the trouble to read *the great book of character so favourably opened before him.*" As he continues, this narrator proves to be the sort that marks off phrases barely edging towards slang—e.g., "latest paper" and "social hall"—in apologetic quotation marks.

Nevertheless, he soon shows he relishes the motley steamboat crowd and popular nicknames: "Here may be seen jostling together the wealthy Southern planter, the pedlar of tin-ware from New England—. . . a venerable bishop and a desperate gambler—. . . Wolverines, Suckers, Hoosiers, Buckeyes, and Corncrackers, besides a 'plentiful sprinkling' of the half-horse and half-alligator species of men, who are peculiar to the 'old Mississippi'. . . ." And when he boards the *Invincible* for a brief trip from New Orleans, he at once notices that the crowd is as miscellaneous as usual and decides that, because of special circumstances, he will not, on this trip anyhow, peruse "the great book of character" they open.

When the second narrator, Jim Doggett, arrives, the writer tells of his offstage shouts, describes and quotes him at length, remarks his pleasant effect on the crowd, and—because he will only see "so singular a personage" briefly—persuades him to tell a long story. Jim's yarnspinning skill delights him:

> His manner was so singular, that half of his story consisted in his excellent way of telling it, the great peculiarity of which was the happy manner he had of emphasizing the prominent parts of his conversation. As near as I can recollect, I have italicized them, and given the story in his own words.

Once Jim gets going, the writer quotes him without interrupting. When Jim ends, the educated narrator describes an aftermath that fascinates him. Stuffy though his language makes him appear, then, this narrator, no aloof and prissy Whig aristocrat, has a lively interest in his fellow passengers and an even livelier one in Jim.

Jim first lifts his voice at the bar, shouting stock frontier boasts. "Hurra for the Big Bar of Arkansaw! [I'm a] horse! [I'm a] screamer! [Alongside me] lightening is slow!" Having noisily identified himself, the Big Bear strolls into the cabin, sits, hoists feet onto the stove, greets the crowd, says he feels at home, and soon charms his motley audience:

> Some of the company at this familiarity looked a little angry, and some astonished; but in a moment every face was wreathed in a smile. There was something about the intruder that won the heart on sight. He appeared to be a man enjoying perfect health and contentment: his eyes were as sparkling as diamonds, and good-natured to simplicity. Then his perfect confidence in himself was irresistibly droll.

Clearly no clownish caricature, this is an interesting personality attractive to men of all "creeds and characters," of all classes and parts of the country.

So close to the stodgy utterances of the writer, Jim's quoted words, phrasings and rhythms are by contrast informal, idiosyncratic, and imaginative. His homage to his dog Bowie-knife is typical:

. . . whew! why the fellow thinks the world is full of bar, he finds them so easy. It's lucky he don't talk as well as think; for with his natural modesty, if he should suddenly learn how much he is acknowledged to be ahead of all other dogs in the universe, he would be astonished to death in two minutes. Strangers, the dog knows a bar's way as well as a horse-jockey knows a woman's; he always barks at the right time, bites at the exact place, and whips without getting a scratch. I never could tell whether he was made expressly to hunt bar, or whether bar was made expressly for him to hunt; any way, I believe they were ordained to go together as naturally as Squire Jones says a man and woman is, when he moralizes in marrying a couple.

Jim's zest creates hyperbole and the flood of details that support wild claims. Affection helps Jim read Bowie-knife's mind and endow the beast with human virtues—intelligence and modesty. One of the unhackneyed similes, the trope which cites the well-informed horse-jockey, signals his worldly wisdom. His praise of the timing of Bowie-knife's bark and bite, and his use of "whips" show his precise knowledge of a great hunting dog's tactics. His philosophical discourse about the predestination of either the hunter or the hunted is distinctive. So is a respect for what is "natural" which comes out two other times as he tells his story.

In addition to being exuberant, an acute observer, and a do-it-yourself philosopher, Jim is a superb yarnspinner. He orders expository details and events in a masterful fashion and marshals hosts of particulars and witty comments on them. Although his story (in large part because of its salty style) seems artless, it makes comical use of two anticlimaxes, mounts to its climax, and then ends.

The introduction of the two narrators, of Jim's audience, and the detailing of Jim's talk with the crowd occupy more than half of Thorpe's pages before the Big Bear begins his account of his greatest hunt. These preliminaries initiate a pattern which Doggett's yarn develops and completes—essentially one of contrasts and expansion.

After saying that he feels entirely at home among the cosmopolitan steamboat crowd, Jim launches talk about a contrast that is analogous to that between his vernacular style and the formal style of the writer:

> "Perhaps," said he, "gentlemen, . . . you have been to New Orleans often; I never made *the first visit before,* and I don't intend to make another in a crow's life. I am thrown away in that ar place, and useless. . . . Some of the gentlemen thar call me *green*—well, perhaps I am, said I, *but I arn't so at home*; and if I ain't off my trail much, the heads of them perlite chaps themselves wern't much the hardest; for according to my notion, they were the real *know-nothings,* green as a pumpkin vine—couldn't, in farming, I'll bet, raise a crop of turnips; and as for shooting, they'd miss a barn if the door was swinging. . . ."

Jim has had trouble talking with these dandies. If they speak of "game," they mean not "Arkansaw poker and high-low jack" but fowl and wild animals, which Jim calls "meat." Moreover, New Orleans game is tiny stuff, "chippenbirds and shite-pokes"—"trash" that Arkansans think beneath contempt. Jim says that at home he will not shoot a bird weighing less than forty pounds.

Arkansas is "the creation state, the finishing-up country. . . . Then its airs—just breathe them, and they will make you snort like a horse." Even when Jim admits that mosquitoes there are enormous, he defends them in a way underlining the contrast between Arkansas and the rest of the world. Natives or settlers are impervious to them, and the one injury they caused was to a Yankee—"a foreigner" who "swelled up and busted, . . . su-per-ated . . . took the ager . . . and finally took a steamboat and left the country."

To end his argument, Jim lists his state's features in the order of their size: mosquitoes, and then—"her varmints are large, her trees are large, her rivers are large." Next—as if climactically—he comes to the bears. They differ not only from bears anywhere else but of any other time: "I read in history that varmints have their fat season and their lean season. That is not the case in Arkansaw, feeding as they do upon the *spontenacious* productions of the sile, they have one continued fat season the year round" and running one "sort of mixes the ile up with the meat," and if you shoot one, "steam comes out of the bullet hole ten feet in a straight line." When a "foreigner" asks, "Whereabouts are these bears so abundant?" Doggett introduces the greatest district in this marvelous Cockayne, Schlaraffenland, Lubberland, Arkansas—"Shirt-tail Bend" on the Forks of Cypress—Jim's own clearing.

Shirt-tail Bend is called "one of the prettiest places on the old Mississippi," but soon this mild claim gives way to claims that "the government ain't got another such place to dispose of" and that three months after planting beets are mistaken for cedar stumps, potato hills for Indian mounds. "*Planting in Arkansaw is dangerous,*" Jim warns. Dangerous for bears are Doggett, "the best bar hunter in the district"; his gun, "*a perfect epidemic among bar*; if not watched closely, it will go off as quick on a warm scent as my dog Bowie-knife will," and the aforesaid super-dog.

Soon after Jim has jocosely praised his settlement, two paragraphs in the highfalutin style of the writer return to the contrasting steamboat cabin. There skeptics briefly dispute with him, but the first narrator asks for "a description of some particular bear hunt," describes the Big Bear's singular manner, then without interrupting, lets him give his account in his own salty words.

Repeating the pattern of contrast and enlargement, Jim mentions two ordinary hunts—ordinary, that is, for the

Forks of Cypress—then promises to give "an idea of a hunt, in which the greatest bar was killed that ever lived, *none excepted.*"

A customary hunt for Jim is "about as much the same to me as drinking." "It is told," he says, "in two sentences—a bar is started, and he is killed." This hunt, by contrast, requires many sentences, since the varmint was the giant beast which eluded Jim, his epidemic gun, and the incomparable Bowie-knife two or three long years.

Jim first learns about this critter by measuring the height of bite marks made on sassafras trees—marks which, experience proves, show "the length of the bar to an inch." These are "about eight inches above any in the forest that I knew of. Says I, 'them marks is a hoax, or it indicates the d——t bar that was ever grown.' In fact, . . . I couldn't believe it was real, and I went on. Again I saw the same marks, . . . and *I knew the thing lived.* That conviction came home to my soul like an earthquake."

Jim tells about hunting the bear and wasting away in flesh because of his frustration over many months before he again happens to mention the critter's size. This time the beast is "a little larger than a horse." Still later, when Jim gets a final shot at him, the bear "loomed up like a *black mist,* he seemed so large." After Jim's shot, "the varmint wheeled, gave a yell, and *walked through the fence* like a falling tree would through a cobweb." Thus, like Cypress Forks beets and potatoes, the bear of bears grows at an astonishing rate.

Though this account has traced the bear's growth by degrees in Jim's narrative to his greatest size, it has not noticed a second climactic development that is not made explicit until the very end.

Soon after that earthquake conviction has proved to Jim that the giant animal lives, he has a startling thought: "Says I, 'here is something a-purpose for me: that bar is mine, or I give up the hunting business.'" The way everything goes wrong during the first pursuit of the bear is disquieting because it is "past my understanding." Other happenings prove to be just as inexplicable. Jim's flesh begins to waste away "faster than the ager." He becomes obsessed—sees the bear in everything he does. But when at last he gets close enough to see the beast plainly, he reacts strangely, exclaiming, "But wasn't he a beauty, though? I loved him like a brother."

A companion's shot strikes the animal's forehead: "The bar shook his head, . . . and then walked down from that tree as gently as a lady would from a carriage. 'Twas a beautiful sight. . . ." Now Jim takes careful aim "at his side just back of his foreleg" and pulls the trigger; his gun snaps. The bear leaps into a lake, has a

fight in the water with the dog, sinks, and stays submerged. Jim dives, brings up the carcass, and thinks all is over. But—

> Stranger, may I be chawed to death by young alligators, if the thing I looked at warn't a she bar, and not the old critter after all. The way matters got mixed . . . was onaccountably curious, and thinking of it made me more than ever convinced that I was hunting the devil himself. I went home that night and took to my bed— the thing was killing me. . . . I grew as cross as a bar with two cubs and a sore tail.

Kidded by his neighbors, Jim decides "to catch that bar, go to Texas, or die," and he makes preparations for a final hunt. But the day before that hunt is planned, at a most inopportune moment the bear comes along. Jim manages to fire a shot. The beast wheels, walks away, and Jim hears him "groaning in a thicket nearby, like a thousand sinners." When Jim reaches him, he is dead.

At this point, ending his story, Jim states a deduction for which his yarning has prepared:

> . . . strangers, I never liked the way I hunted and *missed him.* There is something curious about it, I never could understand,—and I never was satisfied at his giving in so easy at last. Perhaps, he had heard of my preparations to hunt him next day, so he just come in, like Capt. Scott's coon, to save his wind to grunt with in dying; but that ain't likely. My private opinion is, that that bar was an *unhuntable bar, and died when his time come.*

So the biggest bear in Shirt-tail Bend, domicile of the biggest bears in Arkansas, a state which itself is greater than any other country—such a bear in the end is slain not by bullets but by the inscrutable fate which has brought him and the Big Bear of Arkansas together. And from the first sentence to this point a parade of details prepare for this climax.

This climax has some relevance to remarks that Faulkner made during his talk with Professor Shaw and the student about bear stories. Shaw had suggested that the bear in bear stories was "the big test—the medieval dragon." Faulkner agreed: "Yes, the bear was a symbol; he was the wilderness. On the frontier . . . things could be pretty hard. Here was a farmer trying to beat back the woods, trying to make a crop, and not having a very easy time of it; and here was the bear. If he could kill him, he had licked the wilderness."

The comment provides a useful gloss on the work about which Faulkner was talking, his own "The Bear." But since that superb story is a serious one which uses symbols to convey its profound significations, the remarks have relevance to Thorpe's story only as much as a solemn treatise on Mississippi farming would have to Faulkner's hilarious "Spotted Horses." For however noteworthy are the realism and the characterization of **"The Big Bear of Arkansas,"** in essence it is a comic story. Its different narrators and styles, its incongruities and expansions, its fantastic imaginings as well as its initial reception and subsequent history make this clear to all readers except a few thesis-ridden scholars.

Important aids to the humorous effect are the changes in Jim's attitude and that of his listeners while he tells his tall tales, and two strategically placed anticlimaxes.

En route to the cabin, Jim pauses at the bar. Soon he is shouting a cheer for himself, boasting that he is a horse and a screamer, and alleging that compared with him lightning is slow. After he joins fellow passengers, they are at first startled or irritated. But soon "something about the intruder"—his *joie de vivre*, his *Gemütlichkeit* and his "irresistibly droll" self-assurance—win every heart and cause everyone to smile. As he joyously pours out one whopper after another, the listeners' reactions show that they know very well that he is putting them on. When he talks about shooting only forty-pound turkeys, "twenty voices in the cabin at once" proclaim disbelief. When he piles on details about the fatness of one of these birds, "a cynical-looking Hoosier" asks "Where did all that happen?" and a bit later he interrupts Jim's claim that Arkansaw is without a fault by saying, "Excepting mosquitoes." Undeterred, Jim makes even more outrageous claims, whereupon a gentlemanly Englishman, "foreigner" though he is, laughs and voices disbelief, and "a 'live sucker' from Illinois . . . has the daring to say that our Arkansaw friend's stories 'smell rather tall.'"

Jim argues with this skeptic surely in a playful spirit with no hope that he will close yawning credibility gaps. And though the listeners do not interrupt Jim's yarn about his biggest hunt, as he launches it they cannot be unaware of Jim's exaggerations or unappreciative of his witty way of phrasing them.

But as the story moves along, Jim's attitude and that of his listeners change. At the start, fresh from the bar, Jim is high spirited, jocose, humorous. His eyes sparkle as he invents and exaggerates wildly improbable details. But signs that he and his listeners are amused decrease. When he finishes, both he and his audience are solemn:

> When his story was ended, our hero sat some minutes with his auditors in a grave silence; I saw there was a mystery to him connected with the bear whose death he had just related, that had evidently made a strong impression on his mind. It was also evident that there was some superstitious awe connected with the affair,— a feeling common with all "children of the wood," when they meet with any thing out of their everyday experience.

The picture is of a man who tells a beautiful lie—such a superbly imagined and performed work of art that he convinces not only his audience but also himself. Fan-

tastic Cypress Forks, which Jim has created out of thin air (and a fact or two) becomes a reality for him. The bear, which he has imaginatively enlarged beyond all reason and even gifted with supernatural powers, has overawed Jim's auditors and—still more impressive— Jim himself. Thanks to his own soaring eloquence, paradoxically, Jim has confused the real and the imagined.

Overwhelmed though he is, Jim manages to recover before his silenced listeners: "He was the first one, however, to break the silence, and jumping up, he asked all present to 'liquor' before going to bed,—a thing which he did, with a number of companions, evidently to his heart's content."

As the style indicates, after Jim ends his story, his salty language gives way to the stuffy style of the first narrator—latinate words, apologetic quotes, long sentences. Simultaneously, Jim and his audience are plopped down again in the mundane cabin. The final sentence of **"The Big Bear of Arkansas"** rounds out the contrast between Jim's clearing and the world of the writer: "Long before day, I was put ashore at my place of destination, and I can only follow with the reader, in imagination, our Arkansas friend, in his adventures at the 'Forks of Cypress' on the Mississippi."

The shift in style marks an anticlimax. Another anticlimax which occurs earlier was probably even more impressive in 1841.

The period, recall, was by modern standards an incredibly prissy one when the slightest hint of blasphemy or obscenity shocked Americans beyond belief. An instance: Jim, in a passage quoted a few paragraphs back, said that his gigantic bear groaned "like a thousand sinners." Because the simile somehow sounded irreligious, the words were cut out of a number of early reprintings. Whole books have been written about taboos in force against references to sex. Following the publication of Herman Melville's *Typee*—five years after Thorpe's **"Big Bear"** [**"The Big Bear of Arkansas"**]—so many wails would be raised about its frankness that numerous passages would be excised from subsequent editions— passages which readers today often study with complete bewilderment, unable to imagine what the readers of those quaint times found suggestive in them. Even rarer than references—including vague ones—to sex were scatological passages. Melville, in the final chapter of *The Confidence-Man* (1857) would write about what a character called "a life preserver"—described as "a brown stool with curved tin compartment underneath" which smells bad—and alert readers somehow managed to discover that the passage refers to a toilet seat. In our own dear enlightened era when folk are daily uplifted by televised Curses on Constipation and Paeans to Regularity or by bits about bodily functions in respected books, plays, and movies, we need a translation for a passage that in 1841 was unique—part of Jim's story:

. . . I went into the woods near my house, taking my gun and Bowie-knife along, *just from habit,* and there sitting down also from habit, what should I see, getting over my fence, but *the bar!* Yes, the old varmint was within a hundred yards of me, and . . . he walked . . . towards me. I raised myself, took deliberate aim, and fired. Instantly the varmint wheeled . . . I started after, but was tripped up by my inexpressibles, which either from habit, or the excitement of the moment, were about my heels. . . .

This translates: Accompanied by his dog and carrying his gun, as usual, Jim entered the woods to take his daily crap. Squatting there, he looked up, saw the bear approaching, and fired at him. The bear turned. Jim started after him, but his pants ("inexpressibles" in 1841!) fell about his heels and tripped him. Combined with this account, shockingly frank for 1841, were phrases that are indicated above by dots: "the way he walked *over that fence*—stranger, he loomed up like a *black mist,* he seemed so large," and "he *walked through the fence* like a falling tree would through a cobweb." In other words, at the very moment when Jim's imagining carries the picture of the bear to a climax of physical grandeur, he also tells about having a bowel movement, letting his pants fall, and being tripped up by them. And the clauses following the quoted passage are those which tell about the bear's groaning and his mysterious death.

This combination of the earthy with the fantastic makes for a superb anticlimax—an incongruous coalescence that is not only typical of American humor and the tall tale but also one of their superb achievements.

Note

Discussions of the relationship between Thorpe's story and Faulkner's "The Bear" include Carvel Collins, "Faulkner and Certain Southern Fiction," *College English,* 16 (November 1954), 96, and Francis Lee Utley, "Pride and Humility," in *Bear, Man and God* (New York, 1971), pp. 170-171. Early discussions of "The Big Bear" ["The Big Bear of Arkansas"] which were drawn upon include [Walter] Blair, *Native American Humor,* [New York, 1937; San Francisco, 1960,] pp. 91-95, and "The Technique of 'The Big Bear of Arkansas,'" *Southwest Review,* 28 (Summer, 1943), pp. 426-435. A fine biography, supplemented with a detailed bibliography, usefully discusses the story—Milton Rickels, *Thomas Bangs Thorpe, Humorist of the Old Southwest* (Baton Rouge, 1962), pp. 49-62. [Norris] Yates, *William T. Porter and the* Spirit of the Times subtitled "A Study of the 'Big Bear' School of Humor" [Baton Rouge, 1957] and Richard Boyd Hauck's University of Illinois doctoral dissertation, "Literary Content of the New York *Spirit of the Times*" (1965), are good on the tall tale as a genre and on Thorpe's masterpiece. The latter discussion of the story (pp. 226-232) differs somewhat from the one offered here. J. A. Leo Lemay, "The Text, Tradition, and Themes of 'The Big Bear of Arkansas,'" *American Literature,* 47 (November, 1975), 321-42, contains much valuable information about the story and its background. Lemay's reading also differs from ours. Neil Schmitz, "Tall Tale, Tall Talk," *American Literature,* 48 (January, 1977), which appeared after this chapter was completed, discussed Thorpe's story most recently.

Daniel F. Littlefield Jr. (essay date spring 1979)

SOURCE: Littlefield, Daniel F., Jr. "Thomas Bangs Thorpe and the Passing of the Southwestern Wilderness." *Southern Literary Journal* 11, no. 2 (spring 1979): 56-65.

[*In the following essay, Littlefield appraises Thorpe's 1854 story collection* The Hive of "The Bee-Hunter." *In Littlefield's reading, these stories consider the role of the wilderness in shaping the character of the early settlers and represent Thorpe's impassioned indictment of the destruction of the Southwestern frontier. Littlefield claims that, in Thorpe's view, the crudeness and natural beauty of frontier life were more distinctly American than were the more civilized societies on the coast.*]

In his third letter, St. Jean de Crèvecoeur's American Farmer expressed concern for the impact of the wilderness on American character. To the enlightened Farmer, the influence was not entirely good: "He who would wish to see America in its proper light, and have a true idea of its feeble beginnings and barbarous rudiments, must visit our extended line of frontiers where the last settlers dwell, and where he may see the first labours of settlement, the mode of clearing the earth, in all their different appearances; where men are wholly left dependent on their native tempers, and on the spur of uncertain industry, which often fails when not sanctified by the efficacy of a few moral rules."[1] Fifty years later, the theme was still a vital one in the works of American writers such as Cooper and Irving, whose interest in the implications of westward expansion for the wilderness and its inhabitants has been well documented. What these writers did on a national scale was also done on a regional basis in the works of such men as Southwestern humorist Thomas Bangs Thorpe. Although Thorpe was best known among his contemporaries for **"Tom Owen, the Bee-Hunter"** and **"The Big Bear of Arkansas,"** he produced a number of works, including the two for which he was famous, in which he considered the influence of the natural setting on the development of character in the Southwest. In 1854 he published a collection of sketches and stories titled *The Hive of "The Bee-Hunter," A Repository of Sketches, Including Peculiar American Character, Scenery, and Rural*

Sports,[2] in which his concern with the relationship between the wilderness and the American character is flatly stated in the preface. Of the Southwestern forests, Thorpe writes: "Here, in their vast interior solitudes, far removed from trans-Atlantic influences, are alone to be found, in the more comparative infancy of our country, characters truly *sui generis*—truly American. What man would be, uninfluenced by contact with the varied associations of long civilization, is here partially demonstrated in the denizens of the interior of a mighty continent. . . . There are growing up, in these primitive wilds, men, whose daily life and conversation, when detailed, form exaggerations; but whose histories are, after all, only the natural developments of the mighty associations which surround them" (p. 6).

Thorpe had apparently not always had that concern. In 1846, he had published a similar collection called *The Mysteries of the Backwoods; or Sketches of the Southwest; Including Character, Scenery, and Rural Sports,*[3] which contained fourteen of the works later reprinted in *The Hive of "The Bee Hunter."* In the preface, Thorpe tells how the natural beauty of the Southwest impressed him. It inspired him in a way that "the more merely beautiful and familiar scenery of the North" did not.[4] One of his purposes was to "give those personally unacquainted with the scenery of the Southwest, some idea of the country, of its surface, and vegetation."[5] Thorpe, a naturalist, writer, and painter, had come to the Southwest in 1837, and in 1845 he exhibited the naturalist's, writer's, and painter's interest in the natural world of the Southwest. He attached to it none of the larger significance he later placed on the role of the wilderness in the shaping of American character. The preface to *The Hive of "The Bee Hunter"* and the addition of *Peculiar American* before *Character* in the subtitle indicate that the idea was one that matured in Thorpe's mind between 1846 and 1854.

When the reader finishes the preface of *The Hive of "The Bee-Hunter,"* he might assume that Thorpe is suggesting that the largeness and beauty of nature somehow ennoble man. But before he has read far into the volume, he finds in the sketches the sour note of paradox: most contain descriptions of personages who destroy the wilderness from which they draw the very essence of their American character. Throughout the work one finds scenes of the wanton destruction of the forests and of blood and carnage as animals are slaughtered, usually for sport. Thus the sketches, originally intended as realistic, sometimes humorous, accounts of the manners, customs, and natural scenery of the lower Mississippi region, stand as an indictment of the wasteful destruction of natural resources and as a literary lament for the passing of the wilderness frontier.

II

Thorpe's prime concern for the destruction of animal resources is witnessed by the large number of titles containing animal names. **"Wild Turkey Hunting,"** with which the work opens, begins with the statement that the wild turkeys, once found throughout the continent, are still common on the "frontiers." However, each year their numbers decrease, "and as their disappearance always denotes their death, their extermination is progressive and certain" (9). They can exist for a long time to come only because they inhabit regions yet unappealing to the settler. Yet, Thorpe writes, despite unfavorable seasons or devastation by wild animals, the wild turkey's "numbers are also annually lessened by the skill of the pioneer and backwoodsman, and in but comparatively a few more years the bird must have, as a denizen of our border settlements, only a traditionary existence" (10). The skill of the backwoodsman is the point of the sketch, which borders on the ludicrous as Thorpe gets inside the "mind" of the turkey and lets the reader see the "thoughts" of the veteran bird as he is lured into a clearing by what he "thinks" is a lovely young hen. But the reader never laughs outright; in his mind is the frame Thorpe has carefully set around the sketch, and Thorpe never lets the reader forget that the beautiful bird is being lured to his death by the skillful hunter. The sketch ends on a cold note. A shot rings out and sets to flight the squalling jay:

> But our rare and beautiful bird,—our gallant and noble bird,—our cunning and game bird, where is he?
>
> The glittering plumage—the gay step—the bright eye—all—all are gone:—
>
> Without a movement of the muscles, our valorous lover has fallen lifeless to the earth.
>
> (27)

In **"Wild-Cat Hunting,"** Thorpe says that it is the "dense swamps that border on the Mississippi" that "protect this vicious species of game from extermination." He seems not to decrease in numbers because the cat seeks out the "most solitary retreats" to find "protection for itself and its kittens from the destructive hand of man" (155). Though a predator, which Thorpe describes as having a malicious desposition, this animal is beautiful to Thorpe, who praises "its beauty of motion" as it hunts or plays (156). It is pursued by sportsmen, not the hunter, with dogs, and when the animal is cornered, they shoot at it with pistols, not to kill it "but to annoy it" and make it fight the dogs (159). Similarly, in **"Alligator Killing"** Thorpe says that the alligator, denizen of "the lonliest swamp," cannot escape death, for "the pioneer of the forest invades his home—the axe lets in the sunshine upon his hiding-place:—and he frequently finds himself, like the Indian, surrounded by the encroachments of civilization, a mere intruder, in his original domain—and under such circumstances only, does he become an object of rough sport, the incidents of which deserve a passing notice" (184-85). As land is cleared and rivers are opened to navigation, "the alligator, becomes exposed, and falls a victim to the rapacity of man" (185). Thorpe tells a most unflattering story of the destruction of alligators on a Louisiana plantation and describes the most effective way of killing the reptiles and of using pigs or dogs as bait for them.

In **"Buffalo Hunting,"** Thorpe calls the buffalo "one of the noblest victims that is sacrificed to the ardor of the sportsman." Whereas he once roamed all of North America, cities and towns now occupy his haunts, and he has retreated before the "march of civilization" so that he is now found only west of the Mississippi (193). "But the day of his glory is past," writes Thorpe. "The Anglo-Saxon, more wanton of place than the savage himself, possessed of invincible courage and unlimited resources, and feeling adventure a part of life itself, has already penetrated the remotest fastnesses, and wandered over the most extended plains" (194). To the Indian, buffalo hunting takes on a religious connotation. To the white sportsman, "the buffalo hunt is the high consummation of his propensity and power to destroy . . . it is the very unloosing of all the rough passion of our nature, with the conscience entirely at rest" (196). Thorpe describes in gory detail a buffalo hunt and in disgusting detail the nondescript white squatters who first move into the plains. Thorpe continues his description of his first buffalo hunt in **"Scenes in Buffalo Hunting."** Despite the gore of the previous day's hunt, the sportsmen were excited as they "contemplated the sanguinary warfare" they were about to undertake and the "waste of life that would ensue" (214). Thorpe describes the disgusting practice of hamstringing buffaloes on the run by use of razors on the ends of long poles. The senseless killing finally has its effect on the sportsmen; they feast and satisfy the body but not the mind: "There was a waste of life and of food accompanying the hunting of the animal, that, like an ever-present spirit of evil, took away from our enjoyment that zest which is necessary to make it a favorite sport" (224).

In **"Woodcock Fire-Hunting,"** Thorpe describes the method of hunting the birds by torchlight. In the midst of describing the slaughter, he writes, "Heavens, this is murder! Don't load too heavy—let your charges be mere squibs, and murder away,—the sport is fairly up. . . . Thank the stars they do not fly many paces before they again alight, so that you can follow the same bird or birds until every one is destroyed" (229). If one tires of shooting, the birds can be knocked out of the trees with sticks and brought down by the "basketfulls" (230). Thorpe emphasizes the idea of murder by

the following headnote for his sketch: "'Tis murderous, but profitable.'—Tom Owen." Tom, however, makes no such statement in **"Tom Owen, the Bee-Hunter."**

Thorpe tells the reader in **"Opossum Hunting"** that even insignificant and unworthy game such as the opossum is the source of destruction. Its hunters cut down the tree into which the dogs have chased the animal— "let it be a big tree or a small one, it matters not; the growth of a century, or of a few years only, yields to the 'forerunner of civilization,' and comes to the ground" (261).

In the preceding sketches, certain recurring ideas appear. First, Thorpe distinguishes between hunters and those who kill for sport. He makes the distinctions plain in **"Grizzly Bear-Hunting."** The sportsman exaggerates, he says, "but the 'hunter,' surrounded by the magnificence and sublimity of an American forest, earning his bread by the hardy adventure of the chase, meets with too much reality to find room for coloring—too much of the sublime and terrible in the scenes with which he is associated to be boastful of himself. While apart from the favorable effects of civilization, he is also separated from its contaminations; *and boasting and exaggeration are settlement weaknesses,* and not the products of the wild woods" (137). Also, "The hunter follows his object by his own knowledge and instinct, while the sportsman employs the instinct of domesticated animals to assist in his pursuits" (139).

A second recurring idea is the lack of reverence for nature on the part of the backwoodsmen. Tom Owen in **"Tom Owen, the Bee-Hunter"** pursues his occupation with single-minded determination: "'Solitary and alone' has he traced his game through the mazy labyrinth of air; marked, I hunted;—I found;—I conquered;—upon the carcasses of his victims, and then marched homeward with his spoils . . ." (48). It makes no difference to Tom that the bees are lodged in one of the finest trees in the forest. In his mind, the tree "was made expressly for bees to build their nests in, that he might cut them down, and obtain possession of their honeyed treasure . . ." (49-50). To Tom, there was little poetry in the thought that long before the country was formed, his "'bee-hive' had stretched its brawny arms to the winter's blast, and grown green in the summer's sun" (50). The tree becomes a "lordly victim" of his axe, and "Slowly, and majestically, it bowed for the first time towards its mother earth," and "for the first time in at least two centuries" the sun broke "uninterruptedly through the chasm made in the forest . . ." and, Thorpe says sarcastically, shone "with splendor upon the magnificent Tom, standing a conquerer among his spoils" (51).

In **"Summer Retreat in Arkansas"** Thorpe tells us that in the Mississippi Valley in Arkansas, "huge trees seem immortal, their roots look as if they struck to the center of the earth, while the gnarled limbs reach out to the clouds" (29). In this forest is the "retreat," a cane-brake ten miles square, full of birds and bears. Thorpe writes, "The forest, the waste, and the dangers of the cane-brake, but add to the excitement of the Arkansas hunter; he conquers them all, and makes them subservient to his pursuits. Familiar with these scenes, they to him possess no sentiment. . . . The noblest trees to him are only valuable for fence-rails; and the cane-brake is 'an infernal dark hole,' where you can 'see sights,' 'catch bear,' and 'get a fish pole,' ranging in size from a 'penny whistle to that of a young stove pipe'" (30). An *Arkansas* hunter is not the "hunter" Thorpe defined in **"Grizzly Bear-Hunting."** An *Arkansas* hunter is Bob Herring, who squatted on the edge of the "retreat," hunted the bear with thirty dogs, and told tall tales of his exploits.

Jim Doggett, the central figure in **"The Big Bear of Arkansas,"** is likewise an Arkansas hunter. He pretends not to recognize the term *game* in reference to animals (Arkansas call it *meat),* he claims that he would not shoot anything that weighed less than forty pounds, and he pretends to have a reverence for nature: "But mosquitoes is natur, and I never find fault with her. If they ar large, Arkansaw is large, her varmints ar large, her trees ar large, her rivers ar large, and a small mosquito would be of no more use in Arkansaw than preaching in a cane-brake" (77). Doggett reveals his laziness when he says that he does not farm because "planting in Arkansaw is dangerous" (82); things grow too fast. "I don't plant any more: natur intended Arkansaw for a hunting ground, and I go according to natur" (82). Doggett then tells the tale of hunting the big bear. Doggett does not kill the bear; his shot misses, and the bear simply dies. He concludes: "My private opinion is, that that bear was an *unhuntable bear, and died when his time come*" (92). Doggett had called the bear a "creation" bear, and Arkansas "the creation State, the finishing-up country . . ." (76). The reader cannot miss the Edenic implications of the language. Indeed, J. A. Leo Lemay has said that the scatological scene in the story may suggest "a disgust for the act of slaughter, a disgust with the nature of man who is necessarily opposed to nature, as well as a regret for the fall of man, symbolized by the killing of the bear, which marks the end of the reign of the Eden-like wilderness of the Old Southwest." The bear died when his time came, Lemay says, "not because of some abstract idea of fate but because Arkansas had passed its wilderness state."[6]

For Thorpe the wildlife and forests were not the only casualties of the passing of the wilderness. The Indian was a more pitiable one. In **"Familiar Scenes on the Mississippi,"** Thorpe describes scenes aboard a steamboat carrying Seminoles who were being removed from Florida to the Indian Territory west of Arkansas. Since

the aborigines had become "constantly more and more degraded" in the eastern states, the government had undertaken, "as the most merciful policy," the removal of the Indian "from the vicinity of civilization, to homes still wild and primitive, west of the Mississippi," where, says Thorpe, "vast extent of country is still unoccupied, in which he can pursue, comparatively unrestrained, his inclinations, and pluck a few more days of happiness before his sun entirely sets" (114).

The degraded Indian appears in the form of Proud Joe in **"Mike Fink, the Keel-Boatman."** Boatmen such as Mike were of "a character at the present day anomalous" (164). Their problem was that progress had destroyed the wilderness that had made them the heroes they were. Mike complains that he knew the Ohio River before the trees had been cut, a time when he made his living by pulling a trigger and not a sweep. He complains, "What's the use of improvements? When did cutting trees make deer more plentiful? Who ever found wild buffalo, or a brave Indian, in a city? Where's the fun, the frolicking, the fighting? Gone! Gone! The rifle won't make a man a living now—he must turn mule and work. If forests continue this way to be used up, I may yet be smothered in a settlement" (167). Out of boredom Mike shoots the scalplock off Proud Joe, a Cherokee standing on the river bank at Louisville. The act brings on the fight between Indians and the boatmen at the end of the tale and results in the death of Proud Joe.

Thorpe held out little hope for the survival of the Indian or of the wilderness that he inhabited. In **"The Water Craft of the Back-woods"** he predicts the passing of the far western wilderness. As he reflects on the Snake River country, he says that only the "solitary trapper and the wild Indian" inhabit the river's shores, but "the eye of the civilized intruder" is already upon it and envisions on the shores of the river "the city, the village, and the castle." Thus, "Nature reposes like a virgin bride in all her beauty and loveliness, soon to be stripped of her natural charms to fulfil [sic] new offices with a new existence" (232-33).

III

Thomas Bangs Thorpe, a native of New York, came to Louisiana in 1837 for his health and remained there for seventeen years, recording through painting and writing what he saw.[7] However, by the time he published *The Hive of "The Bee-Hunter,"* he was living in New York once more. The scenes of the Old Southwest depicted in the volume were scenes of days gone by. During his years in the Southwest, he had witnessed vast changes. What had been the southwesternmost frontier of America in 1837 was reduced to simply the interior by the Mexican War, to which Thorpe had gone and about which he had written three volumes.[8] Suddenly, the wilderness frontier that had been central to the content of many of his sketches had been projected by the American sense of Manifest Destiny into the West and the New Southwest, far beyond Louisiana and Arkansas. Their wilderness glory had passed. And Thorpe had predicted the passing of the wilderness of the West. Only seldom after 1854 did he return to the Old Southwest as a subject for writing, and then only as it was in former days.[9]

At the time Thorpe published *The Hive of "The Bee-Hunter,"* the volume was a word picture of the Wilderness past. From 1839 on, Thorpe had spoken out thematically against the changes that resulted from the wanton destruction of natural resources. In 1854 he had published a collection of sketches that impressed upon his readers the former beauty and magnitude of the Southwestern wilderness. It was not merely accidental that he dedicated the volume to "the Lovers of Nature, whether residing in the crowded city, pleasant village, or native wild." The volume represents an indictment of the destruction of nature and a lament for the passing of the wilderness frontier. It is also a lament that it was not the beauty and magnitude of nature that shaped American character but, rather, the concept of nature as an object to be tamed or destroyed. When the reader finishes the volume, he realizes a certain irony in Thorpe's prefatory statement that "The discovery of America,—its vast extent,—*and its developing destiny*,—present facts, which far surpass the wildest imagery of the dreamers of the olden times" (6; emphasis added).

Notes

1. J. Hector St. John Crèvecoeur, *Letters from an American Farmer,* based on the 1782 ed. (Gloucester, Mass: Peter Smith, 1968), pp. 52-53.

2. New York: D. Appleton and Company; subsequent references to this work are from this edition and are cited in the text.

3. Philadelphia: Carey and Hart.

4. Thorpe, *The Mysteries of the Backwoods,* p. 7.

5. Ibid., p. 8.

6. J. A. Leo Lemay, "The Text, Tradition, and Themes of 'The Big Bear of Arkansas,'" *American Literature,* 47 (1974), 333.

7. A thorough biography of Thorpe is Milton Rickels, *Thomas Bangs Thorpe, Humorist of the Old Southwest* (Baton Rouge: Louisiana State Univ. Press, 1962). A concise survey of his literary career is Eugene Current-Garcia, "Thomas Bangs Thorpe and the Literature of the Ante-Bellum Southwestern Frontier," *Louisiana Historical Quarterly,* 39 (Apr. 1956), 199-222.

8. *Our Army on the Rio Grande. Being a Short Account of the Important Events Transpiring from the Time of the Removal of the "Army of Occupation" from Corpus Christi, to the Surrender of Matamoros; with Descriptions of the Battles of Palo Alto and Resaca de la Palma, the Bombardment of Fort Brown, and the Ceremonies of the Surrender of Matamoros: With Descriptions of the City, etc. etc.* (Philadelphia: Carey and Hart, 1846); *Our Army at Monterey. Being a Correct Account of the Proceedings and Events which Occurred to the "Army of Occupation" Under the Command of Major General Taylor, from the Time of Leaving Matamoros to the Surrender of Monterey with a Description of The Three Days' Battle and the Storming of Monterey: The Ceremonies Attending the Surrender: Together with the Particulars of the Capitulation* (Philadelphia: Carey and Hart, 1847); and *The Taylor Anecdote Book, Anecdotes and Letters of Zachary Taylor* (New York: D. Appleton and Company, 1848).

9. See e. g., "Bears and Bear Hunting," *Harper's Monthly,* 11 (Oct. 1855), 591-607; "Remembrances of the Mississippi," *Harper's Monthly,* 12 (Dec. 1855), 25-41; "Reminiscences of Tom Owen the Bee Hunter," *Spirit of the Times,* 29 (Feb. 26, 1859), 30.

Alice Hall Petry (essay date winter 1983)

SOURCE: Petry, Alice Hall. "The Common Doom: Thorpe's 'The Big Bear of Arkansas.'" *Southern Quarterly* 21, no. 2 (winter 1983): 24-31.

[*In the following essay, Petry explores symbols of death in Thorpe's "The Big Bear of Arkansas." Petry challenges the views of such critics as Lemay, Rickels, and others who interpret Thorpe's story as an allegory of the conquest of the American wilderness. Instead, Petry asserts, the story represents a more universal lament on the nature of human mortality.*]

Although it has long been regarded as a significant early example of the short story in America, **"The Big Bear of Arkansas"** by Thomas Bangs Thorpe has tended to receive rather superficial critical attention. Taking their cue from such critics as Walter Blair, who sees the story as a "beautiful lie,"[1] or Bernard DeVoto, who has written of a "Big Bear school" of southern humorists,[2] most commentators have regarded the story simply as a comic tall tale, or as a pastiche of tall tales coupled rather incongruously with an account of a mystical hunt for a great bear. But to perceive **"The Big Bear of Arkansas"** as only, or even primarily, a comic piece is not to do it justice. Perhaps the most tenable argument that **"The Big Bear"** functions on a higher level than that of entertainment is offered by Daniel Hoffman, Katherine Simoneaux, J. A. Leo Lemay, and Milton Rickels, all of whom perceive in the story an allegory of the conquest of the frontier.[3] There is much in this thesis, but **"The Big Bear"** owes its perennial appeal and critical attention to something far more universal than the notion of the conquest of the wilderness. Through an exploitation of the traditionally comic qualities of the tall tale, a remarkable use of role reversal, and a skillful utilization of the frame story, Thomas Bangs Thorpe has created a haunting rendering of an event which happens to everyone at some point in life: the realization that someday he or she will die.

First, let us consider the traditionally humorous tall tale elements that Thorpe utilizes in the first half of **"The Big Bear."** Upon first reading the story, one might conclude that **"The Big Bear"** is a broken-backed narrative in which the tall tale elements have no relation to the mystical bear hunt segment, other than to serve as a comic foil to—or scaled-down version of—the latter. In point of fact, however, the tall tale elements are absolutely essential for the characterization of Jim Doggett and the Bear, for an adequate development of the relationship between them, and ultimately for the presentation of the story' theme: Doggett's shocked realization of his own mortality.

Throughout the first half of **"The Big Bear,"** Doggett entertains his audience of riverboat passengers with a series of elements of tall tale humor, which seem to be isolated except for the fact that they all pertain to Arkansas. He tells, for example, of a forty-pound wild turkey, of "rather *enormous*" mosquitoes, and of potatoes and beets which grow so large, so fast that they may be mistaken for Indian mounds and cedar stumps.[4] Clearly these elements are derived from the traditional America-as-Eden mentality.[5] But there is a sinister, virtually demonic dimension to the tall tale elements which qualifies or even negates the Edenic aspects of the region. That forty-pound turkey, for example, meets with a horrible fate: it is shot—significantly by Doggett himself—falls out of the tree in which it has sought refuge, and literally breaks open. The bullet, the fall, or the evisceration would have proved adequate to destroy the unfortunate turkey, but in Doggett's Edenic/demonic Arkansas it meets with all three. Likewise, the giant mosquitoes—even though Doggett maintains that they "take worse to foreigners . . . than they do to natives"—all but kill a Yankee: "But the way they used that fellow up! first they punched him until he swelled up and busted; then he sup-per-a-ted, as the doctor called it, until he was raw as beef; then, owing to the warm weather, he tuck the ager, and finally he tuck a steamboat and left the country." Similarly, Doggett acknowledges that the Arkansas "sile," which "runs down to the centre of the 'arth'," is responsible for a fecun-

dity so extreme that *"'planting in Arkansaw is dangerous'"*; and he cites the incident in which a large sow inadvertently fell asleep on a kernel or two of corn which germinated, grew overnight, and "killed her dead." Clearly these qualities of enormous size and fecundity are Edenic elements characteristic of the humorous tall tale tradition; but Thorpe emphasizes the grotesqueness, injury, and death inherent in these exaggerations, rather than the comedy. One cannot overlook the fact that quite early in the tall tale phase of American literature, Thorpe has seriously and significantly undercut the comedic elements of that genre, and in doing so has cast a distinctive chill over his short story—a chill which becomes progressively more insistent in the course of the narrative. At any rate, it is apparent at the outset that in Thorpe's—as well as in Doggett's—mind, the line between Arkansas-as-Eden and Arkansas-as-Hell is, ultimately, not very clear.

And what of Arkansas's Adamic figure, Doggett himself? Throughout the first half of the story, Doggett swaggers and boasts in the flyting fashion also distinctive of humorous tall tales. He evidently is one of those "half-horse and half-alligator species of men" who may be found on Mississippi steamboats, and he enters the story with "a loud Indian whoop" in "a confused hum of voices, unintelligible, save in such broken sentences as 'horse,' 'screamer,' 'lightning is slow,' & c." Doggett's grand entrance is quite understandable: in a land of bizarre enormity and fecundity, Doggett apparently reigns supreme. It was he who killed the giant turkey, who is unmoved by the enormous mosquitoes, who owns the land where potatoes and beets grow to such grotesque proportions. Moreover, he is the master of Bowie-knife, "acknowledged to be ahead of all other dogs in the universe"; he owns a magical gun which goes off when it detects the scent of a bear; and he is "reckoned a buster, and allowed to be decidedly the best bear hunter in [his] district." Given these attributes, Doggett has every right to swagger and boast—or is he simply whistling in the dark? Are his eyes, "as sparkling as diamonds," a true indication of "perfect health and contentment"—or are they misleading?

If Doggett had never encountered the Big Bear, his role of boastful super-hunter would have remained intact: his home at Shirt-tail Bend would have continued to be lavishly decorated with the skins of the magnificent animals he killed, and he would have continued to eat the creatures he successfully hunted (as he points out, he had given up farming due to the risks involved from giant vegetables). But the series of encounters with the Big Bear have seriously undercut his position in the community, and, more importantly, have caused him to reconsider not only his super-hunter status, but also his precarious status as a mortal. In short, the experience with the Big Bear has provoked a psychic crisis in Jim Doggett.

Consider the genesis of the quest for the Big Bear. Doggett, firmly established in the region as the finest bear hunter, sees the creature's teeth marks at an unusual height in a sassafras tree and automatically concludes that he is destined to hunt it. True to the best-hunter-for-the-best-animal formula, Doggett does not doubt that he can, and must, hunt the Big Bear—but it is of the utmost importance that Doggett comes to this conviction only after he assures himself that *"the thing lived"*—in other words, the one fact which "came home to [his] soul like an earthquake" is that the Big Bear is as mortal as he is. Doggett realizes instinctively that there are some limitations to his abilities as a superhunter (he could not, for example, deal effectively with "a hoax"), but at this stage he does not have a full comprehension of his limitations, and, more precisely, of the implications of his and the Big Bear's mortality. That comprehension comes about only after "two or three" years' experience in hunting the Big Bear; and, I would argue, that comprehension proves damaging to his psyche.

Consider the events of those years. The wonder dog Bowie-knife nearly drowns in the lake into which he has chased the bear; the magical gun misfires when a "greenhorn friend" fails to kill the treed animal; and, as Doggett comes to admit, his knowledge of bears is derived from an old pioneer, from books, and from his accumulated experience in hunting—and being acquired rather than innate, this knowledge is potentially inadequate. In fine, Doggett's experience with the Big Bear put his super-hunter status into proper perspective. He is limited by a decidedly mortal dog, by a gun subject to mechanical failure, by the interference of other people, and, most seriously, by the limitations of his knowledge. One of the most pathetic aspects of Doggett's account to the steamboat audience is his tendency to lament his failure to comprehend his experiences with the Big Bear. The events on the island were "onaccountably curious"; as for the bear's death, "There is something curious about it, that I never could understand." As an apparently well-read man with a considerable knowledge of facts and a surprisingly sophisticated vocabulary (*"spontenacious* productions of the sile," *"quietus"*), Doggett is overwhelmed by his complete inability to comprehend the Big Bear, its pursuit, or its death.

But however much Doggett fails to comprehend the specifics in regard to the Big Bear, he does perceive that there is a lesson for him in the circumstances of its pursuit and death, and the lesson is a chilling one: the fact that he, too, is destined to die. Consider for a moment the similarities between the Big Bear and Doggett, similarities so insistent that ultimately they take the form of a clear role reversal. As noted above, the story follows the best-hunter-for-the-best-animal formula, a tradition which concretely establishes an identification between the man/hunter and the bear/game. But Thorpe goes much farther than this. When he is frustrated in his attempts to kill the Big Bear, the disturbed Doggett asserts that he "grew as cross as a bear"; indeed, he says the Big Bear hunted *him.* Part and parcel of this role reversal is Thorpe's presentation of the Big Bear itself. Apparently endowed with a human-like intelligence, the bear rides the same log which Doggett rode in the incident at the island, and at the time of its death it groans not as animals do, but "like a thousand sinners." The dehumanized hunter/anthropomorphized bear also is reflected in Doggett's remark that he came to love the Big Bear like a brother, but it is most tellingly reflected in Doggett's nickname: he *is* the "Big Bear of Arkansas." Of course, it is traditional for a great hunter/killer to assume the name of the creature he has destroyed (vide Cúchulainn, "the Hound of Ulster"), but in Thorpe's story there is a telling twist to this tradition: as Doggett himself admits, he did *not* kill the Big Bear: "that bear was an *unhuntable bear, and died when his time come.*" Doggett—acknowledged far and wide (and apparently with justice) as the greatest hunter in an extraordinary locale, and himself the killer of forty-pound turkeys, bears, and "cats"—has come face to face with the reality that living things die *only* when they are destined to die; that as a hunter he is simply an agent of forces beyond his comprehension and control; that these forces act even upon giant, mystical, seemingly demonic creatures, let alone humans. He realizes that, by implication, he too—ostensibly as "big" as the Big Bear, but in fact neither so large nor so cunning as "the greatest bear . . . that ever lived, *none excepted*"—will meet his death when his time has come, and neither his wonder dog, his magic gun, nor his knowledge will be able to deter it in the least. Ultimately, the hunter will indeed become the hunted, and he will be no more capable of escaping his fate than was the forty-pound turkey. The circumstances of the Big Bear's demise are especially telling in this regard. The bear dies not according to Doggett's plan, but a day sooner than expected; and it dies when Doggett is relieving himself. This latter earthy detail emphasizes not only the unexpectedness of death, but also man's ludicrous helplessness when faced with its arrival ("I . . . was tripped up by my inexpressibles"). And of even greater significance is the simple fact that few activities more eloquently express the corporality of humans than does "answering Nature's call." As Doggett emphasizes throughout the story, "I go according to natur," an attitude which applies to farming, hunting, excreting, and, as Doggett has come to realize, to dying.[6]

For a fuller comprehension of just how horrible this realization is for Doggett, one must look to the frame story of **"The Big Bear of Arkansas."** The unnamed narrator makes it clear that he feels set apart from the other passengers on the ironically named steamboat, "the Invincible": "I made no endeavors to become acquainted with my fellow-passengers." Given this bit of information, plus the fact that the narrator speaks in an almost stilted, standard English, one might conclude that he would have nothing in common with the apparently sociable, garrulous Doggett. But in point of fact the opposite is true, and herein lies the significance of the frame story. However much he affects to want to be alone, the narrator—far from being "supercilious'"— instinctively feels drawn to Doggett. Furthermore, the narrator is a reader ("I took out of my pocket the 'latest paper,' and more critically than usual examined its contents"), as is Doggett ("I read in history that varmints have their fat season, and their lean season"). Moreover, Doggett apparently sincerely believes that the narrator values experience, precisely as he himself does: "But in the first place, stranger, let me say, I am pleased with you, because you aint ashamed to gain information by asking and listening; and that's what I say to Countess's pups every day when I'm home; and I have got great hopes of them ar pups, because they are continually *nosing* about." In fine, Doggett and the narrator instinctively perceive themselves as kindred spirits—a perception substantiated by the fact that the narrator zeroes in on the one aspect of Doggett's life which he seems to want most to talk about: the *particular* bear hunt. Indeed, the request for the story "seemed to please" Doggett, who "squared himself round" towards the narrator; and it is clear that even though many of the steamboat passengers listen to the story of the hunt of the Big Bear, it is directed only towards the narrator, who requested to hear it. One can imagine that Doggett was disappointed in the reaction to his story: there was a "grave silence," as well there might be; and the narrator comprehended enough of the story to feel compelled to write it down and to notice that "there was a mystery to [Doggett] connected with the bear whose death he had just related, that had evidently made a strong impression on his mind." But Doggett has misjudged the narrator's receptivity to his story, and his capacity to empathize with him: as the narrator remarks, "there was some superstitious awe connected with the affair,—a feeling common with all 'children of the wood,' when they meet with any thing out of their everyday experience." As has been pointed out, Doggett would hardly qualify as a "child of the wood." Well-read and experienced, he can hold his own on a steamboat populated with "men from every State in the Union, and from every portion of the globe." Indeed, it is doubtless this microcosmic quality of the steamboat that attracted Doggett in the first place. Notice how vague the frame-story narrator is about the steamboat. We are told that it is an "up-country" boat which originated in New Orleans, but we do not know why anyone is on it, nor are we told where they are going. Indeed, we never find out why Doggett is on board, and know only that he has just made his first trip to New Orleans. Presumably, he is returning home to Arkansas (his reference to Count-

ess's pups would imply this), but never does he state that this is the case. In point of fact, it is equally likely that he has settled his affairs in New Orleans prior to traveling to Texas, in keeping with his view "to catch that bear, go to Texas, or die," for the first alternative was not realized, and the third alternative is an intolerable reality for him. Another possibility is that he is going nowhere: that, like the post-lapsarian Adam or, more precisely, like the Ishmael figure so common in American literature, Doggett is simply wandering the Mississippi, attempting to run away from death, or at least desperately taking advantage of the microcosmic quality of steamboats to try to find someone sufficiently experienced and empathetic to understand the implications of the Big Bear story and to offer him some consolation for his inability to deal with his mortality. His actual position as wanderer/searcher has displaced his role of super-hunter, for the latter is no longer tenable. All that remains is the pose of the boaster whose "volubility," so "perfectly astonishing," scarcely conceals his despair. As Doggett himself points out, Arkansas is both "the creation State, [and] the finishing-up country"; no matter how attractive the former may be, the harsh reality is that ultimately one must face the latter—and no amount of boasting or fleeing can ever change that.

Through the skillful undercutting of the traditionally comic elements of the tall tale, the utilization of role reversal, and a careful use of a frame story, Thomas Bangs Thorpe has provided a study of a man enmeshed in a psychic crisis. Perhaps what is most frightening about **"The Big Bear of Arkansas"** is precisely what is responsible for the story's longevity. Thorpe is dealing with a crisis which is by no means unique to Jim Doggett. Ultimately we all must face the fact that there is death in Eden.

Notes

1. Walter Blair, "The Technique of 'The Big Bear of Arkansas,'" *Southwest Review,* 28 (1943), 435.

2. Cited in Milton Rickels, *Thomas Bangs Thorpe: Humorist of the Old Southwest* (Baton Rouge: Louisiana State Univ. Press, 1962), p. 51.

3. Writes Hoffman, "Fables such as [*Moby-Dick* and 'The Big Bear'] characterize the form in which American popular culture accepted and transformed the traditional myth of the Huntsman as culture-hero. The quarry, endowed by superstition with magical powers, personifies Nature, against which the American hunter sees himself in a combative relationship. . . . Whether he relies solely on his own magnificent skills, as does the hunter of Mocha Dick, or, as in 'The Big Bear,' these are humorously enhanced with magic aids, there is no doubt of his easy triumph over Nature." *Form and Fable in American Fiction* (New York: Norton,

1973), p. 232. See also Katherine Simoneaux, "Symbolism in Thorpe's 'The Big Bear of Arkansas,'" *The Arkansas Historical Quarterly,* 25 (Autumn 1966), 240-47; J. A. Leo Lemay, "The Text, Tradition, and Themes of 'The Big Bear of Arkansas,'" *American Literature,* 47 (November 1975), 321-42; and Rickels, p. 57.

4. Thorpe, "The Big Bear of Arkansas" in *The Hive of "The Bee-Hunter"* [New York: D. Appleton & Co., 1854], pp. 73-93. All quotations are from this edition. I have retained Thorpe's spelling, punctuation, and underlining.

5. See, for example, Leo Marx, *The Machine in the Garden: Technology and the Pastoral Ideal in America* (New York: Oxford Univ. Press, 1968), especially chapters 2 and 3; and Constance Rourke, *American Humor: A Study of the National Character* (New York: Harcourt, Brace, Jovanovich, 1959), especially chapter 2.

6. One may be reminded of Delmore Schwartz's poem "The Heavy Bear Who Goes With Me," in which the persona's corporeality is symbolized by a bear which "Stumbles, flounders, and strives to be fed / Dragging me with him in his mouthing care."

7. Lemay, p. 324.

FURTHER READING

Biographies

Han, John J. "Thomas Bangs Thorpe." In *Writers of the American Renaissance: An A-to-Z Guide,* edited by Denise D. Knight, pp. 367-71. Westport, Conn.: Greenwood, 2003.

Offers a brief analysis of Thorpe's life and writings.

Rickels, Milton. *Thomas Bangs Thorpe: Humorist of the Old Southwest.* Baton Rouge: Louisiana State University Press, 1962, 275 p.

Provides an overview of Thorpe's life and career, evaluating his influence on the development of nineteenth-century American humor writing.

Criticism

Cox, Leland H., Jr. "T. B. Thorpe's Far West Letters." In *Gyascutus: Studies in Antebellum Southern Humorous and Sporting Writing,* edited by James L. W. West, pp. 121-57. Atlantic Highlands, N.J.: Humanities, 1978.

Examines Thorpe's satirical dispatches on frontier life.

Current-Garcia, Eugene. "Thomas Bangs Thorpe and the Literature of the Ante-Bellum Southwestern Frontier." *Louisiana Historical Quarterly* 39, no. 2 (April 1956): 199-222.

Evaluates Thorpe's romanticized depictions of the primitive, unspoiled beauty of the American wilderness.

Estes, David C. "Folk Humor in Thomas Bangs Thorpe's 'Letters from the Far West.'" *Louisiana Folklore Miscellany* 7 (1992): 50-8.

Analyzes aspects of folk literature in Thorpe's satirical letters.

———. "The Rival Sporting Weeklies of William T. Porter and Thomas Bangs Thorpe." *American Journalist* 2, no. 2 (1985): 135-43.

Examines the circumstances surrounding the creation of Thorpe's short-lived weekly, *Southern Sportsman,* and evaluates the paper's rivalry with William T. Porter's *American Sporting Chronicle.*

———. "Thomas Bangs Thorpe's Backwoods Hunters: Culture Heroes and Humorous Failures." *University of Mississippi Studies in English* 5 (1984): 158-71.

Analyzes the hunter's relationship with the wilderness in Thorpe's frontier sketches.

Higgs, Robert J. "The Sublime and the Beautiful: The Meaning of Sport in Collected Sketches of Thomas B. Thorpe." *Southern Studies: An Interdisciplinary Journal of the South* 25, no. 3 (fall 1986): 235-56.

Examines representations of natural beauty and the sublime in Thorpe's hunting and fishing sketches.

Keller, Mark. "'The Big Bear of—Maine???': Toward the Development of American Humor." *New England Quarterly: A Historical Review of New England Life and Letters* 51, no. 4 (December 1978): 565-74.

Discusses narrative techniques in Thorpe's "The Big Bear of Arkansas," exploring the story's role in the emergence of frontier humor.

———. "T. B. Thorpe's 'Tom Owen, the Bee-Hunter': Southwestern Humor's 'Origin of Species.'" *Southern Studies: An Interdisciplinary Journal of the South* 18 (1979): 89-101.

Evaluates the story's influence on other humor writing of the period.

McDermott, John Francis. "T. B. Thorpe's Burlesque of Far West Sporting Travel." *American Quarterly* 10, no. 2 (summer 1958): 175-80.

Examines elements of parody in Thorpe's satirical travel correspondence.

Rickels, Milton. "Thomas Bangs Thorpe in the Felicianas, 1836-1842." *Louisiana Historical Quarterly* 39 (1956): 169-97.

Discusses the early years of Thorpe's literary career.

Schmitz, Neil. "Tall Tale, Tall Talk: Pursuing the Lie in Jacksonian Literature." *American Literature* 48, no. 4 (winter 1977): 471-91.

Compares qualities of exaggeration and falsehood in the tall tales of Thorpe and Joseph Glover Baldwin.

Simoneaux, Katherine G. "Symbolism in Thorpe's 'The Big Bear of Arkansas.'" *Arkansas Historical Quarterly* 25 (fall 1966): 240-47.

Analyzes the story's symbolic framework.

Additional coverage of Thorpe's life and career is contained in the following sources published by Thomson Gale: *Dictionary of Literary Biography,* **Vols. 3, 11, 248;** *Literature Resource Center*; *Reference Guide to American Literature,* **Ed. 4.**

How to Use This Index

The main references

Calvino, Italo
    1923-1985 .... CLC 5, 8, 11, 22, 33, 39,
                                    73; SSC 3, 48

list all author entries in the following Thomson Gale Literary Criticism series:

AAL = *Asian American Literature*
BG = *The Beat Generation: A Gale Critical Companion*
BLC = *Black Literature Criticism*
BLCS = *Black Literature Criticism Supplement*
CLC = *Contemporary Literary Criticism*
CLR = *Children's Literature Review*
CMLC = *Classical and Medieval Literature Criticism*
DC = *Drama Criticism*
FL = *Feminism in Literature: A Gale Critical Companion*
GL = *Gothic Literature: A Gale Critical Companion*
HLC = *Hispanic Literature Criticism*
HLCS = *Hispanic Literature Criticism Supplement*
HR = *Harlem Renaissance: A Gale Critical Companion*
LC = *Literature Criticism from 1400 to 1800*
NCLC = *Nineteenth-Century Literature Criticism*
NNAL = *Native North American Literature*
PC = *Poetry Criticism*
SSC = *Short Story Criticism*
TCLC = *Twentieth-Century Literary Criticism*
WLC = *World Literature Criticism, 1500 to the Present*
WLCS = *World Literature Criticism Supplement*

The cross-references

See also CA 85-88, 116; CANR 23, 61;
DAM NOV; DLB 196; EW 13; MTCW 1, 2;
RGSF 2; RGWL 2; SFW 4; SSFS 12

list all author entries in the following Thomson Gale biographical and literary sources:

AAYA = *Authors & Artists for Young Adults*
AFAW = *African American Writers*
AFW = *African Writers*
AITN = *Authors in the News*
AMW = *American Writers*
AMWR = *American Writers Retrospective Supplement*
AMWS = *American Writers Supplement*
ANW = *American Nature Writers*
AW = *Ancient Writers*
BEST = *Bestsellers*
BPFB = *Beacham's Encyclopedia of Popular Fiction: Biography and Resources*
BRW = *British Writers*
BRWS = *British Writers Supplement*
BW = *Black Writers*
BYA = *Beacham's Guide to Literature for Young Adults*
CA = *Contemporary Authors*
CAAS = *Contemporary Authors Autobiography Series*
CABS = *Contemporary Authors Bibliographical Series*
CAD = *Contemporary American Dramatists*
CANR = *Contemporary Authors New Revision Series*
CAP = *Contemporary Authors Permanent Series*
CBD = *Contemporary British Dramatists*
CCA = *Contemporary Canadian Authors*
CD = *Contemporary Dramatists*
CDALB = *Concise Dictionary of American Literary Biography*

CDALBS = Concise Dictionary of American Literary Biography Supplement
CDBLB = Concise Dictionary of British Literary Biography
CMW = St. James Guide to Crime & Mystery Writers
CN = Contemporary Novelists
CP = Contemporary Poets
CPW = Contemporary Popular Writers
CSW = Contemporary Southern Writers
CWD = Contemporary Women Dramatists
CWP = Contemporary Women Poets
CWRI = St. James Guide to Children's Writers
CWW = Contemporary World Writers
DA = DISCovering Authors
DA3 = DISCovering Authors 3.0
DAB = DISCovering Authors: British Edition
DAC = DISCovering Authors: Canadian Edition
DAM = DISCovering Authors: Modules
   DRAM: Dramatists Module; **MST:** Most-studied Authors Module;
   MULT: Multicultural Authors Module; **NOV:** Novelists Module;
   POET: Poets Module; **POP:** Popular Fiction and Genre Authors Module
DFS = Drama for Students
DLB = Dictionary of Literary Biography
DLBD = Dictionary of Literary Biography Documentary Series
DLBY = Dictionary of Literary Biography Yearbook
DNFS = Literature of Developing Nations for Students
EFS = Epics for Students
EXPN = Exploring Novels
EXPP = Exploring Poetry
EXPS = Exploring Short Stories
EW = European Writers
FANT = St. James Guide to Fantasy Writers
FW = Feminist Writers
GFL = Guide to French Literature, Beginnings to 1789, 1798 to the Present
GLL = Gay and Lesbian Literature
HGG = St. James Guide to Horror, Ghost & Gothic Writers
HW = Hispanic Writers
IDFW = International Dictionary of Films and Filmmakers: Writers and Production Artists
IDTP = International Dictionary of Theatre: Playwrights
LAIT = Literature and Its Times
LAW = Latin American Writers
JRDA = Junior DISCovering Authors
MAICYA = Major Authors and Illustrators for Children and Young Adults
MAICYAS = Major Authors and Illustrators for Children and Young Adults Supplement
MAWW = Modern American Women Writers
MJW = Modern Japanese Writers
MTCW = Major 20th-Century Writers
NCFS = Nonfiction Classics for Students
NFS = Novels for Students
PAB = Poets: American and British
PFS = Poetry for Students
RGAL = Reference Guide to American Literature
RGEL = Reference Guide to English Literature
RGSF = Reference Guide to Short Fiction
RGWL = Reference Guide to World Literature
RHW = Twentieth-Century Romance and Historical Writers
SAAS = Something about the Author Autobiography Series
SATA = Something about the Author
SFW = St. James Guide to Science Fiction Writers
SSFS = Short Stories for Students
TCWW = Twentieth-Century Western Writers
WLIT = World Literature and Its Times
WP = World Poets
YABC = Yesterday's Authors of Books for Children
YAW = St. James Guide to Young Adult Writers

Anand, Mulk Raj 1905-2004 ..... **CLC 23, 93; 237**
See also CA 65-68; CAAS 231; CANR 32, 64; CN 1, 2, 3, 4, 5, 6, 7; DAM NOV; DLB 323; EWL 3; MTCW 1, 2; MTFW 2005; RGSF 2

Anatol
See Schnitzler, Arthur

Anaximander c. 611B.C.-c. 546B.C. .... **CMLC 22**

Anaya, Rudolfo A. 1937- .... **CLC 23, 148; HLC 1**
See also AAYA 20; BYA 13; CA 45-48; 4; CANR 1, 32, 51, 124; CN 4, 5, 6, 7; DAM MULT, NOV; DLB 82, 206, 278; HW 1; LAIT 4; LLW; MAL 5; MTCW 1, 2; MTFW 2005; NFS 12; RGAL 4; RGSF 2; TCWW 2; WLIT 1

Andersen, Hans Christian 1805-1875 .... **NCLC 7, 79; SSC 6, 56; WLC 1**
See also AAYA 57; CLR 6, 113; DA; DA3; DAB; DAC; DAM MST, POP; EW 6; MAICYA 1, 2; RGSF 2; RGWL 2, 3; SATA 100; TWA; WCH; YABC 1

Anderson, C. Farley
See Mencken, H(enry) L(ouis); Nathan, George Jean

Anderson, Jessica (Margaret) Queale 1916- .... **CLC 37**
See also CA 9-12R; CANR 4, 62; CN 4, 5, 6, 7; DLB 325

Anderson, Jon (Victor) 1940- .... **CLC 9**
See also CA 25-28R; CANR 20; CP 1, 3, 4, 5; DAM POET

Anderson, Lindsay (Gordon) 1923-1994 .... **CLC 20**
See also CA 128; CAAE 125; CAAS 146; CANR 77

Anderson, Maxwell 1888-1959 .... **TCLC 2, 144**
See also CA 152; CAAE 105; DAM DRAM; DFS 16, 20; DLB 7, 228; MAL 5; MTCW 2; MTFW 2005; RGAL 4

Anderson, Poul 1926-2001 .... **CLC 15**
See also AAYA 5, 34; BPFB 1; BYA 6, 8, 9; CA 181; 1-4R, 181; 2; CAAS 199; CANR 2, 15, 34, 64, 110; CLR 58; DLB 8; FANT; INT CANR-15; MTCW 1, 2; MTFW 2005; SATA 90; SATA-Brief 39; SATA-Essay 106; SCFW 1, 2; SFW 4; SUFW 1, 2

Anderson, Robert (Woodruff) 1917- .... **CLC 23**
See also AITN 1; CA 21-24R; CANR 32; CD 6; DAM DRAM; DLB 7; LAIT 5

Anderson, Roberta Joan
See Mitchell, Joni

Anderson, Sherwood 1876-1941 ... **SSC 1, 46, 91; TCLC 1, 10, 24, 123; WLC 1**
See also AAYA 30; AMW; AMWC 2; BPFB 1; CA 121; CAAE 104; CANR 61; CDALB 1917-1929; DA; DA3; DAB; DAC; DAM MST, NOV; DLB 4, 9, 86; DLBD 1; EWL 3; EXPS; GLL 2; MAL 5; MTCW 1, 2; MTFW 2005; NFS 4; RGAL 4; RGSF 2; SSFS 4, 10, 11; TUS

Anderson, Wes 1969- .... **CLC 227**
See also CA 214

Andier, Pierre
See Desnos, Robert

Andouard
See Giraudoux, Jean(-Hippolyte)

Andrade, Carlos Drummond de ..... **CLC 18**
See Drummond de Andrade, Carlos
See also EWL 3; RGWL 2, 3

Andrade, Mario de .... **TCLC 43**
See de Andrade, Mario
See also DLB 307; EWL 3; LAW; RGWL 2, 3; WLIT 1

Andreae, Johann V(alentin) 1586-1654 .... **LC 32**
See also DLB 164

Andreas Capellanus fl. c. 1185- .... **CMLC 45**
See also DLB 208

Andreas-Salome, Lou 1861-1937 ... **TCLC 56**
See also CA 178; DLB 66

Andreev, Leonid
See Andreyev, Leonid (Nikolaevich)
See also DLB 295; EWL 3

Andress, Lesley
See Sanders, Lawrence

Andrewes, Lancelot 1555-1626 .... **LC 5**
See also DLB 151, 172

Andrews, Cicily Fairfield
See West, Rebecca

Andrews, Elton V.
See Pohl, Frederik

Andrews, Peter
See Soderbergh, Steven

Andreyev, Leonid (Nikolaevich) 1871-1919 .... **TCLC 3**
See Andreev, Leonid
See also CA 185; CAAE 104

Andric, Ivo 1892-1975 .... **CLC 8; SSC 36; TCLC 135**
See also CA 81-84; CAAS 57-60; CANR 43, 60; CDWLB 4; DLB 147, 329; EW 11; EWL 3; MTCW 1; RGSF 2; RGWL 2, 3

Androvar
See Prado (Calvo), Pedro

Angela of Foligno 1248(?)-1309 .... **CMLC 76**

Angelique, Pierre
See Bataille, Georges

Angell, Roger 1920- .... **CLC 26**
See also CA 57-60; CANR 13, 44, 70, 144; DLB 171, 185

Angelou, Maya 1928- ... **BLC 1; CLC 12, 35, 64, 77, 155; PC 32; WLCS**
See also AAYA 7, 20; AMWS 4; BPFB 1; BW 2, 3; BYA 2; CA 65-68; CANR 19, 42, 65, 111, 133; CDALBS; CLR 53; CP 4, 5, 6, 7; CPW; CSW; CWP; DA; DA3; DAB; DAC; DAM MST, MULT, POET, POP; DLB 38; EWL 3; EXPN; EXPP; FL 1:5; LAIT 4; MAICYA 2; MAICYAS 1; MAL 5; MBL; MTCW 1, 2; MTFW 2005; NCFS 2; NFS 2; PFS 2, 3; RGAL 4; SATA 49, 136; TCLE 1:1; WYA; YAW

Angouleme, Marguerite d'
See de Navarre, Marguerite

Anna Comnena 1083-1153 .... **CMLC 25**

Annensky, Innokentii Fedorovich
See Annensky, Innokenty (Fyodorovich)
See also DLB 295

Annensky, Innokenty (Fyodorovich) 1856-1909 .... **TCLC 14**
See also CA 155; CAAE 110; EWL 3

Annunzio, Gabriele d'
See D'Annunzio, Gabriele

Anodos
See Coleridge, Mary E(lizabeth)

Anon, Charles Robert
See Pessoa, Fernando (Antonio Nogueira)

Anouilh, Jean 1910-1987 ..... **CLC 1, 3, 8, 13, 40, 50; DC 8, 21**
See also AAYA 67; CA 17-20R; CAAS 123; CANR 32; DAM DRAM; DFS 9, 10, 19; DLB 321; EW 13; EWL 3; GFL 1789 to the Present; MTCW 1, 2; MTFW 2005; RGWL 2, 3; TWA

Anselm of Canterbury 1033(?)-1109 .... **CMLC 67**
See also DLB 115

Anthony, Florence
See Ai

Anthony, John
See Ciardi, John (Anthony)

Anthony, Peter
See Shaffer, Anthony; Shaffer, Peter

Anthony, Piers 1934- .... **CLC 35**
See also AAYA 11, 48; BYA 7; CA 200; 200; CANR 28, 56, 73, 102, 133; CLR 118; CPW; DAM POP; DLB 8; FANT; MAICYA 1; MAICYAS 1; MTCW 1, 2; MTFW 2005; SAAS 22; SATA 84, 129; SATA-Essay 129; SFW 4; SUFW 1, 2; YAW

Anthony, Susan B(rownell) 1820-1906 .... **TCLC 84**
See also CA 211; FW

Antiphon c. 480B.C.-c. 411B.C. .... **CMLC 55**

Antoine, Marc
See Proust, (Valentin-Louis-George-Eugene) Marcel

Antoninus, Brother
See Everson, William (Oliver)
See also CP 1

Antonioni, Michelangelo 1912- .... **CLC 20, 144**
See also CA 73-76; CANR 45, 77

Antschel, Paul 1920-1970
See Celan, Paul
See also CA 85-88; CANR 33, 61; MTCW 1; PFS 21

Anwar, Chairil 1922-1949 .... **TCLC 22**
See Chairil Anwar
See also CA 219; CAAE 121; RGWL 3

Anzaldua, Gloria (Evanjelina) 1942-2004 .... **CLC 200; HLCS 1**
See also CA 175; CAAS 227; CSW; CWP; DLB 122; FW; LLW; RGAL 4; SATA-Obit 154

Apess, William 1798-1839(?) .... **NCLC 73; NNAL**
See also DAM MULT; DLB 175, 243

Apollinaire, Guillaume 1880-1918 .... **PC 7; TCLC 3, 8, 51**
See Kostrowitzki, Wilhelm Apollinaris de
See also CA 152; DAM POET; DLB 258, 321; EW 9; EWL 3; GFL 1789 to the Present; MTCW 2; PFS 24; RGWL 2, 3; TWA; WP

Apollonius of Rhodes
See Apollonius Rhodius
See also AW 1; RGWL 2, 3

Apollonius Rhodius c. 300B.C.-c. 220B.C. .... **CMLC 28**
See Apollonius of Rhodes
See also DLB 176

Appelfeld, Aharon 1932- ... **CLC 23, 47; SSC 42**
See also CA 133; CAAE 112; CANR 86, 160; CWW 2; DLB 299; EWL 3; RGHL; RGSF 2; WLIT 6

Appelfeld, Aron
See Appelfeld, Aharon

Apple, Max (Isaac) 1941- .... **CLC 9, 33; SSC 50**
See also CA 81-84; CANR 19, 54; DLB 130

Appleman, Philip (Dean) 1926- .... **CLC 51**
See also CA 13-16R; 18; CANR 6, 29, 56

Appleton, Lawrence
See Lovecraft, H. P.

Apteryx
See Eliot, T(homas) S(tearns)

Apuleius, (Lucius Madaurensis) c. 125-c. 164 .... **CMLC 1, 84**
See also AW 2; CDWLB 1; DLB 211; RGWL 2, 3; SUFW; WLIT 8

Aquin, Hubert 1929-1977 .... **CLC 15**
See also CA 105; DLB 53; EWL 3

Aquinas, Thomas 1224(?)-1274 ..... **CMLC 33**
See also DLB 115; EW 1; TWA

Aragon, Louis 1897-1982 .... **CLC 3, 22; TCLC 123**
See also CA 69-72; CAAS 108; CANR 28, 71; DAM NOV, POET; DLB 72, 258; EW 11; EWL 3; GFL 1789 to the Present; GLL 2; LMFS 2; MTCW 1, 2; RGWL 2, 3

Arany, Janos 1817-1882 .... **NCLC 34**

Aranyos, Kakay 1847-1910
See Mikszath, Kalman

Aratus of Soli c. 315B.C.-c. 240B.C. .... **CMLC 64**
See also DLB 176

Arbuthnot, John 1667-1735 .... **LC 1**
See also DLB 101

Archer, Herbert Winslow
See Mencken, H(enry) L(ouis)

Archer, Jeffrey 1940- .... **CLC 28**
See also AAYA 16; BEST 89:3; BPFB 1; CA 77-80; CANR 22, 52, 95, 136; CPW; DA3; DAM POP; INT CANR-22; MTFW 2005

Archer, Jeffrey Howard
See Archer, Jeffrey

Archer, Jules 1915- .... **CLC 12**
See also CA 9-12R; CANR 6, 69; SAAS 5; SATA 4, 85

Archer, Lee
See Ellison, Harlan

Archilochus c. 7th cent. B.C.- .... **CMLC 44**
See also DLB 176

Arden, John 1930- .... **CLC 6, 13, 15**
See also BRWS 2; CA 13-16R; 4; CANR 31, 65, 67, 124; CBD; CD 5, 6; DAM DRAM; DFS 9; DLB 13, 245; EWL 3; MTCW 1

Arenas, Reinaldo 1943-1990 .. **CLC 41; HLC 1**
See also CA 128; CAAE 124; CAAS 133; CANR 73, 106; DAM MULT; DLB 145; EWL 3; GLL 2; HW 1; LAW; LAWS 1; MTCW 2; MTFW 2005; RGSF 2; RGWL 3; WLIT 1

Arendt, Hannah 1906-1975 .... **CLC 66, 98**
See also CA 17-20R; CAAS 61-64; CANR 26, 60; DLB 242; MTCW 1, 2

Aretino, Pietro 1492-1556 .... **LC 12**
See also RGWL 2, 3

Arghezi, Tudor .... **CLC 80**
See Theodorescu, Ion N.
See also CA 167; CDWLB 4; DLB 220; EWL 3

Arguedas, Jose Maria 1911-1969 .... **CLC 10, 18; HLCS 1; TCLC 147**
See also CA 89-92; CANR 73; DLB 113; EWL 3; HW 1; LAW; RGWL 2, 3; WLIT 1

Argueta, Manlio 1936- .... **CLC 31**
See also CA 131; CANR 73; CWW 2; DLB 145; EWL 3; HW 1; RGWL 3

Arias, Ron 1941- .... **HLC 1**
See also CA 131; CANR 81, 136; DAM MULT; DLB 82; HW 1, 2; MTCW 2; MTFW 2005

Ariosto, Lodovico
See Ariosto, Ludovico
See also WLIT 7

Ariosto, Ludovico 1474-1533 ... **LC 6, 87; PC 42**
See Ariosto, Lodovico
See also EW 2; RGWL 2, 3

Aristides
See Epstein, Joseph

Aristophanes 450B.C.-385B.C. .... **CMLC 4, 51; DC 2; WLCS**
See also AW 1; CDWLB 1; DA; DA3; DAB; DAC; DAM DRAM, MST; DFS 10; DLB 176; LMFS 1; RGWL 2, 3; TWA; WLIT 8

Aristotle 384B.C.-322B.C. .... **CMLC 31; WLCS**
See also AW 1; CDWLB 1; DA; DA3; DAB; DAC; DAM MST; DLB 176; RGWL 2, 3; TWA; WLIT 8

Arlt, Roberto (Godofredo Christophersen) 1900-1942 .... **HLC 1; TCLC 29**
See also CA 131; CAAE 123; CANR 67; DAM MULT; DLB 305; EWL 3; HW 1, 2; IDTP; LAW

Armah, Ayi Kwei 1939- . **BLC 1; CLC 5, 33, 136**
See also AFW; BRWS 10; BW 1; CA 61-64; CANR 21, 64; CDWLB 3; CN 1, 2, 3, 4, 5, 6, 7; DAM MULT, POET; DLB 117; EWL 3; MTCW 1; WLIT 2

Armatrading, Joan 1950- .... **CLC 17**
See also CA 186; CAAE 114

Armin, Robert 1568(?)-1615(?) .... **LC 120**

Armitage, Frank
See Carpenter, John (Howard)

Armstrong, Jeannette (C.) 1948- .... **NNAL**
See also CA 149; CCA 1; CN 6, 7; DAC; SATA 102

Arnette, Robert
See Silverberg, Robert

Arnim, Achim von (Ludwig Joachim von Arnim) 1781-1831 .. **NCLC 5, 159; SSC 29**
See also DLB 90

Arnim, Bettina von 1785-1859 ...... **NCLC 38, 123**
See also DLB 90; RGWL 2, 3

Arnold, Matthew 1822-1888 ..... **NCLC 6, 29, 89, 126; PC 5; WLC 1**
See also BRW 5; CDBLB 1832-1890; DA; DAB; DAC; DAM MST, POET; DLB 32, 57; EXPP; PAB; PFS 2; TEA; WP

Arnold, Thomas 1795-1842 .... **NCLC 18**
See also DLB 55

Arnow, Harriette (Louisa) Simpson 1908-1986 .... **CLC 2, 7, 18**
See also BPFB 1; CA 9-12R; CAAS 118; CANR 14; CN 2, 3, 4; DLB 6; FW; MTCW 1, 2; RHW; SATA 42; SATA-Obit 47

Arouet, Francois-Marie
See Voltaire

Arp, Hans
See Arp, Jean

Arp, Jean 1887-1966 .... **CLC 5; TCLC 115**
See also CA 81-84; CAAS 25-28R; CANR 42, 77; EW 10

Arrabal
See Arrabal, Fernando

Arrabal (Teran), Fernando
See Arrabal, Fernando
See also CWW 2

Arrabal, Fernando 1932- ... **CLC 2, 9, 18, 58**
See Arrabal (Teran), Fernando
See also CA 9-12R; CANR 15; DLB 321; EWL 3; LMFS 2

Arreola, Juan Jose 1918-2001 .... **CLC 147; HLC 1; SSC 38**
See also CA 131; CAAE 113; CAAS 200; CANR 81; CWW 2; DAM MULT; DLB 113; DNFS 2; EWL 3; HW 1, 2; LAW; RGSF 2

Arrian c. 89(?)-c. 155(?) .... **CMLC 43**
See also DLB 176

Arrick, Fran .... **CLC 30**
See Gaberman, Judie Angell
See also BYA 6

Arrley, Richmond
See Delany, Samuel R., Jr.

Artaud, Antonin (Marie Joseph) 1896-1948 .... **DC 14; TCLC 3, 36**
See also CA 149; CAAE 104; DA3; DAM DRAM; DFS 22; DLB 258, 321; EW 11; EWL 3; GFL 1789 to the Present; MTCW 2; MTFW 2005; RGWL 2, 3

Arthur, Ruth M(abel) 1905-1979 ..... **CLC 12**
See also CA 9-12R; CAAS 85-88; CANR 4; CWRI 5; SATA 7, 26

Artsybashev, Mikhail (Petrovich) 1878-1927 .... **TCLC 31**
See also CA 170; DLB 295

Arundel, Honor (Morfydd) 1919-1973 .... **CLC 17**
See also CA 21-22; CAAS 41-44R; CAP 2; CLR 35; CWRI 5; SATA 4; SATA-Obit 24

Arzner, Dorothy 1900-1979 .... **CLC 98**

Asch, Sholem 1880-1957 .... **TCLC 3**
See also CAAE 105; DLB 333; EWL 3; GLL 2; RGHL

Ascham, Roger 1516(?)-1568 .... **LC 101**
See also DLB 236

Ash, Shalom
See Asch, Sholem

Ashbery, John 1927- ... **CLC 2, 3, 4, 6, 9, 13, 15, 25, 41, 77, 125, 221; PC 26**
See Berry, Jonas
See also AMWS 3; CA 5-8R; CANR 9, 37, 66, 102, 132; CP 1, 2, 3, 4, 5, 6, 7; DA3; DAM POET; DLB 5, 165; DLBY 1981; EWL 3; INT CANR-9; MAL 5; MTCW 1, 2; MTFW 2005; PAB; PFS 11; RGAL 4; TCLE 1:1; WP

Ashdown, Clifford
See Freeman, R(ichard) Austin

Ashe, Gordon
See Creasey, John

Ashton-Warner, Sylvia (Constance) 1908-1984 .... **CLC 19**
See also CA 69-72; CAAS 112; CANR 29; CN 1, 2, 3; MTCW 1, 2

Asimov, Isaac 1920-1992 ..... **CLC 1, 3, 9, 19, 26, 76, 92**
See also AAYA 13; BEST 90:2; BPFB 1; BYA 4, 6, 7, 9; CA 1-4R; CAAS 137; CANR 2, 19, 36, 60, 125; CLR 12, 79; CMW 4; CN 1, 2, 3, 4, 5; CPW; DA3; DAM POP; DLB 8; DLBY 1992; INT CANR-19; JRDA; LAIT 5; LMFS 2; MAICYA 1, 2; MAL 5; MTCW 1, 2; MTFW 2005; RGAL 4; SATA 1, 26, 74; SCFW 1, 2; SFW 4; SSFS 17; TUS; YAW

Askew, Anne 1521(?)-1546 .... **LC 81**
See also DLB 136

Assis, Joaquim Maria Machado de
See Machado de Assis, Joaquim Maria

Astell, Mary 1666-1731 .... **LC 68**
See also DLB 252; FW

Astley, Thea (Beatrice May) 1925-2004 .... **CLC 41**
See also CA 65-68; CAAS 229; CANR 11, 43, 78; CN 1, 2, 3, 4, 5, 6, 7; DLB 289; EWL 3

Astley, William 1855-1911
See Warung, Price

Aston, James
See White, T(erence) H(anbury)

Asturias, Miguel Angel 1899-1974 .... **CLC 3, 8, 13; HLC 1; TCLC 184**
See also CA 25-28; CAAS 49-52; CANR 32; CAP 2; CDWLB 3; DA3; DAM MULT, NOV; DLB 113, 290, 329; EWL 3; HW 1; LAW; LMFS 2; MTCW 1, 2; RGWL 2, 3; WLIT 1

Atares, Carlos Saura
See Saura (Atares), Carlos

Athanasius c. 295-c. 373 .... **CMLC 48**

Bengtsson, Frans (Gunnar)
1894-1954 .... **TCLC 48**
See also CA 170; EWL 3
Benjamin, David
See Slavitt, David R(ytman)
Benjamin, Lois
See Gould, Lois
Benjamin, Walter 1892-1940 .... **TCLC 39**
See also CA 164; DLB 242; EW 11; EWL 3
Ben Jelloun, Tahar 1944-
See Jelloun, Tahar ben
See also CA 135; CWW 2; EWL 3; RGWL 3; WLIT 2
Benn, Gottfried 1886-1956 .. **PC 35; TCLC 3**
See also CA 153; CAAE 106; DLB 56; EWL 3; RGWL 2, 3
Bennett, Alan 1934- .... **CLC 45, 77**
See also BRWS 8; CA 103; CANR 35, 55, 106, 157; CBD; CD 5, 6; DAB; DAM MST; DLB 310; MTCW 1, 2; MTFW 2005
Bennett, (Enoch) Arnold
1867-1931 .... **TCLC 5, 20**
See also BRW 6; CA 155; CAAE 106; CDBLB 1890-1914; DLB 10, 34, 98, 135; EWL 3; MTCW 2
Bennett, Elizabeth
See Mitchell, Margaret (Munnerlyn)
Bennett, George Harold 1930-
See Bennett, Hal
See also BW 1; CA 97-100; CANR 87
Bennett, Gwendolyn B. 1902-1981 .... **HR 1:2**
See also BW 1; CA 125; DLB 51; WP
Bennett, Hal .... **CLC 5**
See Bennett, George Harold
See also CA 13; DLB 33
Bennett, Jay 1912- .... **CLC 35**
See also AAYA 10, 73; CA 69-72; CANR 11, 42, 79; JRDA; SAAS 4; SATA 41, 87; SATA-Brief 27; WYA; YAW
Bennett, Louise 1919-2006 .. **BLC 1; CLC 28**
See also BW 2, 3; CA 151; CAAS 252; CDWLB 3; CP 1, 2, 3, 4, 5, 6, 7; DAM MULT; DLB 117; EWL 3
Bennett, Louise Simone
See Bennett, Louise
Bennett-Coverley, Louise
See Bennett, Louise
Benoit de Sainte-Maure fl. 12th cent.
- .... **CMLC 90**
Benson, A. C. 1862-1925 .... **TCLC 123**
See also DLB 98
Benson, E(dward) F(rederic)
1867-1940 .... **TCLC 27**
See also CA 157; CAAE 114; DLB 135, 153; HGG; SUFW 1
Benson, Jackson J. 1930- .... **CLC 34**
See also CA 25-28R; DLB 111
Benson, Sally 1900-1972 .... **CLC 17**
See also CA 19-20; CAAS 37-40R; CAP 1; SATA 1, 35; SATA-Obit 27
Benson, Stella 1892-1933 .... **TCLC 17**
See also CA 154, 155; CAAE 117; DLB 36, 162; FANT; TEA
Bentham, Jeremy 1748-1832 .... **NCLC 38**
See also DLB 107, 158, 252
Bentley, E(dmund) C(lerihew)
1875-1956 .... **TCLC 12**
See also CA 232; CAAE 108; DLB 70; MSW
Bentley, Eric 1916- .... **CLC 24**
See also CA 5-8R; CAD; CANR 6, 67; CBD; CD 5, 6; INT CANR-6
Bentley, Eric Russell
See Bentley, Eric
ben Uzair, Salem
See Horne, Richard Henry Hengist

Beranger, Pierre Jean de
1780-1857 .... **NCLC 34**
Berdyaev, Nicolas
See Berdyaev, Nikolai (Aleksandrovich)
Berdyaev, Nikolai (Aleksandrovich)
1874-1948 .... **TCLC 67**
See also CA 157; CAAE 120
Berdyayev, Nikolai (Aleksandrovich)
See Berdyaev, Nikolai (Aleksandrovich)
Berendt, John 1939- .... **CLC 86**
See also CA 146; CANR 75, 83, 151
Berendt, John Lawrence
See Berendt, John
Beresford, J(ohn) D(avys)
1873-1947 .... **TCLC 81**
See also CA 155; CAAE 112; DLB 162, 178, 197; SFW 4; SUFW 1
Bergelson, David (Rafailovich)
1884-1952 .... **TCLC 81**
See Bergelson, Dovid
See also CA 220; DLB 333
Bergelson, Dovid
See Bergelson, David (Rafailovich)
See also EWL 3
Berger, Colonel
See Malraux, (Georges-)Andre
Berger, John (Peter) 1926- .... **CLC 2, 19**
See also BRWS 4; CA 81-84; CANR 51, 78, 117; CN 1, 2, 3, 4, 5, 6, 7; DLB 14, 207, 319, 326
Berger, Melvin H. 1927- .... **CLC 12**
See also CA 5-8R; CANR 4, 142; CLR 32; SAAS 2; SATA 5, 88, 158; SATA-Essay 124
Berger, Thomas 1924- .... **CLC 3, 5, 8, 11, 18, 38**
See also BPFB 1; CA 1-4R; CANR 5, 28, 51, 128; CN 1, 2, 3, 4, 5, 6, 7; DAM NOV; DLB 2; DLBY 1980; EWL 3; FANT; INT CANR-28; MAL 5; MTCW 1, 2; MTFW 2005; RHW; TCLE 1:1; TCWW 1, 2
Bergman, (Ernst) Ingmar 1918- ...... **CLC 16, 72, 210**
See also AAYA 61; CA 81-84; CANR 33, 70; CWW 2; DLB 257; MTCW 2; MTFW 2005
Bergson, Henri(-Louis) 1859-1941 . **TCLC 32**
See also CA 164; DLB 329; EW 8; EWL 3; GFL 1789 to the Present
Bergstein, Eleanor 1938- .... **CLC 4**
See also CA 53-56; CANR 5
Berkeley, George 1685-1753 .... **LC 65**
See also DLB 31, 101, 252
Berkoff, Steven 1937- .... **CLC 56**
See also CA 104; CANR 72; CBD; CD 5, 6
Berlin, Isaiah 1909-1997 .... **TCLC 105**
See also CA 85-88; CAAS 162
Bermant, Chaim (Icyk) 1929-1998 ... **CLC 40**
See also CA 57-60; CANR 6, 31, 57, 105; CN 2, 3, 4, 5, 6
Bern, Victoria
See Fisher, M(ary) F(rances) K(ennedy)
Bernanos, (Paul Louis) Georges
1888-1948 .... **TCLC 3**
See also CA 130; CAAE 104; CANR 94; DLB 72; EWL 3; GFL 1789 to the Present; RGWL 2, 3
Bernard, April 1956- .... **CLC 59**
See also CA 131; CANR 144
Bernard, Mary Ann
See Soderbergh, Steven
Bernard of Clairvaux 1090-1153 .. **CMLC 71**
See also DLB 208
Bernard Silvestris fl. c. 1130-fl. c.
1160 .... **CMLC 87**
See also DLB 208
Berne, Victoria
See Fisher, M(ary) F(rances) K(ennedy)

Bernhard, Thomas 1931-1989 ..... **CLC 3, 32, 61; DC 14; TCLC 165**
See also CA 85-88; CAAS 127; CANR 32, 57; CDWLB 2; DLB 85, 124; EWL 3; MTCW 1; RGHL; RGWL 2, 3
Bernhardt, Sarah (Henriette Rosine)
1844-1923 .... **TCLC 75**
See also CA 157
Bernstein, Charles 1950- .... **CLC 142**
See also CA 129; 24; CANR 90; CP 4, 5, 6, 7; DLB 169
Bernstein, Ingrid
See Kirsch, Sarah
Beroul fl. c. 12th cent. - .... **CMLC 75**
Berriault, Gina 1926-1999 .... **CLC 54, 109; SSC 30**
See also CA 129; CAAE 116; CAAS 185; CANR 66; DLB 130; SSFS 7,11
Berrigan, Daniel 1921- .... **CLC 4**
See also CA 187; 33-36R, 187; 1; CANR 11, 43, 78; CP 1, 2, 3, 4, 5, 6, 7; DLB 5
Berrigan, Edmund Joseph Michael, Jr.
1934-1983
See Berrigan, Ted
See also CA 61-64; CAAS 110; CANR 14, 102
Berrigan, Ted .... **CLC 37**
See Berrigan, Edmund Joseph Michael, Jr.
See also CP 1, 2, 3; DLB 5, 169; WP
Berry, Charles Edward Anderson 1931-
See Berry, Chuck
See also CA 115
Berry, Chuck .... **CLC 17**
See Berry, Charles Edward Anderson
Berry, Jonas
See Ashbery, John
See also GLL 1
Berry, Wendell 1934- .... **CLC 4, 6, 8, 27, 46; PC 28**
See also AITN 1; AMWS 10; ANW; CA 73-76; CANR 50, 73, 101, 132; CP 1, 2, 3, 4, 5, 6, 7; CSW; DAM POET; DLB 5, 6, 234, 275; MTCW 2; MTFW 2005; TCLE 1:1
Berryman, John 1914-1972 ... **CLC 1, 2, 3, 4, 6, 8, 10, 13, 25, 62; PC 64**
See also AMW; CA 13-16; CAAS 33-36R; CABS 2; CANR 35; CAP 1; CDALB 1941-1968; CP 1; DAM POET; DLB 48; EWL 3; MAL 5; MTCW 1, 2; MTFW 2005; PAB; RGAL 4; WP
Bertolucci, Bernardo 1940- ...... **CLC 16, 157**
See also CA 106; CANR 125
Berton, Pierre (Francis de Marigny)
1920-2004 .... **CLC 104**
See also CA 1-4R; CAAS 233; CANR 2, 56, 144; CPW; DLB 68; SATA 99; SATA-Obit 158
Bertrand, Aloysius 1807-1841 .... **NCLC 31**
See Bertrand, Louis oAloysiusc
Bertrand, Louis oAloysiusc
See Bertrand, Aloysius
See also DLB 217
Bertran de Born c. 1140-1215 .... **CMLC 5**
Besant, Annie (Wood) 1847-1933 ..... **TCLC 9**
See also CA 185; CAAE 105
Bessie, Alvah 1904-1985 .... **CLC 23**
See also CA 5-8R; CAAS 116; CANR 2, 80; DLB 26
Bestuzhev, Aleksandr Aleksandrovich
1797-1837 .... **NCLC 131**
See also DLB 198
Bethlen, T. D.
See Silverberg, Robert
Beti, Mongo .... **BLC 1; CLC 27**
See Biyidi, Alexandre
See also AFW; CANR 79; DAM MULT; EWL 3; WLIT 2

Bourne, Randolph S(illiman)
   1886-1918 .... **TCLC 16**
   See also AMW; CA 155; CAAE 117; DLB
   63; MAL 5

Bova, Ben 1932- .... **CLC 45**
   See also AAYA 16; CA 5-8R; 18; CANR
   11, 56, 94, 111, 157; CLR 3, 96; DLBY
   1981; INT CANR-11; MAICYA 1, 2;
   MTCW 1; SATA 6, 68, 133; SFW 4

Bova, Benjamin William
   See Bova, Ben

Bowen, Elizabeth (Dorothea Cole)
   1899-1973 . **CLC 1, 3, 6, 11, 15, 22, 118;**
   SSC 3, 28, 66; TCLC 148
   See also BRWS 2; CA 17-18; CAAS 41-
   44R; CANR 35, 105; CAP 2; CDBLB
   1945-1960; CN 1; DA3; DAM NOV;
   DLB 15, 162; EWL 3; EXPS; FW; HGG;
   MTCW 1, 2; MTFW 2005; NFS 13;
   RGSF 2; SSFS 5, 22; SUFW 1; TEA;
   WLIT 4

Bowering, George 1935- .... **CLC 15, 47**
   See also CA 21-24R; 16; CANR 10; CN 7;
   CP 1, 2, 3, 4, 5, 6, 7; DLB 53

Bowering, Marilyn R(uthe) 1949- .... **CLC 32**
   See also CA 101; CANR 49; CP 4, 5, 6, 7;
   CWP

Bowers, Edgar 1924-2000 .... **CLC 9**
   See also CA 5-8R; CAAS 188; CANR 24;
   CP 1, 2, 3, 4, 5, 6, 7; CSW; DLB 5

Bowers, Mrs. J. Milton 1842-1914
   See Bierce, Ambrose (Gwinett)

Bowie, David .... **CLC 17**
   See Jones, David Robert

Bowles, Jane (Sydney) 1917-1973 ..... **CLC 3,**
   68
   See Bowles, Jane Auer
   See also CA 19-20; CAAS 41-44R; CAP 2;
   CN 1; MAL 5

Bowles, Jane Auer
   See Bowles, Jane (Sydney)
   See also EWL 3

Bowles, Paul 1910-1999 ..... **CLC 1, 2, 19, 53;**
   SSC 3, 98
   See also AMWS 4; CA 1-4R; 1; CAAS 186;
   CANR 1, 19, 50, 75; CN 1, 2, 3, 4, 5, 6;
   DA3; DLB 5, 6, 218; EWL 3; MAL 5;
   MTCW 1, 2; MTFW 2005; RGAL 4;
   SSFS 17

Bowles, William Lisle 1762-1850 . **NCLC 103**
   See also DLB 93

Box, Edgar
   See Vidal, Gore
   See also GLL 1

Boyd, James 1888-1944 .... **TCLC 115**
   See also CA 186; DLB 9; DLBD 16; RGAL
   4; RHW

Boyd, Nancy
   See Millay, Edna St. Vincent
   See also GLL 1

Boyd, Thomas (Alexander)
   1898-1935 .... **TCLC 111**
   See also CA 183; CAAE 111; DLB 9;
   DLBD 16, 316

Boyd, William (Andrew Murray)
   1952- .... **CLC 28, 53, 70**
   See also CA 120; CAAE 114; CANR 51,
   71, 131; CN 4, 5, 6, 7; DLB 231

Boyesen, Hjalmar Hjorth
   1848-1895 .... **NCLC 135**
   See also DLB 12, 71; DLBD 13; RGAL 4

Boyle, Kay 1902-1992 .... **CLC 1, 5, 19, 58,**
   121; SSC 5
   See also CA 13-16R; 1; CAAS 140; CANR
   29, 61, 110; CN 1, 2, 3, 4, 5; CP 1, 2, 3,
   4, 5; DLB 4, 9, 48, 86; DLBY 1993; EWL
   3; MAL 5; MTCW 1, 2; MTFW 2005;
   RGAL 4; RGSF 2; SSFS 10, 13, 14

Boyle, Mark
   See Kienzle, William X.

Boyle, Patrick 1905-1982 .... **CLC 19**
   See also CA 127

Boyle, T. C.
   See Boyle, T. Coraghessan
   See also AMWS 8

Boyle, T. Coraghessan 1948- ..... **CLC 36, 55,**
   90; SSC 16
   See Boyle, T. C.
   See also AAYA 47; BEST 90:4; BPFB 1;
   CA 120; CANR 44, 76, 89, 132; CN 6, 7;
   CPW; DA3; DAM POP; DLB 218, 278;
   DLBY 1986; EWL 3; MAL 5; MTCW 2;
   MTFW 2005; SSFS 13, 19

Boz
   See Dickens, Charles (John Huffam)

Brackenridge, Hugh Henry
   1748-1816 .... **NCLC 7**
   See also DLB 11, 37; RGAL 4

Bradbury, Edward P.
   See Moorcock, Michael
   See also MTCW 2

Bradbury, Malcolm (Stanley)
   1932-2000 .... **CLC 32, 61**
   See also CA 1-4R; CANR 1, 33, 91, 98,
   137; CN 1, 2, 3, 4, 5, 6, 7; CP 1; DA3;
   DAM NOV; DLB 14, 207; EWL 3;
   MTCW 1, 2; MTFW 2005

Bradbury, Ray 1920- ... **CLC 1, 3, 10, 15, 42,**
   98, 235; SSC 29, 53; WLC 1
   See also AAYA 15; AITN 1, 2; AMWS 4;
   BPFB 1; BYA 4, 5, 11; CA 1-4R; CANR
   2, 30, 75, 125; CDALB 1968-1988; CN
   1, 2, 3, 4, 5, 6, 7; CPW; DA; DA3; DAB;
   DAC; DAM MST, NOV, POP; DLB 2, 8;
   EXPN; EXPS; HGG; LAIT 3, 5; LATS
   1:2; LMFS 2; MAL 5; MTCW 1, 2;
   MTFW 2005; NFS 1, 22; RGAL 4; RGSF
   2; SATA 11, 64, 123; SCFW 1, 2; SFW 4;
   SSFS 1, 20; SUFW 1, 2; TUS; YAW

Braddon, Mary Elizabeth
   1837-1915 .... **TCLC 111**
   See also BRWS 8; CA 179; CAAE 108;
   CMW 4; DLB 18, 70, 156; HGG

Bradfield, Scott 1955- .... **SSC 65**
   See also CA 147; CANR 90; HGG; SUFW
   2

Bradfield, Scott Michael
   See Bradfield, Scott

Bradford, Gamaliel 1863-1932 .... **TCLC 36**
   See also CA 160; DLB 17

Bradford, William 1590-1657 .... **LC 64**
   See also DLB 24, 30; RGAL 4

Bradley, David (Henry), Jr. 1950- .... **BLC 1;**
   CLC 23, 118
   See also BW 1, 3; CA 104; CANR 26, 81;
   CN 4, 5, 6, 7; DAM MULT; DLB 33

Bradley, John Ed 1958- .... **CLC 55**
   See also CA 139; CANR 99; CN 6, 7; CSW

Bradley, John Edmund, Jr.
   See Bradley, John Ed

Bradley, Marion Zimmer
   1930-1999 .... **CLC 30**
   See Chapman, Lee; Dexter, John; Gardner,
   Miriam; Ives, Morgan; Rivers, Elfrida
   See also AAYA 40; BPFB 1; CA 57-60; 10;
   CAAS 185; CANR 7, 31, 51, 75, 107;
   CPW; DA3; DAM POP; DLB 8; FANT;
   FW; MTCW 1, 2; MTFW 2005; SATA 90,
   139; SATA-Obit 116; SFW 4; SUFW 2;
   YAW

Bradshaw, John 1933- .... **CLC 70**
   See also CA 138; CANR 61

Bradstreet, Anne 1612(?)-1672 .... **LC 4, 30,**
   130; PC 10
   See also AMWS 1; CDALB 1640-1865;
   DA; DA3; DAC; DAM MST, POET; DLB
   24; EXPP; FW; PFS 6; RGAL 4; TUS;
   WP

Brady, Joan 1939- .... **CLC 86**
   See also CA 141

Bragg, Melvyn 1939- .... **CLC 10**
   See also BEST 89:3; CA 57-60; CANR 10,
   48, 89, 158; CN 1, 2, 3, 4, 5, 6, 7; DLB
   14, 271; RHW

Brahe, Tycho 1546-1601 .... **LC 45**
   See also DLB 300

Braine, John (Gerard) 1922-1986 . **CLC 1, 3,**
   41
   See also CA 1-4R; CAAS 120; CANR 1,
   33; CDBLB 1945-1960; CN 1, 2, 3, 4;
   DLB 15; DLBY 1986; EWL 3; MTCW 1

Braithwaite, William Stanley (Beaumont)
   1878-1962 .... **BLC 1; HR 1:2; PC 52**
   See also BW 1; CA 125; DAM MULT; DLB
   50, 54; MAL 5

Bramah, Ernest 1868-1942 .... **TCLC 72**
   See also CA 156; CMW 4; DLB 70; FANT

Brammer, Billy Lee
   See Brammer, William

Brammer, William 1929-1978 .... **CLC 31**
   See also CA 235; CAAS 77-80

Brancati, Vitaliano 1907-1954 .... **TCLC 12**
   See also CAAE 109; DLB 264; EWL 3

Brancato, Robin F(idler) 1936- .... **CLC 35**
   See also AAYA 9, 68; BYA 6; CA 69-72;
   CANR 11, 45; CLR 32; JRDA; MAICYA
   2; MAICYAS 1; SAAS 9; SATA 97;
   WYA; YAW

Brand, Dionne 1953- .... **CLC 192**
   See also BW 2; CA 143; CANR 143; CWP

Brand, Max
   See Faust, Frederick (Schiller)
   See also BPFB 1; TCWW 1, 2

Brand, Millen 1906-1980 .... **CLC 7**
   See also CA 21-24R; CAAS 97-100; CANR
   72

Branden, Barbara .... **CLC 44**
   See also CA 148

Brandes, Georg (Morris Cohen)
   1842-1927 .... **TCLC 10**
   See also CA 189; CAAE 105; DLB 300

Brandys, Kazimierz 1916-2000 .... **CLC 62**
   See also CA 239; EWL 3

Branley, Franklyn M(ansfield)
   1915-2002 .... **CLC 21**
   See also CA 33-36R; CAAS 207; CANR
   14, 39; CLR 13; MAICYA 1, 2; SAAS
   16; SATA 4, 68, 136

Brant, Beth (E.) 1941- .... **NNAL**
   See also CA 144; FW

Brant, Sebastian 1457-1521 .... **LC 112**
   See also DLB 179; RGWL 2, 3

Brathwaite, Edward Kamau
   1930- .... **BLCS; CLC 11; PC 56**
   See also BRWS 12; BW 2, 3; CA 25-28R;
   CANR 11, 26, 47, 107; CDWLB 3; CP 1,
   2, 3, 4, 5, 6, 7; DAM POET; DLB 125;
   EWL 3

Brathwaite, Kamau
   See Brathwaite, Edward Kamau

Brautigan, Richard (Gary)
   1935-1984 .... **CLC 1, 3, 5, 9, 12, 34, 42;**
   TCLC 133
   See also BPFB 1; CA 53-56; CAAS 113;
   CANR 34; CN 1, 2, 3; CP 1, 2, 3, 4; DA3;
   DAM NOV; DLB 2, 5, 206; DLBY 1980,
   1984; FANT; MAL 5; MTCW 1; RGAL
   4; SATA 56

Brave Bird, Mary .... **NNAL**
   See Crow Dog, Mary

Braverman, Kate 1950- .... **CLC 67**
   See also CA 89-92; CANR 141

Brecht, (Eugen) Bertolt (Friedrich)
   1898-1956 ..... **DC 3; TCLC 1, 6, 13, 35,**
   169; WLC 1
   See also CA 133; CAAE 104; CANR 62;
   CDWLB 2; DA; DA3; DAB; DAC; DAM
   DRAM, MST; DFS 4, 5, 9; DLB 56, 124;
   EW 11; EWL 3; IDTP; MTCW 1, 2;
   MTFW 2005; RGHL; RGWL 2, 3; TWA

Brecht, Eugen Berthold Friedrich
See Brecht, (Eugen) Bertolt (Friedrich)
Bremer, Fredrika 1801-1865 .... **NCLC 11**
See also DLB 254
Brennan, Christopher John
1870-1932 .... **TCLC 17**
See also CA 188; CAAE 117; DLB 230;
EWL 3
Brennan, Maeve 1917-1993 ... **CLC 5; TCLC 124**
See also CA 81-84; CANR 72, 100
Brenner, Jozef 1887-1919
See Csath, Geza
See also CA 240
Brent, Linda
See Jacobs, Harriet A(nn)
Brentano, Clemens (Maria)
1778-1842 .... **NCLC 1**
See also DLB 90; RGWL 2, 3
Brent of Bin Bin
See Franklin, (Stella Maria Sarah) Miles
(Lampe)
Brenton, Howard 1942- .... **CLC 31**
See also CA 69-72; CANR 33, 67; CBD;
CD 5, 6; DLB 13; MTCW 1
Breslin, James 1930-
See Breslin, Jimmy
See also CA 73-76; CANR 31, 75, 139;
DAM NOV; MTCW 1, 2; MTFW 2005
Breslin, Jimmy .... **CLC 4, 43**
See Breslin, James
See also AITN 1; DLB 185; MTCW 2
Bresson, Robert 1901(?)-1999 .... **CLC 16**
See also CA 110; CAAS 187; CANR 49
Breton, Andre 1896-1966 .. **CLC 2, 9, 15, 54; PC 15**
See also CA 19-20; CAAS 25-28R; CANR
40, 60; CAP 2; DLB 65, 258; EW 11;
EWL 3; GFL 1789 to the Present; LMFS
2; MTCW 1, 2; MTFW 2005; RGWL 2,
3; TWA; WP
Breton, Nicholas c. 1554-c. 1626 .... **LC 133**
See also DLB 136
Breytenbach, Breyten 1939(?)- .. **CLC 23, 37, 126**
See also CA 129; CAAE 113; CANR 61,
122; CWW 2; DAM POET; DLB 225;
EWL 3
Bridgers, Sue Ellen 1942- .... **CLC 26**
See also AAYA 8, 49; BYA 7, 8; CA 65-68;
CANR 11, 36; CLR 18; DLB 52; JRDA;
MAICYA 1, 2; SAAS 1; SATA 22, 90;
SATA-Essay 109; WYA; YAW
Bridges, Robert (Seymour)
1844-1930 .... **PC 28; TCLC 1**
See also BRW 6; CA 152; CAAE 104; CD-
BLB 1890-1914; DAM POET; DLB 19,
98
Bridie, James .... **TCLC 3**
See Mavor, Osborne Henry
See also DLB 10; EWL 3
Brin, David 1950- .... **CLC 34**
See also AAYA 21; CA 102; CANR 24, 70,
125, 127; INT CANR-24; SATA 65;
SCFW 2; SFW 4
Brink, Andre 1935- .... **CLC 18, 36, 106**
See also AFW; BRWS 6; CA 104; CANR
39, 62, 109, 133; CN 4, 5, 6, 7; DLB 225;
EWL 3; INT CA-103; LATS 1:2; MTCW
1, 2; MTFW 2005; WLIT 2
Brinsmead, H. F(ay)
See Brinsmead, H(esba) F(ay)
Brinsmead, H. F.
See Brinsmead, H(esba) F(ay)
Brinsmead, H(esba) F(ay) 1922- ...... **CLC 21**
See also CA 21-24R; CANR 10; CLR 47;
CWRI 5; MAICYA 1, 2; SAAS 5; SATA
18, 78

Brittain, Vera (Mary) 1893(?)-1970 . **CLC 23**
See also BRWS 10; CA 13-16; CAAS 25-
28R; CANR 58; CAP 1; DLB 191; FW;
MTCW 1, 2
Broch, Hermann 1886-1951 .... **TCLC 20**
See also CA 211; CAAE 117; CDWLB 2;
DLB 85, 124; EW 10; EWL 3; RGWL 2,
3
Brock, Rose
See Hansen, Joseph
See also GLL 1
Brod, Max 1884-1968 .... **TCLC 115**
See also CA 5-8R; CAAS 25-28R; CANR
7; DLB 81; EWL 3
Brodkey, Harold (Roy) 1930-1996 .. **CLC 56; TCLC 123**
See also CA 111; CAAS 151; CANR 71;
CN 4, 5, 6; DLB 130
Brodsky, Iosif Alexandrovich 1940-1996
See Brodsky, Joseph
See also AITN 1; CA 41-44R; CAAS 151;
CANR 37, 106; DA3; DAM POET;
MTCW 1, 2; MTFW 2005; RGWL 2, 3
Brodsky, Joseph . **CLC 4, 6, 13, 36, 100; PC 9**
See Brodsky, Iosif Alexandrovich
See also AAYA 71; AMWS 8; CWW 2;
DLB 285, 329; EWL 3; MTCW 1
Brodsky, Michael 1948- .... **CLC 19**
See also CA 102; CANR 18, 41, 58, 147;
DLB 244
Brodsky, Michael Mark
See Brodsky, Michael
Brodzki, Bella .... **CLC 65**
Brome, Richard 1590(?)-1652 .... **LC 61**
See also BRWS 10; DLB 58
Bromell, Henry 1947- .... **CLC 5**
See also CA 53-56; CANR 9, 115, 116
Bromfield, Louis (Brucker)
1896-1956 .... **TCLC 11**
See also CA 155; CAAE 107; DLB 4, 9,
86; RGAL 4; RHW
Broner, E(sther) M(asserman)
1930- .... **CLC 19**
See also CA 17-20R; CANR 8, 25, 72; CN
4, 5, 6; DLB 28
Bronk, William (M.) 1918-1999 .... **CLC 10**
See also CA 89-92; CAAS 177; CANR 23;
CP 3, 4, 5, 6, 7; DLB 165
Bronstein, Lev Davidovich
See Trotsky, Leon
Bronte, Anne
See Bronte, Anne
Bronte, Anne 1820-1849 ..... **NCLC 4, 71, 102**
See also BRW 5; BRWR 1; DA3; DLB 21,
199; TEA
Bronte, (Patrick) Branwell
1817-1848 .... **NCLC 109**
Bronte, Charlotte
See Bronte, Charlotte
Bronte, Charlotte 1816-1855 ...... **NCLC 3, 8, 33, 58, 105, 155; WLC 1**
See also AAYA 17; BRW 5; BRWC 2;
BRWR 1; BYA 2; CDBLB 1832-1890;
DA; DA3; DAB; DAC; DAM MST, NOV;
DLB 21, 159, 199; EXPN; FL 1:2; GL 2;
LAIT 2; NFS 4; TEA; WLIT 4
Bronte, Emily
See Bronte, Emily (Jane)
Bronte, Emily (Jane) 1818-1848 ... **NCLC 16, 35, 165; PC 8; WLC 1**
See also AAYA 17; BPFB 1; BRW 5;
BRWC 1; BRWR 1; BYA 3; CDBLB
1832-1890; DA; DA3; DAB; DAC; DAM
MST, NOV, POET; DLB 21, 32, 199;
EXPN; FL 1:2; GL 2; LAIT 1; TEA;
WLIT 3

Brontes
See Bronte, Anne; Bronte, Charlotte; Bronte,
Emily (Jane)
Brooke, Frances 1724-1789 .... **LC 6, 48**
See also DLB 39, 99
Brooke, Henry 1703(?)-1783 .... **LC 1**
See also DLB 39
Brooke, Rupert (Chawner)
1887-1915 .. **PC 24; TCLC 2, 7; WLC 1**
See also BRWS 3; CA 132; CAAE 104;
CANR 61; CDBLB 1914-1945; DA;
DAB; DAC; DAM MST, POET; DLB 19,
216; EXPP; GLL 2; MTCW 1, 2; MTFW
2005; PFS 7; TEA
Brooke-Haven, P.
See Wodehouse, P(elham) G(renville)
Brooke-Rose, Christine 1926(?)- ..... **CLC 40, 184**
See also BRWS 4; CA 13-16R; CANR 58,
118; CN 1, 2, 3, 4, 5, 6, 7; DLB 14, 231;
EWL 3; SFW 4
Brookner, Anita 1928- . **CLC 32, 34, 51, 136; 237**
See also BRWS 4; CA 120; CAAE 114;
CANR 37, 56, 87, 130; CN 4, 5, 6, 7;
CPW; DA3; DAB; DAM POP; DLB 194,
326; DLBY 1987; EWL 3; MTCW 1, 2;
MTFW 2005; NFS 23; TEA
Brooks, Cleanth 1906-1994 . **CLC 24, 86, 110**
See also AMWS 14; CA 17-20R; CAAS
145; CANR 33, 35; CSW; DLB 63; DLBY
1994; EWL 3; INT CANR-35; MAL 5;
MTCW 1, 2; MTFW 2005
Brooks, George
See Baum, L(yman) Frank
Brooks, Gwendolyn 1917-2000 .... **BLC 1; CLC 1, 2, 4, 5, 15, 49, 125; PC 7; WLC 1**
See also AAYA 20; AFAW 1, 2; AITN 1;
AMWS 3; BW 2, 3; CA 1-4R; CAAS 190;
CANR 1, 27, 52, 75, 132; CDALB 1941-
1968; CLR 27; CP 1, 2, 3, 4, 5, 6, 7;
CWP; DA; DA3; DAC; DAM MST,
MULT, POET; DLB 5, 76, 165; EWL 3;
EXPP; FL 1:5; MAL 5; MBL; MTCW 1,
2; MTFW 2005; PFS 1, 2, 4, 6; RGAL 4;
SATA 6; SATA-Obit 123; TUS; WP
Brooks, Mel 1926-
See Kaminsky, Melvin
See also CA 65-68; CANR 16; DFS 21
Brooks, Peter (Preston) 1938- .... **CLC 34**
See also CA 45-48; CANR 1, 107
Brooks, Van Wyck 1886-1963 .... **CLC 29**
See also AMW; CA 1-4R; CANR 6; DLB
45, 63, 103; MAL 5; TUS
Brophy, Brigid (Antonia)
1929-1995 .... **CLC 6, 11, 29, 105**
See also CA 5-8R; 4; CAAS 177; CANR
25, 53; CBD; CN 1, 2, 3, 4, 5, 6; CWD;
DA3; DLB 14, 271; EWL 3; MTCW 1, 2
Brosman, Catharine Savage 1934- ..... **CLC 9**
See also CA 61-64; CANR 21, 46, 149
Brossard, Nicole 1943- .... **CLC 115, 169**
See also CA 122; 16; CANR 140; CCA 1;
CWP; CWW 2; DLB 53; EWL 3; FW;
GLL 2; RGWL 3
Brother Antoninus
See Everson, William (Oliver)
Brothers Grimm
See Grimm, Jacob Ludwig Karl; Grimm,
Wilhelm Karl
The Brothers Quay
See Quay, Stephen; Quay, Timothy
Broughton, T(homas) Alan 1936- ..... **CLC 19**
See also CA 45-48; CANR 2, 23, 48, 111
Broumas, Olga 1949- .... **CLC 10, 73**
See also CA 85-88; CANR 20, 69, 110; CP
5, 6, 7; CWP; GLL 2

Broun, Heywood 1888-1939 .... **TCLC 104**
 See also DLB 29, 171
Brown, Alan 1950- .... **CLC 99**
 See also CA 156
Brown, Charles Brockden
 1771-1810 .... **NCLC 22, 74, 122**
 See also AMWS 1; CDALB 1640-1865;
 DLB 37, 59, 73; FW; GL 2; HGG; LMFS
 1; RGAL 4; TUS
Brown, Christy 1932-1981 .... **CLC 63**
 See also BYA 13; CA 105; CAAS 104;
 CANR 72; DLB 14
Brown, Claude 1937-2002 ... **BLC 1; CLC 30**
 See also AAYA 7; BW 1, 3; CA 73-76;
 CAAS 205; CANR 81; DAM MULT
Brown, Dan 1964- .... **CLC 209**
 See also AAYA 55; CA 217; MTFW 2005
Brown, Dee 1908-2002 .... **CLC 18, 47**
 See also AAYA 30; CA 13-16R; 6; CAAS
 212; CANR 11, 45, 60, 150; CPW; CSW;
 DA3; DAM POP; DLBY 1980; LAIT 2;
 MTCW 1, 2; MTFW 2005; NCFS 5;
 SATA 5, 110; SATA-Obit 141; TCWW 1,
 2
Brown, Dee Alexander
 See Brown, Dee
Brown, George
 See Wertmueller, Lina
Brown, George Douglas
 1869-1902 .... **TCLC 28**
 See Douglas, George
 See also CA 162
Brown, George Mackay 1921-1996 ... **CLC 5,
 48, 100**
 See also BRWS 6; CA 21-24R; 6; CAAS
 151; CANR 12, 37, 67; CN 1, 2, 3, 4, 5,
 6; CP 1, 2, 3, 4, 5, 6; DLB 14, 27, 139,
 271; MTCW 1; RGSF 2; SATA 35
Brown, Larry 1951-2004 .... **CLC 73**
 See also CA 134; CAAE 130; CAAS 233;
 CANR 117, 145; CSW; DLB 234; INT
 CA-134
Brown, Moses
 See Barrett, William (Christopher)
Brown, Rita Mae 1944- .... **CLC 18, 43, 79**
 See also BPFB 1; CA 45-48; CANR 2, 11,
 35, 62, 95, 138; CN 5, 6, 7; CPW; CSW;
 DA3; DAM NOV, POP; FW; INT CANR-
 11; MAL 5; MTCW 1, 2; MTFW 2005;
 NFS 9; RGAL 4; TUS
Brown, Roderick (Langmere) Haig-
 See Haig-Brown, Roderick (Langmere)
Brown, Rosellen 1939- .... **CLC 32, 170**
 See also CA 77-80; 10; CANR 14, 44, 98;
 CN 6, 7
Brown, Sterling Allen 1901-1989 ...... **BLC 1;
 CLC 1, 23, 59; HR 1:2; PC 55**
 See also AFAW 1, 2; BW 1, 3; CA 85-88;
 CAAS 127; CANR 26; CP 3, 4; DA3;
 DAM MULT, POET; DLB 48, 51, 63;
 MAL 5; MTCW 1, 2; MTFW 2005;
 RGAL 4; WP
Brown, Will
 See Ainsworth, William Harrison
Brown, William Hill 1765-1793 .... **LC 93**
 See also DLB 37
Brown, William Larry
 See Brown, Larry
Brown, William Wells 1815-1884 ...... **BLC 1;
 DC 1; NCLC 2, 89**
 See also DAM MULT; DLB 3, 50, 183,
 248; RGAL 4
Browne, (Clyde) Jackson 1948(?)- ... **CLC 21**
 See also CA 120
Browne, Sir Thomas 1605-1682 .... **LC 111**
 See also BRW 2; DLB 151

Browning, Robert 1812-1889 . **NCLC 19, 79;
 PC 2, 61; WLCS**
 See also BRW 4; BRWC 2; BRWR 2; CD-
 BLB 1832-1890; CLR 97; DA; DA3;
 DAB; DAC; DAM MST, POET; DLB 32,
 163; EXPP; LATS 1:1; PAB; PFS 1, 15;
 RGEL 2; TEA; WLIT 4; WP; YABC 1
Browning, Tod 1882-1962 .... **CLC 16**
 See also CA 141; CAAS 117
Brownmiller, Susan 1935- .... **CLC 159**
 See also CA 103; CANR 35, 75, 137; DAM
 NOV; FW; MTCW 1, 2; MTFW 2005
Brownson, Orestes Augustus
 1803-1876 .... **NCLC 50**
 See also DLB 1, 59, 73, 243
Bruccoli, Matthew J(oseph) 1931- ... **CLC 34**
 See also CA 9-12R; CANR 7, 87; DLB 103
Bruce, Lenny .... **CLC 21**
 See Schneider, Leonard Alfred
Bruchac, Joseph 1942- .... **NNAL**
 See also AAYA 19; CA 33-36R; CANR 13,
 47, 75, 94, 137, 161; CLR 46; CWRI 5;
 DAM MULT; JRDA; MAICYA 2; MAIC-
 YAS 1; MTCW 2; MTFW 2005; SATA
 42, 89, 131, 176; SATA-Essay 176
Bruin, John
 See Brutus, Dennis
Brulard, Henri
 See Stendhal
Brulls, Christian
 See Simenon, Georges (Jacques Christian)
Brunetto Latini c. 1220-1294 .... **CMLC 73**
Brunner, John (Kilian Houston)
 1934-1995 .... **CLC 8, 10**
 See also CA 1-4R; 8; CAAS 149; CANR 2,
 37; CPW; DAM POP; DLB 261; MTCW
 1, 2; SCFW 1, 2; SFW 4
Bruno, Giordano 1548-1600 .... **LC 27**
 See also RGWL 2, 3
Brutus, Dennis 1924- ... **BLC 1; CLC 43; PC
 24**
 See also AFW; BW 2, 3; CA 49-52; 14;
 CANR 2, 27, 42, 81; CDWLB 3; CP 1, 2,
 3, 4, 5, 6, 7; DAM MULT, POET; DLB
 117, 225; EWL 3
Bryan, C(ourtlandt) D(ixon) B(arnes)
 1936- .... **CLC 29**
 See also CA 73-76; CANR 13, 68; DLB
 185; INT CANR-13
Bryan, Michael
 See Moore, Brian
 See also CCA 1
Bryan, William Jennings
 1860-1925 .... **TCLC 99**
 See also DLB 303
Bryant, William Cullen 1794-1878 . **NCLC 6,
 46; PC 20**
 See also AMWS 1; CDALB 1640-1865;
 DA; DAB; DAC; DAM MST, POET;
 DLB 3, 43, 59, 189, 250; EXPP; PAB;
 RGAL 4; TUS
Bryusov, Valery Yakovlevich
 1873-1924 .... **TCLC 10**
 See also CA 155; CAAE 107; EWL 3; SFW
 4
Buchan, John 1875-1940 .... **TCLC 41**
 See also CA 145; CAAE 108; CMW 4;
 DAB; DAM POP; DLB 34, 70, 156;
 HGG; MSW; MTCW 2; RGEL 2; RHW;
 YABC 2
Buchanan, George 1506-1582 .... **LC 4**
 See also DLB 132
Buchanan, Robert 1841-1901 .... **TCLC 107**
 See also CA 179; DLB 18, 35
Buchheim, Lothar-Guenther
 1918-2007 .... **CLC 6**
 See also CA 85-88

Buchner, (Karl) Georg
 1813-1837 .... **NCLC 26, 146**
 See also CDWLB 2; DLB 133; EW 6;
 RGSF 2; RGWL 2, 3; TWA
Buchwald, Art 1925-2007 .... **CLC 33**
 See also AITN 1; CA 5-8R; CANR 21, 67,
 107; MTCW 1, 2; SATA 10
Buchwald, Arthur
 See Buchwald, Art
Buck, Pearl S(ydenstricker)
 1892-1973 .... **CLC 7, 11, 18, 127**
 See also AAYA 42; AITN 1; AMWS 2;
 BPFB 1; CA 1-4R; CAAS 41-44R; CANR
 1, 34; CDALBS; CN 1; DA; DA3; DAB;
 DAC; DAM MST, NOV; DLB 9, 102,
 329; EWL 3; LAIT 3; MAL 5; MTCW 1,
 2; MTFW 2005; RGAL 4; RHW; SATA
 1, 25; TUS
Buckler, Ernest 1908-1984 .... **CLC 13**
 See also CA 11-12; CAAS 114; CAP 1;
 CCA 1; CN 1, 2, 3; DAC; DAM MST;
 DLB 68; SATA 47
Buckley, Christopher 1952- .... **CLC 165**
 See also CA 139; CANR 119
Buckley, Christopher Taylor
 See Buckley, Christopher
Buckley, Vincent (Thomas)
 1925-1988 .... **CLC 57**
 See also CA 101; CP 1, 2, 3, 4; DLB 289
Buckley, William F., Jr. 1925- ..... **CLC 7, 18,
 37**
 See also AITN 1; BPFB 1; CA 1-4R; CANR
 1, 24, 53, 93, 133; CMW 4; CPW; DA3;
 DAM POP; DLB 137; DLBY 1980; INT
 CANR-24; MTCW 1, 2; MTFW 2005;
 TUS
Buechner, Frederick 1926- ..... **CLC 2, 4, 6, 9**
 See also AMWS 12; BPFB 1; CA 13-16R;
 CANR 11, 39, 64, 114, 138; CN 1, 2, 3,
 4, 5, 6, 7; DAM NOV; DLBY 1980; INT
 CANR-11; MAL 5; MTCW 1, 2; MTFW
 2005; TCLE 1:1
Buell, John (Edward) 1927- .... **CLC 10**
 See also CA 1-4R; CANR 71; DLB 53
Buero Vallejo, Antonio 1916-2000 ... **CLC 15,
 46, 139, 226; DC 18**
 See also CA 106; CAAS 189; CANR 24,
 49, 75; CWW 2; DFS 11; EWL 3; HW 1;
 MTCW 1, 2
Bufalino, Gesualdo 1920-1996 .... **CLC 74**
 See also CA 209; CWW 2; DLB 196
Bugayev, Boris Nikolayevich
 1880-1934 .... **PC 11; TCLC 7**
 See Bely, Andrey; Belyi, Andrei
 See also CA 165; CAAE 104; MTCW 2;
 MTFW 2005
Bukowski, Charles 1920-1994 ... **CLC 2, 5, 9,
 41, 82, 108; PC 18; SSC 45**
 See also CA 17-20R; CAAS 144; CANR
 40, 62, 105; CN 4, 5; CP 1, 2, 3, 4, 5;
 CPW; DA3; DAM NOV, POET; DLB 5,
 130, 169; EWL 3; MAL 5; MTCW 1, 2;
 MTFW 2005
Bulgakov, Mikhail 1891-1940 .... **SSC 18;
 TCLC 2, 16, 159**
 See also AAYA 74; BPFB 1; CA 152;
 CAAE 105; DAM DRAM, NOV; DLB
 272; EWL 3; MTCW 2; MTFW 2005;
 NFS 8; RGSF 2; RGWL 2, 3; SFW 4;
 TWA
Bulgakov, Mikhail Afanasevich
 See Bulgakov, Mikhail
Bulgya, Alexander Alexandrovich
 1901-1956 .... **TCLC 53**
 See Fadeev, Aleksandr Aleksandrovich;
 Fadeev, Alexandr Alexandrovich; Fadeyev,
 Alexander
 See also CA 181; CAAE 117

Bullins, Ed 1935- ... **BLC 1; CLC 1, 5, 7; DC 6**
See also BW 2, 3; CA 49-52; 16; CAD; CANR 24, 46, 73, 134; CD 5, 6; DAM DRAM, MULT; DLB 7, 38, 249; EWL 3; MAL 5; MTCW 1, 2; MTFW 2005; RGAL 4

Bulosan, Carlos 1911-1956 .... **AAL**
See also CA 216; DLB 312; RGAL 4

Bulwer-Lytton, Edward (George Earle Lytton) 1803-1873 .... **NCLC 1, 45**
See also DLB 21; RGEL 2; SFW 4; SUFW 1; TEA

Bunin, Ivan
See Bunin, Ivan Alexeyevich

Bunin, Ivan Alekseevich
See Bunin, Ivan Alexeyevich

Bunin, Ivan Alexeyevich 1870-1953 ... **SSC 5; TCLC 6**
See also CAAE 104; DLB 317, 329; EWL 3; RGSF 2; RGWL 2, 3; TWA

Bunting, Basil 1900-1985 ...... **CLC 10, 39, 47**
See also BRWS 7; CA 53-56; CAAS 115; CANR 7; CP 1, 2, 3, 4; DAM POET; DLB 20; EWL 3; RGEL 2

Bunuel, Luis 1900-1983 ... **CLC 16, 80; HLC 1**
See also CA 101; CAAS 110; CANR 32, 77; DAM MULT; HW 1

Bunyan, John 1628-1688 ... **LC 4, 69; WLC 1**
See also BRW 2; BYA 5; CDBLB 1660-1789; DA; DAB; DAC; DAM MST; DLB 39; RGEL 2; TEA; WCH; WLIT 3

Buravsky, Alexandr .... **CLC 59**

Burckhardt, Jacob (Christoph) 1818-1897 .... **NCLC 49**
See also EW 6

Burford, Eleanor
See Hibbert, Eleanor Alice Burford

Burgess, Anthony . **CLC 1, 2, 4, 5, 8, 10, 13, 15, 22, 40, 62, 81, 94**
See Wilson, John (Anthony) Burgess
See also AAYA 25; AITN 1; BRWS 1; CD-BLB 1960 to Present; CN 1, 2, 3, 4, 5; DAB; DLB 14, 194, 261; DLBY 1998; EWL 3; RGEL 2; RHW; SFW 4; YAW

Burke, Edmund 1729(?)-1797 .... **LC 7, 36; WLC 1**
See also BRW 3; DA; DA3; DAB; DAC; DAM MST; DLB 104, 252; RGEL 2; TEA

Burke, Kenneth (Duva) 1897-1993 ... **CLC 2, 24**
See also AMW; CA 5-8R; CAAS 143; CANR 39, 74, 136; CN 1, 2; CP 1, 2, 3, 4, 5; DLB 45, 63; EWL 3; MAL 5; MTCW 1, 2; MTFW 2005; RGAL 4

Burke, Leda
See Garnett, David

Burke, Ralph
See Silverberg, Robert

Burke, Thomas 1886-1945 .... **TCLC 63**
See also CA 155; CAAE 113; CMW 4; DLB 197

Burney, Fanny 1752-1840 .... **NCLC 12, 54, 107**
See also BRWS 3; DLB 39; FL 1:2; NFS 16; RGEL 2; TEA

Burney, Frances
See Burney, Fanny

Burns, Robert 1759-1796 ... **LC 3, 29, 40; PC 6; WLC 1**
See also AAYA 51; BRW 3; CDBLB 1789-1832; DA; DA3; DAB; DAC; DAM MST, POET; DLB 109; EXPP; PAB; RGEL 2; TEA; WP

Burns, Tex
See L'Amour, Louis

Burnshaw, Stanley 1906-2005 ..... **CLC 3, 13, 44**
See also CA 9-12R; CAAS 243; CP 1, 2, 3, 4, 5, 6, 7; DLB 48; DLBY 1997

Burr, Anne 1937- .... **CLC 6**
See also CA 25-28R

Burroughs, Edgar Rice 1875-1950 . **TCLC 2, 32**
See also AAYA 11; BPFB 1; BYA 4, 9; CA 132; CAAE 104; CANR 131; DA3; DAM NOV; DLB 8; FANT; MTCW 1, 2; MTFW 2005; RGAL 4; SATA 41; SCFW 1, 2; SFW 4; TCWW 1, 2; TUS; YAW

Burroughs, William S. 1914-1997 . **CLC 1, 2, 5, 15, 22, 42, 75, 109; TCLC 121; WLC 1**
See Lee, William; Lee, Willy
See also AAYA 60; AITN 2; AMWS 3; BG 1:2; BPFB 1; CA 9-12R; CAAS 160; CANR 20, 52, 104; CN 1, 2, 3, 4, 5, 6; CPW; DA; DA3; DAB; DAC; DAM MST, NOV, POP; DLB 2, 8, 16, 152, 237; DLBY 1981, 1997; EWL 3; HGG; LMFS 2; MAL 5; MTCW 1, 2; MTFW 2005; RGAL 4; SFW 4

Burroughs, William Seward
See Burroughs, William S.

Burton, Sir Richard F(rancis) 1821-1890 .... **NCLC 42**
See also DLB 55, 166, 184; SSFS 21

Burton, Robert 1577-1640 .... **LC 74**
See also DLB 151; RGEL 2

Buruma, Ian 1951- .... **CLC 163**
See also CA 128; CANR 65, 141

Busch, Frederick 1941-2006 .. **CLC 7, 10, 18, 47, 166**
See also CA 33-36R; 1; CAAS 248; CANR 45, 73, 92, 157; CN 1, 2, 3, 4, 5, 6, 7; DLB 6, 218

Busch, Frederick Matthew
See Busch, Frederick

Bush, Barney (Furman) 1946- .... **NNAL**
See also CA 145

Bush, Ronald 1946- .... **CLC 34**
See also CA 136

Bustos, F(rancisco)
See Borges, Jorge Luis

Bustos Domecq, H(onorio)
See Bioy Casares, Adolfo; Borges, Jorge Luis

Butler, Octavia E. 1947-2006 .... **BLCS; CLC 38, 121, 230**
See also AAYA 18, 48; AFAW 2; AMWS 13; BPFB 1; BW 2, 3; CA 73-76; CAAS 248; CANR 12, 24, 38, 73, 145; CLR 65; CN 7; CPW; DA3; DAM MULT, POP; DLB 33; LATS 1:2; MTCW 1, 2; MTFW 2005; NFS 8, 21; SATA 84; SCFW 2; SFW 4; SSFS 6; TCLE 1:1; YAW

Butler, Octavia Estelle
See Butler, Octavia E.

Butler, Robert Olen, (Jr.) 1945- ...... **CLC 81, 162**
See also AMWS 12; BPFB 1; CA 112; CANR 66, 138; CN 7; CSW; DAM POP; DLB 173; INT CA-112; MAL 5; MTCW 2; MTFW 2005; SSFS 11, 22

Butler, Samuel 1612-1680 .... **LC 16, 43**
See also DLB 101, 126; RGEL 2

Butler, Samuel 1835-1902 .... **TCLC 1, 33; WLC 1**
See also BRWS 2; CA 143; CDBLB 1890-1914; DA; DA3; DAB; DAC; DAM MST, NOV; DLB 18, 57, 174; RGEL 2; SFW 4; TEA

Butler, Walter C.
See Faust, Frederick (Schiller)

Butor, Michel (Marie Francois) 1926- .... **CLC 1, 3, 8, 11, 15, 161**
See also CA 9-12R; CANR 33, 66; CWW 2; DLB 83; EW 13; EWL 3; GFL 1789 to the Present; MTCW 1, 2; MTFW 2005

Butts, Mary 1890(?)-1937 .... **TCLC 77**
See also CA 148; DLB 240

Buxton, Ralph
See Silverstein, Alvin; Silverstein, Virginia B(arbara Opshelor)

Buzo, Alex
See Buzo, Alexander (John)
See also DLB 289

Buzo, Alexander (John) 1944- .... **CLC 61**
See also CA 97-100; CANR 17, 39, 69; CD 5, 6

Buzzati, Dino 1906-1972 .... **CLC 36**
See also CA 160; CAAS 33-36R; DLB 177; RGWL 2, 3; SFW 4

Byars, Betsy 1928- .... **CLC 35**
See also AAYA 19; BYA 3; CA 183; 33-36R, 183; CANR 18, 36, 57, 102, 148; CLR 1, 16, 72; DLB 52; INT CANR-18; JRDA; MAICYA 1, 2; MAICYAS 1; MTCW 1; SAAS 1; SATA 4, 46, 80, 163; SATA-Essay 108; WYA; YAW

Byars, Betsy Cromer
See Byars, Betsy

Byatt, Antonia Susan Drabble
See Byatt, A.S.

Byatt, A.S. 1936- .... **CLC 19, 65, 136, 223; SSC 91**
See also BPFB 1; BRWC 2; BRWS 4; CA 13-16R; CANR 13, 33, 50, 75, 96, 133; CN 1, 2, 3, 4, 5, 6; DA3; DAM NOV, POP; DLB 14, 194, 319, 326; EWL 3; MTCW 1, 2; MTFW 2005; RGSF 2; RHW; TEA

Byrd, William II 1674-1744 .... **LC 112**
See also DLB 24, 140; RGAL 4

Byrne, David 1952- .... **CLC 26**
See also CA 127

Byrne, John Keyes 1926-
See Leonard, Hugh
See also CA 102; CANR 78, 140; INT CA-102

Byron, George Gordon (Noel) 1788-1824 ..... **DC 24; NCLC 2, 12, 109, 149; PC 16; WLC 1**
See also AAYA 64; BRW 4; BRWC 2; CD-BLB 1789-1832; DA; DA3; DAB; DAC; DAM MST, POET; DLB 96, 110; EXPP; LMFS 1; PAB; PFS 1, 14; RGEL 2; TEA; WLIT 3; WP

Byron, Robert 1905-1941 .... **TCLC 67**
See also CA 160; DLB 195

C. 3. 3.
See Wilde, Oscar (Fingal O'Flahertie Wills)

Caballero, Fernan 1796-1877 .... **NCLC 10**

Cabell, Branch
See Cabell, James Branch

Cabell, James Branch 1879-1958 .... **TCLC 6**
See also CA 152; CAAE 105; DLB 9, 78; FANT; MAL 5; MTCW 2; RGAL 4; SUFW 1

Cabeza de Vaca, Alvar Nunez 1490-1557(?) .... **LC 61**

Cable, George Washington 1844-1925 .... **SSC 4; TCLC 4**
See also CA 155; CAAE 104; DLB 12, 74; DLBD 13; RGAL 4; TUS

Cabral de Melo Neto, Joao 1920-1999 .... **CLC 76**
See Melo Neto, Joao Cabral de
See also CA 151; DAM MULT; DLB 307; LAW; LAWS 1

Cabrera Infante, G. 1929-2005 ... **CLC 5, 25, 45, 120; HLC 1; SSC 39**
See also CA 85-88; CAAS 236; CANR 29, 65, 110; CDWLB 3; CWW 2; DA3; DAM MULT; DLB 113; EWL 3; HW 1, 2; LAW; LAWS 1; MTCW 1, 2; MTFW 2005; RGSF 2; WLIT 1

Cabrera Infante, Guillermo
See Cabrera Infante, G.

Cade, Toni
See Bambara, Toni Cade

Cadmus and Harmonia
See Buchan, John

Caedmon fl. 658-680 .... **CMLC 7**
See also DLB 146

Caeiro, Alberto
See Pessoa, Fernando (Antonio Nogueira)

Caesar, Julius .... **CMLC 47**
See Julius Caesar
See also AW 1; RGWL 2, 3; WLIT 8

Cage, John (Milton), (Jr.)
1912-1992 .... **CLC 41; PC 58**
See also CA 13-16R; CAAS 169; CANR 9, 78; DLB 193; INT CANR-9; TCLE 1:1

Cahan, Abraham 1860-1951 .... **TCLC 71**
See also CA 154; CAAE 108; DLB 9, 25, 28; MAL 5; RGAL 4

Cain, G.
See Cabrera Infante, G.

Cain, Guillermo
See Cabrera Infante, G.

Cain, James M(allahan) 1892-1977 .. **CLC 3, 11, 28**
See also AITN 1; BPFB 1; CA 17-20R; CAAS 73-76; CANR 8, 34, 61; CMW 4; CN 1, 2; DLB 226; EWL 3; MAL 5; MSW; MTCW 1; RGAL 4

Caine, Hall 1853-1931 .... **TCLC 97**
See also RHW

Caine, Mark
See Raphael, Frederic (Michael)

Calasso, Roberto 1941- .... **CLC 81**
See also CA 143; CANR 89

Calderon de la Barca, Pedro
1600-1681 . **DC 3; HLCS 1; LC 23, 136**
See also DFS 23; EW 2; RGWL 2, 3; TWA

Caldwell, Erskine 1903-1987 ... **CLC 1, 8, 14, 50, 60; SSC 19; TCLC 117**
See also AITN 1; AMW; BPFB 1; CA 1-4R; 1; CAAS 121; CANR 2, 33; CN 1, 2, 3, 4; DA3; DAM NOV; DLB 9, 86; EWL 3; MAL 5; MTCW 1, 2; MTFW 2005; RGAL 4; RGSF 2; TUS

Caldwell, (Janet Miriam) Taylor (Holland)
1900-1985 .... **CLC 2, 28, 39**
See also BPFB 1; CA 5-8R; CAAS 116; CANR 5; DA3; DAM NOV, POP; DLBD 17; MTCW 2; RHW

Calhoun, John Caldwell
1782-1850 .... **NCLC 15**
See also DLB 3, 248

Calisher, Hortense 1911- ..... **CLC 2, 4, 8, 38, 134; SSC 15**
See also CA 1-4R; CANR 1, 22, 117; CN 1, 2, 3, 4, 5, 6, 7; DA3; DAM NOV; DLB 2, 218; INT CANR-22; MAL 5; MTCW 1, 2; MTFW 2005; RGAL 4; RGSF 2

Callaghan, Morley Edward
1903-1990 ..... **CLC 3, 14, 41, 65; TCLC 145**
See also CA 9-12R; CAAS 132; CANR 33, 73; CN 1, 2, 3, 4; DAC; DAM MST; DLB 68; EWL 3; MTCW 1, 2; MTFW 2005; RGEL 2; RGSF 2; SSFS 19

Callimachus c. 305B.C.-c.
240B.C. .... **CMLC 18**
See also AW 1; DLB 176; RGWL 2, 3

Calvin, Jean
See Calvin, John
See also DLB 327; GFL Beginnings to 1789

Calvin, John 1509-1564 .... **LC 37**
See Calvin, Jean

Calvino, Italo 1923-1985 .... **CLC 5, 8, 11, 22, 33, 39, 73; SSC 3, 48; TCLC 183**
See also AAYA 58; CA 85-88; CAAS 116; CANR 23, 61, 132; DAM NOV; DLB 196; EW 13; EWL 3; MTCW 1, 2; MTFW 2005; RGHL; RGSF 2; RGWL 2, 3; SFW 4; SSFS 12; WLIT 7

Camara Laye
See Laye, Camara
See also EWL 3

Camden, William 1551-1623 .... **LC 77**
See also DLB 172

Cameron, Carey 1952- .... **CLC 59**
See also CA 135

Cameron, Peter 1959- .... **CLC 44**
See also AMWS 12; CA 125; CANR 50, 117; DLB 234; GLL 2

Camoens, Luis Vaz de 1524(?)-1580
See Camoes, Luis de
See also EW 2

Camoes, Luis de 1524(?)-1580 . **HLCS 1; LC 62; PC 31**
See Camoens, Luis Vaz de
See also DLB 287; RGWL 2, 3

Campana, Dino 1885-1932 .... **TCLC 20**
See also CA 246; CAAE 117; DLB 114; EWL 3

Campanella, Tommaso 1568-1639 .... **LC 32**
See also RGWL 2, 3

Campbell, John W(ood, Jr.)
1910-1971 .... **CLC 32**
See also CA 21-22; CAAS 29-32R; CANR 34; CAP 2; DLB 8; MTCW 1; SCFW 1, 2; SFW 4

Campbell, Joseph 1904-1987 .... **CLC 69; TCLC 140**
See also AAYA 3, 66; BEST 89:2; CA 1-4R; CAAS 124; CANR 3, 28, 61, 107; DA3; MTCW 1, 2

Campbell, Maria 1940- .... **CLC 85; NNAL**
See also CA 102; CANR 54; CCA 1; DAC

Campbell, (John) Ramsey 1946- ..... **CLC 42; SSC 19**
See also AAYA 51; CA 228; 57-60, 228; CANR 7, 102; DLB 261; HGG; INT CANR-7; SUFW 1, 2

Campbell, (Ignatius) Roy (Dunnachie)
1901-1957 .... **TCLC 5**
See also AFW; CA 155; CAAE 104; DLB 20, 225; EWL 3; MTCW 2; RGEL 2

Campbell, Thomas 1777-1844 .... **NCLC 19**
See also DLB 93, 144; RGEL 2

Campbell, Wilfred .... **TCLC 9**
See Campbell, William

Campbell, William 1858(?)-1918
See Campbell, Wilfred
See also CAAE 106; DLB 92

Campbell, William Edward March
1893-1954
See March, William
See also CAAE 108

Campion, Jane 1954- .... **CLC 95, 229**
See also AAYA 33; CA 138; CANR 87

Campion, Thomas 1567-1620 .... **LC 78**
See also CDBLB Before 1660; DAM POET; DLB 58, 172; RGEL 2

Camus, Albert 1913-1960 ...... **CLC 1, 2, 4, 9, 11, 14, 32, 63, 69, 124; DC 2; SSC 9, 76; WLC 1**
See also AAYA 36; AFW; BPFB 1; CA 89-92; CANR 131; DA; DA3; DAB; DAC; DAM DRAM, MST, NOV; DLB 72, 321, 329; EW 13; EWL 3; EXPN; EXPS; GFL

1789 to the Present; LATS 1:2; LMFS 2; MTCW 1, 2; MTFW 2005; NFS 6, 16; RGHL; RGSF 2; RGWL 2, 3; SSFS 4; TWA

Canby, Vincent 1924-2000 .... **CLC 13**
See also CA 81-84; CAAS 191

Cancale
See Desnos, Robert

Canetti, Elias 1905-1994 .. **CLC 3, 14, 25, 75, 86; TCLC 157**
See also CA 21-24R; CAAS 146; CANR 23, 61, 79; CDWLB 2; CWW 2; DA3; DLB 85, 124, 329; EW 12; EWL 3; MTCW 1, 2; MTFW 2005; RGWL 2, 3; TWA

Canfield, Dorothea F.
See Fisher, Dorothy (Frances) Canfield

Canfield, Dorothea Frances
See Fisher, Dorothy (Frances) Canfield

Canfield, Dorothy
See Fisher, Dorothy (Frances) Canfield

Canin, Ethan 1960- .... **CLC 55; SSC 70**
See also CA 135; CAAE 131; MAL 5

Cankar, Ivan 1876-1918 .... **TCLC 105**
See also CDWLB 4; DLB 147; EWL 3

Cannon, Curt
See Hunter, Evan

Cao, Lan 1961- .... **CLC 109**
See also CA 165

Cape, Judith
See Page, P(atricia) K(athleen)
See also CCA 1

Capek, Karel 1890-1938 .... **DC 1; SSC 36; TCLC 6, 37; WLC 1**
See also CA 140; CAAE 104; CDWLB 4; DA; DA3; DAB; DAC; DAM DRAM, MST, NOV; DFS 7, 11; DLB 215; EW 10; EWL 3; MTCW 2; MTFW 2005; RGSF 2; RGWL 2, 3; SCFW 1, 2; SFW 4

Capella, Martianus fl. 4th cent. - .. **CMLC 84**

Capote, Truman 1924-1984 . **CLC 1, 3, 8, 13, 19, 34, 38, 58; SSC 2, 47, 93; TCLC 164; WLC 1**
See also AAYA 61; AMWS 3; BPFB 1; CA 5-8R; CAAS 113; CANR 18, 62; CDALB 1941-1968; CN 1, 2, 3; CPW; DA; DA3; DAB; DAC; DAM MST, NOV, POP; DLB 2, 185, 227; DLBY 1980, 1984; EWL 3; EXPS; GLL 1; LAIT 3; MAL 5; MTCW 1, 2; MTFW 2005; NCFS 2; RGAL 4; RGSF 2; SATA 91; SSFS 2; TUS

Capra, Frank 1897-1991 .... **CLC 16**
See also AAYA 52; CA 61-64; CAAS 135

Caputo, Philip 1941- .... **CLC 32**
See also AAYA 60; CA 73-76; CANR 40, 135; YAW

Caragiale, Ion Luca 1852-1912 ...... **TCLC 76**
See also CA 157

Card, Orson Scott 1951- .... **CLC 44, 47, 50**
See also AAYA 11, 42; BPFB 1; BYA 5, 8; CA 102; CANR 27, 47, 73, 102, 106, 133; CLR 116; CPW; DA3; DAM POP; FANT; INT CANR-27; MTCW 1, 2; MTFW 2005; NFS 5; SATA 83, 127; SCFW 2; SFW 4; SUFW 2; YAW

Cardenal, Ernesto 1925- .... **CLC 31, 161; HLC 1; PC 22**
See also CA 49-52; CANR 2, 32, 66, 138; CWW 2; DAM MULT, POET; DLB 290; EWL 3; HW 1, 2; LAWS 1; MTCW 1, 2; MTFW 2005; RGWL 2, 3

Cardinal, Marie 1929-2001 .... **CLC 189**
See also CA 177; CWW 2; DLB 83; FW

Cardozo, Benjamin N(athan)
1870-1938 .... **TCLC 65**
See also CA 164; CAAE 117

Carducci, Giosue (Alessandro Giuseppe)
1835-1907 .... **PC 46; TCLC 32**
See also CA 163; DLB 329; EW 7; RGWL
2, 3

Carew, Thomas 1595(?)-1640 . **LC 13; PC 29**
See also BRW 2; DLB 126; PAB; RGEL 2

Carey, Ernestine Gilbreth
1908-2006 .... **CLC 17**
See also CA 5-8R; CAAS 254; CANR 71;
SATA 2

Carey, Peter 1943- .... **CLC 40, 55, 96, 183**
See also BRWS 12; CA 127; CAAE 123;
CANR 53, 76, 117, 157; CN 4, 5, 6, 7;
DLB 289, 326; EWL 3; INT CA-127;
MTCW 1, 2; MTFW 2005; RGSF 2;
SATA 94

Carleton, William 1794-1869 .... **NCLC 3**
See also DLB 159; RGEL 2; RGSF 2

Carlisle, Henry (Coffin) 1926- .... **CLC 33**
See also CA 13-16R; CANR 15, 85

Carlsen, Chris
See Holdstock, Robert

Carlson, Ron 1947- .... **CLC 54**
See also CA 189; 105, 189; CANR 27, 155;
DLB 244

Carlson, Ronald F.
See Carlson, Ron

Carlyle, Jane Welsh 1801-1866 ... **NCLC 181**
See also DLB 55

Carlyle, Thomas 1795-1881 ..... **NCLC 22, 70**
See also BRW 4; CDBLB 1789-1832; DA;
DAB; DAC; DAM MST; DLB 55, 144,
254; RGEL 2; TEA

Carman, (William) Bliss 1861-1929 ... **PC 34;
TCLC 7**
See also CA 152; CAAE 104; DAC; DLB
92; RGEL 2

Carnegie, Dale 1888-1955 .... **TCLC 53**
See also CA 218

Carossa, Hans 1878-1956 .... **TCLC 48**
See also CA 170; DLB 66; EWL 3

Carpenter, Don(ald Richard)
1931-1995 .... **CLC 41**
See also CA 45-48; CAAS 149; CANR 1,
71

Carpenter, Edward 1844-1929 .... **TCLC 88**
See also CA 163; GLL 1

Carpenter, John (Howard) 1948- ... **CLC 161**
See also AAYA 2, 73; CA 134; SATA 58

Carpenter, Johnny
See Carpenter, John (Howard)

Carpentier (y Valmont), Alejo
1904-1980 . **CLC 8, 11, 38, 110; HLC 1;
SSC 35**
See also CA 65-68; CAAS 97-100; CANR
11, 70; CDWLB 3; DAM MULT; DLB
113; EWL 3; HW 1, 2; LAW; LMFS 2;
RGSF 2; RGWL 2, 3; WLIT 1

Carr, Caleb 1955- .... **CLC 86**
See also CA 147; CANR 73, 134; DA3

Carr, Emily 1871-1945 .... **TCLC 32**
See also CA 159; DLB 68; FW; GLL 2

Carr, John Dickson 1906-1977 .... **CLC 3**
See Fairbairn, Roger
See also CA 49-52; CAAS 69-72; CANR 3,
33, 60; CMW 4; DLB 306; MSW; MTCW
1, 2

Carr, Philippa
See Hibbert, Eleanor Alice Burford

Carr, Virginia Spencer 1929- .... **CLC 34**
See also CA 61-64; DLB 111

Carrere, Emmanuel 1957- .... **CLC 89**
See also CA 200

Carrier, Roch 1937- .... **CLC 13, 78**
See also CA 130; CANR 61, 152; CCA 1;
DAC; DAM MST; DLB 53; SATA 105,
166

Carroll, James Dennis
See Carroll, Jim

Carroll, James P. 1943(?)- .... **CLC 38**
See also CA 81-84; CANR 73, 139; MTCW
2; MTFW 2005

Carroll, Jim 1951- .... **CLC 35, 143**
See also AAYA 17; CA 45-48; CANR 42,
115; NCFS 5

Carroll, Lewis ...... **NCLC 2, 53, 139; PC 18,
74; WLC 1**
See Dodgson, Charles L(utwidge)
See also AAYA 39; BRW 5; BYA 5, 13; CD-
BLB 1832-1890; CLR 2, 18, 108; DLB
18, 163, 178; DLBY 1998; EXPN; EXPP;
FANT; JRDA; LAIT 1; NFS 7; PFS 11;
RGEL 2; SUFW 1; TEA; WCH

Carroll, Paul Vincent 1900-1968 ...... **CLC 10**
See also CA 9-12R; CAAS 25-28R; DLB
10; EWL 3; RGEL 2

Carruth, Hayden 1921- ..... **CLC 4, 7, 10, 18,
84; PC 10**
See also AMWS 16; CA 9-12R; CANR 4,
38, 59, 110; CP 1, 2, 3, 4, 5, 6, 7; DLB 5,
165; INT CANR-4; MTCW 1, 2; MTFW
2005; SATA 47

Carson, Anne 1950- .... **CLC 185; PC 64**
See also AMWS 12; CA 203; CP 7; DLB
193; PFS 18; TCLE 1:1

Carson, Ciaran 1948- .... **CLC 201**
See also CA 153; CAAE 112; CANR 113;
CP 6, 7

Carson, Rachel
See Carson, Rachel Louise
See also AAYA 49; DLB 275

Carson, Rachel Louise 1907-1964 .... **CLC 71**
See Carson, Rachel
See also AMWS 9; ANW; CA 77-80; CANR
35; DA3; DAM POP; FW; LAIT 4; MAL
5; MTCW 1, 2; MTFW 2005; NCFS 1;
SATA 23

Carter, Angela 1940-1992 ..... **CLC 5, 41, 76;
SSC 13, 85; TCLC 139**
See also BRWS 3; CA 53-56; CAAS 136;
CANR 12, 36, 61, 106; CN 3, 4, 5; DA3;
DLB 14, 207, 261, 319; EXPS; FANT;
FW; GL 2; MTCW 1, 2; MTFW 2005;
RGSF 2; SATA 66; SATA-Obit 70; SFW
4; SSFS 4, 12; SUFW 2; WLIT 4

Carter, Angela Olive
See Carter, Angela

Carter, Nick
See Smith, Martin Cruz

Carver, Raymond 1938-1988 ..... **CLC 22, 36,
53, 55, 126; PC 54; SSC 8, 51**
See also AAYA 44; AMWS 3; BPFB 1; CA
33-36R; CAAS 126; CANR 17, 34, 61,
103; CN 4; CPW; DA3; DAM NOV; DLB
130; DLBY 1984, 1988; EWL 3; MAL 5;
MTCW 1, 2; MTFW 2005; PFS 17;
RGAL 4; RGSF 2; SSFS 3, 6, 12, 13, 23;
TCLE 1:1; TCWW 2; TUS

Cary, Elizabeth, Lady Falkland
1585-1639 .... **LC 30**

Cary, (Arthur) Joyce (Lunel)
1888-1957 .... **TCLC 1, 29**
See also BRW 7; CA 164; CAAE 104; CD-
BLB 1914-1945; DLB 15, 100; EWL 3;
MTCW 2; RGEL 2; TEA

Casal, Julian del 1863-1893 .... **NCLC 131**
See also DLB 283; LAW

Casanova, Giacomo
See Casanova de Seingalt, Giovanni Jacopo
See also WLIT 7

Casanova de Seingalt, Giovanni Jacopo
1725-1798 .... **LC 13**
See Casanova, Giacomo

Casares, Adolfo Bioy
See Bioy Casares, Adolfo
See also RGSF 2

Casas, Bartolome de las 1474-1566
See Las Casas, Bartolome de
See also WLIT 1

Casely-Hayford, J(oseph) E(phraim)
1866-1903 .... **BLC 1; TCLC 24**
See also BW 2; CA 152; CAAE 123; DAM
MULT

Casey, John (Dudley) 1939- .... **CLC 59**
See also BEST 90:2; CA 69-72; CANR 23,
100

Casey, Michael 1947- .... **CLC 2**
See also CA 65-68; CANR 109; CP 2, 3;
DLB 5

Casey, Patrick
See Thurman, Wallace (Henry)

Casey, Warren (Peter) 1935-1988 .... **CLC 12**
See also CA 101; CAAS 127; INT CA-101

Casona, Alejandro .... **CLC 49**
See Alvarez, Alejandro Rodriguez
See also EWL 3

Cassavetes, John 1929-1989 .... **CLC 20**
See also CA 85-88; CAAS 127; CANR 82

Cassian, Nina 1924- .... **PC 17**
See also CWP; CWW 2

Cassill, R(onald) V(erlin)
1919-2002 .... **CLC 4, 23**
See also CA 9-12R; 1; CAAS 208; CANR
7, 45; CN 1, 2, 3, 4, 5, 6, 7; DLB 6, 218;
DLBY 2002

Cassiodorus, Flavius Magnus c. 490(?)-c.
583(?) .... **CMLC 43**

Cassirer, Ernst 1874-1945 .... **TCLC 61**
See also CA 157

Cassity, (Allen) Turner 1929- .... **CLC 6, 42**
See also CA 223; 17-20R, 223; 8; CANR
11; CSW; DLB 105

Castaneda, Carlos (Cesar Aranha)
1931(?)-1998 .... **CLC 12, 119**
See also CA 25-28R; CANR 32, 66, 105;
DNFS 1; HW 1; MTCW 1

Castedo, Elena 1937- .... **CLC 65**
See also CA 132

Castedo-Ellerman, Elena
See Castedo, Elena

Castellanos, Rosario 1925-1974 .... **CLC 66;
HLC 1; SSC 39, 68**
See also CA 131; CAAS 53-56; CANR 58;
CDWLB 3; DAM MULT; DLB 113, 290;
EWL 3; FW; HW 1; LAW; MTCW 2;
MTFW 2005; RGSF 2; RGWL 2, 3

Castelvetro, Lodovico 1505-1571 .... **LC 12**

Castiglione, Baldassare 1478-1529 ...... **LC 12**
See Castiglione, Baldesar
See also LMFS 1; RGWL 2, 3

Castiglione, Baldesar
See Castiglione, Baldassare
See also EW 2; WLIT 7

Castillo, Ana 1953- .... **CLC 151**
See also AAYA 42; CA 131; CANR 51, 86,
128; CWP; DLB 122, 227; DNFS 2; FW;
HW 1; LLW; PFS 21

Castle, Robert
See Hamilton, Edmond

Castro (Ruz), Fidel 1926(?)- .... **HLC 1**
See also CA 129; CAAE 110; CANR 81;
DAM MULT; HW 2

Castro, Guillen de 1569-1631 .... **LC 19**

Castro, Rosalia de 1837-1885 ... **NCLC 3, 78;
PC 41**
See also DAM MULT

Cather, Willa (Sibert) 1873-1947 . **SSC 2, 50;
TCLC 1, 11, 31, 99, 132, 152; WLC 1**
See also AAYA 24; AMW; AMWC 1;
AMWR 1; BPFB 1; CA 128; CAAE 104;
CDALB 1865-1917; CLR 98; DA; DA3;
DAB; DAC; DAM MST, NOV; DLB 9,
54, 78, 256; DLBD 1; EWL 3; EXPN;
EXPS; FL 1:5; LAIT 3; LATS 1:1; MAL
5; MBL; MTCW 1, 2; MTFW 2005; NFS
2, 19; RGAL 4; RGSF 2; RHW; SATA
30; SSFS 2, 7, 16; TCWW 1, 2; TUS

Catherine II
See Catherine the Great
See also DLB 150

Catherine the Great 1729-1796 .... **LC 69**
See Catherine II

Cato, Marcus Porcius
234B.C.-149B.C. .... **CMLC 21**
See Cato the Elder

Cato, Marcus Porcius, the Elder
See Cato, Marcus Porcius

Cato the Elder
See Cato, Marcus Porcius
See also DLB 211

Catton, (Charles) Bruce 1899-1978 . **CLC 35**
See also AITN 1; CA 5-8R; CAAS 81-84;
CANR 7, 74; DLB 17; MTCW 2; MTFW
2005; SATA 2; SATA-Obit 24

Catullus c. 84B.C.-54B.C. .... **CMLC 18**
See also AW 2; CDWLB 1; DLB 211;
RGWL 2, 3; WLIT 8

Cauldwell, Frank
See King, Francis (Henry)

Caunitz, William J. 1933-1996 .... **CLC 34**
See also BEST 89:3; CA 130; CAAE 125;
CAAS 152; CANR 73; INT CA-130

Causley, Charles (Stanley)
1917-2003 .... **CLC 7**
See also CA 9-12R; CAAS 223; CANR 5,
35, 94; CLR 30; CP 1, 2, 3, 4, 5; CWRI
5; DLB 27; MTCW 1; SATA 3, 66; SATA-
Obit 149

Caute, (John) David 1936- .... **CLC 29**
See also CA 1-4R; 4; CANR 1, 33, 64, 120;
CBD; CD 5, 6; CN 1, 2, 3, 4, 5, 6, 7;
DAM NOV; DLB 14, 231

Cavafy, C(onstantine) P(eter) .... **PC 36;**
TCLC 2, 7
See Kavafis, Konstantinos Petrou
See also CA 148; DA3; DAM POET; EW
8; EWL 3; MTCW 2; PFS 19; RGWL 2,
3; WP

Cavalcanti, Guido c. 1250-c.
1300 .... **CMLC 54**
See also RGWL 2, 3; WLIT 7

Cavallo, Evelyn
See Spark, Muriel

Cavanna, Betty .... **CLC 12**
See Harrison, Elizabeth (Allen) Cavanna
See also JRDA; MAICYA 1; SAAS 4;
SATA 1, 30

Cavendish, Margaret Lucas
1623-1673 .... **LC 30, 132**
See also DLB 131, 252, 281; RGEL 2

Caxton, William 1421(?)-1491(?) .... **LC 17**
See also DLB 170

Cayer, D. M.
See Duffy, Maureen (Patricia)

Cayrol, Jean 1911-2005 .... **CLC 11**
See also CA 89-92; CAAS 236; DLB 83;
EWL 3

Cela (y Trulock), Camilo Jose
See Cela, Camilo Jose
See also CWW 2

Cela, Camilo Jose 1916-2002 .... **CLC 4, 13,**
59, 122; HLC 1; SSC 71
See Cela (y Trulock), Camilo Jose
See also BEST 90:2; CA 21-24R; 10; CAAS
206; CANR 21, 32, 76, 139; DAM MULT;
DLB 322; DLBY 1989; EW 13; EWL 3;
HW 1; MTCW 1, 2; MTFW 2005; RGSF
2; RGWL 2, 3

Celan, Paul .... **CLC 10, 19, 53, 82; PC 10**
See Antschel, Paul
See also CDWLB 2; DLB 69; EWL 3;
RGHL; RGWL 2, 3

Celine, Louis-Ferdinand .. **CLC 1, 3, 4, 7, 9,**
15, 47, 124
See Destouches, Louis-Ferdinand
See also DLB 72; EW 11; EWL 3; GFL
1789 to the Present; RGWL 2, 3

Cellini, Benvenuto 1500-1571 .... **LC 7**
See also WLIT 7

Cendrars, Blaise .... **CLC 18, 106**
See Sauser-Hall, Frederic
See also DLB 258; EWL 3; GFL 1789 to
the Present; RGWL 2, 3; WP

Centlivre, Susanna 1669(?)-1723 .... **DC 25;**
LC 65
See also DLB 84; RGEL 2

Cernuda (y Bidon), Luis
1902-1963 .... **CLC 54; PC 62**
See also CA 131; CAAS 89-92; DAM
POET; DLB 134; EWL 3; GLL 1; HW 1;
RGWL 2, 3

Cervantes, Lorna Dee 1954- ..... **HLCS 1; PC**
35
See also CA 131; CANR 80; CP 7; CWP;
DLB 82; EXPP; HW 1; LLW

Cervantes (Saavedra), Miguel de
1547-1616 .... **HLCS; LC 6, 23, 93; SSC**
12; WLC 1
See also AAYA 56; BYA 1, 14; DA; DAB;
DAC; DAM MST, NOV; EW 2; LAIT 1;
LATS 1:1; LMFS 1; NFS 8; RGSF 2;
RGWL 2, 3; TWA

Cesaire, Aime 1913- ..... **BLC 1; CLC 19, 32,**
112; DC 22; PC 25
See also BW 2, 3; CA 65-68; CANR 24,
43, 81; CWW 2; DA3; DAM MULT,
POET; DLB 321; EWL 3; GFL 1789 to
the Present; MTCW 1, 2; MTFW 2005;
WP

Chabon, Michael 1963- ... **CLC 55, 149; SSC**
59
See also AAYA 45; AMWS 11; CA 139;
CANR 57, 96, 127, 138; DLB 278; MAL
5; MTFW 2005; SATA 145

Chabrol, Claude 1930- .... **CLC 16**
See also CA 110

Chairil Anwar
See Anwar, Chairil
See also EWL 3

Challans, Mary 1905-1983
See Renault, Mary
See also CA 81-84; CAAS 111; CANR 74;
DA3; MTCW 2; MTFW 2005; SATA 23;
SATA-Obit 36; TEA

Challis, George
See Faust, Frederick (Schiller)

Chambers, Aidan 1934- .... **CLC 35**
See also AAYA 27; CA 25-28R; CANR 12,
31, 58, 116; JRDA; MAICYA 1, 2; SAAS
12; SATA 1, 69, 108, 171; WYA; YAW

Chambers, James 1948-
See Cliff, Jimmy
See also CAAE 124

Chambers, Jessie
See Lawrence, D(avid) H(erbert Richards)
See also GLL 1

Chambers, Robert W(illiam)
1865-1933 .... **SSC 92; TCLC 41**
See also CA 165; DLB 202; HGG; SATA
107; SUFW 1

Chambers, (David) Whittaker
1901-1961 .... **TCLC 129**
See also CAAS 89-92; DLB 303

Chamisso, Adelbert von
1781-1838 .... **NCLC 82**
See also DLB 90; RGWL 2, 3; SUFW 1

Chance, James T.
See Carpenter, John (Howard)

Chance, John T.
See Carpenter, John (Howard)

Chandler, Raymond (Thornton)
1888-1959 .... **SSC 23; TCLC 1, 7, 179**
See also AAYA 25; AMWC 2; AMWS 4;
BPFB 1; CA 129; CAAE 104; CANR 60,
107; CDALB 1929-1941; CMW 4; DA3;
DLB 226, 253; DLBD 6; EWL 3; MAL
5; MSW; MTCW 1, 2; MTFW 2005; NFS
17; RGAL 4; TUS

Chang, Diana 1934- .... **AAL**
See also CA 228; CWP; DLB 312; EXPP

Chang, Eileen 1921-1995 .... **AAL; SSC 28;**
TCLC 184
See Chang Ai-Ling; Zhang Ailing
See also CA 166

Chang, Jung 1952- .... **CLC 71**
See also CA 142

Chang Ai-Ling
See Chang, Eileen
See also EWL 3

Channing, William Ellery
1780-1842 .... **NCLC 17**
See also DLB 1, 59, 235; RGAL 4

Chao, Patricia 1955- .... **CLC 119**
See also CA 163; CANR 155

Chaplin, Charles Spencer
1889-1977 .... **CLC 16**
See Chaplin, Charlie
See also CA 81-84; CAAS 73-76

Chaplin, Charlie
See Chaplin, Charles Spencer
See also AAYA 61; DLB 44

Chapman, George 1559(?)-1634 . **DC 19; LC**
22, 116
See also BRW 1; DAM DRAM; DLB 62,
121; LMFS 1; RGEL 2

Chapman, Graham 1941-1989 .... **CLC 21**
See Monty Python
See also CA 116; CAAS 129; CANR 35, 95

Chapman, John Jay 1862-1933 .... **TCLC 7**
See also AMWS 14; CA 191; CAAE 104

Chapman, Lee
See Bradley, Marion Zimmer
See also GLL 1

Chapman, Walker
See Silverberg, Robert

Chappell, Fred (Davis) 1936- .... **CLC 40, 78,**
162
See also CA 198; 5-8R, 198; 4; CANR 8,
33, 67, 110; CN 6; CP 6, 7; CSW; DLB
6, 105; HGG

Char, Rene(-Emile) 1907-1988 .... **CLC 9, 11,**
14, 55; PC 56
See also CA 13-16R; CAAS 124; CANR
32; DAM POET; DLB 258; EWL 3; GFL
1789 to the Present; MTCW 1, 2; RGWL
2, 3

Charby, Jay
See Ellison, Harlan

Chardin, Pierre Teilhard de
See Teilhard de Chardin, (Marie Joseph)
Pierre

Chariton fl. 1st cent. (?)- .... **CMLC 49**

Charlemagne 742-814 .... **CMLC 37**

Charles I 1600-1649 .... **LC 13**

Charriere, Isabelle de 1740-1805 .. **NCLC 66**
See also DLB 313

Chartier, Alain c. 1392-1430 .... **LC 94**
See also DLB 208

Chartier, Emile-Auguste
See Alain

Charyn, Jerome 1937- .... **CLC 5, 8, 18**
See also CA 5-8R; 1; CANR 7, 61, 101,
158; CMW 4; CN 1, 2, 3, 4, 5, 6, 7;
DLBY 1983; MTCW 1

Chase, Adam
See Marlowe, Stephen

Chubb, Elmer
See Masters, Edgar Lee
Chulkov, Mikhail Dmitrievich
1743-1792 .... **LC 2**
See also DLB 150
Churchill, Caryl 1938- .... **CLC 31, 55, 157;
DC 5**
See Churchill, Chick
See also BRWS 4; CA 102; CANR 22, 46,
108; CBD; CD 6; CWD; DFS 12, 16;
DLB 13, 310; EWL 3; FW; MTCW 1;
RGEL 2
Churchill, Charles 1731-1764 .... **LC 3**
See also DLB 109; RGEL 2
Churchill, Chick
See Churchill, Caryl
See also CD 5
Churchill, Sir Winston (Leonard Spencer)
1874-1965 .... **TCLC 113**
See also BRW 6; CA 97-100; CDBLB
1890-1914; DA3; DLB 100, 329; DLBD
16; LAIT 4; MTCW 1, 2
Chute, Carolyn 1947- .... **CLC 39**
See also CA 123; CANR 135; CN 7
Ciardi, John (Anthony) 1916-1986 . **CLC 10,
40, 44, 129; PC 69**
See also CA 5-8R; 2; CAAS 118; CANR 5,
33; CLR 19; CP 1, 2, 3, 4; CWRI 5; DAM
POET; DLB 5; DLBY 1986; INT
CANR-5; MAICYA 1, 2; MAL 5; MTCW
1, 2; MTFW 2005; RGAL 4; SAAS 26;
SATA 1, 65; SATA-Obit 46
Cibber, Colley 1671-1757 .... **LC 66**
See also DLB 84; RGEL 2
Cicero, Marcus Tullius
106B.C.-43B.C. .... **CMLC 3, 81**
See also AW 1; CDWLB 1; DLB 211;
RGWL 2, 3; WLIT 8
Cimino, Michael 1943- .... **CLC 16**
See also CA 105
Cioran, E(mil) M. 1911-1995 .... **CLC 64**
See also CA 25-28R; CAAS 149; CANR
91; DLB 220; EWL 3
Cisneros, Sandra 1954- .... **CLC 69, 118, 193;
HLC 1; PC 52; SSC 32, 72**
See also AAYA 9, 53; AMWS 7; CA 131;
CANR 64, 118; CN 7; CWP; DA3; DAM
MULT; DLB 122, 152; EWL 3; EXPN;
FL 1:5; FW; HW 1, 2; LAIT 5; LATS 1:2;
LLW; MAICYA 2; MAL 5; MTCW 2;
MTFW 2005; NFS 2; PFS 19; RGAL 4;
RGSF 2; SSFS 3, 13; WLIT 1; YAW
Cixous, Helene 1937- .... **CLC 92**
See also CA 126; CANR 55, 123; CWW 2;
DLB 83, 242; EWL 3; FL 1:5; FW; GLL
2; MTCW 1, 2; MTFW 2005; TWA
Clair, Rene .... **CLC 20**
See Chomette, Rene Lucien
Clampitt, Amy 1920-1994 .... **CLC 32; PC 19**
See also AMWS 9; CA 110; CAAS 146;
CANR 29, 79; CP 4, 5; DLB 105; MAL 5
Clancy, Thomas L., Jr. 1947-
See Clancy, Tom
See also CA 131; CAAE 125; CANR 62,
105; DA3; INT CA-131; MTCW 1, 2;
MTFW 2005
Clancy, Tom .... **CLC 45, 112**
See Clancy, Thomas L., Jr.
See also AAYA 9, 51; BEST 89:1, 90:1;
BPFB 1; BYA 10, 11; CANR 132; CMW
4; CPW; DAM NOV, POP; DLB 227
Clare, John 1793-1864 .. **NCLC 9, 86; PC 23**
See also BRWS 11; DAB; DAM POET;
DLB 55, 96; RGEL 2
Clarin
See Alas (y Urena), Leopoldo (Enrique
Garcia)
Clark, Al C.
See Goines, Donald

Clark, Brian (Robert)
See Clark, (Robert) Brian
See also CD 6
Clark, (Robert) Brian 1932- .... **CLC 29**
See Clark, Brian (Robert)
See also CA 41-44R; CANR 67; CBD; CD
5
Clark, Curt
See Westlake, Donald E.
Clark, Eleanor 1913-1996 .... **CLC 5, 19**
See also CA 9-12R; CAAS 151; CANR 41;
CN 1, 2, 3, 4, 5, 6; DLB 6
Clark, J. P.
See Clark Bekederemo, J.P.
See also CDWLB 3; DLB 117
Clark, John Pepper
See Clark Bekederemo, J.P.
See also AFW; CD 5; CP 1, 2, 3, 4, 5, 6, 7;
RGEL 2
Clark, Kenneth (Mackenzie)
1903-1983 .... **TCLC 147**
See also CA 93-96; CAAS 109; CANR 36;
MTCW 1, 2; MTFW 2005
Clark, M. R.
See Clark, Mavis Thorpe
Clark, Mavis Thorpe 1909-1999 ...... **CLC 12**
See also CA 57-60; CANR 8, 37, 107; CLR
30; CWRI 5; MAICYA 1, 2; SAAS 5;
SATA 8, 74
Clark, Walter Van Tilburg
1909-1971 .... **CLC 28**
See also CA 9-12R; CAAS 33-36R; CANR
63, 113; CN 1; DLB 9, 206; LAIT 2;
MAL 5; RGAL 4; SATA 8; TCWW 1, 2
Clark Bekederemo, J.P. 1935- . **BLC 1; CLC
38; DC 5**
See Bekederemo, J. P. Clark; Clark, J. P.;
Clark, John Pepper
See also BW 1; CA 65-68; CANR 16, 72;
DAM DRAM, MULT; DFS 13; EWL 3;
MTCW 2; MTFW 2005
Clarke, Arthur C. 1917- .... **CLC 1, 4, 13, 18,
35, 136; SSC 3**
See also AAYA 4, 33; BPFB 1; BYA 13;
CA 1-4R; CANR 2, 28, 55, 74, 130; CLR
119; CN 1, 2, 3, 4, 5, 6, 7; CPW; DA3;
DAM POP; DLB 261; JRDA; LAIT 5;
MAICYA 1, 2; MTCW 1, 2; MTFW 2005;
SATA 13, 70, 115; SCFW 1, 2; SFW 4;
SSFS 4, 18; TCLE 1:1; YAW
Clarke, Austin 1896-1974 .... **CLC 6, 9**
See also CA 29-32; CAAS 49-52; CAP 2;
CP 1, 2; DAM POET; DLB 10, 20; EWL
3; RGEL 2
Clarke, Austin C. 1934- . **BLC 1; CLC 8, 53;
SSC 45**
See also BW 1; CA 25-28R; 16; CANR 14,
32, 68, 140; CN 1, 2, 3, 4, 5, 6, 7; DAC;
DAM MULT; DLB 53, 125; DNFS 2;
MTCW 2; MTFW 2005; RGSF 2
Clarke, Gillian 1937- .... **CLC 61**
See also CA 106; CP 3, 4, 5, 6, 7; CWP;
DLB 40
Clarke, Marcus (Andrew Hislop)
1846-1881 .... **NCLC 19; SSC 94**
See also DLB 230; RGEL 2; RGSF 2
Clarke, Shirley 1925-1997 .... **CLC 16**
See also CA 189
Clash, The
See Headon, (Nicky) Topper; Jones, Mick;
Simonon, Paul; Strummer, Joe
Claudel, Paul (Louis Charles Marie)
1868-1955 .... **TCLC 2, 10**
See also CA 165; CAAE 104; DLB 192,
258, 321; EW 8; EWL 3; GFL 1789 to
the Present; RGWL 2, 3; TWA
Claudian 370(?)-404(?) .... **CMLC 46**
See also RGWL 2, 3
Claudius, Matthias 1740-1815 .... **NCLC 75**
See also DLB 97

Clavell, James 1925-1994 .... **CLC 6, 25, 87**
See also BPFB 1; CA 25-28R; CAAS 146;
CANR 26, 48; CN 5; CPW; DA3; DAM
NOV, POP; MTCW 1, 2; MTFW 2005;
NFS 10; RHW
Clayman, Gregory .... **CLC 65**
Cleaver, (Leroy) Eldridge
1935-1998 .... **BLC 1; CLC 30, 119**
See also BW 1, 3; CA 21-24R; CAAS 167;
CANR 16, 75; DA3; DAM MULT;
MTCW 2; YAW
Cleese, John (Marwood) 1939- .... **CLC 21**
See Monty Python
See also CA 116; CAAE 112; CANR 35;
MTCW 1
Cleishbotham, Jebediah
See Scott, Sir Walter
Cleland, John 1710-1789 .... **LC 2, 48**
See also DLB 39; RGEL 2
Clemens, Samuel Langhorne 1835-1910
See Twain, Mark
See also CA 135; CAAE 104; CDALB
1865-1917; DA; DA3; DAB; DAC; DAM
MST, NOV; DLB 12, 23, 64, 74, 186,
189; JRDA; LMFS 1; MAICYA 1, 2;
NCFS 4; NFS 20; SATA 100; YABC 2
Clement of Alexandria
150(?)-215(?) .... **CMLC 41**
Cleophil
See Congreve, William
Clerihew, E.
See Bentley, E(dmund) C(lerihew)
Clerk, N. W.
See Lewis, C.S.
Cleveland, John 1613-1658 .... **LC 106**
See also DLB 126; RGEL 2
Cliff, Jimmy .... **CLC 21**
See Chambers, James
See also CA 193
Cliff, Michelle 1946- .... **BLCS; CLC 120**
See also BW 2; CA 116; CANR 39, 72; CD-
WLB 3; DLB 157; FW; GLL 2
Clifford, Lady Anne 1590-1676 .... **LC 76**
See also DLB 151
Clifton, Lucille 1936- ... **BLC 1; CLC 19, 66,
162; PC 17**
See also AFAW 2; BW 2, 3; CA 49-52;
CANR 2, 24, 42, 76, 97, 138; CLR 5; CP
2, 3, 4, 5, 6, 7; CSW; CWP; CWRI 5;
DA3; DAM MULT, POET; DLB 5, 41;
EXPP; MAICYA 1, 2; MTCW 1, 2;
MTFW 2005; PFS 1, 14; SATA 20, 69,
128; WP
Clinton, Dirk
See Silverberg, Robert
Clough, Arthur Hugh 1819-1861 .. **NCLC 27,
163**
See also BRW 5; DLB 32; RGEL 2
Clutha, Janet Paterson Frame 1924-2004
See Frame, Janet
See also CA 1-4R; CAAS 224; CANR 2,
36, 76, 135; MTCW 1, 2; SATA 119
Clyne, Terence
See Blatty, William Peter
Cobalt, Martin
See Mayne, William (James Carter)
Cobb, Irvin S(hrewsbury)
1876-1944 .... **TCLC 77**
See also CA 175; DLB 11, 25, 86
Cobbett, William 1763-1835 .... **NCLC 49**
See also DLB 43, 107, 158; RGEL 2
Coburn, D(onald) L(ee) 1938- .... **CLC 10**
See also CA 89-92; DFS 23
Cocteau, Jean 1889-1963 ... **CLC 1, 8, 15, 16,
43; DC 17; TCLC 119; WLC 2**
See also AAYA 74; CA 25-28; CANR 40;
CAP 2; DA; DA3; DAB; DAC; DAM
DRAM, MST, NOV; DLB 65, 258, 321;
EW 10; EWL 3; GFL 1789 to the Present;
MTCW 1, 2; RGWL 2, 3; TWA

Conrad, Robert Arnold
See Hart, Moss
Conroy, Pat 1945- .... **CLC 30, 74**
See also AAYA 8, 52; AITN 1; BPFB 1;
CA 85-88; CANR 24, 53, 129; CN 7;
CPW; CSW; DA3; DAM NOV, POP;
DLB 6; LAIT 5; MAL 5; MTCW 1, 2;
MTFW 2005
Constant (de Rebecque), (Henri) Benjamin
1767-1830 .... **NCLC 6, 182**
See also DLB 119; EW 4; GFL 1789 to the
Present
Conway, Jill K(er) 1934- .... **CLC 152**
See also CA 130; CANR 94
Conybeare, Charles Augustus
See Eliot, T(homas) S(tearns)
Cook, Michael 1933-1994 .... **CLC 58**
See also CA 93-96; CANR 68; DLB 53
Cook, Robin 1940- .... **CLC 14**
See also AAYA 32; BEST 90:2; BPFB 1;
CA 111; CAAE 108; CANR 41, 90, 109;
CPW; DA3; DAM POP; HGG; INT CA-
111
Cook, Roy
See Silverberg, Robert
Cooke, Elizabeth 1948- .... **CLC 55**
See also CA 129
Cooke, John Esten 1830-1886 .... **NCLC 5**
See also DLB 3, 248; RGAL 4
Cooke, John Estes
See Baum, L(yman) Frank
Cooke, M. E.
See Creasey, John
Cooke, Margaret
See Creasey, John
Cooke, Rose Terry 1827-1892 ...... **NCLC 110**
See also DLB 12, 74
Cook-Lynn, Elizabeth 1930- .... **CLC 93;**
NNAL
See also CA 133; DAM MULT; DLB 175
Cooney, Ray .... **CLC 62**
See also CBD
Cooper, Anthony Ashley 1671-1713 .. **LC 107**
See also DLB 101
Cooper, Dennis 1953- .... **CLC 203**
See also CA 133; CANR 72, 86; GLL 1;
HGG
Cooper, Douglas 1960- .... **CLC 86**
Cooper, Henry St. John
See Creasey, John
Cooper, J. California (?)- .... **CLC 56**
See also AAYA 12; BW 1; CA 125; CANR
55; DAM MULT; DLB 212
Cooper, James Fenimore
1789-1851 .... **NCLC 1, 27, 54**
See also AAYA 22; AMW; BPFB 1;
CDALB 1640-1865; CLR 105; DA3;
DLB 3, 183, 250, 254; LAIT 5; NFS 9;
RGAL 4; SATA 19; TUS; WCH
Cooper, Susan Fenimore
1813-1894 .... **NCLC 129**
See also ANW; DLB 239, 254
Coover, Robert 1932- .. **CLC 3, 7, 15, 32, 46,**
87, 161; SSC 15
See also AMWS 5; BPFB 1; CA 45-48;
CANR 37, 58, 115; CN 1, 2, 3, 4, 5, 6,
7; DAM NOV; DLB 2, 227; DLBY 1981;
EWL 3; MAL 5; MTCW 1, 2; MTFW
2005; RGAL 4; RGSF 2
Copeland, Stewart (Armstrong)
1952- .... **CLC 26**
Copernicus, Nicolaus 1473-1543 .... **LC 45**
Coppard, A(lfred) E(dgar)
1878-1957 .... **SSC 21; TCLC 5**
See also BRWS 8; CA 167; CAAE 114;
DLB 162; EWL 3; HGG; RGEL 2; RGSF
2; SUFW 1; YABC 1
Coppee, Francois 1842-1908 .... **TCLC 25**
See also CA 170; DLB 217

Coppola, Francis Ford 1939- ... **CLC 16, 126**
See also AAYA 39; CA 77-80; CANR 40,
78; DLB 44
Copway, George 1818-1869 .... **NNAL**
See also DAM MULT; DLB 175, 183
Corbiere, Tristan 1845-1875 .... **NCLC 43**
See also DLB 217; GFL 1789 to the Present
Corcoran, Barbara (Asenath)
1911- .... **CLC 17**
See also AAYA 14; CA 191; 21-24R, 191;
2; CANR 11, 28, 48; CLR 50; DLB 52;
JRDA; MAICYA 2; MAICYAS 1; RHW;
SAAS 20; SATA 3, 77; SATA-Essay 125
Cordelier, Maurice
See Giraudoux, Jean(-Hippolyte)
Corelli, Marie .... **TCLC 51**
See Mackay, Mary
See also DLB 34, 156; RGEL 2; SUFW 1
Corinna c. 225B.C.-c. 305B.C. ...... **CMLC 72**
Corman, Cid .... **CLC 9**
See Corman, Sidney
See also CA 2; CP 1, 2, 3, 4, 5, 6, 7; DLB
5, 193
Corman, Sidney 1924-2004
See Corman, Cid
See also CA 85-88; CAAS 225; CANR 44;
DAM POET
Cormier, Robert 1925-2000 .... **CLC 12, 30**
See also AAYA 3, 19; BYA 1, 2, 6, 8, 9;
CA 1-4R; CANR 5, 23, 76, 93; CDALB
1968-1988; CLR 12, 55; DA; DAB; DAC;
DAM MST, NOV; DLB 52; EXPN; INT
CANR-23; JRDA; LAIT 5; MAICYA 1,
2; MTCW 1, 2; MTFW 2005; NFS 2, 18;
SATA 10, 45, 83; SATA-Obit 122; WYA;
YAW
Corn, Alfred (DeWitt III) 1943- .... **CLC 33**
See also CA 179; 179; 25; CANR 44; CP 3,
4, 5, 6, 7; CSW; DLB 120, 282; DLBY
1980
Corneille, Pierre 1606-1684 .. **DC 21; LC 28,**
135
See also DAB; DAM MST; DFS 21; DLB
268; EW 3; GFL Beginnings to 1789;
RGWL 2, 3; TWA
Cornwell, David
See le Carre, John
Cornwell, Patricia 1956- .... **CLC 155**
See also AAYA 16, 56; BPFB 1; CA 134;
CANR 53, 131; CMW 4; CPW; CSW;
DAM POP; DLB 306; MSW; MTCW 2;
MTFW 2005
Cornwell, Patricia Daniels
See Cornwell, Patricia
Corso, Gregory 1930-2001 .... **CLC 1, 11; PC**
33
See also AMWS 12; BG 1:2; CA 5-8R;
CAAS 193; CANR 41, 76, 132; CP 1, 2,
3, 4, 5, 6, 7; DA3; DLB 5, 16, 237; LMFS
2; MAL 5; MTCW 1, 2; MTFW 2005; WP
Cortazar, Julio 1914-1984 ... **CLC 2, 3, 5, 10,**
13, 15, 33, 34, 92; HLC 1; SSC 7, 76
See also BPFB 1; CA 21-24R; CANR 12,
32, 81; CDWLB 3; DA3; DAM MULT,
NOV; DLB 113; EWL 3; EXPS; HW 1,
2; LAW; MTCW 1, 2; MTFW 2005;
RGSF 2; RGWL 2, 3; SSFS 3, 20; TWA;
WLIT 1
Cortes, Hernan 1485-1547 .... **LC 31**
Corvinus, Jakob
See Raabe, Wilhelm (Karl)
Corwin, Cecil
See Kornbluth, C(yril) M.
Cosic, Dobrica 1921- .... **CLC 14**
See also CA 138; CAAE 122; CDWLB 4;
CWW 2; DLB 181; EWL 3

Costain, Thomas B(ertram)
1885-1965 .... **CLC 30**
See also BYA 3; CA 5-8R; CAAS 25-28R;
DLB 9; RHW
Costantini, Humberto 1924(?)-1987 . **CLC 49**
See also CA 131; CAAS 122; EWL 3; HW
1
Costello, Elvis 1954- .... **CLC 21**
See also CA 204
Costenoble, Philostene
See Ghelderode, Michel de
Cotes, Cecil V.
See Duncan, Sara Jeannette
Cotter, Joseph Seamon Sr.
1861-1949 .... **BLC 1; TCLC 28**
See also BW 1; CA 124; DAM MULT; DLB
50
Couch, Arthur Thomas Quiller
See Quiller-Couch, Sir Arthur (Thomas)
Coulton, James
See Hansen, Joseph
Couperus, Louis (Marie Anne)
1863-1923 .... **TCLC 15**
See also CAAE 115; EWL 3; RGWL 2, 3
Coupland, Douglas 1961- .... **CLC 85, 133**
See also AAYA 34; CA 142; CANR 57, 90,
130; CCA 1; CN 7; CPW; DAC; DAM
POP
Court, Wesli
See Turco, Lewis (Putnam)
Courtenay, Bryce 1933- .... **CLC 59**
See also CA 138; CPW
Courtney, Robert
See Ellison, Harlan
Cousteau, Jacques-Yves 1910-1997 .. **CLC 30**
See also CA 65-68; CAAS 159; CANR 15,
67; MTCW 1; SATA 38, 98
Coventry, Francis 1725-1754 .... **LC 46**
Coverdale, Miles c. 1487-1569 .... **LC 77**
See also DLB 167
Cowan, Peter (Walkinshaw)
1914-2002 .... **SSC 28**
See also CA 21-24R; CANR 9, 25, 50, 83;
CN 1, 2, 3, 4, 5, 6, 7; DLB 260; RGSF 2
Coward, Noel (Peirce) 1899-1973 . **CLC 1, 9,**
29, 51
See also AITN 1; BRWS 2; CA 17-18;
CAAS 41-44R; CANR 35, 132; CAP 2;
CBD; CDBLB 1914-1945; DA3; DAM
DRAM; DFS 3, 6; DLB 10, 245; EWL 3;
IDFW 3, 4; MTCW 1, 2; MTFW 2005;
RGEL 2; TEA
Cowley, Abraham 1618-1667 .... **LC 43**
See also BRW 2; DLB 131, 151; PAB;
RGEL 2
Cowley, Malcolm 1898-1989 .... **CLC 39**
See also AMWS 2; CA 5-8R; CAAS 128;
CANR 3, 55; CP 1, 2, 3, 4; DLB 4, 48;
DLBY 1981, 1989; EWL 3; MAL 5;
MTCW 1, 2; MTFW 2005
Cowper, William 1731-1800 ..... **NCLC 8, 94;**
PC 40
See also BRW 3; DA3; DAM POET; DLB
104, 109; RGEL 2
Cox, William Trevor 1928-
See Trevor, William
See also CA 9-12R; CANR 4, 37, 55, 76,
102, 139; DAM NOV; INT CANR-37;
MTCW 1, 2; MTFW 2005; TEA
Coyne, P. J.
See Masters, Hilary
Cozzens, James Gould 1903-1978 . **CLC 1, 4,**
11, 92
See also AMW; BPFB 1; CA 9-12R; CAAS
81-84; CANR 19; CDALB 1941-1968;
CN 1, 2; DLB 9, 294; DLBD 2; DLBY
1984, 1997; EWL 3; MAL 5; MTCW 1,
2; MTFW 2005; RGAL 4

Cunha, Euclides (Rodrigues Pimenta) da
1866-1909 .... **TCLC 24**
See also CA 219; CAAE 123; DLB 307;
LAW; WLIT 1

Cunningham, E. V.
See Fast, Howard

Cunningham, J(ames) V(incent)
1911-1985 .... **CLC 3, 31**
See also CA 1-4R; CAAS 115; CANR 1,
72; CP 1, 2, 3, 4; DLB 5

Cunningham, Julia (Woolfolk)
1916- .... **CLC 12**
See also CA 9-12R; CANR 4, 19, 36; CWRI
5; JRDA; MAICYA 1, 2; SAAS 2; SATA
1, 26, 132

Cunningham, Michael 1952- .... **CLC 34**
See also AMWS 15; CA 136; CANR 96,
160; CN 7; DLB 292; GLL 2; MTFW
2005; NFS 23

Cunninghame Graham, R. B.
See Cunninghame Graham, Robert
(Gallnigad) Bontine

**Cunninghame Graham, Robert (Gallnigad)
Bontine** 1852-1936 .... **TCLC 19**
See Graham, R(obert) B(ontine) Cunning-
hame
See also CA 184; CAAE 119

Curnow, (Thomas) Allen (Monro)
1911-2001 .... **PC 48**
See also CA 69-72; CAAS 202; CANR 48,
99; CP 1, 2, 3, 4, 5, 6, 7; EWL 3; RGEL
2

Currie, Ellen 19(?)- .... **CLC 44**

Curtin, Philip
See Lowndes, Marie Adelaide (Belloc)

Curtin, Phillip
See Lowndes, Marie Adelaide (Belloc)

Curtis, Price
See Ellison, Harlan

Cusanus, Nicolaus 1401-1464 .... **LC 80**
See Nicholas of Cusa

Cutrate, Joe
See Spiegelman, Art

Cynewulf c. 770- .... **CMLC 23**
See also DLB 146; RGEL 2

Cyrano de Bergerac, Savinien de
1619-1655 .... **LC 65**
See also DLB 268; GFL Beginnings to
1789; RGWL 2, 3

Cyril of Alexandria c. 375-c. 430 . **CMLC 59**

Czaczkes, Shmuel Yosef Halevi
See Agnon, S(hmuel) Y(osef Halevi)

Dabrowska, Maria (Szumska)
1889-1965 .... **CLC 15**
See also CA 106; CDWLB 4; DLB 215;
EWL 3

Dabydeen, David 1955- .... **CLC 34**
See also BW 1; CA 125; CANR 56, 92; CN
6, 7; CP 5, 6, 7

Dacey, Philip 1939- .... **CLC 51**
See also CA 231; 37-40R, 231; 17; CANR
14, 32, 64; CP 4, 5, 6, 7; DLB 105

Dacre, Charlotte c. 1772-1825(?) . **NCLC 151**

Dafydd ap Gwilym c. 1320-c. 1380 ..... **PC 56**

Dagerman, Stig (Halvard)
1923-1954 .... **TCLC 17**
See also CA 155; CAAE 117; DLB 259;
EWL 3

D'Aguiar, Fred 1960- .... **CLC 145**
See also CA 148; CANR 83, 101; CN 7;
CP 5, 6, 7; DLB 157; EWL 3

Dahl, Roald 1916-1990 ...... **CLC 1, 6, 18, 79;
TCLC 173**
See also AAYA 15; BPFB 1; BRWS 4; BYA
5; CA 1-4R; CAAS 133; CANR 6, 32,
37, 62; CLR 1, 7, 41, 111; CN 1, 2, 3, 4;
CPW; DA3; DAB; DAC; DAM MST,

NOV, POP; DLB 139, 255; HGG; JRDA;
MAICYA 1, 2; MTCW 1, 2; MTFW 2005;
RGSF 2; SATA 1, 26, 73; SATA-Obit 65;
SSFS 4; TEA; YAW

Dahlberg, Edward 1900-1977 .. **CLC 1, 7, 14**
See also CA 9-12R; CAAS 69-72; CANR
31, 62; CN 1, 2; DLB 48; MAL 5; MTCW
1; RGAL 4

Daitch, Susan 1954- .... **CLC 103**
See also CA 161

Dale, Colin .... **TCLC 18**
See Lawrence, T(homas) E(dward)

Dale, George E.
See Asimov, Isaac

d'Alembert, Jean Le Rond
1717-1783 .... **LC 126**

Dalton, Roque 1935-1975(?) ..... **HLCS 1; PC
36**
See also CA 176; DLB 283; HW 2

Daly, Elizabeth 1878-1967 .... **CLC 52**
See also CA 23-24; CAAS 25-28R; CANR
60; CAP 2; CMW 4

Daly, Mary 1928- .... **CLC 173**
See also CA 25-28R; CANR 30, 62; FW;
GLL 1; MTCW 1

Daly, Maureen 1921-2006 .... **CLC 17**
See also AAYA 5, 58; BYA 6; CAAS 253;
CANR 37, 83, 108; CLR 96; JRDA; MAI-
CYA 1, 2; SAAS 1; SATA 2, 129; SATA-
Obit 176; WYA; YAW

Damas, Leon-Gontran 1912-1978 .... **CLC 84**
See also BW 1; CA 125; CAAS 73-76;
EWL 3

Dana, Richard Henry Sr.
1787-1879 .... **NCLC 53**

Daniel, Samuel 1562(?)-1619 .... **LC 24**
See also DLB 62; RGEL 2

Daniels, Brett
See Adler, Renata

Dannay, Frederic 1905-1982 .... **CLC 11**
See Queen, Ellery
See also CA 1-4R; CAAS 107; CANR 1,
39; CMW 4; DAM POP; DLB 137;
MTCW 1

D'Annunzio, Gabriele 1863-1938 ... **TCLC 6,
40**
See also CA 155; CAAE 104; EW 8; EWL
3; RGWL 2, 3; TWA; WLIT 7

Danois, N. le
See Gourmont, Remy(-Marie-Charles) de

Dante 1265-1321 .... **CMLC 3, 18, 39, 70; PC
21; WLCS**
See Alighieri, Dante
See also DA; DA3; DAB; DAC; DAM
MST, POET; EFS 1; EW 1; LAIT 1;
RGWL 2, 3; TWA; WP

d'Antibes, Germain
See Simenon, Georges (Jacques Christian)

Danticat, Edwidge 1969- ... **CLC 94, 139, 228**
See also AAYA 29; CA 192; 152, 192;
CANR 73, 129; CN 7; DNFS 1; EXPS;
LATS 1:2; MTCW 2; MTFW 2005; SSFS
1; YAW

Danvers, Dennis 1947- .... **CLC 70**

Danziger, Paula 1944-2004 .... **CLC 21**
See also AAYA 4, 36; BYA 6, 7, 14; CA
115; CAAE 112; CAAS 229; CANR 37,
132; CLR 20; JRDA; MAICYA 1, 2;
MTFW 2005; SATA 36, 63, 102, 149;
SATA-Brief 30; SATA-Obit 155; WYA;
YAW

Da Ponte, Lorenzo 1749-1838 .... **NCLC 50**

d'Aragona, Tullia 1510(?)-1556 .... **LC 121**

Dario, Ruben 1867-1916 .... **HLC 1; PC 15;
TCLC 4**
See also CA 131; CANR 81; DAM MULT;
DLB 290; EWL 3; HW 1, 2; LAW;
MTCW 1, 2; MTFW 2005; RGWL 2, 3

Darley, George 1795-1846 .... **NCLC 2**
See also DLB 96; RGEL 2

Darrow, Clarence (Seward)
1857-1938 .... **TCLC 81**
See also CA 164; DLB 303

Darwin, Charles 1809-1882 .... **NCLC 57**
See also BRWS 7; DLB 57, 166; LATS 1:1;
RGEL 2; TEA; WLIT 4

Darwin, Erasmus 1731-1802 .... **NCLC 106**
See also DLB 93; RGEL 2

Daryush, Elizabeth 1887-1977 ...... **CLC 6, 19**
See also CA 49-52; CANR 3, 81; DLB 20

Das, Kamala 1934- .... **CLC 191; PC 43**
See also CA 101; CANR 27, 59; CP 1, 2, 3,
4, 5, 6, 7; CWP; DLB 323; FW

Dasgupta, Surendranath
1887-1952 .... **TCLC 81**
See also CA 157

**Dashwood, Edmee Elizabeth Monica de la
Pasture** 1890-1943
See Delafield, E. M.
See also CA 154; CAAE 119

da Silva, Antonio Jose
1705-1739 .... **NCLC 114**

Daudet, (Louis Marie) Alphonse
1840-1897 .... **NCLC 1**
See also DLB 123; GFL 1789 to the Present;
RGSF 2

Daudet, Alphonse Marie Leon
1867-1942 .... **SSC 94**
See also CA 217

d'Aulnoy, Marie-Catherine c.
1650-1705 .... **LC 100**

Daumal, Rene 1908-1944 .... **TCLC 14**
See also CA 247; CAAE 114; EWL 3

Davenant, William 1606-1668 .... **LC 13**
See also DLB 58, 126; RGEL 2

Davenport, Guy (Mattison, Jr.)
1927-2005 .... **CLC 6, 14, 38; SSC 16**
See also CA 33-36R; CAAS 235; CANR
23, 73; CN 3, 4, 5, 6; CSW; DLB 130

David, Robert
See Nezval, Vitezslav

Davidson, Avram (James) 1923-1993
See Queen, Ellery
See also CA 101; CAAS 171; CANR 26;
DLB 8; FANT; SFW 4; SUFW 1, 2

Davidson, Donald (Grady)
1893-1968 .... **CLC 2, 13, 19**
See also CA 5-8R; CAAS 25-28R; CANR
4, 84; DLB 45

Davidson, Hugh
See Hamilton, Edmond

Davidson, John 1857-1909 .... **TCLC 24**
See also CA 217; CAAE 118; DLB 19;
RGEL 2

Davidson, Sara 1943- .... **CLC 9**
See also CA 81-84; CANR 44, 68; DLB
185

Davie, Donald (Alfred) 1922-1995 .... **CLC 5,
8, 10, 31; PC 29**
See also BRWS 6; CA 1-4R; 3; CAAS 149;
CANR 1, 44; CP 1, 2, 3, 4, 5, 6; DLB 27;
MTCW 1; RGEL 2

Davie, Elspeth 1918-1995 .... **SSC 52**
See also CA 126; CAAE 120; CAAS 150;
CANR 141; DLB 139

Davies, Ray(mond Douglas) 1944- ... **CLC 21**
See also CA 146; CAAE 116; CANR 92

Davies, Rhys 1901-1978 .... **CLC 23**
See also CA 9-12R; CAAS 81-84; CANR
4; CN 1, 2; DLB 139, 191

Davies, Robertson 1913-1995 .. **CLC 2, 7, 13,
25, 42, 75, 91; WLC 2**
See Marchbanks, Samuel
See also BEST 89:2; BPFB 1; CA 33-36R;
CAAS 150; CANR 17, 42, 103; CN 1, 2,
3, 4, 5, 6; CPW; DA; DA3; DAB; DAC;

De Lisser, H(erbert) G(eorge)
1878-1944 .... **TCLC 12**
See de Lisser, H. G.
See also BW 2; CA 152; CAAE 109
Deloire, Pierre
See Peguy, Charles (Pierre)
Deloney, Thomas 1543(?)-1600 .... **LC 41**
See also DLB 167; RGEL 2
Deloria, Ella (Cara) 1889-1971(?) ..... **NNAL**
See also CA 152; DAM MULT; DLB 175
Deloria, Vine, Jr. 1933-2005 .... **CLC 21, 122;**
NNAL
See also CA 53-56; CAAS 245; CANR 5,
20, 48, 98; DAM MULT; DLB 175;
MTCW 1; SATA 21; SATA-Obit 171
Deloria, Vine Victor, Jr.
See Deloria, Vine, Jr.
del Valle-Inclan, Ramon (Maria)
See Valle-Inclan, Ramon (Maria) del
See also DLB 322
Del Vecchio, John M(ichael) 1947- .. **CLC 29**
See also CA 110; DLBD 9
de Man, Paul (Adolph Michel)
1919-1983 .... **CLC 55**
See also CA 128; CAAS 111; CANR 61;
DLB 67; MTCW 1, 2
DeMarinis, Rick 1934- .... **CLC 54**
See also CA 184; 57-60, 184; CANR 9,
25, 50, 160; DLB 218; TCWW 2
de Maupassant, (Henri Rene Albert) Guy
See Maupassant, (Henri Rene Albert) Guy
de
Dembry, R. Emmet
See Murfree, Mary Noailles
Demby, William 1922- .... **BLC 1; CLC 53**
See also BW 1, 3; CA 81-84; CANR 81;
DAM MULT; DLB 33
de Menton, Francisco
See Chin, Frank (Chew, Jr.)
Demetrius of Phalerum c.
307B.C.- .... **CMLC 34**
Demijohn, Thom
See Disch, Thomas M.
De Mille, James 1833-1880 .... **NCLC 123**
See also DLB 99, 251
Deming, Richard 1915-1983
See Queen, Ellery
See also CA 9-12R; CANR 3, 94; SATA 24
Democritus c. 460B.C.-c. 370B.C. . **CMLC 47**
de Montaigne, Michel (Eyquem)
See Montaigne, Michel (Eyquem) de
de Montherlant, Henry (Milon)
See Montherlant, Henry (Milon) de
Demosthenes 384B.C.-322B.C. ...... **CMLC 13**
See also AW 1; DLB 176; RGWL 2, 3;
WLIT 8
de Musset, (Louis Charles) Alfred
See Musset, Alfred de
de Natale, Francine
See Malzberg, Barry N(athaniel)
de Navarre, Marguerite 1492-1549 ... **LC 61;**
SSC 85
See Marguerite d'Angouleme; Marguerite
de Navarre
See also DLB 327
Denby, Edwin (Orr) 1903-1983 .... **CLC 48**
See also CA 138; CAAS 110; CP 1
de Nerval, Gerard
See Nerval, Gerard de
Denham, John 1615-1669 .... **LC 73**
See also DLB 58, 126; RGEL 2
Denis, Julio
See Cortazar, Julio
Denmark, Harrison
See Zelazny, Roger
Dennis, John 1658-1734 .... **LC 11**
See also DLB 101; RGEL 2

Dennis, Nigel (Forbes) 1912-1989 ...... **CLC 8**
See also CA 25-28R; CAAS 129; CN 1, 2,
3, 4; DLB 13, 15, 233; EWL 3; MTCW 1
Dent, Lester 1904-1959 .... **TCLC 72**
See also CA 161; CAAE 112; CMW 4;
DLB 306; SFW 4
De Palma, Brian 1940- .... **CLC 20**
See also CA 109
De Palma, Brian Russell
See De Palma, Brian
d'Epinay, Louise
See Epinay, Louise d'
See also DLB 313
de Pizan, Christine
See Christine de Pizan
See also FL 1:1
De Quincey, Thomas 1785-1859 ..... **NCLC 4,**
87
See also BRW 4; CDBLB 1789-1832; DLB
110, 144; RGEL 2
Deren, Eleanora 1908(?)-1961
See Deren, Maya
See also CA 192; CAAS 111
Deren, Maya .... **CLC 16, 102**
See Deren, Eleanora
Derleth, August (William)
1909-1971 .... **CLC 31**
See also BPFB 1; BYA 9, 10; CA 1-4R;
CAAS 29-32R; CANR 4; CMW 4; CN 1;
DLB 9; DLBD 17; HGG; SATA 5; SUFW
1
Der Nister 1884-1950 .... **TCLC 56**
See Nister, Der
de Routisie, Albert
See Aragon, Louis
Derrida, Jacques 1930-2004 ...... **CLC 24, 87,**
225
See also CA 127; CAAE 124; CAAS 232;
CANR 76, 98, 133; DLB 242; EWL 3;
LMFS 2; MTCW 2; TWA
Derry Down Derry
See Lear, Edward
Dersonnes, Jacques
See Simenon, Georges (Jacques Christian)
Der Stricker c. 1190-c. 1250 .... **CMLC 75**
See also DLB 138
Desai, Anita 1937- .... **CLC 19, 37, 97, 175**
See also BRWS 5; CA 81-84; CANR 33,
53, 95, 133; CN 1, 2, 3, 4, 5, 6, 7; CWRI
5; DA3; DAB; DAM NOV; DLB 271,
323; DNFS 2; EWL 3; FW; MTCW 1, 2;
MTFW 2005; SATA 63, 126
Desai, Kiran 1971- .... **CLC 119**
See also BYA 16; CA 171; CANR 127
de Saint-Luc, Jean
See Glassco, John
de Saint Roman, Arnaud
See Aragon, Louis
Desbordes-Valmore, Marceline
1786-1859 .... **NCLC 97**
See also DLB 217
Descartes, Rene 1596-1650 .... **LC 20, 35**
See also DLB 268; EW 3; GFL Beginnings
to 1789
Deschamps, Eustache 1340(?)-1404 .. **LC 103**
See also DLB 208
De Sica, Vittorio 1901(?)-1974 .... **CLC 20**
See also CAAS 117
Desnos, Robert 1900-1945 .... **TCLC 22**
See also CA 151; CAAE 121; CANR 107;
DLB 258; EWL 3; LMFS 2
Destouches, Louis-Ferdinand
1894-1961 .... **CLC 9, 15**
See Celine, Louis-Ferdinand
See also CA 85-88; CANR 28; MTCW 1
de Tolignac, Gaston
See Griffith, D(avid Lewelyn) W(ark)

Deutsch, Babette 1895-1982 .... **CLC 18**
See also BYA 3; CA 1-4R; CAAS 108;
CANR 4, 79; CP 1, 2, 3; DLB 45; SATA
1; SATA-Obit 33
Devenant, William 1606-1649 .... **LC 13**
Devkota, Laxmiprasad 1909-1959 . **TCLC 23**
See also CAAE 123
De Voto, Bernard (Augustine)
1897-1955 .... **TCLC 29**
See also CA 160; CAAE 113; DLB 9, 256;
MAL 5; TCWW 1, 2
De Vries, Peter 1910-1993 ..... **CLC 1, 2, 3, 7,**
10, 28, 46
See also CA 17-20R; CAAS 142; CANR
41; CN 1, 2, 3, 4, 5; DAM NOV; DLB 6;
DLBY 1982; MAL 5; MTCW 1, 2;
MTFW 2005
Dewey, John 1859-1952 .... **TCLC 95**
See also CA 170; CAAE 114; CANR 144;
DLB 246, 270; RGAL 4
Dexter, John
See Bradley, Marion Zimmer
See also GLL 1
Dexter, Martin
See Faust, Frederick (Schiller)
Dexter, Pete 1943- .... **CLC 34, 55**
See also BEST 89:2; CA 131; CAAE 127;
CANR 129; CPW; DAM POP; INT CA-
131; MAL 5; MTCW 1; MTFW 2005
Diamano, Silmang
See Senghor, Leopold Sedar
Diamond, Neil 1941- .... **CLC 30**
See also CA 108
Diaz del Castillo, Bernal c.
1496-1584 .... **HLCS 1; LC 31**
See also DLB 318; LAW
di Bassetto, Corno
See Shaw, George Bernard
Dick, Philip K. 1928-1982 ... **CLC 10, 30, 72;**
SSC 57
See also AAYA 24; BPFB 1; BYA 11; CA
49-52; CAAS 106; CANR 2, 16, 132; CN
2, 3; CPW; DA3; DAM NOV, POP; DLB
8; MTCW 1, 2; MTFW 2005; NFS 5;
SCFW 1, 2; SFW 4
Dick, Philip Kindred
See Dick, Philip K.
Dickens, Charles (John Huffam)
1812-1870 .... **NCLC 3, 8, 18, 26, 37, 50,**
86, 105, 113, 161; SSC 17, 49, 88; WLC
2
See also AAYA 23; BRW 5; BRWC 1, 2;
BYA 1, 2, 3, 13, 14; CDBLB 1832-1890;
CLR 95; CMW 4; DA; DA3; DAB; DAC;
DAM MST, NOV; DLB 21, 55, 70, 159,
166; EXPN; GL 2; HGG; JRDA; LAIT 1,
2; LATS 1:1; LMFS 1; MAICYA 1, 2;
NFS 4, 5, 10, 14, 20; RGEL 2; RGSF 2;
SATA 15; SUFW 1; TEA; WCH; WLIT
4; WYA
Dickey, James (Lafayette)
1923-1997 .... **CLC 1, 2, 4, 7, 10, 15, 47,**
109; PC 40; TCLC 151
See also AAYA 50; AITN 1, 2; AMWS 4;
BPFB 1; CA 9-12R; CAAS 156; CABS
2; CANR 10, 48, 61, 105; CDALB 1968-
1988; CP 1, 2, 3, 4, 5, 6; CPW; CSW;
DA3; DAM NOV, POET, POP; DLB 5,
193; DLBD 7; DLBY 1982, 1993, 1996,
1997, 1998; EWL 3; INT CANR-10;
MAL 5; MTCW 1, 2; NFS 9; PFS 6, 11;
RGAL 4; TUS
Dickey, William 1928-1994 .... **CLC 3, 28**
See also CA 9-12R; CAAS 145; CANR 24,
79; CP 1, 2, 3, 4; DLB 5
Dickinson, Charles 1951- .... **CLC 49**
See also CA 128; CANR 141

Dickinson, Emily (Elizabeth)
1830-1886 ..... **NCLC 21, 77, 171; PC 1; WLC 2**
See also AAYA 22; AMW; AMWR 1; CDALB 1865-1917; DA; DA3; DAB; DAC; DAM MST, POET; DLB 1, 243; EXPP; FL 1:3; MBL; PAB; PFS 1, 2, 3, 4, 5, 6, 8, 10, 11, 13, 16; RGAL 4; SATA 29; TUS; WP; WYA

Dickinson, Mrs. Herbert Ward
See Phelps, Elizabeth Stuart

Dickinson, Peter (Malcolm de Brissac)
1927- .... **CLC 12, 35**
See also AAYA 9, 49; BYA 5; CA 41-44R; CANR 31, 58, 88, 134; CLR 29; CMW 4; DLB 87, 161, 276; JRDA; MAICYA 1, 2; SATA 5, 62, 95, 150; SFW 4; WYA; YAW

Dickson, Carr
See Carr, John Dickson

Dickson, Carter
See Carr, John Dickson

Diderot, Denis 1713-1784 .... **LC 26, 126**
See also DLB 313; EW 4; GFL Beginnings to 1789; LMFS 1; RGWL 2, 3

Didion, Joan 1934- . **CLC 1, 3, 8, 14, 32, 129**
See also AITN 1; AMWS 4; CA 5-8R; CANR 14, 52, 76, 125; CDALB 1968-1988; CN 2, 3, 4, 5, 6, 7; DA3; DAM NOV; DLB 2, 173, 185; DLBY 1981, 1986; EWL 3; MAL 5; MBL; MTCW 1, 2; MTFW 2005; NFS 3; RGAL 4; TCLE 1:1; TCWW 2; TUS

di Donato, Pietro 1911-1992 .... **TCLC 159**
See also CA 101; CAAS 136; DLB 9

Dietrich, Robert
See Hunt, E. Howard

Difusa, Pati
See Almodovar, Pedro

Dillard, Annie 1945- ...... **CLC 9, 60, 115, 216**
See also AAYA 6, 43; AMWS 6; ANW; CA 49-52; CANR 3, 43, 62, 90, 125; DA3; DAM NOV; DLB 275, 278; DLBY 1980; LAIT 4, 5; MAL 5; MTCW 1, 2; MTFW 2005; NCFS 1; RGAL 4; SATA 10, 140; TCLE 1:1; TUS

Dillard, R(ichard) H(enry) W(ilde)
1937- .... **CLC 5**
See also CA 21-24R; 7; CANR 10; CP 2, 3, 4, 5, 6, 7; CSW; DLB 5, 244

Dillon, Eilis 1920-1994 .... **CLC 17**
See also CA 182; 9-12R, 182; 3; CAAS 147; CANR 4, 38, 78; CLR 26; MAICYA 1, 2; MAICYAS 1; SATA 2, 74; SATA-Essay 105; SATA-Obit 83; YAW

Dimont, Penelope
See Mortimer, Penelope (Ruth)

Dinesen, Isak ..... **CLC 10, 29, 95; SSC 7, 75**
See Blixen, Karen (Christentze Dinesen)
See also EW 10; EWL 3; EXPS; FW; GL 2; HGG; LAIT 3; MTCW 1; NCFS 2; NFS 9; RGSF 2; RGWL 2, 3; SSFS 3, 6, 13; WLIT 2

Ding Ling .... **CLC 68**
See Chiang, Pin-chin
See also DLB 328; RGWL 3

Diodorus Siculus c. 90B.C.-c.
31B.C. .... **CMLC 88**

Diphusa, Patty
See Almodovar, Pedro

Disch, Thomas M. 1940- .... **CLC 7, 36**
See Disch, Tom
See also AAYA 17; BPFB 1; CA 21-24R; 4; CANR 17, 36, 54, 89; CLR 18; CP 5, 6, 7; DA3; DLB 8; HGG; MAICYA 1, 2; MTCW 1, 2; MTFW 2005; SAAS 15; SATA 92; SCFW 1, 2; SFW 4; SUFW 2

Disch, Tom
See Disch, Thomas M.
See also DLB 282

d'Isly, Georges
See Simenon, Georges (Jacques Christian)

Disraeli, Benjamin 1804-1881 ... **NCLC 2, 39, 79**
See also BRW 4; DLB 21, 55; RGEL 2

Ditcum, Steve
See Crumb, R.

Dixon, Paige
See Corcoran, Barbara (Asenath)

Dixon, Stephen 1936- .... **CLC 52; SSC 16**
See also AMWS 12; CA 89-92; CANR 17, 40, 54, 91; CN 4, 5, 6, 7; DLB 130; MAL 5

Dixon, Thomas, Jr. 1864-1946 ..... **TCLC 163**
See also RHW

Djebar, Assia 1936- .... **CLC 182**
See also CA 188; EWL 3; RGWL 3; WLIT 2

Doak, Annie
See Dillard, Annie

Dobell, Sydney Thompson
1824-1874 .... **NCLC 43**
See also DLB 32; RGEL 2

Doblin, Alfred .... **TCLC 13**
See Doeblin, Alfred
See also CDWLB 2; EWL 3; RGWL 2, 3

Dobroliubov, Nikolai Aleksandrovich
See Dobrolyubov, Nikolai Alexandrovich
See also DLB 277

Dobrolyubov, Nikolai Alexandrovich
1836-1861 .... **NCLC 5**
See Dobroliubov, Nikolai Aleksandrovich

Dobson, Austin 1840-1921 .... **TCLC 79**
See also DLB 35, 144

Dobyns, Stephen 1941- .... **CLC 37, 233**
See also AMWS 13; CA 45-48; CANR 2, 18, 99; CMW 4; CP 4, 5, 6, 7; PFS 23

Doctorow, Edgar Laurence
See Doctorow, E.L.

Doctorow, E.L. 1931- . **CLC 6, 11, 15, 18, 37, 44, 65, 113, 214**
See also AAYA 22; AITN 2; AMWS 4; BEST 89:3; BPFB 1; CA 45-48; CANR 2, 33, 51, 76, 97, 133; CDALB 1968-1988; CN 3, 4, 5, 6, 7; CPW; DA3; DAM NOV, POP; DLB 2, 28, 173; DLBY 1980; EWL 3; LAIT 3; MAL 5; MTCW 1, 2; MTFW 2005; NFS 6; RGAL 4; RGHL; RHW; TCLE 1:1; TCWW 1, 2; TUS

Dodgson, Charles L(utwidge) 1832-1898
See Carroll, Lewis
See also CLR 2; DA; DA3; DAB; DAC; DAM MST, NOV, POET; MAICYA 1, 2; SATA 100; YABC 2

Dodsley, Robert 1703-1764 .... **LC 97**
See also DLB 95; RGEL 2

Dodson, Owen (Vincent) 1914-1983 .. **BLC 1; CLC 79**
See also BW 1; CA 65-68; CAAS 110; CANR 24; DAM MULT; DLB 76

Doeblin, Alfred 1878-1957 .... **TCLC 13**
See Doblin, Alfred
See also CA 141; CAAE 110; DLB 66

Doerr, Harriet 1910-2002 .... **CLC 34**
See also CA 122; CAAE 117; CAAS 213; CANR 47; INT CA-122; LATS 1:2

Domecq, H(onorio Bustos)
See Bioy Casares, Adolfo

Domecq, H(onorio) Bustos
See Bioy Casares, Adolfo; Borges, Jorge Luis

Domini, Rey
See Lorde, Audre
See also GLL 1

Dominique
See Proust, (Valentin-Louis-George-Eugene) Marcel

Don, A
See Stephen, Sir Leslie

Donaldson, Stephen R(eeder)
1947- .... **CLC 46, 138**
See also AAYA 36; BPFB 1; CA 89-92; CANR 13, 55, 99; CPW; DAM POP; FANT; INT CANR-13; SATA 121; SFW 4; SUFW 1, 2

Donleavy, J(ames) P(atrick) 1926- .... **CLC 1, 4, 6, 10, 45**
See also AITN 2; BPFB 1; CA 9-12R; CANR 24, 49, 62, 80, 124; CBD; CD 5, 6; CN 1, 2, 3, 4, 5, 6, 7; DLB 6, 173; INT CANR-24; MAL 5; MTCW 1, 2; MTFW 2005; RGAL 4

Donnadieu, Marguerite
See Duras, Marguerite

Donne, John 1572-1631 ... **LC 10, 24, 91; PC 1, 43; WLC 2**
See also AAYA 67; BRW 1; BRWC 1; BRWR 2; CDBLB Before 1660; DA; DAB; DAC; DAM MST, POET; DLB 121, 151; EXPP; PAB; PFS 2, 11; RGEL 3; TEA; WLIT 3; WP

Donnell, David 1939(?)- .... **CLC 34**
See also CA 197

Donoghue, Denis 1928- .... **CLC 209**
See also CA 17-20R; CANR 16, 102

Donoghue, P. S.
See Hunt, E. Howard

Donoso (Yanez), Jose 1924-1996 ... **CLC 4, 8, 11, 32, 99; HLC 1; SSC 34; TCLC 133**
See also CA 81-84; CAAS 155; CANR 32, 73; CDWLB 3; CWW 2; DAM MULT; DLB 113; EWL 3; HW 1, 2; LAW; LAWS 1; MTCW 1, 2; MTFW 2005; RGSF 2; WLIT 1

Donovan, John 1928-1992 .... **CLC 35**
See also AAYA 20; CA 97-100; CAAS 137; CLR 3; MAICYA 1, 2; SATA 72; SATA-Brief 29; YAW

Don Roberto
See Cunninghame Graham, Robert (Gallnigad) Bontine

Doolittle, Hilda 1886-1961 . **CLC 3, 8, 14, 31, 34, 73; PC 5; WLC 3**
See H. D.
See also AAYA 66; AMWS 1; CA 97-100; CANR 35, 131; DA; DAC; DAM MST, POET; DLB 4, 45; EWL 3; FW; GLL 1; LMFS 2; MAL 5; MBL; MTCW 1, 2; MTFW 2005; PFS 6; RGAL 4

Doppo, Kunikida .... **TCLC 99**
See Kunikida Doppo

Dorfman, Ariel 1942- .... **CLC 48, 77, 189; HLC 1**
See also CA 130; CAAE 124; CANR 67, 70, 135; CWW 2; DAM MULT; DFS 4; EWL 3; HW 1, 2; INT CA-130; WLIT 1

Dorn, Edward (Merton)
1929-1999 .... **CLC 10, 18**
See also CA 93-96; CAAS 187; CANR 42, 79; CP 1, 2, 3, 4, 5, 6, 7; DLB 5; INT CA-93-96; WP

Dor-Ner, Zvi .... **CLC 70**

Dorris, Michael 1945-1997 .... **CLC 109; NNAL**
See also AAYA 20; BEST 90:1; BYA 12; CA 102; CAAS 157; CANR 19, 46, 75; CLR 58; DA3; DAM MULT, NOV; DLB 175; LAIT 5; MTCW 2; MTFW 2005; NFS 3; RGAL 4; SATA 75; SATA-Obit 94; TCWW 2; YAW

Dorris, Michael A.
See Dorris, Michael

Dorsan, Luc
See Simenon, Georges (Jacques Christian)

Dorsange, Jean
See Simenon, Georges (Jacques Christian)

Dorset
See Sackville, Thomas

Dos Passos, John (Roderigo)
1896-1970 ... **CLC 1, 4, 8, 11, 15, 25, 34, 82; WLC 2**
See also AMW; BPFB 1; CA 1-4R; CAAS 29-32R; CANR 3; CDALB 1929-1941; DA; DA3; DAB; DAC; DAM MST, NOV; DLB 4, 9, 274, 316; DLBD 1, 15; DLBY 1996; EWL 3; MAL 5; MTCW 1, 2; MTFW 2005; NFS 14; RGAL 4; TUS

Dossage, Jean
See Simenon, Georges (Jacques Christian)

Dostoevsky, Fedor Mikhailovich
1821-1881 .. **NCLC 2, 7, 21, 33, 43, 119, 167; SSC 2, 33, 44; WLC 2**
See Dostoevsky, Fyodor
See also AAYA 40; DA; DA3; DAB; DAC; DAM MST, NOV; EW 7; EXPN; NFS 3, 8; RGSF 2; RGWL 2, 3; SSFS 8; TWA

Dostoevsky, Fyodor
See Dostoevsky, Fedor Mikhailovich
See also DLB 238; LATS 1:1; LMFS 1, 2

Doty, M. R.
See Doty, Mark

Doty, Mark 1953(?)- .... **CLC 176; PC 53**
See also AMWS 11; CA 183; 161, 183; CANR 110; CP 7

Doty, Mark A.
See Doty, Mark

Doty, Mark Alan
See Doty, Mark

Doughty, Charles M(ontagu)
1843-1926 .... **TCLC 27**
See also CA 178; CAAE 115; DLB 19, 57, 174

Douglas, Ellen .... **CLC 73**
See Haxton, Josephine Ayres; Williamson, Ellen Douglas
See also CN 5, 6, 7; CSW; DLB 292

Douglas, Gavin 1475(?)-1522 .... **LC 20**
See also DLB 132; RGEL 2

Douglas, George
See Brown, George Douglas
See also RGEL 2

Douglas, Keith (Castellain)
1920-1944 .... **TCLC 40**
See also BRW 7; CA 160; DLB 27; EWL 3; PAB; RGEL 2

Douglas, Leonard
See Bradbury, Ray

Douglas, Michael
See Crichton, Michael

Douglas, (George) Norman
1868-1952 .... **TCLC 68**
See also BRW 6; CA 157; CAAE 119; DLB 34, 195; RGEL 2

Douglas, William
See Brown, George Douglas

Douglass, Frederick 1817(?)-1895 ..... **BLC 1; NCLC 7, 55, 141; WLC 2**
See also AAYA 48; AFAW 1, 2; AMWC 1; AMWS 3; CDALB 1640-1865; DA; DA3; DAC; DAM MST, MULT; DLB 1, 43, 50, 79, 243; FW; LAIT 2; NCFS 2; RGAL 4; SATA 29

Dourado, (Waldomiro Freitas) Autran
1926- .... **CLC 23, 60**
See also CA 25-28R; 179; CANR 34, 81; DLB 145, 307; HW 2

Dourado, Waldomiro Freitas Autran
See Dourado, (Waldomiro Freitas) Autran

Dove, Rita 1952- .. **BLCS; CLC 50, 81; PC 6**
See also AAYA 46; AMWS 4; BW 2; CA 109; 19; CANR 27, 42, 68, 76, 97, 132; CDALBS; CP 5, 6, 7; CSW; CWP; DA3; DAM MULT, POET; DLB 120; EWL 3; EXPP; MAL 5; MTCW 2; MTFW 2005; PFS 1, 15; RGAL 4

Dove, Rita Frances
See Dove, Rita

Doveglion
See Villa, Jose Garcia

Dowell, Coleman 1925-1985 .... **CLC 60**
See also CA 25-28R; CAAS 117; CANR 10; DLB 130; GLL 2

Dowson, Ernest (Christopher)
1867-1900 .... **TCLC 4**
See also CA 150; CAAE 105; DLB 19, 135; RGEL 2

Doyle, A. Conan
See Doyle, Sir Arthur Conan

Doyle, Sir Arthur Conan
1859-1930 ..... **SSC 12, 83, 95; TCLC 7; WLC 2**
See Conan Doyle, Arthur
See also AAYA 14; BRWS 2; CA 122; CAAE 104; CANR 131; CDBLB 1890-1914; CLR 106; CMW 4; DA; DA3; DAB; DAC; DAM MST, NOV; DLB 18, 70, 156, 178; EXPS; HGG; LAIT 2; MSW; MTCW 1, 2; MTFW 2005; RGEL 2; RGSF 2; RHW; SATA 24; SCFW 1, 2; SFW 4; SSFS 2; TEA; WCH; WLIT 4; WYA; YAW

Doyle, Conan
See Doyle, Sir Arthur Conan

Doyle, John
See Graves, Robert

Doyle, Roddy 1958- .... **CLC 81, 178**
See also AAYA 14; BRWS 5; CA 143; CANR 73, 128; CN 6, 7; DA3; DLB 194, 326; MTCW 2; MTFW 2005

Doyle, Sir A. Conan
See Doyle, Sir Arthur Conan

Dr. A
See Asimov, Isaac; Silverstein, Alvin; Silverstein, Virginia B(arbara Opshelor)

Drabble, Margaret 1939- ...... **CLC 2, 3, 5, 8, 10, 22, 53, 129**
See also BRWS 4; CA 13-16R; CANR 18, 35, 63, 112, 131; CDBLB 1960 to Present; CN 1, 2, 3, 4, 5, 6, 7; CPW; DA3; DAB; DAC; DAM MST, NOV, POP; DLB 14, 155, 231; EWL 3; FW; MTCW 1, 2; MTFW 2005; RGEL 2; SATA 48; TEA

Drakulic, Slavenka 1949- .... **CLC 173**
See also CA 144; CANR 92

Drakulic-Ilic, Slavenka
See Drakulic, Slavenka

Drapier, M. B.
See Swift, Jonathan

Drayham, James
See Mencken, H(enry) L(ouis)

Drayton, Michael 1563-1631 .... **LC 8**
See also DAM POET; DLB 121; RGEL 2

Dreadstone, Carl
See Campbell, (John) Ramsey

Dreiser, Theodore 1871-1945 .... **SSC 30; TCLC 10, 18, 35, 83; WLC 2**
See also AMW; AMWC 2; AMWR 2; BYA 15, 16; CA 132; CAAE 106; CDALB 1865-1917; DA; DA3; DAC; DAM MST, NOV; DLB 9, 12, 102, 137; DLBD 1; EWL 3; LAIT 2; LMFS 2; MAL 5; MTCW 1, 2; MTFW 2005; NFS 8, 17; RGAL 4; TUS

Dreiser, Theodore Herman Albert
See Dreiser, Theodore

Drexler, Rosalyn 1926- .... **CLC 2, 6**
See also CA 81-84; CAD; CANR 68, 124; CD 5, 6; CWD; MAL 5

Dreyer, Carl Theodor 1889-1968 ...... **CLC 16**
See also CAAS 116

Drieu la Rochelle, Pierre
1893-1945 .... **TCLC 21**
See also CA 250; CAAE 117; DLB 72; EWL 3; GFL 1789 to the Present

Drieu la Rochelle, Pierre-Eugene 1893-1945
See Drieu la Rochelle, Pierre

Drinkwater, John 1882-1937 .... **TCLC 57**
See also CA 149; CAAE 109; DLB 10, 19, 149; RGEL 2

Drop Shot
See Cable, George Washington

Droste-Hulshoff, Annette Freiin von
1797-1848 .... **NCLC 3, 133**
See also CDWLB 2; DLB 133; RGSF 2; RGWL 2, 3

Drummond, Walter
See Silverberg, Robert

Drummond, William Henry
1854-1907 .... **TCLC 25**
See also CA 160; DLB 92

Drummond de Andrade, Carlos
1902-1987 .... **CLC 18; TCLC 139**
See Andrade, Carlos Drummond de
See also CA 132; CAAS 123; DLB 307; LAW

Drummond of Hawthornden, William
1585-1649 .... **LC 83**
See also DLB 121, 213; RGEL 2

Drury, Allen (Stuart) 1918-1998 .... **CLC 37**
See also CA 57-60; CAAS 170; CANR 18, 52; CN 1, 2, 3, 4, 5, 6; INT CANR-18

Druse, Eleanor
See King, Stephen

Dryden, John 1631-1700 ..... **DC 3; LC 3, 21, 115; PC 25; WLC 2**
See also BRW 2; CDBLB 1660-1789; DA; DAB; DAC; DAM DRAM, MST, POET; DLB 80, 101, 131; EXPP; IDTP; LMFS 1; RGEL 2; TEA; WLIT 3

du Bellay, Joachim 1524-1560 .... **LC 92**
See also DLB 327; GFL Beginnings to 1789; RGWL 2, 3

Duberman, Martin (Bauml) 1930- ... **CLC 8**
See also CA 1-4R; CAD; CANR 2, 63, 137; CD 5, 6

Dubie, Norman (Evans) 1945- .... **CLC 36**
See also CA 69-72; CANR 12, 115; CP 3, 4, 5, 6, 7; DLB 120; PFS 12

Du Bois, W(illiam) E(dward) B(urghardt)
1868-1963 ..... **BLC 1; CLC 1, 2, 13, 64, 96; HR 1:2; TCLC 169; WLC 2**
See also AAYA 40; AFAW 1, 2; AMWC 1; AMWS 2; BW 1, 3; CA 85-88; CANR 34, 82, 132; CDALB 1865-1917; DA; DA3; DAC; DAM MST, MULT, NOV; DLB 47, 50, 91, 246, 284; EWL 3; EXPP; LAIT 2; LMFS 2; MAL 5; MTCW 1, 2; MTFW 2005; NCFS 1; PFS 13; RGAL 4; SATA 42

Dubus, Andre 1936-1999 ..... **CLC 13, 36, 97; SSC 15**
See also AMWS 7; CA 21-24R; CAAS 177; CANR 17; CN 5, 6; CSW; DLB 130; INT CANR-17; RGAL 4; SSFS 10; TCLE 1:1

Duca Minimo
See D'Annunzio, Gabriele

Ducharme, Rejean 1941- .... **CLC 74**
See also CAAS 165; DLB 60

du Chatelet, Emilie 1706-1749 .... **LC 96**
See Chatelet, Gabrielle-Emilie Du

Duchen, Claire .... **CLC 65**

Duclos, Charles Pinot- 1704-1772 .... **LC 1**
See also GFL Beginnings to 1789

Ducornet, Erica 1943-
See Ducornet, Rikki
See also CA 37-40R; CANR 14, 34, 54, 82; SATA 7

Ducornet, Rikki .... **CLC 232**
See Ducornet, Erica

Dudek, Louis 1918-2001 .... **CLC 11, 19**
See also CA 45-48; 14; CAAS 215; CANR 1; CP 1, 2, 3, 4, 5, 6, 7; DLB 88

Eberhart, Richard 1904-2005 ...... **CLC 3, 11, 19, 56; PC 76**
See also AMW; CA 1-4R; CAAS 240; CANR 2, 125; CDALB 1941-1968; CP 1, 2, 3, 4, 5, 6, 7; DAM POET; DLB 48; MAL 5; MTCW 1; RGAL 4

Eberhart, Richard Ghormley
See Eberhart, Richard

Eberstadt, Fernanda 1960- .... **CLC 39**
See also CA 136; CANR 69, 128

Echegaray (y Eizaguirre), Jose (Maria Waldo) 1832-1916 .... **HLCS 1; TCLC 4**
See also CAAE 104; CANR 32; DLB 329; EWL 3; HW 1; MTCW 1

Echeverria, (Jose) Esteban (Antonino) 1805-1851 .... **NCLC 18**
See also LAW

Echo
See Proust, (Valentin-Louis-George-Eugene) Marcel

Eckert, Allan W. 1931- .... **CLC 17**
See also AAYA 18; BYA 2; CA 13-16R; CANR 14, 45; INT CANR-14; MAICYA 2; MAICYAS 1; SAAS 21; SATA 29, 91; SATA-Brief 27

Eckhart, Meister 1260(?)-1327(?) .. **CMLC 9, 80**
See also DLB 115; LMFS 1

Eckmar, F. R.
See de Hartog, Jan

Eco, Umberto 1932- .... **CLC 28, 60, 142**
See also BEST 90:1; BPFB 1; CA 77-80; CANR 12, 33, 55, 110, 131; CPW; CWW 2; DA3; DAM NOV, POP; DLB 196, 242; EWL 3; MSW; MTCW 1, 2; MTFW 2005; NFS 22; RGWL 3; WLIT 7

Eddison, E(ric) R(ucker) 1882-1945 .... **TCLC 15**
See also CA 156; CAAE 109; DLB 255; FANT; SFW 4; SUFW 1

Eddy, Mary (Ann Morse) Baker 1821-1910 .... **TCLC 71**
See also CA 174; CAAE 113

Edel, (Joseph) Leon 1907-1997 .. **CLC 29, 34**
See also CA 1-4R; CAAS 161; CANR 1, 22, 112; DLB 103; INT CANR-22

Eden, Emily 1797-1869 .... **NCLC 10**

Edgar, David 1948- .... **CLC 42**
See also CA 57-60; CANR 12, 61, 112; CBD; CD 5, 6; DAM DRAM; DFS 15; DLB 13, 233; MTCW 1

Edgerton, Clyde (Carlyle) 1944- ...... **CLC 39**
See also AAYA 17; CA 134; CAAE 118; CANR 64, 125; CN 7; CSW; DLB 278; INT CA-134; TCLE 1:1; YAW

Edgeworth, Maria 1768-1849 ... **NCLC 1, 51, 158; SSC 86**
See also BRWS 3; DLB 116, 159, 163; FL 1:3; FW; RGEL 2; SATA 21; TEA; WLIT 3

Edmonds, Paul
See Kuttner, Henry

Edmonds, Walter D(umaux) 1903-1998 .... **CLC 35**
See also BYA 2; CA 5-8R; CANR 2; CWRI 5; DLB 9; LAIT 1; MAICYA 1, 2; MAL 5; RHW; SAAS 4; SATA 1, 27; SATA-Obit 99

Edmondson, Wallace
See Ellison, Harlan

Edson, Margaret 1961- ...... **CLC 199; DC 24**
See also CA 190; DFS 13; DLB 266

Edson, Russell 1935- .... **CLC 13**
See also CA 33-36R; CANR 115; CP 2, 3, 4, 5, 6, 7; DLB 244; WP

Edwards, Bronwen Elizabeth
See Rose, Wendy

Edwards, G(erald) B(asil) 1899-1976 .... **CLC 25**
See also CA 201; CAAS 110

Edwards, Gus 1939- .... **CLC 43**
See also CA 108; INT CA-108

Edwards, Jonathan 1703-1758 .... **LC 7, 54**
See also AMW; DA; DAC; DAM MST; DLB 24, 270; RGAL 4; TUS

Edwards, Sarah Pierpont 1710-1758 .. **LC 87**
See also DLB 200

Efron, Marina Ivanovna Tsvetaeva
See Tsvetaeva (Efron), Marina (Ivanovna)

Egeria fl. 4th cent. - .... **CMLC 70**

Egoyan, Atom 1960- .... **CLC 151**
See also AAYA 63; CA 157; CANR 151

Ehle, John (Marsden, Jr.) 1925- ...... **CLC 27**
See also CA 9-12R; CSW

Ehrenbourg, Ilya (Grigoryevich)
See Ehrenburg, Ilya (Grigoryevich)

Ehrenburg, Ilya (Grigoryevich) 1891-1967 .... **CLC 18, 34, 62**
See Erenburg, Il'ia Grigor'evich
See also CA 102; CAAS 25-28R; EWL 3

Ehrenburg, Ilyo (Grigoryevich)
See Ehrenburg, Ilya (Grigoryevich)

Ehrenreich, Barbara 1941- .... **CLC 110**
See also BEST 90:4; CA 73-76; CANR 16, 37, 62, 117; DLB 246; FW; MTCW 1, 2; MTFW 2005

Eich, Gunter
See Eich, Gunter
See also RGWL 2, 3

Eich, Gunter 1907-1972 .... **CLC 15**
See Eich, Gunter
See also CA 111; CAAS 93-96; DLB 69, 124; EWL 3

Eichendorff, Joseph 1788-1857 .... **NCLC 8**
See also DLB 90; RGWL 2, 3

Eigner, Larry .... **CLC 9**
See Eigner, Laurence (Joel)
See also CA 23; CP 1, 2, 3, 4, 5, 6; DLB 5; WP

Eigner, Laurence (Joel) 1927-1996
See Eigner, Larry
See also CA 9-12R; CAAS 151; CANR 6, 84; CP 7; DLB 193

Eilhart von Oberge c. 1140-c. 1195 .... **CMLC 67**
See also DLB 148

Einhard c. 770-840 .... **CMLC 50**
See also DLB 148

Einstein, Albert 1879-1955 .... **TCLC 65**
See also CA 133; CAAE 121; MTCW 1, 2

Eiseley, Loren
See Eiseley, Loren Corey
See also DLB 275

Eiseley, Loren Corey 1907-1977 .... **CLC 7**
See Eiseley, Loren
See also AAYA 5; ANW; CA 1-4R; CAAS 73-76; CANR 6; DLBD 17

Eisenstadt, Jill 1963- .... **CLC 50**
See also CA 140

Eisenstein, Sergei (Mikhailovich) 1898-1948 .... **TCLC 57**
See also CA 149; CAAE 114

Eisner, Simon
See Kornbluth, C(yril) M.

Eisner, Will 1917-2005 .... **CLC 237**
See also AAYA 52; CA 108; CAAS 235; CANR 114, 140; CMTFW 1; MTFW 2005; SATA 31, 165

Ekeloef, (Bengt) Gunnar 1907-1968 .... **CLC 27; PC 23**
See Ekelof, (Bengt) Gunnar
See also CA 123; CAAS 25-28R; DAM POET

Ekelof, (Bengt) Gunnar 1907-1968
See Ekeloef, (Bengt) Gunnar
See also DLB 259; EW 12; EWL 3

Ekelund, Vilhelm 1880-1949 .... **TCLC 75**
See also CA 189; EWL 3

Ekwensi, C. O. D.
See Ekwensi, Cyprian (Odiatu Duaka)

Ekwensi, Cyprian (Odiatu Duaka) 1921- .... **BLC 1; CLC 4**
See also AFW; BW 2, 3; CA 29-32R; CANR 18, 42, 74, 125; CDWLB 3; CN 1, 2, 3, 4, 5, 6; CWRI 5; DAM MULT; DLB 117; EWL 3; MTCW 1, 2; RGEL 2; SATA 66; WLIT 2

Elaine .... **TCLC 18**
See Leverson, Ada Esther

El Crummo
See Crumb, R.

Elder, Lonne III 1931-1996 ..... **BLC 1; DC 8**
See also BW 1, 3; CA 81-84; CAAS 152; CAD; CANR 25; DAM MULT; DLB 7, 38, 44; MAL 5

Eleanor of Aquitaine 1122-1204 ... **CMLC 39**

Elia
See Lamb, Charles

Eliade, Mircea 1907-1986 .... **CLC 19**
See also CA 65-68; CAAS 119; CANR 30, 62; CDWLB 4; DLB 220; EWL 3; MTCW 1; RGWL 3; SFW 4

Eliot, A. D.
See Jewett, (Theodora) Sarah Orne

Eliot, Alice
See Jewett, (Theodora) Sarah Orne

Eliot, Dan
See Silverberg, Robert

Eliot, George 1819-1880 ...... **NCLC 4, 13, 23, 41, 49, 89, 118, 183; PC 20; SSC 72; WLC 2**
See Evans, Mary Ann
See also BRW 5; BRWC 1, 2; BRWR 2; CDBLB 1832-1890; CN 7; CPW; DA; DA3; DAB; DAC; DAM MST, NOV; DLB 21, 35, 55; FL 1:3; LATS 1:1; LMFS 1; NFS 17, 20; RGEL 2; RGSF 2; SSFS 8; TEA; WLIT 3

Eliot, John 1604-1690 .... **LC 5**
See also DLB 24

Eliot, T(homas) S(tearns) 1888-1965 ...... **CLC 1, 2, 3, 6, 9, 10, 13, 15, 24, 34, 41, 55, 57, 113; PC 5, 31; WLC 2**
See also AAYA 28; AMW; AMWC 1; AMWR 1; BRW 7; BRWR 2; CA 5-8R; CAAS 25-28R; CANR 41; CBD; CDALB 1929-1941; DA; DA3; DAB; DAC; DAM DRAM, MST, POET; DFS 4, 13; DLB 7, 10, 45, 63, 245, 329; DLBY 1988; EWL 3; EXPP; LAIT 3; LATS 1:1; LMFS 2; MAL 5; MTCW 1, 2; MTFW 2005; NCFS 5; PAB; PFS 1, 7, 20; RGAL 4; RGEL 2; TUS; WLIT 4; WP

Elisabeth of Schonau c. 1129-1165 .... **CMLC 82**

Elizabeth 1866-1941 .... **TCLC 41**

Elizabeth I 1533-1603 .... **LC 118**
See also DLB 136

Elkin, Stanley L. 1930-1995 ...... **CLC 4, 6, 9, 14, 27, 51, 91; SSC 12**
See also AMWS 6; BPFB 1; CA 9-12R; CAAS 148; CANR 8, 46; CN 1, 2, 3, 4, 5, 6; CPW; DAM NOV, POP; DLB 2, 28, 218, 278; DLBY 1980; EWL 3; INT CANR-8; MAL 5; MTCW 1, 2; MTFW 2005; RGAL 4; TCLE 1:1

Elledge, Scott .... **CLC 34**

Eller, Scott
See Shepard, Jim

Elliott, Don
See Silverberg, Robert

Elliott, George P(aul) 1918-1980 .... **CLC 2**
See also CA 1-4R; CAAS 97-100; CANR 2; CN 1, 2; CP 3; DLB 244; MAL 5

Fecamps, Elise
See Creasey, John

Federman, Raymond 1928- .... **CLC 6, 47**
See also CA 208; 17-20R, 208; 8; CANR 10, 43, 83, 108; CN 3, 4, 5, 6; DLBY 1980

Federspiel, J.F. 1931- .... **CLC 42**
See also CA 146

Federspiel, Juerg F.
See Federspiel, J.F.

Feiffer, Jules 1929- .... **CLC 2, 8, 64**
See also AAYA 3, 62; CA 17-20R; CAD; CANR 30, 59, 129, 161; CD 5, 6; DAM DRAM; DLB 7, 44; INT CANR-30; MTCW 1; SATA 8, 61, 111, 157

Feiffer, Jules Ralph
See Feiffer, Jules

Feige, Hermann Albert Otto Maximilian
See Traven, B.

Feinberg, David B. 1956-1994 .... **CLC 59**
See also CA 135; CAAS 147

Feinstein, Elaine 1930- .... **CLC 36**
See also CA 69-72; 1; CANR 31, 68, 121; CN 3, 4, 5, 6, 7; CP 2, 3, 4, 5, 6, 7; CWP; DLB 14, 40; MTCW 1

Feke, Gilbert David .... **CLC 65**

Feldman, Irving (Mordecai) 1928- ..... **CLC 7**
See also CA 1-4R; CANR 1; CP 1, 2, 3, 4, 5, 6, 7; DLB 169; TCLE 1:1

Felix-Tchicaya, Gerald
See Tchicaya, Gerald Felix

Fellini, Federico 1920-1993 .... **CLC 16, 85**
See also CA 65-68; CAAS 143; CANR 33

Felltham, Owen 1602(?)-1668 .... **LC 92**
See also DLB 126, 151

Felsen, Henry Gregor 1916-1995 ..... **CLC 17**
See also CA 1-4R; CAAS 180; CANR 1; SAAS 2; SATA 1

Felski, Rita .... **CLC 65**

Fenelon, Francois de Pons de Salignac de la Mothe- 1651-1715 .... **LC 134**
See also DLB 268; EW 3; GFL Beginnings to 1789

Fenno, Jack
See Calisher, Hortense

Fenollosa, Ernest (Francisco) 1853-1908 .... **TCLC 91**

Fenton, James 1949- .... **CLC 32, 209**
See also CA 102; CANR 108, 160; CP 2, 3, 4, 5, 6, 7; DLB 40; PFS 11

Fenton, James Martin
See Fenton, James

Ferber, Edna 1887-1968 .... **CLC 18, 93**
See also AITN 1; CA 5-8R; CAAS 25-28R; CANR 68, 105; DLB 9, 28, 86, 266; MAL 5; MTCW 1, 2; MTFW 2005; RGAL 4; RHW; SATA 7; TCWW 1, 2

Ferdowsi, Abu'l Qasem 940-1020(?) .... **CMLC 43**
See Firdawsi, Abu al-Qasim
See also RGWL 2, 3

Ferguson, Helen
See Kavan, Anna

Ferguson, Niall 1964- .... **CLC 134**
See also CA 190; CANR 154

Ferguson, Samuel 1810-1886 .... **NCLC 33**
See also DLB 32; RGEL 2

Fergusson, Robert 1750-1774 .... **LC 29**
See also DLB 109; RGEL 2

Ferling, Lawrence
See Ferlinghetti, Lawrence

Ferlinghetti, Lawrence 1919(?)- .... **CLC 2, 6, 10, 27, 111; PC 1**
See also AAYA 74; BG 1:2; CA 5-8R; CAD; CANR 3, 41, 73, 125; CDALB 1941-1968; CP 1, 2, 3, 4, 5, 6, 7; DA3; DAM POET; DLB 5, 16; MAL 5; MTCW 1, 2; MTFW 2005; RGAL 4; WP

Ferlinghetti, Lawrence Monsanto
See Ferlinghetti, Lawrence

Fern, Fanny
See Parton, Sara Payson Willis

Fernandez, Vicente Garcia Huidobro
See Huidobro Fernandez, Vicente Garcia

Fernandez-Armesto, Felipe .... **CLC 70**
See Fernandez-Armesto, Felipe Fermin Ricardo
See also CANR 153

Fernandez-Armesto, Felipe Fermin Ricardo 1950-
See Fernandez-Armesto, Felipe
See also CA 142; CANR 93

Fernandez de Lizardi, Jose Joaquin
See Lizardi, Jose Joaquin Fernandez de

Ferre, Rosario 1938- ...... **CLC 139; HLCS 1; SSC 36**
See also CA 131; CANR 55, 81, 134; CWW 2; DLB 145; EWL 3; HW 1, 2; LAWS 1; MTCW 2; MTFW 2005; WLIT 1

Ferrer, Gabriel (Francisco Victor) Miro
See Miro (Ferrer), Gabriel (Francisco Victor)

Ferrier, Susan (Edmonstone) 1782-1854 .... **NCLC 8**
See also DLB 116; RGEL 2

Ferrigno, Robert 1948(?)- .... **CLC 65**
See also CA 140; CANR 125, 161

Ferron, Jacques 1921-1985 .... **CLC 94**
See also CA 129; CAAE 117; CCA 1; DAC; DLB 60; EWL 3

Feuchtwanger, Lion 1884-1958 .... **TCLC 3**
See also CA 187; CAAE 104; DLB 66; EWL 3; RGHL

Feuerbach, Ludwig 1804-1872 ..... **NCLC 139**
See also DLB 133

Feuillet, Octave 1821-1890 .... **NCLC 45**
See also DLB 192

Feydeau, Georges (Leon Jules Marie) 1862-1921 .... **TCLC 22**
See also CA 152; CAAE 113; CANR 84; DAM DRAM; DLB 192; EWL 3; GFL 1789 to the Present; RGWL 2, 3

Fichte, Johann Gottlieb 1762-1814 .... **NCLC 62**
See also DLB 90

Ficino, Marsilio 1433-1499 .... **LC 12**
See also LMFS 1

Fiedeler, Hans
See Doeblin, Alfred

Fiedler, Leslie A(aron) 1917-2003 ..... **CLC 4, 13, 24**
See also AMWS 13; CA 9-12R; CAAS 212; CANR 7, 63; CN 1, 2, 3, 4, 5, 6; DLB 28, 67; EWL 3; MAL 5; MTCW 1, 2; RGAL 4; TUS

Field, Andrew 1938- .... **CLC 44**
See also CA 97-100; CANR 25

Field, Eugene 1850-1895 .... **NCLC 3**
See also DLB 23, 42, 140; DLBD 13; MAICYA 1, 2; RGAL 4; SATA 16

Field, Gans T.
See Wellman, Manly Wade

Field, Michael 1915-1971 .... **TCLC 43**
See also CAAS 29-32R

Fielding, Helen 1958- .... **CLC 146, 217**
See also AAYA 65; CA 172; CANR 127; DLB 231; MTFW 2005

Fielding, Henry 1707-1754 .... **LC 1, 46, 85; WLC 2**
See also BRW 3; BRWR 1; CDBLB 1660-1789; DA; DA3; DAB; DAC; DAM DRAM, MST, NOV; DLB 39, 84, 101; NFS 18; RGEL 2; TEA; WLIT 3

Fielding, Sarah 1710-1768 .... **LC 1, 44**
See also DLB 39; RGEL 2; TEA

Fields, W. C. 1880-1946 .... **TCLC 80**
See also DLB 44

Fierstein, Harvey (Forbes) 1954- ..... **CLC 33**
See also CA 129; CAAE 123; CAD; CD 5, 6; CPW; DA3; DAM DRAM, POP; DFS 6; DLB 266; GLL; MAL 5

Figes, Eva 1932- .... **CLC 31**
See also CA 53-56; CANR 4, 44, 83; CN 2, 3, 4, 5, 6, 7; DLB 14, 271; FW; RGHL

Filippo, Eduardo de
See de Filippo, Eduardo

Finch, Anne 1661-1720 ..... **LC 3, 137; PC 21**
See also BRWS 9; DLB 95

Finch, Robert (Duer Claydon) 1900-1995 .... **CLC 18**
See also CA 57-60; CANR 9, 24, 49; CP 1, 2, 3, 4, 5, 6; DLB 88

Findley, Timothy (Irving Frederick) 1930-2002 .... **CLC 27, 102**
See also CA 25-28R; CAAS 206; CANR 12, 42, 69, 109; CCA 1; CN 4, 5, 6, 7; DAC; DAM MST; DLB 53; FANT; RHW

Fink, William
See Mencken, H(enry) L(ouis)

Firbank, Louis 1942-
See Reed, Lou
See also CAAE 117

Firbank, (Arthur Annesley) Ronald 1886-1926 .... **TCLC 1**
See also BRWS 2; CA 177; CAAE 104; DLB 36; EWL 3; RGEL 2

Firdawsi, Abu al-Qasim
See Ferdowsi, Abu'l Qasem
See also WLIT 6

Fish, Stanley
See Fish, Stanley Eugene

Fish, Stanley E.
See Fish, Stanley Eugene

Fish, Stanley Eugene 1938- .... **CLC 142**
See also CA 132; CAAE 112; CANR 90; DLB 67

Fisher, Dorothy (Frances) Canfield 1879-1958 .... **TCLC 87**
See also CA 136; CAAE 114; CANR 80; CLR 71; CWRI 5; DLB 9, 102, 284; MAICYA 1, 2; MAL 5; YABC 1

Fisher, M(ary) F(rances) K(ennedy) 1908-1992 .... **CLC 76, 87**
See also CA 77-80; CAAS 138; CANR 44; MTCW 2

Fisher, Roy 1930- .... **CLC 25**
See also CA 81-84; 10; CANR 16; CP 1, 2, 3, 4, 5, 6, 7; DLB 40

Fisher, Rudolph 1897-1934 . **BLC 2; HR 1:2; SSC 25; TCLC 11**
See also BW 1, 3; CA 124; CAAE 107; CANR 80; DAM MULT; DLB 51, 102

Fisher, Vardis (Alvero) 1895-1968 .... **CLC 7; TCLC 140**
See also CA 5-8R; CAAS 25-28R; CANR 68; DLB 9, 206; MAL 5; RGAL 4; TCWW 1, 2

Fiske, Tarleton
See Bloch, Robert (Albert)

Fitch, Clarke
See Sinclair, Upton

Fitch, John IV
See Cormier, Robert

Fitzgerald, Captain Hugh
See Baum, L(yman) Frank

FitzGerald, Edward 1809-1883 ...... **NCLC 9, 153**
See also BRW 4; DLB 32; RGEL 2

Fitzgerald, F(rancis) Scott (Key) 1896-1940 ... **SSC 6, 31, 75; TCLC 1, 6, 14, 28, 55, 157; WLC 2**
See also AAYA 24; AITN 1; AMW; AMWC 2; AMWR 1; BPFB 1; CA 123; CAAE 110; CDALB 1917-1929; DA; DA3; DAB; DAC; DAM MST, NOV; DLB 4, 9, 86, 219, 273; DLBD 1, 15, 16; DLBY

1981, 1996; EWL 3; EXPN; EXPS; LAIT 3; MAL 5; MTCW 1, 2; MTFW 2005; NFS 2, 19, 20; RGAL 4; RGSF 2; SSFS 4, 15, 21; TUS

Fitzgerald, Penelope 1916-2000 . **CLC 19, 51, 61, 143**
See also BRWS 5; CA 85-88; 10; CAAS 190; CANR 56, 86, 131; CN 3, 4, 5, 6, 7; DLB 14, 194, 326; EWL 3; MTCW 2; MTFW 2005

Fitzgerald, Robert (Stuart)
1910-1985 .... **CLC 39**
See also CA 1-4R; CAAS 114; CANR 1; CP 1, 2, 3, 4; DLBY 1980; MAL 5

FitzGerald, Robert D(avid)
1902-1987 .... **CLC 19**
See also CA 17-20R; CP 1, 2, 3, 4; DLB 260; RGEL 2

Fitzgerald, Zelda (Sayre)
1900-1948 .... **TCLC 52**
See also AMWS 9; CA 126; CAAE 117; DLBY 1984

Flanagan, Thomas (James Bonner)
1923-2002 .... **CLC 25, 52**
See also CA 108; CAAS 206; CANR 55; CN 3, 4, 5, 6, 7; DLBY 1980; INT CA-108; MTCW 1; RHW; TCLE 1:1

Flaubert, Gustave 1821-1880 .... **NCLC 2, 10, 19, 62, 66, 135, 179; SSC 11, 60; WLC 2**
See also DA; DA3; DAB; DAC; DAM MST, NOV; DLB 119, 301; EW 7; EXPS; GFL 1789 to the Present; LAIT 2; LMFS 1; NFS 14; RGSF 2; RGWL 2, 3; SSFS 6; TWA

Flavius Josephus
See Josephus, Flavius

Flecker, Herman Elroy
See Flecker, (Herman) James Elroy

Flecker, (Herman) James Elroy
1884-1915 .... **TCLC 43**
See also CA 150; CAAE 109; DLB 10, 19; RGEL 2

Fleming, Ian 1908-1964 .... **CLC 3, 30**
See also AAYA 26; BPFB 1; CA 5-8R; CANR 59; CDBLB 1945-1960; CMW 4; CPW; DA3; DAM POP; DLB 87, 201; MSW; MTCW 1, 2; MTFW 2005; RGEL 2; SATA 9; TEA; YAW

Fleming, Ian Lancaster
See Fleming, Ian

Fleming, Thomas 1927- .... **CLC 37**
See also CA 5-8R; CANR 10, 102, 155; INT CANR-10; SATA 8

Fleming, Thomas James
See Fleming, Thomas

Fletcher, John 1579-1625 .... **DC 6; LC 33**
See also BRW 2; CDBLB Before 1660; DLB 58; RGEL 2; TEA

Fletcher, John Gould 1886-1950 .... **TCLC 35**
See also CA 167; CAAE 107; DLB 4, 45; LMFS 2; MAL 5; RGAL 4

Fleur, Paul
See Pohl, Frederik

Flieg, Helmut
See Heym, Stefan

Flooglebuckle, Al
See Spiegelman, Art

Flora, Fletcher 1914-1969
See Queen, Ellery
See also CA 1-4R; CANR 3, 85

Flying Officer X
See Bates, H(erbert) E(rnest)

Fo, Dario 1926- .... **CLC 32, 109, 227; DC 10**
See also CA 128; CAAE 116; CANR 68, 114, 134; CWW 2; DA3; DAM DRAM; DFS 23; DLB 330; DLBY 1997; EWL 3; MTCW 1, 2; MTFW 2005; WLIT 7

Foden, Giles 1967- .... **CLC 231**
See also CA 240; DLB 267; NFS 15

Fogarty, Jonathan Titulescu Esq.
See Farrell, James T(homas)

Follett, Ken 1949- .... **CLC 18**
See also AAYA 6, 50; BEST 89:4; BPFB 1; CA 81-84; CANR 13, 33, 54, 102, 156; CMW 4; CPW; DA3; DAM NOV, POP; DLB 87; DLBY 1981; INT CANR-33; MTCW 1

Follett, Kenneth Martin
See Follett, Ken

Fondane, Benjamin 1898-1944 ..... **TCLC 159**

Fontane, Theodor 1819-1898 . **NCLC 26, 163**
See also CDWLB 2; DLB 129; EW 6; RGWL 2, 3; TWA

Fonte, Moderata 1555-1592 .... **LC 118**

Fontenot, Chester .... **CLC 65**

Fonvizin, Denis Ivanovich
1744(?)-1792 .... **LC 81**
See also DLB 150; RGWL 2, 3

Foote, Horton 1916- .... **CLC 51, 91**
See also CA 73-76; CAD; CANR 34, 51, 110; CD 5, 6; CSW; DA3; DAM DRAM; DFS 20; DLB 26, 266; EWL 3; INT CANR-34; MTFW 2005

Foote, Mary Hallock 1847-1938 .. **TCLC 108**
See also DLB 186, 188, 202, 221; TCWW 2

Foote, Samuel 1721-1777 .... **LC 106**
See also DLB 89; RGEL 2

Foote, Shelby 1916-2005 .... **CLC 75, 224**
See also AAYA 40; CA 5-8R; CAAS 240; CANR 3, 45, 74, 131; CN 1, 2, 3, 4, 5, 6, 7; CPW; CSW; DA3; DAM NOV, POP; DLB 2, 17; MAL 5; MTCW 2; MTFW 2005; RHW

Forbes, Cosmo
See Lewton, Val

Forbes, Esther 1891-1967 .... **CLC 12**
See also AAYA 17; BYA 2; CA 13-14; CAAS 25-28R; CAP 1; CLR 27; DLB 22; JRDA; MAICYA 1, 2; RHW; SATA 2, 100; YAW

Forche, Carolyn 1950- .. **CLC 25, 83, 86; PC 10**
See also CA 117; CAAE 109; CANR 50, 74, 138; CP 4, 5, 6, 7; CWP; DA3; DAM POET; DLB 5, 193; INT CA-117; MAL 5; MTCW 2; MTFW 2005; PFS 18; RGAL 4

Forche, Carolyn Louise
See Forche, Carolyn

Ford, Elbur
See Hibbert, Eleanor Alice Burford

Ford, Ford Madox 1873-1939 ... **TCLC 1, 15, 39, 57, 172**
See Chaucer, Daniel
See also BRW 6; CA 132; CAAE 104; CANR 74; CDBLB 1914-1945; DA3; DAM NOV; DLB 34, 98, 162; EWL 3; MTCW 1, 2; RGEL 2; TEA

Ford, Henry 1863-1947 .... **TCLC 73**
See also CA 148; CAAE 115

Ford, Jack
See Ford, John

Ford, John 1586-1639 .... **DC 8; LC 68**
See also BRW 2; CDBLB Before 1660; DA3; DAM DRAM; DFS 7; DLB 58; IDTP; RGEL 2

Ford, John 1895-1973 .... **CLC 16**
See also AAYA 75; CA 187; CAAS 45-48

Ford, Richard 1944- .... **CLC 46, 99, 205**
See also AMWS 5; CA 69-72; CANR 11, 47, 86, 128; CN 5, 6, 7; CSW; DLB 227; EWL 3; MAL 5; MTCW 2; MTFW 2005; RGAL 4; RGSF 2

Ford, Webster
See Masters, Edgar Lee

Foreman, Richard 1937- .... **CLC 50**
See also CA 65-68; CAD; CANR 32, 63, 143; CD 5, 6

Forester, C(ecil) S(cott) 1899-1966 . **CLC 35; TCLC 152**
See also CA 73-76; CAAS 25-28R; CANR 83; DLB 191; RGEL 2; RHW; SATA 13

Forez
See Mauriac, Francois (Charles)

Forman, James
See Forman, James D(ouglas)

Forman, James D(ouglas) 1932- .... **CLC 21**
See also AAYA 17; CA 9-12R; CANR 4, 19, 42; JRDA; MAICYA 1, 2; SATA 8, 70; YAW

Forman, Milos 1932- .... **CLC 164**
See also AAYA 63; CA 109

Fornes, Maria Irene 1930- .... **CLC 39, 61, 187; DC 10; HLCS 1**
See also CA 25-28R; CAD; CANR 28, 81; CD 5, 6; CWD; DLB 7; HW 1, 2; INT CANR-28; LLW; MAL 5; MTCW 1; RGAL 4

Forrest, Leon (Richard)
1937-1997 .... **BLCS; CLC 4**
See also AFAW 2; BW 2; CA 89-92; 7; CAAS 162; CANR 25, 52, 87; CN 4, 5, 6; DLB 33

Forster, E(dward) M(organ)
1879-1970 ...... **CLC 1, 2, 3, 4, 9, 10, 13, 15, 22, 45, 77; SSC 27, 96; TCLC 125; WLC 2**
See also AAYA 2, 37; BRW 6; BRWR 2; BYA 12; CA 13-14; CAAS 25-28R; CANR 45; CAP 1; CDBLB 1914-1945; DA; DA3; DAB; DAC; DAM MST, NOV; DLB 34, 98, 162, 178, 195; DLBD 10; EWL 3; EXPN; LAIT 3; LMFS 1; MTCW 1, 2; MTFW 2005; NCFS 1; NFS 3, 10, 11; RGEL 2; RGSF 2; SATA 57; SUFW 1; TEA; WLIT 4

Forster, John 1812-1876 .... **NCLC 11**
See also DLB 144, 184

Forster, Margaret 1938- .... **CLC 149**
See also CA 133; CANR 62, 115; CN 4, 5, 6, 7; DLB 155, 271

Forsyth, Frederick 1938- .... **CLC 2, 5, 36**
See also BEST 89:4; CA 85-88; CANR 38, 62, 115, 137; CMW 4; CN 3, 4, 5, 6, 7; CPW; DAM NOV, POP; DLB 87; MTCW 1, 2; MTFW 2005

Forten, Charlotte L. 1837-1914 .... **BLC 2; TCLC 16**
See Grimke, Charlotte L(ottie) Forten
See also DLB 50, 239

Fortinbras
See Grieg, (Johan) Nordahl (Brun)

Foscolo, Ugo 1778-1827 .... **NCLC 8, 97**
See also EW 5; WLIT 7

Fosse, Bob 1927-1987
See Fosse, Robert L.
See also CAAE 110; CAAS 123

Fosse, Robert L. .... **CLC 20**
See Fosse, Bob

Foster, Hannah Webster
1758-1840 .... **NCLC 99**
See also DLB 37, 200; RGAL 4

Foster, Stephen Collins
1826-1864 .... **NCLC 26**
See also RGAL 4

Foucault, Michel 1926-1984 . **CLC 31, 34, 69**
See also CA 105; CAAS 113; CANR 34; DLB 242; EW 13; EWL 3; GFL 1789 to the Present; GLL 1; LMFS 2; MTCW 1, 2; TWA

Fouque, Friedrich (Heinrich Karl) de la Motte 1777-1843 .... **NCLC 2**
See also DLB 90; RGWL 2, 3; SUFW 1

Fourier, Charles 1772-1837 .... **NCLC 51**

Fournier, Henri-Alban 1886-1914
See Alain-Fournier
See also CA 179; CAAE 104

Fournier, Pierre 1916-1997 .... **CLC 11**
See Gascar, Pierre
See also CA 89-92; CANR 16, 40

Fowles, John 1926-2005 .... **CLC 1, 2, 3, 4, 6, 9, 10, 15, 33, 87; SSC 33**
See also BPFB 1; BRWS 1; CA 5-8R;
CAAS 245; CANR 25, 71, 103; CDBLB
1960 to Present; CN 1, 2, 3, 4, 5, 6, 7;
DA3; DAB; DAC; DAM MST; DLB 14,
139, 207; EWL 3; HGG; MTCW 1, 2;
MTFW 2005; NFS 21; RGEL 2; RHW;
SATA 22; SATA-Obit 171; TEA; WLIT 4

Fowles, John Robert
See Fowles, John

Fox, Paula 1923- .... **CLC 2, 8, 121**
See also AAYA 3, 37; BYA 3, 8; CA 73-76;
CANR 20, 36, 62, 105; CLR 1, 44, 96;
DLB 52; JRDA; MAICYA 1, 2; MTCW
1; NFS 12; SATA 17, 60, 120, 167; WYA;
YAW

Fox, William Price (Jr.) 1926- .... **CLC 22**
See also CA 17-20R; 19; CANR 11, 142;
CSW; DLB 2; DLBY 1981

Foxe, John 1517(?)-1587 .... **LC 14**
See also DLB 132

Frame, Janet .. **CLC 2, 3, 6, 22, 66, 96, 237; SSC 29**
See Clutha, Janet Paterson Frame
See also CN 1, 2, 3, 4, 5, 6, 7; CP 2, 3, 4;
CWP; EWL 3; RGEL 2; RGSF 2; TWA

France, Anatole .... **TCLC 9**
See Thibault, Jacques Anatole Francois
See also DLB 123, 330; EWL 3; GFL 1789
to the Present; RGWL 2, 3; SUFW 1

Francis, Claude .... **CLC 50**
See also CA 192

Francis, Dick
See Francis, Richard Stanley
See also CN 2, 3, 4, 5, 6

Francis, Richard Stanley 1920- ... **CLC 2, 22, 42, 102**
See Francis, Dick
See also AAYA 5, 21; BEST 89:3; BPFB 1;
CA 5-8R; CANR 9, 42, 68, 100, 141; CD-
BLB 1960 to Present; CMW 4; CN 7;
DA3; DAM POP; DLB 87; INT CANR-9;
MSW; MTCW 1, 2; MTFW 2005

Francis, Robert (Churchill)
1901-1987 .... **CLC 15; PC 34**
See also AMWS 9; CA 1-4R; CAAS 123;
CANR 1; CP 1, 2, 3, 4; EXPP; PFS 12;
TCLE 1:1

Francis, Lord Jeffrey
See Jeffrey, Francis
See also DLB 107

Frank, Anne(lies Marie)
1929-1945 .... **TCLC 17; WLC 2**
See also AAYA 12; BYA 1; CA 133; CAAE
113; CANR 68; CLR 101; DA; DA3;
DAB; DAC; DAM MST; LAIT 4; MAI-
CYA 2; MAICYAS 1; MTCW 1, 2;
MTFW 2005; NCFS 2; RGHL; SATA 87;
SATA-Brief 42; WYA; YAW

Frank, Bruno 1887-1945 .... **TCLC 81**
See also CA 189; DLB 118; EWL 3

Frank, Elizabeth 1945- .... **CLC 39**
See also CA 126; CAAE 121; CANR 78,
150; INT CANR-126

Frankl, Viktor E(mil) 1905-1997 ...... **CLC 93**
See also CA 65-68; CAAS 161; RGHL

Franklin, Benjamin
See Hasek, Jaroslav (Matej Frantisek)

Franklin, Benjamin 1706-1790 .. **LC 25, 134; WLCS**
See also AMW; CDALB 1640-1865; DA;
DA3; DAB; DAC; DAM MST; DLB 24,
43, 73, 183; LAIT 1; RGAL 4; TUS

Franklin, (Stella Maria Sarah) Miles (Lampe) 1879-1954 .... **TCLC 7**
See also CA 164; CAAE 104; DLB 230;
FW; MTCW 2; RGEL 2; TWA

Franzen, Jonathan 1959- .... **CLC 202**
See also AAYA 65; CA 129; CANR 105

Fraser, Antonia 1932- .... **CLC 32, 107**
See also AAYA 57; CA 85-88; CANR 44,
65, 119; CMW; DLB 276; MTCW 1, 2;
MTFW 2005; SATA-Brief 32

Fraser, George MacDonald 1925- ...... **CLC 7**
See also AAYA 48; CA 180; 45-48, 180;
CANR 2, 48, 74; MTCW 2; RHW

Fraser, Sylvia 1935- .... **CLC 64**
See also CA 45-48; CANR 1, 16, 60; CCA 1

Frayn, Michael 1933- .... **CLC 3, 7, 31, 47, 176; DC 27**
See also AAYA 69; BRWC 2; BRWS 7; CA
5-8R; CANR 30, 69, 114, 133; CBD; CD
5, 6; CN 1, 2, 3, 4, 5, 6, 7; DAM DRAM,
NOV; DFS 22; DLB 13, 14, 194, 245;
FANT; MTCW 1, 2; MTFW 2005; SFW
4

Fraze, Candida (Merrill) 1945- .... **CLC 50**
See also CA 126

Frazer, Andrew
See Marlowe, Stephen

Frazer, J(ames) G(eorge)
1854-1941 .... **TCLC 32**
See also BRWS 3; CAAE 118; NCFS 5

Frazer, Robert Caine
See Creasey, John

Frazer, Sir James George
See Frazer, J(ames) G(eorge)

Frazier, Charles 1950- .... **CLC 109, 224**
See also AAYA 34; CA 161; CANR 126;
CSW; DLB 292; MTFW 2005

Frazier, Ian 1951- .... **CLC 46**
See also CA 130; CANR 54, 93

Frederic, Harold 1856-1898 ... **NCLC 10, 175**
See also AMW; DLB 12, 23; DLBD 13;
MAL 5; NFS 22; RGAL 4

Frederick, John
See Faust, Frederick (Schiller)
See also TCWW 2

Frederick the Great 1712-1786 .... **LC 14**

Fredro, Aleksander 1793-1876 .... **NCLC 8**

Freeling, Nicolas 1927-2003 .... **CLC 38**
See also CA 49-52; 12; CAAS 218; CANR
1, 17, 50, 84; CMW 4; CN 1, 2, 3, 4, 5,
6; DLB 87

Freeman, Douglas Southall
1886-1953 .... **TCLC 11**
See also CA 195; CAAE 109; DLB 17;
DLBD 17

Freeman, Judith 1946- .... **CLC 55**
See also CA 148; CANR 120; DLB 256

Freeman, Mary E(leanor) Wilkins
1852-1930 .... **SSC 1, 47; TCLC 9**
See also CA 177; CAAE 106; DLB 12, 78,
221; EXPS; FW; HGG; MBL; RGAL 4;
RGSF 2; SSFS 4, 8; SUFW 1; TUS

Freeman, R(ichard) Austin
1862-1943 .... **TCLC 21**
See also CAAE 113; CANR 84; CMW 4;
DLB 70

French, Albert 1943- .... **CLC 86**
See also BW 3; CA 167

French, Antonia
See Kureishi, Hanif

French, Marilyn 1929- .. **CLC 10, 18, 60, 177**
See also BPFB 1; CA 69-72; CANR 3, 31,
134; CN 5, 6, 7; CPW; DAM DRAM,
NOV; POP; FL 1:5; FW; INT CANR-31;
MTCW 1, 2; MTFW 2005

French, Paul
See Asimov, Isaac

Freneau, Philip Morin 1752-1832 .. **NCLC 1, 111**
See also AMWS 2; DLB 37, 43; RGAL 4

Freud, Sigmund 1856-1939 .... **TCLC 52**
See also CA 133; CAAE 115; CANR 69;
DLB 296; EW 8; EWL 3; LATS 1:1;
MTCW 1, 2; MTFW 2005; NCFS 3; TWA

Freytag, Gustav 1816-1895 .... **NCLC 109**
See also DLB 129

Friedan, Betty 1921-2006 .... **CLC 74**
See also CA 65-68; CAAS 248; CANR 18,
45, 74; DLB 246; FW; MTCW 1, 2;
MTFW 2005; NCFS 5

Friedan, Betty Naomi
See Friedan, Betty

Friedlander, Saul 1932- .... **CLC 90**
See also CA 130; CAAE 117; CANR 72;
RGHL

Friedman, B(ernard) H(arper)
1926- .... **CLC 7**
See also CA 1-4R; CANR 3, 48

Friedman, Bruce Jay 1930- ...... **CLC 3, 5, 56**
See also CA 9-12R; CAD; CANR 25, 52,
101; CD 5, 6; CN 1, 2, 3, 4, 5, 6, 7; DLB
2, 28, 244; INT CANR-25; MAL 5; SSFS
18

Friel, Brian 1929- .... **CLC 5, 42, 59, 115; DC 8; SSC 76**
See also BRWS 5; CA 21-24R; CANR 33,
69, 131; CBD; CD 5, 6; DFS 11; DLB
13, 319; EWL 3; MTCW 1; RGEL 2; TEA

Friis-Baastad, Babbis Ellinor
1921-1970 .... **CLC 12**
See also CA 17-20R; CAAS 134; SATA 7

Frisch, Max 1911-1991 ...... **CLC 3, 9, 14, 18, 32, 44; TCLC 121**
See also CA 85-88; CAAS 134; CANR 32,
74; CDWLB 2; DAM DRAM, NOV; DLB
69, 124; EW 13; EWL 3; MTCW 1, 2;
MTFW 2005; RGHL; RGWL 2, 3

Fromentin, Eugene (Samuel Auguste)
1820-1876 .... **NCLC 10, 125**
See also DLB 123; GFL 1789 to the Present

Frost, Frederick
See Faust, Frederick (Schiller)

Frost, Robert 1874-1963 . **CLC 1, 3, 4, 9, 10, 13, 15, 26, 34, 44; PC 1, 39, 71; WLC 2**
See also AAYA 21; AMW; AMWR 1; CA
89-92; CANR 33; CDALB 1917-1929;
CLR 67; DA; DA3; DAB; DAC; DAM
MST; POET; DLB 54, 284; DLBD 7;
EWL 3; EXPP; MAL 5; MTCW 1, 2;
MTFW 2005; PAB; PFS 1, 2, 3, 4, 5, 6,
7, 10, 13; RGAL 4; SATA 14; TUS; WP;
WYA

Frost, Robert Lee
See Frost, Robert

Froude, James Anthony
1818-1894 .... **NCLC 43**
See also DLB 18, 57, 144

Froy, Herald
See Waterhouse, Keith (Spencer)

Fry, Christopher 1907-2005 ... **CLC 2, 10, 14**
See also BRWS 3; CA 17-20R; 23; CAAS
240; CANR 9, 30, 74, 132; CBD; CD 5,
6; CP 1, 2, 3, 4, 5, 6, 7; DAM DRAM;
DLB 13; EWL 3; MTCW 1, 2; MTFW
2005; RGEL 2; SATA 66; TEA

Frye, (Herman) Northrop
1912-1991 .... **CLC 24, 70; TCLC 165**
See also CA 5-8R; CAAS 133; CANR 8,
37; DLB 67, 68, 246; EWL 3; MTCW 1,
2; MTFW 2005; RGAL 4; TWA

Fuchs, Daniel 1909-1993 .... **CLC 8, 22**
See also CA 81-84; 5; CAAS 142; CANR
40; CN 1, 2, 3, 4, 5; DLB 9, 26, 28;
DLBY 1993; MAL 5

Fuchs, Daniel 1934- .... **CLC 34**
See also CA 37-40R; CANR 14, 48

Author Index

Godwin, Gail 1937- ...... **CLC 5, 8, 22, 31, 69, 125**
See also BPFB 2; CA 29-32R; CANR 15, 43, 69, 132; CN 3, 4, 5, 6, 7; CPW; CSW; DA3; DAM POP; DLB 6, 234; INT CANR-15; MAL 5; MTCW 1, 2; MTFW 2005

Godwin, Gail Kathleen
See Godwin, Gail

Godwin, William 1756-1836 .. **NCLC 14, 130**
See also CDBLB 1789-1832; CMW 4; DLB 39, 104, 142, 158, 163, 262; GL 2; HGG; RGEL 2

Goebbels, Josef
See Goebbels, (Paul) Joseph

Goebbels, (Paul) Joseph
1897-1945 .... **TCLC 68**
See also CA 148; CAAE 115

Goebbels, Joseph Paul
See Goebbels, (Paul) Joseph

Goethe, Johann Wolfgang von
1749-1832 . **DC 20; NCLC 4, 22, 34, 90, 154; PC 5; SSC 38; WLC 3**
See also CDWLB 2; DA; DA3; DAB; DAC; DAM DRAM, MST, POET; DLB 94; EW 5; GL 2; LATS 1; LMFS 1:1; RGWL 2, 3; TWA

Gogarty, Oliver St. John
1878-1957 .... **TCLC 15**
See also CA 150; CAAE 109; DLB 15, 19; RGEL 2

Gogol, Nikolai (Vasilyevich)
1809-1852 .... **DC 1; NCLC 5, 15, 31, 162; SSC 4, 29, 52; WLC 3**
See also DA; DAB; DAC; DAM DRAM, MST; DFS 12; DLB 198; EW 6; EXPS; RGSF 2; RGWL 2, 3; SSFS 7; TWA

Goines, Donald 1937(?)-1974 ... **BLC 2; CLC 80**
See also AITN 1; BW 1, 3; CA 124; CAAS 114; CANR 82; CMW 4; DA3; DAM MULT, POP; DLB 33

Gold, Herbert 1924- ... **CLC 4, 7, 14, 42, 152**
See also CA 9-12R; CANR 17, 45, 125; CN 1, 2, 3, 4, 5, 6, 7; DLB 2; DLBY 1981; MAL 5

Goldbarth, Albert 1948- .... **CLC 5, 38**
See also AMWS 12; CA 53-56; CANR 6, 40; CP 3, 4, 5, 6, 7; DLB 120

Goldberg, Anatol 1910-1982 .... **CLC 34**
See also CA 131; CAAS 117

Goldemberg, Isaac 1945- .... **CLC 52**
See also CA 69-72; 12; CANR 11, 32; EWL 3; HW 1; WLIT 1

Golding, Arthur 1536-1606 .... **LC 101**
See also DLB 136

Golding, William 1911-1993 . **CLC 1, 2, 3, 8, 10, 17, 27, 58, 81; WLC 3**
See also AAYA 5, 44; BPFB 2; BRWR 1; BRWS 1; BYA 2; CA 5-8R; CAAS 141; CANR 13, 33, 54; CD 5; CDBLB 1945-1960; CLR 94; CN 1, 2, 3, 4; DA; DA3; DAB; DAC; DAM MST, NOV; DLB 15, 100, 255, 326, 330; EWL 3; EXPN; HGG; LAIT 4; MTCW 1, 2; MTFW 2005; NFS 2; RGEL 2; RHW; SFW 4; TEA; WLIT 4; YAW

Golding, William Gerald
See Golding, William

Goldman, Emma 1869-1940 .... **TCLC 13**
See also CA 150; CAAE 110; DLB 221; FW; RGAL 4; TUS

Goldman, Francisco 1954- .... **CLC 76**
See also CA 162

Goldman, William 1931- .... **CLC 1, 48**
See also BPFB 2; CA 9-12R; CANR 29, 69, 106; CN 1, 2, 3, 4, 5, 6, 7; DLB 44; FANT; IDFW 3, 4

Goldman, William W.
See Goldman, William

Goldmann, Lucien 1913-1970 .... **CLC 24**
See also CA 25-28; CAP 2

Goldoni, Carlo 1707-1793 .... **LC 4**
See also DAM DRAM; EW 4; RGWL 2, 3; WLIT 7

Goldsberry, Steven 1949- .... **CLC 34**
See also CA 131

Goldsmith, Oliver 1730(?)-1774 .... **DC 8; LC 2, 48, 122; PC 77; WLC 3**
See also BRW 3; CDBLB 1660-1789; DA; DAB; DAC; DAM DRAM, MST, NOV, POET; DFS 1; DLB 39, 89, 104, 109, 142; IDTP; RGEL 2; SATA 26; TEA; WLIT 3

Goldsmith, Peter
See Priestley, J(ohn) B(oynton)

Gombrowicz, Witold 1904-1969 .... **CLC 4, 7, 11, 49**
See also CA 19-20; CAAS 25-28R; CANR 105; CAP 2; CDWLB 4; DAM DRAM; DLB 215; EW 12; EWL 3; RGWL 2, 3; TWA

Gomez de Avellaneda, Gertrudis
1814-1873 .... **NCLC 111**
See also LAW

Gomez de la Serna, Ramon
1888-1963 .... **CLC 9**
See also CA 153; CAAS 116; CANR 79; EWL 3; HW 1, 2

Goncharov, Ivan Alexandrovich
1812-1891 .... **NCLC 1, 63**
See also DLB 238; EW 6; RGWL 2, 3

Goncourt, Edmond (Louis Antoine Huot) de
1822-1896 .... **NCLC 7**
See also DLB 123; EW 7; GFL 1789 to the Present; RGWL 2, 3

Goncourt, Jules (Alfred Huot) de
1830-1870 .... **NCLC 7**
See also DLB 123; EW 7; GFL 1789 to the Present; RGWL 2, 3

Gongora (y Argote), Luis de
1561-1627 .... **LC 72**
See also RGWL 2, 3

Gontier, Fernande 19(?)- .... **CLC 50**

Gonzalez Martinez, Enrique
See Gonzalez Martinez, Enrique
See also DLB 290

Gonzalez Martinez, Enrique
1871-1952 .... **TCLC 72**
See Gonzalez Martinez, Enrique
See also CA 166; CANR 81; EWL 3; HW 1, 2

Goodison, Lorna 1947- .... **PC 36**
See also CA 142; CANR 88; CP 5, 6, 7; CWP; DLB 157; EWL 3; PFS 25

Goodman, Paul 1911-1972 ..... **CLC 1, 2, 4, 7**
See also CA 19-20; CAAS 37-40R; CAD; CANR 34; CAP 2; CN 1; DLB 130, 246; MAL 5; MTCW 1; RGAL 4

GoodWeather, Harley
See King, Thomas

Googe, Barnabe 1540-1594 .... **LC 94**
See also DLB 132; RGEL 2

Gordimer, Nadine 1923- ...... **CLC 3, 5, 7, 10, 18, 33, 51, 70, 123, 160, 161; SSC 17, 80; WLCS**
See also AAYA 39; AFW; BRWS 2; CA 5-8R; CANR 3, 28, 56, 88, 131; CN 1, 2, 3, 4, 5, 6, 7; DA; DA3; DAB; DAC; DAM MST, NOV; DLB 225, 326, 330; EWL 3; EXPS; INT CANR-28; LATS 1:2; MTCW 1, 2; MTFW 2005; NFS 4; RGEL 2; RGSF 2; SSFS 2, 14, 19; TWA; WLIT 2; YAW

Gordon, Adam Lindsay
1833-1870 .... **NCLC 21**
See also DLB 230

Gordon, Caroline 1895-1981 . **CLC 6, 13, 29, 83; SSC 15**
See also AMW; CA 11-12; CAAS 103; CANR 36; CAP 1; CN 1, 2; DLB 4, 9, 102; DLBD 17; DLBY 1981; EWL 3; MAL 5; MTCW 1, 2; MTFW 2005; RGAL 4; RGSF 2

Gordon, Charles William 1860-1937
See Connor, Ralph
See also CAAE 109

Gordon, Mary 1949- .. **CLC 13, 22, 128, 216; SSC 59**
See also AMWS 4; BPFB 2; CA 102; CANR 44, 92, 154; CN 4, 5, 6, 7; DLB 6; DLBY 1981; FW; INT CA-102; MAL 5; MTCW 1

Gordon, Mary Catherine
See Gordon, Mary

Gordon, N. J.
See Bosman, Herman Charles

Gordon, Sol 1923- .... **CLC 26**
See also CA 53-56; CANR 4; SATA 11

Gordone, Charles 1925-1995 .. **CLC 1, 4; DC 8**
See also BW 1, 3; CA 180; 93-96; 180; CAAS 150; CAD; CANR 55; DAM DRAM; DLB 7; INT CA-93-96; MTCW 1

Gore, Catherine 1800-1861 .... **NCLC 65**
See also DLB 116; RGEL 2

Gorenko, Anna Andreevna
See Akhmatova, Anna

Gorky, Maxim .... **SSC 28; TCLC 8; WLC 3**
See Peshkov, Alexei Maximovich
See also DAB; DFS 9; DLB 295; EW 8; EWL 3; TWA

Goryan, Sirak
See Saroyan, William

Gosse, Edmund (William)
1849-1928 .... **TCLC 28**
See also CAAE 117; DLB 57, 144, 184; RGEL 2

Gotlieb, Phyllis (Fay Bloom) 1926- .. **CLC 18**
See also CA 13-16R; CANR 7, 135; CN 7; CP 1, 2, 3, 4; DLB 88, 251; SFW 4

Gottesman, S. D.
See Kornbluth, C(yril) M.; Pohl, Frederik

Gottfried von Strassburg fl. c.
1170-1215 .... **CMLC 10**
See also CDWLB 2; DLB 138; EW 1; RGWL 2, 3

Gotthelf, Jeremias 1797-1854 .... **NCLC 117**
See also DLB 133; RGWL 2, 3

Gottschalk, Laura Riding
See Jackson, Laura (Riding)

Gould, Lois 1932(?)-2002 .... **CLC 4, 10**
See also CA 77-80; CAAS 208; CANR 29; MTCW 1

Gould, Stephen Jay 1941-2002 .... **CLC 163**
See also AAYA 26; BEST 90:2; CA 77-80; CAAS 205; CANR 10, 27, 56, 75, 125; CPW; INT CANR-27; MTCW 1, 2; MTFW 2005

Gourmont, Remy(-Marie-Charles) de
1858-1915 .... **TCLC 17**
See also CA 150; CAAE 109; GFL 1789 to the Present; MTCW 2

Gournay, Marie le Jars de
See de Gournay, Marie le Jars

Govier, Katherine 1948- .... **CLC 51**
See also CA 101; CANR 18, 40, 128; CCA 1

Gower, John c. 1330-1408 .... **LC 76; PC 59**
See also BRW 1; DLB 146; RGEL 2

Guiraldes, Ricardo (Guillermo)
1886-1927 .... **TCLC 39**
See also CA 131; EWL 3; HW 1; LAW;
MTCW 1

Gumilev, Nikolai (Stepanovich)
1886-1921 .... **TCLC 60**
See Gumilyov, Nikolay Stepanovich
See also CA 165; DLB 295

Gumilyov, Nikolay Stepanovich
See Gumilev, Nikolai (Stepanovich)
See also EWL 3

Gump, P. Q.
See Card, Orson Scott

Gunesekera, Romesh 1954- .... **CLC 91**
See also BRWS 10; CA 159; CANR 140;
CN 6, 7; DLB 267, 323

Gunn, Bill .... **CLC 5**
See Gunn, William Harrison
See also DLB 38

Gunn, Thom(son William)
1929-2004 . **CLC 3, 6, 18, 32, 81; PC 26**
See also BRWS 4; CA 17-20R; CAAS 227;
CANR 9, 33, 116; CDBLB 1960 to
Present; CP 1, 2, 3, 4, 5, 6, 7; DAM
POET; DLB 27; INT CANR-33; MTCW
1; PFS 9; RGEL 2

Gunn, William Harrison 1934(?)-1989
See Gunn, Bill
See also AITN 1; BW 1, 3; CA 13-16R;
CAAS 128; CANR 12, 25, 76

Gunn Allen, Paula
See Allen, Paula Gunn

Gunnars, Kristjana 1948- .... **CLC 69**
See also CA 113; CCA 1; CP 6, 7; CWP;
DLB 60

Gunter, Erich
See Eich, Gunter

Gurdjieff, G(eorgei) I(vanovich)
1877(?)-1949 .... **TCLC 71**
See also CA 157

Gurganus, Allan 1947- .... **CLC 70**
See also BEST 90:1; CA 135; CANR 114;
CN 6, 7; CPW; CSW; DAM POP; GLL 1

Gurney, A. R.
See Gurney, A(lbert) R(amsdell), Jr.
See also DLB 266

Gurney, A(lbert) R(amsdell), Jr.
1930- .... **CLC 32, 50, 54**
See Gurney, A. R.
See also AMWS 5; CA 77-80; CAD; CANR
32, 64, 121; CD 5, 6; DAM DRAM; EWL
3

Gurney, Ivor (Bertie) 1890-1937 ... **TCLC 33**
See also BRW 6; CA 167; DLBY 2002;
PAB; RGEL 2

Gurney, Peter
See Gurney, A(lbert) R(amsdell), Jr.

Guro, Elena (Genrikhovna)
1877-1913 .... **TCLC 56**
See also DLB 295

Gustafson, James M(oody) 1925- ... **CLC 100**
See also CA 25-28R; CANR 37

Gustafson, Ralph (Barker)
1909-1995 .... **CLC 36**
See also CA 21-24R; CANR 8, 45, 84; CP
1, 2, 3, 4, 5, 6; DLB 88; RGEL 2

Gut, Gom
See Simenon, Georges (Jacques Christian)

Guterson, David 1956- .... **CLC 91**
See also CA 132; CANR 73, 126; CN 7;
DLB 292; MTCW 2; MTFW 2005; NFS
13

Guthrie, A(lfred) B(ertram), Jr.
1901-1991 .... **CLC 23**
See also CA 57-60; CAAS 134; CANR 24;
CN 1, 2, 3; DLB 6, 212; MAL 5; SATA
62; SATA-Obit 67; TCWW 1, 2

Guthrie, Isobel
See Grieve, C(hristopher) M(urray)

Guthrie, Woodrow Wilson 1912-1967
See Guthrie, Woody
See also CA 113; CAAS 93-96

Guthrie, Woody .... **CLC 35**
See Guthrie, Woodrow Wilson
See also DLB 303; LAIT 3

Gutierrez Najera, Manuel
1859-1895 .... **HLCS 2; NCLC 133**
See also DLB 290; LAW

Guy, Rosa (Cuthbert) 1925- .... **CLC 26**
See also AAYA 4, 37; BW 2; CA 17-20R;
CANR 14, 34, 83; CLR 13; DLB 33;
DNFS 1; JRDA; MAICYA 1, 2; SATA 14,
62, 122; YAW

Gwendolyn
See Bennett, (Enoch) Arnold

H. D. .... **CLC 3, 8, 14, 31, 34, 73; PC 5**
See Doolittle, Hilda
See also FL 1:5

H. de V.
See Buchan, John

Haavikko, Paavo Juhani 1931- .. **CLC 18, 34**
See also CA 106; CWW 2; EWL 3

Habbema, Koos
See Heijermans, Herman

Habermas, Juergen 1929- .... **CLC 104**
See also CA 109; CANR 85; DLB 242

Habermas, Jurgen
See Habermas, Juergen

Hacker, Marilyn 1942- ...... **CLC 5, 9, 23, 72,**
91; PC 47
See also CA 77-80; CANR 68, 129; CP 3,
4, 5, 6, 7; CWP; DAM POET; DLB 120,
282; FW; GLL 2; MAL 5; PFS 19

Hadewijch of Antwerp fl. 1250- ... **CMLC 61**
See also RGWL 3

Hadrian 76-138 .... **CMLC 52**

Haeckel, Ernst Heinrich (Philipp August)
1834-1919 .... **TCLC 83**
See also CA 157

Hafiz c. 1326-1389(?) .... **CMLC 34**
See also RGWL 2, 3; WLIT 6

Hagedorn, Jessica T(arahata)
1949- .... **CLC 185**
See also CA 139; CANR 69; CWP; DLB
312; RGAL 4

Haggard, H(enry) Rider
1856-1925 .... **TCLC 11**
See also BRWS 3; BYA 4, 5; CA 148;
CAAE 108; CANR 112; DLB 70, 156,
174, 178; FANT; LMFS 1; MTCW 2;
RGEL 2; RHW; SATA 16; SCFW 1, 2;
SFW 4; SUFW 1; WLIT 4

Hagiosy, L.
See Larbaud, Valery (Nicolas)

Hagiwara, Sakutaro 1886-1942 .... **PC 18;**
TCLC 60
See Hagiwara Sakutaro
See also CA 154; RGWL 3

Hagiwara Sakutaro
See Hagiwara, Sakutaro
See also EWL 3

Haig, Fenil
See Ford, Ford Madox

Haig-Brown, Roderick (Langmere)
1908-1976 .... **CLC 21**
See also CA 5-8R; CAAS 69-72; CANR 4,
38, 83; CLR 31; CWRI 5; DLB 88; MAI-
CYA 1, 2; SATA 12; TCWW 2

Haight, Rip
See Carpenter, John (Howard)

Haij, Vera
See Jansson, Tove (Marika)

Hailey, Arthur 1920-2004 .... **CLC 5**
See also AITN 2; BEST 90:3; BPFB 2; CA
1-4R; CAAS 233; CANR 2, 36, 75; CCA
1; CN 1, 2, 3, 4, 5, 6, 7; CPW; DAM
NOV, POP; DLB 88; DLBY 1982; MTCW
1, 2; MTFW 2005

Hailey, Elizabeth Forsythe 1938- ..... **CLC 40**
See also CA 188; 93-96, 188; 1; CANR 15,
48; INT CANR-15

Haines, John (Meade) 1924- .... **CLC 58**
See also AMWS 12; CA 17-20R; CANR
13, 34; CP 1, 2, 3, 4, 5; CSW; DLB 5,
212; TCLE 1:1

Ha Jin 1956- .... **CLC 109**
See Jin, Xuefei
See also CA 152; CANR 91, 130; DLB 244,
292; MTFW 2005; SSFS 17

Hakluyt, Richard 1552-1616 .... **LC 31**
See also DLB 136; RGEL 2

Haldeman, Joe 1943- .... **CLC 61**
See Graham, Robert
See also AAYA 38; CA 179; 53-56, 179;
25; CANR 6, 70, 72, 130; DLB 8; INT
CANR-6; SCFW 2; SFW 4

Haldeman, Joe William
See Haldeman, Joe

Hale, Janet Campbell 1947- .... **NNAL**
See also CA 49-52; CANR 45, 75; DAM
MULT; DLB 175; MTCW 2; MTFW 2005

Hale, Sarah Josepha (Buell)
1788-1879 .... **NCLC 75**
See also DLB 1, 42, 73, 243

Halevy, Elie 1870-1937 .... **TCLC 104**

Haley, Alex(ander Murray Palmer)
1921-1992 .... **BLC 2; CLC 8, 12, 76;**
TCLC 147
See also AAYA 26; BPFB 2; BW 2, 3; CA
77-80; CAAS 136; CANR 61; CDALBS;
CPW; CSW; DA; DA3; DAB; DAC;
DAM MST, MULT, POP; DLB 38; LAIT
5; MTCW 1, 2; NFS 9

Haliburton, Thomas Chandler
1796-1865 .... **NCLC 15, 149**
See also DLB 11, 99; RGEL 2; RGSF 2

Hall, Donald 1928- .. **CLC 1, 13, 37, 59, 151;**
PC 70
See also AAYA 63; CA 5-8R; 7; CANR 2,
44, 64, 106, 133; CP 1, 2, 3, 4, 5, 6, 7;
DAM POET; DLB 5; MAL 5; MTCW 2;
MTFW 2005; RGAL 4; SATA 23, 97

Hall, Donald Andrew, Jr.
See Hall, Donald

Hall, Frederic Sauser
See Sauser-Hall, Frederic

Hall, James
See Kuttner, Henry

Hall, James Norman 1887-1951 ..... **TCLC 23**
See also CA 173; CAAE 123; LAIT 1;
RHW 1; SATA 21

Hall, Joseph 1574-1656 .... **LC 91**
See also DLB 121, 151; RGEL 2

Hall, Marguerite Radclyffe
See Hall, Radclyffe

Hall, Radclyffe 1880-1943 .... **TCLC 12**
See also BRWS 6; CA 150; CAAE 110;
CANR 83; DLB 191; MTCW 2; MTFW
2005; RGEL 2; RHW

Hall, Rodney 1935- .... **CLC 51**
See also CA 109; CANR 69; CN 6, 7; CP
1, 2, 3, 4, 5, 6, 7; DLB 289

Hallam, Arthur Henry
1811-1833 .... **NCLC 110**
See also DLB 32

Halldor Laxness .... **CLC 25**
See Gudjonsson, Halldor Kiljan
See also DLB 293; EW 12; EWL 3; RGWL
2, 3

Halleck, Fitz-Greene 1790-1867 .... **NCLC 47**
See also DLB 3, 250; RGAL 4

Halliday, Michael
See Creasey, John

Halpern, Daniel 1945- .... **CLC 14**
See also CA 33-36R; CANR 93; CP 3, 4, 5,
6, 7

Harrison, Tony 1937- .... **CLC 43, 129**
　　See also BRWS 5; CA 65-68; CANR 44,
　　98; CBD; CD 5, 6; CP 2, 3, 4, 5, 6, 7;
　　DLB 40, 245; MTCW 1; RGEL 2
Harriss, Will(ard Irvin) 1922- .... **CLC 34**
　　See also CA 111
Hart, Ellis
　　See Ellison, Harlan
Hart, Josephine 1942(?)- .... **CLC 70**
　　See also CA 138; CANR 70, 149; CPW;
　　DAM POP
Hart, Moss 1904-1961 .... **CLC 66**
　　See also CA 109; CAAS 89-92; CANR 84;
　　DAM DRAM; DFS 1; DLB 7, 266; RGAL
　　4
Harte, (Francis) Bret(t)
　　1836(?)-1902 ... **SSC 8, 59; TCLC 1, 25;**
　　WLC 3
　　See also AMWS 2; CA 140; CAAE 104;
　　CANR 80; CDALB 1865-1917; DA;
　　DA3; DAC; DAM MST; DLB 12, 64, 74,
　　79, 186; EXPS; LAIT 2; RGAL 4; RGSF
　　2; SATA 26; SSFS 3; TUS
Hartley, L(eslie) P(oles) 1895-1972 ... **CLC 2,**
　　22
　　See also BRWS 7; CA 45-48; CAAS 37-
　　40R; CANR 33; CN 1; DLB 15, 139;
　　EWL 3; HGG; MTCW 1, 2; MTFW 2005;
　　RGEL 2; RGSF 2; SUFW 1
Hartman, Geoffrey H. 1929- .... **CLC 27**
　　See also CA 125; CAAE 117; CANR 79;
　　DLB 67
Hartmann, Sadakichi 1869-1944 ... **TCLC 73**
　　See also CA 157; DLB 54
Hartmann von Aue c. 1170-c.
　　1210 .... **CMLC 15**
　　See also CDWLB 2; DLB 138; RGWL 2, 3
Hartog, Jan de
　　See de Hartog, Jan
Haruf, Kent 1943- .... **CLC 34**
　　See also AAYA 44; CA 149; CANR 91, 131
Harvey, Caroline
　　See Trollope, Joanna
Harvey, Gabriel 1550(?)-1631 .... **LC 88**
　　See also DLB 167, 213, 281
Harwood, Ronald 1934- .... **CLC 32**
　　See also CA 1-4R; CANR 4, 55, 150; CBD;
　　CD 5, 6; DAM DRAM, MST; DLB 13
Hasegawa Tatsunosuke
　　See Futabatei, Shimei
Hasek, Jaroslav (Matej Frantisek)
　　1883-1923 .... **SSC 69; TCLC 4**
　　See also CA 129; CAAE 104; CDWLB 4;
　　DLB 215; EW 9; EWL 3; MTCW 1, 2;
　　RGSF 2; RGWL 2, 3
Hass, Robert 1941- ... **CLC 18, 39, 99; PC 16**
　　See also AMWS 6; CA 111; CANR 30, 50,
　　71; CP 3, 4, 5, 6, 7; DLB 105, 206; EWL
　　3; MAL 5; MTFW 2005; RGAL 4; SATA
　　94; TCLE 1:1
Hastings, Hudson
　　See Kuttner, Henry
Hastings, Selina .... **CLC 44**
Hathorne, John 1641-1717 .... **LC 38**
Hatteras, Amelia
　　See Mencken, H(enry) L(ouis)
Hatteras, Owen .... **TCLC 18**
　　See Mencken, H(enry) L(ouis); Nathan,
　　George Jean
Hauptmann, Gerhart (Johann Robert)
　　1862-1946 .... **SSC 37; TCLC 4**
　　See also CA 153; CAAE 104; CDWLB 2;
　　DAM DRAM; DLB 66, 118, 330; EW 8;
　　EWL 3; RGSF 2; RGWL 2, 3; TWA
Havel, Vaclav 1936- ..... **CLC 25, 58, 65, 123;**
　　DC 6
　　See also CA 104; CANR 36, 63, 124; CD-
　　WLB 4; CWW 2; DA3; DAM DRAM;
　　DFS 10; DLB 232; EWL 3; LMFS 2;
　　MTCW 1, 2; MTFW 2005; RGWL 3

Haviaras, Stratis .... **CLC 33**
　　See Chaviaras, Strates
Hawes, Stephen 1475(?)-1529(?) .... **LC 17**
　　See also DLB 132; RGEL 2
Hawkes, John 1925-1998 .. **CLC 1, 2, 3, 4, 7,**
　　9, 14, 15, 27, 49
　　See also BPFB 2; CA 1-4R; CAAS 167;
　　CANR 2, 47, 64; CN 1, 2, 3, 4, 5, 6; DLB
　　2, 7, 227; DLBY 1980, 1998; EWL 3;
　　MAL 5; MTCW 1, 2; MTFW 2005;
　　RGAL 4
Hawking, S. W.
　　See Hawking, Stephen W.
Hawking, Stephen W. 1942- ..... **CLC 63, 105**
　　See also AAYA 13; BEST 89:1; CA 129;
　　CAAE 126; CANR 48, 115; CPW; DA3;
　　MTCW 1; MTFW 2005
Hawkins, Anthony Hope
　　See Hope, Anthony
Hawthorne, Julian 1846-1934 .... **TCLC 25**
　　See also CA 165; HGG
Hawthorne, Nathaniel 1804-1864 ... **NCLC 2,**
　　10, 17, 23, 39, 79, 95, 158, 171; SSC 3,
　　29, 39, 89; WLC 3
　　See also AAYA 18; AMW; AMWC 1;
　　AMWR 1; BPFB 2; BYA 3; CDALB
　　1640-1865; CLR 103; DA; DA3; DAB;
　　DAC; DAM MST, NOV; DLB 1, 74, 183,
　　223, 269; EXPN; EXPS; GL 2; HGG;
　　LAIT 1; NFS 1, 20; RGAL 4; RGSF 2;
　　SSFS 1, 7, 11, 15; SUFW 1; TUS; WCH;
　　YABC 2
Hawthorne, Sophia Peabody
　　1809-1871 .... **NCLC 150**
　　See also DLB 183, 239
Haxton, Josephine Ayres 1921-
　　See Douglas, Ellen
　　See also CA 115; CANR 41, 83
Hayaseca y Eizaguirre, Jorge
　　See Echegaray (y Eizaguirre), Jose (Maria
　　Waldo)
Hayashi, Fumiko 1904-1951 .... **TCLC 27**
　　See Hayashi Fumiko
　　See also CA 161
Hayashi Fumiko
　　See Hayashi, Fumiko
　　See also DLB 180; EWL 3
Haycraft, Anna 1932-2005
　　See Ellis, Alice Thomas
　　See also CA 122; CAAS 237; CANR 90,
　　141; MTCW 2; MTFW 2005
Hayden, Robert E(arl) 1913-1980 ..... **BLC 2;**
　　CLC 5, 9, 14, 37; PC 6
　　See also AFAW 1, 2; AMWS 2; BW 1, 3;
　　CA 69-72; CAAS 97-100; CABS 2;
　　CANR 24, 75, 82; CDALB 1941-1968;
　　CP 1, 2, 3; DA; DAC; DAM MST, MULT,
　　POET; DLB 5, 76; EWL 3; EXPP; MAL
　　5; MTCW 1, 2; PFS 1; RGAL 4; SATA
　　19; SATA-Obit 26; WP
Haydon, Benjamin Robert
　　1786-1846 .... **NCLC 146**
　　See also DLB 110
Hayek, F(riedrich) A(ugust von)
　　1899-1992 .... **TCLC 109**
　　See also CA 93-96; CAAS 137; CANR 20;
　　MTCW 1, 2
Hayford, J(oseph) E(phraim) Casely
　　See Casely-Hayford, J(oseph) E(phraim)
Hayman, Ronald 1932- .... **CLC 44**
　　See also CA 25-28R; CANR 18, 50, 88; CD
　　5, 6; DLB 155
Hayne, Paul Hamilton 1830-1886 . **NCLC 94**
　　See also DLB 3, 64, 79, 248; RGAL 4
Hays, Mary 1760-1843 .... **NCLC 114**
　　See also DLB 142, 158; RGEL 2
Haywood, Eliza (Fowler)
　　1693(?)-1756 .... **LC 1, 44**
　　See also BRWS 12; DLB 39; RGEL 2

Hazlitt, William 1778-1830 ...... **NCLC 29, 82**
　　See also BRW 4; DLB 110, 158; RGEL 2;
　　TEA
Hazzard, Shirley 1931- .... **CLC 18, 218**
　　See also CA 9-12R; CANR 4, 70, 127; CN
　　1, 2, 3, 4, 5, 6, 7; DLB 289; DLBY 1982;
　　MTCW 1
Head, Bessie 1937-1986 ...... **BLC 2; CLC 25,**
　　67; SSC 52
　　See also AFW; BW 2, 3; CA 29-32R; CAAS
　　119; CANR 25, 82; CDWLB 3; CN 1, 2,
　　3, 4; DA3; DAM MULT; DLB 117, 225;
　　EWL 3; EXPS; FL 1:6; FW; MTCW 1, 2;
　　MTFW 2005; RGSF 2; SSFS 5, 13; WLIT
　　2; WWE 1
Headon, (Nicky) Topper 1956(?)- ..... **CLC 30**
Heaney, Seamus 1939- . **CLC 5, 7, 14, 25, 37,**
　　74, 91, 171, 225; PC 18; WLCS
　　See also AAYA 61; BRWR 2; BRWS 2; CA
　　85-88; CANR 25, 48, 75, 91, 128; CD-
　　BLB 1960 to Present; CP 1, 2, 3, 4, 5, 6,
　　7; DA3; DAB; DAM POET; DLB 40,
　　330; DLBY 1995; EWL 3; EXPP; MTCW
　　1, 2; MTFW 2005; PAB; PFS 2, 5, 8, 17;
　　RGEL 2; TEA; WLIT 4
Hearn, (Patricio) Lafcadio (Tessima Carlos)
　　1850-1904 .... **TCLC 9**
　　See also CA 166; CAAE 105; DLB 12, 78,
　　189; HGG; MAL 5; RGAL 4
Hearne, Samuel 1745-1792 .... **LC 95**
　　See also DLB 99
Hearne, Vicki 1946-2001 .... **CLC 56**
　　See also CA 139; CAAS 201
Hearon, Shelby 1931- .... **CLC 63**
　　See also AITN 2; AMWS 8; CA 25-28R;
　　11; CANR 18, 48, 103, 146; CSW
Heat-Moon, William Least .... **CLC 29**
　　See Trogdon, William (Lewis)
　　See also AAYA 9
Hebbel, Friedrich 1813-1863 . **DC 21; NCLC**
　　43
　　See also CDWLB 2; DAM DRAM; DLB
　　129; EW 6; RGWL 2, 3
Hebert, Anne 1916-2000 .... **CLC 4, 13, 29**
　　See also CA 85-88; CAAS 187; CANR 69,
　　126; CCA 1; CWP; CWW 2; DA3; DAC;
　　DAM MST, POET; DLB 68; EWL 3; GFL
　　1789 to the Present; MTCW 1, 2; MTFW
　　2005; PFS 20
Hecht, Anthony (Evan) 1923-2004 .... **CLC 8,**
　　13, 19; PC 70
　　See also AMWS 10; CA 9-12R; CAAS 232;
　　CANR 6, 108; CP 1, 2, 3, 4, 5, 6, 7; DAM
　　POET; DLB 5, 169; EWL 3; PFS 6; WP
Hecht, Ben 1894-1964 ...... **CLC 8; TCLC 101**
　　See also CA 85-88; DFS 9; DLB 7, 9, 25,
　　26, 28, 86; FANT; IDFW 3, 4; RGAL 4
Hedayat, Sadeq 1903-1951 .... **TCLC 21**
　　See also CAAE 120; EWL 3; RGSF 2
Hegel, Georg Wilhelm Friedrich
　　1770-1831 .... **NCLC 46, 151**
　　See also DLB 90; TWA
Heidegger, Martin 1889-1976 .... **CLC 24**
　　See also CA 81-84; CAAS 65-68; CANR
　　34; DLB 296; MTCW 1, 2; MTFW 2005
Heidenstam, (Carl Gustaf) Verner von
　　1859-1940 .... **TCLC 5**
　　See also CAAE 104; DLB 330
Heidi Louise
　　See Erdrich, Louise
Heifner, Jack 1946- .... **CLC 11**
　　See also CA 105; CANR 47
Heijermans, Herman 1864-1924 .... **TCLC 24**
　　See also CAAE 123; EWL 3
Heilbrun, Carolyn G(old)
　　1926-2003 .... **CLC 25, 173**
　　See Cross, Amanda
　　See also CA 45-48; CAAS 220; CANR 1,
　　28, 58, 94; FW

Hostos (y Bonilla), Eugenio Maria de
  1839-1903 .... **TCLC 24**
  See also CA 131; CAAE 123; HW 1

Houdini
  See Lovecraft, H. P.

Houellebecq, Michel 1958- .... **CLC 179**
  See also CA 185; CANR 140; MTFW 2005

Hougan, Carolyn 1943- .... **CLC 34**
  See also CA 139

Household, Geoffrey (Edward West)
  1900-1988 .... **CLC 11**
  See also CA 77-80; CAAS 126; CANR 58;
  CMW 4; CN 1, 2, 3, 4; DLB 87; SATA
  14; SATA-Obit 59

Housman, A(lfred) E(dward)
  1859-1936 .... **PC 2, 43; TCLC 1, 10;
  WLCS**
  See also AAYA 66; BRW 6; CA 125; CAAE
  104; DA; DA3; DAB; DAC; DAM MST,
  POET; DLB 19, 284; EWL 3; EXPP;
  MTCW 1, 2; MTFW 2005; PAB; PFS 4,
  7; RGEL 2; TEA; WP

Housman, Laurence 1865-1959 .... **TCLC 7**
  See also CA 155; CAAE 106; DLB 10;
  FANT; RGEL 2; SATA 25

Houston, Jeanne Wakatsuki 1934- .... **AAL**
  See also AAYA 49; CA 232; 103, 232; 16;
  CANR 29, 123; LAIT 4; SATA 78, 168;
  SATA-Essay 168

Howard, Elizabeth Jane 1923- ..... **CLC 7, 29**
  See also BRWS 11; CA 5-8R; CANR 8, 62,
  146; CN 1, 2, 3, 4, 5, 6, 7

Howard, Maureen 1930- .... **CLC 5, 14, 46,
  151**
  See also CA 53-56; CANR 31, 75, 140; CN
  4, 5, 6, 7; DLBY 1983; INT CANR-31;
  MTCW 1, 2; MTFW 2005

Howard, Richard 1929- .... **CLC 7, 10, 47**
  See also AITN 1; CA 85-88; CANR 25, 80,
  154; CP 1, 2, 3, 4, 5, 6, 7; DLB 5; INT
  CANR-25; MAL 5

Howard, Robert E 1906-1936 .... **TCLC 8**
  See also BPFB 2; BYA 5; CA 157; CAAE
  105; CANR 155; FANT; SUFW 1;
  TCWW 1, 2

Howard, Robert Ervin
  See Howard, Robert E

Howard, Warren F.
  See Pohl, Frederik

Howe, Fanny (Quincy) 1940- .... **CLC 47**
  See also CA 187; 117, 187; 27; CANR 70,
  116; CP 6, 7; CWP; SATA-Brief 52

Howe, Irving 1920-1993 .... **CLC 85**
  See also AMWS 6; CA 9-12R; CAAS 141;
  CANR 21, 50; DLB 67; EWL 3; MAL 5;
  MTCW 1, 2; MTFW 2005

Howe, Julia Ward 1819-1910 .... **TCLC 21**
  See also CA 191; CAAE 117; DLB 1, 189,
  235; FW

Howe, Susan 1937- .... **CLC 72, 152; PC 54**
  See also AMWS 4; CA 160; CP 5, 6, 7;
  CWP; DLB 120; FW; RGAL 4

Howe, Tina 1937- .... **CLC 48**
  See also CA 109; CAD; CANR 125; CD 5,
  6; CWD

Howell, James 1594(?)-1666 .... **LC 13**
  See also DLB 151

Howells, W. D.
  See Howells, William Dean

Howells, William D.
  See Howells, William Dean

Howells, William Dean 1837-1920 ... **SSC 36;
  TCLC 7, 17, 41**
  See also AMW; CA 134; CAAE 104;
  CDALB 1865-1917; DLB 12, 64, 74, 79,
  189; LMFS 1; MAL 5; MTCW 2; RGAL
  4; TUS

Howes, Barbara 1914-1996 .... **CLC 15**
  See also CA 9-12R; 3; CAAS 151; CANR
  53; CP 1, 2, 3, 4, 5, 6; SATA 5; TCLE 1:1

Hrabal, Bohumil 1914-1997 ...... **CLC 13, 67;
  TCLC 155**
  See also CA 106; 12; CAAS 156; CANR
  57; CWW 2; DLB 232; EWL 3; RGSF 2

Hrabanus Maurus 776(?)-856 .... **CMLC 78**
  See also DLB 148

Hrotsvit of Gandersheim c. 935-c.
  1000 .... **CMLC 29**
  See also DLB 148

Hsi, Chu 1130-1200 .... **CMLC 42**

Hsun, Lu
  See Lu Hsun

Hubbard, L. Ron 1911-1986 .... **CLC 43**
  See also AAYA 64; CA 77-80; CAAS 118;
  CANR 52; CPW; DA3; DAM POP;
  FANT; MTCW 2; MTFW 2005; SFW 4

Hubbard, Lafayette Ronald
  See Hubbard, L. Ron

Huch, Ricarda (Octavia)
  1864-1947 .... **TCLC 13**
  See also CA 189; CAAE 111; DLB 66;
  EWL 3

Huddle, David 1942- .... **CLC 49**
  See also CA 57-60; 20; CANR 89; DLB
  130

Hudson, Jeffrey
  See Crichton, Michael

Hudson, W(illiam) H(enry)
  1841-1922 .... **TCLC 29**
  See also CA 190; CAAE 115; DLB 98, 153,
  174; RGEL 2; SATA 35

Hueffer, Ford Madox
  See Ford, Ford Madox

Hughart, Barry 1934- .... **CLC 39**
  See also CA 137; FANT; SFW 4; SUFW 2

Hughes, Colin
  See Creasey, John

Hughes, David (John) 1930-2005 ..... **CLC 48**
  See also CA 129; CAAE 116; CAAS 238;
  CN 4, 5, 6, 7; DLB 14

Hughes, Edward James
  See Hughes, Ted
  See also DA3; DAM MST, POET

Hughes, (James Mercer) Langston
  1902-1967 ..... **BLC 2; CLC 1, 5, 10, 15,
  35, 44, 108; DC 3; HR 1:2; PC 1, 53;
  SSC 6, 90; WLC 3**
  See also AAYA 12; AFAW 1, 2; AMWR 1;
  AMWS 1; BW 1, 3; CA 1-4R; CAAS 25-
  28R; CANR 1, 34, 82; CDALB 1929-
  1941; CLR 17; DA; DA3; DAB; DAC;
  DAM DRAM, MST, MULT, POET; DFS
  6, 18; DLB 4, 7, 48, 51, 86, 228, 315;
  EWL 3; EXPP; EXPS; JRDA; LAIT 3;
  LMFS 2; MAICYA 1, 2; MAL 5; MTCW
  1, 2; MTFW 2005; NFS 21; PAB; PFS 1,
  3, 6, 10, 15; RGAL 4; RGSF 2; SATA 4,
  33; SSFS 4, 7; TUS; WCH; WP; YAW

Hughes, Richard (Arthur Warren)
  1900-1976 .... **CLC 1, 11**
  See also CA 5-8R; CAAS 65-68; CANR 4;
  CN 1, 2; DAM NOV; DLB 15, 161; EWL
  3; MTCW 1; RGEL 2; SATA 8; SATA-
  Obit 25

Hughes, Ted 1930-1998 . **CLC 2, 4, 9, 14, 37,
  119; PC 7**
  See Hughes, Edward James
  See also BRWC 2; BRWR 2; BRWS 1; CA
  1-4R; CAAS 171; CANR 1, 33, 66, 108;
  CLR 3; CP 1, 2, 3, 4, 5, 6; DAB; DAC;
  DLB 40, 161; EWL 3; EXPP; MAICYA
  1, 2; MTCW 1, 2; MTFW 2005; PAB;
  PFS 4, 19; RGEL 2; SATA 49; SATA-
  Brief 27; SATA-Obit 107; TEA; YAW

Hugo, Richard
  See Huch, Ricarda (Octavia)

Hugo, Richard F(ranklin)
  1923-1982 .... **CLC 6, 18, 32; PC 68**
  See also AMWS 6; CA 49-52; CAAS 108;
  CANR 3; CP 1, 2, 3; DAM POET; DLB
  5, 206; EWL 3; MAL 5; PFS 17; RGAL 4

Hugo, Victor (Marie) 1802-1885 ...... **NCLC 3,
  10, 21, 161; PC 17; WLC 3**
  See also AAYA 28; DA; DA3; DAB; DAC;
  DAM DRAM, MST, NOV, POET; DLB
  119, 192, 217; EFS 2; EW 6; EXPN; GFL
  1789 to the Present; LAIT 1, 2; NFS 5,
  20; RGWL 2, 3; SATA 47; TWA

Huidobro, Vicente
  See Huidobro Fernandez, Vicente Garcia
  See also DLB 283; EWL 3; LAW

Huidobro Fernandez, Vicente Garcia
  1893-1948 .... **TCLC 31**
  See Huidobro, Vicente
  See also CA 131; HW 1

Hulme, Keri 1947- .... **CLC 39, 130**
  See also CA 125; CANR 69; CN 4, 5, 6, 7;
  CP 6, 7; CWP; DLB 326; EWL 3; FW;
  INT CA-125; NFS 24

Hulme, T(homas) E(rnest)
  1883-1917 .... **TCLC 21**
  See also BRWS 6; CA 203; CAAE 117;
  DLB 19

Humboldt, Alexander von
  1769-1859 .... **NCLC 170**
  See also DLB 90

Humboldt, Wilhelm von
  1767-1835 .... **NCLC 134**
  See also DLB 90

Hume, David 1711-1776 .... **LC 7, 56**
  See also BRWS 3; DLB 104, 252; LMFS 1;
  TEA

Humphrey, William 1924-1997 .... **CLC 45**
  See also AMWS 9; CA 77-80; CAAS 160;
  CANR 68; CN 1, 2, 3, 4, 5, 6; CSW; DLB
  6, 212, 234, 278; TCWW 1, 2

Humphreys, Emyr Owen 1919- .... **CLC 47**
  See also CA 5-8R; CANR 3, 24; CN 1, 2,
  3, 4, 5, 6, 7; DLB 15

Humphreys, Josephine 1945- ..... **CLC 34, 57**
  See also CA 127; CAAE 121; CANR 97;
  CSW; DLB 292; INT CA-127

Huneker, James Gibbons
  1860-1921 .... **TCLC 65**
  See also CA 193; DLB 71; RGAL 4

Hungerford, Hesba Fay
  See Brinsmead, H(esba) F(ay)

Hungerford, Pixie
  See Brinsmead, H(esba) F(ay)

Hunt, E. Howard 1918-2007 .... **CLC 3**
  See also AITN 1; CA 45-48; CANR 2, 47,
  103, 160; CMW 4

Hunt, Everette Howard, Jr.
  See Hunt, E. Howard

Hunt, Francesca
  See Holland, Isabelle (Christian)

Hunt, Howard
  See Hunt, E. Howard

Hunt, Kyle
  See Creasey, John

Hunt, (James Henry) Leigh
  1784-1859 .... **NCLC 1, 70; PC 73**
  See also DAM POET; DLB 96, 110, 144;
  RGEL 2; TEA

Hunt, Marsha 1946- .... **CLC 70**
  See also BW 2, 3; CA 143; CANR 79

Hunt, Violet 1866(?)-1942 .... **TCLC 53**
  See also CA 184; DLB 162, 197

Hunter, E. Waldo
  See Sturgeon, Theodore (Hamilton)

Hunter, Evan 1926-2005 .... **CLC 11, 31**
  See McBain, Ed
  See also AAYA 39; BPFB 2; CA 5-8R;
  CAAS 241; CANR 5, 38, 62, 97, 149;
  CMW 4; CN 1, 2, 3, 4, 5, 6, 7; CPW;

Ishiguro, Kazuo 1954- . **CLC 27, 56, 59, 110, 119**
See also AAYA 58; BEST 90:2; BPFB 2; BRWS 4; CA 120; CANR 49, 95, 133; CN 5, 6, 7; DA3; DAM NOV; DLB 194, 326; EWL 3; MTCW 1, 2; MTFW 2005; NFS 13; WLIT 4; WWE 1

Ishikawa, Hakuhin
See Ishikawa, Takuboku

Ishikawa, Takuboku 1886(?)-1912 ..... **PC 10; TCLC 15**
See Ishikawa Takuboku
See also CA 153; CAAE 113; DAM POET

Iskander, Fazil (Abdulovich) 1929- .. **CLC 47**
See Iskander, Fazil' Abdulevich
See also CA 102; EWL 3

Iskander, Fazil' Abdulevich
See Iskander, Fazil (Abdulovich)
See also DLB 302

Isler, Alan (David) 1934- .... **CLC 91**
See also CA 156; CANR 105

Ivan IV 1530-1584 .... **LC 17**

Ivanov, V.I.
See Ivanov, Vyacheslav

Ivanov, Vyacheslav 1866-1949 .... **TCLC 33**
See also CAAE 122; EWL 3

Ivanov, Vyacheslav Ivanovich
See Ivanov, Vyacheslav

Ivask, Ivar Vidrik 1927-1992 .... **CLC 14**
See also CA 37-40R; CAAS 139; CANR 24

Ives, Morgan
See Bradley, Marion Zimmer
See also GLL 1

Izumi Shikibu c. 973-c. 1034 .... **CMLC 33**

J. R. S.
See Gogarty, Oliver St. John

Jabran, Kahlil
See Gibran, Kahlil

Jabran, Khalil
See Gibran, Kahlil

Jackson, Daniel
See Wingrove, David

Jackson, Helen Hunt 1830-1885 .... **NCLC 90**
See also DLB 42, 47, 186, 189; RGAL 4

Jackson, Jesse 1908-1983 .... **CLC 12**
See also BW 1; CA 25-28R; CAAS 109; CANR 27; CLR 28; CWRI 5; MAICYA 1, 2; SATA 2, 29; SATA-Obit 48

Jackson, Laura (Riding) 1901-1991 .... **PC 44**
See Riding, Laura
See also CA 65-68; CAAS 135; CANR 28, 89; DLB 48

Jackson, Sam
See Trumbo, Dalton

Jackson, Sara
See Wingrove, David

Jackson, Shirley 1919-1965 . **CLC 11, 60, 87; SSC 9, 39; TCLC 187; WLC 3**
See also AAYA 9; AMWS 9; BPFB 2; CA 1-4R; CAAS 25-28R; CANR 4, 52; CDALB 1941-1968; DA; DA3; DAC; DAM MST; DLB 6, 234; EXPS; HGG; LAIT 4; MAL 5; MTCW 2; MTFW 2005; RGAL 4; RGSF 2; SATA 2; SSFS 1; SUFW 1, 2

Jacob, (Cyprien-)Max 1876-1944 .... **TCLC 6**
See also CA 193; CAAE 104; DLB 258; EWL 3; GFL 1789 to the Present; GLL 2; RGWL 2, 3

Jacobs, Harriet A(nn)
1813(?)-1897 .... **NCLC 67, 162**
See also AFAW 1, 2; DLB 239; FL 1:3; FW; LAIT 2; RGAL 4

Jacobs, Jim 1942- .... **CLC 12**
See also CA 97-100; INT CA-97-100

Jacobs, W(illiam) W(ymark)
1863-1943 .... **SSC 73; TCLC 22**
See also CA 167; CAAE 121; DLB 135; EXPS; HGG; RGEL 2; RGSF 2; SSFS 2; SUFW 1

Jacobsen, Jens Peter 1847-1885 .... **NCLC 34**

Jacobsen, Josephine (Winder)
1908-2003 .... **CLC 48, 102; PC 62**
See also CA 33-36R; 18; CAAS 218; CANR 23, 48; CCA 1; CP 2, 3, 4, 5, 6, 7; DLB 244; PFS 23; TCLE 1:1

Jacobson, Dan 1929- .... **CLC 4, 14; SSC 91**
See also AFW; CA 1-4R; CANR 2, 25, 66; CN 1, 2, 3, 4, 5, 6, 7; DLB 14, 207, 225, 319; EWL 3; MTCW 1; RGSF 2

Jacqueline
See Carpentier (y Valmont), Alejo

Jacques de Vitry c. 1160-1240 ...... **CMLC 63**
See also DLB 208

Jagger, Michael Philip
See Jagger, Mick

Jagger, Mick 1943- .... **CLC 17**
See also CA 239

Jahiz, al- c. 780-c. 869 .... **CMLC 25**
See also DLB 311

Jakes, John 1932- .... **CLC 29**
See also AAYA 32; BEST 89:4; BPFB 2; CA 214; 57-60, 214; CANR 10, 43, 66, 111, 142; CPW; CSW; DA3; DAM NOV, POP; DLB 278; DLBY 1983; FANT; INT CANR-10; MTCW 1, 2; MTFW 2005; RHW; SATA 62; SFW 4; TCWW 1, 2

James I 1394-1437 .... **LC 20**
See also RGEL 2

James, Andrew
See Kirkup, James

James, C(yril) L(ionel) R(obert)
1901-1989 .... **BLCS; CLC 33**
See also BW 2; CA 125; CAAE 117; CAAS 128; CANR 62; CN 1, 2, 3, 4; DLB 125; MTCW 1

James, Daniel (Lewis) 1911-1988
See Santiago, Danny
See also CA 174; CAAS 125

James, Dynely
See Mayne, William (James Carter)

James, Henry Sr. 1811-1882 .... **NCLC 53**

James, Henry 1843-1916 .... **SSC 8, 32, 47; TCLC 2, 11, 24, 40, 47, 64, 171; WLC 3**
See also AMW; AMWC 1; AMWR 1; BPFB 2; BRW 6; CA 132; CAAE 104; CDALB 1865-1917; DA; DA3; DAB; DAC; DAM MST, NOV; DLB 12, 71, 74, 189; DLBD 13; EWL 3; EXPS; GL 2; HGG; LAIT 2; MAL 5; MTCW 1, 2; MTFW 2005; NFS 12, 16, 19; RGAL 4; RGEL 2; RGSF 2; SSFS 9; SUFW 1; TUS

James, M. R. .... **SSC 93**
See James, Montague (Rhodes)
See also DLB 156, 201

James, Montague (Rhodes)
1862-1936 .... **SSC 16; TCLC 6**
See James, M. R.
See also CA 203; CAAE 104; HGG; RGEL 2; RGSF 2; SUFW 1

James, P. D. .... **CLC 18, 46, 122, 226**
See White, Phyllis Dorothy James
See also BEST 90:2; BPFB 2; BRWS 4; CDBLB 1960 to Present; CN 4, 5, 6; DLB 87, 276; DLBD 17; MSW

James, Philip
See Moorcock, Michael

James, Samuel
See Stephens, James

James, Seumas
See Stephens, James

James, Stephen
See Stephens, James

James, William 1842-1910 .... **TCLC 15, 32**
See also AMW; CA 193; CAAE 109; DLB 270, 284; MAL 5; NCFS 5; RGAL 4

Jameson, Anna 1794-1860 .... **NCLC 43**
See also DLB 99, 166

Jameson, Fredric (R.) 1934- .... **CLC 142**
See also CA 196; DLB 67; LMFS 2

James VI of Scotland 1566-1625 ...... **LC 109**
See also DLB 151, 172

Jami, Nur al-Din 'Abd al-Rahman
1414-1492 .... **LC 9**

Jammes, Francis 1868-1938 .... **TCLC 75**
See also CA 198; EWL 3; GFL 1789 to the Present

Jandl, Ernst 1925-2000 .... **CLC 34**
See also CA 200; EWL 3

Janowitz, Tama 1957- .... **CLC 43, 145**
See also CA 106; CANR 52, 89, 129; CN 5, 6, 7; CPW; DAM POP; DLB 292; MTFW 2005

Jansson, Tove (Marika) 1914-2001 ... **SSC 96**
See also CA 17-20R; CAAS 196; CANR 38, 118; CLR 2; CWW 2; DLB 257; EWL 3; MAICYA 1, 2; RGSF 2; SATA 3, 41

Japrisot, Sebastien 1931- .... **CLC 90**
See Rossi, Jean-Baptiste
See also CMW 4; NFS 18

Jarrell, Randall 1914-1965 .... **CLC 1, 2, 6, 9, 13, 49; PC 41; TCLC 177**
See also AMW; BYA 5; CA 5-8R; CAAS 25-28R; CABS 2; CANR 6, 34; CDALB 1941-1968; CLR 6, 111; CWRI 5; DAM POET; DLB 48, 52; EWL 3; EXPP; MAICYA 1, 2; MAL 5; MTCW 1, 2; PAB; PFS 2; RGAL 4; SATA 7

Jarry, Alfred 1873-1907 .... **SSC 20; TCLC 2, 14, 147**
See also CA 153; CAAE 104; DA3; DAM DRAM; DFS 8; DLB 192, 258; EW 9; EWL 3; GFL 1789 to the Present; RGWL 2, 3; TWA

Jarvis, E. K.
See Ellison, Harlan

Jawien, Andrzej
See John Paul II, Pope

Jaynes, Roderick
See Coen, Ethan

Jeake, Samuel, Jr.
See Aiken, Conrad (Potter)

Jean Paul 1763-1825 .... **NCLC 7**

Jefferies, (John) Richard
1848-1887 .... **NCLC 47**
See also DLB 98, 141; RGEL 2; SATA 16; SFW 4

Jeffers, (John) Robinson 1887-1962 .. **CLC 2, 3, 11, 15, 54; PC 17; WLC 3**
See also AMWS 2; CA 85-88; CANR 35; CDALB 1917-1929; DA; DAC; DAM MST, POET; DLB 45, 212; EWL 3; MAL 5; MTCW 1, 2; MTFW 2005; PAB; PFS 3, 4; RGAL 4

Jefferson, Janet
See Mencken, H(enry) L(ouis)

Jefferson, Thomas 1743-1826 . **NCLC 11, 103**
See also AAYA 54; ANW; CDALB 1640-1865; DA3; DLB 31, 183; LAIT 1; RGAL 4

Jeffrey, Francis 1773-1850 .... **NCLC 33**
See Francis, Lord Jeffrey

Jelakowitch, Ivan
See Heijermans, Herman

Jelinek, Elfriede 1946- .... **CLC 169**
See also AAYA 68; CA 154; DLB 85, 330; FW

Jellicoe, (Patricia) Ann 1927- .... **CLC 27**
See also CA 85-88; CBD; CD 5, 6; CWD; CWRI 5; DLB 13, 233; FW

Jones, Louis B. 1953- .... **CLC 65**
See also CA 141; CANR 73
Jones, Madison 1925- .... **CLC 4**
See also CA 13-16R; 11; CANR 7, 54, 83,
158; CN 1, 2, 3, 4, 5, 6, 7; CSW; DLB
152
Jones, Madison Percy, Jr.
See Jones, Madison
Jones, Mervyn 1922- .... **CLC 10, 52**
See also CA 45-48; 5; CANR 1, 91; CN 1,
2, 3, 4, 5, 6, 7; MTCW 1
Jones, Mick 1956(?)- .... **CLC 30**
Jones, Nettie (Pearl) 1941- .... **CLC 34**
See also BW 2; CA 137; 20; CANR 88
Jones, Peter 1802-1856 .... **NNAL**
Jones, Preston 1936-1979 .... **CLC 10**
See also CA 73-76; CAAS 89-92; DLB 7
Jones, Robert F(rancis) 1934-2003 .... **CLC 7**
See also CA 49-52; CANR 2, 61, 118
Jones, Rod 1953- .... **CLC 50**
See also CA 128
Jones, Terence Graham Parry
1942- .... **CLC 21**
See Jones, Terry; Monty Python
See also CA 116; CAAE 112; CANR 35,
93; INT CA-116; SATA 127
Jones, Terry
See Jones, Terence Graham Parry
See also SATA 67; SATA-Brief 51
Jones, Thom (Douglas) 1945(?)- ..... **CLC 81;
SSC 56**
See also CA 157; CANR 88; DLB 244;
SSFS 23
Jong, Erica 1942- .... **CLC 4, 6, 8, 18, 83**
See also AITN 1; AMWS 5; BEST 90:2;
BPFB 2; CA 73-76; CANR 26, 52, 75,
132; CN 3, 4, 5, 6, 7; CP 2, 3, 4, 5, 6, 7;
CPW; DA3; DAM NOV, POP; DLB 2, 5,
28, 152; FW; INT CANR-26; MAL 5;
MTCW 1, 2; MTFW 2005
Jonson, Ben(jamin) 1572(?)-1637 . **DC 4; LC
6, 33, 110; PC 17; WLC 3**
See also BRW 1; BRWC 1; BRWR 1; CD-
BLB Before 1660; DA; DAB; DAC;
DAM DRAM, MST, POET; DFS 4, 10;
DLB 62, 121; LMFS 1; PFS 23; RGEL 2;
TEA; WLIT 3
Jordan, June 1936-2002 .. **BLCS; CLC 5, 11,
23, 114, 230; PC 38**
See also AAYA 2, 66; AFAW 1, 2; BW 2,
3; CA 33-36R; CAAS 206; CANR 25, 70,
114, 154; CLR 10; CP 3, 4, 5, 6, 7; CWP;
DAM MULT, POET; DLB 38; GLL 2;
LAIT 5; MAICYA 1, 2; MTCW 1; SATA
4, 136; YAW
Jordan, June Meyer
See Jordan, June
Jordan, Neil 1950- .... **CLC 110**
See also CA 130; CAAE 124; CANR 54,
154; CN 4, 5, 6, 7; GLL 2; INT CA-130
Jordan, Neil Patrick
See Jordan, Neil
Jordan, Pat(rick M.) 1941- .... **CLC 37**
See also CA 33-36R; CANR 121
Jorgensen, Ivar
See Ellison, Harlan
Jorgenson, Ivar
See Silverberg, Robert
Joseph, George Ghevarughese .... **CLC 70**
Josephson, Mary
See O'Doherty, Brian
Josephus, Flavius c. 37-100 .... **CMLC 13**
See also AW 2; DLB 176; WLIT 8
Josiah Allen's Wife
See Holley, Marietta
Josipovici, Gabriel (David) 1940- ...... **CLC 6,
43, 153**
See also CA 224; 37-40R; 224; 8; CANR
47, 84; CN 3, 4, 5, 6, 7; DLB 14, 319

Joubert, Joseph 1754-1824 .... **NCLC 9**
Jouve, Pierre Jean 1887-1976 .... **CLC 47**
See also CA 252; CAAS 65-68; DLB 258;
EWL 3
Jovine, Francesco 1902-1950 .... **TCLC 79**
See also DLB 264; EWL 3
Joyce, James (Augustine Aloysius)
1882-1941 .... **DC 16; PC 22; SSC 3, 26,
44, 64; TCLC 3, 8, 16, 35, 52, 159;
WLC 3**
See also AAYA 42; BRW 7; BRWC 1;
BRWR 1; BYA 11, 13; CA 126; CAAE
104; CDBLB 1914-1945; DA; DA3;
DAB; DAC; DAM MST, NOV, POET;
DLB 10, 19, 36, 162, 247; EWL 3; EXPN;
EXPS; LAIT 3; LMFS 1, 2; MTCW 1, 2;
MTFW 2005; NFS 7; RGSF 2; SSFS 1,
19; TEA; WLIT 4
Jozsef, Attila 1905-1937 .... **TCLC 22**
See also CA 230; CAAE 116; CDWLB 4;
DLB 215; EWL 3
Juana Ines de la Cruz, Sor
1651(?)-1695 ... **HLCS 1; LC 5, 136; PC
24**
See also DLB 305; FW; LAW; RGWL 2, 3;
WLIT 1
Juana Inez de La Cruz, Sor
See Juana Ines de la Cruz, Sor
Juan Manuel, Don 1282-1348 .... **CMLC 88**
Judd, Cyril
See Kornbluth, C(yril) M.; Pohl, Frederik
Juenger, Ernst 1895-1998 .... **CLC 125**
See Junger, Ernst
See also CA 101; CAAS 167; CANR 21,
47, 106; DLB 56
Julian of Norwich 1342(?)-1416(?) . **LC 6, 52**
See also BRWS 12; DLB 146; LMFS 1
Julius Caesar 100B.C.-44B.C.
See Caesar, Julius
See also CDWLB 1; DLB 211
Junger, Ernst
See Juenger, Ernst
See also CDWLB 2; EWL 3; RGWL 2, 3
Junger, Sebastian 1962- .... **CLC 109**
See also AAYA 28; CA 165; CANR 130;
MTFW 2005
Juniper, Alex
See Hospital, Janette Turner
Junius
See Luxemburg, Rosa
Junzaburo, Nishiwaki
See Nishiwaki, Junzaburo
See also EWL 3
Just, Ward 1935- .... **CLC 4, 27**
See also CA 25-28R; CANR 32, 87; CN 6,
7; INT CANR-32
Just, Ward Swift
See Just, Ward
Justice, Donald (Rodney)
1925-2004 .... **CLC 6, 19, 102; PC 64**
See also AMWS 7; CA 5-8R; CAAS 230;
CANR 26, 54, 74, 121, 122; CP 1, 2, 3, 4,
5, 6, 7; CSW; DAM POET; DLBY 1983;
EWL 3; INT CANR-26; MAL 5; MTCW
2; PFS 14; TCLE 1:1
Juvenal c. 60-c. 130 .... **CMLC 8**
See also AW 2; CDWLB 1; DLB 211;
RGWL 2, 3; WLIT 8
Juvenis
See Bourne, Randolph S(illiman)
K., Alice
See Knapp, Caroline
Kabakov, Sasha .... **CLC 59**
Kabir 1398(?)-1448(?) .... **LC 109; PC 56**
See also RGWL 2, 3
Kacew, Romain 1914-1980
See Gary, Romain
See also CA 108; CAAS 102

Kadare, Ismail 1936- .... **CLC 52, 190**
See also CA 161; EWL 3; RGWL 3
Kadohata, Cynthia (Lynn)
1956(?)- .... **CLC 59, 122**
See also AAYA 71; CA 140; CANR 124;
SATA 155
Kafka, Franz 1883-1924 ... **SSC 5, 29, 35, 60;
TCLC 2, 6, 13, 29, 47, 53, 112, 179;
WLC 3**
See also AAYA 31; BPFB 2; CA 126;
CAAE 105; CDWLB 2; DA; DA3; DAB;
DAC; DAM MST, NOV; DLB 81; EW 9;
EWL 3; EXPS; LATS 1:1; LMFS 2;
MTCW 1, 2; MTFW 2005; NFS 7; RGSF
2; RGWL 2, 3; SFW 4; SSFS 3, 7, 12;
TWA
Kahanovitch, Pinchas
See Der Nister
Kahanovitsch, Pinkhes
See Der Nister
Kahanovitsh, Pinkhes
See Der Nister
Kahn, Roger 1927- .... **CLC 30**
See also CA 25-28R; CANR 44, 69, 152;
DLB 171; SATA 37
Kain, Saul
See Sassoon, Siegfried (Lorraine)
Kaiser, Georg 1878-1945 .... **TCLC 9**
See also CA 190; CAAE 106; CDWLB 2;
DLB 124; EWL 3; LMFS 2; RGWL 2, 3
Kaledin, Sergei .... **CLC 59**
Kaletski, Alexander 1946- .... **CLC 39**
See also CA 143; CAAE 118
Kalidasa fl. c. 400-455 .... **CMLC 9; PC 22**
See also RGWL 2, 3
Kallman, Chester (Simon)
1921-1975 .... **CLC 2**
See also CA 45-48; CAAS 53-56; CANR 3;
CP 1, 2
Kaminsky, Melvin .... **CLC 12, 217**
See Brooks, Mel
See also AAYA 13, 48; DLB 26
Kaminsky, Stuart M. 1934- .... **CLC 59**
See also CA 73-76; CANR 29, 53, 89, 161;
CMW 4
Kaminsky, Stuart Melvin
See Kaminsky, Stuart M.
Kamo no Chomei 1153(?)-1216 .... **CMLC 66**
See also DLB 203
Kamo no Nagaakira
See Kamo no Chomei
Kandinsky, Wassily 1866-1944 .... **TCLC 92**
See also AAYA 64; CA 155; CAAE 118
Kane, Francis
See Robbins, Harold
Kane, Henry 1918-
See Queen, Ellery
See also CA 156; CMW 4
Kane, Paul
See Simon, Paul
Kanin, Garson 1912-1999 .... **CLC 22**
See also AITN 1; CA 5-8R; CAAS 177;
CAD; CANR 7, 78; DLB 7; IDFW 3, 4
Kaniuk, Yoram 1930- .... **CLC 19**
See also CA 134; DLB 299; RGHL
Kant, Immanuel 1724-1804 ..... **NCLC 27, 67**
See also DLB 94
Kantor, MacKinlay 1904-1977 .... **CLC 7**
See also CA 61-64; CAAS 73-76; CANR
60, 63; CN 1, 2; DLB 9, 102; MAL 5;
MTCW 2; RHW; TCWW 1, 2
Kanze Motokiyo
See Zeami
Kaplan, David Michael 1946- .... **CLC 50**
See also CA 187
Kaplan, James 1951- .... **CLC 59**
See also CA 135; CANR 121

Kerouac, Jack 1922-1969 ...... **CLC 1, 2, 3, 5, 14, 29, 61; TCLC 117; WLC**
See Kerouac, Jean-Louis Lebris de
See also AAYA 25; AMWC 1; AMWS 3; BG 3; BPFB 2; CDALB 1941-1968; CP 1; CPW; DLB 2, 16, 237; DLBD 3; DLBY 1995; EWL 3; GLL 1; LATS 1:2; LMFS 2; MAL 5; NFS 8; RGAL 4; TUS; WP

Kerouac, Jean-Louis Lebris de 1922-1969
See Kerouac, Jack
See also AITN 1; CA 5-8R; CAAS 25-28R; CANR 26, 54, 95; DA; DA3; DAB; DAC; DAM MST, NOV, POET, POP; MTCW 1, 2; MTFW 2005

Kerr, (Bridget) Jean (Collins)
1923(?)-2003 .... **CLC 22**
See also CA 5-8R; CAAS 212; CANR 7; INT CANR-7

Kerr, M. E. .... **CLC 12, 35**
See Meaker, Marijane
See also AAYA 2, 23; BYA 1, 7, 8; CLR 29; SAAS 1; WYA

Kerr, Robert .... **CLC 55**

Kerrigan, (Thomas) Anthony 1918- .. **CLC 4, 6**
See also CA 49-52; 11; CANR 4

Kerry, Lois
See Duncan, Lois

Kesey, Ken 1935-2001 .... **CLC 1, 3, 6, 11, 46, 64, 184; WLC 3**
See also AAYA 25; BG 1:3; BPFB 2; CA 1-4R; CAAS 204; CANR 22, 38, 66, 124; CDALB 1968-1988; CN 1, 2, 3, 4, 5, 6, 7; CPW; DA; DA3; DAB; DAC; DAM MST, NOV, POP; DLB 2, 16, 206; EWL 3; EXPN; LAIT 4; MAL 5; MTCW 1, 2; MTFW 2005; NFS 2; RGAL 4; SATA 66; SATA-Obit 131; TUS; YAW

Kesselring, Joseph (Otto)
1902-1967 .... **CLC 45**
See also CA 150; DAM DRAM, MST; DFS 20

Kessler, Jascha (Frederick) 1929- ...... **CLC 4**
See also CA 17-20R; CANR 8, 48, 111; CP 1

Kettelkamp, Larry (Dale) 1933- .... **CLC 12**
See also CA 29-32R; CANR 16; SAAS 3; SATA 2

Key, Ellen (Karolina Sofia)
1849-1926 .... **TCLC 65**
See also DLB 259

Keyber, Conny
See Fielding, Henry

Keyes, Daniel 1927- .... **CLC 80**
See also AAYA 23; BYA 11; CA 181; 17-20R, 181; CANR 10, 26, 54, 74; DA; DA3; DAC; DAM MST, NOV; EXPN; LAIT 4; MTCW 2; MTFW 2005; NFS 2; SATA 37; SFW 4

Keynes, John Maynard
1883-1946 .... **TCLC 64**
See also CA 162, 163; CAAE 114; DLBD 10; MTCW 2; MTFW 2005

Khanshendel, Chiron
See Rose, Wendy

Khayyam, Omar 1048-1131 ... **CMLC 11; PC 8**
See Omar Khayyam
See also DA3; DAM POET; WLIT 6

Kherdian, David 1931- .... **CLC 6, 9**
See also AAYA 42; CA 192; 21-24R, 192; 2; CANR 39, 78; CLR 24; JRDA; LAIT 3; MAICYA 1, 2; SATA 16, 74; SATA-Essay 125

Khlebnikov, Velimir .... **TCLC 20**
See Khlebnikov, Viktor Vladimirovich
See also DLB 295; EW 10; EWL 3; RGWL 2, 3

Khlebnikov, Viktor Vladimirovich 1885-1922
See Khlebnikov, Velimir
See also CA 217; CAAE 117

Khodasevich, V.F.
See Khodasevich, Vladislav

Khodasevich, Vladislav
1886-1939 .... **TCLC 15**
See also CAAE 115; DLB 317; EWL 3

Khodasevich, Vladislav Felitsianovich
See Khodasevich, Vladislav

Kielland, Alexander Lange
1849-1906 .... **TCLC 5**
See also CAAE 104

Kiely, Benedict 1919-2007 . **CLC 23, 43; SSC 58**
See also CA 1-4R; CANR 2, 84; CN 1, 2, 3, 4, 5, 6, 7; DLB 15, 319; TCLE 1:1

Kienzle, William X. 1928-2001 .... **CLC 25**
See also CA 93-96; 1; CAAS 203; CANR 9, 31, 59, 111; CMW 4; DA3; DAM POP; INT CANR-31; MSW; MTCW 1, 2; MTFW 2005

Kierkegaard, Soren 1813-1855 ..... **NCLC 34, 78, 125**
See also DLB 300; EW 6; LMFS 2; RGWL 3; TWA

Kieslowski, Krzysztof 1941-1996 .... **CLC 120**
See also CA 147; CAAS 151

Killens, John Oliver 1916-1987 .... **CLC 10**
See also BW 2; CA 77-80; 2; CAAS 123; CANR 26; CN 1, 2, 3, 4; DLB 33; EWL 3

Killigrew, Anne 1660-1685 .... **LC 4, 73**
See also DLB 131

Killigrew, Thomas 1612-1683 .... **LC 57**
See also DLB 58; RGEL 2

Kim
See Simenon, Georges (Jacques Christian)

Kincaid, Jamaica 1949- ...... **BLC 2; CLC 43, 68, 137, 234; SSC 72**
See also AAYA 13, 56; AFAW 2; AMWS 7; BRWS 7; BW 2, 3; CA 125; CANR 47, 59, 95, 133; CDALBS; CDWLB 3; CLR 63; CN 4, 5, 6, 7; DA3; DAM MULT, NOV; DLB 157, 227; DNFS 1; EWL 3; EXPS; FW; LATS 1:2; LMFS 2; MAL 5; MTCW 2; MTFW 2005; NCFS 1; NFS 3; SSFS 5, 7; TUS; WWE 1; YAW

King, Francis (Henry) 1923- .... **CLC 8, 53, 145**
See also CA 1-4R; CANR 1, 33, 86; CN 1, 2, 3, 4, 5, 6, 7; DAM NOV; DLB 15, 139; MTCW 1

King, Kennedy
See Brown, George Douglas

King, Martin Luther, Jr. 1929-1968 . **BLC 2; CLC 83; WLCS**
See also BW 2, 3; CA 25-28; CANR 27, 44; CAP 2; DA; DA3; DAB; DAC; DAM MST, MULT; LAIT 5; LATS 1:2; MTCW 1, 2; MTFW 2005; SATA 14

King, Stephen 1947- .... **CLC 12, 26, 37, 61, 113, 228; SSC 17, 55**
See also AAYA 1, 17; AMWS 5; BEST 90:1; BPFB 2; CA 61-64; CANR 1, 30, 52, 76, 119, 134; CN 7; CPW; DA3; DAM NOV, POP; DLB 143; DLBY 1980; HGG; JRDA; LAIT 5; MTCW 1, 2; MTFW 2005; RGAL 4; SATA 9, 55, 161; SUFW 1, 2; WYAS 1; YAW

King, Stephen Edwin
See King, Stephen

King, Steve
See King, Stephen

King, Thomas 1943- .... **CLC 89, 171; NNAL**
See also CA 144; CANR 95; CCA 1; CN 6, 7; DAC; DAM MULT; DLB 175; SATA 96

Kingman, Lee .... **CLC 17**
See Natti, (Mary) Lee
See also CWRI 5; SAAS 3; SATA 1, 67

Kingsley, Charles 1819-1875 .... **NCLC 35**
See also CLR 77; DLB 21, 32, 163, 178, 190; FANT; MAICYA 2; MAICYAS 1; RGEL 2; WCH; YABC 2

Kingsley, Henry 1830-1876 .... **NCLC 107**
See also DLB 21, 230; RGEL 2

Kingsley, Sidney 1906-1995 .... **CLC 44**
See also CA 85-88; CAAS 147; CAD; DFS 14, 19; DLB 7; MAL 5; RGAL 4

Kingsolver, Barbara 1955- .... **CLC 55, 81, 130, 216**
See also AAYA 15; AMWS 7; CA 134; CAAE 129; CANR 60, 96, 133; CDALBS; CN 7; CPW; CSW; DA3; DAM POP; DLB 206; INT CA-134; LAIT 5; MTCW 2; MTFW 2005; NFS 5, 10, 12, 24; RGAL 4; TCLE 1:1

Kingston, Maxine Hong 1940- .... **AAL; CLC 12, 19, 58, 121; WLCS**
See also AAYA 8, 55; AMWS 5; BPFB 2; CA 69-72; CANR 13, 38, 74, 87, 128; CDALBS; CN 6, 7; DA3; DAM MULT, NOV; DLB 173, 212, 312; DLBY 1980; EWL 3; FL 1:6; FW; INT CANR-13; LAIT 5; MAL 5; MBL; MTCW 1, 2; MTFW 2005; NFS 6; RGAL 4; SATA 53; SSFS 3; TCWW 2

Kinnell, Galway 1927- ..... **CLC 1, 2, 3, 5, 13, 29, 129; PC 26**
See also AMWS 3; CA 9-12R; CANR 10, 34, 66, 116, 138; CP 1, 2, 3, 4, 5, 6, 7; DLB 5; DLBY 1987; EWL 3; INT CANR-34; MAL 5; MTCW 1, 2; MTFW 2005; PAB; PFS 9; RGAL 4; TCLE 1:1; WP

Kinsella, Thomas 1928- .... **CLC 4, 19, 138; PC 69**
See also BRWS 5; CA 17-20R; CANR 15, 122; CP 1, 2, 3, 4, 5, 6, 7; DLB 27; EWL 3; MTCW 1, 2; MTFW 2005; RGEL 2; TEA

Kinsella, W.P. 1935- .... **CLC 27, 43, 166**
See also AAYA 7, 60; BPFB 2; CA 222; 97-100, 222; 7; CANR 21, 35, 66, 75, 129; CN 4, 5, 6, 7; CPW; DAC; DAM NOV, POP; FANT; INT CANR-21; LAIT 5; MTCW 1, 2; MTFW 2005; NFS 15; RGSF 2

Kinsey, Alfred C(harles)
1894-1956 .... **TCLC 91**
See also CA 170; CAAE 115; MTCW 2

Kipling, (Joseph) Rudyard 1865-1936 . **PC 3; SSC 5, 54; TCLC 8, 17, 167; WLC 3**
See also AAYA 32; BRW 6; BRWC 1, 2; BYA 4; CA 120; CAAE 105; CANR 33; CDBLB 1890-1914; CLR 39, 65; CWRI 5; DA; DA3; DAB; DAC; DAM MST, POET; DLB 19, 34, 141, 156, 330; EWL 3; EXPS; FANT; LAIT 3; LMFS 1; MAICYA 1, 2; MTCW 1, 2; MTFW 2005; NFS 21; PFS 22; RGEL 2; RGSF 2; SATA 100; SFW 4; SSFS 8, 21, 22; SUFW 1; TEA; WCH; WLIT 4; YABC 2

Kircher, Athanasius 1602-1680 .... **LC 121**
See also DLB 164

Kirk, Russell (Amos) 1918-1994 .. **TCLC 119**
See also AITN 1; CA 1-4R; 9; CAAS 145; CANR 1, 20, 60; HGG; INT CANR-20; MTCW 1, 2

Kirkham, Dinah
See Card, Orson Scott

Kirkland, Caroline M. 1801-1864 . **NCLC 85**
See also DLB 3, 73, 74, 250, 254; DLBD 13

Kirkup, James 1918- .... **CLC 1**
See also CA 1-4R; 4; CANR 2; CP 1, 2, 3, 4, 5, 6, 7; DLB 27; SATA 12

Kristeva, Julia 1941- .... **CLC 77, 140**
 See also CA 154; CANR 99; DLB 242;
  EWL 3; FW; LMFS 2
Kristofferson, Kris 1936- .... **CLC 26**
 See also CA 104
Krizanc, John 1956- .... **CLC 57**
 See also CA 187
Krleza, Miroslav 1893-1981 .... **CLC 8, 114**
 See also CA 97-100; CAAS 105; CANR
  50; CDWLB 4; DLB 147; EW 11; RGWL
  2, 3
Kroetsch, Robert (Paul) 1927- .... **CLC 5, 23,
  57, 132**
 See also CA 17-20R; CANR 8, 38; CCA 1;
  CN 2, 3, 4, 5, 6, 7; CP 6, 7; DAC; DAM
  POET; DLB 53; MTCW 1
Kroetz, Franz
 See Kroetz, Franz Xaver
Kroetz, Franz Xaver 1946- .... **CLC 41**
 See also CA 130; CANR 142; CWW 2;
  EWL 3
Kroker, Arthur (W.) 1945- .... **CLC 77**
 See also CA 161
Kroniuk, Lisa
 See Berton, Pierre (Francis de Marigny)
Kropotkin, Peter (Aleksieevich)
  1842-1921 .... **TCLC 36**
 See Kropotkin, Petr Alekseevich
 See also CA 219; CAAE 119
Kropotkin, Petr Alekseevich
 See Kropotkin, Peter (Aleksieevich)
 See also DLB 277
Krotkov, Yuri 1917-1981 .... **CLC 19**
 See also CA 102
Krumb
 See Crumb, R.
Krumgold, Joseph (Quincy)
  1908-1980 .... **CLC 12**
 See also BYA 1, 2; CA 9-12R; CAAS 101;
  CANR 7; MAICYA 1, 2; SATA 1, 48;
  SATA-Obit 23; YAW
Krumwitz
 See Crumb, R.
Krutch, Joseph Wood 1893-1970 ..... **CLC 24**
 See also ANW; CA 1-4R; CAAS 25-28R;
  CANR 4; DLB 63, 206, 275
Krutzch, Gus
 See Eliot, T(homas) S(tearns)
Krylov, Ivan Andreevich
  1768(?)-1844 .... **NCLC 1**
 See also DLB 150
Kubin, Alfred (Leopold Isidor)
  1877-1959 .... **TCLC 23**
 See also CA 149; CAAE 112; CANR 104;
  DLB 81
Kubrick, Stanley 1928-1999 .... **CLC 16;
  TCLC 112**
 See also AAYA 30; CA 81-84; CAAS 177;
  CANR 33; DLB 26
Kumin, Maxine 1925- .... **CLC 5, 13, 28, 164;
  PC 15**
 See also AITN 2; AMWS 4; ANW; CA
  1-4R; 8; CANR 1, 21, 69, 115, 140; CP 2,
  3, 4, 5, 6, 7; CWP; DA3; DAM POET;
  DLB 5; EWL 3; EXPP; MTCW 1, 2;
  MTFW 2005; PAB; PFS 18; SATA 12
Kundera, Milan 1929- . **CLC 4, 9, 19, 32, 68,
  115, 135, 234; SSC 24**
 See also AAYA 2, 62; BPFB 2; CA 85-88;
  CANR 19, 52, 74, 144; CDWLB 4; CWW
  2; DA3; DAM NOV; DLB 232; EW 13;
  EWL 3; MTCW 1, 2; MTFW 2005; NFS
  18; RGSF 2; RGWL 3; SSFS 10
Kunene, Mazisi 1930-2006 .... **CLC 85**
 See also BW 1, 3; CA 125; CAAS 252;
  CANR 81; CP 1, 6, 7; DLB 117
Kunene, Mazisi Raymond
 See Kunene, Mazisi

Kunene, Mazisi Raymond Fakazi Mngoni
 See Kunene, Mazisi
Kung, Hans .... **CLC 130**
 See Kung, Hans
Kung, Hans 1928-
 See Kung, Hans
 See also CA 53-56; CANR 66, 134; MTCW
  1, 2; MTFW 2005
Kunikida Doppo 1869(?)-1908
 See Doppo, Kunikida
 See also DLB 180; EWL 3
Kunitz, Stanley 1905-2006 ..... **CLC 6, 11, 14,
  148; PC 19**
 See also AMWS 3; CA 41-44R; CAAS 250;
  CANR 26, 57, 98; CP 1, 2, 3, 4, 5, 6, 7;
  DA3; DLB 48; INT CANR-26; MAL 5;
  MTCW 1, 2; MTFW 2005; PFS 11;
  RGAL 4
Kunitz, Stanley Jasspon
 See Kunitz, Stanley
Kunze, Reiner 1933- .... **CLC 10**
 See also CA 93-96; CWW 2; DLB 75; EWL
  3
Kuprin, Aleksander Ivanovich
  1870-1938 .... **TCLC 5**
 See Kuprin, Aleksandr Ivanovich; Kuprin,
  Alexandr Ivanovich
 See also CA 182; CAAE 104
Kuprin, Aleksandr Ivanovich
 See Kuprin, Aleksander Ivanovich
 See also DLB 295
Kuprin, Alexandr Ivanovich
 See Kuprin, Aleksander Ivanovich
 See also EWL 3
Kureishi, Hanif 1954- .. **CLC 64, 135; DC 26**
 See also BRWS 11; CA 139; CANR 113;
  CBD; CD 5, 6; CN 6, 7; DLB 194, 245;
  GLL 2; IDFW 4; WLIT 4; WWE 1
Kurosawa, Akira 1910-1998 ..... **CLC 16, 119**
 See also AAYA 11, 64; CA 101; CAAS 170;
  CANR 46; DAM MULT
Kushner, Tony 1956- .... **CLC 81, 203; DC 10**
 See also AAYA 61; AMWS 9; CA 144;
  CAD; CANR 74, 130; CD 5, 6; DA3;
  DAM DRAM; DFS 5; DLB 228; EWL 3;
  GLL 1; LAIT 5; MAL 5; MTCW 2;
  MTFW 2005; RGAL 4; RGHL; SATA 160
Kuttner, Henry 1915-1958 .... **TCLC 10**
 See also CA 157; CAAE 107; DLB 8;
  FANT; SCFW 1, 2; SFW 4
Kutty, Madhavi
 See Das, Kamala
Kuzma, Greg 1944- .... **CLC 7**
 See also CA 33-36R; CANR 70
Kuzmin, Mikhail (Alekseevich)
  1872(?)-1936 .... **TCLC 40**
 See also CA 170; DLB 295; EWL 3
Kyd, Thomas 1558-1594 .. **DC 3; LC 22, 125**
 See also BRW 1; DAM DRAM; DFS 21;
  DLB 62; IDTP; LMFS 1; RGEL 2; TEA;
  WLIT 3
Kyprianos, Iossif
 See Samarakis, Antonis
L. S.
 See Stephen, Sir Leslie
Labe, Louise 1521-1566 .... **LC 120**
 See also DLB 327
Labrunie, Gerard
 See Nerval, Gerard de
La Bruyere, Jean de 1645-1696 .... **LC 17**
 See also DLB 268; EW 3; GFL Beginnings
  to 1789
LaBute, Neil 1963- .... **CLC 225**
 See also CA 240
Lacan, Jacques (Marie Emile)
  1901-1981 .... **CLC 75**
 See also CA 121; CAAS 104; DLB 296;
  EWL 3; TWA

Laclos, Pierre-Ambroise Francois
  1741-1803 .... **NCLC 4, 87**
 See also DLB 313; EW 4; GFL Beginnings
  to 1789; RGWL 2, 3
Lacolere, Francois
 See Aragon, Louis
La Colere, Francois
 See Aragon, Louis
La Deshabilleuse
 See Simenon, Georges (Jacques Christian)
Lady Gregory
 See Gregory, Lady Isabella Augusta (Persse)
Lady of Quality, A
 See Bagnold, Enid
La Fayette, Marie-(Madelaine Pioche de la
  Vergne) 1634-1693 .... **LC 2**
 See Lafayette, Marie-Madeleine
 See also GFL Beginnings to 1789; RGWL
  2, 3
Lafayette, Marie-Madeleine
 See La Fayette, Marie-(Madelaine Pioche
  de la Vergne)
 See also DLB 268
Lafayette, Rene
 See Hubbard, L. Ron
La Flesche, Francis 1857(?)-1932 ...... **NNAL**
 See also CA 144; CANR 83; DLB 175
La Fontaine, Jean de 1621-1695 .... **LC 50**
 See also DLB 268; EW 3; GFL Beginnings
  to 1789; MAICYA 1, 2; RGWL 2, 3;
  SATA 18
LaForet, Carmen 1921-2004 .... **CLC 219**
 See also CA 246; CWW 2; DLB 322; EWL
  3
LaForet Diaz, Carmen
 See LaForet, Carmen
Laforgue, Jules 1860-1887 . **NCLC 5, 53; PC
  14; SSC 20**
 See also DLB 217; EW 7; GFL 1789 to the
  Present; RGWL 2, 3
Lagerkvist, Paer (Fabian)
  1891-1974 ..... **CLC 7, 10, 13, 54; TCLC
  144**
 See Lagerkvist, Par
 See also CA 85-88; CAAS 49-52; DA3;
  DAM DRAM, NOV; MTCW 1, 2; MTFW
  2005; TWA
Lagerkvist, Par .... **SSC 12**
 See Lagerkvist, Paer (Fabian)
 See also DLB 259, 331; EW 10; EWL 3;
  RGSF 2; RGWL 2, 3
Lagerloef, Selma (Ottiliana Lovisa)
  .... **TCLC 4, 36**
 See Lagerlof, Selma (Ottiliana Lovisa)
 See also CAAE 108; MTCW 2
Lagerlof, Selma (Ottiliana Lovisa)
  1858-1940
 See Lagerloef, Selma (Ottiliana Lovisa)
 See also CA 188; CLR 7; DLB 259, 331;
  RGWL 2, 3; SATA 15; SSFS 18
La Guma, Alex 1925-1985 .. **BLCS; CLC 19;
  TCLC 140**
 See also AFW; BW 1, 3; CA 49-52; CAAS
  118; CANR 25, 81; CDWLB 3; CN 1, 2,
  3; CP 1; DAM NOV; DLB 117, 225; EWL
  3; MTCW 1, 2; MTFW 2005; WLIT 2;
  WWE 1
Lahiri, Jhumpa 1967- .... **SSC 96**
 See also AAYA 56; CA 193; CANR 134;
  DLB 323; MTFW 2005; SSFS 19
Laidlaw, A. K.
 See Grieve, C(hristopher) M(urray)
Lainez, Manuel Mujica
 See Mujica Lainez, Manuel
 See also HW 1
Laing, R(onald) D(avid) 1927-1989 . **CLC 95**
 See also CA 107; CAAS 129; CANR 34;
  MTCW 1

Lawler, Raymond Evenor 1922- .... **CLC 58**
See Lawler, Ray
See also CA 103; CD 5, 6; RGEL 2
Lawrence, D(avid) H(erbert Richards)
1885-1930 .... **PC 54; SSC 4, 19, 73;**
TCLC 2, 9, 16, 33, 48, 61, 93; WLC 3
See Chambers, Jessie
See also BPFB 2; BRW 7; BRWR 2; CA
121; CAAE 104; CANR 131; CDBLB
1914-1945; DA; DA3; DAB; DAC; DAM
MST, NOV, POET; DLB 10, 19, 36, 98,
162, 195; EWL 3; EXPP; EXPS; LAIT 2,
3; MTCW 1, 2; MTFW 2005; NFS 18;
PFS 6; RGEL 2; RGSF 2; SSFS 2, 6;
TEA; WLIT 4; WP
Lawrence, T(homas) E(dward)
1888-1935 .... **TCLC 18**
See Dale, Colin
See also BRWS 2; CA 167; CAAE 115;
DLB 195
Lawrence of Arabia
See Lawrence, T(homas) E(dward)
Lawson, Henry (Archibald Hertzberg)
1867-1922 .... **SSC 18; TCLC 27**
See also CA 181; CAAE 120; DLB 230;
RGEL 2; RGSF 2
Lawton, Dennis
See Faust, Frederick (Schiller)
Layamon fl. c. 1200- .... **CMLC 10**
See also DLB 146; RGEL 2
Laye, Camara 1928-1980 ..... **BLC 2; CLC 4,**
38
See Camara Laye
See also AFW; BW 1; CA 85-88; CAAS
97-100; CANR 25; DAM MULT; MTCW
1, 2; WLIT 2
Layton, Irving 1912-2006 ..... **CLC 2, 15, 164**
See also CA 1-4R; CAAS 247; CANR 2,
33, 43, 66, 129; CP 1, 2, 3, 4, 5, 6, 7;
DAC; DAM MST, POET; DLB 88; EWL
3; MTCW 1, 2; PFS 12; RGEL 2
Layton, Irving Peter
See Layton, Irving
Lazarus, Emma 1849-1887 ...... **NCLC 8, 109**
Lazarus, Felix
See Cable, George Washington
Lazarus, Henry
See Slavitt, David R(ytman)
Lea, Joan
See Neufeld, John (Arthur)
Leacock, Stephen (Butler)
1869-1944 .... **SSC 39; TCLC 2**
See also CA 141; CAAE 104; CANR 80;
DAC; DAM MST; DLB 92; EWL 3;
MTCW 2; MTFW 2005; RGEL 2; RGSF
2
Lead, Jane Ward 1623-1704 .... **LC 72**
See also DLB 131
Leapor, Mary 1722-1746 .... **LC 80**
See also DLB 109
Lear, Edward 1812-1888 ..... **NCLC 3; PC 65**
See also AAYA 48; BRW 5; CLR 1, 75;
DLB 32, 163, 166; MAICYA 1, 2; RGEL
2; SATA 18, 100; WCH; WP
Lear, Norman (Milton) 1922- .... **CLC 12**
See also CA 73-76
Leautaud, Paul 1872-1956 .... **TCLC 83**
See also CA 203; DLB 65; GFL 1789 to the
Present
Leavis, F(rank) R(aymond)
1895-1978 .... **CLC 24**
See also BRW 7; CA 21-24R; CAAS 77-
80; CANR 44; DLB 242; EWL 3; MTCW
1, 2; RGEL 2
Leavitt, David 1961- .... **CLC 34**
See also CA 122; CAAE 116; CANR 50,
62, 101, 134; CPW; DA3; DAM POP;
DLB 130; GLL 1; INT CA-122; MAL 5;
MTCW 2; MTFW 2005

Leblanc, Maurice (Marie Emile)
1864-1941 .... **TCLC 49**
See also CAAE 110; CMW 4
Lebowitz, Fran(ces Ann) 1951(?)- ... **CLC 11,**
36
See also CA 81-84; CANR 14, 60, 70; INT
CANR-14; MTCW 1
Lebrecht, Peter
See Tieck, (Johann) Ludwig
le Carre, John 1931- .... **CLC 9, 15**
See also AAYA 42; BEST 89:4; BPFB 2;
BRWS 2; CA 5-8R; CANR 13, 33, 59,
107, 132; CDBLB 1960 to Present; CMW
4; CN 1, 2, 3, 4, 5, 6, 7; CPW; DA3;
DAM POP; DLB 87; EWL 3; MSW;
MTCW 1, 2; MTFW 2005; RGEL 2; TEA
Le Clezio, J. M.G. 1940- .... **CLC 31, 155**
See also CA 128; CAAE 116; CANR 147;
CWW 2; DLB 83; EWL 3; GFL 1789 to
the Present; RGSF 2
Le Clezio, Jean Marie Gustave
See Le Clezio, J. M.G.
Leconte de Lisle, Charles-Marie-Rene
1818-1894 .... **NCLC 29**
See also DLB 217; EW 6; GFL 1789 to the
Present
Le Coq, Monsieur
See Simenon, Georges (Jacques Christian)
Leduc, Violette 1907-1972 .... **CLC 22**
See also CA 13-14; CAAS 33-36R; CANR
69; CAP 1; EWL 3; GFL 1789 to the
Present; GLL 1
Ledwidge, Francis 1887(?)-1917 .... **TCLC 23**
See also CA 203; CAAE 123; DLB 20
Lee, Andrea 1953- .... **BLC 2; CLC 36**
See also BW 1, 3; CA 125; CANR 82;
DAM MULT
Lee, Andrew
See Auchincloss, Louis
Lee, Chang-rae 1965- .... **CLC 91**
See also CA 148; CANR 89; CN 7; DLB
312; LATS 1:2
Lee, Don L. .... **CLC 2**
See Madhubuti, Haki R.
See also CP 2, 3, 4, 5
Lee, George W(ashington)
1894-1976 .... **BLC 2; CLC 52**
See also BW 1; CA 125; CANR 83; DAM
MULT; DLB 51
Lee, Harper 1926- ... **CLC 12, 60, 194; WLC**
4
See also AAYA 13; AMWS 8; BPFB 2;
BYA 3; CA 13-16R; CANR 51, 128;
CDALB 1941-1968; CSW; DA; DA3;
DAB; DAC; DAM MST, NOV; DLB 6;
EXPN; LAIT 3; MAL 5; MTCW 1, 2;
MTFW 2005; NFS 2; SATA 11; WYA;
YAW
Lee, Helen Elaine 1959(?)- .... **CLC 86**
See also CA 148
Lee, John .... **CLC 70**
Lee, Julian
See Latham, Jean Lee
Lee, Larry
See Lee, Lawrence
Lee, Laurie 1914-1997 .... **CLC 90**
See also CA 77-80; CAAS 158; CANR 33,
73; CP 1, 2, 3, 4, 5, 6; CPW; DAB; DAM
POP; DLB 27; MTCW 1; RGEL 2
Lee, Lawrence 1941-1990 .... **CLC 34**
See also CAAS 131; CANR 43
Lee, Li-Young 1957- .... **CLC 164; PC 24**
See also AMWS 15; CA 153; CANR 118;
CP 6, 7; DLB 165, 312; LMFS 2; PFS 11,
15, 17
Lee, Manfred B. 1905-1971 .... **CLC 11**
See Queen, Ellery
See also CA 1-4R; CAAS 29-32R; CANR
2, 150; CMW 4; DLB 137

Lee, Manfred Bennington
See Lee, Manfred B.
Lee, Nathaniel 1645(?)-1692 .... **LC 103**
See also DLB 80; RGEL 2
Lee, Shelton Jackson
See Lee, Spike
See also AAYA 4, 29
Lee, Spike 1957(?)- .... **BLCS; CLC 105**
See Lee, Shelton Jackson
See also BW 2, 3; CA 125; CANR 42;
DAM MULT
Lee, Stan 1922- .... **CLC 17**
See also AAYA 5, 49; CA 111; CAAE 108;
CANR 129; INT CA-111; MTFW 2005
Lee, Tanith 1947- .... **CLC 46**
See also AAYA 15; CA 37-40R; CANR 53,
102, 145; DLB 261; FANT; SATA 8, 88,
134; SFW 4; SUFW 1, 2; YAW
Lee, Vernon .... **SSC 33, 98; TCLC 5**
See Paget, Violet
See also DLB 57, 153, 156, 174, 178; GLL
1; SUFW 1
Lee, William
See Burroughs, William S.
See also GLL 1
Lee, Willy
See Burroughs, William S.
See also GLL 1
Lee-Hamilton, Eugene (Jacob)
1845-1907 .... **TCLC 22**
See also CA 234; CAAE 117
Leet, Judith 1935- .... **CLC 11**
See also CA 187
Le Fanu, Joseph Sheridan
1814-1873 .... **NCLC 9, 58; SSC 14, 84**
See also CMW 4; DA3; DAM POP; DLB
21, 70, 159, 178; GL 3; HGG; RGEL 2;
RGSF 2; SUFW 1
Leffland, Ella 1931- .... **CLC 19**
See also CA 29-32R; CANR 35, 78, 82;
DLBY 1984; INT CANR-35; SATA 65;
SSFS 24
Leger, Alexis
See Leger, (Marie-Rene Auguste) Alexis
Saint-Leger
Leger, (Marie-Rene Auguste) Alexis
Saint-Leger 1887-1975 .. **CLC 4, 11, 46;**
PC 23
See Perse, Saint-John; Saint-John Perse
See also CA 13-16R; CAAS 61-64; CANR
43; DAM POET; MTCW 1
Leger, Saintleger
See Leger, (Marie-Rene Auguste) Alexis
Saint-Leger
Le Guin, Ursula K. 1929- ...... **CLC 8, 13, 22,**
45, 71, 136; SSC 12, 69
See also AAYA 9, 27; AITN 1; BPFB 2;
BYA 5, 8, 11, 14; CA 21-24R; CANR 9,
32, 52, 74, 132; CDALB 1968-1988; CLR
3, 28, 91; CN 2, 3, 4, 5, 6, 7; CPW; DA3;
DAB; DAC; DAM MST, POP; DLB 8,
52, 256, 275; EXPS; FANT; FW; INT
CANR-32; JRDA; LAIT 5; MAICYA 1,
2; MAL 5; MTCW 1, 2; MTFW 2005;
NFS 6, 9; SATA 4, 52, 99, 149; SCFW 1,
2; SFW 4; SSFS 2; SUFW 1, 2; WYA;
YAW
Lehmann, Rosamond (Nina)
1901-1990 .... **CLC 5**
See also CA 77-80; CAAS 131; CANR 8,
73; CN 1, 2, 3, 4; DLB 15; MTCW 2;
RGEL 2; RHW
Leiber, Fritz (Reuter, Jr.)
1910-1992 .... **CLC 25**
See also AAYA 65; BPFB 2; CA 45-48;
CAAS 139; CANR 2, 40, 86; CN 2, 3, 4,
5; DLB 8; FANT; HGG; MTCW 1, 2;
MTFW 2005; SATA 45; SATA-Obit 73;
SCFW 1, 2; SFW 4; SUFW 1, 2

Author Index

Lewis, Matthew Gregory
1775-1818 .... **NCLC 11, 62**
See also DLB 39, 158, 178; GL 3; HGG;
LMFS 1; RGEL 2; SUFW
Lewis, (Harry) Sinclair 1885-1951 . **TCLC 4,
13, 23, 39; WLC 4**
See also AMW; AMWC 1; BPFB 2; CA
133; CAAE 104; CANR 132; CDALB
1917-1929; DA; DA3; DAB; DAC; DAM
MST, NOV; DLB 9, 102, 284, 331; DLBD
1; EWL 3; LAIT 3; MAL 5; MTCW 1, 2;
MTFW 2005; NFS 15, 19, 22; RGAL 4;
TUS
Lewis, (Percy) Wyndham
1884(?)-1957 .. **SSC 34; TCLC 2, 9, 104**
See also BRW 7; CA 157; CAAE 104; DLB
15; EWL 3; FANT; MTCW 2; MTFW
2005; RGEL 2
Lewisohn, Ludwig 1883-1955 .... **TCLC 19**
See also CA 203; CAAE 107; DLB 4, 9,
28, 102; MAL 5
Lewton, Val 1904-1951 .... **TCLC 76**
See also CA 199; IDFW 3, 4
Leyner, Mark 1956- .... **CLC 92**
See also CA 110; CANR 28, 53; DA3; DLB
292; MTCW 2; MTFW 2005
Lezama Lima, Jose 1910-1976 .... **CLC 4, 10,
101; HLCS 2**
See also CA 77-80; CANR 71; DAM
MULT; DLB 113, 283; EWL 3; HW 1, 2;
LAW; RGWL 2, 3
L'Heureux, John (Clarke) 1934- .... **CLC 52**
See also CA 13-16R; CANR 23, 45, 88; CP
1, 2, 3, 4; DLB 244
Li Ch'ing-chao 1081(?)-1141(?) .... **CMLC 71**
Liddell, C. H.
See Kuttner, Henry
Lie, Jonas (Lauritz Idemil)
1833-1908(?) .... **TCLC 5**
See also CAAE 115
Lieber, Joel 1937-1971 .... **CLC 6**
See also CA 73-76; CAAS 29-32R
Lieber, Stanley Martin
See Lee, Stan
Lieberman, Laurence (James)
1935- .... **CLC 4, 36**
See also CA 17-20R; CANR 8, 36, 89; CP
1, 2, 3, 4, 5, 6, 7
Lieh Tzu fl. 7th cent. B.C.-5th cent.
B.C. .... **CMLC 27**
Lieksman, Anders
See Haavikko, Paavo Juhani
Lifton, Robert Jay 1926- .... **CLC 67**
See also CA 17-20R; CANR 27, 78, 161;
INT CANR-27; SATA 66
Lightfoot, Gordon 1938- .... **CLC 26**
See also CA 242; CAAE 109
Lightfoot, Gordon Meredith
See Lightfoot, Gordon
Lightman, Alan P(aige) 1948- .... **CLC 81**
See also CA 141; CANR 63, 105, 138;
MTFW 2005
Ligotti, Thomas (Robert) 1953- ...... **CLC 44;
SSC 16**
See also CA 123; CANR 49, 135; HGG;
SUFW 2
Li Ho 791-817 .... **PC 13**
Li Ju-chen c. 1763-c. 1830 .... **NCLC 137**
Lilar, Francoise
See Mallet-Joris, Francoise
Liliencron, Detlev
See Liliencron, Detlev von
Liliencron, Detlev von 1844-1909 .. **TCLC 18**
See also CAAE 117
Liliencron, Friedrich Adolf Axel Detlev von
See Liliencron, Detlev von
Liliencron, Friedrich Detlev von
See Liliencron, Detlev von

Lille, Alain de
See Alain de Lille
Lillo, George 1691-1739 .... **LC 131**
See also DLB 84; RGEL 2
Lilly, William 1602-1681 .... **LC 27**
Lima, Jose Lezama
See Lezama Lima, Jose
Lima Barreto, Afonso Henrique de
1881-1922 .... **TCLC 23**
See Lima Barreto, Afonso Henriques de
See also CA 181; CAAE 117; LAW
Lima Barreto, Afonso Henriques de
See Lima Barreto, Afonso Henrique de
See also DLB 307
Limonov, Eduard
See Limonov, Edward
See also DLB 317
Limonov, Edward 1944- .... **CLC 67**
See Limonov, Eduard
See also CA 137
Lin, Frank
See Atherton, Gertrude (Franklin Horn)
Lin, Yutang 1895-1976 .... **TCLC 149**
See also CA 45-48; CAAS 65-68; CANR 2;
RGAL 4
Lincoln, Abraham 1809-1865 .... **NCLC 18**
See also LAIT 2
Lind, Jakov .... **CLC 1, 2, 4, 27, 82**
See Landwirth, Heinz
See also CA 4; DLB 299; EWL 3; RGHL
Lindbergh, Anne Morrow
1906-2001 .... **CLC 82**
See also BPFB 2; CA 17-20R; CAAS 193;
CANR 16, 73; DAM NOV; MTCW 1, 2;
MTFW 2005; SATA 33; SATA-Obit 125;
TUS
Lindsay, David 1878(?)-1945 .... **TCLC 15**
See also CA 187; CAAE 113; DLB 255;
FANT; SFW 4; SUFW 1
Lindsay, (Nicholas) Vachel
1879-1931 .... **PC 23; TCLC 17; WLC 4**
See also AMWS 1; CA 135; CAAE 114;
CANR 79; CDALB 1865-1917; DA;
DA3; DAC; DAM MST, POET; DLB 54;
EWL 3; EXPP; MAL 5; RGAL 4; SATA
40; WP
Linke-Poot
See Doeblin, Alfred
Linney, Romulus 1930- .... **CLC 51**
See also CA 1-4R; CAD; CANR 40, 44,
79; CD 5, 6; CSW; RGAL 4
Linton, Eliza Lynn 1822-1898 .... **NCLC 41**
See also DLB 18
Li Po 701-763 .... **CMLC 2, 86; PC 29**
See also PFS 20; WP
Lipsius, Justus 1547-1606 .... **LC 16**
Lipsyte, Robert 1938- .... **CLC 21**
See also AAYA 7, 45; CA 17-20R; CANR
8, 57, 146; CLR 23, 76; DA; DAC; DAM
MST, NOV; JRDA; LAIT 5; MAICYA 1,
2; SATA 5, 68, 113, 161; WYA; YAW
Lipsyte, Robert Michael
See Lipsyte, Robert
Lish, Gordon 1934- .... **CLC 45; SSC 18**
See also CA 117; CAAE 113; CANR 79,
151; DLB 130; INT CA-117
Lish, Gordon Jay
See Lish, Gordon
Lispector, Clarice 1925(?)-1977 .... **CLC 43;
HLCS 2; SSC 34, 96**
See also CA 139; CAAS 116; CANR 71;
CDWLB 3; DLB 113, 307; DNFS 1; EWL
3; FW; HW 2; LAW; RGSF 2; RGWL 2,
3; WLIT 1
Littell, Robert 1935(?)- .... **CLC 42**
See also CA 112; CAAE 109; CANR 64,
115; CMW 4

Little, Malcolm 1925-1965
See Malcolm X
See also BW 1, 3; CA 125; CAAS 111;
CANR 82; DA; DA3; DAB; DAC; DAM
MST, MULT; MTCW 1, 2; MTFW 2005
Littlewit, Humphrey Gent.
See Lovecraft, H. P.
Litwos
See Sienkiewicz, Henryk (Adam Alexander
Pius)
Liu, E. 1857-1909 .... **TCLC 15**
See also CA 190; CAAE 115; DLB 328
Lively, Penelope 1933- .... **CLC 32, 50**
See also BPFB 2; CA 41-44R; CANR 29,
67, 79, 131; CLR 7; CN 5, 6, 7; CWRI
5; DAM NOV; DLB 14, 161, 207, 326;
FANT; JRDA; MAICYA 1, 2; MTCW 1,
2; MTFW 2005; SATA 7, 60, 101, 164;
TEA
Lively, Penelope Margaret
See Lively, Penelope
Livesay, Dorothy (Kathleen)
1909-1996 .... **CLC 4, 15, 79**
See also AITN 2; CA 25-28R; 8; CANR 36,
67; CP 1, 2, 3, 4, 5; DAC; DAM MST,
POET; DLB 68; FW; MTCW 1; RGEL 2;
TWA
Livy c. 59B.C.-c. 12 .... **CMLC 11**
See also AW 2; CDWLB 1; DLB 211;
RGWL 2, 3; WLIT 8
Lizardi, Jose Joaquin Fernandez de
1776-1827 .... **NCLC 30**
See also LAW
Llewellyn, Richard
See Llewellyn Lloyd, Richard Dafydd Viv-
ian
See also DLB 15
Llewellyn Lloyd, Richard Dafydd Vivian
1906-1983 .... **CLC 7, 80**
See Llewellyn, Richard
See also CA 53-56; CAAS 111; CANR 7,
71; SATA 11; SATA-Obit 37
Llosa, Jorge Mario Pedro Vargas
See Vargas Llosa, Mario
See also RGWL 3
Llosa, Mario Vargas
See Vargas Llosa, Mario
Lloyd, Manda
See Mander, (Mary) Jane
Lloyd Webber, Andrew 1948-
See Webber, Andrew Lloyd
See also AAYA 1, 38; CA 149; CAAE 116;
DAM DRAM; SATA 56
Llull, Ramon c. 1235-c. 1316 .... **CMLC 12**
Lobb, Ebenezer
See Upward, Allen
Locke, Alain (Le Roy)
1886-1954 .... **BLCS; HR 1:3; TCLC 43**
See also AMWS 14; BW 1, 3; CA 124;
CAAE 106; CANR 79; DLB 51; LMFS
2; MAL 5; RGAL 4
Locke, John 1632-1704 .... **LC 7, 35, 135**
See also DLB 31, 101, 213, 252; RGEL 2;
WLIT 3
Locke-Elliott, Sumner
See Elliott, Sumner Locke
Lockhart, John Gibson 1794-1854 .. **NCLC 6**
See also DLB 110, 116, 144
Lockridge, Ross (Franklin), Jr.
1914-1948 .... **TCLC 111**
See also CA 145; CAAE 108; CANR 79;
DLB 143; DLBY 1980; MAL 5; RGAL
4; RHW
Lockwood, Robert
See Johnson, Robert

Mandeville, Bernard 1670-1733 .... **LC 82**
   See also DLB 101
Mandeville, Sir John fl. 1350- ...... **CMLC 19**
   See also DLB 146
Mandiargues, Andre Pieyre de .... **CLC 41**
   See Pieyre de Mandiargues, Andre
   See also DLB 83
Mandrake, Ethel Belle
   See Thurman, Wallace (Henry)
Mangan, James Clarence
   1803-1849 .... **NCLC 27**
   See also RGEL 2
Maniere, J.-E.
   See Giraudoux, Jean(-Hippolyte)
Mankiewicz, Herman (Jacob)
   1897-1953 .... **TCLC 85**
   See also CA 169; CAAE 120; DLB 26;
   IDFW 3, 4
Manley, (Mary) Delariviere
   1672(?)-1724 .... **LC 1, 42**
   See also DLB 39, 80; RGEL 2
Mann, Abel
   See Creasey, John
Mann, Emily 1952- .... **DC 7**
   See also CA 130; CAD; CANR 55; CD 5,
   6; CWD; DLB 266
Mann, (Luiz) Heinrich 1871-1950 ... **TCLC 9**
   See also CA 164, 181; CAAE 106; DLB
   66, 118; EW 8; EWL 3; RGWL 2, 3
Mann, (Paul) Thomas 1875-1955 . **SSC 5, 80,**
   82; TCLC 2, 8, 14, 21, 35, 44, 60, 168;
   WLC 4
   See also BPFB 2; CA 128; CAAE 104;
   CANR 133; CDWLB 2; DA; DA3; DAB;
   DAC; DAM MST, NOV; DLB 66, 331;
   EW 9; EWL 3; GLL 1; LATS 1:1; LMFS
   1; MTCW 1, 2; MTFW 2005; NFS 17;
   RGSF 2; RGWL 2, 3; SSFS 4, 9; TWA
Mannheim, Karl 1893-1947 .... **TCLC 65**
   See also CA 204
Manning, David
   See Faust, Frederick (Schiller)
Manning, Frederic 1882-1935 .... **TCLC 25**
   See also CA 216; CAAE 124; DLB 260
Manning, Olivia 1915-1980 .... **CLC 5, 19**
   See also CA 5-8R; CAAS 101; CANR 29;
   CN 1, 2; EWL 3; FW; MTCW 1; RGEL 2
Mannyng, Robert c. 1264-c.
   1340 .... **CMLC 83**
   See also DLB 146
Mano, D. Keith 1942- .... **CLC 2, 10**
   See also CA 25-28R; 6; CANR 26, 57; DLB
   6
Mansfield, Katherine .... **SSC 9, 23, 38, 81;**
   TCLC 2, 8, 39, 164; WLC 4
   See Beauchamp, Kathleen Mansfield
   See also BPFB 2; BRW 7; DAB; DLB 162;
   EWL 3; EXPS; FW; GLL 1; RGEL 2;
   RGSF 2; SSFS 2, 8, 10, 11; WWE 1
Manso, Peter 1940- .... **CLC 39**
   See also CA 29-32R; CANR 44, 156
Mantecon, Juan Jimenez
   See Jimenez (Mantecon), Juan Ramon
Mantel, Hilary 1952- .... **CLC 144**
   See also CA 125; CANR 54, 101, 161; CN
   5, 6, 7; DLB 271; RHW
Mantel, Hilary Mary
   See Mantel, Hilary
Manton, Peter
   See Creasey, John
Man Without a Spleen, A
   See Chekhov, Anton (Pavlovich)
Manzano, Juan Franciso
   1797(?)-1854 .... **NCLC 155**
Manzoni, Alessandro 1785-1873 ... **NCLC 29,**
   98
   See also EW 5; RGWL 2, 3; TWA; WLIT 7
Map, Walter 1140-1209 .... **CMLC 32**

Mapu, Abraham (ben Jekutiel)
   1808-1867 .... **NCLC 18**
Mara, Sally
   See Queneau, Raymond
Maracle, Lee 1950- .... **NNAL**
   See also CA 149
Marat, Jean Paul 1743-1793 .... **LC 10**
Marcel, Gabriel Honore 1889-1973 . **CLC 15**
   See also CA 102; CAAS 45-48; EWL 3;
   MTCW 1, 2
March, William .... **TCLC 96**
   See Campbell, William Edward March
   See also CA 216; DLB 9, 86, 316; MAL 5
Marchbanks, Samuel
   See Davies, Robertson
   See also CCA 1
Marchi, Giacomo
   See Bassani, Giorgio
Marcus Aurelius
   See Aurelius, Marcus
   See also AW 2
Marguerite
   See de Navarre, Marguerite
Marguerite d'Angouleme
   See de Navarre, Marguerite
   See also GFL Beginnings to 1789
Marguerite de Navarre
   See de Navarre, Marguerite
   See also RGWL 2, 3
Margulies, Donald 1954- .... **CLC 76**
   See also AAYA 57; CA 200; CD 6; DFS 13;
   DLB 228
Marie de France c. 12th cent. - ..... **CMLC 8;**
   PC 22
   See also DLB 208; FW; RGWL 2, 3
Marie de l'Incarnation 1599-1672 ...... **LC 10**
Marier, Captain Victor
   See Griffith, D(avid Lewelyn) W(ark)
Mariner, Scott
   See Pohl, Frederik
Marinetti, Filippo Tommaso
   1876-1944 .... **TCLC 10**
   See also CAAE 107; DLB 114, 264; EW 9;
   EWL 3; WLIT 7
Marivaux, Pierre Carlet de Chamblain de
   1688-1763 .... **DC 7; LC 4, 123**
   See also DLB 314; GFL Beginnings to
   1789; RGWL 2, 3; TWA
Markandaya, Kamala .... **CLC 8, 38**
   See Taylor, Kamala
   See also BYA 13; CN 1, 2, 3, 4, 5, 6, 7;
   DLB 323; EWL 3
Markfield, Wallace (Arthur)
   1926-2002 .... **CLC 8**
   See also CA 69-72; 3; CAAS 208; CN 1, 2,
   3, 4, 5, 6, 7; DLB 2, 28; DLBY 2002
Markham, Edwin 1852-1940 .... **TCLC 47**
   See also CA 160; DLB 54, 186; MAL 5;
   RGAL 4
Markham, Robert
   See Amis, Kingsley
Marks, J.
   See Highwater, Jamake (Mamake)
Marks-Highwater, J.
   See Highwater, Jamake (Mamake)
Markson, David M. 1927- .... **CLC 67**
   See also CA 49-52; CANR 1, 91, 158; CN
   5, 6
Markson, David Merrill
   See Markson, David M.
Marlatt, Daphne (Buckle) 1942- .... **CLC 168**
   See also CA 25-28R; CANR 17, 39; CN 6,
   7; CP 4, 5, 6, 7; CWP; DLB 60; FW
Marley, Bob .... **CLC 17**
   See Marley, Robert Nesta
Marley, Robert Nesta 1945-1981
   See Marley, Bob
   See also CA 107; CAAS 103

Marlowe, Christopher 1564-1593 . **DC 1; LC**
   22, 47, 117; PC 57; WLC 4
   See also BRW 1; BRWR 1; CDBLB Before
   1660; DA; DA3; DAB; DAC; DAM
   DRAM, MST; DFS 1, 5, 13, 21; DLB 62;
   EXPP; LMFS 1; PFS 22; RGEL 2; TEA;
   WLIT 3
Marlowe, Stephen 1928- .... **CLC 70**
   See Queen, Ellery
   See also CA 13-16R; CANR 6, 55; CMW
   4; SFW 4
Marmion, Shakerley 1603-1639 .... **LC 89**
   See also DLB 58; RGEL 2
Marmontel, Jean-Francois 1723-1799 .. **LC 2**
   See also DLB 314
Maron, Monika 1941- .... **CLC 165**
   See also CA 201
Marot, Clement c. 1496-1544 .... **LC 133**
   See also DLB 327; GFL Beginnings to 1789
Marquand, John P(hillips)
   1893-1960 .... **CLC 2, 10**
   See also AMW; BPFB 2; CA 85-88; CANR
   73; CMW 4; DLB 9, 102; EWL 3; MAL
   5; MTCW 2; RGAL 4
Marques, Rene 1919-1979 .. **CLC 96; HLC 2**
   See also CA 97-100; CAAS 85-88; CANR
   78; DAM MULT; DLB 305; EWL 3; HW
   1, 2; LAW; RGSF 2
Marquez, Gabriel Garcia
   See Garcia Marquez, Gabriel
Marquis, Don(ald Robert Perry)
   1878-1937 .... **TCLC 7**
   See also CA 166; CAAE 104; DLB 11, 25;
   MAL 5; RGAL 4
Marquis de Sade
   See Sade, Donatien Alphonse Francois
Marric, J. J.
   See Creasey, John
   See also MSW
Marryat, Frederick 1792-1848 .... **NCLC 3**
   See also DLB 21, 163; RGEL 2; WCH
Marsden, James
   See Creasey, John
Marsh, Edward 1872-1953 .... **TCLC 99**
Marsh, (Edith) Ngaio 1895-1982 .. **CLC 7, 53**
   See also CA 9-12R; CANR 6, 58; CMW 4;
   CN 1, 2, 3; CPW; DAM POP; DLB 77;
   MSW; MTCW 1, 2; RGEL 2; TEA
Marshall, Allen
   See Westlake, Donald E.
Marshall, Garry 1934- .... **CLC 17**
   See also AAYA 3; CA 111; SATA 60
Marshall, Paule 1929- .. **BLC 3; CLC 27, 72;**
   SSC 3
   See also AFAW 1, 2; AMWS 11; BPFB 2;
   BW 2, 3; CA 77-80; CANR 25, 73, 129;
   CN 1, 2, 3, 4, 5, 6, 7; DA3; DAM MULT;
   DLB 33, 157, 227; EWL 3; LATS 1:2;
   MAL 5; MTCW 1, 2; MTFW 2005;
   RGAL 4; SSFS 15
Marshallik
   See Zangwill, Israel
Marsten, Richard
   See Hunter, Evan
Marston, John 1576-1634 .... **LC 33**
   See also BRW 2; DAM DRAM; DLB 58,
   172; RGEL 2
Martel, Yann 1963- .... **CLC 192**
   See also AAYA 67; CA 146; CANR 114;
   DLB 326; MTFW 2005
Martens, Adolphe-Adhemar
   See Ghelderode, Michel de
Martha, Henry
   See Harris, Mark
Marti, Jose .... **PC 76**
   See Marti (y Perez), Jose (Julian)
   See also DLB 290

McKay, Festus Claudius 1889-1948
See McKay, Claude
See also BW 1, 3; CA 124; CAAE 104;
CANR 73; DA; DAC; DAM MST, MULT,
NOV, POET; MTCW 1, 2; MTFW 2005;
TUS

McKuen, Rod 1933- .... **CLC 1, 3**
See also AITN 1; CA 41-44R; CANR 40;
CP 1

McLoughlin, R. B.
See Mencken, H(enry) L(ouis)

McLuhan, (Herbert) Marshall
1911-1980 .... **CLC 37, 83**
See also CA 9-12R; CAAS 102; CANR 12,
34, 61; DLB 88; INT CANR-12; MTCW
1, 2; MTFW 2005

McManus, Declan Patrick Aloysius
See Costello, Elvis

McMillan, Terry 1951- .. **BLCS; CLC 50, 61,
112**
See also AAYA 21; AMWS 13; BPFB 2;
BW 2, 3; CA 140; CANR 60, 104, 131;
CN 7; CPW; DA3; DAM MULT, NOV,
POP; MAL 5; MTCW 2; MTFW 2005;
RGAL 4; YAW

McMurtry, Larry 1936- .... **CLC 2, 3, 7, 11,
27, 44, 127**
See also AAYA 15; AITN 2; AMWS 5;
BEST 89:2; BPFB 2; CA 5-8R; CANR
19, 43, 64, 103; CDALB 1968-1988; CN
2, 3, 4, 5, 6, 7; CPW; CSW; DA3; DAM
NOV, POP; DLB 2, 143, 256; DLBY
1980, 1987; EWL 3; MAL 5; MTCW 1,
2; MTFW 2005; RGAL 4; TCWW 1, 2

McMurtry, Larry Jeff
See McMurtry, Larry

McNally, Terrence 1939- ... **CLC 4, 7, 41, 91;
DC 27**
See also AAYA 62; AMWS 13; CA 45-48;
CAD; CANR 2, 56, 116; CD 5, 6; DA3;
DAM DRAM; DFS 16, 19; DLB 7, 249;
EWL 3; GLL 1; MTCW 2; MTFW 2005

McNally, Thomas Michael
See McNally, T.M.

McNally, T.M. 1961- .... **CLC 82**
See also CA 246

McNamer, Deirdre 1950- .... **CLC 70**
See also CA 188

McNeal, Tom .... **CLC 119**
See also CA 252

McNeile, Herman Cyril 1888-1937
See Sapper
See also CA 184; CMW 4; DLB 77

McNickle, (William) D'Arcy
1904-1977 .... **CLC 89; NNAL**
See also CA 9-12R; CAAS 85-88; CANR
5, 45; DAM MULT; DLB 175, 212;
RGAL 4; SATA-Obit 22; TCWW 1, 2

McPhee, John 1931- .... **CLC 36**
See also AAYA 61; AMWS 3; ANW; BEST
90:1; CA 65-68; CANR 20, 46, 64, 69,
121; CPW; DLB 185, 275; MTCW 1, 2;
MTFW 2005; TUS

McPherson, James Alan 1943- . **BLCS; CLC
19, 77; SSC 95**
See also BW 1, 3; CA 25-28R; 17; CANR
24, 74, 140; CN 3, 4, 5, 6; CSW; DLB
38, 244; EWL 3; MTCW 1, 2; MTFW
2005; RGAL 4; RGSF 2; SSFS 23

McPherson, William (Alexander)
1933- .... **CLC 34**
See also CA 69-72; CANR 28; INT
CANR-28

McTaggart, J. McT. Ellis
See McTaggart, John McTaggart Ellis

McTaggart, John McTaggart Ellis
1866-1925 .... **TCLC 105**
See also CAAE 120; DLB 262

Mead, George Herbert 1863-1931 . **TCLC 89**
See also CA 212; DLB 270

Mead, Margaret 1901-1978 .... **CLC 37**
See also AITN 1; CA 1-4R; CAAS 81-84;
CANR 4; DA3; FW; MTCW 1, 2; SATA-
Obit 20

Meaker, Marijane 1927-
See Kerr, M. E.
See also CA 107; CANR 37, 63, 145; INT
CA-107; JRDA; MAICYA 1, 2; MAIC-
YAS 1; MTCW 1; SATA 20, 61, 99, 160;
SATA-Essay 111; YAW

Medoff, Mark (Howard) 1940- .... **CLC 6, 23**
See also AITN 1; CA 53-56; CAD; CANR
5; CD 5, 6; DAM DRAM; DFS 4; DLB
7; INT CANR-5

Medvedev, P. N.
See Bakhtin, Mikhail Mikhailovich

Meged, Aharon
See Megged, Aharon

Meged, Aron
See Megged, Aharon

Megged, Aharon 1920- .... **CLC 9**
See also CA 49-52; 13; CANR 1, 140; EWL
3; RGHL

Mehta, Deepa 1950- .... **CLC 208**

Mehta, Gita 1943- .... **CLC 179**
See also CA 225; CN 7; DNFS 2

Mehta, Ved 1934- .... **CLC 37**
See also CA 212; 1-4R, 212; CANR 2, 23,
69; DLB 323; MTCW 1; MTFW 2005

Melanchthon, Philipp 1497-1560 .... **LC 90**
See also DLB 179

Melanter
See Blackmore, R(ichard) D(oddridge)

Meleager c. 140B.C.-c. 70B.C. ...... **CMLC 53**

Melies, Georges 1861-1938 .... **TCLC 81**

Melikow, Loris
See Hofmannsthal, Hugo von

Melmoth, Sebastian
See Wilde, Oscar (Fingal O'Flahertie Wills)

Melo Neto, Joao Cabral de
See Cabral de Melo Neto, Joao
See also CWW 2; EWL 3

Meltzer, Milton 1915- .... **CLC 26**
See also AAYA 8, 45; BYA 2, 6; CA 13-
16R; CANR 38, 92, 107; CLR 13; DLB
61; JRDA; MAICYA 1, 2; SAAS 1; SATA
1, 50, 80, 128; SATA-Essay 124; WYA;
YAW

Melville, Herman 1819-1891 ..... **NCLC 3, 12,
29, 45, 49, 91, 93, 123, 157, 181; SSC 1,
17, 46, 95; WLC 4**
See also AAYA 25; AMW; AMWR 1;
CDALB 1640-1865; DA; DA3; DAB;
DAC; DAM MST, NOV; DLB 3, 74, 250,
254; EXPN; EXPS; GL 3; LAIT 1, 2; NFS
7, 9; RGAL 4; RGSF 2; SATA 59; SSFS
3; TUS

Members, Mark
See Powell, Anthony

Membreno, Alejandro .... **CLC 59**

Menand, Louis 1952- .... **CLC 208**
See also CA 200

Menander c. 342B.C.-c. 293B.C. .... **CMLC 9,
51; DC 3**
See also AW 1; CDWLB 1; DAM DRAM;
DLB 176; LMFS 1; RGWL 2, 3

Menchu, Rigoberta 1959- .. **CLC 160; HLCS
2**
See also CA 175; CANR 135; DNFS 1;
WLIT 1

Mencken, H(enry) L(ouis)
1880-1956 .... **TCLC 13**
See also AMW; CA 125; CAAE 105;
CDALB 1917-1929; DLB 11, 29, 63, 137,
222; EWL 3; MAL 5; MTCW 1, 2;
MTFW 2005; NCFS 4; RGAL 4; TUS

Mendelsohn, Jane 1965- .... **CLC 99**
See also CA 154; CANR 94

Mendoza, Inigo Lopez de
See Santillana, Inigo Lopez de Mendoza,
Marques de

Menton, Francisco de
See Chin, Frank (Chew, Jr.)

Mercer, David 1928-1980 .... **CLC 5**
See also CA 9-12R; CAAS 102; CANR 23;
CBD; DAM DRAM; DLB 13, 310;
MTCW 1; RGEL 2

Merchant, Paul
See Ellison, Harlan

Meredith, George 1828-1909 .. **PC 60; TCLC
17, 43**
See also CA 153; CAAE 117; CANR 80;
CDBLB 1832-1890; DAM POET; DLB
18, 35, 57, 159; RGEL 2; TEA

Meredith, William (Morris) 1919- .... **CLC 4,
13, 22, 55; PC 28**
See also CA 9-12R; 14; CANR 6, 40, 129;
CP 1, 2, 3, 4, 5, 6, 7; DAM POET; DLB
5; MAL 5

Merezhkovsky, Dmitrii Sergeevich
See Merezhkovsky, Dmitry Sergeyevich
See also DLB 295

Merezhkovsky, Dmitry Sergeevich
See Merezhkovsky, Dmitry Sergeyevich
See also EWL 3

Merezhkovsky, Dmitry Sergeyevich
1865-1941 .... **TCLC 29**
See Merezhkovsky, Dmitrii Sergeevich;
Merezhkovsky, Dmitry Sergeevich
See also CA 169

Merimee, Prosper 1803-1870 ... **NCLC 6, 65;
SSC 7, 77**
See also DLB 119, 192; EW 6; EXPS; GFL
1789 to the Present; RGSF 2; RGWL 2,
3; SSFS 8; SUFW

Merkin, Daphne 1954- .... **CLC 44**
See also CA 123

Merleau-Ponty, Maurice
1908-1961 .... **TCLC 156**
See also CA 114; CAAS 89-92; DLB 296;
GFL 1789 to the Present

Merlin, Arthur
See Blish, James (Benjamin)

Mernissi, Fatima 1940- .... **CLC 171**
See also CA 152; FW

Merrill, James 1926-1995 ...... **CLC 2, 3, 6, 8,
13, 18, 34, 91; PC 28; TCLC 173**
See also AMWS 3; CA 13-16R; CAAS 147;
CANR 10, 49, 63, 108; CP 1, 2, 3, 4;
DA3; DAM POET; DLB 5, 165; DLBY
1985; EWL 3; INT CANR-10; MAL 5;
MTCW 1, 2; MTFW 2005; PAB; PFS 23;
RGAL 4

Merrill, James Ingram
See Merrill, James

Merriman, Alex
See Silverberg, Robert

Merriman, Brian 1747-1805 .... **NCLC 70**

Merritt, E. B.
See Waddington, Miriam

Merton, Thomas (James)
1915-1968 . **CLC 1, 3, 11, 34, 83; PC 10**
See also AAYA 61; AMWS 8; CA 5-8R;
CAAS 25-28R; CANR 22, 53, 111, 131;
DA3; DLB 48; DLBY 1981; MAL 5;
MTCW 1, 2; MTFW 2005

Merwin, W.S. 1927- ..... **CLC 1, 2, 3, 5, 8, 13,
18, 45, 88; PC 45**
See also AMWS 3; CA 13-16R; CANR 15,
51, 112, 140; CP 1, 2, 3, 4, 5, 6, 7; DA3;
DAM POET; DLB 5; EWL 3; INT
CANR-15; MAL 5; MTCW 1, 2; MTFW
2005; PAB; PFS 5, 15; RGAL 4

Metastasio, Pietro 1698-1782 .... **LC 115**
See also RGWL 2, 3

Metcalf, John 1938- .... **CLC 37; SSC 43**
See also CA 113; CN 4, 5, 6, 7; DLB 60;
RGSF 2; TWA
Metcalf, Suzanne
See Baum, L(yman) Frank
Mew, Charlotte (Mary) 1870-1928 .. **TCLC 8**
See also CA 189; CAAE 105; DLB 19, 135;
RGEL 2
Mewshaw, Michael 1943- .... **CLC 9**
See also CA 53-56; CANR 7, 47, 147;
DLBY 1980
Meyer, Conrad Ferdinand
1825-1898 .... **NCLC 81; SSC 30**
See also DLB 129; EW; RGWL 2, 3
Meyer, Gustav 1868-1932
See Meyrink, Gustav
See also CA 190; CAAE 117
Meyer, June
See Jordan, June
Meyer, Lynn
See Slavitt, David R(ytman)
Meyers, Jeffrey 1939- .... **CLC 39**
See also CA 186; 73-76, 186; CANR 54,
102, 159; DLB 111
**Meynell, Alice (Christina Gertrude
Thompson)** 1847-1922 .... **TCLC 6**
See also CA 177; CAAE 104; DLB 19, 98;
RGEL 2
Meyrink, Gustav .... **TCLC 21**
See Meyer, Gustav
See also DLB 81; EWL 3
Michaels, Leonard 1933-2003 ..... **CLC 6, 25;
SSC 16**
See also AMWS 16; CA 61-64; CAAS 216;
CANR 21, 62, 119; CN 3, 45, 6, 7; DLB
130; MTCW 1; TCLE 1:2
Michaux, Henri 1899-1984 .... **CLC 8, 19**
See also CA 85-88; CAAS 114; DLB 258;
EWL 3; GFL 1789 to the Present; RGWL
2, 3
Micheaux, Oscar (Devereaux)
1884-1951 .... **TCLC 76**
See also BW 3; CA 174; DLB 50; TCWW
2
Michelangelo 1475-1564 .... **LC 12**
See also AAYA 43
Michelet, Jules 1798-1874 .... **NCLC 31**
See also EW 5; GFL 1789 to the Present
Michels, Robert 1876-1936 .... **TCLC 88**
See also CA 212
Michener, James A. 1907(?)-1997 . **CLC 1, 5,
11, 29, 60, 109**
See also AAYA 27; AITN 1; BEST 90:1;
BPFB 2; CA 5-8R; CAAS 161; CANR
21, 45, 68; CN 1, 2, 3, 4, 5, 6; CPW; DA3;
DAM NOV, POP; DLB 6; MAL 5;
MTCW 1, 2; MTFW 2005; RHW; TCWW
1, 2
Mickiewicz, Adam 1798-1855 . **NCLC 3, 101;
PC 38**
See also EW 5; RGWL 2, 3
Middleton, (John) Christopher
1926- .... **CLC 13**
See also CA 13-16R; CANR 29, 54, 117;
CP 1, 2, 3, 4, 5, 6, 7; DLB 40
Middleton, Richard (Barham)
1882-1911 .... **TCLC 56**
See also CA 187; DLB 156; HGG
Middleton, Stanley 1919- .... **CLC 7, 38**
See also CA 25-28R; 23; CANR 21, 46, 81,
157; CN 1, 2, 3, 4, 5, 6, 7; DLB 14, 326
Middleton, Thomas 1580-1627 ...... **DC 5; LC
33, 123**
See also BRW 2; DAM DRAM, MST; DFS
18, 22; DLB 58; RGEL 2
Mieville, China 1972(?)- .... **CLC 235**
See also AAYA 52; CA 196; CANR 138;
MTFW 2005

Migueis, Jose Rodrigues 1901-1980 . **CLC 10**
See also DLB 287
Mikszath, Kalman 1847-1910 .... **TCLC 31**
See also CA 170
Miles, Jack .... **CLC 100**
See also CA 200
Miles, John Russiano
See Miles, Jack
Miles, Josephine (Louise)
1911-1985 .... **CLC 1, 2, 14, 34, 39**
See also CA 1-4R; CAAS 116; CANR 2,
55; CP 1, 2, 3, 4; DAM POET; DLB 48;
MAL 5; TCLE 1:2
Militant
See Sandburg, Carl (August)
Mill, Harriet (Hardy) Taylor
1807-1858 .... **NCLC 102**
See also FW
Mill, John Stuart 1806-1873 ... **NCLC 11, 58,
179**
See also CDBLB 1832-1890; DLB 55, 190,
262; FW 1; RGEL 2; TEA
Millar, Kenneth 1915-1983 .... **CLC 14**
See Macdonald, Ross
See also CA 9-12R; CAAS 110; CANR 16,
63, 107; CMW 4; CPW; DA3; DAM POP;
DLB 2, 226; DLBD 6; DLBY 1983;
MTCW 1, 2; MTFW 2005
Millay, E. Vincent
See Millay, Edna St. Vincent
Millay, Edna St. Vincent 1892-1950 ..... **PC 6,
61; TCLC 4, 49, 169; WLCS**
See Boyd, Nancy
See also AMW; CA 130; CAAE 104;
CDALB 1917-1929; DA; DA3; DAB;
DAC; DAM MST, POET; DLB 45, 249;
EWL 3; EXPP; FL 1:6; MAL 5; MBL;
MTCW 1, 2; MTFW 2005; PAB; PFS 3,
17; RGAL 4; TUS; WP
Miller, Arthur 1915-2005 ..... **CLC 1, 2, 6, 10,
15, 26, 47, 78, 179; DC 1; WLC 4**
See also AAYA 15; AITN 1; AMW; AMWC
1; CA 1-4R; CAAS 236; CABS 3; CAD;
CANR 2, 30, 54, 76, 132; CD 5, 6;
CDALB 1941-1968; DA; DA3; DAB;
DAC; DAM DRAM, MST; DFS 1, 3, 8;
DLB 7, 266; EWL 3; LAIT 1, 4; LATS
1:2; MAL 5; RGHL; TUS; WYAS 1
RGAL 4; RGHL; TUS; WYAS 1
Miller, Henry (Valentine)
1891-1980 .... **CLC 1, 2, 4, 9, 14, 43, 84;
WLC 4**
See also AMW; BPFB 2; CA 9-12R; CAAS
97-100; CANR 33, 64; CDALB 1929-
1941; CN 1, 2; DA; DA3; DAB; DAC;
DAM MST, NOV; DLB 4, 9; DLBY
1980; EWL 3; MAL 5; MTCW 1, 2;
MTFW 2005; RGAL 4; TUS
Miller, Hugh 1802-1856 .... **NCLC 143**
See also DLB 190
Miller, Jason 1939(?)-2001 .... **CLC 2**
See also AITN 1; CA 73-76; CAAS 197;
CAD; CANR 130; DFS 12; DLB 7
Miller, Sue 1943- .... **CLC 44**
See also AMWS 12; BEST 90:3; CA 139;
CANR 59, 91, 128; DA3; DAM POP;
DLB 143
Miller, Walter M(ichael, Jr.)
1923-1996 .... **CLC 4, 30**
See also BPFB 2; CA 85-88; CANR 108;
DLB 8; SCFW 1, 2; SFW 4
Millett, Kate 1934- .... **CLC 67**
See also AITN 1; CA 73-76; CANR 32, 53,
76, 110; DA3; DLB 246; FW; GLL 1;
MTCW 1, 2; MTFW 2005
Millhauser, Steven 1943- ... **CLC 21, 54, 109;
SSC 57**
See also CA 111; CAAE 110; CANR 63,
114, 133; CN 6, 7; DA3; DLB 2; FANT;
INT CA-111; MAL 5; MTCW 2; MTFW
2005

Millhauser, Steven Lewis
See Millhauser, Steven
Millin, Sarah Gertrude 1889-1968 ... **CLC 49**
See also CA 102; CAAS 93-96; DLB 225;
EWL 3
Milne, A. A. 1882-1956 .... **TCLC 6, 88**
See also BRWS 5; CA 133; CAAE 104;
CLR 1, 26, 108; CMW 4; CWRI 5; DA3;
DAB; DAC; DAM MST; DLB 10, 77,
100, 160; FANT; MAICYA 1, 2; MTCW
1, 2; MTFW 2005; RGEL 2; SATA 100;
WCH; YABC 1
Milne, Alan Alexander
See Milne, A. A.
Milner, Ron(ald) 1938-2004 ..... **BLC 3; CLC
56**
See also AITN 1; BW 1; CA 73-76; CAAS
230; CAD; CANR 24, 81; CD 5, 6; DAM
MULT; DLB 38; MAL 5; MTCW 1
Milnes, Richard Monckton
1809-1885 .... **NCLC 61**
See also DLB 32, 184
Milosz, Czeslaw 1911-2004 .... **CLC 5, 11, 22,
31, 56, 82; PC 8; WLCS**
See also AAYA 62; CA 81-84; CAAS 230;
CANR 23, 51, 91, 126; CDWLB 4; CWW
2; DA3; DAM MST, POET; DLB 215,
331; EW 13; EWL 3; MTCW 1, 2; MTFW
2005; PFS 16; RGHL; RGWL 2, 3
Milton, John 1608-1674 ..... **LC 9, 43, 92; PC
19, 29; WLC 4**
See also AAYA 65; BRW 2; BRWR 2; CD-
BLB 1660-1789; DA; DA3; DAB; DAC;
DAM MST, POET; DLB 131, 151, 281;
EFS 1; EXPP; LAIT 1; PAB; PFS 3, 17;
RGEL 2; TEA; WLIT 3; WP
Min, Anchee 1957- .... **CLC 86**
See also CA 146; CANR 94, 137; MTFW
2005
Minehaha, Cornelius
See Wedekind, Frank
Miner, Valerie 1947- .... **CLC 40**
See also CA 97-100; CANR 59; FW; GLL
2
Minimo, Duca
See D'Annunzio, Gabriele
Minot, Susan (Anderson) 1956- ...... **CLC 44,
159**
See also AMWS 6; CA 134; CANR 118;
CN 6, 7
Minus, Ed 1938- .... **CLC 39**
See also CA 185
Mirabai 1498(?)-1550(?) .... **PC 48**
See also PFS 24
Miranda, Javier
See Bioy Casares, Adolfo
See also CWW 2
Mirbeau, Octave 1848-1917 .... **TCLC 55**
See also CA 216; DLB 123, 192; GFL 1789
to the Present
Mirikitani, Janice 1942- .... **AAL**
See also CA 211; DLB 312; RGAL 4
Mirk, John (?)-c. 1414 .... **LC 105**
See also DLB 146
Miro (Ferrer), Gabriel (Francisco Victor)
1879-1930 .... **TCLC 5**
See also CA 185; CAAE 104; DLB 322;
EWL 3
Misharin, Alexandr .... **CLC 59**
Mishima, Yukio ... **CLC 2, 4, 6, 9, 27; DC 1;
SSC 4; TCLC 161; WLC 4**
See Hiraoka, Kimitake
See also AAYA 50; BPFB 2; GLL 1; MJW;
RGSF 2; RGWL 2, 3; SSFS 5, 12
Mistral, Frederic 1830-1914 .... **TCLC 51**
See also CA 213; CAAE 122; DLB 331;
GFL 1789 to the Present

POET; DLB 45; DLBD 7; EWL 3; EXPP;
FL 1:6; MAL 5; MBL; MTCW 1, 2;
MTFW 2005; PAB; PFS 14, 17; RGAL 4;
SATA 20; TUS; WP

Moore, Marie Lorena 1957- .... **CLC 165**
See Moore, Lorrie
See also CA 116; CANR 39, 83, 139; DLB
234; MTFW 2005

Moore, Michael 1954- .... **CLC 218**
See also AAYA 53; CA 166; CANR 150

Moore, Thomas 1779-1852 .... **NCLC 6, 110**
See also DLB 96, 144; RGEL 2

Moorhouse, Frank 1938- .... **SSC 40**
See also CA 118; CANR 92; CN 3, 4, 5, 6,
7; DLB 289; RGSF 2

Mora, Pat 1942- .... **HLC 2**
See also AMWS 13; CA 129; CANR 57,
81, 112; CLR 58; DAM MULT; DLB 209;
HW 1, 2; LLW; MAICYA 2; MTFW
2005; SATA 92, 134

Moraga, Cherríe 1952- ...... **CLC 126; DC 22**
See also CA 131; CANR 66, 154; DAM
MULT; DLB 82, 249; FW; GLL 1; HW 1,
2; LLW

Morand, Paul 1888-1976 .... **CLC 41; SSC 22**
See also CA 184; CAAS 69-72; DLB 65;
EWL 3

Morante, Elsa 1918-1985 .... **CLC 8, 47**
See also CA 85-88; CAAS 117; CANR 35;
DLB 177; EWL 3; MTCW 1, 2; MTFW
2005; RGHL; RGWL 2, 3; WLIT 7

Moravia, Alberto .... **CLC 2, 7, 11, 27, 46;
SSC 26**
See Pincherle, Alberto
See also DLB 177; EW 12; EWL 3; MTCW
2; RGSF 2; RGWL 2, 3; WLIT 7

More, Hannah 1745-1833 ...... **NCLC 27, 141**
See also DLB 107, 109, 116, 158; RGEL 2

More, Henry 1614-1687 .... **LC 9**
See also DLB 126, 252

More, Sir Thomas 1478(?)-1535 .... **LC 10, 32**
See also BRWC 1; BRWS 7; DLB 136, 281;
LMFS 1; RGEL 2; TEA

Moréas, Jean .... **TCLC 18**
See Papadiamantopoulos, Johannes
See also GFL 1789 to the Present

Moreton, Andrew Esq.
See Defoe, Daniel

Morgan, Berry 1919-2002 .... **CLC 6**
See also CA 49-52; CAAS 208; DLB 6

Morgan, Claire
See Highsmith, Patricia
See also GLL 1

Morgan, Edwin (George) 1920- .... **CLC 31**
See also BRWS 9; CA 5-8R; CANR 3, 43,
90; CP 1, 2, 3, 4, 5, 6, 7; DLB 27

Morgan, (George) Frederick
1922-2004 .... **CLC 23**
See also CA 17-20R; CAAS 224; CANR
21, 144; CP 2, 3, 4, 5, 6, 7

Morgan, Harriet
See Mencken, H(enry) L(ouis)

Morgan, Jane
See Cooper, James Fenimore

Morgan, Janet 1945- .... **CLC 39**
See also CA 65-68

Morgan, Lady 1776(?)-1859 .... **NCLC 29**
See also DLB 116, 158; RGEL 2

Morgan, Robin (Evonne) 1941- .... **CLC 2**
See also CA 69-72; CANR 29, 68; FW;
GLL 2; MTCW 1; SATA 80

Morgan, Scott
See Kuttner, Henry

Morgan, Seth 1949(?)-1990 .... **CLC 65**
See also CA 185; CAAS 132

**Morgenstern, Christian (Otto Josef
Wolfgang)** 1871-1914 .... **TCLC 8**
See also CA 191; CAAE 105; EWL 3

Morgenstern, S.
See Goldman, William

Mori, Rintaro
See Mori Ogai
See also CAAE 110

Mori, Toshio 1910-1980 .... **AAL; SSC 83**
See also CA 244; CAAE 116; DLB 312;
RGSF 2

Moricz, Zsigmond 1879-1942 .... **TCLC 33**
See also CA 165; DLB 215; EWL 3

Morike, Eduard (Friedrich)
1804-1875 .... **NCLC 10**
See also DLB 133; RGWL 2, 3

Mori Ogai 1862-1922 .... **TCLC 14**
See Ogai
See also CA 164; DLB 180; EWL 3; RGWL
3; TWA

Moritz, Karl Philipp 1756-1793 .... **LC 2**
See also DLB 94

Morland, Peter Henry
See Faust, Frederick (Schiller)

Morley, Christopher (Darlington)
1890-1957 .... **TCLC 87**
See also CA 213; CAAE 112; DLB 9; MAL
5; RGAL 4

Morren, Theophil
See Hofmannsthal, Hugo von

Morris, Bill 1952- .... **CLC 76**
See also CA 225

Morris, Julian
See West, Morris L(anglo)

Morris, Steveland Judkins (?)-
See Wonder, Stevie

Morris, William 1834-1896 . **NCLC 4; PC 55**
See also BRW 5; CDBLB 1832-1890; DLB
18, 35, 57, 156, 178, 184; FANT; RGEL
2; SFW 4; SUFW

Morris, Wright (Marion) 1910-1998 . **CLC 1,
3, 7, 18, 37; TCLC 107**
See also AMW; CA 9-12R; CAAS 167;
CANR 21, 81; CN 1, 2, 3, 4, 5, 6; DLB
2, 206, 218; DLBY 1981; EWL 3; MAL
5; MTCW 1, 2; MTFW 2005; RGAL 4;
TCWW 1, 2

Morrison, Arthur 1863-1945 .... **SSC 40;
TCLC 72**
See also CA 157; CAAE 120; CMW 4;
DLB 70, 135, 197; RGEL 2

Morrison, Chloe Anthony Wofford
See Morrison, Toni

Morrison, James Douglas 1943-1971
See Morrison, Jim
See also CA 73-76; CANR 40

Morrison, Jim .... **CLC 17**
See Morrison, James Douglas

Morrison, John Gordon 1904-1998 ... **SSC 93**
See also CA 103; CANR 92; DLB 260

Morrison, Toni 1931- ...... **BLC 3; CLC 4, 10,
22, 55, 81, 87, 173, 194; WLC 4**
See also AAYA 1, 22, 61; AFAW 1, 2;
AMWC 1; AMWS 3; BPFB 2; BW 2, 3;
CA 29-32R; CANR 27, 42, 67, 113, 124;
CDALB 1968-1988; CLR 99; CN 3, 4, 5,
6, 7; CPW; DA; DA3; DAB; DAC; DAM
MST, MULT, NOV, POP; DLB 6, 33, 143,
331; DLBY 1981; EWL 3; EXPN; FL 1:6;
FW; GL 3; LAIT 2, 4; LATS 1:2; LMFS
2; MAL 5; MBL; MTCW 1, 2; MTFW
2005; NFS 1, 6, 8, 14; RGAL 4; RHW;
SATA 57, 144; SSFS 5; TCLE 1:2; TUS;
YAW

Morrison, Van 1945- .... **CLC 21**
See also CA 168; CAAE 116

Morrissy, Mary 1957- .... **CLC 99**
See also CA 205; DLB 267

Mortimer, John 1923- .... **CLC 28, 43**
See also CA 13-16R; CANR 21, 69, 109;
CBD; CD 5, 6; CDBLB 1960 to Present;
CMW 4; CN 5, 6, 7; CPW; DA3; DAM
DRAM, POP; DLB 13, 245, 271; INT
CANR-21; MSW; MTCW 1, 2; MTFW
2005; RGEL 2

Mortimer, Penelope (Ruth)
1918-1999 .... **CLC 5**
See also CA 57-60; CAAS 187; CANR 45,
88; CN 1, 2, 3, 4, 5, 6

Mortimer, Sir John
See Mortimer, John

Morton, Anthony
See Creasey, John

Morton, Thomas 1579(?)-1647(?) .... **LC 72**
See also DLB 24; RGEL 2

Mosca, Gaetano 1858-1941 .... **TCLC 75**

Moses, Daniel David 1952- .... **NNAL**
See also CA 186; CANR 160

Mosher, Howard Frank 1943- .... **CLC 62**
See also CA 139; CANR 65, 115

Mosley, Nicholas 1923- .... **CLC 43, 70**
See also CA 69-72; CANR 41, 60, 108, 158;
CN 1, 2, 3, 4, 5, 6, 7; DLB 14, 207

Mosley, Walter 1952- .... **BLCS; CLC 97, 184**
See also AAYA 57; AMWS 13; BPFB 2;
BW 2; CA 142; CANR 57, 92, 136; CMW
4; CN 7; CPW; DA3; DAM MULT, POP;
DLB 306; MSW; MTCW 2; MTFW 2005

Moss, Howard 1922-1987 . **CLC 7, 14, 45, 50**
See also CA 1-4R; CAAS 123; CANR 1,
44; CP 1, 2, 3, 4; DAM POET; DLB 5

Mossgiel, Rab
See Burns, Robert

Motion, Andrew 1952- .... **CLC 47**
See also BRWS 7; CA 146; CANR 90, 142;
CP 4, 5, 6, 7; DLB 40; MTFW 2005

Motion, Andrew Peter
See Motion, Andrew

Motley, Willard (Francis)
1909-1965 .... **CLC 18**
See also BW 1; CA 117; CAAS 106; CANR
88; DLB 76, 143

Motoori, Norinaga 1730-1801 .... **NCLC 45**

Mott, Michael (Charles Alston)
1930- .... **CLC 15, 34**
See also CA 5-8R; 7; CANR 7, 29

Mountain Wolf Woman 1884-1960 . **CLC 92;
NNAL**
See also CA 144; CANR 90

Moure, Erin 1955- .... **CLC 88**
See also CA 113; CP 5, 6, 7; CWP; DLB
60

Mourning Dove 1885(?)-1936 .... **NNAL**
See also CA 144; CANR 90; DAM MULT;
DLB 175, 221

Mowat, Farley 1921- .... **CLC 26**
See also AAYA 1, 50; BYA 2; CA 1-4R;
CANR 4, 24, 42, 68, 108; CLR 20; CPW;
DAC; DAM MST; DLB 68; INT CANR-
24; JRDA; MAICYA 1, 2; MTCW 1, 2;
MTFW 2005; SATA 3, 55; YAW

Mowatt, Anna Cora 1819-1870 ..... **NCLC 74**
See also RGAL 4

Moyers, Bill 1934- .... **CLC 74**
See also AITN 2; CA 61-64; CANR 31, 52,
148

Mphahlele, Es'kia
See Mphahlele, Ezekiel
See also AFW; CDWLB 3; CN 4, 5, 6; DLB
125, 225; RGSF 2; SSFS 11

Mphahlele, Ezekiel 1919- ... **BLC 3; CLC 25,
133**
See Mphahlele, Es'kia
See also BW 2, 3; CA 81-84; CANR 26,
76; CN 1, 2, 3; DA3; DAM MULT; EWL
3; MTCW 2; MTFW 2005; SATA 119

O'Donovan, Michael Francis
 1903-1966 .... **CLC 14**
 See O'Connor, Frank
 See also CA 93-96; CANR 84
Oe, Kenzaburo 1935- .. **CLC 10, 36, 86, 187;
 SSC 20**
 See Oe Kenzaburo
 See also CA 97-100; CANR 36, 50, 74, 126;
 DA3; DAM NOV; DLB 182, 331; DLBY
 1994; LATS 1:2; MJW; MTCW 1, 2;
 MTFW 2005; RGSF 2; RGWL 2, 3
Oe Kenzaburo
 See Oe, Kenzaburo
 See also CWW 2; EWL 3
O'Faolain, Julia 1932- .... **CLC 6, 19, 47, 108**
 See also CA 81-84; 2; CANR 12, 61; CN 2,
 3, 4, 5, 6, 7; DLB 14, 231, 319; FW;
 MTCW 1; RHW
O'Faolain, Sean 1900-1991 ...... **CLC 1, 7, 14,
 32, 70; SSC 13; TCLC 143**
 See also CA 61-64; CAAS 134; CANR 12,
 66; CN 1, 2, 3, 4; DLB 15, 162; MTCW
 1, 2; MTFW 2005; RGEL 2; RGSF 2
O'Flaherty, Liam 1896-1984 .... **CLC 5, 34;
 SSC 6**
 See also CA 101; CAAS 113; CANR 35;
 CN 1, 2, 3; DLB 36, 162; DLBY 1984;
 MTCW 1, 2; MTFW 2005; RGEL 2;
 RGSF 2; SSFS 5, 20
Ogai
 See Mori Ogai
 See also MJW
Ogilvy, Gavin
 See Barrie, J(ames) M(atthew)
O'Grady, Standish (James)
 1846-1928 .... **TCLC 5**
 See also CA 157; CAAE 104
O'Grady, Timothy 1951- .... **CLC 59**
 See also CA 138
O'Hara, Frank 1926-1966 .... **CLC 2, 5, 13,
 78; PC 45**
 See also CA 9-12R; CAAS 25-28R; CANR
 33; DA3; DAM POET; DLB 5, 16, 193;
 EWL 3; MAL 5; MTCW 1, 2; MTFW
 2005; PFS 8, 12; RGAL 4; WP
O'Hara, John (Henry) 1905-1970 . **CLC 1, 2,
 3, 6, 11, 42; SSC 15**
 See also AMW; BPFB 3; CA 5-8R; CAAS
 25-28R; CANR 31, 60; CDALB 1929-
 1941; DAM NOV; DLB 9, 86, 324; DLBD
 2; EWL 3; MAL 5; MTCW 1, 2; MTFW
 2005; NFS 11; RGAL 4; RGSF 2
O'Hehir, Diana 1929- .... **CLC 41**
 See also CA 245
Ohiyesa
 See Eastman, Charles A(lexander)
Okada, John 1923-1971 .... **AAL**
 See also BYA 14; CA 212; DLB 312
Okigbo, Christopher 1930-1967 .... **BLC 3;
 CLC 25, 84; PC 7; TCLC 171**
 See also AFW; BW 1, 3; CA 77-80; CANR
 74; CDWLB 3; DAM MULT, POET; DLB
 125; EWL 3; MTCW 1, 2; MTFW 2005;
 RGEL 2
Okigbo, Christopher Ifenayichukwu
 See Okigbo, Christopher
Okri, Ben 1959- .... **CLC 87, 223**
 See also AFW; BRWS 5; BW 2, 3; CA 138;
 CAAE 130; CANR 65, 128; CN 5, 6, 7;
 DLB 157, 231, 319, 326; EWL 3; INT
 CA-138; MTCW 2; MTFW 2005; RGSF
 2; SSFS 20; WLIT 2; WWE 1
Olds, Sharon 1942- .. **CLC 32, 39, 85; PC 22**
 See also AMWS 10; CA 101; CANR 18,
 41, 66, 98, 135; CP 5, 6, 7; CPW; CWP;
 DAM POET; DLB 120; MAL 5; MTCW
 2; MTFW 2005; PFS 17
Oldstyle, Jonathan
 See Irving, Washington

Olesha, Iurii
 See Olesha, Yuri (Karlovich)
 See also RGWL 2
Olesha, Iurii Karlovich
 See Olesha, Yuri (Karlovich)
 See also DLB 272
Olesha, Yuri (Karlovich) 1899-1960 . **CLC 8;
 SSC 69; TCLC 136**
 See Olesha, Iurii; Olesha, Iurii Karlovich;
 Olesha, Yury Karlovich
 See also CA 85-88; EW 11; RGWL 3
Olesha, Yury Karlovich
 See Olesha, Yuri (Karlovich)
 See also EWL 3
Oliphant, Mrs.
 See Oliphant, Margaret (Oliphant Wilson)
 See also SUFW
Oliphant, Laurence 1829(?)-1888 .. **NCLC 47**
 See also DLB 18, 166
Oliphant, Margaret (Oliphant Wilson)
 1828-1897 .... **NCLC 11, 61; SSC 25**
 See Oliphant, Mrs.
 See also BRWS 10; DLB 18, 159, 190;
 HGG; RGEL 2; RGSF 2
Oliver, Mary 1935- ... **CLC 19, 34, 98; PC 75**
 See also AMWS 7; CA 21-24R; CANR 9,
 43, 84, 92, 138; CP 4, 5, 6, 7; CWP; DLB
 5, 193; EWL 3; MTFW 2005; PFS 15
Olivier, Laurence (Kerr) 1907-1989 . **CLC 20**
 See also CA 150; CAAE 111; CAAS 129
Olsen, Tillie 1912-2007 .... **CLC 4, 13, 114;
 SSC 11**
 See also AAYA 51; AMWS 13; BYA 11;
 CA 1-4R; CANR 1, 43, 74, 132;
 CDALBS; CN 2, 3, 4, 5, 6, 7; DA; DA3;
 DAB; DAC; DAM MST; DLB 28, 206;
 DLBY 1980; EWL 3; EXPS; FW; MAL
 5; MTCW 1, 2; MTFW 2005; RGAL 4;
 RGSF 2; SSFS 1; TCLE 1:2; TCWW 2;
 TUS
Olson, Charles (John) 1910-1970 .. **CLC 1, 2,
 5, 6, 9, 11, 29; PC 19**
 See also AMWS 2; CA 13-16; CAAS 25-
 28R; CABS 2; CANR 35, 61; CAP 1; CP
 1; DAM POET; DLB 5, 16, 193; EWL 3;
 MAL 5; MTCW 1, 2; RGAL 4; WP
Olson, Toby 1937- .... **CLC 28**
 See also CA 65-68; 11; CANR 9, 31, 84;
 CP 3, 4, 5, 6, 7
Olyesha, Yuri
 See Olesha, Yuri (Karlovich)
Olympiodorus of Thebes c. 375-c.
 430 .... **CMLC 59**
Omar Khayyam
 See Khayyam, Omar
 See also RGWL 2, 3
Ondaatje, Michael 1943- ..... **CLC 14, 29, 51,
 76, 180; PC 28**
 See also AAYA 66; CA 77-80; CANR 42,
 74, 109, 133; CN 5, 6, 7; CP 1, 2, 3, 4, 5,
 6, 7; DA3; DAB; DAC; DAM MST; DLB
 60, 323, 326; EWL 3; LATS 1:2; LMFS
 2; MTCW 2; MTFW 2005; NFS 23; PFS
 8, 19; TCLE 1:2; TWA; WWE 1
Ondaatje, Philip Michael
 See Ondaatje, Michael
Oneal, Elizabeth 1934-
 See Oneal, Zibby
 See also CA 106; CANR 28, 84; MAICYA
 1, 2; SATA 30, 82; YAW
Oneal, Zibby .... **CLC 30**
 See Oneal, Elizabeth
 See also AAYA 5, 41; BYA 13; CLR 13;
 JRDA; WYA
O'Neill, Eugene (Gladstone)
 1888-1953 ... **DC 20; TCLC 1, 6, 27, 49;
 WLC 4**
 See also AAYA 54; AITN 1; AMW; AMWC
 1; CA 132; CAAE 110; CAD; CANR 131;
 CDALB 1929-1941; DA; DA3; DAB;

DAC; DAM DRAM, MST; DFS 2, 4, 5,
 6, 9, 11, 12, 16, 20; DLB 7, 331; EWL 3;
 LAIT 3; LMFS 2; MAL 5; MTCW 1, 2;
 MTFW 2005; RGAL 4; TUS
Onetti, Juan Carlos 1909-1994 ... **CLC 7, 10;
 HLCS 2; SSC 23; TCLC 131**
 See also CA 85-88; CAAS 145; CANR 32,
 63; CDWLB 3; CWW 2; DAM MULT,
 NOV; DLB 113; EWL 3; HW 1, 2; LAW;
 MTCW 1, 2; MTFW 2005; RGSF 2
O Nuallain, Brian 1911-1966
 See O'Brien, Flann
 See also CA 21-22; CAAS 25-28R; CAP 2;
 DLB 231; FANT; TEA
Ophuls, Max
 See Ophuls, Max
Ophuls, Max 1902-1957 .... **TCLC 79**
 See also CAAE 113
Opie, Amelia 1769-1853 .... **NCLC 65**
 See also DLB 116, 159; RGEL 2
Oppen, George 1908-1984 ..... **CLC 7, 13, 34;
 PC 35; TCLC 107**
 See also CA 13-16R; CAAS 113; CANR 8,
 82; CP 1, 2, 3; DLB 5, 165
Oppenheim, E(dward) Phillips
 1866-1946 .... **TCLC 45**
 See also CA 202; CAAE 111; CMW 4; DLB
 70
Oppenheimer, Max
 See Ophuls, Max
Opuls, Max
 See Ophuls, Max
Orage, A(lfred) R(ichard)
 1873-1934 .... **TCLC 157**
 See also CAAE 122
Origen c. 185-c. 254 .... **CMLC 19**
Orlovitz, Gil 1918-1973 .... **CLC 22**
 See also CA 77-80; CAAS 45-48; CN 1;
 CP 1, 2; DLB 2, 5
O'Rourke, Patrick Jake
 See O'Rourke, P.J.
O'Rourke, P.J. 1947- .... **CLC 209**
 See also CA 77-80; CANR 13, 41, 67, 111,
 155; CPW; DAM POP; DLB 185
Orris
 See Ingelow, Jean
Ortega y Gasset, Jose 1883-1955 ...... **HLC 2;
 TCLC 9**
 See also CA 130; CAAE 106; DAM MULT;
 EW 9; EWL 3; HW 1, 2; MTCW 1, 2;
 MTFW 2005
Ortese, Anna Maria 1914-1998 .... **CLC 89**
 See also DLB 177; EWL 3
Ortiz, Simon J(oseph) 1941- ... **CLC 45, 208;
 NNAL; PC 17**
 See also AMWS 4; CA 134; CANR 69, 118;
 CP 3, 4, 5, 6, 7; DAM MULT, POET;
 DLB 120, 175, 256; EXPP; MAL 5; PFS
 4, 16; RGAL 4; SSFS 22; TCWW 2
Orton, Joe ...... **CLC 4, 13, 43; DC 3; TCLC
 157**
 See Orton, John Kingsley
 See also BRWS 5; CBD; CDBLB 1960 to
 Present; DFS 3, 6; DLB 13, 310; GLL 1;
 RGEL 2; TEA; WLIT 4
Orton, John Kingsley 1933-1967
 See Orton, Joe
 See also CA 85-88; CANR 35, 66; DAM
 DRAM; MTCW 1, 2; MTFW 2005
Orwell, George ...... **SSC 68; TCLC 2, 6, 15,
 31, 51, 128, 129; WLC 4**
 See Blair, Eric (Arthur)
 See also BPFB 3; BRW 7; BYA 5; CDBLB
 1945-1960; CLR 68; DAB; DLB 15, 98,
 195, 255; EWL 3; EXPN; LAIT 4, 5;
 LATS 1:1; NFS 3, 7; RGEL 2; SCFW 1,
 2; SFW 4; SSFS 4; TEA; WLIT 4; YAW
Osborne, David
 See Silverberg, Robert

Pincherle, Alberto 1907-1990 ...... **CLC 11, 18**
See Moravia, Alberto
See also CA 25-28R; CAAS 132; CANR 33, 63, 142; DAM NOV; MTCW 1; MTFW 2005

Pinckney, Darryl 1953- .... **CLC 76**
See also BW 2, 3; CA 143; CANR 79

Pindar 518(?)B.C.-438(?)B.C. .... **CMLC 12; PC 19**
See also AW 1; CDWLB 1; DLB 176; RGWL 2

Pineda, Cecile 1942- .... **CLC 39**
See also CA 118; DLB 209

Pinero, Arthur Wing 1855-1934 .... **TCLC 32**
See also CA 153; CAAE 110; DAM DRAM; DLB 10; RGEL 2

Pinero, Miguel (Antonio Gomez)
1946-1988 .... **CLC 4, 55**
See also CA 61-64; CAAS 125; CAD; CANR 29, 90; DLB 266; HW 1; LLW

Pinget, Robert 1919-1997 .... **CLC 7, 13, 37**
See also CA 85-88; CAAS 160; CWW 2; DLB 83; EWL 3; GFL 1789 to the Present

Pink Floyd
See Barrett, (Roger) Syd; Gilmour, David; Mason, Nick; Waters, Roger; Wright, Rick

Pinkney, Edward 1802-1828 .... **NCLC 31**
See also DLB 248

Pinkwater, D. Manus
See Pinkwater, Daniel Manus

Pinkwater, Daniel
See Pinkwater, Daniel Manus

Pinkwater, Daniel M.
See Pinkwater, Daniel Manus

Pinkwater, Daniel Manus 1941- .... **CLC 35**
See also AAYA 1, 46; BYA 9; CA 29-32R; CANR 12, 38, 89, 143; CLR 4; CSW; FANT; JRDA; MAICYA 1, 2; SAAS 3; SATA 8, 46, 76, 114, 158; SFW 4; YAW

Pinkwater, Manus
See Pinkwater, Daniel Manus

Pinsky, Robert 1940- .... **CLC 9, 19, 38, 94, 121, 216; PC 27**
See also AMWS 6; CA 29-32R; 4; CANR 58, 97, 138; CP 3, 4, 5, 6, 7; DA3; DAM POET; DLBY 1982, 1998; MAL 5; MTCW 2; MTFW 2005; PFS 18; RGAL 4; TCLE 1:2

Pinta, Harold
See Pinter, Harold

Pinter, Harold 1930- .. **CLC 1, 3, 6, 9, 11, 15, 27, 58, 73, 199; DC 15; WLC 4**
See also BRWR 1; BRWS 1; CA 5-8R; CANR 33, 65, 112, 145; CBD; CD 5, 6; CDBLB 1960 to Present; CP 1; DA; DA3; DAB; DAC; DAM DRAM, MST; DFS 5, 7, 14; DLB 13, 310, 331; EWL 3; IDFW 3, 4; LMFS 2; MTCW 1, 2; MTFW 2005; RGEL 2; RGHL; TEA

Piozzi, Hester Lynch (Thrale)
1741-1821 .... **NCLC 57**
See also DLB 104, 142

Pirandello, Luigi 1867-1936 .. **DC 5; SSC 22; TCLC 4, 29, 172; WLC 4**
See also CA 153; CAAE 104; CANR 103; DA; DA3; DAB; DAC; DAM DRAM, MST; DFS 4, 9; DLB 264, 331; EW 8; EWL 3; MTCW 2; MTFW 2005; RGSF 2; RGWL 2, 3; WLIT 7

Pirsig, Robert M(aynard) 1928- ... **CLC 4, 6, 73**
See also CA 53-56; CANR 42, 74; CPW 1; DA3; DAM POP; MTCW 1, 2; MTFW 2005; SATA 39

Pisan, Christine de
See Christine de Pizan

Pisarev, Dmitrii Ivanovich
See Pisarev, Dmitry Ivanovich
See also DLB 277

Pisarev, Dmitry Ivanovich
1840-1868 .... **NCLC 25**
See Pisarev, Dmitrii Ivanovich

Pix, Mary (Griffith) 1666-1709 .... **LC 8**
See also DLB 80

Pixerecourt, (Rene Charles) Guilbert de
1773-1844 .... **NCLC 39**
See also DLB 192; GFL 1789 to the Present

Plaatje, Sol(omon) T(shekisho)
1878-1932 .... **BLCS; TCLC 73**
See also BW 2, 3; CA 141; CANR 79; DLB 125, 225

Plaidy, Jean
See Hibbert, Eleanor Alice Burford

Planche, James Robinson
1796-1880 .... **NCLC 42**
See also RGEL 2

Plant, Robert 1948- .... **CLC 12**

Plante, David 1940- .... **CLC 7, 23, 38**
See also CA 37-40R; CANR 12, 36, 58, 82, 152; CN 2, 3, 4, 5, 6, 7; DAM NOV; DLBY 1983; INT CANR-12; MTCW 1

Plante, David Robert
See Plante, David

Plath, Sylvia 1932-1963 ..... **CLC 1, 2, 3, 5, 9, 11, 14, 17, 50, 51, 62, 111; PC 1, 37; WLC 4**
See also AAYA 13; AMWR 2; AMWS 1; BPFB 3; CA 19-20; CANR 34, 101; CAP 2; CDALB 1941-1968; DA; DA3; DAB; DAC; DAM MST, POET; DLB 5, 6, 152; EWL 3; EXPN; EXPP; FL 1:6; FW; LAIT 4; MAL 5; MBL; MTCW 1, 2; MTFW 2005; NFS 1; PAB; PFS 1, 15; RGAL 4; SATA 96; TUS; WP; YAW

Plato c. 428B.C.-347B.C. .... **CMLC 8, 75; WLCS**
See also AW 1; CDWLB 1; DA; DA3; DAB; DAC; DAM MST; DLB 176; LAIT 1; LATS 1:1; RGWL 2, 3; WLIT 8

Platonov, Andrei
See Klimentov, Andrei Platonovich

Platonov, Andrei Platonovich
See Klimentov, Andrei Platonovich
See also DLB 272

Platonov, Andrey Platonovich
See Klimentov, Andrei Platonovich
See also EWL 3

Platt, Kin 1911- .... **CLC 26**
See also AAYA 11; CA 17-20R; CANR 11; JRDA; SAAS 17; SATA 21, 86; WYA

Plautus c. 254B.C.-c. 184B.C. ...... **CMLC 24; DC 6**
See also AW 1; CDWLB 1; DLB 211; RGWL 2, 3; WLIT 8

Plick et Plock
See Simenon, Georges (Jacques Christian)

Plieksans, Janis
See Rainis, Janis

Plimpton, George 1927-2003 .... **CLC 36**
See also AITN 1; AMWS 16; CA 21-24R; CAAS 224; CANR 32, 70, 103, 133; DLB 185, 241; MTCW 1, 2; MTFW 2005; SATA 10; SATA-Obit 150

Pliny the Elder c. 23-79 .... **CMLC 23**
See also DLB 211

Pliny the Younger c. 61-c. 112 ...... **CMLC 62**
See also AW 2; DLB 211

Plomer, William Charles Franklin
1903-1973 .... **CLC 4, 8**
See also AFW; BRWS 11; CA 21-22; CANR 34; CAP 2; CN 1; CP 1, 2; DLB 20, 162, 191, 225; EWL 3; MTCW 1; RGEL 2; RGSF 2; SATA 24

Plotinus 204-270 .... **CMLC 46**
See also CDWLB 1; DLB 176

Plowman, Piers
See Kavanagh, Patrick (Joseph)

Plum, J.
See Wodehouse, P(elham) G(renville)

Plumly, Stanley (Ross) 1939- .... **CLC 33**
See also CA 110; CAAE 108; CANR 97; CP 3, 4, 5, 6, 7; DLB 5, 193; INT CA-110

Plumpe, Friedrich Wilhelm
See Murnau, F.W.

Plutarch c. 46-c. 120 .... **CMLC 60**
See also AW 2; CDWLB 1; DLB 176; RGWL 2, 3; TWA; WLIT 8

Po Chu-i 772-846 .... **CMLC 24**

Podhoretz, Norman 1930- .... **CLC 189**
See also AMWS 8; CA 9-12R; CANR 7, 78, 135

Poe, Edgar Allan 1809-1849 ..... **NCLC 1, 16, 55, 78, 94, 97, 117; PC 1, 54; SSC 1, 22, 34, 35, 54, 88; WLC 4**
See also AAYA 14; AMW; AMWC 1; AMWR 2; BPFB 3; BYA 5, 11; CDALB 1640-1865; CMW 4; DA; DA3; DAB; DAC; DAM MST, POET; DLB 3, 59, 73, 74, 248, 254; EXPP; EXPS; GL 3; HGG; LAIT 2; LATS 1:1; LMFS 1; MSW; PAB; PFS 1, 3, 9; RGAL 4; RGSF 2; SATA 23; SCFW 1, 2; SFW 4; SSFS 2, 4, 7, 8, 16; SUFW; TUS; WP; WYA

Poet of Titchfield Street, The
See Pound, Ezra (Weston Loomis)

Poggio Bracciolini, Gian Francesco
1380-1459 .... **LC 125**

Pohl, Frederik 1919- .... **CLC 18; SSC 25**
See also AAYA 24; CA 188; 61-64, 188; 1; CANR 11, 37, 81, 140; CN 1, 2, 3, 4, 5, 6; DLB 8; INT CANR-11; MTCW 1, 2; MTFW 2005; SATA 24; SCFW 1, 2; SFW 4

Poirier, Louis 1910-
See Gracq, Julien
See also CA 126; CAAE 122; CANR 141

Poitier, Sidney 1927- .... **CLC 26**
See also AAYA 60; BW 1; CA 117; CANR 94

Pokagon, Simon 1830-1899 .... **NNAL**
See also DAM MULT

Polanski, Roman 1933- .... **CLC 16, 178**
See also CA 77-80

Poliakoff, Stephen 1952- .... **CLC 38**
See also CA 106; CANR 116; CBD; CD 5, 6; DLB 13

Police, The
See Copeland, Stewart (Armstrong); Summers, Andrew James

Polidori, John William
1795-1821 .... **NCLC 51; SSC 97**
See also DLB 116; HGG

Poliziano, Angelo 1454-1494 .... **LC 120**
See also WLIT 7

Pollitt, Katha 1949- .... **CLC 28, 122**
See also CA 122; CAAE 120; CANR 66, 108; MTCW 1, 2; MTFW 2005

Pollock, (Mary) Sharon 1936- .... **CLC 50**
See also CA 141; CANR 132; CD 5; CWD; DAC; DAM DRAM, MST; DFS 3; DLB 60; FW

Pollock, Sharon 1936- .... **DC 20**
See also CD 6

Polo, Marco 1254-1324 .... **CMLC 15**
See also WLIT 7

Polonsky, Abraham (Lincoln)
1910-1999 .... **CLC 92**
See also CA 104; CAAS 187; DLB 26; INT CA-104

Polybius c. 200B.C.-c. 118B.C. ...... **CMLC 17**
See also AW 1; DLB 176; RGWL 2, 3

Pomerance, Bernard 1940- .... **CLC 13**
See also CA 101; CAD; CANR 49, 134; CD 5, 6; DAM DRAM; DFS 9; LAIT 2

Ponge, Francis 1899-1988 .... **CLC 6, 18**
See also CA 85-88; CAAS 126; CANR 40,
86; DAM POET; DLBY 2002; EWL 3;
GFL 1789 to the Present; RGWL 2, 3

Poniatowska, Elena 1932- . **CLC 140; HLC 2**
See also CA 101; CANR 32, 66, 107, 156;
CDWLB 3; CWW 2; DAM MULT; DLB
113; EWL 3; HW 1, 2; LAWS 1; WLIT 1

Pontoppidan, Henrik 1857-1943 .... **TCLC 29**
See also CA 170; DLB 300, 331

Ponty, Maurice Merleau
See Merleau-Ponty, Maurice

Poole, Josephine .... **CLC 17**
See Helyar, Jane Penelope Josephine
See also SAAS 2; SATA 5

Popa, Vasko 1922-1991 . **CLC 19; TCLC 167**
See also CA 148; CAAE 112; CDWLB 4;
DLB 181; EWL 3; RGWL 2, 3

Pope, Alexander 1688-1744 ...... **LC 3, 58, 60,
64; PC 26; WLC 5**
See also BRW 3; BRWC 1; BRWR 1; CD-
BLB 1660-1789; DA; DA3; DAB; DAC;
DAM MST, POET; DLB 95, 101, 213;
EXPP; PAB; PFS 12; RGEL 2; WLIT 3;
WP

Popov, Evgenii Anatol'evich
See Popov, Yevgeny
See also DLB 285

Popov, Yevgeny .... **CLC 59**
See Popov, Evgenii Anatol'evich

Poquelin, Jean-Baptiste
See Moliere

Porete, Marguerite (?)-1310 .... **CMLC 73**
See also DLB 208

Porphyry c. 233-c. 305 .... **CMLC 71**

Porter, Connie (Rose) 1959(?)- .... **CLC 70**
See also AAYA 65; BW 2, 3; CA 142;
CANR 90, 109; SATA 81, 129

Porter, Gene(va Grace) Stratton .. **TCLC 21**
See Stratton-Porter, Gene(va Grace)
See also BPFB 3; CAAE 112; CWRI 5;
RHW

Porter, Katherine Anne 1890-1980 ... **CLC 1,
3, 7, 10, 13, 15, 27, 101; SSC 4, 31, 43**
See also AAYA 42; AITN 2; AMW; BPFB
3; CA 1-4R; CAAS 101; CANR 1, 65;
CDALBS; CN 1, 2; DA; DA3; DAB;
DAC; DAM MST, NOV; DLB 4, 9, 102;
DLBD 12; DLBY 1980; EWL 3; EXPS;
LAIT 3; MAL 5; MBL; MTCW 1, 2;
MTFW 2005; NFS 14; RGAL 4; RGSF 2;
SATA 39; SATA-Obit 23; SSFS 1, 8, 11,
16, 23; TCWW 2; TUS

Porter, Peter (Neville Frederick)
1929- .... **CLC 5, 13, 33**
See also CA 85-88; CP 1, 2, 3, 4, 5, 6, 7;
DLB 40, 289; WWE 1

Porter, William Sydney 1862-1910
See Henry, O.
See also CA 131; CAAE 104; CDALB
1865-1917; DA; DA3; DAB; DAC; DAM
MST; DLB 12, 78, 79; MTCW 1, 2;
MTFW 2005; TUS; YABC 2

Portillo (y Pacheco), Jose Lopez
See Lopez Portillo (y Pacheco), Jose

Portillo Trambley, Estela 1927-1998 .. **HLC 2**
See Trambley, Estela Portillo
See also CANR 32; DAM MULT; DLB
209; HW 1

Posey, Alexander (Lawrence)
1873-1908 .... **NNAL**
See also CA 144; CANR 80; DAM MULT;
DLB 175

Posse, Abel .... **CLC 70**
See also CA 252

Post, Melville Davisson
1869-1930 .... **TCLC 39**
See also CA 202; CAAE 110; CMW 4

Potok, Chaim 1929-2002 ... **CLC 2, 7, 14, 26,
112**
See also AAYA 15, 50; AITN 1, 2; BPFB 3;
BYA 1; CA 17-20R; CAAS 208; CANR
19, 35, 64, 98; CLR 92; CN 4, 5, 6; DA3;
DAM NOV; DLB 28, 152; EXPN; INT
CANR-19; LAIT 4; MTCW 1, 2; MTFW
2005; NFS 4; RGHL; SATA 33, 106;
SATA-Obit 134; TUS; YAW

Potok, Herbert Harold -2002
See Potok, Chaim

Potok, Herman Harold
See Potok, Chaim

Potter, Dennis (Christopher George)
1935-1994 .... **CLC 58, 86, 123**
See also BRWS 10; CA 107; CAAS 145;
CANR 33, 61; CBD; DLB 233; MTCW 1

Pound, Ezra (Weston Loomis)
1885-1972 .. **CLC 1, 2, 3, 4, 5, 7, 10, 13,
18, 34, 48, 50, 112; PC 4; WLC 5**
See also AAYA 47; AMW; AMWR 1; CA
5-8R; CAAS 37-40R; CANR 40; CDALB
1917-1929; CP 1; DA; DA3; DAB; DAC;
DAM MST, POET; DLB 4, 45, 63; DLBD
15; EFS 2; EWL 3; EXPP; LMFS 2; MAL
5; MTCW 1, 2; MTFW 2005; PAB; PFS
2, 8, 16; RGAL 4; TUS; WP

Povod, Reinaldo 1959-1994 .... **CLC 44**
See also CA 136; CAAS 146; CANR 83

Powell, Adam Clayton, Jr.
1908-1972 .... **BLC 3; CLC 89**
See also BW 1, 3; CA 102; CAAS 33-36R;
CANR 86; DAM MULT

Powell, Anthony 1905-2000 ... **CLC 1, 3, 7, 9,
10, 31**
See also BRW 7; CA 1-4R; CAAS 189;
CANR 1, 32, 62, 107; CDBLB 1945-
1960; CN 1, 2, 3, 4, 5, 6; DLB 15; EWL
3; MTCW 1, 2; MTFW 2005; RGEL 2;
TEA

Powell, Dawn 1896(?)-1965 .... **CLC 66**
See also CA 5-8R; CANR 121; DLBY 1997

Powell, Padgett 1952- .... **CLC 34**
See also CA 126; CANR 63, 101; CSW;
DLB 234; DLBY 01

Powell, (Oval) Talmage 1920-2000
See Queen, Ellery
See also CA 5-8R; CANR 2, 80

Power, Susan 1961- .... **CLC 91**
See also BYA 14; CA 160; CANR 135; NFS
11

Powers, J(ames) F(arl) 1917-1999 ..... **CLC 1,
4, 8, 57; SSC 4**
See also CA 1-4R; CAAS 181; CANR 2,
61; CN 1, 2, 3, 4, 5, 6; DLB 130; MTCW
1; RGAL 4; RGSF 2

Powers, John J(ames) 1945-
See Powers, John R.
See also CA 69-72

Powers, John R. .... **CLC 66**
See Powers, John J(ames)

Powers, Richard 1957- .... **CLC 93**
See also AMWS 9; BPFB 3; CA 148;
CANR 80; CN 6, 7; MTFW 2005; TCLE
1:2

Powers, Richard S.
See Powers, Richard

Pownall, David 1938- .... **CLC 10**
See also CA 89-92, 180; 18; CANR 49, 101;
CBD; CD 5, 6; CN 4, 5, 6, 7; DLB 14

Powys, John Cowper 1872-1963 ... **CLC 7, 9,
15, 46, 125**
See also CA 85-88; CANR 106; DLB 15,
255; EWL 3; FANT; MTCW 1, 2; MTFW
2005; RGEL 2; SUFW

Powys, T(heodore) F(rancis)
1875-1953 .... **TCLC 9**
See also BRWS 8; CA 189; CAAE 106;
DLB 36, 162; EWL 3; FANT; RGEL 2;
SUFW

Pozzo, Modesta
See Fonte, Moderata

Prado (Calvo), Pedro 1886-1952 ... **TCLC 75**
See also CA 131; DLB 283; HW 1; LAW

Prager, Emily 1952- .... **CLC 56**
See also CA 204

Pratchett, Terry 1948- .... **CLC 197**
See also AAYA 19, 54; BPFB 3; CA 143;
CANR 87, 126; CLR 64; CN 6, 7; CPW;
CWRI 5; FANT; MTFW 2005; SATA 82,
139; SFW 4; SUFW 2

Pratolini, Vasco 1913-1991 .... **TCLC 124**
See also CA 211; DLB 177; EWL 3; RGWL
2, 3

Pratt, E(dwin) J(ohn) 1883(?)-1964 . **CLC 19**
See also CA 141; CAAS 93-96; CANR 77;
DAC; DAM POET; DLB 92; EWL 3;
RGEL 2; TWA

Premchand .... **TCLC 21**
See Srivastava, Dhanpat Rai
See also EWL 3

Prescott, William Hickling
1796-1859 .... **NCLC 163**
See also DLB 1, 30, 59, 235

Preseren, France 1800-1849 .... **NCLC 127**
See also CDWLB 4; DLB 147

Preussler, Otfried 1923- .... **CLC 17**
See also CA 77-80; SATA 24

Prevert, Jacques (Henri Marie)
1900-1977 .... **CLC 15**
See also CA 77-80; CAAS 69-72; CANR
29, 61; DLB 258; EWL 3; GFL 1789 to
the Present; IDFW 3, 4; MTCW 1; RGWL
2, 3; SATA-Obit 30

Prevost, (Antoine Francois)
1697-1763 .... **LC 1**
See also DLB 314; EW 4; GFL Beginnings
to 1789; RGWL 2, 3

Price, Reynolds 1933- .. **CLC 3, 6, 13, 43, 50,
63, 212; SSC 22**
See also AMWS 6; CA 1-4R; CANR 1, 37,
57, 87, 128; CN 1, 2, 3, 4, 5, 6, 7; CSW;
DAM NOV; DLB 2, 218, 278; EWL 3;
INT CANR-37; MAL 5; MTFW 2005;
NFS 18

Price, Richard 1949- .... **CLC 6, 12**
See also CA 49-52; CANR 3, 147; CN 7;
DLBY 1981

Prichard, Katharine Susannah
1883-1969 .... **CLC 46**
See also CA 11-12; CANR 33; CAP 1; DLB
260; MTCW 1; RGEL 2; RGSF 2; SATA
66

Priestley, J(ohn) B(oynton)
1894-1984 .... **CLC 2, 5, 9, 34**
See also BRW 7; CA 9-12R; CAAS 113;
CANR 33; CDBLB 1914-1945; CN 1, 2,
3; DA3; DAM DRAM, NOV; DLB 10,
34, 77, 100, 139; DLBY 1984; EWL 3;
MTCW 1, 2; MTFW 2005; RGEL 2; SFW
4

Prince 1958- .... **CLC 35**
See also CA 213

Prince, F(rank) T(empleton)
1912-2003 .... **CLC 22**
See also CA 101; CAAS 219; CANR 43,
79; CP 1, 2, 3, 4, 5, 6, 7; DLB 20

Prince Kropotkin
See Kropotkin, Peter (Alekseevich)

Prior, Matthew 1664-1721 .... **LC 4**
See also DLB 95; RGEL 2

Prishvin, Mikhail 1873-1954 .... **TCLC 75**
See Prishvin, Mikhail Mikhailovich

Prishvin, Mikhail Mikhailovich
See Prishvin, Mikhail
See also DLB 272; EWL 3

Pritchard, William H(arrison)
1932- .... **CLC 34**
See also CA 65-68; CANR 23, 95; DLB 111

Pritchett, V(ictor) S(awdon)
1900-1997 ... **CLC 5, 13, 15, 41; SSC 14**
See also BPFB 3; BRWS 3; CA 61-64; CAAS 157; CANR 31, 63; CN 1, 2, 3, 4, 5, 6; DA3; DAM NOV; DLB 15, 139; EWL 3; MTCW 1, 2; MTFW 2005; RGEL 2; RGSF 2; TEA

Private 19022
See Manning, Frederic

Probst, Mark 1925- .... **CLC 59**
See also CA 130

Procaccino, Michael
See Cristofer, Michael

Proclus c. 412-c. 485 .... **CMLC 81**

Prokosch, Frederic 1908-1989 ...... **CLC 4, 48**
See also CA 73-76; CAAS 128; CANR 82; CN 1, 2, 3, 4; CP 1, 2, 3, 4; DLB 48; MTCW 2

Propertius, Sextus c. 50B.C.-c.
16B.C. .... **CMLC 32**
See also AW 2; CDWLB 1; DLB 211; RGWL 2, 3; WLIT 8

Prophet, The
See Dreiser, Theodore

Prose, Francine 1947- .... **CLC 45, 231**
See also AMWS 16; CA 112; CAAE 109; CANR 46, 95, 132; DLB 234; MTFW 2005; SATA 101, 149

Protagoras c. 490B.C.-420B.C. ...... **CMLC 85**
See also DLB 176

Proudhon
See Cunha, Euclides (Rodrigues Pimenta) da

Proulx, Annie
See Proulx, E. Annie

Proulx, E. Annie 1935- .... **CLC 81, 158**
See also AMWS 7; BPFB 3; CA 145; CANR 65, 110; CN 6, 7; CPW 1; DA3; DAM POP; MAL 5; MTCW 2; MTFW 2005; SSFS 18, 23

Proulx, Edna Annie
See Proulx, E. Annie

Proust, (Valentin-Louis-George-Eugene)
Marcel 1871-1922 ..... **SSC 75; TCLC 7, 13, 33; WLC 5**
See also AAYA 58; BPFB 3; CA 120; CAAE 104; CANR 110; DA; DA3; DAB; DAC; DAM MST, NOV; DLB 65; EW 8; EWL 3; GFL 1789 to the Present; MTCW 1, 2; MTFW 2005; RGWL 2, 3; TWA

Prowler, Harley
See Masters, Edgar Lee

Prudentius, Aurelius Clemens 348-c.
405 .... **CMLC 78**
See also EW 1; RGWL 2, 3

Prudhomme, Rene Francois Armand
1839-1907
See Sully Prudhomme, Rene-Francois-Armand
See also CA 170

Prus, Boleslaw 1845-1912 .... **TCLC 48**
See also RGWL 2, 3

Pryor, Aaron Richard
See Pryor, Richard

Pryor, Richard 1940-2005 .... **CLC 26**
See also CA 152; CAAE 122; CAAS 246

Pryor, Richard Franklin Lenox Thomas
See Pryor, Richard

Przybyszewski, Stanislaw
1868-1927 .... **TCLC 36**
See also CA 160; DLB 66; EWL 3

Pseudo-Dionysius the Areopagite fl. c. 5th
cent. - .... **CMLC 89**
See also DLB 115

Pteleon
See Grieve, C(hristopher) M(urray)
See also DAM POET

Puckett, Lute
See Masters, Edgar Lee

Puig, Manuel 1932-1990 .... **CLC 3, 5, 10, 28, 65, 133; HLC 2**
See also BPFB 3; CA 45-48; CANR 2, 32, 63; CDWLB 3; DA3; DAM MULT; DLB 113; DNFS 1; EWL 3; GLL 1; HW 1, 2; LAW; MTCW 1, 2; MTFW 2005; RGWL 2, 3; TWA; WLIT 1

Pulitzer, Joseph 1847-1911 .... **TCLC 76**
See also CAAE 114; DLB 23

Purchas, Samuel 1577(?)-1626 .... **LC 70**
See also DLB 151

Purdy, A(lfred) W(ellington)
1918-2000 .... **CLC 3, 6, 14, 50**
See also CA 81-84; 17; CAAS 189; CANR 42, 66; CP 1, 2, 3, 4, 5, 6, 7; DAC; DAM MST, POET; DLB 88; PFS 5; RGEL 2

Purdy, James (Amos) 1923- .... **CLC 2, 4, 10, 28, 52**
See also AMWS 7; CA 33-36R; 1; CANR 19, 51, 132; CN 1, 2, 3, 4, 5, 6, 7; DLB 2, 218; EWL 3; INT CANR-19; MAL 5; MTCW 1; RGAL 4

Pure, Simon
See Swinnerton, Frank Arthur

Pushkin, Aleksandr Sergeevich
See Pushkin, Alexander (Sergeyevich)
See also DLB 205

Pushkin, Alexander (Sergeyevich)
1799-1837 .... **NCLC 3, 27, 83; PC 10; SSC 27, 55, 99; WLC 5**
See Pushkin, Aleksandr Sergeevich
See also DA; DA3; DAB; DAC; DAM DRAM, MST, POET; EW 5; EXPS; RGSF 2; RGWL 2, 3; SATA 61; SSFS 9; TWA

P'u Sung-ling 1640-1715 .... **LC 49; SSC 31**

Putnam, Arthur Lee
See Alger, Horatio, Jr.

Puttenham, George 1529(?)-1590 ...... **LC 116**
See also DLB 281

Puzo, Mario 1920-1999 .... **CLC 1, 2, 6, 36, 107**
See also BPFB 3; CA 65-68; CAAS 185; CANR 4, 42, 65, 99, 131; CN 1, 2, 3, 4, 5, 6; CPW; DA3; DAM NOV, POP; DLB 6; MTCW 1, 2; MTFW 2005; NFS 16; RGAL 4

Pygge, Edward
See Barnes, Julian

Pyle, Ernest Taylor 1900-1945
See Pyle, Ernie
See also CA 160; CAAE 115

Pyle, Ernie .... **TCLC 75**
See Pyle, Ernest Taylor
See also DLB 29; MTCW 2

Pyle, Howard 1853-1911 .... **TCLC 81**
See also AAYA 57; BYA 2, 4; CA 137; CAAE 109; CLR 22, 117; DLB 42, 188; DLBD 13; LAIT 1; MAICYA 1, 2; SATA 16, 100; WCH; YAW

Pym, Barbara (Mary Crampton)
1913-1980 .... **CLC 13, 19, 37, 111**
See also BPFB 3; BRWS 2; CA 13-14; CAAS 97-100; CANR 13, 34; CAP 1; DLB 14, 207; DLBY 1987; EWL 3; MTCW 1, 2; MTFW 2005; RGEL 2; TEA

Pynchon, Thomas 1937- .. **CLC 2, 3, 6, 9, 11, 18, 33, 62, 72, 123, 192, 213; SSC 14, 84; WLC 5**
See also AMWS 2; BEST 90:2; BPFB 3; CA 17-20R; CANR 22, 46, 73, 142; CN 1, 2, 3, 4, 5, 6, 7; CPW 1; DA; DA3; DAB; DAC; DAM MST, NOV, POP; DLB 2, 173; EWL 3; MAL 5; MTCW 1, 2; MTFW 2005; NFS 23; RGAL 4; SFW 4; TCLE 1:2; TUS

Pythagoras c. 582B.C.-c. 507B.C. . **CMLC 22**
See also DLB 176

Q
See Quiller-Couch, Sir Arthur (Thomas)

Qian, Chongzhu
See Ch'ien, Chung-shu

Qian, Sima 145B.C.-c. 89B.C. .... **CMLC 72**

Qian Zhongshu
See Ch'ien, Chung-shu
See also CWW 2; DLB 328

Qroll
See Dagerman, Stig (Halvard)

Quarles, Francis 1592-1644 .... **LC 117**
See also DLB 126; RGEL 2

Quarrington, Paul (Lewis) 1953- ..... **CLC 65**
See also CA 129; CANR 62, 95

Quasimodo, Salvatore 1901-1968 .... **CLC 10; PC 47**
See also CA 13-16; CAAS 25-28R; CAP 1; DLB 114, 332; EW 12; EWL 3; MTCW 1; RGWL 2, 3

Quatermass, Martin
See Carpenter, John (Howard)

Quay, Stephen 1947- .... **CLC 95**
See also CA 189

Quay, Timothy 1947- .... **CLC 95**
See also CA 189

Queen, Ellery .... **CLC 3, 11**
See Dannay, Frederic; Davidson, Avram (James); Deming, Richard; Fairman, Paul W.; Flora, Fletcher; Hoch, Edward D(entinger); Kane, Henry; Lee, Manfred B.; Marlowe, Stephen; Powell, (Oval) Talmage; Sheldon, Walter J(ames); Sturgeon, Theodore (Hamilton); Tracy, Don(ald Fiske); Vance, Jack
See also BPFB 3; CMW 4; MSW; RGAL 4

Queen, Ellery, Jr.
See Dannay, Frederic; Lee, Manfred B.

Queneau, Raymond 1903-1976 ..... **CLC 2, 5, 10, 42**
See also CA 77-80; CAAS 69-72; CANR 32; DLB 72, 258; EW 12; EWL 3; GFL 1789 to the Present; MTCW 1, 2; RGWL 2, 3

Quevedo, Francisco de 1580-1645 .... **LC 23**

Quiller-Couch, Sir Arthur (Thomas)
1863-1944 .... **TCLC 53**
See also CA 166; CAAE 118; DLB 135, 153, 190; HGG; RGEL 2; SUFW 1

Quin, Ann 1936-1973 .... **CLC 6**
See also CA 9-12R; CAAS 45-48; CANR 148; CN 1; DLB 14, 231

Quin, Ann Marie
See Quin, Ann

Quincey, Thomas de
See De Quincey, Thomas

Quindlen, Anna 1953- .... **CLC 191**
See also AAYA 35; CA 138; CANR 73, 126; DA3; DLB 292; MTCW 2; MTFW 2005

Quinn, Martin
See Smith, Martin Cruz

Quinn, Peter 1947- .... **CLC 91**
See also CA 197; CANR 147

Quinn, Peter A.
See Quinn, Peter

Quinn, Simon
See Smith, Martin Cruz

Quintana, Leroy V. 1944- ...... **HLC 2; PC 36**
See also CA 131; CANR 65, 139; DAM MULT; DLB 82; HW 1, 2

Quintilian c. 40-c. 100 .... **CMLC 77**
See also AW 2; DLB 211; RGWL 2, 3

Quintillian 0035-0100 .... **CMLC 77**

Quiroga, Horacio (Sylvestre)
1878-1937 ... **HLC 2; SSC 89; TCLC 20**
See also CA 131; CAAE 117; DAM MULT; EWL 3; HW 1; LAW; MTCW 1; RGSF 2; WLIT 1

Reeve, Clara 1729-1807 .... **NCLC 19**
See also DLB 39; RGEL 2

Reich, Wilhelm 1897-1957 .... **TCLC 57**
See also CA 199

Reid, Christopher (John) 1949- .... **CLC 33**
See also CA 140; CANR 89; CP 4, 5, 6, 7;
DLB 40; EWL 3

Reid, Desmond
See Moorcock, Michael

Reid Banks, Lynne 1929-
See Banks, Lynne Reid
See also AAYA 49; CA 1-4R; CANR 6, 22,
38, 87; CLR 24; CN 1, 2, 3, 7; JRDA;
MAICYA 1, 2; SATA 22, 75, 111, 165;
YAW

Reilly, William K.
See Creasey, John

Reiner, Max
See Caldwell, (Janet Miriam) Taylor
(Holland)

Reis, Ricardo
See Pessoa, Fernando (Antonio Nogueira)

Reizenstein, Elmer Leopold
See Rice, Elmer (Leopold)
See also EWL 3

Remarque, Erich Maria 1898-1970 . **CLC 21**
See also AAYA 27; BPFB 3; CA 77-80;
CAAS 29-32R; CDWLB 2; DA; DA3;
DAB; DAC; DAM MST, NOV; DLB 56;
EWL 3; EXPN; LAIT 3; MTCW 1, 2;
MTFW 2005; NFS 4; RGHL; RGWL 2, 3

Remington, Frederic S(ackrider)
1861-1909 .... **TCLC 89**
See also CA 169; CAAE 108; DLB 12, 186,
188; SATA 41; TCWW 2

Remizov, A.
See Remizov, Aleksei (Mikhailovich)

Remizov, A. M.
See Remizov, Aleksei (Mikhailovich)

Remizov, Aleksei (Mikhailovich)
1877-1957 .... **TCLC 27**
See Remizov, Alexey Mikhaylovich
See also CA 133; CAAE 125; DLB 295

Remizov, Alexey Mikhaylovich
See Remizov, Aleksei (Mikhailovich)
See also EWL 3

Renan, Joseph Ernest 1823-1892 . **NCLC 26,
145**
See also GFL 1789 to the Present

Renard, Jules(-Pierre) 1864-1910 .. **TCLC 17**
See also CA 202; CAAE 117; GFL 1789 to
the Present

Renart, Jean fl. 13th cent. - .... **CMLC 83**

Renault, Mary .... **CLC 3, 11, 17**
See Challans, Mary
See also BPFB 3; BYA 2; CN 1, 2, 3;
DLBY 1983; EWL 3; GLL 1; LAIT 1;
RGEL 2; RHW

Rendell, Ruth 1930- .... **CLC 28, 48**
See Vine, Barbara
See also BPFB 3; BRWS 9; CA 109; CANR
32, 52, 74, 127; CN 5, 6, 7; CPW; DAM
POP; DLB 87, 276; INT CANR-32;
MSW; MTCW 1, 2; MTFW 2005

Rendell, Ruth Barbara
See Rendell, Ruth

Renoir, Jean 1894-1979 .... **CLC 20**
See also CA 129; CAAS 85-88

Resnais, Alain 1922- .... **CLC 16**

Revard, Carter 1931- .... **NNAL**
See also CA 144; CANR 81, 153; PFS 5

Reverdy, Pierre 1889-1960 .... **CLC 53**
See also CA 97-100; CAAS 89-92; DLB
258; EWL 3; GFL 1789 to the Present

Rexroth, Kenneth 1905-1982 .... **CLC 1, 2, 6,
11, 22, 49, 112; PC 20**
See also BG 1:3; CA 5-8R; CAAS 107;
CANR 14, 34, 63; CDALB 1941-1968;
CP 1, 2, 3; DAM POET; DLB 16, 48, 165,
212; DLBY 1982; EWL 3; INT CANR-
14; MAL 5; MTCW 1, 2; MTFW 2005;
RGAL 4

Reyes, Alfonso 1889-1959 .... **HLCS 2; TCLC
33**
See also CA 131; EWL 3; HW 1; LAW

Reyes y Basoalto, Ricardo Eliecer Neftali
See Neruda, Pablo

Reymont, Wladyslaw (Stanislaw)
1868(?)-1925 .... **TCLC 5**
See also CAAE 104; DLB 332; EWL 3

Reynolds, John Hamilton
1794-1852 .... **NCLC 146**
See also DLB 96

Reynolds, Jonathan 1942- .... **CLC 6, 38**
See also CA 65-68; CANR 28

Reynolds, Joshua 1723-1792 .... **LC 15**
See also DLB 104

Reynolds, Michael S(hane)
1937-2000 .... **CLC 44**
See also CA 65-68; CAAS 189; CANR 9,
89, 97

Reznikoff, Charles 1894-1976 .... **CLC 9**
See also AMWS 14; CA 33-36; CAAS 61-
64; CAP 2; CP 1, 2; DLB 28, 45; RGHL;
WP

Rezzori, Gregor von
See Rezzori d'Arezzo, Gregor von

Rezzori d'Arezzo, Gregor von
1914-1998 .... **CLC 25**
See also CA 136; CAAE 122; CAAS 167

Rhine, Richard
See Silverstein, Alvin; Silverstein, Virginia
B(arbara Opshelor)

Rhodes, Eugene Manlove
1869-1934 .... **TCLC 53**
See also CA 198; DLB 256; TCWW 1, 2

R'hoone, Lord
See Balzac, Honore de

Rhys, Jean 1890-1979 .... **CLC 2, 4, 6, 14, 19,
51, 124; SSC 21, 76**
See also BRWS 2; CA 25-28R; CAAS 85-
88; CANR 35, 62; CDBLB 1945-1960;
CDWLB 3; CN 1, 2; DA3; DAM NOV;
DLB 36, 117, 162; DNFS 2; EWL 3;
LATS 1:1; MTCW 1, 2; MTFW 2005;
NFS 19; RGEL 2; RGSF 2; RHW; TEA;
WWE 1

Ribeiro, Darcy 1922-1997 .... **CLC 34**
See also CA 33-36R; CAAS 156; EWL 3

Ribeiro, Joao Ubaldo (Osorio Pimentel)
1941- .... **CLC 10, 67**
See also CA 81-84; CWW 2; EWL 3

Ribman, Ronald (Burt) 1932- .... **CLC 7**
See also CA 21-24R; CAD; CANR 46, 80;
CD 5, 6

Ricci, Nino (Pio) 1959- .... **CLC 70**
See also CA 137; CANR 130; CCA 1

Rice, Anne 1941- .... **CLC 41, 128**
See Rampling, Anne
See also AAYA 9, 53; AMWS 7; BEST
89:2; BPFB 3; CA 65-68; CANR 12, 36,
53, 74, 100, 133; CN 6, 7; CPW; CSW;
DA3; DAM POP; DLB 292; GL 3; GLL
2; HGG; MTCW 2; MTFW 2005; SUFW
2; YAW

Rice, Elmer (Leopold) 1892-1967 ...... **CLC 7,
49**
See Reizenstein, Elmer Leopold
See also CA 21-22; CAAS 25-28R; CAP 2;
DAM DRAM; DFS 12; DLB 4, 7; IDTP;
MAL 5; MTCW 1, 2; RGAL 4

Rice, Tim(othy Miles Bindon)
1944- .... **CLC 21**
See also CA 103; CANR 46; DFS 7

Rich, Adrienne 1929- ..... **CLC 3, 6, 7, 11, 18,
36, 73, 76, 125; PC 5**
See also AAYA 69; AMWR 2; AMWS 1;
CA 9-12R; CANR 20, 53, 74, 128;
CDALBS; CP 1, 2, 3, 4, 5, 6, 7; CSW;
CWP; DA3; DAM POET; DLB 5, 67;
EWL 3; EXPP; FL 1:6; FW; MAL 5;
MBL; MTCW 1, 2; MTFW 2005; PAB;
PFS 15; RGAL 4; RGHL; WP

Rich, Barbara
See Graves, Robert

Rich, Robert
See Trumbo, Dalton

Richard, Keith .... **CLC 17**
See Richards, Keith

Richards, David Adams 1950- .... **CLC 59**
See also CA 93-96; CANR 60, 110, 156;
CN 7; DAC; DLB 53; TCLE 1:2

Richards, I(vor) A(rmstrong)
1893-1979 .... **CLC 14, 24**
See also BRWS 2; CA 41-44R; CAAS 89-
92; CANR 34, 74; CP 1, 2; DLB 27; EWL
3; MTCW 2; RGEL 2

Richards, Keith 1943-
See Richard, Keith
See also CA 107; CANR 77

Richardson, Anne
See Roiphe, Anne

Richardson, Dorothy Miller
1873-1957 .... **TCLC 3**
See also CA 192; CAAE 104; DLB 36;
EWL 3; FW; RGEL 2

**Richardson (Robertson), Ethel Florence
Lindesay** 1870-1946
See Richardson, Henry Handel
See also CA 190; CAAE 105; DLB 230;
RHW

Richardson, Henry Handel .... **TCLC 4**
See Richardson (Robertson), Ethel Florence
Lindesay
See also DLB 197; EWL 3; RGEL 2; RGSF
2

Richardson, John 1796-1852 .... **NCLC 55**
See also CCA 1; DAC; DLB 99

Richardson, Samuel 1689-1761 ...... **LC 1, 44,
138; WLC 3**
See also BRW 3; CDBLB 1660-1789; DA;
DAB; DAC; DAM MST, NOV; DLB 39;
RGEL 2; TEA; WLIT 3

Richardson, Willis 1889-1977 .... **HR 1:3**
See also BW 1; CA 124; DLB 51; SATA 60

Richler, Mordecai 1931-2001 .... **CLC 3, 5, 9,
13, 18, 46, 70, 185**
See also AITN 1; CA 65-68; CAAS 201;
CANR 31, 62, 111; CCA 1; CLR 17; CN
1, 2, 3, 4, 5, 7; CWRI 5; DAC; DAM
MST, NOV; DLB 53; EWL 3; MAICYA
1, 2; MTCW 1, 2; MTFW 2005; RGEL 2;
RGHL; SATA 44, 98; SATA-Brief 27;
TWA

Richter, Conrad (Michael)
1890-1968 .... **CLC 30**
See also AAYA 21; BYA 2; CA 5-8R;
CAAS 25-28R; CANR 23; DLB 9, 212;
LAIT 1; MAL 5; MTCW 1, 2; MTFW
2005; RGAL 4; SATA 3; TCWW 1, 2;
TUS; YAW

Ricostranza, Tom
See Ellis, Trey

Riddell, Charlotte 1832-1906 .... **TCLC 40**
See Riddell, Mrs. J. H.
See also CA 165; DLB 156

Riddell, Mrs. J. H.
See Riddell, Charlotte
See also HGG; SUFW

Rogers, Will(iam Penn Adair)
1879-1935 .... **NNAL; TCLC 8, 71**
See also CA 144; CAAE 105; DA3; DAM
MULT; DLB 11; MTCW 2

Rogin, Gilbert 1929- .... **CLC 18**
See also CA 65-68; CANR 15

Rohan, Koda
See Koda Shigeyuki

Rohlfs, Anna Katharine Green
See Green, Anna Katharine

Rohmer, Eric .... **CLC 16**
See Scherer, Jean-Marie Maurice

Rohmer, Sax .... **TCLC 28**
See Ward, Arthur Henry Sarsfield
See also DLB 70; MSW; SUFW

Roiphe, Anne 1935- .... **CLC 3, 9**
See also CA 89-92; CANR 45, 73, 138;
DLBY 1980; INT CA-89-92

Roiphe, Anne Richardson
See Roiphe, Anne

Rojas, Fernando de 1475-1541 ... **HLCS 1, 2;**
LC 23
See also DLB 286; RGWL 2, 3

Rojas, Gonzalo 1917- .... **HLCS 2**
See also CA 178; HW 2; LAWS 1

Roland (de la Platiere), Marie-Jeanne
1754-1793 .... **LC 98**
See also DLB 314

Rolfe, Frederick (William Serafino Austin
Lewis Mary) 1860-1913 .... **TCLC 12**
See Al Siddik
See also CA 210; CAAE 107; DLB 34, 156;
RGEL 2

Rolland, Romain 1866-1944 .... **TCLC 23**
See also CA 197; CAAE 118; DLB 65, 284,
332; EWL 3; GFL 1789 to the Present;
RGWL 2, 3

Rolle, Richard c. 1300-c. 1349 ...... **CMLC 21**
See also DLB 146; LMFS 1; RGEL 2

Rolvaag, O(le) E(dvart) .... **TCLC 17**
See Roelvaag, O(le) E(dvart)
See also DLB 9, 212; MAL 5; NFS 5;
RGAL 4

Romain Arnaud, Saint
See Aragon, Louis

Romains, Jules 1885-1972 .... **CLC 7**
See also CA 85-88; CANR 34; DLB 65,
321; EWL 3; GFL 1789 to the Present;
MTCW 1

Romero, Jose Ruben 1890-1952 .... **TCLC 14**
See also CA 131; CAAE 114; EWL 3; HW
1; LAW

Ronsard, Pierre de 1524-1585 . **LC 6, 54; PC**
11
See also DLB 327; EW 2; GFL Beginnings
to 1789; RGWL 2, 3; TWA

Rooke, Leon 1934- .... **CLC 25, 34**
See also CA 25-28R; CANR 23, 53; CCA
1; CPW; DAM POP

Roosevelt, Franklin Delano
1882-1945 .... **TCLC 93**
See also CA 173; CAAE 116; LAIT 3

Roosevelt, Theodore 1858-1919 ..... **TCLC 69**
See also CA 170; CAAE 115; DLB 47, 186,
275

Roper, William 1498-1578 .... **LC 10**

Roquelaure, A. N.
See Rice, Anne

Rosa, Joao Guimaraes 1908-1967 ... **CLC 23;**
HLCS 1
See Guimaraes Rosa, Joao
See also CAAS 89-92; DLB 113, 307; EWL
3; WLIT 1

Rose, Wendy 1948- . **CLC 85; NNAL; PC 13**
See also CA 53-56; CANR 5, 51; CWP;
DAM MULT; DLB 175; PFS 13; RGAL
4; SATA 12

Rosen, R. D.
See Rosen, Richard (Dean)

Rosen, Richard (Dean) 1949- .... **CLC 39**
See also CA 77-80; CANR 62, 120; CMW
4; INT CANR-30

Rosenberg, Isaac 1890-1918 .... **TCLC 12**
See also BRW 6; CA 188; CAAE 107; DLB
20, 216; EWL 3; PAB; RGEL 2

Rosenblatt, Joe .... **CLC 15**
See Rosenblatt, Joseph
See also CP 3, 4, 5, 6, 7

Rosenblatt, Joseph 1933-
See Rosenblatt, Joe
See also CA 89-92; CP 1, 2; INT CA-89-92

Rosenfeld, Samuel
See Tzara, Tristan

Rosenstock, Sami
See Tzara, Tristan

Rosenstock, Samuel
See Tzara, Tristan

Rosenthal, M(acha) L(ouis)
1917-1996 .... **CLC 28**
See also CA 1-4R; 6; CAAS 152; CANR 4,
51; CP 1, 2, 3, 4, 5, 6; DLB 5; SATA 59

Ross, Barnaby
See Dannay, Frederic; Lee, Manfred B.

Ross, Bernard L.
See Follett, Ken

Ross, J. H.
See Lawrence, T(homas) E(dward)

Ross, John Hume
See Lawrence, T(homas) E(dward)

Ross, Martin 1862-1915
See Martin, Violet Florence
See also DLB 135; GLL 2; RGEL 2; RGSF
2

Ross, (James) Sinclair 1908-1996 ... **CLC 13;**
SSC 24
See also CA 73-76; CANR 81; CN 1, 2, 3,
4, 5, 6; DAC; DAM MST; DLB 88;
RGEL 2; RGSF 2; TCWW 1, 2

Rossetti, Christina 1830-1894 ... **NCLC 2, 50,**
66; PC 7; WLC 5
See also AAYA 51; BRW 5; BYA 4; CLR
115; DA; DA3; DAB; DAC; DAM MST,
POET; DLB 35, 163, 240; EXPP; FL 1:3;
LATS 1:1; MAICYA 1, 2; PFS 10, 14;
RGEL 2; SATA 20; TEA; WCH

Rossetti, Christina Georgina
See Rossetti, Christina

Rossetti, Dante Gabriel 1828-1882 . **NCLC 4,**
77; PC 44; WLC 5
See also AAYA 51; BRW 5; CDBLB 1832-
1890; DA; DAB; DAC; DAM MST,
POET; DLB 35; EXPP; RGEL 2; TEA

Rossi, Cristina Peri
See Peri Rossi, Cristina

Rossi, Jean-Baptiste 1931-2003
See Japrisot, Sebastien
See also CA 201; CAAS 215

Rossner, Judith 1935-2005 .... **CLC 6, 9, 29**
See also AITN 2; BEST 90:3; BPFB 3; CA
17-20R; CAAS 242; CANR 18, 51, 73;
CN 4, 5, 6, 7; DLB 6; INT CANR-18;
MAL 5; MTCW 1, 2; MTFW 2005

Rossner, Judith Perelman
See Rossner, Judith

Rostand, Edmond (Eugene Alexis)
1868-1918 .... **DC 10; TCLC 6, 37**
See also CA 126; CAAE 104; DA; DA3;
DAB; DAC; DAM DRAM, MST; DFS 1;
DLB 192; LAIT 1; MTCW 1; RGWL 2,
3; TWA

Roth, Henry 1906-1995 ..... **CLC 2, 6, 11, 104**
See also AMWS 9; CA 11-12; CAAS 149;
CANR 38, 63; CAP 1; CN 1, 2, 3, 4, 5, 6;
DA3; DLB 28; EWL 3; MAL 5; MTCW
1, 2; MTFW 2005; RGAL 4

Roth, (Moses) Joseph 1894-1939 ... **TCLC 33**
See also CA 160; DLB 85; EWL 3; RGWL
2, 3

Roth, Philip 1933- ... **CLC 1, 2, 3, 4, 6, 9, 15,**
22, 31, 47, 66, 86, 119, 201; SSC 26;
WLC 5
See also AAYA 67; AMWR 2; AMWS 3;
BEST 90:3; BPFB 3; CA 1-4R; CANR 1,
22, 36, 55, 89, 132; CDALB 1968-1988;
CN 3, 4, 5, 6, 7; CPW 1; DA; DA3; DAB;
DAC; DAM MST, NOV, POP; DLB 2,
28, 173; DLBY 1982; EWL 3; MAL 5;
MTCW 1, 2; MTFW 2005; RGAL 4;
RGHL; RGSF 2; SSFS 12, 18; TUS

Roth, Philip Milton
See Roth, Philip

Rothenberg, Jerome 1931- .... **CLC 6, 57**
See also CA 45-48; CANR 1, 106; CP 1, 2,
3, 4, 5, 6, 7; DLB 5, 193

Rotter, Pat .... **CLC 65**

Roumain, Jacques (Jean Baptiste)
1907-1944 .... **BLC 3; TCLC 19**
See also BW 1; CA 125; CAAE 117; DAM
MULT; EWL 3

Rourke, Constance Mayfield
1885-1941 .... **TCLC 12**
See also CA 200; CAAE 107; MAL 5;
YABC 1

Rousseau, Jean-Baptiste 1671-1741 ...... **LC 9**

Rousseau, Jean-Jacques 1712-1778 .... **LC 14,**
36, 122; WLC 5
See also DA; DA3; DAB; DAC; DAM
MST; DLB 314; EW 4; GFL Beginnings
to 1789; LMFS 1; RGWL 2, 3; TWA

Roussel, Raymond 1877-1933 .... **TCLC 20**
See also CA 201; CAAE 117; EWL 3; GFL
1789 to the Present

Rovit, Earl (Herbert) 1927- .... **CLC 7**
See also CA 5-8R; CANR 12

Rowe, Elizabeth Singer 1674-1737 ..... **LC 44**
See also DLB 39, 95

Rowe, Nicholas 1674-1718 .... **LC 8**
See also DLB 84; RGEL 2

Rowlandson, Mary 1637(?)-1678 .... **LC 66**
See also DLB 24, 200; RGAL 4

Rowley, Ames Dorrance
See Lovecraft, H. P.

Rowley, William 1585(?)-1626 ... **LC 100, 123**
See also DFS 22; DLB 58; RGEL 2

Rowling, J.K. 1965- .... **CLC 137, 217**
See also AAYA 34; BYA 11, 13, 14; CA
173; CANR 128, 157; CLR 66, 80, 112;
MAICYA 2; MTFW 2005; SATA 109,
174; SUFW 2

Rowling, Joanne Kathleen
See Rowling, J.K.

Rowson, Susanna Haswell
1762(?)-1824 .... **NCLC 5, 69, 182**
See also AMWS 15; DLB 37, 200; RGAL 4

Roy, Arundhati 1960(?)- .... **CLC 109, 210**
See also CA 163; CANR 90, 126; CN 7;
DLB 323, 326; DLBY 1997; EWL 3;
LATS 1:2; MTFW 2005; NFS 22; WWE
1

Roy, Gabrielle 1909-1983 .... **CLC 10, 14**
See also CA 53-56; CAAS 110; CANR 5,
61; CCA 1; DAB; DAC; DAM MST;
DLB 68; EWL 3; MTCW 1; RGWL 2, 3;
SATA 104; TCLE 1:2

Royko, Mike 1932-1997 .... **CLC 109**
See also CA 89-92; CAAS 157; CANR 26,
111; CPW

Rozanov, Vasilii Vasil'evich
See Rozanov, Vassili
See also DLB 295

Rozanov, Vasily Vasilyevich
See Rozanov, Vassili
See also EWL 3

Rozanov, Vassili 1856-1919 .... **TCLC 104**
See Rozanov, Vasilii Vasil'evich; Rozanov,
Vasily Vasilyevich

Saint-Exupery, Antoine Jean Baptiste Marie Roger de
See Saint-Exupery, Antoine de
St. John, David
See Hunt, E. Howard
St. John, J. Hector
See Crevecoeur, Michel Guillaume Jean de
Saint-John Perse
See Leger, (Marie-Rene Auguste) Alexis Saint-Leger
See also EW 10; EWL 3; GFL 1789 to the Present; RGWL 2
Saintsbury, George (Edward Bateman)
1845-1933 .... **TCLC 31**
See also CA 160; DLB 57, 149
Sait Faik .... **TCLC 23**
See Abasiyanik, Sait Faik
Saki .... **SSC 12; TCLC 3; WLC 5**
See Munro, H(ector) H(ugh)
See also BRWS 6; BYA 11; LAIT 2; RGEL 2; SSFS 1; SUFW
Sala, George Augustus 1828-1895 . **NCLC 46**
Saladin 1138-1193 .... **CMLC 38**
Salama, Hannu 1936- .... **CLC 18**
See also CA 244; EWL 3
Salamanca, J(ack) R(ichard) 1922- .. **CLC 4, 15**
See also CA 193; 25-28R, 193
Salas, Floyd Francis 1931- .... **HLC 2**
See also CA 119; 27; CANR 44, 75, 93; DAM MULT; DLB 82; HW 1, 2; MTCW 2; MTFW 2005
Sale, J. Kirkpatrick
See Sale, Kirkpatrick
Sale, John Kirkpatrick
See Sale, Kirkpatrick
Sale, Kirkpatrick 1937- .... **CLC 68**
See also CA 13-16R; CANR 10, 147
Salinas, Luis Omar 1937- ... **CLC 90; HLC 2**
See also AMWS 13; CA 131; CANR 81, 153; DAM MULT; DLB 82; HW 1, 2
Salinas (y Serrano), Pedro
1891(?)-1951 .... **TCLC 17**
See also CAAE 117; DLB 134; EWL 3
Salinger, J.D. 1919- . **CLC 1, 3, 8, 12, 55, 56, 138; SSC 2, 28, 65; WLC 5**
See also AAYA 2, 36; AMW; AMWC 1; BPFB 3; CA 5-8R; CANR 39, 129; CDALB 1941-1968; CLR 18; CN 1, 2, 3, 4, 5, 6, 7; CPW 1; DA; DA3; DAB; DAC; DAM MST, NOV, POP; DLB 2, 102, 173; EWL 3; EXPN; LAIT 4; MAICYA 1, 2; MAL 5; MTCW 1, 2; MTFW 2005; NFS 1; RGAL 4; RGSF 2; SATA 67; SSFS 17; TUS; WYA; YAW
Salisbury, John
See Caute, (John) David
Sallust c. 86B.C.-35B.C. .... **CMLC 68**
See also AW 2; CDWLB 1; DLB 211; RGWL 2, 3
Salter, James 1925- .. **CLC 7, 52, 59; SSC 58**
See also AMWS 9; CA 73-76; CANR 107, 160; DLB 130
Saltus, Edgar (Everton) 1855-1921 . **TCLC 8**
See also CAAE 105; DLB 202; RGAL 4
Saltykov, Mikhail Evgrafovich
1826-1889 .... **NCLC 16**
See also DLB 238:
Saltykov-Shchedrin, N.
See Saltykov, Mikhail Evgrafovich
Samarakis, Andonis
See Samarakis, Antonis
See also EWL 3
Samarakis, Antonis 1919-2003 .... **CLC 5**
See Samarakis, Andonis
See also CA 25-28R; 16; CAAS 224; CANR 36

Sanchez, Florencio 1875-1910 .... **TCLC 37**
See also CA 153; DLB 305; EWL 3; HW 1; LAW
Sanchez, Luis Rafael 1936- .... **CLC 23**
See also CA 128; DLB 305; EWL 3; HW 1; WLIT 1
Sanchez, Sonia 1934- .... **BLC 3; CLC 5, 116, 215; PC 9**
See also BW 2, 3; CA 33-36R; CANR 24, 49, 74, 115; CLR 18; CP 2, 3, 4, 5, 6, 7; CSW; CWP; DA3; DAM MULT; DLB 41; DLBD 8; EWL 3; MAICYA 1, 2; MAL 5; MTCW 1, 2; MTFW 2005; SATA 22, 136; WP
Sancho, Ignatius 1729-1780 .... **LC 84**
Sand, George 1804-1876 ..... **NCLC 2, 42, 57, 174; WLC 5**
See also DA; DA3; DAB; DAC; DAM MST, NOV; DLB 119, 192; EW 6; FL 1:3; FW; GFL 1789 to the Present; RGWL 2, 3; TWA
Sandburg, Carl (August) 1878-1967 . **CLC 1, 4, 10, 15, 35; PC 2, 41; WLC 5**
See also AAYA 24; AMW; BYA 1, 3; CA 5-8R; CAAS 25-28R; CANR 35; CDALB 1865-1917; CLR 67; DA; DA3; DAB; DAC; DAM MST, POET; DLB 17, 54, 284; EWL 3; EXPP; LAIT 2; MAICYA 1, 2; MAL 5; MTCW 1, 2; MTFW 2005; PAB; PFS 3, 6, 12; RGAL 4; SATA 8; TUS; WCH; WP; WYA
Sandburg, Charles
See Sandburg, Carl (August)
Sandburg, Charles A.
See Sandburg, Carl (August)
Sanders, (James) Ed(ward) 1939- .... **CLC 53**
See Sanders, Edward
See also BG 1:3; CA 13-16R; 21; CANR 13, 44, 78; CP 1, 2, 3, 4, 5, 6, 7; DAM POET; DLB 16, 244
Sanders, Edward
See Sanders, (James) Ed(ward)
See also DLB 244
Sanders, Lawrence 1920-1998 .... **CLC 41**
See also BEST 89:4; BPFB 3; CA 81-84; CAAS 165; CANR 33, 62; CMW 4; CPW; DA3; DAM POP; MTCW 1
Sanders, Noah
See Blount, Roy (Alton), Jr.
Sanders, Winston P.
See Anderson, Poul
Sandoz, Mari(e Susette) 1900-1966 .. **CLC 28**
See also CA 1-4R; CAAS 25-28R; CANR 17, 64; DLB 9, 212; LAIT 2; MTCW 1, 2; SATA 5; TCWW 1, 2
Sandys, George 1578-1644 .... **LC 80**
See also DLB 24, 121
Saner, Reg(inald Anthony) 1931- .... **CLC 9**
See also CA 65-68; CP 3, 4, 5, 6, 7
Sankara 788-820 .... **CMLC 32**
Sannazaro, Jacopo 1456(?)-1530 .... **LC 8**
See also RGWL 2, 3; WLIT 7
Sansom, William 1912-1976 . **CLC 2, 6; SSC 21**
See also CA 5-8R; CAAS 65-68; CANR 42; CN 1, 2; DAM NOV; DLB 139; EWL 3; MTCW 1; RGEL 2; RGSF 2
Santayana, George 1863-1952 .... **TCLC 40**
See also AMW; CA 194; CAAE 115; DLB 54, 71, 246, 270; DLBD 13; EWL 3; MAL 5; RGAL 4; TUS
Santiago, Danny .... **CLC 33**
See James, Daniel (Lewis)
See also DLB 122
Santillana, Inigo Lopez de Mendoza, Marques de 1398-1458 .... **LC 111**
See also DLB 286

Santmyer, Helen Hooven
1895-1986 .... **CLC 33; TCLC 133**
See also CA 1-4R; CAAS 118; CANR 15, 33; DLBY 1984; MTCW 1; RHW
Santoka, Taneda 1882-1940 .... **TCLC 72**
Santos, Bienvenido N(uqui)
1911-1996 ... **AAL; CLC 22; TCLC 156**
See also CA 101; CAAS 151; CANR 19, 46; CP 1; DAM MULT; DLB 312; EWL; RGAL 4; SSFS 19
Sapir, Edward 1884-1939 .... **TCLC 108**
See also CA 211; DLB 92
Sapper .... **TCLC 44**
See McNeile, Herman Cyril
Sapphire
See Sapphire, Brenda
Sapphire, Brenda 1950- .... **CLC 99**
Sappho fl. 6th cent. B.C.- ... **CMLC 3, 67; PC 5**
See also CDWLB 1; DA3; DAM POET; DLB 176; FL 1:1; PFS 20; RGWL 2, 3; WLIT 8; WP
Saramago, Jose 1922- ..... **CLC 119; HLCS 1**
See also CA 153; CANR 96; CWW 2; DLB 287, 332; EWL 3; LATS 1:2; SSFS 23
Sarduy, Severo 1937-1993 .... **CLC 6, 97; HLCS 2; TCLC 167**
See also CA 89-92; CAAS 142; CANR 58, 81; CWW 2; DLB 113; EWL 3; HW 1, 2; LAW
Sargeson, Frank 1903-1982 ..... **CLC 31; SSC 99**
See also CA 25-28R; CAAS 106; CANR 38, 79; CN 1, 2, 3; EWL 3; GLL 2; RGEL 2; RGSF 2; SSFS 20
Sarmiento, Domingo Faustino
1811-1888 .... **HLCS 2; NCLC 123**
See also LAW; WLIT 1
Sarmiento, Felix Ruben Garcia
See Dario, Ruben
Saro-Wiwa, Ken(ule Beeson)
1941-1995 .... **CLC 114**
See also BW 2; CA 142; CAAS 150; CANR 60; DLB 157
Saroyan, William 1908-1981 ... **CLC 1, 8, 10, 29, 34, 56; SSC 21; TCLC 137; WLC 5**
See also AAYA 66; CA 5-8R; CAAS 103; CAD; CANR 30; CDALBS; CN 1, 2; DA; DA3; DAB; DAC; DAM DRAM, MST, NOV; DFS 17; DLB 7, 9, 86; DLBY 1981; EWL 3; LAIT 4; MAL 5; MTCW 1, 2; MTFW 2005; RGAL 4; RGSF 2; SATA 23; SATA-Obit 24; SSFS 14; TUS
Sarraute, Nathalie 1900-1999 .... **CLC 1, 2, 4, 8, 10, 31, 80; TCLC 145**
See also BPFB 3; CA 9-12R; CAAS 187; CANR 23, 66, 134; CWW 2; DLB 83, 321; EW 12; EWL 3; GFL 1789 to the Present; MTCW 1, 2; MTFW 2005; RGWL 2, 3
Sarton, May 1912-1995 ... **CLC 4, 14, 49, 91; PC 39; TCLC 120**
See also AMWS 8; CA 1-4R; CAAS 149; CANR 1, 34, 55, 116; CN 1, 2, 3, 4, 5, 6; CP 1, 2, 3, 4, 5, 6; DAM POET; DLB 48; DLBY 1981; EWL 3; FW; INT CANR-34; MAL 5; MTCW 1, 2; MTFW 2005; RGAL 4; SATA 36; SATA-Obit 86; TUS
Sartre, Jean-Paul 1905-1980 . **CLC 1, 4, 7, 9, 13, 18, 24, 44, 50, 52; DC 3; SSC 32; WLC 5**
See also AAYA 62; CA 9-12R; CAAS 97-100; CANR 21; DA; DA3; DAB; DAC; DAM DRAM, MST, NOV; DFS 5; DLB 72, 296, 321, 332; EW 12; EWL 3; GFL 1789 to the Present; LMFS 2; MTCW 1, 2; MTFW 2005; NFS 21; RGHL; RGSF 2; RGWL 2, 3; SSFS 9; TWA

Sassoon, Siegfried (Lorraine)
1886-1967 .... **CLC 36, 130; PC 12**
See also BRW 6; CA 104; CAAS 25-28R;
CANR 36; DAB; DAM MST, NOV,
POET; DLB 20, 191; DLBD 18; EWL 3;
MTCW 1, 2; MTFW 2005; PAB; RGEL
2; TEA

Satterfield, Charles
See Pohl, Frederik

Satyremont
See Peret, Benjamin

Saul, John (W. III) 1942- .... **CLC 46**
See also AAYA 10, 62; BEST 90:4; CA 81-
84; CANR 16, 40, 81; CPW; DAM NOV,
POP; HGG; SATA 98

Saunders, Caleb
See Heinlein, Robert A.

Saura (Atares), Carlos 1932-1998 .... **CLC 20**
See also CA 131; CAAE 114; CANR 79;
HW 1

Sauser, Frederic Louis
See Sauser-Hall, Frederic

Sauser-Hall, Frederic 1887-1961 ...... **CLC 18**
See Cendrars, Blaise
See also CA 102; CAAS 93-96; CANR 36,
62; MTCW 1

Saussure, Ferdinand de
1857-1913 .... **TCLC 49**
See also DLB 242

Savage, Catharine
See Brosman, Catharine Savage

Savage, Richard 1697(?)-1743 .... **LC 96**
See also DLB 95; RGEL 2

Savage, Thomas 1915-2003 .... **CLC 40**
See also CA 132; 15; CAAE 126; CAAS
218; CN 6, 7; INT CA-132; SATA-Obit
147; TCWW 2

Savan, Glenn 1953-2003 .... **CLC 50**
See also CA 225

Sax, Robert
See Johnson, Robert

Saxo Grammaticus c. 1150-c.
1222 .... **CMLC 58**

Saxton, Robert
See Johnson, Robert

Sayers, Dorothy L(eigh) 1893-1957 . **SSC 71;**
TCLC 2, 15
See also BPFB 3; BRWS 3; CA 119; CAAE
104; CANR 60; CDBLB 1914-1945;
CMW 4; DAM POP; DLB 10, 36, 77,
100; MSW; MTCW 1, 2; MTFW 2005;
RGEL 2; SSFS 12; TEA

Sayers, Valerie 1952- .... **CLC 50, 122**
See also CA 134; CANR 61; CSW

Sayles, John (Thomas) 1950- .... **CLC 7, 10,**
14, 198
See also CA 57-60; CANR 41, 84; DLB 44

Scamander, Newt
See Rowling, J.K.

Scammell, Michael 1935- .... **CLC 34**
See also CA 156

Scannell, Vernon 1922- .... **CLC 49**
See also CA 5-8R; CANR 8, 24, 57, 143;
CN 1, 2; CP 1, 2, 3, 4, 5, 6, 7; CWRI 5;
DLB 27; SATA 59

Scarlett, Susan
See Streatfeild, (Mary) Noel

Scarron 1847-1910
See Mikszath, Kalman

Scarron, Paul 1610-1660 .... **LC 116**
See also GFL Beginnings to 1789; RGWL
2, 3

Schaeffer, Susan Fromberg 1941- ..... **CLC 6,**
11, 22
See also CA 49-52; CANR 18, 65, 160; CN
4, 5, 6, 7; DLB 28, 299; MTCW 1, 2;
MTFW 2005; SATA 22

Schama, Simon 1945- .... **CLC 150**
See also BEST 89:4; CA 105; CANR 39,
91

Schama, Simon Michael
See Schama, Simon

Schary, Jill
See Robinson, Jill

Schell, Jonathan 1943- .... **CLC 35**
See also CA 73-76; CANR 12, 117

Schelling, Friedrich Wilhelm Joseph von
1775-1854 .... **NCLC 30**
See also DLB 90

Scherer, Jean-Marie Maurice 1920-
See Rohmer, Eric
See also CA 110

Schevill, James (Erwin) 1920- .... **CLC 7**
See also CA 5-8R; 12; CAD; CD 5, 6; CP
1, 2, 3, 4, 5

Schiller, Friedrich von 1759-1805 ...... **DC 12;**
NCLC 39, 69, 166
See also CDWLB 2; DAM DRAM; DLB
94; EW 5; RGWL 2, 3; TWA

Schisgal, Murray (Joseph) 1926- .... **CLC 6**
See also CA 21-24R; CAD; CANR 48, 86;
CD 5, 6; MAL 5

Schlee, Ann 1934- .... **CLC 35**
See also CA 101; CANR 29, 88; SATA 44;
SATA-Brief 36

Schlegel, August Wilhelm von
1767-1845 .... **NCLC 15, 142**
See also DLB 94; RGWL 2, 3

Schlegel, Friedrich 1772-1829 ...... **NCLC 45**
See also DLB 90; EW 5; RGWL 2, 3; TWA

Schlegel, Johann Elias (von)
1719(?)-1749 .... **LC 5**

Schleiermacher, Friedrich
1768-1834 .... **NCLC 107**
See also DLB 90

Schlesinger, Arthur M., Jr.
1917-2007 .... **CLC 84**
See also AITN 1; CA 1-4R; CANR 1, 28,
58, 105; DLB 17; INT CANR-28; MTCW
1, 2; SATA 61

Schlesinger, Arthur Meier, Jr.
See Schlesinger, Arthur M., Jr.

Schlink, Bernhard 1944- .... **CLC 174**
See also CA 163; CANR 116; RGHL

Schmidt, Arno (Otto) 1914-1979 ...... **CLC 56**
See also CA 128; CAAS 109; DLB 69;
EWL 3

Schmitz, Aron Hector 1861-1928
See Svevo, Italo
See also CA 122; CAAE 104; MTCW 1

Schnackenberg, Gjertrud 1953- ...... **CLC 40;**
PC 45
See also AMWS 15; CAAE 116; CANR
100; CP 5, 6, 7; CWP; DLB 120, 282;
PFS 13, 25

Schnackenberg, Gjertrud Cecelia
See Schnackenberg, Gjertrud

Schneider, Leonard Alfred 1925-1966
See Bruce, Lenny
See also CA 89-92

Schnitzler, Arthur 1862-1931 ..... **DC 17; SSC**
15, 61; TCLC 4
See also CA 104; CDWLB 2; DLB 81,
118; EW 8; EWL 3; RGSF 2; RGWL 2, 3

Schoenberg, Arnold Franz Walter
1874-1951 .... **TCLC 75**
See also CA 188; CAAE 109

Schonberg, Arnold
See Schoenberg, Arnold Franz Walter

Schopenhauer, Arthur 1788-1860 . **NCLC 51,**
157
See also DLB 90; EW 5

Schor, Sandra (M.) 1932(?)-1990 ..... **CLC 65**
See also CAAS 132

Schorer, Mark 1908-1977 .... **CLC 9**
See also CA 5-8R; CAAS 73-76; CANR 7;
CN 1, 2; DLB 103

Schrader, Paul (Joseph) 1946- . **CLC 26, 212**
See also CA 37-40R; CANR 41; DLB 44

Schreber, Daniel 1842-1911 .... **TCLC 123**

Schreiner, Olive (Emilie Albertina)
1855-1920 .... **TCLC 9**
See also AFW; BRWS 2; CA 154; CAAE
105; DLB 18, 156, 190, 225; EWL 3; FW;
RGEL 2; TWA; WLIT 2; WWE 1

Schulberg, Budd (Wilson) 1914- .. **CLC 7, 48**
See also BPFB 3; CA 25-28R; CANR 19,
87; CN 1, 2, 3, 4, 5, 6, 7; DLB 6, 26, 28;
DLBY 1981, 2001; MAL 5

Schulman, Arnold
See Trumbo, Dalton

Schulz, Bruno 1892-1942 .. **SSC 13; TCLC 5,**
51
See also CA 123; CAAE 115; CANR 86;
CDWLB 4; DLB 215; EWL 3; MTCW 2;
MTFW 2005; RGSF 2; RGWL 2, 3

Schulz, Charles M. 1922-2000 .... **CLC 12**
See also AAYA 39; CA 9-12R; CAAS 187;
CANR 6, 132; INT CANR-6; MTFW
2005; SATA 10; SATA-Obit 118

Schulz, Charles Monroe
See Schulz, Charles M.

Schumacher, E(rnst) F(riedrich)
1911-1977 .... **CLC 80**
See also CA 81-84; CAAS 73-76; CANR
34, 85

Schumann, Robert 1810-1856 ...... **NCLC 143**

Schuyler, George Samuel 1895-1977 . **HR 1:3**
See also BW 2; CA 81-84; CAAS 73-76;
CANR 42; DLB 29, 51

Schuyler, James Marcus 1923-1991 .. **CLC 5,**
23
See also CA 101; CAAS 134; CP 1, 2, 3, 4,
5; DAM POET; DLB 5, 169; EWL 3; INT
CA-101; MAL 5; WP

Schwartz, Delmore (David)
1913-1966 ... **CLC 2, 4, 10, 45, 87; PC 8**
See also AMWS 2; CA 17-18; CAAS 25-
28R; CANR 35; CAP 2; DLB 28, 48;
EWL 3; MAL 5; MTCW 1, 2; MTFW
2005; PAB; RGAL 4; TUS

Schwartz, Ernst
See Ozu, Yasujiro

Schwartz, John Burnham 1965- .... **CLC 59**
See also CA 132; CANR 116

Schwartz, Lynne Sharon 1939- .... **CLC 31**
See also CA 103; CANR 44, 89, 160; DLB
218; MTCW 2; MTFW 2005

Schwartz, Muriel A.
See Eliot, T(homas) S(tearns)

Schwarz-Bart, Andre 1928-2006 .... **CLC 2, 4**
See also CA 89-92; CAAS 253; CANR 109;
DLB 299; RGHL

Schwarz-Bart, Simone 1938- . **BLCS; CLC 7**
See also BW 2; CA 97-100; CANR 117;
EWL 3

Schwerner, Armand 1927-1999 .... **PC 42**
See also CA 9-12R; CAAS 179; CANR 50,
85; CP 2, 3, 4, 5, 6; DLB 165

Schwitters, Kurt (Hermann Edward Karl
Julius) 1887-1948 .... **TCLC 95**
See also CA 158

Schwob, Marcel (Mayer Andre)
1867-1905 .... **TCLC 20**
See also CA 168; CAAE 117; DLB 123;
GFL 1789 to the Present

Sciascia, Leonardo 1921-1989 .. **CLC 8, 9, 41**
See also CA 85-88; CAAS 130; CANR 35;
DLB 177; EWL 3; MTCW 1; RGWL 2, 3

Shadwell, Thomas 1641(?)-1692 .... **LC 114**
See also DLB 80; IDTP; RGEL 2

Shaffer, Anthony 1926-2001 .... **CLC 19**
See also CA 116; CAAE 110; CAAS 200;
CBD; CD 5, 6; DAM DRAM; DFS 13;
DLB 13

Shaffer, Anthony Joshua
See Shaffer, Anthony

Shaffer, Peter 1926- ... **CLC 5, 14, 18, 37, 60;
DC 7**
See also BRWS 1; CA 25-28R; CANR 25,
47, 74, 118; CBD; CD 5, 6; CDBLB 1960
to Present; DA3; DAB; DAM DRAM,
MST; DFS 5, 13; DLB 13, 233; EWL 3;
MTCW 1, 2; MTFW 2005; RGEL 2; TEA

Shakespeare, William 1564-1616 .... **WLC 5**
See also AAYA 35; BRW 1; CDBLB Be-
fore 1660; DA; DA3; DAB; DAC; DAM
DRAM, MST, POET; DFS 20, 21; DLB
62, 172, 263; EXPP; LAIT 1; LATS 1:1;
LMFS 1; PAB; PFS 1, 2, 3, 4, 5, 8, 9;
RGEL 2; TEA; WLIT 3; WP; WS; WYA

Shakey, Bernard
See Young, Neil

Shalamov, Varlam (Tikhonovich)
1907-1982 .... **CLC 18**
See also CA 129; CAAS 105; DLB 302;
RGSF 2

Shamloo, Ahmad
See Shamlu, Ahmad

Shamlou, Ahmad
See Shamlu, Ahmad

Shamlu, Ahmad 1925-2000 .... **CLC 10**
See also CA 216; CWW 2

Shammas, Anton 1951- .... **CLC 55**
See also CA 199

Shandling, Arline
See Berriault, Gina

Shange, Ntozake 1948- ... **BLC 3; CLC 8, 25,
38, 74, 126; DC 3**
See also AAYA 9, 66; AFAW 1, 2; BW 2;
CA 85-88; CABS 3; CAD; CANR 27, 48,
74, 131; CD 5, 6; CP 5, 6, 7; CWD; CWP;
DA3; DAM DRAM, MULT; DFS 2, 11;
DLB 38, 249; FW; LAIT 4, 5; MAL 5;
MTCW 1, 2; MTFW 2005; NFS 11;
RGAL 4; SATA 157; YAW

Shanley, John Patrick 1950- .... **CLC 75**
See also AAYA 74; AMWS 14; CA 133;
CAAE 128; CAD; CANR 83, 154; CD 5,
6; DFS 23

Shapcott, Thomas W(illiam) 1935- .. **CLC 38**
See also CA 69-72; CANR 49, 83, 103; CP
1, 2, 3, 4, 5, 6, 7; DLB 289

Shapiro, Jane 1942- .... **CLC 76**
See also CA 196

Shapiro, Karl 1913-2000 ... **CLC 4, 8, 15, 53;
PC 25**
See also AMWS 2; CA 1-4R; 6; CAAS 188;
CANR 1, 36, 66; CP 1, 2, 3, 4, 5, 6; DLB
48; EWL 3; EXPP; MAL 5; MTCW 1, 2;
MTFW 2005; PFS 3; RGAL 4

Sharp, William 1855-1905 .... **TCLC 39**
See Macleod, Fiona
See also CA 160; DLB 156; RGEL 2

Sharpe, Thomas Ridley 1928-
See Sharpe, Tom
See also CA 122; CAAE 114; CANR 85;
INT CA-122

Sharpe, Tom .... **CLC 36**
See Sharpe, Thomas Ridley
See also CN 4, 5, 6, 7; DLB 14, 231

Shatrov, Mikhail .... **CLC 59**

Shaw, Bernard
See Shaw, George Bernard
See also DLB 10, 57, 190

Shaw, G. Bernard
See Shaw, George Bernard

Shaw, George Bernard 1856-1950 ..... **DC 23;
TCLC 3, 9, 21, 45; WLC 5**
See Shaw, Bernard
See also AAYA 61; BRW 6; BRWC 1;
BRWR 2; CA 128; CAAE 104; CDBLB
1914-1945; DA; DA3; DAB; DAC; DAM
DRAM, MST; DFS 1, 3, 6, 11, 19, 22;
DLB 332; EWL 3; LAIT 3; LATS 1:1;
MTCW 1, 2; MTFW 2005; RGEL 2;
TEA; WLIT 4

Shaw, Henry Wheeler 1818-1885 .. **NCLC 15**
See also DLB 11; RGAL 4

Shaw, Irwin 1913-1984 .... **CLC 7, 23, 34**
See also AITN 1; BPFB 3; CA 13-16R;
CAAS 112; CANR 21; CDALB 1941-
1968; CN 1, 2, 3; CPW; DAM DRAM,
POP; DLB 6, 102; DLBY 1984; MAL 5;
MTCW 1, 21; MTFW 2005

Shaw, Robert (Archibald)
1927-1978 .... **CLC 5**
See also AITN 1; CA 1-4R; CAAS 81-84;
CANR 4; CN 1, 2; DLB 13, 14

Shaw, T. E.
See Lawrence, T(homas) E(dward)

Shawn, Wallace 1943- .... **CLC 41**
See also CA 112; CAD; CD 5, 6; DLB 266

Shaykh, al- Hanan
See al-Shaykh, Hanan
See also CWW 2; EWL 3

Shchedrin, N.
See Saltykov, Mikhail Evgrafovich

Shea, Lisa 1953- .... **CLC 86**
See also CA 147

Sheed, Wilfrid (John Joseph) 1930- . **CLC 2,
4, 10, 53**
See also CA 65-68; CANR 30, 66; CN 1, 2,
3, 4, 5, 6, 7; DLB 6; MAL 5; MTCW 1,
2; MTFW 2005

Sheehy, Gail 1937- .... **CLC 171**
See also CA 49-52; CANR 1, 33, 55, 92;
CPW; MTCW 1

Sheldon, Alice Hastings Bradley
1915(?)-1987
See Tiptree, James, Jr.
See also CA 108; CAAS 122; CANR 34;
INT CA-108; MTCW 1

Sheldon, John
See Bloch, Robert (Albert)

Sheldon, Walter J(ames) 1917-1996
See Queen, Ellery
See also AITN 1; CA 25-28R; CANR 10

Shelley, Mary Wollstonecraft (Godwin)
1797-1851 .... **NCLC 14, 59, 103, 170;
SSC 92; WLC 5**
See also AAYA 20; BPFB 3; BRW 3;
BRWC 2; BRWS 3; BYA 5; CDBLB
1789-1832; DA; DA3; DAB; DAC; DAM
MST, NOV; DLB 110, 116, 159, 178;
EXPN; FL 1:3; GL 3; HGG; LAIT 1;
LMFS 1, 2; NFS 1; RGEL 2; SATA 29;
SCFW 1, 2; SFW 4; TEA; WLIT 3

Shelley, Percy Bysshe 1792-1822 .. **NCLC 18,
93, 143, 175; PC 14, 67; WLC 5**
See also AAYA 61; BRW 4; BRWR 1; CD-
BLB 1789-1832; DA; DA3; DAB; DAC;
DAM MST, POET; DLB 96, 110, 158;
EXPP; LMFS 1; PAB; PFS 2; RGEL 2;
TEA; WLIT 3; WP

Shepard, James R.
See Shepard, Jim

Shepard, Jim 1956- .... **CLC 36**
See also AAYA 73; CA 137; CANR 59, 104,
160; SATA 90, 164

Shepard, Lucius 1947- .... **CLC 34**
See also CA 141; CAAE 128; CANR 81,
124; HGG; SCFW 2; SFW 4; SUFW 2

Shepard, Sam 1943- .... **CLC 4, 6, 17, 34, 41,
44, 169; DC 5**
See also AAYA 1, 58; AMWS 3; CA 69-72;
CABS 3; CAD; CANR 22, 120, 140; CD
5, 6; DA3; DAM DRAM; DFS 3, 6, 7,
14; DLB 7, 212; EWL 3; IDFW 3, 4;
MAL 5; MTCW 1, 2; MTFW 2005;
RGAL 4

Shepherd, Jean (Parker)
1921-1999 .... **TCLC 177**
See also AAYA 69; AITN 2; CA 77-80;
CAAS 187

Shepherd, Michael
See Ludlum, Robert

Sherburne, Zoa (Lillian Morin)
1912-1995 .... **CLC 30**
See also AAYA 13; CA 1-4R; CAAS 176;
CANR 3, 37; MAICYA 1, 2; SAAS 18;
SATA 3; YAW

Sheridan, Frances 1724-1766 .... **LC 7**
See also DLB 39, 84

Sheridan, Richard Brinsley
1751-1816 . **DC 1; NCLC 5, 91; WLC 5**
See also BRW 3; CDBLB 1660-1789; DA;
DAB; DAC; DAM DRAM, MST; DFS
15; DLB 89; WLIT 3

Sherman, Jonathan Marc 1968- .... **CLC 55**
See also CA 230

Sherman, Martin 1941(?)- .... **CLC 19**
See also CA 123; CAAE 116; CAD; CANR
86; CD 5, 6; DFS 20; DLB 228; GLL 1;
IDTP; RGHL

Sherwin, Judith Johnson
See Johnson, Judith (Emlyn)
See also CANR 85; CP 2, 3, 4, 5; CWP

Sherwood, Frances 1940- .... **CLC 81**
See also CA 220; 146, 220; CANR 158

Sherwood, Robert E(mmet)
1896-1955 .... **TCLC 3**
See also CA 153; CAAE 104; CANR 86;
DAM DRAM; DFS 11, 15, 17; DLB 7,
26, 249; IDFW 3, 4; MAL 5; RGAL 4

Shestov, Lev 1866-1938 .... **TCLC 56**

Shevchenko, Taras 1814-1861 .... **NCLC 54**

Shiel, M(atthew) P(hipps)
1865-1947 .... **TCLC 8**
See Holmes, Gordon
See also CA 160; CAAE 106; DLB 153;
HGG; MTCW 2; MTFW 2005; SCFW 1,
2; SFW 4; SUFW

Shields, Carol 1935-2003 .. **CLC 91, 113, 193**
See also AMWS 7; CA 81-84; CAAS 218;
CANR 51, 74, 98, 133; CCA 1; CN 6, 7;
CPW; DA3; DAC; MTCW 2; MTFW
2005; NFS 23

Shields, David 1956- .... **CLC 97**
See also CA 124; CANR 48, 99, 112, 157

Shields, David Jonathan
See Shields, David

Shiga, Naoya 1883-1971 .... **CLC 33; SSC 23;
TCLC 172**
See Shiga Naoya
See also CA 101; CAAS 33-36R; MJW;
RGWL 3

Shiga Naoya
See Shiga, Naoya
See also DLB 180; EWL 3; RGWL 3

Shilts, Randy 1951-1994 .... **CLC 85**
See also AAYA 19; CA 127; CAAE 115;
CAAS 144; CANR 45; DA3; GLL 1; INT
CA-127; MTCW 2; MTFW 2005

Shimazaki, Haruki 1872-1943
See Shimazaki Toson
See also CA 134; CAAE 105; CANR 84;
RGWL 3

Shimazaki Toson .... **TCLC 5**
See Shimazaki, Haruki
See also DLB 180; EWL 3

Shirley, James 1596-1666 .... **DC 25; LC 96**
See also DLB 58; RGEL 2
Sholokhov, Mikhail (Aleksandrovich)
1905-1984 .... **CLC 7, 15**
See also CA 101; CAAS 112; DLB 272,
332; EWL 3; MTCW 1, 2; MTFW 2005;
RGWL 2, 3; SATA-Obit 36
Sholom Aleichem 1859-1916 .... **SSC 33;**
TCLC 1, 35
See Rabinovitch, Sholem
See also DLB 333; TWA
Shone, Patric
See Hanley, James
Showalter, Elaine 1941- .... **CLC 169**
See also CA 57-60; CANR 58, 106; DLB
67; FW; GLL 2
Shreve, Susan
See Shreve, Susan Richards
Shreve, Susan Richards 1939- .... **CLC 23**
See also CA 49-52; 5; CANR 5, 38, 69, 100,
159; MAICYA 1, 2; SATA 46, 95, 152;
SATA-Brief 41
Shue, Larry 1946-1985 .... **CLC 52**
See also CA 145; CAAS 117; DAM DRAM;
DFS 7
Shu-Jen, Chou 1881-1936
See Lu Hsun
See also CAAE 104
Shulman, Alix Kates 1932- .... **CLC 2, 10**
See also CA 29-32R; CANR 43; FW; SATA
7
Shuster, Joe 1914-1992 .... **CLC 21**
See also AAYA 50
Shute, Nevil .... **CLC 30**
See Norway, Nevil Shute
See also BPFB 3; DLB 255; NFS 9; RHW;
SFW 4
Shuttle, Penelope (Diane) 1947- .... **CLC 7**
See also CA 93-96; CANR 39, 84, 92, 108;
CP 3, 4, 5, 6, 7; CWP; DLB 14, 40
Shvarts, Elena 1948- .... **PC 50**
See also CA 147
Sidhwa, Bapsi 1939-
See Sidhwa, Bapsy (N.)
See also CN 6, 7; DLB 323
Sidhwa, Bapsy (N.) 1938- .... **CLC 168**
See Sidhwa, Bapsi
See also CA 108; CANR 25, 57; FW
Sidney, Mary 1561-1621 .... **LC 19, 39**
See Sidney Herbert, Mary
Sidney, Sir Philip 1554-1586 .... **LC 19, 39,**
131; PC 32
See also BRW 1; BRWR 2; CDBLB Before
1660; DA; DA3; DAB; DAC; DAM MST,
POET; DLB 167; EXPP; PAB; RGEL 2;
TEA; WP
Sidney Herbert, Mary
See Sidney, Mary
See also DLB 167
Siegel, Jerome 1914-1996 .... **CLC 21**
See Siegel, Jerry
See also CA 169; CAAE 116; CAAS 151
Siegel, Jerry
See Siegel, Jerome
See also AAYA 50
Sienkiewicz, Henryk (Adam Alexander Pius)
1846-1916 .... **TCLC 3**
See also CA 134; CAAE 104; CANR 84;
DLB 332; EWL 3; RGSF 2; RGWL 2, 3
Sierra, Gregorio Martinez
See Martinez Sierra, Gregorio
Sierra, Maria de la O'LeJarraga Martinez
See Martinez Sierra, Maria
Sigal, Clancy 1926- .... **CLC 7**
See also CA 1-4R; CANR 85; CN 1, 2, 3,
4, 5, 6, 7
Siger of Brabant 1240(?)-1284(?) . **CMLC 69**
See also DLB 115

Sigourney, Lydia H.
See Sigourney, Lydia Howard (Huntley)
See also DLB 73, 183
Sigourney, Lydia Howard (Huntley)
1791-1865 .... **NCLC 21, 87**
See Sigourney, Lydia H.; Sigourney, Lydia
Huntley
See also DLB 1
Sigourney, Lydia Huntley
See Sigourney, Lydia Howard (Huntley)
See also DLB 42, 239, 243
Siguenza y Gongora, Carlos de
1645-1700 .... **HLCS 2; LC 8**
See also LAW
Sigurjonsson, Johann
See Sigurjonsson, Johann
Sigurjonsson, Johann 1880-1919 ... **TCLC 27**
See also CA 170; DLB 293; EWL 3
Sikelianos, Angelos 1884-1951 .... **PC 29;**
TCLC 39
See also EWL 3; RGWL 2, 3
Silkin, Jon 1930-1997 .... **CLC 2, 6, 43**
See also CA 5-8R; 5; CANR 89; CP 1, 2, 3,
4, 5, 6; DLB 27
Silko, Leslie 1948- ...... **CLC 23, 74, 114, 211;**
NNAL; SSC 37, 66; WLCS
See also AAYA 14; AMWS 4; ANW; BYA
12; CA 122; CAAE 115; CANR 45, 65,
118; CN 4, 5, 6, 7; CP 4, 5, 6, 7; CPW 1;
CWP; DA; DA3; DAC; DAM MST,
MULT, POP; DLB 143, 175, 256, 275;
EWL 3; EXPP; EXPS; LAIT 4; MAL 5;
MTCW 2; MTFW 2005; NFS 4; PFS 9,
16; RGAL 4; RGSF 2; SSFS 4, 8, 10, 11;
TCWW 1, 2
Sillanpaa, Frans Eemil 1888-1964 ... **CLC 19**
See also CA 129; CAAS 93-96; DLB 332;
EWL 3; MTCW 1
Sillitoe, Alan 1928- .. **CLC 1, 3, 6, 10, 19, 57,**
148
See also AITN 1; BRWS 5; CA 191; 9-12R,
191; 2; CANR 8, 26, 55, 139; CDBLB
1960 to Present; CN 1, 2, 3, 4, 5, 6; CP 1,
2, 3, 4, 5; DLB 14, 139; EWL 3; MTCW
1, 2; MTFW 2005; RGEL 2; RGSF 2;
SATA 61
Silone, Ignazio 1900-1978 .... **CLC 4**
See also CA 25-28; CAAS 81-84; CANR
34; CAP 2; DLB 264; EW 12; EWL 3;
MTCW 1; RGSF 2; RGWL 2, 3
Silone, Ignazione
See Silone, Ignazio
Silver, Joan Micklin 1935- .... **CLC 20**
See also CA 121; CAAE 114; INT CA-121
Silver, Nicholas
See Faust, Frederick (Schiller)
Silverberg, Robert 1935- .... **CLC 7, 140**
See also AAYA 24; BPFB 3; BYA 7, 9; CA
186; 1-4R, 186; 3; CANR 1, 20, 36, 85,
140; CLR 59; CN 6, 7; CPW; DAM POP;
DLB 8; INT CANR-20; MAICYA 1, 2;
MTCW 1, 2; MTFW 2005; SATA 13, 91;
SATA-Essay 104; SCFW 1, 2; SFW 4;
SUFW 2
Silverstein, Alvin 1933- .... **CLC 17**
See also CA 49-52; CANR 2; CLR 25;
JRDA; MAICYA 1, 2; SATA 8, 69, 124
Silverstein, Shel 1932-1999 .... **PC 49**
See also AAYA 40; BW 3; CA 107; CAAS
179; CANR 47, 74, 81; CLR 5, 96; CWRI
5; JRDA; MAICYA 1, 2; MTCW 2;
MTFW 2005; SATA 33, 92; SATA-Brief
27; SATA-Obit 116
Silverstein, Virginia B(arbara Opshelor)
1937- .... **CLC 17**
See also CA 49-52; CANR 2; CLR 25;
JRDA; MAICYA 1, 2; SATA 8, 69, 124
Sim, Georges
See Simenon, Georges (Jacques Christian)

Simak, Clifford D(onald) 1904-1988 . **CLC 1,**
55
See also CA 1-4R; CAAS 125; CANR 1,
35; DLB 8; MTCW 1; SATA-Obit 56;
SCFW 1, 2; SFW 4
Simenon, Georges (Jacques Christian)
1903-1989 ...... **CLC 1, 2, 3, 8, 18, 47**
See also BPFB 3; CA 85-88; CAAS 129;
CANR 35; CMW 4; DA3; DAM POP;
DLB 72; DLBY 1989; EW 12; EWL 3;
GFL 1789 to the Present; MSW; MTCW
1, 2; MTFW 2005; RGWL 2, 3
Simic, Charles 1938- .... **CLC 6, 9, 22, 49, 68,**
130; PC 69
See also AMWS 8; CA 29-32R; 4; CANR
12, 33, 52, 61, 96, 140; CP 2, 3, 4, 5, 6,
7; DA3; DAM POET; DLB 105; MAL 5;
MTCW 2; MTFW 2005; PFS 7; RGAL 4;
WP
Simmel, Georg 1858-1918 .... **TCLC 64**
See also CA 157; DLB 296
Simmons, Charles (Paul) 1924- .... **CLC 57**
See also CA 89-92; INT CA-89-92
Simmons, Dan 1948- .... **CLC 44**
See also AAYA 16, 54; CA 138; CANR 53,
81, 126; CPW; DAM POP; HGG; SUFW
2
Simmons, James (Stewart Alexander)
1933- .... **CLC 43**
See also CA 105; 21; CP 1, 2, 3, 4, 5, 6, 7;
DLB 40
Simms, William Gilmore
1806-1870 .... **NCLC 3**
See also DLB 3, 30, 59, 73, 248, 254;
RGAL 4
Simon, Carly 1945- .... **CLC 26**
See also CA 105
Simon, Claude 1913-2005 ... **CLC 4, 9, 15, 39**
See also CA 89-92; CAAS 241; CANR 33,
117; CWW 2; DAM NOV; DLB 83, 332;
EW 13; EWL 3; GFL 1789 to the Present;
MTCW 1
Simon, Claude Eugene Henri
See Simon, Claude
Simon, Claude Henri Eugene
See Simon, Claude
Simon, Marvin Neil
See Simon, Neil
Simon, Myles
See Follett, Ken
Simon, Neil 1927- .... **CLC 6, 11, 31, 39, 70,**
233; DC 14
See also AAYA 32; AITN 1; AMWS 4; CA
21-24R; CAD; CANR 26, 54, 87, 126;
CD 5, 6; DA3; DAM DRAM; DFS 2, 6,
12, 18; DLB 7, 266; LAIT 4; MAL 5;
MTCW 1, 2; MTFW 2005; RGAL 4; TUS
Simon, Paul 1941(?)- .... **CLC 17**
See also CA 153; CAAE 116; CANR 152
Simon, Paul Frederick
See Simon, Paul
Simonon, Paul 1956(?)- .... **CLC 30**
Simonson, Rick .... **CLC 70**
Simpson, Harriette
See Arnow, Harriette (Louisa) Simpson
Simpson, Louis 1923- ... **CLC 4, 7, 9, 32, 149**
See also AMWS 9; CA 1-4R; 4; CANR 1,
61, 140; CP 1, 2, 3, 4, 5, 6, 7; DAM
POET; DLB 5; MAL 5; MTCW 1, 2;
MTFW 2005; PFS 7, 11, 14; RGAL 4
Simpson, Mona 1957- .... **CLC 44, 146**
See also CA 135; CAAE 122; CANR 68,
103; CN 6, 7; EWL 3
Simpson, Mona Elizabeth
See Simpson, Mona
Simpson, N(orman) F(rederick)
1919- .... **CLC 29**
See also CA 13-16R; CBD; DLB 13; RGEL
2

Snodgrass, W.D. 1926- .... **CLC 2, 6, 10, 18, 68; PC 74**
> See also AMWS 6; CA 1-4R; CANR 6, 36, 65, 85; CP 1, 2, 3, 4, 5, 6, 7; DAM POET; DLB 5; MAL 5; MTCW 1, 2; MTFW 2005; RGAL 4; TCLE 1:2

Snorri Sturluson 1179-1241 .... **CMLC 56**
> See also RGWL 2, 3

Snow, C(harles) P(ercy) 1905-1980 ... **CLC 1, 4, 6, 9, 13, 19**
> See also BRW 7; CA 5-8R; CAAS 101; CANR 28; CDBLB 1945-1960; CN 1, 2; DAM NOV; DLB 15, 77; DLBD 17; EWL 3; MTCW 1, 2; MTFW 2005; RGEL 2; TEA

Snow, Frances Compton
> See Adams, Henry (Brooks)

Snyder, Gary 1930- . **CLC 1, 2, 5, 9, 32, 120; PC 21**
> See also AAYA 72; AMWS 8; ANW; BG 1:3; CA 17-20R; CANR 30, 60, 125; CP 1, 2, 3, 4, 5, 6, 7; DA3; DAM POET; DLB 5, 16, 165, 212, 237, 275; EWL 3; MAL 5; MTCW 2; MTFW 2005; PFS 9, 19; RGAL 4; WP

Snyder, Zilpha Keatley 1927- .... **CLC 17**
> See also AAYA 15; BYA 1; CA 252; 9-12R, 252; CANR 38; CLR 31; JRDA; MAICYA 1, 2; SAAS 2; SATA 1, 28, 75, 110, 163; SATA-Essay 112, 163; YAW

Soares, Bernardo
> See Pessoa, Fernando (Antonio Nogueira)

Sobh, A.
> See Shamlu, Ahmad

Sobh, Alef
> See Shamlu, Ahmad

Sobol, Joshua 1939- .... **CLC 60**
> See Sobol, Yehoshua
> See also CA 200; RGHL

Sobol, Yehoshua 1939-
> See Sobol, Joshua
> See also CWW 2

Socrates 470B.C.-399B.C. .... **CMLC 27**

Soderberg, Hjalmar 1869-1941 ...... **TCLC 39**
> See also DLB 259; EWL 3; RGSF 2

Soderbergh, Steven 1963- .... **CLC 154**
> See also AAYA 43; CA 243

Soderbergh, Steven Andrew
> See Soderbergh, Steven

Sodergran, Edith (Irene) 1892-1923
> See Soedergran, Edith (Irene)
> See also CA 202; DLB 259; EW 11; EWL 3; RGWL 2, 3

Soedergran, Edith (Irene)
> 1892-1923 .... **TCLC 31**
> See Sodergran, Edith (Irene)

Softly, Edgar
> See Lovecraft, H. P.

Softly, Edward
> See Lovecraft, H. P.

Sokolov, Alexander V(sevolodovich) 1943-
> See Sokolov, Sasha
> See also CA 73-76

Sokolov, Raymond 1941- .... **CLC 7**
> See also CA 85-88

Sokolov, Sasha .... **CLC 59**
> See Sokolov, Alexander V(sevolodovich)
> See also CWW 2; DLB 285; EWL 3; RGWL 2, 3

Solo, Jay
> See Ellison, Harlan

Sologub, Fyodor .... **TCLC 9**
> See Teternikov, Fyodor Kuzmich
> See also EWL 3

Solomons, Ikey Esquir
> See Thackeray, William Makepeace

Solomos, Dionysios 1798-1857 .... **NCLC 15**

Solwoska, Mara
> See French, Marilyn

Solzhenitsyn, Aleksandr I. 1918- .. **CLC 1, 2, 4, 7, 9, 10, 18, 26, 34, 78, 134, 235; SSC 32; WLC 5**
> See Solzhenitsyn, Aleksandr Isayevich
> See also AAYA 49; AITN 1; BPFB 3; CA 69-72; CANR 40, 65, 116; DA; DA3; DAB; DAC; DAM MST, NOV; DLB 302, 332; EW 13; EXPS; LAIT 4; MTCW 1, 2; MTFW 2005; NFS 6; RGSF 2; RGWL 2, 3; SSFS 9; TWA

Solzhenitsyn, Aleksandr Isayevich
> See Solzhenitsyn, Aleksandr I.
> See also CWW 2; EWL 3

Somers, Jane
> See Lessing, Doris

Somerville, Edith Oenone
> 1858-1949 .... **SSC 56; TCLC 51**
> See also CA 196; DLB 135; RGEL 2; RGSF 2

Somerville & Ross
> See Martin, Violet Florence; Somerville, Edith Oenone

Sommer, Scott 1951- .... **CLC 25**
> See also CA 106

Sommers, Christina Hoff 1950- ...... **CLC 197**
> See also CA 153; CANR 95

Sondheim, Stephen (Joshua) 1930- . **CLC 30, 39, 147; DC 22**
> See also AAYA 11, 66; CA 103; CANR 47, 67, 125; DAM DRAM; LAIT 4

Sone, Monica 1919- .... **AAL**
> See also DLB 312

Song, Cathy 1955- .... **AAL; PC 21**
> See also CA 154; CANR 118; CWP; DLB 169, 312; EXPP; FW; PFS 5

Sontag, Susan 1933-2004 ... **CLC 1, 2, 10, 13, 31, 105, 195**
> See also AMWS 3; CA 17-20R; CAAS 234; CANR 25, 51, 74, 97; CN 1, 2, 3, 4, 5, 6, 7; CPW; DA3; DAM POP; DLB 2, 67; EWL 3; MAL 5; MBL; MTCW 1, 2; MTFW 2005; RGAL 4; RHW; SSFS 10

Sophocles 496(?)B.C.-406(?)B.C. .... **CMLC 2, 47, 51, 86; DC 1; WLCS**
> See also AW 1; CDWLB 1; DA; DA3; DAB; DAC; DAM DRAM, MST; DFS 1, 4, 8; DLB 176; LAIT 1; LATS 1:1; LMFS 1; RGWL 2, 3; TWA; WLIT 8

Sordello 1189-1269 .... **CMLC 15**

Sorel, Georges 1847-1922 .... **TCLC 91**
> See also CA 188; CAAE 118

Sorel, Julia
> See Drexler, Rosalyn

Sorokin, Vladimir .... **CLC 59**
> See Sorokin, Vladimir Georgievich

Sorokin, Vladimir Georgievich
> See Sorokin, Vladimir
> See also DLB 285

Sorrentino, Gilbert 1929-2006 .... **CLC 3, 7, 14, 22, 40**
> See also CA 77-80; CAAS 250; CANR 14, 33, 115, 157; CN 3, 4, 5, 6, 7; CP 1, 2, 3, 4, 5, 6, 7; DLB 5, 173; DLBY 1980; INT CANR-14

Soseki
> See Natsume, Soseki
> See also MJW

Soto, Gary 1952- ... **CLC 32, 80; HLC 2; PC 28**
> See also AAYA 10, 37; BYA 11; CA 125; CAAE 119; CANR 50, 74, 107, 157; CLR 38; CP 4, 5, 6, 7; DAM MULT; DLB 82; EWL 3; EXPP; HW 1, 2; INT CA-125; JRDA; LLW; MAICYA 2; MAICYAS 1; MAL 5; MTCW 2; MTFW 2005; PFS 7; RGAL 4; SATA 80, 120, 174; WYA; YAW

Soupault, Philippe 1897-1990 .... **CLC 68**
> See also CA 147; CAAE 116; CAAS 131; EWL 3; GFL 1789 to the Present; LMFS 2

Souster, (Holmes) Raymond 1921- .... **CLC 5, 14**
> See also CA 13-16R; 14; CANR 13, 29, 53; CP 1, 2, 3, 4, 5, 6, 7; DA3; DAC; DAM POET; DLB 88; RGEL 2; SATA 63

Southern, Terry 1924(?)-1995 .... **CLC 7**
> See also AMWS 11; BPFB 3; CA 1-4R; CAAS 150; CANR 1, 55, 107; CN 1, 2, 3, 4, 5, 6; DLB 2; IDFW 3, 4

Southerne, Thomas 1660-1746 .... **LC 99**
> See also DLB 80; RGEL 2

Southey, Robert 1774-1843 .... **NCLC 8, 97**
> See also BRW 4; DLB 93, 107, 142; RGEL 2; SATA 54

Southwell, Robert 1561(?)-1595 .... **LC 108**
> See also DLB 167; RGEL 2; TEA

Southworth, Emma Dorothy Eliza Nevitte
> 1819-1899 .... **NCLC 26**
> See also DLB 239

Souza, Ernest
> See Scott, Evelyn

Soyinka, Wole 1934- .. **BLC 3; CLC 3, 5, 14, 36, 44, 179; DC 2; WLC 5**
> See also AFW; BW 2, 3; CA 13-16R; CANR 27, 39, 82, 136; CD 5, 6; CDWLB 3; CN 6, 7; CP 1, 2, 3, 4, 5, 6 ,7; DA; DA3; DAB; DAC; DAM DRAM, MST, MULT; DFS 10; DLB 125, 332; EWL 3; MTCW 1, 2; MTFW 2005; RGEL 2; TWA; WLIT 2; WWE 1

Spackman, W(illiam) M(ode)
> 1905-1990 .... **CLC 46**
> See also CA 81-84; CAAS 132

Spacks, Barry (Bernard) 1931- .... **CLC 14**
> See also CA 154; CANR 33, 109; CP 3, 4, 5, 6, 7; DLB 105

Spanidou, Irini 1946- .... **CLC 44**
> See also CA 185

Spark, Muriel 1918-2006 .... **CLC 2, 3, 5, 8, 13, 18, 40, 94; PC 72; SSC 10**
> See also BRWS 1; CA 5-8R; CAAS 251; CANR 12, 36, 76, 89, 131; CDBLB 1945-1960; CN 1, 2, 3, 4, 5, 6, 7; CP 1, 2, 3, 4, 5, 6, 7; DA3; DAB; DAC; DAM MST, NOV; DLB 15, 139; EWL 3; FW; INT CANR-12; LAIT 4; MTCW 1, 2; MTFW 2005; NFS 22; RGEL 2; TEA; WLIT 4; YAW

Spark, Muriel Sarah
> See Spark, Muriel

Spaulding, Douglas
> See Bradbury, Ray

Spaulding, Leonard
> See Bradbury, Ray

Speght, Rachel 1597-c. 1630 .... **LC 97**
> See also DLB 126

Spence, J. A. D.
> See Eliot, T(homas) S(tearns)

Spencer, Anne 1882-1975 ...... **HR 1:3; PC 77**
> See also BW 2; CA 161; DLB 51, 54

Spencer, Elizabeth 1921- .... **CLC 22; SSC 57**
> See also CA 13-16R; CANR 32, 65, 87; CN 1, 2, 3, 4, 5, 6, 7; CSW; DLB 6, 218; EWL 3; MTCW 1; RGAL 4; SATA 14

Spencer, Leonard G.
> See Silverberg, Robert

Spencer, Scott 1945- .... **CLC 30**
> See also CA 113; CANR 51, 148; DLBY 1986

Spender, Stephen 1909-1995 ..... **CLC 1, 2, 5, 10, 41, 91; PC 71**
> See also BRWS 2; CA 9-12R; CAAS 149; CANR 31, 54; CDBLB 1945-1960; CP 1, 2, 3, 4, 5, 6; DA3; DAM POET; DLB 20; EWL 3; MTCW 1, 2; MTFW 2005; PAB; PFS 23; RGEL 2; TEA

Spengler, Oswald (Arnold Gottfried)
> 1880-1936 .... **TCLC 25**
> See also CA 189; CAAE 118

Spenser, Edmund 1552(?)-1599 ...... **LC 5, 39, 117; PC 8, 42; WLC 5**
See also AAYA 60; BRW 1; CDBLB Before 1660; DA; DA3; DAB; DAC; DAM MST, POET; DLB 167; EFS 2; EXPP; PAB; RGEL 2; TEA; WLIT 3; WP

Spicer, Jack 1925-1965 .... **CLC 8, 18, 72**
See also BG 1:3; CA 85-88; DAM POET; DLB 5, 16, 193; GLL 1; WP

Spiegelman, Art 1948- .... **CLC 76, 178**
See also AAYA 10, 46; CA 125; CANR 41, 55, 74, 124; DLB 299; MTCW 2; MTFW 2005; RGHL; SATA 109, 158; YAW

Spielberg, Peter 1929- .... **CLC 6**
See also CA 5-8R; CANR 4, 48; DLBY 1981

Spielberg, Steven 1947- .... **CLC 20, 188**
See also AAYA 8, 24; CA 77-80; CANR 32; SATA 32

Spillane, Frank Morrison .... **CLC 3, 13**
See Spillane, Mickey
See also BPFB 3; CMW 4; DLB 226; MSW

Spillane, Mickey 1918-2006
See Spillane, Frank Morrison
See also CA 25-28R; CAAS 252; CANR 28, 63, 125; DA3; MTCW 1, 2; MTFW 2005; SATA 66; SATA-Obit 176

Spinoza, Benedictus de 1632-1677 .. **LC 9, 58**

Spinrad, Norman (Richard) 1940- ... **CLC 46**
See also BPFB 3; CA 233; 37-40R, 233; 19; CANR 20, 91; DLB 8; INT CANR-20; SFW 4

Spitteler, Carl 1845-1924 .... **TCLC 12**
See also CAAE 109; DLB 129, 332; EWL 3

Spitteler, Karl Friedrich Georg
See Spitteler, Carl

Spivack, Kathleen (Romola Drucker) 1938- .... **CLC 6**
See also CA 49-52

Spivak, Gayatri Chakravorty 1942- .... **CLC 233**
See also CA 154; CAAE 110; CANR 91; FW; LMFS 2

Spofford, Harriet (Elizabeth) Prescott 1835-1921 .... **SSC 87**
See also CA 201; DLB 74, 221

Spoto, Donald 1941- .... **CLC 39**
See also CA 65-68; CANR 11, 57, 93

Springsteen, Bruce 1949- .... **CLC 17**
See also CA 111

Springsteen, Bruce F.
See Springsteen, Bruce

Spurling, Hilary 1940- .... **CLC 34**
See also CA 104; CANR 25, 52, 94, 157

Spurling, Susan Hilary
See Spurling, Hilary

Spyker, John Howland
See Elman, Richard (Martin)

Squared, A.
See Abbott, Edwin A.

Squires, (James) Radcliffe 1917-1993 .... **CLC 51**
See also CA 1-4R; CAAS 140; CANR 6, 21; CP 1, 2, 3, 4, 5

Srivastava, Dhanpat Rai 1880(?)-1936
See Premchand
See also CA 197; CAAE 118

Stacy, Donald
See Pohl, Frederik

Stael
See Stael-Holstein, Anne Louise Germaine Necker
See also EW 5; RGWL 2, 3

Stael, Germaine de
See Stael-Holstein, Anne Louise Germaine Necker
See also DLB 119, 192; FL 1:3; FW; GFL 1789 to the Present; TWA

Stael-Holstein, Anne Louise Germaine Necker 1766-1817 .... **NCLC 3, 91**
See Stael; Stael, Germaine de

Stafford, Jean 1915-1979 .. **CLC 4, 7, 19, 68; SSC 26, 86**
See also CA 1-4R; CAAS 85-88; CANR 3, 65; CN 1, 2; DLB 2, 173; MAL 5; MTCW 1, 2; MTFW 2005; RGAL 4; RGSF 2; SATA-Obit 22; SSFS 21; TCWW 1, 2; TUS

Stafford, William (Edgar) 1914-1993 .... **CLC 4, 7, 29; PC 71**
See also AMWS 11; CA 5-8R; 3; CAAS 142; CANR 5, 22; CP 1, 2, 3, 4, 5; DAM POET; DLB 5, 206; EXPP; INT CANR-22; MAL 5; PFS 2, 8, 16; RGAL 4; WP

Stagnelius, Eric Johan 1793-1823 . **NCLC 61**

Staines, Trevor
See Brunner, John (Kilian Houston)

Stairs, Gordon
See Austin, Mary (Hunter)

Stalin, Joseph 1879-1953 .... **TCLC 92**

Stampa, Gaspara c. 1524-1554 .. **LC 114; PC 43**
See also RGWL 2, 3; WLIT 7

Stampflinger, K. A.
See Benjamin, Walter

Stancykowna
See Szymborska, Wislawa

Standing Bear, Luther 1868(?)-1939(?) .... **NNAL**
See also CA 144; CAAE 113; DAM MULT

Stanislavsky, Constantin 1863(?)-1938 .... **TCLC 167**
See also CAAE 118

Stanislavsky, Konstantin
See Stanislavsky, Constantin

Stanislavsky, Konstantin Sergeievich
See Stanislavsky, Constantin

Stanislavsky, Konstantin Sergeivich
See Stanislavsky, Constantin

Stanislavsky, Konstantin Sergeyevich
See Stanislavsky, Constantin

Stannard, Martin 1947- .... **CLC 44**
See also CA 142; DLB 155

Stanton, Elizabeth Cady 1815-1902 .... **TCLC 73**
See also CA 171; DLB 79; FL 1:3; FW

Stanton, Maura 1946- .... **CLC 9**
See also CA 89-92; CANR 15, 123; DLB 120

Stanton, Schuyler
See Baum, L(yman) Frank

Stapledon, (William) Olaf 1886-1950 .... **TCLC 22**
See also CA 162; CAAE 111; DLB 15, 255; SCFW 1, 2; SFW 4

Starbuck, George (Edwin) 1931-1996 .... **CLC 53**
See also CA 21-24R; CAAS 153; CANR 23; CP 1, 2, 3, 4, 5, 6; DAM POET

Stark, Richard
See Westlake, Donald E.

Staunton, Schuyler
See Baum, L(yman) Frank

Stead, Christina (Ellen) 1902-1983 ... **CLC 2, 5, 8, 32, 80**
See also BRWS 4; CA 13-16R; CAAS 109; CANR 33, 40; CN 1, 2, 3; DLB 260; EWL 3; FW; MTCW 1, 2; MTFW 2005; RGEL 2; RGSF 2; WWE 1

Stead, William Thomas 1849-1912 .... **TCLC 48**
See also CA 167

Stebnitsky, M.
See Leskov, Nikolai (Semyonovich)

Steele, Richard 1672-1729 .... **LC 18**
See also BRW 3; CDBLB 1660-1789; DLB 84, 101; RGEL 2; WLIT 3

Steele, Timothy (Reid) 1948- .... **CLC 45**
See also CA 93-96; CANR 16, 50, 92; CP 5, 6, 7; DLB 120, 282

Steffens, (Joseph) Lincoln 1866-1936 .... **TCLC 20**
See also CA 198; CAAE 117; DLB 303; MAL 5

Stegner, Wallace (Earle) 1909-1993 .. **CLC 9, 49, 81; SSC 27**
See also AITN 1; AMWS 4; ANW; BEST 90:3; BPFB 3; CA 1-4R; 9; CAAS 141; CANR 1, 21, 46; CN 1, 2, 3, 4, 5; DAM NOV; DLB 9, 206, 275; DLBY 1993; EWL 3; MAL 5; MTCW 1, 2; MTFW 2005; RGAL 4; TCWW 1, 2; TUS

Stein, Gertrude 1874-1946 .... **DC 19; PC 18; SSC 42; TCLC 1, 6, 28, 48; WLC 5**
See also AAYA 64; AMW; AMWC 2; CA 132; CAAE 104; CANR 108; CDALB 1917-1929; DA; DA3; DAB; DAC; DAM MST, NOV, POET; DLB 4, 54, 86, 228; DLBD 15; EWL 3; EXPS; FL 1:6; GLL 1; MAL 5; MBL; MTCW 1, 2; MTFW 2005; NCFS 4; RGAL 4; RGSF 2; SSFS 5; TUS; WP

Steinbeck, John (Ernst) 1902-1968 ... **CLC 1, 5, 9, 13, 21, 34, 45, 75, 124; SSC 11, 37, 77; TCLC 135; WLC 5**
See also AAYA 12; AMW; BPFB 3; BYA 2, 3, 13; CA 1-4R; CAAS 25-28R; CANR 1, 35; CDALB 1929-1941; DA; DA3; DAB; DAC; DAM DRAM, MST, NOV; DLB 7, 9, 212, 275, 309, 332; DLBD 2; EWL 3; EXPS; LAIT 3; MAL 5; MTCW 1, 2; MTFW 2005; NFS 1, 5, 7, 17, 19; RGAL 4; RGSF 2; RHW; SATA 9; SSFS 3, 6, 22; TCWW 1, 2; TUS; WYA; YAW

Steinem, Gloria 1934- .... **CLC 63**
See also CA 53-56; CANR 28, 51, 139; DLB 246; FL 1:1; FW; MTCW 1, 2; MTFW 2005

Steiner, George 1929- .... **CLC 24, 221**
See also CA 73-76; CANR 31, 67, 108; DAM NOV; DLB 67, 299; EWL 3; MTCW 1, 2; MTFW 2005; RGHL; SATA 62

Steiner, K. Leslie
See Delany, Samuel R., Jr.

Steiner, Rudolf 1861-1925 .... **TCLC 13**
See also CAAE 107

Stendhal 1783-1842 .... **NCLC 23, 46, 178; SSC 27; WLC 5**
See also DA; DA3; DAB; DAC; DAM MST, NOV; DLB 119; EW 5; GFL 1789 to the Present; RGWL 2, 3; TWA

Stephen, Adeline Virginia
See Woolf, (Adeline) Virginia

Stephen, Sir Leslie 1832-1904 .... **TCLC 23**
See also BRW 5; CAAE 123; DLB 57, 144, 190

Stephen, Sir Leslie
See Stephen, Sir Leslie

Stephen, Virginia
See Woolf, (Adeline) Virginia

Stephens, James 1882(?)-1950 .... **SSC 50; TCLC 4**
See also CA 192; CAAE 104; DLB 19, 153, 162; EWL 3; FANT; RGEL 2; SUFW

Stephens, Reed
See Donaldson, Stephen R(eeder)

Stephenson, Neal 1959- .... **CLC 220**
See also AAYA 38; CA 122; CANR 88, 138; CN 7; MTFW 2005; SFW 4

Steptoe, Lydia
See Barnes, Djuna
See also GLL 1

Sterchi, Beat 1949- .... **CLC 65**
See also CA 203

Sterling, Brett
See Bradbury, Ray; Hamilton, Edmond

Strugatsky, Boris (Natanovich)
See Strugatskii, Boris (Natanovich)
See also DLB 302
Strummer, Joe 1952-2002 .... **CLC 30**
Strunk, William, Jr. 1869-1946 ...... **TCLC 92**
See also CA 164; CAAE 118; NCFS 5
Stryk, Lucien 1924- .... **PC 27**
See also CA 13-16R; CANR 10, 28, 55,
110; CP 1, 2, 3, 4, 5, 6, 7
Stuart, Don A.
See Campbell, John W(ood, Jr.)
Stuart, Ian
See MacLean, Alistair (Stuart)
Stuart, Jesse (Hilton) 1906-1984 ... **CLC 1, 8,
11, 14, 34; SSC 31**
See also CA 5-8R; CAAS 112; CANR 31;
CN 1, 2, 3; DLB 9, 48, 102; DLBY 1984;
SATA 2; SATA-Obit 36
Stubblefield, Sally
See Trumbo, Dalton
Sturgeon, Theodore (Hamilton)
1918-1985 .... **CLC 22, 39**
See Queen, Ellery
See also AAYA 51; BPFB 3; BYA 9, 10;
CA 81-84; CAAS 116; CANR 32, 103;
DLB 8; DLBY 1985; HGG; MTCW 1, 2;
MTFW 2005; SCFW; SFW 4; SUFW
Sturges, Preston 1898-1959 .... **TCLC 48**
See also CA 149; CAAE 114; DLB 26
Styron, William 1925-2006 .. **CLC 1, 3, 5, 11,
15, 60, 232; SSC 25**
See also AMW; AMWC 2; BEST 90:4;
BPFB 3; CA 5-8R; CANR 6, 33, 74, 126;
CDALB 1968-1988; CN 1, 2, 3, 4, 5, 6,
7; CPW; CSW; DA3; DAM NOV, POP;
DLB 2, 143, 299; DLBY 1980; EWL 3;
INT CANR-6; LAIT 2; MAL 5; MTCW
1, 2; MTFW 2005; NCFS 1; NFS 22;
RGAL 4; RGHL; RHW; TUS
Su, Chien 1884-1918
See Su Man-shu
See also CAAE 123
Suarez Lynch, B.
See Bioy Casares, Adolfo; Borges, Jorge
Luis
Suassuna, Ariano Vilar 1927- .... **HLCS 1**
See also CA 178; DLB 307; HW 2; LAW
Suckert, Kurt Erich
See Malaparte, Curzio
Suckling, Sir John 1609-1642 . **LC 75; PC 30**
See also BRW 2; DAM POET; DLB 58,
126; EXPP; PAB; RGEL 2
Suckow, Ruth 1892-1960 .... **SSC 18**
See also CA 193; CAAS 113; DLB 9, 102;
RGAL 4; TCWW 2
Sudermann, Hermann 1857-1928 .. **TCLC 15**
See also CA 201; CAAE 107; DLB 118
Sue, Eugene 1804-1857 .... **NCLC 1**
See also DLB 119
Sueskind, Patrick 1949- .... **CLC 44, 182**
See Suskind, Patrick
Suetonius c. 70-c. 130 .... **CMLC 60**
See also AW 2; DLB 211; RGWL 2, 3;
WLIT 8
Sukenick, Ronald 1932-2004 ..... **CLC 3, 4, 6,
48**
See also CA 209; 25-28R, 209; 8; CAAS
229; CANR 32, 89; CN 3, 4, 5, 6, 7; DLB
173; DLBY 1981
Suknaski, Andrew 1942- .... **CLC 19**
See also CA 101; CP 3, 4, 5, 6, 7; DLB 53
Sullivan, Vernon
See Vian, Boris
Sully Prudhomme, Rene-Francois-Armand
1839-1907 .... **TCLC 31**
See Prudhomme, Rene Francois Armand
See also DLB 332; GFL 1789 to the Present

Su Man-shu .... **TCLC 24**
See Su, Chien
See also EWL 3
Sumarokov, Aleksandr Petrovich
1717-1777 .... **LC 104**
See also DLB 150
Summerforest, Ivy B.
See Kirkup, James
Summers, Andrew James 1942- .... **CLC 26**
Summers, Andy
See Summers, Andrew James
Summers, Hollis (Spurgeon, Jr.)
1916- .... **CLC 10**
See also CA 5-8R; CANR 3; CN 1, 2, 3;
CP 1, 2, 3, 4; DLB 6; TCLE 1:2
**Summers, (Alphonsus Joseph-Mary
Augustus) Montague**
1880-1948 .... **TCLC 16**
See also CA 163; CAAE 118
Sumner, Gordon Matthew .... **CLC 26**
See Police, The; Sting
Sun Tzu c. 400B.C.-c. 320B.C. ...... **CMLC 56**
Surrey, Henry Howard 1517-1574 ... **LC 121;
PC 59**
See also BRW 1; RGEL 2
Surtees, Robert Smith 1805-1864 .. **NCLC 14**
See also DLB 21; RGEL 2
Susann, Jacqueline 1921-1974 .... **CLC 3**
See also AITN 1; BPFB 3; CA 65-68;
CAAS 53-56; MTCW 1, 2
Su Shi
See Su Shih
See also RGWL 2, 3
Su Shih 1036-1101 .... **CMLC 15**
See Su Shi
Suskind, Patrick .... **CLC 182**
See Sueskind, Patrick
See also BPFB 3; CA 145; CWW 2
Suso, Heinrich c. 1295-1366 .... **CMLC 87**
Sutcliff, Rosemary 1920-1992 .... **CLC 26**
See also AAYA 10; BYA 1, 4; CA 5-8R;
CAAS 139; CANR 37; CLR 1, 37; CPW;
DAB; DAC; DAM MST, POP; JRDA;
LATS 1:1; MAICYA 1, 2; MAICYAS 1;
RHW; SATA 6, 44, 78; SATA-Obit 73;
WYA; YAW
Sutro, Alfred 1863-1933 .... **TCLC 6**
See also CA 185; CAAE 105; DLB 10;
RGEL 2
Sutton, Henry
See Slavitt, David R(ytman)
Suzuki, D. T.
See Suzuki, Daisetz Teitaro
Suzuki, Daisetz T.
See Suzuki, Daisetz Teitaro
Suzuki, Daisetz Teitaro
1870-1966 .... **TCLC 109**
See also CA 121; CAAS 111; MTCW 1, 2;
MTFW 2005
Suzuki, Teitaro
See Suzuki, Daisetz Teitaro
Svevo, Italo .... **SSC 25; TCLC 2, 35**
See Schmitz, Aron Hector
See also DLB 264; EW 8; EWL 3; RGWL
2, 3; WLIT 7
Swados, Elizabeth (A.) 1951- .... **CLC 12**
See also CA 97-100; CANR 49; INT CA-
97-100
Swados, Harvey 1920-1972 .... **CLC 5**
See also CA 5-8R; CAAS 37-40R; CANR
6; CN 1; DLB 2; MAL 5
Swan, Gladys 1934- .... **CLC 69**
See also CA 101; CANR 17, 39; TCLE 1:2
Swanson, Logan
See Matheson, Richard (Burton)

Swarthout, Glendon (Fred)
1918-1992 .... **CLC 35**
See also AAYA 55; CA 1-4R; CAAS 139;
CANR 1, 47; CN 1, 2, 3, 4, 5; LAIT 5;
SATA 26; TCWW 1, 2; YAW
Swedenborg, Emanuel 1688-1772 ..... **LC 105**
Sweet, Sarah C.
See Jewett, (Theodora) Sarah Orne
Swenson, May 1919-1989 ...... **CLC 4, 14, 61,
106; PC 14**
See also AMWS 4; CA 5-8R; CAAS 130;
CANR 36, 61, 131; CP 1, 2, 3, 4; DA;
DAB; DAC; DAM MST, POET; DLB 5;
EXPP; GLL 2; MAL 5; MTCW 1, 2;
MTFW 2005; PFS 16; SATA 15; WP
Swift, Augustus
See Lovecraft, H. P.
Swift, Graham 1949- .... **CLC 41, 88, 233**
See also BRWC 2; BRWS 5; CA 122;
CAAE 117; CANR 46, 71, 128; CN 4, 5,
6, 7; DLB 194, 326; MTCW 2; MTFW
2005; NFS 18; RGSF 2
Swift, Jonathan 1667-1745 ..... **LC 1, 42, 101;
PC 9; WLC 6**
See also AAYA 41; BRW 3; BRWC 1;
BRWR 1; BYA 5, 14; CDBLB 1660-1789;
CLR 53; DA; DA3; DAB; DAC; DAM
MST, NOV, POET; DLB 39, 95, 101;
EXPN; LAIT 1; NFS 6; RGEL 2; SATA
19; TEA; WCH; WLIT 3
Swinburne, Algernon Charles
1837-1909 ... **PC 24; TCLC 8, 36; WLC
6**
See also BRW 5; CA 140; CAAE 105; CD-
BLB 1832-1890; DA; DA3; DAB; DAC;
DAM MST, POET; DLB 35, 57; PAB;
RGEL 2; TEA
Swinfen, Ann .... **CLC 34**
See also CA 202
Swinnerton, Frank (Arthur)
1884-1982 .... **CLC 31**
See also CA 202; CAAS 108; CN 1, 2, 3;
DLB 34
Swinnerton, Frank Arthur
1884-1982 .... **CLC 31**
See also CAAS 108; DLB 34
Swithen, John
See King, Stephen
Sylvia
See Ashton-Warner, Sylvia (Constance)
Symmes, Robert Edward
See Duncan, Robert
Symonds, John Addington
1840-1893 .... **NCLC 34**
See also DLB 57, 144
Symons, Arthur 1865-1945 .... **TCLC 11**
See also CA 189; CAAE 107; DLB 19, 57,
149; RGEL 2
Symons, Julian (Gustave)
1912-1994 .... **CLC 2, 14, 32**
See also CA 49-52; 3; CAAS 147; CANR
3, 33, 59; CMW 4; CN 1, 2, 3, 4, 5; CP 1,
3, 4; DLB 87, 155; DLBY 1992; MSW;
MTCW 1
Synge, (Edmund) J(ohn) M(illington)
1871-1909 .... **DC 2; TCLC 6, 37**
See also BRW 6; BRWR 1; CA 141; CAAE
104; CDBLB 1890-1914; DAM DRAM;
DFS 18; DLB 10, 19; EWL 3; RGEL 2;
TEA; WLIT 4
Syruc, J.
See Milosz, Czeslaw
Szirtes, George 1948- .... **CLC 46; PC 51**
See also CA 109; CANR 27, 61, 117; CP 4,
5, 6, 7
Szymborska, Wislawa 1923- ... **CLC 99, 190;
PC 44**
See also CA 154; CANR 91, 133; CDWLB
4; CWP; CWW 2; DA3; DLB 232, 332;
DLBY 1996; EWL 3; MTCW 2; MTFW
2005; PFS 15; RGHL; RGWL 3

T. O., Nik
See Annensky, Innokenty (Fyodorovich)
Tabori, George 1914- .... **CLC 19**
See also CA 49-52; CANR 4, 69; CBD; CD 5, 6; DLB 245; RGHL
Tacitus c. 55-c. 117 .... **CMLC 56**
See also AW 2; CDWLB 1; DLB 211; RGWL 2, 3; WLIT 8
Tagore, Rabindranath 1861-1941 .... **PC 8; SSC 48; TCLC 3, 53**
See also CA 120; CAAE 104; DA3; DAM DRAM, POET; DLB 323, 332; EWL 3; MTCW 1, 2; MTFW 2005; PFS 18; RGEL 2; RGSF 2; RGWL 2, 3; TWA
Taine, Hippolyte Adolphe 1828-1893 .... **NCLC 15**
See also EW 7; GFL 1789 to the Present
Talayesva, Don C. 1890-(?) .... **NNAL**
Talese, Gay 1932- .... **CLC 37, 232**
See also AITN 1; CA 1-4R; CANR 9, 58, 137; DLB 185; INT CANR-9; MTCW 1, 2; MTFW 2005
Tallent, Elizabeth 1954- .... **CLC 45**
See also CA 117; CANR 72; DLB 130
Tallmountain, Mary 1918-1997 .... **NNAL**
See also CA 146; CAAS 161; DLB 193
Tally, Ted 1952- .... **CLC 42**
See also CA 124; CAAE 120; CAD; CANR 125; CD 5, 6; INT CA-124
Talvik, Heiti 1904-1947 .... **TCLC 87**
See also EWL 3
Tamayo y Baus, Manuel 1829-1898 .... **NCLC 1**
Tammsaare, A(nton) H(ansen) 1878-1940 .... **TCLC 27**
See also CA 164; CDWLB 4; DLB 220; EWL 3
Tam'si, Tchicaya U
See Tchicaya, Gerald Felix
Tan, Amy 1952- ...... **AAL; CLC 59, 120, 151**
See also AAYA 9, 48; AMWS 10; BEST 89:3; BPFB 3; CA 136; CANR 54, 105, 132; CDALBS; CN 6, 7; CPW 1; DA3; DAM MULT, NOV, POP; DLB 173, 312; EXPN; FL 1:6; FW; LAIT 3, 5; MAL 5; MTCW 2; MTFW 2005; NFS 1, 13, 16; RGAL 4; SATA 75; SSFS 9; YAW
Tandem, Carl Felix
See Spitteler, Carl
Tandem, Felix
See Spitteler, Carl
Tanizaki, Jun'ichiro 1886-1965 ... **CLC 8, 14, 28; SSC 21**
See Tanizaki Jun'ichiro
See also CA 93-96; CAAS 25-28R; MJW; MTCW 2; MTFW 2005; RGSF 2; RGWL 2
Tanizaki Jun'ichiro
See Tanizaki, Jun'ichiro
See also DLB 180; EWL 3
Tannen, Deborah 1945- .... **CLC 206**
See also CA 118; CANR 95
Tannen, Deborah Frances
See Tannen, Deborah
Tanner, William
See Amis, Kingsley
Tante, Dilly
See Kunitz, Stanley
Tao Lao
See Storni, Alfonsina
Tapahonso, Luci 1953- .... **NNAL; PC 65**
See also CA 145; CANR 72, 127; DLB 175
Tarantino, Quentin (Jerome) 1963- .... **CLC 125, 230**
See also AAYA 58; CA 171; CANR 125
Tarassoff, Lev
See Troyat, Henri
Tarbell, Ida M(inerva) 1857-1944 . **TCLC 40**
See also CA 181; CAAE 122; DLB 47

Tarkington, (Newton) Booth 1869-1946 .... **TCLC 9**
See also BPFB 3; BYA 3; CA 143; CAAE 110; CWRI 5; DLB 9, 102; MAL 5; MTCW 2; RGAL 4; SATA 17
Tarkovskii, Andrei Arsen'evich
See Tarkovsky, Andrei (Arsenyevich)
Tarkovsky, Andrei (Arsenyevich) 1932-1986 .... **CLC 75**
See also CA 127
Tartt, Donna 1964(?)- .... **CLC 76**
See also AAYA 56; CA 142; CANR 135; MTFW 2005
Tasso, Torquato 1544-1595 .... **LC 5, 94**
See also EFS 2; EW 2; RGWL 2, 3; WLIT 7
Tate, (John Orley) Allen 1899-1979 .. **CLC 2, 4, 6, 9, 11, 14, 24; PC 50**
See also AMW; CA 5-8R; CAAS 85-88; CANR 32, 108; CN 1, 2; CP 1, 2; DLB 4, 45, 63; DLBD 17; EWL 3; MAL 5; MTCW 1, 2; MTFW 2005; RGAL 4; RHW
Tate, Ellalice
See Hibbert, Eleanor Alice Burford
Tate, James (Vincent) 1943- ..... **CLC 2, 6, 25**
See also CA 21-24R; CANR 29, 57, 114; CP 1, 2, 3, 4, 5, 6, 7; DLB 5, 169; EWL 3; PFS 10, 15; RGAL 4; WP
Tate, Nahum 1652(?)-1715 .... **LC 109**
See also DLB 80; RGEL 2
Tauler, Johannes c. 1300-1361 ...... **CMLC 37**
See also DLB 179; LMFS 1
Tavel, Ronald 1940- .... **CLC 6**
See also CA 21-24R; CAD; CANR 33; CD 5, 6
Taviani, Paolo 1931- .... **CLC 70**
See also CA 153
Taylor, Bayard 1825-1878 .... **NCLC 89**
See also DLB 3, 189, 250, 254; RGAL 4
Taylor, C(ecil) P(hilip) 1929-1981 .... **CLC 27**
See also CA 25-28R; CAAS 105; CANR 47; CBD
Taylor, Edward 1642(?)-1729 . **LC 11; PC 63**
See also AMW; DA; DAB; DAC; DAM MST, POET; DLB 24; EXPP; RGAL 4; TUS
Taylor, Eleanor Ross 1920- .... **CLC 5**
See also CA 81-84; CANR 70
Taylor, Elizabeth 1912-1975 ..... **CLC 2, 4, 29**
See also CA 13-16R; CANR 9, 70; CN 1, 2; DLB 139; MTCW 1; RGEL 2; SATA 13
Taylor, Frederick Winslow 1856-1915 .... **TCLC 76**
See also CA 188
Taylor, Henry (Splawn) 1942- .... **CLC 44**
See also CA 33-36R; 7; CANR 31; CP 6, 7; DLB 5; PFS 10
Taylor, Kamala 1924-2004
See Markandaya, Kamala
See also CA 77-80; CAAS 227; MTFW 2005; NFS 13
Taylor, Mildred D. 1943- .... **CLC 21**
See also AAYA 10, 47; BW 1; BYA 3, 8; CA 85-88; CANR 25, 115, 136; CLR 9, 59, 90; CSW; DLB 52; JRDA; LAIT 3; MAICYA 1, 2; MTFW 2005; SAAS 5; SATA 135; WYA; YAW
Taylor, Peter (Hillsman) 1917-1994 .. **CLC 1, 4, 18, 37, 44, 50, 71; SSC 10, 84**
See also AMWS 5; BPFB 3; CA 13-16R; CAAS 147; CANR 9, 50; CN 1, 2, 3, 4, 5; CSW; DLB 218, 278; DLBY 1981, 1994; EWL 3; EXPS; INT CANR-9; MAL 5; MTCW 1, 2; MTFW 2005; RGSF 2; SSFS 9; TUS

Taylor, Robert Lewis 1912-1998 .... **CLC 14**
See also CA 1-4R; CAAS 170; CANR 3, 64; CN 1, 2; SATA 10; TCWW 1, 2
Tchekhov, Anton
See Chekhov, Anton (Pavlovich)
Tchicaya, Gerald Felix 1931-1988 .. **CLC 101**
See Tchicaya U Tam'si
See also CA 129; CAAS 125; CANR 81
Tchicaya U Tam'si
See Tchicaya, Gerald Felix
See also EWL 3
Teasdale, Sara 1884-1933 .... **PC 31; TCLC 4**
See also CA 163; CAAE 104; DLB 45; GLL 1; PFS 14; RGAL 4; SATA 32; TUS
Tecumseh 1768-1813 .... **NNAL**
See also DAM MULT
Tegner, Esaias 1782-1846 .... **NCLC 2**
Teilhard de Chardin, (Marie Joseph) Pierre 1881-1955 .... **TCLC 9**
See also CA 210; CAAE 105; GFL 1789 to the Present
Temple, Ann
See Mortimer, Penelope (Ruth)
Tennant, Emma (Christina) 1937- .. **CLC 13, 52**
See also BRWS 9; CA 65-68; 9; CANR 10, 38, 59, 88; CN 3, 4, 5, 6, 7; DLB 14; EWL 3; SFW 4
Tenneshaw, S. M.
See Silverberg, Robert
Tenney, Tabitha Gilman 1762-1837 .... **NCLC 122**
See also DLB 37, 200
Tennyson, Alfred 1809-1892 ... **NCLC 30, 65, 115; PC 6; WLC 6**
See also AAYA 50; BRW 4; CDBLB 1832-1890; DA; DA3; DAB; DAC; DAM MST, POET; DLB 32; EXPP; PAB; PFS 1, 2, 4, 11, 15, 19; RGEL 2; TEA; WLIT 4; WP
Teran, Lisa St. Aubin de .... **CLC 36**
See St. Aubin de Teran, Lisa
Terence c. 184B.C.-c. 159B.C. .... **CMLC 14; DC 7**
See also AW 1; CDWLB 1; DLB 211; RGWL 2, 3; TWA; WLIT 8
Teresa de Jesus, St. 1515-1582 .... **LC 18**
Teresa of Avila, St.
See Teresa de Jesus, St.
Terkel, Louis .... **CLC 38**
See Terkel, Studs
See also AAYA 32; AITN 1; MTCW 2; TUS
Terkel, Studs 1912-
See Terkel, Louis
See also CA 57-60; CANR 18, 45, 67, 132; DA3; MTCW 1, 2; MTFW 2005
Terry, C. V.
See Slaughter, Frank G(ill)
Terry, Megan 1932- .... **CLC 19; DC 13**
See also CA 77-80; CABS 3; CAD; CANR 43; CD 5, 6; CWD; DFS 18; DLB 7, 249; GLL 2
Tertullian c. 155-c. 245 .... **CMLC 29**
Tertz, Abram
See Sinyavsky, Andrei (Donatevich)
See also RGSF 2
Tesich, Steve 1943(?)-1996 .... **CLC 40, 69**
See also CA 105; CAAS 152; CAD; DLBY 1983
Tesla, Nikola 1856-1943 .... **TCLC 88**
Teternikov, Fyodor Kuzmich 1863-1927
See Sologub, Fyodor
See also CAAE 104
Tevis, Walter 1928-1984 .... **CLC 42**
See also CA 113; SFW 4
Tey, Josephine .... **TCLC 14**
See Mackintosh, Elizabeth
See also DLB 77; MSW

Vosce, Trudie
　　See Ozick, Cynthia
Voznesensky, Andrei (Andreievich)
　　1933- .... **CLC 1, 15, 57**
　　See Voznesensky, Andrey
　　See also CA 89-92; CANR 37; CWW 2;
　　DAM POET; MTCW 1
Voznesensky, Andrey
　　See Voznesensky, Andrei (Andreievich)
　　See also EWL 3
Wace, Robert c. 1100-c. 1175 .... **CMLC 55**
　　See also DLB 146
Waddington, Miriam 1917-2004 .... **CLC 28**
　　See also CA 21-24R; CAAS 225; CANR
　　12, 30; CCA 1; CP 1, 2, 3, 4, 5, 6, 7; DLB
　　68
Wagman, Fredrica 1937- .... **CLC 7**
　　See also CA 97-100; INT CA-97-100
Wagner, Linda W.
　　See Wagner-Martin, Linda (C.)
Wagner, Linda Welshimer
　　See Wagner-Martin, Linda (C.)
Wagner, Richard 1813-1883 ..... **NCLC 9, 119**
　　See also DLB 129; EW 6
Wagner-Martin, Linda (C.) 1936- .... **CLC 50**
　　See also CA 159; CANR 135
Wagoner, David (Russell) 1926- .... **CLC 3, 5,
　　15; PC 33**
　　See also AMWS 9; CA 1-4R; 3; CANR 2,
　　71; CN 1, 2, 3, 4, 5, 6, 7; CP 1, 2, 3, 4, 5,
　　6, 7; DLB 5, 256; SATA 14; TCWW 1, 2
Wah, Fred(erick James) 1939- .... **CLC 44**
　　See also CA 141; CAAE 107; CP 1, 6, 7;
　　DLB 60
Wahloo, Per 1926-1975 .... **CLC 7**
　　See also BPFB 3; CA 61-64; CANR 73;
　　CMW 4; MSW
Wahloo, Peter
　　See Wahloo, Per
Wain, John (Barrington) 1925-1994 . **CLC 2,
　　11, 15, 46**
　　See also CA 5-8R; 4; CAAS 145; CANR
　　23, 54; CDBLB 1960 to Present; CN 1, 2,
　　3, 4, 5; CP 1, 2, 3, 4, 5; DLB 15, 27, 139,
　　155; EWL 3; MTCW 1, 2; MTFW 2005
Wajda, Andrzej 1926- .... **CLC 16, 219**
　　See also CA 102
Wakefield, Dan 1932- .... **CLC 7**
　　See also CA 211; 21-24R, 211; 7; CN 4, 5,
　　6, 7
Wakefield, Herbert Russell
　　1888-1965 .... **TCLC 120**
　　See also CA 5-8R; CANR 77; HGG; SUFW
Wakoski, Diane 1937- ...... **CLC 2, 4, 7, 9, 11,
　　40; PC 15**
　　See also CA 216; 13-16R, 216; 1; CANR 9,
　　60, 106; CP 1, 2, 3, 4, 5, 6, 7; CWP; DAM
　　POET; DLB 5; INT CANR-9; MAL 5;
　　MTCW 2; MTFW 2005
Wakoski-Sherbell, Diane
　　See Wakoski, Diane
Walcott, Derek 1930- .... **BLC 3; CLC 2, 4, 9,
　　14, 25, 42, 67, 76, 160; DC 7; PC 46**
　　See also BW 2; CA 89-92; CANR 26, 47,
　　75, 80, 130; CBD; CD 5, 6; CDWLB 3;
　　CP 1, 2, 3, 4, 5, 6, 7; DA3; DAB; DAC;
　　DAM MST, MULT, POET; DLB 117,
　　332; DLBY 1981; DNFS 1; EFS 1; EWL
　　3; LMFS 2; MTCW 1, 2; MTFW 2005;
　　PFS 6; RGEL 2; TWA; WWE 1
Waldman, Anne (Lesley) 1945- .... **CLC 7**
　　See also BG 1:3; CA 37-40R; 17; CANR
　　34, 69, 116; CP 1, 2, 3, 4, 5, 6, 7; CWP;
　　DLB 16
Waldo, E. Hunter
　　See Sturgeon, Theodore (Hamilton)
Waldo, Edward Hamilton
　　See Sturgeon, Theodore (Hamilton)

Walker, Alice 1944- ...... **BLC 3; CLC 5, 6, 9,
　　19, 27, 46, 58, 103, 167; PC 30; SSC 5;
　　WLCS**
　　See also AAYA 3, 33; AFAW 1, 2; AMWS
　　3; BEST 89:4; BPFB 3; BW 2, 3; CA 37-
　　40R; CANR 9, 27, 49, 66, 82, 131;
　　CDALB 1968-1988; CN 1, 4, 5, 6, 7; CPW;
　　CSW; DA; DA3; DAB; DAC; DAM MST,
　　MULT, NOV, POET, POP; DLB 6, 33,
　　143; EWL 3; EXPN; EXPS; FL 1:6; FW;
　　INT CANR-27; LAIT 3; MAL 5; MBL;
　　MTCW 1, 2; MTFW 2005; NFS 5; RGAL
　　4; RGSF 2; SATA 31; SSFS 2, 11; TUS;
　　YAW
Walker, Alice Malsenior
　　See Walker, Alice
Walker, David Harry 1911-1992 ...... **CLC 14**
　　See also CA 1-4R; CAAS 137; CANR 1;
　　CN 1, 2; CWRI 5; SATA 8; SATA-Obit
　　71
Walker, Edward Joseph 1934-2004
　　See Walker, Ted
　　See also CA 21-24R; CAAS 226; CANR
　　12, 28, 53
Walker, George F(rederick) 1947- .. **CLC 44,
　　61**
　　See also CA 103; CANR 21, 43, 59; CD 5,
　　6; DAB; DAC; DAM MST; DLB 60
Walker, Joseph A. 1935-2003 .... **CLC 19**
　　See also BW 1, 3; CA 89-92; CAD; CANR
　　26, 143; CD 5, 6; DAM DRAM, MST;
　　DFS 12; DLB 38
Walker, Margaret 1915-1998 .. **BLC; CLC 1,
　　6; PC 20; TCLC 129**
　　See also AFAW 1, 2; BW 2, 3; CA 73-76;
　　CAAS 172; CANR 26, 54, 76, 136; CN
　　1, 2, 3, 4, 5, 6; CP 1, 2, 3, 4, 5, 6; CSW;
　　DAM MULT; DLB 76, 152; EXPP; FW;
　　MAL 5; MTCW 1, 2; MTFW 2005;
　　RGAL 4; RHW
Walker, Ted .... **CLC 13**
　　See Walker, Edward Joseph
　　See also CP 1, 2, 3, 4, 5, 6, 7; DLB 40
Wallace, David Foster 1962- ... **CLC 50, 114;
　　SSC 68**
　　See also AAYA 50; AMWS 10; CA 132;
　　CANR 59, 133; CN 7; DA3; MTCW 2;
　　MTFW 2005
Wallace, Dexter
　　See Masters, Edgar Lee
Wallace, (Richard Horatio) Edgar
　　1875-1932 .... **TCLC 57**
　　See also CA 218; CAAE 115; CMW 4;
　　DLB 70; MSW; RGEL 2
Wallace, Irving 1916-1990 .... **CLC 7, 13**
　　See also AITN 1; BPFB 3; CA 1-4R; 1;
　　CAAS 132; CANR 1, 27; CPW; DAM
　　NOV, POP; INT CANR-27; MTCW 1, 2
Wallant, Edward Lewis 1926-1962 ... **CLC 5,
　　10**
　　See also CA 1-4R; CANR 22; DLB 2, 28,
　　143, 299; EWL 3; MAL 5; MTCW 1, 2;
　　RGAL 4; RGHL
Wallas, Graham 1858-1932 .... **TCLC 91**
Waller, Edmund 1606-1687 .... **LC 86; PC 72**
　　See also BRW 2; DAM POET; DLB 126;
　　PAB; RGEL 2
Walley, Byron
　　See Card, Orson Scott
Walpole, Horace 1717-1797 .... **LC 2, 49**
　　See also BRW 3; DLB 39, 104, 213; GL 3;
　　HGG; LMFS 1; RGEL 2; SUFW 1; TEA
Walpole, Hugh (Seymour)
　　1884-1941 .... **TCLC 5**
　　See also CA 165; CAAE 104; DLB 34;
　　HGG; MTCW 2; RGEL 2; RHW
Walrond, Eric (Derwent) 1898-1966 . **HR 1:3**
　　See also BW 1; CA 125; DLB 51

Walser, Martin 1927- .... **CLC 27, 183**
　　See also CA 57-60; CANR 8, 46, 145;
　　CWW 2; DLB 75, 124; EWL 3
Walser, Robert 1878-1956 ..... **SSC 20; TCLC
　　18**
　　See also CA 165; CAAE 118; CANR 100;
　　DLB 66; EWL 3
Walsh, Gillian Paton
　　See Paton Walsh, Jill
Walsh, Jill Paton .... **CLC 35**
　　See Paton Walsh, Jill
　　See also CLR 2, 65; WYA
Walter, Villiam Christian
　　See Andersen, Hans Christian
Walters, Anna L(ee) 1946- .... **NNAL**
　　See also CA 73-76
Walther von der Vogelweide c.
　　1170-1228 .... **CMLC 56**
Walton, Izaak 1593-1683 .... **LC 72**
　　See also BRW 2; CDBLB Before 1660;
　　DLB 151, 213; RGEL 2
Wambaugh, Joseph (Aloysius), Jr.
　　1937- .... **CLC 3, 18**
　　See also AITN 1; BEST 89:3; BPFB 3; CA
　　33-36R; CANR 42, 65, 115; CMW 4;
　　CPW 1; DA3; DAM NOV, POP; DLB 6;
　　DLBY 1983; MSW; MTCW 1, 2
Wang Wei 699(?)-761(?) .... **PC 18**
　　See also TWA
Warburton, William 1698-1779 .... **LC 97**
　　See also DLB 104
Ward, Arthur Henry Sarsfield 1883-1959
　　See Rohmer, Sax
　　See also CA 173; CAAE 108; CMW 4;
　　HGG
Ward, Douglas Turner 1930- .... **CLC 19**
　　See also BW 1; CA 81-84; CAD; CANR
　　27; CD 5, 6; DLB 7, 38
Ward, E. D.
　　See Lucas, E(dward) V(errall)
Ward, Mrs. Humphry 1851-1920
　　See Ward, Mary Augusta
　　See also RGEL 2
Ward, Mary Augusta 1851-1920 ... **TCLC 55**
　　See Ward, Mrs. Humphry
　　See also DLB 18
Ward, Nathaniel 1578(?)-1652 .... **LC 114**
　　See also DLB 24
Ward, Peter
　　See Faust, Frederick (Schiller)
Warhol, Andy 1928(?)-1987 .... **CLC 20**
　　See also AAYA 12; BEST 89:4; CA 89-92;
　　CAAS 121; CANR 34
Warner, Francis (Robert Le Plastrier)
　　1937- .... **CLC 14**
　　See also CA 53-56; CANR 11; CP 1, 2, 3, 4
Warner, Marina 1946- .... **CLC 59, 231**
　　See also CA 65-68; CANR 21, 55, 118; CN
　　5, 6, 7; DLB 194; MTFW 2005
Warner, Rex (Ernest) 1905-1986 ...... **CLC 45**
　　See also CA 89-92; CAAS 119; CN 1, 2, 3,
　　4; CP 1, 2, 3, 4; DLB 15; RGEL 2; RHW
Warner, Susan (Bogert)
　　1819-1885 .... **NCLC 31, 146**
　　See also DLB 3, 42, 239, 250, 254
Warner, Sylvia (Constance) Ashton
　　See Ashton-Warner, Sylvia (Constance)
Warner, Sylvia Townsend
　　1893-1978 .. **CLC 7, 19; SSC 23; TCLC
　　131**
　　See also BRWS 7; CA 61-64; CAAS 77-80;
　　CANR 16, 60, 104; CN 1, 2; DLB 34,
　　139; EWL 3; FANT; FW; MTCW 1, 2;
　　RGEL 2; RGSF 2; RHW
Warren, Mercy Otis 1728-1814 ..... **NCLC 13**
　　See also DLB 31, 200; RGAL 4; TUS

Warren, Robert Penn 1905-1989 .. **CLC 1, 4, 6, 8, 10, 13, 18, 39, 53, 59; PC 37; SSC 4, 58; WLC 6**
See also AITN 1; AMW; AMWC 2; BPFB 3; BYA 1; CA 13-16R; CAAS 129; CANR 10, 47; CDALB 1968-1988; CN 1, 2, 3, 4; CP 1, 2, 3, 4; DA; DA3; DAB; DAC; DAM MST, NOV, POET; DLB 2, 48, 152, 320; DLBY 1980, 1989; EWL 3; INT CANR-10; MAL 5; MTCW 1, 2; MTFW 2005; NFS 13; RGAL 4; RGSF 2; RHW; SATA 46; SATA-Obit 63; SSFS 8; TUS

Warrigal, Jack
See Furphy, Joseph

Warshofsky, Isaac
See Singer, Isaac Bashevis

Warton, Joseph 1722-1800 ... **LC 128; NCLC 118**
See also DLB 104, 109; RGEL 2

Warton, Thomas 1728-1790 .... **LC 15, 82**
See also DAM POET; DLB 104, 109; RGEL 2

Waruk, Kona
See Harris, (Theodore) Wilson

Warung, Price .... **TCLC 45**
See Astley, William
See also DLB 230; RGEL 2

Warwick, Jarvis
See Garner, Hugh
See also CCA 1

Washington, Alex
See Harris, Mark

Washington, Booker T(aliaferro)
1856-1915 .... **BLC 3; TCLC 10**
See also BW 1; CA 125; CAAE 114; DA3; DAM MULT; LAIT 2; RGAL 4; SATA 28

Washington, George 1732-1799 .... **LC 25**
See also DLB 31

Wassermann, (Karl) Jakob
1873-1934 .... **TCLC 6**
See also CA 163; CAAE 104; DLB 66; EWL 3

Wasserstein, Wendy 1950-2006 . **CLC 32, 59, 90, 183; DC 4**
See also AAYA 73; AMWS 15; CA 129; CAAE 121; CAAS 247; CABS 3; CAD; CANR 53, 75, 128; CD 5, 6; CWD; DA3; DAM DRAM; DFS 5, 17; DLB 228; EWL 3; FW; INT CA-129; MAL 5; MTCW 2; MTFW 2005; SATA 94; SATA-Obit 174

Waterhouse, Keith (Spencer) 1929- . **CLC 47**
See also CA 5-8R; CANR 38, 67, 109; CBD; CD 6; CN 1, 2, 3, 4, 5, 6, 7; DLB 13, 15; MTCW 1, 2; MTFW 2005

Waters, Frank (Joseph) 1902-1995 . **CLC 88**
See also CA 5-8R; 13; CAAS 149; CANR 3, 18, 63, 121; DLB 212; DLBY 1986; RGAL 4; TCWW 1, 2

Waters, Mary C. .... **CLC 70**

Waters, Roger 1944- .... **CLC 35**

Watkins, Frances Ellen
See Harper, Frances Ellen Watkins

Watkins, Gerrold
See Malzberg, Barry N(athaniel)

Watkins, Gloria Jean
See hooks, bell

Watkins, Paul 1964- .... **CLC 55**
See also CA 132; CANR 62, 98

Watkins, Vernon Phillips
1906-1967 .... **CLC 43**
See also CA 9-10; CAAS 25-28R; CAP 1; DLB 20; EWL 3; RGEL 2

Watson, Irving S.
See Mencken, H(enry) L(ouis)

Watson, John H.
See Farmer, Philip Jose

Watson, Richard F.
See Silverberg, Robert

Watts, Ephraim
See Horne, Richard Henry Hengist

Watts, Isaac 1674-1748 .... **LC 98**
See also DLB 95; RGEL 2; SATA 52

Waugh, Auberon (Alexander)
1939-2001 .... **CLC 7**
See also CA 45-48; CAAS 192; CANR 6, 22, 92; CN 1, 2, 3; DLB 14, 194

Waugh, Evelyn (Arthur St. John)
1903-1966 .. **CLC 1, 3, 8, 13, 19, 27, 44, 107; SSC 41; WLC 6**
See also BPFB 3; BRW 7; CA 85-88; CAAS 25-28R; CANR 22; CDBLB 1914-1945; DA; DA3; DAB; DAC; DAM MST, NOV, POP; DLB 15, 162, 195; EWL 3; MTCW 1, 2; MTFW 2005; NFS 13, 17; RGEL 2; RGSF 2; TEA; WLIT 4

Waugh, Harriet 1944- .... **CLC 6**
See also CA 85-88; CANR 22

Ways, C. R.
See Blount, Roy (Alton), Jr.

Waystaff, Simon
See Swift, Jonathan

Webb, Beatrice (Martha Potter)
1858-1943 .... **TCLC 22**
See also CA 162; CAAE 117; DLB 190; FW

Webb, Charles (Richard) 1939- .... **CLC 7**
See also CA 25-28R; CANR 114

Webb, Frank J. .... **NCLC 143**
See also DLB 50

Webb, James, Jr.
See Webb, James

Webb, James 1946- .... **CLC 22**
See also CA 81-84; CANR 156

Webb, James H.
See Webb, James

Webb, James Henry
See Webb, James

Webb, Mary Gladys (Meredith)
1881-1927 .... **TCLC 24**
See also CA 182; CAAS 123; DLB 34; FW; RGEL 2

Webb, Mrs. Sidney
See Webb, Beatrice (Martha Potter)

Webb, Phyllis 1927- .... **CLC 18**
See also CA 104; CANR 23; CCA 1; CP 1, 2, 3, 4, 5, 6, 7; CWP; DLB 53

Webb, Sidney (James) 1859-1947 .. **TCLC 22**
See also CA 163; CAAE 117; DLB 190

Webber, Andrew Lloyd .... **CLC 21**
See Lloyd Webber, Andrew
See also DFS 7

Weber, Lenora Mattingly
1895-1971 .... **CLC 12**
See also CA 19-20; CAAS 29-32R; CAP 1; SATA 2; SATA-Obit 26

Weber, Max 1864-1920 .... **TCLC 69**
See also CA 189; CAAE 109; DLB 296

Webster, John 1580(?)-1634(?) ...... **DC 2; LC 33, 84, 124; WLC 6**
See also BRW 2; CDBLB Before 1660; DA; DAB; DAC; DAM DRAM, MST; DFS 17, 19; DLB 58; IDTP; RGEL 2; WLIT 3

Webster, Noah 1758-1843 .... **NCLC 30**
See also DLB 1, 37, 42, 43, 73, 243

Wedekind, Benjamin Franklin
See Wedekind, Frank

Wedekind, Frank 1864-1918 .... **TCLC 7**
See also CA 153; CAAE 104; CANR 121, 122; CDWLB 2; DAM DRAM; DLB 118; EW 8; EWL 3; LMFS 2; RGWL 2, 3

Wehr, Demaris .... **CLC 65**

Weidman, Jerome 1913-1998 .... **CLC 7**
See also AITN 2; CA 1-4R; CAAS 171; CAD; CANR 1; CD 1, 2, 3, 4, 5; DLB 28

Weil, Simone (Adolphine)
1909-1943 .... **TCLC 23**
See also CA 159; CAAE 117; EW 12; EWL 3; FW; GFL 1789 to the Present; MTCW 2

Weininger, Otto 1880-1903 .... **TCLC 84**

Weinstein, Nathan
See West, Nathanael

Weinstein, Nathan von Wallenstein
See West, Nathanael

Weir, Peter (Lindsay) 1944- .... **CLC 20**
See also CA 123; CAAE 113

Weiss, Peter (Ulrich) 1916-1982 .. **CLC 3, 15, 51; TCLC 152**
See also CA 45-48; CAAS 106; CANR 3; DAM DRAM; DFS 3; DLB 69, 124; EWL 3; RGHL; RGWL 2, 3

Weiss, Theodore (Russell)
1916-2003 .... **CLC 3, 8, 14**
See also CA 189; 9-12R, 189; 2; CAAS 216; CANR 46, 94; CP 1, 2, 3, 4, 5, 6, 7; DLB 5; TCLE 1:2

Welch, (Maurice) Denton
1915-1948 .... **TCLC 22**
See also BRWS 8, 9; CA 148; CAAE 121; RGEL 2

Welch, James (Phillip) 1940-2003 ..... **CLC 6, 14, 52; NNAL; PC 62**
See also CA 85-88; CAAS 219; CANR 42, 66, 107; CN 5, 6, 7; CP 2, 3, 4, 5, 6, 7; CPW; DAM MULT, POP; DLB 175, 256; LATS 1:1; NFS 23; RGAL 4; TCWW 1, 2

Weldon, Fay 1931- . **CLC 6, 9, 11, 19, 36, 59, 122**
See also BRWS 4; CA 21-24R; CANR 16, 46, 63, 97, 137; CDBLB 1960 to Present; CN 3, 4, 5, 6, 7; CPW; DAM POP; DLB 14, 194, 319; EWL 3; FW; HGG; INT CANR-16; MTCW 1, 2; MTFW 2005; RGEL 2; RGSF 2

Wellek, Rene 1903-1995 .... **CLC 28**
See also CA 5-8R; 7; CAAS 150; CANR 8; DLB 63; EWL 3; INT CANR-8

Weller, Michael 1942- .... **CLC 10, 53**
See also CA 85-88; CAD; CD 5, 6

Weller, Paul 1958- .... **CLC 26**

Wellershoff, Dieter 1925- .... **CLC 46**
See also CA 89-92; CANR 16, 37

Welles, (George) Orson 1915-1985 .. **CLC 20, 80**
See also AAYA 40; CA 93-96; CAAS 117

Wellman, John McDowell 1945-
See Wellman, Mac
See also CA 166; CD 5

Wellman, Mac .... **CLC 65**
See Wellman, John McDowell; Wellman, John McDowell
See also CAD; CD 6; RGAL 4

Wellman, Manly Wade 1903-1986 ... **CLC 49**
See also CA 1-4R; CAAS 118; CANR 6, 16, 44; FANT; SATA 6; SATA-Obit 47; SFW 4; SUFW

Wells, Carolyn 1869(?)-1942 .... **TCLC 35**
See also CA 185; CAAE 113; CMW 4; DLB 11

Wells, H(erbert) G(eorge) 1866-1946 . **SSC 6, 70; TCLC 6, 12, 19, 133; WLC 6**
See also AAYA 18; BPFB 3; BRW 6; CA 121; CAAE 110; CDBLB 1914-1945; CLR 64; DA; DA3; DAB; DAC; DAM MST, NOV; DLB 34, 70, 156, 178; EWL 3; EXPS; HGG; LAIT 3; LMFS 2; MTCW 1, 2; MTFW 2005; NFS 17, 20; RGEL 2; RGSF 2; SATA 20; SCFW 1, 2; SFW 4; SSFS 3; SUFW; TEA; WCH; WLIT 4; YAW

Whitehead, E(dward) A(nthony)
1933- .... **CLC 5**
See Whitehead, Ted
See also CA 65-68; CANR 58, 118; CBD;
CD 5; DLB 310

Whitehead, Ted
See Whitehead, E(dward) A(nthony)
See also CD 6

Whiteman, Roberta J. Hill 1947- ...... **NNAL**
See also CA 146

Whitemore, Hugh (John) 1936- .... **CLC 37**
See also CA 132; CANR 77; CBD; CD 5,
6; INT CA-132

Whitman, Sarah Helen (Power)
1803-1878 .... **NCLC 19**
See also DLB 1, 243

Whitman, Walt(er) 1819-1892 .. **NCLC 4, 31,
81; PC 3; WLC 6**
See also AAYA 42; AMW; AMWR 1;
CDALB 1640-1865; DA; DA3; DAB;
DAC; DAM MST, POET; DLB 3, 64,
224, 250; EXPP; LAIT 2; LMFS 1; PAB;
PFS 2, 3, 13, 22; RGAL 4; SATA 20;
TUS; WP; WYAS 1

Whitney, Isabella fl. 1565-fl. 1575 ..... **LC 130**
See also DLB 136

Whitney, Phyllis A(yame) 1903- .... **CLC 42**
See also AAYA 36; AITN 2; BEST 90:3;
CA 1-4R; CANR 3, 25, 38, 60; CLR 59;
CMW 4; CPW; DA3; DAM POP; JRDA;
MAICYA 1, 2; MTCW 2; RHW; SATA 1,
30; YAW

Whittemore, (Edward) Reed, Jr.
1919- .... **CLC 4**
See also CA 219; 9-12R, 219; 8; CANR 4,
119; CP 1, 2, 3, 4, 5, 6, 7; DLB 5; MAL
5

Whittier, John Greenleaf
1807-1892 .... **NCLC 8, 59**
See also AMWS 1; DLB 1, 243; RGAL 4

Whittlebot, Hernia
See Coward, Noel (Peirce)

Wicker, Thomas Grey 1926-
See Wicker, Tom
See also CA 65-68; CANR 21, 46, 141

Wicker, Tom .... **CLC 7**
See Wicker, Thomas Grey

Wideman, John Edgar 1941- ... **BLC 3; CLC
5, 34, 36, 67, 122; SSC 62**
See also AFAW 1, 2; AMWS 10; BPFB 4;
BW 2, 3; CA 85-88; CANR 14, 42, 67,
109, 140; CN 4, 5, 6, 7; DAM MULT;
DLB 33, 143; MAL 5; MTCW 2; MTFW
2005; RGAL 4; RGSF 2; SSFS 6, 12, 24;
TCLE 1:2

Wiebe, Rudy 1934- .... **CLC 6, 11, 14, 138**
See also CA 37-40R; CANR 42, 67, 123;
CN 1, 2, 3, 4, 5, 6, 7; DAC; DAM MST;
DLB 60; RHW; SATA 156

Wiebe, Rudy Henry
See Wiebe, Rudy

Wieland, Christoph Martin
1733-1813 .... **NCLC 17, 177**
See also DLB 97; EW 4; LMFS 1; RGWL
2, 3

Wiene, Robert 1881-1938 .... **TCLC 56**

Wieners, John 1934- .... **CLC 7**
See also BG 1:3; CA 13-16R; CP 1, 2, 3, 4,
5, 6, 7; DLB 16; WP

Wiesel, Elie 1928- ...... **CLC 3, 5, 11, 37, 165;
WLCS**
See also AAYA 7, 54; AITN 1; CA 5-8R; 4;
CANR 8, 40, 65, 125; CDALBS; CWW
2; DA; DA3; DAB; DAC; DAM MST,
NOV; DLB 83, 299; DLBY 1987; EWL
3; INT CANR-8; LAIT 4; MTCW 1, 2;
MTFW 2005; NCFS 4; NFS 4; RGHL;
RGWL 2, 3; SATA 56; YAW

Wiesel, Eliezer
See Wiesel, Elie

Wiggins, Marianne 1947- .... **CLC 57**
See also AAYA 70; BEST 89:3; CA 130;
CANR 60, 139; CN 7

Wigglesworth, Michael 1631-1705 .... **LC 106**
See also DLB 24; RGAL 4

Wiggs, Susan .... **CLC 70**
See also CA 201

Wight, James Alfred 1916-1995
See Herriot, James
See also CA 77-80; SATA 55; SATA-Brief
44

Wilbur, Richard 1921- .. **CLC 3, 6, 9, 14, 53,
110; PC 51**
See also AAYA 72; AMWS 3; CA 1-4R;
CABS 2; CANR 2, 29, 76, 93, 139;
CDALBS; CP 1, 2, 3, 4, 5, 6, 7; DA;
DAB; DAC; DAM MST, POET; DLB 5,
169; EWL 3; EXPP; INT CANR-29;
MAL 5; MTCW 1, 2; MTFW 2005; PAB;
PFS 11, 12, 16; RGAL 4; SATA 9, 108;
WP

Wilbur, Richard Purdy
See Wilbur, Richard

Wild, Peter 1940- .... **CLC 14**
See also CA 37-40R; CP 1, 2, 3, 4, 5, 6, 7;
DLB 5

Wilde, Oscar (Fingal O'Flahertie Wills)
1854(?)-1900 .... **DC 17; SSC 11, 77;
TCLC 1, 8, 23, 41, 175; WLC 6**
See also AAYA 49; BRW 5; BRWC 1, 2;
BRWR 2; BYA 15; CA 119; CAAE 104;
CANR 112; CDBLB 1890-1914; CLR
114; DA; DA3; DAB; DAC; DAM
DRAM, MST, NOV; DFS 4, 8, 9, 21;
DLB 10, 19, 34, 57, 141, 156, 190; EXPS;
FANT; GL 3; LATS 1:1; NFS 20; RGEL
2; RGSF 2; SATA 24; SSFS 7; SUFW;
TEA; WCH; WLIT 4

Wilder, Billy .... **CLC 20**
See Wilder, Samuel
See also AAYA 66; DLB 26

Wilder, Samuel 1906-2002
See Wilder, Billy
See also CA 89-92; CAAS 205

Wilder, Stephen
See Marlowe, Stephen

Wilder, Thornton (Niven)
1897-1975 .. **CLC 1, 5, 6, 10, 15, 35, 82;
DC 1, 24; WLC 6**
See also AAYA 29; AITN 2; AMW; CA 13-
16R; CAAS 61-64; CAD; CANR 40, 132;
CDALBS; CN 1, 2; DA; DA3; DAB;
DAC; DAM DRAM, MST, NOV; DFS 1,
4, 16; DLB 4, 7, 9, 228; DLBY 1997;
EWL 3; LAIT 3; MAL 5; MTCW 1, 2;
MTFW 2005; NFS 24; RGAL 4; RHW;
WYAS 1

Wilding, Michael 1942- ...... **CLC 73; SSC 50**
See also CA 104; CANR 24, 49, 106; CN
4, 5, 6, 7; DLB 325; RGSF 2

Wiley, Richard 1944- .... **CLC 44**
See also CA 129; CAAE 121; CANR 71

Wilhelm, Kate .... **CLC 7**
See Wilhelm, Katie
See also AAYA 20; BYA 16; CA 5; DLB 8;
INT CANR-17; SCFW 2

Wilhelm, Katie 1928-
See Wilhelm, Kate
See also CA 37-40R; CANR 17, 36, 60, 94;
MTCW 1; SFW 4

Wilkins, Mary
See Freeman, Mary E(leanor) Wilkins

Willard, Nancy 1936- .... **CLC 7, 37**
See also BYA 5; CA 89-92; CANR 10, 39,
68, 107, 152; CLR 5; CP 2, 3, 4, 5; CWP;
CWRI 5; DLB 5, 52; FANT; MAICYA 1,
2; MTCW 1; SATA 37, 71, 127; SATA-
Brief 30; SUFW 1; TCLE 1:2

William of Malmesbury c. 1090B.C.-c.
1140B.C. .... **CMLC 57**

William of Ockham 1290-1349 ..... **CMLC 32**

Williams, Ben Ames 1889-1953 ..... **TCLC 89**
See also CA 183; DLB 102

Williams, Charles
See Collier, James Lincoln

Williams, Charles (Walter Stansby)
1886-1945 .... **TCLC 1, 11**
See also BRWS 9; CA 163; CAAE 104;
DLB 100, 153, 255; FANT; RGEL 2;
SUFW 1

Williams, C.K. 1936- .... **CLC 33, 56, 148**
See also CA 37-40R; 26; CANR 57, 106;
CP 1, 2, 3, 4, 5, 6, 7; DAM POET; DLB
5; MAL 5

Williams, Ella Gwendolen Rees
See Rhys, Jean

Williams, (George) Emlyn
1905-1987 .... **CLC 15**
See also CA 104; CAAS 123; CANR 36;
DAM DRAM; DLB 10, 77; IDTP; MTCW
1

Williams, Hank 1923-1953 .... **TCLC 81**
See Williams, Hiram King

Williams, Helen Maria
1761-1827 .... **NCLC 135**
See also DLB 158

Williams, Hiram Hank
See Williams, Hank

Williams, Hiram King
See Williams, Hank
See also CA 188

Williams, Hugo (Mordaunt) 1942- ... **CLC 42**
See also CA 17-20R; CANR 45, 119; CP 1,
2, 3, 4, 5, 6, 7; DLB 40

Williams, J. Walker
See Wodehouse, P(elham) G(renville)

Williams, John A(lfred) 1925- . **BLC 3; CLC
5, 13**
See also AFAW 2; BW 2, 3; CA 195; 53-
56, 195; 3; CANR 6, 26, 51, 118; CN 1,
2, 3, 4, 5, 6, 7; CSW; DAM MULT; DLB
2, 33; EWL 3; INT CANR-6; MAL 5;
RGAL 4; SFW 4

Williams, Jonathan (Chamberlain)
1929- .... **CLC 13**
See also CA 9-12R; 12; CANR 8, 108; CP
1, 2, 3, 4, 5, 6, 7; DLB 5

Williams, Joy 1944- .... **CLC 31**
See also CA 41-44R; CANR 22, 48, 97

Williams, Norman 1952- .... **CLC 39**
See also CA 118

Williams, Roger 1603(?)-1683 .... **LC 129**
See also DLB 24

Williams, Sherley Anne 1944-1999 ... **BLC 3;
CLC 89**
See also AFAW 2; BW 2, 3; CA 73-76;
CAAS 185; CANR 25, 82; DAM MULT,
POET; DLB 41; INT CANR-25; SATA
78; SATA-Obit 116

Williams, Shirley
See Williams, Sherley Anne

Williams, Tennessee 1911-1983 . **CLC 1, 2, 5,
7, 8, 11, 15, 19, 30, 39, 45, 71, 111; DC
4; SSC 81; WLC 6**
See also AAYA 31; AITN 1, 2; AMW;
AMWC 1; CA 5-8R; CAAS 108; CABS
3; CAD; CANR 31, 132; CDALB 1941-
1968; CN 1, 2, 3; DA; DA3; DAB; DAC;
DAM DRAM, MST; DFS 17; DLB 7;
DLBD 4; DLBY 1983; EWL 3; GLL 1;
LAIT 4; LATS 1:2; MAL 5; MTCW 1, 2;
MTFW 2005; RGAL 4; TUS

Williams, Thomas (Alonzo)
1926-1990 .... **CLC 14**
See also CA 1-4R; CAAS 132; CANR 2

Williams, William C.
See Williams, William Carlos

Yerby, Frank G(arvin) 1916-1991 ..... **BLC 3; CLC 1, 7, 22**
See also BPFB 3; BW 1, 3; CA 9-12R; CAAS 136; CANR 16, 52; CN 1, 2, 3, 4, 5; DAM MULT; DLB 76; INT CANR-16; MTCW 1; RGAL 4; RHW
Yesenin, Sergei Aleksandrovich
See Esenin, Sergei
Yevtushenko, Yevgeny (Alexandrovich) 1933- ...... **CLC 1, 3, 13, 26, 51, 126; PC 40**
See Evtushenko, Evgenii Aleksandrovich
See also CA 81-84; CANR 33, 54; DAM POET; EWL 3; MTCW 1; RGHL
Yezierska, Anzia 1885(?)-1970 .... **CLC 46**
See also CA 126; CAAS 89-92; DLB 28, 221; FW; MTCW 1; RGAL 4; SSFS 15
Yglesias, Helen 1915- .... **CLC 7, 22**
See also CA 37-40R; 20; CANR 15, 65, 95; CN 4, 5, 6, 7; INT CANR-15; MTCW 1
Yokomitsu, Riichi 1898-1947 .... **TCLC 47**
See also CA 170; EWL 3
Yonge, Charlotte (Mary) 1823-1901 .... **TCLC 48**
See also CA 163; CAAE 109; DLB 18, 163; RGEL 2; SATA 17; WCH
York, Jeremy
See Creasey, John
York, Simon
See Heinlein, Robert A.
Yorke, Henry Vincent 1905-1974 ..... **CLC 13**
See Green, Henry
See also CA 85-88; CAAS 49-52
Yosano, Akiko 1878-1942 ... **PC 11; TCLC 59**
See also CA 161; EWL 3; RGWL 3
Yoshimoto, Banana .... **CLC 84**
See Yoshimoto, Mahoko
See also AAYA 50; NFS 7
Yoshimoto, Mahoko 1964-
See Yoshimoto, Banana
See also CA 144; CANR 98, 160; SSFS 16
Young, Al(bert James) 1939- ... **BLC 3; CLC 19**
See also BW 2, 3; CA 29-32R; CANR 26, 65, 109; CN 2, 3, 4, 5, 6, 7; CP 1, 2, 3, 4, 5, 6, 7; DAM MULT; DLB 33
Young, Andrew (John) 1885-1971 ...... **CLC 5**
See also CA 5-8R; CANR 7, 29; CP 1; RGEL 2
Young, Collier
See Bloch, Robert (Albert)
Young, Edward 1683-1765 .... **LC 3, 40**
See also DLB 95; RGEL 2
Young, Marguerite (Vivian) 1909-1995 .... **CLC 82**
See also CA 13-16; CAAS 150; CAP 1; CN 1, 2, 3, 4, 5, 6
Young, Neil 1945- .... **CLC 17**
See also CA 110; CCA 1
Young Bear, Ray A. 1950- ... **CLC 94; NNAL**
See also CA 146; DAM MULT; DLB 175; MAL 5
Yourcenar, Marguerite 1903-1987 ... **CLC 19, 38, 50, 87**
See also BPFB 3; CA 69-72; CANR 23, 60, 93; DAM NOV; DLB 72; DLBY 1988; EW 12; EWL 3; GFL 1789 to the Present; GLL 1; MTCW 1, 2; MTFW 2005; RGWL 2, 3
Yuan, Chu 340(?)B.C.-278(?)B.C. . **CMLC 36**

Yurick, Sol 1925- .... **CLC 6**
See also CA 13-16R; CANR 25; CN 1, 2, 3, 4, 5, 6, 7; MAL 5
Zabolotsky, Nikolai Alekseevich 1903-1958 .... **TCLC 52**
See Zabolotsky, Nikolay Alekseevich
See also CA 164; CAAE 116
Zabolotsky, Nikolay Alekseevich
See Zabolotsky, Nikolai Alekseevich
See also EWL 3
Zagajewski, Adam 1945- .... **PC 27**
See also CA 186; DLB 232; EWL 3; PFS 25
Zalygin, Sergei -2000 .... **CLC 59**
Zalygin, Sergei (Pavlovich) 1913-2000 .... **CLC 59**
See also DLB 302
Zamiatin, Evgenii
See Zamyatin, Evgeny Ivanovich
See also RGSF 2; RGWL 2, 3
Zamiatin, Evgenii Ivanovich
See Zamyatin, Evgeny Ivanovich
See also DLB 272
Zamiatin, Yevgenii
See Zamyatin, Evgeny Ivanovich
Zamora, Bernice (B. Ortiz) 1938- .. **CLC 89; HLC 2**
See also CA 151; CANR 80; DAM MULT; DLB 82; HW 1, 2
Zamyatin, Evgeny Ivanovich 1884-1937 .... **SSC 89; TCLC 8, 37**
See Zamiatin, Evgenii; Zamiatin, Evgenii Ivanovich; Zamyatin, Yevgeny Ivanovich
See also CA 166; CAAE 105; SFW 4
Zamyatin, Yevgeny Ivanovich
See Zamyatin, Evgeny Ivanovich
See also EW 10; EWL 3
Zangwill, Israel 1864-1926 ... **SSC 44; TCLC 16**
See also CA 167; CAAE 109; CMW 4; DLB 10, 135, 197; RGEL 2
Zanzotto, Andrea 1921- .... **PC 65**
See also CA 208; CWW 2; DLB 128; EWL 3
Zappa, Francis Vincent, Jr. 1940-1993
See Zappa, Frank
See also CA 108; CAAS 143; CANR 57
Zappa, Frank .... **CLC 17**
See Zappa, Francis Vincent, Jr.
Zaturenska, Marya 1902-1982 ..... **CLC 6, 11**
See also CA 13-16R; CAAS 105; CANR 22; CP 1, 2, 3
Zayas y Sotomayor, Maria de 1590-c. 1661 .... **LC 102; SSC 94**
See also RGSF 2
Zeami 1363-1443 .... **DC 7; LC 86**
See also DLB 203; RGWL 2, 3
Zelazny, Roger 1937-1995 .... **CLC 21**
See also AAYA 7, 68; BPFB 3; CA 21-24R; CAAS 148; CANR 26, 60; CN 6; DLB 8; FANT; MTCW 1, 2; MTFW 2005; SATA 57; SATA-Brief 39; SCFW 1, 2; SFW 4; SUFW 1, 2
Zhang Ailing
See Chang, Eileen
See also CWW 2; DLB 328; RGSF 2
Zhdanov, Andrei Alexandrovich 1896-1948 .... **TCLC 18**
See also CA 167; CAAE 117
Zhukovsky, Vasilii Andreevich
See Zhukovsky, Vasily (Andreevich)
See also DLB 205

Zhukovsky, Vasily (Andreevich) 1783-1852 .... **NCLC 35**
See Zhukovsky, Vasilii Andreevich
Ziegenhagen, Eric .... **CLC 55**
Zimmer, Jill Schary
See Robinson, Jill
Zimmerman, Robert
See Dylan, Bob
Zindel, Paul 1936-2003 ...... **CLC 6, 26; DC 5**
See also AAYA 2, 37; BYA 2, 3, 8, 11, 14; CA 73-76; CAAS 213; CAD; CANR 31, 65, 108; CD 5, 6; CDALBS; CLR 3, 45, 85; DA; DA3; DAB; DAC; DAM DRAM, MST, NOV; DFS 12; DLB 7, 52; JRDA; LAIT 5; MAICYA 1, 2; MTCW 1, 2; MTFW 2005; NFS 14; SATA 16, 58, 102; SATA-Obit 142; WYA; YAW
Zinger, Yisroel-Yehoyshue
See Singer, Israel Joshua
Zinger, Yitskhok
See Singer, Isaac Bashevis
Zinn, Howard 1922- .... **CLC 199**
See also CA 1-4R; CANR 2, 33, 90, 159
Zinov'Ev, A.A.
See Zinoviev, Alexander
Zinov'ev, Aleksandr
See Zinoviev, Alexander
See also DLB 302
Zinoviev, Alexander 1922-2006 .... **CLC 19**
See Zinov'ev, Aleksandr
See also CA 133; 10; CAAE 116; CAAS 250
Zinoviev, Alexander Aleksandrovich
See Zinoviev, Alexander
Zizek, Slavoj 1949- .... **CLC 188**
See also CA 201; MTFW 2005
Zoilus
See Lovecraft, H. P.
Zola, Emile (Edouard Charles Antoine) 1840-1902 .. **TCLC 1, 6, 21, 41; WLC 6**
See also CA 138; CAAE 104; DA; DA3; DAB; DAC; DAM MST, NOV; DLB 123; EW 7; GFL 1789 to the Present; IDTP; LMFS 1, 2; RGWL 2; TWA
Zoline, Pamela 1941- .... **CLC 62**
See also CA 161; SFW 4
Zoroaster 628(?)B.C.-551(?)B.C. ... **CMLC 40**
Zorrilla y Moral, Jose 1817-1893 .... **NCLC 6**
Zoshchenko, Mikhail (Mikhailovich) 1895-1958 .... **SSC 15; TCLC 15**
See also CA 160; CAAE 115; EWL 3; RGSF 2; RGWL 3
Zuckmayer, Carl 1896-1977 .... **CLC 18**
See also CA 69-72; DLB 56, 124; EWL 3; RGWL 2, 3
Zuk, Georges
See Skelton, Robin
See also CCA 1
Zukofsky, Louis 1904-1978 ... **CLC 1, 2, 4, 7, 11, 18; PC 11**
See also AMWS 3; CA 9-12R; CAAS 77-80; CANR 39; CP 1, 2; DAM POET; DLB 5, 165; EWL 3; MAL 5; MTCW 1; RGAL 4
Zweig, Paul 1935-1984 .... **CLC 34, 42**
See also CA 85-88; CAAS 113
Zweig, Stefan 1881-1942 .... **TCLC 17**
See also CA 170; CAAE 112; DLB 81, 118; EWL 3; RGHL
Zwingli, Huldreich 1484-1531 .... **LC 37**
See also DLB 179

Literary Criticism Series
Cumulative Topic Index

This index lists all topic entries in Thompson Gale's *Children's Literature Review* (CLR), *Classical and Medieval Literature Criticism* (CMLC), *Contemporary Literary Criticism* (CLC), *Drama Criticism* (DC), *Literature Criticism from 1400 to 1800* (LC), *Nineteenth-Century Literature Criticism* (NCLC), *Short Story Criticism* (SSC), and *Twentieth-Century Literary Criticism* (TCLC). The index also lists topic entries in the Gale Critical Companion Collection, which includes the following publications: *The Beat Generation* (BG), *Feminism in Literature* (FL), *Gothic Literature* (GL), and *Harlem Renaissance* (HR).

NCLC Cumulative Nationality Index

NCLC-183 Title Index

ISBN-13: 978-0-7876-9854-6
ISBN-10: 0-7876-9854-7